GPU Computing Gems
Emerald Edition

Morgan Kaufmann's *Applications of GPU Computing* Series

Computing is quickly becoming the third pillar of scientific research, due in large part to the performance gains achieved through graphics processing units (GPUs), which have become ubiquitous in handhelds, laptops, desktops, and supercomputer clusters. Morgan Kaufmann's *Applications of GPU Computing* series offers training, examples, and inspiration for researchers, engineers, students, and supercomputing professionals who want to leverage the power of GPUs incorporated into their simulations or experiments. Each high-quality, peer-reviewed book is written by leading experts uniquely qualified to provide parallel computing insights and guidance.

Each *GPU Computing Gems* volume offers a snapshot of the state of parallel computing across a carefully selected subset of industry domains, giving you a window into the lead-edge research occurring across the breadth of science, and the opportunity to observe others' algorithm work that might apply to your own projects. Find out more at `http://mkp.com/gpu-computing-gems`.

Recommended Parallel Computing Titles

Programming Massively Parallel Processors
A Hands-on Approach
By David B. Kirk and Wen-mei W. Hwu
ISBN: 9780123814722

GPU Computing Gems: Jade Edition
Editor-in-Chief: Wen-mei W. Hwu
ISBN: 9780123859631
Coming Summer 2011

The Art of Multiprocessor Programming
By Maurice Herlihy and Nir Shavit
ISBN: 9780123705914

GPU Computing Gems
Emerald Edition

Wen-mei W. Hwu

AMSTERDAM • BOSTON • HEIDELBERG • LONDON
NEW YORK • OXFORD • PARIS • SAN DIEGO
SAN FRANCISCO • SINGAPORE • SYDNEY • TOKYO

Morgan Kaufmann Publishers is an imprint of Elsevier

Acquiring Editor: Todd Green
Assistant Editor: Robyn Day
Project Manager: Paul Gottehrer
Designer: Dennis Schaefer

Morgan Kaufmann is an imprint of Elsevier
30 Corporate Drive, Suite 400, Burlington, MA 01803, USA

Library of Congress Cataloging-in-Publication Data
GPU computing gems / editor, Wen-mei W. Hwu.
    p. cm.
  Includes bibliographical references.
  ISBN 978-0-12-384988-5
1. Graphics processing units–Programming. 2. Imaging systems. 3. Computer graphics. 4. Image processing–Digital techniques. I. Hwu, Wen-mei.
  T385.G6875 2011
  006.6–dc22

                    2010047487

British Library Cataloguing-in-Publication Data
A catalogue record for this book is available from the British Library.

For information on all MK publications visit our website at
www.mkp.com

Printed in the United States of America
11 12 13 14 15   11 10 9 8 7 6 5 4 3 2 1

Contents

Editors, Reviewers, and Authors xi
Introduction xix

Wen-mei W. Hwu

SECTION 1 SCIENTIFIC SIMULATION

Robert M. Farber

CHAPTER 1 **GPU-Accelerated Computation and Interactive Display of Molecular Orbitals** 5

John E. Stone, David J. Hardy, Jan Saam, Kirby L. Vandivort, Klaus Schulten

CHAPTER 2 **Large-Scale Chemical Informatics on GPUs** 19

Imran S. Haque, Vijay S. Pande

CHAPTER 3 **Dynamical Quadrature Grids: Applications in Density Functional Calculations** 35

Nathan Luehr, Ivan Ufimtsev, Todd Martinez

CHAPTER 4 **Fast Molecular Electrostatics Algorithms on GPUs** 43

David J. Hardy, John E. Stone, Kirby L. Vandivort, David Gohara, Christopher Rodrigues, Klaus Schulten

CHAPTER 5 **Quantum Chemistry: Propagation of Electronic Structure on a GPU** 59

Jacek Jakowski, Stephan Irle, Keiji Morokuma

CHAPTER 6 **An Efficient CUDA Implementation of the Tree-Based Barnes Hut *n*-Body Algorithm** 75

Martin Burtscher, Keshav Pingali

CHAPTER 7 **Leveraging the Untapped Computation Power of GPUs: Fast Spectral Synthesis Using Texture Interpolation** 93

Richard Townsend, Karthikeyan Sankaralingam, Matthew D. Sinclair

CHAPTER 8 **Black Hole Simulations with CUDA** 103

Frank Herrmann, John Silberholz, Manuel Tiglio

CHAPTER 9 **Treecode and Fast Multipole Method for *N*-Body Simulation with CUDA** 113

Rio Yokota, Lorena A. Barba

CHAPTER 10 Wavelet-Based Density Functional Theory Calculation on Massively
Parallel Hybrid Architectures 133
Luigi Genovese, Matthieu Ospici, Brice Videau, Thierry Deutsch, Jean-François Méhaut

SECTION 2   LIFE SCIENCES

Bertil Schmidt

CHAPTER 11 Accurate Scanning of Sequence Databases with the Smith-Waterman
Algorithm 155
Łukasz Ligowski, Witold R. Rudnicki, Yongchao Liu, Bertil Schmidt

CHAPTER 12 Massive Parallel Computing to Accelerate Genome-Matching 173
Ben Weiss, Mike Bailey

CHAPTER 13 GPU-Supercomputer Acceleration of Pattern Matching 185
Ali Khajeh-Saeed, J. Blair Perot

CHAPTER 14 GPU Accelerated RNA Folding Algorithm 199
Guillaume Rizk, Dominique Lavenier, Sanjay Rajopadhye

CHAPTER 15 Temporal Data Mining for Neuroscience 211
Wu-chun Feng, Yong Cao, Debprakash Patnaik, Naren Ramakrishnan

SECTION 3   STATISTICAL MODELING

Mike Giles

CHAPTER 16 Parallelization Techniques for Random Number Generators 231
Thomas Bradley, Jacques du Toit, Robert Tong, Mike Giles, Paul Woodhams

CHAPTER 17 Monte Carlo Photon Transport on the GPU 247
László Szirmay-Kalos, Balázs Tóth, Milán Magdics

CHAPTER 18 High-Performance Iterated Function Systems 263
Christoph Schied, Johannes Hanika, Holger Dammertz, Hendrik P. A. Lensch

SECTION 4   EMERGING DATA-INTENSIVE APPLICATIONS

Volodymyr Kindratenko

CHAPTER 19 Large-Scale Machine Learning 277
Jerod J. Weinman, Augustus Lidaka, Shitanshu Aggarwal

CHAPTER 20 Multiclass Support Vector Machine 293

Sergio Herrero-Lopez

CHAPTER 21 Template-Driven Agent-Based Modeling and Simulation with CUDA 313

Paul Richmond, Daniela Romano

CHAPTER 22 GPU-Accelerated Ant Colony Optimization 325

Robin M. Weiss

SECTION 5   ELECTRONIC DESIGN AUTOMATION

Sunil P. Khatri

CHAPTER 23 High-Performance Gate-Level Simulation with GP-GPUs 343

Debapriya Chatterjee, Andrew DeOrio, Valeria Bertacco

CHAPTER 24 GPU-Based Parallel Computing for Fast Circuit Optimization 365

Yifang Liu, Jiang Hu

SECTION 6   RAY TRACING AND RENDERING

Austin Robison

CHAPTER 25 Lattice Boltzmann Lighting Models.. 381

Robert Geist, James Westall

CHAPTER 26 Path Regeneration for Random Walks... 401

Jan Novák, Vlastimil Havran, Carsten Dachsbacher

CHAPTER 27 From Sparse Mocap to Highly Detailed Facial Animation 413

Bernd Bickel, Manuel Lang

CHAPTER 28 A Programmable Graphics Pipeline in CUDA for Order-Independent
Transparency 427

Mengcheng Huang, Fang Liu, Xuehui Liu, Enhua Wu

SECTION 7   COMPUTER VISION

James Fung

CHAPTER 29 Fast Graph Cuts for Computer Vision 439

P.J. Narayanan, Vibhav Vineet, Timo Stich

CHAPTER 30 Visual Saliency Model on Multi-GPU... 451

Anis Rahman, Dominique Houzet, Denis Pellerin

CHAPTER 31 Real-Time Stereo on GPGPU Using Progressive Multiresolution Adaptive
Windows 473
Yong Zhao, Gabriel Taubin

CHAPTER 32 Real-Time Speed-Limit-Sign Recognition on an Embedded System
Using a GPU 497
Pinar Muyan-Özçelik, Vladimir Glavtchev, Jeffrey M. Ota, John D. Owens

CHAPTER 33 Haar Classifiers for Object Detection with CUDA 517
Anton Obukhov

SECTION 8 VIDEO AND IMAGE PROCESSING

Timo Stich

CHAPTER 34 Experiences on Image and Video Processing with CUDA and OpenCL 547
Alptekin Temizel, Tugba Halici, Berker Logoglu, Tugba Taskaya Temizel,
Fatih Omruuzun, Ersin Karaman

CHAPTER 35 Connected Component Labeling in CUDA 569
Ondřej Šťava, Bedřich Beneš

CHAPTER 36 Image De-Mosaicing 583
Joe Stam, James Fung

SECTION 9 SIGNAL AND AUDIO PROCESSING

John Roberts

CHAPTER 37 Efficient Automatic Speech Recognition on the GPU 601
Jike Chong, Ekaterina Gonina, Kurt Keutzer

CHAPTER 38 Parallel LDPC Decoding 619
Gabriel Falcao, Vitor Silva, Leonel Sousa

CHAPTER 39 Large-Scale Fast Fourier Transform 629
Yifeng Chen, Xiang Cui, Hong Mei

SECTION 10 MEDICAL IMAGING

Lawrence Tarbox

CHAPTER 40 GPU Acceleration of Iterative Digital Breast Tomosynthesis 647
Dana Schaa, Benjamin Brown, Byunghyun Jang, Perhaad Mistry, Rodrigo Dominguez,
David Kaeli, Richard Moore, Daniel B. Kopans

CHAPTER 41 Parallelization of Katsevich CT Image Reconstruction Algorithm on Generic Multi-Core Processors and GPGPU 659

Abderrahim Benquassmi, Eric Fontaine, Hsien-Hsin S. Lee

CHAPTER 42 3-D Tomographic Image Reconstruction from Randomly Ordered Lines with CUDA 679

Guillem Pratx, Jing-Yu Cui, Sven Prevrhal, Craig S. Levin

CHAPTER 43 Using GPUs to Learn Effective Parameter Settings for GPU-Accelerated Iterative CT Reconstruction Algorithms 693

Wei Xu, Klaus Mueller

CHAPTER 44 Using GPUs to Accelerate Advanced MRI Reconstruction with Field Inhomogeneity Compensation 709

Yue Zhuo, Xiao-Long Wu, Justin P. Haldar, Thibault Marin, Wen-mei W. Hwu, Zhi-Pei Liang, Bradley P. Sutton

CHAPTER 45 $\ell1$ Minimization in $\ell1$-SPIRiT Compressed Sensing MRI Reconstruction 723

Mark Murphy, Miki Lustig

CHAPTER 46 Medical Image Processing Using GPU-Accelerated ITK Image Filters 737

Won-Ki Jeong, Hanspeter Pfister, Massimiliano Fatica

CHAPTER 47 Deformable Volumetric Registration Using B-Splines 751

James Shackelford, Nagarajan Kandasamy, Gregory Sharp

CHAPTER 48 Multiscale Unbiased Diffeomorphic Atlas Construction on Multi-GPUs 771

Linh Ha, Jens Krüger, Sarang Joshi, Cláudio T. Silva

CHAPTER 49 GPU-Accelerated Brain Connectivity Reconstruction and Visualization in Large-Scale Electron Micrographs 793

Won-Ki Jeong, Hanspeter Pfister, Johanna Beyer, Markus Hadwiger

CHAPTER 50 Fast Simulation of Radiographic Images Using a Monte Carlo X-Ray Transport Algorithm Implemented in CUDA 813

Andreu Badal, Aldo Badano

Index 831

Editors, Reviewers, and Authors

Editor-In-Chief
Wen-mei W. Hwu, University of Illinois at Urbana Champaign

Managing Editor
Andrew Schuh, University of Illinois at Urbana Champaign

NVIDIA Editor
Nadeem Mohammad, NVIDIA

Area Editors
Robert M. Farber, Pacific Northwest National Laboratory (Section 1)

James Fung, NVIDIA (Section 7)

Mike Giles, Oxford University (Section 3)

Sunil P. Khatri, Texas A&M University (Section 5)

Volodymyr Kindratenko, University of Illinois at Urbana Champaign (Section 4)

John Roberts, NVIDIA (Section 9)

Austin Robison, NVIDIA (Section 6)

Bertil Schmidt, Nanyang Technical University (Section 2)

Timo Stich, NVIDIA (Section 8)

Lawrence Tarbox, Washington University in St. Louis (Section 10)

Reviewers
François Beaune, /*jupiter jazz*/ visual effects consultants

Jiawen Chen, Massachusetts Institute of Technology

Andrea Di Blas, University of California, Santa Cruz

Roshan Dsouza, University of Wisconsin-Milwaukee

Richard Edgar, Harvard University

Martin Eisemann, Technical University, Braunschweig

John Estabrook, University of Illinois at Urbana-Champaign

Cass Everitt, NVIDIA

Reza Farivar, University of Illinois at Urbana-Champaign

Vladimir Frolov, NVIDIA

Vladimir Glavtchev, BMW Technology Office

Kanupriya Gulati, Intel Corporation

Trym Vegard Haavardsholm, Norwegian Defense Research Establishment

Ken Hawick, University of Auckland, New Zealand

Jared Hoberock, NVIDIA

Tim Kaldewey, Oracle

Vinay Karkala, Advanced Micro Devices

Christian Linz, Technical University, Braunschweig

Christian Lipski, Technical University, Braunschweig

Weiguo Liu, Nanyang Technological University

Dave Luebke, NVIDIA

W. James MacLean, Google

Corey Manders, A*STAR Institute for Infocomm Research

Morgan McGuire, Williams College, Massachusetts

Derek Nowrouzezahrai, Disney Research Zurich

Ming Ouyang, University of Louisville, Kentucky

Steven Parker, NVIDIA

Kalyan Perumalla, Oak Ridge National Laboratory

Nicolas Pinto, Massachusetts Institute of Technology

Tobias Preis, Johannes Gutenberg University

Ramtin Shams, Australian National University

Craig Steffen, University of Illinois at Urbana-Champaign

Andrei Tatarinov, NVIDIA

Cristina Nader Vasconcelos, Instituto de Computação, Universidade Federal Fluminense, Brazil

Ben Weiss, Shell and Slate Software

Ruediger Westermann, Technical University, Munich

Jan Woetzel, MeVis Medical Solutions, AG

Kesheng Wu, Berkeley Lab, University of California

Ren Wu, HP Labs

Weihang Zhu, Lamar University, Texas

Authors

Shitanshu Aggarwal, Grinnell College, Iowa (Chapter 19)

Mike Bailey, Oregon State University (Chapter 12)

Andreu Badal, US Food and Drug Administration (CDRH/OSEL/DIAM) (Chapter 50)

Aldo Badano, US Food and Drug Administration (CDRH/OSEL/DIAM) (Chapter 50)

Lorena A. Barba, Boston University (Chapter 9)

Bedřich Beneš, Purdue University, Indiana (Chapter 35)

Abderrahim Benquassmi, Georgia Institute of Technology (Chapter 41)

Valeria Bertacco, University of Michigan (Chapter 23)

Johanna Beyer, King Abdullah University of Science and Technology (KAUST) (Chapter 49)

Bernd Bickel, Disney Research, Zurich (Chapter 27)

Thomas Bradley, NVIDIA (Chapter 16)

Benjamin Brown, Northeastern University (Chapter 40)

Martin Burtscher, Texas State University, San Marcos (Chapter 6)

Yong Cao, Virginia Tech (Chapter 15)

Debapriya Chatterjee, University of Michigan (Chapter 23)

Yifeng Chen, Peking University (Chapter 39)

Jike Chong, University of California, Berkeley (Chapter 37)

Jing-Yu Cui, Stanford University (Chapter 42)

Xiang Cui, Peking University (Chapter 39)

Carsten Dachsbacher, Karlsruhe Institute of Technology (Chapter 26)

Holger Dammertz, Ulm University (Chapter 18)

Andrew DeOrio, University of Michigan (Chapter 23)

Thierry Deutsch, Laboratoire de Simulation Atomistique (Chapter 10)

Rodrigo Dominguez, Northeastern University (Chapter 40)

Jacques Du Toit, Numerical Algorithms Group (Chapter 16)

Gabriel Falcao, University of Coimbra (Chapter 38)

Massimiliano Fatica, NVIDIA (Chapter 46)

Wu-chu Feng, Virginia Tech and Wake Forest University (Chapter 15)

Eric Fontaine, Georgia Institute of Technology (Chapter 41)

James Fung, NVIDIA (Chapter 36)

Robert Geist, Clemson University (Chapter 25)

Luigi Genovese, European Synchrotron Radiation Facility (Chapter 10)

Mike Giles, Oxford University (Chapter 16)

Vladimir Glavtchev, BMW Group Technology Office (Chapter 32)

David Gohara, Saint Louis University School of Medicine (Chapter 4)

Ekaterina Gonina, University of California, Berkeley (Chapter 37)

Linh Ha, University of Utah (Chapter 48)

Markus Hadwiger, King Abdullah University of Science and Technology (KAUST) (Chapter 49)

Justin P. Haldar, University of Illinois at Urbana-Champaign (Chapter 44)

Tugba Halici, Middle East Technical University (Chapter 34)

Johannes Hanika, Ulm University (Chapter 18)

Imran S. Haque, Stanford University (Chapter 2)

David J. Hardy, University of Illinois at Urbana-Champaign (Chapters 1 and 4)

Vlastimil Havran, Czech Technical University in Prague (Chapter 26)

Sergio Herrero-Lopez, Massachusetts Institute of Technology (Chapter 20)

Frank Herrmann, University of Maryland, College Park (Chapter 8)

Dominique Houzet, GIPSA-lab (Chapter 30)

Jiang Hu, Texas A&M University (Chapter 24)

Mengcheng Huang, Chinese Academy of Sciences (Chapter 28)

Wen-mei W. Hwu, University of Illinois at Urbana-Champaign (Chapter 44)

Stephan Irle, Nagoya University (Chapter 5)

Jacek Jakowski, National Institute for Computational Sciences (Chapter 5)

Byunghyun Jang, Northeastern University (Chapter 40)

Won-Ki Jeong, Harvard University (Chapters 46 and 49)

Sarang Joshi, University of Utah, Salt Lake City (Chapter 48)

David Kaeli, Northeastern University (Chapter 40)

Nagarajan Kandasamy, Drexel University (Chapter 47)

Ersin Karaman, Middle East Technical University (Chapter 34)

Kurt Keutzer, University of California, Berkeley (Chapter 37)

Ali Khajeh-Saeed, University of Massachusetts, Amherst (Chapter 13)

Daniel B. Kopans, Massachusetts General Hospital (Chapter 40)

Jens Krüger, Interactive Visualization and Data Analysis Group, Saarbrücken (Chapter 48)

Manuel Lang, Disney Research, Zurich (Chapter 27)

Dominique Lavenier, École Normale Supérieure de Cachan (Chapter 14)

Hsien-Hsin S. Lee, Georgia Institute of Technology (Chapter 41)

Hendrik Lensch, Ulm University (Chapter 18)

Craig S. Levin, Stanford University (Chapter 42)

Zhi-Pei Liang, University of Illinois at Urbana-Champaign (Chapter 44)

Augustus Lidaka, Grinnell College (Chapter 19)

Łukasz Ligowski, University of Warsaw (Chapter 11)

Fang Liu, Chinese Academy of Sciences (Chapter 28)

Xuehui Liu, Chinese Academy of Sciences (Chapter 28)

Yifang Liu, Texas A&M University (Chapter 24)

Yongchao Liu, Nanyang Technological University (Chapter 11)

Berker Logoglu, Middle East Technical University (Chapter 34)

Nathan Luehr, Stanford University and SLAC National Accelerator Laboratory (Chapter 3)

Miki Lustig, University of California, Berkeley (Chapter 45)

Milán Magdics, Budapest University of Technology and Economics (Chapter 17)

Thibault Marin, Illinois Institute of Technology (Chapter 44)

Todd Martinez, Stanford University and SLAC National Accelerator Laboratory (Chapter 3)

Jean-François Méhaut, Universite Joseph Fourier (Chapter 10)

Hong Mei, Peking University (Chapter 39)

Perhaad Mistry, Northeastern University (Chapter 40)

Richard Moore, Massachusetts General Hospital (Chapter 40)

Keiji Morokuma, Kyoto University (Chapter 5)

Klaus Mueller, State University of New York, Stony Brook (Chapter 43)

Mark Murphy, University of California, Berkeley (Chapter 45)

Pinar Muyan-Özçelik, University of California, Davis (Chapter 32)

P. J. Narayanan, International Institute of Information Technology Hyderabad (Chapter 29)

Jan Novák, Karlsruhe Institute of Technology (Chapter 26)

Anton Obukhov, NVIDIA (Chapter 33)

Fatih Omruuzun, Middle East Technical University (Chapter 34)

Matthieu Ospici, Laboratoire d'Informatique de Grenoble (Chapter 10)

Jeffery M. Ota, BMW Group Technology Office (Chapter 32)

John D. Owens, University of California, Davis (Chapter 32)

Vijay S. Pande, Stanford University (Chapter 2)

Debprakash Patnaik, Virginia Tech (Chapter 15)

Denis Pellerin, GIPSA-lab (Chapter 30)

J. Blair Perot, University of Massachusetts, Amherst (Chapter 13)

Hanspeter Pfister, Harvard University (Chapters 46 and 49)

Keshay Pingali, Texas State University, San Marcos (Chapter 6)

Guillem Pratx, Stanford University (Chapter 42)

Sven Prevrhal, Philips Healthcare (Chapter 42)

Anis Rahman, GIPSA-lab (Chapter 30)

Sanjay Rajopadhye, Colorado State University (Chapter 14)

Naren Ramakrishnan, Virginia Tech (Chapter 15)

Paul Richmond, University of Sheffield (Chapter 21)

Guillaume Rizk, Institut de Recherche en Informatique et Systèmes Aléatoires, Université de Rennes (Chapter 14)

Christopher Rodrigues, University of Illinois at Urbana-Champaign (Chapter 4)

Daniela Romano, University of Sheffield (Chapter 21)

Witold R. Rudnicki, University of Warsaw (Chapter 11)

Jan Saam, University of Illinois at Urbana-Champaign (Chapter 1)

Karthikeyan Sankaralingam, University of Wisconsin-Madison (Chapter 7)

Dana Schaa, Northeastern University (Chapter 40)

Christoph Schied, Ulm University (Chapter 18)

Bertil Schmidt, Nanyang Technological University (Chapter 11)

Klaus Schulten, University of Illinois at Urbana-Champaign (Chapters 1 and 4)

James Shackleford, Drexel University (Chapter 47)

Gregory Sharp, Massachusetts General Hospital (Chapter 47)

John Silberholz, University of Maryland (Chapter 8)

Claudio Silva, University of Utah (Chapter 48)

Vitor Silva, University of Coimbra (Chapter 38)

Matthew D. Sinclair, University of Wisconsin-Madison (Chapter 7)

Leonel Sousa, Technical University of Lisbon (Chapter 38)

Joe Stam, NVIDIA (Chapter 36)

Ondřej Štava, Purdue University (Chapter 35)

Timo Stich, NVIDIA (Chapter 29)

John E. Stone, University of Illinois at Urbana-Champaign (Chapters 1 and 4)

Bradley P. Sutton, University of Illinois at Urbana-Champaign (Chapter 44)

László Szirmay-Kalos, Budapest University of Technology and Economics (Chapter 17)

Gabriel Taubin, Brown University (Chapter 31)

Alptekin Temizel, Middle East Technical University (Chapter 34)

Tugba Taskaya Temizel, Middle East Technical University (Chapter 34)

Manuel Tiglio, University of Maryland (Chapter 8)

Robert Tong, Numerical Algorithms Group(Chapter 16)

Balázs Tóth, Budapest University of Technology and Economics (Chapter 17)

Richard Townsend, University of Wisconsin-Madison (Chapter 7)

Ivan Ufimtsev, Stanford University and SLAC National Accelerator Labortory (Chapter 3)

Kirby L. Vandivort, University of Illinois at Urbana-Champaign (Chapters 1 and 4)

Brice Videau, Laboratoire de Simulation Atomistique, Grenoble (Chapter 10)

Vibhav Vineet, International Institute of Information Technology, Hyderabad (Chapter 29)

Jerod J. Weinman, Grinnell College (Chapter 19)

Ben Weiss, Oregon State University (Chapter 12)

Robin M. Weiss, Macalester College (Chapter 22)

James Westall, Clemson University (Chapter 25)

Paul Woodhams, Numerical Algorithms Group (Chapter 16)

Enhua Wu, Chinese Academy of Sciences (Chapter 28)

Xiao-Long Wu, University of Illinois at Urbana-Champaign (Chapter 44)

Wei Xu, State University of New York, Stony Brook (Chapter 43)

Rio Yokota, Brown University (Chapter 9)

Yong Zhao, Brown University (Chapter 31)

Yue Zhuo, University of Illinois at Urbana-Champaign (Chapter 44)

Introduction

STATE OF GPU COMPUTING

We are entering the golden age of GPU computing. Since the introduction of CUDA in 2007, more than 100 million computers with CUDA-capable GPUs have been shipped to end users. Unlike the previous GPGPU shader programming models, CUDA supports parallel programming in C. From my own experience in teaching CUDA programming, C programmers can begin to write basic CUDA programs after only attending one lecture and reading one textbook chapter. With such a low barrier of entry, researchers all over the world have been engaged in developing new algorithms and applications to take advantage of the extreme floating point execution throughout these GPUs.

Today, there is a large community of GPU computing practitioners. Many of them have reported a 10 to 100 times speedup of their applications with GPU computing. To put this into perspective, with the historical 2X performance growth every 2 years, these researchers are experiencing the equivalent of time travel of 8 to 12 years. That is, they are getting the performance today that they would have to wait for 8 to 12 years if they went for the "free-ride" advancement of performance in microprocessors. Interestingly, such "free ride" advancement is no longer available. Furthermore, once they develop their application in CUDA, they will likely see continued performance growth of 2X for every two years from this day forward.

After discussing with numerous researchers, I have reached the conclusion that many of them are solving similar algorithm problems in their programming efforts. Although they are working on diverse applications, they often end up developing similar algorithmic strategies. The idea of *GPU Computing Gems* is to provide a convenient means for application developers in diverse application areas to benefit from each other's experience. In this volume, we have collected 50 gem articles written by researchers in 10 diverse areas. Each gems article reports a successful application experience in GPU computing. These articles describe the techniques or "secret sauce" that contributed to the success. The authors highlight the potential applicability of their techniques to other application areas. In our editorial process, we have emphasized the accessibility of these gems to researchers in other areas.

When we issued the call for proposals for the first *GPU Computing Gems*, we received more than 280 submissions, an overwhelming response. After careful review, we accepted 110 proposals that have a high likelihood of making valuable contributions to other application developers. Many high-quality proposals were not accepted because of concerns that they may not be accessible to a large audience. With so many accepted proposals, we were forced to divide these gems into two volumes. This volume covers 50 gems in the application areas of scientific simulation, life sciences, statistical modeling, emerging data-intensive applications, electronic design automation, ray tracing and rendering, computer vision, video and image processing, signal and audio processing, and medical imaging.

Each gem is first edited by an area editor who is a GPU computing expert in that area. This is followed by my own editing of these articles.

I would like to thank the people who have worked tirelessly on this project. Nadeem Mohammad at NVIDIA and Andrew Schuh at UIUC have done so much heavy lifting for this project. Without them, it would have been impossible for me to coordinate so many authors and area editors. My area editors, whose names are in front of each section of this volume, have volunteered their valuable time and energy to improve the quality of the gems. They worked closely with the authors to make sure that the gems indeed meet high technical standards while remain accessible to a wide audience. I would like to thank all the authors who have shared their innovative work with the GPU computing community. All authors have worked hard to respond to our requests for improvements. Finally, I would like to acknowledge Manju Hegde, who championed the creation of *GPU Computing Gems* and pursued me to serve as the editor in chief. It has been a true privilege to work with all of these great people.

Online Resources

Visit `http://mkp.com/gpu-computing-gems` and click the ONLINE RESOURCES tab to connect to gpucomputing.net, the vibrant official community site for GPU computing, where you can download source code examples for most chapters and join discussions with other readers and GPU developers. You'll also find links to additional material including chapter walk-through videos and full-color versions of many figures from the book.

Scientific Simulation
Area Editor's Introduction
Robert M. Farber

1 GPU-Accelerated Computation and Interactive Display of Molecular Orbitals 5

2 Large-Scale Chemical Informatics on GPUs 19

3 Dynamical Quadrature Grids: Applications in Density Functional Calculations 35

4 Fast Molecular Electrostatics Algorithms on GPUs 43

5 Quantum Chemistry: Propagation of Electronic Structure on a GPU 59

6 An Efficient CUDA Implementation of the Tree-Based Barnes Hut n-Body Algorithm 75

7 Leveraging the Untapped Computation Power of GPUs: Fast Spectral Synthesis Using Texture Interpolation 93

8 Black Hole Simulations with CUDA 103

9 Treecode and Fast Multipole Method for N-Body Simulation with CUDA 113

10 Wavelet-Based Density Functional Theory Calculation on Massively Parallel Hybrid Architectures 133

THE STATE OF GPU COMPUTING IN SCIENTIFIC SIMULATION

GPU computing is revolutionizing scientific simulation by providing one to two orders of magnitude of increased computing performance per GPU at price points even students can afford. Exciting things are happening with this technology in the hands of the masses, as reflected by the applications, CUDA Gems, and the extraordinary number of papers that have appeared in the literature since CUDA was first introduced in February 2007.

Technology that provides two or more orders of magnitude of increased computational capability is disruptive and has the potential to fundamentally affect scientific research by removing time-to-discovery barriers. I cannot help getting excited by the potential as simulations that previously would have taken a year or more to complete can now be finished in days. Better scientific insight also becomes possible because researchers can work with more data and have the ability to utilize more accurate, albeit computationally expensive, approximations and numerical methods. We are now entering the era where hybrid clusters and supercomputers containing large numbers of GPUs are being built and used around the world. As a result, many researchers (and funding agencies) now have to rethink their computational models and invest in software to create scalable, high-performance applications based on this technology. The potential is there, and some lucky researchers may find themselves with a Galilean first opportunity to see, study, and model using exquisitely detailed data from projects utilizing GPU technology and these hybrid systems.

IN THIS SECTION

The chapters in this section provide gems of insight both in thought and CUDA implementation to map challenging scientific simulation problems to GPU technology. Techniques to work with irregular grids, dynamic surfaces, treecodes, and far-field calculations are presented. All of these CUDA gems can be adapted and should provide food for thought in solving challenging computational problems in many areas. Innovative solutions are discussed, including just-in-time (JIT) compilation; appropriate and effective use of fast on-chip GPU memory resources across GPU technology generations; the application of texture unit arithmetic to augment GPU computational and global memory performance; and the creation of solutions that can scale across multiple GPUs in a distributed environment. General kernel optimization principles are also provided in many chapters. Some of the kernels presented require fewer than 200 lines of CUDA code, yet still provide impressive performance.

In Chapter 1: Evaluating molecular orbitals on 3-D lattices is a common problem in molecular visualization. This chapter discusses the design trade-offs in the popular VMD (visual molecular dynamics) software system plus the appropriate and effective use of fast on-chip GPU memory resources across various generations of GPUs. Several kernel optimization principles are provided. To account for varying problem size and GPU performance regimes, an innovative just-in-time (JIT) kernel compilation technique is utilized.

In Chapter 2: The authors discuss the techniques they used to adapt the LIGO string similarity algorithm to run efficiently on GPUs and avoid the memory bandwidth and conditional operations that limit parallelism in the CPU implementation. These techniques as well as the discussion on minimizing CPU-GPU transfer overhead and exploiting thread level parallelism should benefit readers in many areas; not just those interested in large scale chemical informatics.

In Chapter 3: This chapter discusses a GPU-accelerated dynamic quadrature grid method where the grid points move over the course of the calculation. The merits of several parallelization schemes, mixed precision arithmetic as an optimization technique, and problems arising from branching within a warp are discussed.

In Chapter 4: GPU kernels are presented that calculate electrostatic potential maps on structured grids containing a large amount of fine-grained data parallelism. Approaches to regularize the computation work are discussed along with kernel loop optimizations and implementation notes on how to best use the GPU memory subsystem. All of this is phrased in the context of the popular VMD (visual molecular dynamics) and APBS (Adaptive Poisson-Boltzmann Solver) software packages.

In Chapter 5: Direct molecular dynamics (MD) requires repeated calculation of the potential energy surface obtained from electronic structure calculations. This chapter shows how this calculation can be rethought to propagate the electronic structure without diagonalization — a time-consuming step that is difficult to implement on GPUs. Other topics discussed include efficiently using CUBLAS and the integration of CUDA within a FORTRAN framework.

In Chapter 6: Irregular tree-based data structures are a challenge given the GPGPU memory subsystem likes coalesced memory accesses. This chapter describes a number of techniques — both novel and conventional — to reduce main memory accesses on an irregular tree-based data structure. All the methods run on the GPU.

In Chapter 7: The GRASSY spectral synthesis platform is described, which utilizes GPUs to address the computational needs of asteroseismology. In particular, this chapter demonstrates an innovative use of interpolation by CUDA texture memory to augment arithmetic performance and reduce memory access overhead. The low precision of texture memory arithmetic is discussed and shown to not affect solution accuracy. Mesh building and rasterization are also covered.

In Chapter 8: Exploring the parameter space of a complex dynamical system is an important facet of scientific simulation. Many problems require integration of a coupled set of ordinary differential equations (ODEs). Rather than parallelizing a single integration, the authors use CUDA to turn the GPU into a survey engine that performs many integrations at once. With this technology, scientists can examine more of the phase space of the problem to gain a better understanding of the dynamics of the simulation. In the case of black holes in spirals, GPU technology might have a significant impact in the quest for direct measurement of gravity waves. Robustness across GPUs in a distributed MPI environment is also discussed.

In Chapter 9: As this chapter shows, constructing fast N-body algorithms is far from a formidable task. Basic kernels are discussed that achieve substantial speedups (15x to 150x) in fewer than 200 lines of CUDA code. These same kernels extend previous GPU gems N-body CUDA mappings to encompass parallel far-field approximations that are useful for astrophysics, acoustics, molecular dynamics, particle simulation, electromagnetics, and boundary integral formulations. Other topics include structuring the data to preserve coalesced memory accesses and balancing parallelism and data reuse through the use of tiles.

In Chapter 10: The authors discuss the GPU-specific thought and implementation details for BigDFT, a massively parallel implementation of a full DFT (density functional theory) code for quantum chemistry that runs on hybrid clusters and supercomputers containing many GPUs. From the unconventional use of Daubechies wavelets, which are well suited for GPU-accelerated environments, the authors progress to a discussion of scalability and integration in a distributed runtime environment.

GPU-Accelerated Computation and Interactive Display of Molecular Orbitals

1

John E. Stone, David J. Hardy, Jan Saam, Kirby L. Vandivort, Klaus Schulten

In this chapter, we present several graphics processing unit (GPU) algorithms for evaluating molecular orbitals on three-dimensional lattices, as is commonly used for molecular visualization. For each kernel, we describe necessary design trade-offs, applicability to various problem sizes, and performance on different generations of GPU hardware. We then demonstrate the appropriate and effective use of fast on-chip GPU memory subsystems for access to key data structures, show several GPU kernel optimization principles, and explore the application of advanced techniques such as dynamic kernel generation and just-in-time (JIT) kernel compilation techniques.[1]

1.1 INTRODUCTION, PROBLEM STATEMENT, AND CONTEXT

The GPU kernels described here form the basis for the high-performance molecular orbital display algorithms in VMD [2], a popular molecular visualization and analysis tool. VMD (Visual Molecular Dynamics) is a software system designed for displaying, animating, and analyzing large biomolecular systems. More than 33,000 users have registered and downloaded the most recent VMD software, version 1.8.7. Due to its versatility and user-extensibility, VMD is also capable of displaying other large datasets, such as sequence data, results of quantum chemistry calculations, and volumetric data. While VMD is designed to run on a diverse range of hardware — laptops, desktops, clusters, and supercomputers — it is primarily used as a scientific workstation application for interactive 3-D visualization and analysis. For computations that run too long for interactive use, VMD can also be used in a batch mode to render movies for later use. A motivation for using GPU acceleration in VMD is to make slow batch-mode jobs fast enough for interactive use, thereby drastically improving the productivity of scientific investigations. With CUDA-enabled GPUs widely available in desktop PCs, such acceleration can have a broad impact on the VMD user community. To date, multiple aspects of VMD have been accelerated with the NVIDIA Compute Unified Device Architecture (CUDA), including electrostatic potential calculation, ion placement, molecular orbital calculation and display, and imaging of gas migration pathways in proteins.

Visualization of molecular orbitals (MOs) is a helpful step in analyzing the results of quantum chemistry calculations. The key challenge involved in the display of molecular orbitals is the rapid evaluation

---

[1]This work was supported by the National Institutes of Health, under grant P41-RR05969. Portions of this chapter © 2009 Association for Computing Machinery, Inc. Reprinted by permission [1].

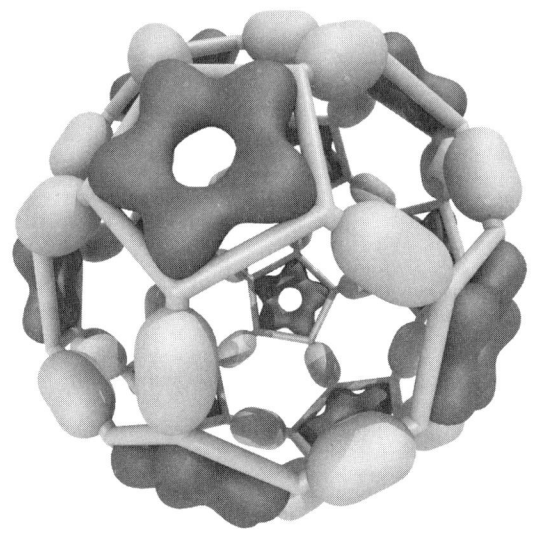

FIGURE 1.1

An example of MO isovalue surfaces resulting from the lattice of wavefunction amplitudes computed for a Carbon-60 molecule. Positive valued isosurfaces are shown in dark grey, and negative valued isosurfaces are shown in light grey.

of these functions on a three-dimensional lattice; the resulting data can then be used for plotting iso-contours or isosurfaces for visualization as shown in Fig. 1.1, and for other types of analyses. Most existing software packages that render MOs perform calculations on the CPU and have not been heavily optimized. Thus, they require runtimes of tens to hundreds of seconds depending on the complexity of the molecular system and spatial resolution of the MO discretization and subsequent surface plots.

With sufficient performance (two orders of magnitude faster than traditional CPU algorithms), a fast real-space lattice computation enables interactive display of even very large electronic structures and makes it possible to smoothly animate trajectories of orbital dynamics. Prior to the use of the GPU, this could be accomplished only through extensive batch-mode precalculation and preloading of time-varying lattice data into memory, making it impractical for everyday interactive visualization tasks. Efficient single-GPU algorithms are capable of evaluating molecular orbital lattices up to 186 times faster than a single CPU core (see Table 1.1), enabling MOs to be rapidly computed and animated on the fly for the first time. A multi-GPU version of our algorithm has been benchmarked at up to 419 times the performance of a single CPU core (see Table 1.2).

1.2 CORE METHOD

Since our target application is visualization focused, we are concerned with achieving interactive rendering performance while maintaining sufficient accuracy. The CUDA programming language enables GPU hardware features — inaccessible in existing programmable shading languages — to be exploited

Table 1.1 Single-GPU comparison of MO kernel performance for the carbon-60 test case relative to CPU reference codes. The devices compared below are 2.4 GHz Intel Core 2 Q6600 CPU (Q6600), 2.6 GHz Intel Xeon X5550 CPU (X5550), NVIDIA GeForce 8800 GTX GPU (G880), NVIDIA GeForce GTX 280 GPU (G280), NVIDIA Tesla C2050 GPU (C2050), and NVIDIA GeForce GTX 480 GPU (G480). Timing results include all host-GPU memory transfers and kernel launches required for evaluation of the molecular orbital for a single combination of parameters and for a single simulation time step. These timings do not include one-time disk I/O and associated sorting and preprocessing associated with the initial loading of simulation log files.

Device	Kernel	CPU Cores	Runtime (sec)	Speedup vs. Q6600	Speedup vs. X5550
Q6600	icc-sse-cephes	1	46.58	1.00	0.65
Q6600	icc-libc	4	37.38	1.24	0.82
Q6600	icc-sse-cephes	4	11.74	3.97	2.61
X5550	icc-sse-cephes	1	30.64	1.52	1.00
X5550	icc-sse-cephes	4	7.82	5.95	3.92
X5550	icc-sse-cephes	8	4.13	11.27	7.42
G8800	tiled-shared	1	0.89	52.0	34.4
G8800	const-cache	1	0.57	81.7	54.7
G280	tiled-shared	1	0.46	100	66.6
G280	const-cache	1	0.37	126	82.8
C2050	tiled-shared	1	0.46	100	66.6
C2050	L1-cache (16 kB)	1	0.33	141	92.8
C2050	const-cache	1	0.31	149	98.8
C2050	const-cache, zero-copy	1	0.30	155	102
G480	tiled-shared	1	0.37	126	82.8
G480	L1-cache (16 kB)	1	0.27	172	113
G480	const-cache	1	0.26	181	117
G480	const-cache, zero-copy	1	0.25	186	122
G480	JIT, const-cache	1	0.142	328	215
G480	JIT, const-cache, zero-copy	1	0.135	345	227

for higher performance, and it enables the use of multiple GPUs to accelerate computation further. Another advantage of using CUDA is that the results can be used for nonvisualization purposes.

Our approach combines several performance enhancement strategies. First, we use the host CPU to carefully organize input data and coefficients, eliminating redundancies and enforcing a sorted ordering that benefits subsequent GPU memory traversal patterns. The evaluation of molecular orbitals on a 3-D lattice is performed on one or more GPUs; the 3-D lattice is decomposed into 2-D planar slices, each of which is assigned to a GPU and computed. The workload is dynamically scheduled across the pool of GPUs to balance load on GPUs of varying capability. Depending on the specific attributes of the problem, one of three hand-coded GPU kernels is algorithmically selected to optimize performance.

Table 1.2 Single-machine multi-GPU performance for computation of a high-resolution ($172 \times 173 \times 169$) molecular orbital lattice for C_{60}. Speedup results are compared against the single-core SSE CPU results presented in Table 1.1.

Device	CPU Workers	Runtime (sec)	Speedup vs. Q6600	Speedup vs. X5550	Multi-GPU Efficiency
Quadro 5800	1	0.381	122	80	100.0%
Tesla C1060	2	0.199	234	154	95.5%
Tesla C1060	3	0.143	325	214	88.6%
Tesla C1060	4	0.111	419	276	85.7%

The three kernels are designed to use different combinations of GPU memory systems to yield peak memory bandwidth and arithmetic throughput depending on whether the input data can fit into constant memory, shared memory, or L1/L2 cache (in the case of recently released NVIDIA "Fermi" GPUs). One useful optimization involves the use of zero-copy memory access techniques based on the CUDA mapped host memory feature to eliminate latency associated with calls to `cudaMemcpy()`. Another optimization involves dynamically generating a problem-specific GPU kernel "on the fly" using just-in-time (JIT) compilation techniques, thereby eliminating various sources of overhead that exist in the three general precoded kernels.

1.3 ALGORITHMS, IMPLEMENTATIONS, AND EVALUATIONS

A molecular orbital (MO) represents a statistical state in which an electron can be found in a molecule, where the MO's spatial distribution is correlated with the associated electron's probability density. Visualization of MOs is an important task for understanding the chemistry of molecular systems. MOs appeal to the chemist's intuition, and inspection of the MOs aids in explaining chemical reactivities. Some popular software tools with these capabilities include MacMolPlt [3], Molden [4], Molekel [5], and VMD [2].

The calculations required for visualizing MOs are computationally demanding, and existing quantum chemistry visualization programs are only fast enough to interactively compute MOs for only small molecules on a relatively coarse lattice. At the time of this writing, only VMD and MacMolPlt support multicore CPUs, and only VMD uses GPUs to accelerate MO computations. A great opportunity exists to improve upon the capabilities of existing tools in terms of interactivity, visual display quality, and scalability to larger and more complex molecular systems.

1.3.1 Mathematical Background

In this section we provide a short introduction to MOs, basis sets, and their underlying equations. Interested readers are directed to seek further details from computational chemistry texts and review articles [6, 7]. Quantum chemistry packages solve the electronic Schrödinger equation $H\Psi = E\Psi$ for a given system. Molecular orbitals are the solutions produced by these packages. MOs are the eigenfunctions Ψ_ν for expression of the molecular wavefunction Ψ, with H the Hamiltonian operator and E the system energy. The wavefunction determines molecular properties, for instance, the one-electron density is $\rho(\mathbf{r}) = |\Psi(\mathbf{r})|^2$. The visualization of the molecular orbitals resulting from quantum chemistry calculations requires evaluating the wavefunction on a 3-D lattice so that isovalue surfaces can be computed and displayed. With minor modifications, the algorithms and approaches we present for evaluating the wavefunction can be adapted to compute other molecular properties such as charge density, the molecular electrostatic potential, or multipole moments.

Each MO Ψ_ν can be expressed as a linear combination over a set of K basis functions Φ_κ,

$$\Psi_\nu = \sum_{\kappa=1}^{K} c_{\nu\kappa} \Phi_\kappa, \tag{1.1}$$

where $c_{\nu\kappa}$ are coefficients contained in the quantum chemistry calculation output files, and used as input for our algorithms. The basis functions used by the vast majority of quantum chemical calculations are atom-centered functions that approximate the solution of the Schrödinger equation for a single hydrogen atom with one electron, so-called atomic orbitals. For increased computational efficiency, Gaussian type orbitals (GTOs) are used to model the basis functions, rather than the exact solutions for the hydrogen atom:

$$\Phi_{i,j,k}^{\text{GTO}}(\mathbf{R}, \zeta) = N_{\zeta ijk} x^i y^j z^k e^{-\zeta R^2}. \tag{1.2}$$

The exponential factor ζ is defined by the basis set; i, j, and k are used to modulate the functional shape; and $N_{\zeta ijk}$ is a normalization factor that follows from the basis set definition. The distance from a basis function's center (nucleus) to a point in space is represented by the vector $\mathbf{R} = \{x, y, z\}$ of length $R = |\mathbf{R}|$.

The exponential term in Eq. 1.2 determines the radial decay of the function. Composite basis functions known as contracted GTOs (CGTOs) are composed of a linear combination of P individual GTO *primitives* in order to accurately describe the radial behavior of atomic orbitals.

$$\Phi_{i,j,k}^{\text{CGTO}}(\mathbf{R}, \{c_p\}, \{\zeta_p\}) = \sum_{p=1}^{P} c_p \Phi_{i,j,k}^{\text{GTO}}(\mathbf{R}, \zeta_p). \tag{1.3}$$

The set of contraction coefficients $\{c_p\}$ and associated exponents $\{\zeta_p\}$ defining the CGTO are contained in the quantum chemistry simulation output.

CGTOs are classified into different *shells* based on the sum $l = i + j + k$ of the exponents of the x, y, and z factors. The shells are designated by letters s, p, d, f, and g for $l = 0, 1, 2, 3, 4$, respectively, where we explicitly list here the most common shell types but note that higher-numbered shells are occasionally used. The set of indices for a shell is also referred to as the *angular momenta* of that shell. We establish an alternative indexing of the angular momenta based on the shell number l and a systematic indexing m over the possible number of sums $l = i + j + k$, where $M_l = \binom{l+2}{l}$ counts the number of combinations and $m = 0, \ldots, M_l - 1$ references the set $\{(i, j, k) : i + j + k = l\}$.

The linear combination defining the MO Ψ_ν must also sum contributions from each of the N atoms of the molecule and the L_n shells of each atom n. The entire expression, now described in terms of the data output from a QM package, for an MO wavefunction evaluated at a point $\mathbf{r}$ in space then becomes

$$\Psi_\nu(\mathbf{r}) = \sum_{\kappa=1}^{K} c_{\nu\kappa}\,\Phi_\kappa$$

$$= \sum_{n=1}^{N} \sum_{l=0}^{L_n-1} \sum_{m=0}^{M_l-1} c_{\nu nlm}\,\Phi_{n,l,m}^{\mathrm{CGTO}}(\mathbf{R}_n,\{c\},\{\zeta\}), \tag{1.4}$$

where we have replaced $c_{\nu\kappa}$ by $c_{\nu nlm}$, with the vectors $\mathbf{R}_n = \mathbf{r} - \mathbf{r}_n$ connecting the position $\mathbf{r}_n$ of the nucleus of atom n to the desired spatial coordinate $\mathbf{r}$. We have dropped the subscript p from the set of contraction coefficients $\{c\}$ and exponents $\{\zeta\}$ with the understanding that each CGTO requires an additional summation over the primitives, as expressed in Eq. 1.3.

The normalization factor $N_{\zeta ijk}$ in Eq. 1.2 can be factored into a first part $\eta_{\zeta l}$ that depends on both the exponent ζ and shell type $l = i+j+k$ and a second part η_{ijk} ($= \eta_{lm}$ in terms of our alternative indexing) that depends only on the angular momentum,

$$N_{\zeta ijk} = \left(\frac{2\zeta}{\pi}\right)^{\frac{3}{4}} \sqrt{(8\zeta)^l} \cdot \sqrt{\frac{i!\,j!\,k!}{(2i)!\,(2j)!\,(2k)!}} = \eta_{\zeta l} \cdot \eta_{ijk}. \tag{1.5}$$

The separation of the normalization factor in Eq. 1.5 allows us to factor the summation over the primitives from the summation over the array of wavefunction coefficients. Combining Eqs. 1.2–1.4 and rearranging terms gives

$$\Psi_\nu(\mathbf{r}) = \sum_{n=1}^{N} \sum_{l=0}^{L_n-1} \left(\sum_{m=0}^{M_l-1} \underbrace{c_{\nu nlm}\eta_{lm}}_{c'_{\nu nlm}}\,\omega_{lm} \right) \times \left(\sum_{p=1}^{P_{nl}} \underbrace{c_p\eta_{\zeta l}}_{c'_p}\exp(-\zeta_p R_n^2) \right). \tag{1.6}$$

We define $\omega_{lm} = x^i\,y^j\,z^k$ using our alternative indexing over l and m explained in the previous section. Both data storage and operation count can be reduced by defining $c'_{valm} = c_{valm}\eta_{lm}$ and $c'_p = c_p\eta_{\zeta l}$. The number of primitives P_{nl} depends on both the atom n and the shell number l. Figure 1.2 shows the organization of the basis set and wavefunction coefficient arrays listed for a small example molecule.

1.3.2 GPU Molecular Orbital Algorithms

Visualization of MOs requires the evaluation of the wavefunction on a 3-D lattice, which can be used to create 3-D isovalue surface renderings, 3-D height field plots, or 2-D contour line plots within a plane. Since wavefunction amplitudes diminish to zero beyond a few Angstroms (due to the radial decay of exponential basis functions), the boundaries of the 3-D lattice have only a small margin beyond the bounding box containing the molecule of interest.

The MO lattice computation is heavily data dependent, consisting of a series of nested loops that evaluate the primitives composing CGTOs and the angular momenta for each shell, with an outer loop over atoms. Since the number of shells can vary by atom and the number of primitives and angular momenta can be different for each shell, the innermost loops traverse variable-length coefficient arrays

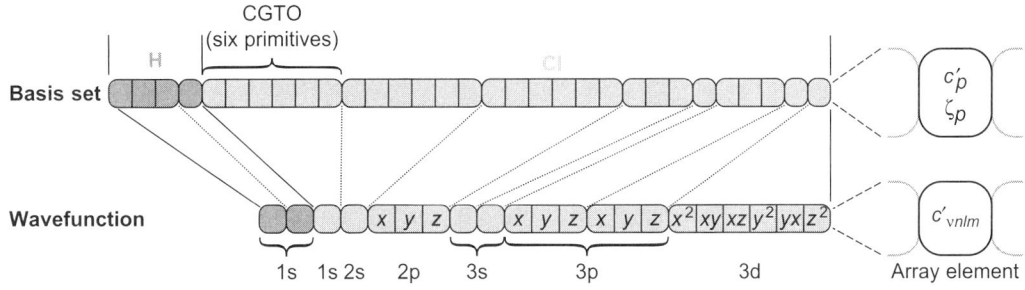

FIGURE 1.2

Structure of the basis set and the wavefunction coefficient arrays for HCl using the 6-31G* basis [8]. Each rounded box contains the data for a single shell. Each square box in the basis set array represents a CGTO primitive composed of a contraction coefficient c_p' and exponent ζ_p. In the wavefunction array the elements signify linear combination coefficients c_{vnlm}' for the basis functions. Despite the differing angular momenta, all basis functions of a shell (marked by x, y, and z) use the same linear combination of primitives (see lines relating the two arrays). For example, the 2p shell in Cl is associated with three angular momenta that all share the exponents and contraction coefficients of the same six primitives. There can be more than one basis function for a given shell type (brackets below array). © 2009 Association for Computing Machinery, Inc. Reprinted by permission [1].

containing CGTO contraction coefficients and exponents, and the wavefunction coefficients. Quantum chemistry packages often produce output files containing redundant basis set definitions for atoms of the same species; such redundancies are eliminated during preprocessing, resulting in more compact data and thus enabling more effective use of fast, but limited-capacity on-chip GPU memory systems for fast access to key coefficient arrays. The memory access patterns that occur within the inner loops of the GPU algorithms can be optimized to achieve peak performance by carefully sorting and packing coefficient arrays as a preprocessing step. Each of the coefficient arrays is sorted on the CPU so that array elements are accessed in a strictly consecutive pattern. The pseudo-code listing in Algorithm 1 summarizes the performance-critical portion of the MO computation described by Eq. 1.6.

The GPU MO algorithm decomposes the 3-D lattice into a set of 2-D planar slices, which are computed independently of each other. In the case of a single-GPU calculation, a simple `for` loop processes the slices one at a time until they are all completed. For a multi-GPU calculation, the set of slices is dynamically distributed among the pool of available GPUs. Each of the GPUs requests a slice index to compute, computes the assigned slice, and stores the result at the appropriate location in host memory.

Each planar slice computed on a GPU is decomposed into a 2-D CUDA grid consisting of fixed-size 8×8 thread blocks. As the size of the 3-D lattice increases, the number of planar slices increases, and the number of thread blocks in each CUDA grid increases accordingly. Each thread is responsible for computing the MO at a single lattice point. For lattice dimensions that cannot be evenly divided by the thread block dimensions or the memory coalescing size, padding elements are added (to avoid unnecessary branching or warp divergence). The padding elements are computed just as the interior lattice points are, but the results are discarded at the end of the computation. Figure 1.3 illustrates the multilevel parallel decomposition strategy and required padding elements.

Algorithm 1: Calculate MO value $\Psi_\nu(\mathbf{r})$ at lattice point $\mathbf{r}$.

1: $\Psi_\nu \Leftarrow 0.0$
2: $ifunc \Leftarrow 0$ {index the array of wavefunction coefficients}
3: $ishell \Leftarrow 0$ {index the array of shell numbers}
4: **for** $n = 1$ to N **do** {loop over atoms}
5:      $(x, y, z) \Leftarrow \mathbf{r} - \mathbf{r}_n$ {$\mathbf{r}_n$ is position of atom n}
6:      $R^2 \Leftarrow x^2 + y^2 + z^2$
7:      $iprim \Leftarrow atom\_basis[n]$ {index the arrays of basis set data}
8:      **for** $l = 0$ to $num\_shells\_per\_atom[n] - 1$ **do** {loop over shells}
9:          $\Phi^{CGTO} \Leftarrow 0.0$
10:          **for** $p = 0$ to $num\_prim\_per\_shell[ishell] - 1$ **do** {loop over primitives}
11:              $c'_p \Leftarrow basis\_c[iprim]$
12:              $\zeta_p \Leftarrow basis\_zeta[iprim]$
13:              $\Phi^{CGTO} \Leftarrow \Phi^{CGTO} + c'_p e^{-\zeta_p R^2}$
14:              $iprim \Leftarrow iprim + 1$
15:          **end for**
16:          **for all** $0 \le i \le shell\_type[ishell]$ **do** {loop over angular momenta}
17:              $jmax \Leftarrow shell\_type[ishell] - i$
18:              **for all** $0 \le j \le jmax$ **do**
19:                  $k \Leftarrow jmax - j$
20:                  $c' \Leftarrow wavefunction[ifunc]$
21:                  $\Psi_\nu \Leftarrow \Psi_\nu + c' \Phi^{CGTO} x^i y^j z^k$
22:                  $ifunc \Leftarrow ifunc + 1$
23:              **end for**
24:          **end for**
25:          $ishell \Leftarrow ishell + 1$
26:      **end for**
27: **end for**
28: **return** Ψ_ν

In designing an implementation of the MO algorithm for the GPU, one must take note of a few key attributes of the algorithm. Unlike simpler forms of spatially evaluated functions that arise in molecular modeling such as Coulombic potential kernels, the MO algorithm involves a comparatively large number of floating-point operations per lattice point, and it also involves reading operands from several different arrays. Since the MO coefficients that must be fetched depend on the atom type, basis set, and other factors that vary due to the data-dependent nature of the algorithm, the control flow complexity is also quite a bit higher than for many other algorithms. For example, the bounds on the loops on lines 10 and 16 of Algorithm 1 are both dependent on the shell being evaluated. The MO algorithm makes heavy use of exponentials that are mapped to the dedicated exponential arithmetic instructions provided by most GPUs. The cost of evaluating e^x by calling the CUDA routines `expf()` or `__expf()`, or evaluating 2^x via `exp2f()`, is much lower than on the CPU, yielding a performance benefit well beyond what would be expected purely as a result of effectively using the massively parallel GPU hardware.

Given the high performance of the various exponential routines on the GPU, the foremost consideration for achieving peak performance is attaining sufficient operand bandwidth to keep the GPU

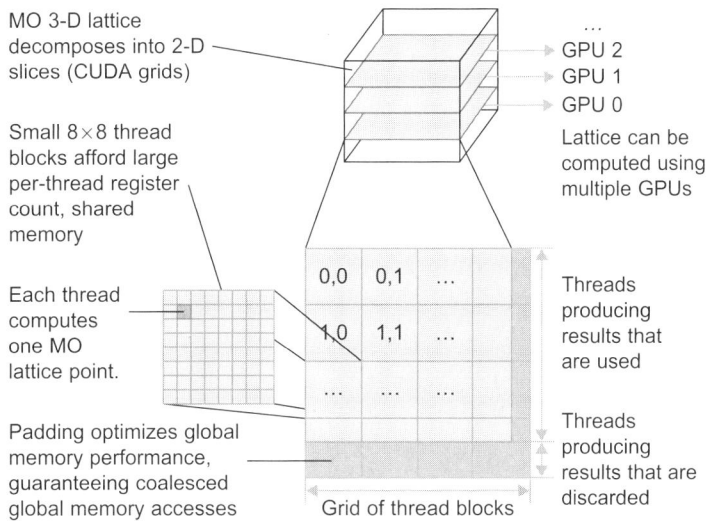

MO 3-D lattice decomposes into 2-D slices (CUDA grids)

Small 8×8 thread blocks afford large per-thread register count, shared memory

Each thread computes one MO lattice point.

Padding optimizes global memory performance, guaranteeing coalesced global memory accesses

GPU 2
GPU 1
GPU 0

Lattice can be computed using multiple GPUs

0,0 | 0,1 | ...
1,0 | 1,1 | ...
... | ... | ...

Threads producing results that are used

Threads producing results that are discarded

Grid of thread blocks

FIGURE 1.3

Molecular orbital multilevel parallel decomposition. The 3-D MO lattice is decomposed into 2-D planar slices that are computed by the pool of available GPUs. Each GPU computes a single slice, decomposing the slice into a grid of 8 × 8 thread blocks, with each thread computing one MO lattice point. Padding elements are added to guarantee coalesced global memory accesses for lattice data.

arithmetic units fully occupied. The algorithms we describe achieve this through careful use of the GPU's fast on-chip caches and shared memory. The MO algorithm's inner loops read varying numbers of coefficients from several different arrays. The overall size of each of the coefficient arrays depends primarily on the size of the molecule and the basis set used. The host application code dispatches the MO computation using one of several GPU kernels depending on the size of the MO coefficient arrays and the capabilities of the attached GPU devices. Optimizations that were applied to all of the kernel variants include precomputation of common factors and specialization and unrolling of the angular momenta loops (lines 16 to 24 of Algorithm 1). Rather than processing the angular momenta with loops, a `switch` statement is used that can process all of the supported shell types with completely unrolled loop iterations, as exemplified in the abbreviated source code shown in Figure 1.4.

Constant Cache

When all of the MO coefficient arrays (primitives, wavefunctions, etc.) will fit within 64 kB, they can be stored in the fast GPU constant memory. GPU constant memory is cached and provides near-register-speed access when all threads in a warp access the same element at the same time. Since all of the threads in a thread block must process the same basis set coefficients and CGTO primitives, the constant cache kernel source code closely follows the pseudo-code listing in Algorithm 1.

Tiled-Shared Memory

If the MO coefficient arrays exceed 64 kB in aggregate size, the host application code dispatches a GPU kernel that dynamically loads coefficients from global memory into shared memory as needed, acting

```
/* multiply with the appropriate wavefunction coefficient */
float tmpshell=0.0f;
switch (shelltype) {
  case S_SHELL:
    value += wave_f[ifunc++] * contracted_gto;
    break;

  case P_SHELL:
    tmpshell += wave_f[ifunc++] * xdist;
    tmpshell += wave_f[ifunc++] * ydist;
    tmpshell += wave_f[ifunc++] * zdist;
    value += tmpshell * contracted_gto;
    break;

  case D_SHELL:
    tmpshell += wave_f[ifunc++] * xdist2;
    tmpshell += wave_f[ifunc++] * xdist * ydist;
    tmpshell += wave_f[ifunc++] * ydist2;
    tmpshell += wave_f[ifunc++] * xdist * zdist;
    tmpshell += wave_f[ifunc++] * ydist * zdist;
    tmpshell += wave_f[ifunc++] * zdist2;
    value += tmpshell * contracted_gto;
    break;
  // abridged for brevity
```

FIGURE 1.4

Example of completely unrolled shell-type-specific angular momenta code.

as a form of software-managed cache for arbitrarily complex problems. By carefully sizing shared memory storage areas (tiles) for each of the coefficient arrays, one can place the code for loading new coefficients outside of performance-critical loops, which greatly reduces overhead. Within the innermost loops, the coefficients in a shared memory tile are read by all threads in the same thread block, reducing global memory accesses by a factor of 64 (for 8×8 thread blocks). For the outer loops (over atoms, basis set indices, the number of shells per atom, and the primitive count and shell type data in the loop over shells) several coefficients are packed together with appropriate padding into 64-byte memory blocks, guaranteeing coalesced global memory access and minimizing the overall number of global memory reads. For the innermost loops, global memory reads are minimized by loading large tiles immediately prior to the loop over basis set primitives and the loop over angular momenta, respectively. Tiles must be sized to a multiple of the 64-byte memory coalescing size for best memory performance, and power-of-two tile sizes greatly simplify shared memory addressing arithmetic. Tiles must also be sized large enough to provide all of the operands consumed by the loops that follow the tile-loading logic. Figure 1.5 illustrates the relationship between coalesced memory block sizes, the portion of a loaded array that will be referenced during subsequent innermost loops, and global memory padding and unreferenced data that exist to simplify shared memory addressing arithmetic and to guarantee coalesced global memory accesses.

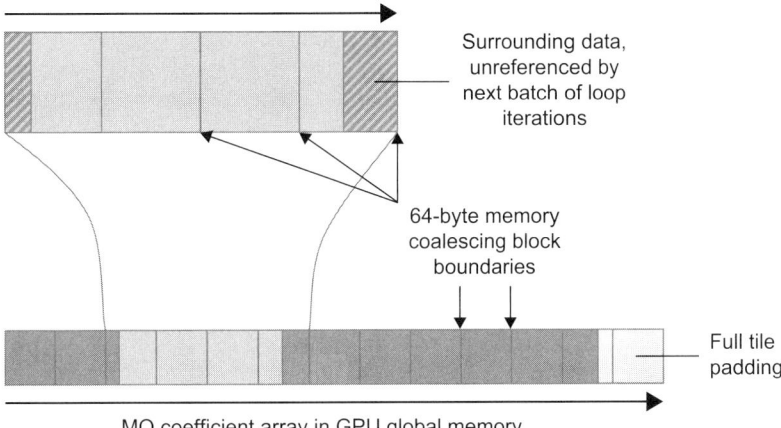

Array tile loaded in GPU shared memory. Tile size is a power two, a multiple of coalescing size, and it allows simple indexing in inner loops. Global memory array indices are merely offset to reference an MO coefficient within a tile loaded in fast on-chip shared memory.

Surrounding data, unreferenced by next batch of loop iterations

64-byte memory coalescing block boundaries

Full tile padding

MO coefficient array in GPU global memory. Tiles are referenced in consecutive order.

FIGURE 1.5

Schematic representation of the tiling strategy used to load subsets of large arrays from GPU global memory, into small regions of the high-performance on-chip shared memory. © 2009 Association for Computing Machinery, Inc. Reprinted by permission [1].

Hardware Global Memory Cache

NVIDIA recently released a new generation of GPUs based on the "Fermi" architecture that incorporate both L1 and L2 caches for global memory. The global memory cache in Fermi-based GPUs enables a comparatively simple kernel that uses only global memory references to run at nearly the speed of the highly tuned constant cache kernel; it outperforms the tiled-shared memory kernel due to the reduction in arithmetic operations encountered within the inner two loop levels of the kernel. The hardware cache kernel can operate on any problem size, with an expected graceful degradation in performance up until the point where the problem size exceeds the cache capacity, at which point it may begin to perform slower than uncached global memory accesses if cache thrashing starts to occur. Even in the situation where the problem size exceeds cache capacity, the strictly consecutive memory access patterns employed by the kernel enable efficient broadcasting of coefficients to all of the threads in the thread block.

Zero-Copy Host-Device I/O

One performance optimization that can be paired with all of the other algorithms is the use of CUDA "host-mapped memory." Host-mapped memory allocations are areas of host memory that are made directly accessible to the GPU through on-demand transparent initiation of PCI-express transfers between the host and GPU. Since the PCI-e transfers incur significant latency and the PCI-e bus can provide only a fraction of the peak bandwidth of the on-board GPU global memory, this technique is a net win only when the host side buffers are read from or written to only once during kernel execution. In this way, GPU kernels can directly access host memory buffers, eliminating the need for explicit host-GPU memory transfer operations and intermediate copy operations. In the case of the MO kernels, the output lattice resulting from the kernel computation can be directly written to the host output buffer, enabling output memory writes to be fully overlapped with kernel execution.

Just-in-Time Kernel Generation

Since Algorithm 1 is very data dependent, we observe that most instructions for loop control and conditional execution could be eliminated for a given molecule by generating a molecule-specific kernel at runtime. A significant optimization opportunity exists based on dynamical generation of a molecule-specific GPU kernel. The kernel is generated when a molecule is initially loaded, and may then be reused. The generation and just-in-time (JIT) compilation of kernels at runtime has associated overhead that must be considered when determining how much code to convert from data-dependent form into a fixed sequence of operations. The GPU MO kernel is dynamically generated by emitting the complete arithmetic sequence normally performed by looping over shells, primitives, and angular momenta for each atom type. This on-demand kernel generation scheme eliminates the overhead associated with loop control instructions (greatly increasing the arithmetic density of the resulting kernel) and allows the GPU to perform much closer to its peak floating-point arithmetic rate. At present, CUDA lacks a mechanism for runtime compilation of C-language source code, but provides a mechanism for runtime compilation of the PTX intermediate pseudo-assembly language through a driver-level interface. OpenCL explicitly allows dynamic kernel compilation from C-language source.

To evaluate the dynamic kernel generation technique with CUDA, we implemented a code generator within VMD and then saved the dynamically generated kernel source code to a file. The standard batch-mode CUDA compilers were then used to recompile VMD incorporating the generated CUDA kernel. We have also implemented an OpenCL code generator that operates in much the same way, but the kernel can be compiled entirely at runtime so long as the OpenCL driver supports online compilation. One significant complication with implementing dynamic kernel generation for OpenCL is the need to handle a diversity of target devices that often have varying preferences for the width of vector types, work-group sizes, and other parameters that can impact the structure of the kernel. For simplicity of the present discussion, we present the results for the dynamically generated CUDA kernel only.

The source code for these algorithms is available free of charge, and they are currently implemented in the molecular visualization and analysis package VMD [1, 2].

1.4 FINAL EVALUATION

The performance of each of the MO algorithms was evaluated on several hardware platforms. The test datasets were selected to be representative of the range of quantum chemistry simulation data that researchers often work with, and to exercise the limits of our algorithms, particularly in the case of the GPU. The benchmarks were run on a Sun Ultra 24 workstation containing a 2.4 GHz Intel Core 2 Q6600 quad core CPU running 64-bit Red Hat Enterprise Linux version 4 update 6. The CPU code was compiled using the GNU C compiler (gcc) version 3.4.6 or Intel C/C++ Compiler (icc) version 9.0. GPU benchmarks were performed using the NVIDIA CUDA programming toolkit version 3.0 running on several generations of NVIDIA GPUs.

1.4.1 Single-GPU Performance Results for Carbon-60

All of the MO kernels presented have been implemented in either production or experimental versions of the molecular visualization program VMD [2]. For comparison of the CPU and GPU implementations, a computationally demanding carbon-60 test case was selected. The C_{60} system was simulated with GAMESS, resulting in an output file (containing all of the wavefunction coefficients, basis set, and atomic element data) that was then loaded into VMD. The MO was computed on a lattice with a 0.075 Å spacing, with lattice sample dimensions of $172 \times 173 \times 169$. The C_{60} test system contained 60 atoms, 900 wavefunction coefficients, 15 unique basis set primitives, and 360 elements in the per-shell primitive count and shell type arrays. The performance results listed in Table 1.1 compare the runtime for computing the MO lattice on one or more CPU cores, and on several generations of GPUs using a variety of kernels.

The CPU "icc-libc" result presented in the table refers to a kernel that makes straightforward use of the `expf()` routine from the standard C library. As is seen in the table, this results in relatively low performance even when using multiple cores, so we implemented our own `expf()` routine. The single-core and multicore CPU results labeled "icc-sse-cephes" were based on a handwritten SIMD-vectorized SSE adaptation of the scalar `expf()` routine from the Cephes [9] mathematical library. The SSE `expf()` routine was hand-coded using intrinsics that are compiled directly into x86 SSE machine instructions. The resulting "icc-sse-cephes" kernel has previously been shown to outperform the CPU algorithms implemented in the popular MacMolPlt and Molekel visualization tools, and it can be taken to be a representative peak-performance CPU reference [1].

The single-core CPU result for the "icc-sse-cephes" kernel was selected as the basis for normalizing performance results because it represents the best-case single-core CPU performance. Benchmarking on a single core results in no contention for limited CPU cache or main memory bandwidth, and performance can be extrapolated for an arbitrary number of cores. Most workstations used for scientific visualization and analysis tasks now contain four or eight CPU cores, so we consider the four-core CPU results to be representative of a typical CPU use-case today.

The CUDA "const-cache" kernel stores all MO coefficients within the 64 kB GPU constant memory. The "const-cache" kernel can be used only for datasets that fit within fixed-size coefficient arrays within GPU constant memory, as defined at compile time. The "const-cache" results represent the best-case performance scenario for the GPU. The CUDA "tiled-shared" kernel loads blocks of the MO coefficient arrays from global memory using fully coalesced reads, storing them in high-speed on-chip shared memory where they are accessed by all threads in each thread block. The "tiled-shared" kernel supports problems of arbitrary size. The CUDA Fermi "L1-cache (16 kB)" kernel uses global memory reads for all MO coefficient data and takes advantage of the Fermi-specific L1/L2 cache hardware to achieve performance exceeding the software-managed caching approach implemented by the "tiled-shared" kernel. The CUDA results for "zero-copy" kernels demonstrate the performance advantage gained by having the GPU directly write orbital lattice results back to host memory rather than requiring the CPU to execute `cudaMemcpy()` operations subsequent to each kernel completion. The CUDA results for the JIT kernel generation approach show that the GPU runs a runtime-generated basis-set-specific kernel up to 1.85 times faster than the fully general loop-based kernels.

All of the benchmark test cases were small enough to reside within the GPU constant memory after preprocessing removed duplicate basis sets, so the "tiled-shared" and "L1-cache (16 kB)" test cases were conducted by overriding the runtime dispatch heuristic, forcing execution using the desired CUDA kernel irrespective of problem size.

1.4.2 Multi-GPU Performance Results for Carbon-60

We ran multi-GPU performance tests on an eight-core system based on 2.6 GHz Intel Xeon X5550 CPUs, containing an NVIDIA Quadro 5800 GPU, and three NVIDIA Tesla C1060 GPUs (both GPU types provide identical CUDA performance, but the Tesla C1060 has no video output hardware). Table 1.2 lists results for a representative high-resolution molecular orbital lattice intended to show scaling performance for a very computationally demanding test case. The four-GPU host benchmarked in Table 1.2 outperforms the single-core SSE results presented in Table 1.1 by up to factors of 419 (vs. Q6600 CPU) and 276 (vs. X5550 CPU). The four-GPU host outperforms the eight-core SSE X5550 CPU result by a factor of 37, enabling interactive molecular visualizations that were previously impossible to be achieved with a single machine.

1.5 FUTURE DIRECTIONS

The development of a range-limited version of the molecular orbital algorithm that uses a distance cutoff to truncate the contributions of atoms that are either far away or that have very rapidly decaying exponential terms can change the molecular orbital computation from a quadratic time complexity algorithm into one with linear time complexity, enabling it to perform significantly faster for display of very large quantum chemistry simulations. Additionally, just-in-time dynamic kernel generation techniques can be applied to other data-dependent algorithms like the molecular orbital algorithm presented here.

References

[1] J.E. Stone, J. Saam, D.J. Hardy, K.L. Vandivort, W.W. Hwu, K. Schulten, High performance computation and interactive display of molecular orbitals on GPUs and multi-core CPUs, in: Proceedings for the 2nd Workshop on General-Purpose Processing on Graphics Processing Units, ACM, New York, 2009, pp. 9–18. http://doi.acm.org/10.1145/1513895.1513897.

[2] W. Humphrey, A. Dalke, K. Schulten, VMD – visual molecular dynamics, J. Mol. Graph. 14 (1996) 33–38.

[3] B.M. Bode, M.S. Gordon, MacMolPlt: a graphical user interface for GAMESS, J. Mol. Graph. Model. 16 (3) (1998) 133–138.

[4] G. Schaftenaar, J.H. Nooordik, Molden: a pre- and post-processing program for molecular and electronic structures, J. Comput. Aided Mol. Des. 14 (2) (2000) 123–134.

[5] S. Portmann, H.P. Lüthi, Molekel: an interactive molecular graphics tool, Chimia 54 (2000) 766–770.

[6] C.J. Cramer, Essentials of Computational Chemistry, John Wiley & Sons, Ltd., Chichester, England, 2004.

[7] E.R. Davidson, D. Feller, Basis set selection for molecular calculations, Chem. Rev. 86 (1986) 681–696.

[8] M.M. Francl, W.J. Pietro, W.J. Hehre, J.S. Binkley, M.S. Gordon, D.J. DeFrees, et al., Self-consistent molecular orbital methods. XXIII. A polarization-type basis set for second-row elements, J. Chem. Phys. 77 (1982) 3654–3665.

[9] S.L. Moshier, Cephes Mathematical Library Version 2.8. http://www.moshier.net/#Cephes, 2000.

Large-Scale Chemical Informatics on GPUs

2

Imran S. Haque, Vijay S. Pande

In this chapter we present the design and optimization of GPU implementations of two popular chemical similarity techniques: Gaussian shape overlay (GSO) and LINGO. GSO involves a data-parallel, arithmetically intensive iterative numerical optimization; we use it to examine issues of thread parallelism, arithmetic optimization, and CPU-GPU transfer overhead minimization. LINGO is a string similarity algorithm that, in its canonical CPU implementation, is bandwidth intensive and branch heavy, with limited data parallelism. We present an algorithmic redesign allowing GPU implementation of such a low arithmetic-intensity kernel and discuss techniques for memory optimization that enable large speedup. Source code for the programs described here is available online: PAPER (for Gaussian shape overlay) can be downloaded at `https://simtk.org/home/paper` under the GPL, and single-instruction, multiple LINGO (SIML) (for LINGO) at `https://simtk.org/home/siml` under a BSD license.

2.1 INTRODUCTION, PROBLEM STATEMENT, AND CONTEXT

Chemical informatics uses computational methods to analyze chemical datasets for applications that include search and classification of known chemicals, virtually screening digital libraries of chemicals to find ones that may be active as potential drugs and predicting and optimizing the properties of existing active compounds. A common computational kernel in cheminformatics is the evaluation of a similarity (using various models of similarity) between a pair of chemicals. Such similarity algorithms are important tools in both academia and industry.

A significant trend in chemical informatics is the increasing size of chemical databases. Public databases listing known chemical matter exceed 30 million molecules in size, the largest exhaustive libraries (listing all possible compounds under certain constraints) are near 1 billion molecules, and virtual combinatorial libraries in use in industry can easily reach the trillions of compounds. Unfortunately, similarity evaluations are often slow, at or below 1000 evaluations/sec on a CPU. Adding to the problem, typical analyses in this field (such as clustering) must execute a number of similarity evaluations that are superlinear in the size of the database. The combination of rapidly growing chemical data-sets and computationally expensive algorithms creates a need for new techniques.

The massive data and task parallelism present in large-scale chemical problems makes GPU reimplementation an attractive acceleration method. In this chapter, we demonstrate 10-100× speedup in large-scale chemical similarity calculations, which allows the analysis of dramatically larger datasets than previously possible. Search problems that formerly would have required use of a cluster can now be efficiently performed on a single machine; alternatively, formerly supercomputer-scale problems can be run on a small number of GPUs. In particular, we show that two commonly used algorithms can be effectively parallelized on the GPU: Gaussian shape overlay (GSO) [5], a three-dimensional shape comparison technique, and LINGO [6], a string comparison method.

2.1.1 Gaussian Shape Overlay: Background

Gaussian shape overlay is an algorithm that measures the similarity of two molecules by calculating the similarity of their shapes in three-dimensional (3-D) space. In this method, a molecule is represented as a scalar field or function in 3-D space, where the value of the function at each point in space indicates whether the point is "inside" the molecule. Given a set of functions $\rho_{Ai}(\mathbf{r})$ that represent the density functions for each atom of a molecule (i.e., functions that are 1 inside the volume of an atom and 0 outside), the function for an entire molecule can be defined using one of the formulae in Eq. 2.1. The first computes interior points by taking the product of the complement of all atoms — defining an "exterior point" as one which is not inside any atom. The latter method uses the principle of inclusion-exclusion between sets to compute the same union of all atoms.

$$\rho_A(\mathbf{r}) \equiv 1 - \prod_{i=1}^{N} (1 - \rho_{Ai}(\mathbf{r}))$$

$$\rho_A(\mathbf{r}) \equiv \sum_i \rho_{Ai} - \sum_{i<j} \rho_{Ai}\rho_{Aj} + \sum_{i<j<k} \rho_{Ai}\rho_{Aj}\rho_{Ak} - \sum_{i<j<k<l} \rho_{Ai}\rho_{Aj}\rho_{Ak}\rho_{Al} + \cdots \qquad (2.1)$$

Equation 2.1 is motivated by considering each atom to be a set of points, and constructing the union of these sets. Defining atomic densities as indicator functions (one inside a given radius around a point and zero outside) generates the "hard-sphere" model of molecular shape. This model has several shortcomings (including nondifferentiability) that makes it difficult to use in computations. Consequently, Grant and Pickup developed the Gaussian model of molecular shape [2], in which each atom's density function is defined not as a hard sphere, but as an isotropic spherical Gaussian function:

$$\rho_{Ak}(\mathbf{r}) = p_k \exp\left(-\alpha_k ||\mathbf{r}_k - \mathbf{r}||^2\right) \qquad (2.2)$$

Such Gaussian functions are smooth and differentiable. Furthermore, simple closed-form expressions for the volumes, volume gradients (with respect to position), and Hessians of the product of an arbitrary number of such Gaussians are known [2]. This enables the calculation of the similarity of two molecules by calculating the maximum overlap possible between their shapes, maximized over all rigid-body transformations (translations and rotations). Mathematically, GSO seeks to maximize Eq. 2.3 over all rigid body transformations. In this integral, the functions ρ_A and ρ_B are the density fields for each molecule, and the integral is taken over all space.

$$\int d\mathbf{r} \rho_A \rho_B \qquad (2.3)$$

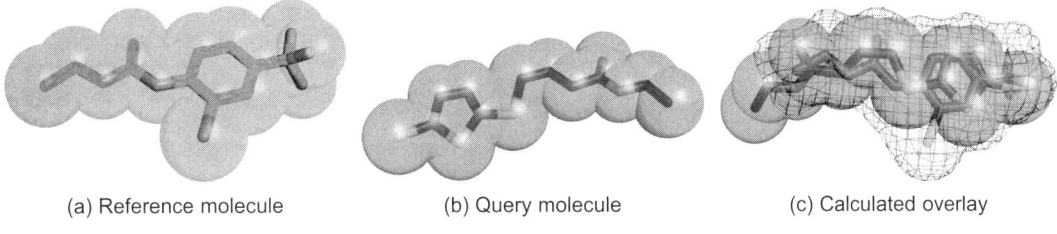

| (a) Reference molecule | (b) Query molecule | (c) Calculated overlay |

FIGURE 2.1

A 3-D shape overlay of molecules. The reference and query molecules are depicted as sticks (to visualize bond structure) embedded within their space-filling representation. GSO rotates the query molecule to maximize its volume overlap (the spheres shown in b and c) with the volume of the reference (the mesh area shown in c).

The computation is performed by numerical optimization to orient a pair of molecules in their optimally overlapping poses and then compute the overlap volume (Figure 2.1) [3]. The objective function in such a calculation is typically a truncated form of Eq. 2.1, including only the single-overlap terms (see Eq. 2.4). Thus, both the objective and gradient calculations are arithmetically intensive and data parallel, involving a double loop over the atoms of each molecule and an exponential evaluation inside the loop body. These aspects make GPUs an attractive platform to implement GSO. In the first half of this chapter, we describe PAPER, our open-source implementation of GSO on NVIDIA GPUs [5].

$$\int d\mathbf{r} \rho_A \rho_B \approx \int d\mathbf{r} \left(\sum_{i,j} \rho_{Ai} \rho_{Bj} \right) \tag{2.4}$$

2.1.2 **LINGO: Background**

Whereas GSO represents a molecule by its three-dimensional shape in space, the LINGO algorithm of Vidal, Thormann, and Pons takes a much simpler, text-based approach [8]. LINGO is a 2-D similarity method: one that operates on molecules as graphs (with vertices representing atoms and edges representing atomic bonds), ignoring their three-dimensional shape. Instead of operating directly on this molecular graph, LINGO processes a linear representation of the graph called a SMILES string, which is constructed by a depth-first traversal of the graph. The characters in the SMILES string represent various graph features, such as atom types, bond orders, ring openings and closings, and branching. Given a SMILES string, LINGO represents a molecule as the set of all overlapping q-character substrings in the SMILES (known as "Lingos," as opposed to "LINGO" for the algorithm as a whole). q is typically set to 4 (i.e., Lingos have length 4), as this has been demonstrated to have superior performance in several applications. Figure 2.2 presents an example of a molecule and its SMILES representation, and its LINGO substrings for $q = 4$.

The similarity between a pair of molecules A and B is defined by the following equation, where $N_{x,i}$ represents the number of Lingos of type i in molecule x:

$$T_{A,B} = \frac{1}{\ell} \sum_{i=1}^{\ell} \left(1 - \frac{|N_{A,i} - N_{B,i}|}{N_{A,i} + N_{B,i}} \right) \tag{2.5}$$

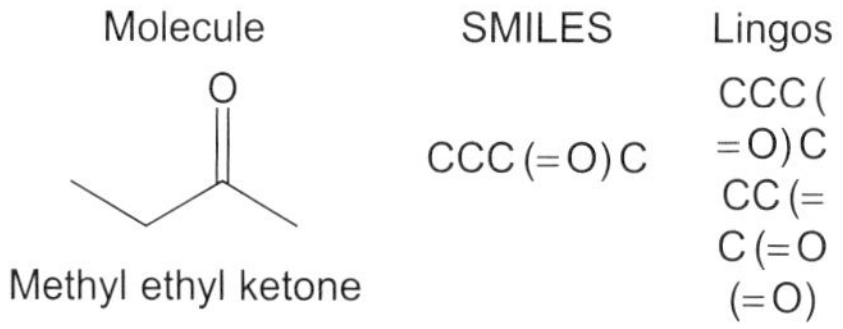

Molecule	SMILES	Lingos
		CCC(
O		=O)C
	CCC(=O)C	CC(=
		C(=O
Methyl ethyl ketone		(=O)

FIGURE 2.2

Chemical graph structure of a common solvent, its SMILES representation, and its constituent Lingos.

The canonical high-performance CPU implementation to rapidly evaluate this similarity on a CPU was presented by Grant *et al.* [4]. This algorithm is optimized for the case in which many SMILES strings must all be compared against one query. The Lingos of the query string are inserted into a trie, a tree data structure allowing fast prefix search of strings. This trie is then converted into a deterministic finite state automaton (DFA) [1]; successive database strings can then be efficiently processed through this DFA. This algorithm suffers from a large amount of branching and poor memory locality in the simulation of the DFA, and it generally has poor data parallelism within each LINGO calculation. It is thus relatively unattractive for GPU implementation. In the latter half of this chapter, we discuss the algorithmic transformations and memory optimizations that enable the high-speed GPU implementation in SIML, our open-source package to calculate LINGO similarities on GPUs [6].

2.2 CORE METHODS

Large-scale chemical informatics calculations involve the calculation of many similarities at the same time, and so they have a large amount of task parallelism; we exploit this structure in both problems by calculating a large number of similarities at a time. The GSO problem in particular is arithmetic bound: its inner loop involves the calculation of $O(MN)$ exponential functions (where M and N are the number of atoms in the molecules being compared), and must be executed many times in a numerical optimization scheme (Eq. 2.4). We make use of SIMD data parallelism and hardware evaluation of exponentials to maximize the arithmetic throughput of GSO on the GPU. LINGO, as implemented for high performance on the CPU, uses a deterministic finite-state automaton algorithm that exhibits large branch penalties and poor memory access locality on the GPU. We describe an algorithmic redesign for LINGO that minimizes branch divergence and makes special use of GPU hardware (texture caching) to maximize memory throughput.

2.3 GAUSSIAN SHAPE OVERLAY: PARALLELIZATION AND ARITHMETIC OPTIMIZATION

The GSO calculation is a numerical maximization of Eq. 2.4 over a seven-dimensional space (three translational coordinates and a four-dimensional quaternion parameterization of a rotation). In this section, we describe the design and optimization of PAPER, our GPU implementation of GSO [5].

PAPER uses the BFGS algorithm [7], a "pseudo-second-order" method that uses evaluations of the objective function and its first derivative (gradient), but no second-derivative evaluations. Because BFGS is a local optimizer and GSO is a global optimization problem, we start each optimization from several initial points. The key computational steps in this calculation are

1. repeatedly evaluate objective at test points along a search direction to find a "sufficiently" improved point (line search);
2. evaluate gradient at new point from line search;
3. update BFGS approximation to inverse Hessian matrix and use this to calculate new search direction.

The primary consideration in software architecture for the GPU is partition of work: what work should be done on the CPU vs. the GPU, how work should be partitioned among independent GPU cores (CUDA thread blocks or OpenCL work groups), and how work can be partitioned among threads or vector lanes in each core. PAPER makes use of the extensive task parallelism in chemical informatics to allocate work to GPU cores. Our target applications focus on searches with hundreds to thousands of comparisons to be performed. Because for each calculation we optimize from several (typically four) starting points, GSO yields a large number (# starting points × # molecules) of independent problems, each of which can be assigned to an independent core (CUDA thread block or OpenCL work-group). Partitioning work among GPU threads and between the CPU and GPU is more involved and is the focus of this section.

2.3.1 Evaluation of the Data-Parallel Objective Function

Equation 2.4 decribes the objective function that must be implemented in GSO. It is inherently data parallel, containing a double loop over the M atoms of the reference molecule and N atoms of the query molecule with an arithmetically intensive loop body. This section describes the parallelization of the objective calculation (which has the same structure as the gradient) and presents several versions illustrating consecutive optimizations.

PAPER uses blocks of 64 threads to maximize the number of registers available to each thread. While it can be advantageous in some cases to use larger thread blocks to hide memory latency, in our application we typically have multiple thread blocks available on each multiprocessor. Since scheduling is done on a per-warp basis, using many smaller thread blocks is sufficient. In typical use cases, the number of terms to be calculated in the objective is larger than the number of available threads: typical molecules are 20-40 atoms, so that normal calculations will have 400-1600 terms. To parallelize the problem, we assign threads to calculate thread-block size "strips" of the interaction matrix consecutively, until the entire set of interactions has been evaluated. Instead of using atomic operations to accumulate the volume among threads, the function keeps an array in shared memory and does a parallel reduction at the end to sum the final overlap volume. Figure 2.3 illustrates the order of the computation, and Listing 2.1 provides code for a simple version of the objective evaluation.

We perform an addressing calculation (lines 12-13) at each loop iteration so that each thread evaluates the correct matrix element. Another strategy would be to disallow thread blocks to span rows of the interaction matrix; however, this has the potential to leave many threads idle, as there are usually more threads than the width of the matrix. Another option would be the use of a two-dimensional thread block. However, because the number of atoms varies by molecule in a batch, and because the number

Query molecule
Atom index (query_idx)

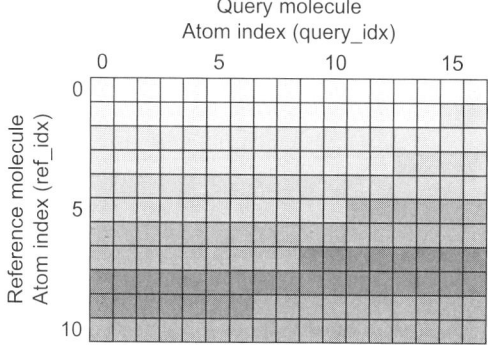

FIGURE 2.3

Thread parallelization scheme in PAPER. Depicted is the full matrix of interactions between a reference molecule of 11 atoms and a query molecule of 17 atoms. Thread blocks of 32 threads process consecutive 32-element strips of the matrix. Each shade represents one iteration of a thread block. Note that no more than a thread block-sized strip of matrix elements must be materialized at any time during the computation.

of atoms is not likely to be a multiple of the GPU warp size, this also is likely to leave the GPU partially idle. Using the given loop structure ensures that all threads do useful work as long as there are terms left to compute.

While the objective function in Listing 2.1 is effectively parallelized across all GPU threads, several changes can be made to improve its performance. The first point of concern is the addressing calculation. Because the number of atoms in either molecule is unlikely to be a power of two, it is necessary to use a division to calculate the row index for each thread. However, integer division is a very expensive operation on current GPUs; when performed in the inner loop, as in the original objective, it adds significant overhead. It is possible to restructure the addressing such that the division is only performed once (Listing 2.2; non-addressing computations have been elided). Restructuring the calculation in this way reduces the in-loop addressing overhead to two adds, a comparison, and two conditional adds, which are much cheaper than the integer division. In the full PAPER implementation, the objective is called multiple times per kernel invocation in the course of a line search; thus, `row_per_block` and `col_per_block` are precalculated at the start of the kernel invocation and stored in shared memory to amortize the cost of the division. Implementing this change to the objective and gradient functions leads to a measured 13% speedup in total optimization time.

With the integer division removed, the runtime becomes dominated by the evaluation of Kij and Vij at lines 18-19 in Listing 2.1, which involves two divides and two transcendental function evaluations — relatively expensive operations. The simplest optimization to apply here is the use of CUDA intrinsic functions for the division and transcendentals. CUDA intrinsics are low-level hardware operations that are often much faster than their library versions, but at the cost of accuracy. In the GSO calculation, experimentation showed that the reduced accuracy of intrinsic functions is not a problem. Listing 2.3 shows the use of the `__expf`, `__powf`, and `__fdividef` intrinsics to speed up the slow operations in the objective core. Adding these three intrinsics more than doubles GSO performance with respect to the previous version (Listing 2.2).

```
1   /* Data: molecules ref and query
2    *           .natoms contains number of atoms in molecule
3    *           .xyz[i] contains coordinates for atom i
4    *           .a[i] is a scalar computed from the van der Waals radius of atom i
5    */
6   float overlap(molecule ref, molecule query) {
7       __shared__ float temp[]; // Has size equal to blockDim.x
8       temp [threadIdx.x] = 0;
9       for (int base = 0; base < ref.natoms * query.natoms; base += blockDim.x) {
10          int mycord = base + threadIdx.x;
11          if (mycord < ref.natoms*query.natoms) {
12              int ref_idx = mycord / query.natoms;
13              int query_idx = mycord − ref_idx*query.natoms;
14
15              float Rij2 = distance_squared(ref.xyz[ref_idx],query.xyz[query_idx]);
16              float ref_a = ref.a[ref_idx], query_a = query.a[query_idx];
17
18              float Kij = expf(−ref_a*query_a*Rij2/(ref_a+query_a));
19              float Vij = Kij * 8 * powf(PI/(ref_a+query_a),1.5f);
20              temp[threadIdx.x] += Vij;
21          }
22      }
23      for (int stride = blockDim.x/2; stride > 0; stride >>=1) {
24          __syncthreads();
25          if (threadIdx.x < stride) temp[threadIdx.x] += temp[threadIdx.x+stride];
26      }
27      __syncthreads();
28      return temp[0];
29  }
```

Listing 2.1: First version of GSO objective function.

However, careful attention to instruction performance shows that this instruction stream can be further improved. In particular, __powf is expensive to evaluate, and it can be replaced in this case by cheaper CUDA intrinsics: reciprocal and reciprocal square root. As is often the case, this optimization produces results that are not numerically identical to the original; however, regression testing showed that the accuracy is sufficient for GSO. The final computational core is provided as Listing 2.4 and is 10% faster than Listing 2.3. Table 2.1 illustrates the performance gains from various tuning strategies on the overlap and gradient kernels, as measured by their effect on the overall program runtime (not just the overlap or gradient evaluation).

2.3.2 Kernel Fusion and CPU/GPU Balancing

It is common in multistage calculations such as GSO to have one or more steps that are not efficiently parallelized on the GPU. In the case of GSO, while the line search/objective evaluation and the gradient evaluation are very efficiently executed on the GPU (because of high data parallelism and arithmetic intensity), the BFGS direction update is not well parallelized. In PAPER, the BFGS update requires a large number of sequential low-dimensional (7-D) vector operations and small (7×7) matrix operations. These operations create a large amount of thread synchronization and many idle threads; it is thus

```
1   float overlap(molecule ref, molecule query) {
2       const int row_per_block = blockDim.x / query.natoms;
3       const int col_per_block = blockDim.x − query.natoms*row_per_block;
4       const int startrow = threadIdx.x / query.natoms;
5       const int startcol = threadIdx.x − startrow * query.natoms;
6       int ref_idx = startrow, query_idx = startcol;
7       /* Shared memory setup goes here */
8       while (ref_idx < ref.natoms) {
9           /* Floating−point core computation goes here */
10
11          ref_idx += row_per_block;
12          query_idx += col_per_block;
13          if (query_idx >= query.natoms) {
14              query_idx −= query.natoms;
15              ref_idx++;
16          }
17      }
18      /* Parallel reduction and return go here */
19  }
```

Listing 2.2: Abbreviated GSO objective function with fast addressing.

```
1   float exp_arg = __fdividef((−ref_a * query_a * Rij2), (ref_a + query_a));
2   float Kij = __expf(exp_arg);
3   float pow_arg = __fdividef(PI,(ref_a + query_a));
4   float Vij = Kij * 8 * __powf(pow_arg,1.5f);
```

Listing 2.3: GSO core computation with CUDA intrinsics.

```
1   const float PIRTPI = 5.56832799683f; // pi^1.5
2   float sum = ref_a + query_a;
3   float inv = 1.0f/sum; // CUDA intrinsic reciprocal
4   float rsq = rsqrtf(sum); // CUDA intrinsic reciprocal square root
5   float Kij = __expf(−ref_a * query_a * Rij2 * inv);
6   float Vij = 8 * PIRTPI * rsq * inv * Kij;
```

Listing 2.4: GSO core computation with restructured CUDA intrinsics.

not attractive to compute them on the GPU. However, moving them to the CPU also imposes a cost. In the case of the BFGS update, the coordinates, gradients, and objective values must be retrieved from the GPU to do the update, and the new direction uploaded to the GPU after the CPU has calculated the update.

Using the CUDA Visual Profiler, it is possible to easily measure the overhead of the two strategies. Table 2.2 shows the timings for various execution stages of PAPER on a 2000-molecule test set.

Table 2.1 Effects of objective/gradient loop tuning on PAPER performance. Measured on GTX 480 with "large" molecule set at 2000 molecules/batch.

Version	Runtime per molecule (μs)	Speedup vs. original
Original	201	—
No-divide addressing	175	1.15$\times$
Intrinsic FP divide/transcendentals	84.9	2.37$\times$
Restructured intrinsics	77.5	2.59$\times$

Table 2.2 Effects of kernel fusion on PAPER performance. Measured on GTX 480 with "large" molecule set at 2000 molecules/batch.

Kernel	Typical execution time, original (μs)	Typical execution time, fused (μs)
Line search	17,000	17,000
Gradient update	4700	5400
GPU-CPU data transfer	2660	10

Measurements examine two versions of PAPER: one in which the gradient kernel only calculates the gradient, with BFGS updates on the host, and one with a "fused" gradient kernel, which both calculates the gradient and does the (poorly parallelized) BFGS update on the GPU. In both versions, a small amount of data is copied from the GPU to the CPU on each iteration to check for convergence.

The results in Table 2.2 demonstrate that on this problem, it is extremely advantageous to keep some poorly parallelized work on the GPU. While the BFGS update takes a significant amount of GPU time (over 12% of the total kernel time, despite having much less arithmetic work than the gradient itself), it is much cheaper than moving the necessary data back to the CPU. The results also show that fusing the line search and gradient+BFGS kernels is unlikely to lead to significant gains: the 10 μs data-transfer overhead in copying completion flags is dominated by the total kernel execution time. This was borne out in testing: a single-kernel version (with all operations in the same kernel call) had essentially identical performance to the two-kernel version.

2.4 LINGO: ALGORITHMIC TRANSFORMATION AND MEMORY OPTIMIZATION

Unlike GSO, which is an arithmetic-bound computation with extensive internal data parallelism, LINGO has few arithmetic operations per memory access and has poor data parallelism. Furthermore, while the GSO algorithm for the GPU is essentially a parallelized version of the CPU GSO algorithm (BFGS), the canonical CPU algorithm for high-performance LINGO is ill suited to the GPU. This algorithm [4] compiles reference strings into a deterministic finite state automaton, which is simulated for each query string. To implement the DFA state transitions requires either significant amounts of branching, or a moderately sized, randomly accessible lookup table (LUT); neither option is good for

GPUs. Branch-heavy code will pay a significant penalty in warp divergence. Worse, none of the memory spaces in the CUDA memory model are well suited to implement a high-performance LUT of the type required: global memory requires aligned, coherent access; texture memory requires spatial locality; constant memory requires that all threads in a warp access the same element for high performance; and shared memory is limited in size. Global, texture, and constant memory are inappropriate for a random-access LUT because different threads are unlikely to use coherent accesses; shared memory is small and may not be able to hold the LUT while maintaining reasonable multiprocessor occupancy (necessary to hide the latency of streaming database Lingos in from global memory). In this section, we discuss the design and optimization of SIML, our algorithm to calculate LINGOs efficiently on the GPU [6].

Consequently, an algorithmic transformation is necessary to implement LINGO efficiently on the GPU. The standard LINGO equation (Eq. 2.5) can be recast into a different form:

$$T_{A,B} = \frac{|A \cap B|}{|A \cup B|} = \frac{|A \cap B|}{|A| + |B| - |A \cap B|} \tag{2.6}$$

In this equation, each molecule (A or B) is represented as a multiset, a generalization of a set in which each element can have cardinality greater than one; the multiset for a molecule contains its Lingos and their counts. The cardinality of each element in a multiset intersection is the minimum of its counts in either set (or maximum, for a multiset union). SIML thus represents each molecule as a pair of integer vectors: one containing the Lingos in sorted order, and one with corresponding counts. Here, the optimality of $q = 4$ is fortuitous, as it allows us to trivially pack a 4-character Lingo into a 32-bit integer (each character is 8 bits). SIML also precalculates the cardinality of each set independently; thus, the only quantity needed to calculate the similarity between two SMILES strings is the size of their multiset intersection. This can be efficiently calculated using the algorithm in the following listing, similar to merging sorted lists (Listing 2.5).

While the simple structure of the algorithm makes it attractive on the GPU, it is not optimal for the CPU. Table 2.3 compares the performance of the SIML multiset algorithm on the CPU against a DFA-based LINGO implementation. The DFA method has nearly twice the throughput of the multiset method. This reflects a common theme in GPU programming — algorithms optimal for the GPU may in fact represent de-optimization for the CPU.

2.4.1 SIML GPU Implementation and Memory Tuning

Because of the poor data parallelism in any single LINGO similarity calculation, we use an individual CUDA thread per similarity; each thread in a block calculates the similarity of its query molecule against a common reference molecule for the entire block. While this approach makes good use of task parallelism in large-scale LINGO calculations, simply running Listing 2.5 per-thread on the GPU results in very poor performance. The first optimization is to load the block's reference molecule into shared memory, rather than global memory. Since all threads access the same reference molecule, this significantly reduces global memory traffic. However, this is sufficient only to reach approximate performance parity with the CPU.

The key to performance in the SIML kernel is memory layout. If multisets were laid out in "molecule-major" order (all elements for a single molecule stored contiguously, followed by the next molecule, etc.), as would be appropriate for the CPU implementation of SIML, consecutive GPU

```
1    /* Data: sorted lists A and B containing Lingos,
2     *        sorted lists A_c and B_c with Lingo counts,
3     *        scalars L_a and L_b the lengths of A/A_c and B/B_c,
4     *        scalars m_a = sum(A_c) and m_b = sum(B_c)
5     */
6    float siml(int* A, int* B, int* A_c, int* B_c,
7              int L_a, int L_b, int m_a, int m_b) {
8        int i = 0, j = 0;
9        int intersection = 0;
10       while ( i < L_a && j < L_b) {
11           if (A[i] == B[j] {
12               intersection += min(A_c[i],B_c[j]);
13               i++, j++;
14           } else if (A[i] < B[j]) {
15               i++;
16           } else {
17               j++;
18           }
19       }
20       return ((float) intersection) / (m_a + m_b − intersection);
21   }
```

Listing 2.5: SIML multiset algorithm for calculating LINGO similarities.

Table 2.3 Multiset vs. DFA algorithm performance on CPU, measured by calculating an 8192×8192 LINGO similarity matrix on a Core i7-920.

Algorithm	Runtime for 8K x 8K (ms)	Throughput (LINGO x 10^3/sec)
DFA	11,875	5651
Multiset/SIML	19,746	2888

threads would read from global memory with a stride equal to the length of the largest multiset (Figure 2.4a). This stride is typically larger than the global memory request size, so a separate read transaction must be dispatched for every thread. This becomes the critical bottleneck: with molecule-major multiset layout, the CUDA Visual Profiler indicates that the kernel's arithmetic throughput is only 15% of peak on a GeForce GTS 250.

Transposing the multiset layout, such that all multisets' first elements are contiguous, followed by the second elements, and so on, nearly solves the problem (Figure 2.4b). However, each thread maintains its own index into its query multiset (a row index in the "Lingo-major" multiset matrix); if these indices differ, then memory access will be uncoalesced. One option is to have a shared row index among all threads: each thread increments its query multiset pointer as far as possible, and then waits at a barrier (__syncthreads) before the block moves on to the next multiset row. While this solution ensures that all global loads are coalesced, it has a relatively high overhead in threads that must wait idle at the barrier; it is able to achieve 80% of peak arithmetic throughput. The best option

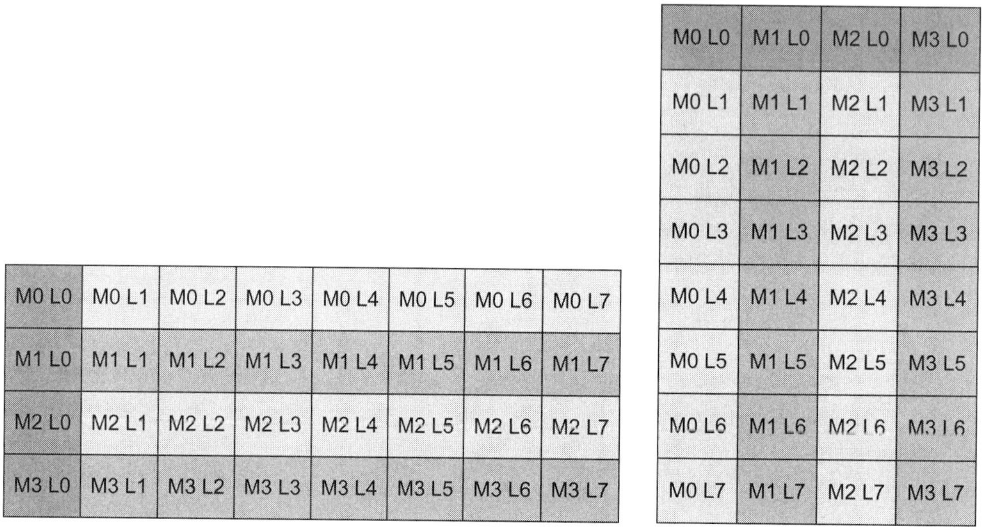

M0 L0	M1 L0	M2 L0	M3 L0
M0 L1	M1 L1	M2 L1	M3 L1
M0 L2	M1 L2	M2 L2	M3 L2
M0 L3	M1 L3	M2 L3	M3 L3
M0 L4	M1 L4	M2 L4	M3 L4
M0 L5	M1 L5	M2 L5	M3 L5
M0 L6	M1 L6	M2 I 6	M3 I 6
M0 L7	M1 L7	M2 L7	M3 L7

M0 L0	M0 L1	M0 L2	M0 L3	M0 L4	M0 L5	M0 L6	M0 L7
M1 L0	M1 L1	M1 L2	M1 L3	M1 L4	M1 L5	M1 L6	M1 L7
M2 L0	M2 L1	M2 L2	M2 L3	M2 L4	M2 L5	M2 L6	M2 L7
M3 L0	M3 L1	M3 L2	M3 L3	M3 L4	M3 L5	M3 L6	M3 L7

(a) Molecule-major layout for CPU. Each thread reads rightwards from a different row, leading to strided, uncoalesced global reads on the GPU without caching.

(b) Lingo-major layout for GPU. Threads read downwards in adjacent columns. Using a barrier on row index, or a 2D texture, ensures that reads stay coalesced as the calculation proceeds.

FIGURE 2.4

"Molecule-major" and "Lingo-major" layouts for storing the Lingos of multiple molecules in memory. Dark gray squares indicate the memory addresses read by consecutive threads. "MX LY" indicates the Yth Lingo of the Xth molecule.

on GPU hardware is to associate a two-dimensional texture with the multiset matrix and use texture loads instead of uncached global loads. Because the texture cache is optimized for spatial locality, it is able to absorb the overhead of the misalignment in row indices between threads. The SIML kernel using a 2-D texture for global memory access is able to achieve 100% of peak single-issue arithmetic throughput (as measured by CUDA Visual Profiler), demonstrating that careful optimization of memory layout and access method can turn a problem traditionally considered to be memory bound into one that is arithmetic bound. An implementation of this transposed, textured kernel is provided as Listing 2.6.

2.5 FINAL EVALUATION

Figure 2.5 compares the performance of the tuned PAPER implementation against OpenEye ROCS, a commercial implementation of Gaussian shape overlay. ROCS supports various "modes," which represent different approximations to the GSO objective function. The objective implemented in PAPER is equivalent to the "Exact" mode in ROCS. ROCS performance was measured on one core of an Intel Core i7-920; PAPER was run on an NVIDIA GeForce GTX 480. Because the complexity of the GSO

```
 1   /* Data:
 2    *  sorted list A containing Lingos for reference molecule (in shared memory)
 3    *  sorted list A_c containing counts for reference molecule (in shared memory)
 4    *  textures B_tex and B_c_tex, pointing to Lingo−major
 5    *          matrices of query Lingos and counts
 6    *  scalars L_a and L_b the lengths of A/A_c and B/B_c,
 7    *  scalars m_a = sum(A_c) and m_b = sum(B_c)
 8    *  scalar maxL_b the longest length of any query molecule
 9    *          list (height of matrix pointed to by B_tex)
10    *  scalar b_offset the column index in B_tex containing data
11    *          for the query molecule to be processed
12    */
13
14   texture<int,2> B_tex;
15   texture<int,2> B_c_tex;
16
17   float siml_colmajor_tex(int* A, int* A_c, int L_a, int m_a,
18                                int m_b, int L_b, int maxL_b, int b_offset) {
19       int i=0,j=0;
20       int intersection=0;
21       int Bj,B_cj;
22
23       // Special−case the empty set
24       if (m_a == 0 || m_b == 0) return 0.0f;
25
26       while (j < maxL_b) {
27           if (j < L_b) {
28               // Use 2D texture to coalesce loads through cache
29               Bj = tex2D(B_tex, b_offset, j);
30               B_cj = tex2D(B_c_tex, b_offset, j);
31
32                   while ( i < L_a && a[i] < Bj) i++;
33
34               // Now a[i] >= bj or i == L_a
35               if (i < L_a && a[i] == Bj) {
36                   intersection += min(A_c[i], B_cj);
37                   i++;
38               }
39               // Now a[i] > b[j] or i == L_a
40           }
41           j++;
42           // If texturing is not used, synchronize here to coalesce loads
43           //__syncthreads();
44       }
45       return intersection/((float)(m_a + m_b − intersection));
46   }
```

Listing 2.6: Transposed SIML algorithm for LINGO using 2-D texturing to coalesce reads on the GPU.

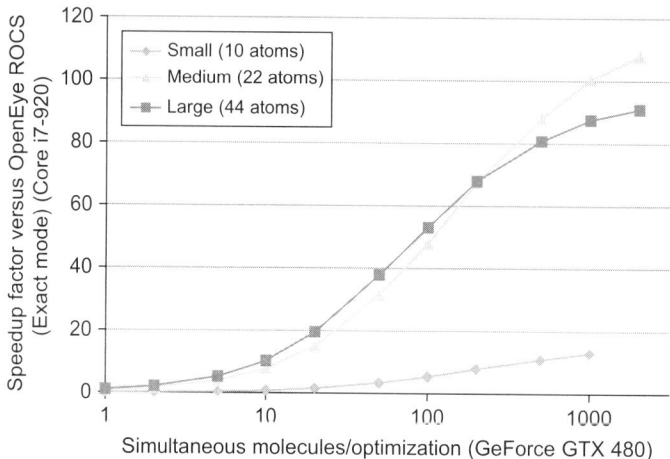

FIGURE 2.5

PAPER performance versus OpenEye ROCS.

kernel varies by the size of the molecules being compared, we present speedup plots for small (10 atoms), medium (22 atoms), and large (44 atoms) molecules. The chosen "medium" size corresponds to the average heavy atom (non-hydrogen) count in a popular chemical screening library.

Two trends are immediately obvious from the graph. First, PAPER requires a large number of molecules to be optimized at the same time for effective speedup. This is typical for GPU algorithms, especially those relying on task parallelism. Because PAPER dispatches only one optimization per thread block, and the GPU can run multiple thread blocks per GPU core (streaming multiprocessor, or SM, in NVIDIA terminology), it is necessary to dispatch many optimizations before the GPU is fully loaded. Performance continues to improve past this lower bound (present around 25 optimizations in the plot) because CPU-GPU copy overhead and kernel dispatch latency can be more effectively amortized with larger batch sizes. The second trend is that the GPU is less effective for very small molecules, which achieve only slightly more than $10\times$ speedup, rather than the $90 - 100\times$ possible on larger molecules. The number of interaction terms is very small for such molecules, so that kernel setup, kernel dispatch time, and idle threads come to dominate performance. Ultimately, however, PAPER is able to demonstrate two orders of magnitude speedup on problem sizes typical in our application domain.

Figure 2.6 illustrates the performance of SIML on three generations of NVIDIA GPU, compared with the performance of a DFA-based LINGO implementation (contributed by NextMove Software) running on one core of an Intel Core i7-920. The benchmark problem for both datasets was the computation of an all-vs.-all similarity matrix on 32,768 molecules. As shown in Table 2.3, the multiset-based algorithm runs at about half the speed of the DFA algorithm on a CPU. However, the multiset algorithm performs very well on a GPU. SIML achieves over $11\times$ greater throughput than the CPU DFA LINGO implementation on a G92-architecture GeForce GTS 250 and over $23\times$ higher throughput on a GF100-based GeForce GTX 480.

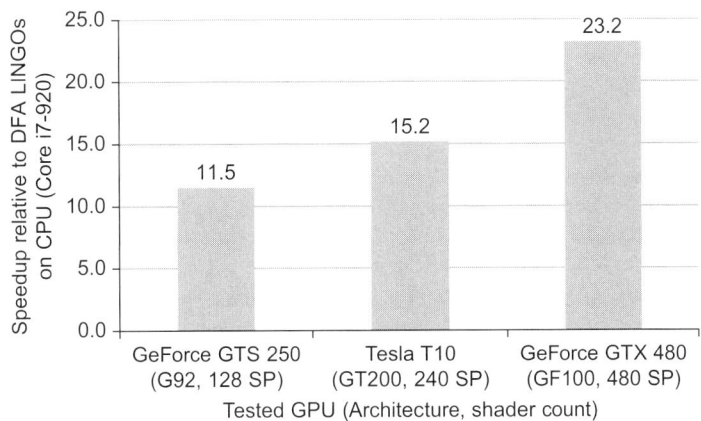

FIGURE 2.6

SIML performance versus DFA-based LINGOs.

2.6 FUTURE DIRECTIONS

We are investigating possible optimizations to both PAPER and SIML. In the PAPER objective/gradient computational core (Listing 2.4), a significant amount of time is spent calculating functions of the reference and query radii that are invariant over the course of the optimization. In particular, the reciprocal and reciprocal square root functions together are as expensive as the following exponential evaluation. One possible option is to precalculate the relevant functions of the radii (`ref_a * query_a * inv` and `8 * PIRTPI * rsq * inv`) and store them in lookup tables in shared memory. This approach has the potential to significantly reduce the number of operations in the core computation, but at the cost of higher memory usage.

The SIML kernel is extremely sensitive to the design of the memory subsystem of the underlying hardware. The version presented has been optimized for the G80/G92 and GT200 NVIDIA architectures, for which texture reads are the only cached reads from global memory. However, the recent GF100 (Fermi) architecture features, in addition to the texture cache, L1 and L2 caches for global memory. It is possible that tuning access methods (such as using non-textured global memory reads) or block sizes (to better fit cache sizes) may significantly affect performance. In general, because LINGO is a memory-sensitive kernel, investigating cache tuning beyond the simple texturing done here is an interesting avenue for future work.

Acknowledgments

We thank Roger Sayle of NextMove Software for his contribution of a DFA-based LINGO implementation for benchmarking and comparison.

References

[1] A.V. Aho, M.J. Corasick, Efficient string matching: an aid to bibliographic search, Commun. ACM, 18 (6) (1975) 333–340.

[2] J.A. Grant, B.T. Pickup, A Gaussian description of molecular shape, J. Phys. Chem. 99 (1995) 3449.

[3] J.A. Grant, M.A. Gallardo, B.T. Pickup, A fast method of molecular shape comparison: a simple application of a Gaussian description of molecular shape, J. Comput. Chem. 17 (1996) 1653.

[4] J.A. Grant, J.A. Haigh, B.T. Pickup, A. Nicholls, R.A. Sayles, Lingos, finite state machines, and fast similarity searching, J. Chem. Inf. Model. 46 (2006) 1912–1918.

[5] I.S. Haque, V.S. Pande, PAPER — accelerating parallel evaluations of ROCS, J. Comput. Chem. 31 (1) (2010) 117–132.

[6] I.S. Haque, V.S. Pande, W.P. Walters, SIML: a fast SIMD algorithm for calculating LINGO chemical similarities on GPUs and CPUs, J. Chem. Inf. Model. 50 (4) (2010) 560–564.

[7] W.H. Press, S.A. Teukolsky, W.T. Vetterling, B.P. Flannery, Numerical Recipes in C, second ed., Cambridge University Press, Cambridge, 1992.

[8] D. Vidal, M. Thormann, M. Pons, LINGO, an efficient holographic text based method to calculate biophysical properties and intermolecular similarities, J. Chem. Inf. Model. 45 (2005) 386–393.

Dynamical Quadrature Grids: Applications in Density Functional Calculations

Nathan Luehr, Ivan Ufimtsev, Todd Martinez

In this chapter we present a GPU accelerated quadrature grid scheme designed for situations where the grid points move in time. We discuss the relative merits of several schemes for parallelization, introduce mixed precision as a valuable optimization technique, and discuss problems arising from necessary branching within a warp.

3.1 INTRODUCTION

Quadrature grids are often custom built to match the topography of a particular integrand. For example, additional points may be allotted near known discontinuities. A subtle complication arises when the integrand evolves in time. In such cases, the quadrature points dynamically follow features of the integrand. As a result the grid depends on the motion of the system and contributes to its gradient. Standard quadrature schemes are unstable in the present context because they assume the grid is static and do not possess well-behaved gradients.

Kohn-Sham density functional theory (DFT) is one application where these considerations arise [1]. DFT replaces the Hamiltonian for interacting electrons in the field of nuclear point charges with a corresponding independent particle Hamiltonian. The independent electrons are then subjected to an additional density-dependent "Kohn-Sham" potential that constrains the noninteracting system to maintain the same charge density as the interacting system it models. Not surprisingly, the form of the Kohn-Sham potential is too complicated for analytical integration, and it must be treated with quadrature grids.

$$\int F(r)d^3r \approx \sum_p \omega_p F(r_p) \qquad (3.1)$$

Here r_p represents an individual quadrature point and ω_p its corresponding weight. Kohn-Sham potentials contain discontinuities owing to their dependence on the electronic density, which itself exhibits a sharp cusp at each nuclear position. As a result, accurate evaluation of the integral requires many quadrature points to be clustered around each nucleus. Now, as the atoms move during a molecular dynamics simulation, they drag their quadrature points with them. As a result, the weights become dependent on the atomic positions and the gradient with respect to the ath atom must be evaluated as follows [2].

$$\nabla_a \sum_p \omega_p F(r_p) = \sum_p \left(\omega_p \nabla_a F(r_i) + F(r_p) \nabla_a \omega_p \right) \tag{3.2}$$

The first term is the usual gradient term for a stationary grid; the second can be understood as a correction for the motion of the quadrature points. Clearly, the overall integral will have a well-defined gradient only if each quadrature weight does as well. In this chapter we will discuss the efficient GPU acceleration of grids appropriate to situations where gradients are essential.

3.2 CORE METHOD

The approach to dynamical grids used in chemical DFT calculations was introduced by Becke [3]. A set of independent and overlapping spherical quadratures with weights λ_I and coordinate offsets r_i are centered at each atomic position, R_a. The independent quadratures are then harmonized with an additional Becke weight, β_{ai}, that allows each atomic-centered quadrature to dominate in the vicinity of its central atom and that forces it to zero in the vicinity of other atoms. In terms of the notation introduced above

$$\omega_p \rightarrow \lambda_i \beta_{ai}$$
$$r_p \rightarrow R_a + r_i \equiv r_{ai} \tag{3.3}$$
$$I \approx \sum_a \sum_i \lambda_i \beta_{ai} F(r_{ai})$$

The spherical quadrature weight, for example, from Lebedev's formulas [4], is a constant so that only the Becke weight needs to be a continuous function of the atomic positions. This is effected by defining the Becke weight in terms of the confocal elliptical coordinate, μ:

$$\mu_{ab}(r) = \frac{|R_a - r| - |R_b - r|}{|R_a - R_b|} = \frac{r_a - r_b}{R_{ab}}$$

where R_a and R_b again represent the locations of the ath and b^{th} atoms, respectively, and r is the position of an arbitrary quadrature point. μ_{ab} is limited to the range $[-1, 1]$ and measures the pair-wise proximity of r to the ath atom. A polynomial cutoff function, $S(\mu)$, is defined that runs smoothly from $S(-1) = 1$ to $S(1) = 0$. The following piecewise form has been recommended for S, along with a value of 0.64 for the parameter a [5], as shown in Figure 3.1.

$$z(\mu; a) = \frac{1}{16} \left[35(\mu/a) - 35(\mu/a)^3 + 21(\mu/a)^5 - 5(\mu/a)^7 \right]$$

$$S(\mu) = \begin{cases} 1 & -1 \leq \mu \leq -a \\ \frac{1}{2}(1 - z(\mu; a)) & -a \leq \mu \leq +a \\ 0 & +a \leq \mu \leq +1 \end{cases}$$

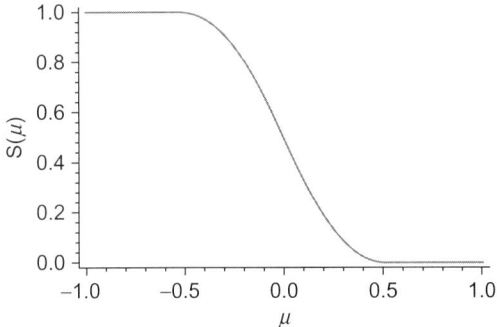

FIGURE 3.1

Plot of cutoff function, $S(\mu)$.

The cutoff function accounts for only a single neighbor atom. To include all of the atoms, a series of cutoff functions are multiplied, each of which accounts for a different neighbor atom. Finally, the cutoff product must be normalized to eliminate double counting from different atomic quadratures.

$$\beta_{ai} = \frac{\prod_{b \neq a} S(\mu_{ab}(r_{ai}))}{\sum_b \prod_{c \neq b} S(\mu_{bc}(r_{ai}))} = \frac{P_a(r_{ai})}{\sum_b P_b(r_{ai})} \qquad (3.4)$$

A naïve approach would allow the atomic indexes in Eq. 3.4 to run over all atoms in the system. Since the number of grid points is proportional to the number of atoms, this leads to a formal scaling of $O(N^3)$ for the calculation of all weights. However, because density functional integrands decay exponentially to zero away from the nuclei, a radial cutoff can be introduced in each of the spherical quadratures. As a result, each point needs to consider only the small set of nearby atoms whose spherical quadratures contain it. For large systems, the number of significant neighbors becomes constant leading to linear scaling.

3.3 IMPLEMENTATION

We have implemented the linear-scaling Becke algorithm within a developmental version of the Tera-Chem quantum chemistry package [6]. Our grids are used to calculate the exchange-correlation component of the total energy and Kohn-Sham Fock matrix.

We chose to use the GPU only for the Becke weight portion of quadrature generation because this step dominates the runtime of the grid setup procedure. Before the kernel is called, the spherical grids are expanded around each atom by table lookup, the points are sorted into spatial bins, and neighbor lists are generated for each bin. These steps are nearly identical for our CPU and GPU implementations. The table lookup and point sorting are already very fast on the CPU, and no GPU implementation is planned. Building atom lists for each bin is more time-consuming and may benefit from further GPU acceleration in the future, but it is not a focus of this chapter.

```
01   for each point in point_array
02        P_a = P_sum = 0.0f
03        list = point.atom_list
04        for each atomA in list
05             Ra = dist(atomA, point)
06             P_tmp = 1.0f
07             for each atomB in list
08                  Rb = dist(atomB, point)
09                  rec_Rab = rdist(atomA, atomB)
10                  mu = (Ra-Rb) * rec_Rab
11                  P_tmp *= S(mu)
12                  if(P_tmp < P_THRE)
13                       break
14             P_sum += P_tmp
15             if(atomA == point.center_atom)
16                  P_a = P_tmp
17        point.weight = point.spherical_weight * P_a/P_sum
```

FIGURE 3.2

Pseudo-code listing of Becke kernel as a serial triple loop.

The GPU is used to calculate the Becke weights given by Eq. 3.4. Since the denominator includes the numerator as one of its terms, we focus on calculating the former, setting aside the numerator in a variable when we come upon it. The serial implementation falls naturally into the triple loop pseudo-code listing in Figure 3.2.

In order to accelerate this algorithm on the GPU, we first needed to locate a fine-grained yet independent task to serve as the basis for our device threads. These arise naturally by dividing loop iterations in the serial implementation into CUDA blocks and threads. Our attempts at optimization fell into two categories. The finest level of parallelism was to have each block cooperate to produce the weight for a single point (block per point). In this scheme CUDA threads were arranged into 2-D blocks. The y-dimension specified the atomA index, and the x-dimension specified the atomB index (following notation from Figure 3.2). The second optimization scheme split the outermost loop and assigned an independent thread to each weight (thread per point).

In addition to greater parallelism, the block-per-point arrangement offered an additional caching advantage. Rather than recalculating each atom-to-point distance (needed at lines 5 and 8), these values were cached in shared memory, avoiding roughly nine floating-point operations in the inner loop.

Unfortunately, this boost was more than offset by the cost of significant block-level cooperation. First, lines 11 and 14 required block-level reductions in the x and y dimensions, respectively. Second, because the number of members in each atom list varies from as few as 2 to more than 80 atoms, any chosen block dimension was necessarily suboptimal for many bins. Finally, the early exit condition at line 12 proved problematic. Since $S(\mu)$ falls between 0.0 and 1.0, each iteration of the atomB loop can only reduce the value of P_tmp. Once it has been effectively reduced to zero, we can safely exit the loop. As a result, calculating multiple "iterations" of the loop in parallel required wasted terms to be calculated before the early exit was reached.

The thread-per-point approach did not suffer from its coarser parallelism. In the optimized kernel each thread required a modest 29 registers and no shared memory. Thus, reasonable occupancies of 16 warps per streaming multiprocessor (SM) were obtained (using a Tesla C1060 GPU). Since a usual calculation requires millions of quadrature points (and thus threads), there was also plenty of work available to saturate the GPU's resources.

The thread-per-point implementation was highly sensitive to branching within a warp. Because each warp is executed in SIMD fashion, neighboring threads can drag each other through nonessential instructions. In the thread-per-point implementation, this can happen in two ways: (1) a warp contains points from bins with varying neighbor list lengths or (2) threads in a warp exit at different iterations of the inner loop. Since many bins have only a few points and thus warps often span multiple bins, case one can become an important factor. Fortunately, it is easily mitigated by presorting the bins such that neighboring warps will have similar loop limits.

The second case was more problematic and limited initial versions of the kernel to only 132 GFLOPS. This was only a third of the Tesla C1060's single issue potential. Removing the early exit and forcing the threads to complete all inner loop iterations significantly improved the GPU's floating-point throughput to 260 GFLOPS, 84% of the theoretical peak. However, the computation time also increased, as the total amount of work more than tripled for our test geometry.

To minimize branching, we need to further sort the points within each bin such that nearest neighbors were executed in nearby threads. In this way, each thread in a warp behaved as similarly as possible under the branch conditions in the code. This adjustment provided a modest performance increase to 149 GFLOPS. Further tweaking ultimately allowed 187 GFLOPS of sustained performance, about 60% of the single-issue peak. However, thread divergence remains a significant barrier to greater efficiency. These results demonstrate the sensitivity of CUDA hardware to even simple branching conditions.

After the bins and points have been sorted on the host, the data is moved to the GPU. We copy each point's Cartesian coordinates, spherical weights (λ_I in Eq. 3.3), central atom index, and bin index to GPU global memory arrays. The atomic coordinates for each bin list are copied to the GPU in bin-major order. This order allows threads across a bin barrier to better coalesce their reads — a step that is necessary since threads working on different bins often share a warp.

Once the data is arranged on the GPU, the kernel is launched, calculates the Becke weight, and combines it with the spherical weight in place. Finally, the weights are copied back to the host and stored for later use in the DFT calculation.

Because the GPU is up to an order of magnitude faster using single- rather than double-precision arithmetic, our kernel was designed to minimize double-precision operations. Double precision is most important when accumulating small numbers into larger ones or when taking differences of nearly equal numbers. With this in mind we were able to improve our single-precision results using only a handful of double-precision operations. Specifically, the accumulation at line 14 and the final arithmetic of line 17 were carried out in double-precision. This had essentially no impact on performance, but improved correlation with the full double-precision results by more than an order of magnitude, as shown in Table 3.1.

3.4 PERFORMANCE IMPROVEMENT

We compared our production mixed precision GPU code with a CPU implementation of the same algorithm. To level the playing field, we had the CPU code use the same mixed precision scheme developed for the GPU. However, the CPU implementation's serial structure limited its computation to a single core. The reference timings were taken using an Intel Xeon X5570 at 2.93 GHz and an

Table 3.1 Comparison of single, mixed, and full double-precision Becke kernels used to integrate the total charge for Olestra, a molecule with 1366 electrons.

Precision	Number of Electrons	Difference from Full Double Precision	Kernel Execution Time
Single	1365.9964166131	3.5×10^{-6}	306.85 (ms)
Mixed	1365.9964131574	3.9×10^{-8}	307.68 (ms)
Double	1365.9964131181	N/A	3076.76 (ms)

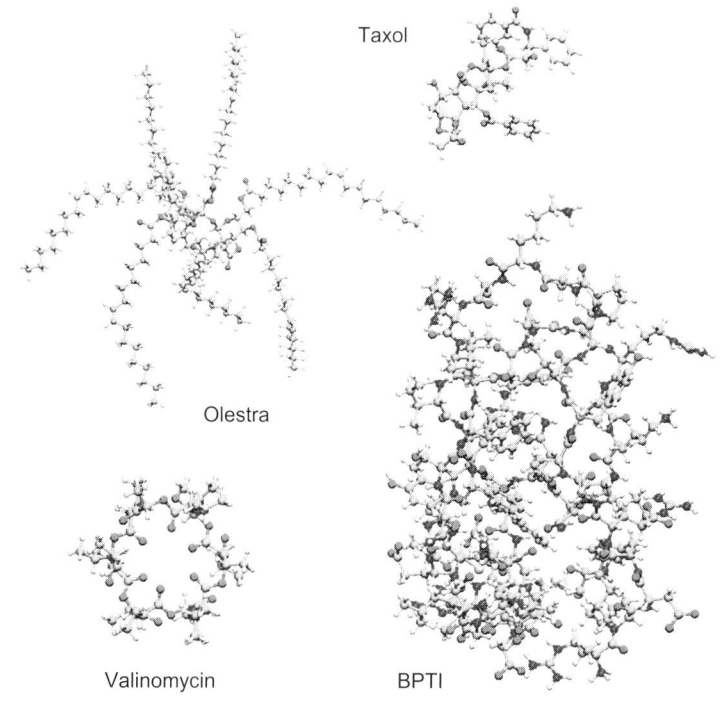

FIGURE 3.3

Test molecules.

NVIDIA Tesla C1060 GPU. Quadrature grids were generated for a representative set of test geometries ranging from about 100 to nearly 900 atoms.

Table 3.2 compares the CPU and GPU Becke kernel implementations (code corresponding to Figure 3.2) for the test molecules shown in Figure 3.3. The observed scaling is not strictly linear with system size. This is because the test molecules exhibit varying atomic densities. When the atoms are more densely packed, more neighbors appear in the inner loops. We can use the average size of the neighbor lists for each system to crudely account for the variation in atomic density. Doing so produces the expected linear result, as shown in Figure 3.4.

Table 3.2 Performance comparison between CPU and GPU Becke kernels; sorting and GPU data transfers are not included.

Molecule	Atoms (Avg. List)	Points	GPU Kernel Time	CPU Kernel Time	Speedup
Taxol	110 (19)	607828	89.1 ms	12145.3 ms	136X
Valinomycin	168 (25)	925137	212.0 ms	26132.2 ms	123X
Olestra	453 (18)	2553521	262.9 ms	30373.6 ms	116X
BPTI	875 (39)	4785813	2330.3 ms	364950.8 ms	157X

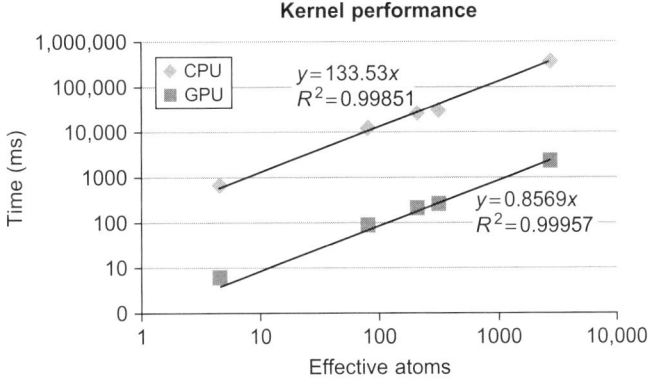

FIGURE 3.4

Plot showing linear scaling of CPU and GPU kernels. Slope of linear fit gives performance in terms of ms per effective atom.

Although a speedup of up to 150X over a state-of-the-art CPU is impressive, it ignores the larger picture of grid generation as a whole. In any real-world application the entire procedure from spherical grid lookup to bin sorting and memory transfers must be taken into account. Table 3.3 provides a timings breakdown for the BPTI test geometry.

The massive kernel improvement translates into a 38X global speedup. Clearly, we have been successful in eliminating the principal bottleneck in the CPU code. The Becke kernel accounts for up to 98% of the total CPU runtime, but on the GPU it is overshadowed by the previously insignificant atom list step. This is a practical example of Amdahl's law, which states that the total speedup is limited by the proportion of code that is left unparallelized.

3.5 FUTURE WORK

From the preceding discussion, the obvious next step will be to implement a GPU accelerated nearest neighbor algorithm to build the atom lists in place on the GPU. Although neighbor listing is not ideally

Table 3.3 Timing breakdown between CPU and GPU implementations for BPTI. Sorting represents the time to sort the bins and points on the host to minimize branching in the GPU kernel. GPU overhead includes packing and transferring point and atom list data for the GPU.

Category	GPU Timing (ms)	CPU Timing (ms)
Atom list generation	6179	6040
Sorting	286	N/A
GPU overhead	316	N/A
Becke kernel	2330	364,951
Total time	9720	371,590

suited for GPU acceleration, use of new features available on NVIDIA's Fermi architecture, such as faster atomics and more robust thread synchronization, should allow a modest speedup. And any gain at this step will amplify the kernel speedup attained thus far.

A second direction for further work is the implementation of GPU accelerated weight gradients (needed in Eq. 3.2). Preliminary tests show that these too are excellent candidates for GPU acceleration.

References

[1] A good overview of DFT can be found in K. Yasuda, Accelerating density functional calculations with graphics processing unit, J. Chem. Theory Comput. 4 (2008) 1230–1236. For detailed coverage see R.G. Parr, W. Yang, Density Functional Theory of Atoms and Molecules, Oxford University Press, New York, 1994.

[2] B.G. Johnson, P.M.W. Gill, J.A. Pople, The performance of a family of density functional methods, J. Chem Phys. 98 (1993) 5612.

[3] A.D. Becke, A multicenter numerical integration scheme for polyatomic molecules, J. Chem. Phys. 88 (1988) 2547.

[4] V.I. Lebedev, D.N. Laikov, A quadrature formula for the sphere of the 131st algebraic order of accuracy, Dokl. Math. 59 (1999) 477–481.

[5] R.E. Stratmann, G.E. Scuseria, M.J. Frisch, Achieving linear scaling in exchange-correlation density functional quadratures, Chem. Phys. Lett. 257 (1996) 213–223.

[6] I.S. Ufimtsev, T.J. Martinez, Quantum chemistry on graphical processing units. 3. Analytical energy gradients, geometry optimization, and first principles of molecular dynamics, J. Chem. Theory Comput. 5 (2009) 2619–2628.

Fast Molecular Electrostatics Algorithms on GPUs

4

David J. Hardy, John E. Stone, Kirby L. Vandivort, David Gohara, Christopher Rodrigues, Klaus Schulten

In this chapter, we present GPU kernels for calculating electrostatic potential maps, which are of practical importance to modeling biomolecules. Calculations on a structured grid containing a large amount of fine-grained data parallelism make this problem especially well suited to GPU computing and a worthwhile case study. We discuss in detail the effective use of the hardware memory subsystems, kernel loop optimizations, and approaches to regularize the computational work performed by the GPU, all of which are important techniques for achieving high performance.[1]

4.1 INTRODUCTION, PROBLEM STATEMENT, AND CONTEXT

The GPU kernels discussed here form the basis for the high-performance electrostatics algorithms used in the popular software packages VMD [1] and APBS [2].

VMD (visual molecular dynamics) is a popular software system designed for displaying, animating, and analyzing large biomolecular systems. More than 33,000 users have registered and downloaded the most recent VMD version 1.8.7. Due to its versatility and user-extensibility, VMD is also capable of displaying other large datasets, such as sequencing data, quantum chemistry data, and volumetric data. While VMD is designed to run on a diverse range of hardware — laptops, desktops, clusters, and supercomputers — it is primarily used as a scientific workstation application for interactive 3D visualization and analysis. For computations that run too long for interactive use, VMD can also be used in a batch mode to render movies for later use. A motivation for using GPU acceleration in VMD is to make slow batch-mode jobs fast enough for interactive use, which can drastically improve the productivity of scientific investigations. With CUDA-enabled GPUs widely available in desktop PCs, such acceleration can have a broad impact on the VMD user community. To date, multiple aspects of VMD have been accelerated with CUDA, including electrostatic potential calculation, ion placement, molecular orbital calculation and display, and imaging of gas migration pathways in proteins.

---

[1]This work was supported by the National Institutes of Health, under grant P41-RR05969.

APBS (Adaptive Poisson-Boltzmann Solver) is a software package for evaluating the electrostatic properties of nanoscale biomolecular systems. The Poisson-Boltzmann Equation (PBE) provides a popular continuum model for describing electrostatic interactions between molecular solutes. The numerical solution of the PBE is important for molecular simulations modeled with implicit solvent (that is, the atoms of the water molecules are not explicitly represented) and permits the use of solvent having different ionic strengths. APBS can be used with molecular dynamics simulation software and also has an interface to allow execution from VMD.

The calculation of electrostatic potential maps is important for the study of the structure and function of biomolecules. Electrostatics algorithms play an important role in the model building, visualization, and analysis of biomolecular simulations; they also are an important component in solving the PBE. One often used application of electrostatic potential maps, illustrated in Figure 4.1, is the placement of ions in preparation for molecular dynamics simulation [3].

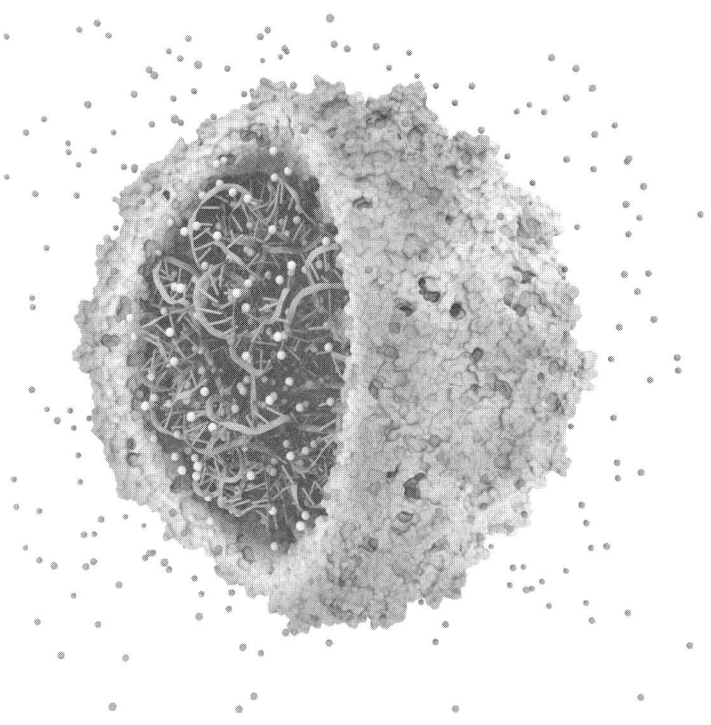

FIGURE 4.1

An early success in applying GPUs to biomolecular modeling involved rapid calculation of electrostatic fields used to place ions in simulated structures. The satellite tobacco mosaic virus model contains hundreds of ions (sodium and chloride ions shown in light grey and dark grey, respectively) that must be correctly placed so that subsequent simulations yield correct results [3]. © 2009 Association for Computing Machinery, Inc. Reprinted by permission [4].

4.2 CORE METHOD

Summing the electrostatic contributions from a collection of charged particles onto a grid of points is inherently data parallel when decomposed over the grid points. Optimized kernels have demonstrated single GPU speeds ranging from 20 to 100 times faster than a conventional CPU core.

We discuss GPU kernels for three different models of the electrostatic potential calculation: a multiple Debye-Hückel (MDH) kernel [5], a simple direct Coulomb summation kernel [3], and a cutoff pair potential kernel [6, 7]. The mathematical formulation can be expressed similarly for each of these models, where the electrostatic potential V_i located at position $\vec{r}_i$ of a uniform 3D lattice of grid points indexed by i is calculated as the sum over N atoms,

$$V_i = \sum_{j=1}^{N} C \frac{q_j}{|\vec{r}_i - \vec{r}_j|} S(|\vec{r}_i - \vec{r}_j|), \tag{4.1}$$

in which atom j has position $\vec{r}_j$ and charge q_j, and C is a constant. The function S depends on the model; the differences in the models are significant enough as to require a completely different approach in each case to obtain good performance with GPU acceleration.

4.3 ALGORITHMS, IMPLEMENTATIONS, AND EVALUATIONS

The algorithms that follow are presented in their order of difficulty for obtaining good GPU performance.

4.3.1 Multiple Debye-Hückel Electrostatics

The Multiple Debye-Hückel (MDH) method (used by APBS) calculates Eq. 4.1 on just the faces of the 3-D lattice. For this model, S is referred to as a "screening function" and has the form

$$S(r) = \frac{e^{-\kappa(r-\sigma_j)}}{1 + \kappa \sigma_j},$$

where κ is constant and σ_j is the "size" parameter for the jth atom. Since the interactions computed for MDH are more computationally intensive than for the subsequent kernels discussed, less effort is required to make the MDH kernel compute bound to achieve good GPU performance.

The atom coordinates, charges, and size parameters are stored in arrays. The grid point positions for the points on the faces of the 3D lattice are also stored in an array. The sequential C implementation utilizes a doubly nested loop, with the outer loop over the grid point positions. For each grid point, we loop over the particles to sum each contribution to the potential.

The calculation is made data parallel by decomposing the work over the grid points. A GPU implementation uses a simple port of the C implementation, implicitly representing the outer loop over grid points as the work done for each thread. The arithmetic intensity of the MDH method can be increased significantly by using the GPU's fast on-chip shared memory for reuse of atom data among threads within the same thread block. Each thread block collectively loads and processes blocks of particle data

```
__global__
void mdh(float * ax, float * ay, float * az,
         float * charge, float * size, float * val,
         float * gx, float * gy, float * gz,
         float pre1, float xkappa, int natoms) {
  extern __shared__ float smem[];
  int igrid = (blockIdx.x * blockDim.x) + threadIdx.x;
  int lsize = blockDim.x;
  int lid = threadIdx.x;
  float lgx = gx[igrid];
  float lgy = gy[igrid];
  float lgz = gz[igrid];
  float v = 0.0f;
  for (int jatom = 0; jatom < natoms; jatom+=lsize) {
    __syncthreads();
    if ((jatom + lid) < natoms) {
      smem[lid ] = ax[jatom + lid];
      smem[lid + lsize] = ay[jatom + lid];
      smem[lid + 2*lsize] = az[jatom + lid];
      smem[lid + 3*lsize] = charge[jatom + lid];
      smem[lid + 4*lsize] = size[jatom + lid];
    }
    __syncthreads();
    if ((jatom+lsize) > natoms) lsize = natoms − jatom;
    for (int i=0; i<lsize; i++) {
      float dx = lgx − smem[i ];
      float dy = lgy − smem[i + lsize];
      float dz = lgz − smem[i + 2*lsize];
      float dist = sqrtf(dx*dx + dy*dy + dz*dz);
      v += smem[i + 3*lsize] *
           expf(−xkappa * (dist − smem[i + 4*lsize])) /
           (1.0f + xkappa * smem[i + 4*lsize])*dist);
    }
  }
  val[igrid] = pre1 * v;
}
```

FIGURE 4.2

In the optimized MDH kernel, each thread block collectively loads and processes blocks of atom data in fast on-chip local memory. Grey-colored program syntax denotes CUDA-specific declarations, types, functions, or built-in variables.

in the fast on-chip memory, reducing demand for global memory bandwidth by a factor equal to the number of threads in the thread block. For thread blocks of 64 threads or more, this enables the kernel to become arithmetic bound. A CUDA version of the MDH kernel is shown in Figure 4.2.

Once the algorithm is arithmetic bound, the GPU performance advantage versus the original CPU code is primarily determined by the efficiency of the specific arithmetic operations contained in the kernel. The GPU provides high-performance machine instructions for most floating-point arithmetic, so the performance gain versus the CPU for arithmetic-bound problems tends to be substantial. This is particularly true for kernels (like the MDH one given) that use special functions such as exp(), which cost only a few GPU machine instructions and tens of clock cycles, rather than the tens of instructions and potentially hundreds of clock cycles that CPU implementations often require. The arithmetic-bound GPU MDH kernel provides a roughly two order of magnitude performance gain over the original C-based CPU implementation.

4.3.2 Direct Coulomb Summation

The direct Coulomb summation has $S(r) \equiv 1$, calculating for every grid point in the 3-D lattice the sum of the q/r electrostatic contribution from each particle. The number of grid points is proportional to the number of atoms N for a typical use case, giving $O(N^2)$ computational complexity, although most applications require a much finer lattice resolution than the average inter-particle spacing between atoms, leading to around 10 to 100 times more grid points than atoms. A sequential algorithm would have a doubly nested loop, with the outer loop over grid points and the inner loop over the atoms. The calculation is made data parallel by decomposing the work over the grid points. A simple GPU implementation might assign each thread to calculate all contributions to a single grid point, in which case the outer loop is expressed implicitly through the parallelization, while the inner loop over atoms is explicitly executed by each thread. However, because the computational intensity of calculating each interaction is so much less than for the MDH kernel, more effort in kernel development is required to obtain high performance on the GPU.

Due to its simplicity, direct Coulomb summation provides an excellent problem for investigating the performance characteristics of the GPU hardware. We have developed and refined a collection of different kernels in an effort to achieve the best possible performance [3]. The particle data x/y/z/q (three coordinates and charge) is optimally stored using the `float4` type. Since the particle data is read only and each particle is to be used by all threads simultaneously, the particles are ideally stored in the GPU constant memory. The limited size of constant memory (just 64 KB with a small part of the upper portion used by the CUDA runtime libraries) means that we are able to store just up to 4000 particles. In practice, this is sufficient to adequately amortize the cost of executing a kernel on the GPU. We decompose the 3-D lattice into 2-D slices, as illustrated in Figure 4.3, with threads assigned to calculate the points for a given slice. The computation proceeds with multiple GPU kernel calls: for each 2-D slice of the lattice, we first zero out its GPU memory buffer, then loop over the particles by filling the constant cache with the next (up to) 4000 particles, invoke the GPU kernel to sum the electrostatic contributions to the slice, and, when finished with the loop over particles, copy the slice to the CPU.

The CUDA thread blocks are assigned to rectangular tiles of grid points. Special cases at the edges of the lattice are avoided by padding the GPU memory buffer for each slice so that it is evenly divisible by the tile size. The padded parts of the calculation are simply discarded after copying the slice back to the CPU. Overall GPU throughput is improved by doing the additional calculations and eliminating the need for conditionals to test for the array boundary.

A simple direct Coulomb summation kernel might calculate a single grid point per thread. Each thread uses its thread and block indices to determine the spatial position of the grid point. The kernel loops over the particles stored in the constant memory cache, calculating the square of the distance between the particle and grid point, followed by a reciprocal square root function accelerated by the GPU special function unit. Figure 4.4 shows part of this simple CUDA kernel.

The GPU performance is sensitive to maintaining coalesced memory reads and writes of the grid point potentials. Each kernel invocation accumulates contributions from another set of atoms, requiring

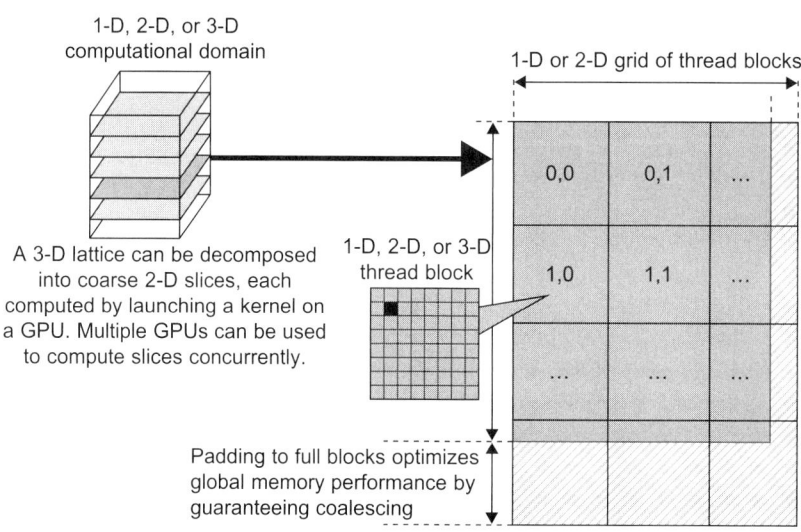

FIGURE 4.3

Each kernel call for direct Coulomb summation operates on a 2-D slice of the 3-D lattice.

that the previously stored values be read and summed with the contributions from the new set of atoms before writing the result. Memory coalescing on earlier GPU architectures (G80 and GT200) required that a half-warp of (16) threads access an aligned, consecutive array of floats. For a 2-D slice, each half-warp-size of threads is assigned to consecutive grid points in the x-dimension. Figure 4.4 shows the read of the previous value (curenergy) into a register being initiated at the beginning of the kernel call, even though this previous value is not needed until the very last sum, in order to better overlap the computation with the memory access. Memory coalescing on the Fermi architecture requires access across the full warp of (32) threads. However, the performance penalty for using the earlier half-warp access is mitigated by the Fermi L1 cache.

Two different optimizations together result in more than doubling the number of interactions evaluated per second. The first optimization, shown to be of lesser benefit for GPU computation than for CPU computation, decreases arithmetic within the kernel loop by exploiting the decomposition of the 3-D lattice into slices. With planar slices taken perpendicular to the z-axis, the jth atom has the same $\Delta z_{ij} = z_i - z_j$ distance to every grid point i on that slice. When buffering the particle data to send to the constant cache memory, the CPU replaces z_j by $(\Delta z_{ij})^2$, which removes a subtraction and a multiplication from each iteration of the kernel loop. Benchmarking shows a slight reduction in FLOPS on the GPU while slightly increasing the number of particle–grid interactions evaluated per second [3].

The second optimization increases the ratio of arithmetic operations to memory references by calculating multiple grid points per thread, with intermediate results stored in registers. We effectively unroll the implicit outer loop over the grid points by a constant UNROLLFACTOR, reusing each atom j read from constant memory multiple times. Unrolling in the x-dimension offers an additional reduction in arithmetic operations, with the y_i's identical for the UNROLLFACTOR grid points permitting just

```
__constant__ float4 atominfo[4000]; // 64kB const memory

__global__ void dcscudasimple(int numatoms, float gridspacing,
                    float * energygrid, float zplane) {
unsigned int xindex = blockIdx.x * blockDim.x + threadIdx.x;
unsigned int yindex = blockIdx.y * blockDim.y + threadIdx.y;
unsigned int outaddr = gridDim.x * blockDim.x * yindex + xindex;

// Start global memory read early, execution continues
// until the first reference of the curenergy variable
// causes hardware to wait for read to complete.
float curenergy = energygrid[outaddr];

float coorx = gridspacing * xindex;
float coory = gridspacing * yindex;
float energyval=0.0f;
for (int atomid=0; atomid<numatoms; atomid++) {
    float dx = coorx − atominfo[atomid].x;
    float dy = coory − atominfo[atomid].y;
    float r_1 = rsqrtf(dx*dx + dy*dy + atominfo[atomid].z);
    energyval += atominfo[atomid].w * r_1;
}
energygrid[outaddr] = curenergy + energyval;
}
```

FIGURE 4.4

A basic direct Coulomb summation GPU kernel. Atom coordinates are stored in the x and y members of the `float4` *atominfo* array elements, with the squared Z distance component from each atom to the current potential map slice stored in the z member, and the partial charge stored in the w member. Grey-colored program syntax denotes CUDA-specific declarations, types, functions, or built-in variables.

one necessary calculation of $(y_i - y_j)^2 + (\Delta z_{ij})^2$ per thread. The unrolled grid points, rather than being arranged consecutively, must skip by the half-warp size in order to maintain coalesced memory reads and writes. A code fragment demonstrating the loop unrolling optimization is shown in Figure 4.5, illustrated by using UNROLLFACTOR = 8.

Loop unrolling optimizations like the one shown here can effectively amplify memory bandwidth by moving costly memory reads into registers, ultimately trading away some amount of parallelism available in the computation. In this case, we reduce the number of thread blocks that will read each atom j from constant memory by a factor of UNROLLFACTOR. Accordingly, the thread block tile size along the x-dimension becomes UNROLLFACTOR × HALFWARPSIZE, which also increases the amount of data padding that might be needed along the x-dimension, and the register use-count per thread expands by almost a factor of UNROLLFACTOR. A schematic for the optimized GPU implementation is presented in Figure 4.6. The increased register pressure caused by unrolling can also decrease the SM occupancy that permits co-scheduling multiple thread blocks (fast context switching between the ready-to-execute warps is used to hide memory transfer latencies). The choice of unrolling factor must balance these considerations; for the direct Coulomb summation, the optimal UNROLLFACTOR is shown to be eight for both the G80 and GT200 architectures [3].

```
__constant__ float4 atominfo[4000]; // 64kB const memory

__global__ void dcscudaopt(int numatoms, float gridspacing,
                   float * energygrid) {
unsigned int xindex = blockIdx.x * blockDim.x * 8 + threadIdx.x;
unsigned int yindex = blockIdx.y * blockDim.y + threadIdx.y;
unsigned int outaddr = gridDim.x * blockDim.x * 8 * yindex + xindex;
float coory = gridspacing * yindex;
float coorx = gridspacing * xindex;
float energyvalx1=0.0f;
// source code abridged for brevity
float energyvalx8=0.0f;
float gridspacing_coalesce = gridspacing * BLOCKSIZEX;
for (int atomid=0; atomid<numatoms; atomid++) {
   float dy = coory - atominfo[atomid].y;
   float dyz2 = (dy * dy) + atominfo[atomid].z;

   float dx1 = coorx - atominfo[atomid].x;
   float dx2 = dx1 + gridspacing_coalesce;
   // source code abridged for brevity
   float dx8 = dx7 + gridspacing_coalesce;

   energyvalx1 += atominfo[atomid].w * rsqrtf(dx1*dx1 + dyz2);
   // source code abridged for brevity
   energyvalx8 += atominfo[atomid].w * rsqrtf(dx8*dx8 + dyz2);
}

energygrid[outaddr ] += energyvalx1;
energygrid[outaddr+1*BLOCKSIZEX] += energyvalx2;
// source code abridged for brevity
energygrid[outaddr+7*BLOCKSIZEX] += energyvalx8;
}
```

FIGURE 4.5

Code optimizations for the direct Coulomb summation GPU kernel, using UNROLLFACTOR = 8. The organization of the `float4` *atominfo* array is the same as for Figure 4.4. Grey-colored program syntax denotes CUDA-specific declarations, types, functions, or built-in variables.

The decomposition of the 3-D lattice into 2-D slices also makes it easy to support multiple GPUs. A round-robin scheduling of the slices to the available GPU devices works well for devices having equal capability, with benchmarks showing near-perfect scaling up to four GPUs [3].

4.3.3 Short-Range Cutoff Electrostatics

The quadratic computational complexity of the direct Coulomb summation makes its use impractical for larger systems. Choosing a "switching" function S that is zero beyond a fixed cutoff distance produces computational work that increases linearly in the number of particles. For molecular modeling applications, the switching function is typically chosen to be a smooth piecewise-defined polynomial.

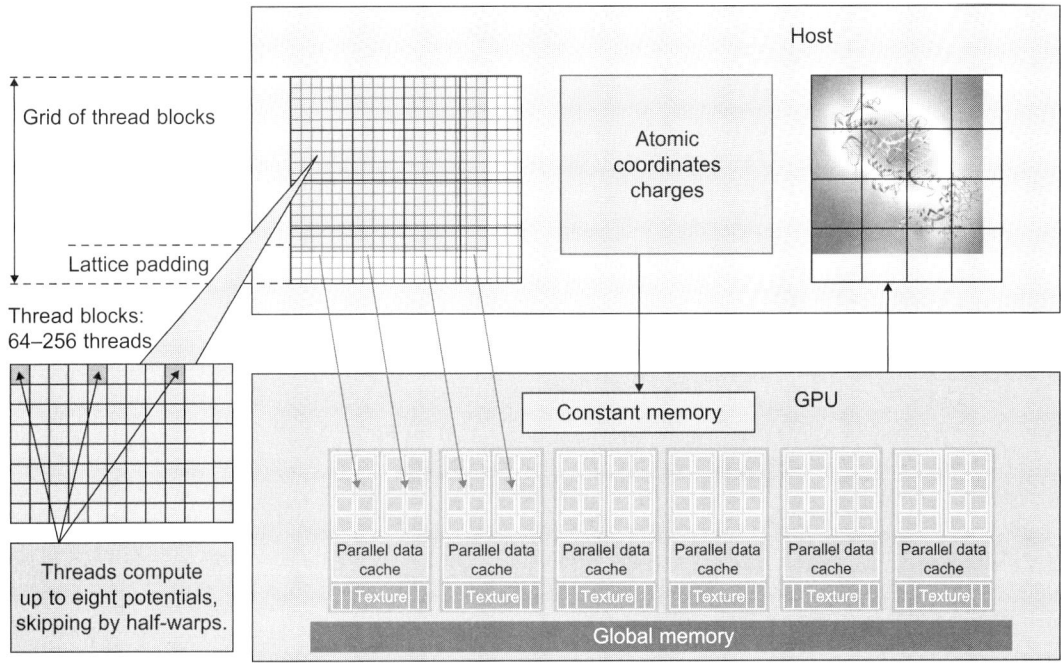

FIGURE 4.6

Illustration of optimized direct Coulomb summation GPU kernel.

A cutoff pair potential is often used as part of a more sophisticated method to approximate the full Coulomb interaction with $O(N)$ or $O(N \log N)$ computational work [7].

A sequential algorithm for calculating a cutoff pair potential might loop over the atoms. For each atom, it is relatively easy to determine the surrounding sphere (or the enclosing cube) of grid points that are within the cutoff distance r_c. The inner loop over these grid points will first test to make sure that the distance to the atom is less than the cutoff distance and will then sum the resulting interaction to the grid point potential. We always test the square of the distance against r_c^2 to avoid evaluating unnecessary square roots. This algorithm is efficient in avoiding the wasteful testing of particle–grid distances beyond the cutoff. However, disorganized memory access can still negatively impact the performance. Good locality of reference in updating the grid potentials can be maintained by performing a spatial sorting of the atoms. Since the density of biomolecules is fairly uniform, or is at least bounded, the spatial sorting is easily done by hashing the atoms into a 3-D array of fixed-size bins.

Adapting the sequential algorithm to the GPU will cause output conflicts from multiple threads, where uncoordinated concurrent memory writes from the threads are likely to produce unpredictable results. Although modern GPUs support atomic updates to global memory, this access is slower than a standard global write and much slower if there is contention between threads. The output conflicts are best eliminated by recasting the scatter memory access patterns into gather memory access patterns. Interchanging the loops produces a gather memory access pattern well suited to the GPU: each grid

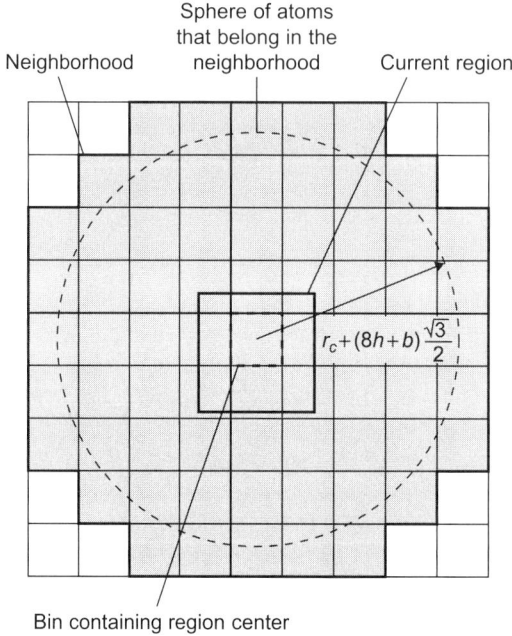

FIGURE 4.7

Cubic region of grid points and surrounding neighborhood of atom bins. Use of small bins allows construction of a neighborhood that more tightly fits to the spherical volume defined by the cutoff distance. © 2008 Association for Computing Machinery, Inc. Reprinted by permission [6].

point loops over the "neighborhood" of all nearby bins that are not beyond the cutoff distance from the grid point.

For GPU computation, each thread will be assigned to calculate the potential for at least one grid point. The bin neighborhood will need to surround not just the grid point(s) for the thread, but the region of grid points designated to each thread block, as depicted in Figure 4.7. An innermost loop over the atoms in a bin evaluates the particle–grid interaction if the pairwise distance is within the cutoff. The performance degrading impact of branch divergence, due to the conditional test of the pairwise distance within the cutoff, is improved if the threads in a warp are calculating potentials at grid points clustered together in space, making it more likely for the threads in the warp to collectively pass or fail the test condition.

Our initial effort to calculate a cutoff pair potential on the GPU adopted the direct Coulomb summation technique of storing the atom data in the GPU constant memory [3], giving rise to a decomposition with coarse granularity. Use of constant memory for the atoms requires repeated kernel calls, each designed to calculate the potentials on a cubic region of grid points, but this region has to be large enough to provide a sufficient amount of work to the GPU. The CPU performs a spatial hashing of the atoms into large bins designed to form a tight-fitting neighborhood around the region of grid points, extending beyond each edge of the region by the length of the cutoff distance. Optimizations include the construction of thread blocks to arrange each half-warp of threads into the tightest possible clusters (of $4 \times 2 \times 2 = 16$ grid points) to reduce the effects of branch divergence. The loop-unrolling optimizations were applied to keep the half-warp clusters together. Best efforts yielded speedup factors of no more than 10 due to the excessive number of failed pairwise distance tests resulting from the coarse spatial hashing.

Redesign of the GPU algorithm and data structures to use a decomposition of finer granularity, with smaller bins of atoms, ultimately resulted in more than doubling the performance over our initial effort. The CPU performs spatial hashing of atoms into bins, and then copies the bins to the GPU main memory. The thread blocks are assigned to calculate potentials for small cubic regions of grid points. Figure 4.7 provides a 2-D schematic of the cubic region of grid points and its surrounding neighborhood of atom bins. Reducing the size of the cubic region of potentials and the volume of atom bins, from those used by the coarse granularity approach, produces a much tighter neighborhood of bins that ultimately results in a much greater success rate for the pairwise distance conditional test. Comparing the two algorithmic approaches by measuring the ratio of the volume of the r_c-sphere to the volume of the enclosed cover of atoms, the success rate of the conditional test increases from about 6.5% for the coarse granularity approach to over 33% for the finer granularity approach. Figure 4.8 illustrates the different CUDA data access patterns between the direct Coulomb summation and the two different approaches to the cutoff pair potential.

In the finer granularity approach, the threads collectively stream each bin in their neighborhood of bins to the GPU shared memory cache and then loop over the particles stored in the current cached bin to conditionally evaluate particle interactions within the cutoff distance. Indexing the bins as a 3-D

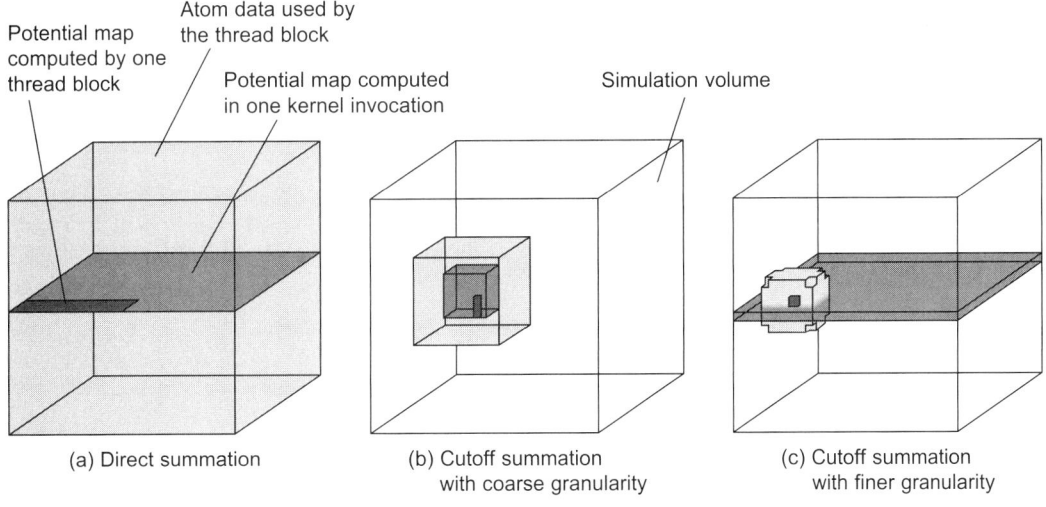

(a) Direct summation   (b) Cutoff summation   (c) Cutoff summation
                                  with coarse granularity   with finer granularity

FIGURE 4.8

Data access patterns of a CUDA grid and thread block for different potential summation implementations. The darkest shade of gray shows the subregion calculated by a single thread block, the medium gray shows the volume calculated by one kernel invocation (or, in the case of direct summation, a set of kernel invocations), and the light gray shows the data needed for calculating each thread block. © 2008 Association for Computing Machinery, Inc. Reprinted by permission [6].

array of cubes allows the "spherical" neighborhood of bins to be precomputed as offsets from a central bin. These offsets are stored in the GPU constant memory cache and accessed optimally at near-register speed, because each consecutive CUDA offset value is read in unison by the thread block. Furthermore, there are no bank conflicts reading from the shared memory cache, because the particle data are read in unison by the thread block.

Coalesced reads and writes significantly reduce the penalty for global memory access. The smallest block size of 128 bytes for global memory coalescing determines a smallest bin depth of 8, with (8 atoms per bin) × (4 coordinates, x/y/z/q, per atom) × (4 bytes per coordinate) = (128 bytes per bin). The bin side length is determined by the density of a system of particles and the expected bin-fill ratio: $binlength = (binfill \times bindepth/density)^{1/3}$. Cubic regions of $8 \times 8 \times 8 = 512$ grid points are assigned to each thread block. The thread blocks themselves are of size $8 \times 2 \times 8$ to use an unrolling factor of 4 in the y-direction, which serves to amortize the cost of caching each bin to shared memory while maximizing reuse of each particle. A code fragment for the loop over the bin neighborhood and the innermost loop over the atoms is shown in Figure 4.9.

The grid potentials calculated by a thread block are, unlike the direct Coulomb summation kernel, accumulated in a single kernel call, which eliminates the need to read partial sums into registers. The potentials of an entire cubic region are written to global memory after completing the loop over the bin neighborhood. To achieve coalesced memory writes, the ordering of each cubic region is transposed to make the memory layout contiguous for the entire region. Upon completion of the GPU kernel calls, the CPU transposes each cubic region of potentials (skipping over the padding) into the 3-D lattice row-major ordering.

Although fixing the bin depth to eight particles optimizes global memory access, it creates a practical limit on the bin side length. Even though the density for a given molecular system is fairly uniform, it is possible for localized clustering of atoms to overfill a bin unless the bin-fill ratio is chosen to be quite small, say $1/4 \leq binfill \leq 1/2$. These overfill cases are instead handled by assigning any extra particles to be calculated asynchronously by the CPU concurrently with the GPU [6, 7]. The use of the CPU to regularize work for the GPU permits larger bin lengths that have a higher average fill, in practice using $binfill = 3/4$, resulting in improved performance as long as the CPU finishes its computation before the GPU does. Multiple GPUs have also been employed by decomposing the 3-D lattice of grid points into slabs of cubic regions of grid points, with the slabs scheduled in parallel to the GPUs.

4.4 FINAL EVALUATION

Performance benchmarks were run on a quiescent test platform with no windowing system, using single cores of a 2.6 GHz Intel Core 2 Extreme QX6700 quad-core CPU, as well as a 2.6 GHz Intel Xeon X5550 quad-core CPU, both running 64-bit Red Hat Enterprise Linux version 4 update 6. The CPU code was compiled using the Intel C/C++ Compiler (ICC) version 9.0. GPU benchmarks were performed using the NVIDIA CUDA programming toolkit version 3.0 running on several generations of NVIDIA GPUs.

Multiple Debye-Hückel (MDH) Electrostatics

The performance of the MDH kernel was benchmarked on CPUs, GPUs, and other accelerators, from multiple vendors, using OpenCL 1.0. When compared against the original serial X5550 SSE CPU code,

```
int tid; // my thread ID
float coorx, coory, coorz; // grid point coordinates
// ... initializations ...
for (nbrid = 0; nbrid < NbrListLen; nbrid++) {
    int ib = myBinIndex.x + NbrList[nbrid].x;
    int jb = myBinIndex.y + NbrList[nbrid].y;
    int kb = myBinIndex.z + NbrList[nbrid].z;
// either clip (ib,jb,kb) to the 3D array of bins or
// wrap around edges, depending on boundary conditions

    // thread block caches bin (ib,jb,kb) into shared memory
    __syncthreads();
    if (tid < bindepth) {
        float4 *bin = bin_global
            + (((kb*yBinDim + jb)*xBinDim + ib)*bindepth);
        bin_shared[tid] = bin[tid];
    }
    __syncthreads();
    for (n = 0; n < bindepth; n++) {
        float q = bin_shared[n].w; // the charge
        if (0.f == q) break; // zero means no more atoms in bin
        float rx = bin_shared[n].x − coorx;
        float rz = bin_shared[n].z − coorz;
        float rxrz2 = rx*rx + rz*rz;
        if (rxrz2 >= cutoff2) continue; // clip to cylinder
        float ry = bin_shared[n].y − coory;
        float r2 = ry*ry + rxrz2;
        if (r2 < cutoff2) {
            s = SF(r2); // implementation−defined function
            energy0 += q*rsqrtf(r2)*s;
        }
        ry −= BLOCK_DIM_Y * gridspacing; // unroll in y
        r2 = ry*ry + rxrz2;
        if (r2 < cutoff2) {
            s = SF(r2); // implementation−defined function
            energy1 += q*rsqrtf(r2)*s;
        }
        // ... subsequent unrolling along y−dimension ...
    }
}
```

FIGURE 4.9

Inner loops of cutoff summation kernel. Grey-colored program syntax denotes CUDA-specific declarations, types, functions, or built-in variables.

the performance increase for an IBM Cell blade (using `float16`) is 5.2× faster, and the AMD Radeon 5870 and NVIDIA GeForce GTX 285 GPUs are 42× faster. With further platform-specific tuning, each of these platforms could undoubtedly achieve even higher performance. Table 4.1 summarizes the performance for OpenCL implementations of the MDH kernel using the standard OpenCL math routines. Table 4.2 contains results for two of the GPUs, using the fast reduced precision device-native

Table 4.1 Multiple Debye-Hückel performance results using standard OpenCL math routines sqrt() and exp(). The benchmark test case consisted of 5,877 atoms and 134,918 grid points.

Device	Runtime (sec)	Speedup vs. QX6700	Speedup vs. X5550
CPU Intel QX6700 SSE	7.15	1.00	0.78
CPU Intel X5550 SSE	5.59	1.27	1.00
OpenCL IBM Cell QS21	1.07	6.68	5.22
OpenCL AMD Radeon 5870	0.134	53.3	41.7
OpenCL NVIDIA GeForce GTX 280	0.133	53.7	42.0
OpenCL NVIDIA Tesla C2050	0.075	95.3	74.0
OpenCL NVIDIA GeForce GTX 480	0.058	123.3	96.4

Table 4.2 Multiple Debye-Hückel performance results using the fast device-native OpenCL math routines native_sqrt() and native_exp() or the associated device-native CUDA math routines. The reduced precision native OpenCL math routines provide a factor of 2.9 performance increase for the AMD Radeon 5870 and a factor of 1.3 performance increase for the NVIDIA GeForce GTX 480, respectively.

Device	Runtime (sec)	Speedup vs. QX6700	Speedup vs. X5550
OpenCL AMD Radeon 5870	0.046	155.4	121.5
OpenCL NVIDIA GeForce GTX 480	0.043	166.3	130.0
CUDA NVIDIA GeForce GTX 480	0.040	178.7	139.7

versions of the OpenCL math routines. The greatly improved AMD Radeon 5870 results shown in Table 4.2 clearly demonstrate the potential benefits of using the OpenCL device-native math routines in cases when precision requirements allow it. The CUDA results using device-native math routines on the GeForce GTX 480 demonstrate that well-written GPU kernels can perform very well in both the CUDA or OpenCL programming languages.

Direct Coulomb Summation (DCS)

The performance results in Table 4.3 compare the performance levels achieved by highly tuned CPU kernels using SSE instructions versus CUDA GPU kernels, all implemented in the C language. It is worth examining the reason for the very minimal increase in performance for the DCS kernels on the Fermi-based GeForce GTX 480 GPU as compared with the GT200-based Tesla C1060, given the significant increase in overall arithmetic performance typically associated with the Fermi-based GPUs. The reason for the rather limited increase in performance is due to the DCS kernel's performance being

Table 4.3 Direct Coulomb summation kernel performance results. The column of GFLOPS results are computed based on multiply-add and reciprocal-sqrt operations counting as two floating-point operations each, with all other floating-point arithmetic operations counting as one operation.

Device	Atom evals per second (billions)	Speedup vs. QX6700	Speedup vs. X5550	GFLOPS
CPU Intel QX6700 SSE	0.89	1.0	0.65	5.3
CPU Intel X5500 SSE	1.36	1.5	1.0	8.2
CUDA GeForce 8800 GTX	39.5	44.4	29.0	291
CUDA Tesla C1060	70.1	78.8	51.5	517
CUDA GeForce GTX 480	82.3	92.5	60.5	607
CUDA 4× Tesla C1060	275.4	309.4	202.5	2031

bound by the execution rate for the reciprocal square root routine `rsqrtf()`. Although the Fermi GPUs are generally capable of outperforming GT200 GPUs by a factor of two on most floating-point arithmetic, the performance of the special function units that execute the machine instructions that implement `rsqrtf()`, `sin()`, `cos()`, and `exp2f()` is roughly the same as the GT200 generation of GPUs; although the effective operations per clock per multiprocessor for Fermi GPUs is double that of GT200 GPUs, the total number of multiprocessors on the device is half that of the GT200 GPUs, leading to overall DCS performance that is only slightly better than break-even with that of GT200 GPUs. Multi-GPU performance measurements were obtained by decomposing the 3-D lattice into 2-D planar slices that are then dynamically assigned to individual GPUs. Each GPU is managed by an associated CPU thread provided by the multi-GPU framework implemented in VMD [1].

Short-Range Cutoff Electrostatics

The performance of the short-range cutoff electrostatic potential kernel was measured for the computation of a potential map for a $1.5 \times 10^7 \, \text{Å}^3$ water box containing 1,534,539 atoms, with a 0.5 Å lattice spacing and a 12 Å cutoff distance. The water box was created with a volume and atom density representative of the biomolecular complexes studied during large-scale molecular dynamics simulations [8] and was generated using the "solvate" plugin included with VMD [1]. A 100-million-atom molecular dynamics simulation has been specified as a model problem for the NSF Blue Waters petascale supercomputer, creating a strong motivation for the development of molecular dynamics analysis tools capable of operating in this regime. The 1.5-million-atom test case is small enough to run in one pass on a single GPU, yet large enough to yield accurate timings and to provide performance predictions for much larger problems such as those targeting Blue Waters.

CUDA benchmarks were performed on three major generations of CUDA-capable GPU devices: G80, GT200, and the Fermi architecture. The results in Table 4.4 demonstrate the tremendous GPU speedups that can be achieved using the combination of memory bandwidth optimization techniques and the use of the CPU to optimize the GPU workload by handling exceptional work units entirely on the host side.

Table 4.4 Comparison of performance for the short-range cutoff kernel tested with a $1.5 \times 10^7\,\text{Å}^3$ water box containing 1,534,539 atoms.

Device	Runtime (sec)	Speedup vs. QX6700	Speedup vs. X5550
CPU Intel QX6700 SSE	480.07	1.00	0.74
CPU Intel X5550 SSE	353.85	1.36	1.00
CUDA C870 (G80)	20.02	23.98	17.67
CUDA GTX 280 (GT200)	14.86	32.30	23.81
CUDA Tesla C2050 (Fermi)	10.06	47.72	35.17

4.5 FUTURE DIRECTIONS

An important extension to the short-range cutoff kernel is to compute the particle–particle nonbonded force interactions — generally the most time-consuming part of each time step in a molecular dynamics simulation. The calculation involves the gradients of the electrostatic and Lennard–Jones potential energy functions. Although more computationally intensive than the electrostatic potential interaction, the problem is challenging due to having a less uniform workload (particles rather than a grid point lattice), extra parameters based on atom types (for the Lennard–Jones interactions), and some additional considerations imposed by the model (e.g., excluding interactions between pairs of atoms that are covalently bonded to each other).

References

[1] W. Humphrey, A. Dalke, K. Schulten, VMD — visual molecular dynamics, J. Mol. Graph. 14 (1996) 33–38.
[2] N.A. Baker, D. Sept, J. Simpson, M.J. Holst, A. McCammon, Electrostatics of nanosystems: application to microtubules and the ribosome, Proc. Natl. Acad. Sci. USA 98 (18) (2001) 10037–10041.
[3] J.E. Stone, J.C. Phillips, P.L. Freddolino, D.J. Hardy, L.G. Trabuco, K. Schulten, Accelerating molecular modeling applications with graphics processors, J. Comput. Chem. 28 (2007) 2618–2640.
[4] J.C. Phillips, J.E. Stone, Probing biomolecular machines with graphics processors, Commun. ACM, 52 (10) (2009) 34–41.
[5] J.E. Stone, D. Gohara, G. Shi, OpenCL: a parallel programming standard for heterogeneous computing systems, Comput Sci Eng. 12 (2010) 66–73.
[6] C.I. Rodrigues, D.J. Hardy, J.E. Stone, K. Schulten, W.W. Hwu, GPU acceleration of cutoff pair potentials for molecular modeling applications, in: Proceedings of the 2008 Conference on Computing Frontiers, 5–7 May 2008, Ischia, Italy, CF'08, ACM, New York, 2008, pp. 273–282.
[7] D.J. Hardy, J.E. Stone, K. Schulten, Multilevel summation of electrostatic potentials using graphics processing units, J. Parallel. Comp. 35 (2009) 164–177.
[8] P.L. Freddolino, A.S. Arkhipov, S.B. Larson, A. McPherson, K. Schulten, Molecular dynamics simulations of the complete satellite tobacco mosaic virus, Structure 14 (2006) 437–449.

Quantum Chemistry: Propagation of Electronic Structure on a GPU

5

Jacek Jakowski, Stephan Irle, Keiji Morokuma

In direct molecular dynamics (MD) methods the nuclei are moving classically, using Newton's equations, on the quantum mechanical potential energy surface obtained from electronic structure calculations [1–3]. This potential energy surface is recalculated every time the nuclei change their positions, or as the chemists and physicists say, it is calculated "on the fly." In order to compute a meaningful trajectory one has to perform several thousands of electronic structure calculations. The electronic structure is a central quantity that contains the information about forces acting on nuclei as well as the energy and chemical reactivity of molecules. The determination of electronic structure and its changes as the nuclei are moving is the central problem of direct dynamics methods [4]. In the typical Born-Oppenheimer MD approaches, the electronic structure is obtained through diagonalization of the Hamiltonian matrix from which the molecular orbitals are found and all chemically interesting properties are derived. This is in contrast to Car-Parrinello MD (CPMD) approaches where molecular orbitals (MOs) are propagated simultaneously with the nuclei, using Lagrangean dynamics in conjunction with a fictitious MO mass [3]. A severe limitation of CPMD is that the orbital occupations are fixed throughout the dynamics. Liouville-von Neumann MD (LvNMD) [5] solves the time-dependent Schrodinger equation for the time propagation of the wavefunction and allows fractional occupation numbers for MOs, which are important to describe mixed quantum states and metallic systems. We show in this chapter (a) how the electronic structure can be propagated without diagonalization in the LvNMD approach, (b) how to cast our problem for GPU in such a way as to utilize the existing pieces of GPU codes, and (c) how to integrate GPU code written in C/CUDA with the main Fortran program. Our implementation combines Fortran with non-thunking CUBLAS (matrix multiplications) and direct CUDA kernels.

5.1 PROBLEM STATEMENT

5.1.1 Background

The physical model for the direct molecular dynamics described here contains nuclei and electrons. All nuclei are treated classically as point particles with mass and electric charge. All electrons are treated quantum mechanically within the so-called independent particle model. The *density functional theories*, *Hartree-Fock* and *tight-binding methods*, are independent particle model methods. In the independent particle model the interaction between electrons is treated in an average way. Each electron can feel only an average field from all other electrons. The interaction between electrons is described by the Fock operator matrix. The Fock operator also contains other information such as the kinetic energy of electrons and the interactions of electrons with nuclei. The determination of electronic structure evolution as the nuclei are moving is the central problem of direct dynamics methods [4].

Electronic structure in quantum chemical applications can be represented by a wave function or equivalently by a density matrix. To construct an electronic wave function or a density matrix, one starts by choosing a physically meaningful set of basis functions χ_k (e.g., Gaussians centered on atoms or plane waves). The behavior of each electron is described through molecular orbitals, ϕ_i, which are linear combinations of basis function

$$\phi_i = \sum_{k=1}^{M} c_k^i \chi_k \tag{5.1}$$

where k runs over all basis functions and i labels different molecular orbitals. The number M of basis functions used corresponds to the size of the system measured in atoms or electrons. The coefficients c_k^i are typically obtained from diagonalization of the Fock operator. The N electronic wavefunction can be constructed as a determinant (or combination thereof) build of occupied molecular orbitals. In an equivalent density matrix representation, instead of using c_k^i coefficients, one can use an M×M matrix to directly describe electronic structure. The relation between molecular orbital coefficients c_k^i and density matrix elements $P_{\mu,\nu}$ is

$$P_{\mu,\nu} = \sum_{i}^{M} \bar{c}_{\mu}^i f_i c_{\nu}^i \tag{5.2}$$

where $\bar{c}$ denotes a complex conjugation of c and f_i is an occupation number (between 0 and 1).

Overview of Direct Dynamics Theory. In direct molecular dynamics, the positions of nuclei are changing with time and the electronic structure adjusts following the time-dependent Schroedinger equation (TDSE). Time dependence of electronic structure is often neglected, and instead, the time-independent Schroedinger equation is solved. This leads to the so-called Born-Oppenheimer approximation [1, 2]. In the density matrix representation of electronic structure, the TDSE becomes the von Neumann equation

$$i\hbar \frac{dP(t)}{dt} = [F(t), P(t)], \tag{5.3}$$

where $P(t)$ and $F(t)$ denote the time-dependent density and Fock operator matrices, respectively [5]. In principle, both $P(t)$ and $F(t)$ are complex square matrices of size $M \times M$. The propagation of density matrix described by Eq. 5.3 is an initial value problem subject to initial density matrix $P(t_0)$. The solution is obtained by time integration of Eq. 5.3 on some discretized time interval $t \in [t_0, t_{final}]$ with the Δt sampling time step. Starting from time $t = t_0$ and initial density $P(t_0)$ we find the density $P(t + \Delta t)$ from $P(t)$ as

$$P(t + \Delta t) = U(t, t')P(t)U^{\dagger}(t, t') = \exp\left[-i\frac{\Delta t}{\hbar}F\right]P(t)\exp\left[+i\frac{\Delta t}{\hbar}F\right] \tag{5.4}$$

where $t' = t + \Delta t$, and F is the Fock operator, and $U(t,t')$ is a quantum mechanical time-evolution operator

$$U(t_0,t_1) = \exp\left[-\frac{\iota}{\hbar} \int_{t_0}^{t_1} F(t)dt \right] \tag{5.5}$$

Here, we approximate the time-evolution operator as $U(t) = \exp\left[-\iota \frac{\Delta t}{\hbar} F \right]$ where F is taken as an average Fock operator on the time interval t and $(t + \Delta t)$.

Now, to obtain the propagated density matrix $P(t + \Delta t)$ from $P(t)$, one can (a.) diagonalize F to obtain the exponential time evolution operator, $U(t) = \exp\left[-\iota \frac{\Delta t}{\hbar} F \right]$, which is then directly applied in Eq. 5.4, or (b.) apply the Baker-Campbell-Hausdorf (BCH) expansion and thus avoid diagonalization. Here, we focus on the latter approach. The final expression for the time evolution of density matrix from $P(t)$ to $P(t + \Delta t)$ is

$$P(t + \Delta t) = P - \iota t[F,P] - \frac{t^2}{2!}[F,[F,P]] + \iota \frac{t^3}{3!}[F,[F,[F,P]]] + \cdots \tag{5.6}$$

where P stands for $P(t)$ and the square bracket denotes matrix commutator $[A,B] = AB-BA$. To propagate the density matrix from time t_0 to t_{final}, one must apply the propagation $P(t) \rightarrow P(t + \Delta t)$ described by Eq. 5.6 or by Eq. 5.4 repeated $(t_{final} - t_0)/\Delta t$ times.

Problem Statement. In this chapter we show that the algorithm based on diagonalization and which also maps poorly to GPU architecture can be replaced by an alternative approach that is based on matrix-matrix multiplication that maps well to GPU architectures. We also show how our density matrix propagation code for GPUs is merged with a main Fortran program. Computational chemists, especially those interested in quantum chemistry, often face the challenge of dealing with large legacy codes written in Fortran. For example, a quantum chemistry package Gaussian was initially released in 1970. Its latest release, Gaussian 09, has 1.5 million lines of Fortran code developed by several authors [6]. It is a formidable challenge to use the features provided in such programs in conjunction with GPU accelerators. Finally, for performance reasons, the authors' philosophy is to use existing efficient libraries whenever possible. This allows to offload the optimization effort to the library vendor. Several efforts are now ongoing toward developing such efficient GPU libraries [7–9]. Although these libraries [8, 9] are not yet fully functional, we anticipate that their role in programmming will be increasing.

In this chapter we discuss the GPU implementation of density matrix propagation via Eq. 5.6. We show (a.) how the electronic structure can be propagated without diagonalization, (b.) how to cast our problem for GPUs in such a way as to utilize the existing pieces of GPU codes, and (c.) how to integrate GPU code written in C/CUDA with the main Fortran program. Our implementation combines Fortran with non-thunking CUBLAS (matrix multiplications) and direct CUDA kernels.

5.2 CORE TECHNOLOGY AND ALGORITHM

5.2.1 Discussion of Technology

The current implementation combines Fortran with C and CUDA. The main program and initialization of the dynamics is written in Fortran. For each time step of MD (Molecular Dynamics) the Fock matrix

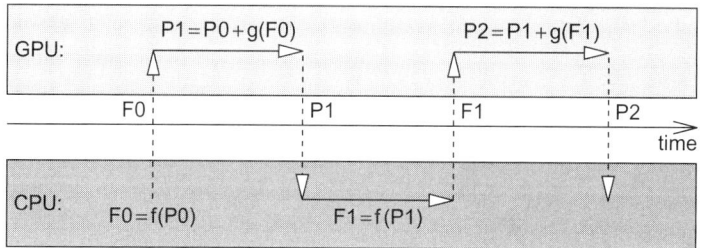

FIGURE 5.1

Main program execution flow for the two consecutive time steps of Liouville-von Neumann molecular dynamics. Operations performed on GPUs (propagation of density matrix) are schematically shown in the light gray box. Operations performed on CPUs (evaluation of Fock matrix and update of nuclei positions) are schematically shown in the dark gray box. Vertical arrows represent transfers of Fock (F) from CPU to GPU and transfer of density matrix (P) in the opposite direction. The MD time is shown as x-axis between the GPU and CPU boxes.

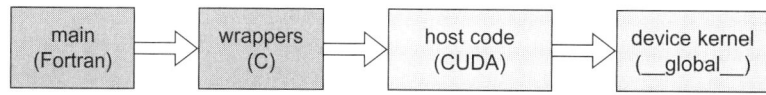

FIGURE 5.2

Schematic description of access to a GPU device from Fortran code. The dark gray boxes denote code compilable with the standard Fortran compiler. The light gray box denotes code written in C/CUDA.

is evaluated on the CPU and transferred to GPU memory. The density matrix is then propagated on the GPU according to Eq. 5.6, and the result is transferred back to CPU for analysis. Thus, two memory transfers between CPU and GPU are performed for each MD time step. Figure 5.1 shows a schematic execution chain of the program for the two consecutive MD time steps.

We analyzed the computational of the density matrix propagation for various GPU programming models. We tested a PGI Accelerator directives-based Open-MP-like programming model [10] and CUDA with the CUBLAS library [7]. The final GPU code combines matrix multiplication from the CUBLAS library with the CUDA kernel for the matrix transpose. The CUDA transpose kernel is a simple implementation optimized for shared memory access, and it uses a thread block size 16×16 (see *CUDA SDK Code Samples* [11]). The discussion describing the chosen programming model is presented in Section 3. We compare the simulation results on the GPU with the best CPU implementation optimized by us.

The CPU host code that directly calls kernels on the device is written in C/CUDA. Wrappers written in C are used to bind the main Fortran code with CUDA code. The hierarchy of code access to the GPU device from Fortran is shown in Figure 5.2. Figure 5.4 shows the code sample that describes the GPU access from Fortran.

Discussion of Algorithm

The overview of the algorithm for the density matrix propagation on the GPU from time t_0 to time t_{final} is presented in Figure 5.3.

Input: Δt, $P(t)$, F, *thrs*
Output: $P(t + \Delta t)$

1 **Initialization:**
2   Allocate GPU device memory for $P(t)$, $P(t + \Delta t)$, ΔP, and F.
3   Transfer $P(t_0)$ from CPU to GPU memory.

4 **foreach** *timestep* $(t < t_{final})$ *starting from* $(t = t_0)$ **do**
5   **Pre-propagation:** Transfer F from CPU to GPU memory
6   **Set:** k =0, and $P(t + \Delta t) = P(t)$, and *err* $= 2 * thrs$
7   **while** $(err > thrs)$ **do**
8 | **Increase counter:** k ++
9 | **Get commutator:** $\Delta P = -\iota \Delta t / k [F, \Delta P]$
10 | **Update P:** $P(t + \Delta t) = P(t + \Delta t) + \Delta P$
11 | **Test convergence:** $err = \max |\Delta P_{i,j}|$
12   **end**
13   **Post-propagation:** Transfer $P(t + \Delta t)$ from GPU to CPU memory
14   Update position of nuclei
15   Update time: $t = t + \Delta t$
16   Calculate F on CPU for new positions of nuclei
17 **end**

FIGURE 5.3

Density matrix propagation via Eq. 5.6. The evaluation of commutator expansion terms is suspended when the convergence is smaller than the threshold *thrs*.aaa

Here are some details and tricks used in the final implementation:

(a) The algorithm requires an allocation of the memory for F (size of real $\times M^2$), initial and final P (size of complex $\times M^2$), a matrix for the intermediate result of commutator $[F, P]$ (size of complex $\times M^2$), and an additional scratch array the same size as F (size of real $\times M^2$).

The expansion in Eq. 5.6 represents a nested commutator. Each higher-order commutator can be obtained recursively from the previous one as

$$\Delta P_k = -\iota \frac{\Delta t}{k} [F, \Delta P_{k-1}] \tag{5.7}$$

for $k > 0$ and $\Delta P_0 = P(0)$.

Each commutator term can be treated as an update to the density matrix

$$P(t + \Delta t) \leftarrow P(t + \Delta t) + \Delta P_k \tag{5.8}$$

Thus, at any given time, it is only necessary to store F, $P(t)$, $P(t + \Delta t)$ and ΔP_k matrices.

(b) The commutator expansion in Eq. 5.6 is truncated when the largest matrix element of P_k is smaller than a preset threshold *thrs*. We use threshold value *thrs* $= 10^{-8}$. Sacrificing accuracy by using a lower threshold would allow the calculation to speed up.

(c) In the current electronic structure model (density functional tight-binding theory [14, 15]), the imaginary part of the Fock operator vanishes. The Fock matrix depends only on the real component of the density matrix [5]. It is currently evaluated on the CPU and transferred to GPU memory. Matrix F is real and symmetric. Matrices P and ΔP_k are complex and self-adjoint with the real part being a symmetric matrix (S) and the imaginary part being an antisymmetric matrix (A). Contrary to this, time evolution matrix $U(t)$ is a general complex.

```
C
C Fortran code: B= transpose(A) ,B-cpu, devB- gpu
C
      subroutine transp (M,N,A,B, devA,devB)
      real *8 A(*), B(*)
      integer stat,devA,devB, M,N, sizeof_real
      sizeof_real=8
      stat = cublas_alloc(M*N, sizeof_real, devA)
      stat = cublas_set_vector(M*N, sizeof_real,A,1,devA,1)
        ...
    call sdotranspose(devB, devA, M,N)
    end
///////////////////////////////////////////////////////////////////////////
// C wrapper: sdotranspose.C
  void sdotranspose_( const devptr_t *devPtrB, const devptr_t *devPtrA,
                      const int *width, const int *height )
  { float *A = (float *)(uintptr_t)(*devPtrA);
    float *B = (float *)(uintptr_t)(*devPtrB);
    sdotranspose_gpu (B,A, *width, *height );
  }
///////////////////////////////////////////////////////////////////////////
// CUDA host code: sdotranspose_gpu.cu
extern "C" {
  void sdotranspose_gpu (float *Bd, float *Ad, int M, int N)
    {   dim3 dimBlockA(min(N,BLOCK_DIM),min(N,BLOCK_DIM));
        dim3 dimGridA(Mblcs,Nblcs);
        stranspose_kernel <<< dimGridA, dimBlockA >>> (Bd, Ad, M,N);
    }
}
///////////////////////////////////////////////////////////////////////////
// CUDA kernel code: stranspospoe_kernel.cu
__global__ void stranspose_kernel(float *odata, float *idata, int width, int height)
  {   __shared__ float block[BLOCK_DIM][BLOCK_DIM+1];
        ...
  }
```

FIGURE 5.4

Code sample for GPU access from Fortran to CUDA. Notice that the "GPU pointer" devA can be passed from transp.F to the calling subroutine as an integer.

(d) All complex quantities are stored and processed as separate, real, and imaginary matrices. For example, the real and imaginary components of hermitian matrix P are stored as a separate symmetric matrix (S) and antisymmetric matrix (A).

$$P = S + \iota A \tag{5.9}$$

Separating real and imaginary components of complex matrices turned out to be beneficial for both efficiency and practical reasons. For example, to perform a matrix product operation between F and P, it is twice as cheap to perform two real matrix multiplications (as FS followed by ιFA), than one matrix product between two complex matrices with the imaginary part of F set to zero.

(e) The basic quantity to be calculated repeatedly in Eq. 5.6 is a matrix commutator $[F,P] = FP - PF$. In principle, to evaluate commutator $[A,B]$ for general matrices A and B, one has to perform two matrix multiplications (AB and BA). However, if A and B are symmetric or antisymmetric, then it is possible to evaluate $[A,B]$ as one matrix multiplication and one transpose. That is $[S',S] = S'S - transpose(S'S)$, $[A',A] = A'A - transpose(A'A)$, and $[S,A] = SA + transpose(SA)$. As we show in the next section of this chapter, the cost of a matrix transpose is significantly lower than the cost of matrix multiplication. We notice that in expression $[F,P]$ the F matrix is symmetric (S) while P is a sum of symmetric (S) and antisymmetric (A) components.

(f) All matrices are treated as super vectors of size M×M, which allows the utilization of level 1 BLAS routines [12] for scalar matrix operations.

5.3 THE KEY INSIGHT ON THE IMPLEMENTATION—THE CHOICE OF BUILDING BLOCKS

In the process of designing a new scientific computing method, one has to answer several questions in order to choose the best possible available building blocks for the program. What is the problem size that one wants to tackle? What is the expected scaling method with respect to the system size? What is the direct and relative cost of different code components in the program for a given problem size (this depends on scaling of the components)? What is the most expensive operation and how often is it used? Are there any preexisting libraries or codes that can be used as building blocks? How efficient are the libraries compared with intrinsic functions and compiler optimized codes? Is there any special structure or pattern to the data that would allow one to modify the algorithm to improve its efficiency? What is the outlook for further improvements or hardware changes? These questions are relevant for both CPU and GPU implementation. We are interested in having the best possible implementation on the CPU as well as the GPU.

The problem size we want to tackle, a quantum chemical simulation of carbon nano-nanomaterials for material science problems, ranges from a few hundred to several thousands of basis functions (see Figure 5.5). The basic operation in the program is the evaluation of the scaled commutator $B \leftarrow \alpha[A,B] = \alpha(AB - BA)$. This can be split into more "primitive" operations such as matrix-matrix multiplication, matrix addition/subtractions, and matrix-scalar product. The computational cost of the

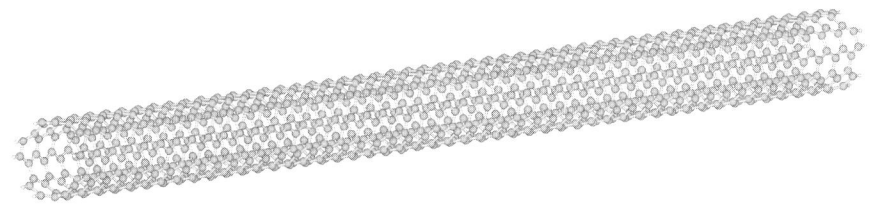

FIGURE 5.5

Single-wall carbon nanotube of (5,5) type with hydrogen-terminated ends. The total number of atoms is 1010. The total number of basis functions for DFTB calculations is 3980. Carbon nanotubes and other carbon-based nanomaterials are very promising materials for the nanotechnology and materials science fields and are hoped to be used as molecular electronic wires in a new generation of electronic devices.

first operation (matrix-matrix multiplication) scales cubically with the matrix size M. The cost of matrix-scalar multiplication and matrix-matrix addition/subtraction scales quadratically with M.

Matrix Multiplication. As was discussed in Section 5.2 of this chapter, matrices A and B in the commutator expression $\alpha(AB - BA)$ can either be symmetric or antisymmetric for the physically meaningful cases. However, the product of symmetric and/or antisymmetric matrices is a general matrix, but its commutator reveals symmetry properties that can be exploited in the implementation. The commutator of matrices of the same type (both symmetric or both antisymmetric) is an antisymmetric matrix. The commutator of a symmetric matrix with an antisymmetric matrix is always a symmetric matrix. Furthermore, once the matrix product AB is known, then the second product can be replaced by its transpose. Specific questions we want to answer are: What is the computational cost of various versions of matrix-matrix multiplications on CPU and on GPU? Is it better to use a matrix transpose or matrix multiplication? The product of two symmetric or general matrices can use specialized routines from BLAS [12]. How expensive is the cost of multiplication for two symmetric [`ssymm()`] versus the product of two general matrices [`sgemm()`]?

First, let us compare the performance of different versions of general matrix multiplication on a CPU and on a GPU. For a CPU, one can test compiler optimization, intrinsic Fortran 90 matrix multiplication, and various versions of BLAS. For the matrix multiplication on a GPU, we tested CUBLAS, a handmade CUDA kernel, and PGI accelerator directives. Some of our test results comparing different versions of general matrix-matrix multiplication are shown in the Table 5.1. Next, we compared the symmetric and general matrix multiplication in Table 5.3. The GPU calculations were performed on a Tesla C1060 with the PGI F90 compiler. All CPU calculations were performed on dual Quad Core Intel Xeon 2.5 GHz Harpertown E5420 (em64t) machine with 16 GB RAM.

The conclusion of our matrix multiplication tests are the following. The best results for the CPU were obtained with Intel's MKL routines [13]. Matrix multiplication with CUBLAS led to superior matrix multiplication results on the GPU. No performance gain was observed by using symmetric versions of matrix multiplication (`ssymm()`) as compared with the general case (`sgemm()`). Table 5.2 compares CUBLAS matrix multiplication for a matrix size as a multiple of 1000 with slightly larger matrices of size equal to multiples of 64. This shows that padding matrices with zero to match the size equal to multiplies of 64 can result in better memory access and decrease the total calculation time by up to 50% in some cases. Overall, we conclude that for CPU implementation one should use multithreaded MKL, while the GPU implementation should be based on CUBLAS matrix multiplication.

Transpose and Other Operations. Finally, we compared the relative cost of matrix multiplication with matrix transpose and other matrix operations that we encounter in our algorithm. The results are presented in Table 5.3. Our tests show that the cost of matrix transpose amounts to no more than a few percent when compared with matrix multiplication. Also, the cost of other matrix operations is very small in comparison to the cost of matrix multiplication.

Based on our knowledge of the properties of matrices, the analysis of the density matrix algorithm, and on the tests we performed, we conclude, thus, that the optimal implementation of density matrix propagation should follow these recommendations:

1. It is beneficial to split the complex P matrix into real and imaginary matrices and then perform two real matrix multiplications of real F with real and imaginary components of P. Using this procedure for the product of real F with complex P saves half of the time.

Table 5.1 Comparison of a single-precision M×M matrix multiplication on CPU and GPU. The upper section shows time in milliseconds while the lower section shows performance in MFLOPS. The "optim" column of data represents the three-nested loops with compiler optimization flag "–fast" enabled. ATLAS library was locally optimized with gfortran. The number at MKL matrix multiplication denotes the number of threads used. The "PGI-acc" symbol stands for the GPU matrix multiplication with PGI accelerator directives. The final column shows the calculation on the GPU with the CUBLAS 2.3 release of NVIDIA SDK.

M	Optim	ATLAS	MKL-1	MKL-8	PGI-acc	CUBLAS
time(msec)						
200	2.8	4.0	3.6	34.3	1.0	0.3
500	44.9	20.0	18.7	36.5	5.5	2.0
1000	360.4	148.0	117.6	59.6	30.9	10.0
2000	11,000.9	1172.0	880.6	184.7	203.7	59.4
4000	87,862.2	9292.5	7003.9	964.1	1503.2	413.3
6000	313,766.7	31,629.9		3124.2	4975.4	1256.7
8000	745,035.5	76,996.8		6915.7	11,489.3	2899.8
10,000	1,450,144.0	159,546.0		13,717.9	22,245.0	5675.8
MFLOPS/sec						
100	4750.1		726.0	65.2	2682.6	21,162.0
200	5600.3	4000.0	4374.2	465.7	15,520.0	58,304.8
500	5560.7	12,499.4	13,336.9	6844.4	45,113.0	153,777.8
1000	5548.0	13,512.7	17,002.6	33,556.4	64,522.3	233,856.0
2000	1454.4	13,651.0	18,169.2	86,618.9	78,529.0	305,888.2
4000	1456.8	13,774.4	18,275.4	132,754.3	85,147.2	343,133.9
6000	1376.8	13,657.9		138,275.1	86,825.5	354,263.0
8000	1374.4	13,299.2		148,067.4	89,125.7	355,924.8
10,000	1379.2	12,535.6		145,795.0	89,907.7	362,263.1

2. The optimal CPU implementation (on our Intel Xeon machine) should use MKL matrix multiplication sgemm(), while the optimal GPU implementation should use its CUBLAS analogue cublas_sgemm() for matrix multiplication.

3. While using CUBLAS matrix multiplication, it is very beneficial to pad matrices so that their leading dimension is a multiple of 64.

4. There is not much gain by using symmetric matrix multiplication routines (ssymm()) rather than general ones (sgemm()).

5. The cost of computing the transpose is very small compared with the cost of matrix multiplication. Also the cost of matrix-scalar multiplication (matrix scaling by sscal()) and other matrix operations that can be mapped to level 1 BLAS routines is much smaller than the matrix-matrix multiplication. Thus, it is of secondary importance which version of transpose or of any other operation is used. However, using BLAS [12] routines guarantees that the code is independent of the machine architecture and the cost of optimization is placed on the library vendor.

6. The optimal implementation of the matrix commutator should use one matrix-matrix multiplication followed by one transpose, rather than two matrix multiplications.

Table 5.2 Comparison of matrix-matrix products for "even" size matrices (500, 1000, etc.) with the corresponding larger matrix with a leading dimension array equal to multiples of 64. For large matrices, slightly increasing the size of the matrix to match a multiple of 64 can significantly decrease calculation time by up to 50%. In real calculations such "increased" matrices can be padded with zeros. Performance is in MFLOPS.

N	Time	Performance	N	Time	Performance
500	2.3	119933.2	$512 = 64 \times 8$	2.0	153777.8
1000	14.0	152077.2	$1024 = 64 \times 16$	10.0	233856.0
2000	96.5	171274.6	$2048 = 64 \times 32$	59.4	305888.2
4000	523.2	250476.1	$4094 = 64 \times 64$	413.3	343133.9
6000	2387.6	183027.3	$6016 = 64 \times 94$	1256.7	354263.0
8000	2899.8	359098.5	$8000 = 64 \times 125$	2899.8	359098.5
10,000	11047.5	182289.3	$10048 = 64 \times 157$	5675.8	362263.1
12,000	14184.6	245522.5	$12032 = 64 \times 188$	9675.2	364111.1
14,000	30374.5	181554.0	$14016 = 64 \times 219$	15203.8	365693.9

Table 5.3 The comparison of time for matrix multiplication with transpose (upper section). The lower section presents timing for level 1 routines of BLAS with a simple 1-loop code for a matrix of size 4000. Single precision is denoted as SP, and DP is double precision. Here the time is multiplied by 100. Clearly, for the system size of our interest, the cost of the matrix multiplication is much higher than all other operations.

Method	Operation	SP	DP
MKL/symm	$A * B$	687.0	1369.0
MKL/gemm	$A * B$	674.0	1340.0
intrinsic	matmul(A,B)	1769.0	4706.0
intrinsic	$B = \text{transpose}(A)$	24.0	26.0
2-loop	$B = \text{transpose}(A)$	13.0	20.0
MKL/copy	$B = A$	4.5	4.5
1-loop	$B = A$	2.7	2.8
MKL/scal	$B = a * A$	2.7	5.3
intrinsic	$B = a * A$	0.3	1.2
1-loop sscal	$B = a * B$	2.7	5.4
MKL/axpy	$a * A + B$	4.4	9.1
1-loop	$a * A + B$	4.4	8.8
MKL/isamax	max$|A|$	3.0	4.9
1-loop	max$|A|$	3.0	4.9

5.4 **FINAL EVALUATION AND BENEFITS**

Following the conclusion of the discussion in Sections 5.2 and 5.3, we implemented and tested both CPU and GPU versions of density matrix propagation. For the CPU implementation we used Intel's MKL as this leads to the best performance on the CPU. For the final evaluation we performed three sets of tests. First, we compared the performance of our GPU implementation of Eq. 5.6 with the analogous CPU implementation based on MKL for random P and F. In the second test, we compared the GPU implementation with CPU propagation based on direct evaluation of the time-evolution operator through diagonalization of the Fock operator. For these tests we also used random F and P matrices. In the final real case test, we compared the timing for density matrix propagation on the GPU for a carbon nanotube containing 1010 atoms (990 carbons + 20 hydrogens). The structure of a carbon nanotube for which we performed the test is shown in Figure 5.5. The corresponding number of basis functions is 3980 for F and P. The matrices for the GPU simulation were padded with zeros to match the size 4032, which is the nearest multiple of 64.

Fock and Density Matrices. For the timing tests we generated random Fock and density matricies of various sizes ranging from M = 500 to M = 4096. To make the density matrix more physical, we scaled the density matrix to make its trace equal to M/2 (the trace of a density matrix is equal to the number of electrons in the molecular system). For a similar reason, we multiplied each randomly generated matrix element of the Fock operator by $-100/(1 + (i - j)^{**}2)$. The chosen values were consistent with our previous simulation of carbon-based nanomaterials performed at the DFTB level of theory [14, 15]. We also chose the value of the threshold for the convergence of the density matrix propagation (see 2.ii) given by Eq. 5.6 to be equal to 10^{-8}. We observed that our commutator expansion converged after around 20 commutator iterations. This, again, was consistent with our previous simulations performed for carbon-based nanomaterials [5]. Thus, we believe that the current tests for random matrices represents the real simulations of carbon nanomaterials well. For the real case test we used armchair (5,5) single-wall carbon nanotubes as well (see Figure 5.5). The test system contained a total of 1010 atoms, including 990 carbons and 20 terminating hydrogens. For the carbon nanotube simulation, we used DFTB theory. The corresponding number of basis functions in DFTB for F and P was 3980. The matrices for the GPU simulation were padded with zeros to match a multiple of 64. Thus, the size of P and F for GPU simulations was 4032. We did not use padding of F and P for the CPU.

Hardware. The CPU tests were performed on a machine with 16 GB RAM and two quad core Intel Xeon model E5420 Harpertown processors with a 2.5 GHz clockspeed and 24 MB L2 cache (6 MB per core pair). Our CPU code used the multithreaded Math Kernel Library (MKL) [13]. Thus, for the CPU tests, we propagated the density matrix in parallel with up to eight cores. Consequently, our CPU code could run in parallel with eight cores. For the GPU tests we used a Tesla C1060 processor and the 2.3 version of the CUDA SDK. The GPU processor C1060 contained 240 single-precision (SP) cores and 30 double-precision (DP) cores clocked at 1.3 GHz. The number of cores had a significant impact on the performance. To see this effect we performed tests for both single-precision (SP) and double-precision (DP) implementations on the GPU and we compared them with analogous CPU implementations.

Discussion. Table 5.4 compares the GPU implementation for the density matrix propagation with the analogous CPU implementation based on multithreaded MKL [13]. In Table 5.5 we compare results

Table 5.4 Comparison of time (in seconds) and speedup for the GPU and CPU implementations of Liouville-von Neumann propagation for different matrix size M×M. The CPU code uses multithreaded Math Kernel Library (MKL). The numbers in the first column correspond to the number of MKL threads used in tests. The symbols SP and DP correspond to single- and double-precision implementations, respectively. The speedup is calculated as the ratio of CPU time over GPU time.

Method	Precision	M = 512	M = 1024	M = 2048	M = 4096
time:					
MKL-1	DP	1.79	14.15	131.54	884.07
MKL-1	SP	0.89	7.35	61.60	466.84
MKL-8	DP	0.62	3.55	26.48	172.34
MKL-8	SP	0.33	2.03	18.36	111.04
GPU	DP	0.25	1.62	12.83	103.85
GPU	SP	0.075	0.42	2.82	21.62
speedup:					
MKL-1/GPU	DP	7.2	8.7	10.3	8.6
MKL-1/GPU	SP	11.9	17.5	21.8	21.6
MKL-8/GPU	DP	2.5	2.2	2.1	1.7
MKL-8/GPU	SP	4.4	4.8	6.5	5.1

Table 5.5 Comparison of time (in seconds) spent for the propagation of the density matrix on the GPU with the similar propagation on the CPU through diagonalization. For the diagonalization we used the `dsyev()` routine from MKL.

dt	Methods	Precision	M = 1024	M = 2048	M = 4096
0.5	GPU	DP	0.81	6.17	48.22
	GPU	SP	0.21	1.36	10.04
	diagonalize	DP	4.44	37.42	295.16
1.0	GPU	DP	1.06	8.55	66.76
	GPU	SP	0.27	1.89	13.90
	diagonalize	DP	4.45	37.43	293.79
2.0	GPU	DP	1.62	12.82	103.84
	GPU	SP	0.42	2.82	21.61
	diagonalize	DP	4.45	37.34	293.94

on the GPU obtained for the BCH algorithm with the CPU results for the single and multithreaded diagonalization (`dsyev()` via MKL) algorithm. As can be seen in Tables 5.4 and 5.5, the density matrix propagation scales cubically with the system size. That is, as the system size (matrix size) increases twice (for example, from 1024 to 2048) we observe a 2^3 times increase in computation time. This is inherently related to the fact that the computing engine for the density matrix propagation relies heavily on the dense matrix-matrix multiplication. The same is true for diagonalization.

We observe an eightfold speedup when using eight MKL threads as compared with a single MKL thread. For example, for M = 4096 in Table 5.4 the CPU time spent on single-threaded MKL calculation is 884 seconds while the same calculation with eight threads takes 111 seconds. When switching from single to double precision on the GPU, we observe about 4–5 times degradation in performance. This roughly corresponds to the 8 to 1 ratio of the number of single- over double-precision cores in the C1060. Our results suggest that the BCH algorithm for density matrix propagation has a strong scaling. This is a very promising indicator since current trends in computer architectures (for both CPU and GPU) is to provide more cores per unit. NVIDIA's Fermi, a new generation GPU, will have a significantly larger number of cores as compared with the Tesla C1060, and we expect a significant speedup of our BCH code on Fermi.

In the case of the BCH algorithm, the computational cost depends on a time step used in molecular dynamics (see Table 5.5). For the larger time steps the more terms of commutator expansion is required to achieve the convergence for a given threshold. Here, we use convergence threshold value $thrs = 10^{-8}$. Thus, overall cost and accuracy in the BCH algorithm can be controlled by the time step and BCH convergence threshold. The cost for the diagonalization-based algorithm is independent of the time step and accuracy versus cost cannot be controlled.

For the final test we propagated the density matrix in a large carbon nanotube (see Figure 5.5) at the DFTB level of theory. The corresponding size of P and F matrices is 3980. For the GPU we increased the size to the nearest multiple of 64 larger than 3980. The computational cost amounts to 10 seconds and 49 seconds for single- and double-precision propagation of the density matrix on the GPU, respectively. Similarly, the CPU time for the propagation of the density matrix via MKL diagonalization is 70 seconds.

Overall, for the double-precision implementations on GPU compared with the CPU we obtain a twofold speedup for 8-thread MKL execution and nine times speedup for the single-thread MKL execution. For the analogous single-precision implementations we obtain a speedup of five times with respect to the 8-thread MKL execution on the CPU and 20 times the speedup for a single-thread MKL run. Our results show that the relative (CPU vs. GPU) computational cost is in good agreement with an estimate from the hardware specification. For the single-precision implementation one can expect that 240 GPU cores of 1.3 GHz, as compared with eight CPU cores clocked at 2.5 GHz, would lead to about 16 times the speedup [(240 cores * 1.3 GHz)/(8 cores * 2.5 GHz)]. Similarly, for double precision one can expect about a twofold speedup [(30 cores * 1.3 GHz)/(8 cores * 2.5 GHz)].

Benefits. The benefits of current implementation are

- Our GPU algorithm shows a reasonable improvement over the CPU implementation and a promising strong scaling;
- The computing engine for propagation of electronic structure can easily be updated by simply replacing the CUBLAS library [7] or transpose subroutine [11];
- The code and GPU subroutines can easily be connected with any Fortran code due to the top layer wrappers Fortran-to-C inferface. This is important considering the fact that a large portion of computational chemistry software is legacy code written in Fortran;
- The propagation scheme is general and does not depend on the specific level of electronic structure used. It can be used with Hartree-Fock, density functional, or tight-binding theories. The general

modular character allows it to connect with any electronic structure method that can provide Fock evaluation;

• The Liouville-von Neumann propagation scheme [5] goes beyond the Born-Oppenheimer approximation.

5.5 CONCLUSIONS AND FUTURE DIRECTIONS

Summary. We described our effort to adapt our quantum dynamics algorithm for the propagation of electronic density matrices on GPU. We showed how the Liouville-von Neumann algorithm can be redesigned to efficiently use vendor-provided library routines in combination with direct CUDA kernels. We discussed the efficiency and computational costs of various components involved that are present in the algorithm. Several benchmark results were shown and the final test simulations were performed for a carbon nanotube containing 1010 atoms, using the DFTB level of theory for electronic structure. Finally, we demonstrated that the GPU code based on a combination of CUDA kernels and CUBLAS routines can be integrated with a main Fortran code.

Here is the summary of the path we followed and the lessons we learned:

• Analyze the theoretical scaling of the algorithm and of its major components. Analyze the computation of various building blocks for the target problem size.
• Focus on the most expensive part (building block) of the algorithm. Use existing efficient libraries if possible. It is generally cheaper and more effective to use existing libraries than to optimize the code by hand.
• If the most expensive building blocks do not exist yet in the form of the efficient library and if no GPU library exists, then focus on the optimization of CUDA code.

Future Directions. We presented our experimental implementation of electronic structure propagation on GPUs. We plan to use this method for the material science simulations. In our future development we will focus on (a) moving the formation of the Fock matrix from the CPU to GPU, (b) adapting the algorithm for multi GPUs, and (c) exploiting sparsity of matrices.

Acknowledgments

The support for this project is provided by the National Science Foundation (grant No. ARRA-NSF-EPS-0919436). NICS computational resources are gratefully acknowledged. We would like to acknowledge the donation of equipment by NVIDIA within the Professor Partnership Program to K.M. J.J. would like to thank Jack Wells for the inspiring discussions. K.M. acknowledges support of AFSOR grants (FA9550-07-1-0395 and FA9550-10-1-030). S.I. acknowledges support by the Program for Improvement of Research Environment for Young Researchers from Special Coordination Funds for Promoting Science and Technology (SCF) commissioned by the Ministry of Education, Culture, Sports, Science and Technology (MEXT) of Japan.

References

[1] W.K. Hase, K. Song, M.S. Gordon, Direct dynamics simulations, Comput. Sci. Eng. 5 (4) (2003) 36–44.

[2] D. Marx, J. Hutter, Ab initio molecular dynamics: theory and implementation, in: J. Grotendorst (Ed.), Modern Methods and Algorithms of Quantum Chemistry Proceedings, Winterschool, Julich, Germany, 21–25 February 2000, John van Neumann Institute fur Computing, 1, 2000, pp. 301–449.

[3] R. Car, M. Parinello, Unified approach for molecular dynamics and density-functional theory, Phys. Rev. Lett. 55 (22) (1985) 2471–2474.

[4] G. Fleming, M. Ratner, Directing Matter and Energy: Five Challenges for Science and the Imagination, A Report from the Basic Energy Sciences Advisory Committee, US Dept. of Energy, http://www.sc.doe.gov/bes/reports/abstracts.html#GC, 2007 (accessed on July 2010).

[5] J. Jakowski, K. Morokuma, Liouville-von Neumann molecular dynamics, J. Chem. Phys. 130 (2009) 224106.

[6] M.J. Frisch, G.W. Trucks, H.B. Schlegel, G.E. Scuseria, M.A. Robb, J.R. Cheeseman, Gaussian 09, Revision A.02, Gaussian, Inc., Wallingford, CT, 2010.

[7] CUDA CUBLAS Library, http://developer.download.nvidia.com/compute/cuda/2_3/toolkit/docs/CUBLAS Library 2.3.pdf.

[8] *CULA, A GPU-Accelerated Linear Algebra Library*, EM Photonics, Newark, DE, http://www.culatools.com/features/.

[9] E. Agullo, J. Demmel, J. Dongarra, B. Hadri, J. Kurzak, J. Langou, et al., Numerical linear algebra on emerging architectures: the PLASMA and MAGMA projects, J. Phys.: Conf. Ser. 180 (2009).

[10] M. Wolfe, PGI Fortran & C Accelerator Programming Model, The Portland Group, http://www.pgroup.com/lit/whitepapers/pgi_accel_prog_model_1.2.pdf, 2010.

[11] G. Reutsch, P. Micikevicius, Optimizing Matrix Transpose in CUDA, CUDA SDK Code Samples, NVIDIA, 2009.

[12] L.S. Blackford, J. Demmel, J. Dongarra, I. Duff, S. Hammarling, G. Henry, et al., An updated set of basic linear algebra subprograms (BLAS), ACM Trans. Math. Soft. 28 (2002) 135–151.

[13] Intel Math Kernel Library 10.2, http://software.intel.com/en-us/intel-mkl/.

[14] D. Porezag, Th. Frauenheim, Th. Köhler, G. Seifert, R. Kaschner, Construction of tight-binding-like potentials on the basis of density-functional theory: application to carbon, Phys. Rev. B 51 (1995) 12947–12957.

[15] M. Elstner, D. Porezag, G. Jungnickel, J. Elsner, M. Haugk, Th. Frauenheim, et al., Self-consistent-charge density-functional tight-binding method for simulations of complex materials properties, Phys. Rev. B 58 (1998) 7260–7268.

An Efficient CUDA Implementation of the Tree-Based Barnes Hut *n*-Body Algorithm

6

Martin Burtscher, Keshav Pingali

This chapter describes the first CUDA implementation of the classical Barnes Hut *n*-body algorithm that runs entirely on the GPU. Unlike most other CUDA programs, our code builds an *irregular* tree-based data structure and performs complex traversals on it. It consists of six GPU kernels. The kernels are optimized to minimize memory accesses and thread divergence and are fully parallelized within and across blocks. Our CUDA code takes 5.2 seconds to simulate one time step with 5,000,000 bodies on a 1.3 GHz Quadro FX 5800 GPU with 240 cores, which is 74 times faster than an optimized serial implementation running on a 2.53 GHz Xeon E5540 CPU.

6.1 INTRODUCTION, PROBLEM STATEMENT, AND CONTEXT

The Barnes Hut force-calculation algorithm [1] is widely used in *n*-body simulations such as modeling the motion of galaxies. It hierarchically decomposes the space around the bodies into successively smaller boxes, called cells, and computes summary information for the bodies contained in each cell, allowing the algorithm to quickly approximate the forces (e.g., gravitational, electric, or magnetic) that the *n* bodies induce upon each other. The hierarchical decomposition is recorded in an octree, which is the three-dimensional equivalent of a binary tree. With *n* bodies, the precise force calculation needs to evaluate $O(n^2)$ interactions. The Barnes Hut algorithm reduces this complexity to $O(n \log n)$ and thus makes interesting problem sizes computationally tractable.

The Barnes Hut algorithm is challenging to implement efficiently in CUDA because (1) it repeatedly builds and traverses an irregular tree-based data structure, (2) it performs a lot of pointer-chasing memory operations, and (3) it is typically expressed recursively. Recursion is not supported by current GPUs, so we have to use iteration. Pointer-chasing codes execute many slow uncoalesced memory accesses. Our implementation combines load instructions, uses caching, and throttles threads to drastically reduce the number of main memory accesses; it also employs array-based techniques to enable some coalescing. Because traversing irregular data structures often results in thread divergence (i.e., detrimental loss of parallelism), we group similar work together to minimize divergence.

Our work shows that GPUs can be used to accelerate even irregular codes. It includes a number of new optimizations, as well as known ones, and demonstrates how to exploit some of the unique architectural features of GPUs in novel ways. For example, because the threads in a warp necessarily run in lockstep, we can have one thread fetch data from main memory and share the data with the other threads without the need for synchronization. Similarly, because barriers are implemented in hardware on GPUs and are therefore very fast, we have been able to use them to reduce wasted work and main memory accesses in a way that is impossible in current CPUs where barriers have to communicate through memory. Moreover, we exploit GPU-specific operations such as thread-voting functions to greatly improve performance and make use of fence instructions to implement lightweight synchronization without atomic operations.

The rest of this chapter is organized as follows: Section 6.2 provides more detail on the Barnes Hut algorithm and how we mapped it to GPU kernels; Section 6.3 describes the operation of each kernel with a focus on tuning; and Section 6.4 evaluates the performance of our implementation, discusses limitations, and draws conclusions.

6.2 CORE METHODS

This section explains the Barnes Hut algorithm. Figure 6.1 shows the high-level steps. Steps 1 through 6, that is, the body of the time step loop, are executed on the GPU. Each of these steps is implemented as a separate kernel (a kernel is a subroutine that runs on the GPU), which is necessary because we need a global barrier between the steps; it is also beneficial because it allows us to individually tune the number of blocks and threads per block for each kernel. Step 4 is not necessary for correctness, but greatly improves performance.

Figures 6.2 through 6.5 illustrate the operation of kernels 1, 2, 3, and 5. Kernel 1 computes a bounding box around all bodies; this box becomes the root node of the octree (i.e., the outermost cell). Kernel 2 hierarchically subdivides this cell until there is at most one body per innermost cell. This is accomplished by inserting all bodies into the octree. Kernel 3 computes, for each cell, the center of gravity and the cumulative mass of all contained bodies (Figure 6.4 shows this for the two shaded

```
0. Read input data and transfer to GPU
for each timestep do {
    1. Compute bounding box around all bodies
    2. Build hierarchical decomposition by inserting each body into octree
    3. Summarize body information in each internal octree node
    4. Approximately sort the bodies by spatial distance
    5. Compute forces acting on each body with help of octree
    6. Update body positions and velocities
}
7. Transfer result to CPU and output
```

FIGURE 6.1

Pseudo code of the Barnes Hut algorithm; bold print denotes GPU code.

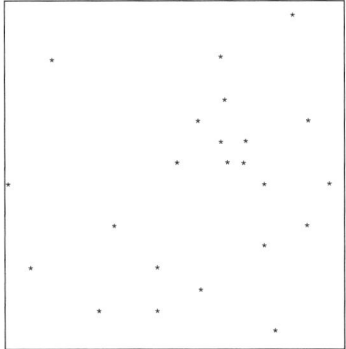

FIGURE 6.2

Bounding box kernel (kernel 1).

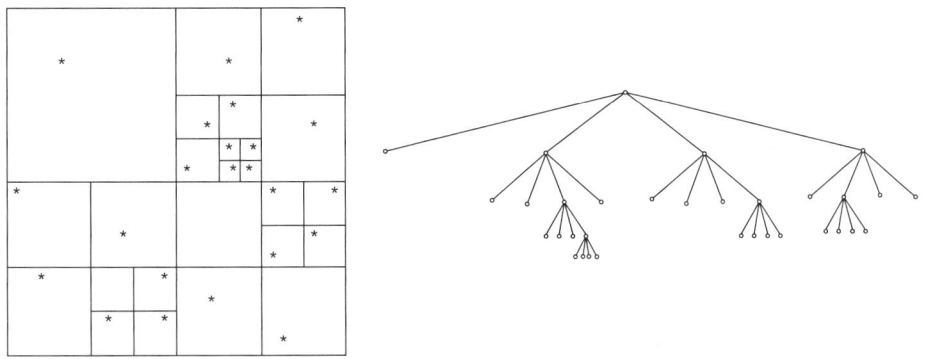

FIGURE 6.3

Hierarchical decomposition kernel (kernel 2); 2-D view on left, tree view on right.

cells). Kernel 4 (no figure) sorts the bodies according to an in-order traversal of the octree, which typically places spatially close bodies close together. Kernel 5 computes the forces acting on each body. Starting from the octree's root, it checks whether the center of gravity is far enough away from the current body for each encountered cell (the current body is located at the source of the arrows in Figure 6.5). If it is not (solid arrow), the subcells are visited to perform a more accurate force calculation (the three dotted arrows); if it is (single dashed arrow), only one force calculation with the cell's center of gravity and mass is performed, and the subcells and all bodies within them are not visited, thus greatly reducing the total number of force calculations. Kernel 6 (no figure) nudges all the bodies into their new positions and updates their velocities.

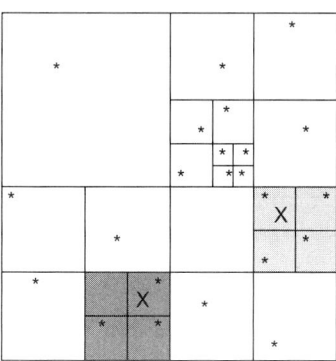

FIGURE 6.4

Center-of-gravity kernel (kernel 3).

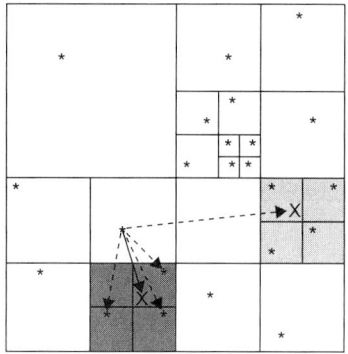

FIGURE 6.5

Force calculation kernel (kernel 5).

6.3 ALGORITHMS AND IMPLEMENTATIONS

This section describes our CUDA implementation of the Barnes Hut algorithm, with a focus on the optimizations we incorporated to make it execute efficiently on a GPU. We start with the global optimizations that apply to all kernels and then discuss each kernel individually. The section concludes with a summary and general optimization patterns that may be useful for speeding up other irregular codes.

6.3.1 Global Optimizations

Dynamic data structures such as trees are typically built from heap objects, where each heap object contains multiple fields, e.g., child-pointer and data fields, and is allocated dynamically. Because dynamic allocation of and accesses to heap objects tend to be slow, we use an array-based data structure. Accesses to arrays cannot be coalesced if the array elements are objects with multiple fields, so we use several aligned scalar arrays, one per field, as outlined in Figure 6.6. As a consequence, our code uses array indexes instead of pointers to tree nodes.

In Barnes Hut, the cells, which are the internal tree nodes, and the bodies, which are the leaves of the tree, have some common fields (e.g., the mass and the position). Other fields are only needed by either the cells (e.g., the child pointers) or the bodies (e.g., the velocity and the acceleration). However, to simplify and speed up the code, it is important to use the same arrays for both bodies and cells.

We allocate the bodies at the beginning and the cells at the end of the arrays, as illustrated in Figure 6.7, and use an index of −1 as a "null pointer." This allocation order has several advantages. First, a simple comparison of the array index with the number of bodies determines whether the index points to a cell or a body. Second, in some code sections, we need to find out whether an index refers to a body or to null. Because −1 is also smaller than the number of bodies, a single integer comparison suffices to test both conditions. Third, we can alias arrays that hold only cell information with arrays that hold only body information to reduce the memory consumption while maintaining a one-to-one correspondence between the indexes into the different arrays, thus simplifying the code. Figure 6.7 shows how arrays A and B are combined into array AB.

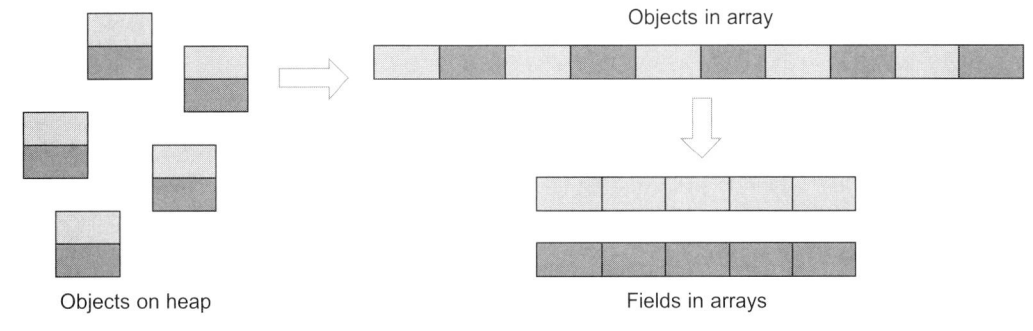

Objects in array

Objects on heap

Fields in arrays

FIGURE 6.6

Using multiple arrays (one per field) instead of an array of objects or separate heap objects.

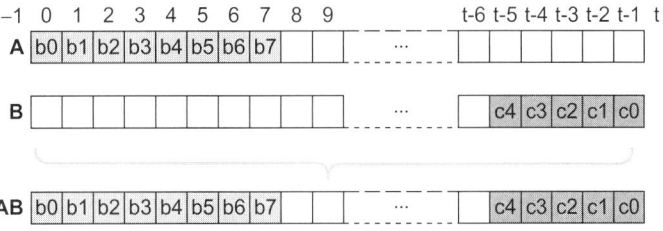

FIGURE 6.7

Array layout and element allocation order for body-only (A), cell-only (B), and combined (AB) arrays; b = body, c = cell, t = array length.

Our implementation requires compute capability 1.2, in particular, a thread-voting function as well as the larger number of registers, which allows launching more threads per block. The thread count per block is maximized and rounded down to the nearest multiple of the warp size for each kernel. All kernels use at least as many blocks as there are streaming multiprocessors in the GPU, which is automatically detected.

Because all parameters passed to the kernels, such as the starting addresses of the various arrays, stay the same throughout the time step loop, we copy them once into the GPU's constant memory. This is much faster than passing them with every kernel invocation.

Our code does not transfer any data between the CPU and the GPU except for one initial transfer to send the input to the GPU and one final transfer to send the result back to the CPU. This approach avoids slow data transfers over the PCI bus during the simulation and is possible because we execute the entire algorithm on one GPU.

Because our code operates on octrees in which nodes can have up to eight children, it contains many loops with a trip count of eight. We use pragmas to unroll these loops, though the compiler does this by default in most cases.

6.3.2 Kernel 1 Optimizations

The first kernel computes a bounding box around all bodies, i.e., the root of the octree. To do that, it has to find the minimum and maximum coordinates in the three spatial dimensions. First, the kernel breaks up the data into equal sized chunks and assigns one chunk to each block. Each block then performs a reduction operation that follows the example outlined in Section B.5 of the CUDA Programming Guide [5]. All the relevant data in main memory are read only once and in a fully coalesced manner. The reduction is performed in shared memory in a way that avoids bank conflicts and minimizes thread divergence [6]. The only thread divergence occurs at the very end when there are fewer than 32 elements left to process per block. Our implementation uses the built-in *min* and *max* functions to perform the reduction operations, since these are faster than *if* statements. The final result from each block is written to main memory. The last block, as is determined by a global *atomicInc* operation, combines these results and generates the root node.

6.3.3 Kernel 2 Optimizations

The second kernel implements an iterative tree-building algorithm that uses lightweight locks, only locks child pointers of leaf cells, and deliberately slows down unsuccessful threads to reduce the memory pressure. The bodies are assigned to the blocks and threads within a block in round-robin fashion. Each thread inserts its bodies one after the other by traversing the tree from the root to the desired last-level cell and then attempts to lock the appropriate child pointer (an array index) by writing an otherwise unused value (-2) to it using an atomic operation, as illustrated in Figures 6.8 and 6.9. If the locking succeeds, the thread inserts the new body, thereby overwriting the lock value, which releases the lock. If a body is already stored at this location, the thread first creates a new cell by atomically requesting the next unused array index, inserts the original and the new body into this new cell, executes a memory fence (*__threadfence*) to ensure the new subtree is visible to the rest of the cores, and then attaches the new cell to the tree, thereby releasing the lock.

The threads that fail to acquire a lock have to retry until they succeed. Allowing them to do so right away would swamp the main memory with requests and slow down the progress of the successful threads, especially in the beginning when the tree is small. As long as at least one thread per warp (a warp is a group of threads that execute together) succeeds in acquiring a lock, thread divergence temporarily disables all the threads in the warp that did not manage to acquire a lock until the successful threads have completed their insertions and released their locks. This process greatly reduces

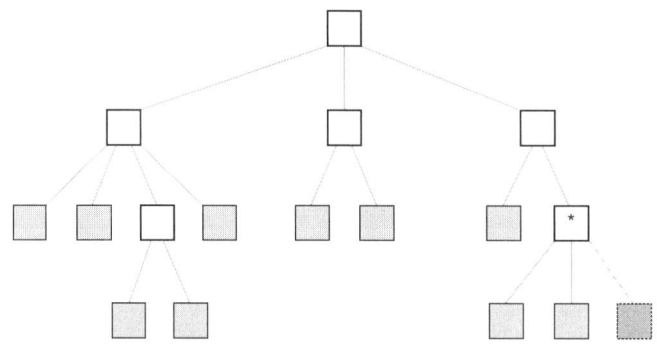

FIGURE 6.8

Locking the dashed child "pointer" of the starred cell to insert a body.

```
// initialize
cell = find_insertion_point(body); // nothing is locked, cell cached for retries
child = get_insertion_index(cell, body);
if (child != locked) {
  if (child == atomicCAS(&cell[child], child, lock)) {
    if (child == null) {
      cell[child] = body; // insert body and release lock
    } else {
      new_cell =...; // atomically get the next unused cell
      // insert the existing and new body into new_cell
      __threadfence(); // make sure new_cell subtree is visible
      cell[child] = new_cell; // insert new_cell and release lock
    }
    success = true; // flag indicating that insertion succeeded
  }
}
__syncthreads(); // wait for other warps to finish insertion
```

FIGURE 6.9

Pseudo code for inserting a body.

the number of retries (i.e., memory accesses), most of which would be useless because they would find the lock to still be unavailable. To also prevent warps in which *all* threads fail to acquire a lock from flooding the memory with lock-polling requests, we inserted an artificial barrier (__syncthreads) into this kernel (the last line in the pseudo code in Figure 6.9) that is not necessary for correctness. This barrier throttles warps that would otherwise most likely not be able to make progress but would slow down the memory accesses of the successful threads. The code shown in Figure 6.9 executes inside of a loop that moves on to the next body assigned to a thread whenever the success flag is true.

In summary, this kernel employs the following optimizations. It caches the root's data in the register file. It employs a barrier to throttle threads that fail to acquire a lock. It minimizes the number of locks by only locking child pointers of leaf cells. It employs lightweight locks that require a single atomic operation to lock and a memory fence followed by a store operation to release the lock. The common case, that is, adding a body without the need to generate a new cell (typically, about one cell is created per three bodies), uses an even faster unlock mechanism that requires only a store operation, but no memory fence.

6.3.4 Kernel 3 Optimizations

The third kernel traverses the unbalanced octree from the bottom up to compute the center of gravity and the sum of the masses of each cell's children. Figure 6.10 shows the octree nodes in the global arrays (bottom) and the corresponding tree representation (top). In this kernel, the cells are assigned to the blocks and to the threads within a block in round-robin fashion. Note that the leftmost cell is not necessarily mapped to the first thread in the first block. Rather, it is mapped to the thread that yields the correct alignment to enable coalescing of memory accesses.

Initially, all cells have negative masses, indicating that their true masses still need to be computed. Because the majority of the cells in the octree have only bodies as children, the corresponding threads

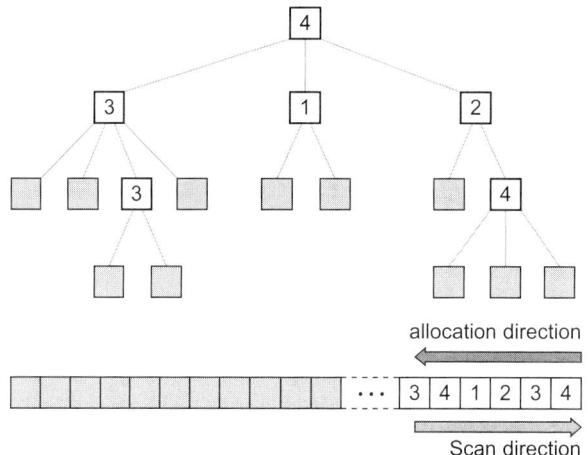

FIGURE 6.10

Allocation of bodies (the shaded nodes) and cells (the white nodes) in the global arrays and corresponding tree representation; the numbers represent thread IDs.

can immediately compute the cell data. In fact, this can be done using coalesced accesses to store the mass and position information until the threads in a warp start processing cells whose children are not yet ready — this step forces threads to wait different amounts of time.

Because the allocation order ensures that a cell's children have lower array indexes than the cell does, it is not possible that a thread will ever attempt to process a cell before it has processed all tree successors of this cell that are assigned to this thread. For example, threads 3 and 4 both have two cells on the same path assigned to them in Figure 6.10, but they are guaranteed to first process the lower-level cell. If this were not the case, the code could deadlock.

As the pseudo code in Figure 6.11 shows, the computed center of gravity is stored first, then a memory fence is executed, and finally the computed mass is stored to indicate that the cell's data are now ready. The memory fence ensures that no other thread in the GPU can see the updated mass before it sees the updated center of gravity. This way, no locks or atomic operations are necessary, and preexisting memory locations (the mass fields) serve as ready flags. Unsuccessful threads have to poll until the "ready flag" is set. Note that the code shown in Figure 6.11 executes inside of a loop that moves on to the next cell assigned to the thread whenever the success flag is set to true.

For performance reasons, the kernel caches all the child pointers of the current cell in shared memory that point to not-ready children. This way, the thread polls only the missing children, which reduces main memory accesses. Moreover, if a child is found to still be unready, thread divergence (due to exiting the do-while loop in Figure 6.11) deliberately forces the thread to wait for a while before trying again to throttle polling requests.

Kernel 3 performs two more functions (not included in Figure 6.11) that piggyback on its bottom-up traversal and therefore incur little additional runtime. The first extra operation is to count the bodies in all subtrees and store this information in the cells. These counts make kernel 4 much faster. The second additional operation is to move all non-null child pointers to the front. In the earlier kernels, the

```
// initialize
if (missing == 0) {
    // initialize center of gravity
    for (/*iterate over existing children*/) {
        if (/*child is ready*/) {
            // add its contribution to center of gravity
        } else {
            // cache child index
            missing++;
    } } }
if (missing != 0) {
    do {
        if (/*last cached child is now ready*/) {
            // remove from cache and add its contribution to center of gravity
            missing−−;
        }
    } while (/*missing changed*/ && (missing != 0));
}
if (missing == 0) {
    // store center of gravity
    __threadfence(); // make sure center of gravity is visible
    // store cumulative mass
    success = true; // local flag indicating that computation for cell is done
}
```

FIGURE 6.11

Pseudo code for computing a cell's center of gravity.

position of each child is essential for correct operation, but the later kernels just need to be able to visit all children. Hence, we can move the existing children to the front of the eight-element child array in each cell and move all the nulls to the end. This makes kernel 5 faster.

In summary, this kernel includes the following optimizations: It maps cells to threads in a way that results in good load balance, avoids deadlocks, allows some coalescing, and enables bottom-up traversals without explicit parent pointers. It does not require any locks or atomic operations, uses a data field in the cells as a ready flag, and sets the flags with a memory fence followed by a simple write operation. It throttles unsuccessful threads, caches data, and polls only missing data to minimize the number of main memory accesses. Finally, it moves the children in each cell to the front and records the number of bodies in all subtrees to accelerate later kernels.

6.3.5 Kernel 4 Optimizations

This kernel sorts the bodies in parallel using a top-down traversal. It employs the same array-based traversal technique as the previous kernel except that the processing order is reversed; i.e., each thread starts with the highest array index assigned to it and works its way down. It also uses a data field as a ready flag. Based on the number of bodies in each subtree, which was computed in kernel 3, it concurrently places the bodies into an array such that the bodies appear in the same order in the array as they would during an in-order traversal of the octree. This sorting groups spatially close bodies together, and these grouped bodies are crucial to speed up kernel 5.

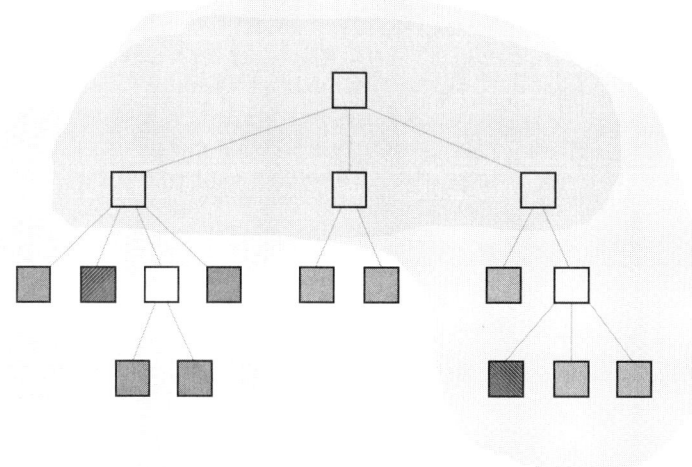

FIGURE 6.12

Tree prefixes that need to be visited for the two marked bodies.

6.3.6 Kernel 5 Optimizations

The fifth kernel requires the vast majority of the runtime and is therefore the most important to optimize. It assigns all bodies to the blocks and threads within a block in round-robin fashion. For each body, the corresponding thread traverses some prefix of the octree to compute the force acting upon this body, as illustrated in Figure 6.12. These prefixes are similar for spatially close bodies, but different for spatially distant bodies. Because threads belonging to the same warp execute in lockstep, every warp in this kernel effectively has to traverse the union of the tree prefixes of all the threads in the warp. In other words, whenever a warp traverses a part of the tree that some of the threads do not need, those threads are disabled due to thread divergence, but they still have to wait for this part to be traversed. As a consequence, it is paramount to group spatially nearby bodies together so that the threads in a warp have to traverse similar tree prefixes, that is, to make the union of the prefixes as small as possible. This is why the sorting in kernel 4 is so important. It eliminates most of the thread divergence and accelerates kernel 5 by an order of magnitude. In fact, we opted to eliminate this kind of thread divergence entirely because it is pointless to make some threads wait when they can, without incurring additional runtime, improve the accuracy of their computation by expanding their tree prefix to encompass the entire union. Determining the union's border can be done extremely quickly using the __all thread-voting function, as illustrated in Figure 6.13.

Having eliminated thread divergence and reduced the amount of work each warp has to do by minimizing the size of the union of the prefixes, we note that main memory accesses still pose a major performance hurdle because this kernel contains very little computation with which to hide them. Moreover, the threads in a warp always access the same tree node at the same time; that is, they always read from the same location in main memory. Unfortunately, multiple reads of the same address are not coalesced by older GPU hardware, but instead result in multiple separate accesses. To remedy this situation, we allow only one thread per warp to read the pertinent data, and then that thread makes the data

```
// precompute and cache info
// determine first thread in each warp
for (/*sorted body indexes assigned to me*/) {
    // cache body data
    // initialize iteration stack
    depth = 0;
    while (depth >= 0) {
        while (/*there are more nodes to visit*/) {
            if (/*I'm the first thread in the warp*/) {
                // move on to next node
                // read node data and put in shared memory
            }
            __threadfence_block();
            if (/*node is not null*/) {
                // get node data from shared memory
                // compute distance to node
                if ((/*node is a body*/) || __all(/*distance >= cutoff*/)) {
                    // compute interaction force contribution
                } else {
                    depth++; // descend to next tree level
                    if (/*I'm the first thread in the warp*/) {
                        // push node's children onto iteration stack
                    }
                    __threadfence_block();
                }
            } else {
                depth = max(0, depth-1); // early out because remaining nodes are also null
            }
        }
        depth--;
    }
    // update body data
}
```

FIGURE 6.13

Pseudo code of the force calculation kernel.

available to the other threads in the same warp by caching the data in shared memory. This introduces brief periods of thread divergence but reduces the number of main memory accesses by a factor of 32, resulting in a substantial speedup of this memory-bound kernel. The code needs a block-local memory fence (*__threadfence_block()*) to prevent data reordering so that the threads in a warp can safely retrieve the data from shared memory. Note that the shared memory allows all threads to simultaneously read the same location without bank conflict.

In addition to these two major optimizations (i.e., minimizing the amount of work per warp and minimizing the number of main memory accesses), kernel 5 incorporates the following optimizations, some of which are illustrated in Figure 6.13. It does not write to the octree and therefore requires no locks or ready flags. It caches information that depends only on the tree-depth of a node in shared memory, it uses the built-in *rsqrtf* function to quickly compute "one over square root," it uses only

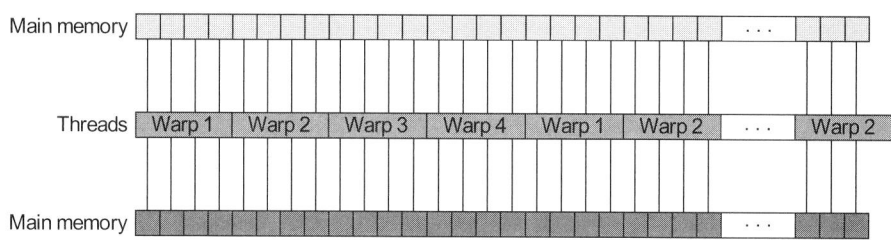

FIGURE 6.14

Fully coalesced streaming updates of the body positions and velocities.

one thread per warp to control the iteration stack (which is necessary to avoid recursion) to reduce the memory footprint enough to make it fit into shared memory, and it takes advantage of the children having been moved to the front in kernel 3 by stopping the processing of a cell's children as soon as the first null entry is encountered. This early termination reduces thread divergence because it makes it likely that all threads in a warp find their first few children to be non-null and their last few children to be null. This is another example of grouping similar work together to minimize divergence and maximize performance.

6.3.7 Kernel 6 Optimizations

The sixth kernel updates the velocity and position of each body based on the computed force. It is a straightforward, fully coalesced, nondivergent streaming kernel, as illustrated in Figure 6.14. As in the other kernels, the bodies are assigned to the blocks and threads within a block in round-robin fashion.

6.3.8 Optimization Summary

This subsection summarizes the optimizations described above and highlights general principles we believe may be useful for tuning CUDA implementations of other irregular pointer-chasing codes. Table 6.1 combines the optimizations from the various Barnes Hut kernels and groups them by category.

In implementing the Barnes Hut algorithm in CUDA and tuning it, we found the following general optimization principles to be important.

Maximizing parallelism and load balance. To hide latencies, particularly memory latencies, it is important to run a large number of threads and blocks in parallel. By parallelizing every step of our algorithm across threads and blocks as well as by using array elements instead of heap objects to represent tree nodes, we were able to assign balanced amounts of work to any number of threads and blocks.

Minimizing thread divergence. To maintain maximum parallelism, it is important for the threads in a warp to follow the same control flow. We found that grouping similar work together can drastically reduce thread divergence, especially in irregular code.

Minimizing main memory accesses. Probably the most important optimization for memory-bound code is to reduce main memory accesses as much as possible, for example, by caching data and by throttling warps that are likely to issue memory accesses that do not contribute to the overall progress.

Table 6.1 Optimizations by category.

MAIN MEMORY

Minimize Accesses
- Let one thread read common data and distribute data to other threads via shared memory
- When waiting for multiple data items to be computed, record which items are ready and only poll the missing items
- Cache data in registers or shared memory
- Use thread throttling (see control-flow section)

Maximize Coalescing
- Use multiple aligned arrays, one per field, instead of arrays of structs or structs on heap
- Use a good allocation order for data items in arrays

Reduce Data Size
- Share arrays or elements that are known not to be used at the same time

Minimize CPU/GPU Data Transfer
- Keep data on GPU between kernel calls
- Pass kernel parameters through constant memory

CONTROL FLOW

Minimize Thread Divergence
- Group similar work together in the same warp

Combine Operations
- Perform as much work as possible per traversal, i.e., fuse similar traversals

Throttle Threads
- Insert barriers to prevent threads from executing likely useless work

Minimize Control Flow
- Use compiler pragma to unroll loops

LOCKING

Minimize Locks
- Lock as little as possible (e.g., only a child pointer instead of entire node, only last node instead of entire path to node)

Use Lightweight Locks
- Use flags (barrier/store and load) where possible
- Use atomic operation to lock but barrier/store or just store to unlock

Reuse Fields
- Use existing data field instead of separate lock field

HARDWARE

Exploit Special Instructions
- Use min, max, __threadfence, __threadfence_block, __syncthreads, __all, rsqft, etc. operations

Maximize Thread Count
- Parallelize code across threads
- Limit shared memory and register usage to maximize thread count

(Continued)

Table 6.1 (*Continued*)
HARDWARE
Avoid Bank Conflicts   • Control the accesses to shared memory to avoid bank conflicts
Use All Multiprocessors   • Parallelize code across blocks   • Make the block count at least as large as the number of streaming multiprocessors

By grouping similar work together in the same warp, we managed to greatly increase sharing and thus reduce main memory accesses. By throttling warps in which all threads failed to acquire a lock and by allowing threads to poll only as-yet unready data, we were able to further reduce the amount of main memory traffic.

Using lightweight locks. If locking is necessary, as few items as possible should be locked and for as short a time as possible. For example, we never lock nodes, only last-level child pointers. The locking is done with an atomic operation, and the unlocking is done with an even faster memory fence and store operation. For maximum speed and minimum space overhead, we use existing data fields instead of separate locks and utilize otherwise unused values to lock them. Writing to these fields releases the lock. In some cases, no atomic operations are needed at all because a fence and store operation suffices to achieve the necessary functionality.

Combining operations. Because pointer-chasing operations are particularly expensive on GPUs, it is probably worthwhile to combine tasks to avoid additional traversals. For example, our code computes the mass and center of gravity, counts the bodies in the subtrees, and moves the non-null children to the front in a single traversal.

Maximizing coalescing. Coalesced memory accesses are difficult to achieve in irregular pointer-chasing codes. Nevertheless, by carefully allocating the node data and spreading the fields over multiple scalar arrays, we have managed to attain some coalescing in several kernels.

Avoiding GPU/CPU transfers. Copying data to or from the GPU is a relatively slow operation. However, data can be left on the GPU between kernels. By implementing the entire algorithm on the GPU, we were able to eliminate almost all data transfers between the host and the device. Moreover, we used the constant memory to transfer kernel parameters — a process that is significantly faster and avoids retransmitting unchanged values.

6.4 EVALUATION AND VALIDATION OF RESULTS, TOTAL BENEFITS, AND LIMITATIONS

6.4.1 Evaluation Methodology

Implementations. In addition to our parallel CUDA version of the Barnes Hut algorithm, we wrote two more implementations for comparison purposes: (1) a serial C version of the Barnes Hut algorithm and

(2) a parallel CUDA version of the $O(n^2)$ algorithm. The three implementations use single precision. The $O(n^2)$ algorithm computes all pair-wise forces and is therefore more precise than the approximate Barnes Hut algorithm. The Barnes Hut implementations are run with a tolerance factor of 0.5. The C and CUDA versions include many of the same optimizations, but also CPU and GPU specific optimizations, respectively.

Inputs. We generated five inputs with 5000, 50,000, 500,000, 5,000,000, and 50,000,000 galaxies (bodies). The galaxies' positions and velocities are initialized according to the empirical Plummer model [2], which mimics the density distribution of globular clusters.

System. We evaluated the performance of our CUDA implementation on a 1.3 GHz Quadro FX 5800 GPU with 30 streaming multiprocessors (240 cores) and 4 GB of main memory. For performance comparison purposes and as host device, we used a 2.53 GHz Xeon E5540 CPU with 48 GB of main memory.

Compilers. We compiled the CUDA codes with *nvcc* v3.0 and the "-O3 -arch=sm_13" flags. For the C code, we used *icc* v11.1 and the "-O2" flag because it generates a faster executable than *nvcc*'s underlying C compiler does.

Metric. We reported the best runtime of three identical experiments. There is typically little difference between the best and the worst runtimes. We measured only the time step loop; that is, generating the input and writing the output is not included in the reported runtimes.

Validation. We compared the output of the three codes to verify that they are computing the same result. Note, however, that the outputs are not entirely identical because the $O(n^2)$ algorithm is more accurate than the Barnes Hut algorithm and because the CPU's floating-point arithmetic is more precise than the GPU's.

6.4.2 Results

Figure 6.15 plots the runtime per time step versus the problem size on a log-log scale for the three implementations (lower numbers are better). With increasing input size, the parallel CUDA Barnes Hut code is 5, 35, 66, 74, and 53 times faster than the serial C code. So even on this irregular code, the GPU has an over 50x performance advantage over a single CPU core for large enough problem sizes. The benefit is lower with small inputs primarily because the amount of parallelism is lower. Our kernels launch between 7680 and 23,040 threads, meaning that many threads receive no work with our smallest input. We are not sure why the performance advantage with the largest input is lower than with the second-largest input. It takes the GPU just over 5 seconds per time step to simulate 5,000,000 bodies and 88 seconds for 50,000,000 bodies.

For problem sizes below about 10,000 bodies, the $O(n^2)$ CUDA implementation is the fastest. On the evaluated input sizes, the Barnes Hut CUDA code is 0.2, 3.3, 35, and 314 times faster than the $O(n^2)$ CUDA code. We did not run the largest problem size with the $O(n^2)$ algorithm as it would have taken almost two days to complete one time step. Because the Barnes Hut algorithm requires only $O(n \log n)$ operations, its benefit over the $O(n^2)$ algorithm increases rapidly with larger problem sizes.

Table 6.2 lists the running times of each kernel and compares them with the corresponding running times on the CPU. The CPU/GPU ratio roughly approximates the number of CPU cores needed to match the GPU performance. Kernel 5 (force calculation) is by far the slowest, followed by kernel 2

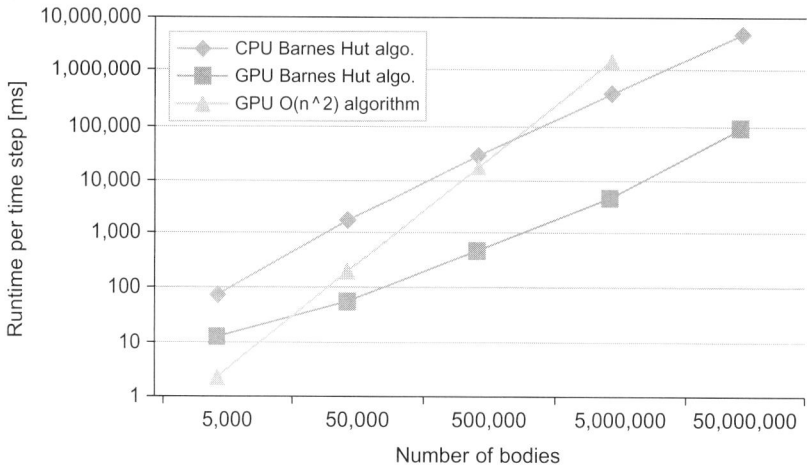

FIGURE 6.15

Runtime per simulated time step in milliseconds.

Table 6.2 CPU (single core) and GPU kernel runtimes in milliseconds for one time step with 5,000,000 bodies.

	Kernel 1	Kernel 2	Kernel 3	Kernel 4	Kernel 5	Kernel 6
CPU runtime	50.0	2,160.0	430.0	310.0	382,840.0	990.0
GPU runtime	0.8	868.0	100.3	38.6	4,202.8	4.1
CPU/GPU	62.5	2.5	4.3	8.0	91.1	241.5

(tree building). The remaining four kernels represent less than 3% of the total running time on the GPU and 0.5% on the CPU. The GPU is faster than a single CPU core on each kernel by a substantial margin. Kernels 2, 3, and 4 are under 10 times faster, whereas the remaining kernels are over 60 times faster. The most important kernel, kernel 5, is over 90 times faster. These results indicate that a hybrid approach, where some of the work is performed on the CPU, is unlikely to result in much benefit, even if the CPU code is parallelized across multiple cores and there is no penalty for transferring data between the CPU and the GPU.

Table 6.3 compares the two CUDA versions in terms of their runtime, floating-point operations per second, and bytes accessed in main memory per second for an input of 5,000,000 bodies. The results are for all kernels combined and show that the very regular $O(n^2)$ code utilizes the GPU hardware at almost maximum effectively, whereas the irregular Barnes Hut code does not. Nevertheless, the Barnes Hut implementation reaches a respectable 75 Gflop/s. Its main memory throughput is low in part because of uncoalesced accesses and in part because we allow only one of the 32 threads in a warp to access main memory on behalf of all threads. The remaining threads operate almost exclusively on data in shared memory.

Table 6.3 Floating-point operations per second (in billions), bytes accessed in main memory per second (in billions), and runtime (in seconds) on the GPU for one time step with 5,000,000 bodies.

	Gflop/s	Gbytes/s	Runtime [s]
Barnes Hut algo.	75.8	2.9	5.2
$O(n^2)$ algorithm	304.9	0.9	1639.9

6.4.3 Limitations

Other than $O(n^2)$ CUDA implementations [3], there are no implementations of an entire n-body algorithm on the GPU that we are aware of. Our approach of running the entire Barnes Hut algorithm on the GPU avoids slow data transfers between the CPU and the GPU, but it also limits the maximum problem size to just over 50,000,000 bodies on our hardware. Other approaches that execute part of the work on the CPU may be more suitable for larger problem sizes. For example, a recent implementation by Hamada *et al.* [4] uses the CPU to construct the tree, traverse the tree, perform the time integration, and send interaction lists to the GPU. The GPU then computes the forces between the bodies in the interaction lists in a streaming fashion that is not limited by the amount of memory on the GPU.

Our implementation is based on the classical Barnes Hut algorithm [1] instead of the newer method by Barnes [7]. The classical method allows only one body per leaf node in the tree, whereas the newer approach allows multiple bodies per node and therefore requires a substantially smaller tree. As a result, the traversal time is much reduced, making the new algorithm a better candidate for a GPU implementation [4]. We opted to use the classical algorithm because we are interested in finding general ways to make tree codes efficient on GPUs as opposed to focusing exclusively on the Barnes Hut algorithm.

6.4.4 Conclusions

The main conclusion of our work is that GPUs can be used to accelerate irregular codes, not just regular codes. However, a great deal of programming effort is required to achieve good performance. We estimate that it took us two person months to port our preexisting C implementation to CUDA and optimize it. In particular, we had to completely redesign the main data structure, convert all the recursive code into iterative code, explicitly manage the cache (shared memory), and parallelize the implementation both within and across thread blocks. The biggest performance win, though, came from turning some of the unique architectural features of GPUs, which are often regarded as performance hurdles for irregular codes, into assets. For example, because the threads in a warp necessarily run in lockstep, we can have one thread fetch data from main memory and share them with the other threads without the need for synchronization. Similarly, because barriers are implemented in hardware on GPUs and are extremely fast, we have been able to use them to reduce wasted work and main memory accesses in a way and to an extent that is impossible in current CPUs because barrier implementations in CPUs have to communicate through memory.

6.5 FUTURE DIRECTIONS

We are actively working on writing high-performing CUDA implementations for other irregular algorithms. The goal of this work is to identify common structures and optimization techniques that can be generalized so that they are ultimately useful for speeding up entire classes of irregular programs.

Acknowledgments

This work was supported in part by NSF grants CSR-0923907, CSR-0833162, CSR-0752845, CSR-0719966, and CSR-0702353 as well as gifts from IBM, Intel, and NEC. The results reported in this chapter have been obtained on resources provided by the Texas Advanced Computing Center (TACC) at the University of Texas at Austin.

References

[1] J. Barnes, P. Hut, A hierarchical O(n log$n$) force-calculation algorithm, Nature, 324 (4) (1986) 446–449.
[2] H.C. Plummer, On the problem of distribution in globular star clusters, Mon. Not. R. Astron. Soc. 71 (1911) 460–470.
[3] L. Nyland, M. Harris, J. Prins, Fast n-body simulation with CUDA, in: H. Nguyen (Ed.), GPU Gems 3, 2007, Addison-Wesley Professional (Chapter 31).
[4] T. Hamada, K. Nitadori, K. Benkrid, Y. Ohno, G. Morimoto, T. Masada, et al., A novel multiple-walk parallel algorithm for the Barnes-Hut treecode on GPUs — towards cost effective, high performance N-body simulation, vol. 24 (1–2), SpringerLink, Computer Science — Research and Development, Springer-Verlag, New York, 2009 (special issue paper).
[5] NVIDIA, CUDA Programming Guide, Version 2.2, NVIDIA Corp., Santa Clara, CA, 2009.
[6] D. Kirk, W.W. Hwu, Lecture 10, http://courses.ece.illinois.edu/ece498/al/lectures/lecture10-control-flow-spring-2010.ppt (accessed 06.11.10).
[7] J. Barnes, A modified tree code: don't laugh; it runs, J. Comput. Phys. 87 (1) (1990) 161–170.

Leveraging the Untapped Computation Power of GPUs: Fast Spectral Synthesis Using Texture Interpolation

7

Richard Townsend, Karthikeyan Sankaralingam, Matthew D. Sinclair

In this chapter we develop a hardware/software platform, GRASSY, that takes a unique approach to computation on GPUs by leveraging the interpolation capability of GPU texture memory. Our solution is motivated by the computational needs of asteroseismology, which we briefly outline. Beyond the specific application to asteroseismology, our work provides the first investigation into the use of texture interpolation functionality for non-graphics computations.

7.1 BACKGROUND AND PROBLEM STATEMENT

7.1.1 Asteroseismology

Asteroseismology is a powerful technique for probing the internal structure of distant stars by study-ing time-varying disturbances on their surfaces. A direct analogy can be drawn to the way that the study of earthquakes (seismology) allows us to infer the internal structure of the Earth. Due to the recent launch of space satellites devoted to discovering and monitoring these surface disturbances in hundreds of thousands of stars, paired with ground-based telescopes capable of high-resolution, high-cadence follow-up spectroscopy, asteroseismology is currently enjoying a golden age. However, there remains a significant computation challenge: how do we analyze and interpret the veritable torrent of new asteroseismic data?

To date, the most straightforward and accurate analysis approach is direct modeling via spectral synthesis (discussed in greater detail later in this chapter). Given a set of observations of the time-varying radiant flux received from a star, we attempt to construct a sequence of synthetic spectra to reproduce these observations. Any given model depends on the assumed parameters describing the star and its surface disturbances. Using an optimization strategy we find the combination of parame-ters that best reproduces the observations, ultimately allowing us to establish constraints on the stellar structure.

7.1.2 Spectral Synthesis

Stellar spectral synthesis is the process of summing up the Earth-directed radiant flux from each region on the visible hemisphere of a star. A typical procedure, e.g., Reference 1, comprises the following steps:

1. *Mesh building.* Decompose the stellar surface into a triangle mesh (Figure 7.1a). A quad $[T, g, v, \mu]$ (see Table 7.1) is associated with each mesh vertex (Figure 7.1b).
2. *Mesh rendering.* Rasterize the view-plane projection of every triangle to produce a set of N_{frag} equal-area fragments (Figure 7.1c). Bilinear interpolation between triangle vertices is used to calculate a quad $[T, g, v, \mu]$ for each fragment.
3. *Flux calculation.* Evaluate the radiant flux spectrum $F(\lambda_j)$ on a uniformly spaced grid of N_λ discrete wavelengths $\lambda_j = \lambda_0 + \Delta\lambda j$ $(j = 0 \ldots N_\lambda - 1)$ for each fragment (Figure 7.1d).
4. *Flux aggregation.* Sum the N_{frag} flux spectra to produce a single synthetic spectrum representing the radiant flux for the whole star (Figure 7.1e).

Steps (1) and (2) are performed once for a star and/or set of stellar and disturbance parameters. The main computational cost comes in step (3), which we now discuss in greater detail.

Over the wavelength grid λ_j the radiant flux is calculated as

$$F(\lambda_j) = \frac{A^2}{D^2} I(T, g, \lambda_j^{rest}, \mu); \tag{7.1}$$

Here, A is the area of the fragment, D the distance to the star, and $I(\ldots)$ the specific intensity of the radiation emerging at rest wavelength λ_j^{rest} and direction cosine μ from a stellar atmosphere with effective temperature T and surface gravity g (see Table 7.1). The rest wavelength is obtained from the Doppler shift formula,

$$\lambda_j^{rest} = \lambda_j\left(1 - \frac{v}{c}\right), \tag{7.2}$$

where v is the line-of-sight velocity of the fragment and c is the speed of light.

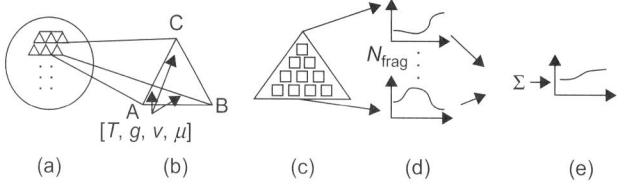

(a)   (b)   (c)   (d)   (e)

FIGURE 7.1

Steps in the spectral synthesis procedure (see Section 7.1.2).

Table 7.1 Definitions of quad variables.	
Variable	**Description**
T	Local effective temperature — a measure of the net radiant flux through the atmosphere.
g	Local surface gravity — a measure of the stratification of the atmosphere.
v	Projection of local surface velocity onto the line of sight.
μ	Projection of local surface normal on the line of sight.

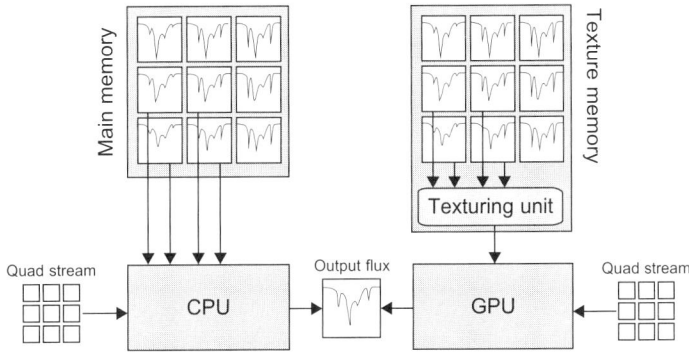

FIGURE 7.2

Schematic comparison of CPU and GPU spectral synthesis.

Calculating the specific intensity $I(\ldots)$ requires detailed modeling of the atomic physics and energy transport within the stellar atmosphere and is far too costly to do on the fly. *Instead, we evaluate this intensity by four-dimensional linear interpolation in precalculated tables.*

7.1.3 Problem Statement

For typical parameters (N_{frag}, $N_\lambda \approx 5{,}000\text{--}10{,}000$) a synthetic spectrum typically takes only a few seconds to generate on a modern CPU. However, with many possible parameter combinations, the overall optimization (see Section 7.1.1) can be computationally expensive, taking many weeks in a typical analysis. The primary bottleneck lies in the 4-D specific intensity interpolations described earlier in this chapter; although algorithmically simple, their arithmetic and memory-access costs quickly add up. This issue motivates us to pose the following question:

How can we use GPUs to accelerate interpolations in the precomputed specific intensity tables?

In addressing this question, we have developed GRASSY (*GR*aphics Processing Unit — *A*ccelerated *S*pectral *SY*nthesis) — a hardware/software platform for fast spectral synthesis that leverages the texture interpolation functionality in CUDA-capable GPUs (see Figure 7.2). In the following section, we establish a more formal basis for the interpolation problem; then, in Section 7.3, we introduce our GRASSY platform. Section 7.4 presents results from initial validation and testing, and in Section 7.5, we discuss future directions for this avenue of GPU computing research.

7.2 FLUX CALCULATION AND AGGREGATION

An example of CPU-oriented pseudo code for the flux calculation and aggregation steps (3 and 4) of the spectral synthesis procedure (Section 7.1.2) is given in Listing 7.1. Input to the code is a stream of quads from the mesh building and rasterization steps (1 and 2); the output is the aggregated synthetic spectrum. The high arithmetic and memory-access costs of the 4-D specific intensity interpolation are evident in the 16-term weighted summation appearing toward the end of the code — this expression must be evaluated $N_{\text{frag}}N_\lambda$ times during the synthesis of a single spectrum.

```
float I_tables[][][][]; // Pre-calculated specific intensity tables

calc_and_agg_flux (input_stream[]) {

    float flux[N_lambda]; // Initialized to zero

    foreach quad in input_stream do {
        for j = 0..N_lambda-1 do {

            // Rest wavelength
            float lambda = lambda_0 + Delta_lambda*j;
            float lambda_rest = lambda*(1 - quad.v/speed_of_light);

            // Accumulate flux
            flux[j] += (A*A)/(D*D)*
                        interpolate_I(quad.T, quad.g, lambda_rest, quad.mu);
        }
    }

    return flux;

}

float interpolate_I (T, g, l, m) {

    // Locate position in tables (assume increments in T, g, l and m are 1.0)
    i_T = floor(T);
    i_g = floor(g);
    i_l = floor(l);
    i_m = floor(m);

    // Set up weights
    w_T = T - i_T;
    w_g = g - i_g;
    w_l = l - i_l;
    w_m = m - i_m;

    // Do the 4-D intensity interpolation (16-term weighted summation)
    I = (1-w_T)*(1-w_g)*(1-w_l)*(1-w_m)*I_tables[i_T  ,i_g  ,i_l  ,i_m  ] +
        (1-w_T)*(1-w_g)*(1-w_l)*(  w_m)*I_tables[i_T  ,i_g  ,i_l  ,i_m+1] +
        ...
        (  w_T)*(  w_g)*(  w_l)*(1-w_m)*I_tables[i_T+1,i_g+1,i_l+1,i_m  ] +
        (  w_T)*(  w_g)*(  w_l)*(  w_m)*I_tables[i_T+1,i_g+1,i_l+1,i_m+1];

    return I;

}
```

Listing 7.1: CPU-oriented pseudo code for the flux spectrum computation and aggregation.

7.3 THE GRASSY PLATFORM

7.3.1 Overview

In this section, we introduce the GRASSY spectral synthesis platform. To leverage the texture interpolation functionality in CUDA-capable GPUs, some modifications to the procedure outlined in Listing 7.1 are necessary. In particular, we decompose the calculations into a series of 2-D interpolations, which are then implemented as fetches (with bilinear filtering) from 2-D textures. This brings the dual benefits of efficient memory access due to use of the texture cache, and "free" interpolation arithmetic provided by the linear filtering mode. One potential pitfall, however, is the limited precision of the linear filtering; we review this issue in Section 7.3.6.

7.3.2 Interpolation Decomposition

The 4-D to 2-D interpolation decomposition is enabled by a CPU-based preprocessing step, whereby quads $[T, g, v, m]$ from step (2) of the spectral synthesis procedure are translated into 10-tuples $[v, \mu, k_0, k_1, k_2, k_3, w_0, w_1, w_2, w_3]$. A single 10-tuple codes for four separate bilinear interpolations, in 2-D tables $I(\lambda^{\text{rest}}, \mu)$ representing the specific intensity for a given combination of effective temperature and surface gravity. The indices $k_0 \ldots k_3$ indicate *which* tables to interpolate within, while the weights $w_0 \ldots w_3$ are used post-interpolation to combine the results together.

7.3.3 Texture Packing

Because CUDA does not support arrays of texture references (which would allow us to place each table into a separate texture), GRASSY packs the 2-D intensity tables $I(\lambda^{\text{rest}}, \mu)$ into a single 2-D texture.[1] For a given interpolation, the floating-point texture coordinates (x, y) are calculated from λ, μ and the table index k via

$$x = \frac{\lambda - \lambda_0^{\text{tab}}}{\Delta \lambda^{\text{tab}}} + 0.5 \tag{7.3}$$

and

$$y = \mu(N_\mu^{\text{tab}} - 1) + kN_\mu^{\text{tab}} + 0.5. \tag{7.4}$$

Here, N_μ^{tab} is the direction cosine dimension of each intensity table, while λ_0^{tab} is the base wavelength and $\Delta \lambda^{\text{tab}}$ the wavelength spacing (not to be confused with λ and $\Delta \lambda$). The offsets by 0.5 come from the recommendations of Appendix F.3 of [10]. Note that these two equations are *not* the actual interpolation, but rather the conversion from physical (wavelength, direction cosine) coordinates to un-normalized texture coordinates.

7.3.4 Division of Labor

To maximize texture cache locality, GRASSY groups calculations into N_b batches of $N = N_\lambda / N_b$ consecutive wavelengths. These batches map directly into CUDA thread blocks, with each thread in a block

---

[1] We considered using a 3-D texture, but the dimension limitations imposed by CUDA are too restrictive.

responsible for interpolating the intensity, and accumulating the flux, at a single wavelength. To ensure adequate utilization of GPU resources, N_b should be an integer multiple of the number of streaming multiprocessors (SMs) in the device.

Every thread block processes the entire input stream of N_{frag} 10-tuples, to build up the aggregated flux spectrum for the wavelength range covered by the block. Upon completion, this spectrum is written to global memory, from where it can subsequently be copied over to the CPU.

7.3.5 Pseudo Code

Listing 7.2 provides pseudo code for the CUDA kernel within GRASSY, which handles the flux calculation and aggregation. Kernel arguments are the input stream of 10-tuples and a pointer to an array in device global memory where the resulting flux spectrum will be placed. Each thread evaluates its own wavelength on the fly from the index j, which in turn is obtained from thread and block indices.

7.3.6 Analysis of Precision Issues

In this subsection we discuss in detail the potential issues arising from the 9-bit precision of the GPU texture interpolation. For exact one-dimensional linear interpolation between two pairs of points, (x_0, f_0) and (x_1, f_1), the interpolant $f(x)$ can be expressed as

$$f(x) = [1 - w(x)]f_0 + w(x)f_1. \tag{7.5}$$

Here,

$$w(x) = \frac{x - x_0}{x_1 - x_0} \tag{7.6}$$

is the weight function, whose linear variation between 0 ($x = x_0$) and 1 ($x = x_1$) gives a corresponding linear change in $f(x)$, from $f = f_0$ to $f = f_1$. In a floating-point implementation of these expressions, the finite precision means that $f(x)$ no longer varies completely smoothly, instead exhibiting step-wise jumps. However, these jumps are typically on the order of a few units of last place and thus not a particularly important source of numerical error.

The situation is different if the weight function $w(x)$ is evaluated using fixed-precision arithmetic. With n bits of precision, there are only 2^n distinct values that $w(x)$ can assume — and, by implication, only 2^n distinct values of $f(x)$ between f_0 and f_1. Then, the step-wise jumps in $f(x)$ can be significant.

Exactly how significant the step-wise jump is depends on the difference between f_0 and f_1. The worst-case scenario occurs when $f_1 = -f_0$, giving a bound on the error in $f(x)$ of

$$|\text{err}[f(x)]| \leq |f| 2^{1-n}. \tag{7.7}$$

For the fixed-precision linear interpolation offered through CUDA texture lookups, $n = 9$ bits, giving an error bound of $|f|/256$. However, in practice the error will be much smaller than this because for an adequately sampled lookup table the worst-case scenario will never arise. If all features in the table have a characteristic width of m points, then the maximum difference between f_0 and f_1 is f/m, giving an error bound

$$|\text{err}[f(x)]| \leq |f| 2^{1-n} m^{-1}. \tag{7.8}$$

```
texture <float, ...> texRef; // Preloaded with 2-D intensity tables

__global__ void calc_and_agg_flux (input_stream[], float dev_flux[]) {

  // Thread wavelength
  int j = blockIdx.x*N + threadIdx.x;
  float lambda = lambda_0 + Delta_lambda*j;

  // Initialize flux
  float flux = 0.f;

  foreach tuple in input_stream do {

    // Rest wavelength
    float lambda_rest = lambda*(1 - tuple.v/speed_of_light);

    // Accumulate flux
    float I = tuple.w_0*interpolate_I(lambda_rest, tuple.mu, tuple.k_0) +
              tuple.w_1*interpolate_I(lambda_rest, tuple.mu, tuple.k_1) +
              tuple.w_2*interpolate_I(lambda_rest, tuple.mu, tuple.k_2) +
              tuple.w_3*interpolate_I(lambda_rest, tuple.mu, tuple.k_3);
    flux += (A*A)/(D*D)*I;

  }

  // Write flux to global memory
  dev_flux[j] = flux;

}

float interpolate_I (l, m, k) {

  float x = (l - LAMBDA_0_TBL)/DELTA_LAMBDA_TBL + 0.5f;
  float y = m*(N_MU_TBL - 1) + k*N_MU_TBL + 0.5f;

  return tex2D(texref, x, y);

}
```

Listing 7.2: Pseudo code for the GRASSY kernel.

Clearly, a more-finely sampled table (i.e., larger m) yields smaller errors, at the cost of consuming more memory.

In the present context of specific intensity interpolation, we use tables sampled at 0.03 Angstrom. Over the optical wavelength range of 3,500–7,500 Angstrom, features in the tables have a typical scale of at least 0.2 Angstrom (the thermal broadening width), six times the sampling interval. This implies an error bound (assuming $n = 9$) of $|f|/1536$. Errors of this magnitude are unimportant when contrasted against uncertainties in the tabulated intensities (due to theoretical approximations) and against the inherent noise in the observations against which synthetic spectra are compared.

7.3.7 **Performance Model**

In anticipation of the performance evaluation in the following section, here we provide a simple model to estimate the expected performance of GRASSY. Let N_{ops} be the number of computational operations required to process one 10-tuple at one wavelength; the total number of operations for synthesis of a complete spectrum is then $N_{tot} = N_{frag}N_\lambda N_{ops}$. For $N_{frag} = N_\lambda = 8192$ (typical values, and the ones adopted in the calculations below), and assuming $N_{ops} = 100$, we estimate $N_{tot} \approx 6.7$ billion operations (GOPS) per spectrum.

A Tesla C1060 GPU has a peak throughput of 933 GOPS/s. Assuming we are able to achieve half of this, we expect a throughput of 70 spectra per second, or 14 ms per spectrum.

7.4 **INITIAL TESTING**

7.4.1 **Platform and Infrastructure**

Our testing and validation platform is a Dell Precision 490 workstation, containing two 2.33 GHz Intel Xeon E5345 quad-core CPUs and a Tesla C1060 GPU. The workstation runs 64-bit Gentoo Linux (kernel 2.6.25) and uses version 3.0 of the CUDA SDK. As a CPU-based comparison code, we adopt a highly optimized Fortran 95 version of the KYLIE code [1], running on the same workstation.

We use specific intensity tables based on the OSTAR2002 and BSTAR2006 grids of model stellar atmospheres [8, 9], with intensities calculated using the SYNSPEC package developed by I. Hubeny and T. Lanz. The input stream of 10 tuples is generated from a modified version of the BRUCE code [1].

7.4.2 **Performance Evaluation**

Table 7.2 summarizes the average time taken by the CPU and GPU platforms to synthesize a spectrum with $N_{frag} = N_\lambda = 8192$. For these calculations, we adopt a GPU thread block size of 128; a gradual performance degradation occurs toward larger values of the block size because of a shortage of blocks to map on to multiprocessors.

As mentioned in Section 7.1, the CPU platform takes on the order of seconds per spectrum. The Tesla C1060 is around 30 times faster than the CPU, although not so fast as we had estimated from our simple analysis in Section 7.3.7. The bottleneck appears to be in the memory accesses; the global memory throughput reported by the CUDAPROF profiler is only 17.1 GB/sec. On closer inspection, it appears that we are not making best use of the texture cache; the ratio of misses to hits is an alarming 90:1! We are currently examining ways in which better cache locality might be achieved, for instance, by altering the texture-packing layout (Section 7.3.3).

Table 7.2 Average calculation times for the test runs.

Platform	Time (ms)
CPU/Xeon E5345	1490
GPU/Tesla C1060	55.1

7.5 IMPACT AND FUTURE DIRECTIONS

7.5.1 Asteroseismology

As we have discussed already in this chapter, specific intensity interpolation currently represents the major bottleneck in synthesizing spectra for asteroseismic analyses. Current CPU-based implementations typically lead to per-star analysis runtimes of weeks. The speedups reported earlier in this chapter — when scaled to multidevice systems — herald the prospect of being able to shorten these times to hours. It goes without saying that this will have a significant impact on the field of asteroseismology, as the analysis throughput and/or resolution of parameter determinations can be greatly increased, in turn allowing stronger constraints to be placed on the internal structures of stars.

7.5.2 Other Areas of Astrophysics

The benefits of accelerated spectral synthesis will also extend to other fields of astrophysics, from the analysis of rotationally flattened stars to the generation of combined spectra for clusters or entire galaxies of stars (so-called population synthesis). Our approach generalizes to other numerical techniques that rely on interpolation as well.

7.5.3 Numerical Analysis

In terms of numerical analysis, our work opens up new avenues. While building this application and investigating the use of textures for computation, we realized several features from a numerical standpoint that introduce trade-offs:

- Sampling: If the data used to populate the interpolation tables are sampled too coarsely, there is loss of precision. However, if sampled too finely the total size of the textures increases.
- Conservative interpolation: Our intensity interpolation scheme is not strictly conservative, in that the integral of the interpolated intensity over a finite wavelength interval will differ somewhat from the corresponding integral of the tabulated intensity. This issue can be resolved by interpolating instead in the cumulative intensity and then taking finite differences. However, such an approach will involve calculating the difference between two large similar numbers, running the risk of catastrophic cancellation. Further research is therefore required to examine how this approach can be implemented safely.

7.5.4 Code Status

Our initial prototype implementation of the code is complete, but optimizations are ongoing. We expect to provide a hosted multiple-device system with remote access for astronomers in the next 12 to 18 months. At this juncture, all source code will be released under the GNU General Public License.

Acknowledgments

We acknowledge support from NSF *Advanced Technology and Instrumentation* grant AST-0904607. The Tesla C1060 GPU used in this study was donated by NVIDIA through its Professor Partnership Program.

References

The most relevant work in terms of asteroseismology is the BRUCE/KYLIE suite of modeling codes [1]. One example of typical analysis using the BRUCE/KYLIE codes is presented in [2]. Other works in astronomy that have used GPUs include [3, 4]. To the best of our knowledge, the present work is the first use of texture units for computation. In terms of experimental data that GRASSY will analyze, current asteroseismic satellite missions include [5–7]. The sources for spectral intensity data we use are [8, 9].

[1] R.H.D. Townsend, Spectroscopic modelling of non-radial pulsation in rotating early-type stars, Mon. Not. R. Astron. Soc. 284 (4) (1997) 839.

[2] Th. Rivinius, D. Baade, S. Štefl, R.H.D. Townsend, O. Stahl, B. Wolf, et al., Stellar and circumstellar activity of the Be star mu Centauri. III, Multiline nonradial pulsation modeling, Astron. Astrophys. A 369 (2001) 1058.

[3] S.F. Portegies Zwart, R.G. Belleman, P.M. Geldof, High-performance direct gravitational N-body simulations on graphics processing units, New Astron. 12 (8) (2007) 641.

[4] T. Hamada, T. Iitaka, The chamomile scheme: an optimized algorithm for n-body simulations on programmable graphics processing units. arXiv.org, Cornell University Library, arXiv:astro-ph 0703100. (accessed 10.11.2010).

[5] J. Christensen-Dalsgaard, T. Arentoft, T.M. Brown, R.L. Gilliland, H. Kjeldsen, W.J. Borucki, et al., Asteroseismology with the Kepler mission, Comm. Astero. 150 (2007) 350.

[6] I. Roxburgh, C. Catala, The PLATO consortium, Comm. Astero. 150 (2007) 357.

[7] G. Handler, Beta Cephei and Slowly Pulsating B stars as targets for BRITE-Constellation, Comm. Astero. 152 (2008), 160.

[8] T. Lanz, I. Hubeny, Grid of NLTE line-blanketed model atmospheres of early B-type stars, Astrophys. J. Suppl. Ser. 169 (1) (2007) 83.

[9] T. Lanz, I. Hubeny, A grid of Non-LTE line-blanketed model atmospheres of O-type stars, Astrophys. J. Suppl. Ser. 146 (2) (2003) 417.

[10] NVIDIA CUDA Programming Guide, version 3.0, (accessed 2.20.10).

Black Hole Simulations with CUDA

8

Frank Herrmann, John Silberholz, Manuel Tiglio

In 1915 Albert Einstein derived the fundamental laws of general relativity that predict the existence of gravitational radiation. While indirect evidence is by now well established and led in 1993 to the Nobel Prize in Physics being awarded to Russel A. Hulse and Joseph H. Taylor, no direct detection has occurred to date. This is because gravitational waves reaching Earth are extremely weak. Recently, researchers have built gravitational wave detectors achieving the required sensitivities to make direct detection possible. A number of laser interferometer experiments are devoted to this task. The currently most sensitive one (LIGO [1]) consists of two crossed laser beams, each of which is 4 km long. Over this distance a typical gravitational wave would change each arm's length by $\sim 10^{-18}$ m — a fraction of the size of an atom. Because the signal to be extracted is very small compared with the background noise, an accurate a priori knowledge of inspiral signals that can be searched for in the data is required.

In this chapter we discuss our CUDA and GPU implementation and results from an approximation to Einstein's equations, the *post-Newtonian* one, which allows us to thoroughly study the inspiral phase-space dynamics of the seven-dimensional parameter space of binary black holes in initial quasi-circular orbit.

8.1 INTRODUCTION

With a number of gravitational wave detectors such as LIGO [1], Virgo [2], and GEO600 [15] now measuring at design sensitivity, the prospect of direct detection of gravitational radiation is becoming increasingly real. Because of the low signal-to-noise ratio encountered at these detectors, researchers need to post-process the data, ideally searching for known signals that would indicate a source of gravitational radiation. One of the most likely sources of detection are stellar-mass binary black hole (BBH) systems. There is a definite need to understand as much as possible about these configurations.

Over recent years numerical solutions of general relativity (GR) have reached the point where accurate and reliable calculations of the interactions of two black holes (BHs) over many orbits can be produced by a number of different groups [3, 4, 12]. These calculations require enormous computational effort, though, and the generation of a large-scale bank of numerical templates that could be used by gravitational wave detectors is currently intractable. Numerical solutions to Einstein's equations require solving a coupled set of nonlinear elliptic-hyperbolic partial differential equations in three spatial dimensions. A single right-hand-side call to advance in time just one point on the three-dimensional spatial grid requires around 13,000 multiplications, 5400 additions, 3400 subtractions, and 69 divisions, excluding derviative calculations. A single simulation can easily take more than 100,000 CPU hours. These simulations are typically running on more than 1024 cores simultaneously so that they can complete in a reasonable amount of time. Here, we report on an approximation to GR, the so-called post-Newtonian expansion (PN), which — as explained in the next section — dramatically reduces the number of computational operations required. Furthermore, recent comparisons between gravitational waveforms obtained from full numerical relativity (that is, numerical solutions of the full Einstein equations) and PN approximations show good agreement until just a few orbits before the two black holes merge [5, 8, 13].

Because of these reasons, performing a large number of PN simulations of BBH systems with different initial configurations is of considerable interest, and it is the focus of our work described in this chapter.

8.2 THE POST-NEWTONIAN APPROXIMATION

The PN approximation leads to a system of coupled ordinary differential equations (ODEs) in time for the orbital frequency ω, the unit orbital angular momentum vector $\hat{\mathbf{L}}$ and the individual spin vectors $\mathbf{S}_i$ for the two BHs. This expansion is valid as long as the two black holes are far separated and slowly moving along a quasi-circular inspiral trajectory. In total this is a seven-dimensional problem as there are three degrees of freedom in each of the spin vectors and one degree of freedom in the mass ratio.

The specific PN expansion and equations that we use are those of Ref. [6] (with Erratum [7]); namely,

$$
\begin{aligned}
\frac{d\omega}{dt} = \omega^2 \frac{96}{5} \eta (M\omega)^{5/3} \Bigg\{ & 1 - \frac{743 + 924\eta}{336}(M\omega)^{2/3} \\
& - \left(\frac{1}{12}\sum_{i=1,2}\left(\chi_i \hat{\mathbf{L}}\cdot\hat{\mathbf{S}}_i\left(\frac{113m_i^2}{M^2} + 75\eta \right) \right) - 4\pi \right)M\omega \\
& + \left(\frac{34103}{18144} + \frac{13661}{2016}\eta + \frac{59}{18}\eta^2 \right)(M\omega)^{4/3} \\
& - \frac{1}{48}\eta\chi_1\chi_2 \left(247(\hat{\mathbf{S}}_1\cdot\hat{\mathbf{S}}_2) - 721(\hat{\mathbf{L}}\cdot\hat{\mathbf{S}}_1)(\hat{\mathbf{L}}\cdot\hat{\mathbf{S}}_2) \right)(M\omega)^{4/3} \\
& - \frac{1}{672}(4159 + 15876\eta)\pi(M\omega)^{5/3} + \left(\left(\frac{16447322263}{139708800} - \frac{1712}{105}\gamma_E + \frac{16}{3}\pi^2 \right) \right. \\
& \left. + \left(-\frac{273811877}{1088640} + \frac{451}{48}\pi^2 - \frac{88}{3}\hat{\theta}\eta \right)\eta \right)
\end{aligned}
$$

$$+ \frac{541}{896}\eta^2 - \frac{5605}{2592}\eta^3 - \frac{856}{105}\log\left(16(M\omega)^{2/3}\right)\Big)(M\omega)^2$$

$$+ \left(-\frac{4415}{4032} + \frac{358675}{6048}\eta + \frac{91495}{1512}\eta^2\right)\pi(M\omega)^{7/3}\Bigg\} \tag{8.1}$$

$$\frac{d\mathbf{S}_i}{dt} = \mathbf{\Omega}_i \times \mathbf{S}_i \tag{8.2}$$

$$\frac{d\hat{\mathbf{L}}}{dt} = -\frac{(M\omega)^{1/3}}{\eta M^2}\frac{d\mathbf{S}}{dt} \tag{8.3}$$

where $\mathbf{S} = \mathbf{S}_1 + \mathbf{S}_2$, $\gamma_E = 0.577\ldots$ is Euler's constant, $\hat{\theta} = 1039/4620$, $M = m_1 + m_2$ is the total mass, $\eta = m_1 m_2/M^2$ the symmetric mass ratio, and the magnitude of the orbital angular momentum is $|\mathbf{L}| = \eta M^{5/3}\omega^{-1/3}$.

The evolution of the individual spin vectors $\mathbf{S}_i$ for the two BHs is described by a precession around $\mathbf{\Omega}_i$, Eq. 8.2, with

$$\mathbf{\Omega}_1 = \frac{(M\omega)^2}{2M}\left(\eta(M\omega)^{-1/3}\left(4 + 3\frac{m_2}{m_1}\right)\hat{\mathbf{L}} + 1/M^2(\mathbf{S}_2 - 3(\mathbf{S}_2 \cdot \hat{\mathbf{L}})\hat{\mathbf{L}})\right), \tag{8.4}$$

and $\mathbf{\Omega}_2$ obtained by the exchange $1 \leftrightarrow 2$. The spin vectors $\mathbf{S}_i$ are related to the unit ones $\hat{\mathbf{S}}_i$ via $\mathbf{S}_i = \chi_i m_i^2 \hat{\mathbf{S}}_i$, with $\chi_i \in [0,1]$ the dimensionless spin parameter of each black hole.

Given mass and spin parameters $(m_1, m_2, \chi_1, \chi_2)$, the aforementioned system of coupled ODEs is evolved from an initial frequency ω_0 to a final one ω_f. We typically choose ω_0 corresponding to an initial separation of $r \approx 40M$ and $\omega_f = 0.05$, which is a conservative estimate of where the PN equations still hold [5, 13].

8.3 NUMERICAL ALGORITHM

The ODEs are integrated in time using Dormand-Prince's method [10]. This ODE integrator uses an adaptive time step h to keep the solution error below a given threshold. Starting from time t, the time integrator updates the state to $t + h$. It computes an approximation to the solution at six intermediate times between t and $t + h$ (referred to as k1 to k6 later in this chapter) and then computes fourth-order and fifth-order accurate solutions at $t + h$ (here denoted y4 and y5). This requires six right-hand-side calls, that is, six evaluations of the right-hand-sides of Eqs. 8.1–8.3. The difference between these solutions is used to estimate the error of y4 and adapt h if the error is below some specified toler-ance. In our simulations we typically set the tolerance to be 5×10^{-7} (i.e., roughly at the level of single-precision accuracy) and start with an adaptive time step of size $h = 10M$. The time step does not change during most of the inspiral. This is crucial for our GPU implementation because — as dis-cussed later in the chapter — it minimizes thread divergences when multiple inspirals are performed in parallel.

8.4 GPU IMPLEMENTATION

Each ODE integration described earlier in this chapter cannot be easily parallelized because the solution at each time step (even for the intermediate `k1` to `k6` values) depends on the previous one. However, if one wants to study an ensemble of BBH inspiral dynamics (for example, in a phase-space study), then a trivial parallelization is available by just performing many inspirals simultaneously.

Figure 8.1 shows a CUDA pseudo-code description of our implementation. The right-hand-side (RHS) expressions of Eqs. 8.1, 8.2, and 8.3 are implemented in the `ode_rhs` function on the GPU. The ODE integration is performed on the CPU. First, GPU storage is allocated in `allocate_gpu_storage`. Then, the initial state data (i.e., ω, $\mathbf{S}_i$ for the two BHs, and the unit orbital angular momentum vector $\hat{\mathbf{L}}$) is set. In the evolution loop the RHS is called, and the different intermediate values `k1` to `k6` are computed in `interm_1`, etc. Next, for each inspiral the time step h is adjusted separately; that is, h is a vector with entries for each parallel inspiral. Finally, the loop is terminated once all the physical configurations have reached a final frequency ω_f to a given precision. At the end the data is copied back from the GPU to the CPU. During each time step a memory copy from the GPU to the CPU is needed to check if all simulations are done. In the profiling Section 8.5 we will see that no significant amount of time is spent in this copying.

Unfortunately, BBH systems interact differently based on their initial state, which describes their relative masses and the orientations of their spins. In particular, this will lead to thread divergence of the different inspirals. This could potentially be a very serious problem as time steps are adjusted in different manners and the load/store patterns of the different threads running in parallel changes. In our simulations we have found, however, that the divergence in the threads appears only toward the very end of the inspirals as only then are the time steps adjusted in a dynamic manner, typically resulting in a runtime difference of at most 10% from just running many copies of the same inspiral. This simplifies the problem significantly, as we do not have to handle thread divergence.

GPUs today provide the most impressive speedups over CPUs for single-precision computations. By comparing single-precision and double-precision CPU results on a number of inspiral configurations,

```
// compute right hand side (rhs) of ODE
__global__ void ode_rhs(state)

// integrate the ODEs
void integrate(initial_state_and_params) {
    allocate_gpu_storage(...);
    while (all_omega>all_omega_final) {
        ode_rhs<<<nBlocks_rhs,nThreads>>>(...);
        checkCUDAError(''first ode_rhs call'');
        interm_1<<<nBlocks_interm,nThreads>>>(...);
        ... // more intermediate values and rhs calls
        adjust_timesteps(...);
    }
    transfer_from_gpu_to_host(...);
}
```

FIGURE 8.1

Pseudo-code describing the parallel ODE integration. The time integration is performed on the CPU with kernels performing the inspirals called on the GPU as described in the text.

we have verified that single-precision processing is sufficient for our problem, yielding a maximum error of just over 5% for any final parameter after the simulation, sufficient for our studies.

8.5 PERFORMANCE RESULTS

We now evaluate the performance advantages GPUs deliver in our application. We executed our code on a single core of a quad-core Intel Xeon E5410 CPU running at 2.33 GHz, which is rated at around 5 GFlops in double-precision. Note that the problem is embarrassingly parallel, and therefore, the CPU would be able to provide excellent scaling over its four cores. We integrated one of our test inspirals 100 times serially and found that we could achieve around 0.057 inspirals per millisecond (ms) on a single core — which we will use for our performance comparison.

For comparison, each of the four GPUs on a high-end unit (the NVIDIA Tesla S1070) is currently rated at 1035 GFlops in single-precision, delivering a theoretical performance advantage of about a *factor 200* over the single-core CPU. We ran our test setup on a single GPU, spawning a large number N of simultaneous inspirals in parallel. Figure 8.2a shows results for the performance of the GPU card. As we increase the number of simultaneously scheduled inspirals N the speed levels off at about 2.7 inspirals/ms. The GPU has 240 processors that work in parallel, but the runtime CUDA scheduler has to be able to keep these 240 processors working simultaneously by switching out threads that would pause while waiting for a memory access to complete. This is the reason why the performance still rises even after $N = 10,000$, as the runtime has a better chance of squeezing the optimal performance out of the card by interleaving different inspirals without having to wait for costly memory transfers. Figure 8.2b shows more detailed profiling information. Listed is the time spent on different routines for one of our simulations run with $N = 50,000$; note the log-scale. The RHS computations dominate, as expected from the arithmetic intensity of Eqs. 8.1, 8.2, and 8.3. The next most expensive routines relate to the time update step. The `y4` and `y5` are the routines performing the estimation updates from the ODE integrator mentioned in Section 8.3, the `k1` to `k6` are the routines for the intermediate computations, while `D.to.H` and `H.to.D` refer to device-to-host and host-to-device `memcopy` operations. Finally, `pois.float`, `pois.int`, and `init` are all initialization steps, which are only run once.

We performed this study using block sizes of 256 threads. We found similar behavior with 128-thread blocks. Based on this data, we achieve a *speedup of about a factor 50*. While this comparison is slightly unfair to the CPU because we only use a single core and double-precision mode on the CPU, there is no doubt that the performance gains are very significant. Note also that for this test problem we integrated the exact same problem in all cases. This means that the individual threads run in perfect lock-step, the best possible case for the GPU. As mentioned earlier in this chapter, we typically see differences of about 10% in the runtime of different inspirals, and this would result in a slight inefficiency on the GPU as some of the threads in a block may finish before others.

8.6 GPU SUPERCOMPUTING CLUSTERS

To further speed our computations, we used the NCSA Lincoln cluster, which is a cluster of 96 NVIDIA Tesla S1070 units connected to 192 eight-core Dell PowerEdge 1950 servers (each scalar unit allows access to two GPUs). To perform these computations, we used a Message Passing Interface (MPI),

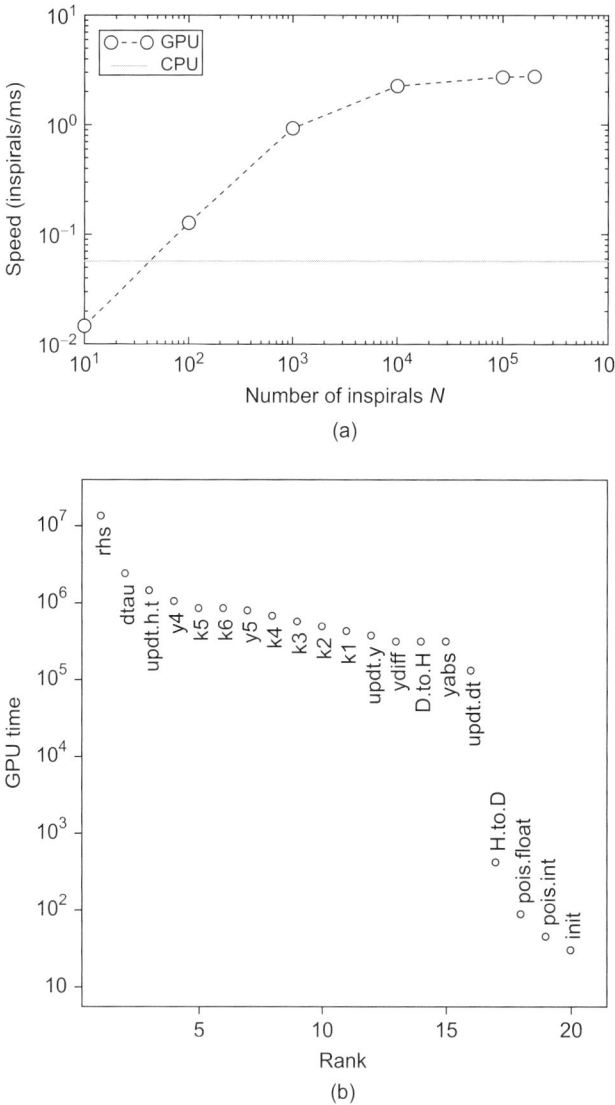

FIGURE 8.2

Performance of the GPU. Figure a shows scaling as we increase the number of inspirals N simultaneously scheduled on the GPU. Figure b shows profiling results — right-hand-side (RHS) computations dominate, as expected.

designating one node as a lead node that delegates tasks to others and keeps track of the progress of the overall job. We subdivided each large computation into a set of smaller jobs, which were completed by individual GPUs. To limit network communication overhead, we sent only basic information about the jobs to the nodes performing the computation, and they calculated the parameters for each of the runs and then performed the computations. On completion of a job, the resulting data file (stored in a binary format to conserve space) was stored on tape storage provided by the cluster. Throughout the course of the run, we would copy files from that storage to a local hard drive so that we had all the files stored locally by the end of the computation.

Several robustness measures were necessary to successfully complete the computation and transfer of the resulting data. Occasionally, a node would never complete a job, blocking completion of the overall computation. To prevent this, we had the lead node reassign abnormally long-running jobs. Further, in our real-time data transfer system, it was sometimes difficult to determine if a file on the tape storage represented a partially or fully transferred data file. To ensure we only copied complete data files to our local hard drive, we added an indicator file to the tape storage to mark that a file had been fully transferred. Last, sometimes our transfers from the tape storage to our local hard drive — using high-performance enabled secure copy (HPN SCP) — only partially completed. We validated the copies by comparing the hash values of the data files on the tape storage to those on the local hard drive.

By using a GPU supercomputing cluster, we were able to significantly speed our investigation on the phase space of a binary black hole system.

8.7 STATISTICAL RESULTS FOR BLACK HOLE INSPIRALS

As described in [14], we can gain significant insight into the interactions of BBH systems through a systematic sampling and evolution of the parameter space of initial configurations. In particular, in a recent statistical study [11], through a principal component analysis of our simulation results, we found quantities that are nearly conserved, both in a statistical sense with respect to parameter variation and as functions of time. Figure 8.3 shows the variance σ^2 with respect to changes in the initial black hole spin orientations for one such quantity,

$$\Delta \mathcal{E}_2^{\text{SO}} = \hat{V}_2^1 \Delta \left(\hat{\mathbf{S}}_1 \cdot \hat{\mathbf{L}} \right) + \hat{V}_2^2 \Delta \left(\hat{\mathbf{S}}_2 \cdot \hat{\mathbf{L}} \right). \tag{8.5}$$

In the previous expression the superscript SO stands for *spin-orbit* interactions, Δ denotes the difference between final and initial quantities, and $\hat{V}_2^i$ ($i = 1, 2$) are the components of the normalized eigenvector of the covariance matrix associated with $\Delta \left(\hat{\mathbf{S}}_1 \cdot \hat{\mathbf{L}} \right)$ and $\Delta \left(\hat{\mathbf{S}}_2 \cdot \hat{\mathbf{L}} \right)$. These components, as well as the variance of $\Delta \mathcal{E}_2^{\text{SO}}$, depend on the black hole masses m_i and spin magnitudes χ_i ($i = 1, 2$). In Figure 8.3 we show the dependence of the variance on these parameters. The range of $\sigma^2 \sim 2 \times 10^{-4} - 10^{-9}$ indicates how narrowly peaked the probability distribution for this quantity is or, in other words, how well it is conserved with respect to variations in initial spin orientations for different masses and spin magnitudes.

8.8 CONCLUSION

In this chapter, we have shown that CUDA and GPUs are well suited for the exploration of the binary black hole system parameter space in the post-Newtonian approximation, enabling significant insights into the binary black hole inspiral phase space. In the future, GPU computing and CUDA have the potential to make a significant impact in the quest for direct measurement of gravitational radiation.

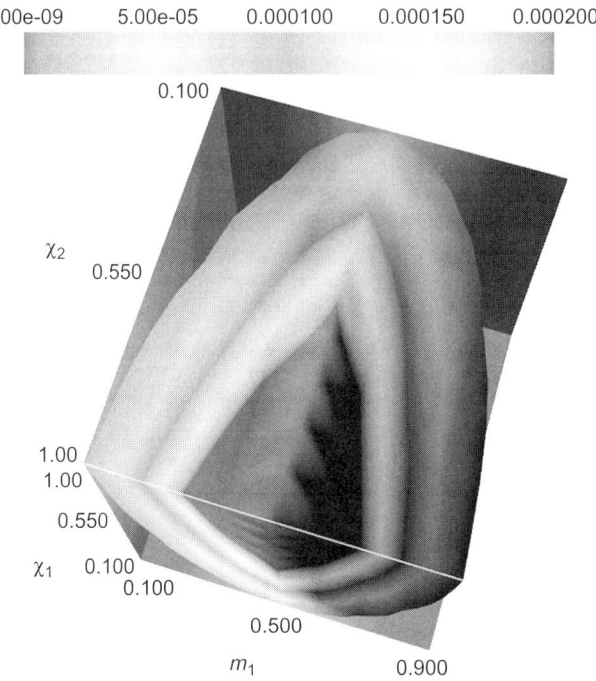

FIGURE 8.3

Variance of the principal component in Eq. 8.5 as a function of the black hole spin magnitudes χ_i ($i = 1, 2$) and one of the black hole masses, m_1 (the total mass was set to $M = m_1 + m_2 = 1$).

Acknowledgments

This work has been supported by NSF Grant PHY0908457 to the University of Maryland and NVIDIA Corporation through a Professor Partnership award. The simulations were carried out at the Teragrid under allocation TG-PHY090080 with some of them using GPUs on the Lincoln cluster.

References

[1]   B. Abbott, et al., LIGO: the laser interferometer gravitational-wave observatory (2007), Rep. Prog. Phys. 72 (7) (2009) 076901.

[2]   F. Acernese, et al., Status of Virgo, Class. Quantum Grav. 25 (2008) 114045.

[3]   B. Aylott, et al., Status of NINJA: the numerical INJection analysis project, Class. Quantum Grav. 26 (2009) 114008.

[4]   B. Aylott, et al., Testing gravitational-wave searches with numerical relativity waveforms: results from the first Numerical INJection Analysis (NINJA) project, Class. Quantum Grav. 26 (2009) 165008.

[5] M. Boyle, A. Buonanno, L.E. Kidder, A.H. Mroue, Y. Pan, H.P. Pfeiffer, et al., High-accuracy numerical simulation of black-hole binaries: computation of the gravitational-wave energy flux and comparisons with post-Newtonian approximants, Phys. Rev. D78 (2008) 104020.

[6] A. Buonanno, Y. Chen, M. Vallisneri, Detecting gravitational waves from precessing binaries of spinning compact objects: adiabatic limit, Phys. Rev. D67 (2003) 104025.

[7] A. Buonanno, Y. Chen, M. Vallisneri, Erratum: detecting gravitational waves from precessing binaries of spinning compact objects: adiabatic limit, Phys. Rev. D74 (2006) 029905.

[8] M. Campanelli, C.O. Lousto, H. Nakano, Y. Zlochower, Comparison of numerical and post-Newtonian waveforms for generic precessing black-hole binaries, Phys. Rev. D79 (2009) 084010.

[9] S. Kee Chung, L. Wen, D. Blair, K. Cannon, A. Datta, Application of graphics processing units to search pipeline for gravitational waves from coalescing binaries of compact objects, Class. Quantum Grav. 27 (2010) 135009.

[10] J.R. Dormand, P.J. Prince, A family of embedded Runge-Kutta formulae, J. Comput. Appl. Math. 6 (1) (1980) 19–26.

[11] C.R. Galley, F. Herrmann, J. Silberholz, M. Tiglio, G. Guerberoff, Statistical constraints on binary black hole inspiral dynamics Cornell University Library, Preprint arXiv.org, Cornell University Library (2010) arXiv:1005.5560.

[12] M. Hannam, Status of black-hole-binary simulations for gravitational-wave detection, Class. Quantum Grav. 26 (2009) 114001.

[13] M. Hannam, S. Husa, B. Bruegmann, A. Gopakumar, Comparison between numerical-relativity and post-Newtonian waveforms from spinning binaries: the orbital hang-up case, Phys. Rev. D78 (2008) 104007.

[14] F. Herrmann, J. Silberholz, M. Bellone, G. Guerberoff, M. Tiglio, Integrating post-Newtonian equations on graphics processing units, Class. Quantum Grav. 27 (2010) 032001.

[15] B. Willke, GEO600: status and plans, Class. Quantum Grav. 24 (2007) S389–S397.

[16] B. Zink, A General Relativistic Evolution Code on CUDA Architectures, Technical Report CCT-TR-2008-1, Louisiana State University, Center for Computation and Technology http://www.cct.lsu.edu/CCT-TR/CCT-TR-2008-1, 2008.

Treecode and Fast Multipole Method for N-Body Simulation with CUDA

9

Rio Yokota, Lorena A. Barba

9.1 INTRODUCTION

The classic N-body problem refers to determining the motion of N particles that interact via a long-distance force, such as gravitation or electrostatics. A straightforward approach to obtaining the forces affecting each particle is the evaluation of all pair-wise interactions, resulting in $\mathcal{O}(N^2)$ computational complexity. This method is only reasonable for moderate-size systems or to compute near-field interactions, in combination with a far-field approximation. In the previous *GPU Gems* volume [21], the acceleration of the all-pairs computation on GPUs was presented for the case of the gravitational potential of N masses. The natural parallelism available in the all-pairs kernel allowed excellent performance on the GPU architecture, and the direct kernel of Reference [24] achieved over 200 Gigaflops on the GeForce 8800 GTX, calculating more than 19 billion interactions per second with $N = 16,384$. In the present contribution, we have addressed the more involved task of implementing the fast N-body algorithms that are used for providing a far-field approximation: the $\mathcal{O}(N \log N)$ treecode [3] and $\mathcal{O}(N)$ fast multipole method [13].

Fast algorithms for N-body problems have diverse practical applications. We have mentioned astrophysics, the paradigm problem. Of great importance is also the calculation of electrostatic (Coulomb) interactions of many charged ions in biological molecules. Proteins and their interactions with other molecules constitute a great challenge for computation, and fast algorithms can enable studies at physiologically relevant scales [4, 26]. Both gravitational and electrostatic problems are mathematically equivalent to solving a Poisson equation for the scalar potential. A general method for the solution of Poisson problems in integral form is described by Greengard and Lee [12], using the FMM in a very interesting way to patch local solutions. In Ethridge and Greengard's work [9], instead, the FMM is applied directly to the volume integral representation of the Poisson problem. These general Poisson solvers based on FMM open the door to using the algorithm in various situations where complex geometries are involved, such as fluid dynamics, and also shape representation and recognition [11].

The FMM for the solution of Helmholtz equations was first developed in Rokhlin's work [25], and is explained in great detail in the book by Gumerov and Duraiswami [14]. The integral-equation formulation is an essential tool in this context, reducing the volumetric problem into one of an integral over a surface. The FMM allows fast solution of these problems by accelerating the computation of dense matrix-vector products arising from the discretization of the integral problem. In fact, the capability of boundary element methods (BEM) is in this way significantly enhanced; see [22] and [19]. These developments make possible the use of the FMM for many physical and engineering problems, such as seismic, magnetic, and acoustic scattering [e.g., 6, 8, 10, 16]. The recent book by Liu [20] covers applications in elastostatics, Stokes flow, and acoustics; some notable applications, including acoustic fields of building and sound barrier combinations, and also a wind turbine model, were presented by Bapart, Shen, and Liu [2].

Because of the variety and importance of applications of treecodes and FMM, the combination of algorithmic acceleration with hardware acceleration can have tremendous impact. Alas, programming these algorithms efficiently is no piece of cake. In this contribution, we aim to present GPU kernels for treecode and FMM in, as much as possible, an uncomplicated, accessible way. The interested reader should consult some of the copious literature on the subject for a deeper understanding of the algorithms themselves. Here, we will offer the briefest of summaries. We will focus our attention on achieving a GPU implementation that is efficient in its utilization of the architecture, but without applying the most advanced techniques known in the field (which would complicate the presentation). These advanced techniques that we deliberately did not discuss in the present contribution are briefly summarized in Section 9.6, for completeness. Our target audience is the researcher involved in computational science with an interest in using fast algorithms for any of the aforementioned applications: astrophysics, molecular dynamics, particle simulation with non-negligible far fields, acoustics, electromagnetics, and boundary integral formulations.

9.2 FAST N-BODY SIMULATION

As in Nyland *et al.* [24], we will use as our model problem the calculation of the gravitational potential of N masses. We have the following expressions for the potential and force, respectively, on a body i:

$$\Phi_i = m_i \sum_{j=1}^{N} \frac{m_j}{r_{ij}}, \qquad \mathbf{F}_i = -\nabla \Phi_i \tag{9.1}$$

Here, m_i and m_j are the masses of bodies i and j, respectively; and $\mathbf{r}_{ij} = \mathbf{x}_j - \mathbf{x}_i$ is the vector from body i to body j. Because the distance vector $\mathbf{r}_{ij}$ is a function of both i and j, an all-pairs summation must be performed. This results in $\mathcal{O}(N^2)$ computational complexity. In the treecode, the sum for the potential is factored into a near-field and a far-field expansion, in the following way,

$$\Phi_i = \sum_{n=0}^{\infty} \sum_{m=-n}^{n} m_i r_i^{-n-1} Y_n^m(\theta_i, \phi_i) \underbrace{\sum_{j=1}^{N} m_j \rho_j^n Y_n^{-m}(\alpha_j, \beta_j)}_{M_n^m}. \tag{9.2}$$

Calculating the summation for M_n^m in this manner can be interpreted as the clustering of particles in the far field. In Eq. 9.2, Y_n^m is the spherical harmonic function, and (r, θ, ϕ); (ρ, α, β) are the distance vectors from the center of the expansion to bodies i and j, respectively. The key is to factor the all-pairs interaction into a part that involves only i and a part that involves only j, hence allowing the summation of j to be performed outside of the loop for i. The condition $\frac{\rho}{r} < 1$, which is required for the series expansion to converge, prohibits the clustering of particles in the near field. Therefore, a tree structure is used to form a hierarchical list of $\log N$ cells that interact with N particles. This results in $\mathcal{O}(N \log N)$ computational complexity.

The complexity can be further reduced by considering cluster-to-cluster interactions.[1] In the FMM, a second series expansion is used for such interactions:

$$\Phi_i = \sum_{n=0}^{\infty} \sum_{m=-n}^{n} m_i r_i^n Y_n^m(\theta_i, \phi_i) \underbrace{\sum_{j=1}^{N} m_j \rho_j^{-n-1} Y_n^{-m}(\alpha_j, \beta_j)}_{L_n^m}, \tag{9.3}$$

where the near-field expansion and far-field expansion are reversed. The condition for this expansion to converge is $\frac{r}{\rho} < 1$, which means that the clustering of particles using L_n^m is only valid in the near field. The key here is to translate multipole expansion coefficients M_n^m of cells in the far field to local expansion coefficients L_n^m of cells in the near field, resulting in a cell-cell interaction. Because of the hierarchical nature of the tree structure, each cell needs to consider only the interaction with a constant number of neighboring cells. Because the number of cells is of $\mathcal{O}(N)$, the FMM has a complexity of $\mathcal{O}(N)$. Also, it is easy to see that keeping the number of cells proportional to N results in an asymptotically constant number of particles per cell. This prevents the direct calculation of the near field from adversely affecting the asymptotic behavior of the algorithm.

The flow of the treecode/FMM calculation is illustrated in Figure 9.1. This schematic shows how the information of all source particles is propagated to a particular set of target particles. The purpose of this figure is to introduce the naming conventions we use for the seven distinct operations (P2P, P2M, M2M, M2P, M2L, L2L, L2P), and to associate these steps to a graphical representation. These naming conventions and graphical representations are used later to describe the GPU implementation and to assess its performance. The difference between the treecode and FMM can be explained concisely using this illustration.

First, the mass/charges of the particles are aggregated into the multipole expansions by calculating M_n^m at the center of all cells (the P2M operation). Next, the multipole expansions are further clustered by translating the center of each expansion to a larger cell and adding their contributions at that level (M2M operation). Once the multipole expansions at all levels of the tree are obtained, the treecode calculates Eq. 9.2 to influence the target particles directly (the M2P operation). In contrast, the FMM first transforms the multipole expansions to local expansions (M2L operation) and then translates the center of each expansion to smaller cells (L2L operation). Finally, the influence of the far field is transmitted from the local expansions to the target particles by calculating Eq. 9.3 in the L2P operation. The influence of the near field is calculated by an all-pairs interaction of neighboring particles (P2P). In the present contribution, all of the aforementioned operations are implemented as GPU kernels.

The schematic in Figure 9.1 shows 2-D representations of the actual 3-D domain subdivisions. There are two levels of cell division shown, one with 16 cells and another with 64 cells. For a typical calculation with millions of particles, the tree is further divided into five or six levels (or more). Recall that the number of cells must be kept proportional to the number of particles for these algorithms to achieve their asymptotic complexity. When there are many levels in the tree, the M2M and L2L

---

[1]The groups or clusters of bodies reside in a subdivision of space for which various authors use the term "box" or "cell"; e.g., "leaf-cell" as used in [24] corresponds to the smallest subdomain.

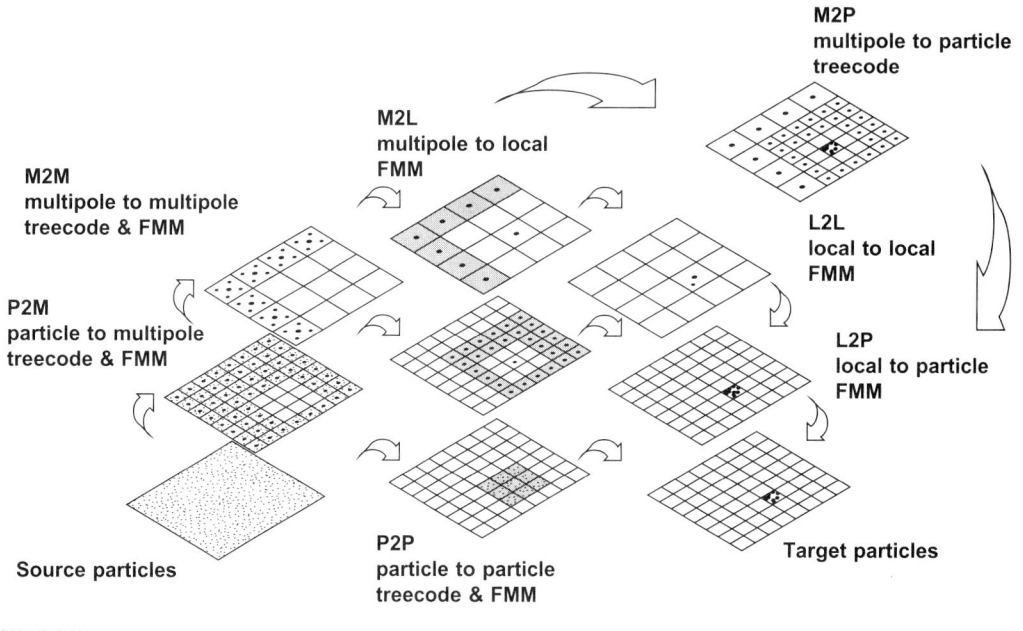

FIGURE 9.1

Flow of the treecode and FMM calculation.

operations are performed multiple times to propagate the information up and down the tree. Also, the M2L and M2P operations are calculated at every level. The P2M, L2P, and P2P are calculated only at the finest (leaf) level of the tree. Since the calculation load decreases exponentially as we move up the tree, the calculation at the leaf level dominates the workload. In particular, it is the M2L/M2P and P2P that consume most of the runtime in an actual program.

9.3 CUDA IMPLEMENTATION OF THE FAST N-BODY ALGORITHMS

In our GPU implementation of the treecode and FMM algorithms, we aim for consistency with the N-body example of Nyland *et al.* [24]. Thus, we will utilize their concept of a computational *tile*: a grid consisting of p rows and p columns representing a subset of the pair-wise interactions to be computed. Consider Figure 9.2, which is adapted from a similar diagram used by the previous authors. Each subset of target particles will be handled by different thread blocks in parallel; the parallel work corresponds to the rows on the diagram. Each subset of source particles is sequentially handled by all thread blocks in chunks of p, where p is the number of threads per thread block. As explained in Nyland *et al.* [24]: "Tiles are sized to balance parallelism with data reuse. The degree of parallelism (that is, the number of rows) must be sufficiently large so that multiple warps can be interleaved to hide latencies in the evaluation of interactions. The amount of data reuse grows with the number of columns, and this parameter also governs the size of the transfer of bodies from device memory into shared memory. Finally, the size of the tile also determines the register space and shared memory required."

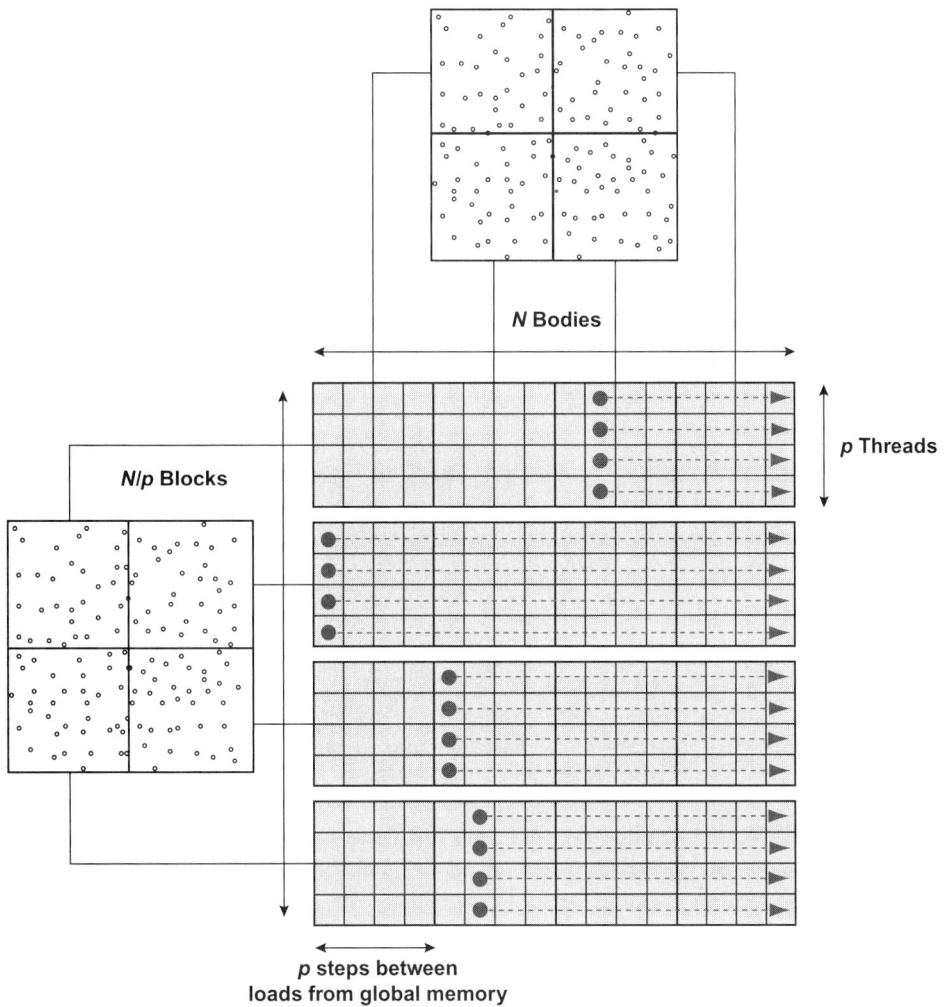

N Bodies

N/p Blocks

p Threads

**p steps between
loads from global memory**

FIGURE 9.2

Thread block model of the direct evaluation on GPU, as in [24].

The particle-to-particle (P2P) interactions of the treecode and FMM are calculated in a similar manner (see Figure 9.3). The entire domain is decomposed into an oct-tree, and each cell at the leaf level is assigned to a thread block. When the number of particles per cell is larger than the size of the thread block, it is split into multiple thread blocks. The main difference with an all-pairs interaction is that each thread block has a different list of source particles. Thus, it is necessary for each thread block to have its unique index list for the offset of source particles. Only the initial offset (for the cells shown in Figure 9.3) is passed to the GPU, and the remaining offsets are determined by increments of p.

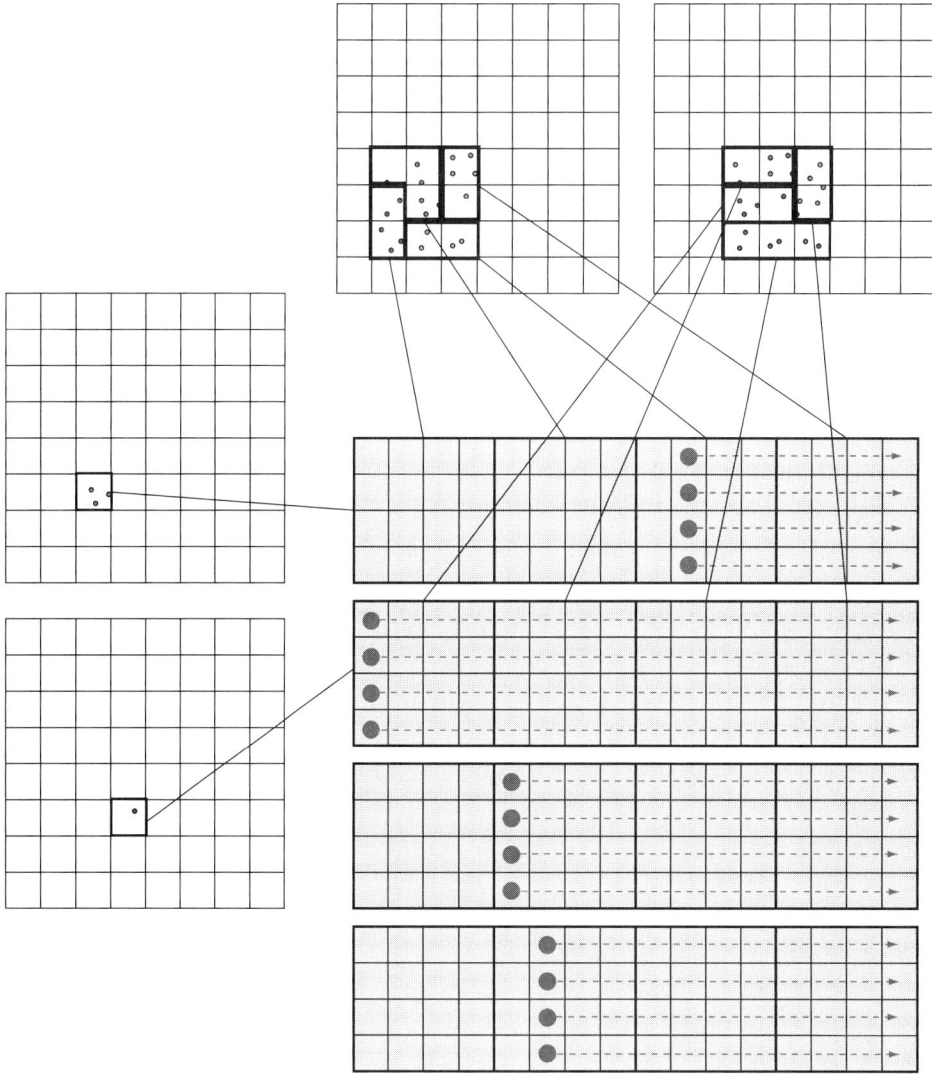

FIGURE 9.3

Thread block model of the particle-particle interaction on GPUs.

In order to ensure coalesced memory access, we accumulate all the source data into a large buffer. On the CPU, we perform a loop over all interaction lists as if we were performing the actual kernel execution, but instead of calculating the kernel, we store the position vector and mass/charge into one large buffer that is passed on to the GPU. This way, the memory access within the GPU kernel is always contiguous because the variables are being stored in exactly the same order that they will be accessed. The time it takes to copy the data into the buffer is less than 1% of the entire calculation. Subsequently, the GPU kernel is called, and all the information in the buffer is processed in one call (if it fits in the global memory of the GPU). The buffer is split up into an optimum size if it becomes too large to fit on the global memory. We also create a buffer for the target particles, which contains the position vectors. Once they are passed to the GPU, the target buffer will be accessed in strides of p, assigning one particle to each thread. Because the source particle list is different for each target cell (see Figure 9.3), having particles from two different cells in one thread block causes branching of the instruction. We avoid this by padding the target buffer, instead of accumulating the particles in the next cell. For example, if there are 2000 particles per box and the thread block size is 128, the target buffer will be padded with 48 particles so that it uses 16 thread blocks of size 128 ($16 \cdot 128 = 2048$) for that cell. In such a case, 1 out of the 16 thread blocks will be doing 37.5% excess work, which is an acceptable trade-off to avoid branching of the instruction within a thread block.

The implementation model used for the P2P calculation can be applied to all other steps in the FMM. An example for the M2L translation kernel is shown in Figure 9.4. Instead of having particle information in each cell, the cell-cell interactions contain many expansion coefficients per cell. Thus, it is natural to assign one target expansion coefficient to each thread while assigning the cell itself to a thread block.

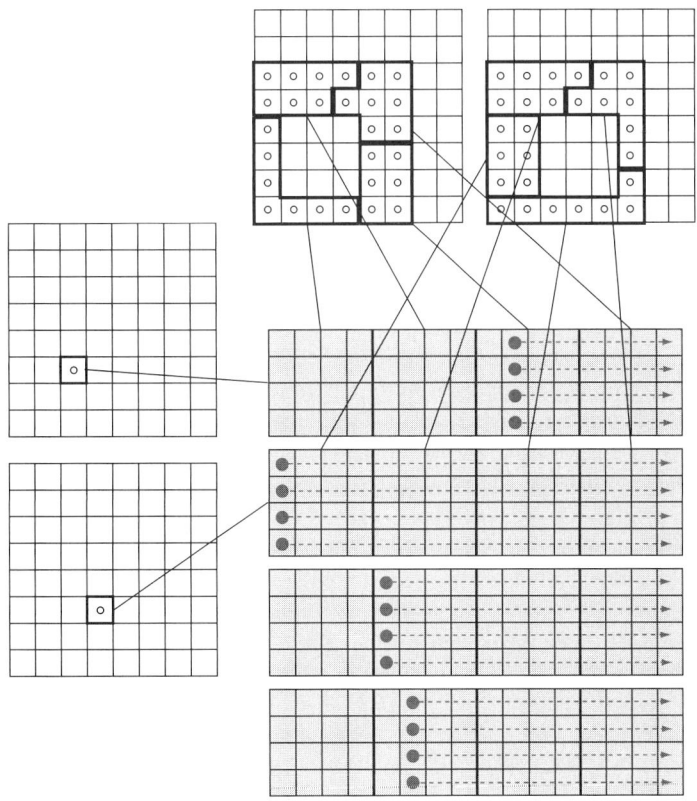

FIGURE 9.4

Thread block model of the cell-cell interaction on GPUs.

The typical number of expansion coefficients is in the order of 10-100, and therefore, the padding issue discussed in the previous paragraph has greater consequences for this case. In the simplest CUDA implementation that we wish to present in this contribution, we simply reduce the thread block size p to alleviate the problem. In the case of particle-cell interactions (P2M) or cell-particles interactions (M2P, L2P), the same logic is applied where either the target expansion coefficients or target particles are assigned to each thread, and the source expansion coefficients or source particles are read from the source buffer in a coalesced manner and sequentially processed in strides of p.

9.4 IMPROVEMENTS OF PERFORMANCE

We consider the performance of the treecode and FMM on GPUs for the same model problem as in Nyland *et al.* [24]. We would like to point out that the performance metrics shown here apply for the very basic and simplified versions of these kernels. The purpose of this contribution is to show the reader how easy it is to write CUDA programs for the treecode and FMM. Therefore, many advanced techniques, which would be considered standard for the expert in these algorithms, are deliberately omitted (see Section 9.6). The performance is reported to allow the readers to reproduce the results and verify that their code is performing as expected, as well as to motivate the discussion about the importance of fast algorithms; we do not claim that the kernels here are as fast as they could be. The CPU tests were run on an Intel Core i7 2.67 GHz processor, and the GPU tests were run on an NVIDIA 295 GTX. The gcc−4.3 compiler with option −O3 was used to compile the CPU codes and nvcc with −use_fast_math was used to compile the CUDA codes.

Figure 9.5 shows the calculation time against the number of bodies for the direct evaluation, treecode, and FMM on a CPU and GPU. The direct calculation is about 300 times faster on the GPU, compared with the single-core CPU. The treecode and FMM are approximately 100 and 30 times faster on the GPU, respectively. For $N < 10^4$, the overhead in the tree construction degrades the performance of the GPU versions. The crossover point between the treecode and direct evaluation is 3×10^3 on the CPU and 2×10^4 on the GPU; the crossover point between the FMM and direct evaluation is 3×10^3 on the CPU and 4×10^4 on the GPU. Note that both for the treecode and FMM, the number of particles at the leaf-level of the tree is higher on the GPU, to obtain a well-balanced calculation (i.e., comparable time should be spent on the near field and on the far field). The crossover point between the treecode and FMM is 3×10^3 on the CPU, but is unclear on the GPU, for the range of our tests.

When the treecode and FMM are performed on the CPU, the P2P and M2P/M2L consume more than 99% of the execution time. When these computationally intensive parts are executed on the GPU, the execution times of the other stages are no longer negligible. This can be seen in the breakdown shown in Figure 9.6 for the $N = 10^7$ case. The contribution of each stage is stacked on top of one another, so the total height of the bar is the total execution time. The legend on the left and right correspond to the treecode and FMM, respectively; "sort" indicates the time it takes to reorder the particles so that they are contiguous within each cell; "other" is the total of everything else, including memory allocation, tree construction, interaction list generation, and so on. The "sort" and "other" operations are performed on the CPU. The depth of the tree in this benchmark is the same for both the treecode and FMM.

As shown in Figure 9.6, the P2P takes the same amount of time for the treecode and FMM. This is due to the fact that we use the same neighbor list for the treecode and FMM. It may be worth noting that the standard treecode uses the distance between particles to determine the clustering threshold (for a

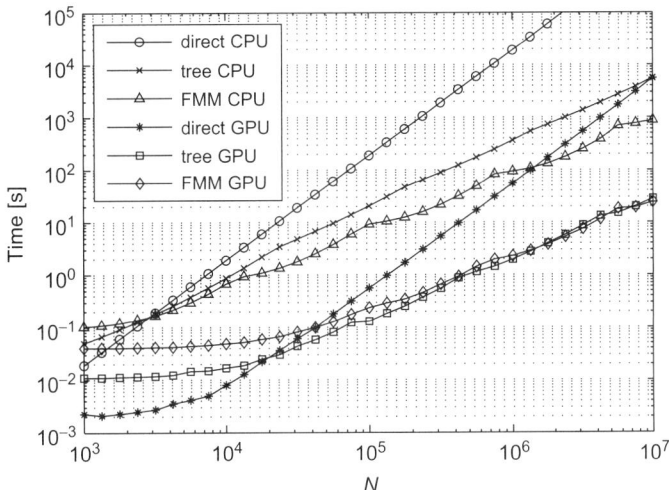

FIGURE 9.5

Calculation time for the direct method, treecode, and FMM on CPU and GPU. (Normalized L^2 norm error of the force is 10^{-4} for both treecode and FMM.)

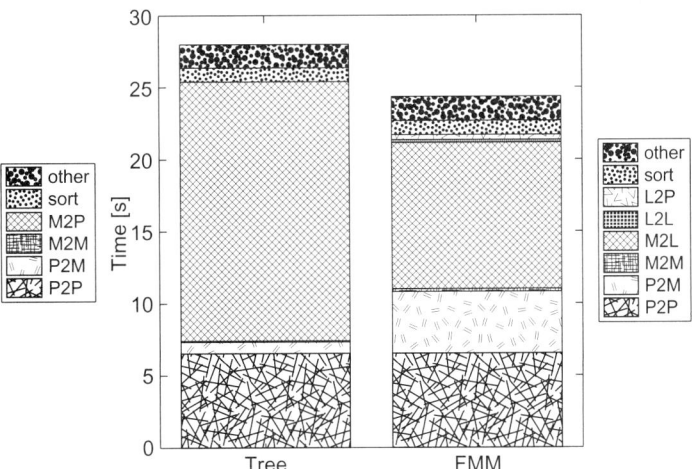

FIGURE 9.6

Breakdown of the calculation time for the treecode and FMM on GPUs using $N = 10^7$ particles.

given desired accuracy) and has an interaction list that is slightly more flexible than that of the FMM. A common measure to determine the clustering in treecodes is the Barnes-Hut multiple acceptance criteria (MAC) $\theta > l/d$ [3], where l is the size of the cell, and d is the distance between the particle and center of mass of the cell. The present calculation uses the standard FMM neighbor list shown in Figure 9.1

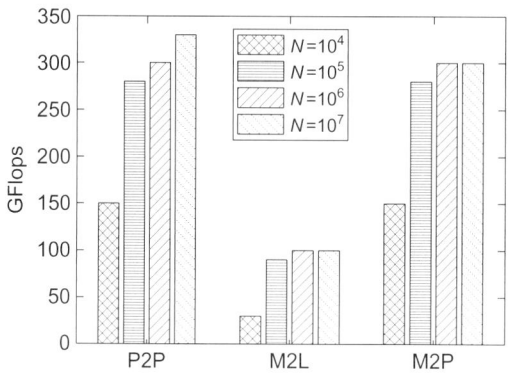

FIGURE 9.7

Actual performance in Gflop/s of three core kernels, for different values of N.

for both the FMM and treecode, which results in a MAC of $\theta = 2/3$. The P2M operation takes longer for the FMM because the order of multipole expansions is larger than in the treecode, to achieve the same accuracy. The calculation loads of M2M, L2L, and L2P are small compared with those of M2P and M2L. The M2P has a much larger calculation load than the M2L, but it has more data parallelism. Therefore, the GPU implementation of these two kernels has a somewhat similar execution time. The high data parallelism of the M2P is an important factor we must consider when comparing the treecode and FMM on GPUs.

Figure 9.7 shows the measured performance on the GPU, measured in Gflop/s; this is actual operations performed in the code, *i.e.*, a `sqrt` counts 1, and so on. Clearly, for $N = 10^4$ the GPU is underutilized, but performance is quite good for the larger values of N. The P2P operation performs very well, achieving in the order of 300 Gflop/s for the larger values of N of these tests. The M2P performs much better than the M2L, owing to the higher inherent parallelism. This explains why we see the treecode accelerating better overall, compared with FMM, in Figure 9.5.

9.5 DETAILED DESCRIPTION OF THE GPU KERNELS

In this section, we provide a detailed explanation of the implementation of the treecode/FMM in CUDA. The code snippets shown here are extracted directly from the code available from the distribution released with this article.[2] In particular, we will describe the implementation of the P2P and M2L kernels, which take up most of the calculation time.

9.5.1 The P2P Kernel Implementation

We start with the simplest kernel for the interaction of a single pair of particles, shown in Listing 9.1. Equation 9.1 is calculated here without the m_i. In other words, it is the acceleration $a_i = F_i/m_i$ that is

---

[2]All source code can be found in `http://code.google.com/p/gemsfmm/`.

```
1    __device__ float3 p2p_kernel_core(float3 accel,
2                                       float3 posTarget, float4 sharedPosSource)
3    {
4        float3 dist;
5        dist.x = posTarget.x − sharedPosSource.x;
6        dist.y = posTarget.y − sharedPosSource.y;
7        dist.z = posTarget.z − sharedPosSource.z;
8        float invDist = rsqrtf(dist.x * dist.x + dist.y * dist.y + dist.z * dist.z + eps);
9        float invDistCube = invDist * invDist * invDist;
10       float s = sharedPosSource.w * invDistCube;
11       accel.x −= dist.x * s;
12       accel.y −= dist.y * s;
13       accel.z −= dist.z * s;
14       return accel;
15   }
```

Listing 9.1: P2P kernel for a single interaction.

being calculated. This part of the code is very similar to that of the nbody example in the CUDA SDK, which is explained in detail in Nyland *et al.* [24]. The only difference is that the present kernel uses the reciprocal square-root function instead of a square root and division. There are 19 floating-point operations in this kernel, counting the three additions, six subtractions, nine multiplications, and one reciprocal square root. The list of variables is as follows:

- posTarget is the position vector of the target particles; it has a float3 data type and is stored in registers.
- sharedPosSource is the position vector and the mass of the source particles; it has a float4 data type and resides in shared memory.
- accel is the acceleration vector of the target particles; it has a float3 data type and is stored in registers.
- the float3 data type is used to store the distance vectors dist.
- eps is the softening factor [1].

The function shown in Listing 9.1 is called from an outer kernel that calculates the pair-wise interactions of all particles in the P2P interaction list. This outer kernel is shown in Listing 9.2, and its graphical representation is shown in Figure 9.3. The input variables are deviceOffset, device-PosTarget, and devicePosSource. The output is deviceAccel. The description of these variables is as follows:

- deviceOffset contains the number of interacting cells and the offset of the particle index for each of these cells.
- devicePosTarget contains the position vector of the target particles.
- devicePosSource is the position vector of the source particles.
- deviceAccel is the acceleration vector of target particles.

All variables that begin with "device" are stored in the device memory. All variables that begin with "shared" are stored in shared memory. Everything else is stored in the registers. Lines 4–10 are declarations of variables; it is possible to reduce register space usage by reusing some of these variables,

```
1    __global__ void p2p_kernel(int* deviceOffset, float3* devicePosTarget,
2                               float4* devicePosSource, float3* deviceAccel)
3    {
4      int jbase, jsize, jblok, numInteraction;
5      int j, ij, jj, jb;
6      const int threadsPerBlock = threadsPerBlockTypeA;
7      const int offsetStride = 2 * maxP2PInteraction + 1;
8      float3 posTarget;
9      float3 accel = {0.0f, 0.0f, 0.0f};
10     __shared__ float4 sharedPosSource[threadsPerBlock];
11     posTarget = devicePosTarget[blockIdx.x * threadsPerBlock + threadIdx.x];
12     numInteraction = deviceOffset[blockIdx.x * offsetStride];
13     for(ij = 0; ij < numInteraction; ij++){
14       jbase = deviceOffset[blockIdx.x * offsetStride + 2 * ij + 1];
15       jsize = deviceOffset[blockIdx.x * offsetStride + 2 * ij + 2];
16       jblok = (jsize + threadsPerBlock - 1) / threadsPerBlock;
17       for(j = 0; j < jblok-1; j++){
18         jb = jbase + j * threadsPerBlock + threadIdx.x;
19         sharedPosSource[threadIdx.x] = devicePosSource[jb];
20         __syncthreads();
21 #pragma unroll 32
22         for(jj = 0; jj < threadsPerBlock; jj++){
23           accel = p2p_kernel_core(accel, posTarget, sharedPosSource[jj]);
24         }
25         __syncthreads();
26       }
27       jb = jbase + j * threadsPerBlock + threadIdx.x;
28       sharedPosSource[threadIdx.x] = devicePosSource[jb];
29       __syncthreads();
30       for(jj = 0; jj < jsize - (j * threadsPerBlock); jj++){
31         accel = p2p_kernel_core(accel, posTarget, sharedPosSource[jj]);
32       }
33       __syncthreads();
34     }
35     deviceAccel[blockIdx.x * threadsPerBlock + threadIdx.x] = accel;
36   }
```

Listing 9.2: The entire P2P kernel.

but for pedagogical purposes we have chosen to declare each variable that has a different functionality. There are four variables that are defined externally. One is the threadsPerBlockTypeA, which is the number of threads per thread block for the P2P kernel. We use a different number of threads per thread block, threadsPerBlockTypeB, for the other kernels that have expansion coefficients as targets. On line 5, threadsPerBlockTypeA is passed to threadsPerBlock as a constant. Another external variable is used on line 7, where maxP2PInteraction (the maximum number of neighbor cells in a P2P interaction) is used to calculate offsetStride (the stride of the data in deviceOffset). The other two externally defined variables are threadIdx and blockIdx, which are thread index and thread-block index provided by CUDA.

On line 11, the position vectors are copied from the global memory to the registers. On line 12, the number of interacting cells is read from the deviceOffset, and on line 13 this number is used to form a loop that goes through all the interacting cells (27 cells for the P2P interaction). Note that each thread block handles (part of) only one target cell, and the interaction list of the neighboring cells is identical for all threads within the thread block. In other words, blockIdx.x identifies which target cell we are looking at, and ij identifies which source cell it is interacting with. On line 14, the offset of the particle index for that source cell is copied from deviceOffset to jbase. On line 15, the number of particles in the source cell is copied to jsize. Now we have the information of the target particles and the offset and size of the source particles that they interact with. At this point, the information of the source particles still resides in the device memory. This information is copied to the shared memory in coalesced chunks of size threadsPerBlock. However, the number of particles per cell is not always a multiple of threadsPerBlock, so the last chunk will contain a remainder that is different from threadsPerBlock. It is inefficient to have a conditional branching to detect if the chunk is the last one or not, and it is a waste of storage to pad for each source cell. Therefore, on line 16 the number of chunks jblok is calculated by rounding up jsize to the nearest multiple of threadsPerBlock. On line 17, a loop is executed for all chunks except the last one. The last chunk is processed separately on lines 27–33. On line 18, the index of the source particle on the device memory is calculated by offsetting the thread index first by the chunk offset j*threadsPerBlock and then by the cell offset jbase. On line 19, this global index is used to copy the position vector of the source particles from device memory to shared memory. Subsequently, __syncthreads() is called to ensure that the copy to shared memory has completed on all threads before proceeding. On lines 21–24, a loop is performed for all elements in the current chunk of source particles, where the p2p_kernel_core is called per pair-wise interaction. The #pragma unroll 32 is the same loop unrolling suggested in Nyland *et al.* [24]. On line 25, __syncthreads() is called to keep sharedPosSource from being overwritten for the next chunk before having been used in the current one. Lines 27–33 are identical to lines 18–25 except for the loop counter for jj, which is the remainder instead of threadsPerBlock. On line 35, the acceleration vector in registers is copied back to the device memory by offsetting the thread index by blockIdx.x * threadsPerBlock.

9.5.2 The M2L Kernel Implementation

As shown in Equations 9.2 and 9.3, the multipole-to-local translation in the FMM is the translation of the multipole expansion coefficients M_n^m in one location to the local expansion coefficients L_n^m at another. If we relabel the indices of the local expansion matrix to L_j^k, the M2L translation can be written as

$$L_j^k = \sum_{n=0}^{p-1} \sum_{m=-n}^{n} \frac{M_n^m i^{|k-m|-|k|-|m|} A_n^m A_j^k Y_{j+n}^{m-k}(\alpha,\beta)}{(-1)^j A_{j+n}^{m-k} \rho^{j+n+1}} \tag{9.4}$$

where i is the imaginary unit, p is the order of the series expansion, A_n^m is defined as

$$A_n^m = \frac{1}{\sqrt{(n-m)!(n+m)!}} \tag{9.5}$$

and Y_n^m is the spherical harmonic

$$Y_n^m(\alpha,\beta) = \sqrt{\frac{(n-|m|)!}{(n+|m|)!}} P_n^{|m|}(\cos\alpha)e^{im\beta}. \tag{9.6}$$

In order to calculate the spherical harmonics, the value of the associated Legendre polynomials P_n^m must be determined. The associated Legendre polynomials have a recurrence relation, which requires only the information of $x = \cos \alpha$ to start. The recurrence relations and identities used to generate the full associated Legendre polynomial are

$$(n - m + 1)P_{n+1}^m(x) = x(2n + 1)P_n^m(x) - (n + m)P_{n-1}^m(x), \tag{9.7}$$

$$P_m^m(x) = (-1)^m (2m - 1)! (1 - x^2)^{m/2}, \tag{9.8}$$

$$P_{m+1}^m = x(2m + 1)P_m^m(x) \tag{9.9}$$

The M2L kernel calculates Equation 9.4 in two stages. First, $Y_n^m/\rho^{n+1}/A_n^m$ is calculated using Equations 9.5–9.9. Then, Equation 9.4 is calculated by substituting this result after switching the indices $n \to j + n$ and $m \to m - k$. Thus, $M_n^m i^{|k-m|-|k|-|m|} A_n^m A_j^k/(-1)^j$ is calculated at the second stage. Furthermore, in the GPU implementation the complex part $e^{im\beta}$ in Equation 9.6 is multiplied at the end of the second stage so that the values remain real until then. At the end of the second stage, we simply put the real and complex part of the L_j^k into two separate variables.

The GPU implementation of the first part for $Y_n^m/\rho^{n+1}/A_n^m$ is shown in Listing 9.3. As was the case with Listing 9.1, this function is called from an outer function that calculates the entire M2L translation for all cells. The inputs are `rho`, `alpha`, and `sharedFactorial`. The output is `sharedYnm`. Because we do not calculate the $e^{im\beta}$ part of the spherical harmonic at this point, `beta` is not necessary. `sharedFactorial` contains the values of the factorials for a given index; i.e., `sharedFactorial[n]`$= n!$. Also, it is $Y_n^m/\rho^{n+1}/A_n^m$ that is stored in `sharedYnm` and not Y_n^m itself. Basically, Equation 9.7 is calculated on line 24, Equation 9.8 is calculated on line 27, and Equation 9.9 is calculated on line 16. `p`, `p1`, and `p2` correspond to P_{n+1}^m, P_n^m, and P_{n-1}^m, respectively. However, `p` is used in lines 14 and 21 before it is updated on lines 16 and 24, so it represents P_n^m at the time of usage. This P_n^m is used to calculate $Y_n^m/\rho^{n+1}/A_n^m$ on lines 14 and 21, although the correspondence to the equation is not obvious at first hand. The connection to the equation will become clear when we do the following transformation,

$$\frac{Y_n^m}{\rho^{n+1}A_n^m} = \frac{\sqrt{(n-m)!/(n+m)!}\,P_n^m e^{im\beta}}{\rho^{n+1}/\sqrt{(n-m)!(n+m)!}} = \frac{(n-m)!\,P_n^m}{\rho^{n+1}} e^{im\beta} \tag{9.10}$$

As mentioned earlier, we do not calculate the $e^{im\beta}$ at this point so `sharedYnm` is symmetric with respect to the sign of m. Therefore, the present loop for the recurrence relation is performed for only $m \geq 0$ and the absolute sign for m in Equation 9.6 disappears. We can also save shared memory consumption by storing only the $m \geq 0$ half of the spherical harmonic in `sharedYnm`.

The second stage of the M2L kernel is shown in Listing 9.4. The inputs are `j`, `beta`, `sharedFactorial`, `sharedYnm`, and `sharedMnmSource`. The output is `LnmTarget`. In this second stage of the M2L, the remaining parts of Equation 9.4 are calculated to obtain L_j^k. Each thread handles a different coefficient in L_j^k. In order to do this, we must associate the `threadIdx.x` to a pair of `j` and `k`. In the outer function, which will be shown later, the index `j` corresponding to `threadIdx.x` is calculated and passed to the present function. Lines 9–11, determine the index `k` from the input `j` and `threadIdx.x`.

We will remind the reader again that this part of the M2L kernel calculates $M_n^m i^{|k-m|-|k|-|m|} A_n^m A_j^k/(-1)^j$. This results in a quadruple loop over the indices j, k, m, and n. However, in the GPU implementation the first two indices are thread parallelized, only leaving m and n as sequential loops

```
1    __device__ void m2l_calculate_ynm(float* sharedYnm,
2                                       float rho, float alpha, float* sharedFactorial)
3    {
4      int i, m, n;
5      float x, s, fact, pn, p, p1, p2, rhom, rhon;
6      x = cosf(alpha);
7      s = sqrt(1 − x * x);
8      fact = 1;
9      pn = 1;
10     rhom = 1.0 / rho;
11     for(m = 0; m < 2 * numExpansions; m++){
12       p = pn;
13       i = m * (m + 1) / 2 + m;
14       sharedYnm[i] = rhom * p;
15       p1 = p;
16       p = x * (2 * m + 1) * p;
17       rhom /= rho;
18       rhon = rhom;
19       for(n = m + 1; n < 2 * numExpansions; n++){
20         i = n * (n + 1) / 2 + m;
21         sharedYnm[i] = rhon * p * sharedFactorial[n − m];
22         p2 = p1;
23         p1 = p;
24         p = (x * (2 * n + 1) * p1 − (n + m) * p2) / (n − m + 1);
25         rhon /= rho;
26       }
27       pn = −pn * fact * s;
28       fact = fact + 2;
29     }
30   }
```

Listing 9.3: Calculation of the spherical harmonic for the M2L kernel.

starting from lines 13, 14, and 28. Lines 14–27 are for negative m, while lines 28–42 are for positive m. $A_j^k/(−1)^j$ is calculated on line 12. We define a preprocessed function "#define ODDEVEN(n) ((n & 1 == 1) ? -1 : 1)", which calculates $(−1)^n$ without using a power function. A_n^m is calculated on lines 19 and 33. $i^{|k−m|−|k|−|m|}$ is calculated on line 34 for the $m \geq 0$ case, and is always 1 for $m < 0$. Because $|k − m| − |k| − |m|$ is always an even number, it is possible to calculate $i^{|k−m|−|k|−|m|}$ as $−1^{(|k−m|−|k|−|m|)/2}$ and use the ODDEVEN function defined previously. Then, anm, ajk, and sharedYnm are multiplied to this result. The complex part $e^{im\beta}$ that was omitted in the first stage is calculated on lines 17–18 and 31–32 using the index $m − k$ instead of m; ere is the real part and eim is the imaginary part. CnmReal and CnmImag in lines 21–22 and 36–37 are the real and imaginary parts of the product of all the terms previously described. Finally, these values are multiplied to M_n^m in lines 23–26 and 38–41, where sharedMnmSource[2*i+0] is the real part and sharedMnmSource[2*i+1] is the imaginary part. We use the relation $M_n^{−m} = \overline{M_n^m}$ to reduce the storage of sharedMnmSource. Therefore, the imaginary part has opposite signs for the $m \geq 0$ case and $m < 0$ case. The real part of L_j^k is accumulated in LnmTarget[0], while the imaginary part is accumulated in LnmTarget[1].

```
1   __device__ void m2l_kernel_core(float* LnmTarget,
2                                    int j, float beta,
3                                    float* sharedFactorial,
4                                    float* sharedYnm,
5                                    float* sharedMnmSource)
6   {
7     int i, k, m, n, jnkm;
8     float ere, eim, anm, ajk, cnm, CnmReal, CnmImag;
9     k = 0;
10    for(i = 0; i <= j; i++) k += i;
11    k = threadIdx.x − k;
12    // using pre−processed function ODDEVEN
13    ajk = ODDEVEN(j) * rsqrtf(sharedFactorial[j − k] * sharedFactorial[j + k]);
14    for(n = 0; n < numExpansions; n++){
15      for(m = −n; m < 0; m++){
16        i = n * (n + 1) / 2 − m;
17        jnkm = (j + n) * (j + n + 1) / 2 − m + k;
18        ere = cosf((m − k) * beta);
19        eim = sinf((m − k) * beta);
20        anm = rsqrtf(sharedFactorial[n − m] * sharedFactorial[n + m]);
21        cnm = anm * ajk * sharedYnm[jnkm];
22        CnmReal = cnm * ere;
23        CnmImag = cnm * eim;
24        LnmTarget[0] += sharedMnmSource[2 * i + 0] * CnmReal;
25        LnmTarget[0] += sharedMnmSource[2 * i + 1] * CnmImag;
26        LnmTarget[1] += sharedMnmSource[2 * i + 0] * CnmImag;
27        LnmTarget[1] −= sharedMnmSource[2 * i + 1] * CnmReal;
28      }
29      for(m = 0; m <= n; m++){
30        i = n * (n + 1) / 2 + m;
31        jnkm = (j + n) * (j + n + 1) / 2 + abs(m − k);
32        ere = cosf((m − k) * beta);
33        eim = sinf((m − k) * beta);
34        anm = rsqrtf(sharedFactorial[n − m] * sharedFactorial[n + m]);
35        cnm = ODDEVEN((abs(k − m) − k − m) / 2);
36        cnm *= anm * ajk * sharedYnm[jnkm];
37        CnmReal = cnm * ere;
38        CnmImag = cnm * eim;
39        LnmTarget[0] += sharedMnmSource[2 * i + 0] * CnmReal;
40        LnmTarget[0] −= sharedMnmSource[2 * i + 1] * CnmImag;
41        LnmTarget[1] += sharedMnmSource[2 * i + 0] * CnmImag;
42        LnmTarget[1] += sharedMnmSource[2 * i + 1] * CnmReal;
43      }
44    }
45  }
```

Listing 9.4: Calculation of L_n^m in the M2L kernel.

The functions in Listings 9.3 and 9.4 are called from an outer function shown in Listing 9.5. This function is similar to the one shown in Listing 9.2. The inputs are `deviceOffset` and `deviceMnmSource`. The output is `deviceLnmTarget`. The definitions are:

- `deviceOffset` contains the number of interacting cells, the offset of the particle index for each of these cells, and the 3D index of their relative positioning;
- `threadsPerBlockTypeB` and `maxM2LInteraction` are defined externally;
- `maxM2LInteraction` is the maximum size of the interaction list for the M2L, which is 189 for the present kernels; and
- `offsetStride`, calculated on line 6, is the stride of the data in `deviceOffset`.

On line 8, the size of the cell is read from `deviceConstant[0]`, which resides in constant memory. On line 10, `LnmTarget` is initialized. Each thread handles a different coefficient in L_j^k. In order to do this, we must associate the `threadIdx.x` to a pair of j and k. `sharedJ` returns the index j when given the `threadIdx.x` as input. It is declared on line 11 and initialized on lines 16–18. The values are calculated on lines 19–24, and then passed to `m2l_kernel_core()` on line 40. `shared-MnmSource` is the copy of `deviceMnmSource` in shared memory. It is declared on line 12 and the values are copied on lines 35–36 before it is passed to `m2l_kernel_core()` on line 41. `sharedYnm` contains the real spherical harmonics. It is declared on line 13, and its values are calculated in the function `m2l_calculate_ynm` on line 39 before they are passed to `m2l_kernel_core` on line 41. `sharedFactorial` contains the factorial for the given index and is declared on line 14 and its values are calculated on lines 25–29 before they are passed to `m2l_kernel_core` on line 41. On line 15, the number of interacting cells is read from `deviceOffset` and its value `numInteraction` is used for the loop on line 30. The offset of particles is read from `deviceOffset` on line 31, and the relative distance of the source and target cell is calculated on lines 32–34. On line 38, this distance is transformed into spherical coordinates using an externally defined function `cart2sph`. The two functions shown in Listings 9.3 and 9.4 are called on lines 39–41. Finally, the results in `LnmTarget` are copied to `deviceLnmTarget` on line 45.

Listings 9.1–9.5 are the core components of the present GPU implementation. We hope that the other parts of the open-source code that we provide along with this article are understandable to the reader without explanation.

9.6 OVERVIEW OF ADVANCED TECHNIQUES

There are various techniques that can be used to enhance the performance of the treecode and FMM. The FMM presented in this article uses the standard translation operator for translating multipole/local expansions. As the order of expansion p increases, the calculation increases as $\mathcal{O}(p^4)$ for this method. There are alternatives that can bring the complexity down to $\mathcal{O}(p^3)$ [5] or even $\mathcal{O}(p^2)$ [14]. In the code that we have released along with this article, we have included an implementation of the $\mathcal{O}(p^3)$ translation kernel by [5] as an extension. We have omitted the explanations in this text, however, and consider the advanced reader able to self-learn the techniques from the literature to understand the code. Some other techniques that can improve the performance are the optimization of the order of expansion for each interaction [7], the use of a more efficient M2L interaction stencil [15], and the use of a treecode/FMM hybrid, as suggested in [5]. It is needless to mention that the parallelization of the

```
1    __global__ void m2l_kernel(int* deviceOffset, float* deviceLnmTarget,
2                               float* deviceMnmSource)
3    {
4      int i, j, k, ij, ib, numInteraction, jbase;
5      const int threadsPerBlock = threadsPerBlockTypeB;
6      const int offsetStride = 4*maxM2LInteraction+1;
7      float3 dist;
8      float boxSize = deviceConstant[0];
9      float rho, alpha, beta, fact;
10     float LnmTarget[2] = {0.0f, 0.0f};
11     __shared__ int sharedJ[threadsPerBlock];
12     __shared__ float sharedMnmSource[2 * threadsPerBlock];
13     __shared__ float sharedYnm[numCoefficients];
14     __shared__ float sharedFactorial[2 * numExpansions];
15     numInteraction = deviceOffset[blockIdx.x * offsetStride];
16     for(i = 0; i < threadsPerBlock; i++){
17       sharedJ[i] = 0;
18     }
19     for(j = 0; j < numExpansions; j++){
20       for(k = 0; k <= j; k++){
21         i = j * (j + 1) / 2 + k;
22         sharedJ[i] = j;
23       }
24     }
25     fact = 1.0;
26     for(i = 0; i < 2 * numExpansions; i++) {
27       sharedFactorial[i] = fact;
28       fact = fact * (i + 1);
29     }
30     for(ij = 0; ij < numInteraction; ij++){
31       jbase = deviceOffset[blockIdx.x * offsetStride + 4 * ij + 1];
32       dist.x = deviceOffset[blockIdx.x * offsetStride + 4 * ij + 2] * boxSize;
33       dist.y = deviceOffset[blockIdx.x * offsetStride + 4 * ij + 3] * boxSize;
34       dist.z = deviceOffset[blockIdx.x * offsetStride + 4 * ij + 4] * boxSize;
35       for(i=0;i<2;i++) sharedMnmSource[2 * threadIdx.x + i] =
36                       deviceMnmSource[2 * (jbase + threadIdx.x) + i];
37       __syncthreads();
38       cart2sph(rho, alpha, beta, dist.x, dist.y, dist.z);
39       m2l_calculate_ynm(sharedYnm, rho, alpha, sharedFactorial);
40       m2l_kernel_core(LnmTarget, sharedJ[threadIdx.x], beta,
41                       sharedFactorial, sharedYnm, sharedMnmSource);
42       __syncthreads();
43     }
44     ib = blockIdx.x * threadsPerBlock + threadIdx.x;
45     for(i=0;i<2;i++) deviceLnmTarget[2 * ib + i] = LnmTarget[i];
46   }
```

Listing 9.5: The entire M2L kernel.

code for multi-GPU calculations [17, 18] is an important extension to the treecode/FMM on GPUs. Again, this is an advanced topic beyond the scope of this contribution.

When you are reporting the GPU/CPU speedup, it is bad form to compare the results against an unoptimized serial CPU implementation. Sadly, this is often done, which negatively affects the credibility of results in the field. For this contribution, we have used a reasonable serial code in C, but it is certainly not so fast as it could be. For example, it is possible to achieve over an order of magnitude performance increase on the CPU by doing single-precision calculations using SSE instructions with inline assembly code [23]. For those who are interested in the comparison between a highly tuned CPU code and highly tuned GPU code, we provide a highly tuned CPU implementation of the treecode/FMM in the code package that we release with this book.

9.7 CONCLUSIONS

This contribution is a follow-on from the previous *GPU Gems 3*, Chapter 31 [24], where the acceleration of the all-pairs computation on GPUs was presented for the case of the gravitational potential of N masses. We encourage the reader to consult that previous contribution, as it will complement the presentation we have given. As can be seen in the results presented here, the cross-over point where fast N-body algorithms become advantageous over direct, all-pairs calculations is in the order of 10^3 for the CPU and in the order of 10^4 for the GPU. Hence, utilizing the GPU architecture moves the cross-over point upward by one order of magnitude, but this size of problem is much smaller than many applications require. If the application of interest involves, say, millions of interacting bodies, the advantage of fast algorithms is clear, in both CPU and GPU hardware. With our basic kernels, about $15\times$ speedup is obtained from the fast algorithm on the GPU for a million particles. For $N = 10^7$, the fast algorithms provide $150\times$ speedup over direct methods on the GPU. However, if the problem at hand requires small systems, smaller than 10^4, say, one would be justified to settle for the all-pairs, direct calculation.

The main conclusion that we would like the reader to draw from this contribution is that constructing fast N-body algorithms on the GPU is far from a formidable task. Here, we have shown basic kernels that achieve substantial speedup over direct evaluation in less than 200 lines of CUDA code. Expert-level implementations will, of course, be much more involved and would achieve more performance. But a basic implementation like the one shown here is definitely worthwhile.

We thank F. A. Cruz for various discussions that contributed to the quality of this chapter.

References

[1] S. Aarseth, Gravitational N-Body Simulations, Cambridge, United Kingdom: Cambridge University Press, 2003.

[2] M.S. Bapat, L. Shen, Y.J. Liu, An adaptive fast multipole boundary element method for three-dimensional half-space acoustic wave problems, Eng. Anal. Bound. Elem. 33 (8–9) (2009) 1113–1123.

[3] J. Barnes, P. Hut, A hierarchical $O(N \log N)$ force-calculation algorithm, Nature 449 (1986) 324–446.

[4] J.A. Board Jr., J.W. Causey, J.F. Leathrum Jr., A. Windemuth, K. Schulten, Accelerated molecular dynamics simulation with the parallel fast multipole algorithm, Chem. Phys. Lett. 198 (1–2) (1992) 89–94.

[5] H. Cheng, L. Greengard, V. Rokhlin, A fast adaptive multipole algorithm in three dimensions, J. Comput. Phys. 155 (1999) 468–498.

[6] E. Darve, P. Have, Efficient fast multipole method for low-frequency scattering, J. Comput. Phys. 197 (2004) 341–363.

[7] H. Daschel, Corrected article: an error-controlled fast multipole method, J. Chem. Phys. 132 (2010) 119901.

[8] K.C. Donepudi, J.-M. Jin, W.C. Chew, A higher order multilevel fast multipole algorithm for scattering from mixed conducting/dielectric bodies, IEEE Trans. Antennas Propag. 51 (10) (2003) 2814–2821.

[9] F. Ethridge, L. Greengard, A new fast-multipole accelerated Poisson solver in two dimensions, SIAM J. Sci. Comput. 23 (3) (2001) 741–760.

[10] H. Fujiwara, The fast multipole method for integral equations of seismic scattering problems, Geophys. J. Int. 133 (1998) 773–782.

[11] L. Gorelick, M. Galun, E. Sharon, R. Basri, A. Brandt, Shape representation and classification using the Poisson equation, IEEE Trans. Pattern Anal. Mach. Intell. 28 (2006) 1991–2005.

[12] L. Greengard, J.-Y. Lee, A direct adaptive Poisson solver of arbitrary order accuracy, J. Comp. Phys. 125 (1996) 415–424.

[13] L. Greengard, V. Rokhlin, A fast algorithm for particle simulations, J. Comput. Phys. 73 (2) (1987) 325–348.

[14] N.A. Gumerov, R. Duraiswami, Fast Multipole Methods for the Helmholtz Equation in Three Dimensions, first ed., Elsevier Ltd., Oxford, 2004.

[15] N.A. Gumerov, R. Duraiswami, Fast multipole methods on graphics processors, J. Comp. Phys. 227 (18) (2008) 8290–8313.

[16] N.A. Gumerov, R. Duraiswami, A broadband fast multipole accelerated boundary element method for the three dimensional Helmholtz equation, J. Acoust. Soc. Am. 125 (1) (2009) 191–205.

[17] T. Hamada, T. Narumi, R. Yokota, K. Yasuoka, K. Nitadori, M. Taiji, 42 TFlops hierarchical N-body simulations on GPUs with applications in both astrophysics and turbulence, in: Proceedings of the Conference on High Performance Computing Networking, November 2009, Portland OR, Storage and Analysis, SC '09, ACM, New York, NY 2009, pp. 1–12.

[18] I. Lashuk, A. Chandramowlishwaran, H. Langston, T.-A. Nguyen, R. Sampath, A. Shringarpure, et al., A massively parallel adaptive fast-multipole method on heterogeneous architectures, in: Proceedings of the Conference on High Performance Computing Networking, November 2009, Portland OR, Storage and Analysis, SC '09, ACM, New York, NY 2009, pp. 1–12.

[19] Y.J. Liu, N. Nishimura, The fast multipole boundary element method for potential problems: a tutorial, Eng. Anal. Bound. Elem. 30 (2006) 371–381.

[20] Y. Liu, Fast Multipole Boundary Element Method: Theory and Applications in Engineering, Cambridge, United Kingdom: Cambridge University Press, 2009.

[21] H. Nguyen, GPU Gems 3, Addison-Wesley Professional, 2007, Available from: http://developer.nvidia.com/object/gpu-gems-3.html.

[22] N. Nishimura, Fast multipole accelerated boundary integral equation methods, Appl. Mech. Rev. 55 (4) (2002) 299–324.

[23] K. Nitadori, K. Yoshikawa, J. Makino, Personal Communication.

[24] L. Nyland, M. Harris, J. Prins, Fast N-body simulation with CUDA, in: GPU Gems 3, Addison-Wesley Professional, 2007, pp. 677–695 (Chapter 31).

[25] V. Rokhlin, Rapid solution of integral equations of scattering theory in two dimensions, J. Comp. Phys. 86 (2) (1990) 414–439.

[26] C. Sagui, A. Darden, Molecular dynamics simulations of biomolecules: long-range electrostatic effects, Annu. Rev. Biophys. Biomol. Struct. 28 (1999) 155–179.

Wavelet-Based Density Functional Theory Calculation on Massively Parallel Hybrid Architectures

10

Luigi Genovese, Matthieu Ospici, Brice Videau, Thierry Deutsch, Jean-François Méhaut

Electronic structure calculations has become in recent years a widespread tool to predict and investigate electronic properties of physics at the nanoscale. Among the different approaches, the Kohn-Sham (KS) formalism [1] in the density functional theory (DFT) framework has certainly become one of the most used. At the same time, the need to simulate systems more and more complex together with the increase in computational power of modern machines pushes the formalism toward limits that were unconceivable just a few years ago. It is thus important to provide reliable solutions to benefit from the enhancements of computational power in order to use these tools in more challenging systems. With this work, we have tried to provide an answer on this direction by exploiting the GPU acceleration of systematic DFT codes. The principal operations of an electronic structure code based on Daubechies wavelets were ported on NVIDIA GPU cards. The CPU version of the code on which our work is based has systematic convergence properties, very high performances, and an excellent efficiency on parallel and massively parallel environments. This code is delivered under the GNU-GPL license and was conceived from the beginning for parallel and massively parallel architectures. For this reason, the questions related to the integration of GPU accelerators into a parallel environment are also addressed. The topics that are presented in this chapter are thus related to efficiently benefiting from GPU acceleration in the context of a complex code made with sections with different runtime behavior. For these reasons, in addition to the technical implementation details of the GPU kernels, a considerable part of the discussion is related to the insertion of these kernels in the context of the full code. The study of GPU accelerations strategies for such a code can be of great interest for a number of groups working on codes with rich and complicated structures.

10.1 INTRODUCTION, PROBLEM STATEMENT, AND CONTEXT

In this contribution, we present an implementation of a full DFT code that can run on massively parallel hybrid CPU-GPU clusters. Our implementation is based on the architecture of NVIDIA GPU cards of compute capability at least of type 1.3, which support double-precision floating-point numbers. This DFT code, named BigDFT, is delivered within the GNU-GPL license either in a stand-alone version or integrated in the ABINIT software package. The formalism of this code is based on Daubechies wavelets [10]. As we will see in the following sections, the properties of this basis set are well suited for an extension on a GPU-accelerated environment. In addition to focusing on the implementation details of a single operation, this chapter also relies of the usage of the GPU resources in a complex code with different kinds of operations.

We start with a brief overview of the BigDFT code in order to describe why and how the use of GPU can be useful for accelerating the code operations.

10.1.1 Overview of the BigDFT Code

In the KS formulation of DFT, the KS wavefunctions $|\Psi_i\rangle$ are eigenfunctions of the KS Hamiltonian operator. The KS Hamiltonian can then be written as the action of three operators on the wavefunction:

$$\left(-\frac{1}{2}\nabla^2 + V + V_{\text{nl}}\right)|\Psi_i\rangle = \epsilon_i|\Psi_i\rangle, \tag{10.1}$$

where $V[\rho] = V_H[\rho] + V_{\text{xc}}[\rho] + V_{\text{ext}} + V_{\text{local}}$ is a real-space-based (local) potential. The KS potential $V[\rho]$ is a functional of the electronic density of the system:

$$\rho(\mathbf{r}) = \sum_{i=1}^{\mathcal{N}_{\text{orbitals}}} n_{\text{occ}}^{(i)} |\Psi_i(\mathbf{r})|^2, \tag{10.2}$$

where $n_{\text{occ}}^{(i)}$ is the occupation number of orbital i.

The KS potential V contains the Hartree potential V_H, solution of the Poisson's equation $\nabla^2 V_H = -4\pi\rho$, the exchange-correlation potential V_{xc}, and the external ionic potential V_{ext} acting on the electrons. In BigDFT code a pseudopotential term is added to the Hamiltonian matrix, that has a local and a nonlocal term, $V_{\text{local}} + V_{\text{nl}}$.

As usual, in a KS DFT calculation, the application of the Hamiltonian matrix is a part of a self-consistent cycle, needed for minimizing the total energy. In addition to the usual orthogonalization routine, in which scalar products $\langle\Psi_i|\Psi_j\rangle$ should be calculated, another operation that is performed on wavefunctions in BigDFT code is the preconditioning. This is calculated by solving the Helmholtz equation

$$\left(-\frac{1}{2}\nabla^2 - \epsilon_i\right)|\tilde{g}_i\rangle = |g_i\rangle, \tag{10.3}$$

where $|g_i\rangle$ is the gradient of the total energy with respect to the wavefunction $|\Psi_i\rangle$, of energy ϵ_i. The solution $|\tilde{g}_i\rangle$ is found by solving Eq. 10.3 by a preconditioned conjugate gradient method.

10.1.2 Daubechies Basis and Convolutions

The set of basis functions used to express the KS orbitals is of key importance for the nature of the computational operations that have to be performed. In the BigDFT code, the KS wavefunctions are expressed on Daubechies wavelets. The latter is a set of localized, real-space-based orthogonal functions that allow for a systematic, multiresolution description. These basis functions are centered on the grid points of a mesh that is placed around the atoms, see Figure 10.1.

We will see in the following section that, thanks to the properties of the basis functions, the action of the KS operators can be written as three-dimensional convolutions with short, separable filters. A more complete description of these operations can be found in the BigDFT reference paper [9].

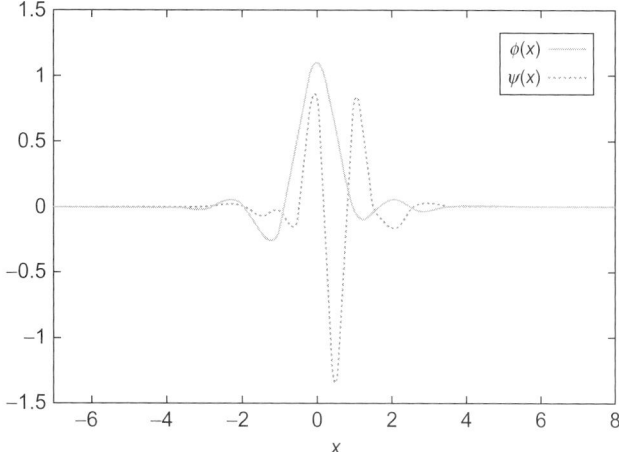

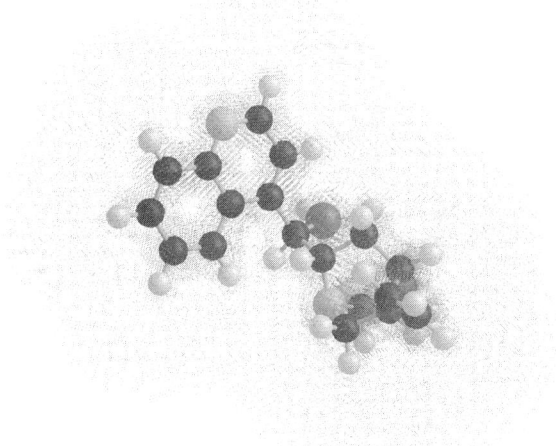

FIGURE 10.1

An example of a simulation domain for a small molecule analyzed with BigDFT code. Both the atoms and the adaptive mesh that is associated to the basis function are indicated. In the top panel the one-dimensional versions of the Daubechies functions that are associated to a given grid point are plotted.

10.2 CORE METHOD

To illustrate the action of the local Hamiltonian operator (laplacian plus local potential), we have to represent a given KS wavefunction Ψ in the so-called fine-scaling function representation, in which the wavefunctions are associated to three-dimensional arrays that express their components. These arrays contain the components $s_{i'_1,i'_2,i'_3}$ of Ψ in the basis of Daubechies scaling functions $\phi_{i'_1,i'_2,i'_3}$:

$$\Psi(\mathbf{r}) = \sum_{i'_1,i'_2,i'_3} s_{i'_1,i'_2,i'_3} \phi_{i'_1,i'_2,i'_3}(\mathbf{r}). \tag{10.4}$$

10.2.1 The Kinetic Operator

The matrix elements of the kinetic energy operator among the basis functions can be calculated analytically [9, 16]. For the pure fine-scaling function representation described in Eq. 10.4, the result of the application of the kinetic energy operator on this wavefunction has the expansion coefficients $\hat{s}_{i'_1,i'_2,i'_3}$, which are related to the original coefficients $s_{i'_1,i'_2,i'_3}$ by a convolution

$$\hat{s}_{i'_1,i'_2,i'_3} = \frac{1}{2} \sum_{j'_1,j'_2,j'_3} K_{i'_1-j'_1,i'_2-j'_2,i'_3-j'_3} s_{j'_1,j'_2,j'_3} \tag{10.5}$$

where

$$K_{i_1,i_2,i_3} = T_{i_1}\delta_{i_2}\delta_{i_3} + \delta_{i_1}T_{i_2}\delta_{i_3} + \delta_{i_1}\delta_{i_2}T_{i_3}, \tag{10.6}$$

and T_i are the filters of the one-dimensional second derivative in Daubechies scaling functions basis, which can be computed analytically.

10.2.2 Application of the Local Potential, Magic Filters

The application of the local potential in Daubechies basis consists of the basis decomposition of the function product $V(\mathbf{r})\Psi(\mathbf{r})$. As explained in [9, 17], the simple evaluation of this product in terms of the point values of the basis functions is not precise enough. A better result may be achieved by performing a transformation to the wavefunction coefficients — this process allows for calculation of the values of the wavefunctions on the fine grid, via a smoothed version of the basis functions. This is the so-called magic filter transformation, which can be expressed as follows:

$$\Psi(\mathbf{r}_{i'_1,i'_2,i'_3}) = \sum_{j'_1,j'_2,j'_3} \omega_{i'_1-j'_1} \omega_{i'_2-j'_2} \omega_{i'_3-j'_3} s_{j'_1,j'_2,j'_3}. \tag{10.7}$$

and allows the potential application to be expressed with better accuracy. After application of the local potential (pointwise product), a transposed magic filter transformation can be applied to obtain Daubechies expansion coefficients of $V|\Psi\rangle$.

10.2.3 The Operations in BigDFT Code

The previously described operations must be combined together for the application of the local Hamiltonian operator $\left(-\frac{1}{2}\nabla^2 + V(\mathbf{r})\right)$. The detailed description of how these operations are chained is beyond the scope of this chapter and can be found in the BigDFT reference paper [9]. Essentially, the three-dimensional convolutions that correspond to the different operators associated to the local part of the Hamiltonian should be chained one after another. Figure 10.2 sketches the chain of operations that is performed.

The density of the electronic system is derived from the square of the point values of the wavefunctions (see Eq. 10.2). As described in Section 10.1.2, a convenient way to express the point values of the wavefunctions is to apply the magic filter transformation to the Daubechies basis expansion coefficients.

The local potential V can be obtained from the local density ρ by solving the Poisson's equation and by calculating the exchange-correlation potential $V_{xc}[\rho]$. These operations are performed via a Poisson Solver based on interpolating scaling functions [19], a basis set tightly connected with Daubechies functions. The properties of this basis are optimal for electrostatic problems, and mixed boundary conditions can be treated explicity. A description of this Poisson solver can be found in papers [20, 21].

The schematic of all these operations is depicted in Figure 10.2.

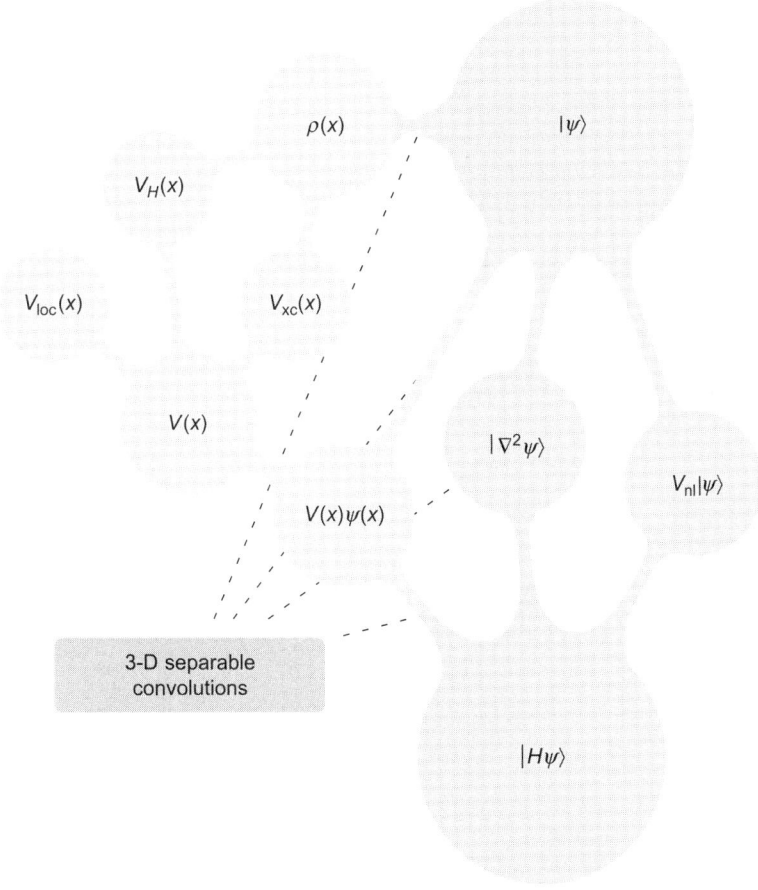

FIGURE 10.2

A schematic of the application of the Hamiltonian in the BigDFT formalism. The operator $H = -\frac{1}{2}\nabla^2 + V + V_{nl}$ is applied on the wavefunction $|\psi\rangle$. The local potential V is derived from charge density ρ, which is built from the wavefunctions. In the BigDFT basis, most of the operations that are needed can be expressed via the action of 3-D convolutions.

10.2.4 The Code Structure: Preliminary CPU Investigation

The application of the Hamiltonian in the BigDFT code is only one of the operations that are performed. During the self-consistent cycle, wavefunctions have to be updated and orthogonalized. Since all the basis functions are orthogonal with each other, the overlap matrices have to be calculated via suitable calls to BLAS routines and then processed with LAPACK subprograms.

An optimized iteration of a KS wavefunction is organized as follows:

1. Local Hamiltonian, construction and application
2. Non-local Hamiltonian
3. Overlap matrix
4. Preconditioning
5. Wavefunction update
6. Orthogonalization (Cholesky factorization)

Steps 1 and 2 have been described in Figure 10.2. The application of the non-local Hamiltonian is not treated here and can be found in Ref. [9]. The preconditioner (step 4) can also be expressed via a kinetic convolution, as described earlier in this chapter. Steps 3, 5, and 6 are performed via BLAS/LAPACK calls. In the current hybrid implementation, we can execute on the GPU the steps 1 and 4 and also all BLAS routines performed in steps 3 (DGEMM), 5, and 6 (DSYRK, DTRMM). However, all other operations, such as LAPACK routines (step 6) or the multiplication with the nonlocal pseudopotentials (step 2), are still executed on the CPU and can be ported on the GPU. We left these implementations to future versions of the hybrid code.

We have evaluated the amount of time spent for a given operation on a typical run. To do this we have profiled the different sections of the BigDFT code for a parallel calculation. In Figure 10.8 we show the percent of time that is dedicated to any of the previously described operations, for runs with different architectures. It should be stressed that for the regimes we have tested, there is no hot-spot operation. This makes GPU accelerations more complicated because they will depend on different factors.

10.3 ALGORITHMS, IMPLEMENTATIONS, AND EVALUATIONS

We have seen that the operations that have to be explicitly ported on GPUs is a set of separable three-dimensional convolutions. In the following section, we will show the design and implementation of these operations on NVIDIA GPUs. We start by considering the magic filter application.

10.3.1 From a Separable 3D Convolution to 1D Convolutions

A three-dimensional array s (input array) of dimension n_1, n_2, n_3 (the dimension of the simulation domain of BigDFT) is transformed into the output array Ψ_r given by

$$\Psi_r(I_1, I_2, I_3) = \sum_{j_1, j_2, j_3=-L}^{U} \omega_{j_1} \omega_{j_2} \omega_{j_3} s(I_1 - j_1, I_2 - j_2, I_3 - j_3). \tag{10.8}$$

With a lowercase index i_p we indicate the elements of the input array, while with a capital index I_p we indicate the indices after application of the magic filters ω_i, which have extension from $-L$ to U. The filter dimension $U + L + 1$ equals to the order of the Daubechies family m, which is 16 in our case. In BigDFT, different boundary conditions (BC) can be applied at the border of the simulation region, which affects the values of the array s in (10.8) when the indices are outside bounds.

The most convenient way to calculate a three-dimensional convolution of this kind is by combining one-dimensional convolutions and array transpositions, as explained in [22]. In fact, the calculation Eq. 10.8 can be cut in three steps:

1. $F_3(I_3, i_1, i_2) = \sum_j \omega_j s(i_1, i_2, I_3 - j) \qquad \forall i_1, i_2;$
2. $F_2(I_2, I_3, i_1) = \sum_j \omega_j F_3(I_3, i_1, I_2 - j) \qquad \forall I_3, i_1;$
3. $\Psi_r(I_1, I_2, I_3) = \sum_j \omega_j F_2(I_2, I_3, I_1 - j) \qquad \forall I_2, I_3.$

The final result is thus obtained by a successive application of the same operation:

$$F(I, a) = \sum_{j=-L}^{U} \omega_j G(a, I - j) \qquad \forall a = 1, \ldots, N, \; I = 1, \ldots, n. \tag{10.9}$$

The lowest level routine that will be ported on GPU is then a set of N separate one-dimensional (periodic) convolutions of arrays of size n, which have to be combined with a transposition. The number N equals $n_1 n_2$, $n_1 n_3$ and $n_2 n_3$, respectively, for each step of the three-dimensional construction, while n_i, $i = 1, 2, 3$, equals the dimension that is going to be transformed. The output of the first step is then taken as the input of the second, and so on.

10.3.2 Kinetic Convolution and Preconditioner

A little, but substantial, difference should be stressed for the kinetic operator application, defined in Eqs. 10.5 and 10.6. In this case the three-dimensional filter is the sum of three different filters. This implies that the kinetic filter operation must be cut differently from the other separable convolutions:

1. $K_3(I_3, i_1, i_2) = \sum_j T_j s(i_1, i_2, I_3 - j) \qquad \forall i_1, i_2$
2. $K_2(I_2, I_3, i_1) = \sum_j T_j s(i_1, I_2 - j, I_3) + K_3(I_3, i_1, I_2) \qquad \forall I_3, i_1$
3. $\hat{s}(I_1, I_2, I_3) = \sum_j T_j s(I_1 - j, I_2, I_3) + K_2(I_2, I_3, I_1) \qquad \forall I_2, I_3$

Also in this case, the three-dimensional kinetic operator can be seen as a result of a successive application of the same operation:

$$K_p(I, a) = \sum_j T_j G_{p-1}(a, I - j) + K_{p-1}(a, I) \quad \text{and} \quad G_p(I, a) = G_{p-1}(a, I) \qquad \forall a, I, \tag{10.10}$$

In other terms, the one-dimensional kernel of the kinetic energy has two input arrays, G_{p-1} and K_{p-1}, and returns two output arrays K_p and the G_p, which is the transposition of G_{p-1}. At the first step ($p = 1$) we put $G_0 = s$ and $K_0 = 0$. Eventually, for $p = 3$, we have $K_3 = \hat{s}$ and $G_3 = s$. One can put instead $K_0 \neq 0$, and in that way, will be $K_3 = \hat{s} + K_0$. This algorithm can be also used for the Helmholtz operator of the preconditioner, by putting $K_0 = -\epsilon_i s$.

10.3.3 Implementation Details

From the GPU parallelism point of view, there is a set of N independent convolutions to be computed. Each of the lines of n elements to be transformed is split in chunks of size N_e. Each multiprocessor of the graphic card computes a group of N_ℓ different chunks and parallellizes the calculation on its computing units. Figure 10.3 shows the data distribution on the grid of blocks during the transposition.

We transfer data from the global to the shared memory of multiprocessors. The shared memory must contain buffers to store the data needed for the convolution computations. In order to perform the convolution for N_e elements, $N_e + N_{\text{buf}}$ elements must be sent to the shared memory for the calculation, where N_{buf} depends of the size of the convolution filter. The shared memory must thus contain buffers to store the data needed for the convolution computations. The desired boundary condition (for example, periodic wrapping) is implemented in the shared memory during the data transfer. Each thread computes the convolution for a subset of N_e elements associated to the block. To avoid bank conflicts, the half-warp size must be a multiple of N_ℓ. Each half-warp thus computes at least $16/N_\ell$ values, and N_e is a multiple of that number, chosen in such a way that the total number of elements $N_\ell(N_e + N_{\text{buf}})$ fits in the shared memory. This data distribution is illustrated in Figure 10.4.

10.3.4 Performance Evaluation of GPU Convolution Routines

To evaluate the performance of 1-D convolution routines described in Eqs. 10.9 and 10.10, together with the analogous operation for the wavelet transformation, we are going to compare the execution times on a CPU and a GPU. We define the GPU speedup with the ratio between CPU and GPU execution times. For these evaluations, we used a computer with an Intel Xeon Processor X5472 (3 GHz) and a NVIDIA Tesla S1070 card. The CPU version of BigDFT is deeply optimized with optimal loop unrolling and compiler options. The GPU code is compiled with the Intel Fortran Compiler (10.1.011) and the most aggressive compiler options (`-O2 -xT`). With these options the magic filter convolutions run at about 3.4 GFlops. All benchmarks are performed with double precision floating-point numbers.

The GPU versions of the one-dimensional convolutions are about one order of magnitude faster than their CPU counterparts. We can then achieve an effective performance rate of the GPU convolutions of about 40 GFlops, by also considering the data transfers in the card. We are not close to peak performance because, on GPU, a considerable fraction of time is still spent in data transfers rather than in calculations. This appears since data should be transposed between input and output array, and the arithmetic needed to perform convolutions is not heavy enough to hide the latency of all the memory transfers. However, we will later show that these results are really satisfying for our purposes.

The performance graphs for the three aforementioned convolutions, together with the compression-decompression operator, are indicated in Figure 10.5 as a function of the size of the corresponding three-dimensional array.

10.3.5 Three-Dimensional Operators, BLAS Routines

As described in the previous sections, to build a three-dimensional operation one must chain three times the corresponding one-dimensional GPU kernels. We obtain in this way the three-dimensional wavelet transformations as well as the kinetic operator and the magic filter transformation (direct and transposed). The multiplication with the potential and the calculation of the square of the wavefunction are performed via the application of some special GPU kernels, based on the same guidelines of the others. The GPU speedup of the local density construction, as well as the local Hamiltonian application and the

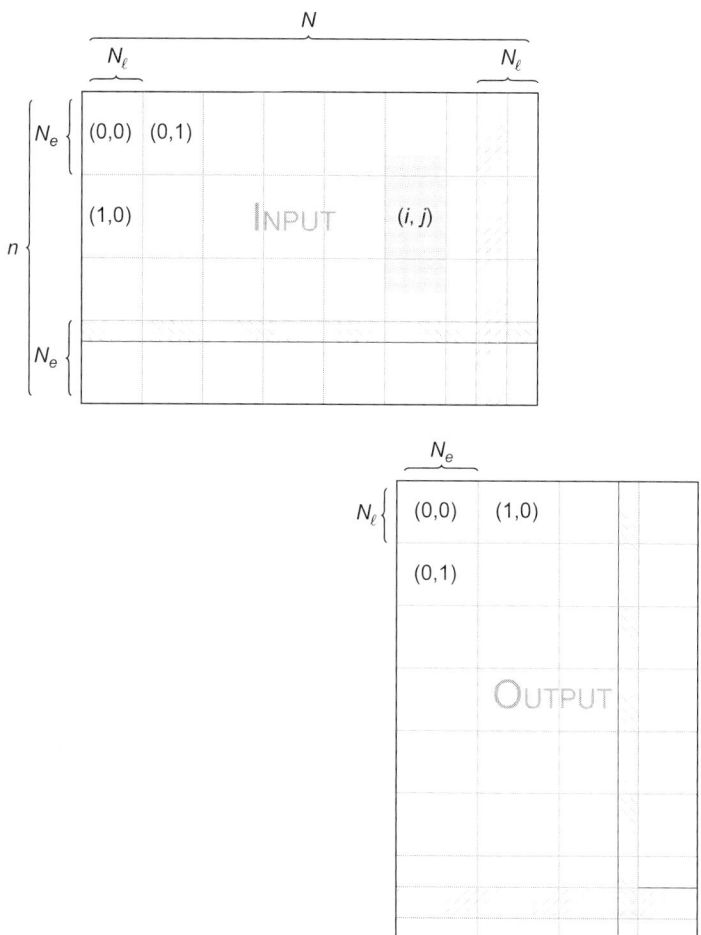

FIGURE 10.3

Data distribution for 1-D convolution+transposition on the GPU. Input data (left panel) are ordered along the N-axis, while output (right panel) is ordered in n-axis direction; see Eq. 10.9. When one is executing a GPU convolution kernel, each block (i,j) of the execution grid is associated to a set of N_ℓ (N-axis) times N_e (n-axis) elements. The size of the data fed to each block is identical (such as to avoid block-dependent treatment); hence, when N and n are not multiples of N_ℓ and N_e, some data treated by different blocks may overlap. This is indicated with the filled patterns in the figure. Behind the (i,j) label, in light gray, it is indicated the portion of data that should be copied to the shared memory for treating the data in the block. See Figure 10.4 for a detail of that part.

preconditioning operation, is represented in Figure 10.6 as a function of the compressed wavefunction size.

Also the linear algebra operation can be executed on the card thanks to the CUBLAS routines. In Figure 10.7 we present the speedups we obtain for double-precision calls to CUBLAS routines for a

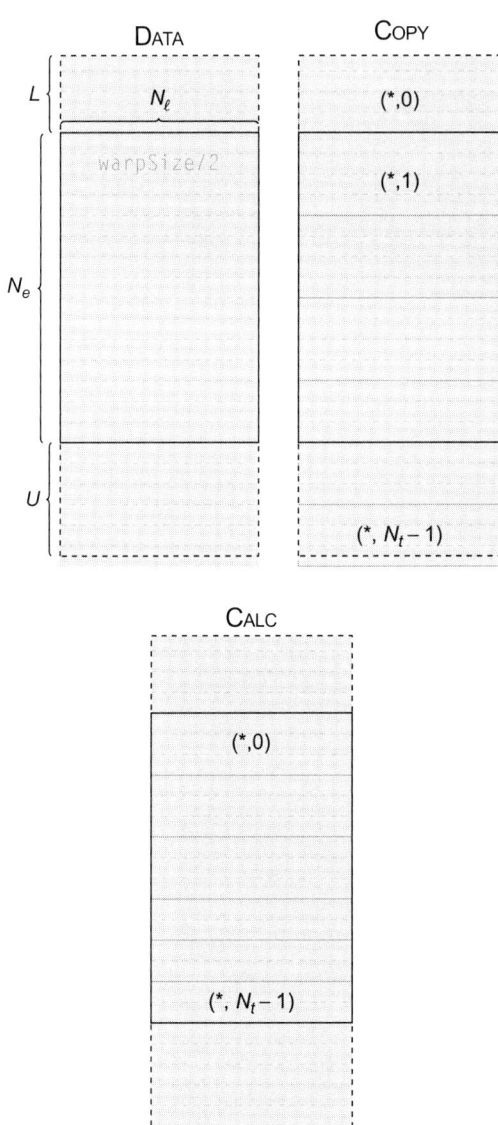

FIGURE 10.4

Data arrangement in shared memory for a given block. The number of lines N_ℓ is chosen to be a divisor of the half-warp size. Data are then treated in units of `warpSize/2`. The thread index has (`warpSize/2`, N_t) elements, with $N_t \leq 16$ (left panel). Each group of threads $(*, i)$ of the half-warp i treats a definite number of elements, either for copying the data (center panel) or for performing the calculation (right panel). This data arrangement ensures the avoiding of bank conflicts in the shared memory access. For calcuating the convolution, two buffers of sizes $N_\ell L$ and $N_\ell U$ must be created in shared memory. This figure reproduces the portion of the input data higlighted in gray in Figure 10.3.

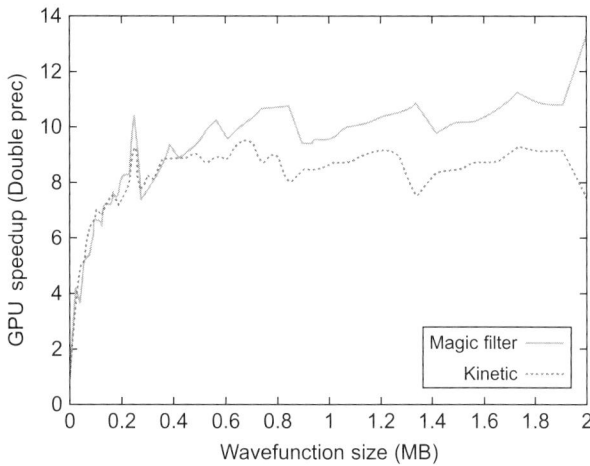

FIGURE 10.5

Double-precision speedup for the GPU version of the fundamental operations on the wavefunctions as a function of the single wavefunction size.

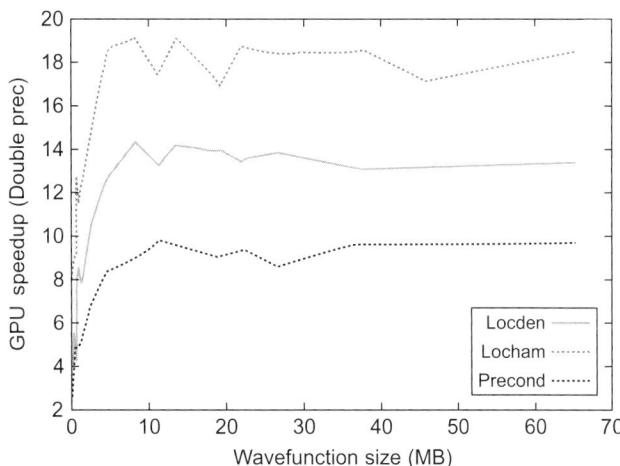

FIGURE 10.6

Double-precision speedup for the GPU version of the three-dimensional operators used in the BigDFT code as a function of the single wavefunction size.

typical wavefunction size of a BigDFT run as a function of the number of orbitals. These results take into account the amount of time needed to transfer the data of the card.

From these tests, we can see that both the GPU-ported sections are an order of magnitude (or more) faster than the corresponding CPU counterpart. We will now consider this behavior in the framework of the complete BigDFT code.

10.4 **FINAL EVALUATION AND VALIDATION OF RESULTS, TOTAL BENEFITS, AND LIMITATIONS**

For a code with the complexity of BigDFT, the evaluation of the benefits of using a GPU-accelerated code must be performed at three different levels. First, one has to evaluate the effective speedup provided by the GPU kernels with respect to the corresponding CPU routines that perform the same operations. This is the bare speedup, which, of course, for a given implementation, depends on the computational power that the device can provide us. For the BigDFT code, these results are obtained by analyzing the performances of the GPU kernels that perform the convolutions and the linear algebra (BLAS) operations, as provided by the CUBLAS library. As discussed earlier in this chapter such results can be found in Figures 10.6 and 10.7. At the second level, the complete speedup has to be evaluated; the performances of the whole hybrid CPU/GPU code should be analyzed with respect to the pure CPU executions. Clearly, this result depends on the actual importance of the ported routines in the context of the whole code (i.e., following the Amdahl's law). This is the first reliable result of the actual performance enhancements of the GPU porting of the code. For a hybrid code that originates from a monocore CPU program, this is the last level of evaluation. For a parallel code, there is still another step that has to be evaluated. This is the behavior of the hybrid code in a parallel (or massively parallel) environment. Indeed, for parallel runs, the picture is complicated by two things. The first one is the management of the extra level of communication that is introduced by the PCI-express bus, which may interact negatively with the underlying code communication scheduling (MPI or OpenMP par example). The second is the behavior of the code for a number of GPU devices — this number can be lower than the number of CPU processes that are running. In this case the GPU resource is not homogeneously

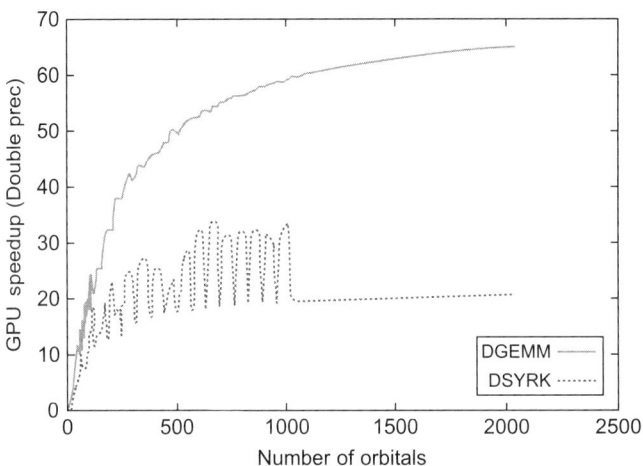

FIGURE 10.7

Double-precision speedup for the CUBLAS operations used in the code for a typical wavefunction size (300 KB) as a function of the number of orbitals.

distributed and the management of this fact adds an extra level of complexity. The evaluation of the code at this stage contributes at the user-level speedup, which is the real time-to-solution speedup.

10.4.1 Parallelization for Homogeneous Computing Clusters (CPU Code)

In its CPU version, two data distribution schemes are used for parallelizing the code. In the orbital distribution scheme (used for Hamiltonian application, preconditioning), each processor works on one or a few orbitals for which it holds all its scaling function and wavelet coefficients. Operations like linear algebra are performed in the coefficient distribution scheme, where each processor holds a certain subset of the coefficients of all the orbitals. The switch between the two different schemes is done via suitable calls to the MPI global transposition routine MPI_ALLTOALLV. This communication scheme, based more on bandwith than latency, guarantees optimal efficiency on parallel and massively parallel architectures.

10.4.2 Performance Evaluation of Hybrid Code

As a test system, we used the ZnO crystal, which has a wurtzite bulk-like structure. Such a system has a relatively high density of valence electrons so that the number of orbitals is rather large even for a moderate number of atoms.

We performed two kinds of tests. For the first one we used the hybrid part of the CINES IBLIS machine, which has 12 nodes, connected with an Infiniband 4X DDR connectX network, each node (2 Xeon X5472 quadri-core) connected with two GPUs on a Tesla S1070 card. To check the behavior of the code for systems of increasing size, we performed a set of calculations for different supercells with an increasing number of processors such that the number of orbitals per MPI processes is kept constant. We performed a comparison for the same runs in which all the CPU cores have a GPU associated. The hybrid code is around 5.5 times faster than its pure CPU couterpart, regardless of the system size.

For the second test we used the hybrid section of the CCRT Titane machine, similar to IBLIS, but with Intel X5570 (Nehalem) CPUs. In this test we kept fixed the size of the system and increased the number of MPI processes in order to decrease the number of orbitals per core. We then controlled the speedup of each run with the hybrid code. The parallel efficiency of the code is not particularly affected by the presence of the GPU. For this machine, owing to the better CPU technology, the time-to-solution speedup is around 3.

Results of the two tests are shown in Figure 10.8. Because there is no hot-spot operation, the actual time-to-solution speedup of the complete code is influenced by the features of the code. In other words, a performance evaluation based on the Amdahl's law is of great importance for evaluating the final benefit that a partially accelerated code may have.

These results are interesting and seem very promising for a number of reasons. First of all, as already discussed, not all the routines of the code were ported on the GPU. We focus our efforts to the operators that can be written via a convolution. Also, the application of the nonlocal part of the Hamiltonian (the potential Vnl presented in Section 10.1.1) can be performed on the GPU, and we are planning to do this in further developments. Moreover, the actual implementation of the GPU convolutions can be further optimized.

The linear algebra operations also can be further optimized. For the moment, only the calls to the BLAS routines were accelerated on the GPU, via suitable calls to the corresponding CUBLAS routines.

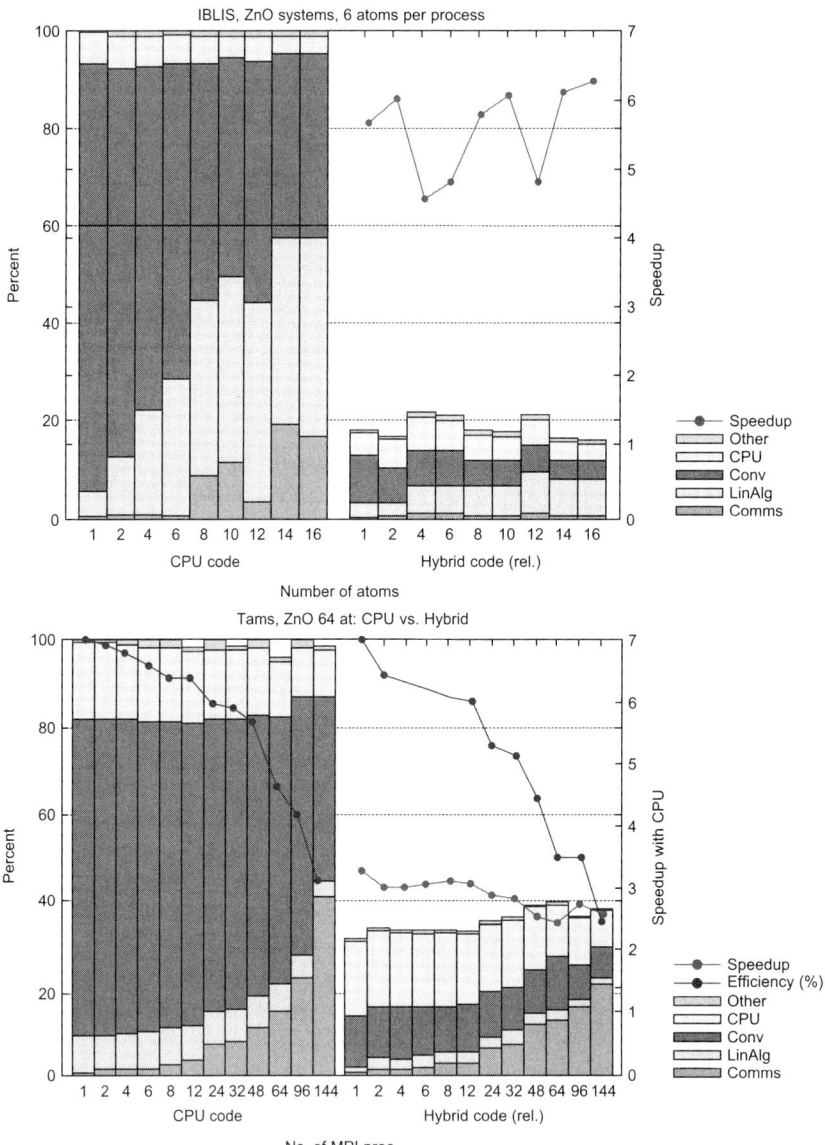

FIGURE 10.8

Relative speedup of the hybrid DFT code with respect to the equivalent pure CPU run. In the top panel, different runs for systems of increasing size have been done on an Intel X5472 3 GHz (Harpertown) machine. In the bottom panel, a given system has been tested with an increasing number of processors on an Intel X5570 2.93 GHz (Nehalem) machine. The scaling efficiency of the calculation is also indicated. In the right side of each panel, the same calculation has been done by accelerating the code via one Tesla S1070 card per CPU core used for both architectures. The speedup is around a value of 6 for a Harpertown and around 3.5 for a Nehalem-based calculation.

Also the LAPACK routines, which are needed to perform the orthogonalization process, can be ported on a GPU, with a considerable gain. Indeed, the linear algebra operations represent the most expensive part of the code for very large systems [9]. An optimization of this section is then crucial for future improvements of the hybrid code.

10.4.3 Parallel Distribution

A typical example of a hybrid architecture may be composed of two quad-core processors and two NVIDIA GPUs. So, in this case, the two GPUs have to be shared among the eight CPU cores. The problem of data distribution and load balancing is a major issue to achieve optimal performance. The operators implemented on the GPU are parallelized within the orbital distribution scheme (see Section 10.4.1). This means that each core may host a subset of the orbitals and apply the operators of Section 10.3.5 only to these wavefunctions.

A possible solution to the GPU sharing is to dedicate statically one GPU to one CPU core. So, in the common configuration, two CPU cores are more powerful because they have access to the GPU. The six other CPU cores do not interact with the GPU. Because the number of orbitals that may be assigned to each core can be adjusted, a possible way to handle the fact that the CPU cores and GPU are in different number would be to assign more orbitals to the cores that have a GPU associated. This kind of approach can be realized owing to the flexibility of the data distribution scheme of BigDFT. However, it may be difficult for the end user to define an optimal repartition of the orbitals between the different cores for a generic system.

For this reason, we have designed an alternative approach where the GPUs are completely shared by all CPU cores. The major consequence is that the set of orbitals is equally distributed to CPU cores. Essentially, each of the CPU cores of a given node is allowed to use one of the GPU cards that are associated to the node so that each card dialogues with a group of CPU cores. Each GPU is associated to two semaphores, which control the memory transfers and the calculations. In this way, the memory transfers of the data between the different cores and the card can be executed asynchronously and overlapped with the calculations. This is optimal because each orbital is processed independently. The schematics of this approach are depicted in Figure 10.9.

For a system of 128 ZnO atoms, we performed different runs for different repartitions of the card per core in order to check the speedup by varying the ratio GPU/CPU on a hybrid run. We then compared this solution with the inhomogeneous data repartition scheme, in which the GPUs are associated statically to two out of eight cores.

Results are plotted in Table 10.1. The shared GPU solution provides better performances and speedups than the best possible inhomogeneous data repartition, which is system dependent and much more difficult to tune for the end user. These results are particularly encouraging because at the moment only the convolutions operators are desyncronized by the semaphores (see Section 10.4.3), and the BLAS routines are executed at the same time on the card. Future improvements in this direction may allow us to better optimize the load on the cards in order to further increase the efficiency.

10.5 CONCLUSIONS AND FUTURE DIRECTIONS

The port of the principal sections of an electronic structure code over graphic processing units (GPUs) has been shown. Such GPU sections have been inserted in the complete code in order to have a

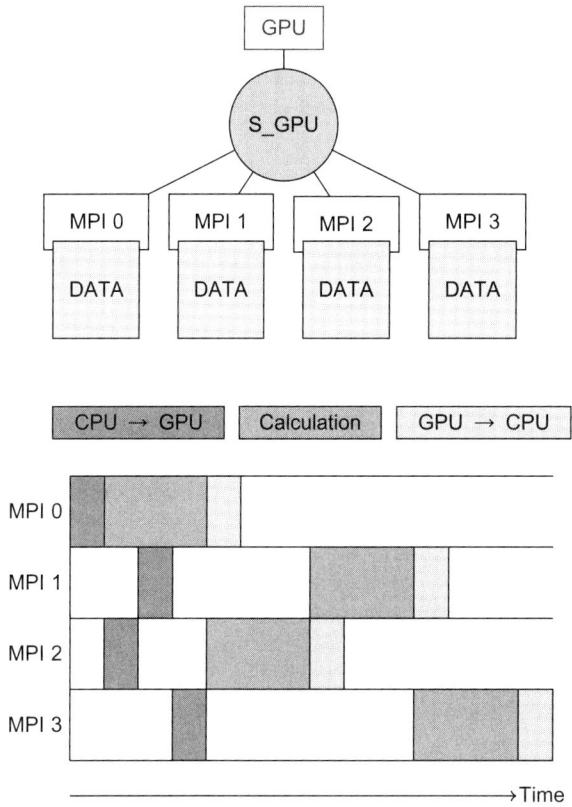

FIGURE 10.9

Schematic of the management of the association of the same GPU to multiple cores. The time spent on calculation is such that the time needed for data transfer can be hidden by the calculations.

Table 10.1 Speedup of the full DFT code as a function of the number of CPU cores (i.e., MPI processes) for inhomogeneous repartitions of the number of GPU cards per core. The shared GPU solution always provides better or similar speedups.

CPU-GPU	8-1	8-2	4-2	2-2
S_GPU	1.96	3.69	3.73	5.09
Inhomogeneous (best)	2.08	2.64	2.32	2.40

production DFT code that is able to run in a multi-GPU environment. The DFT code we used, named BigDFT, is based on Daubechies wavelets, and has high systematic convergence properties, very good performances, and excellent efficiency on parallel computation. The GPU implementation of the code we propose fully respects these properties. We used double-precision calculations, and we might have achieved considerable speedup for the converted routines (up to a factor of 20 for some operations). Our developments are fully compatible with the existing parallellization of the code, and the communication between CPU and GPU does not affect the efficiency of the existing implementation. The data transfers between the CPU and the GPU can be optimized in such a way to allow that more than one CPU core is associated to the same card. This is optimal for modern hybrid supercomputer architectures in which the number of GPU cards is generally smaller than the number of CPU cores. We test our implementation by running systems of variable numbers of atoms on a 12-node hybrid machine, with two GPU cards per node. These developements produce an overall speedup on the whole code of a factor of around six, also for a fully parallel run. It should be stressed that, for these runs, our code has no hot-spot operations, and that all the sections that are ported on the GPU contribute to the overall speedup.

At present, developments in several directions are under way to further increase the efficiency of the usage of the GPU in the context of BigDFT. Different developments are active at present, including the following ones:

- With the advent of the Nehalem processor, we have seen that the CPU power is increased to an extent as to renormalize the cost of the CPU operations that have been GPU ported. The evaluation of the hybrid code with the new generation of Fermi card is thus of great importance to understand the better implementation strategies for the next generation of architectures. Also the combination of GPU acceleration with OMP parallelization (which exists in pure CPU BigDFT code) should be exploited.
- The OpenCL specifications is a great opportunity to build an accelerated code that can be potentially multiplatform. To this aim, an OpenCL version of BigDFT is under finalization, and it has already been tested with new NVIDIA drivers. The development of this version will allow us to implement new functionalities (e.g., different boundary conditions) that have not been implemented in the CUDA version because of lack of time. On the other hand, other implementations of the convolutions routines can be tested, which may fit better with the specifications of the new architectures. In Figure 10.10 we show some preliminary results in these directions. We have profiled the whole code for different parallelization strategies (OpenMP, MPI), with the addition of GPU acceleration, with CUDA or OpenCL written routines. Two platforms have been used, a Nehalem processor plus an S1070 card, and a Harpertown processor plus a Fermi C2050 card. In both cases, better performances are achieved while combining MPI parallelization with GPU acceleration. In particular, in the Fermi card, we are starting to experience benefits from the concurrent kernel execution. Different strategies are under analysis to show how to efficiently profit from this feature.
- For the same reasons, the strategy of the repartition of the GPU resource also should be reworked. In particular, the possiblity of the concurrent kernel execution should be allowed whenever possible, and the strategies of GPU repartition should be adapted accordingly.

The hybrid BigDFT code, like its pure CPU counterpart, is available under the GNU-GPL license and can be downloaded from the site shown in reference [9].

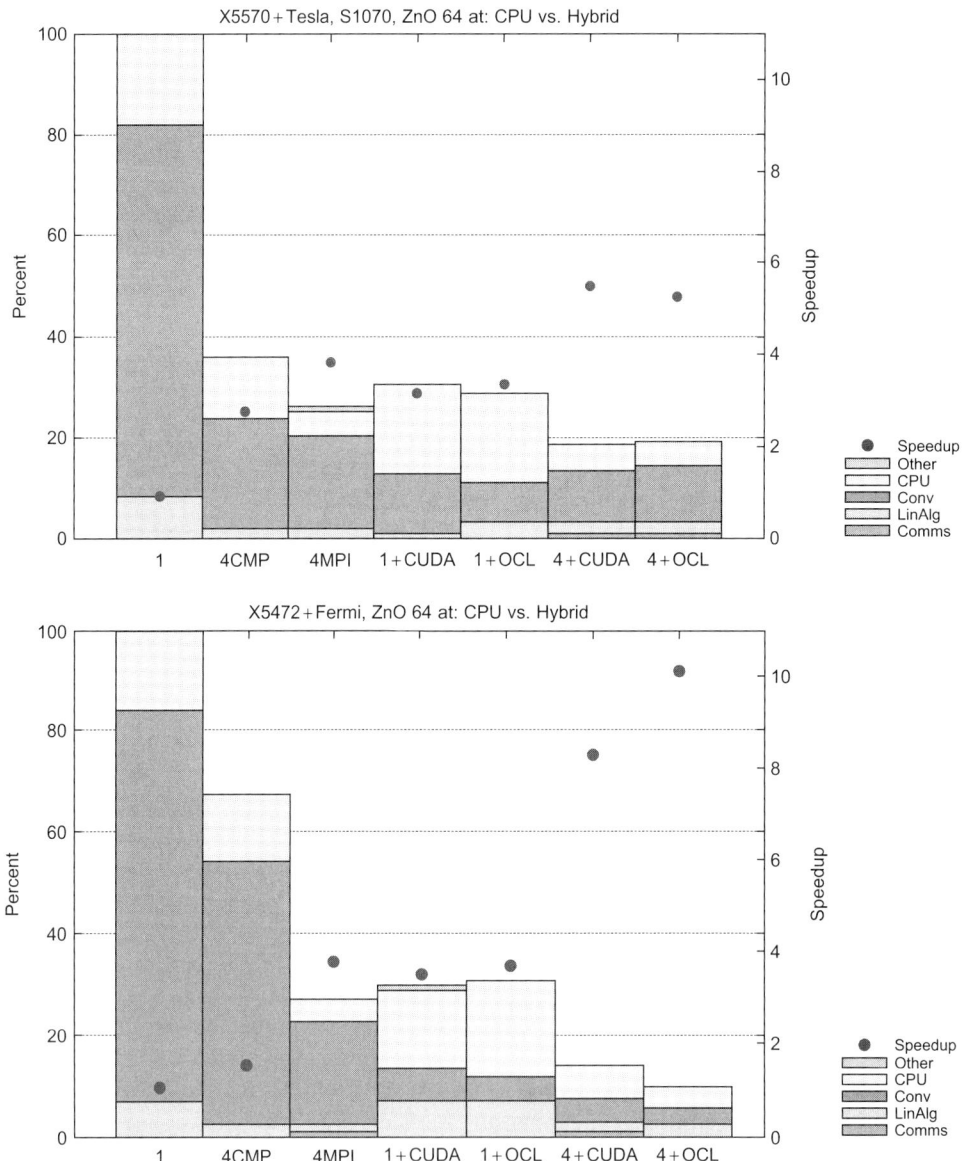

FIGURE 10.10

Top panel: performances of a run of the BigDFT code for a 64-atom ZnO system on a platform with one Nehalem quad-core and a Tesla S1070 card. The maximum speedup is obtained with combined usage of MPI and CUDA routines, distributed via an S_GPU approach. Bottom panel: the same runs on a platform of one Harpertown and a Fermi C2050. In that case, the concurrent kernel execution, exploited on the OpenCL version of the code, is providing us a benefit, and the speedup grows up to a factor of 10. The study of the exploitation of these strategies for a massively parallel architecture is under way.

References

[1]   W. Kohn, L.J. Sham, Phys. Rev. 140 (1965) A1133.

[2]   NVIDIA CUDA Programming Guide, version 3.1, Available from: `http://www.nvidia.com/object/cuda_home.html`.

[3]   J. Yang, et al., J. Comput. Phys. 221 (2007) 779.

[4]   A. Anderson, et al., Comput. Phys. Commun. 177 (2007) 298.

[5]   K. Yasuda, J. Chem. Theory Comput. 4 (2008) 1230.

[6]   K. Yasuda, J. Comput. Chem. 29 (2008) 334–342.

[7]   `http://www.nvidia.com/object/computational_chemistry.html`

[8]   D. Göddeke, et al, Parall. Comput. 33 (2007) 10685.

[9]   L. Genovese, et al., J. Chem. Phys 129 (2008) 014109. L. Genovese, et al., J. Chem. Phys. 131 (2009) 034103. Available from: `http://inac.cea.fr/sp2m/L_Sim/BigDFT`.

[10] I. Daubechies, Ten Lectures on Wavelets, SIAM, Philadelphia, PA, 1992.

[11] X. Gonze, J.-M. Beuken, R. Caracas, F. Detraux, M. Fuchs, G.-M. Rignanese, et al., Comput. Mater. Sci. 25 (2002) 478–492. Available from: `http://www.abinit.org`.

[12] S. Goedecker, M. Teter, J. Hutter, Phys. Rev. B 54 (1996) 1703.

[13] C. Hartwigsen, S. Goedecker, J. Hutter, Phys. Rev. B 58 (1998) 3641.

[14] M. Krack, Theor. Chem. Acc. 114 (2005) 145.

[15] S. Goedecker, Wavelets and their Application for the Solution of Partial Differential Equations (ISBN 2-88074-398-2), Presses Polytechniques Universitaires Romandes, Lausanne, Switzerland, 1998.

[16] G. Beylkin, SIAM J. Numer. Anal. 6 (1992) 1716.

[17] A.I. Neelov, S. Goedecker, J. Comput. Phys. 217 (2006) 312–339.

[18] J.R. Shewchuk, An Introduction to the Conjugate Gradient Method Without the Agonizing Pain, Unpublished Draft, Carnegie Mellon University, Pittsburgh, PA, Technical Report CS-94-125, (1994). Available from: `http://www.cs.cmu.edu/ quake-papers/painless-conjugate-gradient.pdf`.

[19] G. Deslauriers, S. Dubuc, Constr. Approx. 5 (1989) 49.

[20] L. Genovese, T. Deutsch, A. Neelov, S. Goedecker, G. Beylkin, Efficient solution of Poisson's equation with free boundary conditions, J. Chem. Phys. 125 (2006) 074105.

[21] L. Genovese, T. Deutsch, S. Goedecker, Efficient and accurate three-dimensional Poisson solver for surface problems, J. Chem. Phys. 127 (2007) 054704.

[22] S. Goedecker, Rotating a three-dimensional array in optimal positions for vector processing: case study for a three-dimensional fast Fourier transform, Comput. Phys. Commun. 76 (1993) 294.

[23] S. Goedecker, A. Hoisie, Performance Optimization of Numerically Intensive Codes (ISBN 0-89871-484-2), SIAM, Philadelphia, PA, 2001.

Life Sciences
Area Editor's Introduction
Bertil Schmidt

11 Accurate Scanning of Sequence Databases with the Smith-Waterman Algorithm 155

12 Massive Parallel Computing to Accelerate Genome-Matching 173

13 GPU-Supercomputer Acceleration of Pattern Matching 185

14 GPU Accelerated RNA Folding Algorithm 199

15 Temporal Data Mining for Neuroscience 211

STATE OF GPU COMPUTING IN LIFE SCIENCES

Life sciences have emerged as a primary application area for the use of GPU computing. This is mainly caused by the large amount of publicly available sequence, expression, and structure data. The amount of available data will grow even further in the near future owing to advances in high-throughput technologies leading to a data explosion. Because GPU performance grows faster than CPU performance, the use of GPUs in the life sciences is therefore a perfect match.

A particular area of interest in this context is next-generation sequencing (NGS) technology, which can now produce billions of sequences (reads) on a daily basis. The usage of GPUs can thus play a key role in NGS, and its future applications (such as personal genomics) by providing the necessary computing power to process and analyze this data.

IN THIS SECTION

Chapter 11 by Ligowski, Rudnicki, Liu, and Schmidt describes how the popular Smith-Waterman algorithm for protein sequence database scanning can be optimized on GPUs. Starting from a basic CUDA implementation, several optimization techniques using shared memory, registers, loop unrolling, and CPU/GPU partitioning are presented. The combination of these techniques leads to a fivefold performance improvement on the same hardware.

How CUDA can be used to accelerate the folding of an RNA sequence is shown by Rizk, Lavenier, and Rajopadhye in Chapter 14. The authors achieve a highly efficient CUDA implementation by introducing a reordering of the given sequential algorithm that allows tiled computations and data reuse on the GPU.

In Chapter 12, Weiss and Bailey explore the process of optimizing mapping of short read data produced by NGS technologies to a reference genome. By using a number of techniques, such as new data layouts, an improvement of two orders of magnitude over the initial CUDA implementation is achieved.

Khajeh-Saeed and Perot describe the computation of a single very large pattern matching search on a large GPU cluster in Chapter 13. The authors reformulate the Smith-Waterman algorithm in a way that allows the use of parallel scan operations across multiple GPUs, resulting in an efficient implementation even for slow GPU interconnection links.

Finally, in Chapter 15 Feng, Cao, Patnaik, and Ramakrishnan present a solution for mining spike train datasets produced by multielectrode arrays on GPUs. Two strategies for efficiently mapping the problem onto CUDA are described: one thread per occurrence and two-pass elimination.

Accurate Scanning of Sequence Databases with the Smith-Waterman Algorithm

11

Łukasz Ligowski, Witold R. Rudnicki, Yongchao Liu, Bertil Schmidt

Because of the advances in high-throughput sequencing technologies, publicly available protein sequence databases continue to grow rapidly. Biologists frequently need to scan these databases to find similar sequences in order to annotate a query sequence of unknown functionality. In this chapter we present how the dynamic programming-based Smith-Waterman (SW) algorithm for protein sequence database scanning can be optimized on GPUs. Starting from a basic CUDA implementation, we discuss several optimization techniques using shared memory, registers, loop unrolling, and CPU/GPU partitioning. The combination of these techniques leads to a fivefold performance improvement on the same hardware. Smith-Waterman is one of the most popular algorithms in bioinformatics, and therefore, the optimization techniques presented in this chapter are beneficial and instructive to researchers in this area.

11.1 INTRODUCTION, PROBLEM STATEMENT, AND CONTEXT

Let us assume that a biologist has just obtained the sequence of a protein that is important for the biological problem under scrutiny. The first question to be asked is whether the function of the protein is already known. This can be answered by aligning this new sequence (query) to the database of all protein sequences with known functionalities to detect similar sequences. Pairwise sequence similarity may be defined by edit distance; that is, the number of edit operations (substitutions, deletions, insertions) required for transforming one sequence into the other [1]. Another definition of similarity is based on a so-called substitution matrix and gap penalties. A substitution matrix is a symmetric, pairwise measure of similarity between amino acids (the basic building blocks of proteins) [2]. Similar amino acid pairs correspond to positive entries and dissimilar ones to negative entries. The best possible alignment of two sequences is the one with the highest similarity score obtained for any pair of substrings from the two input sequences. The algorithm for finding such a pair of substrings was proposed by Smith and Waterman [3]. The Smith-Waterman algorithm is based on dynamic programming (DP). Unfortunately, the algorithm has a quadratic time complexity in terms of the lengths of the two input sequences and is therefore rather slow. Consequently, there has been significant effort to improve the speed of SW for scanning large databases using various techniques, including vectorization on standard multicores [4–6], Field Programmable Gate Arrays (FPGAs) [7–10], Cell/BE [11–14], and GPUs [15–19]. The goal of this chapter is to show various approaches for implementing the SW algorithm on GPUs using

CUDA and explain various optimization techniques that lead to a fivefold performance improvement of the basic CUDA implementation on the same hardware.

11.2 CORE METHOD

The SW algorithm computes the optimal local pairwise alignment of two given sequences Q (query) and T (target) of length $l1$ and $l2$ using DP with the following recurrence relations:

$$E[i,j] = \max\{H[i,j-1] - \alpha, E[i,j-1] - \beta\}$$

$$F[i,j] = \max\{H[i-1,j] - \alpha, F[i-1,j] - \beta\}$$

$$H[i,j] = \max\{0, E[i,j], F[i,j], H[i-1,j-1] + sbt(Q[i-1], T[j-1])\}$$

where $sbt()$ is a substitution matrix, α is the gap opening penalty, and β is the gap extension penalty. The above recurrences are computed for $1 \leq i \leq l1$ and $1 \leq j \leq l2$ and are initialized as $H[0][,j] = H[i][0] = E[0][j] = E[i][0] = F[0][j] = F[i][0] = 0$ for $0 \leq i \leq l1, 0 \leq j \leq l2$. Typical values for the gap penalties would be $\alpha = 10$ and $\beta = 2$. An example of a simple substitution matrix is $sbt(x,y) = +5$ if $x = y$ and $sbt(x,y) = -3$ if $x \neq y$. However, in practice, more complex substitution matrices (such as BLOSUM62 [2]) that model biochemical properties of amino acids are used.

The score of the optimal local pairwise alignment is the maximal score in matrix H (*maxScore*). The actual alignment can be found by a trace-back procedure. However, for SW-based protein sequence database scanning, we just need to compute *maxScore* for each query/database sequence pair. Database sequences are then ranked according to their *maxScore* value and the top hits are displayed to the user. Note that the score-only computation can be done in linear space and does not require storing the full DP matrix.

The described algorithm is embarrassingly parallel because each target/query alignment can be performed independently. GPU ports of SW are specifically designed to improve the speed of scanning of large databases. The main problem during the design of a CUDA algorithm is to find the most efficient use of various types of memory as well as registers to achieve highest possible performance.

11.3 CUDA IMPLEMENTATION OF THE SW ALGORITHM FOR IDENTIFICATION OF HOMOLOGOUS PROTEINS

The SW algorithm can be used for two applications:

1. Computing an optimal pairwise alignment
2. Scanning a database with a query sequence

The first application usually takes a negligible amount of time even for very long sequences. The second application, however, is highly time-consuming owing to the enormous growth of sequence databases. Acceleration of this task can be achieved in two ways: either by improving the speed of individual alignment or by computing a large number of alignments in parallel. In this chapter we present the design of a massively parallel SW algorithm for database scanning on GPUs.

Our design concentrates on the SW algorithm for protein sequences. Three examples of protein databases that scientists routinely scan are:

- The NR database from NCBI. NR currently consists of 10.8 million sequences comprising 3.7 billion residues;
- The SwissProt database from SIB and EBI. SwissProt currently contains 516,000 sequences comprising 182 million residues; and
- The ASTRAL.SCOP database contains sequences of protein domains with known 3-D structures obtained from the Protein Data Bank. It currently contains 16.7 thousand sequences comprising 2.9 million residues.

The average sequence length in NR and SwissProt is around 350 residues and the longest sequence length is around 35,000 residues.

Assume that the length of the query length is between 100 and 1000 residues. Then the total number of DP matrix cells to be computed is in the range 370–3700 G for NR, 18–180 G for SwissProt, and 0.29–2.9 G for ASTRAL.SCOP. Performance of the SW algorithm is commonly measured in cell updates per second (CUPS). A nonvectorized and single-threaded C implementation of SW achieves a performance of around 0.1 GCUPS (giga CUPS) on a standard CPU. This would translate in a scanning time of up to 10 hours for the NR database. In the following section, we will show how CUDA and a GPU can be used to significantly improve this runtime.

Our approach takes advantage of inherent data parallelism: each database sequence can be aligned independently. Therefore, each CUDA thread can separately perform a different pairwise query-database alignment. Overall scanning speed will then depend on clever organization and implementation of memory access and computation.

In order to achieve good load balancing, database sequences are sorted with respect to their length in decreasing order as a preprocessing step. This guarantees that all threads within the same thread block can work on sequences with similar lengths. We load these sequences into the CUDA shared memory for fast high-bandwidth access. Because of the limited shared memory capacity, special care might be necessary for very long sequences. In our description we will initially skip those cases, assuming that they are processed by the standard CPU algorithm. Later on we will return to this issue and propose a method that can take care of sequences of arbitrary length.

After sorting the database, we split it into chunks consisting of sequences with similar length. Each chunk can be processed by a single kernel. Naturally, the number of sequences in the single chunk should be equal to the optimal number of threads running concurrently on the GPU. For example, let us assume that we use a GTX 280 card with 30 multiprocessors and that the optimal number of threads is 256 per multiprocessor. Then each database chunk should consist of 7680 sequences. With 10.8 million sequences in the NR database, this provides about 1400 chunks, and 1400 kernels are required to process the entire database. We further assume that the card has sufficient memory to hold the entire database.

11.3.1 Version 1 — Simple Implementation of the SW Algorithm on GPU Using CUDA

We fill the DP matrices vertically, in column-major order. The substitution matrix is located in the shared memory; all other matrices are located in the global memory. Other variables are located in registers. We start with initialization of the first row and first column with zeros.

```
for (i=0;i<=db_sequence_len;i++) H[0][i]=0;
for (i=0;i<=query_equence_len;i++) H[i][0]=0;
//
for (i=1;i<=db_sequence_len;i++) do
    aa_db = db[i]
    F_local = 0;
    H_local = 0;
    for (j=0;j<query_sequence_len;j++) do
        aa_query = query[j]
        A = sbt[aa_db,aa_query];
        // read H and E from previous step
        // Compute auxiliary variables
        E_local = max(E[i][j-1]-beta,H[i][j-1]-alpha);
        F_local = max(F_local-beta,H_local-alpha);
        // Compute H
        H_local = max(0,E_local);
        H_local = max(H_local,F_local);
        H_local = max(H_local,H[i-1][j-1]+A);
        H_max = max(H_max,H_local)
        H[i][j] = H_local;
        E[i][j] = E_local;
    done
done
```

One should notice that formally in the SW algorithm E, F, and H are two-dimensional arrays, but the algorithm utilizes only a single column of E and H and a single value of F. This is particularly important for an SW CUDA implementation because the quadratic space required by the two-dimensional matrices E, F, and H would easily exhaust the available global memory. In the pseudo code above we denote E and H by two-dimensional arrays for clarity; however, in the real code only one-dimensional matrices are used.

It is useful to make a simple analysis of the algorithm to identify bottlenecks. To this end one counts useful instructions performed in the kernel — arithmetic operations, operations on the memory, etc. The maximal theoretical performance of the code is the number of instructions which can be executed by all processors of GPU divided by number of instructions required by algorithm. The real world performance is always lower, due to multiple factors, including memory bandwidth and latency, memory access conflicts, shuffling of data between registers, synchronisation, etc. Very often the memory bandwidth, and not the operation count, is limiting the performance of the algorithm. Therefore, one should always check whether memory bandwidth is sufficient to deliver all data required by the algorithm.

In the preceding pseudo-code operation count in the inner loop is following:

max − 6, add − 9, **shared** load/store 2, **global** load/store 4, 21 instructions in total, assuming that processor does not need any auxiliary instructions.

The theoretical peak memory bandwidth of a single GPU on a Tesla C1070 board is 102 GB/s. Realistically, one can achieve at most about 70% efficiency of bandwidth usage on applications as simple as copying data; more complicated tasks yield even less bandwidth efficiency. Therefore, taking into account the number of memory operations required by the algorithm, the bandwidth limits the performance of the simple implementation to about 4.5 GCUPS. On the other hand, the theoretical maximal performance of the code, assuming ideal timing of instructions and assuming that the executable code, assuming ideal timing of instructions and assuming that the executable code contains a minimal number of instructions, is roughly 14.8 GCUPS (240×1.3 GHz/ 21 instructions). The implementation is therefore memory bound.

The practical implementation based on this algorithm achieves about 1.7 GCUPS on a Tesla C1070 board. The code of the kernel executing the simple implementation of the SW algorithm in CUDA is shown in Figure 11.1.

The preceding analysis shows that the optimization of the memory usage is the most effective method for improved performance. A simple way to reduce the amount of data to be accessed from the global memory is to use short integers to represent values of the matrices E, F, and H. This approach halves the number of transactions with the global memory at the price of increased operation count (for reading/storing two short integers in a 32-bit word). After this modification the operation count therefore increases to 25. Thus, the performance limit that is due to operation count decreases to 12.5 GCUPS, whereas the performance limit that is due to memory bandwidth increases to about 9 GCUPS,

```
__global__ void sw(int qs, int* base, int base_size, int gap_open,\
                int gap_extend, int* result){
  int i = threadIdx.x + blockIdx.x * blockDim.x;
  int step = blockDim.x * gridDim.x;
  int e_tmp[max_qs], h_tmp[max_qs];
  __shared__ int shared_score_matrix[alphabet_len * alphabet_len];

  for (int i = 0; i < alph_len * alphabet_len; i++) \
      shared_score_matrix[i] = score_matrix_gpu[i];
  for (int i = 0; i < qs; i++) h_tmp[i] = 0;
  for (int i = 0; i < qs; i++) e_tmp[i] = 0;
  int h_max = 0;

  for (; i < base_size; i+= step){
      int* score_line = shared_score_matrix + base[i] * alphabet_len;
      int f_top = 0, h_topleft = 0, h_top = 0;
      for (unsigned int j = 0; j < qs; j++){
          int e_left = e_tmp[j];
          int h_left = h_tmp[j];
          int f = max(f_top - gap_extend, h_top - gap_open);
          int e = max(e_left - gap_extend, h_left - gap_open);
          int h = max(0, max(e, max(f, h_topleft + score_line[query_gpu[j]])));
          f_top = f;
          h_topleft = h_left;
          h_top = h;
          e_tmp[j] = e;
          h_tmp[j] = h;
          h_max = max(h, h_max);
      };
  };
  result[threadIdx.x + blockIdx.x * blockDim.x] = h_max;
};
```

FIGURE 11.1

The code for the kernel using a straightforward port of the SW algorithm to the GPU.

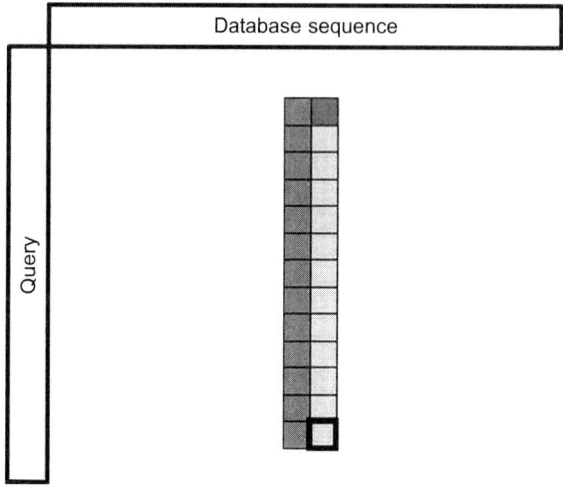

FIGURE 11.2

An illustration of the use of shared memory. Each thread sequentially computes $k = 12$ matrix cells in column j (*light gray*) in shared memory. The $k + 1$ required cells of column $j - 1$ (*dark gray*) have been computed in the previous iteration and are therefore already stored in shared memory. However, the upper neighboring cell (*black*) needs to be read from global memory. At the end of the computation only the bottom cell (*fat, light gray*) needs to be written to global memory.

which is still not satisfactory. A better approach is redesigning of the code to take advantage of fast shared memory.

11.3.2 Version 2 — Shared Memory Implementation

The shared memory implementation is based on the following idea. The DP matrix is processed in the vertical stripes, parallel to the query. The innermost loop is processing a short column parallel to the query (see Figure 11.2). Global memory is accessed only upon entering and exiting this loop. On entrance, the initialization requires reading the relevant values of H and F from global memory, and on exit, the same variables are stored in the global memory for initialization of the subsequent stripe. All matrices are located either in global memory (suffix Global) or in shared memory (suffix Shared). Other variables are located in registers. Pseudo code for this algorithm is presented below.

```
H_up=Global_H[j];// read from global memory
F_up=Global_F[j];//
H_upleft = H_init;// register operation

aa_db = db_seq[j];// this operation performed once per column
for (k=0;k<12;k++) do
    // read similarity score from the shared memory
    aa_query = query[i];
    A = sbt[aa_query,aa_db]; // shared memory
    // read H and E from previous sweep
```

```
H_left=Shared_H[k]; // shared memory
E_left=Shared_E[k]; // shared memory
// Compute auxiliary variables
E = max(E_left-beta,H_left-alpha);
F = max(F_up-beta,H_up-alpha);
// Compute H
H = max(0,E);
H = max(H,F);
H = max(H,H_upleft+A);
// if this is a first step store H_up in a register
// for initializing next column
if (k==0) H_init = H_up;
// initialize variables for the next step
    Shared_H[k]=H;
    Shared_E[k]=E;
    H_upleft = H_left;
    H_up = H;
    F_up = F;
  done
done
// Write variables to global memory for next sweep
Global_H[j]=H;
Global_F[j]=F;
```

In the pseudo code above the operation count is as follows:

- main loop per 14 steps:
  - load /store from global memory: 4 (2 if H and F are represented by short int)
  - load/store from shared memory: 2 (1 if H and F are represented by short int)
- per single step
  - load/store from shared memory 4
  - add: 4
  - max: 6
  - TOTAL 14
- total per 14 steps
  - load/store from global memory: 4 (2)
  - load/store from shared memory: 58 (57)
  - add: 56
  - max: 84
  - TOTAL: 202 (199)

The theoretical performance limit resulting from the instruction count is $(240 \times 1.3 \text{ GHz}/202) \times 14 = 21.6$ GCUPS. The performance limit that is due to bandwidth is 102 GBs per second/16 bytes per 14 cell updates $\times 0.7 = 62.5$ GCUPS. We can see that by using shared memory, we were able to reduce both the number of instructions and usage of global memory. As a result we obtain much higher theoretical bounds on performance. One should note, however, that the limit that is due to memory bandwidth is now higher than the limit that is due to operation count; that is, the algorithm is bound by the amount of instructions that can be issued by processor, not by the memory. The actual performance of the code is 11 GCUPS on a Tesla C1070 board. The computational kernel is displayed in Figure 11.3.

```
__constant__ int gap_open; __constant__ int gap_extend;
__constant__ int profile_matrix[constant_query_max][alphabet_len];

__global__ void psi_sw_block_3(int* base, int* base_helper, int* base_r,\
                               int block_len, int query_len, int buf_single){
  const int i = threadIdx.x + blockIdx.x * blockDim.x;
  const int step = blockDim.x * gridDim.x;
  const int buf_len = buf_single_max * BLOCK_SIZE;
  __shared__ short2 eh_tmp_base[buf_len];
  __shared__ int score[buf_line_max][alphabet_len];
  short2* eh_tmp = eh_tmp_base + threadIdx.x;
  for (int z = 0; z < block_len; z++){ base_helper[z * step + i] = 0; };
  int z = 0, h_max = 0;

  while (z < query_len){
    int strip = min(query_len - z, buf_single);
    for (int j = 0; j < buf_single; j++) eh_tmp[BLOCK_SIZE * j] = make_short2(0, 0);
    if (threadIdx.x == 0){ // dumb
      for (int j = 0; j < buf_single_max; j++) for (int k = 0; k < alphabet_len;
          k++) \ score[j][k] = profile_matrix[z + j][k];
    };
    __syncthreads();
    int h_toplast = 0;
    for (int k = 0; k < block_len; k++){
      int offset = k * step + i;
      int letter = base[offset];
      short2 data = (*((short2**)&(base_helper)))[offset];
      int f_top = data.x, h_top = data.y;
      int h_topleft = h_toplast;
      h_toplast = h_top;

    #pragma unroll 4
      for (int j = 0; j < strip; j++){
        short2 tmp = eh_tmp[blockDim.x * j];
        int e_left = tmp.x, h_left = tmp.y;
        int f = max(f_top - gap_extend, h_top - gap_open);
        int e = max(e_left - gap_extend, h_left - gap_open);
        int h = max(0, max(e, max(f, h_topleft + score[j][letter])));
        f_top = f;
        h_topleft = h_left;
        h_top = h;
        tmp.x = e; tmp.y = h;
        eh_tmp[blockDim.x * j] = tmp;
        h_max = max(h, h_max);
        };
        data.x = f_top; data.y = h_top;
        (*((short2**)&(base_helper)))[offset] = data;
    };
    z += strip;
  };
};
```

FIGURE 11.3

The code of the kernel utilizing shared memory.

11.3.3 **Version 3 — Efficient Use of Registers, Loop Unrolling**

Some additional optimizations are still possible. Load/store operations on shared memory are more than one order of magnitude faster than those on global memory. However, access to the shared memory still requires issuing load/store instructions and can possibly generate access conflicts. Some of the load/store operations can be avoided by explicit loop unrolling. The previous implementation is therefore modified in the following way. The DP matrix is still partitioned in horizontal stripes, but within the innermost loop, we process a rectangular tile of cells. The tile consists of 14·8 cells. The access to the shared memory is performed only for the first (reading) and last (writing) column of the tile. This allows for reducing the number of operations per cell from 14 to 12.

We start by defining the hierarchical set of functions performing computations on different scales of the dynamic programming matrix:

- single() — performs an update for a single cell
- do_8step() — performs an update for eight adjacent cells (segment) in a single row of the matrix
- strip_update() — performs an update for a strip 14 cells high for an entire database sequence length
- read_helper_data() — reads data from global memory; this is an auxiliary function reading data required in strip_update()
- write_helper_data() — writes processed variables to global memory; this is an auxiliary function which writes data to global memory
- DO_STEP(x) — actually it is a macro, useful to unroll the loop over rows of the tile without actually writing all code manually. The macro is expanded to the do_8step() function.

All variables are accessed by reference and therefore their modifications are nonlocal.

```
def function single()(H_left,H_topleft,H_top,E,F,Hmax,Score)
    E=max(E-beta,H_left-alpha);
    F = max(F-beta,H_up-alpha);
    // Compute H
    H = max(0,E);
    H = max(H,F);
    H = max(H,H_upleft+Score);
    H_max=max(H,H_max);
    H_left=H;
    E_left=E;

def function do_8step(\
i,j,E_left,H_left,H_topleft,H_t1...H_t8,F_t1...F_t8)
    E_left=Shared_E[i];
    H_left=Shared_H[i];
    Score = QueryProfile[i][j];
    single(H_left,H_topleft,Ht1,E_left,F_t1,H_max,Score)
    Score = QueryProfile[i][j+1];
    single(H_left,H_t1,Ht2,E_left,F_t2,H_max,Score)
    Score = QueryProfile[i][j+1];
    single(H_left,H_t1,Ht2,E_left,F_t2,H_max,Score)
    ...
    Score = QueryProfile[i][j+7];
    single(H_left,H_t7,Ht8,E_left,F_t8,H_max,Score)
```

```
#define DO_STEP(x) do_8step(..., BLOCK_SIZE * x);

def function strip_update()
    for (i=0;i<number_of_tiles;i++) do
        read_helper_data()
        DO_STEP(0)
        DO_STEP(1)
        ...
        DO_STEP(13)
        write_helper_data()
    done
```

The previously described implementation enables us to reduce the number of operations per cell update to 12. The theoretical performance limit therefore increases to 26 GCUPS. The CUDA program based on this idea achieves 17 GCUPS on a single GPU of a Tesla S1070. One should note, however, that while the theoretical performance limit increased from 21.6 to 26 GCUPS (20%), the performance of the actual code increased by 55% (from 11 to 17 GCUPS) and reached 65% of the theoretical limit. The essential fragments of this kernel are displayed in Figure 11.4. One may note that the volume of the code is increased significantly, despite our use of macros for reduction of most repetitive parts. In the actual implementation the additional functions are introduced for the first and last strip.

```
___device___ void single(int& h_max, int& f_top, int& h_top, int& e, int& h, int&
h_topleft, const int& score){
    int f = max(f_top - gap_extend, h_top - gap_open);
    e = max(e - gap_extend, h - gap_open);
    h = max(0, max(e, max(f, h_topleft + score)));
    f_top = f; h_topleft = h_top;
    h_top = h; h_max = max(h, h_max);
};

___device___ void do_8step(short2* eh_tmp, int& h_topleft, int& h_top_0, int& f_top_0,
int& h_top_1, int& f_top_1, ..., int& f_top_7, int& h_max, const int& score_0, const
int& score_1, ..., const int& offset){
    short2 tmp = eh_tmp[offset];
    int e_left = tmp.x;
    int h_left = tmp.y;
    int tmp_h_left = h_left;
    single(h_max, f_top_0, h_top_0, e_left, h_left, h_topleft, score_0);
    ...
    single(h_max, f_top_7, h_top_7, e_left, h_left, h_topleft, score_7);
    h_topleft = tmp_h_left; tmp.x = e_left; tmp.y = h_left; eh_tmp[offset] = tmp;
};
___device___ void load_letters(int k, int i, int step, uchar4* base_u, int& letter_0,
int& letter_1, ..., int& letter_7){
    int offset = 2 * k * step + i;
    int offset2 = offset + step;
    uchar4 letter_container = base_u[offset];
    uchar4 letter_container2 = base_u[offset2];
```

```
      letter_0 = letter_container.x; . . . letter_7 = letter_container2.w;
};

__device__ void read_helper_data(int& offset, int step, int* base_helper, int& f_top_0,
int& h_top_0, ..., int& f_top_7, int& h_top_7){
      short4 f_data = (*((short4**)&(base_helper)))[offset];   offset += step;
      short4 h_data = (*((short4**)&(base_helper)))[offset];   offset += step;
      short4 f_data_2 = (*((short4**)&(base_helper)))[offset];    offset += step;
      short4 h_data_2 = (*((short4**)&(base_helper)))[offset];    offset += step;

      f_top_0 = f_data.x;   h_top_0 = h_data.x; ... ; h_top_3 = h_data.w;
      f_top_4 = f_data_2.x; h_top_4 = h_data_2.x;...; h_top_7 = h_data_2.w;
};

__device__ void init_helper_data(int& offset, int step, int* base_helper, int& f_top_0,
int& h_top_0, ..., int& f_top_7, int& h_top_7){
      f_top_0 = h_top_0 = ... = 0;
      offset += 4 * step;
};
__device__ void dump_helper_data(int& offset, int step, int* base_helper, int& f_top_0,
int& h_top_0, int& f_top_1, ..., int& f_top_7, int& h_top_7){
      short4 f_data, f_data_2, h_data, h_data_2;
      f_data.x = f_top_0; h_data.x = h_top_0; ...;       h_data.w = h_top_3;
      f_data_2.x = f_top_4; h_data_2.x = h_top_4; ...;   h_data_2.w = h_top_7;
      offset -= 4*step;

      (*((short4**)&(base_helper)))[offset] = f_data;    offset += step;
      (*((short4**)&(base_helper)))[offset] = h_data;    offset += step;
      (*((short4**)&(base_helper)))[offset] = f_data_2;  offset += step;
      (*((short4**)&(base_helper)))[offset] = h_data_2;  offset += step;
};

__device__ void do_strip(int z, short2* eh_tmp, int i, int block_len, int step, int
strip, uchar4* base_u, int& h_max, int* base_helper, int
score[buf_line_max][alphabet_len]){
    for (int j=0;j<buf_single_max;j++) eh_tmp[BLOCK_SIZE * j] = make_short2(0, 0);
    __syncthreads();

    if (threadIdx.x < buf_single_max){
        for (int k = 0; k < alphabet_len; k++){
           score[threadIdx.x][k] = profile_matrix[z + threadIdx.x][k];
        };
    };
    __syncthreads();
    int h_toplast = 0;
    int off = i;
    for (int k = 0; k < block_len/8; k++){ // IMPORTANT
       int letter_0, ..., letter_7;
       load_letters(k, i, step, base_u, letter_0, ..., letter_7);
       int f_top_0, h_top_0, ..., f_top_/, h_top_7;
```

(continued)

```
        read_helper_data(off, step, base_helper, f_top_0, h_top_0, ..., h_top_7);
        int h_topleft = h_toplast;   h_toplast = h_top_7;
        #define DO_STEP(x) do_8step(eh_tmp, h_topleft, h_top_0, f_top_0, ..., f_top_7,
    h_max, score[x][letter_0], ..., score[x][letter_7], BLOCK_SIZE * x);
        DO_STEP(0)
...
        DO_STEP(13)
        #undef DO_STEP
        dump_helper_data(off, step, base_helper, f_top_0, h_top_0, ..., h_top_7);
    };
};

__device__ void do_init_strip(int z, short2* eh_tmp, int i, int block_len, int step,
int strip, uchar4* base_u, int& h_max, int* base_helper, int
score[buf_line_max][alphabet_len]){

    for (int j=0;j<buf_single_max;j++) eh_tmp[BLOCK_SIZE * j] = make_short2(0, 0);
    __syncthreads();
    if (threadIdx.x < buf_single_max) for (int k = 0; k < alphabet_len; k++){
        score[threadIdx.x][k] = profile_matrix[z + threadIdx.x][k];
    };
    __syncthreads();
    int h_toplast = 0;   int off = i;
    for (int k = 0; k < block_len/8; k++){ // IMPORTANT
        int letter_0, letter_1, ..., letter_7;
        load_letters(k, i, step, base_u, letter_0, ..., letter_7);
        int f_top_0, h_top_0, ..., f_top_7, h_top_7;
        init_helper_data(off, step, base_helper, f_top_0, h_top_0, ..., h_top_7);
        int h_topleft = h_toplast;   h_toplast = h_top_7;
        // DO_STEP(x) defined as above
        #define DO_STEP(x)
...
        #undef DO_STEP

        dump_helper_data(off, step, base_helper, f_top_0, h_top_0, ..., h_top_7);
    };
};

template<int leftover>
__ device __ void do_last_strip(int z, short2* eh_tmp, int i, int block_len, int step,
int strip, uchar4* base_u, int& h_max, int* base_helper, int
score[buf_line_max][alphabet_len]){

    for (int j=0;j<buf_single_max;j++)  eh_tmp[BLOCK_SIZE * j] = make_short2(0, 0);
    __syncthreads();
    if (threadIdx.x < buf_single_max) for (int k = 0; k < alphabet_len; k++){
        score[threadIdx.x][k] = profile_matrix[z + threadIdx.x][k];
    };
    __syncthreads();
    int h_toplast = 0;
    int off = i;
```

                                                                    (continued)

```
    for (int k = 0; k < block_len/8; k++){ // <- zwrocic na to uwage
        int letter_0, ..., letter_7;
        load_letters(k, i, step, base_u, letter_0, ..., letter_7);
        int f_top_0, h_top_0, ..., f_top_7, h_top_7;
        read_helper_data(off, step, base_helper, f_top_0, h_top_0, ..., h_top_7);
        int h_topleft = h_toplast;
        h_toplast = h_top_7;
        #define DO_STEP(x) do_8step(eh_tmp, h_topleft, ..., f_top_7, h_max,
    score[x][letter_0], ..., score[x][letter_7], BLOCK_SIZE * x);
        for (int i = 0; i < leftover; i++) DO_STEP(i);
        #undef DO_STEP
    };
};

template<int leftover>
__global__ void psi_sw_block_3_template(int* base, int* base_helper, \
int* base_r, int block_len, int query_len, int buf_single){

    const int i = threadIdx.x + blockIdx.x * blockDim.x;
    const int step = blockDim.x * gridDim.x;
    const int buf_len = buf_single_max * BLOCK_SIZE;

    __shared__ short2 eh_tmp_base[buf_len];
    short2* eh_tmp = eh_tmp_base + threadIdx.x;
    uchar4* base_u = (uchar4*)base;
    __shared__ int score[buf_line_max][alphabet_len];

    int h_max = 0;
    int z = 0;

    do_init_strip(z, eh_tmp, i, block_len, step, 14, base_u, h_max, \
                    base_helper, score);
    z += 14;

    while (z < query_len){
        do_strip(z, eh_tmp, i, block_len, step, 14, base_u, h_max, \
                    base_helper, score);
        z += 14;
    };

    do_last_strip<leftover>(z, eh_tmp, i, block_len, step, leftover, \
                    base_u, h_max, base_helper, score);
    base_r[i] = h_max;
};
extern "C" void run_psi_sw_block_3(int BLOCKS, int THREADS, void* base, void*
base_helper, void* base_r, int block_len, int query_len, int buf_single,
cudaStream_t stream){

    int q_org = query_len;

    if (query_len % 14 != 0) query_len -= query_len % 14;
```

(continued)

```
switch (q_org % 14){
    case 0: { psi_sw_block_3_template<0><<<BLOCKS, THREADS, 0, 0>>>
            ((int*)base,\
            (int*)base_helper, (int*)base_r, block_len,
            query_len, 14); }
    break;
    case 1: { psi_sw_block_3_template<1><<<BLOCKS, THREADS, 0, 0>>>
            ((int*)base,\ (int*)base_helper, (int*)base_r, block_len,
            query_len, 14); }
    break;
    ...
    case 13: { psi_sw_block_3_template<13><<<BLOCKS,THREADS,0,0>>>
            ((int*)base,\ (int*)base_helper, (int*)base_r, block_len,
            query_len, 14); }
    break;
    };
};
```

FIGURE 11.4

Listing of the optimized kernel. Repetitive parts of the code replaced by "...".

11.3.4 Version 4 — Loose Ends — Long Sequences

Initially, we left the problem of long sequences for later. Now, when the code of the basic kernel has been optimized to the last instruction, it is time to handle this problem as well. Initially, we assumed that all sequences processed by a single kernel have similar length, and therefore all threads within all blocks process (almost) identical matrices. When sequence databases are being processed, this is true most of the time, but not all the time. The distribution of the sequence lengths in the SwissProt database has a broad maximum for sequence lengths in the range between 100 and 250. There are about 1000 different sequences at each length in this range.

Then the the number of sequences at given length decreases gradually. This is a distribution with a long thin tail, with longest sequence having over 35000 residues. Unfortunately, one cannot simply ignore these very long sequences.

A sequence block accommodating the longest sequence would take 192 MB, which can be compared with just 182 MB of the entire database. Most of this block would be empty, and the entire kernel performing computations on such a block would wait idling for the single thread performing alignment of the longest sequence. Certainly, it doesn't make sense to put much effort in optimization of the kernels and leave such nonoptimal design.

There are two possible solutions for this problem. One is a modification of the GPU kernel to accommodate long sequences. There are many possible ways to modify the kernel. The easiest one is quite simple. Instead of aligning sequences within a whole kernel, we can align sequences only within blocks (or even individual warps within the block). The corresponding kernel may process several sequence blocks within each thread block. The sequence blocks processed by a single-thread block are selected in such a way that the sum of their sizes is similar for all thread blocks within the kernel. In particular, the longest sequence block processed by the first kernel will have a length of about 35,000 residues and will be processed by a single block of threads. The remaining thread blocks process multiple sequence blocks where the sum of the lengths of these blocks will be close to 35,000. In particular, with such kernels the entire SwissProt database can be processed by a single kernel.

The following pseudo code illustrates this kernel. We define a new function, do_sequence_block — this function is equivalent to the old kernel. The new_kernel function performs computations for several sequence blocks at once.

```
new_kernel(...)
    // We first find how many sequences we need to process in
    // given block
    seq_blocks_to_process = seq_block_count[block_id];
    // Then we get the pointer to the data for given block
    data_ptr = seq_block_ptr[block_id];
    // And now we do processing
    for (int i = 0; i < seq_blocks_to_process; i++) do
        set_block_parameters(data_ptr, i, ...)
        do_block(data_ptr, block_len, ...)
    done
```

This solution will work best for large databases, but it will not scale well for smaller ones. Another option is to develop a version of the code in which multiple threads would work on a single sequence, taking advantage of the independence of cells located on the antidiagonal. This solution introduces overhead because some threads must wait for several cell update cycles, until all threads processing higher rows are initialized, but fortunately, this overhead is relatively small for long sequences. One would then call two versions of kernels to process a database containing very long sequences. The kernel with a single thread per sequence would be used for the bulk of the database, whereas the kernel with block per sequence would be used to handle long sequences.

The second method to optimize the kernel for long sequences is radical and simple. One should simply avoid processing these sequences on a GPU in the first place. Instead of developing a more complicated kernel for handling long sequences, one could apply a CPU version of the algorithm running on a CPU for this task. In this way the CPU could be used in parallel to the GPU, instead of sitting idle and waiting until the GPU finishes the task.

11.4 DISCUSSION

Because of the importance of SW in bioinformatics, there have been several attempts to improve its performance using a variety of parallel architectures. The highest performance of the multithreaded SSE2-vectorized CPU version [6] is about 15 GCUPS on a modern quad-core CPU [17]. This is similar to the performance of the best optimized version of the algorithm described here. Nevertheless, there are some significant disadvantages of the vectorized CPU version. First, its performance drops significantly for short sequences. Second, its performance drops when aligning a query to a large number of similar sequences. Third, its performance is sensitive to the utilized scoring system (i.e., gap penalties and a substitution matrix). In all these situations the GPU algorithm works perfectly well with only minor performance variations.

Even though the optimal alignment scores of the SW algorithm can be used to detect related sequences, the scores are biased by sequence length and composition. The Z-value [20] has been proposed to estimate the statistical significance of these scores. However, the computation of Z-value requires the calculation of a large set of pairwise alignments between random permutations of the sequences compared — a process that is highly time-consuming. The acceleration of Z-value computation with CUDA is therefore part of our future work.

Table 11.1 Performance comparison for different versions of algorithm on two generations of GPUs.

Hardware	Version Ia	Version Ib	Version II	Version III
Tesla C1070	1.7	2.7	11.0	17.0
GeForce 480 GTX	7.9	7.9	22.6	42.6

Other possible application areas are, for example, next-generation sequencing, profile-based methods, and multiple alignment.

11.5 FINAL EVALUATION

The algorithms described in this chapter were developed on and optimized for a Tesla C1070 card. The new Fermi architecture of NVIDIA hardware was available for tests after completing the work. We have been able to evaluate performance of the various versions of the algorithm on the GeForce GTX 480 card. Performance in GCUPS is reported in Table 11.1.

Version Ia of Table 11.1 is the implementation with all variables located in the global memory, and Version Ib is the implementation with the similarity matrix located in the shared memory and query in the constant memory. The performance is roughly 2.5 times higher on the Fermi architecture for the optimized version of the code and 4.6 times higher for the simple port. This is probably due to the cache memory introduced by Fermi. One can see that the difference between both variants of the naive port disappeared because the frequently accessed data from global memory resides in cache. A quick estimate shows that both versions achieve 70% of the theoretical performance limit set by the theoretical global memory bandwidth. Apparently, Fermi performs load/store operations within cache memory, and the memory controller transfers data between cache and global memory with maximal practically achievable speed.

On the other hand, speed increase of the optimized versions of the algorithm is more in line with the difference in raw performance between a Tesla C1070 and a GeForce 480 GTX. The conclusion from this little experiment is that the introduction of the new Fermi architecture significantly improved performance of the naive version, which suggests that automatic porting of applications to CUDA will have a better chance of success than for the previous generations of CUDA-enabled chips. Nevertheless, the code optimized by hand still achieves more than a five-fold speedup in comparison with a naive port.

References

[1]   D. Gusfield, Algorithms on Strings, Trees, and Sequences: Computer Science and Computational Biology, Cambridge University Press, Cambridge, UK, 1997.
[2]   S. Henikoff, J.G. Henikoff, Amino acid substitution matrices from protein blocks, Proc. Natl. Acad. Sci. U.S.A. 89 (1992) 10915–10919.
[3]   T. Smiths, M. Waterman, Identification of common molecular subsequences, J. Mol. Biol. 147 (1981) 195–197.

[4]   A. Wozniak, Using video-oriented instructions to speed up sequence comparison, Comput. Appl. Biosci. 13 (1997) 145–150.

[5]   T. Rognes, E. Seeberg, Six-fold speed-up of Smith-Waterman sequence database searches using parallel processing on common microprocessors, Bioinformatics 16 (8) (2000) 699–706.

[6]   M. Farrar, Striped Smith-Waterman speeds database searches six times over other simd implementations, Bioinformatics 23 (2) (2007) 156–161.

[7]   S. Dydel, P. Bała, Large scale protein sequence alignment using FPGA reprogrammable logic devices, in: Field Programmable Logic and Application, Lecture Notes in Computer Science, vol. 3204, 2004, pp. 23–32.

[8]   T. Oliver, B. Schmidt, D. Nathan, R. Clemens, D. Maskell, Using reconfigurable hardware to accelerate multiple sequence alignment with ClustalW, Bioinformatics 21 (16) (2005) 3431–3432.

[9]   T. Oliver, B. Schmidt, D.L. Maskell, Reconfigurable architectures for biosequence database scanning on FPGAs. IEEE Trans, Circuits Syst. II 52 (2005) 851–855.

[10] T.I. Li, W. Shum, K. Truong, 160-fold acceleration of the Smith-Waterman algorithm using a field programmable gate array (FPGA), BMC Bioinformatics 8 (2007) 185.

[11] M.S. Farrar, Optimizing Smith-Waterman for the Cell broadband engine. http://sites.google .com/site/farrarmichael/SW-CellBE.pdf

[12] A. Szalkowski, C. Ledergerber, P. Krahenbuhl, C. Dessimoz, SWPS3 — fast multi-threaded vectorized Smith-Waterman for IBM Cell/B.E. and x86/SSE2, BMC Res. Notes 1 (2008) 107.

[13] A. Wirawan, C.K. Kwoh, N.T. Hieu, B. Schmidt, CBESW: sequence alignment on Playstation 3, BMC Bioinformatics 9 (2008) 377.

[14] W.R. Rudnicki, A. Jankowski, A. Modzelewski, A. Piotrowski, A. Zadrożny, The new SIMD implementation of the Smith-Waterman algorithm on Cell microprocessor, Fundamenta Informaticae 96 (2009) 181–194.

[15] W. Liu, B. Schmidt, G. Voss, W. Muller-Wittig, Streaming algorithms for biological sequence alignment on GPUs, IEEE Trans. Parallel Distrib. Syst. 18 (9) (2007) 1270–1281.

[16] S.A. Manavski, G. Valle, CUDA compatible GPU cards as efficient hardware accelerators for Smith-Waterman sequence alignment, BMC Bioinformatics 9 (Suppl. 2) (2008) S10.

[17] Y. Liu, D.L. Maskell, B. Schmidt, CUDASW++: optimizing Smith-Waterman sequence database searches for CUDA-enabled graphics processing units, BMC Res. Notes 2 (2009) 73.

[18] L. Ligowski, W. Rudnicki, An efficient implementation of Smith-Waterman algorithm on GPU using CUDA, for massively parallel scanning of sequence databases, in: IEEE International Workshop on High Performance Computational Biology, HiCOMB 2009, Rome, Italy, May 25, 2009.

[19] Y. Liu, B. Schmidt, D.L. Maskell, CUDASW++2.0: enhanced Smith-Waterman protein database search on CUDA-enabled GPUs based on SIMT and virtualized SIMD abstractions, BMC Res. Notes 3 (2010) 93.

[20] J.P. Comet, J.C. Aude, E. Glémet, J.L. Risler, A. Hénaut, P.P. Slonimski, *et al.* Significance of Z-value statistics of Smith–Waterman scores for protein alignments, Comput. Chem. 23 (3, 4) (1999) 317–331.

Massive Parallel Computing to Accelerate Genome-Matching

Ben Weiss, Mike Bailey

INTRODUCTION

This chapter explores the process of defining and optimizing a relatively simple matching algorithm in CUDA. The project was designed to be a tool to explore the process of developing algorithms from start to finish with CUDA in mind; it also intended to highlight some of the differences between development in a massively parallel GPU-based architecture and a more traditional CPU-based single- or multi-threaded one. Framed in the context of a real-world genetic sequence alignment problem, we explored and quantified the effect of various attempts to speed up this code, ultimately achieving more than two orders of magnitude of improvement over our original CUDA implementation and over three orders of magnitude of improvement over our original CPU version.

12.1 INTRODUCTION, PROBLEM STATEMENT, AND CONTEXT

Because exploration and learning were the primary goals, we chose to explore the development of a solution to a well-understood computational genetics problem that seeks to align short sequences of genetic material against a larger fully sequenced genome or chromosome. This choice originated with a desire to support Michael Freitag's (Oregon State University) genetics research. This provided a real-world customer with real datasets and requirements. However, in the broader aspect, the lessons learned throughout the development of this code will act as a guide to anyone trying to write any high-efficiency comparison algorithms on CUDA, beyond computational genetics. Our hope is that the lessons we learned can save others time and effort in understanding at least one way of using and optimizing for the CUDA platform. We attempt to present the give and take between optimizing the algorithm and tweaking the problem statement itself to better suit the CUDA platform; several of our most significant improvements came as we rephrased the problem to more accurately suit CUDA's abilities within the context of our customers' needs.

As sequencing machines produce larger and larger datasets, the computational requirements of aligning the reads into a reference genome have become increasingly great [8]. Modern sequencing machines can produce batches of millions of short (<100 base pair) reads, here referred to as "targets" for clarity, which need to be aligned against a known reference genome. Several CPU-based solutions

```
For every short target sequence:
      For every genome base−pair:
            Compare the target to the genome subsequence starting at this base pair
            Record any matches
      Next genome base pair
Next target
```

Listing 12.1: Basic problem pseudo code.

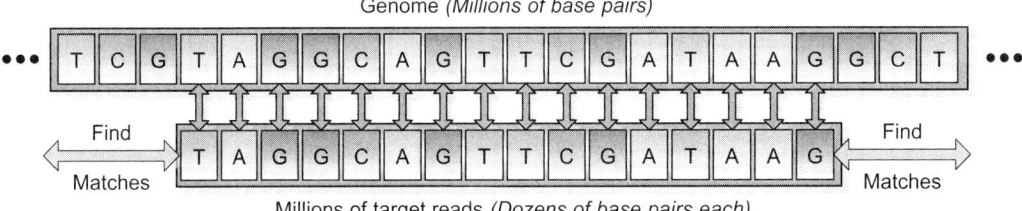

FIGURE 12.1

Illustration of the basic problem being solved. A large genome is searched for matches to a long list of target reads.

have been developed to address this issue, a few of which have been ported to CUDA, but we chose instead to present a method developed with CUDA in mind from the very beginning. A small snippet of pseudo code (Listing 12.1) and an illustrative graphic (Figure 12.1) provide a naive solution that clarifies the fundamental problem that we have solved.

This problem appeared to be a good match for implementation in CUDA because the code is highly parallelizable and fits well into an Single Instruction, Multiple Data (SIMT) paradigm. Additionally, the cost-effectiveness of using NVIDIA hardware to solve this problem made a CUDA solution appealing: a traditional cluster could have cost 10 times what an equivalent desktop GPU solution might cost. Hashing the genome and target sequences, one of the standard techniques for solving a problem like this, was implemented very late in the development of our solution in part because it complicates the algorithm's data access patterns significantly and makes it more difficult to optimize.

For the development phase of our specific algorithm, a benchmark set of 5000 real-world 36 base pair (BP) targets (reads) was replicated many times and matched against an already-sequenced map of linkage group VII of *Neurospora crassa* (3.9 million BP). This was used as a baseline to gauge the performance of the algorithm, which had to run on inexpensive hardware and scale to problems with millions or even billions of reads and tens of millions of genome base pairs.

12.2 CORE METHODS

The algorithm presented here, which currently reports only exact matches of the target reads onto the references genome, differs significantly in structure from many previously available codes because instead of seeking to port a CPU-centric algorithm to the GPU, we built the solution entirely with CUDA 1.1 in mind. In this section, we present a brief overview of our comparison kernel.

The first few steps of each kernel involved rearranging memory on the GPU. Though somewhat mundane, these tasks received a great deal of time in the optimization process because the various memory access pathways and caches available in CUDA are strikingly different than the cache layers of a CPU. First, a section of genome was loaded from global memory into shared memory; this section of genome persisted throughout the comparison operation. The load operation was designed to create a series of coalesced memory transfers that maximized speed, and each block takes a different section of the genome.

Next, each thread loaded a target into a different section of shared memory. In each kernel, all blocks checked the same series of several thousand targets, so targets were stored in constant memory to take advantage of on-chip caching. Once loaded, each thread checked its target against the portions of the genome stored locally in each block's shared memory, recording matches in a global memory array. After a target had been checked, a new one was loaded from constant memory to replace it, and the comparison repeated until all designated targets had been handled. In successive kernel calls, the constant memory was reloaded with new targets.

A simple example clarifies the process. Suppose we have a short section of genome and a list of four targets that we match using a kernel with two blocks and three threads per block (see Figure 12.2). First, each block loads a section of genome into shared memory; then each thread grabs a target and compares it against the cached portion of the genome. Most threads do not find matches, but thread 3 in block 1 does, and records the target identifier and genome offset in global memory. When the first three targets have been handled, the next three are loaded and checked. All matches are recorded. The process continues until all targets for the run have been handled. Of course, CUDA does this with dozens of threads in hundreds of blocks at a time.

Late in the development of the algorithm, a hash table was implemented, sorting each genome offset and target based on the first eight BPs. This, vaguely similar to Maq's seed index table [7], [2], allows the algorithm to consider only genome/target matches where the first few base pairs already match, increasing the probability by several orders of magnitude that a comparison will succeed. Most commercial CPU-based alignment algorithms use a hash table of some form. No advantage was gained

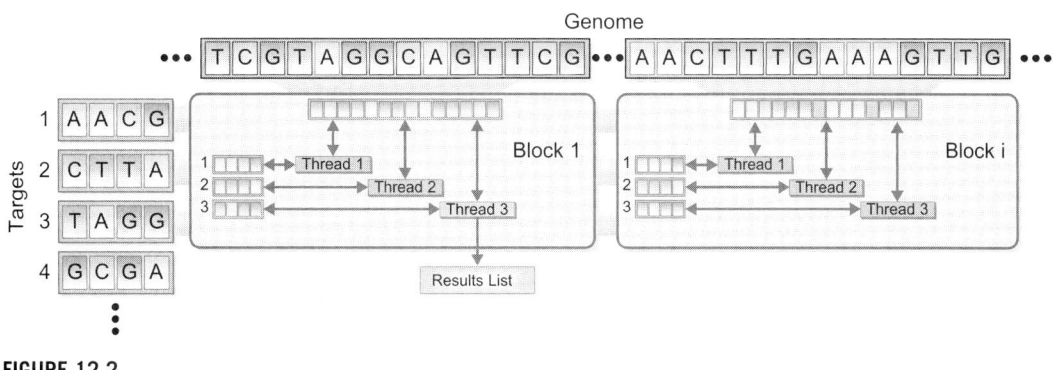

FIGURE 12.2

Example of a kernel of three threads doing a comparison.

by computing target reverse-complements on the fly, so when enabled, complements are precomputed on the CPU and added to the target list.

In addition to the CUDA kernel, a multithreaded CPU version was built with a similar formulation, though organized and optimized somewhat differently to cater to the differences between the architectures, especially in the way that memory is allocated and arranged. Details of these differences are discussed later in this chapter. Running both CPU and CUDA versions of the comparison in parallel provided still greater speed, but also presented additional challenges.

In the following sections, we will explore some of the specific changes made, but major lessons learned are summarized here. As expected, multiprocessor occupancy was found to be important, though on more recent hardware this parameter is easier to keep high because of increases in the number of available registers in each multiprocessor. Additionally, optimizing and utilizing the various memory pathways are critical for this kind of high-throughput code. In order to maximize these indicators of performance, both algorithm design and kernel parameter settings must be carefully selected. Also as expected, wrap cohesion was found to be important, but if the basic kernel flow is cohesive, the NVCC compiler handles this without much need for programmer involvement.

With its complex memory pathways and computation architecture, CUDA is fundamentally different than the CPU for performance applications, and one should approach CUDA carefully, with the understanding that some conventional wisdom from single-threaded programming does not work in an SIMT environment.

12.3 ALGORITHMS, IMPLEMENTATIONS, AND EVALUATIONS

A main goal of the project was to determine the characteristics of CUDA algorithms that have the greatest influence on execution speed. Thus, our improvements in performance were measured against previous versions of the same code, not the results of other researchers' solutions, to allow for quantification of the effectiveness of algorithmic changes in increasing efficiency. Most industry-standard codes for this kind of problem support mismatches between target reads and a reference genome, as well as gaps of a few BPs.

Our development occurred on a Pentium 4 3.0 GHz dual-core system with 2 GB of RAM running a single 256 MB GeForce 8600 graphics card, Windows XP Professional, and CUDA 1.1. All performance statistics reported here were based on this system, but we expect that they would scale very well to the newer, faster generations of NVIDIA hardware available.

Throughout the development of the code, the speed improvements and their associated algorithmic changes were carefully tracked to give us an idea of the effectiveness of various strategies in speeding up CUDA code (see Figure 12.3). "Targets per second" is representative of the number of targets processed per second during the comparison stage of the algorithm; setup and post-processing time were assumed to be small compared with the computation time for real-world problems, and this metric provided a more direct measure of the performance of the algorithm, rather than the system, making performance improvements in CUDA easier to distinguish.

Some changes involved optimizations to the code itself while retaining the overall structure of the algorithm; others pertained to changes in the way the problem was solved or (in a few cases) a modification of the problem statement itself. This seems typical of any project developed in CUDA and shows the interplay between the hardware's capabilities and the software's requirements as they

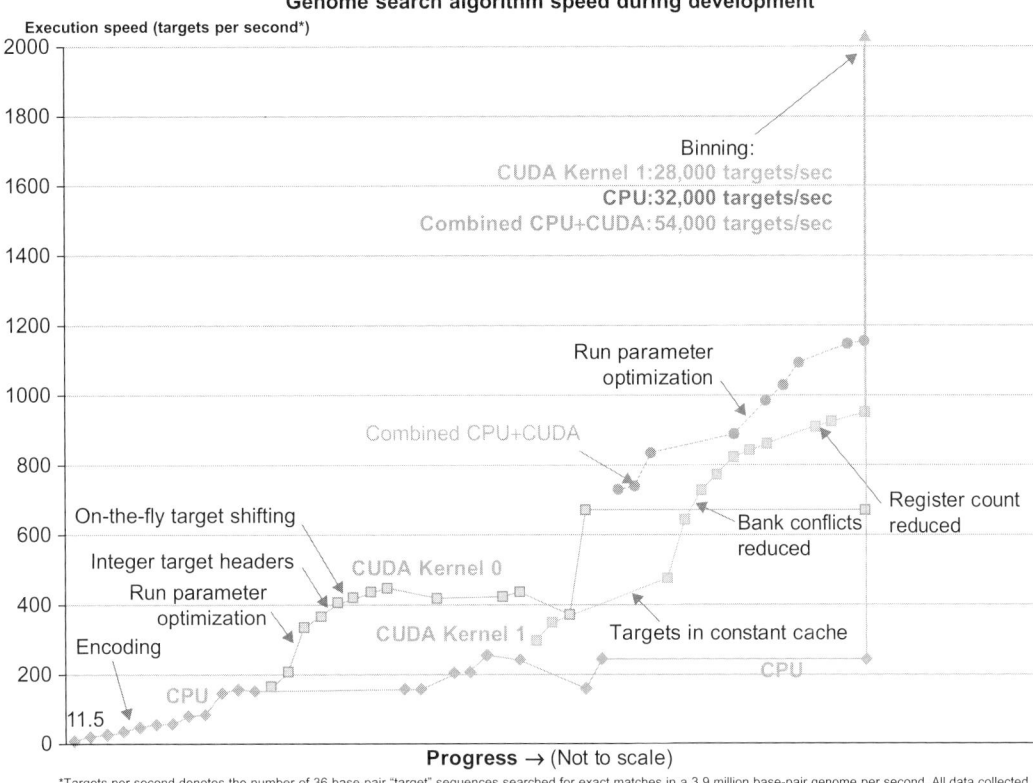

FIGURE 12.3

Genome search algorithm speed during development, for two different versions of the CUDA kernel and the optimized CPU version of the same algorithm. Points represent significant changes made to the code.

relate to overall speed. In the following sections, we describe some of the most interesting and effective optimizations that we employed.

12.3.1 Genome Encoding

Obviously, reading genetic data in 8-bit ASCII character format is a significant waste of space. Encoding the A's, C's, T's, and G's into a more compact form provided a significant speedup: With each base pair requiring only two bits, four could be packed into each byte and compared at once. Though easily implemented, an algorithmic problem presented itself: The bytes of genome and target data lined up only one-quarter of the time. To resolve this we created four "subtargets" for every target sequence (read), each with a different sub-byte offset, and introduced a bitwise mask to filter out the unused BPs in any comparison. All told, this change (which occurred while still investigating the problem on the CPU before initial implementation in CUDA) improved performance only by about 10%, but significantly reduced memory usage and paved the way for more effective changes. Although search algorithms in other disciplines may not have such an obvious encoding scheme, this result still indicates that for high-throughput applications like this, packing the relevant data even though it consumes a bit more GPU horsepower can provide a significant speedup. Figure 12.4 demonstrates the compression and masking process.

12.3.2 Target Headers

Another inherent inefficiency was addressed: The code runs on a 32-bit multiprocessor, but all comparisons were single-byte operations. Very significant speed gains were made by encoding the genome into char arrays and then typecasting them to integers to more fully utilize the pipeline width. In this revision, "headers" were created for each subtarget, containing 4-byte (16-BP) integer versions of the target itself and the accompanying mask, and then the appropriate section of genome was typecast to int and compared with the header. Used as a pre-filter for the remainder of the comparison process, this reduced the likelihood of a target passing the header check but not being an actual match to about one in 50 million compares on our test dataset. The result was a speed increase of more than 25% in CPU mode, slightly less under CUDA, which complicates typecasting of char to int because of its shared memory layout. Figure 12.5 illustrates a 2-byte target header in action.

Our CUDA kernel stores the genome in shared memory. Shared memory is arranged in 16 banks, each 32 bits wide [5]. Presumably because of this unique layout, the NVCC compiler behaves in an unusual way when typecasting from char arrays to int. When an address for an int lies on an even multiple of four bytes, the typecast proceeds as expected. However, when the address is not aligned this

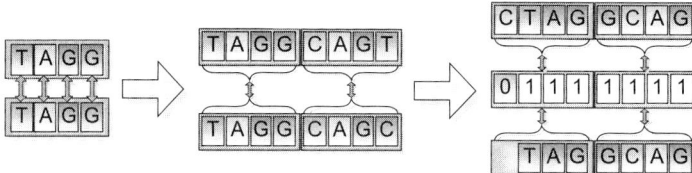

FIGURE 12.4

A switch from single BP compares to encoded BPs comparing whole bytes at a time. When the genome and target don't align at byte boundaries, a mask filters out the unused base pairs.

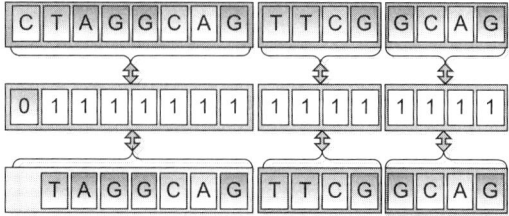

FIGURE 12.5

A target header in action. If the 16-bit (8 BP) header comparison succeeds, then the compare operation proceeds.

way, the word returned is the next-lowest aligned `int` to the address requested. For example, given an array `char q[8]` that spans two banks: `0xAABBCCDD` is stored in Bank 1 and `0xEEFF1122` in Bank 2, we try the typecast `*(int*)(q + 2)`, which we expect to return `0x1122AABB`. We instead obtain `0xAABBCCDD` — the contents of Bank 1. This makes some sense: The compiler requests memory from one bank at a time to maximize speed, and this fringe case occurs very seldom in practice. However, it extends to other typecasts as well — if a `char` array is typecast to `shorts`, only typecasts to even-numbered bytes give the expected result. Compensating for this behavior requires bit fiddling two bank-aligned integers into the desired portion of the encoded genome for comparison and reduces performance gains significantly. Once we understood this, working with it was not a problem.

12.3.3 Data Layout

Even though CUDA is fundamentally a stream-processing engine, the best access patterns for this kind of problem appeared more like a spider web: The many available memory pathways made moving data around a complex task with easily overlooked subtleties. Table 12.1 provides an overview of where the data structures needed by the algorithm were stored. Because the comparison mask was fixed, we stored that information in constant memory, which was heavily cached, while the genome resided in global memory and was copied into shared (local) memory for comparison. The entire target list is kept in global memory, but because each kernel uses relatively few targets, a subset is copied to the remaining constant memory for each kernel. Targets are then further cached in shared memory for each compare operation. The texture memory pathway was initially unused, then later pressed into service for loading target and genome hash information, which attempts to take advantage of its spatial locality caching.

Table 12.1 Data storage locations.

Data	Location	Access pattern
Entire genome	Global memory	Subset cached to local memory once per kernel in a cohesive transfer.
Entire target list	Global memory	Subset loaded to constant memory before each kernel.
Kernel target list	Constant memory	Targets loaded as needed from constant memory.
Active genome section	Shared memory	Frequent random access throughout kernel.
Active target list	Shared memory	Frequent sequential access throughout kernel, reloaded many times from constant memory.
Target masks	Constant memory	Very frequent access to a few dozen bytes of information.
Hash offsets	Texture memory	Somewhat frequent access to clusters of nearby entries.
Results table	Global memory	Written two by threads in different blocks once per match (relatively rare).

The advantage of pulling from different memory sources is a smaller utilization of global memory bandwidth, decreasing the load on one of the weakest links in data-intensive CUDA kernels like ours. On the CPU, however, experiments indicated that the highest speed could be provided by actually replicating the mask set many times and interleaving the target data so that target headers and their associated masks are very close together. Placing the masks in their own array, even though it means almost half as much data is streamed into and out of the CPU, actually slows performance down very significantly (a 35% speed increase for the interleaved scheme).

CUDA's shared memory is arranged in banks capable of serving only one 4-byte word every two clock cycles [5]. Successive 32-bit ints of shared memory are stored in successive banks, so word 1 is stored in bank 1, word 2 in bank 2, and so on. The importance of understanding this layout was driven home in one design iteration that had the targets arranged in 16-byte-wide structures. Every iteration in all 32 threads read just the first word (the header) from the structure, which resided in only four banks and created an eight-way "bank conflict" — it took 16 GPU clock cycles to retrieve all the data and continue. To alleviate this problem, the target headers were segregated in their own block of shared memory so that every bank was used on every read and presented at most a two-way bank conflict per iteration. This change alone gave us a 35% speed increase.

Each CUDA multiprocessor on the GeForce 8600 graphics card that we used has only 8192 registers, although later architectures have more. This meant that the number of registers a given thread used was very important (a block of 256 threads all wanting 24 registers requires $256 \times 24 = 6114$ registers, so only one block would be able to execute at a time). A variety of efforts were made to reduce the number of registers in use in the program, the most successful of which involved passing permutations on kernel parameters as additional kernel parameters instead of using extra registers to compute them. Generally, though, the NVCC compiler seemed to do a good job of optimizing for low register count where possible, and almost nothing we tried successfully reduced the number further.

12.3.4 Target Processing

Because so little time is required to do a simple comparison operation, the algorithm was bottlenecked in the global memory bus. A significant performance increase was obtained by creating the subtargets (sub-byte shifts of targets to compensate for the encoding mechanism discussed earlier in this chapter) on the fly on the GPU instead of pregenerating them on the CPU and then reading them in. On the CPU, of course, the extra steps were a significant drain; *not* doing on-the-fly shifting increased performance by roughly 30%. On CUDA, *doing* on-the-fly preprocessing increased performance by about 3% initially, with much more significant benefit later owing to the decreased memory bandwidth involved in moving only one-quarter as much target data into local shared memory.

12.3.5 CUDA Kernel Parameter Settings

The single most significant change in the development of the CUDA version of the algorithm occurred when the kernel parameters (threads per block, targets per kernel, and cache size per block) were first optimized. To do this, a massive systematic search of the entire kernel parameter space was made, seeking a global optimum operating point. The resulting optimum parameters are listed in Table 12.2.

Great care needs to be exercised when selecting these options for a number of reasons. First, there are limited amounts of cache and registers available to each multiprocessor, so setting threads/block

Table 12.2 Optimized kernel execution parameters.

Threads/block	64
Shared cache size	7950 bytes/block
Blocks/kernel	319

or cache size too large can result in processors having to idle because memory resources are taxed. Additionally, the overhead required to get each block started incurred a penalty for blocks that do too little work, so very small blocks are not advisable. Finally, if blocks ran too long, the OS watchdog timer interfered with execution and manually yanked back control, crashing the kernel and providing impetus to keep blocks/kernel relatively small. One aid we used in setting these parameters was the CUDA Occupancy Calculator, which predicts the effects of execution parameters on GPU utilization [4]. The advice of this calculator should be taken with a grain of salt, however, as it cannot know how parameter changes affect the speed of the code itself within each block, but it provides a good indication of how fully the device is being utilized.

12.3.6 Additional Smaller Threads

Midway through the project, the CUDA kernel underwent a significant overhaul (the difference between Kernel 0 and Kernel 1 in Figure 12.3). The biggest change came from a desire to reduce the workload of each individual thread. Additional, smaller threads tend to perform better in CUDA, especially if each thread is linked to a proportionate amount of shared memory — the smaller the task, the less shared memory it requires, and the more threads can run. In Kernel 1, targets and subtargets were cached in shared memory, so having each thread do just one subtarget instead of an entire target resulted in a very significant speedup in the long term. Eventually, however, genome hashing forced Kernel 1 to be changed back to one target per thread because the genome locations for successive comparisons were not consecutive.

12.3.7 Combined CUDA and CPU Execution

Using both CUDA and the CPU version of the algorithm seemed like a logical next step, and indeed, doing this improved performance. Some issues became apparent, however, in the loop that waits for CUDA to finish. Out of the box, CUDA is set up to "hot idle" the CPU until the kernel is done, keeping CPU usage at 100% and prohibiting it from doing other tasks. To mitigate this, we used a different approach that queried the device for kernel completion only once every 2–6 ms, using the rest of the time to run comparisons with the CPU version of the algorithm. In this mode, both CPU and GPU see a slight performance hit, but the combined totals still outweigh either individually in our development dataset.

12.3.8 Gaps and Mismatches

Commercial implementations of the short read genome matching problem allow a set number of mismatches between the target and the genome match location, as well as "gaps" — regions of code

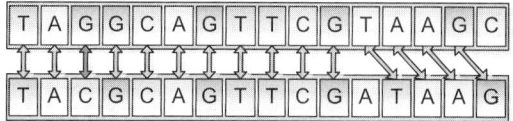

FIGURE 12.6

Example of a compare operation containing a gap and a mismatch.

inserted in either the genome or the target before the match continues (see Figure 12.6). A little binary trickery [1] allowed mismatches to be implemented beyond the 16 BP header region with only a slight performance hit. However, to find mismatches in the target header with hashing enabled, all targets would need to be requeried using a header and hash key from a different part of the target (see Figure 12.6). This would require all targets to be compared twice to find a mismatch, once for each header, and would reduce performance by more than 50%. This feature has not yet been fully implemented, and so is not reported in any other results, but the fundamental challenges have been overcome. The current code also does not yet support gaps, but once multiple headers for mismatches are in place, it simply makes the comparison operation more complex, reducing performance by an unpleasant, but tolerable, measure.

12.3.9 Genome/Target Hashing

The greatest single performance improvement throughout the development of the algorithm came when the genome was hashed into bins, with each bin containing a list of offsets where the sequence matches the same first eight base pairs. This approach is taken by the majority of commercial solutions to this problem, and for good reason. Once targets were similarly binned, only compare operations in the same bin needed to be executed, reducing the total number of comparison operations 2^{16}-fold. Information about the genome offsets for each bin was given to the kernel in a texture, utilizing the GPU's cache locality to try to ensure that the next offset needed was readily available in cache. Even just a crude first-round implementation of this feature increased performance by nearly 10x, though the hashing process (which is actually quite quick) was treated as a preprocess, and thus is not included in the performance metrics in Figure 12.3.

12.3.10 Scaling Performance

In order to gauge how well this solution scales to larger problems, we tested the algorithm against two real-world datasets that push our GeForce 8600's memory resources to their limit. In each case, wild cards ("N"s) within the genome were ignored, and targets were required to contain no wild cards. The first dataset uses our development test genome (used to create Figure 12.3), Linkage Group VII from the sequenced *Neurospora crassa* genome, and searches a target list of slightly more than 3.4 million 36 base-pair segments. The second dataset consists of the first 5.0 million base pairs of chromosome 1 of *N. crassa* and a list of 1.0 million 76 base-pair targets. Table 12.3 shows the compare times with the most recent version of the algorithm running in CUDA-only mode as well as both CUDA and CPU combined. For reference, one run of the first dataset was limited to only 1.0 million base pairs as well.

Table 12.3 Large dataset performance results.

Dataset	Genome BP	Target Count	Target Length (BP)	Compare Time (CUDA)	Targets/ Second (CUDA)	Compare Time (Both)	Targets/ Second (Both)
1*	3,938,688	1,000,000	36	24.7 s	40,400	9.7 s	103,000
1*	3,938,688	3,419,999	76	48.2 s	70,900	22.3 s	153,000
2+	5,000,000	1,000,000	76	62.2 s	16,100	38.8 s	25,800

*Linkage group VII of Neurospora crassa. +First 5 MBP of chromosome 1 of Neurospora crassa.

These numbers appear significantly higher than the numbers reported in Figure 12.3 because of the comparatively few exact matches present in these datasets, which reduces the number of expensive writes to global memory. This is to be expected for this application.

12.4 FINAL EVALUATION AND VALIDATION OF RESULTS, TOTAL BENEFITS, AND LIMITATIONS

Our application provided an excellent platform to explore the tuning characteristics of this relatively new computing platform. Much was learned about memory access and kernel execution parameters, which are sensitive aspects of CUDA programs that differ significantly from traditional CPU design problems, but can both have a large impact on performance.

Even after over a year of development, we believe that the algorithm is still far from optimized and that more performance gains can still be expected. Limitations in the handling of gaps and mismatches and in the size of datasets can be overcome with additional development. Additionally, the handling of wild card "N" base pairs in the genome is implemented, but requires further validation. Handling of wild cards in targets is theoretically possible, but was omitted to simplify the algorithm and because it was not one of our customer's requirements.

Ultimately, this project serves as an example to other CUDA developers solving similar search-and-match problems. It seeks to provide ideas of ways to optimize such codes, as well as information about the relative effectiveness of these techniques in this specific case.

12.5 FUTURE DIRECTIONS

Then next steps for this algorithm are fairly obvious. Final verification and benchmarking of mismatches and support for gaps and larger datasets are the immediate next steps. Farther down the road, implementing gaps and benchmarking against industry-standard solutions to this problem present themselves as important future objectives. As new generations of CUDA hardware and the NVCC compiler are released, the optimizations presented here must be tweaked and updated, adjusting to new intricacies on new hardware.

References

[1] S.E. Anderson, Bit Twiddling Hacks, Stanford University. Available from: `http://www.graphics.stanford.edu/~seander/bithacks.html`.

[2] H. Li, J. Ruan, R. Durbin, Mapping short DNA sequencing reads and calling variants using mapping quality scores, Genome Res. 18 (2008) 1851–1858.

[3] Y. Liu, D.L. Maskell, B. Schmidt, CUDASW++: optimizing Smith-Waterman sequence database searches for CUDA-enabled graphics processing units, BMC Res. Notes 2 (1) (2009) 73. Available from: `http://www.biomedcentral.com/1756-0500/2/73/citation`.

[4] CUDA Occupancy Calculator, NVIDIA (2008). Available from: `http://developer.download.nvidia.com/compute/cuda/CUDA_Occupancy_calculator.xls`.

[5] NVIDIA CUDA Compute Unified Device Architecture Programmers Guide, NVIDIA Corp. (1.1) (2009) 56–61. Available from: `http://developer.download.nvidia.com/compute/cuda/1_1/NVIDIA_CUDA_Programming_Guide_1.1.pdf`.

[6] T.F. Smith, M.S. Waterman, Identification of common molecular subsequences, J. Mol. Biol. 147 (1) (1981) 195–197.

[7] C. Trapnell, S. Salzberg, How to map billions of short reads onto genomes, Nat. Biotechnol. 27 (5) (2009) 455–457.

[8] C. Trapnell, M.C. Schatz, Optimizing data intensive GPGPU computations for DNA sequence alignment, Parallel Comput. 35 (8–9) (2009) 429–440.

GPU-Supercomputer Acceleration of Pattern Matching

13

Ali Khajeh-Saeed, J. Blair Perot

This chapter describes the solution of a single very large pattern-matching search using a supercomputing cluster of GPUs. The objective is to compare a query sequence that has a length on the order of $10^2 - 10^6$ with a "database" sequence that has a size on the order of roughly 10^8, and find the locations where the test sequence best matches parts of the database sequence. Finding the optimal matches that can account for gaps and mismatches in the sequences is a problem that is nontrivial to parallelize. This study examines how to achieve efficient parallelism for this problem on a single GPU and between the GPUs when they have a relatively slow interconnect.

13.1 INTRODUCTION, PROBLEM STATEMENT, AND CONTEXT

Pattern matching in the presence of noise and uncertainty is an important computational problem in a variety of fields. It is widely used in computational biology and bioinformatics. In that context DNA or amino acid sequences are typically compared with a genetic database. More recently optimal pattern-matching algorithms have been applied to voice and image analysis, as well as to the data mining of scientific simulations of physical phenomena.

The Smith-Waterman (SW) algorithm is a dynamic programming algorithm for finding the optimal alignment between two sequences once the relative penalty for mismatches and gaps in the sequences is specified. For example, given two RNA sequences, CAGCCUCGCUUAG (the database) and AAUGC-CAUUGCCGG (the test sequence), the optimal region of overlap (when the gap penalties are specified according to the SSCA #1 benchmark) is shown below in bold

CAGCC-UCGCUUAG

AAUGCCAUUGCCGG

The optimal match between these two sequences is eight items long and requires the insertion of one gap in the database and the toleration of one mismatch (the third-to-last character in the match) as well as a shifting of the starting point of the query sequence. The SW algorithm determines the optimal alignment by constructing a table that involves an entry for the combination of every item of the query sequence and in the database sequence. When either sequence is large, constructing this table is a computationally intensive task. In general, it is also a relatively difficult algorithm to parallelize because every item in the table depends on all the values above it and to its left.

This chapter discusses the algorithm changes necessary to solve a single very large SW problem on many Internet-connected GPUs in a way that is scalable to any number of GPUs and to any problem size. Prior work on the SW algorithm on GPUs [1] has focused on the quite different problem of solving many (roughly 400,000) entirely independent small SW problems of different sizes (but averaging about 1k by 1k) on a single GPU [2].

Within each GPU this chapter shows how to reformulate the SW algorithm so that it uses a memory-efficient parallel scan to circumvent the inherent dependencies. Between GPUs, the algorithm is modified in order to reduce inter-GPU communication.

13.2 CORE METHOD

Given two possible sequences (A and B), such as those shown in the preceding section, sequence alignment strives to find the best matching subsequences from the original pair. The best match is defined by the formula

$$J = \sum_{i=a}^{b} [S(A(i), B(i+c))] - W(G_s, G_e)$$

where W is a gap function that can insert gaps in either or both sequences A and B for some penalty, and S is a similarity score. The goal in sequence alignment is to find the start and end points (a and b) and the shift (c) that maximizes the alignment score J.

This problem can be solved by constructing a table (as in Figure 13.1) where each entry in the table, $H_{i,j}$, is given by the formula,

$$H_{i,j} = Max \begin{cases} Max\left(H_{i-1,j-1} + S_{i,j}, 0\right) \\ \underset{0<k<i}{Max}\left(H_{i-k,j} - (G_s + kG_e)\right) \\ \underset{0<k<j}{Max}\left(H_{i,j-k} - (G_s + kG_e)\right) \end{cases}$$

where G_s is the gap start penalty, G_e is the gap extension penalty, and k is the gap length. Each table entry has dependencies on other H values (shown in Figure 13.2) that makes parallel calculations of the H values difficult.

Prior work on GPUs has focused on problems that involve solving many independent SW problems. For example the Swiss-Prot protein database (release 56.6) consists of 405,506 separate protein sequences. The proteins in this database have an average sequence length of 360 amino acids each. In this type of alignment problem, it is possible to perform many separate SW tests in parallel (one for each of the many proteins). Each thread (or sometimes a thread block) independently calculates a separate table. Performing many separate SW problems is a static load-balancing problem because the many problems are different sizes. But having many separate problems to work on removes the dependency issue.

However, in this work we wish to solve a single large SW problem. For example, each human chromosome contains on the order of 10^8 nucleic acid base pairs. When one is interested in the interstitial sequences between the active genes, there are no clear breaks in this sequence, and it must be searched in its entirety. Similarly, searching a voice sequence for a particular word generally requires searching the entire voice stream (also roughly 10^8 long) in its entirety.

	0	C	A	G	C	C	U	C	G	C	U	U	A	G
0	0	0	0	0	0	0	0	0	0	0	0	0	0	0
A	0	0	5	0	0	0	0	0	0	0	0	0	5	0
A	0	0	5	2	0	0	0	0	0	0	0	0	5	2
U	0	0	0	2	0	0	5	0	0	0	5	5	0	2
G	0	0	0	5	0	0	0	2	5	0	0	2	2	5
C	0	5	0	0	10	5	0	5	0	10	1	0	0	0
C	0	5	2	0	5	15	6	5	4	5	7	1	0	0
A	0	0	10	1	0	6	12	3	2	1	2	4	6	0
U	0	0	1	7	0	5	11	9	1	0	6	7	1	3
U	0	0	0	0	4	4	10	8	6	0	5	11	4	1
G	0	0	0	5	0	3	1	7	13	4	3	2	8	9
C	0	5	0	0	10	5	0	6	4	18	9	8	7	6
C	0	5	2	0	5	15	6	5	4	9	15	6	5	4
G	0	0	2	7	0	6	12	3	10	8	6	12	3	10
G	0	0	0	7	4	5	3	9	8	7	5	3	9	8

FIGURE 13.1

Similarity table and best alignment for two small sequences CAGCCUCGCUUAG (top) and AAUGCCAUUGCCGG (left). The best alignment is highlighted in light gray values terminated by the Bold value (maximal) score.

Unlike prior work, this chapter on parallelizing the SW algorithm for GPUs does not assume the database can be split into many parallel tasks. We desire to present a parallel formulation that is applicable to an arbitrarily large query sequence or database sequence and to any number of GPUs.

13.3 ALGORITHMS, IMPLEMENTATIONS, AND EVALUATIONS

There are a number of optimizations to the SW algorithm that are relevant to this discussion. They are detailed in the next sections.

13.3.1 Reduced Dependency

The dependency requirements (and work) of the SW algorithm can be significantly reduced at the expense of using additional memory by using the three-variable formula,

$$E_{i,j} = Max\left(E_{i,j-1}, H_{i,j-1} - G_s\right) - G_e$$
$$F_{i,j} = Max\left(F_{i-1,j}, H_{i-1,j} - G_s\right) - G_e$$
$$H_{i,j} = Max\left(H_{i-1,j-1} + S_{i,j},\ E_{i,j}, F_{i,j}, 0\right)$$

where $E_{i,j}$ is the modified row maximum and $F_{i,j}$ is the modified column maximum. The dependencies for this algorithm are shown in Figure 13.3. Figure 13.3 shows the $H_{i,j}$ values for the table, but each

	0	C	A	G	C	C	U	C	G	C	U	U	A	G
0	0	0	0	0	0	0	0	0	0	0	0	0	0	0
A	0	0	5	0	0	0	0	0	0					
A	0	0	5	2	0	0	0	0	0					
U	0	0	0	2	0	0	5	0	0					
G	0	0	0	5	0	0	0	2	5					
C	0	5	0	0	10	5	0	5	0					
C	0	5	2	0	5	15	6	5	4					
A														
U														
U														
G														
C														
C														
G														
G														

FIGURE 13.2

Dependency of the values in the Smith-Waterman table. The gray values in the tables determine the value in the lower right corner.

table entry now actually stores a triplet of values ($H_{i,j}$, $E_{i,j}$, and $F_{i,j}$). This algorithm nominally requires reading five items and writing three items for every cell update. The five additions and three *Max* operations are very fast compared with the memory operations, so the SW algorithm is typically memory bound.

13.3.2 Antidiagonal Approach

The SW algorithm can be parallelized by operating along the antidiagonal. Figure 13.4 shows (in gray) the cells that can be updated in parallel. If the three-variable approach is used, then the entire table does not need to be stored. An antidiagonal row can be updated from the previous E and F antidiagonal row, and the previous two antidiagonal rows of H. The algorithm can then store the i and j location of the maximum H value so far. When the entire table has been searched, it is then possible to return to the maximum location and rebuild the small portion of the table necessary to reconstruct the alignment subsequences.

The antidiagonal method has start-up and shut-down issues that make it somewhat unattractive to program. It is inefficient (by a factor of roughly 50%) if the two input sequences have similar sizes. For very dissimilar sized input sequences, the maximum length of the antidiagonal row is the minimum of the two input sequence lengths. On a GPU we would like to operate with roughly 128 to 256 threads

	0	C	A	G	C	C	U	C	G	C	U	U	A	G
0	0	0	0	0	0	0	0	0	0	0	0	0	0	0
A	0	0	5	0	0	0	0	0	0					
A	0	0	5	2	0	0	0	0	0					
U	0	0	0	2	0	0	5	0	0					
G	0	0	0	5	0	0	0	2	5					
C	0	5	0	0	10	5	0	5	0					
C	0	5	2	0	5	15	6	5	4					
A														
U														
U														
G														
C														
C														
G														
G														

FIGURE 13.3

Dependencies in the three-variable Smith-Waterman table. The gray values in the tables determine the value in the lower right corner.

per block and at least two blocks per multiprocessor (32-60 blocks). This means that we need query sequences of length 10^4 or greater to efficiently occupy the GPU using the antidiagonal method. This is an order of magnitude larger than a typical query sequence.

The antidiagonal method can not operate entirely with just registers and shared memory. The inherent algorithm dependencies still require extensive communication of the values of H, F, and E between the threads.

13.3.3 Row (or Column) Parallel Approach

If a parallel scan is used, the SW algorithm can be parallelized along rows or columns [3]. The row/column parallel algorithm takes three steps. The first step involves a temporary variable, $\tilde{H}_{i,j}$. A row of $\tilde{H}$ is computed in parallel from previous row data via

$$F_{i,j} = Max\left(F_{i-1,j}, H_{i-1,j} - G_s\right) - G_e$$
$$\tilde{H}_{i,j} = Max\left(H_{i-1,j-1} + S_{i,j}, F_{i,j}, 0\right)$$

	0	C	A	G	C	C	U	C	G	C	U	U	A	G
0	0	0	0	0	0	0	0	0	0	0	0	0	0	0
A	0	0	5	0	0	0	0	0	0	0	?			
A	0	0	5	2	0	0	0	0	0	?				
U	0	0	0	2	0	0	5	0	?					
G	0	0	0	5	0	0	0	?						
C	0	5	0	0	10	5	?							
C	0	5	2	0	5	?								
A	0	0	10	1	?									
U	0	0	1	?										
U	0	0	?											
G	0	?												
C	0													
C	0													
G	0													
G	0													

FIGURE 13.4

Antidiagonal parallelism. All the question table entries can be computed in parallel, using the prior two antidiagonals and the sequence data.

The variable $\tilde{E}_{i,j}$ is then used instead of $E_{i,j}$ and is given by $\tilde{E}_{i,j} = \underset{1<k<j}{Max}\left(\tilde{H}_{i,j-k} - kG_e\right)$ which can be computed efficiently using a modified parallel maximum scan of the previous $\tilde{H}$ row. Finally, the values of H are computed in parallel for the new row using the expression

$$H_{i,j} = Max\left(\tilde{H}_{i,j}, \tilde{E}_{i,j} - G_s\right)$$

In this algorithm the first step and the last steps are entirely local. Data from a different thread is not required. The dependency problem is forced entirely into the parallel scan. Efficient methods to perform this scan on the GPU are well understood. We simply need to modify them slightly to account for the gap extension penalty G_e. These code modifications are presented in the Appendix. The row parallel SW algorithm is also attractive on GPUs because it leads to sequential coalesced memory accesses. One row of the calculation is shown in Figure 13.5.

The parallel scan can be adapted to work on many GPUs. It requires sending one real number from each GPU in the middle of the scan (between the up and the down sweeps of the scan algorithm). The results presented in this chapter do not use this approach. Although the amount of data being sent is small, this approach still produces a synchronization point between the GPUs that can

		0	C	A	G	C	C	U	C	G	C	U	U	A	G
H	C	0	5	0	0	10	5	0	5	0	10	1	0	0	0
F		0	-4	-4	-4	-4	-4	-4	-4	-4	-4	-4	-4	-4	-4
$\widetilde{H}$		0	5	2	0	5	15	2	5	2	5	7	0	0	0
$\widetilde{\widetilde{E}}$	C	0	-1	4	3	2	4	14	13	12	11	10	9	8	7
H		0	5	2	0	5	15	6	5	4	5	7	1	0	0
F		0	-5	-5	-4	-5	-5	-5	-5	-4	-5	-5	-5	-5	-4

FIGURE 13.5

An example of the calculations in a row-parallel scan Smith-Waterman algorithm. This example is calculating the sixth row from the fifth row data (of the example problem shown in Figure 13.1).

reduce the parallel efficiency. Instead, the idea of overlapping, described next, is used for the inter-GPU parallelism.

13.3.4 Overlapping Search

If an upper bound is known a priori for the length of the alignment subsequences that will result from the search, it is possible to start the SW search algorithm somewhere in the middle of the table. This allows an entirely different approach to parallelism. Figure 13.6 shows an example where the database sequence has been broken into four overlapping parts. If the region of overlap is wider than any subsequence that is found, then each part of the database can be searched independently. The algorithm will start each of the four searches with zeros in the left column. This is correct for the first section, but not for the other sections. Nevertheless, by the time that the end of the overlap region has been reached, the table values computed by the other sections will be the correct values.

This means that in the overlap region the values computed from the section on the overlap region's left are the correct values. The values computed at the beginning of the section that extends to the right are incorrect and are ignored (in the overlap region) for the purposes of determining best alignment subsequences.

This approach to parallelism is attractive for partitioning the problem onto the different GPUs. It does not require any communication at all between the GPUs except a transfer of the overlapping part of the database sequence at the beginning of the computation and a collection (and sorting) of the best alignments at the very end. This approach also partitions a large database into much more easily handled/accessed database sections. The cost to be paid lies in the duplicate computation that is occurring in the overlap regions and the fact that the amount of overlap must be estimated before the computation occurs.

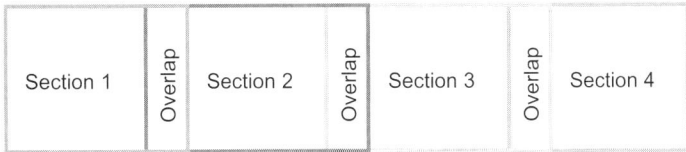

FIGURE 13.6

Example of the overlapping approach to parallelism.

For a 10^8 long database on 100 GPUs, each GPU handles a database section of a million items. If the expected subsequence alignments are less than 10^4 long, the overlap is less than 1% of the total computation. However, if we were to try to extend this approach to produce parallelism at the block level (with 100 blocks on each GPU), the amount of overlap being computed would be 100%, which would be quite inefficient. Thread-level parallelism using this approach (assuming 128 threads per block and no more than 10% overlap) would require that subsequences be guaranteed to be less than eight items long. This is far too small, so thread-level parallelism is not possible using overlapping. The approach used in this chapter, which only uses overlapping at the GPU level, can efficiently handle potential subsequence alignments that are comparable to the size of the database section being computed on each GPU (sizes up to 10^6 in our current example). For larger alignments, the GPU parallel scan would be necessary.

13.3.5 Data Packing

Because the SW algorithm is memory constrained, one simple method to improve the performance significantly is to pack the sequence data and the intermediate table values. For example, when one is working with DNA or RNA sequences, there are only four possibilities (2 bits) for each item in the sequence. Sixteen RNA items can therefore be stored in a single 32-bit integer, increasing the performance of the memory reads to the sequence data by a factor of 16. Similarly, for protein problems 5 bits are sufficient to represent one amino acid resulting in 6 amino acids per 32-bit integer read (or write).

The bits required for the table values are limited by the maximum expected length of the subsequence alignments and by the similarity scoring system used for a particular problem. The Scalable Synthetic Compact Application (SSCA) No. 1 benchmark sets the similarity value to 5 for a match, so the maximum table values will be less than or equal to 5* (the alignment length). Therefore, 16 bits are sufficient for sequences of length up to 10^4.

Data packing is problem dependent, so we have not implemented it in our code distribution (web site), or used it to improve the speed of the results presented in the subsequent sections.

13.3.6 Hash Tables

Some commonly used SW derivatives (such as FASTA and BLAST) use heuristics to improve the search speed. One common heuristic is to insist upon perfect matching of the first n items before a subsequence is evaluated as a potential possibility for an optimal alignment. This step and some preprocessing of the database allow the first n items of each query sequence to be used as a hash table to reduce the search space.

For example, if the first four items are required to match perfectly, then there are 16 possibilities for the first four items. The database is then preprocessed into a linked list with 16 heads. Each linked list head points to the first location in the database of that particular four-item string, and each location in the database points to the next location of that same type.

In theory this approach can reduce the computational work by roughly a factor of 2^n. It also eliminates the optimality of the SW algorithm. If the first eight items of a 64-item final alignment must match exactly, there is roughly a 12.5% chance that the alignment found is actually suboptimal. On a single CPU, the BLAST and FASTA programs typically go about 60 times faster than optimal SW.

Because this type of optimization is very problem dependent and is difficult to parallelize, we have not included it in our code or the following results.

13.4 **FINAL EVALUATION**

Lincoln is a National Science Foundation (NSF) Teragrid GPU cluster located at National Center for Supercomputing Applications (NCSA). Lincoln has 96 Tesla S1070 servers (384 Tesla GPUs). Each of Lincoln's 192 servers holds two Intel 64 (Harpertown) 2.33 GHz dual-socket quad-core processors with 2 × 6 MB L2 cache and 2 GB of RAM per core. Each server CPU (with four cores) is connected to one of the Tesla GPUs via PCI-e Gen2 X8 slots. All code was written in C++ with NVIDIA's CUDA language extensions for the GPU. The results were compiled using Red Hat Enterprise Linux 4 (Linux 2.6.19) and the GCC compiler.

The SW algorithm is implemented as two kernels. The first kernel identifies the end points of the best sequence matches by constructing the SW table. This is the computationally intensive part of the algorithm. The best end-point locations are saved but not the table values. Once the best sequences end points are found (200 of them in this test), the second kernel goes back and determines the actual sequences by reconstructing small parts of the table and using a trace-back procedure. The second kernel is less amenable to efficient implementation on the GPU (we devote one GPU block to each trace-back operation), but it is also not very computationally intensive. Splitting the two tasks, rather than identifying the sequences on the fly as they are found, prevents the GPUs from getting stalled during the computationally expensive task.

Timings for five different NVIDIA GPUs and one core of an AMD CPU (quad-core Phenom II X4 CPU operating at 3.2 GHz, with 4 × 512 KB of L2 cache, 6 MB of L3 cache) are shown in Figure 13.7. Speedups over the CPU of close to a factor of 100 can be obtained on table sizes (query sequence size times database size) that are larger than 1B. The CPU code has been compiled with optimization on (−03), but the algorithm itself was not hand optimized (by using MMX instructions, for example).

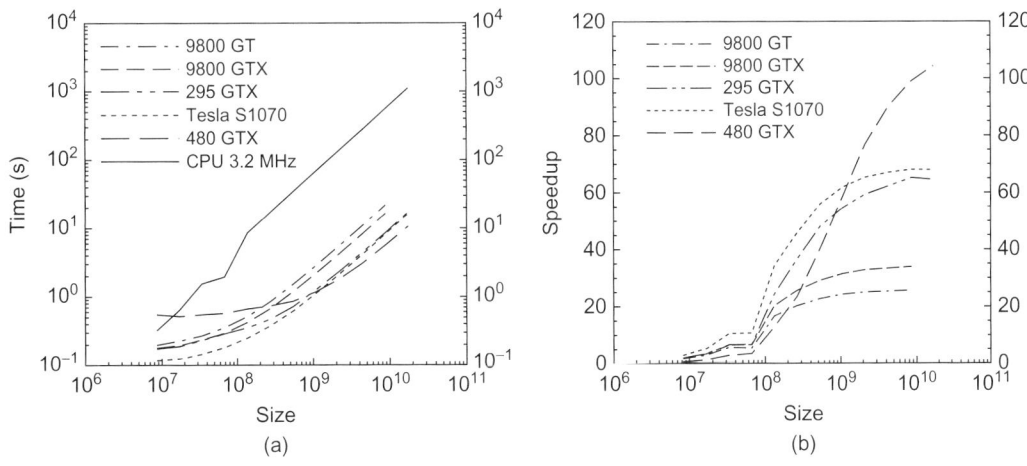

FIGURE 13.7

Performance of a single GPU for the Smith-Waterman algorithm (kernel 1) for a test sequence of 1024 and various database sizes. The size axis refers to the total table size. (a) Time. (b) Speedup versus one core of a 3.2 GHz AMD quad-core Phenom II X4 CPU.

A single GPU can search for an optimal match of a 1000 long query sequence in a 1M long database in roughly 1 second. In contrast the time to determine the 200 sequences corresponding to the 200 best matches (kernel 2) is about 0.02 seconds on the CPU, and this calculation is independent of the database size. The GPUs were programmed to perform this task, but they took 0.055 seconds (for the 8800 GT) to 0.03 seconds for the 295 GTX. With shorter query sequences, 128 long instead of the 512 long sequences quoted earlier in this chapter, the GPU outperforms the CPU on kernel 2 by about three times. The impact of kernel 2 on the total algorithm time is negligible in all cases.

When the problem size is held constant and the number of processors is varied, we obtain strong scaling results. Figure 13.8 shows the speedup obtained when a 16M long database is searched with a 128 long query sequence on Lincoln. Ideally, the speedup in this case should be linear with the number of GPUs. In practice, as the number of GPUs increases, the problem size per GPU decreases, and small problem sizes are less efficient on the GPU. When 120 GPUs are working on this problem, each GPU is only constructing a subtable of roughly size 10^7. From Figure 13.7 it is clear that this size is an order of magnitude too small to be reasonably efficient on the GPU.

Weak scaling allows the problem size to grow proportionally with the number of GPUs so that the work per GPU remains constant. The cell updates per second (GCUPS) for this weak-scaled problem are shown in Figure 13.9a, when 2 M elements per GPU are used for the database size, and a 128-element query sequence is used. Because the amount of work being performed increases proportionally with the number of GPUs used, the GCUPS should be linear as the number of GPUs is increased. However, the time increases slightly because of the increased communication burden between GPUs as their number is increased. The total time varies from 270 ms to 350 ms, and it increases fairly slowly with the number of GPUs used. Figure 13.9b shows speedups for kernel 1 on the Lincoln supercomputer

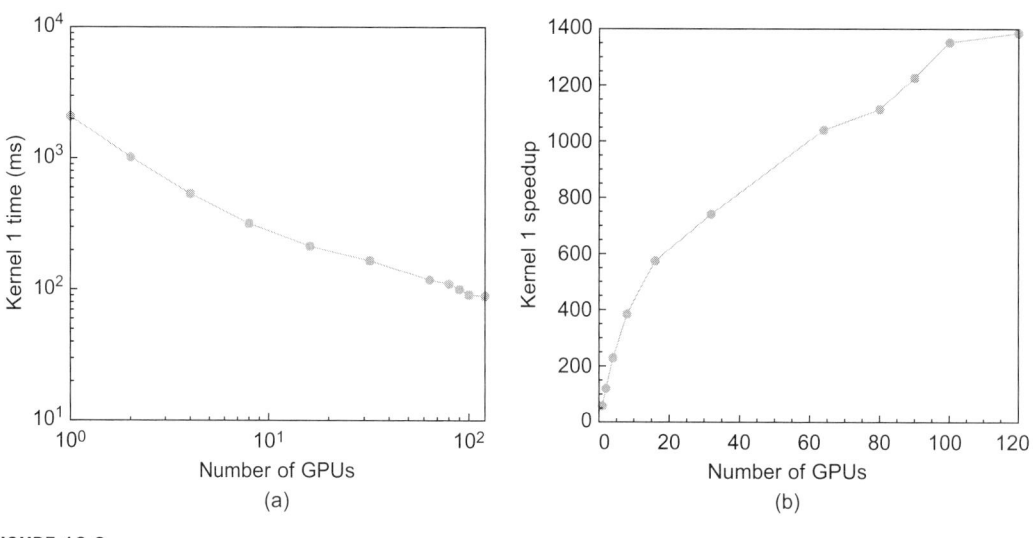

(a)   (b)

FIGURE 13.8

Strong scaling timings with 16 M for database and 128 for test sequence. (a) Time. (b) Speedup versus one core of a 3.2 GHz AMD quad-core Phenom II X4 CPU.

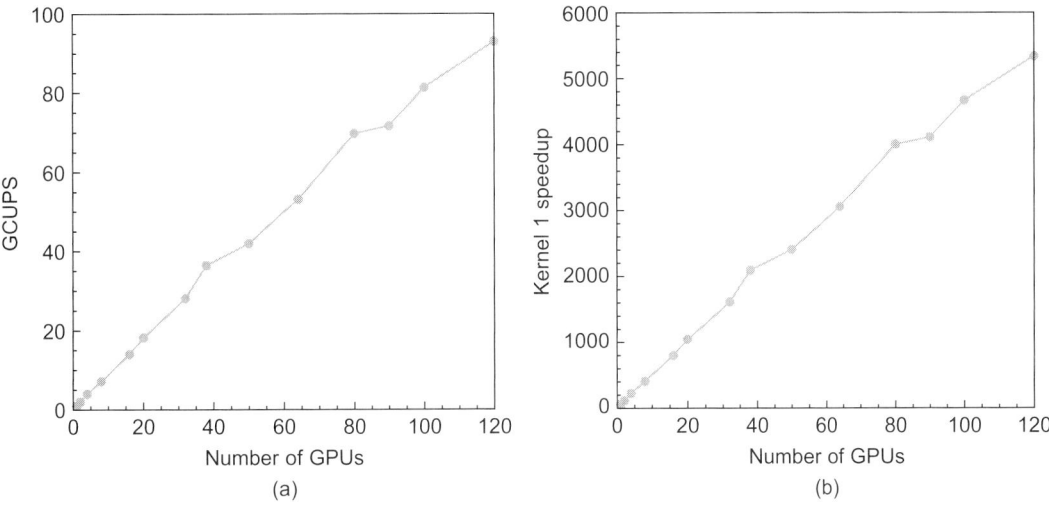

FIGURE 13.9

Weak scaling GCUPS (a) and speedups (b) for kernel 1 using various numbers of GPUs on Lincoln with 2 M elements per GPU for the database size and a 128-element test sequence.

compared with a single-CPU core of an AMD quad-core. Compared with a single CPU core, the speedup is almost 56x, for a single GPU, and 5335x, for 120 GPUs (44x faster per GPU).

The current implementation keeps track of the location of the highest 200 alignment scores on each GPU. This list changes dynamically as the algorithm processes the rows of the table. The first few rows cause many changes to this list. The changes are then less frequent, but still require continual sorting of the list. This portion of the code takes about 2% of the total time. The breakdown for the other three steps of the algorithm is shown in Table 13.1.

The scan is the most expensive part of the three steps. This scan was adapted from an SDK distribution that accounts for bank conflicts and is probably performing at close to the peak possible efficiency. If a single SW problem is being solved on the GPU, then the problem is inherently coupled. The row-parallel algorithm isolates the dependencies in the Smith-Waterman problem as much as is possible, and solves for those dependencies as efficiently as possible, using the parallel scan.

The maximum memory bandwidth that can be achieved on Lincoln is close to 85 GB/s for a single GPU. Based on our algorithm (7 memory accesses per cell) the maximum theoretical GCUPS is close to 3.0 (85/4/7) for a single GPU. Since this code obtains 1.04 GCUPS per GPU, the algorithm is

Table 13.1 Breakdown of the Smith-Waterman algorithm.

	Top 200	$\tilde{H}$ and F	Scan for $\tilde{E}$	H
295 GTX	2%	30%	48%	20%
480 GTX	3%	27%	54%	16%

reasonably efficient (34% of the peak memory throughput). Higher GCUPS rates for a single GPU would be possible by using problem dependent optimizations such as data packing or hash tables.

The row parallel algorithm doesn't have any limitation on the query or database sequence sizes. For example, a database length of 4M per GPU was compared with a query sequence of 1M. This query took 4229 seconds on Lincoln and 2748 seconds on the 480 GTX. This works out to 1.03 and 1.6 GCUPS per GPU for the Tesla S1070 and 480 GTX GPUs respectively. This is very similar to the performance obtained for smaller test sequences, because the algorithm works row by row and is therefore independent of the number of rows (which equals the query or test sequence size).

13.5 FUTURE DIRECTION

One way to optimize this algorithm further is to combine the three steps into a single GPU call. The key to this approach is being able to synchronize the threads within the kernel, because each step of the algorithm must be entirely completed (for all threads) before the next step can be executed. The first synchronization point is after finishing the up-sweep step of the parallel scan, and second one is after finding the value for H. At both GPU synchronization points one number per block must be written to the global memory. All other data items are then kept in the shared memory (it is possible to use registers for some data), so the number of access to the global memory is reduced to 3 per cell update. Early indications have been that within experimental error, this approach is not faster than the approach of issuing separate GPU kernel calls to enforce synchronization of the threads.

Because the algorithm operates row-by-row the query size (number of rows) is entirely arbitrary and limited only by the patience of the user. In contrast, the database size is restricted by the total memory available from all the GPUs (so less than 10^{11} when using 100 Tesla GPUs). In practice human patience expires before the database memory is exhausted.

Acknowledgments

This work was supported by the Department of Defense and used resources from the Extreme Scale Systems Center at Oak Ridge National Laboratory. Some of this work occurred on the NSF Teragrid supercomputer, Lincoln, located at NCSA.

Appendix

The most important part of a row parallel approach for the GPU is the contiguous and coalesced access to the memory that this algorithm allows and the fact that the level of small-scale parallelism is now equal to the *maximum* of the query sequence and the database lengths.

Each step of the row parallel approach can be optimized for the GPU. In the first step (when calculating $\tilde{H}_{i,j}$), two H values are needed ($H_{i-1,j-1}$, $H_{i-1,j}$). To enable coalesced memory accesses and minimize accesses to the global memory, H values are first copied to the shared memory. The second step of the algorithm (that calculates the $\tilde{E}_{i,j}$) uses a modification of the *scanLargeArray* code found in the SDK of CUDA 2.2. This code implements a work-efficient parallel sum scan [4]. The work-efficient parallel scan has two sweeps, an Up-Sweep and a Down-Sweep. The formulas for the original Up-sweep sum scan (from the SDK) and for our modified scan are shown at the end of this paragraph. The major change is to change the sum to a max, and then to modify the max arguments (terms in bold).

Sum Scan	Modified Scan
for d = 0 to Log₂n − 1 *in parallel for k = 0 to n − 1 by* 2^{d+1} $\tilde{E}[k + 2^{d+1} − 1] += \tilde{E}[k + 2^d − 1]$	*for d = 0 to Log₂n − 1* *in parallel for k = 0 to n − 1 by* 2^{d+1} $\tilde{E}[k + 2^{d+1} − 1] = Max\left(\begin{matrix} \tilde{E}[k + 2^d − 1], \\ \tilde{E}[k + 2^{d+1} − 1] + \mathbf{2^d \times G_e} \end{matrix} \right)$

The formulas for down-sweep for both scans are

Sum Scan	Modified Scan
$\tilde{E}[n − 1] = 0$ *for d = Log₂n − 1 to 0* *in parallel for k = 0 to n − 1 by* 2^{d+1} $Temp = \tilde{E}[k + 2^d − 1]$ $\tilde{E}[k + 2^d − 1] = \tilde{E}[k + 2^{d+1} − 1]$ $\tilde{E}[k + 2^{d+1} − 1] += Temp$	$\tilde{E}[n − 1] = 0$ *for d = Log₂n − 1 to 0* *in parallel for k = 0 to n − 1 by* 2^{d+1} $Temp = \tilde{E}[k + 2^d − 1]$ $\tilde{E}[k + 2^d − 1] = \tilde{E}[k + 2^{d+1} − 1]$ $\tilde{E}[k + 2^{d+1} − 1] = Max\left(\begin{matrix} Temp, \\ \tilde{E}[k + 2^{d+1} − 1] \end{matrix} \right) − \mathbf{2^d \times G_e}$

Detailed implementation of these scan algorithms is presented in reference [5]. This reference explains how this algorithm uses shared memory and avoids bank conflicts. In the *scanLargeArray* code in the SDK, the scan process is recursive. The values in each block are scanned individually and then are corrected by adding the sum from the previous block (this is the *uniformAdd* kernel in the SDK). Our implementation does not perform this last step of the scan. Instead, every block needs the scan result from the previous block (we assume that no alignment sequence has a gap length greater than 1024 within it). Before putting zero in the down-sweep scan for the last element, we save this final number (one for each block) in global memory, and the next block uses this number instead of forcing it to be zero. Only the first block uses zero; the other blocks use the previous block's result.

If one needed to assume gaps greater than 1024 are possible, it is not difficult to modify the existing scan code. *uniformAdd* would need to be replaced with a *uniformMax* subroutine. This would save the last number at the end of the up-sweep, $(G_e)_{old}$. The new value of G_e is related to the number of threads in a block and the level of the recursive scan call. For example, if one uses 512 threads per block for the scan, then

$$(G_e)_{new} = 1024 \times (G_e)_{old}$$

Then in *uniformMax*, the correction is given by

$$\tilde{E} = Max\left(\tilde{E}, \tilde{E}_{Block} - (G_e)_{old} \times ThreadIx\right)$$

$$\tilde{E} = Max\left(\tilde{E}, \tilde{E}_{Block} - (G_e)_{old} \times (ThreadIx + BlockDim)\right)$$

where $\tilde{E}_{Block}$ is the result of the block scan and $(G_e)_{old}$ is the previous gap extension penalty. This *uniformMax* subroutine must be applied to all the elements. In our test cases, *uniformMax* would never cause any change in the results (because all sequences have far fewer than 1024 gaps). The *Max* always returns the first argument.

After the 200 best alignments in kernel 1 are found, sequence extraction is done in kernel 2 with each thread block receiving one sequence end point to trace back. By starting from the end point and constructing the similarity table backward for a short distance, one can actually extract the sequences. For kernel 2 the antidiagonal method is used within each thread block. Because the time is small for kernel 2 and because this kernel is not sensitive to the length of the database, global memory was used. The trace back procedure is summarized below.

$$
\begin{aligned}
&\textit{in parallel for all blocks} \\
&\textit{for } k = 0 \textit{ to } (L_A + L_B - 1) \\
&\quad \textit{if } (k < L_A) \quad iStart = 0 \\
&\quad \textit{else} \qquad\quad iStart = iStart + 1 \\
&\quad iEnd = Min(k+1, L_B) \\
&\quad \textit{in parallel for all threads in block } i = iStart \textit{ to } i = iEnd \\
&\qquad j = k - i \\
&\qquad E_{i+1,j+1} = Max(E_{i+1,j}, H_{i+1,j} - G_s) - G_e \\
&\qquad F_{i+1,j+1} = Max(F_{i,j+1}, H_{i,j+1} - G_s) - G_e \\
&\qquad H_{i+1,j+1} = Max(H_{i,j} + S_{i+1,j+1}, E_{i+1,j+1}, F_{i+1,j+1}, 0)
\end{aligned}
$$

References

[1]   Y. Liu, B. Schmidt, D.L Maskell, CUDASW++2.0: enhanced Smith-Waterman protein database search on CUDA-enabled GPUs based on SIMT and virtualized SIMD abstractions, BMC Res. Notes 3 (2010) 93.

[2]   L. Ligowski, W. Rudnicki, An efficient implementation of Smith Waterman algorithm on GPU using CUDA, for massively parallel scanning of sequence databases, in: 23rd IEEE International Parallel and Distributed Processing Symposium, May 25–29, Aurelia Convention Centre & Expo Rome, Italy, 2009.

[3]   A. Khajeh-Saeed, S. Poole, J.B. Perot, Acceleration of the Smith–Waterman algorithm using single and multiple graphics processors, J. Comput. Phys. 229 (2010) 4247–4258.

[4]   M. Harris, S. Sengupta, J.D. Owens, Parallel prefix sum (scan) with CUDA, in: GPU Gems 3, Chapter 39. NVIDIA Corporation, USA, December 2007.

[5]   S. Sengupta, M. Harris, Y. Zhang, J.D. Owens, Scan primitives for GPU computing, in: Graph. Hardware 2007, San Diego, CA, August 4–5, 2007.

GPU Accelerated RNA Folding Algorithm*

14

Guillaume Rizk, Dominique Lavenier, Sanjay Rajopadhye

In this chapter, we present an implementation of the main kernel in the widely used RNA folding package Unafold. Its key computation is a dynamic programming algorithm with complex dependency patterns, making it an a priori bad match for GPU computing. This study, however, shows that reordering computations in such a way to enable tiled computations and good data reuse can significantly improve GPU performance and yields good speedup compared with optimized CPU implementation that also uses the same approach to tile and vectorize the code.

14.1 PROBLEM STATEMENT

RNA, or ribonucleic acid, is a single-stranded chain of nucleotide units. There are four different nucleotides, also called *bases*: adenine (A), cytosine (C), guanine (G), and uracil (U). Two nucleotides can form a bond, thus forming a *base pair*, according to the Watson-Crick complementarity: A with U, G with C; but also the less stable combination G with U, called wobble base pair. Because RNA is single stranded, it does not have the double-helix structure of DNA. Rather, all the base pairs of a sequence force the nucleotide chain to fold in "on itself" into a system of different recognizable domains like hairpin loops, bulges, interior loops, or stacked regions.

This 2-D space conformation of RNA sequences is called the secondary structure, and many bioinformatics studies require detailed knowledge of this.

Algorithms computing this 2-D folding runs in $\mathcal{O}(n^3)$ complexity, which means computation time quickly becomes prohibitive when dealing with large datasets of long sequences. The first such algorithm was introduced in 1978 by Nussinov, which finds the structure with the largest number of base pairs [1]. In 1981 Zuker and Stiegler proposed an algorithm with a more realistic energy model than simply the count of the number of pairs [2]. It is still widely used today and is available in two packages, ViennaRNA [3] and Unafold [4]. Our goal is to write a GPU efficient algorithm with the same usage and results as the one in the Unafold implementation.

---

*Work performed while the first author was visiting Colorado State University and supported in part by NSF grant CCF-0917319, "Simplifying Reductions," and in part by French ANR BioWIC: ANR-08-SEGI-005.

RNA folding algorithms compute the most stable structure of an RNA sequence; that is, the structure maximizing a given scoring system, or rather, minimizing the total free energy of the RNA molecule.

Although this may seem like a daunting task because there is an exponential number of different possible structures, a key observation makes it computationally feasible in reasonable time: the optimal score of the whole sequence can be defined in terms of optimal scores of smaller subsequences, leading to a simple dynamic programming formulation.

Let us look at the optimal score E of the whole sequence. As shown in recursion Figure 14.1(a), there are two possible ways it can be constructed: the last base n is either paired or unpaired. If it is unpaired, the scoring system implies that E can be directly derived from the score of sequence $1 \ldots n - 1$. In the second case, it is paired with some base k, thus breaking the sequence in two parts: subsequences $1 \ldots k - 1$ and $k \ldots n$, with k, n forming a base pair. The scoring system implies that E is the sum of the score of these two constituent parts. Now, if determining optimal scores of both parts are self-contained subproblems, meaning they are independent of the rest of the sequence, then they need to be computed only once, and then stored and reused wherever the subsequence occurs again. This opens the path to dynamic programming; E is computed as the optimal way to construct it recursively with the equation:

$$E_j = \min\left\{ E_{j-1}, \min_{1 < k < j} (E_{k-1} + QP_{k,j}) \right\} \tag{14.1}$$

with E_j the optimal score of subsequence $1 \ldots j$ and $QP_{k,j}$ the optimal score of subsequence $k \ldots j$ when k, j form a base pair. The assumption that subproblems are self-contained implies that there cannot exist a base pair d, e with $d < k$ and $k < e < j$, i.e., something that would make their scores dependent on exterior elements. Such forbidden base pairs are called pseudoknots.

Quantity $QP_{i,j}$ is also broken down in smaller subproblems, as shown in recursion Figure 14.1(b). Either subsequence $i \ldots j$ contains no other base pairs — i, j is then called a *hairpin loop* — or there exists one internal base pair k, l forming the *interior loop* i, j, k, l, or there are at least two interior base pairs, forming a *multiloop*. The recursion can then be conceptually written in the simplified form:

$$QP_{i,j} = \begin{cases} \min \begin{cases} \text{Hairpin loop} \\ \text{Interior loops} \\ \text{Multiloops} \end{cases} & \text{if pair } i \cdot j \text{ is allowed} \\ \infty & \text{if pair } i \cdot j \text{ is not allowed} \end{cases} \tag{14.2}$$

14.2 CORE METHOD

The main computation is a dynamic programming algorithm, the majority of whose time is spent in a triply nested loop with complex, affine dependency patterns. Despite the complexity, dependency patterns nevertheless allow a parallelization scheme with one of the triply nested loops parallelized, and another expressing a reduction operation. However, with this parallelization, the threads work on different data, preventing us from using shared memory. This lack of a good memory access scheme

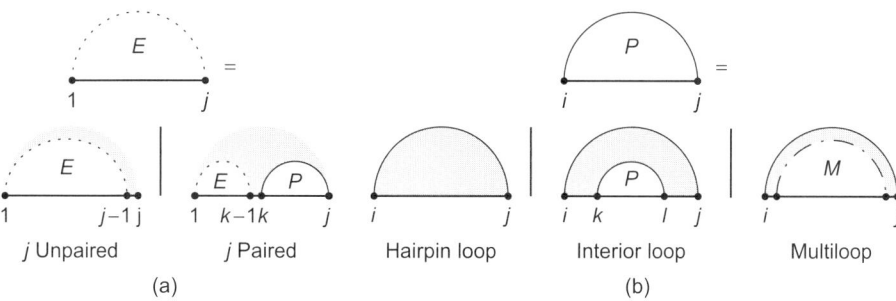

FIGURE 14.1

Recursion diagrams [5] represent the recursive equations of the dynamic programming algorithm. The flat line represents the backbone of an RNA sequence. A base pair is indicated by a solid curved line, and a dashed curved line represents a subsequence with terminal bases that may be paired or unpaired. Shaded regions are parts of the structure fixed by the recursion, while white regions denote substructures whose scores have already been computed and stored in previous steps of the recursion. (a) Recursion of subsequence $1 \ldots j$ assuming no exterior dependence. Last base j is either paired or unpaired. (b) Recursion for subsequence $i \ldots j$ assuming i, j are paired. The subsequence either contains none, one, or several internal base pairs. This corresponds, respectively, to hairpin loops, interior loops, and multiloops. In the case of multiloops another quantity, QM, is introduced and computed through another recursion.

leads to a low ratio between computation and memory loads and thus mediocre performance. It is illegal to tile the loops as written in this direct implementation.

Our main idea is to exploit associativity to change the algorithm. We reorder the accumulations in such a way to make it legal to tile the code. This new tiled approach exhibits a lot of data reuse between threads. This technique therefore allows us to move from a memory-bound algorithm to a compute-bound kernel, thus fully unleashing raw GPU power. We note that our algorithmic modification also enables tiling and subsequent vectorization of the standard CPU implementation. This will allow us to a do a fair apples-to-apples comparison of the CPU and GPU implementations in Section 14.4.2 and avoid the hype surrounding GPGPU.

14.3 ALGORITHMS, IMPLEMENTATIONS, AND EVALUATIONS
14.3.1 Recurrence Equations

We first describe with more details the principles of the folding algorithm as implemented in the Unafold package in the function *hybrid-ss-min* [4]. Recurrence equations of the RNA folding algorithm are well known in the bioinformatic community [2, 3]; we describe them here to make our paper self-contained. Recurrence Eq. 14.1 shows that finding the most stable structure of an RNA sequence involves computing table $QP_{i,j}$, itself constructed in three possible ways, as shown in Eq. 14.2. The first possibility is a hairpin loop, whose score is given by a function Eh mainly depending on loop length. The second possibility is interior loops, containing the special case where $k = i + 1$ and

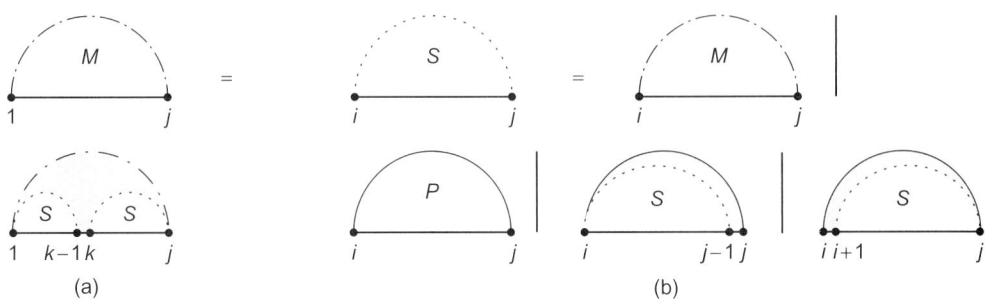

FIGURE 14.2

(a) Recursion of subsequence $i\ldots j$ containing at least two internal base pairs. Both subsequences $i\ldots k-1$ and $k\ldots j$ each contain at least one base pair. (b) Recursion for subsequence $i\ldots j$ containing at least one internal base pair. It contains either several or one base pair on i,j, or on $i,j-1$ or $i-1,j$ if i or j are unpaired.

$l = j - 1$ corresponding to a stacked base pair. Functions Es and Ei give, respectively, the scores of stacked pairs and interior loops. The last possibility is when subsequence $i\ldots j$ contains at least two internal base pairs, forming a multiloop. Another quantity, QM, is introduced, representing the score of a subsequence assuming it is forming a multiloop. Recursive Eq. 14.2 can then be detailed as:

$$QP_{i,j} = \begin{cases} \min \begin{cases} Eh(i,j) \\ Es(i,j) + QP_{i+1,j-1} \\ \displaystyle\min_{\{k,l|i<k,l<j\}} Ei(i,j,k,l) + QP_{k,l} \\ QM_{i+1,j-1} \end{cases} & \text{if pair } i\cdot j \text{ is allowed} \\ \\ \infty & \text{if pair } i\cdot j \text{ is not allowed} \end{cases} \tag{14.3}$$

The value QM represents the score of a subsequence with at least two internal base pairs. It is simply broken down as two subsequences $i\ldots k$ and $k+1\ldots j$ containing both at least one internal base pair. A third value, QS, is introduced to represent the score of such subsequences. $QS_{i,j}$ decomposition is then straightforward: either a pair is on i,j giving $QP_{i,j}$, or there are several pairs giving $QM_{i,j}$, or i or j are unpaired, giving $QS_{i+,j}$ or $QS_{i,j-1}$.

Recursion Figures 14.2(a) and (b) show their decomposition patterns. Their recurrence equations are written as:

$$QM_{i,j} = \min_{i<k<j}(Q_{i,k} + Q_{k+1,j}) \tag{14.4}$$

$$QS_{i,j} = \min\{QM_{i,j}, \min(QS_{i+1,j}, QS_{i,j-1}), QP_{i,j}\} \tag{14.5}$$

The third term of Eq. 14.3 is computed over the four variables i, j, k, l, hence implying a complexity of $\mathcal{O}(n^4)$. However, a common approximation is to limit internal loop sizes to $K = 30$, thus reducing complexity to $\mathcal{O}(n^2 \cdot K^2)$. Equation 14.4 is in $\mathcal{O}(n^3)$, leading to an overall $\mathcal{O}(n^2 \cdot K^2 + n^3)$ complexity. The corresponding secondary structure is then obtained by a traceback procedure, which will not be parallelized on the GPU since its computing time is negligible for large sequences.

14.3.2 **Related Work**

GTfold is a multicore implementation conducted with OpenMP and reports a 19x speedup on a 16 dual-core 1.9 GHz server over the sequential CPU code for a sequence of 9781 nucleotides [6]. Jacob *et al.* report a 103x speedup with an FPGA implementation over a single core of a 3.0 GHz Core 2 duo, but their implementation is limited to 273-nucleotide-long sequences [7]. Other previous efforts were aimed toward parallelization over multiple computers via MPI [8, 9].

14.3.3 **General Parallelization Scheme**

Figure 14.3 shows the data dependencies coming from the recursion Eqs. 14.3 to 14.5. They imply that, once all previous diagonals are available, all cells of a diagonal can be processed independently. Three kernels are designed for the computation of $QP_{i,j}$, $QM_{i,j}$, and $QS_{i,j}$, corresponding to Eqs. 14.3 to 14.5. Each one computes one full diagonal. The whole matrix is then processed sequentially through a loop over the diagonals. The next step corresponding to Eq. 14.1 is a combination of reductions (search of the minimum of an array) which is parallelized in another kernel. The pseudo code for the host side of this parallelization scheme is given in Algorithm 1.

14.3.4 $\mathcal{O}(n^2)$ **Part: Internal Loops**

The third term of Eq. 14.3 corresponds to the computation of internal loops. Their size is usually limited to $K = 30$, which means the minimization is conducted over the domain defined by (k,l) with $i < k < l < j$ and $(k - i) + (j - l) < K$. This domain is represented by the dashed triangle in Figure 14.3. This term is therefore responsible in total for $\mathcal{O}(n^2 \cdot K^2)$ computations. The kernel GPU_QP is designed to compute all cells $QP(i,j)$ over a diagonal d.

One major issue with this kernel is the divergence caused by the two branches in Eq. 14.3: if pair i,j is not allowed, then $QP(i,j)$ is assigned the score ∞ and no computations are required. Different cells of the diagonal are following different code paths, causing a huge loss in performance. To tackle this problem we compute on the CPU an index of all diagonal cells i,j where the base pair i,j is allowed. The kernel computation domain is then the set of cells pointed by this index.

14.3.5 $\mathcal{O}(n^3)$ **Part: Multiloops**

Equation 14.4 computes the most stable multiloop formed by subsequence i,j, and requires $\mathcal{O}(n)$ computations per cell, thus $\mathcal{O}(n^3)$ overall for the n^2 cells of the matrix. It requires the knowledge of the

---

Algorithm 1: Host code, first implementation.

1: **Input**: sequence of length N
2: **Output**: minimal energy of the sequence
3: **for** diagonal d in $[1;N]$ **do**
4:     launch kernel $GPU\_QP(i \in [1;N-d], j = i+d)$
5:     launch kernel $GPU\_QM(i \in [1;N-d], j = i+d)$
6:     launch kernel $GPU\_QS(i \in [1;N-d], j = i+d)$
7: **end for**
8: launch kernel GPU_reduction E_N

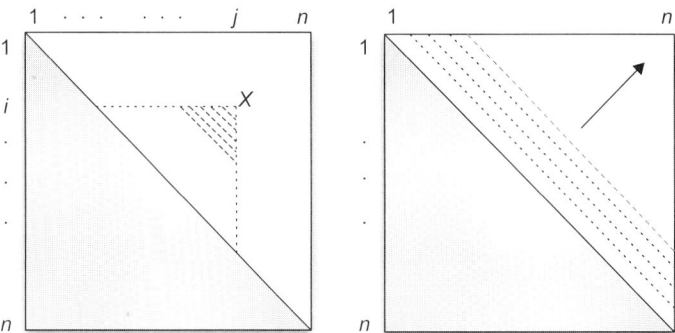

FIGURE 14.3

Left: Data dependency relationship. Each cell of the matrix contains the three values: QP, QM, and QS. As subsequence i,j is the same as subsequence j,i only the upper half of the matrix is needed. The computation of cell i,j needs the lower left dashed triangle and the two vertical and horizontal dotted lines. **Right: Parallelization.** According to the data dependencies, all cells along a diagonal can be computed in parallel from all previous diagonals.

line and column represented by dotted lines in Figure 14.3 and is simply computed by finding the minimum of $(QS_{i,k} + QS_{k+1,j})$ over $k \in [i;j]$. Although it is a simple computation, it is the only $\mathcal{O}(n^3)$ part of the algorithm and as such the most important one for large sequences.

First Implementation

The obvious way to implement the multiloop computation is to compute cells of a diagonal in parallel, with the reduction computation of each cell being itself parallelized over several threads. This way is implemented in kernel GPU_QM, shown in Algorithm 2 and used in our first implementation. The scheme is simple: BX threads cooperate to compute the reduction, with each thread sequentially accessing memory locations BX cells apart so that the memory accesses to $QS(i,k)$ are coalesced among threads. The code shows that each thread does two operations for every two global memory elements accessed, on line 7. This is a very poor ratio, worsened by the fact that accesses $QS(k+1,j)$ are not coalesced. Performance for this piece of code is measured at only 4.5 GOPS (giga operations per second) and a bandwidth usage of 17 GB/s for a 10 Kb sequence. It is obviously severely bandwidth limited. It may be possible to improve and coalesce the second reference in the loop body by storing QS and its transpose in global memory, but we did not pursue this approach because tiling leads to significantly higher performance as we shall see next.

Reduction Split and Reordering

The main issue with our first implementation is that it requires a lot of memory bandwidth, as each cell of the diagonal requires $\mathcal{O}(n)$ data, and there is no reuse of data between the computation of different cells. Theoretically, there is a lot of data reuse, as a single value $QS(i,k)$ will be used for the computation of all cells $QM(i,j)$ with $j \in [k;n]$. Unfortunately, the dependency pattern makes it a priori impossible to take advantage of this, as the set of cells $QM(i,j)$ $j \in [k;n]$ are located on different diagonals and thus computed in separate kernel calls.

Algorithm 2: QM kernel, first implementation.

1: **BlockSize**: One dimension $= BX$
2: **Block Assignment**: Computation of one cell $QM_{i,j}$
3: $tx \leftarrow threadIdx.x$
4: $k \leftarrow i + tx$
5: Shared_data[tx] $\leftarrow \infty$
6: **while** $k < j$ **do**
7:     Shared_data[tx] $\leftarrow$ min (Shared_data[tx] , QS(i,k) + QS(k+1,j))
8:         $k \leftarrow k + BX$
9: **end while**
10: Syncthreads
11: $QM_{i,j} \leftarrow$ Minimum of array Shared_data

In our "tiled implementation," we designed a way to exploit this data reuse. The key observation is that the computation of a single cell is a minimization over $i < k < j$, which can be split into several parts. Our approach is inspired by the systolic array implementation of the optimum string parenthesization problem by Guibas-Kung-Thompson [10, 11], which completely splits reductions in order to have a parallelization scheme working for an array of $\mathcal{O}(n^2)$ processors. Although our approach does not go this far, it exploits the same idea: we split and reorder the reductions, in order to obtain a parallelization scheme better suited for a GPU.

Let's say we have already computed all cells up to a given diagonal d_0, meaning that all cells (i,j) such that $j < i + d_0$ are known. For a given (i_1, j_1) outside of the known area (marked with an x in Figure 14.4) with $j_1 = i_1 + d_0 + T, T > 0$, the whole computation $\min_{i_1 < k < j_1} (QS_{i_1,k} + QS_{k+1,j_1})$ is not possible as many QS values are still unknown.

Nevertheless, we can compute a *part* of the minimization for which QS values are already known: for $\delta_1 < k < \delta_2$ with $\delta_1 = j - d_0$ and $\delta_2 = i + d_0$. Similar "portions" of the accumulations of all the points in the tile can be computed in parallel. This means that by taking apart the range that violates the dependency pattern, we can compute in parallel a tile of cells and thus benefit from a good memory reuse scheme. Figure 14.4 shows such a tile and how the minimization is split.

Tiling Scheme
We still move sequentially diagonal after diagonal, but we compute "in advance" the middle part of the minimization of Eq. 14.4 in tiles. This tiled computation is implemented in the kernel *GPU_QM_tiled*, and called every *Tile_Size* diagonal. The remaining part of the minimization is done in kernel *GPU_finish_QM* and called every diagonal, as shown in Algorithm 3 and depicted in the right part of Figure 14.4.

GPU Implementation
The tiled implementation allows for a very efficient GPU program: each tile is computed by a thread block, which can sequentially load into shared memory blocks of lines and columns, similar to a standard tiled matrix-matrix multiplication. Kernel code of *GPU_QM_tiled* is shown in Algorithm 4. QS values are stored in shared memory lines 9, 10 and reused BS times each, on line 13. Bandwidth

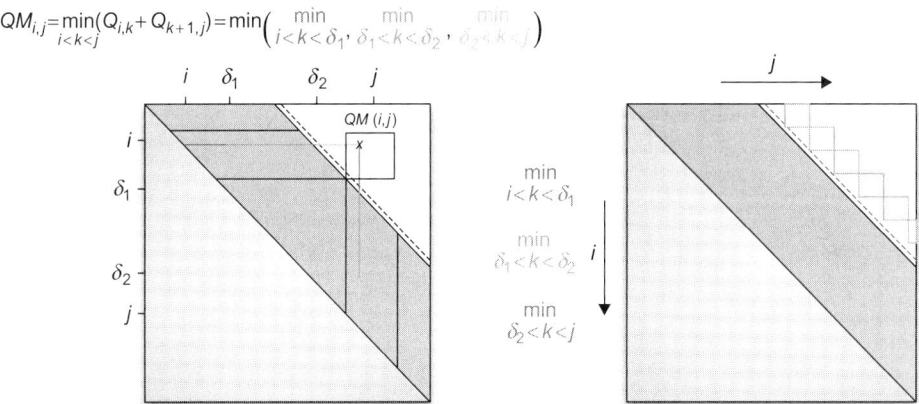

FIGURE 14.4

Left: Reduction split. All shaded cells in the upper part of the matrix are already available. For a point (i,j) located outside of the known area, the middle part of the reduction represented by the thin line between δ_1 and δ_2 can be computed. **Right: Tiling scheme.** The middle part of the reduction is done "in advance" in the square tiles. The remaining part is done on the dashed cells, diagonal after diagonal.

Algorithm 3:   Host code, tiled implementation.

1: **Input**: sequence of length N
2: **Output**: minimal energy of the sequence
3: **for** diagonal d in $[1;N]$ **do**
4:      launch kernel $GPU\_QP(i \in [1;N-d], j = i+d)$
5:      **if** (d modulo Tile_Size $==0$) **then**
6:          launch kernel $GPU\_QM\_tiled(d)$
7:      **end if**
8:      launch kernel $GPU\_finish\_QM(i \in [1;N-d], j = i+d)$
9:      launch kernel $GPU\_QS(i \in [1;N-d], j = i+d)$
10: **end for**
11: launch kernel $GPU\_reductionE_N$

---

requirement is therefore reduced by a factor of $Tile\_Size = BS$ compared with the first implementation. Performance of this kernel is now 90 GOPS with a bandwidth usage of 23 GB/s.

14.3.6 Related Algorithms

We also applied the technique presented here to the computation of suboptimal foldings and the partition function of a sequence, whose algorithms are similar to the one presented here. Suboptimal foldings and partition function are very useful to give a more accurate view of a sequence ensemble of possible foldings, because the unique "optimal" folding is not necessarily always representative of biological reality.

Algorithm 4: QM kernel, tiled implementation.

1: **BlockSize**: Two dimension $= BS \cdot BS$
2: **Block Assignment**: Computation of "middle part" of QM for a tile of $BS \cdot BS$ cells, with upper left corner (i_0, j_0)
3: $tx \leftarrow threadIdx.x$, $ty \leftarrow threadIdx.y$
4: $iter \leftarrow$ beginning of "middle part"
5: $bound \leftarrow$ end of "middle part"
6: $temp \leftarrow \infty$
7: **while** $iter < bound$ **do**
8:     *Load blocks in shared memory:*
9:     Shared_L $[tx][ty] \leftarrow QS(i_0 + ty, iter + tx)$
10:     Shared_C $[tx][ty] \leftarrow QS(iter + 1 + ty, j_0 + tx)$
11:     Syncthreads
12:     **for** $k = 0, k \leq BS, k++$ **do**
13:         $temp \leftarrow \min(temp, \text{Shared\_L } [ty][k] + \text{Shared\_C } [k][tx])$
14:     **end for**
15:     $iter \leftarrow iter + BS$
16: **end while**
17: $QM_{i_0+tx, j_0+ty} \leftarrow temp$

14.4 FINAL EVALUATION

14.4.1 Results

Our GPU implementation uses exactly the same thermodynamic rules as Unafold, thus the results and accuracy obtained on a GPU are exactly the same as for the standard CPU Unafold function. We therefore compare only the execution time between programs, including the host-to-device transfer for the GPU implementation. Our tests are run on a Xeon E5450 @ 3.0 GHz and a Tesla C1060. CPU code is running on Fedora 9, compiled with the GCC 4.3.0 compiler with -O3 optimization level.

14.4.2 Tiled Implementation

Figure 14.5(a) shows the speedup obtained by the tiled implementation on a Tesla C1060 over the standard Unafold algorithm running on one core of a Xeon E5450 for randomly generated sequences of different lengths. Tests are run with a large enough number of sequences, ensuring that GPU starting costs are amortized. The speedup starts at around 20x for short sequences and goes up to 150x for large sequences. For small sequences, the $\mathcal{O}(n^2)$ part of the algorithm is preponderant, so the overall speedup is roughly that of the kernel computing internal loops, called *GPU_QP* and explained in Section 14.3.4. As sequence size increases, the $\mathcal{O}(n^3)$ multiloop computation becomes more important, so the speedup approaches that of kernel *GPU_QM_tiled*, which is very efficient thanks to our tiled code.

In order to do a fair, "apples-to-apples" comparison, we applied our tiling technique on the CPU and used SSE vectorized instructions to get the full potential of CPU performance. Execution speed of the vectorized part of the code is 5.4 GOPS for a 10 Kb sequence, which is quite high considering first GPU implementation speed was only 4.5 GOPS. Speedup obtained by the second GPU implementation

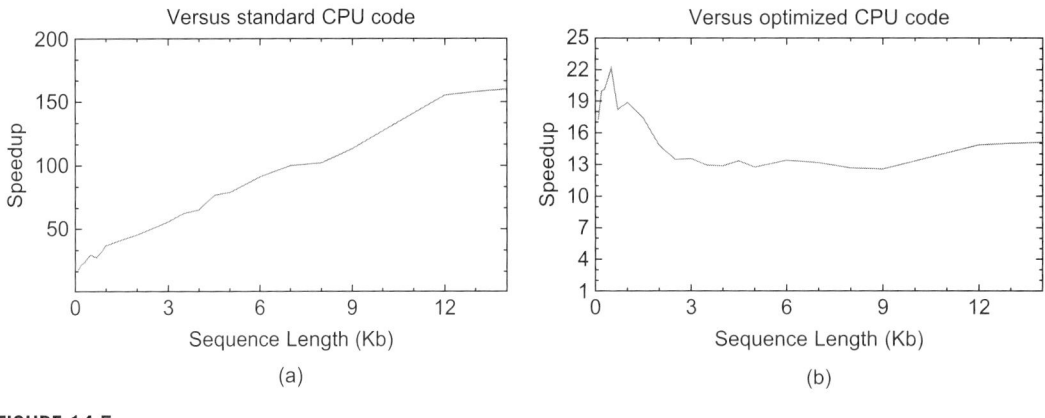

FIGURE 14.5

Tesla C1060 speedup against one core of Xeon E5450 @ 3.0 GHz for various sequence lengths. (a) Speedup against standard Unafold code. (b) Speedup against tiled and vectorized CPU code.

against this optimized code is presented Figure 14.5(b). Here speedup is more stable across sequence lengths because like the GPU, CPU tiled code is very efficient. GPU speedup of the $\mathcal{O}(n^3)$ part of the code compared with CPU code using the same tiling technique and vectorized code is 90 GOPS / 5.4 GOPS = 16.6x. This is therefore the theoretical maximum speedup that can be achieved when running on very large sequences when the $\mathcal{O}(n^2)$ part — exhibiting different speedup — becomes negligible.

14.4.3 Overall Comparison

Figure 14.6 compares performance on a 9781-nucleotide-long virus sequence on a larger set of programs: on the first untiled GPU implementation, the tiled one, the standard Unafold CPU code [4], the GTfold algorithm [6] running on eight CPU cores, and the new SSE-optimized CPU code running on one or eight threads.

We can see that our new CPU code is running 10 times faster than the regular Unafold code, thanks to both SSE and better memory locality of the tiled code. Even against this fast CPU code, the Tesla C1060 is still more than 11 times faster than the Xeon. It is also worth noting the 6x speedup obtained between the GPU tiled and untiled code. For the CPU tiled and vectorized, however, going from one to eight threads yielded a 6.2x speedup. We measured memory bandwidth usage of the tiled part of the code at 0.6 GB/s when running on one CPU core; therefore, running eight cores at full potential would require 4.8 GB/s, exceeding the memory bandwidth limit of the Xeon E5450. As a result, the single GPU tested is approximately two times faster than this eight-CPU system. This may seem a low speedup, especially to those used to seeing hyped-up GPU performance gains. However, this is a more reasonable expectation — for example, the commercially released CULA package for linear algebra is "only" about three to five times faster than a vectorized and optimized linear algebra library on a four-core CPU. Also, note that GPU computing provides significant advantages for dealing with huge numbers of sequences; a single system fitted with several GPUs rivals with a small cluster at a fraction of the cost.

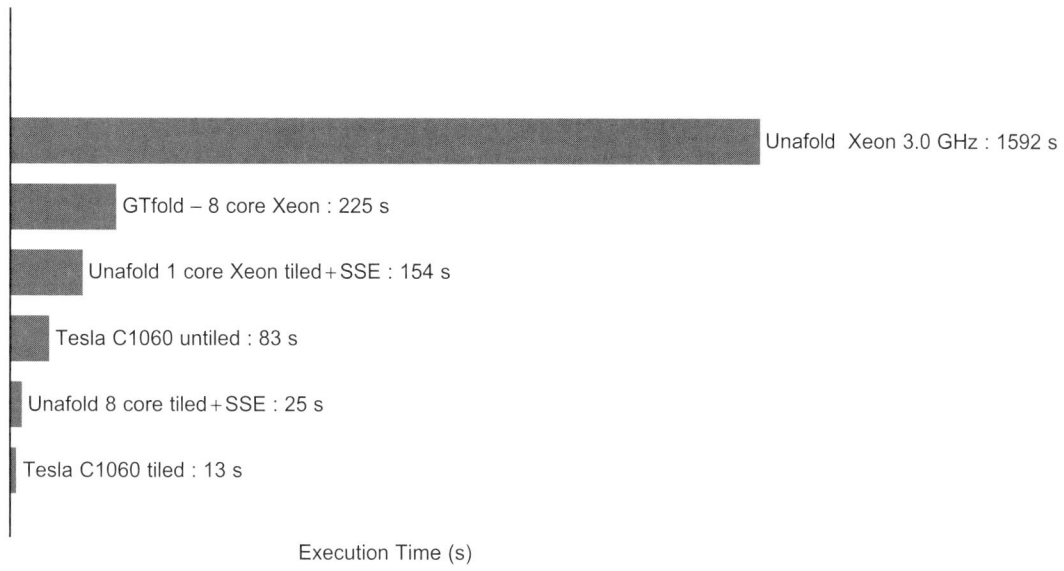

FIGURE 14.6

Execution time on a 9781-nucleotide-long virus sequence.

14.5 FUTURE DIRECTIONS

For the $\mathcal{O}(n^3)$ part of the code, it seems difficult to get much better performance than our tiled approach. Some work could in theory be done to get a little closer to the peak 312 GOPS of the Tesla. However, code profiling shows that now that this part is well optimized, it has become a non-preponderant part of total time even for large 10 Kb sequences. Therefore, future optimizations should focus on the $\mathcal{O}(n^2)$ part computing interior loops, which is bandwidth limited with a complex memory access pattern.

References

[1] R. Nussinov, G. Pieczenik, J. Griggs, D. Kleitman, Algorithms for loop matchings, SIAM, J. Appl. Math. 35 (1) (1978) 68–82.

[2] M. Zuker, P. Stiegler, Optimal computer folding of large RNA sequences using thermodynamics and auxiliary information, Nucleic Acids Res. 9 (1) (1981) 133–148.

[3] I.L. Hofacker, W. Fontana, P.F. Stadler, L.S. Bonhoeffer, M. Tacker, P. Schuster, Fast folding and comparison of RNA secondary structures, Monatsh. Chem. 125 (1994) 167–188.

[4] N. Markham, M. Zuker, DINAMelt web server for nucleic acid melting prediction, Nucleic Acids Res. 33 (2005) W577–W581.

[5] E. Rivas, S. Eddy, A dynamic programming algorithm for RNA structure prediction including pseudoknots1, J. Mol. Biol. 285 (5) (1999) 2053–2068.

[6]   A. Mathuriya, D. Bader, C. Heitsch, S. Harvey, GTfold: a scalable multicore code for RNA secondary struc-
      ture prediction, in: Proceedings of the 2009 ACM Symposium on Applied Computing, Honolulu, Hawaii,
      March 2009, ACM, New York, 2009, pp. 981–988.
[7]   A. Jacob, J. Buhler, R. Chamberlain, Rapid RNA folding: analysis and acceleration of the Zuker recurrence,
      in: Proceedings of the 2010 IEEE Symposium on Field-Programmable Custom Computing Machines, IEE,
      New York, May 2010, Charlotte NC, 2010, pp. 87–94.
[8]   I. Hofacker, M. Huynen, P. Stadler, P. Stolorz, RNA folding on parallel computers: the minimum free energy
      structures of complete HIV genomes, Working Papers, Santa Fe Institute Tech Report, 95-10-089, 1995.
[9]   F. Almeida, R. Andonov, D. Gonzalez, L. Moreno, V. Poirriez, C. Rodriguez, Optimal tiling for the RNA
      base pairing problem, in: Proceedings of the Fourteenth Annual August 2002, Winnipeg, Manitoba, Canada
      ACM Symposium on Parallel Algorithms and Architectures, New York, 2002, pp. 182.
[10] L. Guibas, H. Kung, C. Thompson, Direct VLSI implementation of combinatorial algorithms, in: Proceed-
      ings of the Caltech Conference on Very Large Scale Integration, January 22–24, California Institute of
      Technology, Caltech Computer Science Dept., 1979, pp. 509.
[11] S.V. Rajopadhye, Synthesizing systolic arrays with control signals from recurrence equations, Distrib.
      Comput. 3 (1989) 88–105.

Temporal Data Mining for Neuroscience

15

Wu-chun Feng, Yong Cao, Debprakash Patnaik, Naren Ramakrishnan

Today, multielectrode arrays (MEAs) capture neuronal spike streams in real time, thus providing dynamic perspectives into brain function. Mining such spike streams from these MEAs is critical toward understanding the firing patterns of neurons and gaining insight into the underlying cellular activity. However, the acquisition rate of neuronal data places a tremendous computational burden on the subsequent temporal data mining of these spike streams. Thus, computational neuroscience seeks innovative approaches toward tackling this problem and eventually solving it efficiently and in real time.

In this chapter, we present a solution that uses graphics processing units (GPUs) to mine spike train datasets. Specifically, our solution delivers a novel mapping of a "finite state machine for data mining" onto the GPU while simultaneously addressing a wide range of neuronal input characteristics. This solution ultimately transforms the task of temporal data mining of spike trains from a batch-oriented process towards a real-time one.

15.1 INTRODUCTION

Brain-computer interfaces have made massive strides in recent years [1]. Scientists are now able to analyze neuronal activity in living organisms, understand the intent implicit in these signals and, more importantly, use this information as control directives to operate external devices. Technologies for modeling and recording neuronal activity include functional magnetic resonance imaging (fMRI), electroencephalography (EEG), and multielectrode arrays (MEAs).

In this chapter, we focus on event streams gathered through MEA chips for studying neuronal function. As shown in Figure 15.1, an MEA records spiking action potentials from an ensemble of neurons, and after various preprocessing steps, these neurons yield a spike train dataset that provides a real-time dynamic perspective into brain function. Key problems of interest include identifying sequences of firing neurons, determining their characteristic delays, and reconstructing the functional connectivity of neuronal circuits. Addressing these problems can provide critical insights into the cellular activity recorded in the neuronal tissue.

In only a *few minutes* of cortical recording, a 64-channel MEA can easily capture *millions* of neuronal spikes. In practice, such MEA experiments run for *days* or even months [8] and can result in

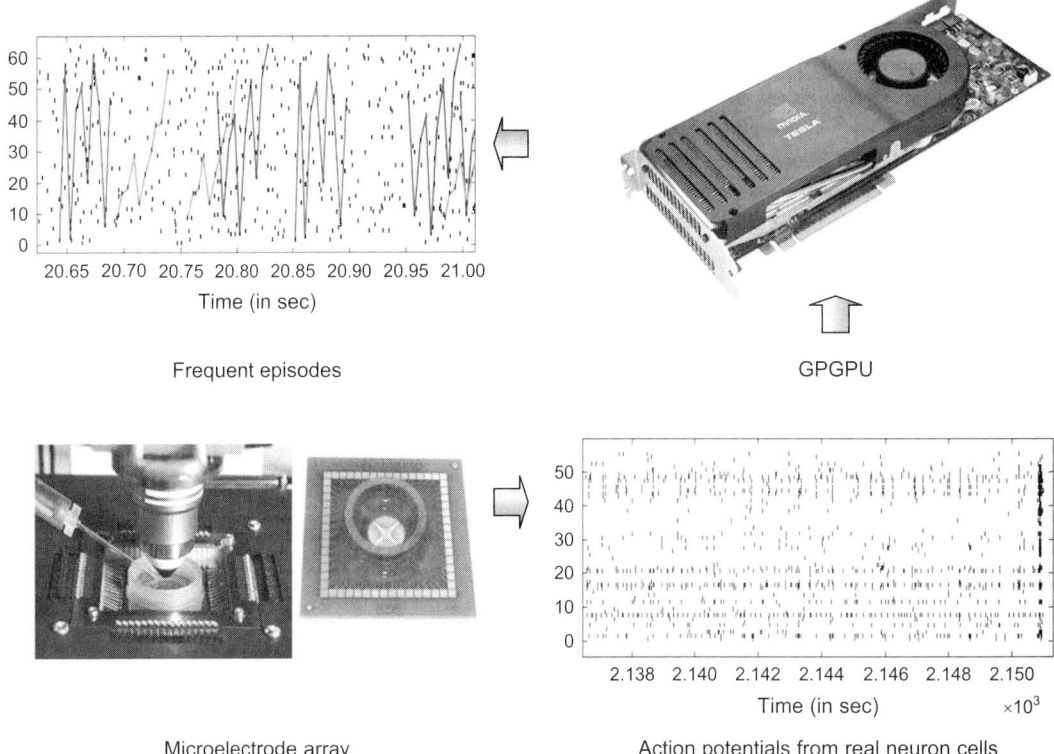

Frequent episodes

GPGPU

Microelectrode array

Action potentials from real neuron cells

FIGURE 15.1

Spike trains recorded from a multielectrode array (MEA) are mined by a GPU to yield frequent episodes, which can be summarized to reconstruct the underlying neuronal circuitry.

trillions to *quadrillions* of neuronal spikes. From these neuronal spike streams, we seek to identify (or mine for) *frequent episodes* of repetitive patterns that are associated with higher-order brain function. The mining algorithms of these patterns are usually based on finite state machines [3, 5] and can handle temporal constraints [6]. The temporal constraints add significant complexity to the state machine algorithms as they must now keep track of what part of an episode has been seen, which event is expected next, and when episodes interleave. Then, they must make a decision of which events to be used in the formation of an episode.

15.2 CORE METHODOLOGY

We model a spike train dataset as an event stream, where each symbol/event type corresponds to a specific neuron (or clump of neurons). In addition, the dataset encodes the occurrence times of these events.

Temporal data mining of event streams aims to discover interesting patterns that occur frequently in the event stream, subject to certain timing constraints. More formally, each pattern (i.e., episode) is an ordered tuple of event types with temporal constraints. For example, the episode shown below describes a pattern where event B must occur at least t_{low}^1 after event A and at most t_{high}^1 after event A and event C must occur at least t_{low}^2 after event B and at most t_{high}^2 after event B.

$$\left(A \xrightarrow{(t_{low}^1, t_{high}^1]} B \xrightarrow{(t_{low}^2, t_{high}^2]} C \right)$$

The preceding is a size-three episode because it contains three events.

Episodes are mined by a generate-and-test approach; that is, we generate numerous candidate episodes that are counted to ascertain their frequencies. This process happens levelwise: search for one-node episodes (single symbols) first, followed by two-node episodes, and so on. At each level, size-N candidates are generated from size-$(N-1)$ frequent episodes, and their frequencies (i.e., counts) are determined by making a pass over the event sequence. Only those candidate episodes whose count is greater than a user-defined threshold are retained. The most computationally expensive step in each level is the counting of all candidate episodes for that level. At the initial levels, there are a large number of candidate episodes to be counted in parallel; the later levels only have increasingly fewer candidate episodes.

The frequency of an episode is a measure that is open to multiple interpretations. Note that episodes can have "junk" symbols interspersed; for example, an occurrence of event A followed by B followed by C might have symbol D interspersed, whereas a different occurrence of the same episode might have symbol F interspersed. Example ways to define frequency include counting all occurrences, counting only nonoverlapped occurrences, and so on. We utilize the nonoverlapped count, which is defined as the maximum number of nonoverlapped instances of the given episode. This measure has the advantageous property of *antimonotonicity*; that is, the frequency of a subepisode cannot be less than the frequency of the given episode. Antimonotonicty allows us to use levelwise pruning algorithms in our search for frequent episodes.

Our approach is based on a state machine algorithm with interevent constraints [6]. Algorithm 1 shows our serial counting procedure for a single episode α. The algorithm maintains a data structure s, which is a list of lists. Each list $s[k]$ in s corresponds to an event type $E_{(k)} \in \alpha$ and stores the times of occurrences of those events with event type $E_{(k)}$ that satisfy the interevent constraint $(t_{low}^{(k-1)}, t_{high}^{(k-1)}]$ with at least one entry $t_j \in s[k-1]$. This requirement is relaxed for $s[0]$, thus every time an event $E_{(0)}$ is seen in the data, its occurrence time is pushed into $s[0]$.

When an event of type $E_{(k)}, 2 \le k \le N$ at time t is seen, we look for an entry $t_j \in s[k-1]$ such that $t - t_j \in (t_{low}^{(k-1)}, t_{high}^{(k-1)}]$. Therefore, if we are able to add the event to the list $s[k]$, it implies that there exists at least one previous event with event type $E_{(k-1)}$ in the data stream for the current event that satisfies the interevent constraint between $E_{(k-1)}$ and $E_{(k)}$. After we apply this argument recursively, if we can add an event with event type $E_{(|\alpha|)}$ to its corresponding list in s, then there exists a sequence of events corresponding to each event type in α satisfying the respective interevent constraints. Such an event marks the end of an occurrence, after which the *count* for α is incremented and the data structure s is reinitialized. Figure 15.2 illustrates the data structure s for counting $A \xrightarrow{(5,10]} B \xrightarrow{(10,15]} C$.

Algorithm 1: Serial Episode Mining.

Input: Candidate N-node episode $\alpha = \langle E_{(1)} \xrightarrow{(t_{low}^{(1)}, t_{high}^{(1)}]} \ldots E_{(N)} \rangle$ and event sequence $S = \{(E_i, t_i) | i = 1 \ldots n\}$.
Output: Count of nonoverlapped occurrences of α satisfying interevent constraints
1: $count = 0; s = [[], \ldots, []]$ //List of $|\alpha|$ lists
2: **for all** $(E, t) \in S$ **do**
3:     **for** $i = |\alpha|$ down to 1 **do**
4:         $E_{(i)} = i^{th}$ event type of α
5:         **if** $E = E_{(i)}$ **then**
6:             $i_{prev} = i - 1$
7:             **if** $i > 1$ **then**
8:                 $k = |s[i_{prev}]|$
9:                 **while** $k > 0$ **do**
10:                     $t_{prev} = s[i_{prev}, k]$
11:                     **if** $t_{low}^{(i_{prev})} < t - t_{prev} \leq t_{high}^{(i_{prev})}$ **then**
12:                         **if** $i = |\alpha| - 1$ **then**
13:                             $count + +; s = [[], \ldots, []];$ **break** Line: 1.2
14:                         **else**
15:                             $s[i] = s[i] \cup t$
16:                         **break** Line: 1.2
17:                     $k = k - 1$
18:                 **else**
19:                     $s[i] = s[i] \cup t$
20: RETURN count

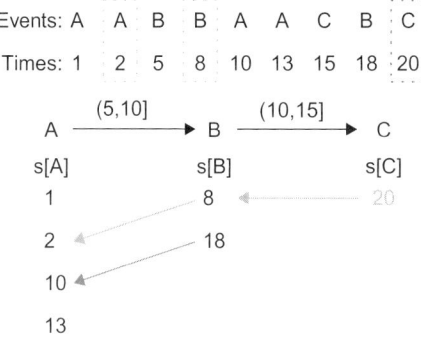

FIGURE 15.2

An illustration of the data structure s for counting $A \xrightarrow{(5,10]} B \xrightarrow{(10,15]} C$.

15.3 GPU PARALLELIZATION: ALGORITHMS AND IMPLEMENTATIONS

To parallelize the aforementioned sequential counting approach on a GPU, we segment the overall computation into independent units that can be mapped onto GPU cores and executed in parallel to fully utilize GPU resources. Different computation-to-core mapping schemes can result in different levels of parallelism, which are suitable for different inputs for the episode counting algorithm. Next, we present two computation-to-core mapping strategies, which are suitable for different scenarios with different sizes of input episodes. The first strategy, one thread per occurrence of an episode, is used for mining a very few episodes. The second strategy is used for counting many episodes.

15.3.1 Strategy 1: One Thread per Occurrence

Problem Context

This mapping strategy handles the case when we have a few input episodes to count. In the limit, mining one episode with one thread severely underutilizes the GPU. Thus, we seek an approach to increase the level of parallelism. The original sequential version of the mining algorithm uses a state-machine approach with a substantial amount of data dependencies. Hence, it is difficult to increase the degree of parallelism by optimizing this algorithm directly. Instead, we transform the algorithm by discarding the state-machine approach and decomposing the problem into two subproblems that can be easily parallelized using known computing primitives. The mining of an episode entails counting the frequency of nonoverlapped neuronal patterns of event symbols. It represents the size of the largest set of nonoverlapped occurrences. Based on this definition, we design a more data-parallel solution.

Basic Idea

In our new approach, we find a superset of the nonoverlapped occurrences that could potentially be overlapping. Each occurrence of an episode has a start time and an end time. If each episode occurrence in this superset is viewed as a task/job with fixed start and end times, then the problem of finding the largest set of nonoverlapped occurrences transforms itself into a job-scheduling problem, where the goal is to maximize the number of jobs or tasks while avoiding conflicts. A greedy $O(n)$ algorithm solves this problem optimally where n is the number of jobs. The original problem now decomposes into two subproblems:

1. Find a superset of nonoverlapped occurrences of an episode
2. Find the size of the largest set of nonoverlapped occurrences from the set of occurrences

The first subproblem can be solved with a high degree of parallelism as will be shown later in this chapter. We design a solution where one GPU thread can mine one occurrence of an episode. To preprocess the data, however, we perform an important compaction step between the searches of the next query event in the episode. This entailed us to investigate both a lock-based compaction method using atomic operations in CUDA as well as a lock-free approach with the CUDPP library. However, the performance of both compaction methods was unsatisfactory. Thus, in order to further improve performance, we adopted a counterintuitive approach that divided the counting process into three parts. First, each thread looks up the event sequence for suitable next events, but instead of recording the events found, it merely counts and writes the count to global memory. Second, an exclusive scan is performed on the recorded counts. This gives the offset into the global memory where each thread can write its "next events" list. The actual writing is done as the third step. Although each thread looks up the event sequence twice (first to count and second to write), we show that we nevertheless achieve better performance.

The second subproblem is the same as the task or interval scheduling problem where tasks have fixed times. A fast greedy algorithm is well known to solve the problem optimally.

Algorithmic Improvements

We first preprocess the entire event stream, noting the positions of events of each event type. Then, for a given episode, beginning with the list of occurrences of the start event type in the episode, we find occurrences satisfying the temporal constraints in parallel. Finally, we collect and remove overlapped occurrences in one pass. The greedy algorithm for removing overlaps requires the occurrences to be sorted by end time, and the algorithm proceeds as shown in Algorithm 2. Here, for every set of consecutive occurrences, if the start time is after the end time of the last selected occurrence, then we select this occurrence; otherwise, we skip it and go to the next occurrence.

Next, we explore different approaches of solving the first subproblem, as presented earlier. The aim here is to find a superset of nonoverlapped occurrences in parallel. The basic idea is to start with all events of the first event-type in parallel for a given episode and find occurrences of the episode starting at each of these events. There can be several different ways in which this can be done. We shall present two approaches that showed the most performance improvement. We shall use the episode $A \overset{(5-10]}{\longrightarrow} B \overset{(5-10]}{\longrightarrow} C$ as our running example and explain each of the counting strategies using this example. This example episode specifies event occurrences where an event A is to be followed by an event B within 5–10 ms and event B is to be followed by an event C within 5–10 ms delay. Note again that the delays have both a lower and an upper bound.

Parallel Local Tracking

In the preprocessing step, we have noted the locations of each of the event-types in the data. In the counting step, we launch as many threads as there are events in the event stream of the start event type (of the episode). In our running example these are all events of type A. Each thread searches the event stream starting at one of these events of type A and looks for an event of type B that satisfies the inter event time constraint $(5 - 10]$; that is, $5 < t_{B_j} - t_{A_i} \leq 10$ where i, j are the indices of the events of type A and B. One thread can find multiple B's for the same A. These are recorded in a preallocated array assigned to each thread. Once all the events of type B (with an A before them) have been collected by the threads (in parallel), we need to compact these newfound events into a contiguous array/list. This is necessary because in the next kernel launch we will find all the events of type C that satisfy the interevent constraints with this set of B's. This is illustrated in Figure 15.3.

Algorithm 2: Obtaining the Largest Set of Nonoverlapped Occurrences.

Input: List C of occurrences with start and end times (s_i, e_i) sorted by end time, e_i.
Output: Size of the largest set of nonoverlapped occurrences.
    Initialize $count = 0$
    $prev_e = 0$
    for all $(s_i, e_i) \in C$ **do**
        if $prev_e < s_i$ **then**
            $prev_e = e_i$; $count = count + 1$
    return $count$

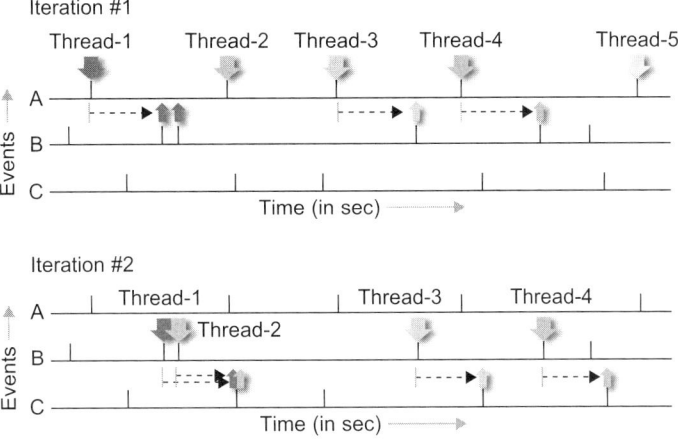

FIGURE 15.3

Illustration of the parallel local tracking algorithm (i.e., Algorithm 3), showing two iterations for the episode $A \rightarrow B \rightarrow C$ with implicit interevent constraints. Note that each thread can find multiple next events. Furthermore, a thread stops scanning the event sequence when event times go past the upper bound of the interevent constraint.

Algorithm 3: Kernel for Parallel Local Tracking.

Input: Iteration number i, Episode α, $\alpha[i]$: i^{th} event-type in α, Index list $I_{\alpha[i]}$, Data sequence S.
Output: $I_{\alpha[i+1]}$: Indices of events of type $\alpha[i+1]$.
   for all threads with distinct identifiers *tid* **do**
      Scan S starting at event $I_{\alpha[i]}[tid]$ for event-type $\alpha[i+1]$ satisfying inter-event constraint $(t_{low}^{(i)}, t_{high}^{(i)}]$.
      Record all such events of type $\alpha[i+1]$.
   Compact all found events into the list $I_{\alpha[i+1]}$. $I_{\alpha[i+1]}$

Algorithm 3 presents the work done in each kernel launch. In order to obtain the complete set of occurrences of an episode, we need to launch the kernel $N - 1$ times where N is the size of an episode. The list of qualifying events found in the ith iteration is passed as input to the next iteration. Some amount of bookkeeping is also done to keep track of the start and end times of an occurrence. After this phase of parallel local tracking is completed, the nonoverlapped count is obtained using Algorithm 2. The compaction step in Algorithm 3 presents a challenge because it requires concurrent updates into a global array.

Implementation Notes
Lock-Based Compaction
NVIDIA graphics cards with CUDA compute capability 1.3 support atomic operations on shared and global memory. Here, we use atomic operations to perform compaction of the output array into the global memory. After the counting step, each thread has a list of next events. Subsequently, each thread adds the size of its next events list to the block-level counter using an atomic add operation and, in

return, obtains a local offset (which is the previous value of the block-level counter). After all threads in a block have updated the block-level counter, one thread from a block updates the global counter by adding the value of the block-level counter to it and, as before, obtains the offset into global memory. Now, all threads in the block can collaboratively write into the correct position in the global memory (resulting in overall compaction). A schematic for this operation is shown for two blocks in Figure 15.4. In the results section, we refer to this method as *AtomicCompact*.

Because there is no guarantee for the order of atomic operations, this procedure requires sorting. The complete occurrences need to be sorted by end time for Algorithm 2 to produce the correct result.

Lock-Free Compaction

Prefix scan is known to be a general-purpose, data-parallel primitive that is a useful building block for algorithms in a broad range of applications. Given a vector of data elements $[x_0, x_1, x_2, \ldots]$, an associative binary function $\oplus$ and an identity element i, exclusive prefix scan returns $[i, x_0, x_0 \oplus x_1, x_0 \oplus x_1 \oplus x_2, \ldots]$. The first parallel prefix-scan algorithm was proposed in 1962 [4]. With increasing interest in general-purpose computing on the GPU (GPGPU), several implementations of scan algorithms have been proposed for the GPU, the most recent ones being [2] and [7]. The latter implementation is available as the *CUDPP: CUDA Data Parallel Primitives Library* and forms part of the CUDA SDK distribution.

Our lock-free compaction is based on prefix sum, and we reuse the implementation from the CUDPP library. Because the scan-based operation guarantees ordering, we modify our counting procedure to count occurrences backward starting from the last event. This results in the final set of occurrences to be automatically ordered by end time and therefore completely eliminates the need for sorting (as required by the approach based on atomic operations).

The CUDPP library provides a compact function that takes an array d_{in}, an array of 1/0 flags, and returns a compacted array d_{out} of corresponding only the "valid" values from d_{in} (it internally uses cudppScan). In order to use this, our counting kernel is now split into three kernel calls. Each thread

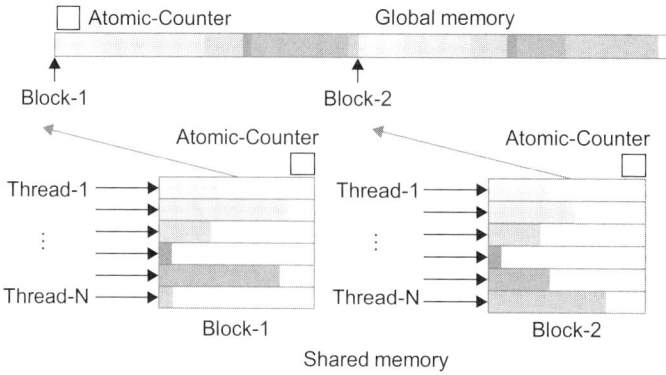

FIGURE 15.4

Illustration of output compaction using atomicAdd operations. Note that we use atomic operations at both block and global level. These operations return the correct offset into global memory for each thread to write its next-event list into.

is allocated a fixed portion of a larger array in global memory for its next events list. In the first kernel, each thread finds its events and fills up its next-events list in global memory. The `cudppCompact` function, implemented as two GPU kernel calls, compacts the large array to obtain the global list of next-events. A difficulty of this approach is that the array on which `cudppCompact` operates is very large, resulting in a scattered memory access pattern. We refer to this method as *CudppCompact*.

In order to further improve performance, we adopt a counterintuitive approach. We again divide the counting process into three parts. First, each thread looks up the event sequence for suitable next events but instead of recording the events found, it merely counts and writes the count to global memory. Then, an exclusive scan is performed on the recorded counts. This gives the offset into the global memory where each thread can write its next-events list. The actual writing is done as the third step. Although each thread looks up the event sequence twice (first to count, and second to write), we show that we nevertheless achieve better performance. This entire procedure is illustrated in Figure 15.5. We refer to this method of compaction as *CountScanWrite* in the ensuing results section.

Note that prefix scan is essentially a sequential operator applied from left to right to an array. Hence, the memory writes operations into memory locations generated by prefix scan preserve order. The sorting step (i.e., sorting occurrences by end time) required in the lock-based compaction can be completely avoided by counting occurrences backward, starting from the last event type in the episode.

15.3.2 Strategy 2: A Two-Pass Elimination Approach

Problem Context

When mining a large number of input episodes, we can simply assign one GPU thread for each episode. Because there are enough episodes, the GPU computing resource will be fully utilized. The state-machine-based algorithm is very complex and requires a large amount of shared memory and a large number of GPU registers for each GPU thread. For example, if the length of the query is 5, each thread requires 220 bytes of shared memory and 97 bytes of register file. It means that only 32 threads can be allocated on a GPU multiprocessor, which has 16 kB of shared memory and register file. As each thread

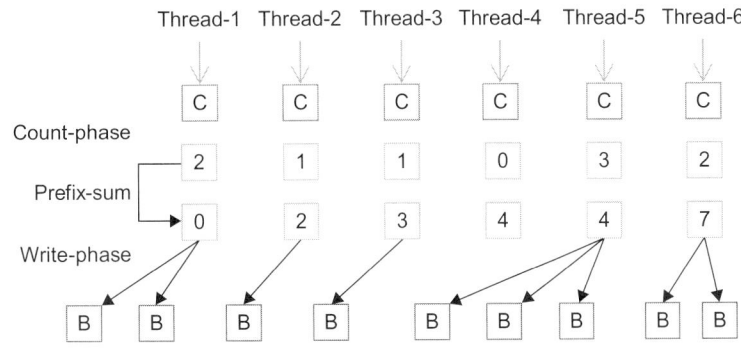

FIGURE 15.5

An illustration of output compaction using the scan primitive. Each iteration is broken into three kernel calls: Counting the number of next events, using scan to compute offset into global memory, and finally launching count-procedure again but this time allowing write operations to the global memory.

requires more resources, fewer threads can run on GPU at the same time, resulting in longer execution time for each thread.

Basic Idea

To address this problem, we sought to reduce the complexity of the algorithm without losing correctness. Our idea was to use a simpler algorithm that we call *PreElim* to eliminate most of the nonsupported episodes, and only use the more complex algorithm to determine if the rest of the episode is supported or not. To introduce the algorithm *PreElim*, we consider the solution to a slightly relaxed problem, which plays an important role in our two-pass elimination approach. In this approach, algorithm *PreElim* is simpler and runs faster than the more complex algorithm because it reduces the time complexity of the interevent constraint. As a result, when the number of episodes is very large and the number of episodes culled in the first pass is also large, the performance of our two-pass elimination algorithm is significantly better than the more complex original algorithm.

Algorithmic Improvements

Less-Constrained Mining: Algorithm PreElim

Let us consider a constrained version of Problem 1. Instead of enforcing both lower limits and upper limits on interevent constraints, we design a counting solution that enforces only upper limits.

Let α' be an episode with the same event types as in α, where α uses the original episode definition from Problem 1. The lower bounds on the interevent constraints in α are relaxed for α' as shown here.

$$\alpha' = \langle E_{(1)} \xrightarrow{(0,t_{high}^{(1)}]} E_{(2)} \dots \xrightarrow{(0,t_{high}^{(N-1)}]} E_{(N)} \rangle \tag{15.1}$$

Observation 1 In Algorithm 1, if lower-bounds of interevent constraints in episode α are relaxed as α', the list size of $s[k], 1 \leq k \leq N$ can be reduced to 1.

Proof. In Algorithm 1, when an event of type $E_{(k)}$ is seen at time t while going down the event sequence, $s[E_{(k-1)}]$ is looked up for at least one t_i^{k-1}, such that $t - t_i^{k-1} \in (0, t_{high}^{(k-1)}]$. Note that t_i^{k-1} represents the ith entry of $s[E_{(k-1)}]$ corresponding the $(k-1)^{th}$ event-type in α.

Let $s[E_{(k-1)}] = \{t_1^{k-1} \dots t_m^{k-1}\}$ and t_i^{k-1} be the first entry that satisfies the interevent constraint $(0, t_{high}^{(k-1)}]$, i.e.,

$$0 < t - t_i^{k-1} \leq t_{high}^{(k-1)} \tag{15.2}$$

Also Eq. 15.3 below follows from the fact that t_i^{k-1} is the first entry in $s[E_{(k-1)}]$ matching the time constraint.

$$t_i^{k-1} < t_j^{k-1} \leq t, \forall j \in \{i+1 \dots m\} \tag{15.3}$$

From Eq. 15.2 and Eq. 15.3, Eq. 15.4 follows.

$$0 < t - t_j^{k-1} \leq t_{high}^{(k-1)}, \forall j \in \{i+1 \dots m\} \tag{15.4}$$

This shows that every entry in $s[E_{(k-1)}]$ following t_i^{k-1} also satisfies the interevent constraint. This follows from the relaxation of the lower bound. Therefore, it is sufficient to keep only the latest time stamp

---

Algorithm 4: Less-Constrained Mining: *PreElim.*

Input: Candidate episode $\alpha = \langle E_{(1)} \xrightarrow{(0,t_{high}^{(1)}]} \ldots E_{(N)} \rangle$ is a N-node episode, event sequence $S = \{(E_i, t_i)\}, i \in \{1 \ldots n\}$.
Output: Count of nonoverlapped occurrences of α
  1: $count = 0; s = []$ //List of $|\alpha|$ time stamps
  2: **for all** $(E, t) \in S$ **do**
  3:    **for** $i = |\alpha|$ to 1 **do**
  4:      $E_{(i)} = i^{th}$ event type $\in \alpha$
  5:      **if** $E = E_{(i)}$ **then**
  6:        $i_{prev} = i - 1$
  7:        **if** $i > 1$ **then**
  8:          **if** $t - s[i_{prev}] \leq t_{high}^{(i_{prev})}$ **then**
  9:            **if** $i = |\alpha|$ **then**
10:              $count + +; s = []$; **break** Line: 1.3.2
11:            **else**
12:              $s[i] = t$
13:        **else**
14:          $s[i] = t$
15: **Output**: count

---

t_m^{k-1} only in $s[E_{(k-1)}]$ because it can serve the purpose for itself and all entries above/before it, thus reducing $s[E_{(k-1)}]$ to a single time stamp rather than a list (as in Algorithm 1). ■

    Combined Algorithm: Two-Pass Elimination. Now, we can return to the original mining problem (with both upper and lower bounds). By combining Algorithm *PreElim* with our hybrid algorithm, we can develop a two-pass elimination approach that can deal with the cases on which the hybrid algorithm cannot be executed. The two-pass elimination algorithm is as follows:

Algorithm 5: Two-Pass Elimination Algorithm.

  1: (First pass) For each episode α, run *PreElim* on its less-constrained counterpart, α'.
  2: Eliminate every episode α, if $count(\alpha') < CTh$, where CTh is the support count threshold.
  3: (Second Pass) Run the hybrid algorithm on each remaining episode, α, with both interevent constraints enforced.

    The two-pass elimination algorithm yields the correct solution for Problem 1. Although the set of episodes mined under the less constrained version are not a superset of those mined under the original problem definition, we can show the following result:

Theorem 1 $count(\alpha') \geq count(\alpha)$, i.e., the count obtained from Algorithm PreElim is an upperbound on the count obtained from the hybrid algorithm.

Proof. Let h be an occurrence of α. Note that h is a map from event types in α to events in the data sequence S. Let the time stamps for each event type in h be $\{t^{(1)} \ldots t^{(k)}\}$. Since h is an occurrence of α, it follows that

$$t_{low}^{i} < t^{(i)} - t^{(i-1)} \le t_{high}^{i}, \forall i \in \{1 \ldots k-1\} \tag{15.5}$$

Note that $t_{low}^{i} > 0$. The inequality in Eq. 15.5 still holds after we replace t_{low}^{i} with 0 to get Eq. 15.6.

$$0 < t^{(i)} - t^{(i-1)} \le t_{high}^{i}, \forall i \in \{1 \ldots k-1\} \tag{15.6}$$

The preceding corresponds to the relaxed interevent constraint in α'. Therefore, every occurrence of α is also an occurrence of α', but the opposite may not be true. Hence, we have that $count(\alpha') \ge count(\alpha)$. ∎

In our two-pass elimination approach, algorithm *PreElim* is less complex and runs faster than the hybrid algorithm because it reduces the time complexity of the interevent constraint check from $O(|s[E_{(k-1)}]|)$ to $O(1)$. Therefore, the performance of the two-pass elimination algorithm is significantly better than the hybrid algorithm when the number of episodes is very large and the number of episodes culled in the first pass is also large, as shown by our experimental results described next.

15.4 EXPERIMENTAL RESULTS

15.4.1 Datasets and Testbed

Our datasets are drawn from both mathematical models of spiking neurons as well as real datasets gathered by Wagenar *et al.* [8] in their analysis of cortical cultures. Both these sources of data are described in detail in [6]. The mathematical model involves 26 neurons (event types) whose activity is modeled via inhomogeneous Poisson processes. Each neuron has a basal firing rate of 20 Hz and two causal chains of connections — one short and one long — are embedded in the data. This dataset (*Sym26*) involves 60 seconds with 50,000 events. The real datasets (*2-1-33, 2-1-34, 2-1-35*) observe dissociated cultures on days 33, 34, and 35 from over five weeks of development. The original goal of this study was to characterize bursty behavior of neurons during development.

We evaluated the performance of our GPU algorithms on a machine equipped with Intel Core 2 Quad 2.33 GHz and 4 GB of system memory. We used a NVIDIA GTX280 GPU, which has 240 processor cores with a 1.3 GHz clock for each core and 1 GB of device memory.

15.4.2 Performance of the One Thread per Occurrence

The best GPU implementation is compared with the CPU by counting a single episode. This is the case where the GPU was weakest in previous attempts, owing to the lack of parallelization when the episodes are few.

In terms of the performance of our best GPU method, we achieve a 6x speedup over the CPU implementation on the largest dataset, as shown in Figure 15.6.

Figure 15.7 contains the timing information of three compaction methods of our redesigned GPU algorithm with varying episode length. Compaction using CUDPP is the slowest of the GPU implementations, owing to its method of compaction. It requires each data element to be either in or out of the final compaction and does not allow for compaction of groups of elements. For small episode lengths, the *CountScanWrite* approach is best because sorting can be completely avoided. However, with longer episode lengths, compaction using lock-based operators shows the best performance. This method of

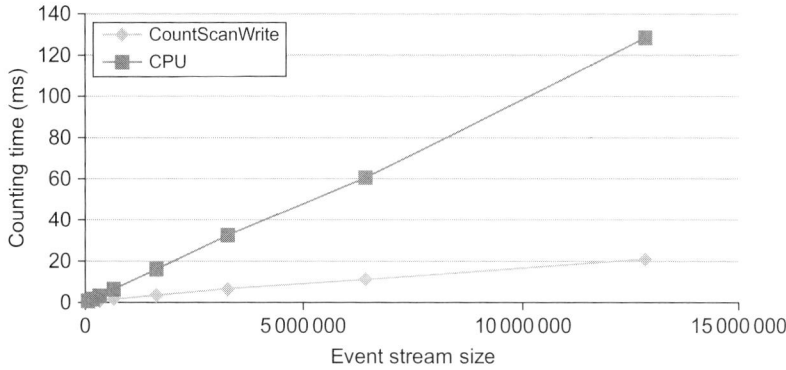

FIGURE 15.6

Performance comparison of the CPU and best GPU implementation, counting a single episode in datasets 1 through 8.

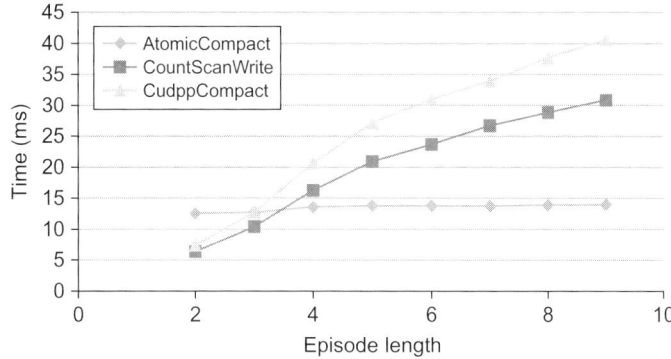

FIGURE 15.7

Performance of algorithms with varying episode length in dataset 1.

compaction avoids the need to perform a scan and a write at each iteration, at the cost of sorting the elements at the end. The execution time of the *AtomicCompact* is nearly unaffected by episode length, which seems counterintuitive because each level requires a kernel launch. However, each iteration also decreases the total number of episodes to sort and schedule at the end of the algorithm. Therefore, the cost of extra kernel invocations is offset by the final number of potential episodes to sort and schedule.

We find that counting time is related to episode frequency, as shown in Figure 15.8. There is a linear trend, with episodes of higher frequency requiring more counting time. The lock-free compaction methods follow an expected trend of slowly increasing running time because there are more potential episodes to track. The method that exhibits an odd trend is the lock-based compaction, *AtomicCompact*. As the frequency of the episode increases, there are more potential episodes to sort and schedule. The running time of the method becomes dominated by the sorting time as the episode frequency increases.

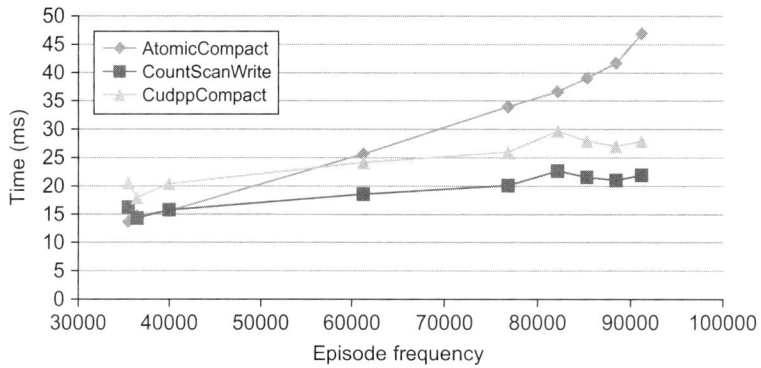

FIGURE 15.8

Performance of algorithms with varying episode frequency in dataset 1.

Another feature of Figure 15.8 that requires explanation is the bump where the episode frequency is slightly greater than 80,000. This is because it is not the final nonoverlapped count that affects the running time; it is the total number of overlapped episodes found before the scheduling algorithm is applied to remove overlaps. The x-axis is displaying nonoverlapped episode frequency, where the runtime is actually affected more by the overlapped episode frequency.

We used the CUDA Visual Profiler on the other GPU methods. They had similar profiler results as the *CountScanWrite* method. The reason is that the only bad behavior exhibited by the method is divergent branching, which comes from the tracking step. This tracking step is common to all of the GPU methods of the redesigned algorithm.

15.4.3 Performance of the Two-Pass Elimination Algorithm

The performance of the hybrid algorithm suffers from the requirement of large shared memory and large register file, especially when the episode size is big. So we introduce algorithm *PreElim*, which can eliminate most of the nonsupported episodes and requires much less shared memory and register file, and then the complex hybrid algorithm can be executed on much fewer episodes, resulting in performance gains. The amount of elimination that *PreElim* conducts can greatly affect the execution time at different episode sizes. In segment (a) of Figure 15.9, the *PreElim* algorithm eliminates over 99.9% (43,634 out of 43,656) of the episodes of size four. The end result is a speedup of 3.6× over the hybrid algorithm for this episode size and an overall speedup for this support threshold of 2.53×. Speedups for three different datasets at different support thresholds are shown in segment (b) of Figure 15.9 where in every case, the two-pass elimination algorithm outperforms the hybrid algorithm with speedups ranging from 1.2× to 2.8×.

We also use *CUDA Visual Profiler* to analyze the execution of the hybrid algorithm and *PreElim* algorithm to give a quantitative measurement of how *PreElim* outperforms the hybrid algorithm on the GPU. We have analyzed various GPU performance factors, such as GPU occupancy, coalesced global memory access, shared memory bank conflict, divergent branching, and local memory loads and

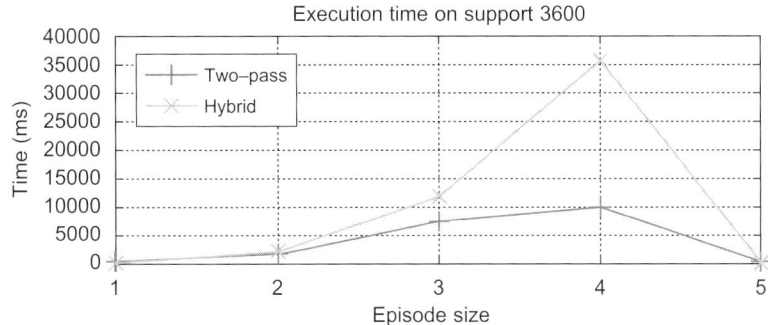

(a) Execution time of two-pass elimination and hybrid algorithms for
support = 3600 on dataset 2-1-35 at different episode sizes.

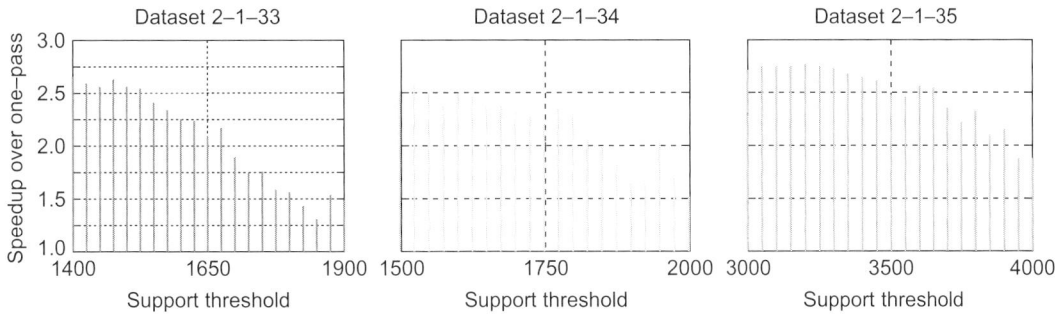

(b) Speedup of two-pass elimination over hybrid algorithm for multiple support thresholds on multiple datasets.

FIGURE 15.9

Execution time and speedup comparison of the hybrid algorithm versus the two-pass elimination algorithm.

stores. We find the last two factors are primarily attributed to the performance difference between the hybrid algorithm and *PreElim* (see Figure 15.10). The hybrid algorithm requires 17 registers and 80 bytes of local memory for each counting thread, whereas *PreElim* algorithm only requires 13 registers and no local memory. Because local memory is used as a supplement for registers and mapped onto global memory space, it is accessed very frequently and has the same high memory latency as global memory. In segment (a) of Figure 15.10, the total amount of local memory access of both the two-pass elimination algorithm and the hybrid algorithm comes from the hybrid algorithm. Because the *PreElim* algorithm eliminates most of the nonsupported episodes and requires no local memory access, the local memory access of the two-pass approach is much less than the one-pass approach when the size of the episode increases. At the size of four, the *PreElim* algorithm eliminates all episode candidates; thus, there is no execution for the hybrid algorithm and no local memory access, resulting in a large performance gain for the two-pass elimination algorithm over the hybrid algorithm. As shown in segment (b) of Figure 15.10, the amount of divergent branching also affects the GPU performance difference between the two-pass elimination algorithm and the hybrid algorithm.

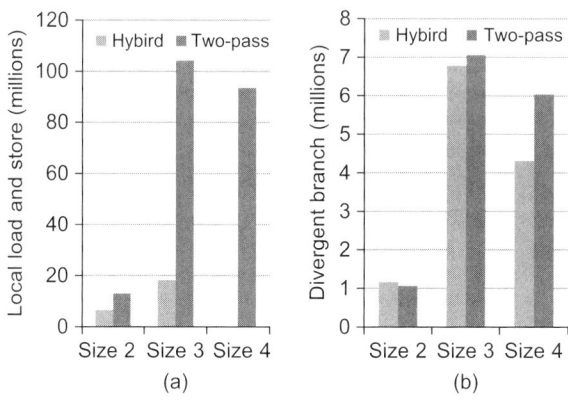

FIGURE 15.10

Comparison between the hybrid algorithm and two-pass elimination algorithm for support threshold 1650 on dataset *2-1-33*. (a) Total number of loads and stores of local memory. (b) Total number of divergent branches.

15.5 DISCUSSION

We have presented a powerful and nontrivial framework for conducting frequent episode mining on GPUs and shown its capabilities for mining neuronal circuits in spike train datasets. For the first time, neuroscientists can enjoy the benefits of data mining algorithms without needing access to costly and specialized clusters of workstations. Our supplementary website (http://neural-code.cs.vt.edu/gpgpu) provides auxiliary plots and videos demonstrating how we can track evolving cultures to reveal the progression of neural development in real time.

Our future work is in four areas. First, our experiences with the neuroscience application have opened up the interesting topic of mapping finite state machine algorithms onto the GPU. A general framework to map any finite state machine algorithm for counting will be extremely powerful not just for neuroscience, but for many other areas such as (massive) sequence analysis in bioinformatics and linguistics. Second, the development of the hybrid algorithm highlights the importance of developing new programming abstractions specifically geared toward data mining on GPUs. Third, we found that the two-pass approach performs significantly better than running the complex counting algorithm over the entire input. The first pass generates an upper bound that helps reduce the input size for the complex second pass, speeding up the entire process. We seek to develop tighter bounds that incorporate more domain-specific information about neuronal firing rates and connectivities. Finally, we wish to integrate more aspects of the application context into our algorithmic pipeline, such as candidate generation, streaming analysis, and rapid "fast-forward" and "slow-play" facilities for visualizing the development of neuronal circuits.

References

[1] S. Adee, Mastering the brain-computer interface, IEEE Spectrum (2008). Available from: `http://spectrum.ieee.org/biomedical/devices/mastering-the-braincomputer-interface`.

[2] M. Harris, S. Sengupta, J.D. Owens, GPU Gems 3, Addison Wesley, Pearson Education Inc., Upper Saddle River, 2007 (Chapter 39).

[3] P. Hingston, Using finite state automata for sequence mining, Aust. Comput. Sci. Commun. 24 (1) (2002) 105–110.

[4] K.E. Iverson, A Programming Language, John Wiley & Sons, Inc., New York, 1962.

[5] S. Laxman, P. Sastry, K. Unnikrishnan, A fast algorithm for finding frequent episodes in event streams, in: Proceedings of the 13th ACM SIGKDD International Conference on Knowledge Discovery and Data Mining (KDD 2007), San Jose, CA, August 2007, pp. 410–419.

[6] D. Patnaik, P. Sastry, K. Unnikrishnan, Inferring neuronal network connectivity from spike data: a temporal data mining approach, Sci. Program. 16 (1) (2008) 49–77.

[7] S. Sengupta, M. Harris, Y. Zhang, J.D. Owens, Scan primitives for GPU computing, in: Graphics Hardware, ACM, New York, 2007, pp. 97–106.

[8] D.A. Wagenaar, J. Pine, S.M. Potter, An extremely rich repertoire of bursting patterns during the development of cortical cultures, BMC Neurosci. (2006), doi:10.1186/1471-2202-7-11.

Statistical Modeling
Area Editor's Introduction
Mike Giles

3

16 Parallelization Techniques for Random Number Generators 231

17 Monte Carlo Photon Transport on the GPU 247

18 High-Performance Iterated Function Systems 263

STATE OF GPU COMPUTING IN STATISTICAL MODELING

Many kinds of statistical modeling are naturally suited for GPU computing owing to their inherent parallelism. For example, in Monte Carlo simulation there are usually many independent simulations to be done, and each can be performed by a separate thread. The challenges lie in coping with unusual features that could lead to warp divergence or poor memory coalescence, or require a global reduction operation. Nevertheless, this is an area with rapid adoption of GPU technology within universities.

Banks and other financial organizations have also been actively investigating the potential of GPUs. Computational finance has been a major HPC growth area in the past 20 years, and with the development of commercial random number-generation software for GPUs, I think we are likely to see widespread use of GPUs in the near future.

IN THIS SECTION

Chapter 16, written by Thomas Bradley, Mike Giles, Jacques Du Toit, Robert Tong, and Paul Woodhams, concerns techniques for parallel random number generation. Three of the most widely used generators are implemented, and interestingly, the different mathematical features of the three generators lead to different approaches for efficient GPU execution.

Chapter 17, written by Laszlo Szirmay-Kalos, Balazs Toth, and Milan Magdics, discusses a physical application, the Monte Carlo simulation of photon transport in an inhomogeneous medium. The implementation has to be structured carefully to avoid excessive warp divergence owing to the large variation in the lifetime of different photons. The efficiency is also enhanced by using a coarse grid to represent the inhomogeneous properties of the medium.

Chapter 18, written by Christoph Schied, Johannes Hanika, Holger Dammertz, and Hendrik Lensch, deals with an application from computer graphics using random functions to generate fractal images. Here, the key idea is the use of presorting to eliminate branch divergence.

Parallelization Techniques for Random Number Generators

Thomas Bradley, Jacques du Toit, Robert Tong, Mike Giles, Paul Woodhams

In this chapter, we discuss the parallelization of three very popular random number generators. In each case, the random number sequence that is generated is identical to that produced on a CPU by the standard sequential algorithm. The key to the parallelization is that each CUDA thread block generates a particular block of numbers within the original sequence, and to do this step, it needs an efficient skip-ahead algorithm to jump to the start of its block.

Although the general approach is the same in the three cases, there are significant differences in the details of the implementation owing to differences in the size of the state information required by each generator. This point is perhaps of most general interest, the way in which consideration of the number of registers required, the details of data dependency in advancing the state, and the desire for memory coalescence in storing the output lead to different implementations in the three cases.

16.1 INTRODUCTION

Random number generation [3] is a key component of many forms of simulation, and fast parallel generation is particularly important for the naturally parallel Monte Carlo simulations that are used extensively in computational finance and many areas of computational science and engineering.

In this chapter we present CUDA implementations of three of the most popular generators that appear in major commercial software libraries: L'Ecuyer's multiple recursive generator MRG32k3a, the Mersenne Twister MT19937, and the Sobol quasi-random generator. Although there is much in common in the underlying mathematical formulation of these three generators, there are also very significant differences, and one of our aims in this chapter is to explain to layman readers why these differences lead to quite different implementations.

In all three cases, there is a *state* Y_n, consisting of one or more variables, which can be advanced, step-by-step, by some algorithm

$$Y_{n+1} = f_1(Y_n)$$

from an initial value Y_0. In addition, there is an output process

$$x_n = g(Y_n)$$

which generates an approximately uniformly distributed random number x_n.

The parallel implementations are made possible by the fact that each generator can efficiently "skip ahead" a given number of points using a state advance algorithm of the form

$$Y_{n+p} = f_p(Y_n),$$

with a cost which is $O(\log p)$ in general. The question then becomes how such a skip ahead should be used. In a broad sense, there are three possible strategies:

- Simple skip ahead: each thread in each CUDA thread block performs a skip ahead to a specified point in the generator sequence, and then generates a contiguous segment of points. The skip aheads are chosen so that the segments are adjacent and do not overlap.
- Strided (or "leapfrog") skip ahead: the n-th thread (out of N) generates points $n, n+N, n+2N$, and so on.
- Hybrid: a large skip ahead is performed at the thread block level, and then within a block, each thread does strided generation.

In outline, the approaches used in the three cases are as follows:

- MRG32k3a has a very small state and a very efficient skip ahead, so the simple skip-ahead approach is used. However, care must be taken to achieve memory coalescence in writing the random outputs to device memory.
- The Sobol generator has a very small state and very efficient skip ahead. It could be implemented efficiently using the simple skip-ahead approach, but it is slightly more efficient to use the hybrid approach to achieve simple memory coalescence when writing the output data.
- MT19937 has a very large state and a very slow skip ahead. However, special features of the state advance algorithm make it possible for the threads within a block to work together to advance a shared state. Hence, the hybrid approach is adopted.

The next three sections examine each generator in detail and explain the CUDA implementation. We then present some benchmark figures comparing our implementations against the equivalent parallel generators in the Intel MKL/VSL libraries.

The software described in this chapter is available from The Numerical Algorithms Group (NAG); please see `www.nag.co.uk/numeric/gpus/` or contact `support@nag.co.uk`. In addition, the CUDA SDK example "SobolQRNG" has the source code for an implementation of the Sobol generator.

16.2 L'ECUYER'S MULTIPLE RECURSIVE GENERATOR MRG32K3A

16.2.1 Formulation

L'Ecuyer studied combined multiple recursive generators (CMRG) in order to produce a generator that had good randomness properties with a long period, while at the same time being fairly straightforward to implement. The best known CMRG is MRG32k3a [4], which is defined by the set of equations

$$y_{1,n} = \left(a_{12} y_{1,n-2} + a_{13} y_{1,n-3}\right) \qquad \bmod m_1,$$
$$y_{2,n} = \left(a_{21} y_{2,n-1} + a_{23} y_{2,n-3}\right) \qquad \bmod m_2, \qquad (16.1)$$
$$x_n = \left(y_{1,n} + y_{2,n}\right) \qquad \bmod m_1,$$

for all $n \geq 3$ where

$$a_{12} = 1403580 \quad a_{13} = -810728 \quad m_1 = 2^{32} - 209,$$
$$a_{21} = 527612 \quad a_{23} = -1370589 \quad m_2 = 2^{32} - 22853.$$

The sequence of integers $x_3, x_4, x_5 \ldots$ are the output of this generator. When divided by m_1 they give pseudorandom outputs with a uniform distribution on the unit interval $[0, 1)$. These may then be transformed into various other distributions.

At any point in the sequence the state can be represented by the pair of vectors

$$Y_{i,n} = \begin{pmatrix} y_{i,n} \\ y_{i,n-1} \\ y_{i,n-2} \end{pmatrix}$$

for $i = 1, 2$. It follows that the two recurrences in Eq. 16.1 can be represented as

$$Y_{i,n+1} = A_i Y_{i,n} \quad \bmod m_i$$

for $i = 1, 2$ where each A_i is a 3×3 matrix, and therefore

$$Y_{i,n+p} = A_i^p Y_{i,n} \quad \bmod m_i \qquad (16.2)$$

for any $p \geq 0$.

16.2.2 Parallelization

The parallel MRG generator has a small state (only six 32-bit integers) and requires few registers. The simple skip-ahead strategy whereby each thread has its own copy of state and produces a contiguous segment of the MRG32k3a sequence (as specified in Eq. 16.4) independently of all other threads works well, provided we have a very efficient way to skip ahead to an arbitrary number of points. To efficiently compute A_i^p for large values of p, one can use the classic "divide-and-conquer" strategy of iteratively squaring the matrix A_i [5, 8] . It begins by writing

$$p = \sum_{j=0}^{k} g_j 2^j,$$

where $g_j \in \{0, 1\}$ and then computing the sequence

$$A_i, A_i^2, A_i^4, A_i^8, A_i^{16}, \ldots, A_i^{2^k}, \quad \bmod m_i$$

by successively squaring the previous term found. It is then a simple matter to compute

$$A_i^p Y_i = \prod_{j=0}^{k} A^{g_j 2^j} Y_i \mod m_i$$

for $i = 1, 2$ and the entire process can be completed in approximately $O(\log_2 p)$ steps.

We can improve the speed of this procedure at the cost of more memory by expanding the exponent p in a base higher than two so that

$$p = \sum_{j=0}^{k} g_j b^j,$$

for some $b > 2$ and $g_j \in \{0, 1, \ldots, b-1\}$. This improves the "granularity" of the expansion. To illustrate, suppose $b = 10$ and $p = 7$. Then computing $A^p Y$ requires only a single lookup from memory; namely, the precomputed value A^7, and a single matrix-vector product. However, if $b = 2$, then $A^7 Y = A^4(A^2(A Y))$, requiring three lookups and three matrix-vector products.

16.2.3 Implementation

We take $b = 8$ and precompute the set of matrices $A_i^{g_j b^k}$ for $g_j = 1, \ldots, 7$ and $k = 0, \ldots, 20$; namely,

$$
\begin{array}{cccc}
A_i & A_i^2 & \cdots & A_i^7 \\
A_i^8 & A_i^{2 \cdot 8} & \cdots & A_i^{7 \cdot 8} \\
A_i^{8^2} & A_i^{2 \cdot 8^2} & \cdots & A_i^{7 \cdot 8^2} \\
\vdots & \vdots & \cdots & \vdots \\
A_i^{8^{20}} & A_i^{2 \cdot 8^{20}} & \cdots & A_i^{7 \cdot 8^{20}} & A_i^{8^{21}}
\end{array}
$$

for $i = 1, 2$ on the host. Because the state is so small, only 10,656 bytes of memory are used, and both sets of matrix powers are copied to constant memory on the GPU. Selecting from this large store of pre-computed matrix powers allows us to compute $A_i^p Y_i$, roughly three times faster than using $b = 2$.

To generate a total of N random numbers, a kernel can be launched with any configuration of threads and blocks. Using T threads in total, the i-th thread for $1 \leq i \leq T$ will advance its state by $(i-1)N/T$ and will then generate N/T numbers.

The most efficient way to use the numbers generated in this manner is to consume them as they are produced, without writing them to global memory. Because any configuration of threads and blocks can be used, and because the MRG generator is so light on resources, it can be embedded directly in an application's kernel. If this is not desired, output can be stored in global memory for subsequent use. Note that each thread generates a contiguous segment of random numbers, and therefore, writes to global memory will *not* be coalesced if they are stored to correspond to the sequence produced by the serial algorithm described in [4]; in other words, if the j-th value (counting from zero) produced by a given thread is stored at

```
storage[j+p*threadIdx.x+p*blockIdx.x*blockDim.x]
```

where $p = N/T$ and blocks and grids are one dimensional. Coalesced access can be regained either by reordering output through shared memory, or by simply writing the j-th number from each thread to

```
storage[threadIdx.x+j*blockDim.x+p*blockIdx.x*blockDim.x].
```

This will result in a sequence in global memory that has a different ordering to the MRG32k3a sequence described in [4].

16.3 SOBOL GENERATOR

Sobol [12] proposed his sequence as an alternative method of performing numerical integration in a unit hypercube. The idea is to construct a sequence that fills the cube in a regular manner. The integral is then approximated by a simple average of the function values at these points. This approach is very successful in higher dimensions where classical quadrature techniques are very expensive.

Sobol's method for constructing his sequence was improved by Antonov and Saleev [1]. Using Gray code, they showed that if the order of the points in the sequence is permuted, a recurrence relation can be found whereby the $i+1$-th point can be generated directly from the i-th point in a simple manner. Using this technique, Bratley and Fox [2] give an efficient C algorithm for generating Sobol sequences, and this algorithm was used as the starting point for our GPU implementation.

16.3.1 Formulation

We will briefly discuss how to generate Sobol sequences in the unit cube. For more details and further discussion we refer to [2]. A D-dimensional Sobol sequence is composed of D different one-dimensional Sobol sequences. We therefore examine a one-dimensional sequence.

When one is generating at most 2^{32} points, a Sobol sequence is defined by a set of 32-bit integers $m_i, 1 \leq i \leq 32$ known as *direction numbers*. Using these direction numbers, one can compute the sequence $y_1, y_2, \ldots$ from

$$y_n = g_1 m_1 \oplus g_2 m_2 \oplus g_3 m_3 \oplus \cdots \qquad (16.3)$$
$$= y_{n-1} \oplus m_{f(n-1)}$$

starting from $y_0 = 0$. Here $\oplus$ denotes the binary exclusive-or operator, and the g_i's are the bits in the binary expansion of the Gray code representation of n. The Gray code of n is given by $n \oplus (n/2)$, and so $n \oplus (n/2) = \ldots g_3 g_2 g_1$. The function $f(n)$ in Eq. 16.3 returns the index of the rightmost zero bit in the binary expansion of n. Finally, to obtain our Sobol sequence $x_1, x_2, \ldots$ we set $x_n = 2^{-32} y_n$.

To obtain multidimensional Sobol sequences, different direction numbers are used for each dimension. Care must be taken in choosing these because poor choices can easily destroy the multidimensional uniformity properties of the sequence. For more details we refer to [10].

16.3.2 Parallelization

The first expression in Eq. 16.3 gives a formula for directly computing y_n, whereas the second expression gives an efficient algorithm for computing y_n from the value of y_{n-1}. The first formula therefore allows us to skip ahead to the point y_n. This skip ahead is quite fast as it requires a loop with at most

32 iterations, and each iteration performs a bit shift and (possibly) an xor. We could therefore have parallelized this generator along the same lines as the MRG32k3a generator described earlier in this chapter with threads performing a skip ahead and then generating a block of points. However, there is another option.

Recall the second expression in Eq. 16.3, fix $n \geq 1$ and consider what happens as n increases to $n+8$. If $n = \ldots b_3 b_2 b_1$ denotes the bit pattern of n, clearly the last three bits $b_3 b_2 b_1$ remain unchanged when we add 8 to n: adding 1 to n eight times results in flipping b_1 eight times, flipping b_2 four times and flipping b_3 twice. It follows that $b_3 b_2 b_1$ will enumerate all permutations of 3 bits as n increases to $n+8$. Consider now what happens to $f(n+i)$ for $1 \leq i \leq 8$: because we are enumerating all permutations of $b_3 b_2 b_1$ we will have $f(n+i) = 1$ four times, $f(n+i) = 2$ twice, $f(n+i) = 3$ once, and $f(n+i) > 3$ once. Returning to Eq. 16.3 and recalling that two exclusive-ors cancel (i.e., $y_n \oplus m_i \oplus m_i = y_n$), we see that

$$y_{n+8} = y_n \oplus \overbrace{m_1 \cdots m_1}^{\text{four times}} \oplus \overbrace{m_2 \cdots m_2}^{\text{twice}} \oplus m_3 \oplus m_{q_n}$$

$$= y_n \oplus m_3 \oplus m_{q_n}$$

for some $q_n > 3$. This analysis can be repeated for any power of 2: in general,

$$y_{n+2^p} = y_n \oplus m_p \oplus m_{q_n} \tag{16.4}$$

for some $q_n > p$ given by $q_n = f(n|(2^p - 1))$ where | denotes the bitwise or operator. This gives an extremely efficient algorithm for strided (or "leapfrog") generation, which in turn is good for memory coalescing (see the next section).

16.3.3 Implementation

Our algorithm works as follows. The m_i values are precomputed on the host and copied to the device. In a 32-bit Sobol sequence, each dimension requires at most 32 of the m_i values. Since individual dimensions of the D dimensional Sobol sequence are independent, it makes sense to use one block to compute the points of each dimension (more than one block can be used, but suppose for now there is only one). For each Sobol dimension then, a block is launched with 2^p threads for some $p \geq 6$ and the 32 m_i values for that dimension are copied to shared memory. Within the block, the i-th thread skips ahead to the value y_i using the first expression in Eq. 16.3. Because p is typically small (around 6 or 7), the skip-ahead loop will have few iterations (around 6 or 7) because the bit pattern of $i \oplus i/2$ will contain mostly zeros. The thread then iteratively generates points $y_i, y_{i+2^p}, y_{i+2 \cdot 2^p}, \ldots$ using Eq. 16.4. Note that m_p is fixed throughout this iteration: all that is needed at each step is the previous y value and the new value of q_n. Writes to global memory are easily coalesced because successive threads in a warp generate successive values in the Sobol sequence. In global memory we store all the numbers for the first Sobol dimension first, then all the numbers for the second Sobol dimension, and so on. Therefore, if N points were generated from a D dimensional Sobol sequence and stored in an array x, the i-th value of the d-th dimension would be located at x[d*N+i] where $0 \leq i < N$ and $0 \leq d < D$.

As a final tuning of the algorithm, additional blocks can be launched for each dimension as long as the number of blocks cooperating on a given dimension is a power of 2. In this case if 2^b blocks cooperate, the i-th thread in a block simply generates the points $y_i, y_{i+2^{p+b}}, y_{i+2 \cdot 2^{p+b}}, \ldots$.

16.4 MERSENNE TWISTER MT19937

The Mersenne Twister (MT19937) is a pseudorandom number generator proposed by Matsumoto and Nishumira [11]. It is a twisted generalized feedback shift register (TGFSR) generator featuring state bit reflection and tempering. The generator has a very long period of $2^{19937} - 1$ and good multidimensional uniformity and statistical properties. The generator is also relatively fast compared with similar quality algorithms, and therefore, it is widely used in simulations where huge quantities of high-quality random numbers are required.

We start by discussing the rather complex-looking mathematical formulation. We then present the relatively simple sequential implementation, which some readers may prefer to take as the specification of the algorithm, before proceeding to the parallel implementation.

16.4.1 Formulation

TGFSR generator is based on the linear recurrence

$$X_{k+N} = X_{k+M} \oplus X_k D$$

for all $k \geq 0$ where $M < N \in \mathbb{N}$ are given and fixed. Each value X_i has a word length of w that is represented by w 0–1 bits. The value D is a $w \times w$ matrix with 0–1 entries, the matrix multiplication in the last term is performed modulo 2, and $\oplus$ is again bitwise exclusive-or, which corresponds to bitwise addition modulo 2. These types of generators have several advantages: they are easy to initialize (note that we need N seed values), they have very long periods, and they have good statistical properties.

The Mersenne Twister defines a family of TGFSR generators with a separate output function for converting state elements into random numbers. The output function applies a *tempering transform* to each generated value X_k before returning it (see [11] for further details) where the transform is chosen to improve the statistical properties of the generator. The family of generators is based on the recurrence

$$X_{k+N} = X_{k+M} \oplus (X_k^u | X_{k+1}^\ell)D \tag{16.5}$$

for all $k \geq 0$ where $M < N \in \mathbb{N}$ are fixed values and each X_i has a word length of w. The expression $(X_k^u | X_{k+1}^\ell)$ denotes the concatenation of the $w - r$ most significant bits of X_k and the r least significant bits of X_{k+1} for some $0 \leq r \leq w$, and the $w \times w$ bit-matrix D is given by

$$D = \begin{pmatrix} 0 & 1 & 0 & 0 & \cdots & 0 & 0 \\ 0 & 0 & 1 & 0 & \cdots & 0 & 0 \\ 0 & 0 & 0 & 1 & \cdots & 0 & 0 \\ \vdots & \vdots & \vdots & \vdots & \cdots & \vdots & \vdots \\ 0 & 0 & 0 & 0 & \cdots & 0 & 1 \\ d_{w-1} & d_{w-2} & d_{w-3} & d_{w-4} & \cdots & d_1 & d_0 \end{pmatrix}$$

where all the entries d_i are either zero or one. The matrix multiplication in Eq. 16.5 is performed bitwise modulo 2.

The popular Mersenne Twister MT19937 [11] is based on this scheme with $w = 32$, $N = 624$, $M = 397, r = 31$, $d_{31}d_{30} \ldots d_1 d_0 = 2567483615$, and has a period equal to the Mersenne prime

$2^{19937} - 1$. The state vector of MT19937 consists of 19,937 *bits* — 623 unsigned 32-bit words plus one bit — and is stored as 624 32-bit words. We denote this state vector by

$$Y_k = \begin{pmatrix} X_{N-1+k} \\ X_{N-2+k} \\ \vdots \\ X_k \end{pmatrix}$$

for all $k \geq 0$ where Y_0 denotes the initial seed. When read from top to bottom, the first 19,937 bits are used and the bottom 31 bits (the 31 least significant bits of X_k) are ignored. If the generator is considered as an operation on individual *bits*, it can be recast in the form

$$Y_{k+1} = A Y_k \quad \text{and} \quad Y_k = A^k Y_0 \tag{16.6}$$

where A is a matrix of dimension 19,937 with elements having value 0 or 1 and the multiplication is performed mod 2. For the explicit form of this matrix, see [11].

Matsumoto and Nishimura give a simple C implementation of their algorithm that is shown in Listing 16.1. Their implementation updates all 624 elements of state at once so that the `state` variable contains $A^{624n} Y_0$ for $n \geq 0$. The subsequent 624 function calls each produce a single random number without updating any state, and the 625-th call will again update the state.

16.4.2 Parallelization

The state size of the Mersenne Twister is too big for each thread to have its own copy. Therefore, the per-thread parallelization strategy used for the MRG32k3a is ruled out, as is the strided generation strategy used for the Sobol generator. Instead, threads within a block have to cooperate to update state and generate numbers, and the level to which this can be achieved determines the performance of the generator. Note from Eq. 16.5 that the process of advancing state is quite cheap, involving three state elements and 7 bit operations.

We follow a hybrid strategy. Each block will skip the state ahead to a given offset, and the threads will then generate a contiguous segment of points from the MT19937 sequence by striding (or leapfrogging). There are three main procedures: skipping ahead to a given point, advancing the state, and generating points from the state. We will examine how to parallelize the latter two procedures first, and then return to the question of skipping ahead.

16.4.3 Updating State and Generating Points

Generating X_{k+N} for any $k \geq 0$ requires the values of X_k, X_{k+1}, X_{k+M} where $N = 624$ and $M = 397$. In particular, $X_{(N-M)+N}$ requires $X_{(N-M)+M} = X_N$. If there are T threads in a block and the i-th thread generates $X_{N+i}, X_{N+i+T}, X_{N+i+2T}, \ldots$ for $0 \leq i < T$, then we see that we must have $T \leq N - M = 227$; otherwise, thread $N - M$ would require X_N, a value that will be generated by thread 0. To avoid dependence between threads, we are limited to fewer than 227 threads per block. We will use 1-D blocks with 224 threads because this is a multiple of 32.

```
1  #define N 624
   #define M 397
3  #define UPPER_MASK 0x80000000UL   /* most significant w-r bits */
   #define LOWER_MASK 0x7fffffffUL   /* least significant r bits */
5  static unsigned long state[N];    /* the array for the state vector  */
   static int stateIdx = N+1;        /* stateIdx==N+1 means state[N] uninitialized */
7
   /* Generates a random number in [0, 0xffffffff] */
9  unsigned int genrand_int32(void) {
       static unsigned long constants[2]={0x0UL, 0x9908b0dfUL};
11     unsigned long y;
       /* UPDATING STATE */
13     if (stateIdx >= N) { /* generate N words at one time */
           int k;
15         for (k=0; k<N-M; k++) {
               y = (state[k]&UPPER_MASK) | (state[k+1]&LOWER_MASK);
17             state[k] = state[k+M] ^ (y >> 1) ^ constants[y&0x1UL];
           }
19         for (; k<N-1; k++) {
               y = (state[k]&UPPER_MASK) | (state[k+1]&LOWER_MASK);
21             state[k] = state[k+(M-N)] ^ (y >> 1) ^ constants[y&0x1UL];
           }
23         y = (state[N-1]&UPPER_MASK) | (state[0]&LOWER_MASK);
           state[N-1] = state[M-1] ^ (y >> 1) ^ constants[y&0x1UL];
25         stateIdx = 0;
       }
27     /* GENERATING */
       y = state[stateIdx++];
29     /* Tempering */
       y ^= (y >> 11);
31     y ^= (y << 7)  & 0x9d2c5680UL;
       y ^= (y << 15) & 0xefc60000UL;
33     y ^= (y >> 18);
       return y;
35 }
```

Listing 16.1: Serial implementation of MT19937.

We implement state as a circular buffer in shared memory of length $N + 224$, and we update 224 elements at a time. We begin by generating 224 random numbers from the initial seed and then updating 224 elements of state and storing them at locations state[N...N+223]. This process repeats as often as needed, with the writing indices wrapping around the buffer. All indices except writes to global memory are computed modulo $N + 224$. The code is illustrated in Listing 16.2. As was the case with the Sobol generator, writes to global memory are easily coalesced because the threads cooperate in a leapfrog manner.

```
 1  #define N2    (N+224)
        /* ... kernel function signature, etc ... */
 3      __shared__ unsigned int state[N2];
        /* ... copy values into state from global memory ... */
 5      output_start = ... // determine where block starts generating points

 7      int k1 = threadIdx.x;
        int k2 = k1 + 1;
 9      int k3 = k1 + M;
        int k4 = k1 + N;
11      int k5 = output_start + k1;
        int num_loops = ... // Number of 224-updates of state
13      for(; num_loops>0; num_loops--) {
            /* GENERATING */
15          y = state[k1];
            y ^= (y >> 11);
17          y ^= (y << 7) & 0x9d2c5680UL;
            y ^= (y << 15) & 0xefc60000UL;
19          y ^= (y >> 18);
            global_mem_storage[k5] = y; // Modify to change output distributions
21
            /* UPDATING STATE */
23          y = (state[k1]&UPPER_MASK) | (state[k2]&LOWER_MASK);
            state[k4] = state[k3] ^ (y >> 1) ^ constants[y&0x1UL];
25
            k1 += 224;  k2 += 224;  k3 += 224;  k4 += 224;  k5 += 224;
27          if (k1>=N2) k1 -= N2;
            if (k2>=N2) k2 -= N2;
29          if (k3>=N2) k3 -= N2;
            if (k4>=N2) k4 -= N2;
31          __syncthreads();
        }
33      // Tidy up the last few points ...
```

Listing 16.2: CUDA code for generating points and updating state for MT19937. The code follows the general notation of Listing 16.1.

16.4.4 Skipping Ahead

We now consider how blocks can skip ahead to the correct point in the sequence. Given a certain number of Mersenne points to generate, we wish to determine how many points each block should produce and then skip that block ahead by the number of points all the preceding blocks will generate. For this we need a method to skip a single block ahead by a given number of points in the Mersenne sequence.

Such a skip-ahead algorithm was presented by Haramoto *et al.* [9]. Recall that $Y_n = A^n Y_0$ for $n \geq 0$ where A is a $19{,}937 \times 19{,}937$ matrix. However computing A^n even through a repeated squaring (or "divide-and-conquer") strategy is prohibitively expensive and would require a lot of memory. Instead, a different approach is followed in [9] based on polynomials in the field $\mathbb{F}_2$ (the field with elements $\{0, 1\}$ and where all operations are performed modulo 2). Briefly, they show that for any $v \in \mathbb{N}$ we have

$$A^v Y_0 = g_v(A) Y_0 \tag{16.7}$$
$$= \left(a_k A^{k-1} + a_{k-1} A_{k-2} + \cdots + a_2 A + a_1 I \right) Y_0$$
$$= a_k Y_{k-1} + a_{k-1} Y_{k-2} + \cdots + a_2 Y_1 + a_1 Y_0$$

where $k = 19,937$ and $g_v(x) = a_k x^{k-1} + \cdots + a_2 x + a_1$ is a polynomial over $\mathbb{F}_2$ that depends on v. A formula is given for determining g_v for any $v \geq 1$ given and fixed. Note that each of the coefficients a_i of g_v are either zero or one.

Figure 16.1 shows the time taken for a single block to perform the various tasks in the MT19937 algorithm: calculate g_v on the host, compute $g_v(A) Y_0$, perform v updates of state (not generating points from state), and generating v values with all updates of state. Although evaluating $g_v(A) Y_0$ is

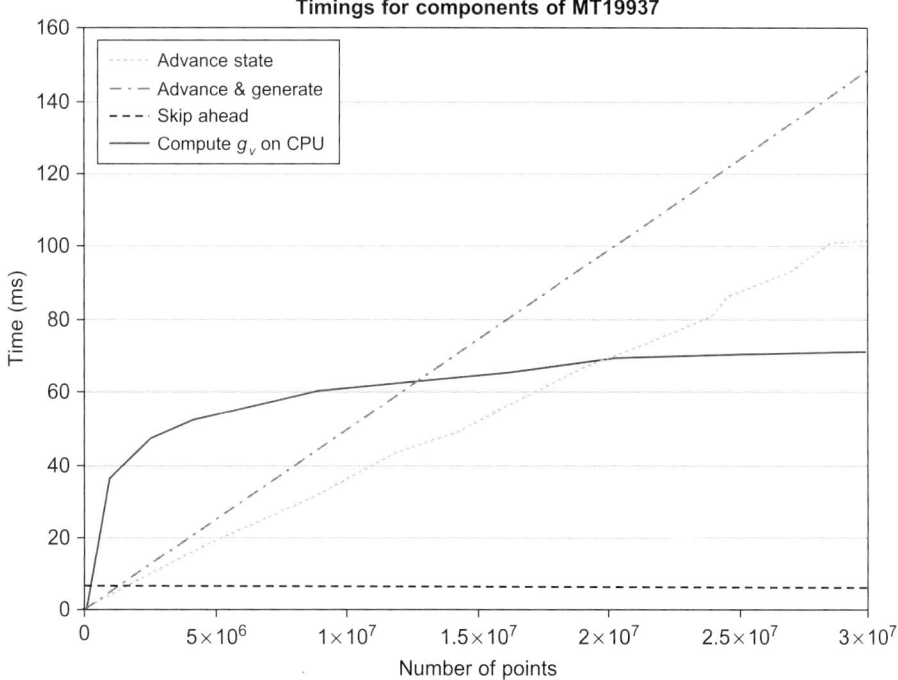

FIGURE 16.1

Time (in ms) for one block of 224 threads to (a) advance state v times (without generating points); (b) advance state v times and generate points; (c) apply the skip-ahead algorithm in Eq. 16.7; and (d) compute the skip-ahead polynomial $g_v(x)$ on the CPU (Xeon E5502). Number of points v ranges from 1000 to 30 million and GPU code was run on a Quadro FX5800.

fairly expensive (equivalent to generating about 2 million points and advancing state about 2.3 million times), computing the polynomial g_v is is much more so: one could generate almost 13 million points in the same time, and advance state almost 20 million times. Updating state and generating points scale linearly with v.

Clearly, we would prefer not to calculate g_v on the fly. We would also prefer not to perform the calculation $g_v(A)Y_0$ in a separate kernel because the first block never has to skip ahead and this would prevent it from generating points until the calculation was finished. However, there is the question of load balance: the first block can generate around 2 million points in the time it takes the second block to skip ahead. Because the total runtime is equal to the runtime of the slowest block, if the number of blocks equals the number of streaming multiprocessors in the GPU, it is clear that blocks should not all generate the same number of points. A mathematical analysis of the runtimes of each block, coupled with experimental measurements, can be done, and this yields formulae for the optimal number of points each block should generate as well as how far the block should skip ahead. This depends on the sample size and so requires us to calculate g_v on the fly.

There are a number of options when choosing a skip-ahead strategy for the Mersenne Twister, and it is not completely clear which approach is best:

- When a huge number of points are to be generated, the only option may be to generate the necessary polynomials on the fly and perform Eq. 16.7 on the device. In this case the generator will typically be embedded in a larger application so that the cost of computing the polynomials is small compared with the total runtime.
- When a small number of points are to be generated it may be more efficient to have a producer-consumer model where one (or a few) blocks advance state and write the values to global memory, while other blocks read these values in and generate points from the necessary distributions. This requires rather sophisticated interblock communication using global memory locks and relies on the update of state shown in Eq. 16.5 being much cheaper than converting state into a given distribution. It is not clear how useful this would be, and indeed for smaller samples, it will probably be faster (and simpler) to compute the numbers on the host.
- When a medium number of points are to be generated, it is possible to precompute and store a selection of polynomials $\{g_v\}_{v \in \mathcal{V}}$ for some $\mathcal{V} \subset \mathbb{N}$. At runtime a suitable subset of these can be chosen and copied to the device where the skip ahead is then performed. This is the approach we have adopted. The difficulty here is deciding on $\mathcal{V}$ and on which subset to choose at runtime. Formulae can be developed to help with this, but it is still a rather tricky problem.
- Lastly, we can always calculate g_{v_i} and $g_{v_i}(A)Y_0$ for all necessary skip points v_i on the host and then copy the advanced states to the device to generate random numbers. This is currently impractical, but the upcoming Westmere family of Intel CPUs contains a new instruction `PCLMULQDQ` — a bitwise carry-less multiply — that is ideally suited to this task; see [7] for further details.

16.5 PERFORMANCE BENCHMARKS

We compared our CUDA implementations with the Intel MKL/VSL library's random number generators. Benchmarks were done in both single and double precision on a Tesla C1060 and a Tesla

Table 16.1 Test systems used for benchmarking. Tesla C2050 uses the new Fermi micro architecture.

Hardware	Intel Xeon E5410 2.33 GHz with 8 GB RAM for Tesla C1060
	Intel Core i7 860 2.80 GHz with 8 GB RAM for Tesla C2050
Operating System	Windows XP 64-bit SP2 for Tesla C1060
	Windows 7 Professional for Tesla C2050
C++ Compiler	Intel C++ Compiler Pro v11.1
C++ Options	`/O2 /Og /Ot /Qipo /D "WIN32" /D "NDEBUG" /EHsc /MD`
	`/D "_CONSOLE" /D "_UNICODE" /D "UNICODE" /nologo`
	`/GS- /fp:strict /Qfp-speculation:off /W3 /Wp64 /Zi`
	`/Qopenmp /QxHost /Quse-intel-optimized-headers`
NVIDIA Toolkit	CUDA 2.3 for Tesla C1060
	CUDA 3.0 for Tesla C2050
NVIDIA GPU	Tesla C1060 using NVIDIA Driver v190.38
	Tesla C2050 using NVIDIA Driver v197.68
NVCC Options	`-O2 -D_CONSOLE -arch compute_13 -code sm_13`
	`--host-compilation C++ -Xcompiler /MT -m 64`

C2050 (that uses the new Fermi micro architecture). The test system configuration is detailed in Table 16.1.

The Intel random number generators are contained in the vector statistical library (VSL). This library is not multithreaded, but is thread safe and contains all the necessary skip-ahead functions to advance the generators' states. We used OpenMP to parallelize the VSL generators and obtained figures when running one, two, three and four CPU threads. Timing of the CPU code was done using hardware high-resolution performance counters; the GPU code was timed using CUDA events and `cudaEvent ElapsedTime`. Ideally, an application would consume the random numbers on the GPU, however, if the random numbers were required by CPU code, then there may be an additional cost to copy the data back from the GPU to the host. A fixed problem size of 2^{25} was chosen so that each generator produced $33,554,432$ floating-point numbers. This corresponds to 134 MB of data in single precision and 268 MB in double precision. For the Sobol generators we chose $2^7 = 128$ dimensions and generated $2^{18} = 262,144$ multidimensional points. Note that the VSL does not have skip-ahead functions for the MT19937 generator, so it was not possible to parallelize this generator.

We produced uniform exponential and normal random numbers. For the MRG the normal random numbers were obtained through a Box-Muller transform whereas for the Sobol and Mersenne generators the normal random numbers were obtained by inverting the cumulative normal distribution function using an efficient implementation of the inverse error function [6]. Exponential numbers were obtained by inverting the cumulative exponential distribution function. The results are given in Tables 16.2 and 16.3.

All benchmarks were performed after a clean reboot of the workstation, with only a command prompt open. There does seem to be some variability in the figures across different runs, depending on system load, but this is small enough to be ignored. For the Mersenne Twister we precomputed

Table 16.2 Benchmark figures for Tesla C1060 vs. Intel Xeon E5410. Values in **bold type** are double precision; other values are single precision. Columns "1 Thread" through "4 Threads" show speedup of GPU vs. CPU, i.e., (GPU pts/ms)÷(CPU pts/ms). Generators produced 2^{25} points: Sobol generators produced 2^{18} points of 2^7 dimensions each. The test system is as detailed in Table 16.1.

Generators		Tesla GPU	Intel MKL on Xeon E5410			
		GPU pts/ms	1 Thread	2 Threads	3 Threads	4 Threads
MRG	Unif	3.6151E+06	41.161x	24.774x	19.639x	16.247x
		3.1202E+06	**45.528x**	**31.094x**	**30.887x**	**29.889x**
	Exp	2.8280E+06	39.545x	23.222x	17.882x	14.964x
		6.8651E+05	**12.329x**	**7.634x**	**6.724x**	**6.468x**
	Norm	2.6647E+06	47.043x	25.619x	18.498x	15.188x
		6.5853E+05	**18.012x**	**10.257x**	**7.463x**	**6.215x**
Sobol	Unif	1.5790E+07	100.51x	93.976x	94.179x	64.556x
		9.2006E+06	**7.591x**	**90.396x**	**84.130x**	**88.832x**
	Exp	6.8723E+06	52.591x	41.702x	33.784x	32.251x
		7.8709E+05	**10.622x**	**8.683x**	**7.398x**	**7.432x**
	Norm	7.4239E+06	57.079x	45.129x	35.896x	34.820x
		4.0799E+05	**5.516x**	**4.578x**	**3.915x**	**3.856x**
Mersenne	Unif	2.6721E+06	25.051x			
		2.5762E+06	**40.320x**			
	Exp	2.0741E+06	24.758x			
		5.9492E+05	**19.728x**			
	Norm	2.0657E+06	24.856x			
		3.1229E+05	**5.8127x**			

the skip-ahead polynomials g_v for $v = 1 \times 10^6, 2 \times 10^6, \ldots, 32 \times 10^6$ and then used a combination of redundant state advance (without generating points) and runtime equations to find a good workload for each thread block.

The Fermi card is roughly twice as fast as the Tesla in single precision, and roughly four times as fast in double precision. The exception to this is the Sobol single precision figures, which are very similar between the two cards. It may be that the Sobol generator is bandwidth limited because Sobol values (in single precision) are so cheap to compute.

Acknowledgments

Jacques du Toit thanks the UK Technology Strategy Board for funding his KTP Associate position with the Smith Institute, and Mike Giles thanks the Oxford-Man Institute of Quantitative Finance for its support.

Table **16.3** Benchmark figures for Tesla C2050 vs. Intel Xeon E5410. Values in **bold type** are double precision; other values are single precision. Columns "1 Thread" through "4 Threads" show speedup of GPU vs. CPU; i.e., (GPU pts/ms)÷(CPU pts/ms). Generators produced 2^{25} points: Sobol generators produced 2^{18} points of 2^7 dimensions each. Test system is as detailed in Table 16.1.

		Fermi GPU	Intel MKL on Xeon E5410			
Generators		GPU pts/ms	1 Thread	2 Threads	3 Threads	4 Threads
MRG	Unif	7.7127E+06	88.108x	52.854x	41.900x	34.622x
		7.4453E+06	**108.64x**	**74.197x**	**73.703x**	**71.321x**
	Exp	5.4368E+06	76.024x	44.643x	34.378x	28.767x
		2.6696E+06	**47.935x**	**29.682x**	**26.143x**	**25.148x**
	Norm	4.6129E+06	81.436x	44.348x	32.022x	26.291x
		2.4418E+06	**66.789x**	**38.034x**	**27.673x**	**23.044x**
Sobol	Unif	1.7434E+07	110.97x	103.76x	103.98x	71.724x
		1.3452E+07	**142.68x**	**132.16x**	**123.00x**	**129.88x**
	Exp	7.9361E+06	60.732x	48.157x	39.014x	37.243x
		3.2094E+06	**43.312x**	**35.404x**	**30.168x**	**30.304x**
	Norm	8.6020E+06	66.137x	52.291x	41.593x	40.346x
		1.6202E+06	**21.904x**	**18.179x**	**15.547x**	**15.314x**
Mersenne	Unif	2.9077E + 06	27.260x			
		2.8728E+06	**44.961x**			
	Exp	2.2352E+06	26.680x			
		1.2465E+06	**23.097x**			
	Norm	2.1965E+06	26.430x			
		8.8145E+05	**16.407x**			

References

[1] I.A. Antonov, V.M. Saleev, An economic method of computing LP_τ sequences, USSR J. Comput. Math. Math. Phys. 19 (1979) 252–256.
[2] P. Bratley, B. Fox, Algorithm 659: implementing Sobol's quasirandom sequence generator, ACM Trans. Model. Comput. Simul. 14 (1) (1988) 88–100.
[3] P. L'Ecuyer, Uniform random number generation, in: S.G. Henderson, B.L. Nelson (Eds.), Simulation Handbooks in Operation Research and Management Science, Elsevier Inc., Amsterdam, 2006, pp. 55–81.
[4] P. L'Ecuyer, Good parameter sets for combined multiple recursive random number generators, Ops. Rsch. 47 (1) (1999) 159–164.
[5] P. L'Ecuyer, R. Simar, E.J. Chen, W.D. Kelton, An object oriented random number package with many long streams and substreams, Ops. Rsch. 50 (6) (2002) 1073–1075.
[6] M. Giles, Approximating the `erfinv` function, in: GPU Gems 4, vol. 2.

[7] S. Gueron, M.E. Kounavis, Intel carry-less multiplication instruction and its usage for computing the GCM mode, Intel White Paper, http://software.intel.com/en-us/articles/intel-carry-less-multiplication-instruction-and-its-usage-for-computing-the-gcm-mode/.

[8] D. Knuth, *The Art of Computer Programming, vol. 2, third ed.*, Addison-Wesley Professional, Reading, MA, 1997.

[9] H. Haromoto, M. Matsumoto, T. Nishumira, F. Panneton, P. L'Ecuyer, Efficient jump ahead for $\mathbb{F}_2$-linear random number generators, INFORMS J. Comput. 20 (3) (2008) 385–390.

[10] S. Joe, F.Y. Kuo, Constructing Sobol sequences with better two dimensional projects, SIAM J. Sci. Comput. 30 (2008) 2635–2654.

[11] M. Matsumoto, T. Nishumira, Mersenne Twister: a 623-dimensionally equidistributed uniform pseudo-random number generator, ACM Trans. Mod. Comput. Simul. 8 (1) (1998) 3–30.

[12] I.M. Sobol, On the distribution of points in a cube and the approximate evaluation of integrals, USSR Comput. Math. Math. Phys. 16 (1967) 1332–1337.

Monte Carlo Photon Transport on the GPU

17

László Szirmay-Kalos, Balázs Tóth, Milán Magdics

This chapter presents a fast parallel Monte Carlo method to solve the radiative transport equation in inhomogeneous participating media for light and gamma photons. Light transport is relevant in computer graphics while higher-energy gamma photons play an essential role in medical or physical simulation. Real-time graphics applications are speed critical because we need to render more than 20 images per second in order to provide the illusion of continuous motion. Fast simulation is also important in interactive systems like radiotherapy or physical experiment design where the user is allowed to place the source and expects an instant feedback about the resulting radiation distribution. The speed of multiple scattering simulation is also crucial in iterative tomography reconstruction where the scattered radiation is estimated from the actually reconstructed data, removed from the measurements, and reconstruction is continued for the residual that is assumed to represent only the unscattered component.

17.1 PHYSICS OF PHOTON TRANSPORT

Computing multiple scattering and rendering inhomogeneous participating media in a realistic way are challenging problems. The most accurate approaches are based on Monte Carlo quadrature and simulate the physical phenomena by tracing photons randomly in the medium and summing up their contribution.

The conditional probability density that a photon collides with the particles of the material provided that the photon arrived at this point is defined by the *extinction coefficient* $\sigma_t(v,\vec{x})$, which may depend on the photon's frequency v and also on the location $\vec{x}$ if the particle density is not homogeneous. The extinction coefficient can usually be expressed by the product of the material density $C(\vec{x})$ and a factor depending just on the frequency.

Upon collision, the photon may get reflected or absorbed. The probability of reflection is called the *albedo* and is denoted by $a(v)$.

The random reflection direction is characterized by two spherical coordinates, *scattering angle* θ and *azimuth angle* φ (Figure 17.1). The probability density of *scattering angle* θ that is between the original and the new directions may depend on the frequency and is described by the physical model (we use the *Rayleigh scattering* [12] model for light photons and the *Klein-Nishina formula* [11], [13] for gamma photons). The probability density of the azimuth angle is uniform due to the rotational symmetry.

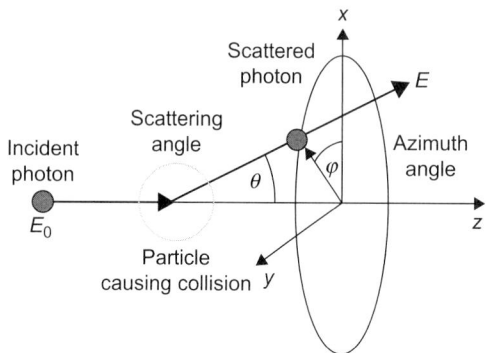

FIGURE 17.1

Photon scattering in participating media. The incident photon of energy E_0 collides with a particle of the material. Because of this collision the photon's direction and energy may change. The new direction is specified by scattering angle θ and azimuth angle φ. The new photon energy E is determined by the incident photon energy and the scattering angle.

The photon's energy $E = hv$ is proportional to its frequency and the ratio of the proportionality is the *Planck constant h*. The energy (i.e., the frequency of a higher energy gamma photon) may change as a result of scattering. According to the Compton law, there is a unique correspondence between the scattering angle and the relative change of the photon energy:

$$E = \frac{E_0}{1 + \frac{E_0}{m_e c^2}(1 - \cos\theta)}$$

where E is the scattered photon energy, E_0 is the incident photon energy, m_e is the rest mass of the electron, and c is the speed of light. Examining the Compton formula, we can conclude that the energy change at scattering is significant when E_0 is nonnegligible with respect to the energy of the electron ($m_e c^2$). This is not the case for photons of visible wavelengths, when $E_0 = hv << m_e c^2$; thus, their scattered energy will be similar to the incident energy. Consequently, we can decompose the simulation of low-energy radiation (light photons) to different frequencies, but on higher energies (gamma photons), the frequency will be an attribute of each simulated photon.

In computer simulation, the photon is traced according to the basic laws mentioned so far. The inputs of the simulation are the density of the participating medium, which is defined by a 3-D scalar density field $C(\vec{x})$, the frequency dependent albedo function, and the probability density of the scattering angle. The density field is assumed to be available in a discrete form as a 3-D texture of voxels. The frequency dependent albedo and scattering density functions may be defined either by tables stored in textures or by algebraic formulae.

In order to simulate the photon transport process, the collision, the absorption, and the scattering direction should be generated with the probability densities defined by the physical model. One approach to generate random variables with prescribed probability densities is the *inversion method*. The inversion method first calculates the *cumulative probability distribution* (*CDF*) as the integral of the probability density and then generates the discrete samples by inverting the CDF for values that are uniformly distributed in the unit interval. Formally, if the cumulative probability distribution of a random variable is $P(x)$, then a random sample x can be generated by solving equation

$$P(x) = r$$

where r is a random variable uniformly distributed in the unit interval and is usually obtained by calling the random number generator.

17.2 PHOTON TRANSPORT ON THE GPU

Photons travel in space independently of each other and thus can be simulated in parallel, thereby revealing the inherent parallelism of the physical simulation (nature is a massively parallel machine). The algorithm of simulating the path of a single photon is a nested loop. Both the outer and the inner loops are dynamic, and their number of executions cannot be predicted. The body of the outer loop is responsible for finding the next scattering point, then sampling absorption and the new scattering direction in case of survival. This loop is terminated when the photon is absorbed or it leaves the simulation volume. The number of scattering events of different photons will range on a large interval, and so will the number of outer loop executions. The inner loop visits voxels until the next scattering point is located; this process depends on the drawn random number and also on the density of medium along the ray of the photon path. Both the random number and the density vary, thus again the number of visited voxels may be different for different samples (Figure 17.2).

The problem of executing different numbers of iterations in parallel threads becomes crucial on the GPU. If we assigned a photon to a computational thread of the GPU, then the longest photon path and the longest ray of all paths in each warp will limit the computational speed. In order to maintain warp coherence, the execution lengths of the threads must be similar, and the threads are preferred to

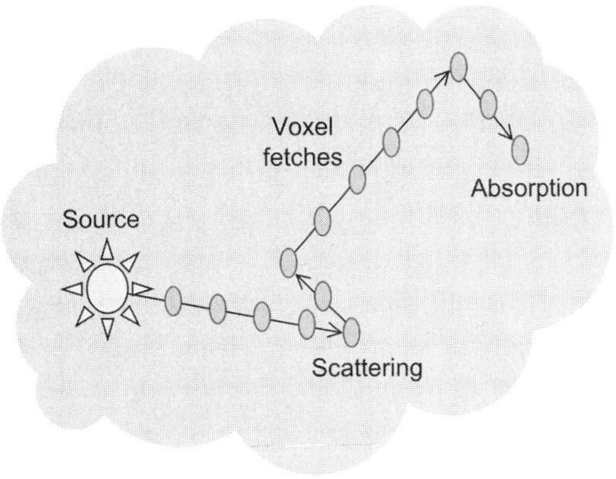

FIGURE 17.2

Causes of control path divergence in photon transport simulation. A photon path has a random number of scattering points and between two scattering points there may be a different number of voxels.

always execute the same instruction sequence. To attack these problems, we restructure the transport simulation according to the requirements of efficient GPU execution; that is, we develop algorithms that can be implemented with minimal conditional instructions.

To solve the problem of different numbers of scattering events, we iterate photon steps, that is, rays in computational threads. A step includes identifying the next scattering point, making the decision on termination, and sampling the new direction if the photon survived the collision, or generating a new photon at the source otherwise. This strategy keeps all threads busy at all times.

After this restructuring, threads may still diverge. Determining whether the photon is absorbed and sampling the new scattering direction are based on the local properties of the medium; thus, these tasks require the solution of an equation that contains just a few variables, which can be determined from the actual position. Even this simple problem becomes difficult if the CDF cannot be analytically computed and symbolically inverted. In these cases, numerical methods should be used. Free path sampling is even worse because it requires the exploration of a larger part of the medium, which corresponds to a lot of memory accesses being relatively slow on current GPUs. Both iterative numerical root finding and the exploration of the volume in regions of different density lead to thread divergence and eventually poor GPU utilization.

As different photons are traced randomly, they visit different parts of the simulated volume, resulting in parallel accesses of far parts of the data memory. This kind of memory accesses degrades cache utilization. To solve this problem, one might propose the assignment of those photons to a warp that possibly has similar paths. Because random paths are computed from sequences of uniformly distributed random numbers, this would mean the clustering of vectors of random numbers. A complete path may be associated with many (e.g., more than 20) random numbers, so the clustering operation should work in very high dimensional spaces, which is not feasible in practice. So photons are sorted according to only the first random number and assigned to warps in the sorted sequence. This step provides little initial data access coherence, but sooner or later, threads will inevitably fetch different parts of the volume.

In order to guarantee the coherence of threads tracing rays in the medium, we develop a conditional instruction-free solution for sampling absorption and scattering direction. To solve the free-path-sampling problem and also to limit the data access divergence, we present a technique that uses a low-resolution voxel array in addition to the original high-resolution voxel array. This technique significantly reduces the number of texture fetches to the high-resolution array as well as the number of iterations needed to find the next scattering point.

17.2.1 Free Path Sampling

The first step of simulating a photon of current location $\vec{x}$, direction $\vec{\omega}$, and frequency v is the sampling of the *free path* s that the photon can fly without collision, that is, the determination of the next interaction point along the ray $\vec{p}(s) = \vec{x} + \vec{\omega}s$ of its path. The probability density that photon-particle collision happens is the extinction coefficient. From this, the cumulative probability distribution of the free path length can be expressed in the form of an exponential decay; thus free path sampling is equivalent to the solution of the following equation for scalar r that is uniformly distributed in the unit interval:

$$1 - \exp\left(-\int_0^s \sigma_t(v, \vec{p}(l)) dl\right) = r.$$

The integral of the extinction coefficient is called the *optical depth*, for which the following equation can be derived:

$$\tau(0,s) = \int_0^s \sigma_t(v,\vec{p}(l))dl = -\log(1-r). \tag{17.1}$$

Free path sampling, that is, the solution of this equation, is simple when the medium is homogeneous; in other words, when the extinction coefficient is the same everywhere:

$$s = \frac{-\log(1-r)}{\sigma_t(v)}.$$

When the medium is inhomogeneous, the extinction coefficient is not constant but is represented by a voxel array. In this case, the usual approach is *ray marching* that takes small steps Δs along the ray and finds step number n when the Riemann sum approximation of the optical depth gets larger than $-\log(1-r)$:

$$\sum_{i=0}^{n-1}\sigma_t(v,\vec{p}(i\Delta s))\Delta s \leq -\log(1-r) < \sum_{i=0}^{n}\sigma_t(v,\vec{p}(i\Delta s))\Delta s.$$

Step size Δs is set to the edge length of the voxel in order not to skip voxels during the traversal. Unfortunately, this algorithm requires a lot of voxel array fetches, especially when the voxel array is large and the average extinction is small. To make it even worse, the number of texture fetches vary significantly, depending on the random length of the ray. Recall that free path sampling is the evaluation of a simple formula when the optical depth is a simple algebraic expression, as in the case of homogeneous volumes. However, if the optical depth can be computed only from many data, which happens when the extinction coefficient is specified by a high-resolution voxel array, then the sampling process will be slow. Fortunately, we do not have to pay the full cost if we have at least partial information about the extinction coefficient, which can be utilized to reduce the number of fetches. This is the basic idea of our method.

Free path sampling is equivalent to the solution of Eq. 17.1 for path length s, where we want to replace the optical depth by a simpler function that can be computed from a few variables. To reach this goal, we modify the volume by adding virtual "material" or particles in a way that the total density will follow a simple function. One might think that mixing additional material into the original medium would also change the radiation intensity inside the volume, resulting in a bad solution, which is obviously not desired. Fortunately, this is not necessarily the case if the other two free properties of the virtual material — namely the albedo and the probability density of the scattering angle — are appropriately defined.

Virtual particles must not alter the radiation intensity inside the medium; that is, they must not change the energy and the direction of photons during scattering. This requirement is met if the virtual particle has *albedo* 1, that is, it reflects photons with probability 1, and the probability density of the scattering angle is a Dirac-delta at zero — in other words, it does not change the photon's direction with probability 1.

More formally, we handle heterogeneous volumes by mixing additional virtual particles into the medium to augment the extinction coefficient to a simpler upper-bounding function $\sigma_{max}(v,\vec{x})$. For

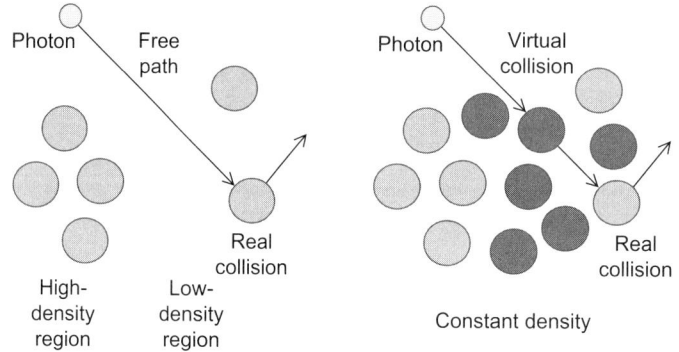

FIGURE 17.3

The application of virtual particles. In the left image the free path sampling of the original volume of real particles (colored as light gray) is shown. The right image depicts the total volume containing both the real and the virtual (dark gray) particles. Collision with a virtual particle does not alter the photon direction.

original extinction coefficient $\sigma_t(v,\vec{x})$, we have to find the extinction coefficient $\sigma_v(v,\vec{x})$ of the virtual particles so that in the *combined medium* of real and virtual particles the extinction coefficient is $\sigma_{max}(v,\vec{x}) = \sigma_t(v,\vec{x}) + \sigma_v(v,\vec{x})$.

When a collision occurs in the combined medium, we have to determine whether it happened on a real or on a virtual particle. Sampling is required to generate random points with a prescribed probability density, and therefore, it is enough to solve this problem randomly with the proper probabilities. As the extinction parameters define the probability density of scattering, ratios $\sigma_t(v,\vec{x})/\sigma_{max}(v,\vec{x})$ and $\sigma_v(v,\vec{x})/\sigma_{max}(v,\vec{x})$ give us the probabilities whether scattering happened on a real or on a virtual particle, respectively.

Having added the virtual particles, we can execute free path sampling in the following steps (Figure 17.3):

1. Generate tentative path length s and *tentative collision point* $\vec{p}(s)$ using the upper-bounding extinction coefficient function $\sigma_{max}(v,\vec{x})$. This requires the solution of the sampling equation using the maximum extinction:

$$\tau_{max}(0,s) = \int_0^s \sigma_{max}(v,\vec{p}(l))dl = -\log(1-r). \tag{17.2}$$

2. When a tentative collision point $\vec{p}$ is identified, we decide randomly with probability $\sigma_t(v,\vec{p})/\sigma_{max}(v,\vec{p})$ whether scattering happened on a real or on a virtual particle. If only virtual scattering occurred, then the particle's direction is not altered and a similar sampling step is repeated from the scattering point. This loop is terminated when a real scattering is found.

Note that the samples declared as real by the algorithm are generated with a conditional probability density of the original extinction coefficient no matter what upper-bounding extinction coefficient is built into the sampling. However, the efficiency of the sampling is greatly affected by the proper choice of the upper-bounding coefficient. On one hand, the upper-bounding coefficient should offer a simple

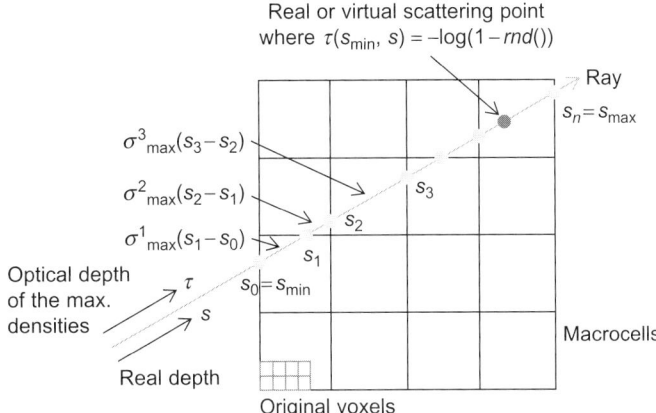

FIGURE 17.4

Free path sampling with virtual particles. We execute a 3-D DDA voxel traversal in the grid of macrocells and analytically obtain the optical depth τ corresponding to the extinction coefficient σ_{max} of the combined medium of the real and virtual particles.

solution for Eq. 17.2. On the other hand, if the difference of the upper-bounding coefficient and the real coefficient, that is, the density of virtual particles, is high, then the probability of virtual scattering events will also be high, thus requiring many additional sampling steps until the real scattering is found. Thus, an optimal upper-bounding coefficient offers an easy solution of Eq. 17.2 and is a tight upper bound of the real extinction coefficient.

To find a simple, but reasonably accurate upper bound, we use a piecewise constant function that is defined in a low-resolution grid of *macrocells* (Figure 17.4) as proposed in [8] and assign the maximum extinction coefficient of its original voxels to each macrocell. If only one macrocell is defined that contains the whole volume, then the method becomes equivalent to *Woodcock tracking* [10].

In order to solve Eq. 17.2, we execute a 3-D DDA-like voxel traversal [4] on the macrocell grid to visit all macrocells that are intersected by the ray. The 3-D DDA algorithm is based on the recognition that the boundaries of the cells are on three collections of parallel planes, which are orthogonal to the respective coordinate axes. The algorithm maintains three ray parameters representing the next intersection points with these plane collections. The minimum of the three ray parameters represents the exit point of the current cell. To step on to the next cell, an increment is added to this ray parameter. The increments corresponding to the three plane collections are constants for a given ray and should be calculated only once.

During traversal, ray parameters s_i corresponding to points when the ray crosses the macrocell boundaries are found. We visit macrocells one by one until the current macrocell contains the root of Eq. 17.2 (Figure 17.4).

The inequalities selecting the macrocell n that contains the scattering point are:

$$\sum_{i=0}^{n-1} \sigma_{max}^i(v)\Delta s_i \leq -\log(1-r) < \sum_{i=0}^{n} \sigma_{max}^i(v)\Delta s_i$$

where $\sigma_{max}^i(v)$ is the constant extinction coefficient of the augmented volume in macrocell i.

The important differences of ray marching and the proposed approach are that steps Δs_i are not constant but are obtained as the length of the intersection of the ray and the macrocells.

When in step n the inequalities are first satisfied, the macrocell of the scattering point is located. As $\sigma_{max}^n(\nu)$ is constant in the identified macrocell, its integral in Eq. 17.2 is linear; thus, the free path sampling becomes equivalent to the solution of a linear equation:

$$s = s_{n-1} + \Delta s_n = s_{n-1} - \frac{\log(1-r) + \sum_{i=0}^{n-1} \sigma_{max}^i(\nu)\Delta s_i}{\sigma_{max}^n(\nu)}.$$

The proposed free-path-sampling method causes significantly smaller warp divergence than ray marching or Woodcock tracking. In ray marching, the number of iteration cycles would be proportional to the length of the free path, which may range from 1 to the linear resolution of the voxel array (e.g., 512). In Woodcock tracking, the average step size is inversely proportional to the global maximum of the extinction coefficient. The probability of nonvirtual collisions is equal to the ratio of the actual and the maximum extinction coefficients, so the algorithm would take many small steps and find only virtual collisions in low-density regions. In the proposed method, however, the probability of nonvirtual collisions is the ratio of actual coefficient and the maximum of this macrocell, so it corresponds to how accurately the piecewise constant bound of macrocells represents the true extinction coefficient. Increasing the resolution of the macrocell grid, this accuracy can be controlled paying the price of more macrocell steps. For example, in the head dataset (Figure 17.9) of 128^3 voxels, with 8^3 macrocell grid resolution, the average number of virtual collisions before finding a real one is 0.95, whereas the average number of macrocell steps is 1.7. If the macrocell resolution is increased to 16^3, then the average number of virtual collisions reduces to 0.92, but the average number of visited macrocells increases to 3.7. Generally, very few (at the most one or two virtual collisions) may happen before finding the real collision point, and the possible number of macrocell steps is far smaller than that of the steps of a ray-marching algorithm.

17.2.2 Absorption Sampling

When the photon collides with a real particle, we should determine whether or not absorption happened and also the new direction if the photon survived the collision. The probability of survival is defined by the albedo; thus, this random decision is made by checking whether the albedo is larger than a random number uniformly distributed in the unit interval:

$$r < a(\nu).$$

In our implementation the frequency dependent albedo function is stored in a 1-D texture addressed by the frequency normalized by maximum frequency ν_{max} that is the frequency of emitted photons. Turning linear interpolation on, the albedo is smoothly interpolated in between the representative frequencies. For light photons, the albedo is stored just on the frequencies corresponding to the red, green, and blue light.

17.2.3 Scattering Direction

If the photon survives the collision, a new continuation direction needs to be sampled, which is defined by scattering angle θ and azimuth angle φ.

The azimuth angle φ is uniformly distributed; thus, it is generated as $\varphi = 2\pi r_1$ where r_1 is a uniform random number in the unit interval. The scattering angle is sampled by solving the sampling equation

$$P_{\cos\theta}(\nu, \cos\theta) = r_2$$

where $P_{\cos\theta}(\nu, \cos\theta)$ is the cumulative probability distribution of the cosine of the scattering angle on a given frequency, and r_2 is another uniform random number. The probability density of the scattering angle is usually defined by the physical model and is a moderately complex algebraic expression (we use Rayleigh scattering for light photons and the Klein-Nishina differential cross section for gamma photons, but other phase functions can also be handled in the discussed way), from which the cumulative distribution can be obtained by integration. Unfortunately, for most of the models, the integral cannot be expressed in a closed form, and the sampling equation cannot be solved analytically. On the other hand, numerical solutions, like the midpoint or the false position methods, would execute a loop and would be slow.

To attack this problem, we find regularly placed samples for $r_2 = 0, 1/N, 2/N, \ldots, 1$ and $\nu = 0$, $\nu_{\max}/M, 2\nu_{\max}/M, \ldots, \nu_{\max}$, and solve the sampling equation for these samples offline (we set N and M to 128). The solutions are stored in a 2-D texture that can be addressed by r_2 and $\nu/\nu_{\max}$. The content of this texture is the cosine of the scattering angle corresponding to the given frequency and random number (Figure 17.5). During the simulation, we just obtain the cosine of the sampling direction by

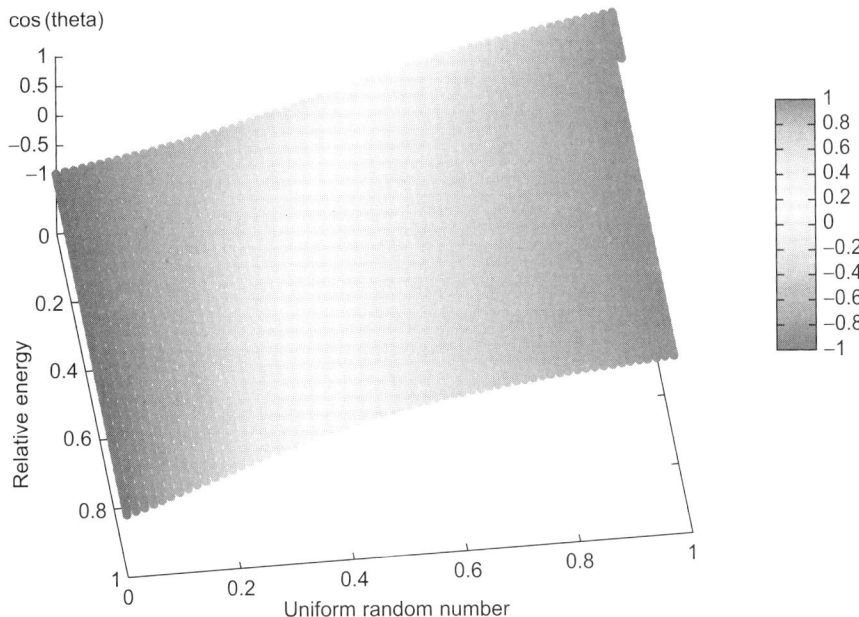

FIGURE 17.5

The table used for the sampling of the scattering angle assuming Compton scattering and the Klein-Nishina phase function. The table is parameterized with a random variable uniformly distributed in [0,1] and the relative energy of the photon with respect to the energy of the electron (512 keV), and provides the cosine of the scattering angle.

looking up this texture addressed by the current values of the uniform random number and the photon frequency. Because for light photons the scattering angle is independent of the frequency, we can use just a 1-D texture for the solutions of the sampling problem.

17.2.4 Parallel Random Number Generation

All discussed sampling steps transform random numbers that are uniformly distributed in the unit interval. Free path sampling needs as many random numbers as virtual scattering events happen until the first real scattering point. Absorption sampling requires just one additional random variable, but direction sampling uses two. Because different steps of the photon path are statistically independent, every step should use a new set of random numbers. Furthermore, different photons behave statistically independently, and therefore, the simulation of every photon should be based on a new random number sequence. Clearly, if we used the same random number generator in all parallel threads simulating different photons, then we would unnecessarily repeat the very same computation many times.

The typical solution of this problem is the allocation of a private random number generator for each parallel thread. To guarantee that their sequences are independent, the private random number generators are initialized with random seeds. The private random number generators run on the GPU and are assigned to parallel threads, whereas their random initial seeds are generated on the CPU using the random number generator of the C library.

We note that the mathematical analysis and the construction of robust parallel random number generators (and even nonparallel ones) are hard problems, which are out of the scope of this chapter. The interested reader should consult the literature, for example, a CUDA implementation [6], which is also used in our program, and [7] for the mathematical background.

17.3 THE COMPLETE SYSTEM

The discussed method has been integrated into a photon-mapping global illumination application, which decomposes the rendering into a shooting and a gathering phase. During shooting, multiple scattering of photons is calculated in the volume, registering the collision points, photon powers, and incident directions. The powers of photon hits are accumulated in cells defined by a 3-D array called the *illumination buffer*. The gathering phase visualizes the illumination buffer by standard alpha blending.

The inputs of the simulation system are the position of the isotropic radiation source, the position of the virtual camera, and the three-dimensional texture of the density field.

The shooting phase iteratively updates three arrays (Figure 17.6):

1. The one-dimensional *seed buffer* that stores the seeds of the parallel random number generators. This buffer is initialized by the CPU and is updated when a new random number is generated by its respective thread.
2. The one-dimensional *photon buffer* representing the currently simulated photons with their current position, direction, and energy.
3. The three-dimensional *illumination buffer*.

The photon buffer and the seed buffer have the same size, which is equal to the number of concurrently simulated photons, that is, the number of threads, and there is a one-to-one mapping between the threads and the items of the photon buffer and the seed buffer.

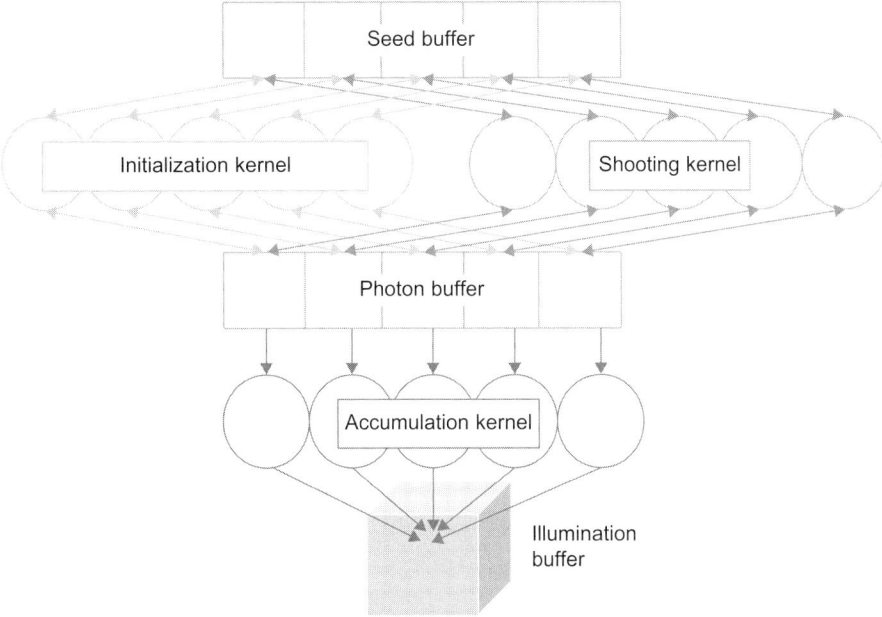

FIGURE 17.6

The architecture of the shooting phase of the simulation program. A thread is built of three functions: initialization, shooting, and accumulation. The seed buffer contains the seeds of the random number generators, which are initialized by the CPU and are updated by the initialization and the shooting functions. The initialization function processes the photon buffer and executes two operations, depending on whether the photon exists and is alive. It samples the scattering direction of already existing and living photons, and sets the initial position and direction of newly born ones that replace the dead photons. The shooting function finds the next collision location and decides on termination. A thread is assigned to its own items of the seed buffer and the photon buffer, so no synchronization is needed here. The accumulation function adds the power of the photon to a cell of the illumination buffer selected by the photon's location.

The photon buffer is managed by three functions of the thread that are called in a cyclic manner:

1. The *initialization function* puts newly emitted photons into the places of dead or uninitialized photons in the photon buffer and samples the scattering direction of existing or living ones. In the place of dead photons, a new photon is generated at the position of the source with uniformly distributed random direction and assigning the source's energy level to the photon. If the photon already exists and is alive, then its position is not altered, but a new scattering direction is sampled, and its energy level is modified according to the Compton law. Generating a new photon and sampling the scattering direction may seem conceptually different, but these processes have very similar control paths. Both types of random direction sampling require two new uniform random numbers in the unit interval. If the scattering is uniform, then the only difference is that the location of newly born photons is set to the source position. In the general case, the different formulae of initial direction and scattering direction may cause small warp divergence.

2. The *shooting function* simulates one step of the photons stored in the photon buffer. It calculates the next scattering event of its own photon executing free path sampling and then decides whether absorption occurs. If the photon leaves the volume without collision, or the absorption check tells us that the photon is absorbed, then its status is set to "dead," to get the next initialization operation to generate a new emitted photon in its place. The thread finally writes out the modified location and the status of the photon.

3. The *accumulation function* gathers the incident photon powers from the photon buffer and adds them to the illumination buffer shared by all threads. The illumination buffer is a 3D grid, where an item represents the total irradiance arriving at the respective grid cell. The quantized Cartesian coordinates of the photon's actual position serves as an index into the accumulation buffer where the incident power is added. Not only scattered photons but also absorbed photons are considered because they also arrived at this point. Note that this is the only place in our algorithm where different threads may write to the same memory location, and synchronization problems might occur. The correct implementation requires semaphores or atomic add operations to guarantee that no photon power gets lost. If we remove the mutual exclusion, then the power of some photons may not be added to the buffer. As the number of active threads is far smaller than the number of data items in the illumination buffer, the probability of such missing photons is rather small. Moreover, the simulation process will trace millions of photons, so a few missing photons cause just a negligible error.

For the visualization of the simulation results, we implemented two methods. The first option assigns a pseudocolor to each illumination buffer item, which is determined by the *irradiance*, and renders the volume with standard alpha blending. This kind of visualization is appropriate in medical systems where we are interested in the radiation dose of body tissues. Irradiance $I(\vec{x})$ is computed from the in-scattered flux [5]:

$$I(\vec{x}) = \frac{\sum_i E_i}{\Delta V},$$

where E_i is the power of the ith photon arriving at this cell, and ΔV is the volume of the cell. In order to visualize not only the total energy but also the spectrum, a separate irradiance value is computed in different frequency ranges, and a photon is added only to that irradiance where its frequency fits.

The second method computes the radiance arriving at a virtual camera and can be used, for example, in global illumination rendering. To compute the radiance, the irradiance is multiplied by the albedo of the material, and the probability density that the inscattered photon gets reflected to the direction of the virtual camera.

17.4 RESULTS AND EVALUATION

The implementation of the discussed method is based on CUDA and runs entirely on the GPU. We tested the system on an NVIDIA GeForce 260 GTX graphics card. The current version assumes a single isotropic point source and runs on a single GPU, but the extension to more general sources and the exploitation of multi-GPU cards and GPU clusters are straightforward. In our application the radiation source can be placed interactively in the volume represented by a 3-D texture fitting into the GPU texture memory.

Simulations executed by our photon transport program at interactive rates can also be done by commercially available and widely used Monte Carlo tools, like Geant4 [2], GATE (http://www.opengatecollaboration.org), MCNP (http://mcnp-green.lanl.gov/), SimSet (http://depts.washington.edu/simset), or PeneloPET [3], but the computation of the same problem in these systems takes hours or even days.

An optimized, multithreaded CPU (Intel Q8200) program is able to trace 0.4 million photons in each second with Woodcock tracking according to [14]. Our implementation simulates 36 million and 166 million photons in a second on NVIDIA GeForce 260 GTX and NVidia GeForce 480 GTX GPUs; these rates correspond to 90 times and 415 times speedups, respectively. The shares of the main functions in the execution time are 30% for initialization, 60% for shooting, and 10% for accumulation. According to the profiler results, the GPU program is memory bandwidth bound.

We used the GATE package to validate our program. We took the same density field and simulated the photon transport, and then finally compared the results. Of course, in a Monte Carlo simulation we cannot expect the two results to be exactly the same; thus, we also computed the variance of the results and checked whether the difference is smaller than the standard deviation. For light photons, there is another possibility for validation. If the medium is optically dense, then the diffusion equation is a good approximation of the radiance transfer, which can be solved analytically for homogeneous medium and a single isotropic radiation source [9]. Our application has passed both tests.

Figures 17.7 and 17.8 show the rendering results of our program when light photons are transported. The images show the radiance levels encoded by pseudocolor superimposed onto the image of the density field. Generally, the error of Monte Carlo methods is inversely proportional to the square root of the number of simulated paths, whereas the rendering time is proportional to the number of paths. In our implementation, noisy initial results are generated at high-frame rates, and even visually converged images (the relative error is less than 1%) are obtained at interactive speed.

Figure 17.8 demonstrates that the method scales well for higher-resolution models as well. Here, the density is taken from the visible human dataset converted to a 512^3 resolution voxel array. Volumes of this size are the largest that fit into the memory of our GPU.

Figure 17.9 depicts the results of gamma photon transport assuming two different sources emitting photons on 512 keV and 256 keV energy levels, respectively. Note that the simulation time of gamma photons is practically the same as for light photons, although the equations are slightly more complicated.

17.5 FUTURE DIRECTIONS

The presented implementation has several limitations that were necessary to keep the system simple and small. For example, the Rayleigh and Klein-Nishina models are hardwired into the code, so is the single isotropic source that emits either 512 keV photons or a photon triplet on the frequencies of red, green, and blue colors. Although, these settings are very common, the 512 keV level corresponds to positron-electron annihilation, while the light photon triplet to the standard selection in computer graphics, a more general user interface could widen the field of applications.

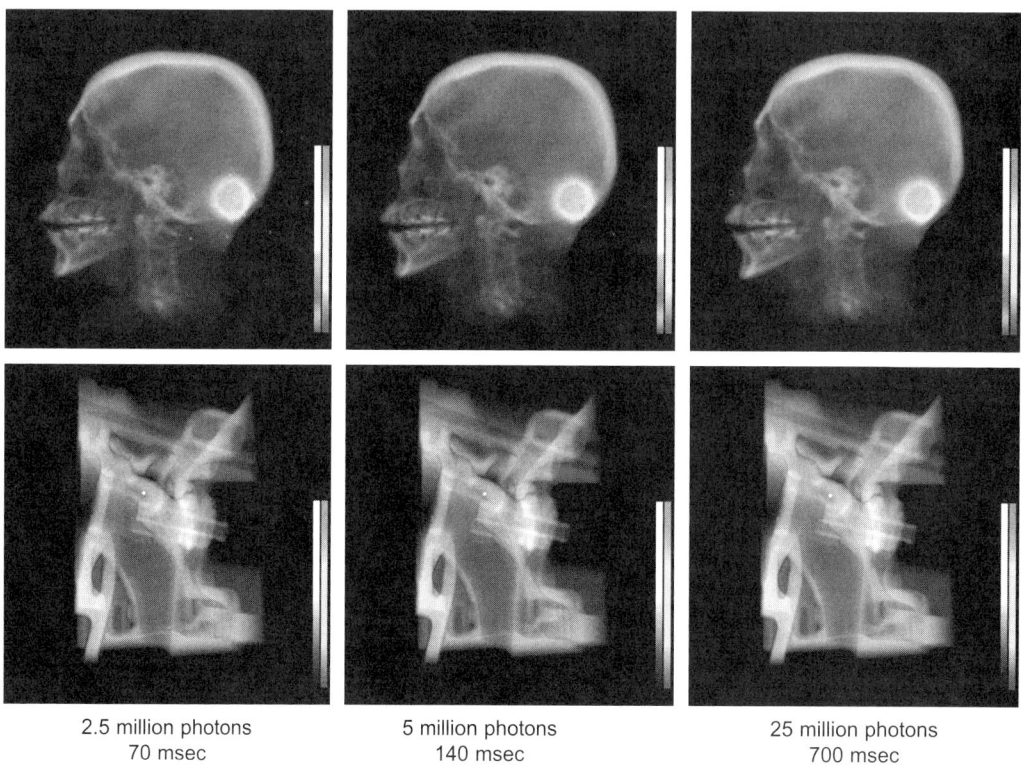

| 2.5 million photons | 5 million photons | 25 million photons |
| 70 msec | 140 msec | 700 msec |

FIGURE 17.7

Visualization of the radiation dose caused by a point source emitting lower energy photons in isotropic material. The volumes are defined by 128^3 resolution voxel arrays; the macrocell grid has 16^3 cells.

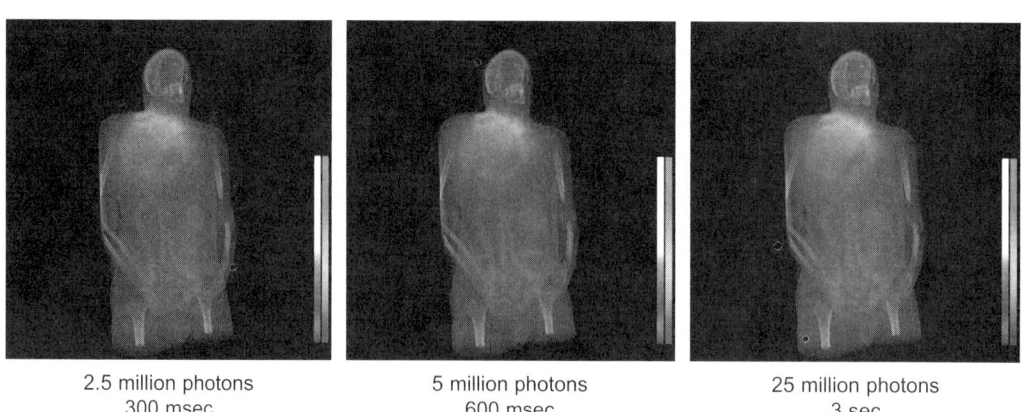

| 2.5 million photons | 5 million photons | 25 million photons |
| 300 msec | 600 msec | 3 sec |

FIGURE 17.8

Visualization of the radiation dose caused by a point source emitting lower-energy photons in isotropic material. The volume is defined by a 512^3 resolution voxel array.

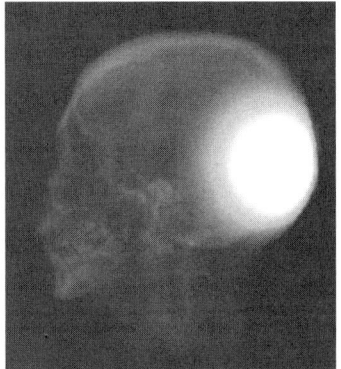 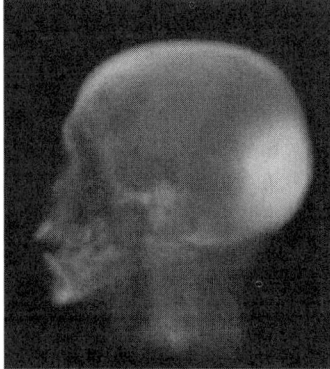

512 keV initial photon energy   256 keV initial photon energy

FIGURE 17.9

Visualization of the radiation dose owing to gamma photon transfer. The volume is defined by a 128^3 resolution voxel array.

The limitation that the density field should fit into the GPU memory is even more challenging. Because our proposed method accesses the high-resolution array just to decide whether a real collision happened and otherwise uses only the low-resolution array of macrocells, it is a natural extension to store only the low-resolution array of macrocells in the GPU memory and copy the real extinction coefficients from the CPU memory only when they are needed. This extension would allow practically arbitrarily high-resolution models to be simulated; these models are badly needed in medical diagnosis. However, the data access pattern of the high-resolution array is very incoherent, so realizing a caching scheme for it in the GPU memory is not simple. We consider this as our most important future work.

Another possibility is the consideration of procedurally generated models, which represent the high-resolution model as an algorithm instead of a high-resolution array. For such models, arbitrary virtual resolutions can be achieved.

References

[1] K. Assie, B. Breton, et al., Monte Carlo simulation in PET and SPECT instrumentation using GATE, Nucl. Instrum. Methods Phy. Res. 527 (1–2) (2004) 180–189.

[2] Geant, Physics Reference Manual, Version 4 9.1, CERN (2007) (Technical report).

[3] S. Espana, J. Herraiz, et al., PeneloPET, a monte carlo PET simulation toolkit based on PENELOPE: features and validation, in: IEEE Nuclear Science Symposium Conference, IEEE, 2006, pp. 2597–2601.

[4] A. Fujimoto, T. Takayuki, I. Kansei, Arts: accelerated ray-tracing system, IEEE Comput. Graph. Appl. 6 (4) (1986) 16–26.

[5] H.W. Jensen, P.H. Christensen, Efficient simulation of light transport in scenes with participating media using photon maps, in: Proceedings of SIGGRAPH '98, 1998, pp. 311–320.

[6] L. Howes, D. Thomas, Efficient random number generation and application using CUDA, in: GPU Gems 3, Addison Wesley, Upper Saddle Creek, 2007.

[7] D.E. Knuth, The Art of Computer Programming, vol. 2 (Seminumerical Algorithms), Addison-Wesley, Upper Saddle Creek, 1981.

[8] L. Szirmay-Kalos, B. Tóth, M. Magdics, B. Csébfalvi, Efficient free path sampling in inhomogeneous media, Poster from Eurographics, 3–7 May, 2010, Norrköping, Sweden.

[9] L. Szirmay-Kalos, G. Liktor, T. Umenhoffer, B. Tóth, S. Kumar, G. Lupton, Parallel iteration to the radiative transport in inhomogeneous media with bootstrapping, IEEE Trans. Vis. Comput. Graph. (in press).

[10] E. Woodcock, T. Murphy, P. Hemmings, S. Longworth, Techniques used in the GEM code for Monte Carlo neutronics calculation, in: Proceedings of the Conference Applications of Computing Methods to Reactors, ANL-7050, 1965.

[11] C.N. Yang, The Klein-Nishina formula & quantum electrodynamics, Lect. Notes Phys. 746 (2008) 393–397.

[12] http://en.wikipedia.org/wiki/Rayleigh_scattering.

[13] http://en.wikipedia.org/wiki/Klein-Nishina_formula.

[14] A. Wirth, A. Cserkaszky, B. Kári, D. Légrády, S. Fehér, S. Czifrus, et al., Implementation of 3D Monte Carlo PET reconstruction algorithm on GPU, in: IEEE Medical Imaging Conference '09, IEEE, The Nuclear and Plasma Sciences Society of the Institute of Electrical and Electronic Engineers, 25-31 October, Orlando, FL, 2009, pp. 4106–4109.

High-Performance Iterated Function Systems

18

Christoph Schied, Johannes Hanika, Holger Dammertz, Hendrik P. A. Lensch

This chapter presents an interactive implementation of the Fractal Flames algorithm which is used to create intriguing images such as Figure 18.1. It uses CUDA and OpenGL to take advantage of the computational power of modern graphics cards. GPUs use a SIMT (single-instruction multiple-thread) architecture. To achieve good performance, it is needed to design programs in a way which avoids divergent branching. The Fractal Flames algorithm involves random function selection that needs to be calculated in each thread. The algorithm thus would cause heavy branch divergence, which leads to $O(n)$ complexity in the number of functions. Current implementations suffer severely from this problem and address it by restricting the number of functions to a value with acceptable computational overhead.

The implementation presented in this chapter changes the algorithm in a way that leads to $O(1)$ complexity and therefore allows an arbitrary number of active functions. This is done by applying a presorting algorithm that removes the random function selection and thus eliminates branch divergence completely.

18.1 PROBLEM STATEMENT AND MATHEMATICAL BACKGROUND

Fractal Flames is an algorithm to create fractal images based on Iterated Function Systems (IFS) with a finite set of functions. The algorithm uses the *Chaos Game* [1], which is an iteration scheme that picks one random function for each data point and iteration, evaluates it, and continues with the next iteration. This scheme is visualized in Figure 18.2. The larger the number of different functions, the

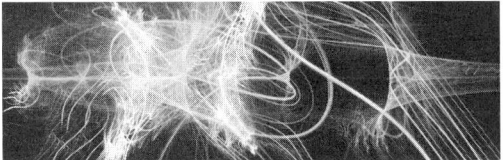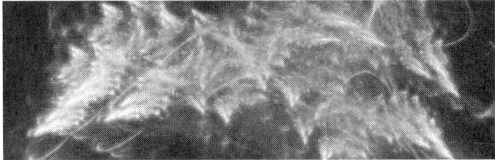

FIGURE 18.1

A crop from a Fractal Flames image rendered using $2 \cdot 10^6$ points at a resolution of 1280×800 with 40 Hz on a GTX280.

GPU Computing Gems

263

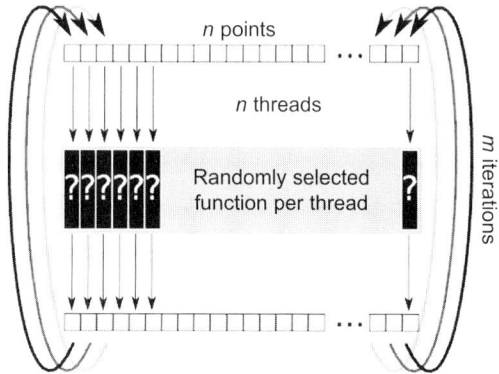

FIGURE 18.2

Naive parallelizing approach of the Chaos Game. The parallelization is realized by assigning a thread to each data point. Every thread chooses a random function and replaces the point by the computed value. This process is repeated *m* times.

more interesting the images that can be rendered. It is therefore a goal to allow for as many functions as possible.

Selecting a random function per sample results in a different branch per thread, if the algorithm is implemented on graphics hardware. One needs to consider that these devices execute the same instruction in lockstep within a *warp* of 32 threads. That is, the multiprocessor can execute a single branch at a time, and therefore, diverging branches are executed in serial order.

The random function selection causes very heavy branch divergence as every thread needs to evaluate a different function in the worst case. This results in linear runtime complexity in the number of functions, thus severely restricting the number of functions that can be used in practice, owing to the computational overhead involved.

18.1.1 **Iterated Function Systems**

As described in [1], an IFS consists of a finite set of affine contractive functions

$$F = \{f_i : X \rightarrow X | i = 1, 2, \ldots, N\}, \quad N \in \mathbb{N}. \tag{18.1}$$

The set $F_s = \{f_1^s, f_2^s, f_3^s\}$ for example forms a Sierpinski triangle with

$$f_1^s(p) = \frac{p}{2}, \quad f_2^s(p) = \frac{1}{2}\left(p + \begin{pmatrix} 0 \\ 1 \end{pmatrix}\right), \quad f_3^s(p) = \frac{1}{2}\left(p + \begin{pmatrix} 1 \\ 0 \end{pmatrix}\right), \tag{18.2}$$

where p is a vector.

The associated set S is the fixed point of Hutchinsons's recursive set equation

$$S = \bigcup_{i=1}^{N} f_i(S). \tag{18.3}$$

```
p = a random point in [−1, 1]²
iterate m times {
    i := random integer from 0 to N − 1 inclusive
    p := fᵢ(p)
    if iteration > 17
        plot(p)
}
```

FIGURE 18.3

The Chaos Game Monte Carlo algorithm. It chooses a random point and starts its iteration phase. Every iteration, a random function f_i is selected and evaluated for p which is then assigned to p.

It is not possible to directly evaluate the set, as the Hutchinson Equation (Eq. 18.3) describes an infinite recursion. An approximate approach is the Chaos Game [1], which solves the Hutchinson Equation by a Monte Carlo method. Figure 18.3 shows it in a basic version. The Chaos Game starts by selecting a random point of the bi-unit square $p = (x, y)$ with $|x| \leq 1, |y| \leq 1$ and starts its iterating phase by choosing a random function f_i in each iteration and evaluates $p := f_i(p)$. With increasing numbers of calculated iterations, p converges closer to the set [6]. After a sufficient number of steps, the point can be plotted in every iteration.

Iterated Function Systems have numerous applications, as outlined in [3], such as graphs of functions, dynamical systems, and brownian motion. Furthermore, this approach could be used in multilayer material simulations in ray tracing. In this chapter, we concentrate on IFS for the simulation of Fractal Flames.

We chose to start with a random point and to select a function at random, even though randomness is not a requirement of the algorithm. The initial point is actually arbitrary; and it will still converge to the set, given that the last iterations contain all possible combinations of functions. As we aim for real-time performance, we can evaluate only a very limited number of iterations, but on a lot of points, exploiting parallelization. Should the resulting fractal be too complicated to achieve subpixel convergence, the random initialization still creates a uniform appearance. This is, especially over the course of some frames, more visually pleasing than deterministic artifacts.

18.1.2 Fractal Flames

Fractal Flames, as described in [2], extend the IFS algorithm by allowing a larger class of functions that can be in the set F. The only restriction that is imposed on the functions f_i is the contraction on average. These functions can be described by:

$$f_i(x, y) = P_i \left(\sum_j v_{ij} V_j (a_i x + b_i y + c_i, \ d_i x + e_i y + f_i) \right) \tag{18.4}$$

with $P_i(x, y) = (\alpha_i x + \beta_i y + \gamma_i, \delta_i x + \epsilon_i y + \chi_i)$, where $a_i \cdots g_i$ and $\alpha_i \cdots \chi_i$ express affine transformations on 2-D points, while V_j, so-called *variations* apply nonlinear transformations, which are scaled by the factors v_{ij}. Typically, each function has its own set of up to 20 variations V_j. A few variation functions can be found in Figure 18.4. An extensive collection of those variations can be found in [2].

$$\psi : \text{random number} \in [0,1], \Omega : \text{random number} \in [0,\pi]$$
$$r = \sqrt{x^2 + y^2}, \theta = arctan(x/y)$$
$$V_0(x,y) = (x,y)$$
$$V_1(x,y) = (sin\, x, sin\, y)$$
$$V_2(x,y) = \frac{1}{r^2}(x,y)$$
$$V_3(x,y) = (x\, sin(r^2) - y\, cos(r^2),\, x\, cos(r^2) + y\, sin(r^2))$$
$$V_{13}(x,y) = \sqrt{r} \cdot (cos(\theta/2 + \Omega),\, sin(\theta/2 + \Omega))$$
$$V_{18}(x,y) = e^{x-1} \cdot (cos(\pi y), sin(\pi y))$$
$$V_{19}(x,y) = r^{sin\,\theta} \cdot (cos\theta, sin\theta)$$

FIGURE 18.4

A few selected variation functions. Ω and ψ are new random numbers in each evaluation of the variation function.

Every function is assigned a weight w_i that controls the probability that f_i is chosen in a Chaos Game iteration. This parameter controls the influence of a function in the computed image. Furthermore, a color $c_i \in [0,1]$ is assigned. Every point has a third component that holds the current color c, which is updated by $c := (c + c_i)/2$ in each iteration and is finally mapped into the output color space.

The computed points are visualized by creating a colored histogram. Because the computed histogram has a very high dynamic range, a tone-mapping operator is applied.

18.2 CORE TECHNOLOGY

In order to remove branch divergence, we replace the randomness of the function selection by randomized data access. This way, instructions can be optimally and statically assigned to threads.

Warps are assigned to a fixed function and every thread randomly selects a data point in each iteration. This selection is realized by a random bijective function mapping between the data and the thread indices. A fixed set of precomputed permutations is used, as they don't depend on dynamic data and may be cyclic, for it doesn't matter if the generated images repeat after a few rendered frames.

Every thread calculates its assigned function and indirectly accesses the data array by its permuted index. It then evaluates the function and writes back the result. A new permutation is picked in each iteration. Figure 18.5 shows the iteration scheme.

18.3 IMPLEMENTATION

The optimized algorithm and the divergent approach have been implemented to benchmark both of them. The implementation uses CUDA to be able to tightly control the thread execution that would not have been possible with traditional shading languages.

All variation functions have been implemented in a large switch statement. A struct containing variation indices and the scalar factor is stored in the constant memory. To evaluate a function f_i, a loop

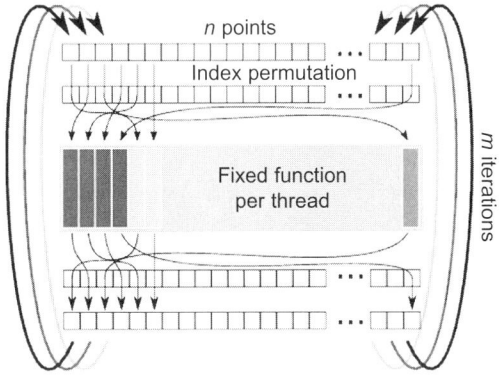

FIGURE 18.5

Optimized parallel algorithm. Instead of indexing directly into the data array as in Figure 18.2, the data is shuffled randomly in every iteration. This allows one to statically assign threads to functions and thereby remove the branch divergence.

over all those indices is performed that is used to index in the switch statement. The results are summed up according to Eq. 18.4.

18.3.1 The Three Phases

The optimized Chaos Game algorithm requires synchronization across all threads and blocks after each iteration because the data gets shuffled across all threads. Because of CUDA's lack of such a synchronization instruction, the Chaos Game had to be split into three kernels to achieve synchronization by multiple kernel executions (see Figures 18.6 and 18.7).

The initialization kernel performs one iteration of the Chaos Game on the randomly permuted Hammersley point set. The warm-up kernel performs one Chaos Game iteration and is called multiple times until the output data points converged to the fractal. The last kernel generates a larger set of points by randomly transforming each of the previously generated points 64 times, producing 64 independent samples for each input sample. The generated points are recorded in a vertex buffer object (VBO), which is then passed to the rendering stage. From those kernels, the point-generation kernel takes by far the most computation time. Those runtimes on a GTX280 are $34.80\,\mu s$ init, $43.12\,\mu s$ warm-up, and $1660.59\,\mu s$ generate points. The init kernel occupies 1.5% of the total Chaos Game runtime; the warm-up kernel is called 15 times and thus takes 27.6%, whereas the point-generation kernel takes 70.9%.

18.3.2 Memory-Access Patterns

The point-generation kernel needs to select a point from the point buffer multiple times, calculate one iteration, and write the result into the VBO. As the input point array does not change, texture caching can be used. The effect of this optimization is a 6.9% speed improvement for the 9500GT and 18% for the GTX280. The access pattern is pretty bad for the texture-caching mechanisms of a GPU because it completely lacks locality. Because the memory consumption of the samples is approximately 200 kB,

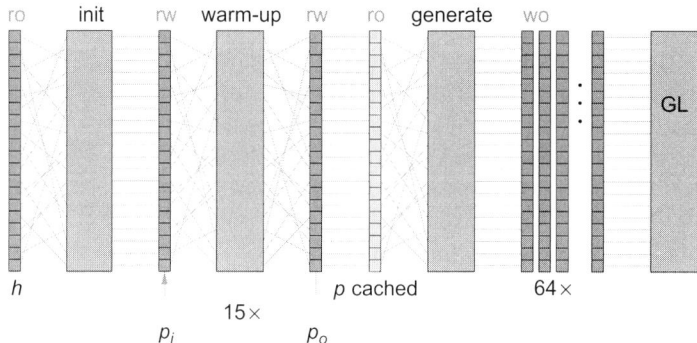

FIGURE 18.6

Illustration of the pseudo-code listing in Figure 18.7. The left three large boxes are the kernels (init, warm-up, generate), the last representing rendering in OpenGL. Memory access patterns are indicated by the gray lines. On the left, h indicates the Hammersley point set as the input.

f : fixed function **for** each thread
i : thread index
$h :=$ Hammersley point set in the bi$-$unit square
p : the point buffer
$\phi :=$ random permutation

// phase one: initialization
$p[i] := f(h[\phi(i)])$

// phase two: warm$-$up
iterate 15 times {
    $\phi :=$ next random permutation
    $p[\phi(i)] := f(p[\phi(i)])$
}

// phase three: generate points
iterate 64 times {
    $\phi :=$ next random permutation
    $\text{plot}(f(p[\phi(i)]))$
}

FIGURE 18.7

The three phases of the GPU version of the Chaos Game. First, p is initialized by transforming the Hammersley points by one function evaluation. Second, the warm-up phase assures that the points p are sufficiently close to the fractal. Finally, the point set is transformed 64 times more. In this last phase, the transformed points are displayed, but not written back to p.

the cache of a GPU seems to be big enough to hold a large number of samples; therefore, this method yields a major performance improvement. Benchmarks have been conducted to measure the effect of the number of samples on the texture caching. As shown in Figure 18.8, the number of threads — and therefore the number of samples in the texture cache — doesn't have a huge impact: the runtime stays

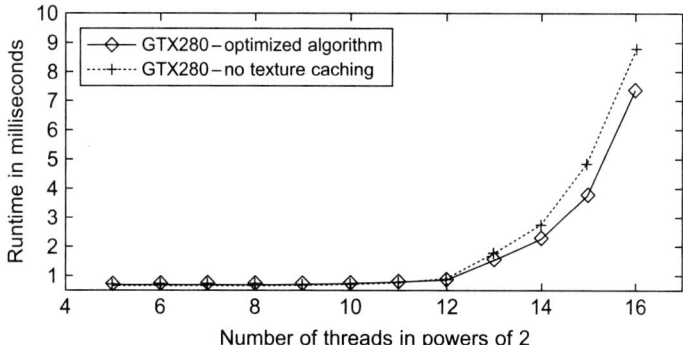

FIGURE 18.8

Runtime on the GTX280 in dependence of number of running threads. Each thread generates 64 samples. The runtime stays almost constant to 2^{12} threads and subsequently increases linearly with the number of threads.

constant up to 2^{12} threads and then increases linearly with the number of threads; the cached version is constantly faster.

Note that only the warm-up kernel has a completely random memory-access pattern during read and write. It needs to randomly access the point array to read a point for the iteration and to write out its result. To avoid race conditions on write accesses, either data has to be written back to the position the point was read from, or else a second array storing points is needed. The former approach involves random reads and writes, whereas the latter one has higher memory use. The initialization kernel needs to randomly select a starting point, but it can write the iterated points in a coalesced manner. Because of its low runtime, there is no need to optimize it further.

18.3.3 **Rendering**

The generated points are rendered as a tone-mapped histogram using OpenGL. This step consumes approximately 70% of the total time, depending on the particular view.

The 1-D color component needs to be mapped into the RGBA(red, green, blue, alpha) representation. This is done by a 1-D texture look-up in a shader. To create the colored histogram, the points are rendered using the OpenGL point primitive and using an additive blending mode. This yields brighter spots where multiple points are drawn in the same pixel. To cope with the large range of values, a floating-point buffer is employed. The resulting histogram is then tone mapped and gamma corrected, because the range between dark and bright pixel values is very high. For the sake of simplicity and efficiency, we use $L' = L/(L+1)$ to calculate the new pixel lightness L' from the input lightness L, but more sophisticated operators are possible [2].

Monte Carlo-generated images are typically quite noisy. This is especially true for the real-time implementation of Fractal Flames because only a limited number of samples can be calculated in the given time frame. Using temporal antialiasing smoothes out the noise by blending between the actual frame and the previously rendered ones. This is implemented by using frame buffer objects and it increases the image quality significantly.

18.3.4 Static Data

Some static data is needed during runtime; this data is calculated by the host during program start-up. A set of Hammersley Points [4] is used as the starting-point pattern to ensure a stratified distribution, which increases the quality of the generated pictures. The presorting algorithm needs permutations that are generated by creating multiple arrays containing the array index and a random number calculated by the Mersenne Twister [5]. These arrays are then sorted by the random numbers, which can be discarded afterwards. The resulting set of permutations is uploaded onto the device. Since some of the implemented functions need random numbers, a set of random numbers also is created and uploaded onto the device. All of this generated data is never changed during runtime.

In the runtime phase, it is necessary to specify various parameters that characterize the fractal. Every function needs to be evaluated in $p(f_i) \cdot num\_threads$ threads, where $p(f_i)$ is the user-specified probability that function f_i is chosen in the Chaos Game. The number of functions is small compared to the number of threads, and therefore, it doesn't matter if this mapping is done in warp size granularity instead of thread granularity. Each thread is mapped to a function by an index array that is compressed into a prefix sum. A thread can find out which function it has to evaluate by performing a binary search on this array. This search does not introduce a performance penalty in our experiments, but reduces the memory requirements significantly. The parameters and the prefix sum are accumulated in a struct that is uploaded into the constant memory each frame.

18.4 FINAL EVALUATION

The naive parallel implementation degenerates to an $O(n)$ algorithm in the number of functions on graphics hardware due to the branch divergence issues. The proposed algorithm turns the function evaluation in the naive Chaos Game algorithm to an $O(1)$ solution. This is shown in Figure 18.9 and Figure 18.10, where the optimized algorithm is benchmarked against the naive parallel implementation on a 9500GT and a 280GTX, respectively. In the benchmark, 20 randomly selected variation functions V_j were used in each f_i. The evaluation time of the optimized algorithm stays constant, whereas the naive solution increasingly suffers from branch divergence issues. When the CUDA profiler is employed, the branch divergence can be measured. The amount of branch divergence with 20 activated functions is at 23.54% for the divergent approach, whereas the optimized algorithm shows branch divergence only inside the function evaluation (0.05%).

The optimization doesn't come without cost, though. The algorithm basically trades branch divergence for completely random memory-access patterns. As the benchmark shows, GPUs handle this surprisingly well. Different GPUs have been benchmarked to show that this behavior isn't restricted to high-end GPUs (the speed impact of permuted read-and-write access versus completely linear operations was 3.1% for the 9500GT and 5.3% for the 280GTX).

In Figure 18.11, it is shown that the Chaos Game runtime is not monotonically decreasing with increasing block size. The best runtime is achieved with 64 threads per block. It is not entirely clear from where this behavior arises, but it may be that the scheduler has a higher flexibility with smaller block sizes.

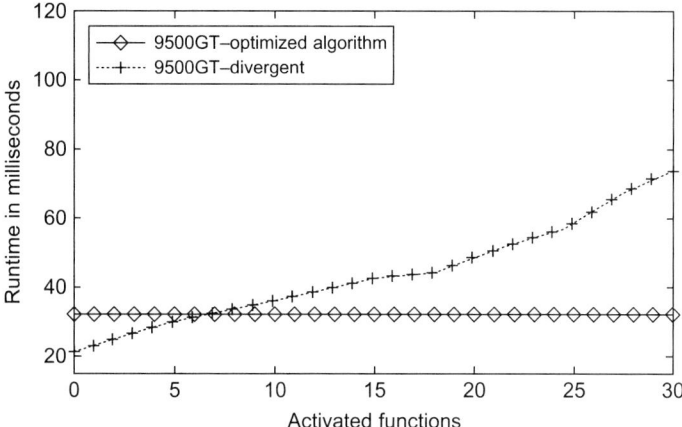

FIGURE 18.9

Runtime comparison between divergent and optimized Chaos Game on a 9500GT in dependence on the number of activated functions. The divergent implementation shows linearly increasing runtime in the number of activated functions, while the optimized algorithm shows constant runtime. The optimized version beats the divergent solution when eight or more functions are activated.

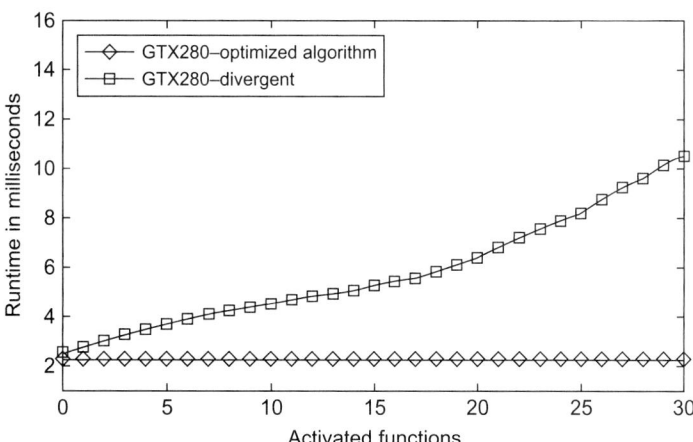

FIGURE 18.10

A runtime comparison between divergent and optimized Chaos Game on a GTX280 in dependence on the number of activated functions. The performance characteristics are the same as with the 9500GT shown in Figure 18.9, with a smoother increase in the divergent graph. The optimized version is always faster.

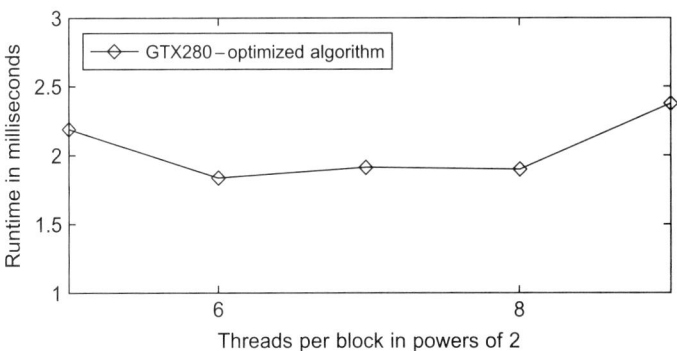

FIGURE 18.11

Runtime changing with increasing block size and constant number of threads. The fastest configuration is a block size of 2^6.

In our implementations, the occupancy as reported by the CUDA profiler is 0.25. This is due to high-register usage of the function evaluation code. Enforcing a lower-register usage at compile time increases the occupancy to 1.0 but reduces the performance by 51.3%.

We additionally implemented a CPU version to verify the benefits of using graphics hardware. Benchmarks have shown that a GTX285 is able to perform the Chaos Game iterations, without the rendering, at about 60 times faster than a single-core Opteron CPU clocked at 2.8 GHz (240 Hz vs. 3.7 Hz).

18.5 CONCLUSION

A presorting approach has been presented that completely eliminates branch divergence in Monte Carlo algorithms that use random-function selection and evaluation. Furthermore, it was shown that the approach is sufficiently fast for real-time rendering at high-frame rates, while it is necessary to keep an eye on the imposed performance penalty owing to high-memory bandwidth costs.

The optimized approach allows us to change all parameters in real time and to observe their effects; it thus can effectively help in getting an understanding of Iterated Function Systems. This also makes it possible to use the Fractal Flames algorithm in live performances by changing the parameters in real time, conducting interactive animations.

References

[1] M. Barnsley, Fractals Everywhere: The First Course in Deterministic Fractal Geometry, Academic Press, Boston, 1988.
[2] S. Draves, E. Reckase, The fractal flame algorithm. http://flam3.com/flame_draves.pdf, 2008.

[3]   K. Falconer, K.J. Falconer, Fractal Geometry: Mathematical Foundations and Applications, Wiley, New York, 1990 (Chapters 9–18).

[4]   C. Lemieux, Monte Carlo and Quasi-Monte Carlo sampling, Springer Verlag, Berlin, 2009.

[5]   M. Matsumoto, T. Nishimura, Mersenne twister: a 623-dimensionally equidistributed uniform pseudo-random number generator, ACM Trans. Model. Comput. Simul. (TOMACS) 8 (1) (1998) 3–30.

[6]   B. Silverman, Density Estimation for Statistics and Data Analysis, Chapman & Hall/CRC, London, 1998.

Emerging Data-Intensive Applications

Area Editor's Introduction

Volodymyr Kindratenko

4

19 Large-Scale Machine Learning 277

20 Multiclass Support Vector Machine 293

21 Template-Driven Agent-Based Modeling and Simulation with CUDA 313

22 GPU-Accelerated Ant Colony Optimization 325

THE STATE OF GPU COMPUTING IN DATA-INTENSIVE APPLICATIONS

Many of today's data-intensive problems, such as data mining and machine learning, push the boundaries of conventional computing architectures with ever-increasing requirements for greater performance. GPUs are a good match for these applications because of their high memory bandwidth and massive computation power. But achieving high performance for this class of applications using GPUs can be quite challenging because of irregular data access patterns and complex heuristics employed in many of the data processing algorithms. Only a few recent efforts have resulted in productive GPU implementations of data-intensive applications, some of which are included in this section.

The use of GPUs in data-intensive applications is poised to explode in the near future. Although in the past many scientific communities focused on how to obtain more experimental or observed data, today scientists are concerned about what to do with the flood of data produced by modern scientific instruments. Fast analysis of very large volumes of data is now of paramount importance in astronomy, biology, finance, and medicine, and software developers are more and more inclined to take advantage of the GPU hardware to achieve the desirable level of performance.

IN THIS SECTION

Chapter 19, written by Jerod J. Weinman, Augustus Lidaka, and Shitanshu Aggarwal, describes a discriminative maximum entropy learning algorithm, a machine-learning technique that builds a probability model from known data to make predictions about previously unseen data. CUBLAS library is used for one of the stages; other stages involve finding maximum value in an array for which the authors present two solutions. The program is implemented as a back end to Matlab.

Chapter 20, written by Sergio Herrero-Lopez, describes the support vector machine, a supervised learning technique for classification and regression. The sequential minimal optimization algorithm is used to solve the multiclass classification problem. The implementation is decomposed into map and reduce stages realized as separate GPU kernels. Multi-GPU cascaded implementation is also presented.

Chapter 21, written by Paul Richmond and Daniela Romano, describes a large-scale agent-based simulation framework for modeling the behavior of complex interacting systems. The GPU code for modeling individual agents is autogenerated from XML templates using a finite state machine-based abstract model of an agent. The formulation of agents' behavior as distinct states reduces thread divergence and results in simple memory access patterns for better memory access coalescing. Real-time agent visualization is also presented.

Chapter 22, written by Robin Weiss, describes a GPU implementation of an ant colony optimization algorithm, a rule-based classification technique used to solve a range of hard optimization problems. Major simulation steps are mapped into separate GPU kernels, with each ant modeled by a single GPU thread.

Large-Scale Machine Learning

19

Jerod J. Weinman, Augustus Lidaka, Shitanshu Aggarwal

A typical machine-learning algorithm creates a classification function that inductively generalizes from training examples — input features and associated classification labels — to previously unseen examples requiring labels. Optimizing the prediction accuracy of the learned function for complex problems can require massive amounts of training data. This chapter describes a GPU-based implementation of a discriminative maximum entropy learning algorithm that can improve runtime on large datasets by a factor of over 200.

19.1 INTRODUCTION

Machine learning is used on a variety of problems, including time series prediction for financial forecasting [2], machine translation [1], character and speech recognition [8, 11], and even conservation biology [9]. Although there are many techniques for performing such classifications, the aforementioned approaches all use one type of model: the maximum entropy classifier, also known as multinomial logistic regression. The maximum entropy (hence, MaxEnt) technique builds a probability model that is consistent with training data, but is otherwise maximally noncommittal [6]. This property makes it theoretically ideal when training data is scant, but its superb performance when supplied with massive amounts of training data enhances its practical appeal as well. Such a probability model may then be used for making predictions about previously unseen data.

Train time for a MaxEnt classifier scales linearly with the size of the dataset. Because some effects can be seen only when training data is plentiful, running experiments with a MaxEnt classifier in the loop can be time-consuming. Fortunately, the training algorithm for MaxEnt can be parallelized, drastically reducing turnaround time for experiments. With this development, researchers can get results more quickly, and practitioners can deploy classifiers trained on much larger datasets.

Our motivation for employing MaxEnt has been to improve character recognition in arbitrary images of natural scenes [10, 11]. This task is more complex than typical document-based character recognition because it involves a wide variety of fonts and uncontrolled viewing conditions. As we demonstrate, gaining even a logarithmic performance improvement requires exponentially more data. Therefore, the training process should be parallelized to stay ahead of the computational demands of so much data.

19.2 CORE TECHNOLOGY

A maximum entropy model consists of an $L \times D$ matrix $\mathbf{W}$ that determines how much weight to assign each of D features in an input vector for each of L potential category labels. A $D \times 1$ column vector of input features $\mathbf{x}$ to be classified must simply be multiplied by the weight matrix. The label with the largest value in the product $\mathbf{Wx}$ can be taken as the assigned or predicted value. Thus, classification is a relatively efficient task. The goal of the learning algorithm is to find a weight matrix $\mathbf{W}$ that gives high values to correct labels and relatively low values to the rest for all input vectors.

The learning process involves optimizing a convex function of $\mathbf{W}$ for a fixed $D \times N$ matrix $\mathbf{X}$ of N training instances. The $L \times D$ matrix requires an optimization over many parameters. Though the optimization problem is convex, representing the second derivative of the objective function with the Hessian matrix is space prohibitive. Therefore, limited-memory quasi-Newton optimization algorithms (e.g., L-BFGS [3]) must be used to find the optimal weights. The bottleneck in the process is simply evaluating the objective function and its gradient when the number of training instances N is extremely large.

Fortunately, both the objective function and the gradient (detailed later in this chapter) are sums over the N training instances involving matrix products, vector sums, a vector max, and other straight-forward computations. To parallelize the process, the data may be divided into smaller pieces whose contributions are repeatedly added to result accumulators.

The source code for the system described here is available under the GNU GPLv3 license.[1] A MATLAB implementation of a learning MaxEnt model is provided with the requisite CUDA kernels, as well as the optimization routines necessary for training.

19.2.1 Background: Maximum Entropy Theory

As its name suggests, the maximum entropy model is intimately related to probability theory. We now give details on the model in order to understand and implement the objective function being optimized. Let $\mathbf{X}$ be the $D \times N$ matrix of training data, as before, so that $\mathbf{x}_j$ is a column vector formed by the jth column of $\mathbf{X}$. Let $\mathbf{W}$ be the $L \times D$ weight matrix, with $\mathbf{w}_i$ the row vector formed by the ith row of $\mathbf{W}$. The probability of category label i given the data $\mathbf{x}_j$ is

$$p_{i,j} = \frac{1}{Z_j} \exp\left(\mathbf{w}_i \mathbf{x}_j\right). \tag{19.1}$$

The constant Z_j is the sum of the exponentiated inner products for all the category labels,

$$Z_j = \sum_{i=1}^{L} \exp\left(\mathbf{w}_i \mathbf{x}_j\right), \tag{19.2}$$

so that $\mathbf{p}_j$ represents a properly normalized probability distribution over labels with $\sum_{i=1}^{L} p_{i,j} = 1$.

---

[1] Available from http://www.cs.grinnell.edu/~weinman/code.

The training examples must have category labels assigned to the data. Let $\mathbf{y}$ be a $N \times 1$ column vector with entries $y_j \in \{1, \ldots, L\}$. With all of this, the objective function is the conditional log-likelihood of the labels given the observed data,

$$\mathcal{L}(\mathbf{W}; \mathbf{y}, \mathbf{X}) \equiv \sum_{j=1}^{N} \log p_{y_j, j}$$

$$= \sum_{j=1}^{N} \left(\mathbf{w}_{y_j} \mathbf{x}_j - \log Z_j \right), \tag{19.3}$$

where $p_{y_j, j}$ indicates the probability of the correct label y_j for the jth instance and $\mathbf{w}_{y_j}$ is the vector of weights for the correct label of the instance. Typically, a regularization term is added to the function in order to prevent overfitting [4, 7]. We omit the details of this practice and point out where in the parallel implementation they are handled. For a particular label i and feature k, the gradient of the objective function, needed by the optimization routine, is given by

$$g_{i,k} \equiv \frac{\partial}{\partial w_{i,k}} \mathcal{L}(\mathbf{W}; \mathbf{y}, \mathbf{X})$$

$$= \sum_{j=1}^{N} \left(\delta_{i, y_j} x_{k,j} - p_{i,j} x_{k,j} \right)$$

$$= \sum_{j: y_j = i} x_{k,j} - \sum_{j=1}^{N} p_{i,j} x_{k,j}, \tag{19.4}$$

where $\delta_{a,b}$ is the Kronecker delta.

19.2.2 Base Algorithm

Seeing the individual values used in the system, such as $p_{i,j}$ and $g_{i,k}$, is helpful for understanding the meaning of the computations. However, for economy many of these computations are calculated as matrix products. The inner products of Eq. 19.1 necessary to calculate the objective of Eq. 19.3 can be calculated at once with a matrix product. In addition, the gradient can also be calculated as two matrix products. In summary, the major computations involve

1. calculating a large matrix product $\mathbf{U} = \mathbf{WX}$;
2. log-normalizing the columns of $\mathbf{U}$ to create an $L \times N$ matrix of log probabilities, $\mathbf{L}$;
3. summing one entry from each column of $\mathbf{L}$ to find the objective function value and exponentiating the entire matrix to produce the probabilities $\mathbf{P}$; and then finally
4. calculating the gradient as a matrix product $\mathbf{G} = \left(\mathbf{XP}^\top \right)^\top$.

We note that the first term in the gradient Eq. 19.4 is a category-specific sum over the columns of $\mathbf{X}$. Much like the second term of the gradient can be implemented as a matrix product between the data $\mathbf{X}$ and the probabilities $\mathbf{P}$, the first term may be implemented as a sparse matrix product. Instead of $\mathbf{P}$,

---

Algorithm 1: Core value and gradient calculation for training a maximum entropy model in MATLAB.

```
 1:   function [V, G] = value(Y, X, W, G0)
 2:   % Calculate the raw energy (LxN)
 3:   U = W*X;
 4:   % Find the largest energy for each instance (1xN)
 5:   umax = max(U);
 6:   % Repeat for all labels (LxN)
 7:   umax = repmat(umax, [size(W,1) 1]);
 8:   % Log normalization (1xN)
 9:   logZ = umax + log(sum(exp(U-umax)));
10:   % Repeat for all labels (LxN)
11:   logZ = repmat(logZ, [size(W,1) 1]);
12:   % Normalized log probability (LxN)
13:   L = U − logZ;
14:   % Indices in L of labels Y (1xN)
15:   index = sub2ind(size(L), 1:length(Y), Y');
16:   % Value: sum of log probabilities (1x1)
17:   V = sum(L(index));
18:   % Probabilities (LxN)
19:   P = exp(L);
20:   % Gradient (LxD)
21:   G = G0 − (X*P')';
```

---

a sparse $L \times N$ matrix containing a 1 (one) at the appropriate row (the given label) for each column (instance) is used to calculate the first gradient term en masse. Because one factor of the matrix product is very sparse, the default MATLAB implementation for this calculation is sufficiently fast. Furthermore, this product needs to be calculated only once at the outset of training because it does not depend on the weights **W**.

For numerical stability in calculating Z_j, the largest entry in the energy (for each instance) is found and subtracted before exponentiating in Eq. 19.2. All of these computations can be easily "vectorized" (i.e., written without any explicit loops) in MATLAB. An example implementation is shown in Algorithm 1. The first term of the gradient is precalculated and given as the input G0. In practice, to conserve memory the same variable can be used for U, L, and P, because they are the same size and are never needed simultaneously. We use separate variable names in this example to emphasize their connection to the mathematics outlined earlier in this chapter.

19.3 GPU ALGORITHM AND IMPLEMENTATION

Our program has been implemented as a back end to a MATLAB-based learning object. There are four calls to CUDA kernels, which are labeled energy, probabilities, values, and gradient in Figure 19.1. Each of these implements one of the four major computations listed in Section 19.2.2

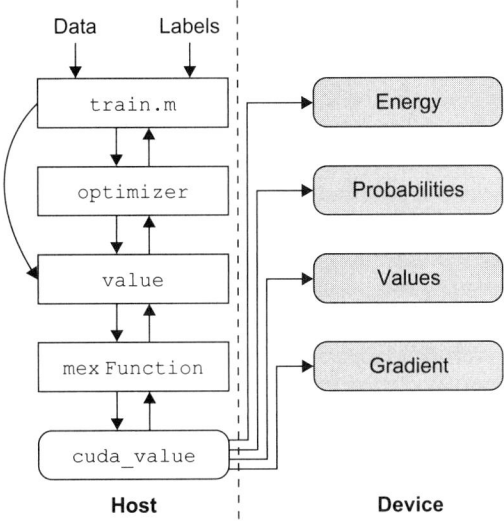

FIGURE 19.1

Overall program architecture. MATLAB routines and MEX functions are shown in square boxes, while CUDA functions are shown in rounded boxes. Shaded boxes indicate kernels that run exclusively on the CUDA device.

for a small piece of the training data. These kernels are called by another main procedure, cuda_value, that manages the division of the overall training data on the host system into pieces that are transferred to the CUDA device(s) for processing. The cuda_value wrapper procedure returns the total objective function value and gradient to a MATLAB mexFunction. In turn, the MEX gateway routine passes the result off to a MATLAB function value called by the overall optimization routine. It is the optimizer that uses the objective function value and gradient returned by value to calculate an updated weight matrix for subsequent evaluation, repeating the learning process as it maximizes the objective. After giving an overview of the communication patterns and module responsibilities, we explain each of these operations in more detail.

19.3.1 Training Overview

The training data $\mathbf{X}$ and category labels $\mathbf{y}$ are given to train, a MATLAB object method, along with any optional parameters relating to the learning process. Since $\mathbf{X}$ and $\mathbf{y}$ are fixed during the optimization process, these are cached in the value function, which calculates the objective function value and gradient when the optimizer passes in a weight matrix $\mathbf{W}$ for evaluation. The value function then forwards the request to a MEX gateway routine to be handled by our parallel CUDA implementation.

It is common to prevent overfitting by adding a regularization term for the weights to the objective function. This can easily be done in the value method. Because the regularization depends solely on $\mathbf{W}$ and a few other other higher-level parameters given to the training method, no parallelization is needed. The regularization term's value and gradient can be quickly calculated in value on the host system and added to the objective function value and gradient determined by the data.

19.3.2 Host-Device Interface

The interface between the host system and the CUDA device(s) is the `cuda_value` function. It is responsible for allocating memory on the device for the weights, the data, and intermediate results (i.e., the probabilities and the gradient). Host memory is much larger than the device memory, so we must partition the training data into smaller slices (several columns of **X**), transferring each to the device and calculating their contributions to the objective function value and gradient one slice at a time. All four steps (energy through gradient calculation) must be completed on the device for the given slice of instances before the next slice is processed.

Because the value and gradient are sums over the N instances, this is a straightforward process of adding results to accumulator variables. The partial sum for the objective function value is calculated on the device and then accumulated on the host. The partial sums for the gradient matrix are accumulated on the CUDA device and copied back to the host when all the data has been processed. This is because the gradient is calculated using the CUBLAS library, which makes it easy to accumulate matrix products in parallel.

We assume that N will be the dominating term of the data over D and L. The number of labels L is unlikely to be extremely large because the number of instances N required to train an accurate classifier would need to be (nonlinearly) much larger. It is possible for the number of features D to be rather large, although overfitting may result. In some cases using fewer features can yield better prediction performance (e.g., [7]). In any case, we assume device memory will hold the full $L \times D$ weight and gradient matrices along with an intermediate $L \times N'$ probability matrix and the partial $D \times N'$ data matrix for several columns ($1 \ll N' < N$) of the full $D \times N$ data matrix **X**.

For the most common ranges of L and D, the slice size N' will almost always exceed the number of independent streaming multiprocessors (SMs) on the device. Therefore, in the hopes of maximizing parallelism in the most common cases, we take the approach of processing the N' instances on the device in parallel, rather than maximally parallelizing the operations for processing each instance serially.

19.3.3 Calculating the Energy

The major computation of the MaxEnt model is the inner product between the weights and the data, called the energy. When viewed as matrices, these terms may easily be related via the matrix product $\mathbf{U} = \mathbf{WX}$. The weights and part of the data have been copied to the CUDA device, so the product **U**, which is kept on the device, is easily calculated via a CUBLAS library call (`cublasSgemm`), the first exploitation of the device's parallelism. In order to calculate the objective function value, these raw energies must be converted into log probabilities, a normalization process that is performed in the next kernel function.

19.3.4 Normalizing Probabilities

Recall that the original data matrix has already been divided into slices, with one slice copied to the CUDA device. A column of the slice represents a training instance, each of which is assigned a block of threads for an SM. This partitioning of data is illustrated in Figure 19.2.

To calculate the probabilities used for the value and the gradient, the log-normalization term $\log Z_j$ must be calculated. This process requires three passes: finding a maximum, totaling exponentiated energies, and finally normalizing.

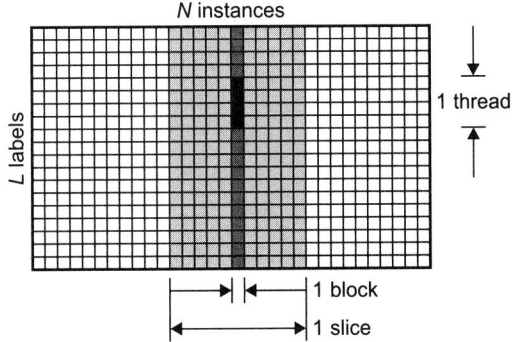

FIGURE 19.2

Partitioning of energy/probability matrix among blocks and threads.

```
_shared_ _device float mxarr[MAX_THREADS_PER_BLOCK];

...

float local_umx = P[start];

for (unsigned int i = start+1 ; i < end ; i++)
  local_umx = fmaxf(local_umx, P[i]);

mxarr[threadIdx.x] = local_umx;
```

FIGURE 19.3

Local maximum computation for a thread. The array P holds the instance's raw energies for the block, while start and end indicate the thread's partition bounds.

In the first pass, the the maximum value of the raw energy $u_{i,j}$ is found for all labels i of the instance j. This is ultimately to avoid exponentiating large values, which can give unreliable results, especially with the single precision floating-point numbers used in this implementation. We have tested two methods for finding the maximum float value in the vector. One makes use of comparisons and conditional assignment, while the other uses an order-preserving bijection between unsigned int and float types, so that comparisons can be made with the CUDA atomicMax function. First, we describe the simpler method and then an enhancement of it using the bijection and atomic functions.

Finding the Maximum Energy Without Atomics

We can use a simple butterfly reduction to find the maximum energy [5, 2.4.1]. An array is shared among the threads in the block. Because there may be more labels than threads, the labels are divided evenly among the block's threads, and each thread then finds the max among its partition of the data. This process is demonstrated in Figure 19.3.

```
unsigned int i;
for (i = powf(2,floorf(log2f(blockDim.x−1))); i > 0; i >>= 1)
{
  if (threadIdx.x < i && threadIdx.x + i < blockDim.x)
    if (mxarr[threadIdx.x] < mxarr[threadIdx.x + i])
      mxarr[threadIdx.x] = mxarr[threadIdx.x + i];

  _syncthreads();
}
float umax = mxarr[0];
```

FIGURE 19.4

Max-reduction butterfly code for a thread.

The butterfly reduction then proceeds by allocating one thread to two entries in the shared array and assigning one of the entries to the greater of the two. With the number of entries effectively halved, the process is repeated until the maximum entry is found.

One subtle detail that must be handled is when the number of threads is not a power of two. Let T be the number of threads, which is also the number of valid values in the butterfly. The value $2^{\lfloor \log_2(T-1) \rfloor}$ is thus the highest power of two strictly less than T. To ensure that no invalid data is accessed, we also check that the second index used belongs to a valid thread. This is demonstrated in Figure 19.4.

Finding the Maximum Using Atomics and Bijection

Rather than using conditional assignment, we may try using the CUDA atomicMax function to atomically assign the maximum value to one of the entries. This also performs assignment only as necessary. Because all threads in a butterfly must complete before advancing to the next level, a synchronization barrier is still required. However, the atomicMax function accepts only integral values. Fortunately, we can use an order-preserving bijection between unsigned int, a type supported by atomicMax, and float, the type of values in our vector.

As Herf reports,[2] the binary representation of a float number (regardless of denormalization) has two primary issues that prevent direct bitwise comparison, as would be done with unsigned ints. First and foremost, negative numbers use a leading sign bit, so that they are interpreted as larger than any positive number. Second, the signed-magnitude representation means the smaller (i.e., more negative) the number, the larger the bit interpretation. Because inverting the bits of both the exponent and mantissa reverses their ordering, we will want to do this for any negative number, but not positive numbers. To solve the first problem, we always flip the sign bit. The pair of methods for doing such a conversion in both directions is given in Figure 19.5.

With this conversion in hand, we can now re-tool our previous local max and butterfly algorithms. The only changes to Figure 19.3 are that the type of mxarr would be defined as unsigned int, and the final assignment to the array uses the forward bijection conversion:

```
mxarr[threadIdx.x] = floatFlip(local_umx);
```

---

[2] http://stereopsis.com/radix.html (accessed June 9, 2010).

```
_device_ unsigned int floatFlip(float theFloat)
{
  unsigned int mask = (_float_as_int(theFloat) >> 31) | 0x80000000;
  return _float_as_int(theFloat) ^ mask;
}

_device_ float invFloatFlip(unsigned int theUint)
{
  unsigned int mask = ((theUint >> 31) — 1) | 0x80000000;
  return_int_as_float((int)(theUint ^ mask));
}
```

FIGURE 19.5

A pair of routines for a bijection between `float` and `unsigned int` types. Note that the `_float_as_int_` and `_int_as_float` procedures are needed for doing bit-preserving conversions and that the leading (i.e., sign) bit is copied on a shift.

```
unsigned int i;
for (i = powf(2,floorf(log2f(blockDim.x—1))); i > 0; i >>= 1)
{
  if (threadIdx.x < i && threadIdx.x + i < blockDim.x)
    atomicMax(&(mxarr[threadIdx.x]), mxarr[threadIdx.x + i]);
  _syncthreads();
}
float umax = invFloatFlip(mxarr[0]);
```

FIGURE 19.6

Max-reduction butterfly code for a thread using CUDA atomics.

The butterfly reduction is changed to replace the conditional assignment with calls to `atomicMax`, and the final assignment of the max inverts the bijection, as shown in Figure 19.6.

While we have found only a very slight improvement in performance using atomics, we include this approach for completeness. If the design changed so that the partition spread an instance across multiple blocks, maximum values may need to be calculated in global memory, requiring greater use of atomics for `float` values.

Calculating the Normalizer: A Butterfly Sum Reduction

The second pass computes the sum for calculating Z_j, as in Eq. 19.2, subtracting the largest energy found in the previous pass before exponentiating. The same basic approach for calculating the maximum is used to calculate a sum involving the same data. Each thread computes a total for its partition, and then these subtotals are accumulated in a butterfly pattern to yield Z_j. We can finally compute the log of this sum and add back the maximum energy to give $\log Z_j$. This is demonstrated in Figure 19.7.

```
_shared_ _device_ float Z[MAX_THREADS_PER_BLOCK];

...

unsigned int i;

float local_Z = 0;

for (i = start; i < end; i++)
  local_Z += expf(P[i] - umax);

Z[threadIdx.x] = local_Z;

_syncthreads();

for (i = powf(2,floorf(log2f(blockDim.x-1))); i > 0; i >>= 1)
{
  if (threadIdx.x < i && threadIdx.x + i < blockDim.x)
    Z[threadIdx.x] += Z[threadIdx.x + i];

  _syncthreads();
}

float logZ = umax + logf(Z[0]);
```

FIGURE 19.7

Sum-reduction with thread-local computations and the butterfly for a thread. The array P holds the instance's raw energies for the block, while start and end indicate the thread's partition bounds. The maximum value umax has already been computed.

Calculating the Probability

The final pass uses the previous result to log-normalize the column of probabilities by subtracting $\log Z_j$ from every row (label) of the raw energy $u_{i,j}$. Because the raw energy is no longer needed, all of this computation is done in place to avoid extensive memory use. This helps to reduce the number of host-device data transfers because more space is available on the device for each slice.

In addition, we need to add the log probability of the correct label for each instance. Because there is only one for each block/instance, we allow a leader thread to make this calculation, which stores the result in a shared array that has one element for each block.

The final calculation is to normalize the log probability using the previously totalled log normalizer logZ (for $\log Z_j$ in Eq. 19.3) and exponentiate the result. This is done for every label assigned to the thread's partition, as shown in Figure 19.8.

19.3.5 **Summing the Values**

The third step is to total the value of the instances in the current slice. This is also a simple sum reduction. Because the number of instances in a slice is typically much smaller than the total memory on the device, this step is unlikely to be a bottleneck unless L and D are *very* small. Thus, we use a simple trick that is slightly suboptimal, but easy to implement. Because probabilities are between

```
for (unsigned int i = start ; i<end ; i++)
  P[i] = expf(P[i] - logZ);
```

FIGURE 19.8

Calculating the final normalized probability in one thread.

0 and 1, the log probability should be nonpositive. We can thus use the `cublasSasum` procedure to total the absolute values of the entries (which always flips the sign), and negate the result. The total for the slice is added to an accumulator on the host.

19.3.6 Calculating the Gradient

Like the first and third kernels, the final kernel is a straightforward CUBLAS call. To calculate the first term of the gradient Eq. 19.4, we use MATLAB's built-in sparse matrix multiplication routine with no significant speed loss. At each call to `cuda_value`, the gradient accumulator on the device is initialized to that pre-calculated matrix; subsequent gradient calculations simply add to it.

Because the number of features is typically much larger than the number of category labels ($D \gg L$), we avoid taking the transpose of the large slice of the data matrix $\mathbf{X}$ and instead prefer to transpose $\mathbf{P}$. Therefore, the product between the data and the probabilities is formatted as $\mathbf{G} = \left(\mathbf{XP}^\top\right)^\top$, rather than the mathematically equivalent $\mathbf{G} = \mathbf{PX}^\top$, to minimize data-processing overhead. Our implementation requires the outer transpose to occur only once on the host device after the gradients for all N instances have been accumulated. Despite this, there is a substantial performance improvement in avoiding the transpose of $\mathbf{X}$.

19.4 IMPROVEMENTS OF PERFORMANCE

To establish a baseline, we compare our CUDA-based GPU implementation of the training algorithm with a previous implementation using MATLAB (R2009a) matrix multiplications and other vectorized operations on a 64-bit platform with dual Intel Xeon Quad-Core 2.26 GHz CPUs and 48 GB of 1066 MHz DDR3 RAM. The parallel version is currently designed for a single GPU, but more could be utilized with relatively little effort. Our experiments are based on the same host system using an NVIDIA C1060 Tesla having 240 streaming processors (SPs) running at 1.3 GHz arranged in 30 streaming multiprocessors (SMs) with 4 GB DDR3 RAM.

MATLAB uses the extremely efficient LAPACK/BLAS routines, many of which are automatically multithreaded over a host system's available multicore processors (eight cores in this case). The vectorized operations $+$, $-$, `exp`, and `log` are also parallelized. Because many of our algorithm's most computationally intensive operations are parallelized, the comparison is reasonable. The notable exceptions are `sum` and `max`.

19.4.1 General Benchmarks

To measure the speedup of our parallel implementation, we use a variety of configurations of N, L, and D on random data, shown in Figure 19.9. We achieve a maximum speedup of $205\times$ when $N = 2^{15}$ and

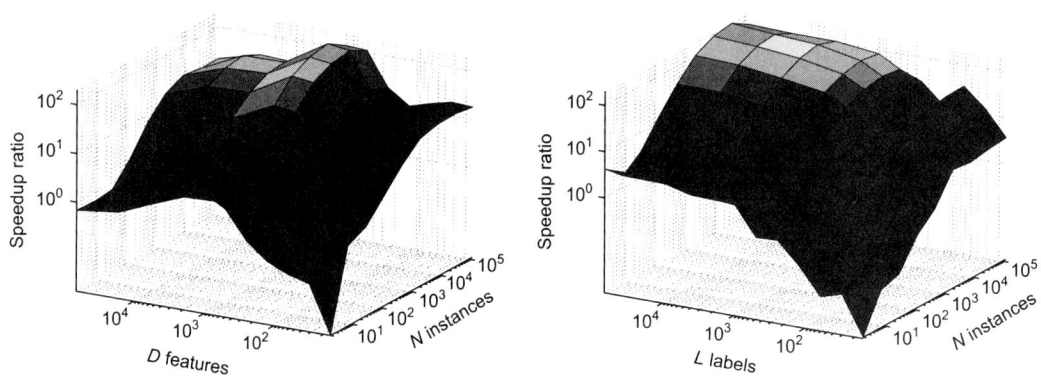

FIGURE 19.9

Speedup of GPU vs. CPU implementations when the number of labels is $L = 1024$ (left) and the number of features of the input is $D = 1024$ (right). The ratio of the average times over 10 runs are shown.

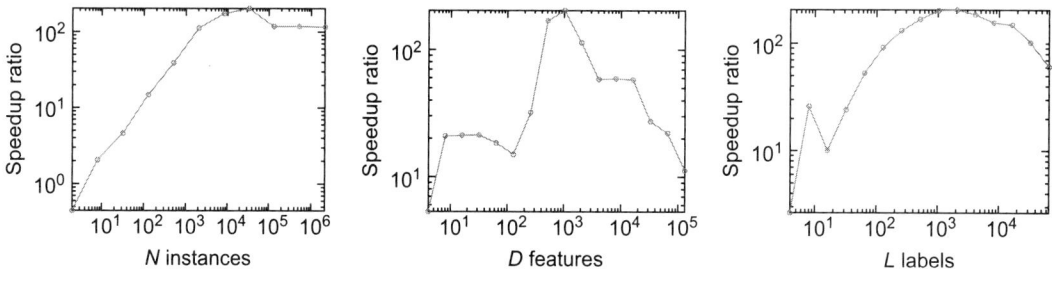

FIGURE 19.10

Saturation of improvement when the number of labels is $L = 1024$ and the number of features of the input is $D = 1024$ (left), $L = 1024$ and $N = 32768$ (center), and $D = 1024$ and $N = 32768$ (right).

$D = 2^{10}$ with $L = 2^{11}$. This simply measures the ratio of the time to run a single iteration of training (i.e., calculation of the objective function value and its gradient). There are likely to be more complex interactions between the optimizer and the amount of training data. We do not explore those interactions because they will depend heavily on the nature of the data, making it difficult to generalize. Our experience suggests that if additional training data requires more training iterations, the growth is more likely to be additive than multiplicative.

Additional experiments indicate that after the peak along the N axis there is a slight drop-off that then flattens out, as shown in Figure 19.10. There is a similar peak performance with respect to L, which gradually tapers. This is the dimension where our GPU implementation is more parallelized than MATLAB. The sum and max functions over the L labels in Algorithm 1 are not parallelized. Thus, we expect the parallelization of the kernel snippets in Figures 19.3, 19.6, and 19.7 to be most apparent when the matrix multiplication for the energy is not the dominant term, as shown in Figure 19.10.

After the peak along the D axis, performance drops more rapidly. This is because, for sufficiently large L, as the inner dimension of the matrix products grows (D in our case), the matrix multiplication

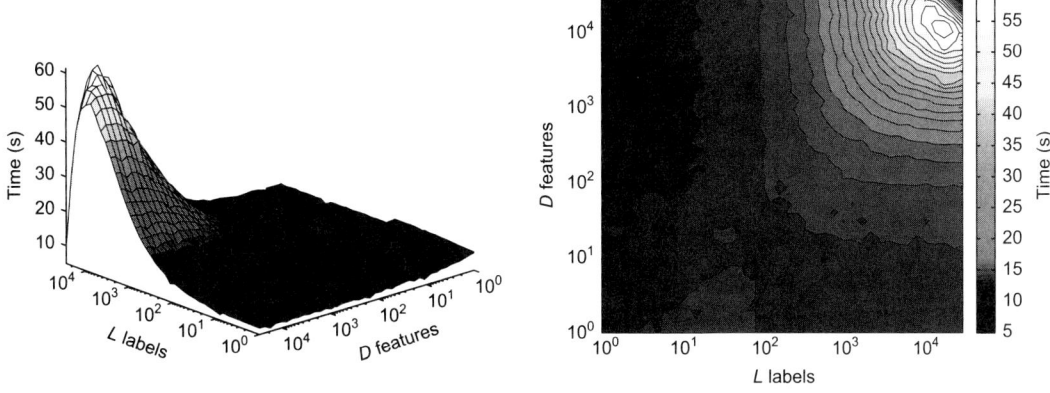

FIGURE 19.11

Two views of the time to calculate a matrix product between $L \times D$ and $D \times N$ matrices using CUBLAS SGEMM. The total amount of memory required is held constant so that N is determined by L and D.

(in CUBLAS) takes longer, even with a concomitant drop in the outer dimension N. We demonstrate this in Figure 19.11, where we measure the time to calculate the product of an $L \times D$ matrix and a $D \times N$ matrix using the CUBLAS SGEMM call. As we vary L and D, the remaining dimension N is set so that the matrix factors and product occupy as much of the device memory as possible. The product time increases with D until N is forced to be close to one, degenerating to a much faster operation.

19.4.2 Character Recognition Application

The parallel training algorithm is now a part of a larger character recognition system [10]. A character image is processed by a wavelet filter bank, whose responses undergo post-processing for invariance and numerical stability. In addition, a simple binarization algorithm is applied to the image. In this context, the number of features is $D = 32$ pixels $\times$ 32 pixels $\times$ 25 images $= 25600 \approx 2^{14.64} \approx 10^{4.41}$. Our classifier must recognize 63 character categories (upper- and lower-case letters, digits, and space) in one of 7 quantized character widths, as well as a "null," non-text category. This gives rise to $L = 63 \times 7 + 1 = 442 \approx 2^{8.79} \approx 10^{2.65}$ categories. We use examples of characters from 1600 fonts rendered with various distortions, neighboring characters, and other contextual elements modeled on the intended deployed application environment. With 1600 base fonts, four distortions for each of the 62 characters and 3 spaces (of varying width), we have $N = 409600 \approx 2^{18.64} \approx 10^{5.61}$ training instances. Only N is determined by our system capability (host memory); L and D are driven by the application.

In these circumstances, our GPU implementation measures a sustained speedup of 30.6$\times$ over the MATLAB implementation (the ratio of average times over 5 runs). With these values of N, L, and D, the bottleneck of the computation is the energy calculation, a large matrix multiplication. Presumably, both the MATLAB and CUDA implementations of the BLAS function SGEMM are highly optimized. Despite the large difference in core processor speed (2.26 GHz on the host vs. 1.3 GHz GPU), the approximately 30$\times$ speedup here can largely be attributed to the use of 30 times as many cores for processing on the GPU (240 cores) over the host (eight cores).

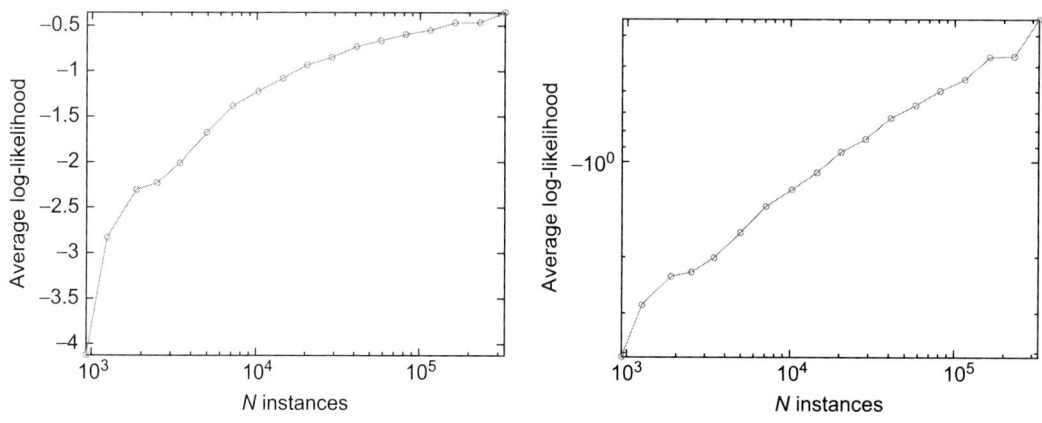

FIGURE 19.12

Performance of a character recognition model on a held-out dataset of over 100,000 characters. The size of the training set is gradually increased and the average log-likelihood of the validation data is measured. The right-hand figure is a log-log plot of the data on the left, which is plotted log-linear.

In real terms, the time drops from 56.6 minutes per iteration to 111 seconds per iteration. With just over 1000 iterations necessary to complete training with parameter validation, the CUDA implementation allows us to perform experiments in just over a day that would have taken more than a month otherwise.

The rapid turnaround time means that more data can be used to generate improved results. To measure the impact of increased training data in the character recognition domain, we used a simpler problem having $L = 62$ categories (only the digits and characters) with the same $D = 25600$ features. We assess the average log-likelihood of the model (the objective function) on a *different*, held-out dataset as N varies. Since the recognition model is used as part of a larger system where the relative probabilities of the various categories are important, the log-likelihood is a more useful metric than raw accuracy. Figure 19.12 shows a logarithmic improvement in log-likelihood as the training data increases in size exponentially.

19.5 CONCLUSIONS AND FUTURE WORK

Although MATLAB is highly optimized for the kinds of computations that must be performed in training a maximum entropy classifier, its host platform does not support the degree of parallelism necessary for learning from large datasets. We have therefore implemented such a learner that utilizes the parallelism of a GPU for the most common scenarios (large numbers of training instances and a moderate number of features). It is likely that in the cases where matrix multiplication is not the bottleneck, performance can be improved even further by optimizing the max and sum reductions at the heart of the other kernels. Unrolling loops and/or initializing extraneous values for non-power of two block sizes so that special cases can be eliminated should yield improved runtimes.

Acknowledgments

Augustus Lidaka and Shitanshu Aggarwal received support from Grinnell College and an HHMI Undergraduate Science Education Award for this work. The authors wish to thank NVIDIA corporation for a hardware grant, Michael Herf for the original float/unsigned integer bijection, Colin Sprinkle for his tutorial on atomics, Gernot Ziegler for early assistance with CUDA, and anonymous reviewers for suggestions that have improved this manuscript.

References

[1] A.L. Berger, S.A. Della Pietra, V.J. Della Pietra, A maximum entropy approach to natural language processing, Comput. Linguist. 22 (1) (1996) 39–71.

[2] P.W. Buchen, M. Kelly, The maximum entropy distribution of an asset inferred from option prices, J. Financ. Quant. Anal. 31 (1) (1996) 143–159.

[3] R.H. Byrd, J. Nocedal, R.B. Schnabel, Represenations of quasi-Newton matrices and their use in limited memory methods, Math. Program. 63 (1994) 129–156.

[4] S. Chen, R. Rosenfeld, A Gaussian Prior for Smoothing Maximum Entropy Models, Technical Report CMU-CS-99-108, Carnegie Mellon University, 1999.

[5] I.T. Foster, Designing and Building Parallel Programs, Addison-Wesley, Reading, MA, 1995.

[6] E.T. Jaynes, Information theory and statistical mechanics, Phys. Rev. 106 (4) (1957) 620–630.

[7] B. Krishnapuram, L. Carin, M.A.T. Figueiredo, A.J. Hartemink, Sparse multinomial logistic regression: fast algorithms and generalization bounds, IEEE Trans. Pattern Anal. Mach. Intell. 27 (6) (2005) 957–968.

[8] J.K. Hong-Kwang, Y. Gao, Maximum entropy direct models for speech recognition, IEEE Trans. Audio. Speech. Lang. Processing 14 (3) (2006) 873–881.

[9] S.J. Phillips, M. Dudík, R.E. Schapire, A maximum entropy approach to species distribution modeling, in: Proceedings International Conference on Machine Learning, Banff, A., Canada, July 4–8, 2004, New York: Association for Computing Machinery, p. 83.

[10] J.J. Weinman, E. Learned-Miller, A. Hanson, A discriminative semi-Markov model for robust scene text recognition, in: 19th International Conference on Pattern Recognition, Tampa, Florida, 2008, IEEE Computer Society, pp. 1–5.

[11] J.J. Weinman, E. Learned-Miller, A. Hanson, Scene text recognition using similarity and a lexicon with sparse belief propagation, IEEE Trans. Pattern Anal. Mach. Intell. 31 (10) (2009) 1733–1746.

Multiclass Support Vector Machine

20

Sergio Herrero-Lopez

In this chapter we present the GPU implementation of the support vector machine (SVM). The SVM is a set of supervised learning methods used for classification and regression. Given a set of training examples, the SVM algorithm builds a model that predicts the class of new unseen examples. This algorithm is considered essential in both machine-learning and data-mining curriculums and is frequently used by practitioners. Besides, its utilization spans to a wide variety of applied research fields such as computer vision, neuroscience, text categorization, and finance. This study shows that the GPU implementation of the dual form of the SVM using the sequential minimal optimization algorithm leads to performance improvements of an order of magnitude in both training and classification. Finally, a technique that coordinates multiple GPUs to solve even larger classification problems is presented at the end of this chapter.

20.1 INTRODUCTION, PROBLEM STATEMENT, AND CONTEXT

The multiclass classification problem based on SVMs is presented as follows: In multiclass classification, given ln-dimensional examples and their corresponding labels $(\bar{x}_1, y_1), \ldots, (\bar{x}_l, y_l)$ with $\bar{x}_i \in R^n, y_i \in Y, \forall i$ and $Y = \{1, \ldots, M\}$, the goal is to construct a classifier $f(\bar{x})$ that predicts the label $y \in Y$ of a new unseen example $\bar{x} \in R^n$. The process of designing the classifier $f(\bar{x})$ from a set of training examples is called the *training phase*, while the process of evaluating the generalization performance of the classifier with a separate dataset of testing examples is known as the *testing phase* [1].

The success of SVMs solving classification tasks in a wide variety of fields, such as text or image processing and medical informatics, has stimulated practitioners to do research on the execution performance and scalability of the training phase of serial versions of the algorithm. Nevertheless, the training phase of the SVM remains a computationally expensive task, and the training time of a binary problem composed by 100,000 points with hundreds of dimensions can often take on the order of hours of serial execution.

In this chapter, our contribution is twofold: (1) we provide a single-device implementation of a multiclass SVM classifier that reduces the training and testing time of the algorithm an order of magnitude compared with a popular multiclass solver, LIBSVM, while guaranteeing the same accuracy and (2) we provide an adaptation of the cascade SVM algorithm that uses multiple CPU threads to orchestrate multiple GPUs and confront larger-scale classification tasks [2].

20.2 CORE METHOD

A classical method to solve multiclass SVM classification problems is to decompose it into the combination of N independent binary SVM classification tasks [3].

20.2.1 Binary SVM

A binary classification task is the one that given l n-dimensional examples and their corresponding labels $(\bar{x}_1, y_1), \ldots, (\bar{x}_l, y_l)$ with $\bar{x}_i \in R^n$, $y_i \in Y, \forall i$ and $Y = \{-1, 1\}$, constructs a classifier $f(\bar{x})$ that predicts the binary label $y \in \{-1, 1\}$ of a new unseen example $\bar{x} \in R^n$. The binary classifier $f(\bar{x})$ is obtained by solving the following regularization problem:

$$\min_{f \in H} C \sum_{i=1}^{1} (1 - yf(\bar{x}))_+ + \frac{1}{2}||f||_k^2, \quad \text{where:} (k)_+ = \max(k, 0) \text{ and } C > 0 \qquad (20.1)$$

The introduction of slack variables ξ_i allows classifying nonseparable data and leads to the *Primal* form:

$$\min_{f \in H} C \sum_{i=1}^{1} \xi_i + \frac{1}{2}|f|_K^2, \quad \text{subject to} : y_i f(x_i) \geq 1 - \xi_i \text{ and } \xi_i \geq 0 \, i = 1, \ldots, l. \qquad (20.2)$$

The *Dual* form, which is derived from the Primal, has simpler constraints to be solved:

$$\max_{\alpha \in R} l \sum_{i=1}^{l} \alpha_i - \frac{1}{2}\alpha^T K\alpha, \quad \text{subject to} : \sum_{i=1}^{l} y_i \alpha_i = 0 \text{ and } 0 \leq \alpha_i \leq C \, i = 1, \ldots, l \qquad (20.3)$$

where $K_{ij} = y_i y_j k(\bar{x}_i, \bar{x}_j)$ is the kernel function. Common kernel functions are shown in Table 20.1. The Dual form (Eq. 20.3) is a quadratic programming optimization problem, and solving it defines the classification function: $f^*(\bar{x}) = \sum_{i=1}^{l} y_i \alpha_i k(\bar{x}, \bar{x}_i) + b$ where b is an unregularized bias term. Geometrically, obtaining $f^*(\bar{x})$ corresponds to finding the maximum margin hyperplane. Figure 20.1 (left) illustrates the geometrical interpretation of the binary SVM classifier, and Figure 20.1 (right) shows the introduction of slack variables when data is not separable. The samples on the margin ($\alpha_i > 0$) are called the support vectors (SVs).

Table 20.1 Kernel functions.

Linear kernel	$k(x_i, \bar{x}_j) = \bar{x}_i \bar{x}_j$
Polynomial kernel	$k(\bar{x}_i, \bar{x}_j) = (c_1 \bar{x}_i \bar{x}_j + c_2)^{c_3}$
Radial basis kernel	$k(\bar{x}_i, \bar{x}_j) = e^{-\beta \|\bar{x}_i - \bar{x}_j\|^2}$
Sigmoid kernel	$k(\bar{x}_i, \bar{x}_j) = \tanh(c_1 \bar{x}_i \bar{x}_j + c_2)$

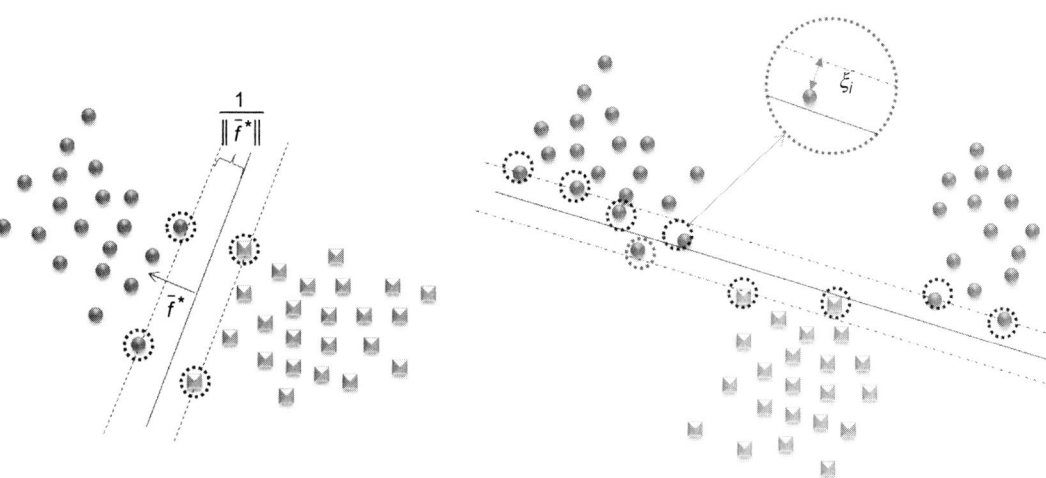

FIGURE 20.1

Left: Binary SVM. Right: Binary SVM with nonseparable data.

20.2.2 Multiclass SVM

Classical approaches construct the multiclass classifier as the combination of N independent binary classification tasks. Binary tasks are defined in the output code matrix R of size $M \times N$, where M is the number of classes, N is the number of tasks, and $R_{ij} \in \{-1, 0, 1\}$. Each column in matrix R represents how multiclass labels are mapped to binary labels for each specific binary task. There are three common types of output codes:

- One-vs-All (OVA): M classifiers are needed. For the $f^i(\bar{x})$ classifier, the positive examples are all the points in class i, and the negative samples all the points not in class i.
- All-vs-All (AVA): $\binom{M}{2}$ classifiers are needed, one classifier to distinguish each pair of classes i and j. $f^{ij}(\bar{x})$ is the classifier where class i has positive samples and class j negative.
- Error-correcting codes: Often error-correcting codes are applied to reconstruct labels from noisy predicted binary labels.

Figure 20.2 (left) illustrates the hyperplanes generated from the resolution of a multiclass SVM problem using AVA output codes, while Figure 20.2 (right) represents the result using OVA output codes.

Then each $f^k(\bar{x})$ is trained separately with $(\bar{x}_1, R_{y1k}), \ldots, (\bar{x}_l, R_{y_1 k})$ where $k = 1 \ldots N$. The outputs of trained binary classifiers $f^{*k}(\bar{x})$, along with the output codes R_{yk} and a user-specified loss function V are used to calculate the multiclass label that best agrees with the binary predictions:

$$f^*(\bar{x}) = \underset{y \in Y}{\operatorname{argmin}} \left\{ \sum_{k=1}^{N} V\left(R_{yk}, f^{*k}(\bar{x})\right) \right\} \tag{20.4}$$

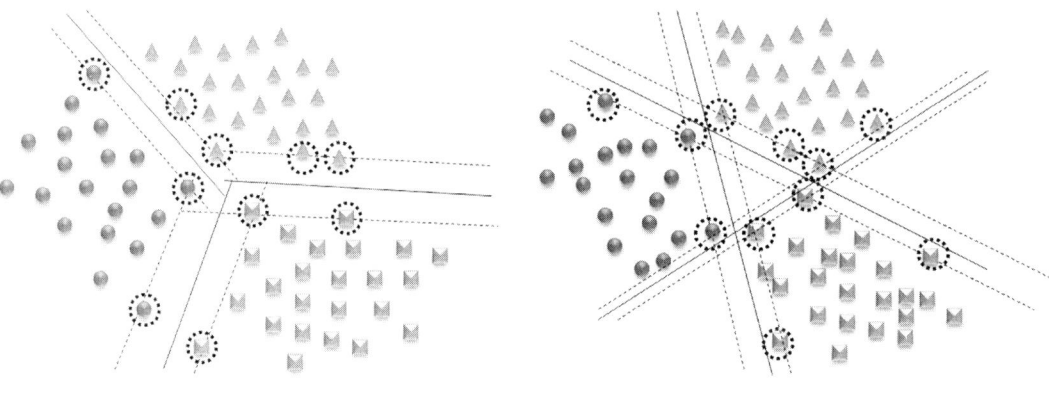

FIGURE 20.2

Left: All-vs-All (AVA) output code. Right: One-vs-All (OVA) output code.

20.3 ALGORITHMS, IMPLEMENTATIONS, AND EVALUATIONS

Our approach to solve the multiclass classification problem utilizes the sequential minimal optimization (SMO) algorithm [4]. This approach was also successfully used by [5] on the implementation of binary classifier for the GPU. Our work takes this previous solution a step further and generalizes the construction of N binary classifiers concurrently on the GPU grid. On this section the implementation details of the algorithm are presented.

20.3.1 Sequential Minimal Optimization (SMO)

In order to construct the set of N binary classifiers $f^{*k}(\bar{x}), k = 1 \ldots N$, we need to solve N quadratic programming (QP) optimization programs on the same set of kernel evaluations K, but with different binary labels:

$$\max_{\bar{\alpha} \in R^l} \sum_{i=1}^{l} \alpha_i^k - \frac{1}{2} \bar{\alpha}^{k^T} K \bar{\alpha}^k \tag{20.5}$$

subject to: $\sum_{i=1}^{l} R_{(y_i, k)} \alpha_i^k = 0$ and $0 \leq \alpha_i^k \leq C^k, i = 1, \ldots, l, k = 1, \ldots, N$. We will use the sequential minimal optimization (SMO) algorithm. SMO solves large-scale QP optimization problems by choosing the smallest optimization problem at every step, which involves only two Lagrange multipliers $\left(\alpha_{I_{low}}^k, \alpha_{I_{up}}^k \right)$. For two Lagrange multipliers the QP problem can be solved analytically without the need of numerical QP solvers. At each iteration, the two Lagrange multipliers are used to obtain the updated function values f_i^k. The SMO algorithm can be directly decomposed into iterations of *Map* and *Reduce* primitives, which have been proven to be very useful extracting parallelism on machine-learning algorithms [6], [7]. Different QP programs will have different convergence rates, and the algorithm finishes when the last QP program has converged. Early convergence of some of the QP programs allows binary tasks that are lagging to find a larger number of stream processors available. These are the key steps of the algorithm:

1. **Map**: Calculates the new values of the function $f_i^k, i = 1, \ldots, l, k = 1, \ldots, N$. This step is entirely executed on the device.
2. **Reduce**: The Reduce step combines both host and device segments. These are the substeps that compose the Reduce:
   a. *Local Reduce*: Performs reduction operations (*max/min* and *argmax/argmin*) on the device thread blocks.
   b. *Global Reduce*: The global reduction is carried out on the host using the output of each device thread block.
   c. *Kernel Evaluation*: The calculation of the Lagrange multipliers requires the evaluation of multiple rows of the Gram Matrix K. In SVM problems with large numbers of samples and dimensions the storage of matrix K in device memory might not be feasible. Consequently, a kernel-caching mechanism was implemented [8]. The kernel-cache is managed by the host and stores pointers to the locations of the requested rows of K on the device memory.
   d. *Update Alphas*: Using the kernel values the Lagrange multipliers are updated on the device so that they are available for the next iteration $\left(\alpha_{I_{low}}^k, \alpha_{I_{up}}^k\right)$.

The core of the algorithm is illustrated in Figure 20.3. In the next subsections we include additional details for each step.

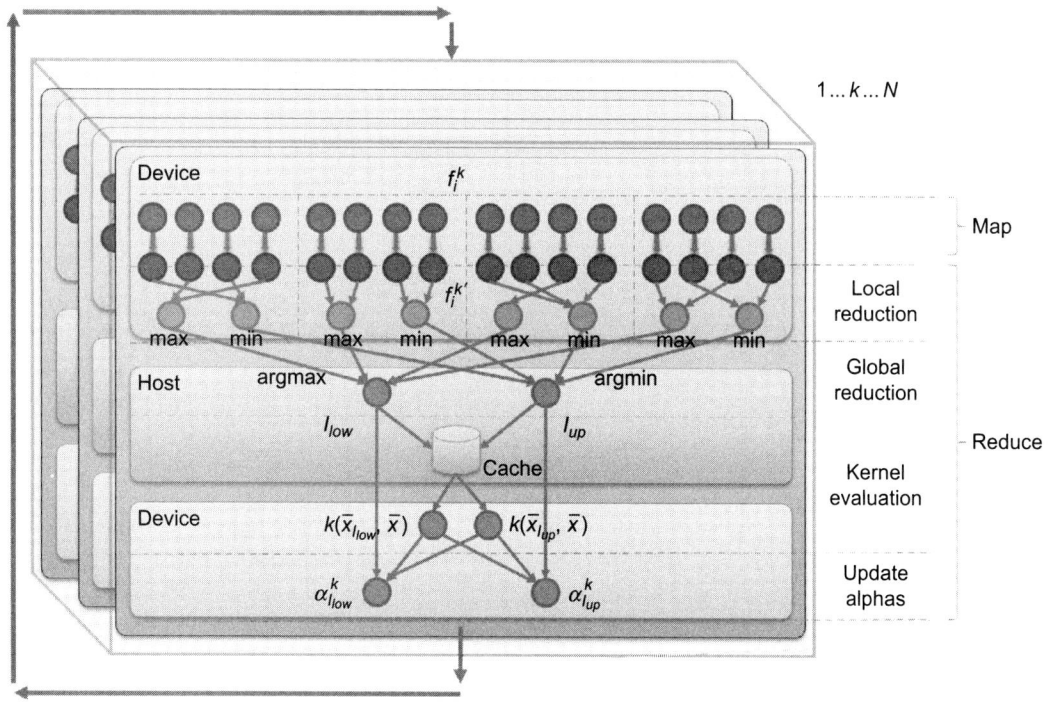

FIGURE 20.3

SMO algorithm.

20.3.2 Map Step

The Map step updates the values of the classifier function f_i^k based on the variation of the two Lagrange multipliers, $\Delta\alpha_{I_{low}}^k = \alpha_{I_{low}}^{k'} - \alpha_{I_{low}}^k, \Delta\alpha_{I_{up}}^k = \alpha_{I_{up}}^{k'} - \alpha_{I_{up}}^k$ and the corresponding kernel evaluations:

$$f_i^{k'} = f_i^k + \Delta\alpha_{I_{up}}^k y_{I_{up}}^k k\left(\bar{x}_{I_{up}^k}, \bar{x}_l\right) + \Delta\alpha_{I_{low}}^k y_{I_{low}}^k k\left(\bar{x}_{I_{low}^k}, \bar{x}_l\right) \tag{20.6}$$

with $i = 1,\ldots,l, k = 1,\ldots,N$. The initialization values for the first iteration of the SMO algorithm are $f_i^k = -y_i^k, \Delta\alpha_{I_{low}}^k = \Delta\alpha_{I_{up}}^k = 0, \alpha_{I_{low}}^k = \alpha_{I_{up}}^k = 0, I_{up}^k = I_{low}^k = 0$. Figure 20.4 presents the code of the kernel function that executes the Map step. The function takes the following arguments: (1) Input arrays: the function values d_f, the binary labels d_y, K matrix rows d_k and the variation of the Lagrange multipliers d_delta_a. (2) Indices: the indices of the global locations of the two Lagrange multipliers (d_Iup_global, d_Ilow_global) and the indices of the cached rows that store the required kernel evaluations (d_Iup_cache, d_Ilow_cache). (3.) Other parameters: An array pointing to the non-converged binary tasks d_active and the number of training samples in the dataset ntraining. The Map kernel is launched on a 2-D grid where the blocks along the x dimension select specific subsets of the training samples, and the y dimension specifies the binary task to work on.

```
__global__ void Map_Kernel(float* d_f,float* d_k,int* d_y,float* d_delta_a,
                unsigned int* d_Iup_global,unsigned int* d_Ilow_global,
                    unsigned int* d_Iup_cache,unsigned int* d_Ilow_cache,
                    int* d_active,int ntraining)
{
        unsigned int blockSize= blockDim.x;
        unsigned int i = blockIdx.x* blockSize + threadIdx.x;
        unsigned int gridSize= blockSize* gridDim.x;
        unsigned int bidy= d_active[blockIdx.y];
        unsigned int g_Iup_cache= d_Iup_cache [bidy];
        unsigned int g_Ilow_cache= d_Ilow_cache [bidy];
        float delta_alpha_low= d_delta_a[bidy*2];
        float delta_alpha_up= d_delta_a[bidy*2+1];
        int y_up= d_y[bidy*ntraining + d_Iup_global[bidy]];
        int y_low= d_y[bidy*ntraining + d_Ilow_global[bidy]];

        while (i < ntraining)
        {
                d_f[bidy*ntraining +i]+=        delta_alpha_low* y_low*
                                               d_k [g_Ilow_cache * ntraining +i] +
                                               delta_alpha_up* y_up*
                                               d_k [g_Iup_cache * ntraining +i];
                i += gridSize;
        }
}
```

FIGURE 20.4

The Map step GPU kernel.

20.3.3 Reduce Step

The Reduce step finds the indices I_{up}^k and I_{low}^k $k = 1 \ldots N$ of the Lagrange multipliers that need to be optimized in each iteration and calculates the new values for $\alpha_{I_{low}}^k$ and $\alpha_{I_{up}}^k$. This step interleaves host and device segments. The calculation of the indices is as follows:

$$I_0^k = \{i : y_i^k = 1, 0 < \alpha_i^k < C^k\} \cup \{i : y_i^k = -1, 0 < \alpha_i^k < C^k\}$$

$$I_1^k = \{i : y_i^k = 1, \alpha_i^k = 0\}, \quad I_2^k = \{i : y_i^k = -1, \alpha_i^k = C^k\} \tag{20.7}$$

$$I_3^k = \{i : y_i^k = 1, \alpha_i^k = C^k\}, \quad I_4^k = \{i : y_i^k = -1, \alpha_i^k = 0\}$$

$$b_{up}^k = \min\{f_i^k : i \in I_0^k \cup I_1^k \cup I_2^k\}, \quad I_{up}^k = \underset{i \in I_0^k \cup I_1^k \cup I_2^k}{\operatorname{argmin}} \ f_i^k$$

$$b_{low}^k = \max\{f_i^k : i \in I_0^k \cup I_3^k \cup I_4^k\}, \quad I_{low}^k = \underset{i \in I_0^k \cup I_3^k \cup I_4^k}{\operatorname{argmin}} \ f_i^k \tag{20.8}$$

The indices are obtained by filtering Eq. 20.7 and reducing Eq. 20.8 the f_i^k $i = 1, \ldots, l, k = 1, \ldots, N$ array. The Local Reduce is carried out on the device and the Global Reduce is performed by the host. Figure 20.5 shows the Local Reduce kernel function utilized to obtain the I_{up}^k Lagrange multiplier using *min* and *argmin* reductions. The kernel function for the I_{low}^k multiplier is analogous, but using *max* and *argmax* operations instead.

Both kernel functions take similar arguments: (1) Input arrays: the binary labels d_y, the current Lagrange multiplier values d_a, the function values d_f. (2) Output arrays: the value and index of the locally reduced Lagrange multiplier (d_Bup_local, d_Iup_local) for the *min* reduction and (d_Blow_local, d_Ilow_local) for the *max* reduction. (3) Other parameters: an array pointing to the regularization parameter values d_c, an array pointing to the nonconverged binary tasks d_active, and the number of training samples in the dataset ntraining. The parallel reduction is carried out using a shared memory array, extern__shared__ float reducearray[]. The length of this array is specified at kernel launch time. The first half of the array is used to store the reduced values and the second half for the indices. Both reduce kernels are launched on a 2-D grid in which the blocks along the *x* dimension select specific subsets of the training samples, and the *y* dimension specifies the binary task to work on.

After the Local Reduce has been performed in the device, the host finalizes the reduction by finding the global minimum and global maximum with their corresponding indices, which indicate the Lagrange multipliers to be optimized. These two indices per binary task, I_{up}^k and I_{low}^k $k = 1 \ldots N$, also point to the rows of the Gram matrix K that will be required in order to calculate the new values of the Lagrange multipliers. A host-controlled LRU (Least Recently Used) cache indicates whether these rows have been previously calculated and are kept in the device memory. A cache hit simply returns the memory location of the required row, whereas a cache miss invokes the CUBLAS *sgemv* routine to calculate the new row and returns its location. In any case, the required $2N$ rows will be in memory before the Lagrange multipliers are updated. The fact that different binary tasks may require the same rows of the Gram matrix K increases the cache hit rate.

```
__global__ void Local_Reduce_KernelMin(int* d_y,float* d_a,float* d_f,float*
                    d_bup_local,unsigned
                                     int* d_Iup_local,float* d_C,int* d_active,int
                                     ntraining)
{
     extern __shared__ float reducearray[];
     unsigned int tid = threadIdx.x;
     unsigned int bidy= d_active[blockIdx.y];
     unsigned int blockSize= blockDim.x;
     unsigned int gridSize = blockSize* gridDim.x;
     unsigned int i = blockIdx.x*(blockSize) + threadIdx.x;
     float* minreduction = (float*)reducearray;
     int* minreductionid = (int*)&reducearray[blockSize];
     minreduction[tid]= (float)FLT_MAX;
     minreductionid[tid]= i;
     float C= d_C[bidy];
     float alpha_i;
     int y_i;

     while (i < ntraining)
     {
          alpha_i = d_a[bidy* ntraining + i];
          y_i= d_y[bidy* ntraining + i];

          if((    (y_i==1 && alpha_i>0 && alpha_i<C) ||
                  (y_i== −1 && alpha_i>0 && alpha_i<C)) ||
                  (y_i==1 && alpha_i==0) || (y_i== −1 && alpha_i==C) )
        {
                  if(minreduction[tid] >= d_f[bidy* ntraining +i])
                  {
                          minreduction[tid]= d_f[bidy* ntraining +i];
                          minreductionid[tid]= i;
                  }
        }
        i += gridSize;
     }
__syncthreads();
if(blockSize>=512){if(tid<256){if(minreduction[tid] >= minreduction[tid+256])
                          {minreduction[tid]= minreduction[tid +256];
                          minreductionid[tid]= minreductionid[tid+256];}}
                  __syncthreads();}
if(blockSize>=256){if(tid<128){if(minreduction[tid] >= minreduction[tid+128])
                          {minreduction[tid]= minreduction[tid +128];
                          minreductionid[tid]= minreductionid[tid +128];}}
                  __syncthreads();}
if(blockSize>=128){if(tid<64) {if(minreduction[tid] >= minreduction[tid+64])
                          {minreduction[tid]= minreduction[tid +64];
                          minreductionid[tid]= minreductionid[tid +64];}}
                  __syncthreads();}
```

(Continued)

```
if(tid<32){if(blockSize >= 64){if(minreduction[tid] >= minreduction[tid+32])
                                {minreduction[tid]= minreduction[tid +32];
                                 minreductionid[tid]= minreductionid[tid +32];}}
            if(blockSize >= 32){if(minreduction[tid] >= minreduction[tid+16])
                                {minreduction[tid]= minreduction[tid +16];
                                 minreductionid[tid]= minreductionid[tid +16];}}
            if(blockSize >= 16){if(minreduction[tid] >= minreduction[tid+8])
                                {minreduction[tid]= minreduction[tid +8];
                                 minreductionid[tid]= minreductionid[tid +8];}}
            if(blockSize >= 8){if(minreduction[tid] >= minreduction[tid+4])
                                {minreduction[tid]= minreduction[tid +4];
                                 minreductionid[tid]= minreductionid[tid +4];}}
            if(blockSize >= 4){if(minreduction[tid] >= minreduction[tid+2])
                                {minreduction[tid]= minreduction[tid +2];
                                 minreductionid[tid]= minreductionid[tid +2];}}
            if(blockSize >= 2){if(minreduction[tid] >= minreduction[tid+1])
                                {minreduction[tid]= minreduction[tid +1];
                                 minreductionid[tid]= minreductionid[tid +1];}}}
    if(tid==0)
    {
        d_bup_local [bidy * gridDim.x + blockIdx.x]=minreduction[tid];
        d_Iup_local [bidy * gridDim.x + blockIdx.x]= minreductionid[tid];
    }
}
```

FIGURE 20.5

Kernel function for the reduction of the "Up" Lagrange multiplier.

Using the values of these rows of the K matrix, we obtain the new values of the Lagrange multipliers:

$$\alpha_{I_{up}}^{k'} = \alpha_{I_{up}}^{k} - \frac{y_{I_{up}}^{k}\left(f_{I_{low}}^{k} - f_{I_{up}}^{k}\right)}{\eta}, \qquad \alpha_{I_{low}}^{k'} = \alpha_{I_{low}}^{k} + y_{I_{up}}^{k}y_{I_{low}}^{k}\left(\alpha_{I_{up}}^{k} - \alpha_{I_{up}}^{k'}\right) \qquad (20.9)$$

where $\eta = 2k\left(\bar{x}_{I_{low}}, \bar{x}_{I_{up}}\right) - k\left(\bar{x}_{I_{low}}, \bar{x}_{I_{low}}\right) - k\left(\bar{x}_{I_{up}}, \bar{x}_{I_{up}}\right)$. Because all the information required to update the Lagrange multipliers resides on the device memory and the Lagrange multipliers themselves will be required by the Map task to be on the device memory as well, $\left(\alpha_{low}^{k'}, \alpha_{I_{up}}^{k'}\right)$ are calculated on the device using the kernel function in Figure 20.6.

The Update kernel function takes the following arguments: (1) Input arrays: K matrix rows d_k, the binary labels d_y, the function values d_f. (2) Output arrays: the Lagrange multiplier values d_a, the variation of the Lagrange multipliers d_delta_a. (3) Indices: the indices of the global locations of the two Lagrange multipliers (d_Iup_global, d_Ilow_global) and the indices of the cached rows that keep the required kernel evaluations (d_Iup_cache, d_Ilow_cache). (4) Other parameters: an array pointing to the regularization parameter values d_c, an array pointing to the nonconverged binary tasks d_active, the number of training samples in the dataset ntraining and the number of nonconverged binary tasks activeTasks. Both reduce kernels are launched on a 2-D grid where the blocks along

```
__global__ void Update_Kernel(float* d_k,int* d_y,float* d_f,float* d_a,float* d_delta_a,
                              unsigned int* d_Iup_global, unsigned int* d_Ilow_global,
                              unsigned int* d_Iup_cache, unsigned int* d_Ilow_cache,
                              float* d_C,int* d_active,int ntraining,int activetasks)
{
        unsigned int blockSize= blockDim.x;
        unsigned int tid = blockIdx.x* blockSize + threadIdx.x;

        if(tid<activetasks)
        {
                unsigned int j= d_active[tid];
                float C= d_C[j];
                int g_Iup=d_Iup_global[j];
                int g_Ilow=d_Ilow_global[j];
                int y_up= d_y[j*ntraining + g_Iup];
                int y_low= d_y[j*ntraining + g_Ilow];
                float alpha_up_old= d_a[j*ntraining + g_Iup];
                float alpha_low_old= d_a[j*ntraining + g_Ilow];

                float alpha_up_new= fmaxf(0, fminf(alpha_up_old +
                                (y_up*(d_f[j*ntraining + g_Ilow] - d_f[j*ntraining + g_Iup])/
                                (d_k[d_Ilow_cache[j]*ntraining + g_Ilow]+
                                d_k[d_Iup_cache[j]*ntraining + g_Iup]-
                                2*d_k[d_Ilow_cache[j]*ntraining + g_Iup]))), C));

        float alpha_low_new= fmaxf(0, fminf(alpha_low_old +
                                y_up*y_low*(alpha_up_old - alpha_up_new), C));

        d_delta_a[j*2]= alpha_low_new-alpha_low_old;
        d_delta_a[j*2 +1]= alpha_up_new-alpha_up_old;
        d_a[j*ntraining + g_Ilow]=alpha_low_new;
        d_a[j*ntraining + g_Iup]=alpha_up_new;
    }
    __syncthreads();
}
```

FIGURE 20.6

Update Alpha kernel function.

the x dimension select specific subsets of the training samples, and the y dimension specifies the binary task to work on.

Finally, once the new Lagrange multiplier values have been calculated, we check for convergence of the QP program: If $b_{low}^k \leq b_{up}^k + 2\tau$, task k has converged, where τ is the tolerance parameter. The algorithm finishes when all the N tasks have converged.

20.3.4 Testing Phase

In the testing phase, we need to calculate $f^{*k}(\bar{z}) = \sum_{i=1}^{l} y_i^k \alpha_i^k k(\bar{z},\bar{x}_i) + b^k$, for $k = 1 \ldots N$ and $\bar{z} \in Z$. For each test sample $\bar{z}$, it is required to evaluate an entire row $k(\bar{z},\bar{x}_i)\, i = 1..l$ of the kernel matrix, this row will be shared by all N binary tasks. In order to increase the efficiency of the calculation, we classify as many test samples $\bar{z}$ simultaneously as allowed by the device memory.

We estimate the maximum number P of test samples that we can classify at a time based on the available device memory, and we break the test dataset into partitions of P samples. For each of these partitions we calculate $\bar{z}_p \bar{x}_i\, i = 1..l, p = 1..P$ using CUBLAS *sgemm*. Then for each sample $p = 1 \ldots P$, we carry out a parallel reduction on the device to calculate $\sum_{i=1}^{l} y_i^k \alpha_i^k k\left(\bar{z}_p, \bar{x}_i\right)$. This step is called *Test Reduce* and is illustrated in Figure 20.7. Finally, back in the host, we add the unregularized bias parameter b^k to obtain $f^{\times k}\left(\bar{z}\right)$, and calculate (4).

The Test Reduce kernel function takes the following arguments: (1) Input arrays: the binary labels d_y, the Lagrange multiplier values d_a, an array with the dot products of the training samples d_Xdot1, an array with the dot products of the testing samples d_Xdot2, an array with the results of the *sgemm* operation d_ReductionF. (2) Output arrays: the array that will store the results of the reduction d_ReducedF. (3) Other parameters: the number of training samples in the dataset ntraining, the index of the test sample local to the partition being processed ii, the index of the test sample global to the test dataset iRow, the parameters kernel functions beta, c1, c2, and c3 and the indicator of the kernel function used kernelcode. The kernel is launched on a 2-D grid where the blocks along the x dimension select specific subsets of the testing samples, and the y dimension specifies the binary task to work on.

20.3.5 Size of Device Blocks and Grids

In general, maximum multiprocessor occupancy does not necessarily guarantee best performance. Nevertheless, we chose the number of threads per block and the number of blocks per grid to maximize the device multiprocessor occupancy, but then searched the performance peak experimentally. Fortunately, for the case of multiclass SVMs, maximum occupancy and higher performance resulted to be aligned. Because of the similar nature of the Map, the Local Reduce, and Test Reduce kernel functions, the same block and grid sizes were used in all three cases.

- **Grid size**: Devices with CUDA Compute Capability 1.2 that have eight thread blocks per multiprocessor. Hence, on a device with eight multiprocessors 64 thread blocks can be executed simultaneously. For this reason we set the maximum number of blocks on the x dimension of the grid to 64. The y dimension of the grid is imposed by the number of nonconverged binary tasks. This arrangement ensures that all the blocks corresponding to the same binary task are being processed simultaneously.
- **Block size**: The register and shared memory usage determine the maximum number of threads per block. The Map_kernel uses 11 registers per thread and 92 bytes of shared memory per block. Both Local_Reduce_KernelMin and Local_Reduce_KernelMax use 13 registers per thread and 1104 bytes of shared memory per block. The Test_Reduce_kernel uses 14 registers per thread and 608 bytes of shared memory per block. In all three cases, 100% of multiprocessor occupancy is achieved by setting the maximum number of threads per block to 128.

Large classification problems achieve maximum occupancy by using 128 threads per block and 64 blocks per binary task. This implementation will also work for small classification problems by launching kernel functions with less of blocks and less threads. However, these cases might not result on a 100% of multiprocessor occupancy and consequently would be suboptimal.

```
__global__ void TestReduce_Kernel( int* d_y,float* d_a,float* d_ReductionF,float* ReducedF,
                              float* d_Xdot1,float* d_Xdot2,int ntraining,int ii, int iRow,
                              float beta,float c1, float c2,float c3,int kernelcode)
{
        extern __shared__ float reduction[];
        unsigned int blockSize= blockDim.x;
        unsigned int tid = threadIdx.x;
        unsigned int bidx= blockIdx.x;
        unsigned int bidy = blockIdx.y;
        unsigned int i = blockIdx.x*blockSize + threadIdx.x;
        unsigned int gridSize = blockSize*gridDim.x;
        reduction[tid]= 0;
        while (i < ntraining)
        {
                if(kernelcode==0){reduction[tid] += d_a[bidy*ntraining +i]*d_y[bidy*ntraining +i]*
                                            expf(2*beta* d_ReductionF[ii*ntraining+i] -
                                            beta* (d_Xdot1[i] + d_Xdot2[iRow]));}
                else if (kernelcode==1){reduction[tid] +=d_a[bidy*ntraining i]*d_y[bidy*ntraining+i]*
                                                    d_ReductionF[ii*ntraining+i];}
                else if (kernelcode==2){reduction[tid] +=d_a[bidy*ntraining +i]*d_y[bidy*ntraining +i]*
                                                    powf(c1* d_ReductionF[ii*ntraining+i]+c2,c3);}
                else if (kernelcode==3){reduction[tid] +=d_a[bidy*ntraining +i]*d_y[bidy*ntraining +i]*
                                                    tanhf(c1* d_ReductionF[ii*ntraining+i]+c2);}
                i += gridSize;
        }
        __syncthreads();
        if(blockSize>=512)    {if(tid<256){reduction[tid] += reduction[tid + 256];}__syncthreads();}
        if(blockSize>=256)    {if(tid<128){reduction[tid] += reduction[tid + 128];}__syncthreads();}
        if(blockSize>=128)    {if(tid<64) {reduction[tid] += reduction[tid + 64];}__syncthreads();}
        if(tid<32){      if(blockSize >= 64) {reduction[tid] += reduction[tid + 32];}
                              if(blockSize >= 32) {reduction[tid] += reduction[tid + 16];}
                              if(blockSize >= 16) {reduction[tid] += reduction[tid + 8];}
                              if(blockSize >= 8) {reduction[tid] += reduction[tid + 4];}
                              if(blockSize >= 4) {reduction[tid] += reduction[tid + 2];}
                              if(blockSize >= 2) {reduction[tid] += reduction[tid + 1];} }
        if(tid==0){d_ReducedF[bidy*gridDim.x + bidx]=reduction[tid];}
}
```

FIGURE 20.7

Test Reduce kernel function.

The Update kernel function launches one thread per nonconverged binary task on a one-dimensional grid of blocks. The maximum number of threads per block is set to 128. In practice most classification problems involve less than 128 binary tasks; hence, a single block will be launched. This leads to low multiprocessor occupancy, but it is still faster than moving the computation of the Lagrange multiplier update to the host.

20.3.6 Multi-GPU Cascade SVM

Graf *et al.* proposed an algorithm that would allow solving large-scale classification problems on clusters using individual instances of SVMs on a *Cascade* topology [2]. The characteristics of different topologies were investigated by Lu *et al.* [12]. In both cases, parallelism was achieved by distributing the SVM problem across multiple machines running single-threaded SVM solvers. In this section, we explain how we adapted the *Cascade SVM* algorithm to run on a multicore and multi-GPU scenario.

In order to orchestrate the operation of multiple devices, a *port-based asynchronous messaging* pattern was used. Typically, *ports* are communication end points associated to a *state*. The posting of a *message* to a port is followed by a predefined *handler* receiving and processing the message based on the actual state. Each port is composed by a queue and a thread pool that manages the messages as they arrive. The existence of this queue makes posting a nonblocking call, letting the sender thread proceed to do other work [9].

In the Multi-GPU Cascade SVM algorithm, each SVM instance is associated to a single device and the state of the SVM is composed by all the variables involved in the training and testing phases. We added a port with the corresponding queue and thread pool on top of the SVM to handle messages asynchronously. Finally, message handlers invoke device kernels based on the SVM state and the message type and its content. In general, thread pools in charge of absorbing the messages accumulated in the queue are composed by multiple threads. Nevertheless, some multiprocessor devices only allow being managed by the same host thread during the entire execution of the program in order to maintain the context between device calls. This is the case for devices with CUDA Compute Capability 1.2; therefore, our thread pools were limited to a single thread, thus guaranteeing that communication with the device would be always performed by the same thread. Latest devices enable concurrent kernel execution to be allowed to increase the number of threads in the thread pool. We call the host thread, the *Master* thread, and the threads assigned to each of the devices, *Slave* threads. Figure 20.8 illustrates the structure of the port used to invoke SVM functions asynchronously; this is the basic building block of the Cascade SVM.

The Multi-GPU Cascade SVM algorithm is composed by a series of *scatter-gather* iterations initiated by the host that work as follows:

1. Given P devices the Master thread breaks the training set into P subsets and scatters these among available SVM nodes by posting a message containing training samples, training phase parameters, and the response port in which the host will collect all the responses. Each device solves its local multiclass classification problem using the single-device solver described in this chapter. When finished, the obtained SVs are posted back to the response port. The Master thread waits to gather all SVs from P devices before proceeding to the next step.
2. The next layer is composed by $P/2$ devices. Each of the devices receives the SVs generated by two devices in the upper level combined pairwise. Each device in this layer solves the local multiclass classification problem using the single-device solver. The values of the Lagrange multipliers are initialized with the SV values of the upper layer. The SVs generated are posted back to the response port of the Master thread. Step 2 is repeated until only a single device is left.
3. The SVs generated by the only device composing the last layer are fed again to the first layer along with shuffled subsets of the non-SV samples. The Lagrange multipliers of the single-device solvers of the first layer are initialized with the SVs provided by the last layer. Convergence is obtained when the set of SVs returned by the last layer remains unchanged. Typically, a single iteration provides comparable accuracy to the single-device solver.

Figure 20.9 illustrates the structure of the Multi-GPU Cascade SVM and its modular composition using multiple instances of the single-device solver.

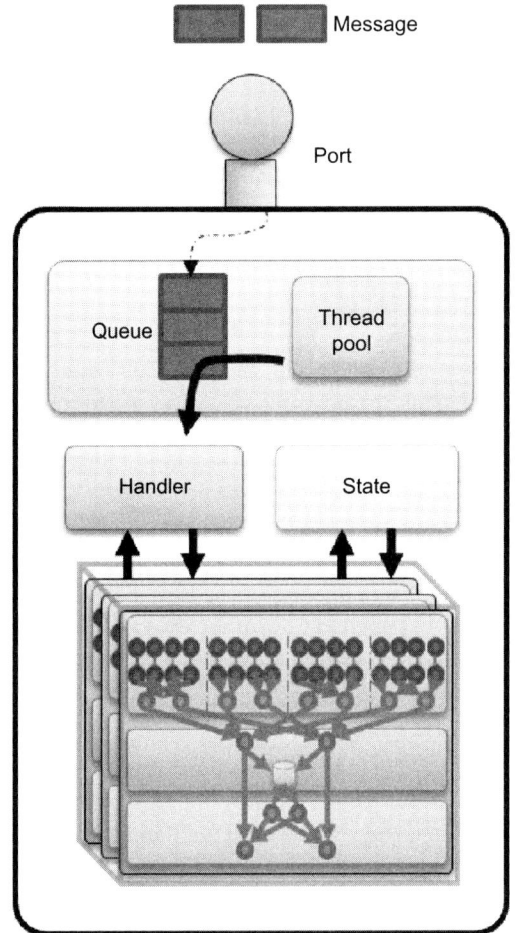

FIGURE 20.8

GPU SVM instance port.

20.4 FINAL EVALUATION

Experimental results show that the single-GPU multiclass-SVM solver can reduce the training phase and testing phase time an order of magnitude compared to LIBSVM, a de facto established reference serial implementation for SVM training and classification [10]. In addition to increased performance, test results with multiple benchmark datasets demonstrate that the GPU implementation guarantees the same accuracy as LIBSVM. Furthermore, the orchestration of multiple GPUs following the *Cascade SVM* algorithm can introduce an additional order of magnitude of acceleration on top of the already-gained time reduction. In order to provide a representative comparison, special attention was given to use the same configuration parameters for both the GPU and the serial implementation.

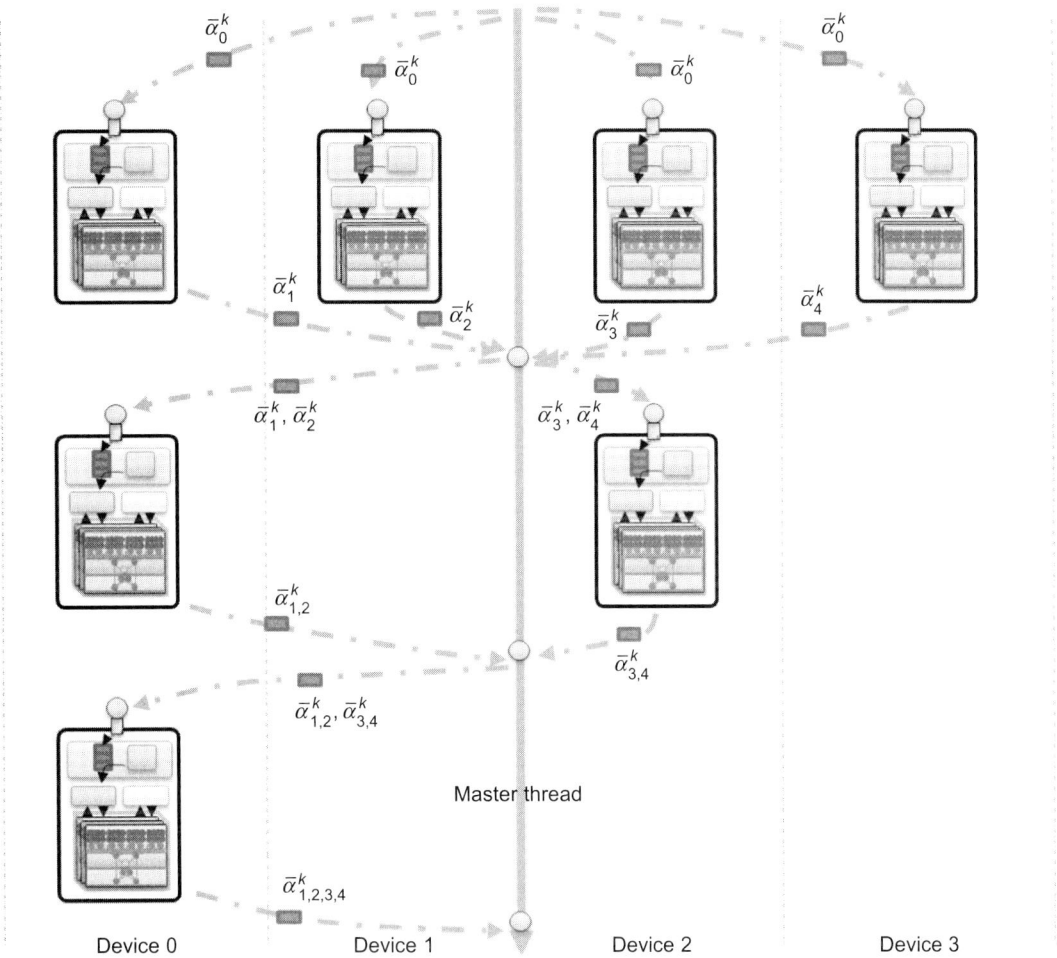

FIGURE 20.9

Multi-GPU Cascade SVM.

- Same kernel types: Radial Basis Function: $k\left(\bar{x}_i, \bar{x}_j\right) = e^{-\beta \| \bar{x}_i - \bar{x}_j \|^z}$
- Same regularization parameter C.
- Same stopping criteria.
- Both SMO based.
- Both use One-vs-All (OVA) output codes.
- Same kernel cache size 1GB.
- Both consider I/O an intrinsic part of the classifier.

The performance measurements were carried out using publicly available benchmark datasets. ADULT [13], WEB [4], MNIST [14], and USPS [15] datasets were used to test the correctness of

Table 20.2 Dataset characteristics.

Dataset	Application	No. Training Points	No. Testing Points	No. Features	No. Classes	C	β
ADULT	Household income classification	32,561	16,281	123	2	100	0.5
WEB	Web browsing classification	49,749	14,951	300	2	64	7.813
MNIST	Handwritten digit classification	60,000	10,000	780	10	10	0.125
USPS	Handwritten digit classification	7291	2007	256	10	10	1/256
SHUTTLE	Shuttle measurement classification	43,500	14,500	9	7	2048	8
LETTER	English character image classification	15,000	5000	16	26	16	12

single-binary classifications tasks. MNIST and USPS datasets were converted from multiclass to binary problems considering only even versus odd values. Then, MNIST, USPS, SHUTTLE, and LETTER [16] datasets were used to analyze the accuracy and performance in multiclass problems. The sizes of these datasets and the parameters used for training are indicated in Table 20.2.

20.4.1 GPU SVM Performance

The performance tests measured in this subsection were carried out in a single machine with Intel Core i7 920 @ 2.67 GHz and 6 GB of RAM running Ubuntu 9.04 (64 bit). The graphics processor model used was a NVIDIA Tesla C1060 with 240 stream processors—each of them with a frequency of 1.3 GHz. The card had 4 GB of memory and a memory bandwidth of 102 GB/s.

Table 20.3 shows the measured training and testing time for both binary and multiclass-SVM problems compared with LIBSVM. All datasets resulted on reductions of the training and testing times. It is observed that the GPU implementation benefited particularly classification problems with the largest numbers of dimensions. MNIST and USPS datasets, which have samples with hundreds of dimensions, resulted in the largest speedup both during the training phase and the testing phase.

The training time was reduced for these datasets in the range of (16x-57x), while the testing time was reduced (13x-112x). Nevertheless, binary and multiclass problems composed by samples with tens of dimensions, such as SHUTTLE or LETTER, obtained a reduced but still respectable acceleration, (3x-25x) for training and (2x-3x) for testing. These results are consistent with the binary SVM in [5].

Table 20.4 shows the comparison of accuracy results for binary and multiclass classification. Results show that classification accuracy in the GPU does as well as the LIBSVM solver. Even if both optimization algorithms run with a tolerance value $\tau = 0.001$, there is some variation in the number of support vectors, the value of the offset, and the number of iterations. It is speculated that this difference might be due to the application of second-order heuristics [11] or shrinking techniques [8] in LIBSVM.

Table 20.3 Single-GPU SVM solver performance.

Dataset	Tasks	Phase	GPU (sec)	LIBSVM (sec)	Speedup
ADULT	Binary (2)	Training	32.68	341.5	10.45x
		Testing	1.1	42.7	38.77x
WEB	Binary (2)	Training	157	2350	14.97x
		Testing	2.51	75	29.88x
MNIST	Binary (2)	Training	425.9	13,963	32.79x
		Testing	4.43	496.5	112.19x
USPS	Binary (2)	Training	1.65	27	16.36x
		Testing	0.07	1	13.72x
MNIST	OVA(10)	Training	2067	118,916	57.52x
		Testing	14	683.9	48.86x
USPS	OVA(10)	Training	1.28	21.3	16.59x
		Testing	0.13	3.62	27.49x
SHUTTE	OVA(7)	Training	5.85	18.88	3.23x
		Testing	0.49	1.43	2.94x
LETTER	OVA(26)	Training	19.04	479.9	25.2x
		Testing	2.02	6.77	3.35x

Table 20.4 Single-GPU SVM solver accuracy comparison.

Dataset		SVM	Accuracy	No. SVs	Avg (b)	No. Iterations
ADULT	Binary (2)	GPU	82.70%	18,667		115,177
		LIBSVM	82.70%	19,058	−0.0018%	43,735
WEB	Binary (2)	GPU	99.45%	35,220		76,242
		LIBSVM	99.45%	35,232	−0.0137%	85,299
MNIST	Binary (2)	GPU	95.32%	43,731		68,038
		LIBSVM	95.32%	43,753	−0.0452%	76,104
USPS	Binary (2)	GPU	97.06%	684		7518
		LIBSVM	97.06%	684	−0.0042%	4614
MNIST	OVA (10)	GPU	95.76%	48,510		
		LIBSVM	95.76%	684	−0.0511%	N/A
USPS	OVA (10)	GPU	95.01%	1557		
		LIBSVM	95.01%	1706	−0.0097%	N/A
SHUTTLE	OVA (7)	GPU	99.90%	348		
		LIBSVM	99.90%	428	−0.0112%	N/A
LETTER	OVA (26)	GPU	97.16%	12,667		
		LIBSVM	97.16%	12,807	−0.0742%	N/A

The number of iterations for multiclass problems is not comparable because the GPU solver runs all SMO instances concurrently, whereas LIBSVM does it sequentially.

20.4.2 Multi-GPU Cascade SVM Performance

The execution of the Multi-GPU Cascade SVM algorithm on two layers (four multiprocessor devices) resulted on an additional speedup for the largest and widest datasets. Smaller datasets will not gain additional acceleration, and the parallelization will be affected by the coordination overhead.

The WEB (binary) dataset reduced the SVM training time from 157 s to 106 s (1.48x) resulting on a total acceleration of 22.16x over LIBSVM, while MNIST (OVA 10) reduced the training time from 2067 s to 1180 s (1.75x) resulting on a total of 100.77x over LIBSVM.

20.5 FUTURE DIRECTION

In has been shown in this chapter that a naive implementation of a multiclass classifier based on the SMO algorithm running on a single-multiprocessor device can lead to dataset dependent speedups in the range of 3-57x for training and 3-112x for classification. These results reduced the training time more than an order of magnitude while maintaining accuracy of the classification tasks. Datasets with the largest number of training samples and largest number of dimensions resulted on considerable speedups, while smaller datasets also resulted on a notable acceleration. Furthermore, we have shown that multiple devices can be orchestrated effectively using port-based asynchronous programming in order to further increase the acceleration of the training phase or tackle larger classification problems.

The future direction of this work is threefold: first, the sparse nature of many classification problems requires investigating the effect of the integration of sparse data structures and sparse matrix and vector multiplications on the GPU SVM implementation. Second, it is necessary to extend this GPU SVM implementation in order to be able to learn from data streams. For this purpose it is necessary to revisit the possibilities of exploitation of structural parallelism in online SVM solvers both in the primal [18] and dual [17] forms. Third, it is necessary to investigate the distribution of online SVM solvers across multiple devices in order to be able scale out the data stream classification problem.

References

[1] V.N. Vapnik, The Nature of Statistical Learning Theory (Information Science and Statistics), Springer, 1999.
[2] H.P. Graf, E. Cosatto, L. Bottou, I. Durdanovic, V. Vapnik, Parallel support vector machines: the cascade svm, in: Advances in Neural Information Processing Systems, vol. 17, 2005, pp. 521–528.
[3] R. Rifkin, A. Klautau, In defense of one-vs-all classification, J. Mach. Learn. Res. 5 (2004) 101–141.
[4] J.C. Platt, Fast Training of Support Vector Machines Using Sequential Minimal Optimization, MIT Press, Cambridge, MA, 1999.
[5] B. Catanzaro, N. Sundaram, K. Keutzer, Fast support vector machine training and classification on graphics processors, in: Proceedings of the 25th International Conference on Machine Learning, Helsinki, Finland, July 5–9, 2008, ICML '08, vol. 307, New York, ACM, 2008, pp. 104–111.
[6] J. Dean, S. Ghemawat, Mapeduce: simplified data processing on large clusters, Commun. ACM 51 (1) (2008) 107–113.

[7] C. Chu, S. Kim, Y.A. Lin, Y.Y. Yu, G. Bradski, A. Ng, et al., Map-reduce for machine learning on multicore, NIPS 19 (2007).

[8] T. Joachims, Making Large-Scale Support Vector Machine Learning Practical, MIT Press, Cambridge, MA, 1999.

[9] D.W. Holmes, J.R. Williams, P. Tilke, An events based algorithm for distributing concurrent tasks on multi-core architectures, Comput. Phys. Commun. 181 (2) (2010).

[10] C. Chang, C. Lin, LIBSVM: a library for support vector machines. Software available at http://www.csie.ntu.edu.tw/~cjlin/libsvm/, 2001.

[11] S.S. Keerthi, S.K. Shevade, C. Bhattacharyya, K.R.K. Murthy, Improvements to platt's SMO algorithm for SVM classifier design, Neural Comput. 13 (3) (2001) 637–649.

[12] Y. Lu, V. Roychowdhury, L. Vandenberghe, Distributed parallel support vector machines in strongly connected networks, IEEE Trans. Neural Netw. 19 (7) (2008) 1167–1178.

[13] A. Frank, A. Asuncion, UCI Machine Learning Repository. Irvine, CA, University of California, School of Information and Computer Science. http://archive.ics.uci.edu/ml, 2010.

[14] Y. Lecun, L. Bottou, Y. Bengio, P. Haffner, Gradient-based learning applied to document recognition, Proc. IEEE 86 (11) (1998) 2278–2324.

[15] J. Hull, A database for handwritten text recognition research, IEEE Trans. Patten Anal. Mach. Intell. 16 (5) (1994) 550–554.

[16] C.-W. Hsu, C.-J. Lin, A comparison of methods for multiclass support vector machines, IEEE Trans. Neural Netw. 13 (2) (2002) 415–425.

[17] G. Cauwenberghs, T. Poggio, Incremental and decremental support vector machine learning, NIPS (2000) (Online Paper) 409–415.

[18] Z. Liang, Y. Li, Incremental support vector machine learning in the primal and applications, Neurocomputing 72 (10–12) (2009), Lattice Computing and Natural Computing (JCIS 2007) / Neural Networks in Intelligent Systems Designn (ISDA 2007), June 2009.

Template-Driven Agent-Based Modeling and Simulation with CUDA

21

Paul Richmond, Daniela Romano

This chapter describes a number of key techniques that are used to implement a flexible agent-based modeling (ABM) framework entirely on the GPU in CUDA. Performance rates equaling or bettering that of high-performance computing (HPC) clusters can easily be achieved, with obvious cost-to-performance benefits. Massive population sizes can be simulated, far exceeding those that can be computed (in reasonable time constraints) within traditional ABM toolkits. The use of data parallel methods ensures that the techniques used within this chapter are applicable to emerging multicore and data parallel architectures that will continue to increase their level of parallelism to improve performance. The concept of a flexible architecture is built around the use of a neutral modeling language (XML) for agents. The technique of template-driven dynamic code generation specifically using XML template processing is also general enough to be effective in other domains seeking to solve the issue of portability and abstraction of modeling logic from simulation code.

21.1 INTRODUCTION, PROBLEM STATEMENT, AND CONTEXT

Agent-based modeling is a technique for computational simulation of complex interacting systems through the specification of the behavior of a number of autonomous individuals acting simultaneously. The focus on individuals is considerably more computationally demanding than top-down system-level simulation, but provides a natural and flexible environment for studying systems demonstrating emergent behavior. Despite the potential for parallelism, traditionally frameworks for agent-based modeling are often based on highly serialized agent simulation algorithms operating in a discrete space environment. Such an approach has serious implications, placing stringent limitations on both the scale of models and the speed at which they may be simulated and analyzed. Serial simulation frameworks are also unable to exploit architectures such as the GPU that are shown within this article to demonstrate enormous performance potential for the agent modeling field.

Previous state-of-the-art work that demonstrates agent-based simulation on the GPU [4, 5] is also either very task specific or limited to only discrete spaced environments and is therefore unsuitable for a wider range of agent-based simulation. Little focus has previously been given to general techniques for agent modeling on the GPU, particularly those that address the issue of allowing heterogeneous agents without introducing large amounts of divergent code execution. This chapter presents a summary of techniques used to implement the Flexible Large-Scale Modeling Environment (FLAME) framework for GPU simulation that is both extendible and suitable for a wide range of agent simulation examples.

21.1.1 **Core Method**

This chapter describes a technique for using template-generated CUDA code for simulation of large-scale agent-based models on the GPU using CUDA. More specifically, it describes the FLAME process of translating formally specified XML descriptions of agent systems into CUDA code through the use of templates. The use of templates within work is essential because it allows the specification of agent systems to be abstracted from the simulation code and described using a common and portable specification format. Likewise, the use of multiple template sets also offers the potential to target multiple architectures (such as more traditional high-performance processing clusters or grids) that are used for comparison with our GPU implementation. With respect to agent modeling in CUDA, common parallel routines are described that achieve essential agent-based functionality, including agent birth and death processing as well as various interagent communication patterns. Most importantly, the issue of agent heterogeneity is addressed through the use of state machine-based agent representation. This representation allows agents to be separated into associated state lists that are processed in batches to allow very diverse agents while avoiding large divergence in parallel code kernels.

21.1.2 **Algorithms and Implementations**

A key aspect of implementing thread-level agents on the GPU in CUDA is to ensure heterogeneous agents can be simulated without introducing large amounts of thread-level divergence. Such divergence occurs during simulation when not all threads (or agents) within a processing group of 32 threads (a warp) fail to follow the same instruction path.

21.1.3 **State-Based Agent Simulation in CUDA**

Part of the solution to this is the expression of agents using a technique that allows a state-based grouping of agents that are likely to perform similar behaviors. To achieve this, FLAME GPU uses an abstract model of an agent that is based on finite state machines. More specifically a formal definition known as the X-Machine can be used to represent an agent that adds to the finite state machine definition a persistent internal memory. The addition of memory allows a state transition to include the mapping of a memory set (M) to a new set (M') that is implemented in CUDA using a kernel. The separation of agents into distinct states reduces divergence and ensures agents can be processed efficiently. In addition to this, storage and processing of agents within state lists ensures that memory accesses from consecutive threads are linear and are therefore coalesced. Using this formal-based definition a simulation can be derived from a list of ordered transition functions that occur during each simulation step.

Because the movement of agents from one state to another occurs as a direct result of performing a state transition (or agent function), it is important to allow a filtering mechanism that may restrict the execution of a transition depending on some condition of the simulation or the agent's memory. This ensures that agents are free to follow heterogeneous paths between states independent of their initial state and neighboring agents. Within the FLAME GPU this is implemented using a *function condition kernel* (Figure 21.1) for each state transition. This kernel outputs a flag for each agent thread indicative of the result of performing the filtering process for the current list of agents. A parallel prefix sum algorithm [6] is then used to produce two new compact lists that represent a working list (agents that met the transition function condition) and a list with remaining agents that replaces the original state list. The working list is then able to perform the agent transition function (mapping of memory from M to M') before the agents are finally appended to the state transitions next state list. The prefix sum technique is not limited to filtering of agents during transition functions and is also employed through

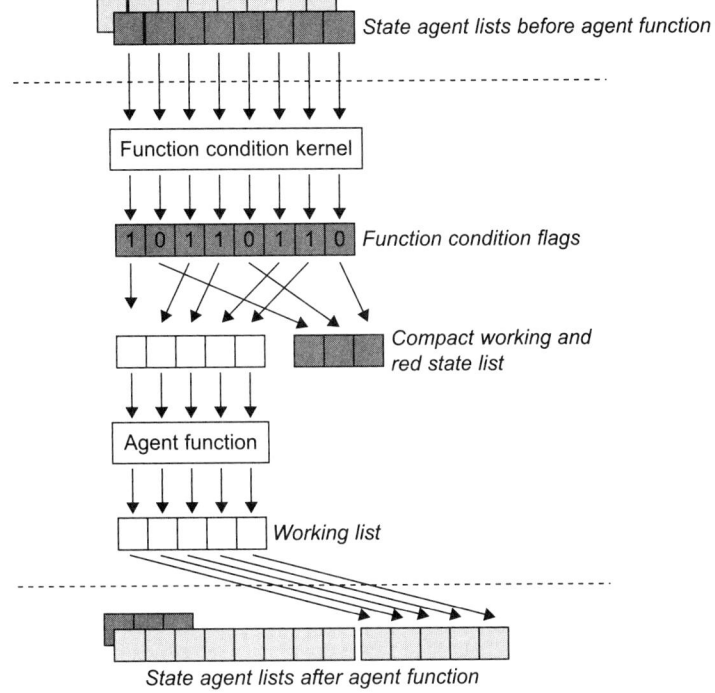

State agent lists before agent function

Function condition kernel

Function condition flags

Compact working and red state list

Agent function

Working list

State agent lists after agent function

FIGURE 21.1

Use of function condition filters to compact an agent state list into a working list for transition function processing. Agents in the start state that meet the function condition are finally appended to the end state.

the simulation process to compact lists containing dead agents and on sparse lists containing new agents (agent births).

21.1.4 XML-Driven CUDA Code Generation

Representation of agents in a flexible and portal format is essential in ensuring agent models are suitable for simulation on a wide range of hardware architectures (including the GPU, HPC grids, and more traditional CPU architectures). XML-based technologies form a large part of providing this functionality and are used extensively with the FLAME GPU to both specify an agent model and generate agent code. Model specification is achieved through XML representation of agent structure, including agent memory variables, states, and transition functions. The syntax of this specification is guarded through a number of extendible XML schemas that based on polymorphic extension, allow a base specification to be extended with a number of GPU-specific elements. The base specification in this case forms the structure of a basic X-Machine agent model compatible with HPC and CPU versions of the FLAME framework. The GPU schema extensions add some specific information, such as the maximum population size (used to preallocate GPU memory), as well as some optional elements that indicate additional model details used to select between a number of lower-level algorithms at the code-generation stage. These details include a distinction between discrete and continuous agents and the type of communication that may exist between agents.

Given an XML-based agent model definition, template-driven code generation has been achived through Extensible Stylesheet Transformations (XSLT). XSLT is a flexible functional language based on XML and is most commonly used in the translation of XML documents into other HTML or other XML document formats on the Web. Despite this there is no limitation on the type of file that may be generated from an XSLT template, and it is hence suitable for the generation of source code (Figure 21.2). Translation of XSLT documents is possible through any compliant processor (such as Saxon, Xalan, Visual Studio, and even many common Web browsers) that will also validate the template itself using a W3C specified schema. The XSLT code sample in Figure 21.3 demonstrates how the iterative for-each control is used to generate a C structure for each agent and an agent list used for state-based global storage within the XML model document. The select attribute uses an XPath expression to match nodes in the document. Likewise, XPath expressions are used with XSLT to match nodes within the value-of attributes and any other XSLT elements that require XML document querying. Within FLAME GPU any global memory is stored using the Structure of Array (SoA) format rather than the Array of Structure format to ensure all memory access is coalesced. Data can then be translated into more accessible and logical structure format within registers or shared memory (so long as appropriate padding is used to avoid bank conflicts) without any performance penalties.

21.1.5 Agent Communication and Transition Function Behavior Scripting

While agents perform independent actions, interagent communication is essential in the emergence of group behavior. Communication between agents using the X-Machine notation within FLAME GPU

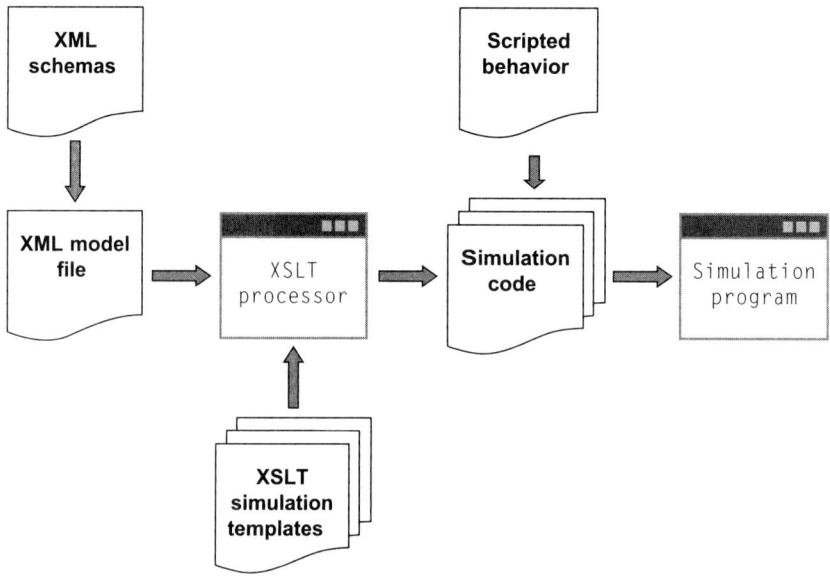

FIGURE 21.2

The FLAME GPU modeling and code-generation process.

```
//agent structure
<xsl:for-each select="gpu:xmodel/xmml:xagents/gpu:xagent"> struct
_align_(16) xagent_memory_<xsl:value-of select="xmml:name"/> {
    <xsl:for-each select="xmml:memory/gpu:variable">
     <xsl:value-of select="xmml:type"/><xsl:text></xsl:text>
     <xsl:value-of select="xmml:name"/>;
    </xsl:for-each>
};
</xsl:for-each>

//agent list structure (AoS)
<xsl:for-each select="gpu:xmodel/xmml:xagents/gpu:xagent"> struct
xagent_memory_<xsl:value-of select="xmml:name"/>_list {
    //Holds agents position in the 1D agent list
    int _position [<xsl:value-of select="gpu:maxPopulationSize"/>];
    <xsl:for-each select="xmml:memory/gpu:variable">
     <xsl:value-of select="xmml:type"/><xsl:text></xsl:text>
     <xsl:value-of select="xmml:name"/>[<xsl:value-of
                          select=" gpu:maxPopulationSize"/>];
    </xsl:for-each>
};
</xsl:for-each>
```

FIGURE 21.3

An example of XSLT template code used to generate an structure representing an agent's memory and a structure of arrays representing a list of agent memory data.

is introduced through the use of messages stored in global message lists. Agent transition functions are able to both output and input messages that in the case of the latter, requires a message iteration loop for the agent to process message information. The use of only indirect message-based communication between agents ensures that the scheduling of agents can in no way introduce bias or any other simulation artifacts based on the order of agent updates. Figures 21.4 and 21.5 show examples of two agent transition functions that demonstrate message output and a message input loop, respectively. The ordering of transition functions is used to ensure global synchronization of messages between consecutive transition functions, and as a result, a single-transition function can never perform both input and output of the same message type. Each agent transition function performs the memory mapping of M to M′ by updating the agent memory structure argument directly. Agent deaths can be signaled by the return value flag by returning any value other than 0 (the flag can then be used to compact the working list of agents).

Integration of the transition functions within automatically generated simulation code is made possible by wrapping the transition functions with global kernels (generated through the XSLT templates) that are responsible for loading and storing agent data from the SoA format into registers. The custom message functions (Figures 21.4 and 21.5) are also template generated, depending on the definition of a message within the XML model file. The custom message functions hide the same data-loading techniques as used for agent storage with each message having a structure and SoA definition consisting of a number of memory variables.

```
_FLAME_GPU_FUNC_
int outputdata(xagent_memory_Circle* memory,
              message_location_list* location_messages)
{
      /* Output a location message */
      add_location_message(location_messages,
                           xmemory—>x,
                           xmemory—>y,
                           xmemory—>z);
      return 0;
}
```

FIGURE 21.4

An example of a scripted agent transition function demonstrating message output.

```
_FLAME_GPU_FUNC_
int inputdata(xagent_memory_Circle* memory,
              message_location_list* location_messages)
{
      /* Get the first message */
      message_location* message;
      message = get_first_location_message(location_messages);

      while(message)
      {
            /* Process the message */
            ...

            /* Get the next message in the iteration*/
            message = get_next_location_message(message,
                                                location_messages);
      }

      /* Update agent memory */
      memory—>x += 1;
      ...

      /* Agent is not flagged to die */
      return 0;
}
```

FIGURE 21.5

An example of a scripted agent transition function showing message iteration through the template-generated custom message functions.

The use of message functions to hide the iteration of messages is particularly advantageous because it abstracts the underlying algorithms from the behavioral agent scripting. This allows the same functional syntax to be used for a number of different communication techniques between agents. The most general of these techniques is that of brute-force communication where an agent will read every single message of a particular type. Technically, this is implemented through the use of tiled batching

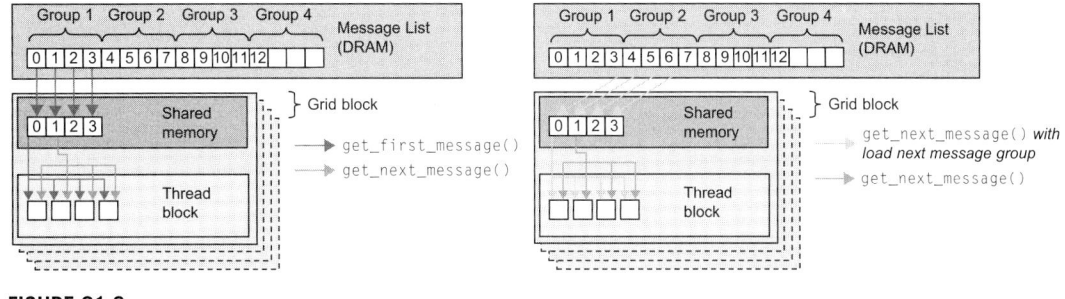

FIGURE 21.6

Brute-force message group loading when requesting the first and next message (left). Brute-force message group loading when requesting the next message from a new message group (right).

of messages into shared memory [8]. The message iteration functions are responsible for performing this tiled loading into shared memory that occurs at the beginning of the iteration loop and after each message from within a group has been serially accessed. Figure 21.6 demonstrates how this is performed and shows the access pattern from shared memory for the iteration functions, particularly when iteration through shared memory has been exhausted.

In addition to brute-force message communication, the FLAME GPU templates provide both a spatially partitioned message iteration technique and a discrete message partitioning technique. In the case of spatially partitioned messages, a 2-D or 3-D regular grid is used to partition the agent/message environment, depending on a prespecified message interaction range (the range in which agents read the message if it is used as a input during a transition function). When we use a parallel radix sort and texture cached lookups [7], the message iteration loop can ensure far higher performance for limited range interactions. Within discrete message communication, messages can be output only by discrete spaced agents (cellular automaton) with the message iteration functions operating by cycling through a fixed range in a discrete message grid. For discrete agents, the message iteration through the discrete grid is accelerated by loading a single large message block into shared memory. Interaction between continuous and discrete agents is possible by continuous agents using a texture cache implementation of discrete message iteration.

21.1.6 Real-Time Instanced Agent Visualization

In addition to improving the performance of simulation, simulation on the GPU provides the obvious benefit of maintaining agent information directly where it is required for visualization. The first step to performing visualization is making the agent data available to the rendering pipeline from CUDA. This can be achieved through the use of OpenGL Buffer Objects, which are able to share the same memory space as CUDA global memory. Simple agent visualization can be accomplished with a single draw call, rendering the positions as either OpenGL points or axis-aligned point sprites (which give the appearance of more complex geometry). By default the FLAME GPU visualization templates provide rendering of agents using more complex geometry. This requires an instancing-based technique that displaces sets of vertices for each agent rather than a single-vertex position. This is implemented by using a CUDA kernel to pass positional agent data to a texture buffer object (TBO) and then rendering instances of geometry with a vertex attribute (or index), which corresponds to the agent's position in the TBO texture data. The vertex shader uses this attribute to look up the agent position and applies the

```
uniform samplerBuffer displacementMap;
attribute in float index;
varying vec3 normal, lightDir;
void main()
{
    vec4 position = gl_Vertex;
    vec4 displacement = texelFetchBuffer(displacementMap, (int)index);

    //offset instanced gemotery by agent position
    displacement.w = 1.0;
    position += displacement;
    gl_Position = gl_ModelViewProjectionMatrix * position;

    //lighting
    vec3 mvPosition = vec3(gl_ModelViewMatrix * position);
    lightDir = vec3(gl_LightSource[0].position.xyz − mvPosition);

    //normal
    normal = gl_NormalMatrix * gl_Normal;
}
```

FIGURE 21.7

GLSL vertex program for instanced agent rendering used to displace agents depending on their location.

vertex transformations, with a further fragment shader providing per-pixel lighting. To minimize data transfer to the GPU model, data can be stored within a VBO; instances of the same model can then be created with a single draw call minimizing GPU data transfer. Figure 21.7 shows a GLSL (Open GL Shading Language) shader program that is used to displace instanced agents and perform the model view projection.

More advanced visualization is available within the FLAME GPU by extending the basic visualization source code produced by the templates (Figure 21.8). Levels of detail, where the fidelity of agent representation is varied with respect to the viewer position, can be integrated by considering the distance to the camera within an agent transition function. This distance can then be used to store an appropriate detail level within a single-agent memory variable with the total for the population of each level being calculated through a number of prefix sum operations. The FLAME GPU simulation templates generate a per-agent sort function that can be then used to sort the population by detail level allowing host code to draw the correct number of instances for each level sequentially. Simple keyframe animation of agents such as fish (Figure 21.8) can be further added by considering a number of model representations for each detail level and updating the vertex shaders to perform interpolation between these key frames depending on some agent memory variable such as velocity.

21.2 FINAL EVALUATION AND VALIDATION OF RESULTS

Performance and quality of the FLAME GPU framework can be measured through reduction in modeling/analysis time and directly through quantitative simulation performance and cost performance (when compared with supercomputing alternatives). Measuring the reduction in modeling time as a result of

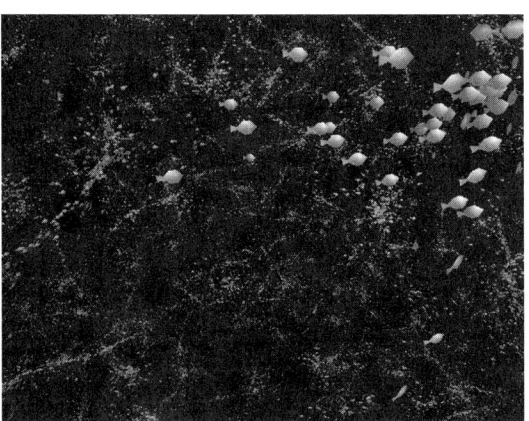

FIGURE 21.8

Agent-based simulation of flocking within the FLAME GPU showing 65,000 low-resolution agents (left) and 5000 dynamically detailed (level of detail) agents (right).

using the FLAME GPU framework is difficult to quantify; however, the volume of modeling code provides a good indication of what is required to produce a complete simulation. For the case of a simple Boids [9] flocking model, the model can be described within 91 elements of XML code (roughly 100 lines, depending on formatting) and fewer than 100 lines of agent function script. The script consists of two agent state transition functions, of which the first outputs location information and a second cycles the location information to influence the Boids velocity and movement. After the full simulation code is generated from the simulation templates, the resulting source code (including real-time visualization) consists of roughly 2500 lines of C and CUDA code (2000 lines without visualization), of which about 660 lines consists of CUDA kernels. The ability to generate complete GPU-enabled agent simulations with such a small amount of time investment is massively advantageous and allows models to be developed without prior knowledge of the GPU architecture or CUDA. Likewise, the use of templates to produce CUDA-enabled code removes vast amounts of code repetition for common agent-based functionality (such as communication and birth and death allocation) that occurs when writing agent simulations from scratch.

Simulation performance of the FLAME GPU can be compared directly with similar FLAME implementations that exist for both a single CPU processor and a grid-based supercomputing architecture. For the purposes of benchmarking, a simple force resolution model (referred to as the Circles model) has been benchmarked (without visualization) on a single GPU core of an NVIDIA 9800GX2 and also on an NVIDIA GTX480. For the latter, full double precision was used for agent memory variables and arithmetic operations, whereas the former utilizes single precision floats throughout. The model consists of only a single agent and message type with three agent functions, which output and input a message containing location information with a final function that moves the agent according to inter-agent repulsive forces. Figure 21.9 shows a comparison of the FLAME GPU and FLAME for the CPU (AMD Athlon 2.51 GHz dual-core processor with 3 GB of RAM). Relative speedup is the percentage of performance improvement over the CPU timings calculated by considering the iteration time of a single time step of the Circles model at various population sizes.

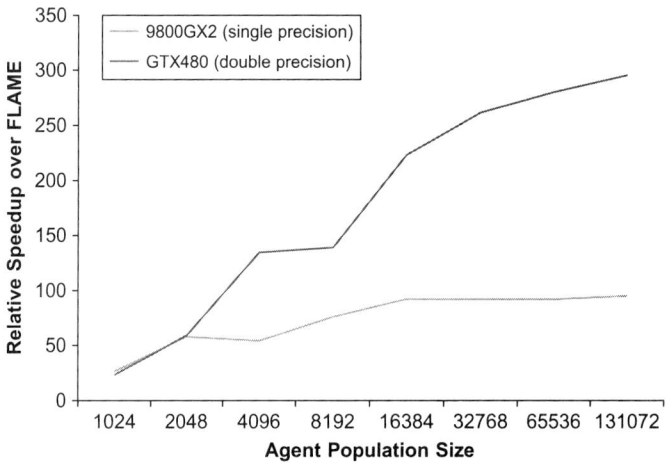

FIGURE 21.9

Relative speedup of the Circles benchmarking model for brute-force message iteration in both single and full precision on a NVIDIA 9800GX2 and a NVIDIA GTX480, respectively.

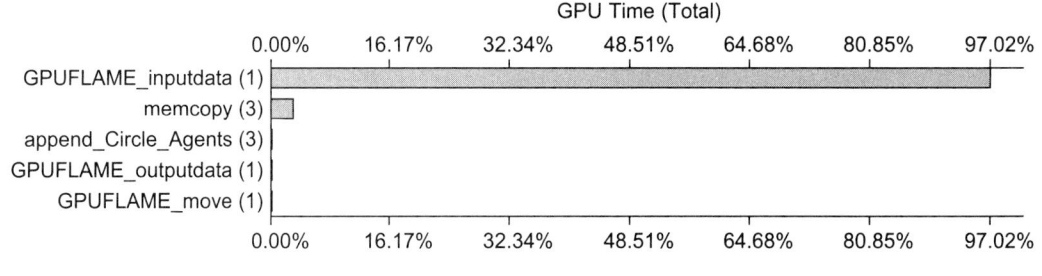

FIGURE 21.10

Breakdown of simulation time during a single simulation step of the Circles benchmarking model.

The initial fluctuation of the simulation performance in Figure 21.9 can be attributed to the fact that, at (relatively) low agent counts, the multiprocessors are underutilized during the most computationally expensive stage of the simulation (the inputdata function, shown in Figure 21.10), resulting in unpredictable amounts of idle time and global memory access latency coverage. In fact, for the 9800GX2, population sizes up to and including 4096 (and a thread block size of 128), the maximum number of thread blocks per multiprocessor is limited by the register count (of 8192 for compute capability 1.1 cards), to 2. This suggests that 4096 agents (or 32 blocks of 128 agent threads) are the minimum number required to fill all 16 of the multiprocessors. In the case of the GTX480 the number of thread blocks per multiprocessor is limited by shared memory to 6, suggesting that 11,520 agents (90 blocks of 128 agent threads) is the minimum number required to fill the 15 multiprocessors.

Performance of the FLAME GPU in contrast with the performance of the Circles model on distributed HPC architectures is considered by comparing FLAME GPU's spatially partitioned message functionality with a technique that partitions agents across multiple nodes on an HPC grid. Within the

Table 21.1 Simulation performance of spatially partitioned message iteration for the Circles benchmarking model.

Population Size	9800GX2 – Single Precision (ms)	GTX480 – Double Precision (ms)
1024	0.94	1.59
4096	1.24	2.75
16,384	2.45	2.12
65,536	9.09	5.19
262,144	33.74	10.53
1,048,576	136.28	34.41

HPC implementation each grid node processes a subset of agents and corresponding communication messages. Messages spanning multiple nodes are communicated through the use of a message board library (which is optimized to reduce transfer costs by communicating messages in batches rather than independently). Although the Circles model has been benchmarked on multiple architectures, both the SCARF and HAPU architectures show the best performance and are able to perform a single simulation step consisting of 1 million agents in double precision in just over 6 seconds, using a total of 100 processing cores.

Table 21.1 shows the performance timing of a single iteration of the Circles model using a thread block size of 32. Although some larger thread block size results in higher occupancy, experimentation shows that a smaller block size results in a higher-texture cache hit rate (and faster overall performance) during message reading owing to an increased locality between threads. Future work will improve upon this further through the use of space-filling curves, such as that demonstrated by Anderson et al. [2] which have been shown to dramatically increase the cache hit rate in molecular dynamics modeling. In summary, Table 21.1 demonstrates that 1 million agents can be simulated in single precision using a single GPU in less than 0.14 seconds. If we use full double-precision support within the Fermi architecture of the GTX480, it is possible to simulate a million agents in little over 0.03 seconds, a speedup of 200 times the SCARF and HAPU architectures. From this it is clear that the GPU is easily able to compete with and outperform supercomputing solutions for large population agent modeling using the FLAME GPU framework.

In the case of more complex continuous spaced agent models, the FLAME GPU has also shown massive potential, especially in the case of cell-based tissue modeling [10] where simulation performance in contrast with previous MATLAB models has improved from hours to seconds in the most extreme cases. Such performance improvements allow real-time visualization (which using instancing has a minimal performance effect) where it was previously not possible. This in turn allows a mechanism for fast parameter exploration and immediate face validation with the possibility of real-time steering (manipulation) of models by extending the dynamically produced simulation code.

21.3 CONCLUSIONS, BENEFITS AND LIMITATIONS, AND FUTURE WORK

This chapter has presented the FLAME GPU for large-scale agent-based simulation on GPU hardware using CUDA. Benchmarking has demonstrated a considerable performance advantage to using the

GPU for agent-based simulation. Future work will focus on addressing some of the current limitations of the framework. Specifically, the framework will be extended to support multi-GPU configurations. This will be possible by using concepts from the HPC FLAME code to perform distribution of agents and MPI-based communication between hardware devices. Recent work in performance optimization across multiple nodes connected by a network [1, 3] highlights performance potential for discrete/grid-based agent systems. The suitability of this toward more general state-based agent execution will have to be considered.

The use of multiple program multiple data kernel execution within the NVIDIA Fermi architecture is particularly exciting and lends itself well to the state-based storage and processing of agents within the FLAME GPU. The effect of this on performance will almost certainly be explored in future work. Currently, the framework's reliance on CUDA allows it to be used only on NVIDIA hardware. The introduction of OpenCL may offer a solution toward increased portability across heterogeneous core platforms and will be explored in the future. This will not require any major change in the framework and will be possible by simply specifying a new set of compatible templates.

References

[1]   B.G. Aaby, K.S. Perumalla, S.K. Seal, Efficient simulation of agent-based models on multi-GPU and multi-core clusters, in: SIMUTools '10: Proceedings of the 3rd International ICST Conference on Simulation Tools and Techniques, ICST (Institute for Computer Sciences, Social-Informatics and Telecommunications Engineering), Brussels, Belgium, Torremolinos, Malaga, Spain, 2010, pp. 1–10. Available from: http://dx.doi.org/10.4108/ICST.SIMUTOOLS2010.8822.

[2]   J. Anderson, D. Lorenz, A. Travesset, General purpose molecular dynamics simulations fully implemented on graphics processing units, J. Comput. Phys. 227 (2008) 5342–5359.

[3]   K. Datta, M. Murphy, V. Volkov, S. Williams, J. Carter, L. Oliker, et al., Stencil computation optimization and auto-tuning on state-of-the-art multicore architectures, in: Proceedings of the 2008 ACM/IEEE Conference on Supercomputing, Austin, TX, IEEE Press, Piscataway, NJ, 2008, pp. 1–12.

[4]   R.M. D'Souza, M. Lysenko, K. Rahmani, SugarScape on steroids: simulating over a million agents at interactive rates, in: Proceedings of the Agent 2007 Conference on Complex Interaction and Social Emergence, Chicago, IL, 2007. Available from: http://www.me.mtu.edu/~rmdsouza/Papers/2007/SugarScape_GPU.pdf

[5]   U. Erra, B. Frola, V. Scarano, I. Couzin, An efficient GPU implementation for large scale individual-based simulation of collective behavior, in: HIBI '09: Proceedings of the 2009 International Workshop on High Performance Computational Systems Biology, IEEE Computer Society, Washington, DC, Trento, Italy, 2009, pp. 51–58. Available from: http://dx.doi.org/10.1109/HiBi.2009.11

[6]   M. Harris, S. Sengupta, J.D. Owens, Parallel prefix sum (scan) with CUDA, in: H. Nguyen (Ed.), GPU Gems 3, Addison Wesley, 2007, Chapter 39, pp. 851–876.

[7]   S. Le Grand, Broad-phase collision detection with CUDA, in: H. Nguyen (Ed.), GPU Gems 3, Addison Wesley, 2007, Chapter 39, pp. 677–695.

[8]   L. Nyland, M. Harris, J. Prins, Fast N-Body simulation with CUDA, in: H. Nguyen (Ed.), GPU Gems 3, Addison Wesley, 2007, Chapter 39, pp. 677–695.

[9]   C. Reynolds, Flocks, herds and schools: a distributed behavioral model, in: M.C. Stone (Ed.), Proceedings of the 14th Annual Conference on Computer Graphics and Interactive Techniques, SIGGRAPH '87, ACM, New York, 1987, pp. 25–34.

[10] P. Richmond, D. Walker, S. Coakley, D. Romano, High performance cellular level agent-based simulation with FLAME for the GPU, Brief. Bioinform. 11 (3) (2010) 334–347.

GPU-Accelerated Ant Colony Optimization

Robin M. Weiss

In this chapter we discuss how GPGPU computing can be used to accelerate ant colony optimization (ACO) algorithms. To this end, we present the AntMinerGPU algorithm, a GPU-based implementation of the AntMiner+ algorithm for rule-based classification. Although AntMinerGPU is a special-purpose ACO algorithm, the general implementation strategy presented here is applicable to other ACO systems, swarm intelligence algorithms, and other algorithms that exhibit a similar execution pattern.

22.1 INTRODUCTION, PROBLEM STATEMENT, AND CONTEXT

In the past decade, the field of swarm intelligence has become a hot topic in the areas of computer science, collective intelligence, and robotics. ACO is a general term used to describe the subset of swarm intelligence algorithms that are inspired by the behaviors exhibited by colonies of real ants in nature. Current literature has shown that ACO algorithms are viable methods for tackling a wide range of hard optimization problems including the traveling salesman, quadratic assignment, and network routing problems [1–3].

In nature, ants are simple organisms. Individually, each has very limited perceptual capabilities and intelligence. However, ants are social insects, and it has been observed that groups of ants can exhibit highly intelligent collective behaviors that surpass the capabilities of any given individual. It is these emergent behaviors of ant colonies that ACO algorithms reproduce with colonies of virtual "ant agents" and use for solving computational problems.

In general, ACO algorithms are characterized by a repeated process of probabilistic solution generation, evaluation, and reinforcement. Over time, the solutions generated by ant agents converge to a (near) optimal solution. By generating a larger number of solutions each iteration (which requires a similarly larger population of ant agents), a more complete exploration of solution space can be achieved and thus better solutions can be found in less time. However, the population of ant agents in sequential ACO algorithms is a large factor in overall running time and therefore makes very large ant populations infeasible.

Because ant colonies, both real and virtual, are a type of distributed and self-organizing system, there is a large amount of implicit parallelism. In this chapter we investigate how the GPGPU computing model can take advantage of this parallelism to achieve large populations of ant agents while also reducing overall running time. It is our hope to show that with GPU-based implementations, ACO algorithms will be seen as competitive with traditional methods for a range of problems. As a case study, we present the GPU-based AntMinerGPU algorithm, an ACO algorithm for rule-based classification, and show how the GPGPU computing model can be leveraged to improve overall performance.

22.2 CORE METHOD

Perhaps the most well-explored feature of ant systems is their ability to locate optimal paths through an environment. This phenomenon forms the basis of the standard ACO metaheuristic. The path-finding ability of ant colonies can be extended to solve problems from a wide range of domains so long as the solution space of the target problem can be expressed as a graph where paths represent solutions. The reader is referred to [1, 2], and [3] for examples of how various problems can be represented as such.

In ACO, virtual ant agents make explorations of the solution space of a target problem in an attempt to locate the optimal solution. A solution is defined by a path traveled by an ant agent through a graph-based representation of solution space called the "construction graph." After each solution construction phase, candidate solutions are evaluated with respect to a quantitative fitness function. The path that describes the "best" solution (maximizes the fitness function) is reinforced with "pheromone," which attracts ant agents in subsequent iterations to a similar path. Over time and with the introduction of random variations in the movements of ant agents, the repeated explorations of solution space often leads to a convergence of the swarm as a whole to the optimal solution. This generalized control flow of ACO algorithms is depicted in Figure 22.1.

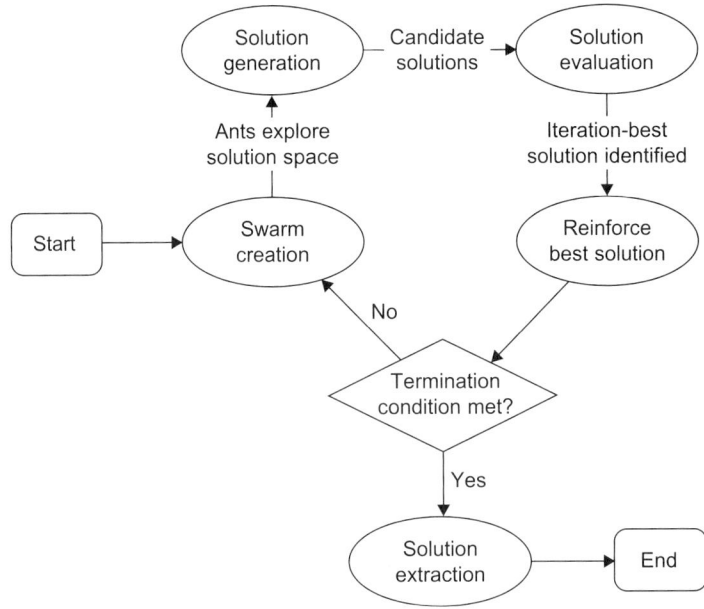

FIGURE 22.1

The basic scheme of an ACO swarm.

22.3 ALGORITHMS, IMPLEMENTATIONS, AND EVALUATIONS

22.3.1 Ant Colony Optimization and GPU Computing

The three main phases of ACO algorithms are shown in the high-level pseudo code for ACO given in Figure 22.2 and further described in the context of AntMinerGPU in the following subsections.

It is our hypothesis that with a larger population of ant agents than suggested by current literature, higher-quality solutions will be found in less time because more candidate solutions are generated each iteration. However, achieving large populations of ant agents can present a problem with respect to running time. Because each ant is a completely independent agent and requires its own memory and control logic, a sequential implementation forces ants to "take turns" on the processor, each generating a candidate solution one after the next. This is a sub-optimal implementation strategy for ACO algorithms because overall running time will grow directly with the number of ant agents in the system.

With a GPU-based parallel implementation, the computational complexity of ACO can be greatly reduced and can thus allow for efficient execution with very large ant populations. Furthermore, a parallelized implementation in which each ant is allocated its own control thread allows the virtual ant colony to achieve the asynchronous nature of the real ant colonies on which the model is based.

22.3.2 AntMinerGPU Overview

The AntMinerGPU algorithm is an extension of the MAX-MIN Ant System [8] and the AntMiner+ algorithm [6]. The creators of the original AntMiner algorithm show how the solution space of the rule-based classification problem can be conceived of as a graph and in doing so prove that the ACO technique can be applied [5].

AntMiner+ is the fourth version of the AntMiner algorithm and has been shown to produce higher-quality results and offers a less complex implementation than previous versions [6]. For these reasons, AntMiner+ is the version adopted here for GPU-based implementation. The AntMinerGPU algorithm extends AntMiner+ by offloading its implicitly parallel steps to a GPU device. Most notably, we use the multithreading capabilities of the GPU to allocate each ant agent its own thread. In this way, the overall running time of the algorithm is much less affected by the population of ant agents, and therefore, much larger populations can be used.

The input to AntMinerGPU is a training dataset where the class of each data point is known. From this, AntMinerGPU iteratively builds up a set of classification rules that can be used to predict the class of new data points. The implementation presented here is concerned with only binary classification (i.e., data points are a member of one of two possible classes). Therefore, rules generated by

```
GenerateConstructionGraph()
while (not terminated)
     ConstructSolutions()
     DaemonTasks() {optional, not used in AntMinerGPU}
     UpdatePheromone()
done
```

FIGURE 22.2

High-level pseudo-code overview of the general ACO approach.

if (*Variable*$_1$ *op Value*$_1$) *AND* (*Variable*$_2$ *op Value*$_2$) *... AND* (*Variable*$_i$ *op Value*$_k$)
then Class $= 1$
else Class $= 0$

where op ϵ $(=, \leq, \geq)$

FIGURE 22.3

The general form of classification rules generated by AntMinerGPU.

AntMinerGPU always attempt to identify the predictive characteristics of data points of class 1, using an explicit "else" statement as the final rule to indicate that any data point not covered by a rule must be of class 0. Figure 22.3 shows the general form of rules produced by AntMinerGPU.

The basic task of ants in AntMinerGPU is to probabilistically select a subset of terms (*Variable*$_i$ *op Value*$_k$) where $op \in \{=, \leq, \geq\}$ from the set of all possible terms (as given by the data being classified) such that when conjoined with the logical AND operator, classification rules that maximize confidence and coverage are produced. The reader is referred to [9] for a detailed explanation of rule-based classification and the metrics of confidence and coverage that are used as the quantitative evaluation of solution quality in our algorithm.

The Construction Graph

The AntMinerGPU algorithm uses a directed acyclic graph (DAG) as the representation of solution space. The construction graph, $Gc(V,E)$, is generated in such a way that the vertices represent the set of all possible solution components and the existence of some edge $E_{i,j}$ represents the ability to select solution component j after having selected i. With this configuration, a path through Gc can be taken as a solution to the target problem, and good solutions can be found by exploiting the collectively intelligent behaviors of ant colonies that allow them to find optimal paths through an environment.

In the case of rule-based classification, the construction graph is generated in such a way that it captures the dimensionality of the feature space of the data to be classified. That is, the construction graph is created by generating one node group for each variable in the training dataset. These node groups are shown as vertical rectangles in Figure 22.4. Each group contains nodes representing all possible values that the respective variable may possess.

Nominal variables are represented by one node group, containing a node for each value the variable may possess, as well as an additional node representing "does not matter." This "dummy" node can be selected by the ants and signifies that the variable has no bearing on the class that is predicted by the rule. An ant visiting vertex k in the group representing nominal variable i will add the term (*Variable*$_i$ $=$ *Value*$_k$) to its candidate rule.

The AntMinerGPU algorithm also allows for ordinal variables to be used in the data mining process. For this type of variable, we allow for the selection of terms that can specify a range of values. That is, we allow for terms such as (*Variable*$_i$ $>=$ *Value*$_k$) and (*Variable*$_i$ $<=$ *Value*$_l$). To realize this, ordinal variables are represented by two node groups that represent a lower and upper bound that can be placed on the given variable in candidate classification rules. $V2$ in Figure 22.4 is an example of this structure.

The movements of ants through the construction graph are restricted by requiring that each variable appear at most once in the final classification rule. This is accomplished by using directed edges in

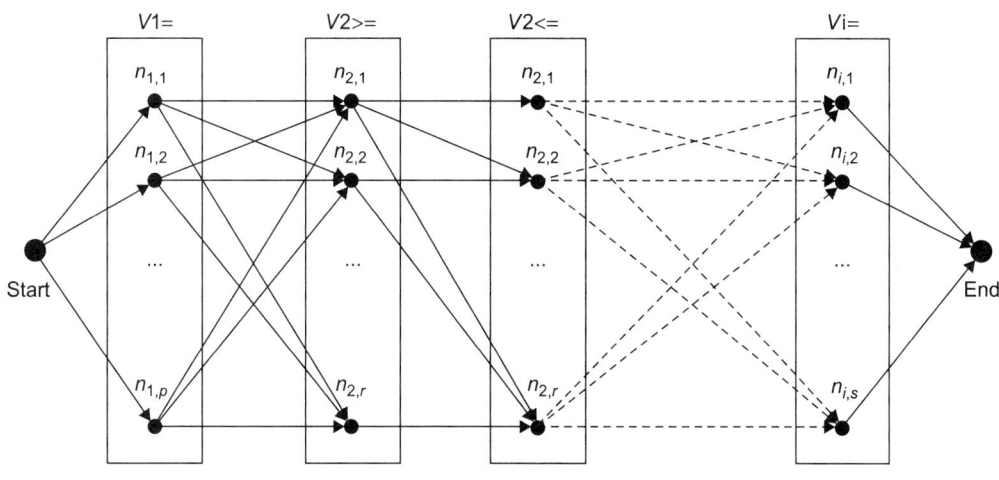

FIGURE 22.4

The general form of the construction graph for AntMinerGPU.

the construction graph. In the case of nodes representing ordinal variables, the choice of paths is also restricted such that rules that lead to logically unsatisfiable conditions cannot be produced. Specifically, we wish to avoid the situation where a rule specifies (*Variable$_i$* <= x) *AND* (*Variable$_i$* >= y) where $y > x$. To prevent this, we simply remove edges from the construction graph that would allow for this type of path (note that node $n_{2,2}$ does not connect to node $n_{2,1}$).

Solution Construction

In the solution construction phase, a set of m ant agents generates candidate classification rules from a finite set of terms (represented by the vertices of GC). Solution construction for each ant begins with an empty partial classification rule, $R_p = \emptyset$. At each construction step, R_p is extended by adding an available term to the partial classification rule. This is achieved as ant agents repeatedly move from some node i to some node j in the construction graph, appending the term represented by j to R_p, and continuing in this fashion until reaching the end node. The choice of term to add to R_p from the set of feasible terms is a probabilistic choice with the probability of selecting term j after having selected term i given by:

$$P_{(i,j)} = \frac{[\tau_{i,j}]^\alpha \cdot [\eta_j]^\beta}{\sum [\tau_{i,j}]^\alpha \cdot [\eta_j]^\beta}$$

Equation 22.1. Edge probability calculation.

where $\tau_{i,j}$ is the pheromone associated with edge $E_{i,j}$, and η is the heuristic value of term j (α and β being parameters that weight the relative influence of τ and η). As mentioned, pheromone levels reflect the quality of classification rules produced when other ants traversed the edge, and these pheromones are used to attract ants toward potentially rich areas in the construction graph. The heuristic value of j (η_j) indicates the importance of node j in final solutions. This value is supplied by a problem-dependent function and is derived from a priori knowledge of the problem. The reader is referred to [6] for a description of the heuristic value used by the AntMiner class of algorithms.

Pheromone Updating

An ant will select a term to add to its candidate classification rule with a probability that is proportional to the amount of pheromone on the edge leading to it. The objective of pheromone updating is to increase the pheromone levels on paths associated with good solutions (by reinforcement) and to decrease pheromone levels on paths associated with bad solutions (by evaporation). Reinforcing the pheromone levels on edges that comprise "good" solutions attracts ants in later iterations to similar areas of solution space (which are likely to contain other good, if not better, solutions). Evaporation is the process whereby pheromone levels on all graph edges are diminished over time. This allows for trails that were reinforced earlier in the exploration phase, and that may represent suboptimal solutions, to be slowly "forgotten."

The MAX-MIN Ant System on which AntMinerGPU is based specifies a few requirements for pheromone levels. Before the first exploration of the construction graph by ant agents, all edges are initialized with a pheromone level equal to the parameter τ_{max}. This allows for a more complete exploration of solution space in the early iterations of the algorithm because all edges appear equally attractive with respect to pheromone level.

Pheromone updating is achieved in two phases, evaporation and reinforcement. First, pheromone evaporation is applied to all edges in the construction graph. In this phase, all pheromone levels are multiplied by an evaporation factor (ϱ) that normally lies in the range between 0.8 and 0.99. The pheromone levels on all edges are bounded to a minimum value (τ_{min}) such that edges are prevented from having such a small amount of pheromone on them that they become unexplored altogether.

The process of pheromone reinforcement occurs after evaporation. This phase begins by evaluating the quality of each ant agent's candidate solution with respect to some quantitative fitness function. The MAX-MIN Ant System indicates that only the path representing the iteration-best solution be reinforced with an amount of pheromone proportional to the quality of that solution [8]. To realize this, an amount of pheromone is added to all edges of the iteration-best solution equal to the quantitative measure of quality of that solution. The maximum amount of pheromone on an any given edge is bounded by the parameter τ_{max}.

22.3.3 Operational Overview and Implementation Details

The basic operation of the AntMinerGPU algorithm is as follows. At the start of every iteration, ants begin in the start node and walk through the construction graph until reaching the end node. As an ant walks, it makes a probabilistic choice of which edge to traverse based on the amount of pheromone on each available edge, and the heuristic value of the node to which each available edge connects. An ant records the nodes it visits, with each node representing a logical term that is added to the ant's candidate classification rule. Once all ants in a generation reach the end node, each ant's rule is evaluated, and the rule with the best quality is reinforced with pheromone. This process repeats until there is no improvement of the global-best rule for some predefined number of iterations. Then, the global-best rule is outputted, and training data points that are "covered" by that rule are removed from the training dataset. This whole process is then repeated until some minimum percentage of training data points remain. This process is given in pseudo code in Figure 22.5.

```
generate construction graph
do until (min. percentage of training data remains)
    calculate heuristic values of nodes
    initial pheromone levels
    calculate edge probabilities
    while (no improvement to global-best solution for X iterations)
        create ants
        let ants walk from start node to end node
        evaporate pheromone from edges
        identify iteration-best ant
        reinforce path of iteration-best ant
        if necessary, update global-best solution
        kill ants
            re-calculate edge probabilities
    end
    record global-best solution
    remove data points covered by global-best solution from training data
    reset global-best solution
end
```

FIGURE 22.5

Pseudo-code overview of AntMinerGPU.

The overall operation of AntMinerGPU is broken down into eight GPU kernel functions. The control flow of AntMinerGPU is diagrammed in Figure 22.6. A description of each kernel function and implementation considerations for each follow this diagram.

Data Structures and General Implementation Considerations

To capture the structure of the construction graph, we implement two structs, Node and Link. The output of the host-side initialization code is two arrays, d_nodes and d_links, each a 1-D array containing all Node and Link structs generated to represent the construction graph for the input dataset.

Node structs keep track of which edges emanate from each node in order to allow ants to identify which edges are available to them during each stage of solution construction. The Node struct contains two int values, allowing a Node to be read as a single 64-bit chunk. This also alleviates alignment issues as Node structs can be neatly packed in memory and accesses can be coalesced.

The important information pertaining to edges (pheromone level, heuristic value of terminal node, and probability of traversal) are stored as float values in three separate arrays (d_pheromone, d_heuristic, and d_probability). Keeping these values separate allows kernels that may need some combination of them to fetch them individually. Additionally, separating this data as such allows Link structs to only contain 4 int values, allowing them to be aligned neatly in memory. Because there are a number of kernel functions that operate over all links, the d_pheromone, d_heuristic, and d_probability arrays are padded so that their sizes are a multiple of 512 elements. In this way, we can avoid the overhead of checking to see if threads are working within the bounds of the array, and a number of threads equal to the number of links in the padded array can always be safely invoked.

In addition to reading in training data and generating the corresponding construction graph, host-side code also generates an array of the training data itself because this will be needed by the

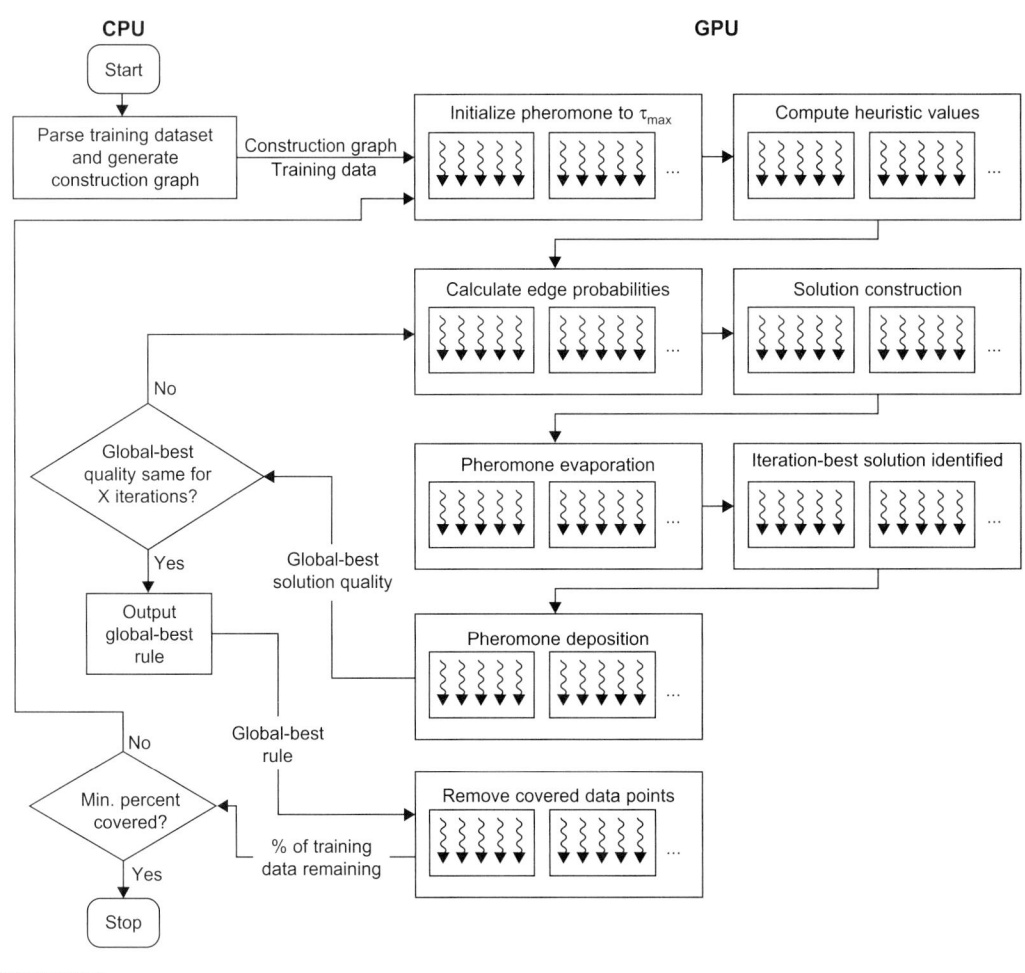

FIGURE 22.6

The CPU-GPU control flow of AntMinerGPU.

`evaluateTours` and `calculateHeuristic` kernels to compute the quality of candidate solutions and heuristic values of nodes, respectively. Because training data is static, we are able to leverage the performance benefits of caching by binding the training data to a 1-D texture and accessing the data through texture fetch calls. The use of texture caching will be discussed in the following subsections in the context of particular kernel functions.

Pheromone Initialization

This very simple kernel function initializes the pheromone level on all edges in the construction graph to the value supplied by the parameter `tMax`. The `initializePheromones` kernel is passed a pointer to the padded array of pheromone levels, `d_pheromone`, and the parameter `tMax`. Because adjacent threads store tMax to adjacent memory locations, very strong memory coalescing is achieved by this kernel.

```
__global__ void initializePheromones(float* d_pheromone, float tMax){

    int linkID = blockIdx.x * blockDim.x + threadIdx.x;

    d_pheromone[linkID] = tMax;

}
```

Heuristic Value Computation

The heuristic value of a node in the construction graph attempts to capture the importance of that node's value for its variable in classification rules. The heuristic value of a given node is given in Equation 22.2. We use the notation |*condition*| to refer to the number of elements in the set of all data points that satisfy *condition*.

$$\eta_{n_{i,k}} = \frac{|(Variable_i = Value_k) \cap (class = 1)|}{|Variable_i = Value_k|}$$

Equation 22.2: Heuristic value of a given node.

Equation 22.2 is realized by the kernel calculateHeuristic in the following way. We pass calculateHeuristic pointers to the array of links, d_links, and training data, d_translatedData. Each Link in d_links specifies the node to which the link connects.

calculateHeuristic is invoked with a number of threads equal to the size of d_links arranged in a 1-D grid of 1-D blocks. A thread identifies which link it is responsible for based on its position in the grid. Each thread then iterates over the training data in d_translatedData and calculates the heuristic value of the node to which its edge connects to, recording this value in the d_heuristic array in the location of the link it is working with.

Edge Probabilities

As detailed earlier in this chapter, the solution-generation process carried out by ant agents is probabilistic. That is, when located on a given node, an ant will elect to traverse a connected edge with some probability as given by Eq. 22.1. The task of the calculateProbabilities kernel is to precompute edge probabilities. This requires computing the product of the amount of pheromone on an edge and the heuristic value of the node to which the edge connects, divided by the sum of this value computed for all edges emanating from the source node.

The abstraction we make in this kernel is between nodes and blocks. Each node in the construction graph is allocated a block of threads where each thread calculates the probability for an edge emanating from its block's node.

The calculateProbabilities kernel is actually quite simple. Each thread identifies which node it is working with based on its block's index in the grid. Then, based on its index within the block, each thread calculates the product of the amount of pheromone and heuristic value associated with its link, retrieving these values from the d_pheromone and d_heuristic arrays, respectively. The resultant value is then stored in a shared memory array. Once all threads calculate this value for their respective link, each thread sums these values from shared memory, storing the result in a register. All threads then divide the value it calculated for its link by the sum, storing the result in the d_probability array located in global memory. Abbreviated source code for the calculateProbabilities kernel is offered below.

```
extern __shared__ float choices[];

Node n = d_nodes[blockIdx.x];

int idx = threadIdx.x;

if (idx < n.numLinks){

        choices[idx] = __powf(d_pheromone[n.firstLink + idx],alpha) *
                        __powf(d_heuristic[n.firstLink + idx], beta);

        __syncthreads();

        float sum = 0.0f;
        for (int i = 0; i < n.numLinks; i++){
            sum += choices[i];
        }

        d_probability[n.firstLink + idx] = choices[idx] / sum;

}
```

It should be noted that the calculateProbabilities kernel is usually invoked with a relatively small number of threads per block. Thus, the occupancy of the calculateProbabilities kernel is usually small. However, this abstraction of graph structure to grid organization is the most natural and has been selected here.

Solution Generation

Exploration of the construction graph by the population of ant agents is carried out by the runGeneration kernel. The runGeneration kernel illustrates one of the most challenging aspects of ACO for GPGPU computing, namely, the probabilistic path selection process. Because each ant may take a different path through the construction graph and because these paths are impossible to predict, little can be done to ensure orderly memory transactions and concurrency.

The runGeneration kernel is passed a pointer to d_nodes, d_probability, and an array of random number seeds, d_random. It is invoked with a number of threads equal to the number of ants in the system, arranged into a 1-D grid of 1-D blocks. Each thread calculates which ant it represents based on its position in the grid.

All threads enter a loop for a number of iterations equal to the number of node groups in the construction graph. In each pass of the loop, a new link is added to each ant's tour. Threads generate a new random number based on their seeds and a simple Park-Miller pseudorandom number generator. This pseudorandom number is then used in a roulette-wheel selection process to probabilistically select an edge to traverse. When an ant selects an edge to traverse, it adds the index of the edge it traverses to an array in global memory that records the paths of all ants in the generation.

Pheromone Evaporation

The `evaporizePheromone` kernel is very similar to the `initializePheromone` kernel in that a simple function is being applied to all values in the `d_pheromone` array. In this case, the kernel must read in each value from `d_pheromone`, multiply it by a supplied parameter, and store the result back to `d_pheromone`. As in `initializePheromone`, adjacent threads in `evaporizePheromone` read and write values to adjacent memory locations and, therefore, strong memory coalescing is achieved in this kernel as well. The source code for this kernel is provided here. It should be noted that the array `d_pLevels` contains the values of parameters $\langle tau \rangle\_min$ and $\langle tau \rangle\_max$ in locations 0 and 1, respectively.

```
__global__ void evaporizePheromone(float evaporize,float* d_pLevels, float* d_pheromone){

        int linkID = blockIdx.x * blockDim.x + threadIdx.x;

        float p = d_pheromone[linkID] *= evaporize;

        if (p < d_pLevels[0]){
                d_pheromone[linkID] = d_pLevels[0];

        }

}
```

Solution Evaluation

Solution evaluation is the most costly portion of the AntMinerGPU algorithm. This phase necessitates comparing each ant's tour to the entirety of the training dataset to identify how many training data points each ant's tour accurately describes. Thus, this kernel requires a very large amount of memory transactions because each training data point must be analyzed.

The implementation strategy we have adopted here is depicted in Figure 22.7. The abstraction we make is between ants and blocks. That is, the threads of one block are collectively responsible for evaluating the respective ant's tour against all training data points. Each block contains a number of helper threads equal to the number of data points, m, in the training dataset (or the maximum number of threads per block if m is greater than this value).

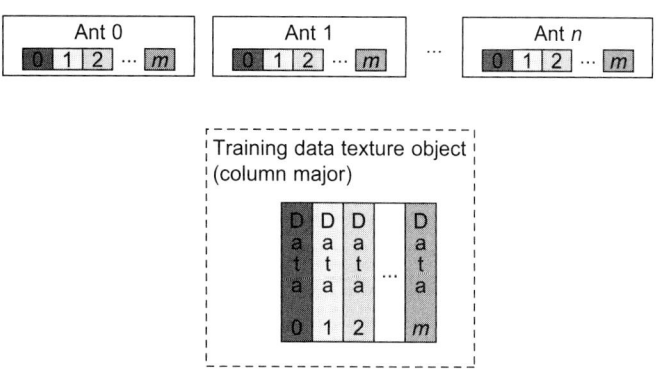

FIGURE 22.7

Thread allocation abstraction for solution-evaluation kernel.

The heart of the `evaluateTours` kernel is a for-loop that iterates over each term in the block's candidate classification rule. For each term, the helper thread must determine whether its training data point is accurately described by its ant's candidate classification rule. By storing the training dataset in column major form, consecutive helper threads access consecutive memory locations. Because of the spatial locality exhibited by this access pattern, we have found that texture caching provides performance benefits. In fact, testing reveals an average texture cache hit rate of ~40% in the `evaluateTours` kernel and running time of this kernel is reduced by nearly 25%.

Recall that the goal of the `evaluateTours` kernel is to determine how many training data points are described by each ant's rule. In our implementation strategy, we use an atomic add operation on a shared memory location to accumulate this value across all helper threads. That is, once each helper thread evaluates whether or not the ant's tour accurately predicts its designated data point, the helper thread will increment the shared memory accumulator atomically. Although this method implies some degree of serialization will occur, we have found the performance impact to be small compared with other approaches.

After the result of each helper thread is recorded, a thread will select a new data point to consider if m is greater than the maximum number of threads allowed per block. Here is abbreviated source code for this kernel function.

```
int antID = blockIdx.x;
int idx = threadIdx.x;

// shared data structures
int* s_tour;           // the tour of the ant this block is responsible for
int* s_covered;        // how many data points are covered by the solution
int* s_correct;        // how many data points are accurately described by the solution
int* s_graphVarType;   // what type of term (==, <=, or >=) each term is
int* s_graphVarID;     // what variable in the training data each term pertains to


...
__syncthreads();
int dataID = idx;
while (dataID < dataCount){
    int test = 0;
    if (d_classOf[dataID] != -1){
        for (int j = 0; j < graphVarCount; j++){
            int tourValue = s_tour[j];
            int varType = s_graphVarType[j];
            int dataValue = tex1Dfetch(translatedDataTEX, s_graphVarID[j] * dataCount
                                                                        + dataID);

        // Test tourValue against dataValue
        // if tourValue == dataValue, test++
        }
        if (test == graphVarCount){
            atomicAdd(s_covered, 1);
            if (d_classOf[dataID] == 1){
                atomicAdd(s_correct, 1);
            }
        }
    }

    }
```

```
      dataID += blockDim.x;
}

__syncthreads();

if (idx == 0){

    // Implement fitness function, storing result in d_quality[antID]

}
```

Pheromone Deposition

AntMinerGPU deposits pheromone only on the best path of all ants in a generation. Therefore, the quality of each ant's path must be considered to determine which ant generated the "best" solution. This is accomplished by a kernel function that copies the quality of each ant's tour into shared memory and then applies a reduction to determine which ant generated the best quality tour. Once the iteration-best ant has been identified, a number of threads equal to the number of node groups in the construction graph adds an amount of pheromone to the links in the iteration-best ant's tour.

Remove Covered Data Points

Once a predefined number of iterations pass with no improvement to the global-best solution, the global-best rule is outputted, and data points described by that rule must be removed from the training dataset. To accomplish this, we invoke the kernel `flagCoveredCases` with a number of threads equal to the number of training data points. Each thread checks to see if the global-best solution describes the data point it is responsible for. If so, the class of that data point is set to -1, indicating that the data point has been covered. The internal workings of this kernel are very similar to that of the `evaluateTours` kernel.

22.4 FINAL EVALUATION

To evaluate the performance benefits of our GPU-based implementation of AntMiner+, we ran AntMinerGPU on two simple datasets to compare the accuracy and running time against that given by a CPU-based implementation of AntMinerGPU. The datasets used were the Wisconsin Breast Cancer (WBC) and Tic-Tac-Toe (TTT), both of which were downloaded from the UCI Machine Learning Repository [7].

To split the datasets into training and testing sets, the order of data points in each set was first randomized, and then the first two-thirds of the data points were taken as training data with the remaining data points used as testing data. Because AntMinerGPU is a stochastic algorithm, results can vary from run to run. For this reason, the metrics we report are average values derived from 15 independent runs on three different random splits of the given dataset. The same random splits were used on both CPU and GPU implementations. Results presented later in this chapter were gathered on a desktop computer system with a 2.4 GHz Intel Core 2 Quad processor and 3 GB of DDR3 memory. The GPU device used was an NVIDIA Tesla C1060.

To determine the effect of ant population, we ran AntMinerGPU with a range of populations, plotting this variable against accuracy of rules generated for the WBC dataset (in Figure 22.8a) and the TTT dataset (in Figure 22.9a). We also plotted the effect of ant population on running time in

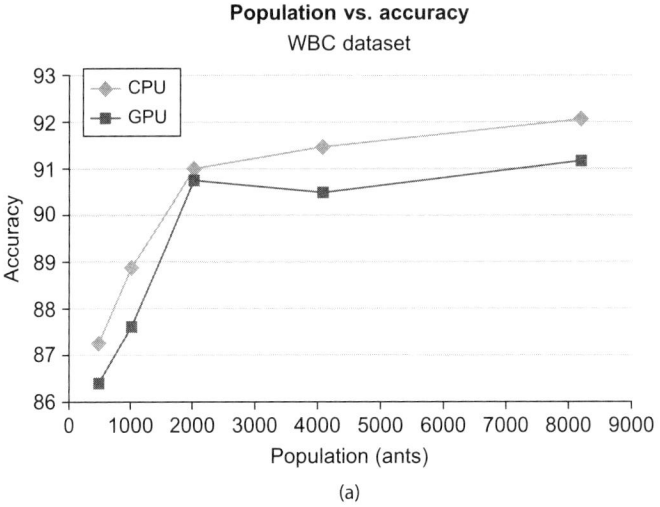

(a)

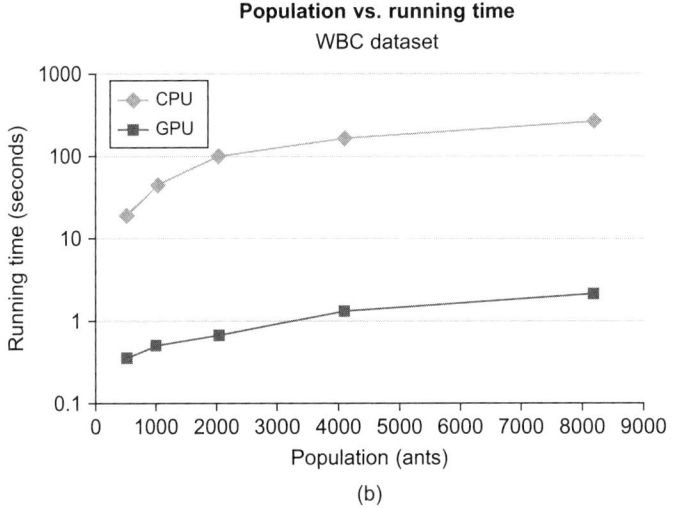

(b)

FIGURE 22.8

(a) Comparison of the effect of population size on accuracy of classification rules for the WBC dataset for both CPU- and GPU-based implementations. (b) Comparison of the effect of population size on running time of the AntMinerGPU algorithm for the WBC dataset for both CPU- and GPU-based implementations.

Figures 22.8b and 22.9b for the WBC and TTT datasets, respectively. Also included in these plots are results obtained from a CPU-based implementation of AntMinerGPU for comparison.

We found that in general, the accuracy of GPU- and CPU-based implementations were very similar. In terms of running time, we found that the GPU-based implementation is up to 100x faster than the simple CPU-based implementation for large populations of ants.

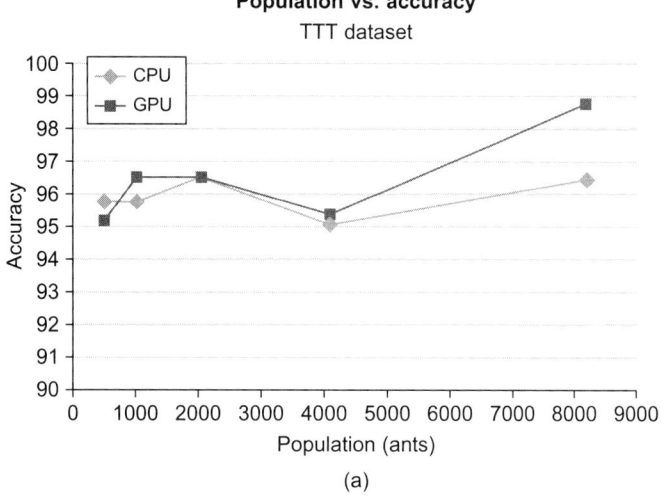

(a)

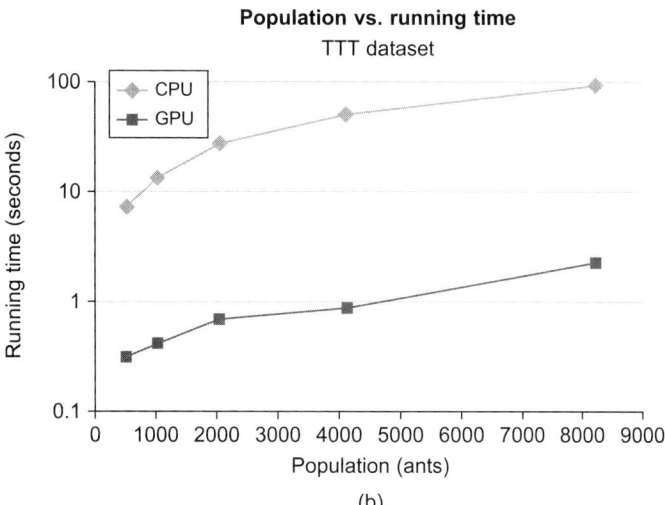

(b)

FIGURE 22.9

(a) Comparison of the effect of population size on accuracy of classification rules for the TTT dataset for both CPU- and GPU-based implementations. (b) Comparison of the effect of population size on running time of the AntMinerGPU algorithm for the TTT dataset for both CPU- and GPU-based implementations.

22.5 **FUTURE DIRECTION**

Perhaps the most promising area of exploration for GPU-based ACO algorithms is in multi-colony implementations on multiple GPUs. ACO algorithms are notoriously dependent on parameter settings, and therefore, running multiple ACO algorithms with varying parameters on multiple GPUs could allow for the optimal settings to be found for a given problem. Additionally, because ACO algorithms are stochastic, some runs are better than others. To take advantage of this, it is possible that multiple instances of AntMinerGPU may be run concurrently, perhaps on a multi-GPU computer system, and the instance with the best performance be taken as the final solution.

Another area for improvement of AntMinerGPU is in the boundary placed on it by limited GPU memory. In order to store much larger training datasets in GPU memory, we propose that a pre-processing step could be used to translate the values of the input dataset into `short int` values. This step would generate a lookup table that would be stored in CPU memory and could be used to translate between these short integer "value codes" and the actual values that they represent. By translating input data to `short int` form, we can load twice the amount of data onto the GPU as compared with using `int` or `float` data types. This step would, of course, introduce more running time because preprocessing and postprocessing are required, but would allow for larger datasets to be classified.

Acknowledgments

Support for this research was provided by NSF grants for Mathematics and Geophysics (CMG) and an equipment grant from CRI awarded to the LCSE of the University of Minnesota. I would also like to thank my advisors David Yuen, Witold Dzwinel, and Marcin Kurdziel for their ideas and advice throughout the development process of this software.

References

[1]   M. Dorigo, G.D. Caro, Ant algorithms for discrete optimization, Artif. Life 5 (1999) 137–172.
[2]   M. Dorigo, G. Di Caro, The ant colony optimization meta-heuristic, in: D. Corne, M. Dorigo, F. Glover (Eds.), New Ideas in Optimization, McGraw-Hill, Maidenhead, UK, England, 1999, pp. 11–32.
[3]   M. Dorigo, T. Stützle, Ant colony optimization, MIT Press, Cambridge, MA, 2004.
[4]   R.S. Parpinelli, H.S. Lopes, A.A. Freitas, An ant colony based system for data mining: application to medical data, in: L. Spector, E. Goodman et al. (Eds.), Proceedings of the Genetic and Evolutionary Computation Conference, Morgan Kaufmann Publishers, San Francisco, CA, San Francisco, CA, July 7–11, 2001, pp. 791–797.
[5]   B. Liu, H.A. Abbass, B. McKay, Classification rule discovery with ant colony optimization, IEEE Comput. Intell. Bull. 3 (1) (2004) 31–35.
[6]   D. Martens, M.D. Backer, R. Haesen, B. Baesens, T. Holvoet, Ants constructing rule-based classifiers, Stud. Comput. Intell. 34 (2006) 21–43.
[7]   UCI Machine Learning Repository, University of California, School of Information and Computer Science, Irvine, CA. http://archive.ics.uci.edu/ml/, 2010 (accessed 20.03.10).
[8]   T. Stutzle, H. Hoos, Improving the ant-system: a detailed report on the max-min ant system (Technical Report), FG Intellektik, FB Informatik, TU Darmstadt, Germany, 1996.
[9]   P. Tan, M. Steinbach, V. Kumar, Introduction to data mining, first ed., Pearson, Boston, MA, 2006, pp. 207–223.

Electronic Design Automation
Area Editor's Introduction
Sunil P. Khatri

23 High-Performance Gate-Level Simulation with GP-GPUs 343

24 GPU-Based Parallel Computing for Fast Circuit Optimization 365

THE STATE OF GPU COMPUTING IN ELECTRONIC DESIGN AUTOMATION

The success of very large-scale integrated (VLSI) design hinges heavily on design automation techniques to speed up the design process. Electronic design automation (EDA) software utilizes several key underlying algorithms, and an efficient implementation of these algorithms holds the key to our ability to design highly integrated, complex integrated circuits (ICs) of the future. Over the last few years, GPUs have received close attention by EDA practitioners, and significant speedups have been obtained by implementations of several key algorithms on the GPU. Some of these algorithms include logic simulation, Boolean satisfiability, fault simulation, and state space exploration.

In the future, it is expected that GPU computing will hold a key role in EDA advances. As more EDA algorithms are sped up using GPUs, it is conceivable that users of EDA tools will have the ability to quickly perform what-if analyses when different optimization options are invoked. Such an ability is not available today owing to the large runtimes associated with several steps of the EDA flow. More flexible GPU architectures will hold the key to making this possible.

IN THIS SECTION

In this section, we present two chapters that utilize GPUs to accelerate specific EDA algorithms.

Chapter 23 addresses logic simulation at the gate level, using GPU-based algorithms. Logic simulation is a key step in the design automation process, allowing the designer to verify whether their design meets specifications. The approach employs gate levelization and then maps the independent computations of each level on a GPU, thereby leveraging the parallelism available. This is combined with a technique that performs event-driven simulation at a higher level of circuit granularity.

Chapter 24 addresses performance and power optimization (by simultaneous gate sizing and theshold voltage adjustment). This is a key step in automatic circuit optimization after technology mapping. The approach employs clever task scheduling in order to maximize the speedup available from a GPU-based algorithm.

High-Performance Gate-Level Simulation with GP-GPUs

23

Debapriya Chatterjee, Andrew DeOrio, Valeria Bertacco

A successful, correctly functioning product is the goal of every semiconductor design. However, correctness is an elusive goal, complicated by ever-increasing complexity of hardware designs. This complexity is enabled by continually shrinking semiconductor technology, enabling designs that incorporate more and more components and functionality with each new generation. Verifying a complex chip is the most time-consuming process in the design flow, typically carried out through logic simulation, a computationally intensive process where the nascent design is tested for correct functionality. Logic simulation is traditionally run on large server farms of computers to counter its low performance and throughput. Unfortunately, protracted simulations, especially at the gate-level, significantly limit the portion of the design that can be verified. Improvements in simulation performance have great potential to boost verification capabilities, thereby decreasing the number of bugs in a design that escape into the final manufactured product. We approach this goal by leveraging recent GP-GPU technology, thus enabling massive parallelism in logic simulation. Our techniques enable large, complex designs to be mapped onto a GP-GPU leading to order-of-magnitude performance improvement and efficiency of current server farms.

23.1 INTRODUCTION

The vast complexity of modern semiconductor systems is challenging all aspects of their development. Among these, functional verification is the most critical one, absorbing more than 70% of the effort and resources of the entire development. Incomplete or limited verification leads to the discovery of functional errors (bugs), late in the development process, or aftermarket release of a silicon product. The impact of these bugs may lead to development delays, financial losses, and product recalls.

The majority of verification methodologies in industry rely heavily on the use of logic simulation tools. These tools simulate the design's functional behavior at different levels of abstraction, ranging from high-level behavioral to low-level structural gate-level descriptions. A typical simulation will rely on a model of the design, stimulating it with inputs and then checking the outputs for correctness. Unfortunately, this approach is very slow: even in the face of decades of improvements in the performance of these tools by the EDA industry, they still lack the horsepower required to tackle today's complex digital designs, especially when simulating gate-level netlists, where the system's description is fairly detailed, leading to a large design model.

In a typical digital design flow, a system is first described in a high-level behavioral fashion with a hardware description language (HDL), then it is automatically synthesized to a netlist, consisting of structural logic elements such as logic gates and flip-flops. To ensure that the gate-level design provides the same functionality as the behavioral design, the former must be validated by thorough simulation and comparison with the behavioral model. These structural netlists can easily consist of tens of millions of gates in modern digital systems. A logic simulator takes this netlist as input, converting it to internal data structures: feedback loops are opened by disconnecting the sequential storage elements in the design, thus allowing to simulate the design one cycle at a time, storing the value of latches and flip-flops in internal data structures of the simulator software. The remaining logic, that is, the combinational portion, is then levelized according to the dependencies implied by the gates input-ouput connections. Simulation proper can now begin: the simulator generates input values and then computes the outputs of the internal logic gates, one level at a time, until the design's output values are produced. In subsequent simulation cycles, the values computed for the design's storage elements are looped back and used as part of the next cycle's inputs.

Logic simulators comes in two flavors: oblivious and event driven. In an oblivious simulation, the simpler of the two, all gates in the design are computed at every cycle. Although the program's control flow for this approach is low overhead, computing for every gate at every cycle can be time-consuming and, most importantly, unnecessary for all those gates whose inputs have not changed from the previous cycle. Event-driven simulation, on the other hand, takes advantage precisely of this fact: the output of a gate will not change unless its inputs have changed. Large portions of the design are often quiescent during a given simulation cycle; thus event-driven simulation can spare a large amount of redundant computation. Note, however, that the key to a successful event-driven simulation lies in the effective management of the additional program control overhead, necessary to track which gates must be recomputed and which are quiescent.

Structural gate-level simulation benefits from inherent parallelism because the logic corresponding to different outputs can be simulated in parallel. However, available commercial simulators operate primarily on single-threaded processors; thus, they do not exploit this potential for concurrent computation available in the data structure representing the netlist. In this chapter, we investigate how the parallelism available in the problem structure can be mapped to that of the execution hardware of GP-GPUs. To this end, we use novel algorithmic solutions to address a netlist's structural irregularity, as well as techniques to exploit a GPU's memory locality in an optimal manner. The parallelism of netlists matches well with the parallel computational power available in GPUs, but there are a number of problems that must be addressed to enable GPU-based logic simulation. First, a netlist must be partitioned into portions that can be mapped and simulated concurrently and efficiently on a GPU. The partitioning must be aware of the GPU architecture and its memory model. Additionally, we need low-overhead algorithms to efficiently control the simulation of all the design's portions.

Our GPU-based simulator leverages novel solutions to the partitioning and mapping problems, enabling large designs to be simulated on GPU hardware. Keeping GPU nuances in mind, we are able to efficiently use this hardware platform for event-driven simulation. In this chapter we present our solutions and explore several simulation techniques and algorithms, noting the trade-offs and optimizations. Our final simulator is capable of achieving over an order-of-magnitude speedup over traditional approaches.

23.2 SIMULATOR OVERVIEW

The logic simulation of a gate-level netlist applies input values to an internal representation of the netlist and then propagates these values through each internal logic gate to compute binary values for the outputs and state registers. This process is akin to value propagation through a directed acyclic graph, where each vertex represents a logic gate. This computation is repeated for each clock cycle of the simulation: at the beginning of each new cycle, new input values are applied, and new output values are computed. Storage elements in the netlist are modeled by variables in the simulator software, storing the output values of the last cycle to be used as input values for the next cycle. Thus, the central component of a logic simulator is the block that simulates the combinational logic portion: this block is often executed millions of times during a simulation, and its performance drives the overall simulator performance. To this end, the graph representing the circuit's netlist is sorted topologically so that each gate is computed after its inputs have been generated. This sorting is called "levelization." Note, in addition, that all the gates within a same "level" in the topological order can be computed concurrently because all their input values have been previously generated. Hence, gate-level simulation has naturally good potential for a concurrent execution model. However, to derive performance benefits from this concurrency, we need to understand and tune the algorithm to the underlying hardware architecture, that is, CUDA.

A CUDA-compatible GPU architecture consists of a set of multiprocessors (see Figure 23.1), each comprising several stream processors (SPs), which can execute multiple program threads concurrently (up to 512). Threads are organized into blocks, with one or more blocks executing concurrently on individual multiprocessors. All threads belonging to the same thread block have exclusive fast access (within 1 clock cycle of hardware execution) to a small shared local memory (typically, 16 kB per multiprocessor, to be shared among resident thread blocks on that multiprocessor). All threads can access a much larger and much higher latency device memory (up to 2 GB – 300–400 cycles latency for access). The aforementioned memory sizes and latency are typical of a GeForce8-generation GPU. The CUDA architecture can be programmed using a C language extension in an SIMT (single-instruction,

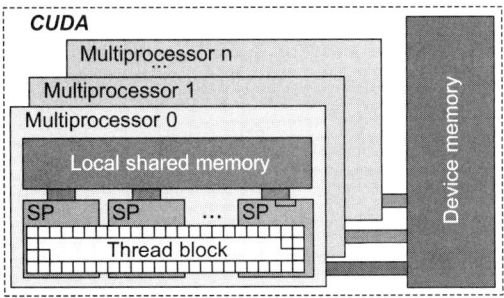

FIGURE 23.1

NVIDIA CUDA architecture. A GPU includes a number of multiprocessors, each consisting of several stream processors. Several threads belonging to the same thread block may execute concurrently within a multiprocessor and communicate through a small shared memory bank with fast access latency. The larger device memory has also a much higher access latency.

multiple-thread) fashion. In designing a gate-level logic simulator, we must note the importance of being aware of this memory layout and organization of the execution units so that we can derive the most performance benefits. For instance, a group of closely coupled gates is most efficiently simulated within a same thread block, which can store the intermediate logic values in shared memory for quick repeated accesses.

The simulation method outlined before is called "oblivious logic simulation" because all logic gates are simulated during each simulated clock cycle. However, it is often the case that, while propagating values through the netlist, for at least some gates the inputs have not changed from the previous cycle. As a result the output of those gates will also remain the same, and the computation is indeed redundant. This observation is the central idea of "event-driven simulation," where only those gates whose input values are different from the previous simulation cycle are computed. To monitor internal value changes and determine which gates should be computed, event-driven simulation incurs a fairly large control-flow overhead. Many commercial logic simulators today are based on an event-driven scheme because the benefits from a reduced amount of gate computation well offset the cost of a centralized scheduler to manage the simulation's control flow. However, this scheduler is inherently sequential; thus, its impact is particularly negative in a massively concurrent environment such as CUDA. In our solution we wished to reap the benefits of reduced computation of the event-driven approach, while bypassing most of the associated control-flow overhead. Thus, we devised a hybrid oblivious/event-driven scheme that applies event-driven simulation at a coarse netlist granularity, that is, for large monolithic blocks of gates, and oblivious simulation within each block.

Traditional event-driven simulators rely on a centralized event queue to schedule gates that must be computed within a simulation cycle. In the context of the CUDA architecture such a queue would incur

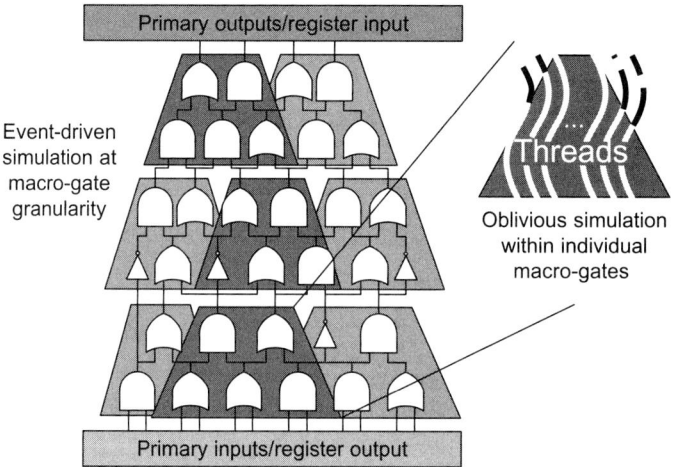

FIGURE 23.2

Hybrid event-driven simulator. The novel simulator architecture is event driven at the granularity of macro-gates, while the macro-gates themselves are simulated in an oblivious fashion. The macro-gates with a darker shade are the only ones scheduled for simulation during a possible simulation cycle.

high latency delays — most probably higher than the computation of the gates themselves. However, we noted that a dynamic scheduling approach can still be valuably exploited as long as it operates at the granularity of thread blocks, and it is thus accessed much more infrequently. As a result, we assign clusters of gates from the circuit's netlist to individual thread blocks. Each of these clusters is simulated by the assigned thread block in an oblivious fashion. At the same time, we monitor the input values of the cluster, and we use an event-driven approach in scheduling a cluster for simulation or bypassing it if none of its inputs have changed.

A high-level schematic of the approach described is presented in Figure 23.2, showing a pool of clusters for a netlist and a possible simulation requiring to schedule only three of the clusters for computation. Note that we call the clusters of gates "macro-gates." To implement this design we must develop a segmentation algorithm to create macro-gates of appropriate size, striking a trade-off between performance and memory locality requirements, and additional optimizing algorithms to ensure as regular of an execution as possible within each macro-gate's oblivious simulation.

23.3 COMPILATION AND SIMULATION

The GPU-based simulation operates in a compiled-code fashion: a compilation process is performed, mapping the netlist to internal data structures suited to the GPU memory hierarchy. Following compilation, in the simulation phase, the GPU accesses these internal data structures and updates them according to the inputs provided by the test bench. The same mapped design can be reused while running several times with many distinct test benches, allowing the compilation time to be amortized over multiple simulation runs.

Compilation consists of two phases (see Figure 23.3): the first phase is *system-level compilation*, where a gate-level netlist is considered as input. During this phase segmentation is applied to the netlist to partition it into a set of levelized *macro-gates*: each macro-gate includes several gates within the netlist connected by input/output relations. Companion data structures are also created for each macro-gate to facilitate event-driven simulation. The second phase is *macro-gate balancing*. During this phase each macro-gate is reshaped for efficient simulation on the GPU platform. Once compilation is completed, the data structures and the GPU kernels generated can be transferred to the GPU and simulation may begin.

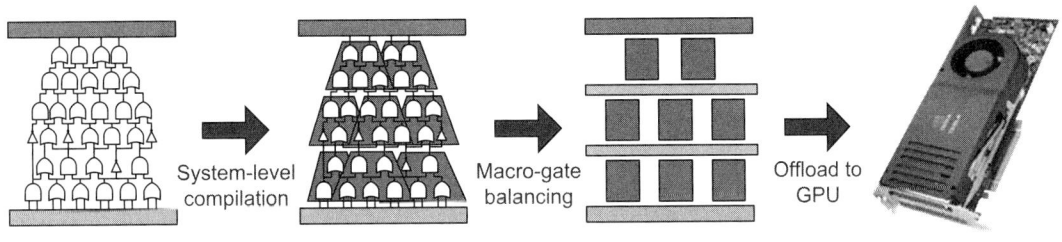

FIGURE 23.3

Simulator organization. The simulator performs a two-phase compilation, after which data structures and GPU kernels are transferred to the GPU, which in turn performs the simulation.

During the execution of the GPU program, that is, during simulation, the test bench reads the outputs generated at the end of each clock cycle and provides inputs for the next cycle. Test benches can be implemented using a variety of strategies, the most efficient of which is a direct GPU implementation, which avoids costly communication with the host CPU. Once the stimuli are exhausted, simulation comes to an end.

23.3.1 System-Level Compilation

The goal of system-level compilation is to segment the netlist into macro-gates, groups of gates that will be simulated in an oblivious fashion by a single-thread block, while different macro-gates are scheduled in an event-driven fashion. Before macro-gates can be extracted, three preprocessing steps are required: *synthesis*, *combinational logic extraction*, and *levelization*. Finally, macro-gate segmentation can be performed, producing a set of macro-gates and their associated sensitivity lists (that is, the set of inputs a macro-gate depends on).

Synthesis

The first compilation step considers a digital design and synthesizes it to a flattened netlist using a target technology library, such as the GTECH library by Synopsys in our experiments. We chose GTECH for its generality and simplicity; however, any other library may be used for this task because the simulator will replace each gate type with functional primitives; thus, a different library will simply lead to a different set of primitives. In order to enable cycle-by-cycle simulation, we used a subset of the GTECH library excluding nonclocked latches. When the netlist is read into our compiler, a functional primitive of each gate is created, internally represented by a four-valued (0, 1, X, Z) truth table. In order to maintain uniform program execution paths, all primitives use a uniform format to indicate inputs, outputs, and functionality. The primitives are frequently accessed, once for each time a gate type is simulated. To minimize the memory bandwidth required to access them, we leverage bit-level packing in storing the truth tables. As a result, the output of a gate can be determined by performing fast, efficient bit-wise operations on the packed data.

Extraction of Combinational Logic

Once the design is synthesized and mapped into internal functional primitives, the combinational portion is extracted. Because the design is simulated cycle by cycle, the contents of registers that retain state across clock cycles can be modeled as program variables. These variables store the circuit's register values: they are updated at the end of the cycle with the values computed for the register's input nets, and they are accessed for reading at the beginning of each cycle to determine the values at the register's output nets. Thus, the entire circuit can be viewed as a combinational network from the simulator's point of view. If we assume absence of combinational loops, this consists of a directed acyclic graph (DAG), a representation leveraged later during macro-gate segmentation.

Levelization

After combinational logic extraction, the combinational netlist is then *levelized*. Logic gates are organized into levels based on their topological order, so that the fan-in of all gates in one level is computed in previous levels. With this organization, it is possible to simulate the entire netlist one level at a time, from inputs to outputs, without concern for backward dependencies. In our prototype implementation, we used an ALAP (as-late-as-possible) levelization, though other solutions are also possible.

Macro-Gate Segmentation

Once the design has been synthesized and the combinational logic has been extracted and levelized, macro-gate segmentation may be applied. When we view the preprocessed design as a levelized DAG, this phase partitions the graph, carving out blocks of logic referred to as macro-gates (see Figure 23.4). In addition to the segmentation itself, wires at the periphery of macro-gates are annotated with their relation to other macro-gates and grouped into a sensitivity list used to inform event-driven simulation.

Three important factors govern the process of macro-gate segmentation: (1) because the objective of forming macro-gates is to perform event-driven simulation at a coarse granularity (compared with individual gates), the time required to simulate a given macro-gate should be substantially larger than the overhead to decide which macro-gates to activate. (2) The multiprocessors in the GPU can communicate only through high-latency device memory, and thus for best performance, there should be no communication among them. This can be ensured if the tasks executing on distinct multiprocessors are independent of each other. To this end, macro-gates that are simulated concurrently must be independent of each other. To achieve this goal, we duplicate small portions of logic that occasionally create overlap among macro-gates, eliminating the need of communication. (3) Finally, we want to avoid cyclic dependencies between macro-gates so that we can simulate each macro-gate at most once per cycle; to this end, we levelize the netlist at the granularity of macro-gates as well.

Segmentation begins by partitioning the netlist into *layers*: each layer encompasses a fixed number of the netlist's levels, as shown in Figure 23.4. Macro-gates are then defined by selecting a set of nets at the top boundary of a layer and including their cone of influence back to the input nets of the layer. The number of nets used to generate each macro-gate is a parameter called *lid*; its value is selected so that the number of logic gates in each macro-gate is approximately the same. The number of levels within each layer is called *gap*, and it corresponds to the height of the macro-gate. In Section 23.3.4 we discuss how to select a suitable value for gap and lid in order to achieve a high level of parallelism during simulation, as well as maintain the event-driven structure of simulation.

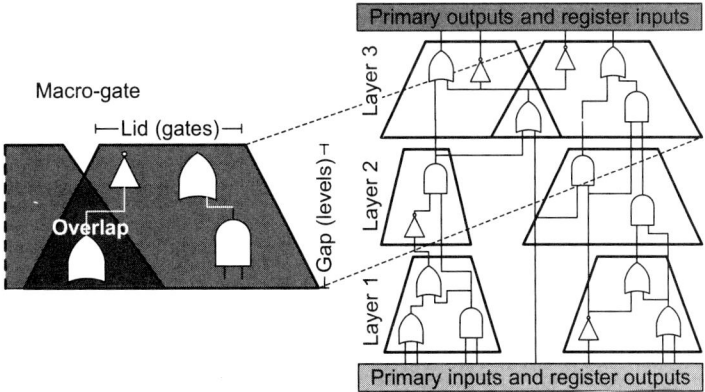

FIGURE 23.4

Macro-gate segmentation. The levelized netlist is partitioned into layers, each encompassing a fixed number of levels (gap). Macro-gates are then carved out by extracting the transitive fan-in from a set of nets (lid) at the output of a layer, back to the layer's input. If an overlap occurs, the gates involved are replicated for all associated macro-gates.

```
segmentation (netlist, gap, lid) {
  levelized_netlist = ALAP_levelize(netlist);
  layers = gap_partition(levelized_netlist);
  for (layer in layers) {
    macro-gates = lid_partition(layer);
    macro-gates_pool = append(macro-gates);
    compute_monitored_nets (layer);
  }
  return macro-gates_pool; }
```

FIGURE 23.5

Macro-gate segmentation algorithm. First, the netlist is levelized, and the resulting levels are grouped into layers. Each layer is then partitioned into macro-gates, which are then added to the pool to be simulated. The nets to be monitored for switching activity (which indicate the need for a macro-gate to be scheduled for simulation) are also collected at this stage.

While we are collecting the gates that belong to a logic cone, it is possible that gates may be assigned to two or more macro-gates. Duplication of a few gates allows macro-gates to be simulated independently, without sharing any data with other macro-gates. There can be several possible policies for selecting the output nets, whose cones of influence are clustered in a single macro-gate. In our case we aim at minimizing duplication; thus, we cluster together those nets whose cones of influence have the most gates in common. This policy is implemented in our prototype. Figure 23.5 presents the pseudocode of the algorithm discussed in this section.

23.3.2 Macro-Gate Balancing

After macro-gate segmentation, each macro-gate is treated as an independent block of logic gates to be simulated by concurrent threads. The threads operating on an individual macro-gate must belong to the same thread block for resource sharing, and thus, they execute in the same multiprocessor of a GPU. The macro-gate balancing step, presented in this section, reshapes each macro-gate to enable the best use of execution resources.

To maximize resource usage, all threads should be busy for the entire execution of a macro-block simulation. This efficiency goal is challenged by the typical shape of macro-gates: a large base (many gates) close to the primary inputs and a narrower tip (very few gates toward the outputs), resulting in a trapezoidal shape. This shape is the by-product of the macro-gate generation process, that is, the selection of a few output wires and their fan-in logic cones, as discussed in macro-gate segmentation in Section 23.3.1. Thus, a large number of active threads are required at the lower levels and just a few in the levels close to the top, where just a few gates must be simulated. The process of macro-gate balancing is illustrated qualitatively in Figure 23.6: balancing moves gates toward the upper levels of the netlist, within the slack allowed by their input/output connections. The result after balancing is a macro-gate where the number of gates at each level is equalized as much as possible. Note also that balancing may increase the overall gap of the macro-gate.

The macro-gate balancing algorithm outlined in Figure 23.7 exploits the slack available in the levelized netlist within each macro-gate and reshapes it to have approximately the same number of logic gates in each level. The algorithm processes all the gates in a bottom-up fashion, filling every slot in the macro-gate with logic gates, with the goal of assigning each gate to the lowest level possible, while

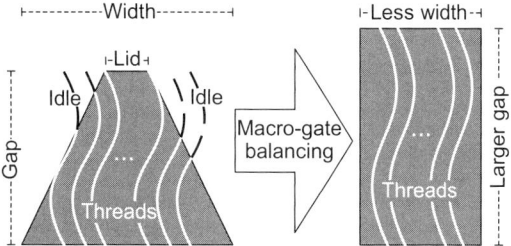

FIGURE 23.6

Macro-gate balancing. The balancing algorithm restructures each macro-gate to minimize the number of concurrent execution threads required. The result is a more efficient utilization of thread-block resources.

```
balance_macro-gate() {
  for each (level in height)
    for each (column in width)
      balanced_macro-gate[level][column] = select_gate();
    }
  }
  return balanced_macro-gate;
}

select_gate() {
  sort gates in macro-gates by increasing level;
  for each (gate in macro-gate) {
    if(not assigned_to_balanced_macro-gate(gate))
      return gate;
  }
}
```

FIGURE 23.7

Macro-gate balancing algorithm. Macro-gates are considered one at a time and reshaped to fit into a thread block with a preset maximum number of threads, while trying to minimize the number of logic levels. The algorithm proceeds in a bottom-up fashion, filling each level of the macro-gate with logic gates.

maintaining the restriction on maximum width. Note that this might also lead to an increase in the height of a particular macro-gate and thus its simulation latency. Hence, there is an inherent trade-off between execution latency and thread utilization.

23.3.3 Simulation Phase

Simulation is carried out directly on the GPU coprocessor, evaluating the gates within each macro-gate in an oblivious fashion and using event-driven scheduling for macro-gates. Event-driven scheduling is informed by sensitivity lists, used to determine which macro-gates to activate in the subsequent layer. During simulation, concurrency is exploited at two different levels of abstraction: several macro-gates can be simulated in parallel using distinct thread blocks (and multiprocessors); in addition, within each macro-gate, gates at the same level can be computed concurrently by different individual threads.

Event-Driven Simulation of Macro-Gates

Each macro-gate is assigned to a distinct thread-block; thread blocks are then grouped and scheduled to distinct multiprocessors by the CUDA scheduler. Macro-gates are scheduled layer by layer, simulating all the activated macro-blocks in one layer before proceeding to the next, as shown in Figure 23.8. The sensitivity list of each macro-gate (that is, its monitored nets) informs the event-driven simulation scheduler, which determines which macro-gates in a layer require simulation.

Simulation is driven by two kernels (GPU programs) alternating their execution on the GPU. First, the *simulation kernel* simulates all active macro-gates in a layer. Execution of the *scheduling kernel* follows, evaluating the array of monitored nets to determine which macro-gates should be activated in the next layer. This array is organized as a bit vector, with each monitored net being implicitly mapped to a unique location in the array. If a macro-gate simulation from a previous layer modifies the value of any of these nets, its corresponding array index is tagged. Each macro-gate has a corresponding *sensitivity list* where all the input nets triggering its activation are tagged. With this structure, a simple bit-wise AND operation between the monitored net's array and a macro-gate's sensitivity list determines if any input change has occurred and whether the macro-gate should be activated. A schematic overview of this process is illustrated in Figure 23.8; in addition, Figure 23.9 provides a simple pseudocode of the flow just presented.

Data placement for simulation is organized so that primary inputs, outputs, register values, and monitored nets are mapped to device memory because they must be shared among several macro-gates (multiprocessors). The netlist structure is also stored in device memory and accessed during each macro-gate simulation.

Oblivious Simulation within Macro-Gates

Individual macro-gates are simulated by a thread block; each thread within the block is responsible for computing the output of one distinct logic gate. All threads in the thread block synchronize after

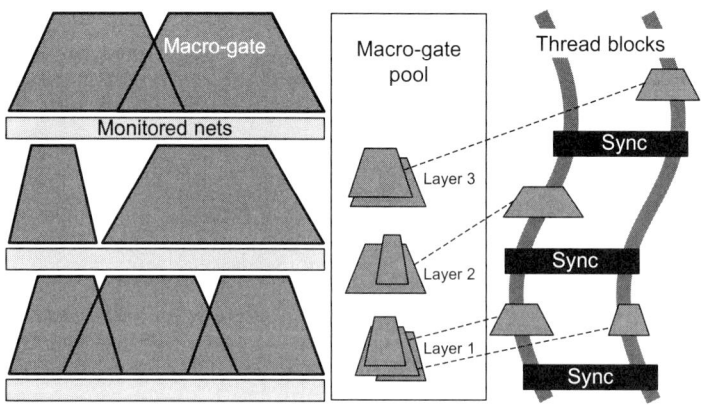

FIGURE 23.8

Event-driven simulation proceeds layer by layer at the macro-gate granularity. Within each layer, activated macro-gates are simulated, and monitored nets are analyzed to activate a subset of the next layer's macro-gates. Activated macro-gates are transferred by the CUDA scheduler to an available multiprocessor for simulation.

```
scheduler (layer, monitored_nets) {
  switching_monitored_nets = monitored_nets.previous
                             xor monitored_nets.current;
  for each (macro_gate in layer){
    macro—gate.to_schedule = macro—gate.sensitivity_list
                             and switching_monitored_nets;
    if(macro—gate.to_schedule!=0){
      active_list.append(macro_gate);
    }
  }
  return active_list;
}
```

FIGURE 23.9

Event-driven simulation scheduler. The scheduling algorithm considers all macro-gates in the next layer of simulation and intersects their sensitivity list with the monitored nets that have switched during the current simulation cycle. Each macro-gate that finds a nonzero intersection is then scheduled for simulation in the next layer.

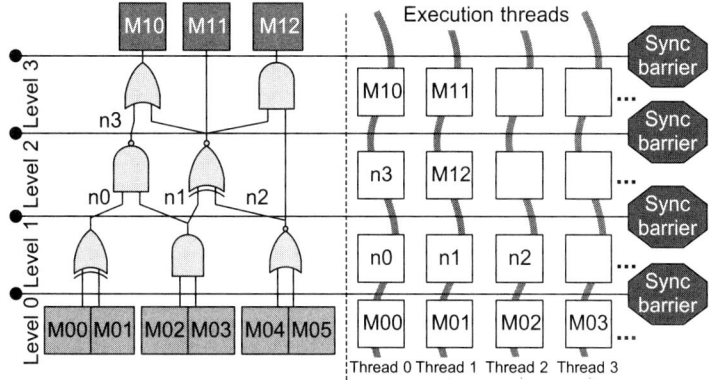

FIGURE 23.10

Oblivious simulation within a macro-gate. The logic gates within a macro-gate are simulated in an oblivious fashion. Each thread is responsible for computing the output of one gate at a time: vertical waved lines connect the set of logic gates for which a single thread is responsible at subsequent time intervals. Note that each level is kept synchronized within the block by a synchronization barrier.

the simulation of each netlist level of the macro-gate is completed so that all the output values from previous levels are updated before the next level's gates are computed. Figure 23.10 illustrates this process by showing which gate output values are computed by each thread during the simulation. Note that in the right part of the figure, distinct threads are spread horizontally, while time progresses vertically. The shared memory associated with each multiprocessor is used to store the truth tables for all gates in the technology library and internal net values for the macro-gate. Truth tables are stored in shared memory because of their frequent access during simulation. Intermediate nets values (internal

```
simulate_macro-gate(){
  for each (level) {
    launch_gate_simulation(assigned_gate);
    sync_gate_simulation();
  }
  sync_gate_simulation();
}
```

FIGURE 23.11

Oblivious simulation routine for an individual thread. The routine is executed by each thread within a thread block. Each thread operates on a different set of gates, and a complete macro-gate is simulated after the last synchronization step.

gates outputs) are also potentially accessed by several gates (and, thus, threads) during a macro-gate simulation. However, macro-gate topologies are stored in device memory, and each thread fetches its corresponding gate information from there. In device memory, logic gates are stored in a regular matrix-like fashion and the location of each gate corresponds to the position of the output nets of the logic gates of a balanced macro-gate.

They also correspond to the layout of the nets in shared memory, thus creating the scope of very regular execution suited for GPU. Each thread simulating a gate gathers the relevant information from device memory, that is, location of input nets and type of logic function. Note, however, that balanced macro-gates have a fairly regular structure; thus all this information can be coalesced to limit the number of device memory accesses. Input net values are then retrieved from shared memory and a truth table access determines the output value of this gate, which is subsequently written to shared memory. Upon completion of a macro-gate simulation, output values are transferred to device memory to determine if a value change has occurred since the previous simulation cycle. The oblivious simulation kernel (one thread's designated work) is presented in the pseudocode of Figure 23.11. Concurrent execution of this kernel by all threads within a thread block results in the simulation of a complete macro-gate.

Test Benches
Test benches are an important part of simulation because simulation is only useful when the design is validated with a relevant sequence of stimuli. Hence, we need to provide methods of incorporating test benches. Because the simulator is cycle based, the task of the test bench is to read the outputs computed at the end of every cycle and provide suitable inputs for the next cycle. In our solution, test benches are implemented as separate GPU kernels: during simulation, the kernels for simulation proper and those for the test bench alternate execution on the GP-GPU device. At the completion of each simulation cycle, the outputs produced by the netlist are read from device memory, and suitable inputs are computed and written there to be consumed during the following simulation cycle. We developed several ways of implementing the test bench kernels, each appropriate for different types of designs and simulation setups. The two fundamental types of test-bench kernels are synthesizable ones and software kernels emulating a behavioral hardware description.

Synthesizable Test Benches
These test benches can be expressed by synthesizable hardware descriptions. As a result they can be synthesized and represented by a netlist, similarly to the design under simulation. In these situations the alternating of test-bench and simulation kernels can be viewed as a cosimulation: the two kernels are

identical; they simply operate on different netlists. The result is very high-performance kernels, which can completely reside on the GPU device.

Software Test Benches

In other situations, test benches can be described as GPU's software programs reading input values from device memory at each clock cycle and producing outputs for the next simulation step. A classic example of this type of test bench is a microprocessor test kernel, a simple kernel that is often used when simulating a microprocessor design executing a binary program. The test bench is responsible for providing instructions from the binary program to the microprocessor design as well as processing its load/store data memory accesses. The program is stored in device memory: at each simulation cycle the test bench also serves memory requests by the microprocessor.

Other Test Benches

Other complex test benches involving constructs that cannot be expressed in a CUDA kernel can still be executed on the host CPU, but an additional communication penalty is incurred with every simulation cycle.

23.3.4 Macro-Gate Sizing Heuristics

The key to simulation performance lies in the quality of macro-gate partitioning. Event-driven simulation is most efficient when only a small fraction of macro-gates are active in each given cycle. Consequently, the selection of which gates to include in each macro-gate is a critical aspect of our simulator architecture, as discussed in macro-gate segmentation in Section 23.3.1.

The size of a macro-gate is governed by two parameters, gap and lid, which control the granularity of the event-driven mechanism. The goal in selecting the values for these parameters is to create macro-gates with low-activation rates. Gap and lid values are selected during the compilation phase by evaluating a range of candidate <gap,lid> value pairs; for each candidate pair, we collect several metrics: number of macro-gates generated, number of monitored nets, size of macro-gates, and their activation rate. The activation rate is obtained by a simulation mock-up on a micro test bench. We then select optimal values among those considered and perform detailed segmentation. Figure 23.12 shows an example of this selection process for one of our experimental evaluation designs, reporting simulation times. In this example, the best performance is achieved at <gap,lid>=<5,100>.

Boundaries for the range of gap values considered are derived from the number of monitored nets generated: we consider gap values only for which no more than 50% of the total nets are monitored. In practice, small gap values tend to generate many monitored nets, while large gap values trigger high-activation rates. In selecting the range of lid values to consider, we bound the analysis by estimating how many macro-gates will be created at each layer, striving to run all the macro-gates concurrently in the GPU, even in the worst case. The GPU used for our evaluation (8800GT) included 14 multiprocessors, and the CUDA scheduler allowed for at most three thread blocks executing concurrently on the same multiprocessor. Thus, we considered only lid values that generate no more than $14 \times 3 = 42$ macro-gates per layer. Note that this analysis is performed only once per compilation.

23.4 EXPERIMENTAL RESULTS

We evaluated the performance of our simulator on a broad set of designs, ranging from purely combinational circuits, such as a low-density parity check (LDPC) encoder, to a multicore SPARC design

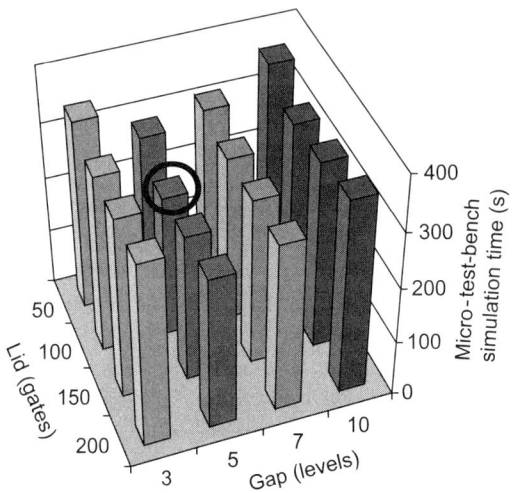

FIGURE 23.12

Optimal gap and lid estimation for a low-density parity check (LDPC) encoder design. The figure plots the execution time of a micro test-bench simulation with a range of gap and lid values. The dark circle highlights the optimal selection of values among those considered.

containing over 1 million logic gates. Designs were obtained from the OpenCores suite [12] and from the Sun OpenSPARC project [15]; we also considered two Alpha ISA-based microprocessors and two network-on-chip (NoC) systems developed in advanced digital design courses by student teams at the University of Michigan.

We report in Table 23.1 the key aspects of these designs: number of gates, flip-flops and type of stimulus that was used during simulation. The complexity of the test benches is expressed in terms of lines of code in the original verilog test bench (see the column named No. LOC). The first two designs are processors implementing the Alpha instruction set; the first can execute one instruction at a time, whereas the second is a five-stage pipelined architecture. Both were simulated executing a binary program that computed Fibonacci series recursively. The LDPC encoder outputs an encoded version of its input; for this design, we developed a random stimulus generator that runs directly on the GPU platform. The JPEG decompressor decodes an image provided as input. The NoC designs consist of a network of five-channel routers connected in a torus topology and simulated with a random stimulus generator transmitting packets across the network. Finally, the OpenSPARC designs are composed of processor cores from the OpenSPARC T1 multicore chip (excluding caches) and run a conglomeration of assembly regressions provided with Sun's open source distribution. We built several versions of this processor: single core, two cores, and four cores; and we emulated local cache activity by leveraging playback of prerecorded signal traces from processor-crossbar and processor-cache interactions.

23.4.1 Macro-Gates

Macro-gate segmentation partitions the design into clusters to be simulated in an event-driven fashion, while gates within each macro-gate are simulated in an oblivious fashion. Thus, the effectiveness of the

Table 23.1 **Test-bench designs for evaluation of the GPU-based logic simulator.**
The table reports the designs considered for the experimental evaluation and the related test bench applied for simulation. For each design we report the number of logic gates and flip-flops, and for test benches we report the lines of codes of the corresponding Verilog description.

Design	No. Gates	No. Flops	Test Bench	No. LOC
Alpha no pipeline	17,546	2,795	Recursive Fibonacci program	287
Alpha pipeline	18,222	2,804	Recursive Fibonacci program	293
LDPC encoder	62,515	0	Random stimulus	170
JPEG decompressor	93,278	20,741	1920 × 1080 image	365
3 × 3 NoC routers	64,432	13,698	Random legal traffic	105
4 × 4 NoC routers	144,098	23,875	Random legal traffic	105
OpenSPARC core	262,201	62,001	OpenSPARC regression suite	902
OpenSPARC-2 cores	610,670	124,002	OpenSPARC regression suite	902
OpenSPARC-4 cores	1,221,340	248,004	OpenSPARC regression suite	902

Table 23.2 **Macro-gate segmentation statistics.** The table reports the parameters used in macro-gate segmentation for each design, the resulting number of macro-gates, and their sizes.

Design	Gap	Lid	No. Layers	No. Macro-gates	Size of Macro-gate Avg.	Max.	Min.
Alpha no pipeline	7	100	23	56	350	423	33
Alpha pipeline	7	100	26	60	341	406	29
LDPC encoder	5	100	7	140	458	767	128
JPEG decompressor	5	150	28	282	412	689	50
3 × 3 NoC routers	5	100	7	250	333	593	254
4 × 4 NoC routers	5	100	7	451	342	569	169
OpenSPARC core	5	150	28	756	446	574	23
OpenSPARC-2 cores	5	150	28	1489	453	577	31
OpenSPARC-4 cores	5	150	28	2955	456	582	33

macro-gate segmentation process has a strong impact on performance. We studied several aspects of the compilation phase of our simulator, including the number of macro-gates resulting from segmentation and their size. Additionally, we explored the extent of gate replication among macro-gates.

Table 23.2 presents the characteristics of the macro-gates that result from segmentation of each design. We report the gap and lid values used to segment the designs, as determined by the process described in Section 23.3.4. Additionally, the fourth column indicates the number of layers obtained by segmenting with the reported gap. The total number of macro-gates that were formed as a result of segmentation for each design is also reported, as well as their average, maximum, and minimum size in terms of logic gates. Note that the largest design, OpenSPARC-4 cores, includes many more

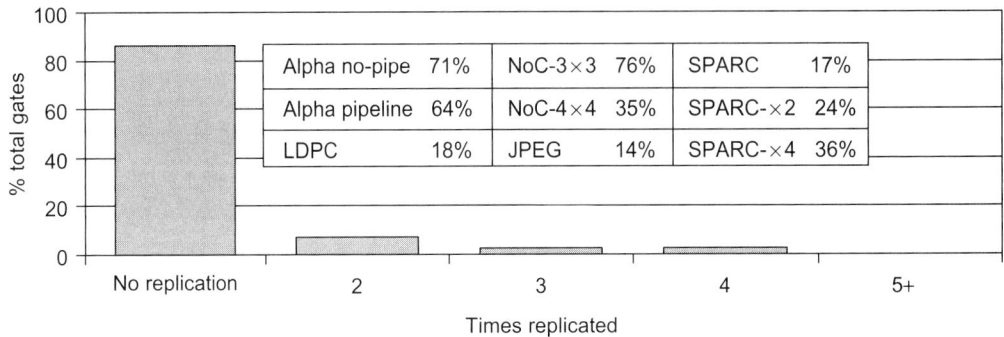

FIGURE 23.13

Gate replication resulting from macro-gate overlap. The graph reports the number of times that gates have been replicated in order to obtain independent macro-gates. The inset table indicates the gate inflation that each design incurred as a result of this process.

macro-gates in each layer that could be simulated concurrently (42 as computed in Section 23.3.4) because it has 2955 macro-gates distributed over only 28 layers.

As mentioned in macro-gate segmentation in Section 23.3.1, gate replication is a necessary consequence of the high communication latency between multiprocessors. However, we strive to keep replication low, so as not to inflate the number of simulated gates during each cycle. Figure 23.13 plots the fraction of gates that incurred replication, averaged over all our experimental designs: more than 80% incurred no replication, less than 10% were simply duplicated, and very few incurred a higher degree of replication. The table inset reports the rate of "gate inflation" for each design, resulting in an overall average of 39%.

23.4.2 Monitored Nets

The number of monitored nets has a high impact on simulator performance; thus, segmentation strives to keep the fraction of nets that are monitored low. As an example, in Figure 23.14, we plot the structure of the LDPC encoder design after segmentation: for each layer, we plot the corresponding number of macro-gates and monitored nets. Note how middle layers tend to have more macro-gates than peripheral layers and how lower layers tend to generate the most monitored nets. Finally, we analyzed the fraction of total nets in the design that requires monitoring because they cross layer boundaries. The compilation phase should strive to keep this fraction low because it directly relates to the size of the sensitivity list. Figure 23.15 reports our findings for the designs in our evaluation pool.

23.4.3 Design Compilation

As part of our experimental evaluation, we consider the time spent in compiling the design for simulation on the GPU-based simulator. Table 23.3 reports separate times for the system-level compilation phase and for the balancing phase in compiling each design. The table also indicates the total compilation time and compares that data against that of a commercial logic simulator executing on a general processor machine. The commercial simulator that we used for the comparison is considered among the fastest available in the market today. Note that the compilation time is not a critical aspect in the

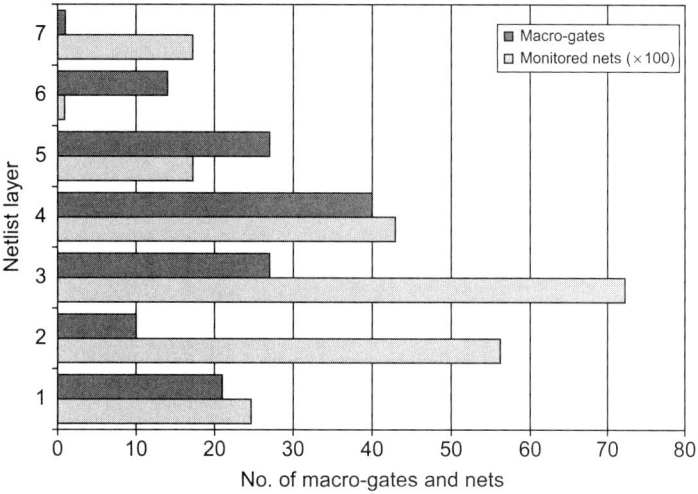

FIGURE 23.14

Segmented structure for LDPC encoder design. The plot shows the geometry of the LDPC encoder after segmentation. For each layer we report the number of macro-gates and of monitored nets in hundreds.

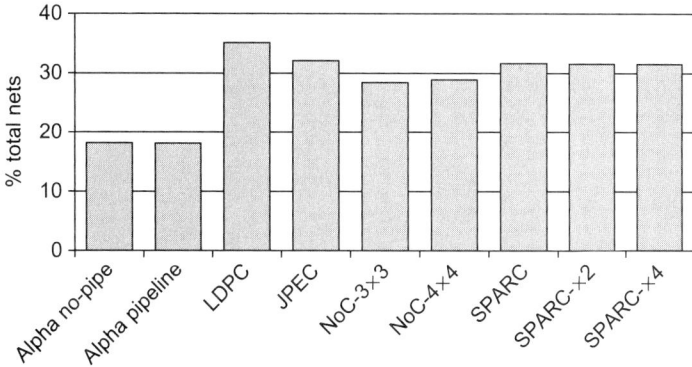

FIGURE 23.15

Fraction of monitored nets. Percentage of all nets that must be monitored for each design in our experimental evaluation.

performance of a simulator because this time can be amortized over many simulations and over very long (hours or days) simulation runs. However, we felt it was relevant to convey information on the timescale of compilation performance.

23.4.4 Macro-Gate Activity

The activation rate of macro-gates is an important metric for event-driven simulation; by comparison, an oblivious simulator has an activation rate of 100% on any design. The goal of an event-driven

Table 23.3 Performance of design compilation for our GPU-based simulator and comparison with a commercial logic simulator. The table reports the time in seconds required for system-level compilation and macro-gate balancing for our simulator. It also compares the total compilation time with that of a commercial logic simulator.

| Design | GPU-based Simulator | | | |
	System Level (s)	Balancing (s)	Total (s)	Commercial Simulator (s)
Alpha no pipeline	13	8	21	7
Alpha pipeline	21	15	36	13
LDPC encoder	78	47	125	63
JPEG decompressor	245	92	337	156
3 × 3 NoC routers	212	164	376	189
4 × 4 NoC routers	302	130	432	237
OpenSPARC core	456	187	643	275
OpenSPARC-2 cores	873	259	1132	504
OpenSPARC-4 cores	1670	575	2245	1278

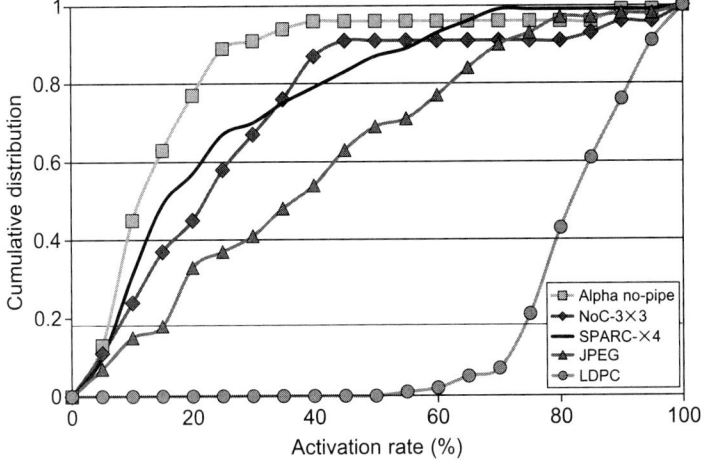

FIGURE 23.16

Macro-gates activation. Cumulative distribution of macro-gates with respect to the activation rate. The plots show the fraction of macro-gates with an activation rate below the threshold indicated on the horizontal axis. For most designs, a majority of the macro-gates have an activation rate below 30%, indicating that the segmentation parameters selected are effective in reducing the amount of computation in event-driven simulation.

simulator is to keep this rate as low as possible, thus leveraging the fact that not all gates in a netlist switch on every cycle. Figure 23.16 reports the macro-gate activation rates for a number of the evaluation designs. Individual plots show the cumulative distribution of activation rates among all the macro-gates for a given design. Note that, for most designs, most macro-gates have an activation rate of only 10 to 30%. However, for LDPC, most macro-gates experience a high-activation rate (> 80%): this is due to the inherent nature of the design, which requires evaluation of all the bits positions for each parity check. The designs that are not reported have a cumulative distribution similar to that of the OpenSPARC and NoC designs. Note that the activation rate for our solution does not directly relate to performance gain over oblivious simulation. As an example, the JPEG decoder has an average activation rate of 40%. This does not mean that, on average, the JPEG decoder is simulated 2.5 times faster when compared against an oblivious simulation. Indeed, even if very few macro-gates are activated, one for each layer, the performance would be just the same as if several macro-gates were simulated in each layer. This is because of the parallelism of the underlying hardware, capable of simulating many macro-gates in a same layer simultaneously, coupled with synchronization barriers that force macro-gates to be simulated in layer order. In the end, the overall performance of the JPEG design in event-driven simulation is 1.55 times faster than in oblivious simulation.

23.4.5 Performance Evaluation

Finally, we evaluated the performance of our prototype event-driven simulator against that of a commercial, event-driven simulator for a general-purpose processor system. The commercial simulator we selected is known to be among the fastest (or the fastest) available in the market today. Our graphics coprocessor was a CUDA-enabled 8800GT GPU with 14 multiprocessors and 512 MB of device memory, operating at 600 MHz for the cores and at 900 MHz for the memory. Device memory size was not a limitation in any of our experiments, as all data structures, including stimuli data, occupied always less than 200 MB. However, it is possible that, for even larger designs, device memory becomes a storage bottleneck. The commercial simulator executed on a 2.4 GHz Intel Core 2 Quad running Red Hat Enterprise Linux 5, using four parallel simulation threads. Table 23.4 shows the performance evaluation results: for each design we report the number of cycles simulated, the runtimes in seconds for both the GPU-based simulator and the commercial simulator (compilation times are excluded), and the

Table 23.4 GPU-based simulator performance. Performance comparison between our GPU-based event-driven simulator and a commercial event-driven simulator. Our prototype simulator outperforms the commercial simulator by 13 times on average.

Design	Simulation Cycles	Commercial Simulator (s)	GPU-based Simulator (s)	Relative Speedup
Alpha no pipeline	12,889,495	31,678	2,567	**12.34x**
Alpha pipeline	13,423,608	54,789	7,781	**7.04x**
LDPC encoder	1,000,000	115,671	2,578	**44.87x**
	10,000,000	>48 h	25,973	**43.49x**
JPEG decompressor	2,983,674	12,146	599	**20.28x**
3 × 3 NoC routers	1,967,155	3,532	397	**8.90x**
4 × 4 NoC routers	10,000,001	28,867	3,935	**7.34x**
sparc core × 1	1,074,702	27,894	6,077	**4.59x**
sparc core × 2	1,074,702	40,378	8,229	**4.91x**
sparc core × 4	1,074,702	61,678	10,983	**5.62x**

relative speedup. Note that our prototype simulator outperforms the commercial simulator by 4 to 44 times, depending on the design. Note that, despite the LDPC encoder having a very high-activation rate, we report the best performance improvement for this design. As mentioned earlier, most gates in this design are switching every cycle: while this affects our activation rates, it also hampers the sequential simulator performance. Thus, the improvement obtained for this design is due to sheer parallelism of our simulator architecture.

23.5 FUTURE DIRECTIONS

Through our experience in the design and evaluation of the hybrid event-driven logic simulator, we noted that the formation of macro-gates has a strong impact on the performance of the simulator. In particular, macro-gates containing even a single frequently activated logic gate will trigger frequent simulation of the entire macro-gate, degrading overall system performance. As an alternative strategy, we plan to consolidate these logic cones with frequently activated logic gates into the same macro-gate, basically clustering based on activity instead of logic sharing.

Our baseline clustering algorithm, which considers only the degree of logic sharing, results in many macro-gates with a high-activation frequency. In Figure 23.17(a) we illustrate this problem qualitatively, by shading in dark gray logic cones that are activated more frequently. The proposed algorithm is illustrated in Figure 23.17(b), where clustering is based on switching activity profiles, thus resulting in some highly activated macro-gates and other rarely activated ones. Activity-based clustering creates a higher separation between the activation frequency of distinct macro-gates, leading to overall improved performance.

The potential downside of this approach is in the higher gate duplication that would result from activity-based clustering. However, we expect that this cost will be negligible when compared with the significant reduction in the total number of macro-gates (and gates) dynamic simulations. This can be seen as a trade-off, shown in the figure by the lesser overlap of the cones. This trade-off is amortized by the significant reduction in the total number of macro-gate simulations that must be performed. We

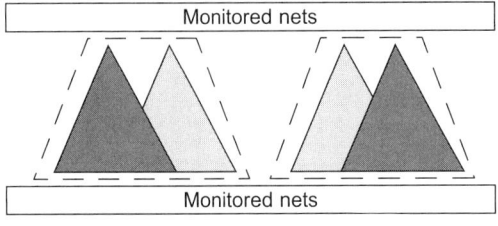
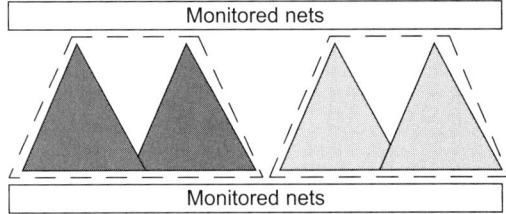

| (a) Clustering based on logic sharing | (b) Clustering based on activity profile |

FIGURE 23.17

Activity-based clustering compared against the baseline solution. (a) Our baseline solution clusters logic gates by degree of sharing, while (b) activity-based clustering is based on the activation frequency of logic cones. The darkness of a cone in the picture is qualitatively proportional to its activation frequency. Clustering based on activity profile results in the consolidation of frequently activated logic cones.

plan to use profiling to estimate activity profiles, first simulating a micro test bench on a segmented circuit using the baseline clustering policy based on logic sharing. Once activity estimates of individual cones are computed, the segmentation process will be applied again, but this time cones will be added to macro-gates based on activation frequency. Future plans include a detailed study of the performance gain that can be obtained by this enhanced clustering method.

We also intend to explore the possible advantages of a more flexible segmentation scheme where the value of gap and lid are not constant throughout the entire netlist. Indeed, by allowing varying gap and lid values, we should be able to generate macro-gates with a narrower size range, leading to an even better thread utilization during simulation.

Related Work

For several decades the majority of the validation effort in industry has revolved around logic simulators. Initial works from the 1980s addressed several key algorithmic aspects that are still utilized in modern commercial solutions, including netlist compilation, scheduling solutions for event-driven simulators, propagation delays, and so on [2, 10]. The exploration of parallel algorithms for simulation started at approximately the same time: Baker *et al.* [1] provide a comparative analysis of early attempts to parallelize event-driven simulation by partitioning the processing of individual events across multiple machines with fine granularity. Both shared memory multiprocessors [9] and distributed memory systems [11] have been targeted as the underlying parallel execution resource.

Only recently the effort of parallelizing simulation algorithms has started to target data-streaming architectures (single-instruction, multiple-data), as in the solution proposed by Perinkulam, *et al.* [13]. However, the communication overhead of that system had a high impact on overall performance, leading to no overall benefit. Another recent solution in this space introduced parallel fault simulation on a CUDA GPU target [7], which derives its parallelism by simulating distinct fault patterns on distinct processing units, with no partitioning within individual simulations, nor in the design. In contrast, we target fast simulation of complex designs, which requires specialized algorithms to partition the netlist and leverages solutions to stress memory locality in order not to lose the performance advantage on memory access latency. We have performed preliminary studies in this direction using oblivious [4] and event-driven [3] simulation architectures. Moreover, we focus on optimizing the performance of individual simulation runs, in contrast with [7], which optimizes over all faults simulations.

Recently, acceleration of many diverse computation-intensive processes using general-purpose graphics processing units (GP-GPU) has been explored, in several domains of EDA, such as power grid analysis [14], statistical timing analysis [8], and fault table generation [6]. Utilizing GP-GPUs to accelerate few core algorithms that are shared across many EDA applications has also been proposed in [5].

References

[1] W. Baker, A. Mahmood, B. Carlson, Parallel event-driven logic simulation algorithms: tutorial and comparative evaluation, IEEE J. Circuits Devices Syst. 143 (4) (1996) 177–185.

[2] Z. Barzilai, J. Carter, B. Rosen, J. Rutledge, HSS–a high-speed simulator, IEEE Trans. Comput. Aided. Des. 6 (4) (1987) 601–617.

[3] D. Chatterjee, A. DeOrio, V. Bertacco, Event-driven gate-level simulation with GP-GPUs, in: Proceedings of the 46th Annual Design Automation Conference, 26–31 July 2009, San Francisco, California, DAC'09, ACM, New York, 2009, pp. 557–562.

[4] D. Chatterjee, A. DeOrio, V. Bertacco, GCS: high-performance gate-level simulation with GP-GPUs, in: Proceedings of the Design, Automation & Test in Europe Conference & Exhibition, 20–24 April 2009, Nice, France, DATE'09, IEEE Computer Society, Washington, DC, 2009, pp. 1332–1337.

[5] Y.S. Deng, B.D. Wang, S. Mu, Taming irregular EDA applications on GPUs, in: Proceedings of the 2009 International Conference on Computer-Aided Design, 02–05 November 2009, San Jose, California, ICCAD'09. ACM, New York, 2009, pp. 539–546.

[6] K. Gulati, S. Khatri, Fault table generation using graphics processing units, in: Proceedings High Level Design Validation and Test Workshop, 2009. 4–6 November 2009, San Francisco, California, HLDVT, IEEE Computer Society, Washington, DC, 2009, pp. 60–67.

[7] K. Gulati, S.P. Khatri, Towards acceleration of fault simulation using graphics processing units, in: Proceedings of the 45th Annual Design Automation Conference, 08–13 June 2008, Anaheim, California, DAC'08. ACM, New York, 2008, pp. 822–827.

[8] K. Gulati, S.P. Khatri, Accelerating statistical static timing analysis using graphics processing units, in: Proceedings of the 2009 Asia and South Pacific Design Automation Conference, 19–22 January 2009, Yokohama, Japan, IEEE Press, Piscataway, NJ, 2009, pp. 260–265.

[9] H.K. Kim, S.M. Chung, Parallel logic simulation using time warp on shared-memory multiprocessors, in: Proceedings of the 8th International Symposium on Parallel Processing, April 1994, Cancún, Mexico, IEEE Computer Society, Washington, DC, 1994, pp. 942–948.

[10] D. Lewis, A hierarchical compiled code event-driven logic simulator, IEEE Trans. Comput. Aided. Des. 10 (6) (1991) 726–737.

[11] Y. Matsumoto, K. Taki, Parallel logic simulation on a distributed memory machine, in: Proceedings of the 3rd European Conference on Design Automation, 16–19 March 1992 Brussels, Belgium, EDAC'92, IEEE Computer Society, Washington, DC, 1992, pp. 76–80.

[12] Opencores, http://www.opencores.org/.

[13] A. Perinkulam, S. Kundu, Logic simulation using graphics processors, in: Proceedings 14th International Test Synthesis Workshop, 5–7 March 2007, San Antonio, Texas, ITSW'07.

[14] J. Shi, Y. Cai, W. Hou, L. Ma, S. X.-D. Tan, P.-H. Ho, et al., GPU friendly fast Poisson solver for structured power grid network analysis, in: Proceedings of the 46th Annual Design Automation Conference, 26–31 July 2009, San Francisco, California, DAC'09, ACM, New York, 2009, pp. 178–183.

[15] Sun microsystems OpenSPARC, http://opensparc.net/.

GPU-Based Parallel Computing for Fast Circuit Optimization

24

Yifang Liu, Jiang Hu

The progress of GPU (graphics processing unit) technology opens a new avenue for boosting computing power. This chapter exploits the GPU to accelerate VLSI circuit optimization. We present GPU-based parallel computing techniques and apply them on solving simultaneous gate sizing and threshold voltage assignment problem, which is often employed in practice for performance and power optimization. These techniques are aimed at utilizing the benefits of GPU through efficient task scheduling and memory organization. Compared against conventional sequential computation, our techniques can provide up to $56\times$ speedup without any sacrifice on solution quality.

24.1 INTRODUCTION, PROBLEM STATEMENT, AND CONTEXT

Fast circuit optimization technique is used during chip design. Although the pressure of time-to-market is almost never relieved, design complexity keeps growing along with transistor count. In addition, more and more issues need to be considered — from conventional objectives like performance and power to new concerns like process variability and transistor aging. On the other hand, the advancement of chip technology opens new avenues for boosting computing power. One example is the amazing progress of GPU technology. In the past five years, the computing performance of GPU has grown from about the same as a CPU to about 10 times that of a CPU in term of GFLOPS [4]. GPU is particularly good at coarse-grained parallelism and data-intensive computations. Recently, GPU-based parallel computation has been successfully applied for the speedup of fault simulation [3] and power-grid simulation [2].

In this work, we propose GPU-based parallel computing techniques for simultaneous gate sizing and threshold voltage assignment. Gate sizing is a classic approach for optimizing performance and power of combinational circuits. Different size implementations of a gate realize the same gate logic, but present a trade-off between the gate's input capacitance and output resistance, thus affecting the signal propagation delay on the gate's fan-in and fan-out paths, as well as the balance between timing performance and power dissipation of the circuit. Threshold voltage (V_t) assignment is a popular technique for reducing leakage power while meeting a timing performance requirement. It is a trade-off factor between the signal propagation delay and power consumption at a gate. Because both of these two circuit optimization methods essentially imply a certain implementation for a logic gate, it is not difficult to perform them simultaneously. It is conceivable that a simultaneous approach is often superior to a separated one in terms of solution quality.

To demonstrate the GPU-based parallelization techniques, we use as an example of the simultaneous gate sizing and V_t assignment problem, which minimizes the power dissipation of a combinational circuit under timing (performance) constraint. The problem is formulated as follows.

Timing-Constrained Power Optimization: Given the netlist of a combinational logic circuit $G(V, E)$, arrival times (AT) at its primary inputs, required arrival times (RAT) at its primary outputs, and a cell library, in which each gate v_i has a size implementation set W_i and a V_t implementation set U_i, select an implementation (a specific size and V_t level) for each gate to minimize the power dissipation under timing constraints, that is,

$$\text{Min:} \sum_{v_i \in V} p(v_i)$$

$$\text{s.t.:} \quad RAT(v_i) \geq AT(v_i), \qquad\qquad \forall v_i \in I(G)$$

$$RAT(v_i) \geq RAT(v_j) + D(v_j, v_i), \qquad \forall (v_j, v_i) \in E$$

$$w_i \in W_i, \qquad\qquad\qquad\qquad \forall v_i \in V$$

$$u_i \in U_i, \qquad\qquad\qquad\qquad \forall v_i \in V$$

where w_i and u_i are the size and the V_t level of gate v_i, respectively, $D(v_j, v_i)$ is the signal propagation delay from gate v_j to gate v_i, p_i is the power consumption at gate v_i, and $I(G)$ is the primary inputs of the circuit.

For the optimization solution, we focus on discrete algorithm because (1) it can be directly applied with cell library-based timing and power models, and (2) V_t assignment is a highly discrete problem. Discrete gate sizing and V_t assignment faces two interdependent difficulties. First, the underlying topology of a combinational circuit is typically a DAG (directed acyclic graph). The path reconvergence of a DAG makes it difficult to carry out a systematic solution search like dynamic programming (DP). Second, the size of a combinational circuit can be very large, sometimes with dozens of thousands of gates. As a result, most of the existing methods are simple heuristics [1]. Recently, a Joint Relaxation and Restriction (JRR) algorithm [5] was proposed to handle the path reconvergence problem and enable a DP-like systematic solution search. Indeed, the systematic search [5] remarkably outperforms its previous work. To address the large problem size, a grid-based parallel gate sizing method was introduced in [10]. Although it can obtain high-solution quality with very fast speed, it concurrently uses 20 computers and entails significant network bandwidth. In contrast, GPU-based parallelism is much more cost-effective. The expense of a GPU card is only a few hundreds of dollars, and the local parallelism obviously causes no overhead on network traffic.

It is not straightforward to map a conventional sequential algorithm onto GPU computation and achieve desired speedup. In general, parallel computation implies that a large computation task needs to be partitioned to many threads. For the partitioning, one needs to decide its granularity levels, balance the computation load, and minimize the interactions among different threads. Managing data and memory is also important. One needs to properly allocate the data storage to various parts of the memory system of a GPU. Apart from general parallel computing issues, the characteristics of the GPU should be taken into account. For example, the parallelization should be SIMD (single instruction multiple data) in order to better exploit the advantages of GPU. In this work, we propose task-scheduling techniques for performing gate-sizing/V_t assignment on the GPU. To the best of our knowledge, this is the first work on GPU-based combinational circuit optimization. In the experiment, we compare our parallel version of the joint relaxation and restriction algorithm [5] with its original sequential implementation. The results show that our parallelization achieves speedup of up to $56\times$ and $39\times$ on average. At the same time, our techniques can retain the exact same solution quality as [5]. Such speedup will allow many systematic optimization approaches, which were slow and previously regarded as impractical, to be widely adopted in realistic applications.

24.2 CORE METHOD

24.2.1 Algorithm for Simultaneous Gate Sizing and V_t Assignment

We briefly review the simultaneous gate sizing and V_t assignment algorithm proposed in [5], because the parallel techniques proposed here are built upon this algorithm. This algorithm has two phases: relaxation phase and restriction phase. It is called Joint Relaxation and Restriction (JRR). Each phase consists of two or more circuit traversals. Each traversal is a solution search in the same spirit as dynamic programming. The main structure of the algorithm is outlined in Algorithm 1. For the ease of description, we call a combination of certain size and V_t level as an implementation of a gate (or a node in the circuit graph).

The relaxation phase includes two circuit traversals: history consistency relaxation and history consistency restoration. The history consistency relaxation is a topological order traversal of the given circuit, from its primary inputs to its primary outputs. In the traversal, a set of partial solutions is propagated. Each solution is characterized by its arrival time (a) and resistance (r). A solution is pruned without further propagation if it is inferior on both a and r. This is very similar to the dynamic programming-based buffer insertion algorithm [10]. However, the topology here is a DAG as opposed to a tree in buffer insertion. Therefore, two fan-in edges e_1 and e_2 of a node v_i may have a common ancestor node v_j. When solutions from e_1 and e_2 are merged, normally one needs to ensure that they are based on the same implementation at v_j. This is called history consistency constraint. When a DP-like algorithm is applied directly on a DAG, this constraint requires all history information to be kept or traced, and consequently causes substantial computation and memory overhead. To overcome this difficulty, Liu and Hu [5] suggest to relax this constraint in the initial traversal; that is, solutions are allowed to be merged even if they are based on different implementations of their common ancestor

---

Algorithm 1:   Outline of the Joint Relaxation and Restriction (JRR) Algorithm.

Phase I: Relaxation
    history consistency relaxation;
    history consistency restoration;
Phase II: Restriction
  repeat
    topological order search;
    reverse topological order search;
  until improvement $< \sigma$ in current iteration;

---

nodes. Although the resulting solutions are not legitimate, they provide a lower bound to the a at each node, which is useful for subsequent solution search.

In the second traversal of the relaxation phase, any history inconsistency resulted from the first iteration is resolved in a reverse topological order, from the primary outputs to the primary inputs. When a node is visited in the traversal, only one implementation is selected for the node. Hence, no history inconsistency should exist after the traversal is completed. The implementation selection at each node is to maximize the timing slack at the node. The slack can be easily calculated by the required arrival time (q), which is propagated along with the traversal, and the a obtained in the previous traversal.

The solution at the end of the relaxation phase can be further improved. This is because the solution is based on the a obtained in the relaxation, which is not necessarily an accurate one. Because of the relaxation, the a is just a lower bound, which implies optimistic deviations. Such deviations are compensated in the restriction phase. In contrast to relaxation, where certain constraints are dropped, restriction imposes additional constraints to a problem. Both relaxation and restriction are for the purpose of making the solution search easy. A restricted search provides a pessimistic bound to the optimal solution. Using pessimistic bounds in the second phase can conceivably compensate the optimistic deviation of the relaxation phase.

The restriction phase consists of multiple circuit traversals with one reverse topological order traversal following each topological order traversal. Each topological order traversal generates a set of candidate solutions at each node, with certain restrictions. Each reverse topological order traversal selects only one solution in the same way as the history consistency restoration traversal in the relaxation phase. A topological order traversal starts with an initial solution inherited from the previous traversal. The candidate solution generation is also similar to the DP-based buffer insertion algorithm. The restriction is that only those candidate solutions based on the initial solution are propagated at every multifan-out node. For example, at a multifan-out node v_i, candidate solutions are generated according to their implementations, but only the candidates that are based on the initial solution of v_i are propagated toward their child nodes. By doing so, the history consistency can be maintained throughout the traversal. The candidate solutions that are not based on the initial solution are useful for the subsequent reverse topological order traversal.

The description so far is for the problem of maximizing timing slack. For problem formulations where timing performance, power consumption, and/or other objectives are considered simultaneously, one can apply the Lagrangian relaxation technique together with the algorithm of Joint Relaxation and Restriction [5].

24.2.2 **GPU-Based Parallelization**

A GPU is usually composed of an array of multiprocessors, and each multiprocessor consists of multiple processing units (or ALUs). Each ALU is associated with a set of local registers, and all the ALUs of a multiprocessor share a control unit and some shared memory. There is normally no synchronization mechanism between different multiprocessors. A typical GPU may have over 100 ALUs. GPU is designed for SIMD parallelism. Therefore, an ideal usage of GPU is to execute identical instructions on a large volume of data, each element of which is processed by one thread.

The software program applied on GPU is called kernel function, which is executed on multiple ALUs in the basic unit of thread. The threads are organized in a two-level hierarchy. Multiple threads form a warp, and a set of warps constitutes a block. All warps of the same block run on the same

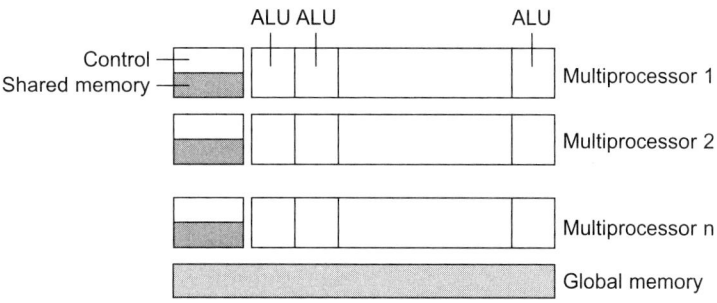

FIGURE 24.1

A generic GPU hardware architecture.

multiprocessor. This organization is for convenience of sharing memory and synchronization among thread executions. The thread blocks are often organized in a three-dimensional grid, just as threads in themselves are. The global memory for a GPU is usually a DRAM off the GPU chip, but on the same board as GPU. The latency of global memory access can be very high, owing to the small cache size. Similarly, loading the kernel function onto the GPU also takes a long time. In order to improve the efficiency of GPU usage, one needs to load data infrequently and make the ALUs dominate the overall program runtime.

Two-Level Task Scheduling: Our GPU-based parallelism for gate sizing and V_t assignment is motivated by the observation that the algorithm repeats a few identical computations on many different gates. When evaluating the effect of an implementation (a specific gate and V_t level) for a gate, we compute its corresponding AT, RAT, and power dissipation. These few computations are repeated for many gates, sometimes hundreds of thousands of gates, and for multiple iterations [5]. Evidently, such repetitive computations on a large number of objects fit very well with SIMD parallelism.

We propose a two-level task-scheduling method that allocates the computations to multiple threads. At the first level, the computations for each gate are allocated to a set of thread blocks. The algorithm, software, and hardware units of this level are gate, thread block, and multiprocessor, respectively. Because different implementations of a gate share the same context (fan-in and fan-out characteristics), such allocation matches the shared context information with the shared memory for each thread block. At the second level, the evaluation of each gate implementation is assigned to a set of threads. The algorithm, software, and hardware units of this level are gate implementation, thread, and ALU, respectively. For each gate, the evaluations for all of its implementation options are independent of each other. Hence, it is convenient to parallelize them on multiple threads. The two-level task scheduling will be described in detail in the subsequent sections.

24.3 ALGORITHMS, IMPLEMENTATIONS, AND EVALUATIONS

24.3.1 Gate-Level Task Scheduling

We describe the gate-level task scheduling in the context of topological order traversal of the circuit. The techniques for reverse topological order traversal are almost the same. In a topological order traversal, a gate is a *processed gate* if the computation of delay/power for all of its implementations is completed. A gate is called a *current gate* if all of its fan-in gates are processed gates. We term a gate as a *prospective gate* when all of its fan-in gates are either current gates or processed gates. In GPU-based parallel computing, multiple current gates can be processed at the same time because there is no inter-dependency among their computations. Current gates are also called *independent current gates* (ICG) because there is no computational interdependency among them. Because of the restriction of GPU computing bandwidth, the number of current gates that can be processed at the same time is limited. A critical problem here is how to select a subset of independent current gates for parallel processing. This subset is designated as *concurrent gate group*, which has a maximum allowed size.

The way of forming a concurrent gate group may greatly affect the efficiency of utilizing the GPU-based parallelism. This can be illustrated by the example in Figure 24.2. In Figure 24.2, the processed gates, independent current gates, and prospective gates are represented by dashed, gray, and white rectangles, respectively. If the maximum group size is four, there could be at least two different ways of forming a concurrent gate group for the scenario of Figure 24.2(a). In Figure 24.2(b), $\{G1, G2, G3, G4\}$ are selected to be the concurrent gate group. After they are processed, any four gates among $\{G5, G6, G7, G8, G9\}$ may become the next concurrent gate group. Alternatively, we can choose $\{G2, G3, G4, G5\}$ as in Figure 24.2(c). However, after $\{G2, G3, G4, G5\}$ are processed, we can include at most three gates $\{G1, G9, G10\}$ for the next concurrent gate group because a fan-in gate for $\{G6, G7, G8\}$ has not been processed yet. The selection of concurrent gates in Figure 24.2(c) is inferior to that in Figure 24.2(b) because Figure 24.2(c) cannot fully utilize the bandwidth of concurrent group size 4.

The problem of finding a concurrent gate group among a set of independent current gates can be formulated as a max-throughput problem, which maximizes the minimum size of all concurrent gate groups. The max-throughput problem is very difficult to solve. Therefore, we will focus on a reduced problem: max-succeeding-group. Given a set of independent current gates, the max-succeeding-group problem asks to choose a subset of them as the concurrent gate group such that the size of the succeeding independent gate group is maximized. We show in the last section of this chapter that the max-succeeding-group problem is NP-complete.

Because the max-succeeding-group problem is NP-complete, we propose a linear-time heuristic to solve it. This heuristic iteratively examines the prospective gates and puts a few independent current gates into the concurrent gate group. For each prospective gate, we check its fan-in gates that are independent current gates. The number of such fan-in gates is called ICG (independent current gate) fan-in size. In each iteration, the prospective gate with the minimum ICG fan-in size is selected. Then, all of its ICG fan-in gates are put into the concurrent gate group. Afterward, the selected prospective gate will no longer be considered in subsequent iterations. At the same time, the selected ICG fan-in gates are not counted in the ICG fan-in size of the remaining prospective gates.

In the example in Figure 24.2, the prospective gate with the minimum ICG fan-in size is $G9$. When it is selected, gate $G3$ is put into the concurrent gate group. Then, the ICG fan-in size of $G7$ becomes 1, which is the minimum. This requires gate $G1$ to be put into the concurrent gate group. Next, any two of $G2$, $G4$, and $G5$ can be selected to form the concurrent gate group of size four.

Here is the rationale behind the heuristic. The maximum allowed size of a concurrent gate group can be treated as a budget. The goal is to maximize the number of succeeding ICGs. If a prospective gate has a small ICG fan-in size, selecting its ICG fan-in gates can increase the number of succeeding ICGs with the minimum usage of concurrent gate group budget.

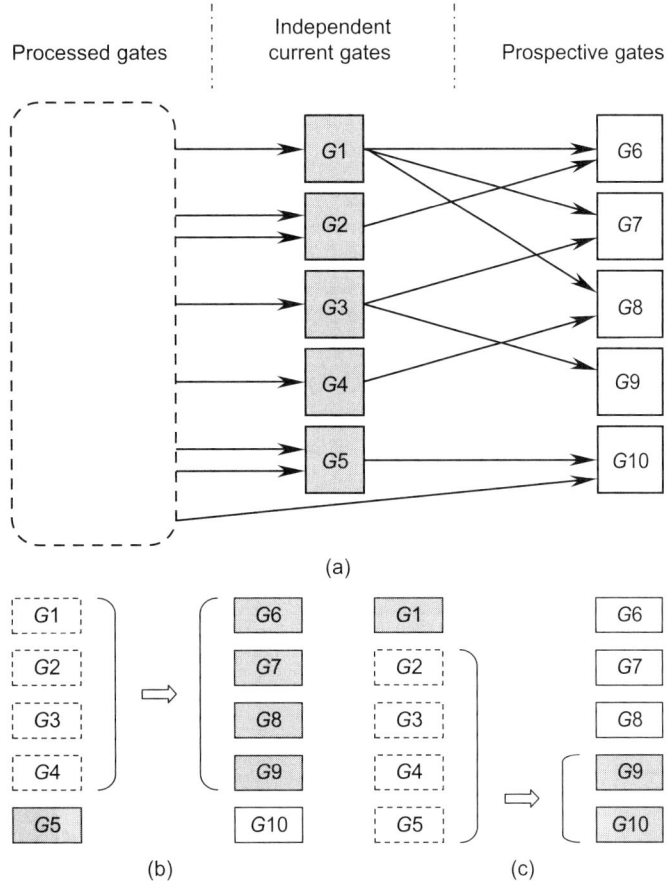

FIGURE 24.2

Processed gates: dashed rectangles; independent current gates: gray rectangles; prospective gates: solid white rectangles. For the scenario in (a), one can choose at most four independent current gates for the parallel processing. In (b): if $G1, G2, G3$, and $G4$ are selected, we may choose another four gates in $G5, G6, G7, G8$, and $G9$ for the next parallel processing. In (c): if $G2, G3, G4$, and $G5$ are selected, only three independent current gates $G1, G9$, and $G10$ are available for the next parallel processing.

This heuristic is performed on the CPU once. The result, which is the gate-level scheduling, is saved because the same schedule is employed repeatedly in the traversals of the JRR algorithm (see Section 2). The pseudocode for the concurrent gate selection heuristic is given in Algorithm 2. The minimum ICG fan-in size is updated each time an ICG fan-in size is updated, so the computation time is dominated by fan-in size updating. If the maximum fan-in size among all gates is F_i, each gate can be updated on its ICG fan-in size for at most F_i times. Thus, the time complexity of this heuristic is $O(|V|F_i)$, where V denotes the set of nodes in the circuit.

Algorithm 2: Concurrent Gate Group Selection.

$\texttt{Input:}$ *current_grp*, *prospective_grp*
$\texttt{Output:}$ *concurrent_grp*

1 *concurrent_grp* ← ∅;
2 $\texttt{repeat}$
3 │ *prop_gate* ← $\texttt{gate}$(*min_ICGfanin*);
4 │ *prospective_grp* ← *prospective_grp* − *prop_gate*;
5 │ *concurrent_grp* ← *concurrent_grp* $\bigcup$($\texttt{inputs}$(*prop_gate*)$\bigcap$*current_grp*);
6 │ *current_grp* ← *current_grp* − $\texttt{inputs}$(*prop_gate*) + *prop_gate*;
7 │ $\texttt{update\_ICGfanin}$ ($\texttt{outputs}$($\texttt{inputs}$(*prop_gate*)));
8 $\texttt{until}$ |*concurrent_grp*| ≥ *concurrent_budget*

24.3.2 Parallel Gate Implementation Evaluation

When processing a gate, we need to evaluate all of its implementations. It is not difficult to see that the evaluations for different implementations of the same gate are independent of each other. Therefore, we can allocate these evaluations into multiple threads without worrying about interdependence. These evaluations include a few common computations: the timing and power estimation for each implementation. Different implementations of the same gate also share some common data such as the parasitics of the fan-in and fan-out. According to this observation, the evaluations of implementations for the same gate are assigned to the same thread block and the same multiprocessor. Because all the ALUs of the same multiprocessor have access to a fast on-chip shared memory (see Figure 24.3), the shared data can be saved in the shared memory to reduce memory access time. Because the evaluation for an implementation of a gate involves computing it with all the implementations of gates on its fan-in.

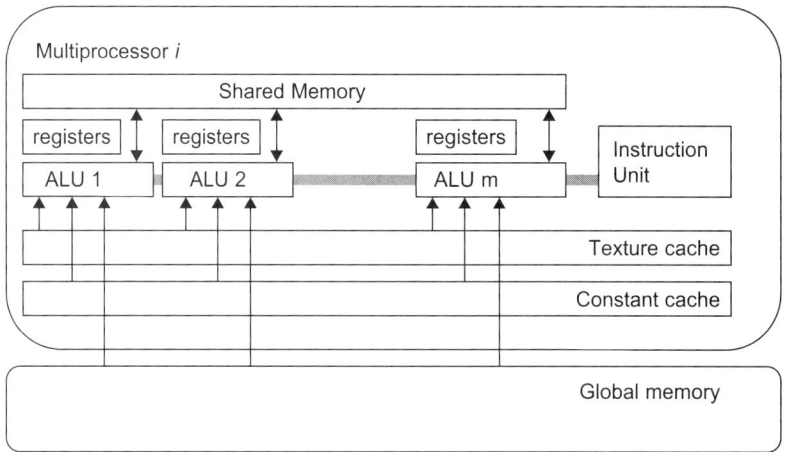

FIGURE 24.3

A multiprocessor with on-chip shared memory. Device memory is connected to the processors through on-chip caches.

Therefore, the number of parallel threads needed in one gate's implementation evaluation is the square of the number of implementations for each gate. For example, in the experiments in the Final Evaluation section, each gate has 24 possible implementations (4 V_t levels and 6 sizes); thus, there are 576 threads in a thread block.

In order to facilitate simultaneous memory access, the shared memory is usually divided into equal-sized banks. Memory requests on addresses that fall in different banks are able to be fulfilled simultaneously, while requested addresses falling in the same bank cause a bank conflict and the conflicting requests have to be serialized. In order to reduce the chance of bank conflict and avoid the cost of serialized access, we store all information of a gate in the same bank and separate it from that of other gates in other banks.

GPU global memory often has a memory-coalescing mechanism for improved access efficiency. When the data of connected gates in the circuit are saved to adjacent locations in the global memory, memory access requests from different threads in a warp would have a greater chance to be coalesced, and the access latency is thereby reduced. However, because of complex multiple-multiple connections between gates in the circuit, it is difficult to achieve efficient coalesced memory access. Therefore, we employ simple random memory access in this work.

GPU global memory contains a constant memory, which is a read-only region. This constant memory can be accessed by all ALUs through a constant cache (see Figure 24.3), which approximately halves the access latency if there is a hit in the cache. We save cell library data, which are constant, in the constant memory so that the data access time can be largely reduced.

Loading the kernel function to GPU can be very time-consuming. Sometimes, the loading time is comparable to time of all computations and memory access for one gate. Therefore, it is highly desirable to reduce the number of calls to the kernel function. Because the computation operations for all gates are the same, we load the computation instructions only once and apply them to all of the gates in the circuit. This is made possible by the fine-grained parallel threads and the precomputed gate-level task schedule (see Section 3.3). In other words, the gate-level task schedule is computed before the circuit optimization and saved in the GPU global memory. Once the kernel function is called, the optimization follows the schedule saved on GPU, and no kernel reloading is needed.

To reduce the idle time of the multiprocessors during memory access, we assign multiple thread blocks to a multiprocessor for concurrent execution. This arrangement has a positive impact on the performance because memory access takes a large portion of the total execution time of the kernel function.

24.4 FINAL EVALUATION

In our experiment, the test cases are the ISCAS85 combinational circuits. They are synthesized by SIS [8] and their global placement is obtained by mPL [9]. The global placement is for the sake of including wire delay in the timing analysis. The cell library is based on 70 nm technology. Each gate has six different sizes and four V_t levels so that it has 24 options of implementation.

In order to test the runtime speedup of our parallel techniques, we compare our parallel version of the JRR algorithm [5] with its original sequential implementation. Regarding solution quality, we compare the results with another previous work [6] in addition to ensuring that the parallel JRR solutions are identical with those of sequential JRR. The method of Nguyen *et al.* [6] starts with gate sizing that maximizes timing slack. Then, the slack is allocated to each gate using a linear programming guided by delay/power sensitivity. The slack allocated to each gate is further converted to power reduction by greedily choosing a gate implementation. We call this a method based on slack allocation (SA). The problem formulation for all these methods is to minimize total power dissipation subject to timing constraints. The power dissipation here includes both dynamic and leakage power. The timing evaluation accounts for both gate and wire delay. Because we do not have lookup table-based timing and power information for the cell library, we use the analytical model for power [5] and the Elmore model for delay computation. However, the JRR algorithm and our parallel techniques can be easily applied with lookup table-based models.

The SA method and sequential JRR algorithm are implemented in C++. The parallel JRR implementation includes two parts: one part is in C++ and runs on the host CPU; the other part runs on the GPU through CUDA (Compute Unified Device Architecture), a parallel programming model and interface developed by NVIDIA [7]. The major components of the parallel programming model and software environment include thread groups, shared memory, and thread synchronization. The experiment was performed on a Windows XP-based machine with an Intel core 2 duo CPU of 2.66 GHz and 2 GB of memory. The GPU is NVIDIA GeForce 9800GT, which has 14 multiprocessors, and each multiprocessor has eight ALUs. The GPU card has 512 MB of off-chip memory. We set the maximum number of gates being parallel processed to four. Therefore, at most, 96 gate implementations are evaluated at one time.

The main results are listed in Table 24.1. Because all of these methods can satisfy the timing constraints, timing results are not included in the table. The solution quality can be evaluated by the results of power dissipation. One can see that JRR can reduce power by about 24% on average when compared with SA [6]. The parallel JRR achieves exactly the same power as the sequential JRR. Our parallel techniques provide runtime speedup from 10× to 56×. One can see that the speedup tends to be more significant when the circuit size grows. One of the reasons is that both small and large circuits have similar overhead for setup.

Table 24.1 Comparison on power (μW) and runtime (seconds). All solutions satisfy timing constraints.

Circuit	No. gates	SA [6]		Sequential JRR [5]		Parallel JRR	
		Power	Runtime	Power	Runtime	Runtime	Speedup
c432	289	703	1.7	701	3.25	0.317	10×
c499	539	1669	4.9	1590	6.27	0.295	21×
c880	340	1817	5.1	1050	3.61	0.328	11×
c1355	579	1385	3.3	1076	7.36	0.218	34×
c1908	722	2502	10.7	2296	9.20	0.327	28×
c2670	1082	3412	18.6	2509	15.70	0.376	42×
c3540	1208	4645	22.3	3830	21.30	0.515	41×
c5315	2440	8406	26.8	5023	64.88	1.156	56×
c6288	2342	13,685	19.2	12,356	53.47	1.295	41×
c7552	3115	9510	46.1	5949	67.44	1.595	42×
Average		4773	15.87	3638	25.25	0.64	39×
Norm.		1.0		0.76			

Figure 24.4 shows the ratio between the GPU runtime and the total runtime. Here, the GPU runtime is the runtime of the code on GPU after it is parallelized from a part of the sequential code. The ratio is mostly between 0.4 and 0.6 among all circuits, which means a majority of the sequential runtime is parallelized into GPU computing. Usually, larger circuits have higher GPU runtime percentage. This may be due to the higher parallel efficiency of larger circuits.

In Figure 24.5, the total runtime and GPU memory usage versus circuit size are plotted to show the runtime and memory scalability of our techniques. The main trend of the runtime curve indicates a linear dependence on circuit size. There are a few nonmonotone parts in the curve that can be explained by the fact that the runtime depends on not only the circuit size but also circuit topology. The memory curve exhibits a strong linear relationship with circuit size. At least for ISCAS85 benchmark circuits, we can conclude that our techniques scale well on both runtime and memory.

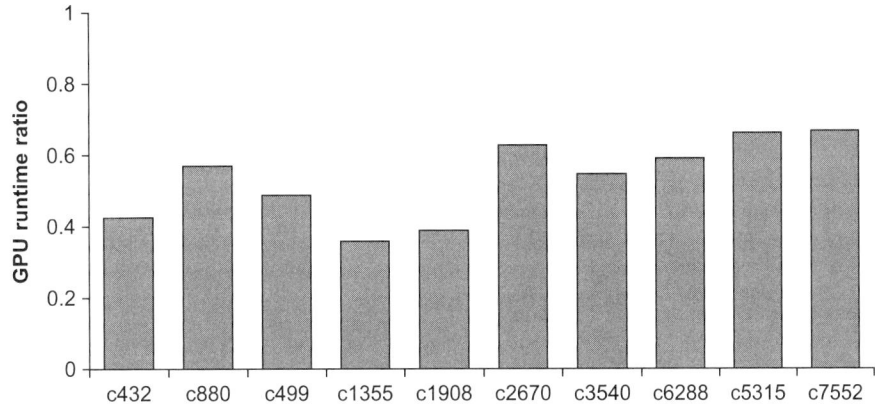

FIGURE 24.4

The ratio of GPU runtime over overall runtime.

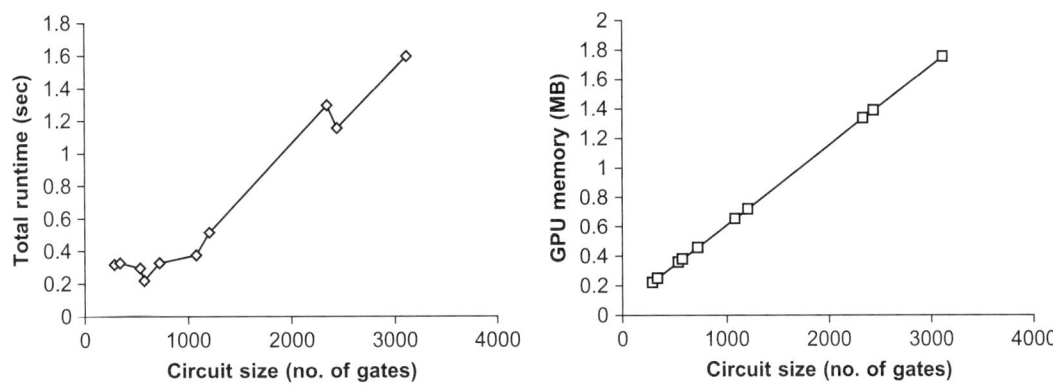

FIGURE 24.5

Runtime and GPU memory scalability.

24.5 FUTURE DIRECTION

It has long been a challenge to optimize a combinational circuit in a systematic, yet fast manner owing to its topological reconvergence and large size. A recent progress [5] suggests an effective solution to the reconvergence problem. This work addresses the large problem size by exploiting GPU-based parallelism. The proposed parallel techniques are integrated with the state-of-the-art gate sizing and V_t assignment algorithm [5]. These techniques and the integration effectively solve the challenge of combinational circuit optimization. A circuit with thousands of gates can be optimized with high quality in less than 2 seconds. The parallel techniques provide up to 56× runtime speedup. They also show an appealing trend that the speedup is more significant on large circuits. In the future, we will test these techniques on larger circuits, for example, circuits with hundreds of thousands of gates.

The problem of simultaneous gate sizing and V_t assignment is used in this work as an example to demonstrate the application of our GPU-based parallelization techniques. However, more general problems in circuit optimization can be solved by these techniques in combination with the optimization algorithm in [5]. Candidate problems, such as technology mapping, voltage assignment, and cell placement, will be explored with the method in future.

NP-Completeness

The NP-completeness of **max-succeeding-group** is proved by reducing the **CLIQUE** problem to an auxiliary problem **MIN-EDGECOVER**, which in turn is reduced to **MIN-DEPCOVER**. Then, we show that MIN-DEPCOVER is equivalent to max-succeeding-group.

Before getting into the first part of our proof, we introduce the concept of edge cover. An edge is covered by a node, if the node is its source or sink. The problem MIN-EDGECOVER asks if b nodes from the node set V in a graph $G(V,E)$ can be selected, such that the number of edges covered by the nodes is at most a.

Lemma 1 **MIN-EDGECOVER** *is NP-complete.*

Proof. First, MIN-EDGECOVER $\in$ NP, because checking if a set of b nodes covers at most a edges takes linear time.

Second, MIN-EDGECOVER is NP-hard, because CLIQUE is polynomial-time reducible to MIN-EDGECOVER, i.e., CLIQUE $\leq_P$ MIN-EDGECOVER. We construct a function to transform a CLIQUE problem to a MIN-EDGECOVER problem. For a problem that asks if a b-node complete subgraph can be found in $G(V,E)$, the corresponding MIN-EDGECOVER problem is whether there exists a set of $|V| - b$ nodes in $G(V,E)$ that covers at most $|E| - b(b-1)/2$ edges. If the answer to the first question is true, then the $|V| - b$ nodes apart from the b nodes in the complete subgraph found in the first question are nodes that cover the $|E| - b(b-1)/2$ edges outside the complete subgraph. In this case, the answer to the second question is also true. On the other hand, if the answer to the second question is true, then at least $b(b-1)/2$ edges other than the $|E| - b(b-1)/2$ edges found in second question are between the rest b nodes. Then, the b nodes make a complete graph. Thus, the answer to the first question is true. Therefore, the answer to each of the two aforementioned problems is true if and only if the answer to the other is positive, too.

Because of the simple arithmetic calculation, the transform of the aforementioned reduction clearly runs in $O(1)$ time. Therefore, CLIQUE $\leq_P$ MIN-EDGECOVER.

By the preceding two steps of reasoning, it is proved that MIN-EDGECOVER problem is NP-complete. ∎

Next, in the second part of our proof, we show that MIN-EDGECOVER is polynomial-time reducible to the problem MIN-DEPCOVER, which is equivalent to MAX-INDEPSET. An independent graph is a directed graph $G(V, E')$ with two sets of nodes V_1 and V_2 ($V = V_1 \bigcup V_2$, $V_1 \bigcap V_2 = \emptyset$), and every edge $e' \in E'$ originates from a node in V_1 and ends at a node in V_2. A node v_2 in V_2 is said to be dependently covered by a node v_1 in V_1, if there is an edge from v_1 to v_2. MIN-DEPCOVER asks if a set of b nodes can be selected from V_1, so that at most a nodes in V_2 are dependently covered.

Lemma 2 MIN-DEPCOVER *is NP-complete.*

Proof. First, MIN-DEPCOVER $\in$ NP, because checking if a set of b nodes in V_1 dependently cover at most a nodes in V_2 takes polynomial time.

Second, we verify that MIN-DEPCOVER is NP-hard by showing MIN-EDGECOVER $\leq_P$ MIN-DEPCOVER. We transform any given MIN-EDGECOVER problem on $G(V, E)$ into a MIN-DEPCOVER problem on $G(V_1 \bigcup V_2, E')$. Each node in V corresponds to a node in V_1, and each edge in E corresponds to a node in V_2. An edge $e' \in E'$ from node $v_1 \in V_1$ to $v_2 \in V_2$ exists if and only if the node v corresponding to v_1 is adjacent to the edge e corresponding to v_2. If the answer to the first question is true, then there are b nodes in V_1 that dependently cover at most a nodes in V_2, therefore, the answer to the second question is true, too. And vice versa, if the answer to the second question is true, then there are b nodes in V that cover at most a edges corresponding to a nodes in V_2. So the answer to the first question is true. Therefore, each of the positive answers to the two problems holds if and only if the other one holds.

During the construction of the corresponding MIN-DEPCOVER problem, given a MIN-EDGECOVER problem, going through every edge in $G(V, E)$ and its adjacent nodes takes $O(E)$ time. So the transform takes polynomial time. Consequently, MIN-EDGECOVER $\leq_P$ MIN-DEPCOVER.

By the two steps of reasoning that we just described, it is proved that MIN-DEPCOVER problem is NP-complete. ∎

In the final part of our proof, we show that max-succeeding-group problem is NP-complete. Before getting into it, we review the concept in max-succeeding-group problem. The decision problem of max-succeeding-group asks if a set of b gates from current gate group can be chosen as concurrent gate group so that the size of the succeeding independent group is at least a.

Theorem 1 max-succeeding-group is NP-complete.

Proof. First, max-succeeding-group $\in$ NP because it takes polynomial time to check if a set of b independent gates enable at least a prospective gates to become independent gates.

Second, we verify that max-succeeding-group is NP-hard by showing MIN-DEPCOVER $\leq_P$ max-succeeding-group. It is true simply because max-succeeding-group is equivalent to MIN-DEPCOVER. The situation that at least a gates in the prospective group are made independent by selecting b gates from the independent current set is the same as the situation that at most $|prospective\_group| - a$ gates in the prospective group are prevented from becoming independent gates by excluding $|independent\_current\_group| - b$ independent gates from entering the concurrent group. The two aforementioned statements above are sufficient and necessary conditions to each other because they are equivalent.

Clearly, the preceding transform takes $O(1)$ time; therefore, MIN-DEPCOVER $\leq_P$ max-succeeding-group.

By the two steps of reasoning above, it is proved that max-succeeding-group problem is NP-complete. ∎

In fact, the NP-completeness of MAX-THROUGHPUT can be verified by a straightforward polynomial-time transform that reduces max-succeeding-group to MAX-THROUGHPUT.

References

[1] O. Coudert, Gate sizing for constrained delay/power/area optimization, IEEE Trans. Very Large Scale Integr. Syst. 5 (4) (1997) 465–472.

[2] Z. Feng, P. Li, Multigrid on GPU: tackling power grid analysis on parallel SIMT platforms, in: ICCAD '08: Proceedings of the 2008 IEEE/ACM International Conference on Computer-Aided Design, IEEE Press, Piscataway, NJ, 2008, pp. 647–654.

[3] K. Gulati, S. Khatri, Towards acceleration of fault simulation using graphics processing units, in: DAC '08: Proceedings of the 45th Annual Design Automation Conference, ACM, New York, 2008, pp. 822–827.

[4] J. Owens, D. Luebke et al., A survey of general-purpose computation on graphics hardware, in: Eurographics '05: Proceedings of 2005 Eurographics, Eurographics Association, 1207 Geneve, Switzerland.

[5] Y. Liu, J. Hu, A new algorithm for simultaneous gate sizing and threshold voltage assignment, in: ISPD '09: Proceedings of the 2009 International Symposium on Physical Design, ACM, New York, pp. 27–34.

[6] D. Nguyen, A. Davare et al., Minimization of dynamic and static power through joint assignment of threshold voltages and sizing optimization, in: ISLPED '03: Proceedings of the 2003 International Symposium on Low Power Electronics and Design, ACM, New York, 2003, pp. 158–163.

[7] NVIDIA CUDA homepage, http://www.nvidia.com/.

[8] E.M. Sentovich, SIS: A System for Sequential Circuit Synthesis, Memorandum No. UCB/ERL M92/41, UCB Memorandum, University of California, Berkeley, 1992.

[9] UCLA. CPMO-constrained placement by multilevel optimization, University of California at Los Angeles, http://ballade.cs.ucla.edu/cpmo.

[10] L. Van Ginneken, Buffer placement in distributed RC-tree networks for minimal elmore delay, in: ISCS '90: Proceedings of the 1990 International Symposium on Circuits and Systems, IEEE Press, Piscataway, NJ, 1990.

[11] T.-H. Wu, A. Davoodi, Pars: fast and near-optimal grid-based cell sizing for library-based design, in: ICCAD '08: Proceedings of the 2008 IEEE/ACM International Conference on Computer-Aided Design, IEEE Press, Piscataway, NJ, 2008, pp. 107–111.

Ray Tracing and Rendering
Area Editor's Introduction

Austin Robison

25 Lattice Boltzmann Lighting Models 381

26 Path Regeneration for Random Walks... 401

27 From Sparse Mocap to Highly Detailed Facial Animation 413

28 A Programmable Graphics Pipeline in CUDA for Order-Independent Transparency 427

THE STATE OF GPU COMPUTING IN RAY TRACING AND RENDERING

We are on the cusp of a rendering renaissance. Although GPUs have traditionally been used to drive hardware rasterization pipelines, and GPU computing has ventured into many different fields as a general computing platform, it is not to be forgotten that computer graphics stands to greatly benefit from these new programming models.

As GPUs continue to become more powerful and flexible, we will see an explosion of hybrid rendering techniques running on these processors: graphics pipelines that do not rely on a single rendering algorithm to produce their final images, but rather use the algorithms that are best suited to the needs of the desired images. As we are more and more able to use the right rendering tool for the job, the results will be spectacular, and GPUs will take us there.

We have begun to see the components of these pipelines being created, several of which are detailed in this section, and as new algorithms are developed, we will continue to experience increases in rendering quality and speed, enabling a new generation of fantastic imagery.

IN THIS SECTION

Chapter 25, written by Geist and Westall, describes a method using Lattice Boltzmann methods for simulating light transport. The work formulates the scattering of photons through a scene as a diffusion process that can be efficiently solved in parallel on the GPU.

In Chapter 26, Novak *et al.* describe a system for efficiently implementing randomized walks on the wide execution units of the GPU. They combat the main problem of these randomized walks, low processor utilization, by regenerating paths on the fly in otherwise terminated threads and apply the result to path tracing.

Bickel and Lang, in Chapter 27, describe an animation system that combines sparse motion-capture data with fine wrinkle models to produce realistic facial animation. By parallelizing the operations required to construct a facial animation and running on the GPU, real-time rates are achieved.

Chapter 28, by Huang *et al.* describes a rasterization pipeline implemented in CUDA. This pipeline, similar to traditional hardware rasterization pipelines, renders triangles at real-time rates and is specifically optimized for handling order-independent transparency.

Lattice Boltzmann Lighting Models

25

Robert Geist, James Westall

In this chapter, we present a GPU-based implementation of a photon transport model that is particularly effective in global illumination of participating media, including atmospheric geometry such as clouds, smoke, and haze, as well as densely placed translucent surfaces. The model provides the "perfect" GPU application in the sense that the kernel code can be structured to minimize control flow divergence and yet avoid all memory bank conflicts and uncoalesced accesses to global memory. Thus, the speedups over single-core CPU execution are dramatic. Example applications include clouds, plants, and plastics.

25.1 INTRODUCTION, PROBLEM STATEMENT, AND CONTEXT

Quickly and accurately capturing the the process of light scattering in a volume filled with a participating medium remains a challenging problem, but often it is one that must be solved to achieve photo-realistic rendering. The scattering process can be adequately described by the standard volume radiative transfer equation

$$(\vec{\omega} \cdot \bigtriangledown + \sigma_t) L(\vec{x}, \vec{\omega}) = \sigma_s \int p(\vec{\omega}, \vec{\omega}') L(\vec{x}, \vec{\omega}') d\vec{\omega}' + Q(\vec{x}, \vec{\omega}) \tag{25.1}$$

where $\vec{x}$ is a position in space, $\vec{\omega}$ is a spherical direction, $p(\vec{\omega}, \vec{\omega}')$ is the phase function, σ_s is the scattering coefficient, σ_a is the absorption coefficient, $\sigma_t = \sigma_s + \sigma_a$ is the extinction coefficient, and $Q(\vec{x}, \vec{\omega})$ is any emissive field within the volume [1]. This simply says that the change in radiance along any path includes the loss due to absorption and out-scattering (coefficient $-\sigma_t$) and the gain due to in-scattering from other paths (coefficient σ_s).

Radiative transfer in volumes is a well-studied topic, and many methods for solving Eq. 25.1 have been suggested. Most are a variation on one of a few central themes. Rushmeier and Torrance [25] used a *radiosity* (finite-element) technique to model energy exchange between environmental zones and hence capture isotropic scattering. Their method requires computing form factors between all pairs of volume elements. Bhate and Tokuta [2] extended this approach to anisotropic scattering, at the cost of additional form-factor computation.

The most popular approach is undoubtedly the *discrete ordinates method* [3] in which Eq. 25.1 is discretized to a spatial lattice with a fixed number of angular directions in which light may propagate.

The need to compute only local lattice point interactions, rather than form factors between all volumes, substantially reduces the computational complexity. Max [21] and Languénou *et al.* [20] were able to capture anisotropic effects using early variations on this technique. It is well known, however, that this discretization leads to two types of potentially visible errors: (1) light smearing caused by repeated interpolations and (2) spurious beams, called the ray effect. Fattal [8] has recently suggested a method that significantly ameliorates both. Successive iteration across six collections of 2-D maps of rays, along which light is propagated, is employed. The 2-D maps are detached from the 3-D lattice, thus allowing a much finer granularity in the angular discretization. Execution time for grids of reasonable size (e.g., 128^3) is several minutes. Kaplanyan and Dachsbacher [17] have recently provided a real-time variation on the discrete ordinates method that is principally aimed at single-bounce, indirect illumination. The method propagates virtual point lights along axial cells by projecting illumination to the walls of an adjacent cell and then constructing a new point light in the adjacent cell that would deliver exactly that effect. It is not immune to either light smearing or the ray effect, and thus the authors restrict its use to low-frequency lighting. The method is extremely fast, largely owing to relatively low-resolution nested grids that are fixed in camera space and give higher resolution close to the viewer.

A third central theme, and that to which our own method may be attached, is the *diffusion approximation*. Stam [27], motivated by earlier work of Kajiya and Von Herzen [16] in lighting clouds, observed that a two-term Taylor expansion of diffuse intensity in the directional component only could be substituted into Eq. 25.1 to ultimately yield a diffusion process that is an accurate approximation for highly scattering (optically thick) media. Jensen *et al.* [15] showed that a simple two-term approximation of radiance naturally leads to a diffusion approximation that is appropriate for a highly scattering medium. This was later extended to include thin translucent slabs and multilayered materials [7].

In [11] we introduced an approach to solving Eq. 25.1 based on a Lattice Boltzmann technique and showed how this might be applied to lighting participating media such as clouds, smoke, and haze. In [12] we extended this approach to capture diffuse transmission, interobject scattering, and ambient occlusion, such as needed in photo-realistic rendering of dense forest ecosystems. Most recently, we showed that the technique could be parameterized to allow real-time relighting of scenes in response to movement of light sources [28].

As originally described in [11], the technique was effective, but slow. The technique is grid based, and a steady-state solution for a grid of reasonable size (128^3 nodes) originally required more than 30 minutes on a single CPU. Our goal here is to provide the details of a GPU-based implementation that, for this same size grid, will run on a single GPU in 2 seconds. Example lighting tasks will include clouds, plants, and plastics.

25.2 CORE METHODS

Lattice Boltzmann (LB) methods are a particular class of *cellular automata* (CA), a collection of computational structures that can trace their origin at least back to John Conway's famous *Game of Life* [10], which models population changes in a hypothetical society that is geographically located on a rectangular grid. In Conway's game, each grid site follows only local rules, based on nearest-neighbor population, in synchronously updating itself as populated or not, and yet global behavior emerges in the form of both steady-state colonies and migrating bands of "beings" who can generate new colonies or destroy existing ones.

Arbitrary graphs and sets of rules for local updates can be postulated in a general CA, but those that are most interesting exhibit a global behavior that has some provable characteristic. Lattice Boltzmann methods also employ synchronous, neighbor-only update rules on a discrete grid, but the discrete populations have been replaced by continuous distributions of some quantity of interest. The result is that the provable characteristic is often quite powerful: the system is seen to converge, as lattice spacing and time step approach zero, to a solution of a targeted class of partial differential equations (PDEs).

Lattice Boltzmann methods are thus often regarded as computational alternatives to finite-element methods (FEMs) for solving coupled systems of PDEs. The methods have provided significant successes in modeling fluid flows and associated transport phenomena [4, 13, 26, 29, 31]. They provide stability, accuracy, and computational efficiency comparable to finite-element methods, but they realize significant advantages in ease of implementation, parallelization, and an ability to handle interfacial dynamics and complex boundaries.

The principal drawback to the methods, compared with FEMs, is the counterintuitive direction of the derivation they require. Differential equations describing the macroscopic system behavior are derived (emerge) from a postulated computational update (the local rules), rather than the reverse. Thus, a relatively simple computational method must be justified by a derivation that is often fairly intricate.

In the section titled "Derivation of the Diffusion Equation," we provide the derivation of the parameterized diffusion equation for our lighting model. On one hand, the derivation itself is totally irrelevant to the implementation of the LB lighting technique proposed here, and users of the technique may feel free to skip it entirely. On the other hand, if the processes of interest to the user vary, beyond simple parameter changes, from our basic diffusion process, a new derivation will be required, and it is extremely valuable to have such a sample derivation at hand.

25.3 ALGORITHMS, IMPLEMENTATION, AND EVALUATION

Lattice Boltzmann methods are grid based, and so, we begin with a standard 3-D lattice, a rectangular collection of points with integer coordinates in 3-D space. A complication of LB methods in three dimensions is that isotropic flow, whether it is water or photon density, requires that all neighboring lattice points of any site (lattice point) be equidistant. A standard approach, owing to d'Humières, Lallemand, and Frisch [6], is to use 24 points equidistant from the origin in 4-D space and project onto 3-D. The points are:

$$(\pm 1, 0, 0, \pm 1) \quad (0, \pm 1, \pm 1, 0) \quad (0, \pm 1, 0, \pm 1)$$
$$(\pm 1, 0, \pm 1, 0) \quad (0, 0, \pm 1, \pm 1) \quad (\pm 1, \pm 1, 0, 0)$$

and projection is truncation of the fourth component, which yields 18 directions, that is, the vectors from the origin in 3-D space to each of the projected points. Axial directions then receive double weights. Representation of several phenomena, including energy absorption and energy transmission, is facilitated by adding a direction from each lattice point back to itself, which thus yields 19 directions, the non-corner lattice points of a cube of unit radius.

The key quantity of interest is the per-site photon density. We store this value at each lattice point and then simulate transport by synchronously updating all the values in discrete time steps according to a single update rule. Let $f_m(\vec{r}, t)$ denote the density at lattice site $\vec{r} \in \Re^3$ at simulation time t that is moving in cube direction $\vec{c}_m$, $m \in \{0, 1, \dots, 18\}$. If the lattice spacing is λ and the simulation time step is τ, then the update (local rule) is:

$$f_m(\vec{r} + \lambda\vec{c}_m, t + \tau) - f_m(\vec{r}, t) = \Omega_m \cdot f(\vec{r}, t) \tag{25.2}$$

where Ω_m denotes row m of a 19×19 matrix, Ω, that describes scattering, absorption, and (potentially) wavelength shift at each site. If $\rho(\vec{r}, t) = \sum_m f_m(\vec{r}, t)$ denotes total site density, then the derivation in the the section titled "Derivation of the Diffusion Equation" shows that the limiting case of Eq. 25.2 as $\lambda, \tau \to 0$ is the diffusion equation

$$\frac{\partial \rho}{\partial t} = D \nabla_{\vec{r}}^2 \rho \tag{25.3}$$

where the diffusion coefficient

$$D = \left(\frac{\lambda^2}{\tau}\right)\left[\frac{(2/\sigma_t) - 1}{4(1 + \sigma_a)}\right] \tag{25.4}$$

As noted, this is consistent with previous approaches to modeling multiple photon scattering events [15, 27], which have invariably led to diffusion processes.

For any Lattice Boltzmann method, the choice of the so-called collision matrix, Ω, is not unique. Standard constraints are conservation of mass, $\sum_m (\Omega_m \cdot f) = 0$, and conservation of momentum, $\sum_m (\Omega_m \cdot f)\vec{v}_m = \tau\vec{F}$, where $\vec{v}_m = (\lambda/\tau)\vec{c}_m$ and $\vec{F}$ represents any site external force. Here, as in [11–13, 28], for the case of isotropic scattering, we specify Ω as follows:

For row 0:

$$\Omega_{0j} = \begin{cases} -1 & j = 0 \\ \sigma_a & j > 0 \end{cases} \tag{25.5}$$

For the axial rows, $i = 1, \dots, 6$:

$$\Omega_{ij} = \begin{cases} 1/12 & j = 0 \\ \sigma_s/12 & j > 0, \quad j \neq i \\ -\sigma_t + \sigma_s/12, & j = i \end{cases} \tag{25.6}$$

For the nonaxial rows, $i = 7, \dots, 18$:

$$\Omega_{ij} = \begin{cases} 1/24 & j = 0 \\ \sigma_s/24 & j > 0, \quad j \neq i \\ -\sigma_t + \sigma_s/24, & j = i \end{cases} \tag{25.7}$$

Entry i, j controls scattering from direction $\vec{c}_j$ into direction $\vec{c}_i$, and thus the nondiagonal entries are scaled values of the scattering coefficient for the medium, σ_s. Diagonal entries must include out-scattering, $-\sigma_t$, and, as noted earlier, isotropic flow requires double weights (scale factors) on the axial directions. Directional density f_0 holds the absorption/emission component. On update, that is, $\Omega \cdot f$, fraction σ_a from each directional density will be moved into f_0. The entries of Ω are then multiplied by the density of the medium at each lattice sight so that a zero density yields a pass-through in Eq. 25.2, and a density of 1 yields a full scattering.

Of course, in general, scattering is anisotropic and wavelength dependent. Anisotropic scattering is incorporated by multiplying σ_s that appears in entry $\Omega_{i,j}$ by a normalized phase function:

$$pn_{i,j}(g) = \frac{p_{i,j}(g)}{\left(\sum_{i=1}^{6} 2p_{i,j}(g) + \sum_{i=7}^{18} p_{i,j}(g)\right)/24} \tag{25.8}$$

where $p_{i,j}(g)$ is a discrete version of the Henyey-Greenstein phase function [14],

$$p_{i,j}(g) = \frac{1 - g^2}{(1 - 2g\vec{n}_i \cdot \vec{n}_j + g^2)^{3/2}} \tag{25.9}$$

Here $\vec{n}_i$ is the normalized direction, $\vec{c}_i$. Parameter $g \in [-1, 1]$ controls scattering direction. Value $g > 0$ provides forward scattering, $g < 0$ provides backward scattering, and $g = 0$ yields isotropic. Mie scattering [9] is generally considered preferable, but the significant approximations induced here by a relatively coarse grid render the additional complexity unwarranted. Note that Eq. 25.8, which first appeared in [12], differs from the treatment in [11], in that setting $\sigma_a = 0$ and $g = 1$ yields an effect that is identical to a pass-through.

If the media in the model are presumed to interact with all light wavelengths in an identical way, then $f_m(\vec{r}, t)$ can be considered to be the luminance density. In our cloud lighting example of Section 25.3.2, this is the case.

Otherwise, as in our other examples, each discrete wavelength to be modeled is characterized by appropriate scattering parameters and phase function. The Lattice Boltzmann model is run once for each parameter set, and the results are combined in a post-processing (ray-tracing) step.

An alternative approach is to implement $\vec{f}_m(\vec{r}, t)$ as a vector of per-wavelength densities and run the model one time. This approach can be used to incorporate wavelength shifts during the collision process.

The model is thus completely specified by a choice of g, σ_a, and σ_s, any of which can be wavelength-dependent.

Initial conditions include zero photon density in all directions at all interior nodes in the lattice. For each node in the lattice boundary, directions that have positive dot products with the external light source direction will receive initial photon densities that are proportional to these dot products. These directional photon densities on boundary nodes are fixed for the duration of the execution. Any flow (movement of photon density) into a boundary node is ignored, as is any flow out of a boundary node that goes off lattice.

25.3.1 An OpenCL Implementation

The fundamental update in Eq. 25.2 must be synchronous. Each lattice site must read 19 values and write 19 values at each time step, but the layout is particularly well suited to GPU architectures in that there is no overlap in sites read or sites written between or among sites. We have implemented kernels for the update in both CUDA and OpenCL for the NVIDIA GTX 480, and we find, after optimizations of both, essentially no speed difference. Thus, in the interest of greater portability, we present the OpenCL solution here.

We use two copies of the directional densities, $f_m(\vec{r},t)$, and ping-pong between them as we advance the time step, t. Experience indicates that a final time of $n \times \tau$, where n is twice the longest edge dimension of the lattice, will suffice to achieve near-equilibrium values.

Both the collision matrix, Ω, and the per-site density of the medium are constant for the duration of the computation. The Ω matrix, which is 19×19, easily fits in constant memory, and so we can take advantage of the caching effects there. The medium density is one float per lattice site, which is too large for constant memory, but each lattice site reads only one medium density value per update, and that value can be stored in a register.

In addition to storage for Ω and storage for the per-site medium density, GPU-side storage includes two arrays for the flows:

```
cl_mem focl[2][WIDTH*HEIGHT*DEPTH*DIRECTIONS];
```

and a single integer array

```
dist[WIDTH*HEIGHT*DEPTH*DIRECTIONS];
```

which holds, for each lattice site and each direction, the flow array index where exiting flow should be placed. The values for *dist[ ]* can be calculated and stored by the CPU during initialization.

On the CPU side, the entire update, using kernel *mykrn_update*, command queue *mycq*, and lattice dimension *LDIM* is then given by:

```
void run_updates()
{
int t, from = 0;
cl_event wait[1];

for(t=0;t<FINAL_TIME;t++,from = 1-from){
    clSetKernelArg(mykrn_update,0,sizeof(cl_mem),(void *)&focl[from]);
    clSetKernelArg(mykrn_update,1,sizeof(cl_mem),(void *)&focl[1-from]);
    clEnqueueNDRangeKernel(mycq,mykrn_update,3,0,ws,lws,0,0,&wait[0]);
    clWaitForEvents(1,wait);
    }
clEnqueueReadBuffer(mycq,focl[from],CL_TRUE,0,LDIM*sizeof(float),&f[0],
  0,NULL,NULL);
return;
}
```

The work size, *ws*, is a three-dimensional integer vector with value (WIDTH, HEIGHT, DEPTH), the dimensions of the the grid. The local work size, *lws*, which specifies threads per scheduled block, is (1, 1, DEPTH), for reasons to be specified shortly.

A naive but conceptually straightforward kernel is then given by

```
__kernel void update(__global float* from, __global float* to,__global
  int* dist, __global float* omega, __global float* density)
{
int i = get_global_id(0);
int j = get_global_id(1);
int k = get_global_id(2);
```

```
int m, n;
float medium_density, new_flow;

medium_density = density(i,j,k);
for(m=0;m<DIRECTIONS;m++){
  new_flow = 0.0f;
  for(n=0;n<DIRECTIONS;n++) new_flow += omega(m,n)*from(i,j,k,n);
  to[dist(i,j,k,m)] = from(i,j,k,m) + new_flow*medium_density;
  }
}
```

The *from* and *to* arguments hold addresses of the two copies of the flow values. Macros *from(i,j,k,n)*, *dist(i,j,k,m)*, and *omega(m,n)* simply provide convenient indexing into the arrays of the same names, which are necessarily one-dimensional in GPU storage. Both the *from* and *to* arrays hold an extra index, a "sink," and if the exiting flow from any site in any direction would be off lattice, the value of the *dist(i,j,k,m)* index is this "sink."

This kernel is attractive in its simplicity, and it offers zero control flow divergence because there are no conditionals. Nevertheless, although the kernel will produce correct results, its performance advantage over a CPU implementation is modest. For the $256 \times 128 \times 128$ array used in the first example of the next section, a CPU implementation running on an Intel i7 X980 3.33 GHz processor required 19.5 minutes. The OpenCL implementation with this kernel required 2.8 minutes. With kernel modifications, the total execution time can be reduced to 6 seconds, of which 1 second is CPU initialization and 5 seconds are GPU execution.

The first important modification is to avoid reloading the values, *from(i,j,k,n)*, from global device memory. Instead, we force storage into registers by declaring 19 local variables,

```
float f00, f01, ..., f18
```

We then load each directional value once, unroll the interior loop, and use these local variable values instead of *from(i,j,k,n)*.

The second important modification is to rearrange storage to facilitate coalescing of memory requests. Because we have WIDTH×HEIGHT×DEPTH lattice sites, and each of these has 19 DIRECTIONS, it is natural to access linear storage as

```
from[(((((i)*HEIGHT+(j))*DEPTH+(k))*DIRECTIONS+(m))]
```

but this leads to relatively poor performance. Instead, since DEPTH is usually a large power of 2, we interchange DEPTH and DIRECTIONS so that the DEPTH index varies most rapidly in linear storage:

```
from[(((((i)*HEIGHT+(j))*DIRECTIONS+(m))*DEPTH+(k))]
```

This rearrangement applies to both copies of the photon density values, *focl[2]*, and the integer *dist[]* array.

The third modification, though least important in terms of performance gained, is probably the most surprising. Performance improves when we add conditionals and extra computation to this kernel! In particular, if we eliminate the *dist[]* array, instead pass only the 19 directions, and calculate the indices for the exiting photon density on the fly, performance improves by a small amount. The conditionals and the index computations, which are required to avoid indices that would be off lattice, are less expensive than accesses to the global *dist[]* array. Because flow divergence then occurs only between boundary nodes and interior nodes, and we place each DEPTH stripe in a single thread block using local work size (1, 1, DEPTH), the effect of divergence is really minimal.

The final kernel is then given by

```
#define nindex(i,j,k) (((i)*HEIGHT+(j))*DEPTH+(k))
#define bindex(i,j,k) ((((i)*HEIGHT+(j))*DIRECTIONS*DEPTH)+(k))
#define dindex(i,j,k,m) (((((i)*HEIGHT+(j))*DIRECTIONS+(m))*DEPTH+(k))
#define inbounds(q,r,s) ((q>0)&&(q<(WIDTH-1))&&(r>0)&&(r<(HEIGHT-1))&&\
    (s>0)&&(s<(DEPTH-1)))

__kernel void update(__global float* from,__global float* to,__constant
    int* direction, __constant float* omega,__global float* density)
{
const int i = get_global_id(0);
const int j = get_global_id(1);
const int k = get_global_id(2);
const int lnindex = nindex(i,j,k);
const int lbindex = bindex(i,j,k);
int m;
float cloud_density, new_flow;
float f00, f01, f02, f03, ..., f18;
int outi, outj, outk;

cloud_density = density[lnindex];
f00 = from[lbindex+0*DEPTH];
f01 = from[lbindex+1*DEPTH];
f02 = from[lbindex+2*DEPTH];
f03 = from[lbindex+3*DEPTH];
...
f18 = from[lbindex+18*DEPTH];

for(m=0;m<DIRECTIONS;m++){
     outi = i+direction[3*m+0];
     outj = j+direction[3*m+1];
     outk = k+direction[3*m+2];
     if(inbounds(outi,outj,outk)){
          new_flow = 0.0f;
          new_flow += omega(m,0)*f00;
          new_flow += omega(m,1)*f01;
          new_flow += omega(m,2)*f02;
          new_flow += omega(m,3)*f03;
          ...
          new_flow += omega(m,18)*f18;
          to[dindex(outi,outj,outk,m)] = from[lbindex+m*DEPTH] +
               new_flow*cloud_density;
     }
   }
}
```

Profiling this kernel shows 100% coalesced global memory reads and writes and an occupancy of 0.5. Transfer from/to global memory is measured at 67 GB/sec., which is a significant portion of the available bandwidth for the GTX 480 as reported by the *oclBandwidthTest* utility, 115 GB/sec. Note that this does not include transfer from (cached) constant memory, which is significantly larger, 718 GB/sec.

On devices of lower compute capability, this kernel can generate a significant number of unco-alesced global memory writes. Nevertheless, with a simple kernel modification we can force these writes to be coalesced as well. Because we use a local work size vector of (1, 1, DEPTH), we can collect DEPTH output values, one for each *outk*, in a local (shared) memory array of size DEPTH, synchronize the threads using a *barrier()* command, and then write the entire DEPTH stripe in order. The final kernel, revised for this lower compute capability, is then:

```
#define nindex(i,j,k) (((i)*HEIGHT+(j))*DEPTH+(k))
#define bindex(i,j,k) ((((i)*HEIGHT+(j))*DIRECTIONS*DEPTH)+(k))
#define dindex(i,j,k,m) ((((i)*HEIGHT+(j))*DIRECTIONS+(m))*DEPTH+(k))
#define inbounds(q,r,s) ((q>0)&&(q<(WIDTH-1))&&(r>0)&&(r<(HEIGHT-1))&&\
      (s>0)&&(s<(DEPTH-1)))

__kernel void update(__global float* from,__global float* to,__constant
      int* direction, __constant float* omega,__global float* density)
{
const int i = get_global_id(0);
const int j = get_global_id(1);
const int k = get_global_id(2);
const int lnindex = nindex(i,j,k);
const int lbindex = bindex(i,j,k);
__local float getout[DEPTH];
float cloud_density, new_flow;
float f00, f01, f02, f03, ..., f18;
int m, outi, outj, outk;

cloud_density = density[lnindex];
f00 = from[lbindex+0*DEPTH];
f01 = from[lbindex+1*DEPTH];
f02 = from[lbindex+2*DEPTH];
...
f18 = from[lbindex+18*DEPTH];

for(m=0;m<DIRECTIONS;m++){
      outk = k+direction[3*m+2];
      if(outk>0 && outk<(DEPTH-1){
            new_flow = 0.0f;
            new_flow += omega(m,0)*f00;
            new_flow += omega(m,1)*f01;
            new_flow += omega(m,2)*f02;
            ...
            new_flow += omega(m,18)*f18;
            getout[outk] = from[lbindex+m*DEPTH] +
                  new_flow*cloud_density;
      }
```

```
        barrier(CLK_LOCAL_MEM_FENCE);
        outi = i+direction[3*m+0];
        outj = j+direction[3*m+1];
        if(inbounds(outi,outj,k))
            to[dindex(outi,outj,outk,m)] = getout[k];
        }
    }
```

Testing this modified kernel on a Quadro FX 5600 (compute capability 1.0) shows that it entirely eliminates the uncoalesced writes generated by the original kernel. Execution time performance improves
by slightly more than 25%. Nevertheless, on the GTX 480, where there were no uncoalesced writes,
the modified kernel provides no improvement over the original. In fact, the overhead of the added
conditional and the added barrier causes a small execution time penalty, and the modified kernel is
actually slower than the original.

25.3.2 Examples

We have applied this technique to a wide variety of rendering tasks. We find compelling lighting effects
in those cases where the object geometry is both reflective and significantly transmissive across a
reasonably wide band of the visible spectrum. We include three examples here.

Clouds

In Figure 25.1 we show a synthetic cloud lighted with this technique. The cloud density here was
also generated by a Lattice Boltzmann model, in this case a model of the interaction between water
vapor and thermal energy. (Details of that model may be found in [13].) Key parameter values are the
Henyey-Greenstein parameter, $g = 0.9$, which provides significant forward scattering, and $\sigma_a = 0.008$,
and $\sigma_s = 0.792$, that together give a relatively high scattering albedo, $\sigma_s/\sigma_t = 0.99$, which is appropriate
for clouds.

For rendering, we use a standard path-integrating volume tracer that samples the medium density
and the LB lighting solution along each ray. The medium density sample is used to determine opacity.
We use trilinear interpolation from the surrounding lattice point values for sampling both quantities.
Watt and Watt [30] provide a detailed description of this algorithm.

Plants

In [12] we first conjectured that a leafy plant or even a forest might be regarded as a "leaf cloud,"
to which LB lighting might be effectively applied. Of course, polygonal mesh models must first be
voxelized [22, 23] to produce the lattice densities, which are then used as coefficient multipliers in the
collision matrix.

The ray tracer here differs from the path-integrating volume tracer used for clouds. It is essentially
a conventional ray tracer that incorporates the LB lighting as an ambient source. For each fragment, it
samples the Lattice Boltzmann solution at the nearest grid point to obtain an illumination value that is
then modulated by the fragment's ambient response color, attenuated by viewer distance, and added to
the direct diffuse and specular components to produce final fragment color.

The example plant model used in Figure 25.2 is a dogrose bush (Rosa canina) from the Xfrog Plants
collection [24].

FIGURE 25.1

Synthetic cloud with Lattice Boltzmann lighting.

FIGURE 25.2

Synthetic plant (dogrose) with Lattice Boltzmann lighting.

A visualization of the Lattice Boltzmann lighting alone is shown in Figure 25.3. Here each fragment is colored with the three-component photon density from the nearest grid node. The virtual sun is located on the left. This produces significant mid-band illumination that causes the right side to appear darker than the left. Thus, we are capturing both transmission and ambient occlusion.

The key parameter values here were derived from the values reported in the remarkable study by Knapp and Carter [19] that showed that the reflective and transmissive properties of plants are essentially constant across species. The wavelength-dependent values used are shown in Table 25.1. Visible energy loss due to absorption was modeled by zeroing out the f_0 component at each site on each iteration.

FIGURE 25.3

Visualization of Lattice Boltzmann lighting for the dogrose plant.

Table 25.1 Parameters used in lighting the dogrose plant.

	Red	Green	Blue
Henyey–Greenstein g	−0.231	0.103	−0.750
σ_a	0.109	0.091	0.118
σ_s	0.891	0.909	0.882

Table 25.2 Parameters used in lighting the PMMA teapot.

	Red	Green	Blue
Henyey – Greenstein g	0.80	−0.88	−0.88
σ_a	0.01	0.01	0.01
σ_s	0.99	0.99	0.99

Plastics

The reflective and transmissive properties of polymethyl methacrylate (PMMA) are well known. It is a lightweight, shatter-resistant alternative to glass that is often used in automobile taillights. To push the limits of our lighting technique, we fashioned a (hypothetical) PMMA teapot and applied LB lighting. The results are shown in Figure 25.4. The key model parameter values are shown in Table 25.2.

Although the effects of LB lighting here are admittedly minimal, we find that it offers a small, but believable "glow" that is not available with conventional lighting. In Figure 25.5 we show the same teapot, rendered with conventional lighting, where the ambient surface color is set equal to the diffuse surface color.

FIGURE 25.4

Lattice Boltzmann lighting for the PMMA teapot.

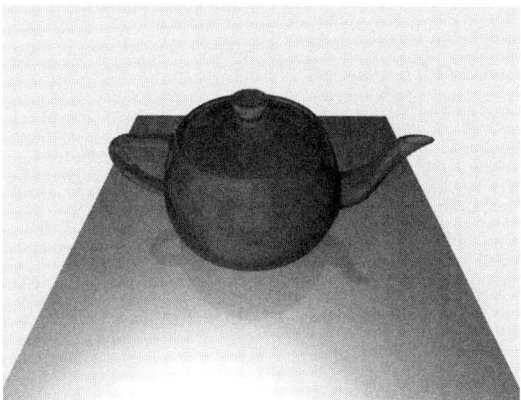

FIGURE 25.5

The PMMA teapot with conventional lighting.

25.4 FINAL EVALUATION

In Table 25.3 we compare timings for solutions of our LB lighting model as applied to the 256×128^2 grid used in the cloud lighting example of Section 25.3.2. Because each line includes a 1-second CPU overhead for loading, the available speedup (without resorting to SSE instructions or multithreading) is from 1169 s to 5 s, or 234x.

It is interesting to note that by resorting to SSE instructions and multithreading on the i7 X980, we can achieve an execution time that is better than that of the naive kernel running on the GTX 480.

Table 25.3 Execution time for lighting the 256×128^2 cloud model.

Platform	Time (Seconds)
Intel i7 X980	1170
Intel i7 X980 with SSE	281
Intel i7 X980 with SSE and four-way threading	100
NVIDIA GTX 480 naive kernel	167
NVIDIA GTX 480 final kernel	6

Table 25.4 Execution time for lighting a 128^3 cloud model.

Platform	Time (Seconds)
Intel i7 X980	292
Intel i7 X980 with SSE	70
Intel i7 X980 with SSE and four-way threading	26
NVIDIA GTX 480 naive kernel	41
NVIDIA GTX 480 final kernel	2

Results scale linearly with available resources. It should be expected that doubling the longest edge dimension would increase execution time by a factor of four. There are twice as many nodes, but achieving steady-state requires twice as many iterations. In Table 25.4 we show execution times for a cloud model of size 128^3. Results are as expected. Of the 2 seconds required for the final kernel on the 128^3 problem, approximately 0.7 seconds may be attributed to CPU loading, and thus the expected factor of $\times 4$ holds for all entries.

Although the computational structure of our method is similar to that which would be used in a parallel implementation of the discrete ordinates method, it is important to remember that our simulation-like structure is actually a numerical solution of an approximating diffusion equation. Thus, like Stam's approach [27], its value is probably restricted to highly scattering geometry. Nevertheless, on the other side of this same coin, one should not expect any ray effects, as seen in the discrete ordinates derivatives.

We believe that our LB lighting model is effective in quickly lighting scenes with highly scattering geometry, such as clouds or forests. It is best used to capture diffuse transmission, interobject scattering, and ambient occlusion, all of which are important to photo-realism.

There are limitations. Because the technique models photon transport as a diffusion process, it is inappropriate for most direct illumination effects. Thus, it must be augmented with other techniques to capture such effects. Another limitation is the memory requirement. Because the grid state is maintained as floats:

```
cl_mem focl[2][WIDTH*HEIGHT*DEPTH*DIRECTIONS];
```

a grid of size 256^3 would require 2.5 GB, and larger grids would exceed available GPU memory. To light a scene with more than a single cloud or a single tree and yet capture interobject, indirect illumination requires a grid hierarchy, such as the one suggested in [28].

25.5 FUTURE DIRECTIONS

More effective use of grids of limited size is under investigation. The impressive real-time performance achieved by Kaplanyan and Dachsbacher [17] can be attributed to their use of nested grids of varying resolution positioned in camera space. Their grid hierarchy is more sophisticated than our own [28], and could offer significant performance benefits. Another approach is the use of dynamic grids. In [5] we proposed a spring-loaded vertex model for 2-D radiosity computations. The grids were represented as point masses interconnected by zero-rest-length springs. Spring forces were dynamically determined by the current best lighting solution until equilibrium, with an attendant deformed grid, was achieved. This approach allowed high-quality lighting solutions with relative small grid sizes. Application of this approach to 3-D lighting appears most promising.

25.6 DERIVATION OF THE DIFFUSION EQUATION

The purpose of this section is to show that, as the lattice spacing, λ, and the time step, τ, both approach 0, the limiting behavior of the fundamental update in Eq. 25.2 is the diffusion Eq. 25.3. A sketch of the derivation originally appeared in [11]. The present treatment includes significantly more detail. As noted earlier, the principal value of this derivation is as a prototype for related derivations.

We begin by expanding the left side of Eq. 25.2 in a Taylor series with respect to the differential operator

$$\nabla = (\partial/\partial\vec{r}, \partial/\partial t) = (\partial/\partial x, \partial/\partial y, \partial/\partial z, \partial/\partial t) \tag{25.10}$$

which handles three spatial dimensions and one temporal. This gives us

$$[(\lambda\vec{c_m}, \tau) \cdot \nabla]f_m(\vec{r}, t) + \frac{[(\lambda\vec{c_m}, \tau) \cdot \nabla]^2}{2!}f_m(\vec{r}, t) + \cdots = \Omega_m \cdot (f(\vec{r}, t)) \tag{25.11}$$

For the diffusion behavior we seek, it will be important for the time step to approach 0 faster than the lattice spacing. Specifically, we write

$$t = \frac{t_0}{\epsilon^2} \quad \text{where} \quad t_0 = o(\epsilon^2)$$

that is, t_0 is a term that approaches 0 faster than ϵ^2, and

$$\vec{r} = \frac{\vec{r_0}}{\epsilon} \quad \text{where} \quad \|\vec{r_0}\| = o(\epsilon)$$

It follows from the chain rule for differentiation that

$$\frac{\partial}{\partial t} = \epsilon^2 \frac{\partial}{\partial t_0}$$

and

$$\frac{\partial}{\partial r_\alpha} = \epsilon \frac{\partial}{\partial r_{0\alpha}} \quad \text{for} \quad \alpha \in \{x, y, z\}$$

As is standard practice in Lattice Boltzmann modeling, we also assume that we can write $f(\vec{r}, t)$ as a small perturbation on this same scale about some local equilibrium, $f^{(0)}$, i.e.,

$$f(\vec{r}, t) = f^{(0)}(\vec{r}, t) + \epsilon f^{(1)}(\vec{r}, t) + \epsilon^2 f^{(2)}(\vec{r}, t) + \cdots \tag{25.12}$$

where the local equilibrium carries the total density, i.e., $\rho(\vec{r}, t) = \sum_{m=0}^{18} f_m^{(0)}(\vec{r}, t)$. Equation 25.12 is the Chapman-Enskog expansion from statistical mechanics [4], wherein it is assumed that any flow that is near equilibrium can be expressed as a perturbation in the so-called Knudsen number, ϵ, which represents the mean free path (expected distance between successive density collisions) in lattice spacing units.

Equation 25.11 now becomes:

$$\left[\left[\epsilon\lambda \left(\vec{c}_m \cdot \frac{\partial}{\partial \vec{r}_0} \right) + \epsilon^2 \tau \frac{\partial}{\partial t_0} \right] + \frac{\left[\epsilon\lambda \left(\vec{c}_m \cdot \frac{\partial}{\partial \vec{r}_0} \right) + \epsilon^2 \tau \frac{\partial}{\partial t_0} \right]^2}{2} + \cdots \right] \left(f_m^{(0)} + \epsilon f_m^{(1)} + \cdots \right)$$

$$= \Omega_m \cdot \left(f^{(0)} + \epsilon f^{(1)} + \cdots \right) \tag{25.13}$$

Equating coefficients of ϵ^0 in (25.13), we obtain:

$$0 = \Omega_m \cdot (f^{(0)}(\vec{r}, t)) \tag{25.14}$$

i.e., $f^{(0)}$ is indeed a local equilibrium. In general, a local equilibrium need not be unique, and the choice can affect the speed of convergence [18]. Nevertheless, in this case it turns out that Ω has a one-dimensional null space. We observe that

$$\vec{v} = (\sigma_a, 1/12, \ldots, 1/12, 1/24, \ldots, 1/24)$$

(where entries 1–6 are $1/12$) satisfies $\Omega_m \cdot \vec{v} = 0$, all m, and so we must have

$$f_m^{(0)} = K v_m$$

where the scaling coefficient, K, is determined by the requirement that $\rho = \sum_m f_m^{(0)} = K \sum_m v_m = K(1 + \sigma_a)$. Thus, we have:

$$f_m^{(0)}(\vec{r}, t) = \frac{v_m}{1 + \sigma_a} \rho(\vec{r}, t) \tag{25.15}$$

Similarly, equating coefficients of ϵ^1 in (25.13), we obtain:

$$\lambda \left(\vec{c}_m \cdot \frac{\partial}{\partial \vec{r}_0} \right) f_i^{(0)}(\vec{r}, t) = \Omega_m \cdot f^{(1)}(\vec{r}, t) \tag{25.16}$$

that is, after substituting Eq. 25.15,

$$\frac{\lambda v_m}{1 + \sigma_a} \left(\vec{c_m} \cdot \frac{\partial}{\partial \vec{r_0}} \right) \rho(\vec{r}, t) = \Omega_m \cdot f^{(1)}(\vec{r}, t) \tag{25.17}$$

We would like to solve Eq. 25.17 for $f^{(1)}$, but we cannot simply invert Ω, since it is singular. Nevertheless, we can observe that any vector comprising lattice direction components,

$$(c_{0_\alpha}, c_{1_\alpha}, \ldots, c_{18_\alpha}) \quad \text{where} \quad \alpha \in \{x, y, z\}12pt]$$

as well as any of

$$(v_0 c_{0_\alpha}, v_1 c_{1_\alpha}, \ldots, v_{18} c_{18_\alpha}) \quad \text{where} \quad \alpha \in \{x, y, z\}$$

is an eigenvector of Ω with eigenvalue $-\sigma_t$. Thus, if we write

$$f_m^{(1)}(\vec{r}, t) = K v_m \left(\vec{c_m} \cdot \frac{\partial}{\partial \vec{r_0}} \right) \rho(\vec{r}, t)$$

and substitute into (25.17), we can determine that $K = -\lambda/((1 + \sigma_a)\sigma_t)$ and so

$$f_m^{(1)}(\vec{r}, t) = \frac{-\lambda v_m}{(1 + \sigma_a)\sigma_t} \left(\vec{c_m} \cdot \frac{\partial}{\partial \vec{r_0}} \right) \rho(\vec{r}, t) \tag{25.18}$$

Finally, we need to equate ϵ^2 terms in Eq. 25.13, but here it will suffice to sum over all directions. We obtain:

$$\sum_{m=0}^{18} \left[\tau \frac{\partial f_i^{(0)}}{\partial t_0} + \lambda \left(\vec{c_m} \cdot \frac{\partial}{\partial \vec{r_0}} \right) f_m^{(1)} + \frac{\lambda^2}{2} \left(\vec{c_m} \cdot \frac{\partial}{\partial \vec{r_0}} \right)^2 f_m^{(0)} \right] = 0 \tag{25.19}$$

Substituting Eqs. 25.15 and 25.18 into Eq. 25.19 and observing that

$$\sum_{m=0}^{18} v_m c_{m_\alpha} c_{m_\beta} = (1/2)\delta_{\alpha\beta} \quad \text{for} \quad \alpha, \beta \in \{x, y, z\}$$

we obtain

$$\frac{\partial \rho}{\partial t_0} - \frac{\lambda^2 (1/\sigma_t - 1/2)}{2\tau (1 + \sigma_a)} \left(\frac{\partial^2 \rho}{\partial r_{0_x}^2} + \frac{\partial^2 \rho}{\partial r_{0_y}^2} + \frac{\partial^2 \rho}{\partial r_{0_z}^2} \right) = 0 \tag{25.20}$$

which, if we multiply through by ϵ^2, yields the standard diffusion equation,

$$\frac{\partial \rho}{\partial t} = D \nabla_{\vec{r}}^2 \rho \tag{25.21}$$

with diffusion coefficient

$$D = \left(\frac{\lambda^2}{\tau}\right)\left[\frac{(2/\sigma_t) - 1}{4(1 + \sigma_a)}\right]$$

The critical step is clearly a choice of Ω that both represents plausible collision events and has readily determined eigenvectors that can be used to solve for the first few components in the Chapmann-Enskog expansion.

Acknowledgments

This work was supported in part by the National Science Foundation under Award 0722313 and by an equipment donation from NVIDIA Corporation.

References

[1] J. Arvo, Transfer equations in global illumination, in: Global Illumination, SIGGRAPH '93 Course Notes, vol. 42, 1993.

[2] N. Bhate, A. Tokuta, Photorealistic volume rendering of media with directional scattering, in: Third Eurographics Workshop on Rendering, Bristol, 1992, pp. 227–245.

[3] S. Chandrasekhar, Radiative Transfer, Clarendon Press, Oxford, 1950.

[4] B. Chopard, M. Droz, Cellular automata modeling of physical systems, Cambridge University Press, Cambridge, 1998.

[5] R. Danforth, R. Geist, Automatic mesh refinement and its application to radiosity computations, Int. J. Robot. Autom. 15 (1) (2000) 1–8.

[6] D. d'Humières, P. Lallemand, U. Frisch, Lattice gas models for 3d hydrodynamics, Europhys. Lett. 2 (1986) 291–297.

[7] C. Donner, H. Jensen, Light diffusion in multi-layered translucent materials, ACM Trans. Graph. 24 (3) (2005) 1032–1039.

[8] R. Fattal, Participating media illumination using light propagation maps, ACM Trans. Graph. 28 (1) (2009) 1–11.

[9] J.R. Frisvad, N.J. Christensen, H.W. Jensen, Computing the scattering properties of participating media using Lorenz-Mie theory, in: SIGGRAPH '07: ACM SIGGRAPH 2007 ACM, New York, 2007, pp. 60-1–60-10.

[10] M. Gardner, Mathematical games: John Conway's game of life, Sci. Am. (223) (1970) 120–123.

[11] R. Geist, K. Rasche, J. Westall, R. Schalkoff, Lattice-Boltzmann lighting, in: Rendering Techniques 2004 (Proc. Eurographics Symposium on Rendering), Norrköping, Sweden, 2004, pp. 355–362, 423.

[12] R. Geist, J. Steele, A lighting model for fast rendering of forest ecosystems, in: Proceeding of the IEEE Symposium on Interactive Ray Tracing (RT08), Los Angeles, CA, 2008, pp. 99–106 (also back cover).

[13] R. Geist, J. Steele, J. Westall, Convective clouds, in: Natural Phenomena 2007 (Proceeding of the Eurographics Workshop on Natural Phenomena), Prague, Czech Republic, 2007, pp. 23–30, 83 (and back cover).

[14] G. Henyey, J. Greenstein, Diffuse radiation in the galaxy, Astrophys. J. 88 (1940) 70–73.

[15] H. Jensen, S. Marschner, M. Levoy, P. Hanrahan, A practical model for subsurface light transport, in: Proceedings of SIGGRAPH 2001, ACM, New York, 2001, pp. 511–518.

[16] J. Kajiya, B. von Herzen, Ray tracing volume densities, ACM Comput. Graph. (SIGGRAPH '84) 18 (3) (1984) 165–174.

[17] A. Kaplanyan, C. Dachsbacher, Cascaded light propagation volumes for real-time indirect illumination, in: I3D '10: Proceedings of the 2010 ACM SIGGRAPH Symposium on Interactive 3D Graphics and Games, ACM, New York, 2010, pp. 99–107.

[18] I. Karlin, A. Ferrante, C. Ottinger, Perfect entropy functions of the lattice boltzmann method, Europhys. Lett. 47 (1999) 182–188.

[19] A. Knapp, G. Carter, Variability in leaf optical properties among 26 species from a broad range of habitats, Am. J. Bot. 85 (7) (1998) 940–946.

[20] E. Languénou, K. Bouatouch, M. Chelle, Global illumination in presence of participating media with general properties, in: Fifth Eurographics Workshop on Rendering, Darmstadt, Germany, 1994, pp. 69–85.

[21] N.L. Max, Efficient light propagation for multiple anisotropic volume scattering, in: Fifth Eurographics Workshop on Rendering, Darmstadt, Germany, 1994, pp. 87–104.

[22] P.M. Binvox, http://www.cs.princeton.edu/~min/binvox/binvox.html, 2003.

[23] F. Nooruddin, G. Turk, Simplification and repair of polygonal models using volumetric techniques, IEEE Trans. Visual. Comput. 9 (2) (2003).

[24] Greenworks Organic-Software, Xfrogplants v 2.0, http://www.xfrogdownloads.com/greenwebNew/products/productStart.htm, 2008.

[25] H. Rushmeier, K. Torrance, The zonal method for calculating light intensities in the presence of a participating medium, in: Proceeding SIGGRAPH '87, ACM, New York, 1987, pp. 293–302.

[26] X. Shan, G. Doolen, Multicomponent lattice-boltzmann model with interparticle interaction. J. Stat. Phys. 81 (1/2) (1995) 379–393.

[27] J. Stam, Multiple scattering as a diffusion process, in: Proceeding of the 6th Eurographics Workshop on Rendering, Dublin, Ireland, Eurographics Association, Aire-la-Ville, Switzerland, 1995, pp. 51–58.

[28] J. Steele, R. Geist, Relighting forest ecosystems, in: G. Bebis et al. (Eds.), ISVC 2009 Part I, LNCS 5875 (Proceedings of the 5th International Symposium on Visual Computing), Las Vegas, NV, Springer, Heidelberg, 2009, pp. 55–66.

[29] N. Thürey, U. Rüde, M. Stamminger, Animation of open water phenomena with coupled shallow water and free surface simulations, in: SCA '06: Proceedings of the 2006 ACM SIGGRAPH/Eurographics Symposium on Computer animation, Vienna, Austria, Eurographics Association, Aire-la-Ville, Switzerland, 2006, pp. 157–164.

[30] A. Watt, M. Watt, Advanced animation and rendering techniques: Theory and practice, Addison-Wesley, Wokingham, England, 1992.

[31] X. Wei, W. Li, K. Mueller, A. Kaufman, The Lattice-Boltzmann method for gaseous phenomena, IEEE Trans. Visual. Comput. 10 (2) (2004).

Path Regeneration for Random Walks

26

Jan Novák, Vlastimil Havran, Carsten Dachsbacher

In this chapter, we present a method for efficiently generating random walks on the GPU. We analyze the main drawback of naive random walk generators resulting in a low GPU utilization over time, and propose an intuitive scheme for keeping all the processing units busy during the entire computation. The algorithm does not require interthread communication, collective operations, or intricate handling of work queues. Instead, the improved utilization is achieved by intelligently regenerating terminated walks. We discuss our optimization in the context of rendering global illumination images where random walks are used to compute the propagation of energy between light sources and cameras. Algorithms such as (bidirectional) path tracing, photon mapping, and irradiance caching directly benefit from the higher throughput; however, our technique is also applicable to nongraphical problems that explore the domain of interest by random walks.

26.1 INTRODUCTION

When rendering photo-realistic images, we need to estimate the amount of light that is emitted from the light sources and scattered by objects in the scene toward the camera. The propagation of light is a fairly complex high-dimensional problem, and thus, many image-synthesis algorithms use numeric Monte Carlo integration. This is based on creating a number of random walks along which the light transport is measured. A random walk is a Markov chain describing a trajectory of a walker (e.g., a molecule in fluid simulations, an animal in foraging behavior studies, or a photon in light tracing) that takes a number of successive random steps, thus forming a path through the domain. To sufficiently explore the domain, we need to compute a vast number of such paths. Even worse, the length of the walk is generally not known prior to execution because the termination criteria are probabilistic. Straightforward porting of such methods to SIMD architectures results in poor hardware utilization: although some walks are still being constructed, others have already been terminated, and the corresponding processing units are idle. This prevents the algorithm from exploiting the entire hardware throughput.

A well-known method for rendering photo-realistic images that suffers from this problem is path tracing [5]. The algorithm traces a high number of random walks (paths) from the camera in order to determine the color of each pixel in the image. The walker in such cases is an importance that is emitted from the camera and traced through the scene gathering light from light sources, as shown in Figure 26.1. The paths are terminated using Russian roulette: given some probability, we either

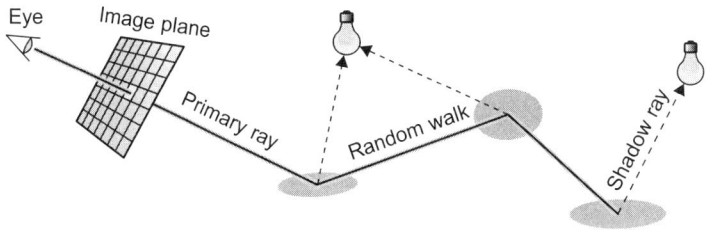

FIGURE 26.1

Path tracing computes the color of each pixel by tracing random walks gathering light and estimating the energy transported along the path.

terminate the walk or allow construction of the next segment of the path. Because the termination is probabilistic and depends on local surface properties, such as albedo (hemispherical reflectance), the paths are highly divergent in length ranging from two up to a few tens of steps. This leads to the previously mentioned problem of poor hardware utilization, when some threads are still tracing paths, while others are inactive because the corresponding paths were terminated.

26.2 PATH TRACING AS CASE STUDY

Our intention to use path tracing for the demonstration of the regeneration technique stems from two important characteristics of the algorithm. First, path tracing is motivated by the physical nature of light propagation: the algorithm is well described by a set of fundamental equations that are frequently used as a starting point for deriving more advanced global illumination techniques. For brevity we omit the mathematical description and refer the reader to [2]. Second, path tracing provides an intuitive and conceivable demonstration of the proposed optimizations. As previously mentioned, the algorithm computes a 2-D picture of a 3-D virtual scene by constructing random walks connecting the camera and the light sources. A vast amount of research has already been devoted to improving the convergence of the algorithm by various sampling and caching schemes. In this chapter we focus on the second important component of path tracing, which is an efficient random walk generator that fully utilizes the GPU. In the next section we briefly describe the algorithm, analyze the drawbacks of naive straightforward implementation, and propose three optimization strategies for regenerating terminated paths. We then describe the implementation details and measured results. The chapter concludes by comparing the path regeneration with other optimization techniques.

26.3 RANDOM WALKS IN PATH TRACING

In path tracing, the construction of each random walk starts by shooting a primary ray through a pixel on the image plane. The algorithm then traces this ray in the scene searching for the closest intersection with one of the surfaces. Once the hit point is found, we sample its bidirectional scattering distribution function (BSDF) and select an outgoing direction to shoot the next path segment, that is, a new ray.

The process of tracing rays and sampling outgoing directions is repeated until the path is terminated. In order to terminate the path without introducing bias, we use Russian roulette: with a probability derived from local surface properties, we either continue constructing the path or terminate it at the current location. As the purpose of the path is gathering the energy from light sources, the algorithm explicitly samples direct illumination of each discovered intersection (vertex) and estimates the amount of energy transported along the path to the corresponding pixel.

Because the main idea of path tracing resides in figuring out where the light is coming from, we have to explore the whole scene space with many different paths; otherwise, the resulting image contains a high amount of noise. When we are porting the algorithm to parallel SIMD architectures, a straight-forward approach is to use one thread for constructing all N paths for a single pixel. In order to trace these N paths, we execute the parallel construction of paths in N subsequent batches. The computation starts by tracing the primary rays. For this first path segment, all processing units are equally and fully utilized; however, as the threads construct further segments, some of them become inactive when the corresponding paths are terminated.

Figure 26.2 shows two subsequent batches of simultaneously computed paths in the conference room scene. The illustration at the bottom emphasizes the utilization of individual processing units over time. Once a path is terminated, the corresponding GPU thread becomes inactive until a new batch is executed. Notice that before starting a new path, all the threads must wait until the last path terminates. This results in a tremendous waste of resources: first, the length of the longest path can be much higher than the average length, causing the majority of threads to be inactive most of the time. Second, after every step we need to check whether there is at least one nonterminated path, which

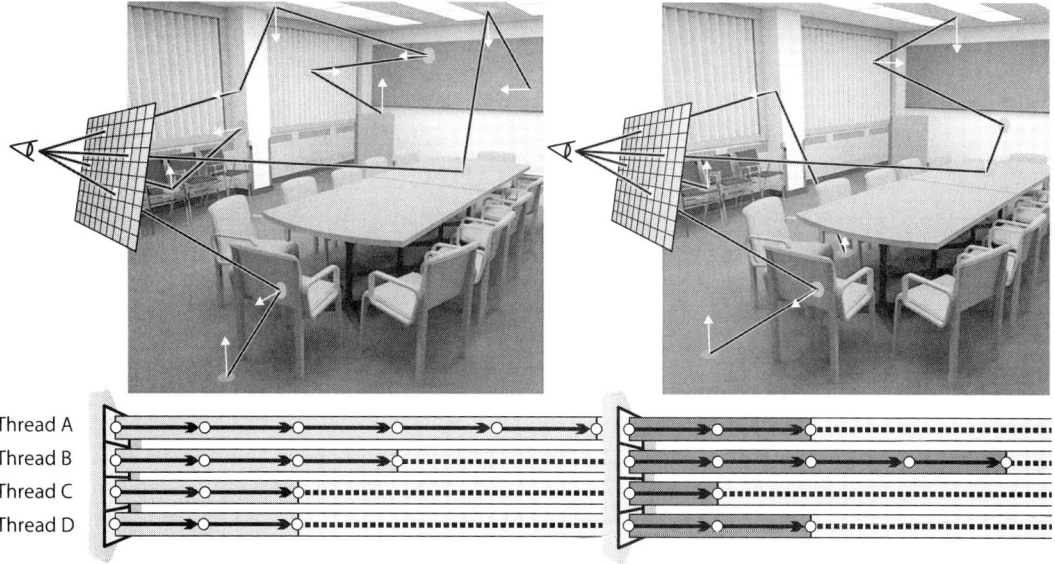

FIGURE 26.2

Poor utilization of processing units in a naive GPU path tracing.

would require a parallel reduction and GPU-to-CPU transfer.[1] Obviously, both issues have a negative impact on the performance.

One solution to reduce the disproportion in path lengths, and to completely avoid the reduction, is to forcedly terminate all paths after a fixed number of iterations. This is the most common workaround in many current GPU path tracers. Unfortunately, this results in biasing the integration: by setting an upper limit on the path length to K, we will never capture effects that require more than K light bounces. This becomes an issue when rendering participating media with multiple scattering, complex caustics, or scenes with many reflections. Furthermore, the utilization of the processing units is still low because many threads become inactive much earlier than after K iterations.

26.3.1 Sparse Warps

Interesting observations arise from the analysis of the inactivity of individual threads. As the termination probability of the Russian roulette is derived from the albedo of the hit surface, the average path length is also dependent on the material properties. This allows us to estimate the number of steps, after which only a certain amount of paths are still active. For this, we compute the overall scene reflectance α_S as the area weighted average of all N scene albedos α_i:

$$\alpha_S = \frac{1}{S} \sum_{i=1}^{N} S_i \alpha_i,$$

where S_i is the surface area of material i and S the total surface area. The number of steps required for the Russian roulette to terminate C percent of paths is then set to $\log_{\alpha_S}(1 - C/100)$. The equation allows adjusting the amount of forcedly terminated paths, enabling to control the amount of bias in the naive implementation of path tracing.

Figure 26.3 shows the measurements of the relative number of active and inactive threads over time. The dark columns represent the numbers of threads that are active and trace the paths. Light columns show the total number of threads that occupy the multiprocessors (either actively or inactively). As soon as the Russian roulette starts terminating paths, some of the threads in a warp (simultaneously processed group of threads) become inactive. Therefore, each warp containing at least one active thread will be further processed by the GPU with the inactive threads not contributing to the computation, thus decreasing the potential throughput. We will refer to such warps as *sparse*. The difference between the light and dark columns in Figure 26.3 refers to the amount of inactive threads (wasted resources) in sparse warps. Notice that this also depends on the average albedo of the scene. Minimizing the difference between the bars means higher utilization of the processing units and can be achieved using the path regeneration technique introduced in the next section.

26.3.2 Path Regeneration

In order to avoid sparse warps we modify the random walk generation so that we can create new paths immediately after the termination. Once a path P_i is terminated, we generate a new path P_{i+1}, assign

---

[1]Here we assume that the algorithm is implemented using multiple kernels. More details are provided in the section about implementation.

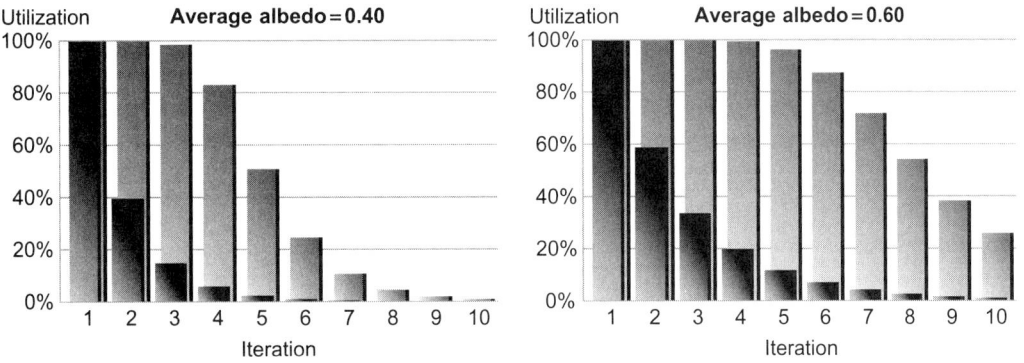

FIGURE 26.3

The relative number of all (light) and actively working (dark) threads in sparse warps when rendering the Conference Room scene with darker (left) and brighter (right) materials.

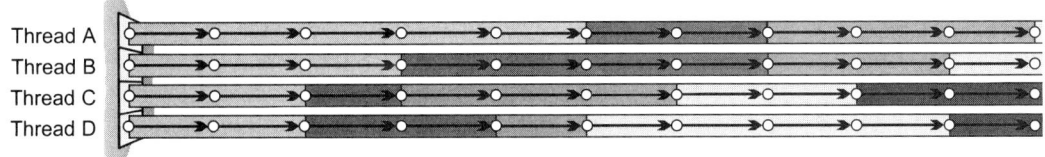

FIGURE 26.4

Regeneration of paths immediately after they were terminated by the Russian roulette.

it to the inactive thread, and continue the computation with all threads having a valid path to trace. The regeneration technique avoids constructing the paths in batches and strives to tightly pack the computation as shown in Figure 26.4. An important advantage of the regeneration is that we avoid the forced termination of paths preserving an unbiased integration. In general, we have three options for regenerating the paths:

Restart in the origin: This is the simplest option for creating new random walks without inheriting any information from the previously terminated ones. In our case this means that new paths are created independently starting directly from the camera.

Restart at the first hit point: The second strategy focuses on the main source of noise in path tracing: the indirect illumination. It is computed by paths having at least three segments (primary ray + secondary ray + shadow ray). To address this issue, we create new paths that inherit the primary ray and the estimation of direct illumination from the previous one, and continue gathering the indirect illumination from the first hit point of the previous path.

Restart at any point: This technique is the most general one. In cases where new paths are allowed to reuse any part of the previous random walk, we can construct new paths by appending segments to a prefix of the previous path. This can be particularly beneficial in bidirectional path tracing [7] for regenerating light paths with high-potential contribution, and the technique can provide faster convergence in complicated scenes, for example, two connected rooms, one containing the camera, the other containing a light source.

The restarting strategies differ in what part of previous paths is reused, but all enforce full utilization of the processing units during the computation. As shown in the results section, the optimization is capable of improving the throughput and ensuring that the performance remains stable and immune to material properties. The measurements also show that the average scene albedo greatly affects the performance of naive path tracing.

26.4 IMPLEMENTATION DETAILS

The source code accompanying this chapter includes a naive implementation as well as an optimized version of a path tracer using the regeneration technique. For accelerating the ray-triangle intersection tests, we use a kd-tree that is built in a preprocessing step on the CPU. The GPU threads traverse the kd-tree using a limited-size stack stored in the local thread memory. For generating random numbers, each thread maintains its own instance of a Mersenne Twister random number generator.

Naive path tracing: The straightforward implementation of path tracing is based on the following concept: for each image pixel, we create a single GPU thread that constructs the required number of paths to obtain a (largely) noise-free image. The computation is partitioned into a sequence of N batches in which each thread computes exactly one path. A batch starts with generating an initial primary ray and then the algorithm enters a loop for constructing the path. In every iteration we find the closest intersection of the ray with the scene, sample direct illumination, create a new ray for constructing the next path segment, and possibly terminate the path using Russian roulette. All the previously described tasks can be concentrated in a single large kernel; however, we achieved higher throughput with a number of specialized kernels. Such kernels benefit from higher occupancy, and the performance penalty resulting from additional global memory accesses for exchanging data between kernels is negligible in our case. Multiple lightweight kernels are also easier to debug and profile. The pipeline of the naive algorithm is show in Figure 26.5 on the left. Kernels suffering from low utilization (e.g., Trace rays) are emphasized by dark background.

Path regeneration: In order to regenerate terminated paths, we have to slightly adjust the loop over the kernels. We will need to execute an additional kernel after the Russian roulette that regenerates the terminated paths. Supposing that we always want to restart the paths in the origin (camera), we can call a slightly modified *Generate Camera Rays* kernel that first stores the contribution of the terminated path and then generates a new primary ray for each inactive thread. Once we exit the loop, the accumulated contribution is divided by the total number of paths traced for the respective pixel.

Our second strategy — restart the paths at the first hit point — is suited to devote the majority of computation time to the main source of noise, that is, to indirect illumination. This option requires executing a simple kernel that stores the sampled direct illumination and vertex parameters when the first vertex of a path is found. Instead of generating new primary rays, we will restore these values and sample the BSDF to find the new outgoing direction for gathering indirect illumination. The illustration in Figure 26.5 shows pipelines of both regeneration options.

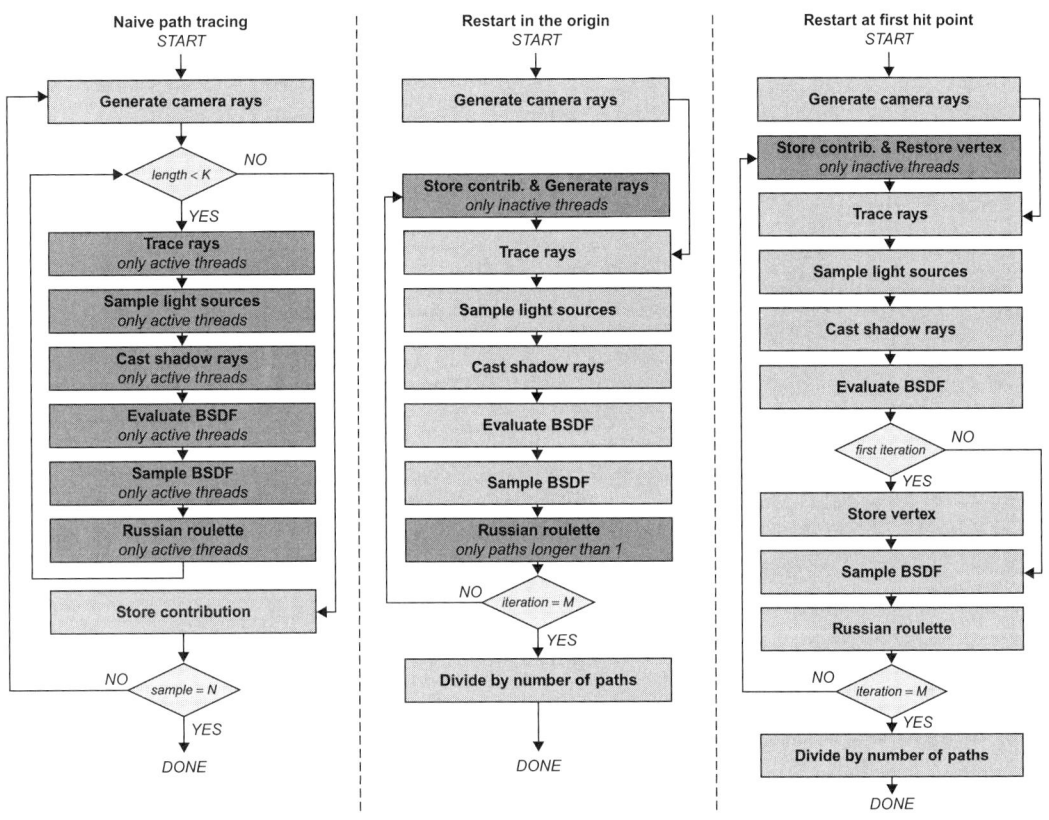

FIGURE 26.5

Pipelines of a naive path tracing (left), path tracing that restarts in the origin (middle), and a version that regenerates the paths at the first hit point (right). The demonstration source code combines both regeneration strategies to trade between computation of direct and indirect illumination. Light and dark background emphasizes entire and low utilization of processing units, respectively.

Because it is often required to multisample direct illumination (e.g., in scenes with area light sources), using only a single sample estimate of direct illumination is not sufficient. To this end, we combine both regeneration strategies: according to a user-defined rate, we create new paths (by executing the kernel for creating primary rays), whereas in all the other cases, we regenerate the paths at the previously stored first hit point. This approach allows the user to adjust the ratio of complete paths to those built only by appending a path suffix.

The last important modification in the optimized implementation is the number of iterations that the algorithm loops over the kernels. The naive path tracer executes N batches (one for each sample) consisting of K iterations required to unbiasedly terminate C percent of paths. With the regeneration scheme we replace the two nested loops by a single loop that creates all the paths. The algorithm iterates over the kernels in two phases. The first *regeneration phase* is responsible for creating the majority of

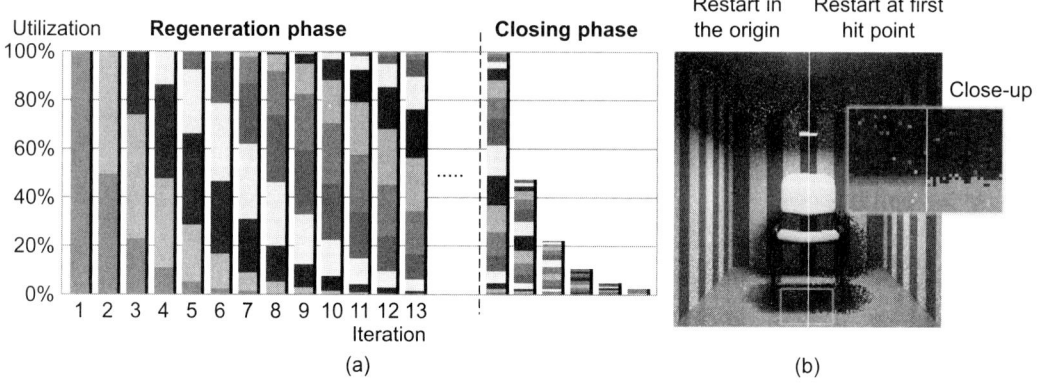

FIGURE 26.6

Figure 26.6a (left): Utilization of processing units when the regeneration of paths is used (the color coding distinguishes different path generations). Figure 26.6b (right): Regenerating at the origin (left half) helps to reduce the noise from direct illumination and minimizes aliasing artifacts. Regenerating at the first vertex (right half) is better suited to reduce the noise that is due to indirect illumination.

paths required for synthesizing the final image. Any path terminated during this phase is immediately replaced by a new path using one of the previously described strategies. As the paths are terminated only by the Russian roulette, no bias is introduced.

The length of the regeneration phase is computed as a product of the average path length and the number of per-pixel samples. Subsequently, the algorithm enters a *closing phase*, which omits the regeneration to let the existing paths gradually terminate. The length of the closing phase is set to the length of one batch from the naive implementation. The total number of iterations M for any regeneration technique therefore equals the total length of both phases.

In practical applications, the regeneration phase is several magnitudes longer than the closing phase. The utilization of processing units with the optimized algorithm is illustrated in Figure 26.6a. Figure 26.6b shows a rendering of a chair in a room, where the left half of the image is computed by restarting the paths in the origin only, and the right half, using the regeneration at the first vertex. In both cases, the number of iterations is identical. Notice the difference in the amount of noise from direct lighting (chair shadow) and indirect illumination (reflections on the floor and area below the chair).

26.5 RESULTS

In order to compare the throughput of the naive and path regeneration versions, we have conducted a number of tests with various scenes and materials affecting the termination probability of the Russian roulette. More precisely, we have always adjusted the material properties so that the average scene albedo ranges from 0.1 (dark scene) to 0.9 (bright scene). Figure 26.7 reports the throughput of our implementation running on an NVIDIA GeForce GTX 285 and an NVIDIA GeForce GTX 470. Without the regeneration technique (dark curves), the overall throughput, measured as the number of constructed path segments per unit time, is much more dependent on the average albedo. If the albedo is low,

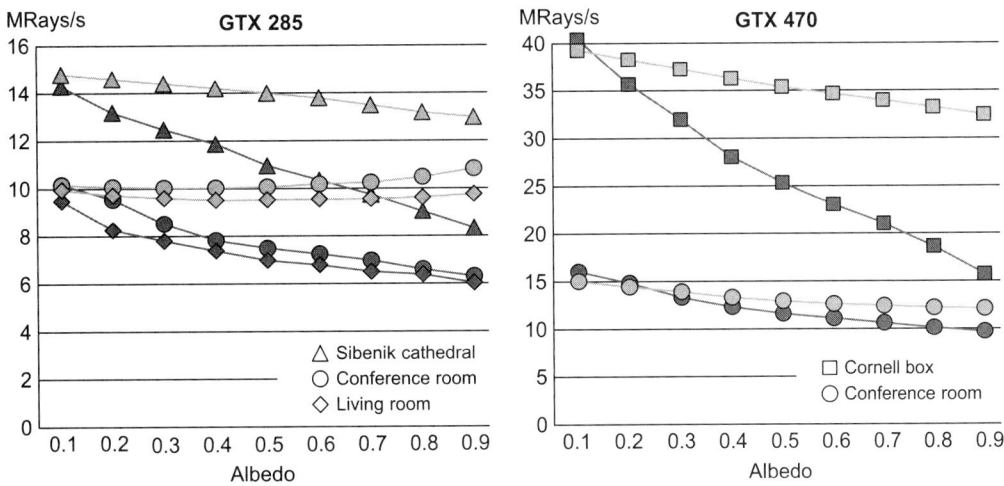

FIGURE 26.7

Throughput of the naive (dark) and optimized (light) path tracing on GeForce GTX 285 (left) and GeForce GTX 470 (right).

the Russian roulette terminates the paths more aggressively, requiring less iterations, during which the hardware is still well utilized. As the albedo increases, the termination probability of the Russian roulette becomes lower, producing longer walks that require more iterations to construct the paths. This results in wider inactivity gaps of some threads, and the utilization of the processing units is low. The conference room and the living room scenes used for testing are shown in Figure 26.8.

One of the main drawbacks of the naive path tracer is that the number of active threads is dropping with each subsequent iteration. This means that the whole effort of executing kernels is spent on constructing less and less path segments during later iterations. The overhead of launching kernels is more notable in the case of the GTX 285, where the difference in performance of the naive and regeneration path tracing is larger. The GTX 470, with its improved hardware architecture, significantly decreases the time required for kernel execution, and therefore, the difference between both implementations is not so dramatic in cases with bandwidth-bound kernels (conference room). Because the demonstration source code contains only simple shaders, the main bottleneck of the computation is the tracing of rays. For the conference room the traversal of the kd-tree together with ray-triangle intersection tests represents more than 90% of the computation time and the performance is mostly dependent on the total number of global memory accesses. In such cases the throughput is limited by the GPU bandwidth and the impact of poor utilization on the overall performance is marginal.

Because photo-realistic renderers typically use more involved shading and sampling techniques, we have also investigated the outcomes of regenerating the paths in situations similar to production rendering. We used a modified version of the Cornell box scene with computationally intensive multilayer Cook Torrance BRDFs, both helping to narrow the performance gap between tracing and shading kernels. In this case, the regeneration proved to be much more rewarding. With increasing albedo the performance of the naive implementation dropped to less than 40% of the original throughput, whereas the regeneration technique helped to retain stable throughput with only a minor descent owing to the

(a)   (b)

FIGURE 26.8

Conference room (with glossy floor) (a) and living room (b) scenes used for testing the performance.

Table 26.1 Performance of the naive (NPT) and path regeneration path tracing (PRPT) in 10^6 rays/sec. Columns l_a and l_m report the average and maximum path length (for forcedly terminating the naive version). Column S states the relative speedup of the optimized algorithm (PRPT/NPT).

	Faces	Albedo	l_a	l_m	NPT	PRPT	S
Cornell box	32	0.32	1.5	5	30.0	48.5	**1.6**
Office	36.0K	0.43	1.8	6	10.3	15.4	**1.5**
Sibenik	80.5K	0.67	3.0	12	9.0	17.2	**1.9**
Theatre	163.3K	0.60	2.5	10	5.4	8.9	**1.6**
Conference room	298.9K	0.44	1.8	6	6.6	9.6	**1.5**

higher fraction of secondary (highly incoherent) rays that are more expensive to trace than the coherent primary rays.

Table 26.1 provides measurements from an advanced path tracer supporting multiple different materials, shaders, and types of light sources. The performance measured on the GTX 285 is slightly lower than in the case of the demonstration source code, but the reported speedup is reliable as the conditions are closer to production rendering (for details please refer to [8]). We made the observation that the regeneration attains much higher speedup with arithmetically intensive (compute bound) kernels. In cases when the throughput is conditional to memory bandwidth, the utilization of processing units is less important, and the technique brings only marginal improvements.

The amount of saved computation that is due to reusing the primary rays can be estimated from the average length of paths. In the actual tests, the rendering time was reduced by 10% to 20%, which is a little less than the theoretical prediction. This is to be expected because the primary rays are coherent, taking greater advantage of memory caching than the highly incoherent secondary rays.

26.6 DISCUSSION

Thanks to its simplicity, path regeneration can be easily applied to existing implementations of GPU photon mapping [4] or instant radiosity [6] that require distributing a lot of photons and virtual point lights (VPL) in the scene. Many implementations targeting interactive performance restrict all the random walks to have the same length producing many photons and VPLs with negligible energy. For instance, if a photon hits a black surface, the random walk should be terminated because it will not transport any energy. Here, the path regeneration enables achieving the same throughput as the restrictive version, but with better distribution thanks to the usage of the Russian roulette. Furthermore, the regeneration will produce a densely packed array of photons because every thread will produce one photon at each step. Without the regeneration the resulting array will be sparse, requiring additional code for packing the photons into a linear array.

The path regeneration technique is orthogonal to other optimizations that target fast ray-primitive intersection and traversal algorithms. Furthermore, it does not pose any requirements on the shared memory, enabling its usage for other purposes of the algorithm. Another option for keeping all the processing units busy is to use only a number of persistent threads that repeatedly fetch paths from a queue [1]. This is essentially very similar to our concept, with the difference being that we do not need to manage the queues: the new path is (re)generated on demand whenever a thread becomes inactive. A completely different approach has been shown in [3], which minimizes the amount of sparse warps by compacting the rays before tracing them. Furthermore, the authors also sort the rays according to their origin and direction to achieve more coherent memory accesses. Notice that both previous techniques (persistent threads, ray sorting) are complementary to our optimization, allowing them to be combined. The regeneration technique improves the workload of individual processing units by regenerating terminated paths; therefore, it does not solve the underutilization that is due to divergent branching that occurs during the kd-tree traversal and shading. In order to avoid warp divergence, another technique has to be incorporated.

Even though we have demonstrated the path regeneration on algorithms used mainly in computer graphics, the technique is sufficiently general and can be applied to other areas whenever a vast number of random walks has to be computed (e.g., Monte Carlo simulations of flow in heterogeneous porous media).

Acknowledgments

This work is partially funded by the Deutsche Forschungs-gemeinschaft (DFG), as part of the Collaborative Research Centre SFB 627; the Ministry of Education, Youth and Sports of the Czech Republic, under research programs MSM 6840770014, LC-06008 (Center for Computer Graphics), and MEB-060906 (Kontakt OE/CZ); and the Grant Agency of the Czech Technical University in Prague, grant No. SGS10/289/OHK3/3T/13.

References

[1] T. Aila, S. Laine, Understanding the efficiency of ray traversal on GPUs, in: Proceedings of the Conference on High Performance Graphics 2009, ACM, New York, NY, USA, 2009, pp. 145–149.

[2] P. Dutre, K. Bala, P. Bekaert, Advanced Global Illumination, A.K. Peters, Ltd., Natick, MA, USA, 2002.

[3] K. Garanzha, C. Loop, Fast ray sorting and breadth-first packet traversal for GPU ray tracing, Comput. Graph. Forum. 29 (2) (2010) 289–298.

[4] H.W. Jensen, Global illumination using photon maps, in: Proceedings of the Eurographics Workshop on Rendering Techniques '96, London, UK, 1996, pp. 21–30.

[5] T. Kajiya, The rendering equation, in: Computer Graphics Proceedings of SIGGRAPH '86, vol. 20 (4), ACM, New York, NY, USA, 1986, pp. 143–150.

[6] A. Keller, Instant radiosity, in: Proceedings of the 24th Annual Conference on Computer Graphics and Interactive Techniques, ACM Press/Addison-Wesley Publishing Co., New York, NY, 1997, pp. 49–56.

[7] E.P. Lafortune, Y.D. Willems, Bi-directional path tracing, in: Compugraphics '93, Alvor, Portugal, 1993, pp. 145–153.

[8] J. Novák, V. Havran, C. Dachsbacher, Path regeneration for interactive path tracing, in: Eurographics 2010 Annex: Short Paper, Eurographics Association, Norrköping, Sweden, 2010, pp. 61–64.

From Sparse Mocap to Highly Detailed Facial Animation

27

Bernd Bickel, Manuel Lang

The face conveys the most relevant visual characteristics of human identity and expression. Hence, realistic facial animations or interactions with virtual avatars are important for storytelling and gameplay. However, current approaches are either computationally expensive, require very specialized capture hardware, or are extremely labor intensive. In our article, we present a method for real-time animation of highly detailed facial expressions based on sparse motion capture data and a limited set of static example poses. This data can be easily obtained by traditional capture hardware. The proposed in-game algorithm is fast. It also is easy to implement and maps well onto programmable GPUs.

27.1 SYSTEM OVERVIEW

Our method for real-time animation of highly detailed facial expressions decomposes geometry into large-scale motion and fine-scale details, such as expression wrinkles.

First, large-scale deformations are computed with a fast and simple linear deformation model, which is intuitively and accurately controlled by a sparse set of motion-capture markers or user-defined handle points. Our GPU implementation for this step is only a couple of lines long and already results in a convincing facial animation by exactly interpolating the given marker points.

In the second step, fine-scale facial details, like wrinkles, are incorporated using a pose-space deformation technique. In a precomputation step, the correlation of wrinkle formation to sparsely measured skin strain is learned. At runtime, given an arbitrary facial expression, our algorithm computes the skin strain from the relative distance between marker points and derives fine-scale corrections for the large-scale deformation. During gameplay only the sparse set of marker-point positions is transmitted to the GPU. The face animation is entirely computed on the GPU where the resulting mesh can directly be used as input for the rendering stages.

Our method features real-time animation of highly detailed faces with realistic wrinkle formation and allows both large-scale deformations and fine-scale wrinkles to be edited intuitively. Furthermore, our pose-space representation enables the transfer of facial details to novel expressions or other facial models. Both large- and fine-scale deformation algorithms run entirely on the GPU, and our implementation based on CUDA achieves an overall performance of about 30 fps on an NVIDIA 8800 GTX graphics card for a mesh of 530,000 vertices and more than a million faces.

27.2 BACKGROUND

Modeling, acquisitions, and animation of the human face are topics largely explored in computer graphics and related fields like computer vision. We will quickly review and compare the current state-of-the-art methods for real-time facial animation before we dive into the specifics of our method.

One large family of face animation methods evolved around a technique called blend shapes. As the name suggests, a facial expression is obtained by linearly combining ("blending") a set of example shapes. As demonstrated by Lorach [6], this operation can be performed very efficiently on the GPU. Blend shapes are a very flexible and powerful tool, but the example shapes have to be created and selected very carefully because the method is able to produce only facial expressions spanned by those examples. Therefore, the number of required input poses tends to be high. All of these input poses have to be modeled or scanned. Our two-scale approach allows a significant reduction in the required number of example poses. In contrast to blend shapes, we start with a single pose. Using a simple, but powerful deformation technique, we obtain the large-scale deformation. The method ensures that given motion capture marker positions are exactly matched; therefore, we obtain already in the first step an accurate overall pose approximation, which has to be enriched only by the specific fine-scale details distinctive for the given pose. This is done by our fine-scale enrichment. A few example input poses are sufficient for learning the formation of high-resolution details based on local skin strain.

Alternatively, Borshukov *et al.* [7] presents a stunning method for reproducing realistic animated faces called Playable Universal Capture. In addition to a marker-based motion capture system, they use high-definition color cameras to record an animated texture. The animated texture contains fine details and "baked-in" ambient occlusion. Although this technique is already successfully applied in various computer games, it requires very specialized capture hardware and is restricted to playback of captured sequences. When the animation is split in three parts, a single mesh in undeformed state, the large-scale, and the fine-scale deformation allow us to perform editing operations on each of them independently and even reuse fine-scale details on different facial models. This gives artists and animators the freedom to combine any facial model with any other dataset of facial details and even enrich artificial characters with real-life captured wrinkle data. For a storage-critical application, this may also allow reduction of the number of different facial details and save memory by reusing the same details on multiple characters.

27.3 CORE TECHNOLOGY AND ALGORITHMS

We start with an overview of the input data and the workflow of our face animation pipeline, depicted in Figure 27.1, before describing the large-scale and fine-scale deformations in more detail in the following sections. In contrast to blend shapes, which linearly combine several facial poses, we use a single high-resolution face mesh of the rest pose ($\sim$1 M triangles), and generate all frames of the animation by deforming this mesh from its rest pose.

We compute the large-scale facial motion using a linear thin shell model. Figuratively, it approximates the face as a rubber shell and minimizes bending and stretching energies. Its deformation is controlled through a set of approximately 100 handle vertices, which may correspond to a set of face points tracked during an actor's performance or may be interactively controlled by an animator.

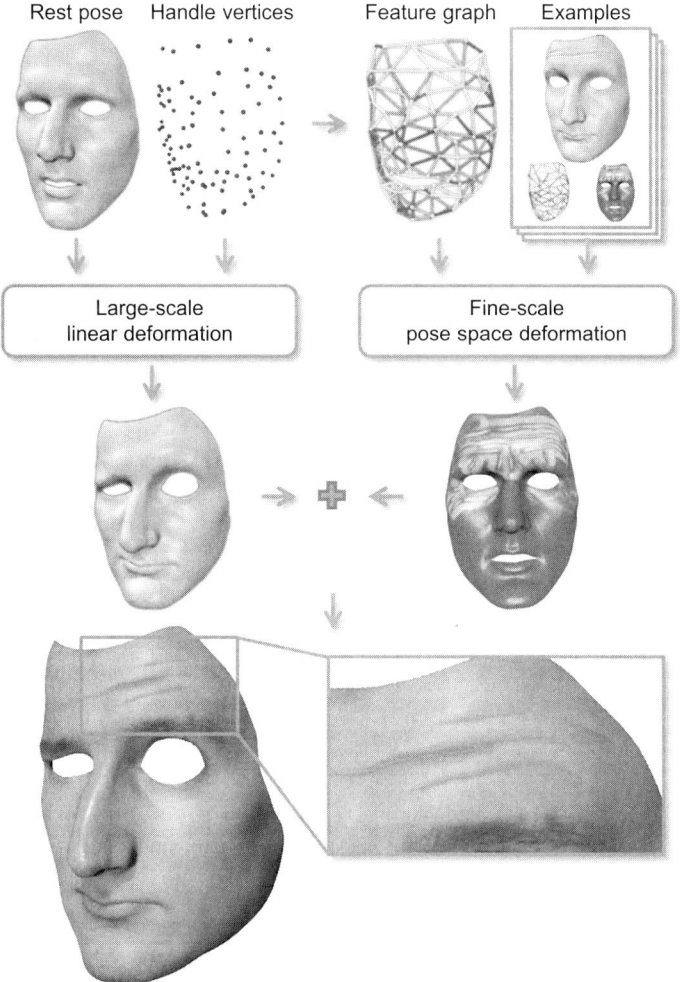

FIGURE 27.1

Our animation pipeline computes the large-scale facial motion from a linear deformation model and adds fine-scale details from a set of example poses. Image from Bickel et al., 2008.

The resulting large-scale deformation successfully captures the overall facial expression, but lacks fine-scale facial details such as expression wrinkles.

The nonlinear behavior that goes beyond the linear large-scale motion is learned in a preprocess from a set of example poses. These examples are represented by high-resolution triangle meshes in full-vertex correspondence with the rest pose mesh. In practice, example poses can, for instance, be created manually by an artist or by capturing an actor's face with a high-resolution scanner. Given the example poses, the corresponding fine-scale details are extracted per-vertex as the difference between the examples and the results of the large-scale deformation for the same poses.

In order to synthesize the fine-scale corrections for an arbitrary facial pose, we learn the correlation of skin strain to the formation of skin details such as wrinkles. The skin strain is approximated by the relative distance change of neighboring marker points. These discrete measurements are sufficient for locally controlling the fine-scale corrections on a per-vertex basis (Figure 27.1, right).

27.3.1 Large-Scale Deformation

For the large-scale face deformation we employ the method of Bickel *et al.* [1], which demonstrates that the displacements of a set of sparse handle vertices provides sufficient geometric constraints for capturing the large-scale facial motion in a plausible way. Given as input constraints the 3-D displacements $u_H \in R^{H \times 3}$ of the H handle vertices, the large-scale deformation is computed by minimizing a simplified quadratic thin shell energy. The deformation is represented as a vector u, containing the displacement of all free vertices from their rest pose position. A comprehensive overview of linear surface deformation methods can be found in Botsch and Sorkine [2].

Setting Up the Equations
This amounts to solving the equations

$$-k_s \Delta u + k_b \Delta^2 u = 0,$$

under the constraints u_H imposed by handle vertices. In this equation, k_s and k_b denote the stiffness for surface stretching and bending, respectively, and Δ is the Laplace-Beltrami operator. It can be discretized using the following form:

$$\Delta u_i = w_i \sum_{v_j \in N_1(v_i)} W_{ij} (u_j - u_i),$$

where u_i is the displacement of the i'th vertex v_i, and $v_i \in N_1(v_i)$ are its incident one-ring neighbors. For the per-vertex normalization weights and the edge weights, we are using the de facto standard cotangent discretization [2].

$$w_i = \frac{1}{A_i}, \quad w_{ij} = \frac{1}{2\left(\cot \alpha_{ij} + \cot \beta_{ij}\right)},$$

where α_{ij} and β_{ij} are the two angles opposite to the edge (v_i, v_j), and A_i is the Voronoi area of vertex v_i as shown in Figure 27.2.

Setting up this equation at every free vertex yields the linear system

$$(A \quad A_H) \begin{pmatrix} u \\ u_H \end{pmatrix} = 0$$

to be solved for the unknown displacements $u \in \mathbf{R}^{(V-H) \times 3}$ of the $(V - H)$ free vertices. The matrix A is of size $(V - H) \times (V - H)$, and A_H is of size $(V - H) \times H$.

Implementation — Solving It in Real Time
The standard way of computing the displacements would be directly solving the preceding linear equation system. However, we found that precomputing a "basis function" matrix $Bu_H = u$ allows a very

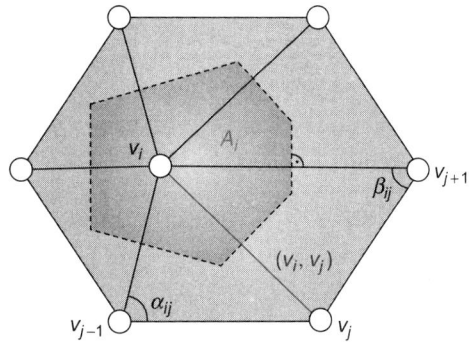

FIGURE 27.2

The cotangent discretization. The weights of the Laplacian operator at a vertex v_i are computed by considering the Voronoi area A_i and the edge weights W_{ij} based on the cotangents of the angles α_{ij} and β_{ij} opposite to the edge.

efficient evaluation of the large-scale deformation during runtime on the GPU. Basically, the required computation during runtime boils down to a simple matrix-vector multiplication of the basis function matrix B with the handle positions u_H.

The basis function matrix $B = -A^{-1}A_H$ depends only on the rest pose mesh and the selection of handle vertices. Each column b_i of B is computed by solving a sparse linear system $Ab_i = h_i$ involving A and the corresponding column h_i of A_H.

At runtime, the large-scale deformation u is obtained from the handle displacement u_H by the matrix product $Bu_H = u$, which can efficiently be computed in a parallel GPU implementation. The kernel for the matrix multiplication is given in Listing 27.1.

Before starting the animation sequence, we load all required static data to GPU memory. In the case of the large-scale deformation, this comprises the position of all vertices in their rest pose (float4 *in) and the basis function matrix B^T (float *basis). During animation only the current handle displacements u_H have to be copied to the GPU (float3 *handles) and the `LargeScaleKernel` kernel function has to be invoked for all face vertices in parallel. The function first copies the commonly accessed handles to fast on-chip shared memory. After that step is completed, the matrix vector multiplication can be carried out in a simple for-loop, and the resulting displacements can be added to rest pose positions. Please note that matrix B is stored transposed to achieve a coalesced memory access pattern.

27.3.2 Fine-Scale Deformation

The linear deformation model described in the last section approximates the facial motion well at a large scale. However, nonlinear fine-scale effects, such as the bulging produced by expression wrinkles, cannot be reproduced. These fine-scale deformations are highly nonlinear with respect to the positions of the handle vertices. However, they vary smoothly as a function of facial pose; hence, we have opted for learning, as a preprocess, the fine-scale displacement d from a set of example poses, and then at runtime compute it by interpolation in a suitable facial pose space.

We first define a facial pose space based on a rotation-invariant feature vector of skin strain and formulate the learning problem as scattered-data interpolation in this pose space. We extend the basic

```
extern__shared_float3shared_handles[];
__global__void LargeScaleKernel(      float4 *out,           // ouput: vertex pos
                                      float4 * in,           // rest pose vert. Pos
                                      unsignedint vertex_count,
                                      float3 *handles, //displacements handles
                                      unsignedint handle_count,
                                      float *basis, // basis function matrix
                                      unsignedint stride) //alignment for basis
{

        ////2D Grid and 1D block
        unsignedint n = (blockIdx.y *gridDim.x * blockDim.x)
                + blockIdx.x * blockDim.x + threadIdx.x;

        // Copy handles to shared memory
        if (threadIdx.x<handle_count) {
                shared_handles[threadIdx.x] = handles[threadIdx.x];
        }
        __syncthreads();
        if (n<vertex_count) {
                float4 vertex = in[n];       // vertexrest pose position

                for (int i= 0 ; i<handle_count; i++) {
                        float3 uh = shared_handles[i];
                        float b = basis[i*stride + n];
                        //float3 += float3 * float
                        VECSCAL_EXPR( vertex, +=, uh, *, b);
                }
                out[n] = vertex;
        }
}
```

Listing 27.1: The large-scale deformation can be implemented as a matrix vector multiplication.

method to weighted pose-space deformation, segmenting the face implicitly into individual regions and thereby allowing for a more compact basis.

Skin Strain Is a Good Descriptor for Facial Pose

We require a suitable space and descriptor that controls the interpolation of fine-scale displacements from a set of example poses. At each animation frame, the raw input data describing a pose consists of the positions of the handle vertices. These data are not invariant under rigid transformations; hence, it does not constitute an effective pose descriptor.

As everybody can observe, bulging effects of wrinkles appear due to lateral compression of skin patches. Therefore, we suggest a feature vector that measures skin strain between various points across the face. We define a set of F edges between handle vertices, which yields an F-dimensional feature vector $f = [f_1 \ldots f_F]$ of a pose. The entry f_i represents the relative stretch of the i'th feature edge, which can be regarded as a measure of strain. Specifically, given the positions of the end points $p_{i,1}$ and $p_{i,2}$

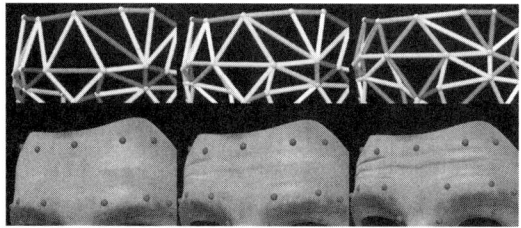

FIGURE 27.3

Wrinkle formation and skin strain. Close-up of the forehead for three input examples (bottom) and the corresponding strain on the feature edges (top), showing the correlation between skin strain and wrinkle formation. Image from Bickel et al., 2008.

and the rest length l_i, we define

$$f_i = \frac{\|\, p_{i,1} - p_{i,2}\,\| - l_i}{l_i}.$$

Figure 27.3 shows the correlation between the feature vector and wrinkle formation.

Mathematical Background — Blending in High-Resolution Details

Our goal is to use a data-driven approach and learn the connection of skin strain to wrinkle formation. We represent each facial expression by its rotation-invariant feature vector f as described in the last section. Hence, each facial expression corresponds to a point in an F-dimensional pose space, which constitutes the domain of the function we want to learn. Its range is the fine-scale detail correction d, represented as well in a rotation-invariant manner by storing it in per-vertex local frames.

Each of the P example poses corresponds to a feature vector f with its associated fine-scale displacement d. Our goal is now to come up with a function that fulfills the following properties:

- Given an arbitrary facial pose, compute efficiently the fine-scale displacements by smart interpolation and extrapolation of the details contained in the example poses.
- Given an input facial pose, it should accurately reproduce the corresponding input detail.
- It should vary smoothly and should not contain any discontinuities.

This corresponds to a scattered data interpolation problem, for which we employ radial basis functions (RBFs). Hence, the function $d : \mathbf{R}^F \rightarrow \mathbf{R}^{3V}$, mapping a facial pose to 3-D fine-scale displacement, has the form

$$d(f) = \sum_{j=1}^{P} W_j \cdot \varphi\left(\|\, f - f_j \,\|\right),$$

where φ is a scalar basis function, and $w_j \in \mathbf{R}^{3V}$ and f_j are the weight and feature vectors for the j'th example pose. We employ the biharmonic RBF kernel $\varphi(r) = r$, because it allows for smooth interpolation of sparsely scattered example poses and does not require any additional parameter tuning. More information on smooth scattered data interpolation using RBFs can be found in Carr *et al.* [5].

Local Blending

In our basic definition of a function for blending in details, every input example influences all vertices of the face mesh in the same manner because we compute a single feature distance $\| f - f_i \|$ per example pose j. This feature distance is constant over the whole face. Consequently, the set of example poses is required to grow exponentially to sufficiently sample the combinations of independent deformations (e.g., raising both eyebrows versus raising just one eyebrow). As an answer to this problem, we follow the idea of [4]. We break the face into several overlapping areas. Every vertex will be affected only by a small set of nearby strain measurements. This requires us to redefine the function $d(f)$ to compute feature distances in a per-vertex manner, replacing the global Euclidean metric $\| f - f_i \|$ with a weighted distance metric per vertex v:

$$
\varphi_{f,v} := \| f - f_j \|_v := \left(\sum_{i=1}^{F} \alpha_{v,i} \left(f_i - f_{j,i} \right)^2 \right)^{\frac{1}{2}},
$$

where $f_{j,i}$ is the strain of the i'th strain edge in the j'th pose. We exploit the fact that every edge measures a local property (i.e., relative stretch of feature edges), and therefore, assign weights $\alpha_{v,i}$ based on proximity to the edges. Specifically, for a vertex v we define the weight of the i'th feature edge as a exponentially decaying weight

$$
\alpha_{(v,i)} = \overline{\alpha}_{(v,i)} / \left(\sum_i a_{(v,i)} \right) \text{ with } \overline{\alpha}_{v,i} = e^{-\beta(L_{v,i} - l_i)},
$$

where l_i is the rest length of the feature edge, and $L_{v,i}$ is the sum of rest pose distances from vertex v to the edge end points. This weight is 1 on the edge and decays smoothly everywhere else, as shown in Figure 27.4. The parameter β can be used to control the rate of decay, based on the local density of handle vertices. In our experiments we discard weights $\overline{\alpha} < 0.025$, and set β so that a vertex is influenced by at most 16 edges.

Precomputation

As a preprocess, the RBF weights w_j have to be computed. We compute the weights so that the displacements of the example poses are interpolated exactly; that is, $d(f_i) = d_i$. This reduces to solving $3 \cdot V$ linear $P \times P$ systems, which differ in their right-hand side only.

27.3.3 Implementation — Synthesizing High-Resolution Details on the GPU

Calculating the high-resolution details during runtime is done by evaluating $d(f)$ for every vertex independently, as shown in Listing 27.2. First, the scalar basis function $\varphi_{f,v}$ is evaluated and multiplied with the corresponding precomputed weight w_j. The sum of those yields the displacement correction in the local tangent frame. These are transformed into global coordinates and applied to the vertex positions.

Evaluating $\varphi_{f,v}$ efficiently is done by precomputing the $\alpha_{v,i}$'s and storing them on GPU memory (`alphas_v`). To achieve real-time performance, we consider only the 16 (`alpha_size = 16`) closest strain measurements. Therefore, for every vertex, we store the `alpha_size` non-zero $\alpha_{v,i}$ values. We utilize another `alpha_size` large array (`alpha_indices_v`) per vertex to store the indices pointing to the corresponding feature vector (`poses_f`) entries. The feature vector of all example poses is stored in the `arrayposes_f`. This data structure is randomly accessed from all vertices and fits into fast shared

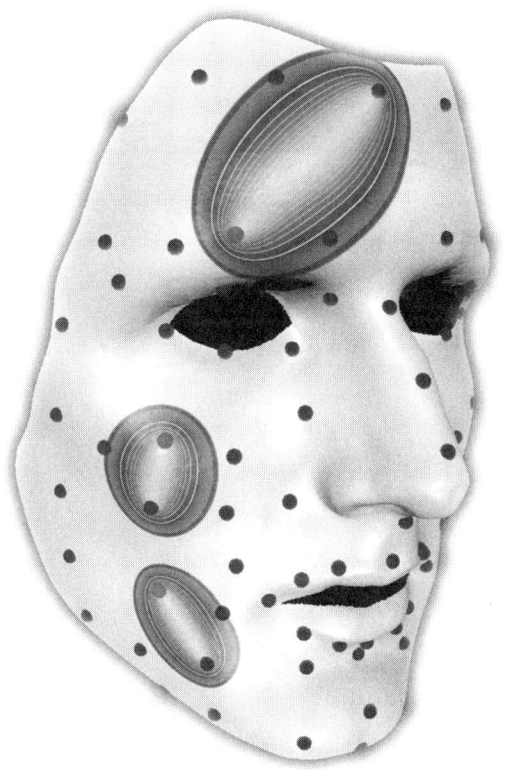

FIGURE 27.4

For three edges, the exponentially dropping local influence weight $\alpha_{v,i}$ is shown. The weights decay in a way such that every face vertex is influenced by at most 16 feature edges.

memory. After we have calculated the weighted distance $\varphi_{f,v}$ (phi_fv), we multiply it with w_j's of each vertex. Because w_j's (poses_w) is large and the entries are accessed only once per vertex, we store it in a way that coalesced reads are used.

Now, the computed fine-scale displacements $d(f)$ have to be applied onto the vertex positions (vertex) resulting from the previous large-scale deformation. $d(f)$ is represented in a local coordinate frame at each vertex. We defined the local coordinate frame by assigning each mesh vertex a specific neighbor vertex. This neighbor vertex position, together with the vertex normal, is sufficient to span a consistent local coordinate frame. Based on the local frame, we compute and apply the global high-resolution details.

27.3.4 **Results and Evaluation**

Our method is designed for parallel GPU computation. All computations are carried out on the GPU, and the resulting geometry is directly passed to the rendering stage, without transferring a large amount of data. During runtime, the animation is controlled by the motion-capture marker position, and only these data have to be sent to the GPU.

```
if (n<vertex_count) {
    float3 df = {0.0f,0.0f,0.0f};

    // evaluating d(f)
    for(unsignedint j = 0 ; j<poses_count; j++) {
        float phi_fv = 0.0f;
        //only the alpha_size highest term of sum phi_f are considered
        for(unsignedint i=0; i<alpha_size; i++) {
                unsignedint idx = alpha_indices_v[i*joint_stride + n];
                float alpha = alphas_v[i*joint_stride + n];    //alpha_{vi}

                //difference f_i −f_{ij}
                float reg = (features[idx] − poses_f[j * poses_dim + idx]);
                phi_fv += reg *  reg * alpha;
        }
        phi_fv = sqrtf(phi_fv);

        float3 w_j = *((float3*) (&poses_w[j*poses_w_stride + n * 3]));

        VECSCAL_EXPR( df, +=, w_j, * , phi_fv);
    }

    //apply offset in right local frame:
    //calculate frame
    float4 normal = normals[n];
    float4 nb = neighbors[n];//'first' neighbor
    float4 v = vertex[n];

    VECVEC_EXPR ( nb, = , nb, − , v );

    float dot = VEC_DOT( nb, normal);
    VECSCAL_EXPR ( nb, −=, normal, * , dot);

    float normaliz = VEC_DOT ( nb, nb);
    normaliz = rsqrtf (normaliz );

    VECSCAL_EXPR ( nb, =, nb, * , normaliz);

    float4 y;
    VEC_CROSS( y, normal, nb);

    //apply fine−scale detail
    VECSCAL_EXPR ( v, +=, normal, * , df.x );
    VECSCAL_EXPR ( v, +=, nb, * , df.y  );
    VECSCAL_EXPR ( v, +=, y, * , df.z );

    vertex[n] = v;
    }
```

Listing 27.2: This CUDA kernel computes the fine-scale details for a given a set of approximated local skin strain measurements.

27.3.5 **Parallelization**

The significant speedup compared with a single-core CPU (about a factor of 80, factor of 10 on an eight core) is possible because our method is parallelized over the large number of vertices of the face mesh. The position and displacement of vertices can be computed independently from each other. We need three CUDA kernels to perform the animation. First, the large-scale kernel computes new positions for all face vertices; these positions are simply obtained by three dot products (for x, y, z coordinates) of weights with handle positions. Then, the normals of the face vertices have to be updated. This is done in one kernel with the help of a simple data structure enumerating one ring of vertices around every vertex. Then, the fine-scale enrichment kernel calculates the local displacement for each vertex and computes all new vertex positions in parallel. This is followed by a second final vertex normal update for rendering. In our current implementation, we utilize the CPU to synchronize the kernel invokes of the aforementioned steps.

27.3.6 **Memory Access Strategy**

We found that an optimized memory access pattern is crucial to achieve the required interactive performance. In the following, we will quickly summarize the applied strategies. Most of them will be very familiar to experienced GPU programmers, and some of them are less important on newer hardware (compute capability 2.0).

Large-Scale Deformation

For the large-scale deformation, it is important to note that the same handle position is accessed simultaneously by all threads. Therefore, the handle positions should be either placed in shared memory or in constant memory. Because all threads address the same location at the same time, both methods will be almost as fast as accessing a register (after caching).

Furthermore, every element in the basis matrix is accessed only once per kernel invocation; therefore, it is not helpful to copy it first into shared memory. Only a neighborhood-aware caching could improve performance. This would be exactly what texture-caching units could achieve. However, our large-scale deformation basis matrix is too large to fit into a CUDA array (texture). It is also too big to fit into cached constant memory. Therefore, we can optimize only the access pattern for global memory. Luckily, this is straightforward. The matrix is stored transposed so that the information for each thread (vertex) is next to each other. This way, the number of rows in the matrix is equal to the number of handles. It is also important to use a correct padding between the rows to achieve coalesced memory access also on older GPUs. In this context, one can also benefit from NVIDA GF100's L1 cache that enhances memory locality.

Fine-Scale Deformation

Finding the right memory access patterns for the fine-scale deformation kernel is a bit more involved. The per-frame input of this stage is the feature vector composed out of approximately 250 scalar float values (the strain measurements). In contrast to the large-scale deformation, not all input components are accessed exactly once by all vertices. Multiple threads in one block will likely access some of the components multiple times. Therefore, these reads should be cached. In this case we opt in for shared memory. We assume that simultaneously running threads will randomly access 16 of the feature vector components. By placing them into shared memory, we observed that random bank conflicts are not too frequent. The other option would be constant memory, but because threads will likely not access the same address at the same time, a bank-conflict-free shared memory access is faster. We apply the same strategy for the feature vectors of all example poses. Luckily, all feature vectors together fit into shared memory.

All other data in this kernel is accessed only once per vertex, and therefore, we just utilized coalesced memory reads.

Normal Updates

We have to update all vertex normals twice in our algorithm. The data accessed by the normal update kernel are the vertex positions and a list of indices per vertex to help finding the first ring of neighbor vertices (the list is terminated with a-1 index). For older computing architectures it is beneficial to interleave the neighbor list so that vertices running in the same warp will have a coalesced access pattern.

27.3.7 **Performance**

We tested the performance of our method with a detailed facial model. The face model is composed from 530,000 vertices and more than one million triangles. To achieve convincing animation results we required only six example poses. The animation sequence was captured by motion capturing with 89 mocap markers that were directly painted on the actor's face. The 89 markers were directly used to drive the large-scale deformation and additionally they were used to compute 243 discrete local strain measurements. These 243 float values were used as per-frame input to the fine-scale kernel. Overall, we stored 137 floats and 24 integers per face vertex on the GPU memory. For this setup we obtained an overall performance of about 30 fps on an NVIDIA 8800 GTX graphics card on Windows XP. The large-scale deformation required about 4 ms and fine-scale deformation was performed in 13 ms. Additionally, we had to update the vertex normals twice (one after large-scale deformation and one before rendering). This was also done in CUDA and required about 5 ms per update. A subsequent simple untextured Gouraud shading in OpenGL required 4 ms. With an additional skin rendering providing real-time subsurface scattering, as described by D'Eon et al. [8], the final rendering took about 36 ms/frame for our highly detailed mesh.

Table 27.1 shows a comparison of performance numbers. Our algorithm was 10 times faster than an OpenMP CPU implementation. The CPU implementation would also require an additional copy of the entire face onto the GPU every frame before rendering (+2 ms GTX480, not included in the measured timings). We also observed that the user space driver model in Windows 7 influenced our

Table 27.1 Performance numbers for a different configuration and comparison with the CPU. Face model with 530,000 vertices.

	GTX8800 Windows XP	GTX480 Windows 7	CPU i7920 QuadCore*
Large-scale kernel	4 ms	6 ms	65 ms
Medium-scale kernel	13 ms	11 ms	80 ms

The CPU implementation uses OpenMP to utilize eight logical cores.

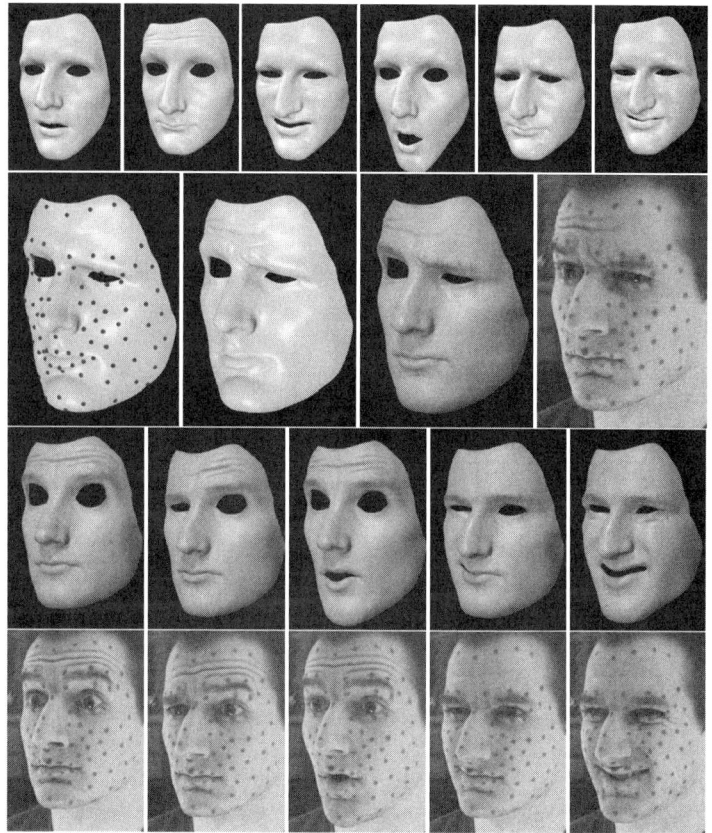

FIGURE 27.5

Results. The first row shows the six example poses used. The second row shows the intermediate large-scale result and the final result. The third and fourth rows show some additional results with asymmetric deformations not present in the input examples. Image from Bickel et al., 2008.

timings significantly. One solution to reduce the kernel invocation overhead would be to implement everything in a single kernel and use global GPU synchronization techniques. However, those features are only available on newer architectures.

27.4 FUTURE DIRECTIONS

Although we focused on animating human faces, the presented algorithms are not inherently limited to this application area. Theoretically, our approach can be applied for deforming arbitrary surfaces, but large local rotations would require special handling owing to linearization artifacts that we do not address in this chapter.

There is room for further speeding up of the algorithm. All timings were measured on a dense, uniformly sampled mesh. Although in regions such as the forehead and around the eyes, complex wrinkle structures might show up, other regions, such as the cheek or chin, are less affected. Adaptive mesh decimation depending on the frequency of the high-resolution features could lead to significant speedups.

CUDA is a perfect environment to implement the algorithms presented in this chapter in a highly parallelized way on a GPU without being limited by the API of a traditional graphics pipeline. However, future work could investigate how the algorithms could be mapped onto traditional shader architectures. Large-scale and fine-scale deformation are both parallelized over the vertices; therefore, a vertex shader could be a natural choice for both. The large-scale deformation could be implemented in vertex shader straightforward, but extra care has to be given to the large basis matrix. A single texture (often restricted to $8k \times 8k$) might not be able to store the entire matrix for a large face with many handles. Also a high number of handles may not fit into an available number of uniform registers. Modern extensions to graphics APIs, like DirectCompute or OpenCL, could also be an alternative for a GPU vendor-independent implementation, as often required for commercial products.

Acknowledgments

This chapter is based on the paper "Pose-Space Animation and Transfer of Facial Details" by Bickel et al., 2008. Figure 27.1 and Figure 27.3, Eurographics Association 2008. Reproduced by kind permission of the Eurographics Association.

References

[1] B. Bickel, M. Lang, M. Botsch, M. Otaduy, M. Gross, Pose-space animation and transfer of facial details, in: M. Gross, D. James (Eds.), Proceedings of the 2008 ACM SIGGRAPH/Eurographics Symposium on Computer Animation, July 7–9, 2008, Dublin, Ireland, 2008, pp. 57–66.

[2] M. Meyer, M. Desbrun, P. Schrder, A.H. Barr, Discrete differential-geometry operators for triangulated 2-manifolds, in: Visualization and Mathematics III, Springer-Verlag, 2003, pp. 35–57.

[3] J.P. Lewis, M. Cordner, N. Fong, Pose spaced deformations: a unified approach to shape interpolation and skeleton-driven deformation, in: K. Akeley (Ed.), Proceedings of SIGGRAPH 00, New Orleans, 2000, pp. 165–172.

[4] T. Rhee, J.P. Lewis, U. Neumann, Real-time weighted pose-space deformation on the GPU, in: Proceedings of Eurographics, Comput. Graph. Forum 25 (3) (2006) 439–448.

[5] J.C. Carr, R.K. Beatson, J.B. Cherrie, T.J. Mitchell, W.R. Fright, B.C. McCallum et al., Reconstruction and representation of 3D objects with radial basis functions in: E. Fiume (Ed.), Proceedings of SIGGRAPH 01, Los Angeles, CA, 2001, pp. 67–76.

[6] T. Lorach, K. Akeley (Eds.), DirectX10 blend shapes: breaking the limit, in: H. Nguyen (Ed.), GPU Gems 3, Addison Wesley, Boston, MA, 2007, pp. 53–67.

[7] G. Borshukov, J. Montgomery, J. Hable, K. Akeley (Eds.), Playable universal capture, in: H. Nguyen (Ed.), GPU Gems 3, Addison Wesley, Boston, MA, 2007, pp. 349–371.

[8] E. D'eon, D. Luebke, E. Enderton, Efficient rendering of human skin, in: J. Kautz, S. Pattanaik (Eds.), Proceedings of Eurographics Symposium on Rendering, Grenoble, France, 2007, pp. 147–157.

A Programmable Graphics Pipeline in CUDA for Order-Independent Transparency

28

Mengcheng Huang, Fang Liu, Xuehui Liu, Enhua Wu

In this chapter we present a rasterization-rendering pipeline using CUDA. We discuss the implementation details of the basic functionalities in a hardware-rendering pipeline, with a focus on triangle rasterization and raster operations. Within this architecture, we propose two single-pass algorithms for efficient rendering of order-independent transparency. The results demonstrate significant performance speedups in comparison to the state-of-the-art methods that are based on traditional graphics pipelines.

28.1 INTRODUCTION, PROBLEM STATEMENT, AND CONTEXT

In recent years the graphics hardware has undergone tremendous growth in processing power and functionality. Early GPUs were built based on fixed-function pipelines with only a few adjustable parameters. With demands on more realistic visual effects, graphics hardware began to support programmable shading, where some stages of the pipeline can execute a user-defined program to generate customized effects. However, the triangle rasterization and raster operations (ROP) remain fixed functions on chip, making it difficult to implement many rendering algorithms efficiently.

Order-independent transparency is a classical problem in 3-D computer graphics; it requires the geometry to be sorted and composited in a back-to-front order from the viewpoint. Depth peeling [1] is the state-of-art solution to order-independent transparency that peels off one surface layer in each rendering pass. This method requires a number of iterations equal to the maximum depth complexity of transparent surfaces. For complex scenes, multiple geometry rasterizations are quite expensive. Ideally, we prefer to perform fragment sorting in a single-geometry pass. K-buffer [3] and bucket depth peeling [7] try to perform parallel insert sorting and bucket sorting on the GPU, but suffer from read/write race conditions and fragment collisions. As a result, it is difficult to implement fragment sorting with the traditional graphics pipeline in a single-geometry pass.

We implement the rasterization-based graphics pipeline using NVIDIA CUDA [8]. CUDA provides more flexible control over the GPU as a general-purpose parallel computing architecture. Some research work uses CUDA to implement other rendering architectures, such as ray tracing, and REYES-style micropolygon rendering, but CUDA implementation of a rasterization-rendering pipeline has received little attention by far. This work is based on our SI3D paper [2], with more emphasis on implementation issues. We show two modifications to the raster operations stage in the traditional graphics pipeline, with significant performance speedup compared with previous work based on the traditional pipeline.

28.2 CORE METHOD

We mapped the traditional graphics pipeline to the CUDA programming model, with each thread projecting a single triangle onto the screen and rasterizing it by an advanced scan-line algorithm [8]. On each pixel location covered by the projected triangle, a fragment will be generated with interpolated attributes, such as depth, color, and so on. A fixed-size array is allocated per pixel in global memory of GPU for storage. We then describe two schemes to store and sort the fragments per pixel using the atomic operations in CUDA to avoid the read-modify-write hazards. The first scheme stores the depth and color of the fragments into the array of the corresponding pixel and sorts them on the fly using the 64-bit *atomicCAS* operation in CUDA. The second scheme starts by setting a fragment counter initialized to 0 per pixel in global memory. Each incoming fragment will atomically increase the counter by 1 using the *atomicInc* operation and route the fragment into the corresponding entry of the array in rasterization order. In postprocessing, the fragments per pixel array will be sorted by insert sort or bitonic sort for further applications.

28.3 ALGORITHMS, IMPLEMENTATIONS, AND EVALUATIONS

28.3.1 System Overview

We implemented an OpenGL-like rendering pipeline, as shown in Figure 28.1. It takes three-dimensional scene geometry and camera parameters as input. The attributes of each vertex and the vertex indices of each triangle are packed into two textures for memory coherency. The modelview-projection matrix is computed according to the scene configurations in each frame and loaded to constant memory for low memory latency.

The traditional graphics pipeline can be mapped to the GPU with each thread processing a single triangle. The vertex transformation from model space to screen space can be performed by multiplying the modelview-projection matrix in vertex shader. After projection, if back face culling is enabled, the triangle will be tested according to its normal, and back faces will be discarded. Otherwise, the vertex order is reversed for consistency. The back-face culling test is performed with double precision, or some faces might be culled or reversed by error owing to the limited precision of the floating-point arithmetic. Frustum clipping is done by calculating the axis-aligned bounding volume of the triangle in screen space according to its three vertices. If the bounding volume is totally out of the view frustum, the triangle will be discarded, and the thread will terminate. Otherwise, the bounding box of the triangle on the screen plane will be clipped according to the size of the screen.

We then perform rasterization using an advanced scan-line algorithm that is optimized for small triangles [8]. Pixel locations covered by the clipped triangle bounding box will be tested, and each pixel inside the triangle will generate a fragment with interpolated attributes. In our system the fragment is represented by a data structure that encodes its color and depth. A customized routine is then executed to shade each fragment. We allocated a screen-aligned buffer in global memory as the frame buffer, and the shaded fragments will be directed to the corresponding pixel locations.

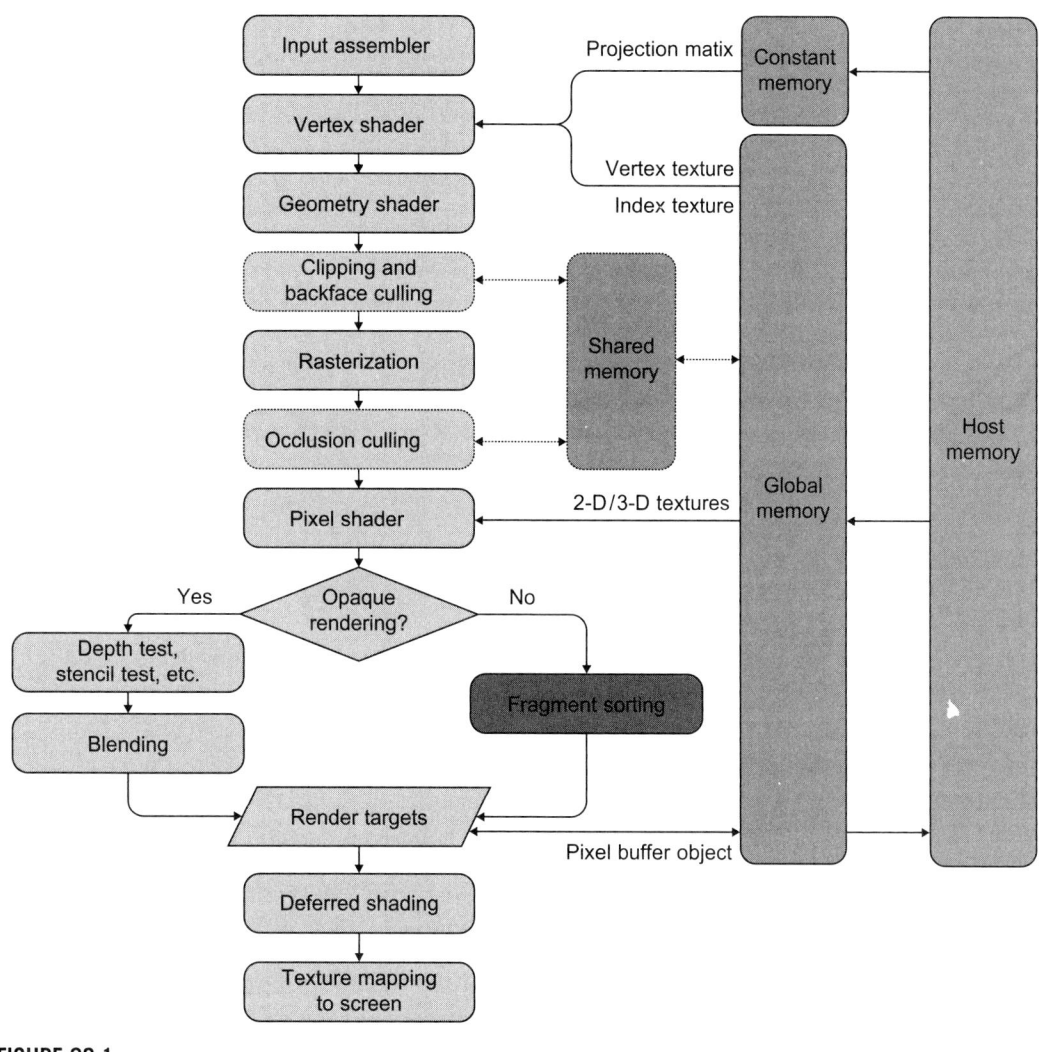

FIGURE 28.1

System overview.

The raster operations (ROP) stage will perform a set of per-fragment operations before updating the frame buffer. The depth test compares the depth value of incoming fragments to that stored in the depth buffer and discards occluded fragments. Transparent fragments are blended in the alpha-blending process. It's nontrivial to implement the ROP stage using CUDA because the built-in ROP stage in graphics hardware is not yet exposed to programmers. In our system, the depth test is simulated by multiple threads simultaneously reading and updating the same entry in the frame buffer. Inspired by RenderAnts [4], we describe a method using 64-bit *atomicCAS* operation to partially address this problem.

```
__device__ long long DepthTest(DepthColorBuffer,x,y,Depth,Color)
1       ZNew  ← ( (long long) Depth <<32 ) || Color;
2       ZOld ← DepthColorBuffer[x][y];
3       while( ZOld > ZNew )
4           ZTemp ← atomicCAS(&DepthColorBuffer[x][y],ZOld,ZNew);
5           if( ZOld == ZTemp )
6               break;
7           end if
8           ZOld ← ZTemp;
9       end while
10      return ZOld;
```

Listing 28.1: Pseudo code of depth test.

The *atomicCAS(*address, compare , val)* stores the *val* in global memory *address* if *compare* equals the old value stored at *address*. These operations can be executed in one atomic transaction without interference from other threads. The depth test can be simulated in the following algorithm as summarized in Listing 28.1.

In this case, the depth and color buffer will be allocated in the global memory and initialized to the maximum 64-bit integer (0x7FFFFFFFFFFFFFFF). In CUDA runtime API, the *cudaMemset* function initializes the device memory to a specific value, but it's less efficient to initialize such as a large amount of GPU memory. Instead, we use a simple CUDA kernel with each thread initializing a single entry of the array. In this way, the initializing operation can be performed entirely on the GPU without the involvement of the CPU, and the GPU gains more throughput.

The depth and color values of incoming fragments are packed into a 64-bit ZNew, with depth value located in the higher 32 bits. If ZNew is smaller than the current value ZOld in the depth buffer, it will try to store ZNew into the buffer using *atomicCAS* operation. Note that when multiple fragments are trying to update, the same pixel location simultaneously, the read/write race conditions will occur. *atomicCAS* will serialize the update and we use a *while()* loop to guarantee each fragment completes the test. As an example, suppose two fragments f_a and f_b with depth value $d_{old} > d_a > d_b$, d_{old} is the current value in the depth buffer. They simultaneously read d_{old} into ZOld and try to update the depth buffer because their depth value is smaller (line 3). The update is serialized by *atomicCAS*. Because fragment f_a comes earlier, the update is succeeded. Fragment f_b failed, however, because the value in depth buffer has changed to d_a and no longer equals to ZOld. We changed the ZOld to the returned value d_a so that fragment f_b will succeed in the next loop. Finally, the frame buffer will contain the fragment with the smallest depth value.

This strategy ensures coherent update of depth and color buffers. In postprocessing, the color buffer will be separated from the depth buffer and rendered to the screen using texture mapping. The whole pipeline of our system can be summarized in Listing 28.2.

Our system is flexible and offers full programmability in all stages, as shown in Figure 28.2. For order-independent transparency, we modify the blending stage of the pipeline and develop two efficient schemes to capture and sort multiple fragments per pixel in a single-geometry pass. The first scheme is called a multidepth test scheme, and it is an extension of the aforementioned depth test scheme. The second scheme is called A-buffer scheme, which captures all fragments per pixel in submission order via *atomicInc* operation and post-sorts them before deferred shading.

```
texture < float4, 1, cudaReadModeElementType> VertexTex;
texture < int4, 1, cudaReadModeElementType> IndexTex;
__constant__ int ScreenWidth,ScreenHeight,DepthArraySize;
__constant__ float MVP[16]; //Modelview−projection matrix
__global__ CUDARenderingPipeline(DepthColorBufferr)
1        [V1,V2,V3] = VertexShader(VertexTex,IndexTex,MVP,ThreadID);
2        if( !isFrontFace(V1,V2,V3) )
3            swap(V1,V2); // Reverse the vertex order of back face if back face culling is disabled
4        end if
5        BV ← GetBoungingVolume(V1,V2,V3);
6        FrustumClipping(BV,ScreenWidth,ScreenHeight);
7        for y = BV.miny : BV.maxy
8            for x = BV.minx : BV.maxx
9                if( isInsideTriangle(x,y,V1,V2,V3) )
10                   Depth ←__float _ as _int(InterpolateDepth());
11                   Color ← __float _ as _int(InterpolateColor());
12                   DepthTest(DepthColorBuffer,x,y,Depth,Color);
13               end if
14           end for
15       end for
```

Listing 28.2: Pseudo code of the pipeline.

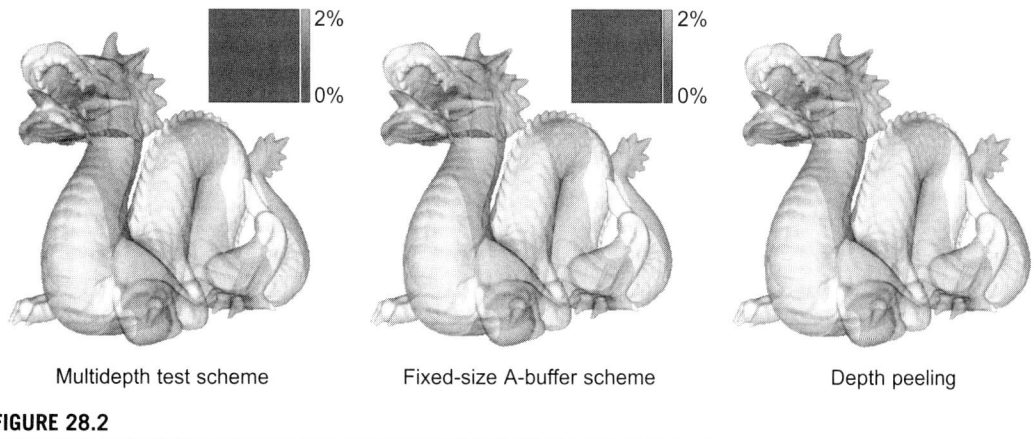

Multidepth test scheme	Fixed-size A-buffer scheme	Depth peeling

FIGURE 28.2

Transparency on the Stanford Dragon.

28.3.2 Multidepth Test Scheme

This scheme extends the depth test scheme to multiple levels and performs fragment sorting on the GPU using a novel parallel sorting algorithm for unpredictable data. The algorithm begins by allocating a fixed-size buffer array as storage with a 64-bit format in global memory. The size can be set to the maximum depth complexity in all view angles to avoid overflow, provided sufficient memory is available. Each entry of the buffer array will be initialized to the maximum value in the same way as described earlier in this chapter. As the buffer array is layered at the screen size, we can take it as a group of arrays per pixel. During rasterization, an incoming fragment will loop through the pixel array at a corresponding pixel location and store the depth value to the first empty entry via the depth test scheme described in Listing 28.1. For a nonempty entry, if its value is smaller than the current depth value, the entry will be left unchanged, and the fragment will continue to test the next entry. Otherwise, the depth value operation assures the current depth value to be stored into that entry and the returned source value will be used as a reference value to test the next entry. This operation loops until the fragment is stored into the first empty entry. Otherwise, it will be discarded at the end of the array. The algorithm can be summarized in Listing 28.3.

For applications that need only depth values, we can explore the *atomicMin* operation in CUDA to act as the depth test instead. In particular, we can substitute code line 3 by line 4 for simplicity and redefine MAX_VALUE as 0x7FFFFFFF in Listing 28.3.

This strategy guarantees correct ascending depth order under concurrent updates of the array per pixel without read-modify-write hazards. For a certain pixel location, suppose there are N threads generating N fragments in rasterization order. They will concurrently execute with each one loops to store its depth value into the array on that pixel location (denoted as A for short). Each thread will early or late begin the first iteration of the loop and try to store its depth value into A[0]. The first executed thread will always succeed to store its value into A[0] and exit the loop with the maximum value returned. The others will sequentially compare their values with A[0] and swap if their values are less than A[0]. After all the threads end the first iteration, the minimum fragment depth will be stored into A[0], while the rest N-1 threads will hold the rest N-1 values. In the second round they will compete for A[1] in the same way: the thread that first compares with A[1] will store its value into A[1] and exit the loop with the maximum integer returned, and the second minimum fragment depth will be stored into A[1], with the rest N-2 threads holding the rest N-2 values, and so on. After all the threads have exited the loop,

```
__device__ DepthSortWithColor(DepthColorBuffer,x,y,Depth,Color)
1        ZNew ← ( (long long)Depth <<32 ) || Color;
2        for i = 0 : DepthColorBufferSize − 1
3            ZOld ← DepthTest(DepthColorBuffer[i],x,y,ZNew);
4            // ZOld ← atomicMin(& DepthColorBuffer[i][x][y],ZNew);
5            if( ZOld == MAX _ VALUE ) // 0x7FFFFFFFFFFFFFFF
6                break;
7            end if
8        ZNew ← max(ZNew, ZOld);
9        end for
```

Listing 28.3: Pseudo code of multi depth test scheme.

all the depth values of the fragments will be stored into the array in ascending order. They can also be sorted on the fly in descending order in a similar way with the array initialized to 0. Then the sorted depth array per pixel can be passed to a following CUDA kernel for postprocessing.

Given an array of fixed-size N, the multidepth test scheme can correctly capture and sort the minimum N fragment depth values. In other words, it is capable of peeling off N front-most layers. This is useful for some applications when only the first N layers of the scene are needed, such as shadow mapping.

28.3.3 Fixed-Size A-Buffer Scheme

The multidepth test scheme performs fragment sorting in a time complexity of $O(N^2)$. It will suffer from high memory latency for complex scenes because the sort is performed in global memory. In addition, only one fragment attribution can be captured together with depth. So we resort to a second scheme to alleviate the problems.

Inspired by Carpenter [5], we allocate a fixed-size struct (such as *float2* for depth and color in order of independent transparency) array per pixel in global memory. We also set up a fragment counter for each pixel location. The counter is initialized to 0 by a CUDA kernel in a similar way for better throughput. Each incoming fragment will first increase the corresponding counter by 1 using the *atomicInc* operation. The *atomicInc* operation reads a 32-bit word located in global or shared memory, increases its value by 1, stores the result back to the memory at the same address, and returns the source value. In other words, the kth incoming fragment of a pixel will atomically increase the counter to $k + 1$ and return the source value k. Then the depth value and the additional attributes of the kth fragment can be stored into the kth entry of the array in submission order without read-modify-write hazards. The captured fragments will be sent to a post-sort CUDA kernel, with each thread handling only one pixel. All fragments per pixel will be loaded into an array allocated in the registers of that thread and sorted by insert sort or bitonic sort. The results then can be directly accessed in correct depth order for deferred shading in postprocessing without global memory access.

This scheme overcomes the problem of the multidepth test scheme in that it can capture multiple fragment attributes simultaneously. Meanwhile, the sorting is performed at the register level without memory latency, making it more efficient than sorting in global memory, especially for scenes with high-depth complexity.

28.4 FINAL EVALUATION

The experimental results of our two fragment-sorting schemes have demonstrated great speed improvement over previous methods that were based on the traditional graphics pipeline. We also compare them with the ground truth rendered by depth peeling, k-buffer, and bucket depth peeling. All the results were taken from a commodity PC, Intel Duo Core 2.4 GHz with 3 GB of memory and an NVIDIA Geforce 280 GTX (compute capability 1.3) with Windows XP Pro SP2 32-bit and CUDA version 2.1(181.20).

Figure 28.1 shows an order-independent transparent effect on the Stanford Dragon rendered by our two schemes for a 512×512 viewport. The depth values and the corresponding color attributes are captured and sorted in ascending order in a single-geometry pass, and blended in front-to-back order during postprocessing. Both results of our two schemes are almost identical to depth peeling, with only slight differences, as shown in the difference maps in Figure 28.1. This is mainly caused by different implementation details as well as the quantization errors of the color attribute.

The performance of our algorithm is evaluated by comparison to k-buffer [3], bucket depth peeling [7], and the classical depth peeling on a set of common models. The system configuration is the same as described earlier in this chapter. The analysis demonstrates that our algorithm produces faithful results with significant speed improvement, especially for large scenes.

For a scene with depth complexity N, both the multidepth test scheme (MDTS) and the fixed-size A-buffer scheme (FABS) gain an accelerate rate of about N times to depth peeling (see Table 28.1). Both k-buffer and bucket depth peeling have similar speedup as ours, but the former suffers from severe read-modify-write hazards, while the latter is subject to fragment collisions. The speedups of the two schemes compared with the two-pass (BDP2) and the adaptive (ADP) extensions of bucket depth peeling are more than two times owing to the two-geometry passes needed for these methods. Both schemes gain significant speedup to depth peeling, especially for large scenes because most memory access latency of the atomic operations on global memory overlaps that of vertex fetching during rasterization, and thus can be hidden by the thread scheduler. MDTS is a little slower than FABS because the sorting stage in MDTS is performed in global memory with high latency. In contrast, the array per pixel of FABS will first be loaded onto the registers of each thread and sorted by insert sort or bitonic sort with zero memory latency. As the screen resolution increases, the performance of both schemes will degrade consequently.

Current implementation is a proof-of-concept prototype, with the following limitations: First, the rasterization strategy used is efficient only when input triangles occupy a small number of pixels. If the scene contains large triangles, or the scene is scaled, each thread will loop through a large number of pixels covered by the triangle, resulting in heavy serialization. Second, when scene geometry contains fewer triangles, such as the Bunny case in Table 28.1, the speedup of our renderer will degrade rapidly. For a single large triangle at the extreme, the performance will be seriously degraded because all the fragments are shaded by only one thread without any parallelism. Third, our system is less efficient to handle geometries with too many layers, such as hair, grass, and transparent particle effects. The proposed two schemes will result in a serious performance bottleneck and memory consumption.

Table 28.1 Comparison of frame rates (fps) by different methods.

Model Name	Triangle Number	MDTS	FABS	K-buffer	BDP	BDP2	ADP	Depth Peeling	N
Bunny	70 K	455 fps	616 fps	875 fps	645 fps	317 fps	183 fps	141 fps	8
Armadillo	349 K	339 fps	422 fps	294 fps	258 fps	116 fps	107 fps	20 fps	13
Dragon	871 K	244 fps	316 fps	262 fps	256 fps	141 fps	106 fps	29 fps	10
Buddha	1.0 M	208 fps	275 fps	248 fps	253 fps	128 fps	98 fps	24 fps	10
Lion	1.3 M	152 fps	209 fps	163 fps	183 fps	91 fps	80 fps	11 fps	16
Lucy	2.0 M	152 fps	98 fps	149 fps	160 fps	80 fps	75 fps	18 fps	12
Neptune	4.0 M	87 fps	105 fps	46 fps	47 fps	23 fps	22 fps	5 fps	8

28.5 **FUTURE DIRECTION**

The CUDA implementation of the traditional rendering pipeline shows some promise. However, because of its limitations, the performance cannot catch up with highly optimized hardware implementation in general. It will be interesting to expect the change in future graphics hardware that exposes the rasterization and blending stages to programmers.

We believe that many other graphics applications, such as occlusion culling and antialiasing, could potentially benefit from the CUDA rendering system. We would like to investigate these extensions in the future.

References

[1] C. Everitt, Interactive order-independent transparency, Technical Report, NVIDIA Corporation, Santa Clara, CA, 2001.

[2] F. Liu, M.C. Huang, X.H, Liu, E.H. Wu, Freepipe: a programmable parallel rendering architecture for efficient multi-fragment effects, in: S.N. Spencer (Ed.), Symposium on Interactive 3d Graphics, Proceedings of the 2010 ACM SIGGRAPH Symposium on Interactive 3D Graphics and Games, Washington, D.C., ACM, New York, 2010, pp. 75–82.

[3] L. Bavoil, S.P. Callahan, A. Lefohn, J.L.D. Comba, C.T. Silva, Multi-fragment effects on the GPU using the k-buffer, in: S.N. Spencer (Ed.), Symposium on Interactive 3D Graphics, Proceedings of the 2007 ACM SIGGRAPH symposium on Interactive 3D graphics and games, Seattle, WA, ACM, New York, 2007, pp. 97–104.

[4] K. Zhou, Q. Hou, Z. Ren, M. Gong, X. Sun, B. Guo, Renderants: interactive REYES rendering on GPUs, in: ACM Transactions on Graphics, vol. 28, Proceedings of ACM SIGGRAPH, Asia, 2009, pp. 1–11.

[5] L. Carpenter, The A-buffer, an antialiased hidden surface method, in: H. Christiansen (Ed.), Proceedings of the 11th Annual Conference on Computer Graphics and Interactive Techniques, SIGGRAPH '84, ACM, New York, pp. 103–108.

[6] F. Liu, M.C. Huang, X.H. Liu, E.H. Wu, Efficient depth peeling via bucket sort, in: S.N. Spencer (Ed.), Proceedings of the 1st Conference on High Performance Graphics 2009, New Orleans, LA, ACM, New York, 2009, pp. 51–57.

[7] Nick, Advanced rasterization, DevMaster.net. Http://www.devmaster.net/forums/showthread.php?t=1884 (accessed 15.03.09).

[8] NVIDIA, CUDA: Compute Unified Device Architecture, NVIDIA Corporation, Santa Clara, CA, 2009.

Computer Vision
Area Editor's Introduction
James Fung

7

29 Fast Graph Cuts for Computer Vision 439

30 Visual Saliency Model on Multi-GPU 451

31 Real-Time Stereo on GPGPU Using Progressive Multiresolution Adaptive Windows 473

32 Real-Time Speed-Limit-Sign Recognition on an Embedded System Using a GPU 497

33 Haar Classifiers for Object Detection with CUDA 517

THE STATE OF GPU COMPUTING IN COMPUTER VISION

The GPU has found a natural fit for accelerating computer vision algorithms. With its high performance and flexibility, GPU computing has seen its application in computer vision evolve from providing fast early vision results to new applications in the middle and late stages of vision algorithms. Completely "GPU-resident" computer vision pipelines are being constructed owing to the high degree of programmability of the GPU. The GPU is now allowing high-quality vision algorithms to operate at interactive frame rates.

Real-time computation aids the developer by providing faster algorithm testing and feedback and by bringing previously impractically large datasets or complex algorithms into the realm of possibility. As a widely adopted commodity processor, the GPU makes the previously intractable real-time computation required in computer vision achievable in a home PC or even portable laptop computer, and this brings computer vision out of the lab and into everyday application. As a result, GPU computing is enabling fast, intelligent image analysis and interpretation of the personal images, video, and media that we produce and view each day. In the context of larger applications, the GPU is providing the platform for creating interactive computer vision-based experiences and interfaces.

IN THIS SECTION

The chapters in this section present a cross section of GPU computing as applied in computer vision. The chapters range from efficient implementations of specific algorithms of wide applicability to examples of implementing full-vision algorithms as pipelines of processing on the GPU.

Narayanan, Vineet, and Stich implement a GPU graph cuts algorithm in Chapter 29. GPU graph cuts provides high-quality image segmentation in a fraction of the time as on the CPU. In this chapter, Narayanan *et al.* demonstrate how to implement a graph algorithm in a data-parallel fashion efficiently on the GPU to create a fast graph cuts algorithm that can find widespread use in applications from video processing to panorama stitching.

Chapter 30, written by Rahman, Houzet, and Pellerin, applies the GPU to identify areas of visual saliency. The authors implement a wide range of image-processing filters to create a vision system that identifies areas of visual interest. By applying the GPU, the authors develop an ensemble of filters that operate extremely fast, allowing the system to analyze the scene in a variety of ways while maintaining a high processing throughput.

Chapter 31, written by Zhao and Taubin, develops a stereo depth recovery algorithm based on CUDA. Recovering stereo disparity provides valuable 3-D scene information, but is computationally intense. Its data-parallel nature, however, makes it well suited for the GPU. This chapter shows an algorithm that achieves high frame-rate stereo depth estimation for images with large disparity ranges.

In Chapter 32, Muyan-Özçelik, Glavtchev, and Ota develop real-time speed-limit sign recognition using mobile GPU hardware and demonstrate an end-to-end working vision system on the GPU. The system combines both OpenGL graphics and CUDA to recognize speed-limit signs. This shows the applicability of the GPU in mobile and resource-constrained applications.

In Chapter 33, Anton Obhukov develops a GPU face-detection algorithm by creating a fast implementation of the well-known Haar classifier. This chapter demonstrates how the varying workloads in the Haar cascade can be accommodated on the GPU by processing successive stages in different ways to maintain data parallelism. The detection scheme presented can be further applied to more general object recognition.

Fast Graph Cuts for Computer Vision

29

P.J. Narayanan, Vibhav Vineet, Timo Stich

In this chapter we present an implementation of Graph Cuts with CUDA C. The computation pattern of this application is iterative with varying workloads and data dependencies between neighbors. We explore techniques to scale workload per iteration and how to parallelize the computation with the nontrivial data dependencies efficiently. This study shows the practical use of these techniques and reports the achieved performance on datasets for binary image segmentation and gives an outlook on how to extend the implementation to solve multilabel problems.

29.1 INTRODUCTION, PROBLEM STATEMENT, AND CONTEXT

The work is done in the context of image segmentation. The task of cutting out arbitrary-shaped objects from images is very common in computer vision and image-processing applications. Graph Cuts have become a powerful and popular approach to solve this problem with minimal user input. The range of applications that can be solved with Graph Cuts also includes stereo vision, image restoration, panorama stitching, and so on [4].

Graph Cuts solve energy minimization problems on integer Markov-Random-Fields (MRF). An MRF is a grid of variables where the solution for a single variable is also dependent on the solution of variables in its neighborhood. For example, in image segmentation the MRF has the shape of the image with a one-to-one correspondence between pixels and variables. The solution assigns to each pixel a label that signals if it belongs to the object to cut out or not. The MRF can be thought of as encoding the increased probability for a pixel to belong to the object if its neighbors belong to the object. By taking the solution of neighboring variables into account, we can significantly improve the results of the segmentation. Unfortunately, this also makes the problem NP-hard in the general case. The best reported serial CPU implementation takes 99 milliseconds on a standard dataset of size 640×480 for two labels. Our parallel GPU implementation solves the same problem in 7.5 ms, and hence, makes it possible to get the quality improvement Graph Cuts provided into real-time image-processing applications.

29.2 CORE METHOD

To solve the energy minimization problem, a flow network is constructed that represents the MRF. Finding the maximum flow/minimum cut of the network solves the binary energy minimization problem over the MRF [3]. Our implementation follows the Push-Relabel algorithm introduced by Goldberg and Tarjan [1]. The algorithm exhibits good data parallelism and maps well to the CUDA programming model. The computation proceeds by repetitively alternating operations push and relabel on the network until a termination criterion is met. The computations update two properties assigned to each variable of the flow network: excess flow and height. The push operations push excess flow from a variable to its neighbors. The relabel operation updates the height property. The convergence of the computation is sped up in practice by periodically performing a special case of breadth-first search on the network to reset the height property [2].

29.3 ALGORITHMS, IMPLEMENTATIONS, AND EVALUATIONS

Figure 29.1 shows pseudo code for the push and the relabel operations, which are the main parts of the Graph Cut algorithm. Both these operations loop over all variables of the network, but update different properties. First, it should be noted that both operations update only active variables. A variable is active if it has positive excess flow and a height less than infinite. Push transports available excess flow to one or more of eligible neighbors. The operation updates the excess flow and edge capacities, while the height property stays constant. Relabel computes the minimum heights of eligible neighbors and the current height of a variable to update this property. Excess flow and edge capacities stay constant.

For both operations the results for a single variable are dependent on neighboring data values. This makes their parallelization nontrivial. For now we assume that the computation can be split into quadratic tiles such that there are only data dependencies inside the tiles but none between tiles. There

```
void push(excess_flow, edge_capacity, const height) {
  for( x=0; x<N; ++x) {
    if ( active(x) ) {
      foreach( y=neighbor(x) ) {
        if( height(y) == height(x) − 1) {
          flow = min(edge_capacity(x,y), excess_flow(x));
          excess_flow(x) −= flow; excess_flow(y) += flow;
          edge_capacity(x,y) −= flow; edge_capacity(y,x) += flow;
}}}}}

void relabel(height, const excess_flow, const edge_capacity) {
  for( x=0; x<N; ++x) {
    if( active(x) ) {
      my_height = INF;
      foreach( y=neighbor(x) ) {
        if(edge_capacity(x,y) > 0 ) {
          my_height = min(my_height, height(y)+1);
      }}
      height(x) = my_height;
}}}
```

FIGURE 29.1

Pseudo code for the push and relabel operations.

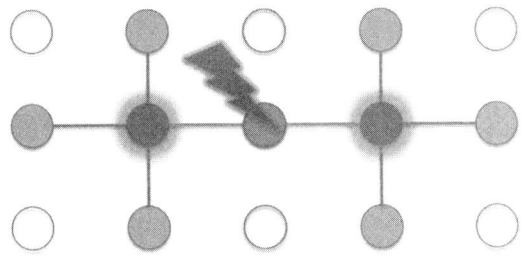

FIGURE 29.2

Potential data race conditions during updates of the excess flow when flow is pushed from multiple directions into a single variable.

are different options to achieve this, and we will discuss them in more detail separately. With this tiling, we get a perfect mapping to the CUDA programming model by launching one CUDA block per tile. The threads of one CUDA block cooperate to handle the intratile data dependencies, while there are no interblock dependencies. We set the tile edge length to the GPU warp size of 32. We also assume the neighborhood of the MRF to be the standard 4-neighborhood.

29.3.1 Parallel Push Implementation

For the discussion of the implementation of the push operation, we focus on a single tile and discuss the handling of intertile dependencies at the end of the section. As stated before we launch one CUDA block to handle one tile of the flow network. Although the operation in serial code is simple, we need to be cautious when parallelizing the outer loop because of intratile data dependencies. Looking at the code reveals that a single push from variable x to its neighbor y updates the excess flow for both x and y, as well as the edge capacities for $x -> y$ and $y <- x$. First, it is important to note that there will actually be no data access collisions when updating the edge capacities in parallel. The reason for this comes first from the fact that the height property is constant and the if(height(y) == height(x) $-$ 1) condition meaning that flow between neighbors will be pushed only in one direction and never back in one push iteration. Still a one-to-one mapping of variables to threads requires atomic operations to avoid any RAW or WAR hazards when updating the excess flow properties because flow is pushed in multiple directions and can converge into a single variable (see Figure 29.2). However, this would not be the optimal choice because atomic operations have reduced achievable peak memory bandwidth and do not support all data types, as, for example, 16-bit integers. A rewrite of the serial push operation, however, shows an alternative to achieve parallel data updates without the need of atomic operations. The idea is to change the order of the loops by looping first over the directions of the neighborhood as follows:

```
void push(excess_flow, edge_capacity, const height) {
    foreach( dir=direction) {
        for( x=0; x<N; ++x) {
            if ( active(x) ) {
                y = neighbor(x,dir);
                if( height(y) == height(x) − 1) {
                    flow = min(edge_capacity(x,y), excess_flow(x));
```

```
                excess_flow(x) −= flow; excess_flow(y) += flow;
                edge_capacity(x,y) −= flow; edge_capacity(y,x) += flow
    }}}}}
```

In this version the data dependencies in the inner loop are reduced to one neighbor, the one in the current direction being processed, instead of all neighbors as in the original version. The second idea is to process the variables in the inner loop in the order of the neighbor direction being considered. So for the right neighbor we process like this:

```
    void push_right(row, excess_flow, edge_capacity, const height) {
        for( x=row; x<row+Width−1;) {
            y = (x+1); // Right neighbor
            if ( active(x) ) {
                if( height(y) == height(x) − 1) {
                    flow = min(edge_capacity(x,y), excess_flow(x));
                    excess_flow(x) −= flow; excess_flow(y) += flow;
                    edge_capacity(x,y) −= flow; edge_capacity(y,x) += flow
            }}
            x = y; // Process in the direction of the neighbor
    }}
```

The code for the other directions is analogous. This rewrite makes it clear that for a single direction first, there are no data dependencies in the directions *orthogonal* to the current neighbor direction. Second, if we further subdivide the processing of a single direction into multiple chunks that are processed in parallel, there is a potential hazard only when accessing the excess flow of the first element of each chunk. This leads to our proposed processing of tiles with one CUDA block. We launch four warps (128 threads) where each thread transports flow over a chunk of 8 pixels per direction, as shown in Figure 29.3.

The update of the neighbor outside of the assigned chunk is done after all threads are synchronized. This step ensures that no data hazard will occur. At this point we also need to discuss how updates to neighbors outside of the current tile are handled. One could argue that using atomic operations just for those is a good choice. However, still atomics are not supported for all data types on all compute devices and also add additional complexity to the code. Instead, we store the updates outside the tiles into a special border array and use a separate kernel to add the border array to the excess flow after each push kernel to avoid data hazards.

So far we have discussed how the parallelization of the push operation is implemented. The next step to achieving good performance is optimizing the memory accesses. During the push operations, the excess flow of the variables is accessed four times for each direction. Hence, we read it once from global memory and process in shared memory to reduce the global memory footprint. Because the height stays constant, the different edge capacities are accessed only once for one push operation, as discussed earlier. Hence, there is no benefit of staging the edge capacities to shared memory, and we read and write to global memory directly. However, during the horizontal waves, the threads of a warp need to access different rows of the edge capacities, resulting in uncoalesced memory accesses. To avoid this we store the horizontal edge capacities in transposed form. This way, accessing the rows in horizontal directions maps to adjacent addresses in global memory, and hence, fully coalesced memory reads and writes.

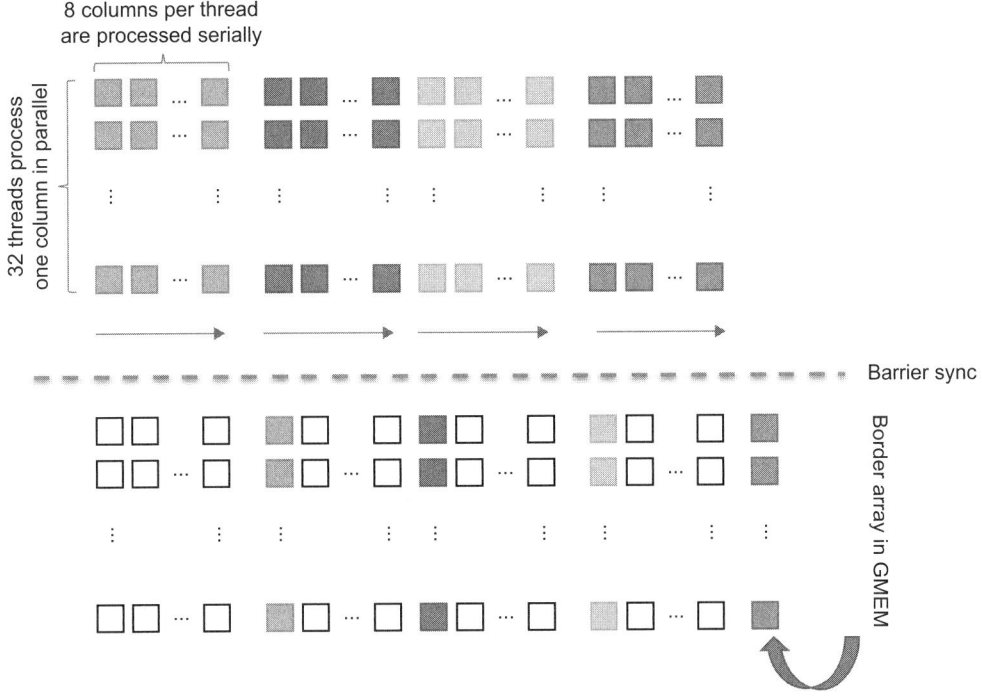

FIGURE 29.3

In this diagram, 128 threads are pushing flow to the right in a tile of 32 × 32 elements. Each warp of 32 threads transports excess flow in a wavelike pattern. First, each warp transports flow over eight elements in the current direction. After synchronizing, the ninth element in this direction is updated. This avoids data hazards and increases the flow transport distance per operation. The processing is repeated for the other three directions.

Finally, the height array must also be accessed read-only during the push operation. Each height value is read multiple times during the push operation, so again, staging to shared memory seems sensible. Unfortunately, the increased shared memory footprint significantly reduces occupancy on pre-Fermi GPUs. Alternatively, because read-only access is sufficient, we can resort to texture fetches on bound linear memory and make use of the texture cache instead. On Fermi GPUs with 48 KB of shared memory per multiprocessor available, the height array is staged to shared memory that results in a slight performance improvement over the texture approach.

29.3.2 Parallel Relabel Implementation

The parallelization of the relabel operation is straightforward. The height properties can all be updated in parallel, and we could launch one thread per variable without having to worry about race conditions. The first idea in improving this naive approach becomes apparent when analyzing the memory accesses. For each thread we check edge capacities to and heights of its neighbors and itself and compute a minimum. Hence, the ratio of memory to arithmetic operations is very high, and the performance of

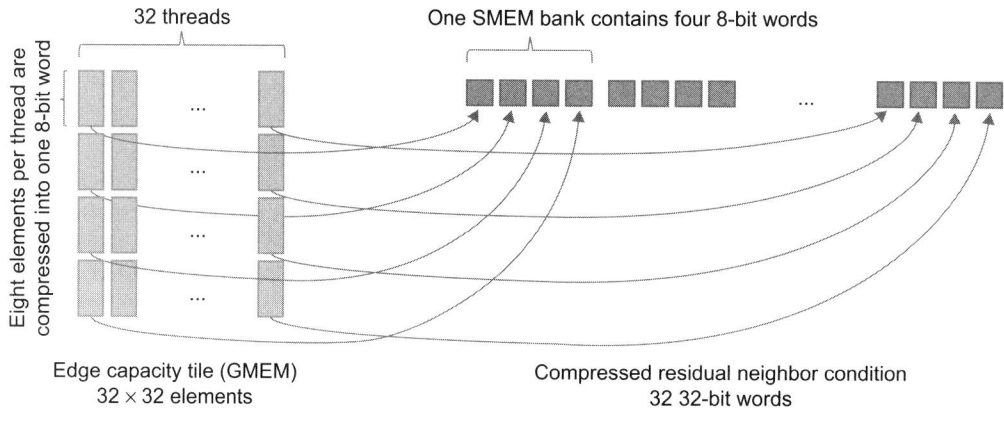

FIGURE 29.4

Coalesced bank-conflict-free compression of the residual neighbor condition for one direction. Four warps cooperate to compute the result in parallel.

the kernel is memory bound. To improve, we make use of the fact that a variable y is a neighbor in the residual flow network if it is in the 4-neighborhood of x *and if* the edge between x and y has a capacity greater than 0. If the residual neighbor condition is stored with one bit per neighbor, we can reduce the memory footprint and consequently improve performance.

Although not complex, the implementation of the compression needs some attention to make it right. To enable thread cooperation, we store the compressed residual neighbor condition in shared memory. The smallest memory entities a thread can access are 8-bit words. Hence, we choose to let each thread congest 8-neighbor conditions into one 8-bit word. Another restriction to consider is that on pre-Fermi GPUs, accessing consecutive 8-bit words in shared memory within one warp will cause a four-way bank conflict. This leads us to the computation pattern shown in Figure 29.4 to achieve a coalesced bank-conflict-free implementation of the compression. Four warps cooperate to compute the result. Each warp processes 32 columns of the edge capacity array, with each thread reading eight rows to build the compressed 8-bit word. The 8-bit words are then scattered into shared memory with a stride of 4 bytes, so bank conflicts are avoided. After the four warps are synchronized, four adjacent 8-bit words computed by the different warps represent 32 compressed elements of one full column. The same pattern is repeated for the other three different edge directions. Because the horizontal edge capacities are stored in transposed form, four adjacent 8-bit words will represent one row of the tile.

29.3.3 Efficient Workload Management

The optimization considerations so far focused on making most efficient use of the GPU and its resources from the implementation point of view. However, these optimizations do not take into account properties of the algorithm and specific workloads. In this section we look at improvements to make the implementation more work efficient as the computation converges toward the final solution.

The key observation is that most of the excess flow that is pushed through the network during processing has reached its final location after a few iterations [8]. Still, we continue to process all variables, even if the majority is not active anymore. This step results in very inefficient utilization of the resources from the algorithmic point of view even though the implementation itself is efficient. What we would like to achieve instead, is to process only those variables that are active per the current iteration and skip the ones that are inactive completely. Although implementing such a scaling of the workload per kernel efficiently on the per-variable level is not trivial, there is an easy approach that we can follow instead to achieve a slightly less efficient work scaling. Because we are launching one CUDA block per flow network tile, it is easy to scale the workload on the per-tile level. Instead of launching the CUDA blocks in the full 2-D grid configuration representing the flow network, we build a list of active tiles that are active and launch just enough CUDA blocks to process this list. The active tile list is built using a kernel that stores a 1 for every tile that has any active variables and 0 for others. Compaction is then used to build the list of active tiles. For the push kernel to make use of this, we need to modify it only slightly. First, a new argument, the pointer to the list in GPU memory, is added. Second, we replace the code to compute the 2-D tile offset from the block indices with code to read the assigned list entry and compute the tile offset from the entry instead:

Device:
```
__global__
void push_2D_config(...) {

int tile_x = blockIdx.x * 32;
int tile_y = blockIdx.y * 32;
...
```

Host:
```
...
dim3 grid(Width/32, Height/32);
dim3 block(32,4);
push_2D_config<<<grid,block>>>(...);
...
```

Device:
```
__global__
void push_list_config(unsigned int* tile_list, ...) {

unsigned int tile_id = tile _list[blockIdx.x];

int tile_x = ((tile_id & 0x0ffff0000) >> 16)* 32;
int tile_y = ((tile_id & 0x00000ffff) * 32;
...
```

Host:
```
...
dim3 grid(tile_list_length);
dim3 block(32,4);
push_list_config<<<grid,block>>>(d_tile_list, ...);
...
```

29.3.4 Global Relabeling

The final optimization of the basic Graph Cut implementation we consider in this chapter is again motivated from algorithmic observations. First, we point out that the height field is a lower-bound estimate of the geodesic distance of each pixel to the sink in the residual flow network. It has been shown that the more accurate the current estimate, the more effective the push operation will bring the solution toward the final one. Unfortunately, the relabel operation as we implemented it so far can lead to quite poor estimates owing to their local nature. Only direct neighbors are considered, and hence, topological changes can take many kernel invocations to propagate throughout the network. To mitigate this issue, we note that the additional costs of periodically computing the exact distances are more than compensated for with less total iterations and will result in a significant overall speedup. This is also referred to as global relabeling in the literature. In this section we discuss our implementation of global relabeling with CUDA C.

```
void global_relabel_tile(height) {
    done = 0;
    while( !done ) {
        done = 1;
        foreach( x of tile ) {
            my_height = height(x);
            foreach( y=neighbor(x) ) {
                if(edge_capacity(x,y) > 0 ) {
                    my_height = min(my_height, height(y)+1);
                }
                if( height(x) != my_height ) {
                    height(x) = my_height;
                    done = 0;
}}}}
```

The correct distances can be computed with a breadth-first search (BFS) of the residual flow network starting from the sink node. The depths in the search tree are the geodesic distances that we are looking for. Discussing a general BFS implementation with CUDA C would fill a separate chapter, but our implementation fortunately has to cover only a special case. The graph we search on is known to have a maximum of four outbound edges per node, and nodes are laid out in a regular grid. The only exception we have to deal with is the sink node that is unbounded and typically has a large number of outbound edges in computer vision problems [11]. We handle this exception during the initialization of the search once so that the implementation of the actual search can make use of the regular bounded grid property. During initialization the height is set to 0 if there is an inbound edge from sink (excess `flow<0`), thus taking the first step in the search at this point, and to infinity if a node has no inbound edge from sink (excess `flow>=0`). See Figure 29.5.

The parallelization of the BFS is then straightforward. We again launch one CUDA block per tile where each block updates the heights of the tile in parallel, as detailed in Figure 29.5, until the heights inside the tile do not change anymore. This guarantees that after each kernel execution there will be no gaps in tiles, but only between tiles. A gap in the height field is a height difference between neighbors in the residual graph that is larger than one. In an outer loop we launch this kernel until there are no gaps left and thus the height field contains the solution of the BFS.

Again, the global relabeling implementation can be optimized by applying the strategies from optimizing the push operation. Most obvious, because heights are updated multiple times during operation, it is again beneficial to stage the height tile into shared memory to reduce the traffic to global memory.

Initialization — Tiles with intragaps highlighted

∞	∞	∞	∞	∞	∞	∞	∞
∞	∞	∞	∞	∞	∞	∞	∞
∞	∞	0	0	∞	∞	0	∞
∞	∞	0	0	∞	∞	0	∞
∞	∞	0	∞	0	0	0	∞
∞	∞	∞	∞	∞	∞	0	∞
∞	∞	∞	0	∞	∞	0	∞
∞	∞	∞	∞	∞	∞	∞	∞

After first iteration — Tiles with intergaps highlighted

∞	∞	∞	∞	∞	∞	∞	∞
∞	∞	∞	∞	∞	∞	∞	∞
∞	∞	0	0	∞	∞	0	1
∞	∞	0	0	∞	∞	0	1
∞	∞	0	1	0	0	0	1
∞	∞	1	2	1	1	0	1
∞	∞	1	0	∞	∞	0	1
∞	∞	2	1	∞	∞	1	2

After second iteration — Tiles with intergaps highlighted

∞	∞	2	2	∞	∞	2	3
∞	∞	1	1	∞	∞	1	2
2	1	0	0	1	1	0	1
2	1	0	0	1	1	0	1
2	1	0	1	0	0	0	1
3	2	1	1	1	1	0	1
3	2	1	0	1	1	0	1
4	3	2	1	2	2	1	2

After third iteration — No gaps left, we are done.

4	3	2	2	3	3	2	3
3	2	1	1	2	2	1	2
2	1	0	0	1	1	0	1
2	1	0	0	1	1	0	1
2	1	0	1	0	0	0	1
3	2	1	1	1	1	0	1
3	2	1	0	1	1	0	1
4	3	2	1	2	2	1	2

FIGURE 29.5

Computation pattern of the Global Relabel implementation. Each tile is processed by one CUDA block. Each block updates the heights until there is no change. Tiles at gaps are processed only to achieve efficient workload scaling per iteration.

Also, instead of launching one thread per variable of the tile, we use the same wave processing that we introduced with the push kernel. This time we don't use it to avoid hazards, but to benefit from its balancing of directed serial updates, which increase information propagation speed throughout the tile, with data parallelism favorably. Finally, we note that launching a 2-D grid of blocks to process all tiles per iteration is similarly work inefficient as it was for the push operation. Changes will proceed as waves through the height field, and only a few tiles will actually change per iteration. So again, we build a list of tiles instead and launch just enough CUDA blocks to process the tiles of the list in each kernel invocation. For the first iteration after initialization, the list contains all tiles that contain height gaps inside the tile itself. Afterward, only the tile boundaries have to be checked for gaps, and only the tiles at intertile height gaps are scheduled for processing in the next iteration (see Figure 29.5). The BFS is done when the tile list is empty.

29.4 FINAL EVALUATION AND VALIDATION OF RESULTS

Table 29.1 summarizes the performance figures for computing the Graph Cut for graphs that represent binary image segmentation problems. The segmentation is based on color models for the foreground and background and also take the image gradients into account. The models are initialized by user input [12] as shown in Figure 29.6. For the presented figures we did not include the time to compute the data and neighborhood terms. We also compare this performance with that of a CPU implementation that is a different, serial algorithm to compute Graph Cuts [11]. Because Graph Cuts find the global optimal solution, the final results are the same.[1] The comparison with the CPU results was also used to verify correctness of our implementation. The average speedup over the test set of an NVIDIA GTX470 in comparison with an Intel Core2 @ 3 GHz is 12x, varying from 4x to 30x.

---

[1]For some datasets there exist multiple solutions with the same total global minimal energy (e.g., the Sponge dataset). Graph Cuts return only one of the possibly multiple solutions to a given optimization problem. Hence, we compare the energy of the GPU and the CPU results rather than the two results pixel by pixel.

Table 29.1 Performance figures for binary image segmentation datasets. The measured timings are the average measured over 10 repetitions. The computation has been performed on the Middlebury standard dataset (Person, Flower, Sponge) as well as nine additional image segmentation problems to explore a larger range of image sizes.

Image	GTX470 (ms)	C1060 (ms)	Intel Core2 @ 3 GHz (ms)	CPU vs. C1060	CPU vs. GTX470	C1060 vs. GTX470	Width	Height
Person	14.9	22.1	102.8	4.7	6.9	1.5	600	450
Flower	7.9	13.7	101.5	7.4	12.7	1.7	600	450
Sponge	7.4	11.8	99.2	8.4	13.4	1.6	640	480
Insect	129.1	179.6	552.9	3.1	4.3	1.4	1000	664
Bird	13.9	20.2	439.0	21.8	31.6	1.5	1500	1087
White flower	67.9	94.4	825.1	8.7	12.1	1.4	1946	1749
Bird2	99.5	143.1	1059.6	7.4	10.6	1.4	2038	1918
Smile fruit	151.6	216.7	1202.6	5.6	7.9	1.4	1712	2288
Bees	103.1	166.4	1337.5	8.0	13.0	1.6	2434	2302
Thistle	145.9	220.4	2476.8	11.2	17.0	1.5	2592	3888
Fan	310.6	478.5	2948.8	6.2	9.5	1.5	3507	3507
Space shuttle	514.3	785.1	3747.6	4.8	7.3	1.5	4164	3123

FIGURE 29.6

Example application of Graph Cuts. Left: Flower image from the Middlebury dataset with user input overlaid. Right: Binary image segmentation solution computed with Graph Cuts.

29.5 MULTILABEL GRAPH CUTS

Many problems in computer vision can be modeled as the problem to assign a label from a set of labels to each pixel. Examples include stereo correspondence, image restoration, and so on. The labels partition the image into multiple, disjoint sets of pixels. Assigning multiple labels can be mapped to a general multiway cut operation on the graph. Unfortunately, the globally optimal multiway cuts problem is

NP-hard. However, there are algorithms of polynomial complexity that find a local minima solution. One such algorithm is alpha expansion [10], which proceeds in cycles and iterations, each of which involves solving a binary label assignment problem.

Alpha-Expansion Method

The alpha-expansion algorithm is described in this section. The outer loop (steps 2 to 10) forms a cycle, which consists of multiple iterations (steps 3 to 6):

```
1    Initialize the MRF with an arbitrary labeling f.
2      for each label alpha ⟩ \ ← L {
3
4          Construct the graph on the current labeling and the label alpha.
5          Perform graph cuts to separate vertices of the graph into two disjoint sets.
6          Assign label alpha to each pixel in the source set to get the current configuration f′.
7          Calculate the energy value E(f′) of the current configuration f′.
8      }
9      if E(f′) < ψE(f) {
10        goto 2
11     }
12     return f′;
```

The algorithm starts from an initial random labeling with each pixel in the image getting a random label from the label set. Iteration alpha (between 1 and L) decides if a pixel gets the label *alpha* or not. This is formulated as a two-level graph cut in which all pixels with a label other than *alpha* participate. After each iteration, each variable retains its current label or takes the label *alpha*. Once all L labels are cycled through, the energy of the current configuration is evaluated. This cycle is repeated until no further decrease in energy values is possible.

Step 4 of the algorithm involves a binary graph cut, which can use the parallel GPU implementation described earlier. There are two formulations of the graph for this step. Boykov's formulation [10] introduces auxiliary variables, which disturbs the grid structure of the graph. We use Kolmogorov's formulation [12], which maintains the grid structure, but has an additional flag bit for each node to indicate if it takes part in a particular graph cuts step or not.

Incremental Alpha Expansion

Energy minimization algorithms converge faster if the starting point is close to the minima. Intelligent initialization can have a huge impact on the computation time. Reusing the flow as in Kohli and Torr [6] is one of the successful methods to initialize better. Alahari *et al.* [5] extend this concept to multilabel problems and Vineet and Narayanan [9] present a way to exploit relationships within cycles and across cycles in incremental alpha expansion. The final graph of the push-relabel method and the final residual graph of the Ford-Fulkerson method are the same. Each graph is reparametrized based on the final graph of the previous iteration or cycle, as shown in Figure 29.7. This incurs additional memory requirements to store L graphs, one at the end of each iteration, including their excess flows. Reparametrization is applied to the stored final excess flow from the previous iteration, based on the difference between the initial graphs of the iterations.

Incremental alpha expansion on the GPU results in an average speedup of 5–6 times compared with conducting alpha expansion on the CPU. For more details we refer the interested reader to [9].

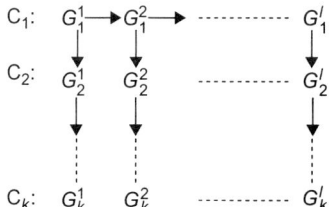

FIGURE 29.7

Incremental alpha expansion. Arrows indicate the direction of recycling and reparameterization of graphs. G_i^j means iteration j and cycle i.

References

[1]   A.V. Goldberg, R.E. Tarjan, A new approach to the maximum-flow problem, J. ACM 35 (4) (1988) 921–940.

[2]   B.V. Cherkassky, A.V. Goldberg, On implementing push-relabel method for the maximum flow problem, in: Proceedings of the 4th International IPCO Conference on Integer Programming and Combinatorial Optimization, Lecture Notes in Computer Science, vol. 920, Springer, 1995, pp. 157–171.

[3]   D.M. Greig, B.T. Porteous, A.H. Seheult, Exact maximum a posteriori estimation for binary images, J. R. Stat. Soc. Series B 51 (2) (1989) 271–279.

[4]   Middlebury MRF page, Results (plots, images, and code) to accompany, R. Szeliski, R. Zabih, D. Scharstein, O. Veksler, V. Kolmogorov, A. Agarwala, et al., A comparative study of energy minimization methods for Markov random fields with smoothness-based priors, IEEE Trans. Pattern Anal. Mach. Intell. (TPAMI) 30 (6) (2008) 1068–1080. Available from: `http://vision.middlebury.edu/MRF`.

[5]   K. Alahari, P. Kohli, P.H.S. Torr, Reduce, reuse & recycle: efficiently solving multi-label MRFs, in: IEEE Conference on Computer Vision and Pattern Recognition, 23–28 June, 2008, Lecture Notes in Computer Science, vol. 5996, Springer, Anchorage, AK, 2008, pp. 1–8.

[6]   P. Kohli, P.H.S. Torr, Dynamic graph cuts for efficient inference in Markov random fields, IEEE Trans. Pattern Anal. Mach. Intell. 29 (12) (2007) 2079–2088.

[7]   V. Kolmogorov, R. Zabih, What energy functions can be minimized via graph cuts? IEEE Trans. Pattern Anal. Mach. Intell. 26 (2) (2004) 147–159.

[8]   V. Vineet, P.J. Narayanan, CUDA cuts: fast graph cuts on the GPU, in: CVGPU08, CVPR Workshops. IEEE, 2008, pp. 1–8.

[9]   V. Vineet, P.J. Narayanan, Solving multilabel MRFs using incremental alpha-expansion on the GPUs, in: Proceedings of the Ninth Asian Conference on Computer Vision (ACCV 09), 23–27 September, 2009, Lecture Notes in Computer Science, vol. 5996, Springer, Xian, China, 2009, pp. 633-643.

[10] Y. Boykov, O. Veksler, R. Zabih, Fast approximate energy minimization via graph cuts, IEEE Trans. Pattern Anal. Machine Intell. 23 (11) (2001) 1222–1239.

[11] Y. Boykov, V. Kolmogorov, An experimental comparison of min-cut/max-flow algorithms for energy minimization in vision, IEEE Trans. Pattern Anal. Machine Intell. 26 (9) (2004) 1124–113.

[12] C. Rother, V. Kolmogorov, A. Blake, GrabCut — interactive foreground extraction using iterated graph cuts, ACM Trans. Graph. 23 (2004) 309–314.

Visual Saliency Model on Multi-GPU

30

Anis Rahman, Dominique Houzet, Denis Pellerin

30.1 INTRODUCTION

Visual attention models translate the capability of human vision to concentrate only on smaller regions of the visual scene. More precisely, such regions are the spotlight of focus, which either may be an object or a portion of the scene. A number of modalities are used to locate regions of attention like intensity, color, orientation, motion, and many others. The attention model acts as an information-processing bottleneck to reduce the overall information into a region of useful information. When guided by salient stimuli, this model falls into a category of a bottom-up approach, which is fast and primitive. On the other hand, models driven by cognition using variable selection criteria are the basis for top-down approaches, and they are slower and more complex. The human visual system uses either a saliency-based or a top-down approach, or the combination of both these approaches to find the spotlight of focus.

The bottom-up visual saliency model [7, 11] implemented on GPU mimics the human vision system all the way from the retina to the visual cortex. The model uses a saliency map to determine where the source of attention lies within the input scene, which may further be used to initiate other tasks. Also, it is linearly modeled and based on the human visual system. The forking of the entire pathway into different subpaths using various modalities is more efficient to compute. In the end, the output of both pathways is combined into a final saliency map using several adaptive coefficients, like mean, maximum, and skewness. The model is validated against large datasets of images, and the results are compared against that of a human visual system using an eye tracker. The model is efficient, and results in a stable prediction of eye movements.

This model to predict the areas of concentration finds its worth in applications like ones used for video content analysis to perform structural decomposition to build indexes, for video reframing to deliver comforting viewing experiences on mobile devices, for video compression to reduce the bandwidth required to transmit, and for realistic video synthesis. The notion of sketching a biologically inspired model is to build robust and all-purpose vision systems adaptable to various environmental conditions, users, and tasks.

30.2 **VISUAL SALIENCY MODEL**

The cortical organization of the primate visual system has two central pathways: ventral and dorsal. Each pathway carries distinct information regarding what an object is and where an object is. More precisely, the ventral pathway carries information about static object properties like shape and color, whereas the dorsal pathway carries information about dynamic object properties, such as motion and spatial relationships.

The bottom-up model [7, 11] illustrated in Figure 30.1 is inspired from the primate's visual system and is subdivided into two distinct pathways: static and dynamic.

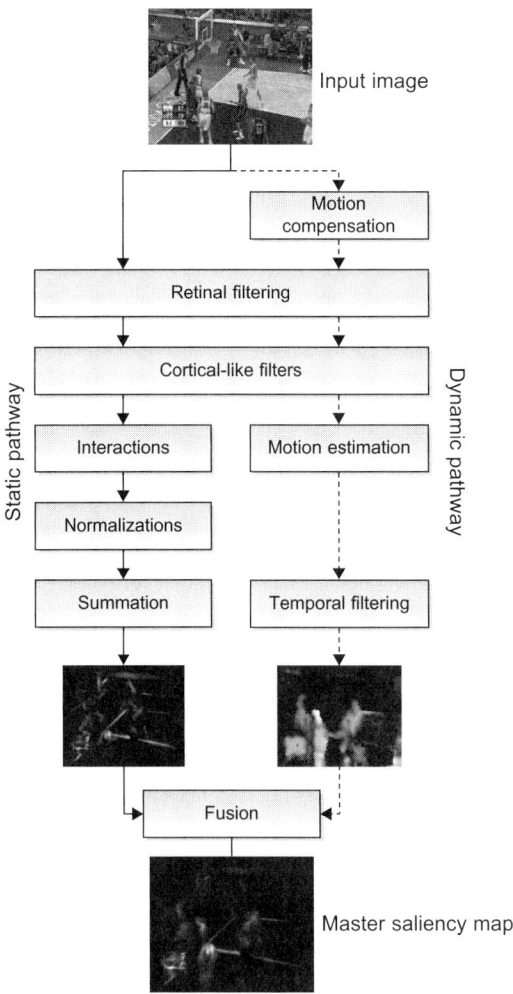

FIGURE 30.1

The bottom-up visual saliency model.

30.2.1 **Static Pathway**

The retinal model is primarily based on the primate's retina, which imitates the photoreceptor, horizontal, bipolar, and ganglion cells. It takes an input visual scene, and decomposes it into two types of information: the parvocellular output that enforces equalization of the visual by increasing its contrast. Next in the order, the magnocellular that responds to higher temporal and lower spatial frequencies. Analogous to a primate's retina, the ganglion cells respond to high contrast, whereas the parvocellular output highlights the borders among the homogeneous regions, thus exposing more detail in the visual input.

The primary visual cortex is a model of simple cell receptive fields that are sensitive to visual signal orientations and spatial frequencies. This can be imitated using a bank of Gabor filters organized in two dimensions, which is closely related to the processes in the primary visual cortex. The retinal output is convolved to these Gabor filters in the frequency domain.

In the primate's visual system, the response of a cell is dependent on its neuronal environment, that is, its lateral connections. Therefore, this activity can be modeled as a linear combination of simple cells interacting with their neighbors. This interaction may be inhibitory or excitory, depending on the orientation or the frequency: excitory when in the same direction; otherwise, it is inhibitory. The energy maps from the visual cortical filters and interaction phase are normalized. This model uses a technique [6] proposed by Itti for strengthening the intermediate results.

Ultimately, a saliency map for the static pathway is extracted for the input visual, simply by summing up all the energy maps. It is significant that the resulting map has salient regions, that is, those with the highest energies, which can be observed in Figure 30.2 by energy located on such objects.

30.2.2 **Dynamic Pathway**

On the other hand, the dynamic pathway finds salient regions in a moving scene. The dynamic pathway uses camera motion compensation [8] for compensation of dominant motion against its background. This compensation is followed by retinal filtering to illuminate the salient regions before motion estimation.

After the preprocessing, two-dimensional estimation [2] is used to find local motion with respect to the background. The algorithm is based on Gabor filters to decompose the image into its sub-bands. These equations are then used to estimate the optical flow between two images. After Gabor filtering, we calculate a system of N equations for each pixel at each time t using spatial and temporal gradients to get an overconstrained system. To resolve this system, which is fairly noisy, we use the method of iterated weighted least squares within the motion estimator. In the end, temporal filtering is performed on the sequence of images, often used to remove extraneous information. Finally, we get the dynamic saliency map.

30.2.3 **Fusion**

The saliency maps from both the static and dynamic pathways exhibit different characteristics; for example, the first map has larger salient regions based on textures, whereas the other map has smaller regions, depending on the moving objects. Based on these features, the maps are modulated using maximum and skewness, respectively, and fused together to get a final saliency map.

(a) Visual input

(b) Static saliency map

(c) Dynamic saliency map

(d) Master saliency map

FIGURE 30.2

Results of the visual saliency model.

30.3 GPU IMPLEMENTATION

Often visual saliency models incorporate a number of complex tasks that make a real-time solution quite difficult to achieve. This objective is only achievable by simplification of the overall model as done by Itti [5] and Ouerhani [9]. Consequently, including other processes into the existing model is impossible. Over the years, GPUs have evolved from fixed-function architecture into completely programmable shader architecture. All together with a mature programming model like CUDA [1] makes the GPU platform a preferable choice for acquiring high-performance gains. Generally, vision algorithms are a sequence of filters that are relatively easier to implement on the GPU's massively data-parallel architecture. The graphics device is also cheaper and easier to program than its counterparts. In addition, the graphics device is accessible to everyone.

Algorithm 1: Static pathway of visual saliency model.

```
   input : An image Im of size w × l
   output: A saliency map
 1 map ← RetinalFilter(Im);
 2 map ← FFT(map);
 3 for i ← 1 to orientations do
 4     for j ← 1 to frequencies do
 5         maps[i,j] ← GaborFilter(map,i,j);
 6         maps[i,j] ← IFFT(maps[i,j]);
 7         maps[i,j] ← Interactions(maps[i,j]);
 8         maps[i,j] ← Normalizations(maps[i,j]);
 9     end
10 end
11 saliency ← Fusion (maps);
```

30.3.1 **The Static Pathway**

To start with the mapping of the Algorithm 1 onto GPU, it is partitioned into data-parallel portions of code that are isolated into separate kernels. Then, the input data is transferred and stored on the device memory, which afterward is used by the kernels. After all the memory declarations on the device, the host sequentially initiates all the data-parallel kernels. First, some preprocessing using a retinal filter and Hanning mask is done that gives more detail to the visual input. Second, this data in the frequency domain is treated with a 2-D Gabor filter bank using six orientations and four frequency bands, resulting in 24 partial maps. Third, the pathway is moved back to the spatial domain before interactions among these maps. These interactions inhibit or excite the data values, depending on the orientation and frequency band of a partial map. Fourth, the resulting values are normalized between a dynamic range before applying Itti's method for normalization, and suppressing values lower than a certain threshold. Finally, all the partial maps are accumulated into a single map that is the saliency map from the static pathway.

30.3.2 **The Dynamic Pathway**

Similar to the implementation of the static pathway, we first perform task distribution of the algorithm and realize its sequential version. Some of the functional units are recursive Gaussian filter, Gabor filter bank to break the image into sub-bands of different orientations, Biweight Tuckey motion estimator, Gaussian prefiltering for pyramids, spatial and temporal gradient maps for estimation, and bilinear interpolation. After testing these functions separately, we put them together to give a complete sequential code. The algorithm being intrinsically parallel allows it to be easily ported to CUDA.

Algorithm 2 describes the dynamic pathway, where first camera motion compensation and retinal filtering are done as a preprocessing on the visual input. Afterward, the preprocessed input is passed on to the motion estimator implemented using third-order Gabor filter banks. The resulting motion vectors are normalized using temporal information to get a dynamic saliency map.

The saliency maps from both the static and dynamic pathways are copied back onto the host CPU, where they are fused together outputting a saliency map. The two saliency maps from different

---

Algorithm 2: Dynamic pathway of visual saliency model.

```
input : An image Im of size w × l
output: A dynamic saliency map
```
1 map [*t*] ← MotionCompensation(*Im*);
2 map [*t*] ← RetinalFilter(*map*[*t*]);
3 map [*t*] ← MotionEstimation(*map*[*t*]);

4 *saliency* ← TemporalFilter(*map*[*t*], *map*[*t* − 1]);

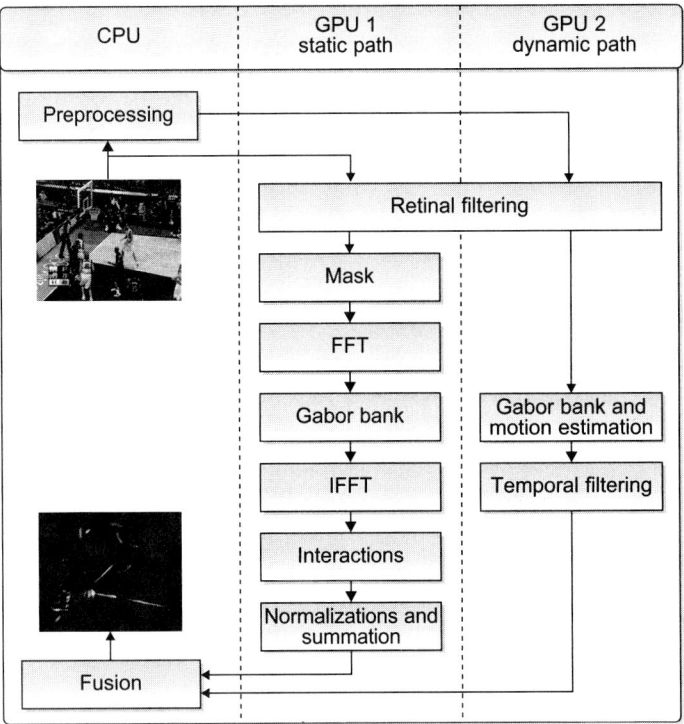

FIGURE 30.3

GPU implementation of the visual saliency model.

pathways and the final output saliency map are shown in Figure 30.2. Moreover, Figure 30.3 illustrates the block diagram of the GPU implementation of the visual saliency model.

Importance of Optimizations

One of the biggest challenges in optimizing GPU code for data-dominated applications is the management of the memory accesses, which is a key performance bottleneck. Memory latency can be several hundreds, or even thousands, of clock cycles. This can be improved first by memory coalescing when memory accesses of different threads are consecutive in memory addresses. This process allows the global memory controllers to execute burst memory accesses. The second optimization is to avoid such memory accesses through the use of a cache memory, internal shared memories, or registers. Most important, shared memory is an on-chip high-bandwidth memory shared among all the threads on a single SM. It has several uses: as a register extension, to avoid global memory accesses, to give fast communication among threads, and as a data cache.

30.3.3 Various CUDA Kernels

The static pathway includes the retina filter with low-pass filters using 2-D convolutions, the normalizations with reduction operations, simple shifts operations, and fourier transforms. On the other hand, the dynamic pathway involves recursive guassian filters, projection, modulation/demodulation, and kernels for calculation of spatial and temporal gradients that are simple and classically implemented. Notabaly, the kernels that are compute intensive and interesting to be implemented on the GPU are the interactions kernel and Gabor filter bank from the static pathway, as well as the motion estimator kernel from the dynamic pathway. Hence, we present these kernels because they can be potentially improved by employing various optimizations and making several adjustments to the kernel launch configurations.

Interactions Kernel

In the primate's visual system, the response of a cell is dependent on its neuronal environment, that is, its lateral connections. This activity can be modeled as a linear combination of simple cells interacting with their neighbors.

$$E_{int}(f_i, \theta_j) = E(f_i, \theta_j) \times w$$

$$\text{where, } w = \begin{cases} 0.0 & -0.5 & 0.0 \\ 0.5 & 1.0 & 0.5 \\ 0.0 & -0.5 & 0.0 \end{cases}$$

The resulting partial maps E_{int} after taking into account interactions among different orientation maps E from the Gabor filter bank are the visual input's energy as a function of spatial frequency f and orientation θ.

The block diagram in Figure 30.4 shows the simple interactions kernel for 32 complex numbers for 32 partial maps from the Gabor filter bank that are first accessed from the global memory in a coalesced manner and placed in shared memory *"maps"* in separate regions for real and complex portions of the number. These numbers are then accessed in a random manner and converted into 16 real numbers. These results are stored in the *"buf"* shared memory variable, which is afterward used as prefetched data for the next phase of neuronal interactions.

We'll now discuss coalescing using shared memory. A method to avoid noncoalesced memory accesses is by reordering the data in shared memory. To demonstrate the uses of shared memory, we take an example kernel, as shown in Listing 30.1, which is illustrated using a block diagram shown in Figure 30.4. Here, the data values are in a complex format consisting of two floats. The very first step is fetching the values into shared memory, where each float is read by a separate thread as shown in line 12 in Listing 30.1. These global memory accesses are coalesced, as contiguous floats are read shown in line 24 in Listing 30.1. Furthermore, we use two shared buffers, one for real part, and the other for imaginary part. This arrangement provides uncoalesced shared memory accesses during computation in lines 30 and 31 in Listing 30.1 to convert the complex numbers into real and also to scale down the

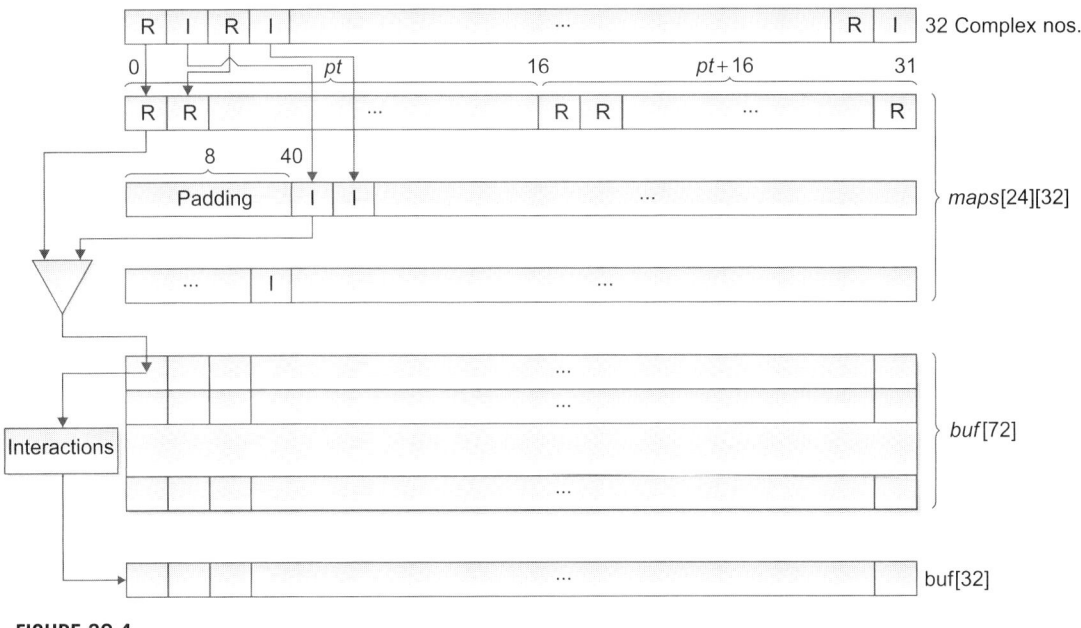

FIGURE 30.4

A block diagram of a data-parallel interaction kernel.

output from the unnormalized Fourier transforms done using the CUFFT library. Table 30.1 shows the performance gains after coalescing global memory accesses.

Multiple threads accessing the same bank may cause conflicts. In the case of shared memory bank conflicts, these conflicting accesses are required to be serialized either using an explicit stride based on the thread's ID or by allocating more shared memory. In our case, when the thread's ID is used to access shared memory, a conflict occurs, as thread 0 and thread 1 access the same bank. Thus, we use a stride of 8 to avoid any conflicts, as shown in line 13 in Listing 30.1. Although a multiprocessor takes only 4 clock cycles doing a shared memory transaction for an entire half warp, bank conflicts in the shared memory can degrade the overall performance, as shown in Table 30.2.

Another use of shared memory is to prefetch data from global memory and cache it. In the example kernel, the data after conversion and rescaling are cached, as shown in line 29 in Listing 30.1. and this prefetched data is used in the next phase of interactions.

30.3.4 Motion Estimator Kernel

The motion estimator [2] presented here employs a differential method using Gabor filters to estimate local motion. The estimated speeds are obtained by solving a robust system of equations of optical flow. It works on the principle of conservation of brightness; that is, the luminance of any pixel remains the same for a certain interval of time. Consider that $I(x, y, t)$ represents the brightness function for the sequence of images, and then according to the hypothesis of conversation of total luminance, its time

```
1   __global__ void STA_ker_short_interaction ( Complex* in, unsigned int width
2                   ,unsigned int height, float* out) {
3    __shared__ float maps[ NO_OF_ORIENTS * NO_OF_BANDS ][32];
4    __shared__ float buf [72];
5
6    unsigned int x1 = blockIdx.x*blockDim.x + threadIdx.x/2;
7    unsigned int x2 = blockIdx.x*blockDim.x + threadIdx.x;
8    unsigned int y  = blockIdx.y*blockDim.y + threadIdx.y;
9
10   if ( x1 >= width || x2 >= width || y>= height) return;
11
12   unsigned int mod  = threadIdx.x1%2;
13   unsigned int pt   = threadIdx.x1/2 + 40* mod;
14   unsigned int size = width*height;
15
16   for ( unsigned int j=0 ; j< NO_OF_ORIENTS ; ++j) {
17     for ( unsigned int i=0 ; i< NO_OF_BANDS ; ++i) {
18       /* *******************************************************
19        * 32 threads process 16 complex numbers in parallel
20        * every thread stores them with real and imaginary interlaced
21        * 32 threads produce 32 real products in parallel
22        ******************************************************** */
23       buf[pt] = // first 16 complex numbers
24         in[(j* NO_OF_BANDS+i)*size+(y*width+x1)][mod]/(float)(size);
25       buf[pt+16] = // next 16 complex numbers
26         in[(j*NO_OF_BANDS+i)*size+(y*width+x1+16)][mod]/(float)(size);
27       __syncthreads();
28
29       maps[j* NO_OF_BANDS + i][ threadIdx.x] = abs
30         buf[threadIdx.x ]*buf[threadIdx.x ] +
31         buf[threadIdx.x + 40]* buf[threadIdx.x + 40]);
32       __syncthreads ();
33     }
34   }
35   // prefetched data in shared memory is used by interactions
36 }
```

Listing 30.1: The interactions kernel in the static pathway.

Table 30.1 A profile of the interaction kernel for memory coalescing using shared memory.

	GPU time	Occupancy	Shared memory per block (bytes)
Uncoalesced memory accesses	38 ms	0.125	0
Coalesced memory accesses	12 ms	0.125	288

Table 30.2 A profile of the interaction kernel for bank conflicts.

	GPU time	Occupancy	Warp serialize
With bank conflicts	8.13 ms	0.125	75,529
Without bank conflicts	7.9 ms	0.125	0

derivative is zero. Therefore, the motion vector $v(p) = (v_x, v_y)$ can be found using the equation of optical flow:

$$\frac{dI(p,t)}{dt} = \nabla I(p,t) \cdot v(p) + \frac{\partial I(p,t)}{\partial t} = 0$$

where $\nabla I(x,y,t)$ is the spatial gradient of luminance $I(x,y,t)$. Using this equation, we get a velocity component parallel to this spatial gradient. The information from the spatial gradients in different directions can be used to find the actual movement of an object. If the intensity gradient is $\nabla I = 0$, then the motion is negligible, whereas motion in one direction represents the edges.

To perform a proper estimation of motion, we average the movement corresponding to its spatial neighborhood. This spatial neighborhood is required to be large enough to avoid any ambiguous resulting motion vectors. Thus, to get a spatial continuity within the optical flow, we convolve the spatio-temporal image sequence with a Gabor filter bank:

$$v_x \cdot \frac{\partial (I * G_i)}{\partial x} + v_y \cdot \frac{\partial (I * G_i)}{\partial y} + \frac{\partial (I * G_i)}{\partial t} = 0$$

The bank consists of N filters G_i with the same radial frequency. The result is a system of N equations for each pixel with a velocity vector composed of two components (v_x, v_y). This system of equations can be represented as:

$$\begin{pmatrix} \Omega_2^x & \Omega_1^y \\ \Omega_2^x & \Omega_2^y \\ & \cdots \\ \Omega_n^x & \Omega_n^y \end{pmatrix} \cdot \begin{pmatrix} v_x \\ v_y \end{pmatrix} = \begin{pmatrix} \Omega_2^t \\ \Omega_2^t \\ \cdots \\ \Omega_n^t \end{pmatrix}$$

This overdetermined system of equations is solved by using the method of least squares (Biweight Tuckey test) [2].

The estimator uses multiresolution patterns to allow robust motion estimation over a wide range of speeds. Here, the image is subsampled into multiple scales resulting in a pyramid, where the approximation begins with the subsampled version of the image at the highest level. This process is iterated until applied to the image with original resolution. This multiscale approach is equivalent to applying a Gabor bank of several rings with different scales. The final result for the estimator is a motion vector for each pixel.

In the motion estimator prefetch kernel, we use spatial and temporal gradient values to get $N(2N-1)$ solutions that are used to perform iterative weighted least-square estimations. These numerous intermediate values are stored as array variables because the register count is already high. Unfortunately, this process leads to costly global memory accesses that can be avoided by placing some values in shared memory as shown in line 7 in Listing 30.4. Consequently, we get a solution with the lesser memory accesses and efficient use of limited resources on the device. We achieved performance gains by carefully selecting the amount of shared memory without compromising the optimal number of active blocks residing on each SM.

In the motion estimator kernel illustrated in Listing 30.2, there is a limitation of higher register count owing to the complexity of the algorithm; hence, using the motion estimator kernel results in a reduced number of active thread blocks per SM. In our naive solution, the register count is 22, and this number can be considerably reduced to 15 registers per thread block using shared memory for some local variables as done in line 6 of Listing 30.2. Consequently, the occupancy increased from 0.33

```
1   texture<float, 1, cudaReadModeElementType> tex_dx, tex_dy, tex_wi;
2   __global__ void DYN_ker_motion_estimator( float *vx, float *vy, int w, int h)
3   {
4     unsigned int i, j, m;
5     float _wi, _ri;
6     __shared__ float _dx, _dy, Mx, My, W, mxp, myp;
7
8     m = threadIdx.x + blockIdx.x*blockDim.x; if( m>=(w*h)) return;
9
10    for( j=0 ; j<NO_OF_STEPS ; ++j){
11      mxp[threadIdx.x] = Mx[threadIdx.x]; myp[threadIdx.x] = My[threadIdx.x];
12      Mx[threadIdx.x] = 0; My[threadIdx.x] = 0; W[threadIdx.x] = 0;
13      syncthreads();
14
15      for( i=0 ; i<N*(2*N-1) ; ++i){
16        _dx[threadIdx.x] = tex1Dfetch( tex_dx, m + i*(w*h));
17        _dy[threadIdx.x] = tex1Dfetch( tex_dy, m + i*(w*h));
18        _wi = tex1Dfetch( tex_wi, m + i*(w*h));
19        syncthreads();
20
21        _ri = sqrtf( powf( _dx[threadIdx.x]-mxp[threadIdx.x],2) +
22          powf( _dy[threadIdx.x]-myp[threadIdx.x],2));
23
24        if( fabsf(_ri)<C && _wi!=0){ _wi=( _ri*_ri - C*C)/(C*C); _wi*=_wi;}
25
26        Mx[threadIdx.x]+=_wi*_dx[threadIdx.x];
27        My[threadIdx.x]+=_wi*_dy[threadIdx.x];
28         W[threadIdx.x]+=_wi;
29        syncthreads();
30      }
31      if ( W[threadIdx.x]!=0){
32        Mx[threadIdx.x]/=W[threadIdx.x]; My[threadIdx.x]/=W[threadIdx.x];
33      }
34      syncthreads();
35    }
36    vx[m] += Mx[threadIdx.x]; vy[m] += My[threadIdx.x];
37  }
```

Listing 30.2: The motion estimator kernel.

```
1   float eqx[2*N], eqy[2*N];
2   __shared__ float eqt[2*N][64];
```

Listing 30.3: Using shared memory to reduce global memory accesses.

Table 30.3 A profile of the motion estimator kernel.

	No. of registers	Occupancy	GPU time %
Naive solution	18	0.75	32
Shared memory	29	0.50	31.5
Shared + prefetching	32	0.50	31.7
Shared + textures	17	0.375	32

to 0.67 with eight active thread blocks residing on each SM. These variables to be placed in shared memory are carefully selected to reduce the number of synchronization barriers needed.

Texture memory provides an alternative path to device memory, which is faster. This is because of specialized on-chip texture units with internal memory to allow buffering of data from device memory. It can be very useful to reduce the penalty incurred for nearly coalesced accesses.

In our implementation, the main motion estimation kernel exhibits a pattern that requires the data to be loaded from device memory multiple times; that is, we calculate an $N(2N - 1)$ system of equations for 2*N levels of spatial and temporal gradients. Because of memory limitations of the device, it is not feasible to keep the intermediate values. Therefore, we calculate these values at every pass of the estimator leading to performance degradation because of higher device memory latency. As a solution, the estimation kernel can be divided into two parts: one calculates the system of equations, while the other uses these equations for estimation through texture memory. Here, texture memory's caching mechanism is employed to prefetch the data calculated in the prefetch kernel shown in Listing 30.3, thereby reducing global memory latency and yielding up to a 10% performance improvement. The profile of the gains due to various optimizations is illustrated in Table 30.3.

30.3.5 Gabor Kernel

Cortical-like filters are a model of simple cell receptive fields that are sensitive to visual signal orientations and spatial frequencies. This can be imitated using a bank of Gabor filters organized in two dimensions; that is, closely related to the processes in the primary visual cortex. A Gabor function is defined as:

$$G(u,v) = exp\left\{-\left(\frac{(u\prime - f_0)^2}{2\theta_u^2} + \frac{v\prime^2}{2\theta_v^2}\right)\right\}$$

$$where, \; u\prime = u\cos\theta + v\sin\theta$$

$$v\prime = v\cos\theta - u\sin\theta$$

```
1   texture<float, 1, cudaReadModeElementType> tex_gx, tex_gy, tex_gt;
2   __global__ void DYN_ker_motion_estimator_prefetch ( float *dx, float *dy, float *wi,
3       int w, int h)
4   {
5     float dif, _dx, _dy, _wi;
6     float eqx[2*N], eqy[2*N];
7     __shared__ float eqt[2*N][64];
8     unsigned int x = threadIdx.x + blockIdx.x*blockDim.x;
9     unsigned int y = threadIdx.y + blockIdx.y*blockDim.y;
10    if( x>=w || y>=h )return;
11    for( unsigned int j=0 ; j<2*N ; j++){
12      eqx[j] = tex1Dfetch(tex_gx, (x + y*w) + j*(w*h));
13      eqy[j] = tex1Dfetch(tex_gy, (x + y*w) + j*(w*h));
14      eqt[j][threadIdx.x] = tex1Dfetch(tex_gt, (x + y*w) + j*(w*h));
15    }
16    syncthreads();
17    for( unsigned int i=0, unsigned int j=0 ; j<2*N ; j++ ){
18      for( unsigned int k=0 ; k<j ; k++, i++ ){
19          dif = eqx[k]*eqy[j] - eqy[k]*eqx[j];
20          _dx = _dy = 0.0f;
21          if( dif!=0.0f ){
22            _dx = ( eqy[k]*eqt[j][threadIdx.x]-eqt[k][threadIdx.x]*eqy[j] ) / dif;
23            _dy = ( eqt[k][threadIdx.x]*eqx[j]-eqx[k]*eqt[j][threadIdx.x] ) / dif;
24        }
25          dx[(x + y*w) + i*(w*h)] = _dx;
26          dy[(x + y*w) + i*(w*h)] = _dy;
27          wi[(x + y*w) + i*(w*h)] = (( fabsf(_dx)>Mmax || fabsf(_dy)>Mmax) ? 0.0f :
                1.0f);
28      }
29    }
30  }
```

Listing 30.4: The prefetch motion estimator kernal.

The retinal output is filtered using Gabor filters implemented in the frequency domain after applying a mask. The mask is similar to a Hanning function to produce non-uniform illumination approaching zero at the edges. The visual information is processed in different frequencies and orientations in the primary cortex; that is, the model uses six orientations and four frequencies to obtain 24 partial maps as shown in Figure 30.5. These filters demonstrate optimal localization properties and a good compromise of resolution between frequency and spatial domains. Finally, the Listing 30.5 illustrates the kernel of the Gabor filters using constant and texture memories.

30.3.6 **Multi-GPU Implementation**

Multi-GPU implementation is quite interesting to increase the computational efficiency of the entire visual saliency model. We have employed a shared-system GPU model, where multiple GPUs are installed on a single CPU. If the devices need to communicate, they do it through the CPU with no

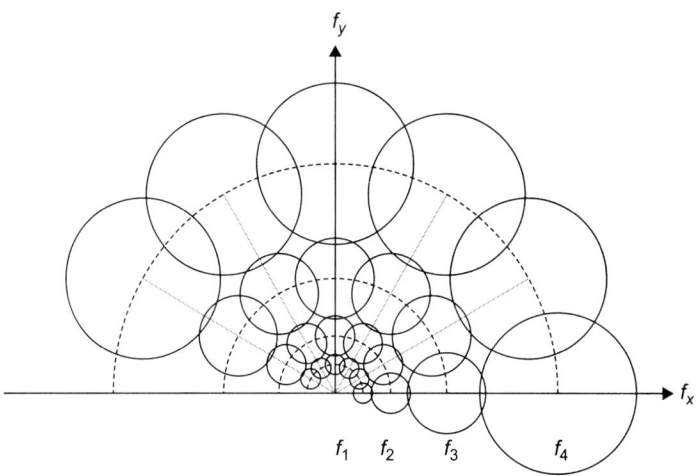

FIGURE 30.5

Gabor filter bank configuration.

```
1   texture<float, 2, cudaReadModeElementType> texGaborU, texGaborV;
2   __constant__ float d_frequencies[NO_OF_BANDS], d_sig_hor[NO_OF_BANDS];
3
4   __global__ void STA_k_gabor_bank(cmplx* in, unsigned int width, unsigned int height,
        ↩ cmplx* maps)
5   {
6     unsigned int x   = threadIdx.x/2 + blockIdx.x*blockDim.x/2;
7     unsigned int y   = threadIdx.y   + blockIdx.y*blockDim.y;
8     unsigned int mod = threadIdx.x%2;
9
10    for ( unsigned int j = 0; j < NO_OF_ORIENTS ; j++ ){
11      for ( unsigned int i = 0 ; i < NO_OF_BANDS ; i++ ){
12        maps[(j*NO_OF_BANDS + i) * (width*height) + (y*width + x)][mod] =
13          in[y*width + x][mod] *
14          __expf( -(
15          powf( tex2D(texGaborU, x, j*height + y) - d_frequencies[i], 2)
16          / ( 2.0f * d_sig_hor[i]*d_sig_hor[i])
17          + powf( tex2D(texGaborV ,x ,j*height + y), 2)
18          / ( 2.0f * d_sig_hor[i]*d_sig_hor[i])
19          ));
20      }
21    }
22  }
```

Listing 30.5: A Gabor bank filtering kernel producing 24 partial maps.

inter-GPU communication. A CPU thread is created to invoke kernel execution on a GPU; accordingly, we will have a CPU thread for each GPU. To successfully execute our single GPU solution on multi-GPUs, the parallel version must be deterministic. Our first implementation, the two pathways of the visual saliency model — static and dynamic — are completely separate with no inter-GPU communication required. The resultant saliency maps are simply copied back to the host, where they can be fused together into the final saliency map.

Pipeline Model

In this multi-GPU implementation, we employ a simple domain decomposition technique by assigning separate portions of the task to different threads. As soon as any thread finds an available device, it fetches the input image from the RAM to device memory and invokes the execution of the kernel. The threads wait until the execution of the kernel is complete and then gather their respective results back.

In our implementation as illustrated in Figure 30.6, we have three threads that are assigned different portions of the visual saliency model. For instance, thread 0 calculates the static saliency map; thread 1 does the retinal filtering and applies the Gabor filters bank; and thread 2 performs the motion estimation

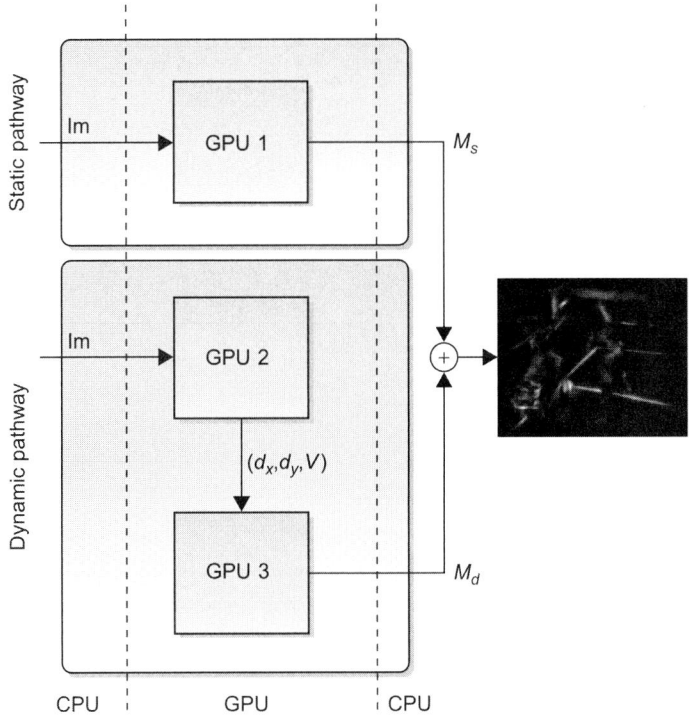

FIGURE 30.6

A block diagram of the multi GPU pipeline model.

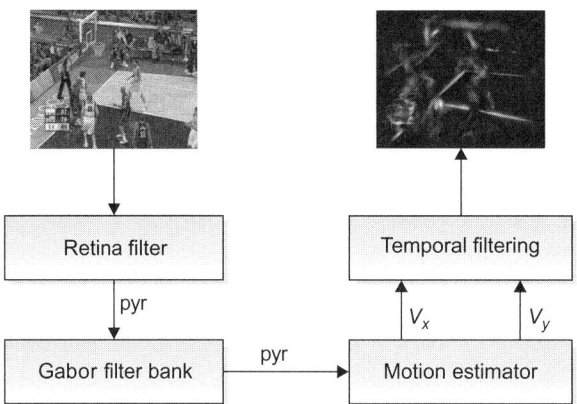

FIGURE 30.7

A block diagram of the decompose dynamic pathway.

outputting the dynamic saliency map to the host. The division of the dynamic pathway is done based on computational times of different kernels; we find that the suitable cut will be after recursive Gaussian filters that are followed by the motion estimator, as shown in Figure 30.7. Each half of this cut takes ~60 ms, which is half of 130 ms for the entire pathway. The inter-GPU communication between thread 1 and thread 2 involves the transfer of the N-level pyramid for the input image treated with the retinal filter and Gabor bank. Afterward, thread 2 is responsible for the estimation. Finally, the static and dynamic saliency maps from thread 0 and thread 2 are fused into the final visual saliency map. Consequently, using a pipeline cuts off the time to calculate the entire model to ~50 ms instead of 150 ms for the simple solution.

In such a multithreaded model, there is complexity involved in selecting an efficient strategy for creation and destruction of threads, resource utilization, and load balancing. Also, inter-GPU communication between GPUs might be an overhead affecting the overall performance. This overhead can be tackled by overlapping communications with computations using streaming available in the CUDA programming model.

30.4 RESULTS

All implementations were tested on a 2.80 GHz system with 1 GB of main memory, and Windows 7 running on it. On the other hand, the parallel version was implemented using the latest CUDA v3.0 programming environment on NVIDIA GTX285 series graphics cards.

30.4.1 Speedup of Static Pathway

In the algorithm, a saliency map is produced at the end of the static pathway, which identifies the salient regions in the visual input. These stages include a Hanning mask, Retinal filter, Gabor filter

Table 30.4 Speedups after optimizations to static pathway.

Case	Over MATLAB	Over	Mpixels/sec First CUDA
First implementation	396x	1.00x	4.11
Textures used	421x	1.06x	5.93
No bank conflicts	429x	1.08x	6.08
Fast math used	440x	1.11x	6.25

bank, interaction, normalization, and fusion. All these stages show a great potential to be parallelized and are isolated within separate kernels. Initially, the model is implemented using MATLAB that happens to be extremely slow because it involves a number of compute-intensive operations; for example, 2-D convolutions, conversions between frequency and spatial domains, and Gabor banks producing 24 partial maps that are further processed. As a result, a single image would take about 18 s to pass through the entire pathway in our MATLAB code, making it unfeasible for real-time applications. The target of the second implementation in C is to identify the data-parallel portions after writing it in a familiar language. It includes many optimizations and also the use of a highly optimized FFTW library for Fourier transforms, but the speedup witnessed is only 2.17x.

At first, the porting of the data-parallel portions into separate kernels for the GPU can be simple. But the code requires many tweaks to achieve the promised speedup, and tweaking the code happens to be the most complex maneuver. Although the very first implementation involved partitioning into data-parallel portions, which resulted in a speedup of about 396x, the peak performance topped over to 440x after we made various optimizations. Table 30.5 shows timings for the different kernels, while performance gains after optimizations are presented in Table 30.4. To test the performance of this pathway, we use an image size of 640×480 pixels.

30.4.2 Speedup of Dynamic Pathway

To evaluate the performance gains of the dynamic pathway, we compare the timings on the GPU against the sequential C and MATLAB code, as shown in Table 30.6. Table 30.7 shows times for the various kernels in the pathway. We used three datasets of images "Treetran," "Treediv," and "Yosemite" for comparison, the first two with resolution of 150×150 pixels, while 316×252 pixels for the last one.

30.4.3 Precision

The vision algorithm implemented in CUDA is ported from MATLAB code, where all the computations are done entirely in double precision; fortunately, the effects of low precision in parallel implementation are not obvious. The main reason is the type of algorithm, that is, whether it can produce acceptable results, or ones that are usable. Here, the resultant saliency map may be inaccurate, but visually fine

Table 30.5 Computational cost of each step in static pathway.

Kernel	Geforce GTX 285 (ms)
Mask	0.08
FFT	0.59
Shift	0.09
24 × Gabor	1.47
24 × Inverse shift	1.13
24 × IFFT	10.76
24 × Interaction	3.13
24 × Normalize	3.33
24 × Normalize Itti	3.34
24 × Normalize Fusion	2.89
Total	26.81

Table 30.6 Timings for the dynamic pathway after optimizations.

	Treetran	Treediv	Yosemite
MATLAB	13.30 s	12.86 s	46.61 s
C	1.75 s	1.76 s	6.28 s
CUDA	0.12 s	0.12 s	0.30 s

Table 30.7 Computational cost of each step in dynamic pathway.

Kernel	Geforce GTX 285 (ms)
Retinal filtering	21.5
Modulation	2.6
Demodulation	3.1
Interpolation	0.3
Projection	0.2
Vertical Gaussian recursive	33.2
Horizontal Gaussian recursive	21.7
Gradients	6.2
Motion estimator	39.1
Median filtering	0.2
Total	128.1

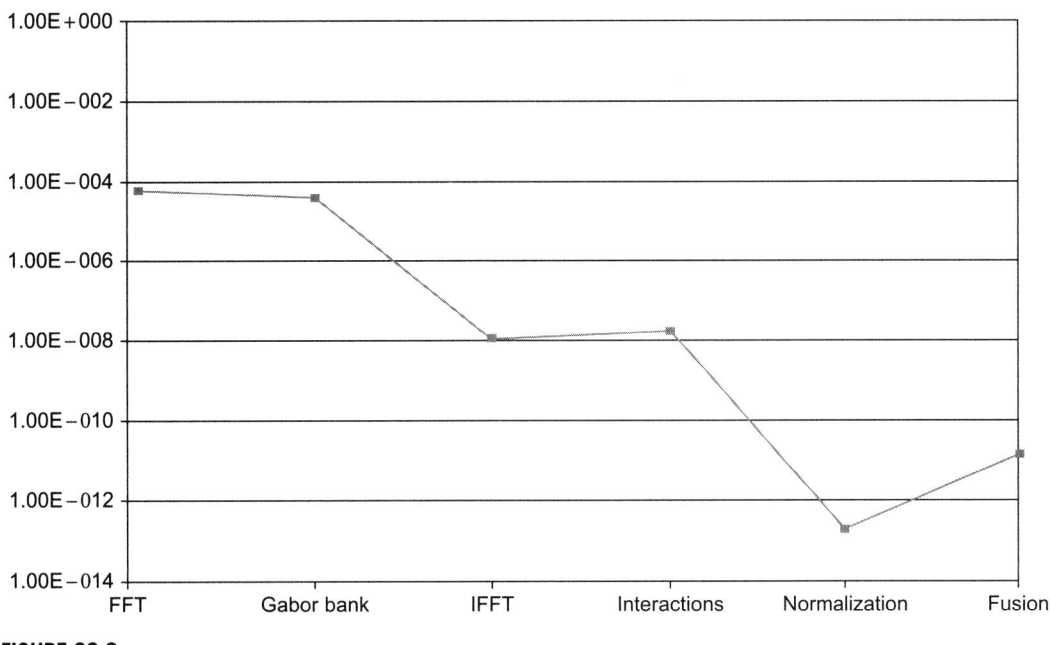

FIGURE 30.8

The effect of lower-precision support on the result.

with a universal image quality index [12] of 99.66% and two digit precision among the 24 bits of a float mantissa. Figure 30.8 shows the mean error with respect to the reference during different stages of the pathway. We observe that the accuracy increases along the progressing stages because of the reduction of information, more evident during Gabor filtering and normalization phases until finally ending up in regions that are salient.

30.4.4 Evaluation of Results

To evaluate the correctness of the motion estimator, we calculate the error between estimated and real optical flows using the equation below:

$$\alpha_e = \arccos \left(\frac{uu_r + vv_r + 1}{\sqrt{u^2 + v^2 + 1}\sqrt{u_r^2 + v_r^2 + 1}} \right)$$

where a_e is the angular error for a given pixel with (u, v) the estimated and (u_r, v_r) the real motion vectors. We used "treetran" and "treediv" image sequences for the evaluation, showing translational and divergent motion, respectively [2]. The results shown in Table 30.8 are obtained using "treetran" and "treediv" image sequences of sizes 150×150 pixels.

Table 30.8 Evaluating the estimator using angular error.

	Treetran		Treediv	
	$\bar{x}$	σ	$\bar{x}$	σ
Matlab	1.63	5.27	6.06	8.22
C	1.10	0.99	4.15	2.69
CUDA	1.19	1.00	5.73	3.91

Table 30.9 Mean NSS value for the static, dynamic, and fused saliency maps.

Saliency maps	M_s	M_d	M_{sd}
Real eye movements	0.68	0.87	0.96
Partially randomized eye movements	0.33	0.14	0.14

30.4.5 Evaluation

The results of the visual saliency model can be evaluated using Normalized Scanpath Saliency (NSS) [10] as shown in Table 30.9. This criteria compares the eye fixations of the subjects with the salient areas in the resulting saliency map. The NSS metric corresponds to a Z-score that expresses the divergence of experimental results (eye fixations) compared with model mean as a number of standard deviations of the model. The higher value of the Z-score suggests a correspondence between the eye fixations and locations calculated by the model. We calculate the NSS with the equation:

$$NSS(k) = \frac{\overline{M_h(x,y,k) \times M_m(x,y,k)} - \overline{M_h(x,y,k)}}{\sigma_{M_h(x,y,k)}}$$

where $M_h(x,y,k)$ is the human eye position density map normalized to unit mean, and $M_m(x,y,k)$ is a model saliency map. The value of NSS is zero if there is no correspondence between eye positions and salient regions. Whereas, if positive then strong correspondence, and the rest show anti-correspondence.

30.4.6 Real-Time Streaming Solution

OpenVIDIA [4] is an open source platform that provides an interface for video input, display, and programming on the GPU that is facilitated with a bunch of high-level implementations of a number of image-processing and computer vision algorithms using OpenGL, Cg, and CUDA. These implementations include feature detection and tracking, skin tone tracking, and projective panoramas.

After the parallel implementation of the visual saliency algorithm, we used OpenVIDIA to demonstrate the real-time processing. The demonstration is done on a quad-core machine with three GPUs installed, and the library is used to interface with the webcam. This resulted in execution of the static

FIGURE 30.9

A platform for a real-time solution.

pathway at 28 fps on the platform shown in Figure 30.9. Finally, the performance gains on GPU will enable our model to be used for various applications such as the automatic video reframing process [3]. This application extracts a cropping window using the regions of interest from the model. These windows are then smooth to increase the viewing experience.

30.5 CONCLUSION

In this chapter, we presented the multi-GPU implementation of a visual saliency model to identify the areas of attention. The main advantage of the performance gain accomplished will allow the inclusion of face recognition, stereo, audio, and other complex processes. Consequently, this real-time solution finds a wide application for several research and industrial problems, such as video compression, video reframing, frame quality assessment, visual telepresence and surveillance, automatic target detection, robotics control, super-resolution, and computer graphics rendering.

References

[1] NVIDIA Corporation: NVIDIA CUDA compute unified device architecture programming guide v3.0. NVIDIA Corporation. http://developer.nvidia.com/cuda (accessed 12.31.10).
[2] E. Bruno, D. Pellerin, Robust motion estimation using spatial gabor-like filters, Signal Process. 82 (2002) 297–309.

[3] C. Chamaret, O. Le Meur, Attention-based video reframing: validation using eye-tracking, in: Pattern Recognition, 2008. ICPR 2008. 19th International Conference on, IEEE, Tampa, FL, December 2008, pp. 1–4.

[4] J. Fung, S. Mann, C. Aimone, Openvidia: parallel gpu computer vision, in: MULTIMEDIA '05: Proceedings of the 13th Annual ACM International Conference on Multimedia, ACM, New York, 2005, pp. 849–852.

[5] L. Itti, Real-time high-performance attention focusing in outdoors color video streams, in: B. Rogowitz, T.N. Pappas (Eds.), Proceedings of SPIE Human Vision and Electronic Imaging VII, HVEI '02, SPIE Press, San Jose, 2002, pp. 235–243.

[6] L. Itti, C. Koch, E. Niebur, A model of saliency-based visual attention for rapid scene analysis, IEEE Trans. Pattern Anal. Mach. Intell. 20 (1998) 1254–1259.

[7] S. Marat, T. Ho Phuoc, L. Granjon, N. Guyader, D. Pellerin, A. Guérin-Dugué, Modelling spatio-temporal saliency to predict gaze direction for short videos, Int. J. Comput. Vision 82 (2009) 231–243.

[8] J.M. Odobez, P. Bouthemy, Robust multiresolution estimation of parametric motion models applied to complex scenes. J. Vis. Commun. Image Represent. 6 (1994) 348–365.

[9] N. Ouerhani, H. Hgli, Real-time visual attention on a massively parallel simd architecture, Real-Time Imaging 9 (2003) 189–196.

[10] R.J. Peters, A. Iyer, L. Itti, C. Koch, Components of bottom-up gaze allocation in natural images, Vision Res. 45 (2005) 2397–2416.

[11] T. Ho-Phuoc, A. Guérin-Dugué, N. Guyader, P. Encarnação, A. Veloso (Ed.), A computational saliency model integrating saccade programming, in: BIOSIGNALS, INSTICC Press, 2009, 57–64.

[12] Z. Wang, A.C. Bovik, A universal image quality index, IEEE Signal Process. Lett. 9 (2002) 81–84.

Real-Time Stereo on GPGPU Using Progressive Multiresolution Adaptive Windows

31

Yong Zhao, Gabriel Taubin

In this chapter, a new GPGPU-based real-time dense stereo-matching algorithm is presented. The algorithm is based on a progressive multiresolution pipeline that includes background modeling and dense matching with adaptive windows. For applications in which only moving objects are of interest, this approach effectively reduces the overall computation cost quite significantly and preserves the high-definition details. Running on an off-the-shelf commodity graphics card, our implementation achieves a high speed that is effectively the same as 7200 M disparity evaluations per second. The current implementation achieves 36 Hz stereo matching on 1024×768 stereo video with a fine 256-pixel disparity range. We envision a number of potential applications, such as real-time motion capture, as well as tracking, recognizing and identifying moving objects.

31.1 INTRODUCTION, PROBLEM STATEMENT, AND CONTEXT

Estimating depth from stereo is a classic computer vision problem, which has received tremendous attention since the early days. Recovering 3-D information from a pair of stereo cameras has been a popular topic because the additional 3-D information provided by this technology contains significantly more information than 2-D information produced by traditional cameras. Some believe that this technology will fundamentally revolutionize the computer vision signal processing pipeline, as well as how future cameras will be built.

However, this 2-D to 3-D evolution has always faced many challenges, which can be grouped into two main categories: accuracy and efficiency. Accuracy becomes an important concern in applications such as precise 3-D surface modeling, especially when dealing with object surfaces with complex reflectance behavior, rich geometric structure, a significant amount of occlusion, and poor texture. Efficiency is the main concern when the stereo system is employed in real-time applications such as robot navigation, video surveillance, or interactive human-computer interaction (HCI).

Unfortunately, these challenges often conflict with each other: in order to improve the quality of stereo matching, people usually cast the problem as a global optimization problem, which results in high-computation cost and poor efficiency. On the other hand, most efficient stereo-matching

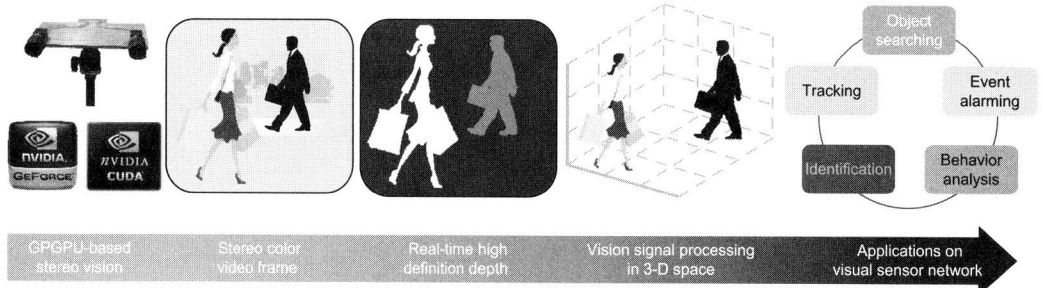

FIGURE 31.1

Processing a computer vision signal in 3-D.

algorithms are based on only local information, which leads to poor accuracy under some difficult situations.

The focus of our work is to provide efficient high-resolution stereo algorithms for real-time applications in which only foreground moving objects are of interest, such as motion capture, object tracking, and recognition and identification in a surveillance scenario, shown in Figure 31.1. These applications usually have some special performance requirements to their stereo engines: first, being able to estimate depth in real-time speed is essential for the whole system to be able to work in real-time; second, high resolution is very important for applications that have large working volumes, and very crowded scenes, where attention to detail information is necessary; third, fine scanning range (maximum disparity) is necessary for applications that have to deal with big depth of view; after all, stereo is usually only one part of a real-time computer vision processing pipeline. In order to make the overall pipeline real time, the stereo system must work faster than real time and save a significant amount of processing time (CPU time and GPU time) for other higher-level processing tasks. In the following sections, we will explain in detail how this daunting task can be fulfilled with commodity computer graphic hardware.

During the past 20 years, many stereo systems have been successfully developed with high flexibility, compact size, and acceptable cost. The overall stereo-matching literature is too large to be surveyed here. We refer interested readers to [1] for a taxonomy and evaluation. In this chapter, we focus only on real-time stereo algorithms. A number of real-time stereo algorithms have been presented in recent years such as [2–10]. The algorithm presented in this chapter is based on the adaptive window approach introduced by Yang and Pollefeys [4]. Instead of using the traditional fixed-size square window, such as the one shown in Figure 31.2(a), the "adaptive window" approach, which is illustrated in Figure 31.2(b), computes matching costs in five subwindows. The final matching cost is determined by the cost from the center window and two surrounding windows whose matching costs are among the two lowest ones. The resulting shape can be any one of six possibilities, as shown in Figure 31.2(c). In practice, the adaptive window can change its shape adaptively to reflect the local image content such as edges and corners. Yang and Pollefeys have shown comparison results that this approach not only provides higher accuracy but also leads to more efficient computing. This work successfully pushed the stereo-matching speed record up to 289 Mde/s using more modern computer graphics hardware.

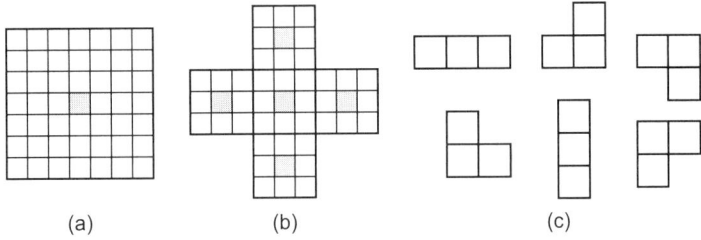

FIGURE 31.2

The cost aggregation window. (a) A 7 × 7 pixel square window; (b) adaptive window; (c) all six possible resulting shapes of adaptive windows.

31.2 CORE METHOD

Figure 31.3(a) shows the pipeline of our stereo algorithm. Stereo video frames are captured and rectified so that a pair of row-aligned images can be obtained to reduce the computation cost of matching. However, the matching doesn't start at the original resolution of the input stereo images. Instead, a pyramid of down-sampled images are generated from the rectified pair, denoted by $\{I_1, I_2, \ldots, I_N\}$. N is the number of total resolutions. I_N is the stereo frame at its original full resolution, and each I_i is the half sample of I_{i+1}. Before stereo matching starts, a multiresolution background modeling on both views, denoted by $\{B_1, B_2, \ldots, B_n\}$, is applied on stereo views to detect the multiresolution foreground mask $\{F_1, F_2, \ldots, F_N\}$. The foreground detection result is used to constrain the image area on which stereo matching is operated. This will not only reduce the matching error but also improve the speed performance. The stereo dense matching will be processed on the lowest resolution I_1 first, then progressively on other higher resolutions.

During this process, the disparity searching is operated only on a small range suggested by the disparity result from lower resolution. This iteration continues until the processing on the original full-resolution I_N is finished. Figure 31.3(b) shows some intermediate results from this coarse-to-fine multiresolution process. Once the stereo matching on the original resolution is finished, subpixel disparity refinement is optionally applied in applications where higher precision is needed.

Design ideas to make our algorithm a GPU-friendly one will be articulated in following sections. These ideas include how to minimize the global memory traffic during the disparity scan process, how to accelerate matching aggregation by using an in-kernel integral image, as well as how to maximize the homogeneity of an individual thread's memory access pattern.

31.2.1 Algorithms, Implementations, and Evaluations
Multiresolution Background Modeling
A foreground segmentation is embedded in our stereo-matching pipeline because in many applications, only moving objects are of interest. In these cases, the uninteresting background part of the image results not only in a waste of processing time but also in additional sources of matching errors.

Our foreground detection algorithm is based on the algorithm introduced by K. Jain *et al.* [11], which is an efficient variation of Gaussian background modeling [12]. This background modeling is applied on Hue-Saturation-Value (HSV) color space instead of Red-Green-Blue (RGB) color space in order

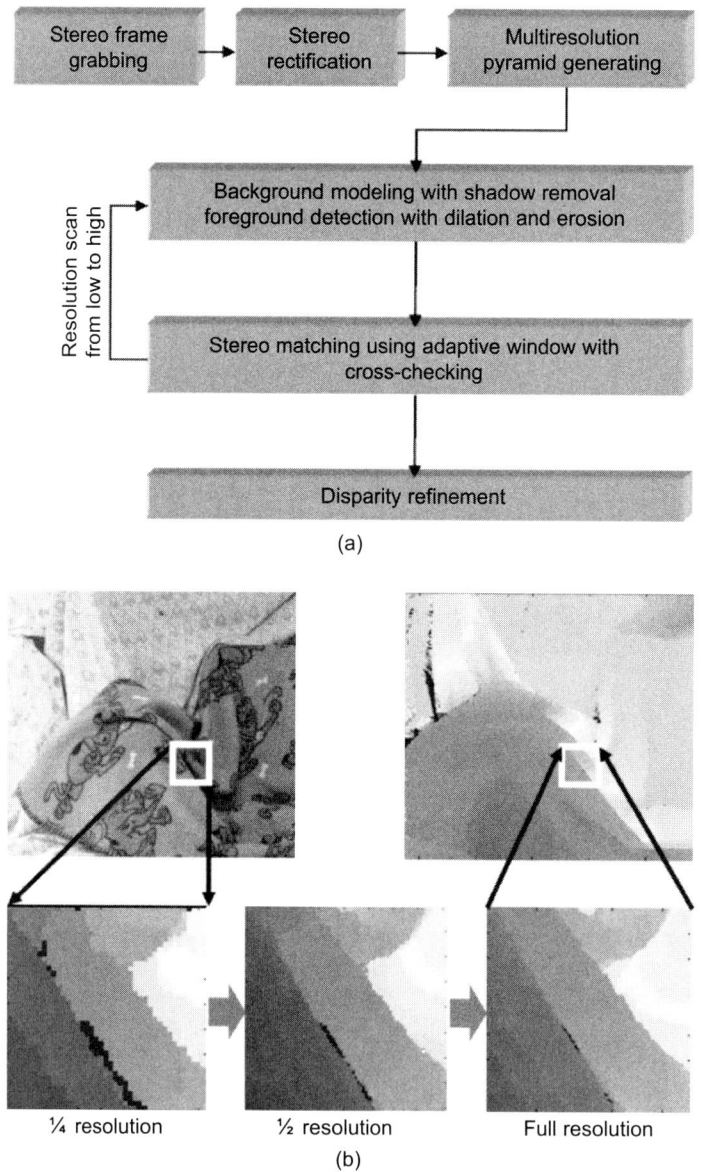

FIGURE 31.3

(a) The processing pipeline of a proposed stereo algorithm. (b) Coarse-to-fine matching on multiple resolutions.

to reduce shadow effects. This background-modeling algorithm works fine with most indoor scenarios and is computational economic enough for real-time applications. However, any other background-modeling algorithms can be used in our stereo-matching pipeline as long as they can produce a binary mask indicating a foreground or background decision.

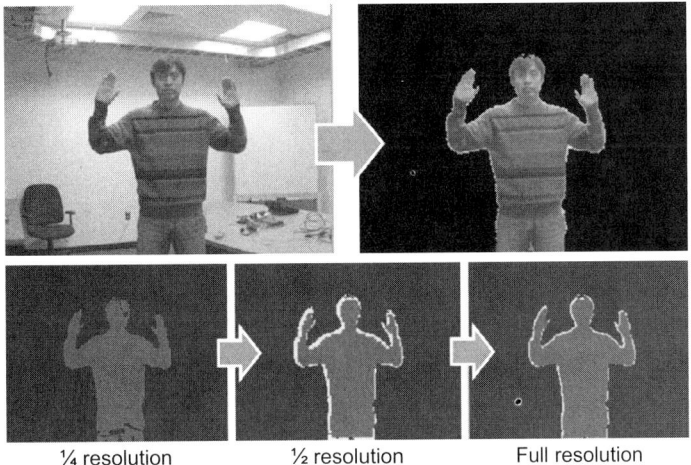

¼ resolution   ½ resolution   Full resolution

FIGURE 31.4

Foreground detection is performed on multiple resolutions, from low to high. On higher resolutions, the actual foreground detections take place only at the boundary blocks of foreground blobs. Only the white pixels on the boundary region of foreground masks shown in Figure 31.4 represent the foreground pixels actually detected by the pixelwise comparison to the background model.

In our multiresolution pipeline, the foreground detection algorithm is applied on the pyramid, progressively from low to high resolution. In addition, we take two extra steps to accelerate the processing on multiple resolutions and improve the smoothness of foreground detection, respectively.

First, stereo images on different resolutions are divided into square blocks in the foreground detection. For each pixel block from $I_i (i > 1)$, the foreground detection results F_{i-1} from the lower resolution $I_i - 1$ are checked. If all the pixels of the corresponding block in $I_i - 1$ have uniform detection results (either all foreground or all background), then this result will be copied to all the pixels of the block on I_i. Otherwise, pixelwise comparison between I_i and B_i is applied to decide whether it is a foreground pixel or not. This process is illustrated in Figure 31.4. By doing this, only pixels of the foreground boundary blocks are actually tested against the background model. At the same time most noises on foreground blobs at high resolutions are removed. In practice, this technique can effectively reduce the total number of pixels that need to be tested by up to 90%.

Second, foreground dilation and erosion are applied on the foreground detection result, which fills the holes inside foreground blobs. After this, a pyramid of nice and smooth foreground detections are obtained and will be used in the matching step.

The CUDA implementation of this multiresolution foreground detection algorithm comprises multiple passes, each of which works on a different resolution. In each pass, the steps of background update, foreground detection, foreground dilation, and foreground erosion are all performed by one CUDA kernel function. As illustrated in Figure 31.5(a), each 16×16 thread block takes care of loading and processing a 16×16 pixel square block. However, only the center 8×8 pixel square is saved. This mapping gives each 8×8 pixel block a 4-pixel-wide "apron" that overlaps with surrounding blocks. The overlapped part of the image is processed redundantly so that the foreground dilation and erosion

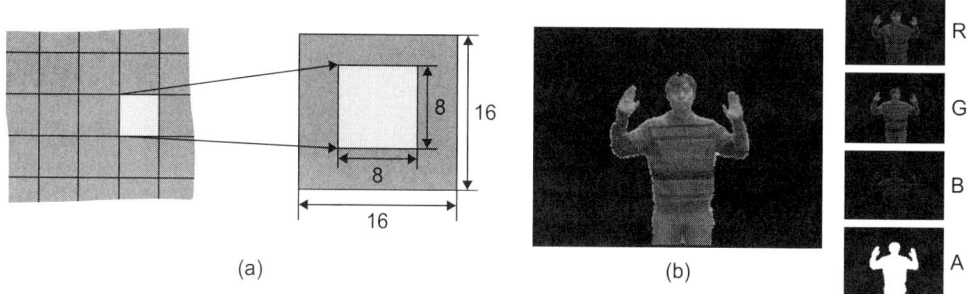

FIGURE 31.5

(a) A CUDA implementation of foreground detection. (b) The foreground mask is packed with the color image at the A channel of the RGBA-formatted image.

would not cause artifacts at the block boundary area. The result of foreground detection is saved in the alpha channel of the rectified input images, which are represented in RGBA format, as indicated in Figure 31.5(b).

Multiresolution Stereo Matching

In our algorithm, stereo matching starts from the lowest resolution. The adaptive window approach introduced by Yang and Pollefeys [4] is adopted here. The reason for adopting this approach now is because it results in higher matching accuracy compared with the fixed-window approaches, given the same number of involved neighboring pixels. However, as the resolution of image and range of disparity scan increases, the 4×4 subwindow configuration in this algorithm eventually becomes insufficient. This is why this approach is used only on the lowest resolution I_1.

For example, consider a stereo pair with full-resolution $W_N \times H_N$, and disparity-searching range S_N. The lowest resolution of this stereo input is $\frac{W_N}{2^{N-1}} \times \frac{H_N}{2^{N-1}}$, and the corresponding disparity-searching range $S_1 = \frac{S_N}{2^{N-1}}$. For each pixel on the left view of the lowest resolution, denoted by $I_1(left, x, y)$ (*left* means left view of stereo pair; x and y are pixel coordinates on horizontal and vertical direction, respectively), the process of computing its disparity $D_1(left, x, y)$ is as follows:

- If $F_1(left, x, y) = 1$, continue; otherwise, no disparity for $I_1(left, x, y)$.
- For $s \in [x, x + S_1]$, compute the matching cost $C(s)$ using the adaptive window approach if $F_1(right, x + s, y) = 1$. If $F_1(right, x + s, y) = 0$, set the matching cost $C(s) = \infty$.
- Disparity $D_1(left, x, y) = \arg\min_s C(s)$, where $s \in [x, x + S_1]$.

Once the stereo matching on the lowest resolution is done, stereo matching is performed on higher resolutions progressively. For each pixel of left view at resolution i, denoted by $I_i(left, x, y)$, the process of computing its disparity $D_i(left, x, y)$ is as follows:

- If $F_i(left, x, y) = 1$, continue; otherwise, no disparity value for $I_i(left, x, y)$.
- For $s \in \left[2 \cdot D_{i-1}\left(left, \frac{x}{2}, \frac{y}{2}\right) - 2, 2 \cdot D_{i-1}\left(left, \frac{x}{2}, \frac{y}{2}\right) + 2\right]$, compute the matching cost $C(s)$ using the adaptive window approach if $F_i(right, x + s, y) = 1$. If $F_i(right, x + s, y) = 0$, set the matching cost $C(s) = \infty$.
- Disparity $D_i(left, x, y) = \arg\min_s C(s)$, where $s \in \left[2 \cdot D_{i-1}\left(left, \frac{x}{2}, \frac{y}{2}\right) - 2, 2 \cdot D_{i-1}\left(left, \frac{x}{2}, \frac{y}{2}\right) + 2\right]$.

Notice that two steps are taken to minimize the disparity searching range: (1) the foreground detection result is used in this process in such a way that only foreground pixels from both views are considered for possible matching; (2) for each resolution $I_i(i > 1)$, the searching is limited to a 4-pixel span centered at the suggestion from the disparity result on the lower-resolution D_{i-1}. By doing these steps, we significantly accelerate the matching process and improve the matching accuracy.

Here we want to discuss how our approach is different from one of the most well-known multi-resolution real-time stereo approaches [3]. In that work, Yang *et al.* propose that for each pixel, a matching cost is aggregated on a number of different resolutions, and the final disparity is decided by first summing up the matching cost on all these resolutions and searching for the minimum overall cost. This basically means using the average matching costs on multiple different resolutions to decide high-resolution disparity. Their approach generates a good-looking disparity map, but they usually lose the high-resolution detail because of a smoothing factor introduced by the results from lower resolutions. Also their approach computes matching cost along the full disparity-searching range on all resolutions, and saves all the immediate matching cost results in global memory, placing a tremendous burden on the global memory bandwidth.

Our approach, on the other hand, uses the disparity results from lower resolution to guide the searching range at higher resolution. The matching costs do not need to be computed exhaustively on every possible test disparity along the searching range. Therefore, time is saved from both computing and global memory access. And the final high-resolution disparity is directly determined only by the high-resolution matching cost aggregation. Therefore, our approach tends to preserve high-resolution details. Of course, there exist chances where once a wrong decision has been made at low resolution, it cannot be corrected at higher resolution. However, in practice, the chance of erroneous matching at low resolution is quite low. Besides, cross-checking can always be used to detect most low-resolution matching errors, and these problematic pixels will get opportunities to be corrected on higher resolutions later.

Single CUDA Kernel Implementation of Stereo Matching

It's worth mentioning some of our CUDA implementation details because an elaborate job of mapping processing and data to the CUDA concurrent thread array (CTA) is extremely important for achieving optimal performance. As illustrated in Figure 31.6, each thread block loads a 16×16 pixel block from the reference image, but only the disparities of the center 8×8 pixels are evaluated. All the input data — rectified image pairs with foreground masks embedded in the alpha channel — are bound with CUDA texture so that fast access can be achieved through a cached memory interface.

Each thread block also loads two 16×16 square blocks from the nonreference image. Then, for each of the 8×8 pixels from the reference image, cost aggregation is computed using the adaptive window approach with a 3×3 subwindow size. If the searching range is bigger than 16 pixels, the thread block just loads another 16×16 square block from the nonreference image and repeats the cost aggregation process. The disparity evaluation finishes only after the entire searching range is covered.

Figures 31.7 and 31.8 demonstrate how our stereo-matching algorithm is implemented at a certain resolution, using just a single-kernel CUDA function.

In Figure 31.7(a), rectified stereo images (left and right view) with a foreground mask at resolution i, as well as the left-view disparity map at resolution $i - 1$, are displayed on the upper row. Given this information, we will show how a single CUDA kernel function can be used to estimate the left-view

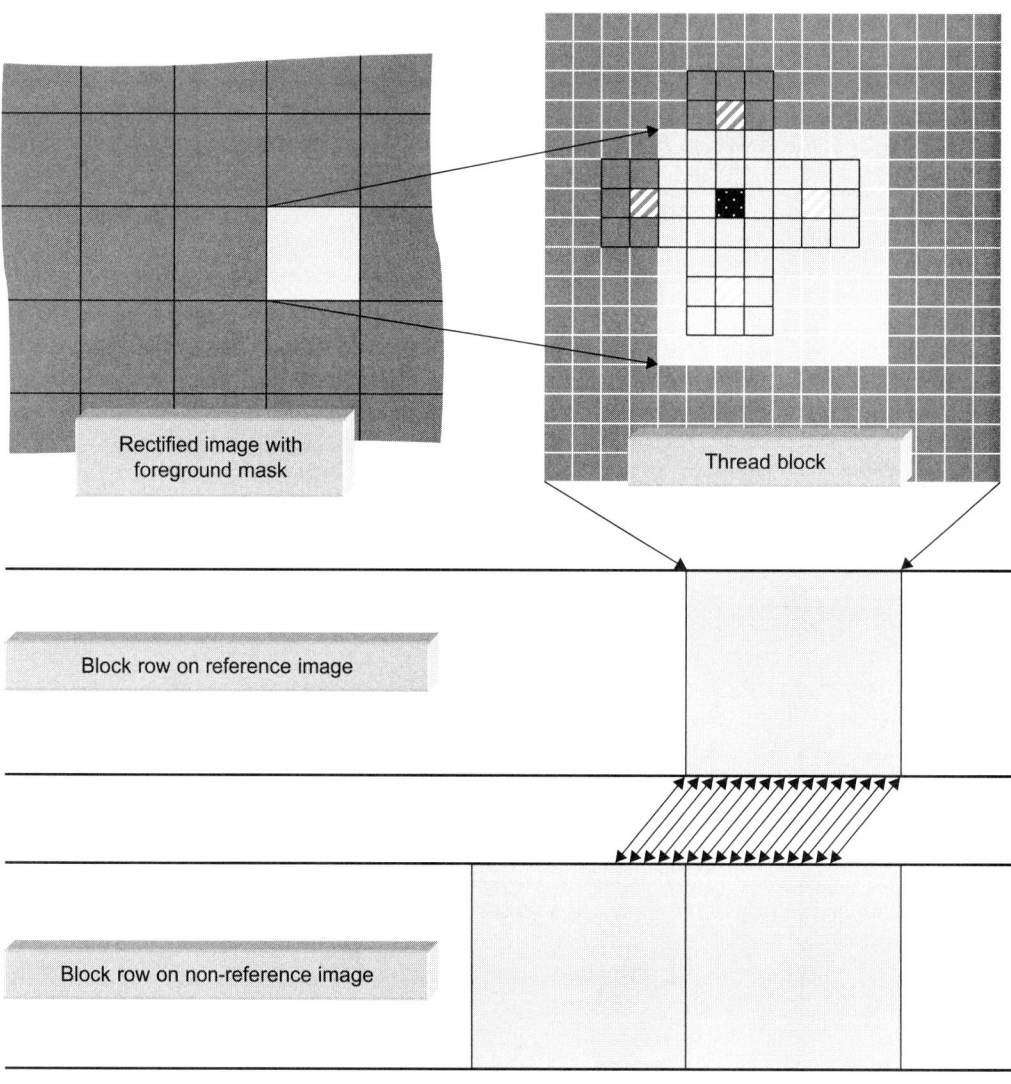

FIGURE 31.6

CUDA implementation of dense matching using an adaptive window.

disparity map at resolution i. In the lower-left section of this diagram is a CUDA thread block, or so-called cooperative thread array (CTA) taking care of estimating disparity at an 8×8 pixel block region. But in order to compute the matching cost using an adaptive window, this CTA actually needs to load a bigger 16×16 pixel block, which is centered on the 8×8 pixel block. Before the stereo matching starts, this CTA first reads the lower-resolution disparity map at the corresponding region shown in

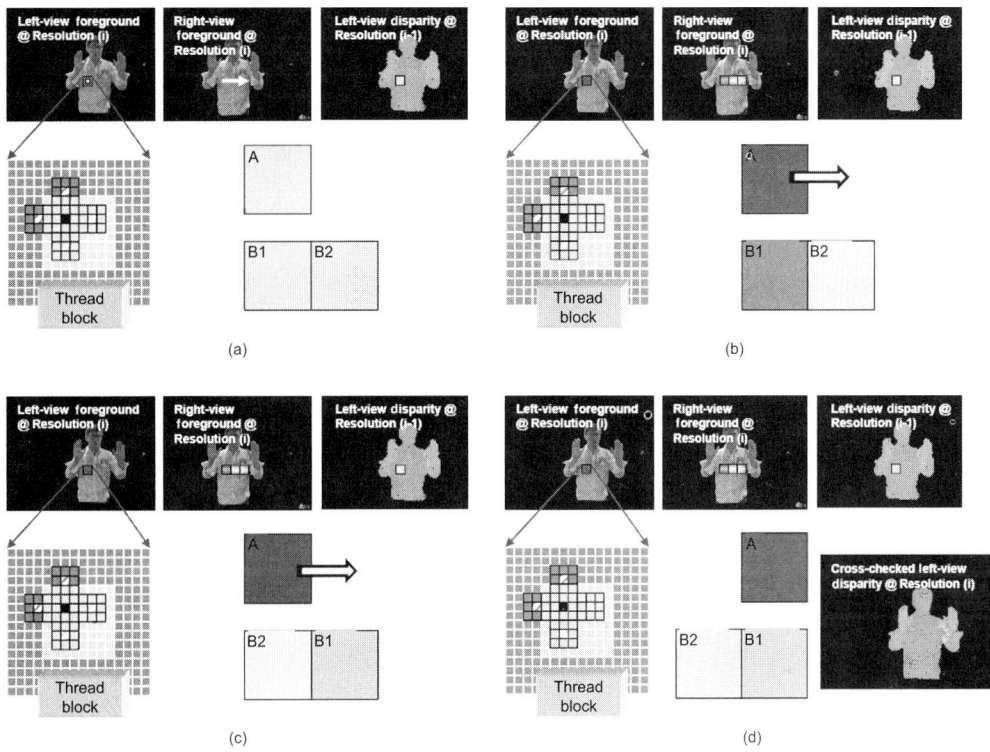

FIGURE 31.7

CUDA implementation of dense matching using an adaptive window.

the upper-right section of Figure 31.7(a). From the lower-resolution disparity map, a lower and upper boundary of the disparity values of this pixel block at current higher resolution can be obtained. For example, if the lower-resolution disparity map at this region varies in $[21, 42]$, then at the current resolution, the disparity-searching range should be in $[42 - 2, 84 + 2]$. Notice that an extra 4-pixel padding is added on both ends. On the upper-center part of Figure 31.7(a), a white arrow indicates the suggested disparity-searching range at resolution i. Each CTA creates three 16×16 RGBA buffers in its shared memory, denoted by A, B1, and B2.

In Figure 31.7(b), the CTA fills three RGBA buffers — A, B1, and B2 — with 16×16 pixel blocks from left view and right view. The pixel block from left view is loaded in buffer A; the first and second pixel block along the disparity-searching line are loaded in buffers B1 and B2, respectively. Once the data are ready in these fast internal buffers, a so-called disparity sweeping can be performed. The big white horizontal arrow on top of buffer A indicates the direction of this sweeping.

Figures 31.8(a) through 31.8(f) illustrate the "disparity-sweeping" process: Buffer A is loaded with a 16×16 pixel block from the left view; buffers B1 and B2 are loaded with the first and second 16×16 pixel blocks of the right view initially. Buffers B1 and B2 are combined as a 16×32 pixel block. Buffer

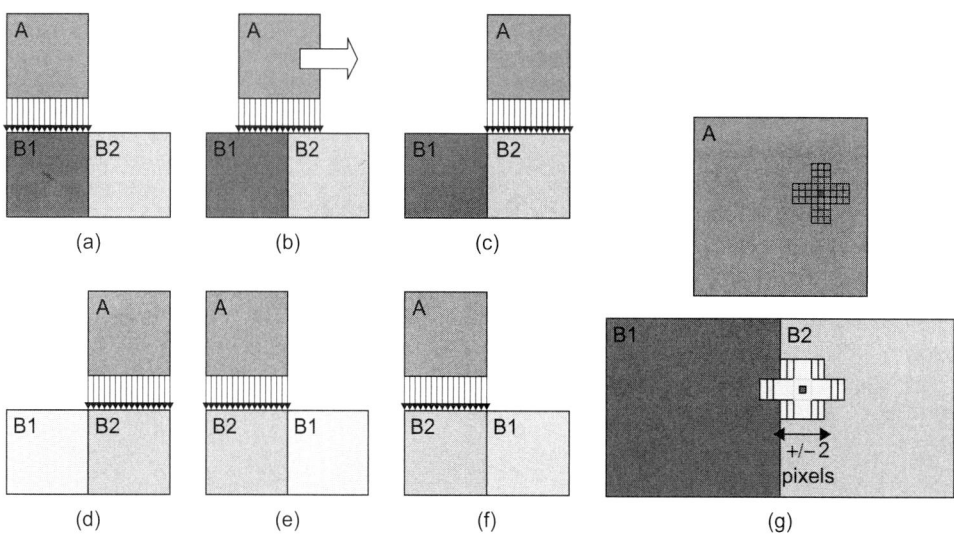

FIGURE 31.8

CUDA implementation of dense matching using an adaptive window. (a) Disparity sweeping starts after buffers B1 and B2 are loaded with the first and second pixel block. (b) During each step of disparity sweeping, each pixel of the 8 × 8 pixel block in the center part of buffer A is compared with the pixels in the corresponding region in the B1-B2 combined buffer. After each step, a 1-pixel offset is applied on the horizontal direction. (c) The disparity sweeping keeps proceeding until it reaches the end of the B1-B2 combined buffer. (d) Buffer B1 is cleared. (e) A new B2-B1 combination is formed. (f) The next 16 × 16 pixel block from the right view is loaded in Buffer B1, and then the disparity sweeping keeps going (g) the life of one pixel during the disparity sweep.

A is used to "sweep" along the combined B1-B2 buffer. At each step of this "sweeping," the matching costs of the center 8 × 8 pixel block are computed using the adaptive window approach. When sweeping reaches the end of the B1-B2 combined buffer, B1 is cleared and reloaded with the next pixel block from the right view. Then, B1 is attached at the trailing end of B2 to form a B2-B1 combined buffer. Then, "sweeping" can keep going until the whole disparity searching is finished.

Figure 31.8(g) shows what actually happens for each pixel in the left view during the disparity sweeping. One pixel and its five surrounding sub-windows are shown in buffer A, whose disparity will be estimated by the disparity sweeping. From the corresponding location in the lower-resolution disparity map, the suggested disparity of this pixel at higher resolution can be obtained. During the disparity sweeping, each CTA travels a much longer distance. Only when the sweeping proceeds into a small 4-pixel range that is centered at the suggested high-resolution disparity, the adaptive window matching cost will be computed for this pixel. Please notice that foreground detection information that is embedded at the alpha channel will also be used to constrain the matching cost computing during the disparity sweeping process.

Figures 31.7(c) and 31.7(d) show how disparity sweeping is performed on the example stereo image pair with swapping buffer B1 and B2 in the combined buffer. Finally, a left-view disparity map, which

v_lane (threadIdx.x)

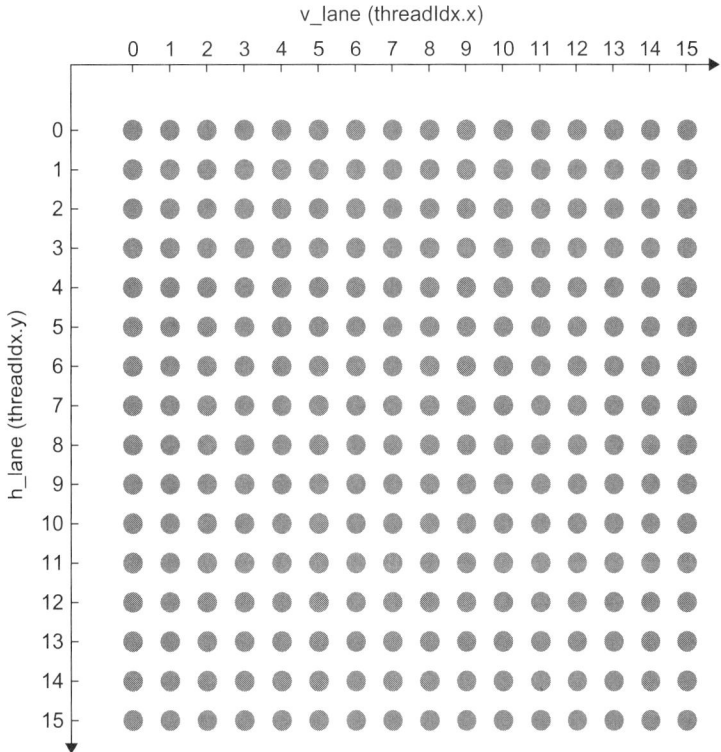

FIGURE 31.9

Integrating a 16 × 16 2-D image block in a CUDA thread block.

is shown in the lower-right section of Figure 31.7(d) at resolution i is created by this single CUDA kernel function.

Here, we want to mention an important CUDA implementation technique that significantly improves the speed performance of the disparity-sweeping process — using an integral image to accelerate computing-matching costs in subwindows. An integral image is a useful technique to compute the sum of values from a rectangular block efficiently. The definition of an integral image is that for an image N, the integral image of N is I. The value of each pixel of I must satisfy $I(x,y) = \sum_{x'=0}^{x} \sum_{y'=0}^{y} N(x',y')$. However, computing an integral image can be quite expensive. Here, a very simple CUDA implementation of a 2-D-image integration is presented.

Figure 31.9 shows a 16 × 16 Sum-of-Absolute-Difference (SAD) image block stored in shared memory, which will be processed by a thread block with 16 × 16 threads. Each thread has a 2-D thread ID (threadIdx.x, threadIdx.y). And each pixel has a 2-D coordinate (h_lane, v_lane). In this example, the integral image of this SAD image is computed so that it can be used to efficiently compute the matching cost of each subwindow. A two-pass approach is used to integrate the SAD image: first, integrate each row, and then integrate each column.

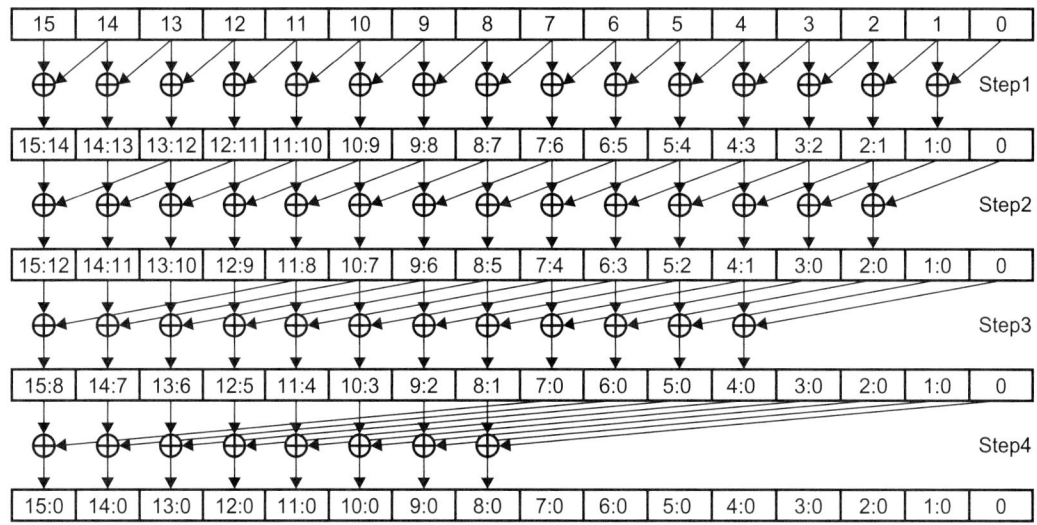

FIGURE 31.10

Integrating a 1-D pixel array with 16 pixels by a CUDA half-warp.

Figure 31.10 illustrates the process of integrating a 1-D pixel array with 16 pixels using 16 threads from the same half-warp of a CUDA thread block. It takes four steps to finish this 1-D integration. During each step, some thread replaces the value of a pixel using the sum of this pixel with the value of another pixel. Because all the threads from the same half-warp are automatically synchronized, each step can be executed simultaneously without using an extra buffer. It doesn't take a "__syncthreads()" command to synchronize the whole thread block until the horizontal integration is finished. And then the vertical integration is done by using the same four steps. A sample CUDA device function of this 2-D integration is shown in Figure 31.11.

Compared with Yang's GPU implementation in [4], the most remarkable improvement of our implementation is that, for each pixel, the entire disparity searching takes place within one kernel function, and only the final disparity result is stored in global memory just once. This helps to speed up the processing quite significantly because writing to global memory in the GPGPU is one of the most time-consuming operations because there is no outbound caching in current GPGPU architecture.

Cross-Checking

Cross-checking was first introduced by Cochran *et al.* [13]. When we use a different view from the stereo pair as the reference image, the two disparity maps may not be entirely identical. This problem may be caused by occlusion, reflection, differences caused by non-Lambertian surfaces, and sampling noise. Cross-checking is a process to check the consistency of disparity estimation when the reference view is changed. For example, after stereo matching at two different reference views, we note that there are two resulting disparity maps: $D(left)$ and $D(right)$. For a pixel of the left-view disparity map at position (x,y), the disparity value is $D(left,x,y)$; this means the corresponding pixel at the right image is at position $(x + D(left,x,y),y)$; the actual disparity value of this pixel at the right-view

```
_device_ inline void integrate_2D(float* im_block, int v_lane, int h_lane)
{
    // scan along horizontal direction
    if (v_lane>=1) im_block[h_lane*16+v_lane] += im_block[h_lane*16+v_lane-1]; // step1
    if (v_lane>=2) im_block[h_lane*16+v_lane] += im_block[h_lane*16+v_lane-2]; // step2
    if (v_lane>=4) im_block[h_lane*16+v_lane] += im_block[h_lane*16+v_lane-4]; // step3
    if (v_lane>=8) im_block[h_lane*16+v_lane] += im_block[h_lane*16+v_lane-8]; // step4

    _syncthreads();

    // scan along vertical direction
    if (v_lane>=1) im_block[v_lane*16+h_lane] += im_block[v_lane*16+h_lane-1]; // step1
    if (v_lane>=2) im_block[v_lane*16+h_lane] += im_block[v_lane*16+h_lane-2]; // step2
    if (v_lane>=4) im_block[v_lane*16+h_lane] += im_block[v_lane*16+h_lane-4]; // step3
    if (v_lane>=8) im_block[v_lane*16+h_lane] += im_block[v_lane*16+h_lane-8]; // step4

    _syncthreads();
    return;
}
```

FIGURE 31.11

Sample code of a CUDA device function to integrate a 16 × 16 2-D image block.

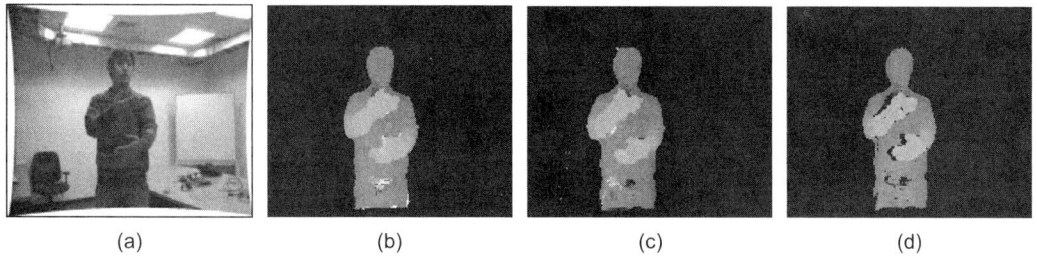

(a)   (b)   (c)   (d)

FIGURE 31.12

(a) Input image. (b) Depth map after cross-checking. A matching error is caused by occlusion, and poor texture is successfully removed. (c) A disparity map from stereo matching with the left view as the reference image. (d) A disparity map from stereo matching with the right view as the reference image.

disparity map, which is $D(right, x + D(left, x, y), y)$, is checked. The sum of two disparity values should be zero, which means the stereo-matching results on this pair of pixels when disparity is estimated from two different reference views are consistent. By doing cross-checking, we can effectively detect most matching errors, and the matching accuracy can be improved. Figure 31.12 shows how cross-checking removes the matching errors.

In general, cross-checking can detect erroneous matching results, but also leave some holes whose disparity values are missing. In a multiresolution framework like ours, pixels from these holes at the lower-resolution disparity map will be searched at the maximum disparity range defined by the whole CTA. In practice, this would provide opportunities to these holes to be filled at higher resolution. Therefore, the holes from lower resolution will not be passed or even enlarged at higher resolution.

31.2.2 **Final Evaluation**
Middlebury Evaluation

Comparing our method with other stereo algorithms is not straightforward. The reason is that our method works only on moving objects that are detected by a background model. In order to appropriately measure the performance of our method, a reference stereo video dataset with ground truth information is needed. Unfortunately, such a dataset is not available. In order to compare our method with other regular stereo algorithms that work on a pair of static stereo images, we use the Middlebury static stereo datasets [1], with the assumption that the whole image area is foreground. The output disparity maps are shown in Figure 31.13, and the error rates for different pictures are shown in Table 31.1.

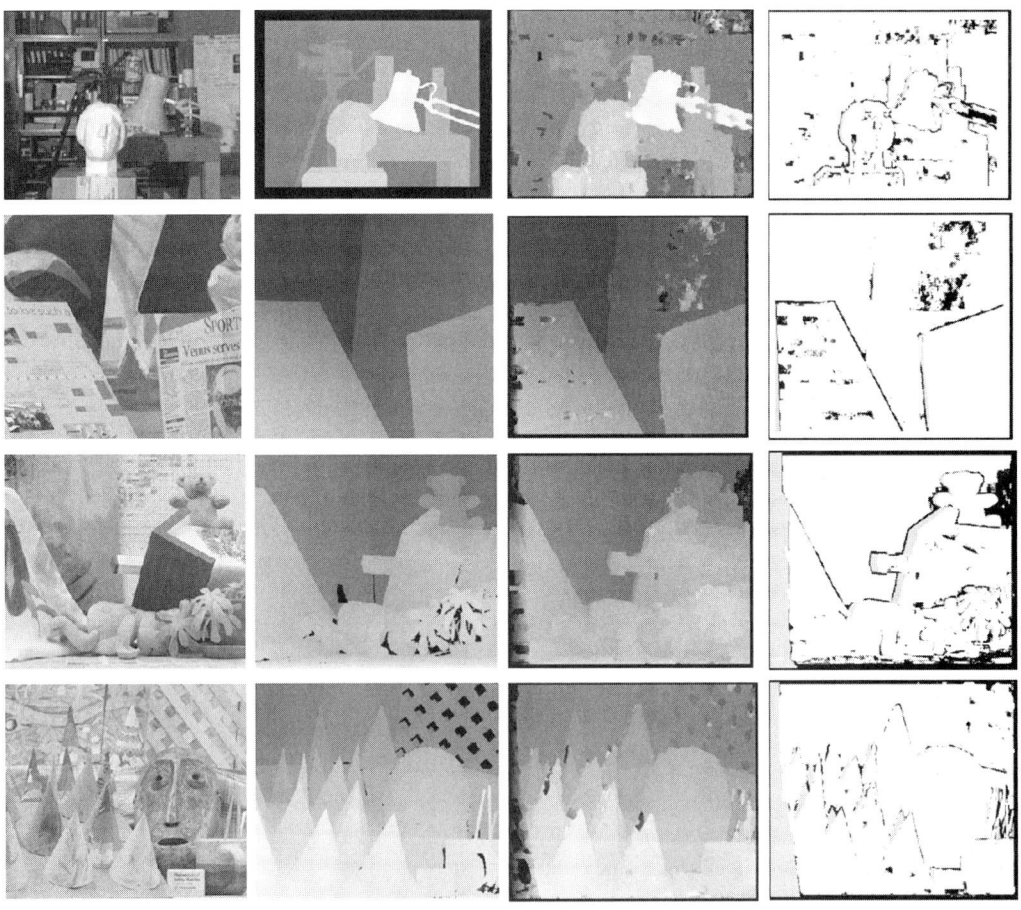

FIGURE 31.13

The disparity maps of the benchmark stereo image pairs on the Middlebury Website obtained by our multiresolution adaptive window algorithm. The first row — Tsukuba; the second — Venus; the third — Teddy; and the fourth — Cones. The first column — reference image; the second — ground truth; the third — our results; and the fourth — matching errors.

Table 31.1 Error rate of our method on Middelbury dataset. Error rate is defined as the percentage of the bad pixels.

		Tsukuba			Venus			
Algorithm	Avg. Rank	nonocc	all	disc	nonocc	all	disc	% of bad pixels
Our Method	73.0	8.29	10.3	22.4	6.20	7.51	26.6	14.3

		Teddy			Cones			
Algorithm	Avg. Rank	nonocc	all	disc	nonocc	All	Disc	% of bad pixels
Our Method	73.0	12.5	21.2	25.7	5.83	14.5	10.3	14.3

Table 31.2 shows the performance comparison of 23 different stereo algorithms, including our method. This comparison covers all kinds of algorithms: belief propagation-based algorithms, segmentation-based algorithms, dynamic programming-based algorithms, correlation-based local algorithms, as well as some semiglobal algorithms. Some of these algorithms also operate on multiple resolutions. The comparison is made both on accuracy and speed. Figure 31.14 visualizes the result of this comparison on a 2-D chart. Notice that the vertical axis of this chart is in logarithmic scale. Our algorithm is at the top of this chart and is more than 100,000 times faster than the slowest algorithm. In general, it is obvious that more accurate algorithms tend to be slower. Compared with all the global or semi-global algorithms, our algorithm is much faster, but also less accurate; however, compared with some other local algorithms, such as MultiResSSD [3] and AdaptiveWin [4], our algorithm is much faster and more accurate. This proves that the coarse-to-fine process in our multiresolution framework works better than just averaging the matching results from multiple resolutions in [3]; it also proves that using adaptive window on multiresolution can achieve better accuracy than AdaptiveWin [4]. On the right side of Figure 31.14, the frame rates of the stereo algorithm when applied on a 1024×768 stereo pair with a 256-pixel disparity range are indicated. This is the exact configuration used in our human detection, tracking, and identification system. Almost every algorithm faster than 0.5 fps is implemented on the GPU. And our algorithm is the only one that achieves 30+ fps — a commonly used video frame rate.

Multiresolution vs. Single Resolution

Just like the original adaptive window approach [4], our approach is also a purely local algorithm, in the sense that the disparity decision for each pixel is made purely based on the local matching cost for this pixel alone. However, our method differs from the original one in the sense that the decision at each resolution is directly constrained by the decision from previous lower resolution. At the original resolution, the decision on each pixel is affected by the visual content of its neighborhood at all the different lower resolutions. Therefore, compared with the original single-resolution adaptive window approach, our approach is somewhat more "global."

This advantage is confirmed by the experimental results. Both our approach and the original approach are applied on the same stereo image pair at three different resolutions: $325 \times 275, 650 \times 550$,

Table 31.2 Accuracy and speed performance comparison of different algorithms using the Middlebury dataset. The unit of speed performance measurement is million disparity estimations per second, or MDE/s. The accuracy performances are all evaluated using the Middlebury benchmark images. Algorithms followed by the * sign do not report Middlebury benchmark results. For these algorithms, the error rate results are from our own implementation on a PC. All speed performance numbers are from the original papers. This comparison includes the following algorithms: AdaptOvrSegBP [14], SymBP+occ [15], DoubleBP [16], EnhancedBP [17], LocallyConsist [18], CoopRegion [19], AdaptingBP [20], C-SemiGlob [21], FastAggreg [22], OptimizedDP [23], SegTreeDP [24], RealtimeVar [25], RealtimeBP [26], RealtimeGPU [27], MultiResSSD [3], PlaneFitBP [28], RealtimeDP [29], ESAW [30], ConnectivityCons [31], AdaptiveWin [4], CSBP [32], RTCensus [33], and our method.

Algorithm Name	Percentage of Bad Pixels	Speeds (MDE/s)	Hardware Platform
AdaptOvrSegBP	5.59	0.04	3.2 GHz CPU
SymBP+occ	5.92	0.08	2.8 GHz CPU
DoubleBP	4.19	0.1	PC
EnhancedBP	6.69	0.13	PC
LocallyConsist	6.33	0.15	2.5 GHz CPU
CoopRegion	4.41	0.18	1.6 GHz CPU
AdaptingBP	4.23	0.2	2.21 GHz Athlon 64 bit
C-SemiGlob	5.76	0.4	2.8 GHz CPU
FastAggreg	8.24	6.14	2.14 GHz CPU
OptimizedDP	8.83	9.95	1.8 GHz CPU
SegTreeDP	6.82	10.2	2.4 GHz CPU
RealtimeVar	9.05	13.9	2.85 GHz CPU
RealtimeBP	7.69	19.7	Geforece 7900 GTX
RealtimeGPU	9.82	53	ATI Radeon XL1800
MultiResSSD*	17.32	117	Nvidia Geforce4
PlaneFitBP	5.78	170	Nvidia Geforce 8800 GTX
RealtimeDP	10.7	187	AthlonXP 2400+ CPU
ESAW	8.2	194.8	Nvidia Geforece 7900 GTX
ConnectivityCons*	15.62	280	Nvidia Geforce 6800 GT GPU
AdaptiveWin*	19.69	289	ATI Radeon 9800
CSBP	11.4	460	Nvidia Geforece 8800 GTX
RTCensus	9.73	1300	Nvidia Geforce GTX 280
Our Method	14.3	7200	Nvida Geforce GTX 280

and 1300×1100, as shown in Figure 31.15. The disparity search range is always one-fourth of the image width. The same 3×3 pixel subwindow is used in both algorithms. The error rates are shown under each resulting disparity map in Figure 31.15. It turns out that, at lower resolution, two algorithms produce similarly accurate results. This is because the scene texture at that resolution is just about enough to differentiate each pixel from other pixels on the same epipolar line. As the resolution goes

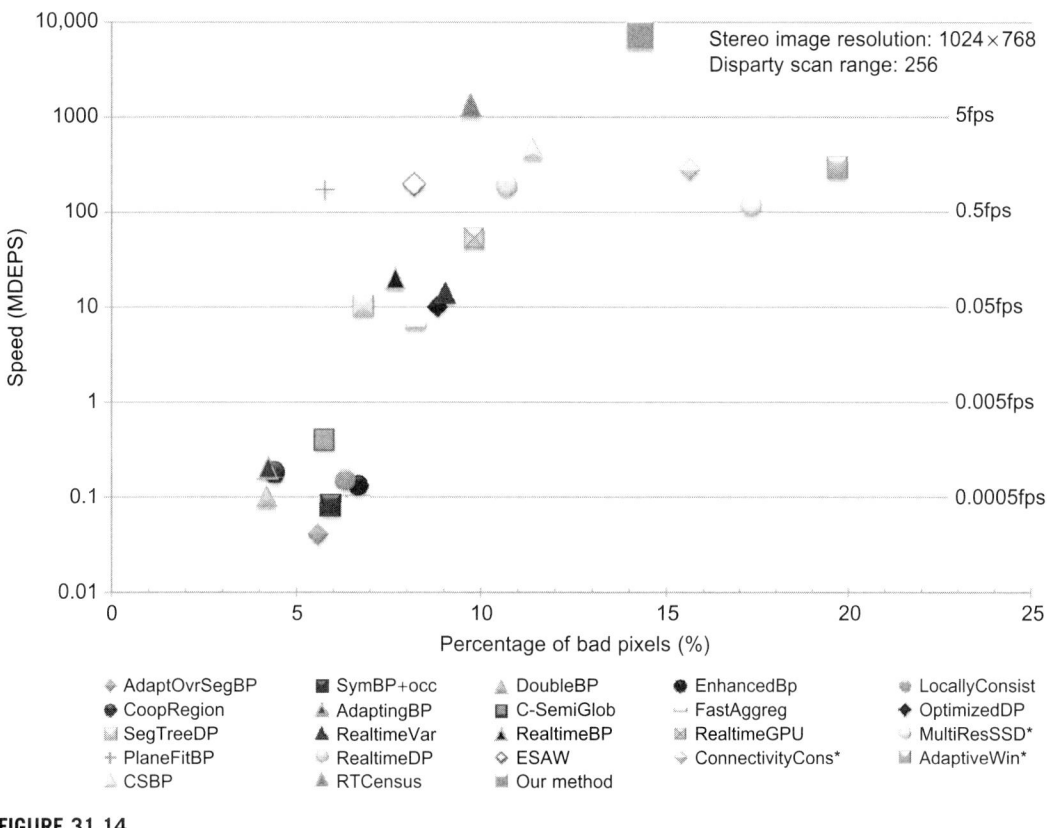

FIGURE 31.14

An accuracy and speed performance comparison of different algorithms.

up, our approach produces higher and higher accuracy than the original algorithm. Increasing the size of the subwindow will not help because it introduces too much error at the depth discontinuity region of the image.

Improved accuracy is not the only advantage of our approach over the original one. Our approach also performs much faster than the original approach does. The reason is obvious: in the multiresolution approach, the full-range disparity search is applied only at the lowest resolution; on higher resolutions, the disparity search is applied in a 4-pixel range for each pixel, thereby significantly reducing the computational cost. On an SIMD architecture GPGPU device, memory traffic is the most significant part of computing costs for most processing tasks. The comparison of memory traffic on our approach versus the original approach is shown in Figure 31.16. Again, the experiment is done on three different resolutions; the disparity search range is one-fourth of the image width. At the original resolution, which is 1300×1100 pixel, our approach is more than 30 times cheaper than the original approach on memory access.

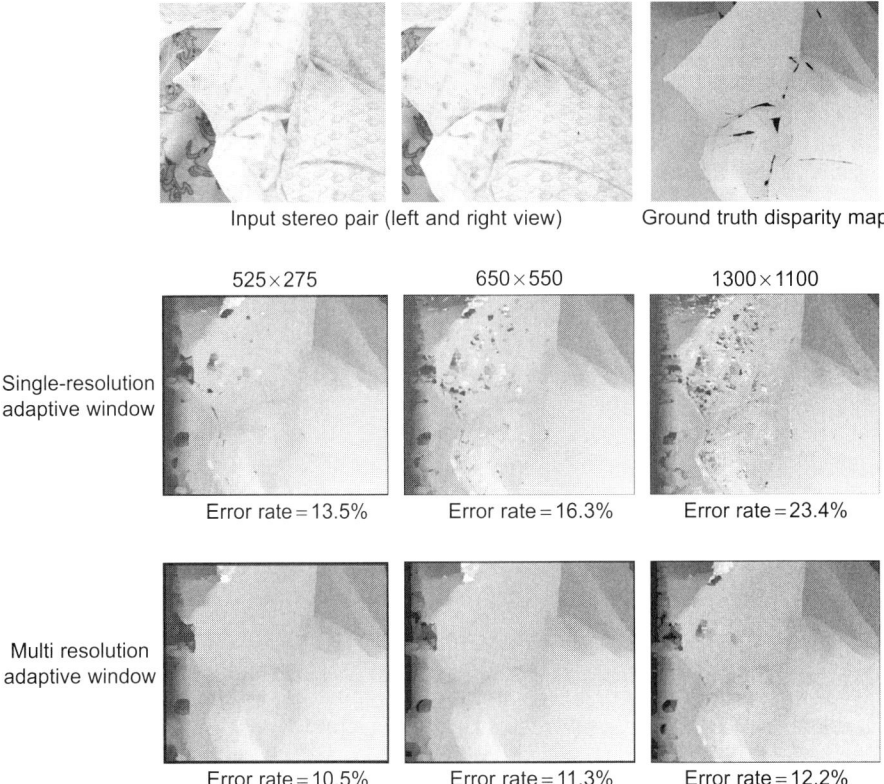

Input stereo pair (left and right view)   Ground truth disparity map

525×275	650×550	1300×1100

Single-resolution adaptive window

Error rate = 13.5%   Error rate = 16.3%   Error rate = 23.4%

Multi resolution adaptive window

Error rate = 10.5%   Error rate = 11.3%   Error rate = 12.2%

FIGURE 31.15

An accuracy comparison of the multiresolution adaptive window approach and the single-resolution adaptive window approach. First row: stereo pairs and ground truth disparity map; second row: disparity maps obtained by the original single-resolution adaptive window approach [4], on the same stereo pair at different resolutions: left — 325 × 275, middle — 650 × 550, right — 1300 × 1100; third row: disparity maps obtained by our multiresolution adaptive window approach on different resolutions: left — 325 × 275, middle — 650 × 550, right — 1300 × 1100. The disparity-search range is one-fourth of the image width. The error rates are displayed at the bottom of each resulting disparity map.

Therefore, the effectiveness of using multiresolution on a purely local stereo algorithm is clearly proven by the significant improvement on both accuracy and speed.

Stereo on Foreground vs. Stereo on Full Image

The reason that the foreground detection is used to constrain our stereo-matching algorithm is that only moving objects are of interest in our target applications. Therefore, there is no need to spend computing resources on those uninteresting background regions of the image. In reality, the texture of an indoor background is usually poor, and therefore, is a major source of the overall matching errors. Many

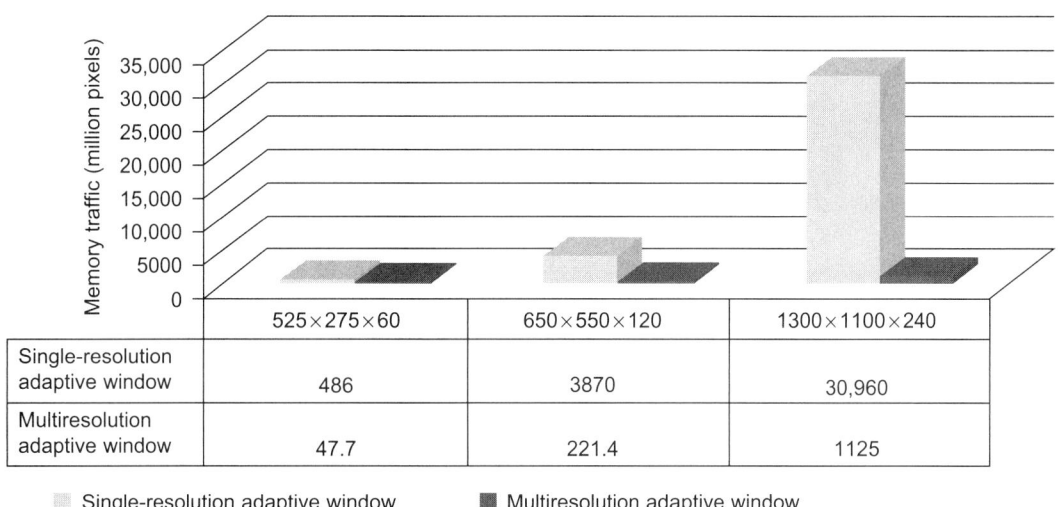

	525×275×60	650×550×120	1300×1100×240
Single-resolution adaptive window	486	3870	30,960
Multiresolution adaptive window	47.7	221.4	1125

Single-resolution adaptive window   ■ Multiresolution adaptive window

FIGURE 31.16

A memory traffic comparison of the multiresolution adaptive window approach and the single-resolution adaptive window approach with different resolutions.

previous applications use a full-image stereo algorithm and then use the foreground detection result to filter the full-image depth map. However, using foreground detection results at the early stage of the stereo-matching algorithm would be more efficient both in cost and quality.

Computing stereo matching only on the foreground region not only saves computing time but also improves the accuracy of the stereo matching, especially at the boundary regions of foreground blobs, which are also the depth discontinuity regions between foreground objects and their backgrounds. The reason is simple: without foreground information, a decision has to be made at the depth discontinuity region: which side does each pixel belong to? This decision is often difficult for the local algorithms because the matching window they use is usually bigger than one pixel. Foreground information can make this decision extremely easy: all foreground pixels belong to the foreground region.

In order to verify this advantage, the following experiment is conducted: some foreground objects (the lamp and the statue) are manually segmented out in one of the Middlebury benchmark stereo images, Tsukuba, as shown in Figures 31.17(c) and (d). Also, the depth discontinuity regions around the foreground objects are manually defined, as shown in Figure 31.17(i). First our multiresolution adaptive window approach is applied on the full-image area to obtain the full-image disparity map shown in Figure 31.17(f); then, our stereo-matching algorithm with the constraint that only foreground pixels can be matched to each other is applied, and the foreground disparity map is obtained. See Figure 31.17(h). Finally, the error rates (percentage of bad pixels) of two different results only at the discontinuity region are checked. The error maps are shown in Figures 31.17(j) and (k), and the error rates are listed in Figure 31.17(l). This experiment clearly shows that using foreground information

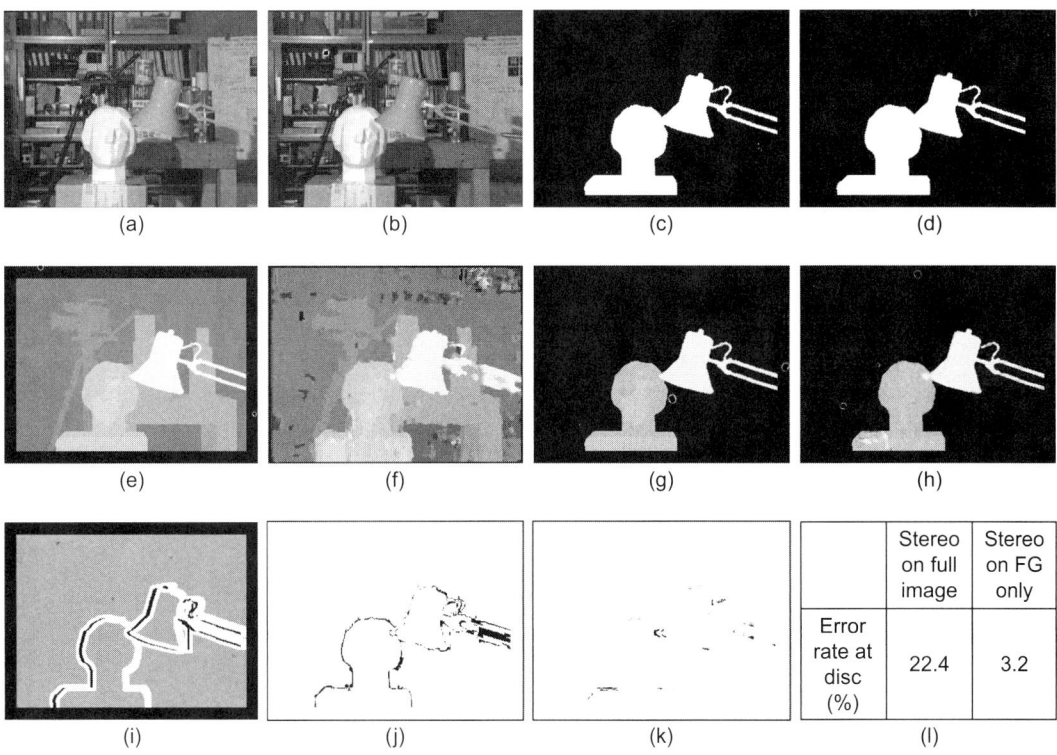

FIGURE 31.17

Stereo matching on the foreground region vs. stereo matching on a full image. (a), (b) Left and right view of
stereo pair; (c), (d) left and right view of foreground region; (e) full-image ground truth disparity map;
(f) full-image disparity map obtained from our method without using foreground information;
(g) foreground-only ground truth disparity map; (h) foreground-only disparity map obtained from our method
using foreground information; (i) depth discontinuity map: black means boundary and occluded regions, white
means boundary regions on the depth discontinuity, gray means nonoccluded regions; (j), (k) error map of
full-image stereo matching and foreground-only stereo matching on the depth discontinuity regions; (l) error
rate (percentage of bad pixels) only on the depth discontinuity regions around foreground blobs.

significantly improves the quality of a disparity map on foreground regions. The disparity values on the
boundary of these objects are smooth and accurate.

Some screenshots of our system working with live video in real time are shown in Figure 31.18.

In order to evaluate speed performance, we tested our system on an 1024 × 768 stereo camera pair
with various kinds of moving objects: single person, multiple people, a basketball being tossed in the
air, and so on. We tested our system using one NVIDIA Geforce GTX 280 graphics card that has 240
streaming processor cores. The average speed we achieved was 36 frames per second with a 256-pixel
disparity range, which is effectively same as 7200MDE/s.

FIGURE 31.18

Screenshots of our real-time stereo system working on the field.

References

[1] D. Scharstein, R. Szeliski, A taxonomy and evaluation of dense two-frame stereo correspondence algorithms, Int. J. Comput. Vis. 47 (1) (2002) 7–42.

[2] L. Di Stefano, M. Marchionni, S. Mattoccia, A pc-based real-time stereo vision system, Mach. Graph. Vis. Int. J. Arch. 13 (3) (2004) 197–220.

[3] R. Yang, M. Pollefeys, Multi-resolution real-time stereo on commodity graphics hardware, in: Proceedings of Conference on Computer Vision and Pattern Recognition, 2003, pp. 211–218.

[4] R. Yang, M. Pollefeys, Improved real-time stereo on commodity graphics hardware, in: Proceedings of Conference on Computer Vision and Pattern Recognition Workshop on Real-time 3D Sensors and Their Use, 2004.

[5] M. Gong, Y.-H. Yang, Near real-time reliable stereo matching using programmable graphics hardware, in: Proceedings of Conference on Computer Vision and Pattern Recognition, 2005, pp. 924–931.

[6] M. Gong, R. Yang, Image-gradient-guided real-time stereo on graphics hardware, in: Proceedings of the Fifth International Conference on 3-D Digital Imaging and Modeling, 2005, pp. 548–555.

[7] N. Cornelis, L.V. Cool, Real-time connectivity constrained depth map computation using programmable graphics hardware, in: Proceedings of Conference on Computer Vision and Pattern Recognition, 2005, pp. 1099–1104.

[8] S.J. Kim, D. Gallup, J.M. Frahm, A. Akbarzadeh, Q. Yang, R. Yang et al., Gain adaptive real-time stereo streaming, in: Proceedings of International Conference on Computer Vision System, 2007.

[9] J. Gibson, O. Marques, Stereo depth with a unified architecture GPU, in: Proceedings of Conference on Computer Vision and Pattern Recognition Workshop on CVGPU, 2008.

[10] D. Gallup, J.M. Frahm, P. Mordohai, Q. Yang, M. Pollefeys, Real-time plane-sweeping stereo with multiple sweeping directions, in: Proceedings of Conference on Computer Vision and Pattern Recognition, 2007.

[11] U. Park, A. Jain, I. Kitahara, K. Kogure, N. Hagita, Vise: visual search engine using multiple networked cameras, in: Proceedings of IEEE Computer Society Conference on Pattern Recognition, 2006, pp. 1204–1207.

[12] C. Stauffer, W. Grimson, Adaptive background mixture models for real-time tracking, in: IEEE Conference on Computer Vision and Pattern Recognition, 1999, pp. 246–252.

[13] S.D. Cochran, G. Medioni, 3D surface description from binocular stereo, in: IEEE Transactions on Pattern Analysis and Machine Intelligence, 1992, pp. 981–994.

[14] Y. Taguchi, B. Wilburn, C.L. Zitnick, Stereo reconstruction with mixed pixels using adaptive over-segmentation, in: IEEE Conference on Computer Vision and Pattern Recognition, 2008.

[15] J. Sun, Y. Li, S.B. Kang, H.-Y. Shum, Symmetric stereo matching for occlusion handling, in: IEEE Conference on Computer Vision and Pattern Recognition, 2005, pp. 399–406.

[16] Q. Yáng, L. Wang, R. Yang, H. Stewnius, D. Nistr, Stereo matching with color-weighted correlation, hierarchical belief, in: CVPR, IEEE Computer Society, 2006, pp. 2347–2354.

[17] E. Larsen, P. Mordohai, M. Pollefeys, H. Fuchs, Temporally consistent reconstruction from multiple video streams using enhanced belief propagation, in: Proceedings of IEEE International Conference on Computer Vision, 2007, pp. 1–8.

[18] S. Mattoccia, A locally global approach to stereo correspondence, in: Proceedings of 3DIM, 2009.

[19] Z. Wang, Z. Zheng, A region based stereo matching algorithm using cooperative optimization, in: IEEE Conference on Computer Vision and Pattern Recognition, 2008, pp. 1–8.

[20] A. Klaus, M. Sormann, K. Karner, Segment-based stereo matching using belief propagation and a self-adapting dissimilarity measure, in: Proceedings of the 18th International Conference on Pattern Recognition, IEEE Computer Society, ICPR '06, Washington, DC, 2006, pp. 15–18.

[21] H. Hirschmuller, Stereo vision in structured environments by consistent semi-global matching, in: IEEE Computer Society Conference on Computer Vision and Pattern Recognition, vol. 2, 2006, pp. 2386–2393.

[22] F. Tombari, S. Mattoccia, E. Addimanda, Near real-time stereo based on effective cost aggregation, in: Proceedings of the 18th International Conference on Pattern Recognition, ICPR '06, 2006.

[23] J. Salmen, M. Schlipsing, J. Edelbrunner, S. Hegemann, S. Luke, Real-time stereo vision: Making more out of dynamic programming, in: CAIP '09, 2009, pp. 1096–1103.

[24] Y. Deng, X. Lin, A fast line segment based dense stereo algorithm using tree dynamic programming, in: ECCV '06, 2006, pp. 201–212.

[25] S. Kosov, T. Thormahlen, H. Seidel, Accurate real-time disparity estimation with variational methods, in: ISVC '09, 2009, pp. 796–807.

[26] Q. Yang, L. Wang, R. Yang, Real-time global stereo matching using hierarchical belief propagation, in: BMVC '06, 2006, p. III:989.

[27] L. Wang, M. Liao, M. Gong, R. Yang, D. Nister, High-quality real-time stereo using adaptive cost aggregation and dynamic programming, in: Proceedings of the Third International Symposium on 3D Data Processing, Visualization, and Transmission, 3DPVT'06, IEEE Computer Society, Washington, DC, 2006, pp. 798–805.

[28] Q. Yang, C. Engels, A. Akbarzadeh, Near real-time stereo for weakly-textured scenes, in: BMVC '08, 2008.

[29] S. Forstmann, Y. Kanou, J. Ohya, S. Thuering, A. Schmitt, Real-time stereo by using dynamic programming, in: Proceedings of the 2004 Conference on Computer Vision and Pattern Recognition Workshop, CVPRW'04, 3, IEEE Computer Society, Washington, DC, 2004, p. 29.

[30] W. Yu, T. Chen, F. Franchetti, J. Hoe, High performance stereo vision designed for massively data parallel platforms, IEEE Trans. Circuits Syst. Video Technol.

[31] N. Cornelis, L.V. Gool, Real-time connectivity constrained depth map computation using programmable graphics hardware, in: Proceedings of the 2005 IEEE Computer Society Conference on Computer Vision and Pattern Recognition, CVPR'05, vol. 1, IEEE Computer Society, Washington, DC, 2005, pp. 1099–1104.

[32] Q. Yang, L. Wang, N. Ahuja, A constant-space belief propagation algorithm for stereo matching, in: IEEE Conference on Computer Vision and Pattern Recognition, 2010.

[33] M. Humenberger, C. Zinner, M. Weber, W. Kubinger, M. Vincze, A fast stereo matching algorithm suitable for embedded real-time systems, Comput. Vis. Image Unders.

Real-Time Speed-Limit-Sign Recognition on an Embedded System Using a GPU

Pinar Muyan-Özçelik, Vladimir Glavtchev, Jeffrey M. Ota, John D. Owens

We address the challenging problem of detecting and classifying speed-limit signs in a real-time video stream using an embedded, low-end GPU. We implement three pipelines to address this problem. The first is a detection-only feature-based method that finds objects with radial symmetry (suitable for circular EU-speed-limit signs). In this implementation, we leverage the graphics part of the GPU pipeline to perform the radial-symmetry voting step. The second is a template-based method that searches for image templates in the frequency domain using Fast Fourier Transform (FFT) correlations, suitable for both EU and US speed-limit signs. This method performs recognition (both detection and classification); it incorporates contrast-enhancement, composite filters, frequency-domain detection and classification, and temporal integration to aggregate results over many frames in its implementation. The third is the classic GPU-based SIFT approach that provides a basis for evaluation of recognition results of the template-based approach. We show 88% detection accuracy using the feature-based pipeline on an embedded system (Intel Atom CPU + NVIDIA GeForce 9200 M GS GPU) running at 33 fps. In addition, we show 90% recognition accuracy using the template-based pipeline on an Intel Core2 Duo P8600 2.4 GHz CPU and an NVIDIA GeForce 9600 M GT GPU (a low-end GPU that can be used in an embedded automotive system) running at 18 fps, superior in both accuracy and frame rate to the SIFT-based approach.

32.1 INTRODUCTION

Graphics processing units (GPUs) have been increasingly used for applications beyond traditional graphics that are well suited for their capabilities [11]. One of these fields is automotive computing. Today's cars provide many features with significant compute requirements and upcoming automotive tasks need even more compute. GPUs are a good fit for performing most of these applications. One group of the automotive tasks well suited for GPU's data-parallel architecture are computer vision-related applications, such as speed-limit-sign recognition.

In this chapter, we present different GPU-based techniques for performing real-time speed-limit-sign recognition on a resource-constrained system with a low-end GPU that can be embedded in a car. The input to our system is a video sequence of EU or US roads taken from a moving vehicle. We process this video in real time to detect and classify speed-limit signs as depicted in Figure 32.1.

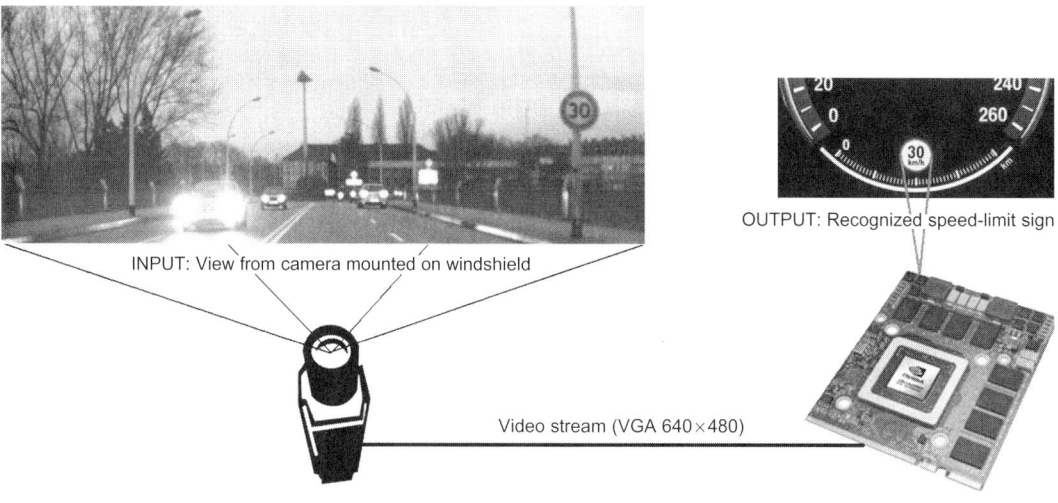

FIGURE 32.1

Embedded speed-limit-sign recognition system using the GPU.

The main challenge of our study is achieving real-time performance while adhering to the resource constraints imposed by an embedded system. To address this challenge we need efficient use of the available resources. Exploiting parallelism is a great method for providing this efficiency. Hence, in our study, we leverage the inherent parallelism in the recognition process by working with algorithms that are data parallel or can easily be modified to be suitable for the GPU architecture.

We pursue three different approaches and indicate how we map them to the GPU architecture. We highlight their weaknesses and strengths and compare them in terms of their success rate and runtime. To provide better insight to our comparisons and results, we present example scenes where our pipelines have failed or succeeded. In addition, we indicate how we can tune our parameters to obtain optimum performance, if we are given less/more compute power. Finally, we present scalability results of our approaches by running them on different GPUs with varying compute power.

By performing GPU-based speed-limit-sign recognition, this study serves as a proof of concept for the use of GPU computing in automotive tasks. Today's cars use a combination of digital systems for performing many automotive tasks that are a possible fit for the GPU architecture. Using GPUs instead of these technologies has the following advantages: (1) GPUs allow consolidation that simplifies vehicle design, (2) because of economies of scale, adding a GPU to the production line is cheap, and (3) with their programmability, GPUs offer the ability to rapidly prototype and improve functionality with software updates.

Finally, this study contributes to the field of computer vision by providing different GPU implementations of real-time object recognition on embedded systems. Although we present an application from the automotive computing domain, our approach can also be used to perform similar real-time recognition tasks in different embedded vision domains, such as cell phones and robotics.

32.2 **METHODS**

In order to investigate the full potential of the GPU for performing speed-limit-sign recognition and to evaluate our results, we pursue three different implementations: (1) a symmetry-focused feature-based approach (referred to as a feature-based approach in the rest of the chapter) that utilizes the fast radial symmetry algorithm [8] for detecting circular signs in the scene, (2) a template-based approach that performs FFT correlation between the scene and composite filters generated from the speed-limit-sign templates, and (3) an approach based on the Scale Invariant Feature Transform (SIFT) [6] that performs matching of SIFT features extracted from speed-limit-sign templates and the scene.

Currently, we use the feature-based approach to detect only circular shapes. However, as demonstrated by Loy and Barnes [7], fast radial symmetry can be extended to recognize other symmetric shapes, such as octagonal stop signs, diamond-shaped warning signs, and rectangular traffic information signs. On the other hand, the template-based and SIFT-based pipelines are applicable for recognition of planar objects with any shape and text. In addition, the feature-based approach only detects the location of candidate signs, whereas the other two approaches perform recognition of the signs by implementing classification as well as detection. It is possible to combine different stages of these approaches and generate hybrid pipelines. For instance, EU sign detection can be performed by the feature-based pipeline, and then to recognize the sign, the classification stage of the template-based pipelines can be utilized, as shown in Figure 32.2.

32.2.1 **Feature-Based Pipeline**

We have designed a feature-based pipeline to detect circular EU speed-limit signs. Hence, to find locations of these signs, this pipeline finds circular shapes in the scene. Barnes and Zelinsky propose using the fast radial symmetry algorithm to detect circular Australian signs [1]. In collaboration with NVIDIA engineers James Fung and Joe Stam, we develop a hardware-accelerated version of this algorithm in this pipeline.

The pipeline consists of three main stages, as shown in Figure 32.2. In the first stage, we perform Sobel edge detection with thresholding to extract the edges in the scene. In the next stage, for each edge pixel we perform radial-symmetry voting that outputs an intensity map. Finally, in the last stage, we perform a reduction operation to find maximum intensity values that indicate candidate locations of speed-limit signs. Stages of the feature-based pipeline applied to an example scene are shown in Figure 32.3.

Sobel edge detection involves a convolution operation to approximate the absolute gradient magnitude at each pixel. Because convolution is performed for each pixel, this algorithm is data parallel and very suitable to be implemented on the GPU. We use a modified version of the Sobel implementation found in the CUDA Vision Workbench [2] to perform edge detection. Likewise, the radial-symmetry algorithm requires a given computation to be performed per edge pixel. In addition to using GPU for performing data-parallel operations of radial-symmetry voting, we also use it to provide hardware acceleration using graphics operations as we will further discuss in Section 32.3.1. Finally, reduction can be performed in parallel, as shown in the NVIDIA CUDA SDK, and therefore, we also use the GPU for this operation.

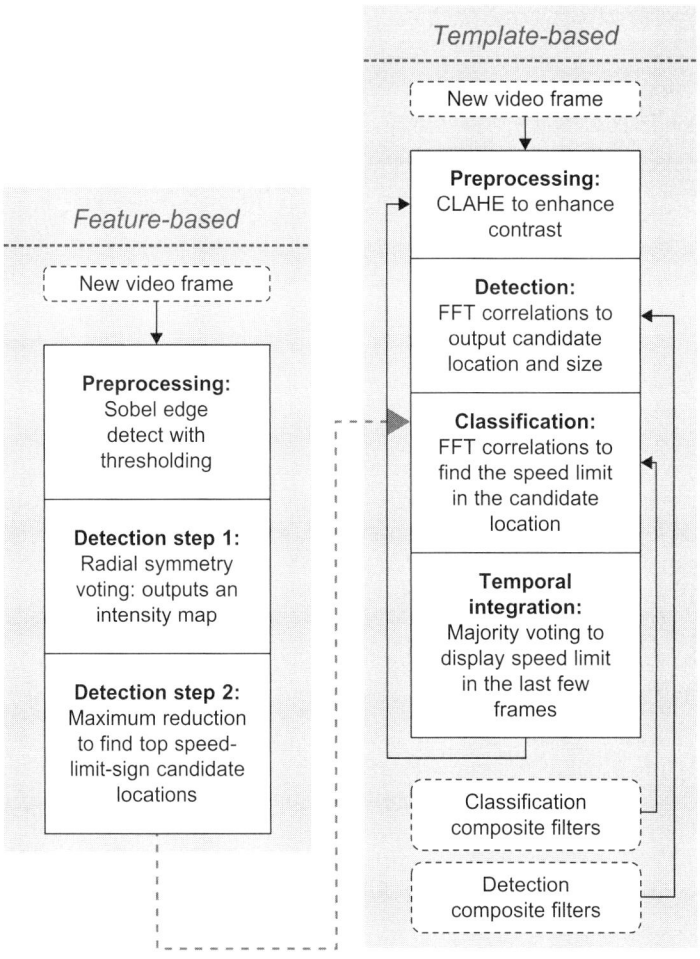

FIGURE 32.2

Stages of feature-based and template-based approaches. The hybrid pipeline can be constructed by combining the approaches as shown by the dashed line.

We make an important contribution to computer vision literature by providing a novel hardware-accelerated version of the fast radial-symmetry algorithm. Other vision applications, which need to detect symmetric shapes, can employ this version of the algorithm to achieve a faster runtime.

32.2.2 Template-Based Pipeline

To recognize a speed-limit sign, we look for specific images (i.e., speed-limit signs) in the scenes. A natural thing to do is to use these images as templates and match them with the scene. This is our motivation for pursuing a template-based approach. Template matching can be done in the spatial domain with convolution-type operations or in the frequency domain with FFT correlation. In our

FIGURE 32.3

Feature-based pipeline stages. (a) An input image from a camera is mounted in a vehicle. (b) An edge map is extracted using a 3 × 3 Sobel filter. (c) Voting results of the radial-symmetry detector. (d) Detected speed-limit signs.

approach, we have chosen to perform matching in the frequency space because it provides a faster runtime. This is because performing one multiplication required by FFT correlation is less expensive than computing many match values required by a convolution operation. In addition, we can perform some operations in the frequency domain to improve the performance (i.e., kth-Law nonlinearity, which will be explained later in this section), which is not applicable in the spatial domain.

We further reduce our matching runtime by using composite filters instead of individual templates. Composite filters are generated from several templates and can be thought of as a "combination template." Using composite filters reduces the number of correlations we need to perform. For instance, we would like to recognize objects when they are seen from different viewpoints. We can search for the object by performing several correlations between the scene and templates that are generated by viewing the object from different viewpoints. However, if we generate a composite filter from these templates, we would need to perform only one correlation instead of performing a correlation for each template. We generate our filters using kth-Law nonlinear extension [4] of the minimum average correlation energy (MACE) [9] filter synthesis algorithm. Using these filters, Javidi *et al.* [3] performed the offline recognition of US speed-limit signs with an approach that is similar in spirit to our implementation.

The template-based pipeline has four main stages: preprocessing, detection, classification, and temporal integration, as shown in Figure 32.2. We generate composite filters off-line and input them to the detection and classification stages of the system.

Composite filters used in the detection stage are more general than the ones used in the classification stage. They are generated from multiple templates. For instance, to detect EU speed-limit signs,

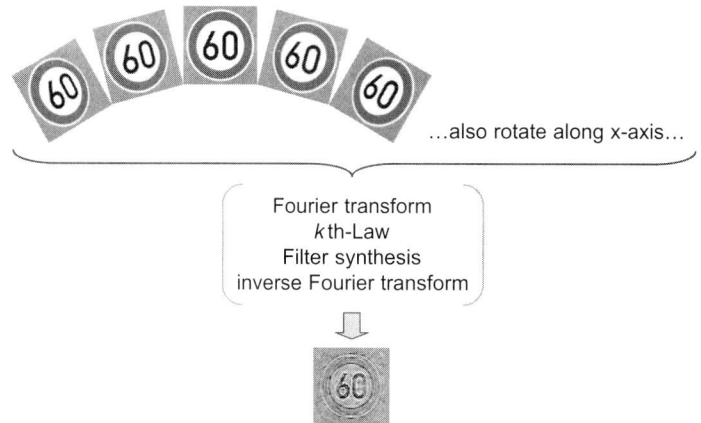

...also rotate along x-axis...

Fourier transform
kth-Law
Filter synthesis
inverse Fourier transform

(Composite filter in spatial domain)

FIGURE 32.4

Overview of kth-Law MACE composite filter generation that integrates different out-of-plane rotations of the template.

we use templates 00 and 100, which helps with detecting two-digit and three-digit signs, respectively. The detection composite filter used on EU roads is shown in Figure 32.5(b). On the other hand, each classification composite filter is generated from one specific speed-limit-sign template. The classification composite filter generated for EU speed-limit 60 km/h is shown in Figure 32.5(c). We generate a different group of classification composite filters for each speed-limit sign we would like to recognize. Composite filters in each group have different sizes and in-plane rotations. For each size, we have composite filters with different in-plane rotations. Detection composite filters consist of only one group because all of them are generated from the same templates. This group consists of different sizes of detection composite filters. Both detection and classification composite filters integrate different out-of-plane rotations of the templates, as shown in Figure 32.4.

Performing an FFT correlation between the scene and the kth-Law MACE filter produces a sharp, distinct peak in the correlation plane where the candidate speed-limit sign is located as depicted in Figure 32.5. To measure the goodness of the match returned by this correlation, we use peak-to-sidelobe ratio (PSR) [12].

The preprocessing stage enhances the contrast of the scene, and hence, improves the visibility of the signs, by applying Contrast Limited Adaptive Histogram Equalization (CLAHE) [14], as shown in Figure 32.6. In the detection stage, we find the location and the size of the candidate sign. We achieve this by performing FFT correlations between the scene and the detection composite filters and then determining the detection filter that returns the maximum PSR. In the classification stage, we perform FFT correlations between the classification composite filters and the part of the scene that includes the candidate sign. We use only the classification filters that have the same size as the candidate sign. If the maximum PSR value is below a certain threshold, we conclude that there are no speed-limit signs in the scene and start processing the next frame. If not, the classification filter with maximum PSR indicates the number displayed by the speed-limit sign in the current scene. An overview of these stages is depicted in Figure 32.7.

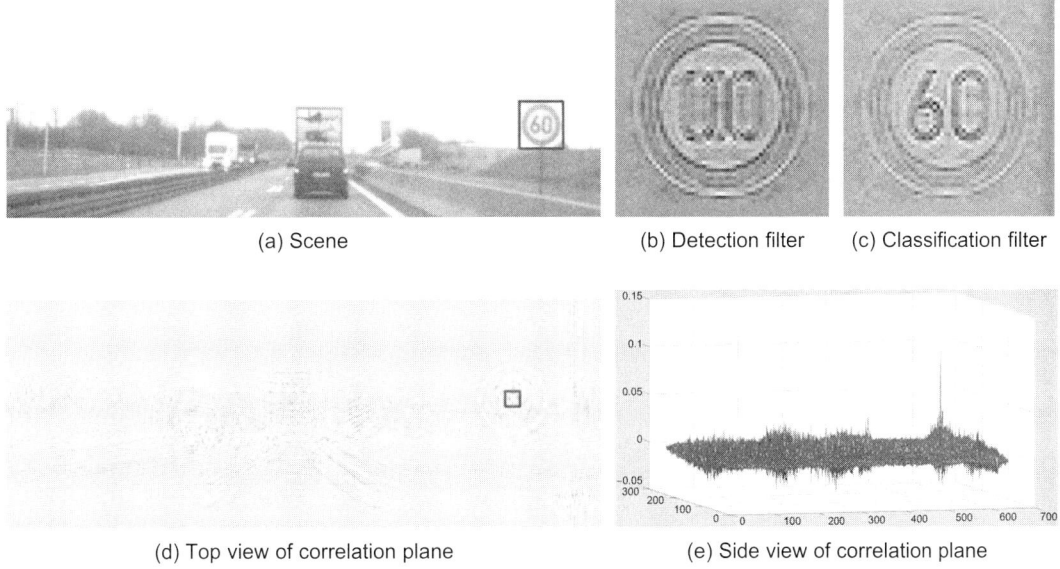

(a) Scene

(b) Detection filter

(c) Classification filter

(d) Top view of correlation plane

(e) Side view of correlation plane

FIGURE 32.5

FFT correlation between scene and kth-Law MACE detection composite filter produces a sharp peak in correlation plane.

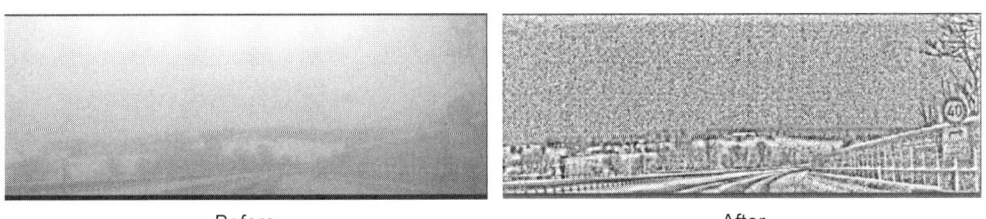

Before

After

FIGURE 32.6

After CLAHE is applied, the EU speed-limit 40 km/h becomes more visible.

In the temporal integration stage, we increase the reliability of our results by accumulating the findings from the sequence of frames. For this purpose, we employ a majority-voting technique similar to the one used by Keller *et al.* [5]. Each frame votes for the speed-limit number indicated by its classification stage. The maximum PSR determined at this stage is used as the base vote value. If the previous frame also voted for the same number, the vote is increased by multiplying the base value with a constant factor, when one or both of the following conditions are met: (1) the size of the sign is not decreasing or (2) in-plane rotation of the sign remains the same. After all the frames in the sequence are processed, we display the speed-limit number that collected the most votes over a given threshold as the final result. The example in Figure 32.8 shows how the temporal integration stage helps us display the correct results (i.e., 80 km/h) when some frames return misclassifications (i.e., 30 km/h).

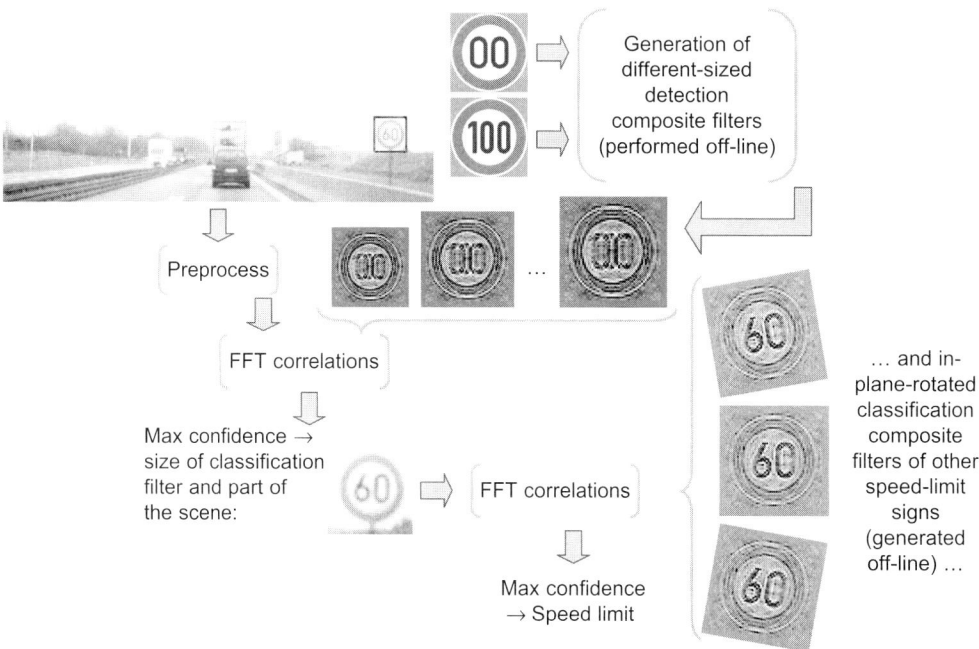

FIGURE 32.7

Overview of preprocessing, detection, and classification stages of the template-based pipeline for performing EU speed-limit-sign recognition.

Frame	n	n+1	n+2	n+3	...	n+9	n+10
Sign	(30)	(80)	(30)	(80)		(80)	(80)
PSR value	9	10	9.5	11		14	13.5
Size	25×25	25×25	30×30	35×35		45×45	45×45
In-plane rot	−6°	0°	+6°	0°		0°	0°
Total vote	9	10	30.3	37.5		70	93.6

FIGURE 32.8

An example that shows how the temporal-integration stage of the template-based pipeline works. The results are determined as 80 km/h because it collected the maximum total vote as indicated by the thick-dashed box.

Currently, we use optimized C code to apply CLAHE. However, this operation has several data-parallel parts and could be mapped to the GPU to improve runtime. Performing FFT correlations between the scene and kth-Law MACE filters also involve data-parallel computations; hence, they are a very good fit for the GPU architecture as will be further discussed in Section 32.3.2. In addition, we use the GPU to find the peak in the correlation plane by performing a reduction operation.

Although we present recognition of speed-limit signs with our template-based approach, this pipeline can easily be modified to recognize planar objects with different shapes or text (e.g., other road signs, gas station logos, etc.) as long as we have a template for it. Recognition techniques, which look for particular features of the object, such as shape or color, lack this ability. Hence, we contribute to the computer vision literature by providing a GPU-based implementation of template-based object recognition, which can also be utilized in other application domains.

32.2.3 SIFT-Based Pipeline

In the computer vision literature, Scale Invariant Feature Transform (SIFT) is a commonly used method for performing object recognition. Hence, in order to evaluate our approach, we also implement a SIFT-based speed-limit-sign recognition system on the GPU and compare it with our pipeline.

The SIFT-based pipeline has three main stages: SIFT feature extraction, SIFT matching, and temporal integration. We perform feature extraction and matching by utilizing SiftGPU [13], an open source GPU-based SIFT project. In addition to performing the last stage of this pipeline, we employ a similar technique used in the temporal integration stage of the template-based pipeline. We provide details of the SIFT-based pipeline in a different publication [10].

32.3 IMPLEMENTATION

In this section, we present implementation details of important parts of the feature-based and template-based pipelines. We explain the computation performed in these parts and indicate how we map them to the GPU architecture.

32.3.1 GPU-Accelerated Fast Radial Symmetry

In the feature-based pipeline, both preprocessing and detection are highly parallel processes. Each algorithm operates on a per-pixel basis with no data or control dependencies. Thus, we map both of these algorithms entirely on the GPU in order to take advantage of its many processing cores.

The incoming image is copied over to the GPU's video memory and is mapped as a texture. The first stage, Sobel filter, is a CUDA kernel that runs per pixel. Each pixel samples its immediate neighbors (3×3 pixel border) using fast texture sampling. The input image remains as a texture and is unmodified, as it might be needed for classification after successful detection. The result of the Sobel filter is an edge map containing gradient angles and is saved to global video memory. Then, a per-pixel radial symmetry kernel runs using the gradient angle image as its input. Each nonzero element uses the gradient angle stored in the input location to calculate its voting areas. The values calculated at this stage are (x, y) coordinate pairs for the vertices of the voting triangles. Each pixel stores its result in an OpenGL vertex buffer object (VBO). Once the radial-symmetry kernel finishes, OpenGL uses this VBO to draw triangles defined by the (x, y) pairs. When the CUDA-OpenGL interoperability is used, there are no memory transfers between these two stages.

OpenGL binds a pixel buffer object to a texture. The pixel buffer is chosen as the rendering target. With blending enabled, each triangle is rendered with a high-transparency (lowest nonzero alpha) value onto the pixel buffer. The graphics hardware blends together all overlapping triangles, causing these areas to appear brighter. The result here is an intensity map with the accumulated votes of the radial symmetry stage. A large gain here comes from the drawing and blending hardware of the GPU. A high

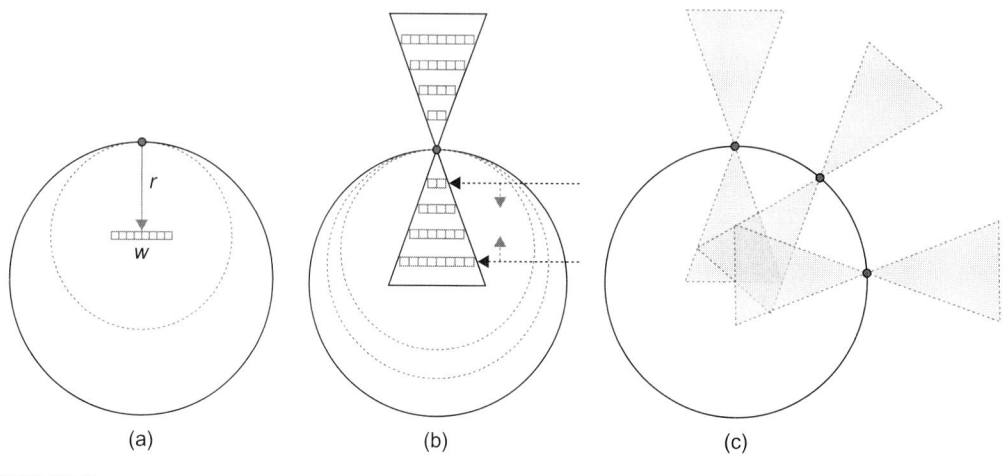

FIGURE 32.9

Radial symmetry voting. (a) Each pixel votes a distance r away with a width w. (b) Voting is performed throughout a range of radii. (c) The overall voting pattern of several edge pixels. Note the accumulating votes in the overlapping regions.

number of overlapping incremental votes causes contention and serialization in most architectures, but the GPU hardware is optimized for this operation. In this stage, our technique takes full advantage of the present resources in a highly efficient voting strategy. We diagram radial-symmetry voting in Figure 32.9.

For the final stage (maxima detection), we use a block maximum reduction where the cumulative voting image V is divided into blocks. The reduction is performed per block and returns the index and value of the element with the highest vote total within each block. This process is also parallelized where possible, but becomes serial in its final stages. First, each thread finds the maximum element among its elements in serial. This process occurs concurrently among the b blocks covering the entire voting image V. This process is applied iteratively until the output is reduced to a desired number of speed-sign candidates. The results are candidate centroids (in x, y pairs) and are copied back to the host processor. On the host, a reduction is performed to locate the block with the maximum value. That block is then marked as used and is further invalid. The maximum reduction that is performed on the CPU is only an 80×60 pixel block and executes fast enough on the host processor as to not affect the overall runtime of the detection process.

The main gain in performance here is the hardware acceleration achieved during the voting stage — calculating voting areas and accumulating the results. The first stage is accelerated by fast texture lookups that do not exhibit many of the common memory drawbacks, such as expensive uncoalesced accesses and boundary condition checking. In the second stage of the voting process, the graphics pipeline performs all interpolating and accumulating calculations. The need for sine and cosine calculations throughout the triangular voting process is completely eliminated and is handled seamlessly by the native rendering hardware of the GPU. This voting process is similar to the Hough Transform calculations performed using the rendering hardware in the OpenVIDIA project [2].

32.3.2 GPU-Based FFT Correlation with Nonlinear Filters

In the detection and classification stages of the template-based pipeline, we perform FFT correlations. Equation 32.1 shows the formula for computing FFT correlation between a scene and an individual template, where $\overline{C}$ indicates the complex conjugate of complex number C, *FFT*/*invFFT* denotes forward/inverse Fast Fourier Transforms, $\times$ indicate complex multiplication, and *norm* is the FFT normalization.

$$\text{correlation plane} = invFFT(norm(FFT(\text{scene}) \times \overline{FFT(\text{template})})) \quad (32.1)$$

Instead of using individual templates, we use kth-Law nonlinear MACE composite filters as explained in Section 32.2.2. Using kth-Law nonlinearity in our system improves correlation-peak sharpness, illumination invariance, and discrimination ability against impostor objects that look similar to speed-limit signs. In order to compute an FFT correlation between the scene and a kth-Law composite filter, we apply a kth-Law nonlinear operation to the FFT of the scene before it is multiplied with the complex conjugate of the filter. The nonlinear operation raises the magnitude of the Fourier transform to the power of k, while keeping its original phase, as shown in Equation 32.2, where complex number C is represented in its trigonometric form. In this equation $|C|$ and $arg(C)$ indicate magnitude and phase of C, respectively.

$$kthLaw(C) = |C|^k \times (\cos(arg(C)) + i\sin(arg(C))) \quad (32.2)$$

Hence, combining Equations 32.1 and 32.2, in order to perform FFT correlation between scene and kth-Law nonlinear MACE composite filters, we need to perform the computation shown in Equation 32.3.

$$\text{correlation plane} = invFFT(norm(kthLaw(FFT(\text{scene})) \times \overline{FFT(\text{filter})})) \quad (32.3)$$

Computation shown in Equation 32.3 is a good fit for a GPU architecture because all operations can be done in a data-parallel fashion. To implement this computation on the GPU, we use NVIDIA's CUFFT library to take inverse and forward FFTs. In addition, we use CUDA kernels to apply kth-Law nonlinearity to the FFT of the scene, take the complex conjugate of the composite filter in the frequency domain, multiply these two FFTs, and normalize the result of this product; all these processes involve per-pixel operations.

32.4 RESULTS AND DISCUSSION

This section consists of several parts. First, we present success rates and runtimes of all pipelines on the footage captured on EU roads. We also provide our initial recognition results of the template-based pipeline on US roads. Next, drawing on the EU speed-limit-sign recognition results, we compare the pipelines by highlighting their strengths and weaknesses. We present interesting scenes from EU roads where both template-based and SIFT-based pipelines performed well/poorly or one of the pipelines outperformed the other. We provide additional interesting scenes from US roads to provide better evaluation of the template-based pipeline. We also explain why template-based and/or SIFT-based approaches failed or succeeded in these particular cases and what kinds of improvements are done to overcome these challenges. Then, we talk about parameters we use in feature-based and template-based pipelines and how we would tune our parameters if we are given less or more compute power. This is followed by a discussion of scalability results that presents runtimes of the feature-based and template-based pipelines on different GPUs, while performing EU-speed-limit-sign recognition.

32.4.1 Recognition Results

Both EU and US videos we used to report our results are grayscale and filmed under a variety of weather conditions (e.g., rainy, snowy, foggy) and on different road types (country road, highway, city).

The feature-based pipeline returned an 88% detection rate for the footage captured on EU roads. The footage is 43 minutes, includes 164 signs, and consists of 80 clips shot in both daylight and nighttime. The video resolution is 640×480. Our detection runtime is 33 fps on an embedded system with an Intel Atom 230 @ 1.67 GHz CPU and an NVIDIA GeForce 9200M GS GPU. Both of these processors are found in low-end laptops and owing to their ultra-low power requirements, are an ideal match for an embedded automotive system.

We have collected results of template-based and SIFT-based pipelines on footage captured from 45 minutes of driving that consists of 69 clips and includes 120 EU speed-limit signs. The video size is 640×240. In this dataset we have included only daytime videos (e.g., early morning, noon, late afternoon) in our test set. However, we can also recognize speed-limit signs in nighttime videos if the parameters of the pipelines are properly tuned. We process the footage on a laptop equipped with an Intel Core2 Duo P8600 2.4 GHz CPU and an NVIDIA GeForce 9600M GT GPU, a laptop graphics card comparable in performance to next-generation embedded GPUs. With the template-based approach, we achieved a runtime of 18.5 fps. Our success rate is 90% with no misclassification and false positives. The runtime for the SIFT-based pipeline increases with the number of keypoints extracted from an image. For a frame with moderate complexity, the runtime is around 8 fps. Because the camera capture rate was faster than the runtime of the SIFT-based pipeline, we could not achieve a real-time performance with this approach. An off-line run of the SIFT-based pipeline provided a 75% success rate and returned four misclassifications and nine false positives. A summary of these results is presented in Table 32.1.

In order to demonstrate that the template-based pipeline can be used to recognize different road signs other than EU speed-limit signs, we have also performed recognition of US speed-limit signs. Unlike circular EU speed-limit signs that include only numbers, US ones are rectangular and also include text, as shown in Figure 32.11(e). We have collected our initial results from 54 clips captured on US roads, which include 41 US speed-limit signs. Our success rate is 88% with one misclassification and no false positives. As expected, these results are very similar to the template-based pipeline results collected on EU roads.

32.4.2 Evaluation of Pipelines

Although it can be used only to detect symmetric shapes, the feature-based approach has an advantage of providing a very fast detection rate. The SIFT-based pipeline has the slowest runtime because

Table 32.1 Template-based and SIFT-based pipeline results.

Pipeline	Runtime	Success Rate	Misclassifications	False Positives
Template-based	18.5 fps	90%	0	0
SIFT-based	8 fps	75%	4	9

it consists of different stages that are computationally intensive. In addition, the SIFT-based approach has a lower success rate mainly for two reasons: (1) SIFT recognition works best when objects have some complexity. However, speed-limit signs have simple shapes and constant color regions. They also mostly appear small in videos. Thus, usually few features can be extracted from these signs, and often the same number of feature matches are returned by different templates, which makes the recognition hard. (2) Because the test videos have low contrast, in the template-based pipeline we employ a pre-processing stage and apply CLAHE to the scene. Applying CLAHE on the template-based pipeline improved our success rate from 65% to 90% and eliminated all misclassifications and false positives. However, we could not use CLAHE in SIFT-based pipelines because CLAHE creates noise that the SIFT-based approach could not handle.

We gain insight on the relative advantages and disadvantages of the template-based and SIFT-based pipelines by comparing their performances on a variety of scenes. On some scenes, both pipelines perform well:

- Both methods reject signs with a dominant difference. For instance, in Figure 32.10(a), the thick line that crosses over the whole sign differentiates the end-of-50 sign from a speed-limit sign. Hence, both pipelines reject this sign.
- Both methods also recognize signs with insignificant modifications. For example, in Figure 32.10(b), the small stain in the digit "0" does not affect its recognition.

The template-based pipeline recognizes several scenes where the SIFT-based pipeline fails:

- The template-based approach is better at recognizing small signs (Figure 32.10(c)). Many of our tests begin with a small sign that becomes a larger sign as it approaches. However, as the sign

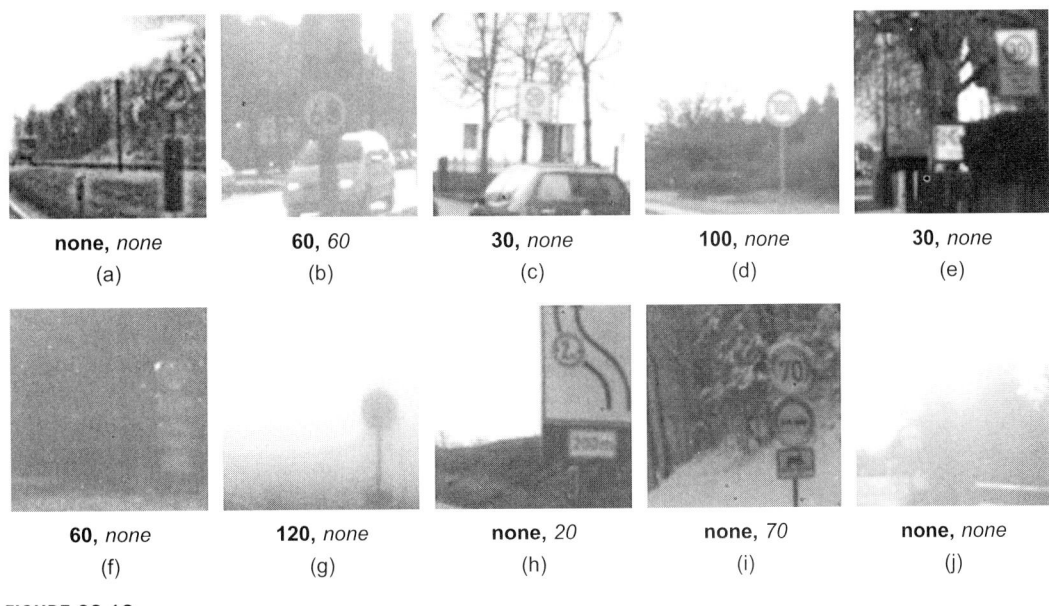

| **none**, *none* | **60**, *60* | **30**, *none* | **100**, *none* | **30**, *none* |
| (a) | (b) | (c) | (d) | (e) |

| **60**, *none* | **120**, *none* | **none**, *20* | **none**, *70* | **none**, *none* |
| (f) | (g) | (h) | (i) | (j) |

FIGURE 32.10

Template-based and SIFT-based pipeline results shown in **bold** and italic, respectively.

gets closer in succeeding frames, we see increasing viewpoint change, making recognition more difficult. The SIFT-based pipeline suffers in this scenario because it does not benefit from an initial recognition of the sign at small sizes. Although doubling the image size and reducing the initial Gaussian blur in the SIFT-based pipeline helps recognize moderately small signs, these improvements are not effective enough to succeed in smaller signs that can be recognized by the template-based approach.

- Noisy images, caused by effects such as motion blur (Figure 32.10(d)) and partial shade (Figure 32.10(e)), are a challenge for vision algorithms. The template-based pipeline is better at handling these different types of noise. Tolerance to noise also allows the template-based approach to use CLAHE as mentioned earlier in this chapter. Applying CLAHE allows the template-based pipeline to succeed in hard cases with very low contrast, such as the sun behind the sign (Figure 32.10(f)) or a light beam effect (Figure 32.10(g)). The SIFT-based pipeline benefits from decreasing the threshold used to select potential keypoints in low-contrast cases, but the template-based approach still has superior performance, particularly in very low-contrast scenes.

- The template-based approach also wins in recognizing signs as a whole. The SIFT-based pipeline uses local features to recognize objects; thus, if part of the sign looks like a speed-limit sign, SIFT may misclassify it. Figure 32.10(h) shows a 2-meter-width-limit sign that SIFT misclassifies as a 20 km/h speed-limit sign, because of the similarity between the digit "2" in both signs.

However, the SIFT-based method succeeds and the template-based pipeline fails in the following cases:

- Although concentrating on local features causes the SIFT-based approach to miss global features and fail in the preceding case, local features are beneficial for recognizing partially occluded signs. Figure 32.10(i) shows a partially occluded sign because of snow where the SIFT-based pipeline succeeds and the template-based pipeline fails.

- The "SI" in "SIFT" stands for scale invariance: indeed, the SIFT-based pipeline better recognizes signs that initially appear large in the videos as well as the ones with large rotations. To match its performance, the template-based pipeline must be augmented with bigger sizes and larger rotations in our composite filters, which in turn would increase our runtime.

Finally, some cases cause both pipelines to fail:

- Although the template-based pipeline is better at recognizing small signs, very small signs perform equally poorly on both pipelines. We tried introducing additional composite filters with smaller sizes in the template-based pipeline, but we found this was counterproductive as it introduced misclassifications and false positives.

- Both pipelines perform poorly when a significant part of the sign is missing. Bright sunshine in Figure 32.10(j) results in failure for both approaches.

To provide a better evaluation of the template-based pipeline, we show interesting scenes captured from US roads in Figure 32.11. There are several hard cases where the template-based pipeline succeeds. For instance, our system performs well even if the shape of the sign is slightly deformed, as in Figure 32.11(a) where the sign is bent along the horizontal axis. It also succeeds in recognizing signs that have large rotations, as in Figure 32.11(b). In addition, Figure 32.11(c) demonstrates that our system can recognize signs located in different parts of the scene.

On the other hand, there are some hard scenes where our template-based approach fails. Because in some cases, US speed-limit signs have nonuniform shapes and fonts, our system cannot successfully

FIGURE 32.11

Template-based pipeline results of example scenes on US roads.

recognize them. For instance, our system uses filters generated from standard templates (like the one shown in Figure 32.11(e)) to recognize Figure 32.11(d). However, in order to successfully recognize a sign like this, we need to include templates with wider text and smaller numbers. Our system also fails in Figure 32.11(f) because the sign has a very small size. Figure 32.11(g) shows another scene where our system is not successful. In order to recognize this sign, we need to expand the range of in-plane rotations we cover with our filters.

Finally, in some US scenes (Figure 32.11(h–j)) speed limits are indicated with several different special signs. In order to make our system applicable to these cases, we can easily add filters generated from templates of these signs. This flexibility of the template-based pipeline makes our approach a good fit for speed-limit-sign recognition on US roads involving several different sign types.

32.4.3 Parameters and Tuning for Less/More Compute Power

We can make the best use of the limited resources of underlying hardware by fine-tuning the parameters of our pipelines based on the trade-off between the runtime and success rate. If given a GPU with less or more compute power, we can contract or extend parameters of the pipelines to achieve the optimum real-time performance.

To leverage the fast detection rate of the feature-based pipeline, we can use a hybrid pipeline for the recognition of EU speed-limit signs, as shown in Figure 32.2. In this pipeline, the detection is performed by the feature-based approach, and classification is performed by the classification stage of the template-based pipeline. In such an approach, increasing the number of examined candidates improves the recognition rate. Because of the parallel implementation of the maximum reduction stage, the runtime of the feature-based detection is invariant to the number of candidates detected. However, there is an increase in the overall execution time because the classification stage needs to process an increasing number of candidates. Thus, in the hybrid pipeline, if we are given less/more compute power, we can adjust the number of candidates detected to make the best use of hardware resources.

The template-based pipeline consists of modular components and the parameters of these components can be adjusted to achieve the optimum performance. In this pipeline, we compute FFT correlations between the scene and composite filters that have different sizes and in-plane rotations. We used five different sizes and three different in-plane rotations while performing EU speed-limit-sign recognition. Additionally, in the generation of composite filters, we used three different out-of-plane rotations along the X axis and seven different rotations along the Y axis. We include more rotations along the Y axis because signs usually have larger rotations along the vertical axis than the horizontal one.

There are few differences between the template-based pipeline parameters that we used for US and EU roads. US signs are rectangular, and therefore, we have noticed that in-plane rotations produce bigger energy changes in US signs than they do in circular EU signs. Hence, for US roads we have reduced in-plane rotations of our classification filters. To further improve accuracy, we could expand the range of in-plane rotations that we cover by generating in-plane rotations of detection filters. Another difference is that we used different templates for generating EU and US detection filters. This is because EU signs have two and three digits that always end with 0, whereas US signs always have two digits that end with 0 or 5. As on EU roads, we also have used five different filter sizes on US roads.

In the template-based approach, if we are given less compute power, it is better to reduce our runtime by dropping bigger sizes from the parameter list than to decrease the number of frames we process per second. We prefer to drop bigger sizes than the smaller ones because signs in the videos usually appear small and get bigger as we get closer. Hence, if we can successfully classify the signs while they are small, we may not need the bigger sizes to correctly recognize most of them. If we are given more compute power to pursue the template-based approach, we can achieve a higher success rate in the following ways: (1) increase the processing frame rate, (2) add larger sizes of signs to our parameter list, (3) generate additional composite filters that cover larger OOP rotations that current filters do not cover, and (4) strengthen the statistical model of the temporal integration stage by employing techniques like a hidden Markov model. We would add bigger sizes rather than smaller ones because the ones that are smaller than what we currently have in our parameter list are too small to successfully discriminate the signs, and they introduce misclassifications and false positives. In addition, we would not add larger OOP rotations to current filters because it also hurts the discrimination capability of the filters by introducing high-energy changes.

32.4.4 Scalability of Feature-Based and Template-Based Pipelines

We perform EU speed-limit-sign recognition on different GPUs with varying compute power to measure the scalability of our approaches.

Performance of the feature-based pipeline scales close to ideal, as shown in Table 32.2. We do not achieve an ideal speedup (i.e., 4x speedup in runtime for a 4x increase in the number of processing cores) because there are several overheads and bottlenecks introduced in a larger device. First, there is a larger overhead for scheduling threads across four streaming-multiprocessors (SMs), as opposed to just a single SM. Second, distributing operands to the threads awaiting them involves a more complicated on-chip network. Third, with more threads executing at once, there is higher memory contention and certain reads or writes could end up being serialized if the memory controller cannot service all requests simultaneously.

We also measure the effect of changing the number of SMs on the GPU runtime and performance of the template-based pipeline, as shown in Table 32.3. Our base configuration runs on a GeForce

Table 32.2 Scalability of the feature-based pipeline across a variety of NVIDIA GeForce GPUs. Speedup is shown with respect to a 9200M GS.

GPU	SMs	Speedup
9200M GS	1	–
9400M G	2	1.8x
9600M GS	4	3.2x

Table 32.3 Scalability of template-based pipeline across a variety of NVIDIA GeForce GPUs. Speedup is shown with respect to 9600M GT.

GPU	SMs	Change in SMs	Speedup	Frames Used	Success Rate	Misclassifications	False Positives
9600M GT	4	–	–	100%	90%	0	0
8400M GS	2	0.5x	0.3x	60%	83.33%	1	1
8800 GTX	16	4x	2.3x	100%	90%	0	0

9600M GT, a GPU with four SMs. Our GPU runtime is $3\times$ lower when we run our code on a GeForce 8400M GS GPU that has two SMs. Even though we have $2\times$ fewer SMs, we are getting more than $2\times$ slowdown because we replaced the GT model of the 4-SM GPU with the GS model of the 2-SM GPU. The extra slowdown can be explained by the fact that GS models have slower clock rates and memory. The overall runtime on the GeForce 8400M GS is 8 fps. With this speed we can process only 60% of the frames in real time. Because we process fewer frames, we lower the threshold that we use in the temporal integration stage to get an accurate performance measure. Even though we cannot process 40% of the frames, the success rate is decreased by only 6.67%. In addition, only one misclassification and one false positive are introduced. These results show that our system can still return reliable and high performance, even if we have a 2-SM GPU.

To measure the effect of having more SMs on the GPU runtime, we run our code on a GeForce 8800 GTX GPU, which has 16 SMs. Even though we have 4x more SMs in this architecture, our runtime is only 2.3x faster. The reason for not getting a speedup closer to 4x is that in the classification stage, we cannot utilize the full power of the 16-SM GPU. In this stage we perform many small FFT correlations between different classification filters, and the small part of the scene that has the potential sign. Running the kernels on this small amount of data does not create enough work to fill the 16-SM GPU. Hence, in order to get a higher speedup on this architecture, we can perform a batch computation in the classification stage. We can achieve this by gathering the small amounts of data into one big chunk and performing one big FFT correlation instead of many small ones.

32.5 CONCLUSION AND FUTURE WORK

We performed real-time speed-limit-sign recognition on a resource-constrained embedded system with a low-end GPU as the main processing unit. To provide fast runtimes and make efficient use of the underlying limited hardware resources, we exploited the inherent parallelism in the recognition process using data-parallel algorithms that are suitable for the GPU architecture. We pursued three different pipelines in order to evaluate our results and investigate the full potential of the GPU for performing speed-limit-sign recognition. The feature-based and template-based pipelines returned real-time performance using a low-end GPU, which could not be achieved by their CPU-based implementations. The SIFT-based pipeline provided a basis for evaluation of recognition results of our template-based approach, which achieved a higher success rate with a faster runtime. By providing results of US speed-limit-sign recognition, in addition to the results collected from EU roads, we demonstrated that the template-based approach can easily be adapted to recognize road signs with different shapes and the inclusion or exclusion of text. We contributed to the computer vision literature by presenting a novel GPU-accelerated implementation of the fast radial-symmetry algorithm and GPU-based implementation of template matching in the frequency domain that utilizes nonlinear composite filters.

This study serves as a proof of concept for the use of GPU computing in automotive tasks. However, in order to make the best use of an embedded GPU in the cars, we should be able to simultaneously run multiple other automotive tasks that are a good fit for the GPU architecture. Examples of such tasks include other computer vision applications, such as performing optical flow for pedestrian detection; signal processing applications, such as speech recognition; and graphics applications, such as infotainment systems. Using the GPU over the digital systems that currently perform these tasks has several advantages, as explained in Section 32.1. Hence, in the future, we would like to work on developing software support for our data-parallel embedded system that can run multiple tasks simultaneously while delivering real-time throughput and/or latency guarantees, which we believe is an understudied research area in the field of GPU computing.

References

[1] N. Barnes, A. Zelinsky, Real-time radial symmetry for speed sign detection, in: Proceedings of the 2004 IEEE Intelligent Vehicles Symposium, Parma, Italy, IEEE, Los Alamitos, CA, 2004, pp. 566–571.

[2] J. Fung, S. Mann, C. Aimone, OpenVIDIA: parallel GPU computer vision, in: Proceedings of the 13th Annual ACM International Conference on Multimedia, Singapore, ACM, New York, 2005, pp. 849–852.

[3] B. Javidi, M.-A. Castro, S. Kishk, E. Perez, Automated detection and analysis of speed limit signs, Technical Report, University of Connecticut, Storrs, CT, JHR 02 (2002) 285.

[4] B. Javidi, D. Painchaud, Distortion-invariant pattern recognition with fourier-plane nonlinear filters, Appl. Opt. 35 (2) (1996) 318–331.

[5] C.G. Keller, C. Sprunk, C. Bahlmann, J. Giebel, G. Baratoff, Real-time recognition of U.S. speed signs, in: Proceedings of the 2008 IEEE Intelligent Vehicles Symposium, IEEE, Los Alamitos, CA, 2008, pp. 518–523.

[6] D.G. Lowe, Distinctive image features from scale-invariant keypoints, Int. J. Comput. Vision 60 (2) (2004) 91–110.

[7] G. Loy, N. Barnes, Fast shape-based road sign detection for a driver assistance system, in: Proceedings of the 2004 IEEE/RSJ International Conference on Intelligent Robots and Systems (IROS), IEEE, Los Alamitos, CA, 2004, pp. 70–75.

[8] G. Loy, A. Zelinsky, Fast radial symmetry for detecting points of interest, Trans. Pattern Anal. Mach. Intell. 25 (8) (2003) 959–973.

[9] A. Mahalanobis, B.V.K. Vijaya Kumar, D. Casasent, Minimum average correlation energy filters, Appl. Opt. 26 (17) (1987) 3633–3640.

[10] P. Muyan-Özçelik, V. Glavtchev, J.M. Ota, J.D. Owens, A template-based approach for real-time speed-limit-sign recognition on an embedded system using GPU computing, in: Proceedings of the 32nd Annual German Association for Pattern Recognition (DAGM) Symposium, Springer-Verlag, Berlin, Heidelberg, Germany, 2010, LNCS 6376, pp. 162–171.

[11] J.D. Owens, D. Luebke, N. Govindaraju, M. Harris, J. Krger, A.E. Lefohn, et al., A survey of general-purpose computation on graphics hardware, Comput. Graph. Forum. 26 (1) (2007) 80–113.

[12] M. Savvides, B.V.K. Vijaya Kumar, P. Khosla, Face verification using correlation filters, in: Proceedings of the Third IEEE Conference on Automatic Identification Advanced Technologies (AutoID), IEEE, Los Alamitos, CA, 2002, pp. 56–61.

[13] C. Wu, SiftGPU: A GPU Implementation of Scale Invariant Feature Transform (SIFT), University of North Carolina at Chapel Hill, Chapel Hill, NC, http://cs.unc.edu/~ccwu/siftgpu, 2007.

[14] K. Zuiderveld, Contrast limited adaptive histogram equalization, in: Graphics Gems IV, Academic Press, Boston, MA, 1994, pp. 474–485.

Haar Classifiers for Object Detection with CUDA

33

Anton Obukhov

This gem covers aspects of the approach to object detection proposed by Viola and Jones [1]. The algorithm is discussed along with its well-known implementation from the OpenCV library. We describe the creation process of the GPU-resident object detection pipeline step by step and provide analysis of intermediate results and the pseudo code. Finally, we evaluate the CUDA implementation and discuss its properties.

The gem is targeted at the users and programmers of computer vision algorithms. The implementation and analysis sections require basic knowledge of C/C++ programming languages and CUDA architecture.

33.1 INTRODUCTION

Object detection in still images and video is among the most-demanded techniques that originate from computer vision. Paul Viola and Michael Jones came up with their framework for object detection in early 2001 [1] and since that time, the framework has not changed significantly. It is widely used in a variety of software and hardware applications that incorporate elements of computer vision, like the face detection module in video conferencing, human-computer interaction, and digital photo cameras.

Although the original framework provides several optimizations that allow rejection of the greater part of potential workload on early stages of processing, the algorithm is still considered to be computationally expensive. At the dawn of high-definition imaging sensors and hybrid CPU-GPU architectures, the problem of performing fast and accurate object detection becomes especially important.

33.2 VIOLA-JONES OBJECT DETECTION RETROSPECTIVE

The core algorithm of object detection, as described in [1], consists of two steps:

- Creation of the object classifier
- Application of this classifier to an image

Hereby, an **object classifier** is a function applied to a region of pixels. The function evaluates to 1 in case the region is likely to be a representation of the object, and to 0 otherwise.

Throughout the chapter, the term "**object**" will stand for *a constrained view of any tangible object of some predefined structure, material, and shape.* Such elaborate definition comes as a constraint of the mathematical model, serving as the basis for the object detection algorithm. In this context, a "human head" is not an object because several views of a human head exist that differ in structure from each other: the front view, the profile view, the view from the back (Figure 33.1), and so on. The "frontal face view" is much closer to the correct definition, but it still needs specification of the view constraints, like sufficient lighting conditions and horizontal alignment. As for the structure, material, and shape, the counterexamples of the previous definition are demonstrated in Figure 33.2.

In order to accomplish the training step and create an object classifier, one needs to collect a training set of images that contain depiction of the object of interest (Figure 33.3) and images containing

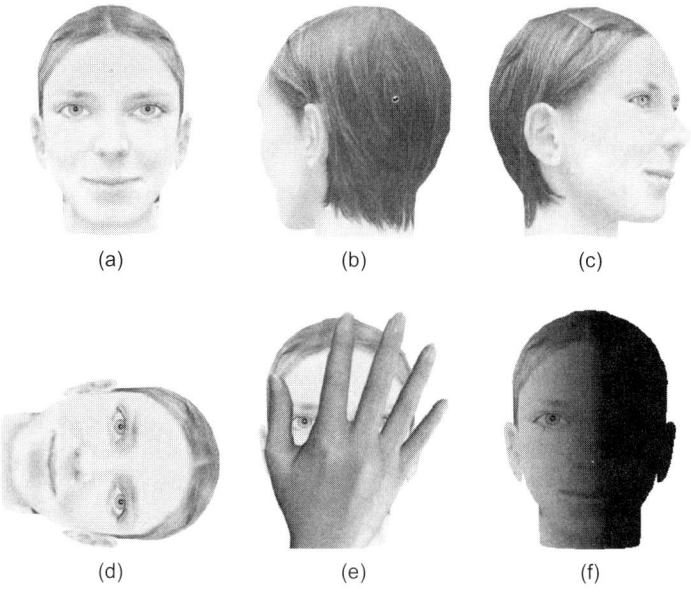

(a)   (b)   (c)

(d)   (e)   (f)

FIGURE 33.1

(a) A properly aligned fully visible frontal face. (b), (c) Unconstrained viewpoint. (d) Unconstrained alignment. (e) Unconstrained occlusion conditions. (f) Unconstrained lighting conditions.

(a)   (b)

FIGURE 33.2

(a) Varying shape. (b) Undefined structure.

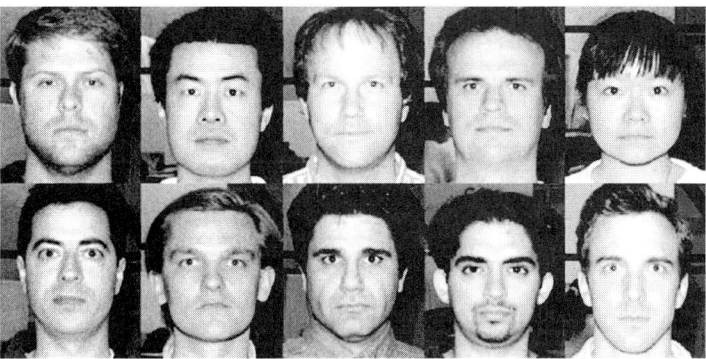

FIGURE 33.3

Example of the face detector training database entries (from the Yale Face Database B).

anything else. The typical size of such a training set can start from several thousand images. The process of object classifier creation is very computationally expensive: a training program loads all images into the memory and performs a thorough search of similarities between images of the object. The training process needs to be done only once, and its output is a compact representation of the data, that according to the training model represents a set of formal rules for distinguishing between an image of the object of interest and any other image. This data is the object classifier itself.

In the original work, Viola and Jones trained the frontal face classifier for images of 24×24 pixels size. Such a small size of the test region appears to be optimum for the task of face detection because it contains a reasonable amount of details and at the same time keeps training time to about a week using a modern workstation PC.

Later, Rainer Lienhart created his own set of frontal face classifiers for the Open Source Computer Vision library (OpenCV), which were trained to classify regions of 20×20 pixels size. Those classifiers are stored as XML files of an average size of 1 MB. With the wide adoption of OpenCV in open source and commercial products, Lienhart's classifiers have become a de facto standard for general-purpose frontal face detection. They are well studied and usually meet requirements for a face detection system. In case the requirements are not met (for instance, if a user wants to create a classifier for some other object like faces in profile), OpenCV provides the training framework for the new classifier creation.

Although there is a certain interest in increasing the speed of classifier creation (for instance, for semiautomatic video annotation and tagging), this gem concentrates on the second step of the object detection task — the object classifier application. OpenCV and the Lienhart frontal face classifier will be used as references for the implementation using NVIDIA CUDA technology.

33.2.1 The Core Algorithm

Now, when a user has an object classifier trained on images of size $M \times N$ and an input image of much higher dimensions, it is possible to detect all instances of the object of interest in the image. This is achieved by applying the classifier to every region of pixels of size $M \times N$ on a large set of scales of the input image (Figure 33.4a). OpenCV implements this algorithm in the `CascadeClassifier::detectMultiScale` function, which also takes the image buffer, scale step,

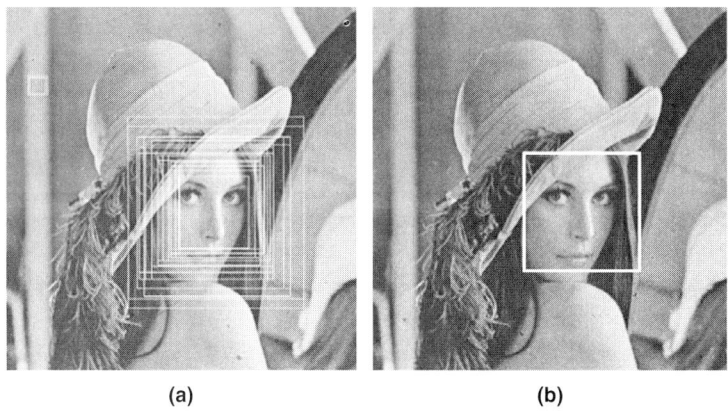

(a)   (b)

FIGURE 33.4

(a) Multiple detections at various scales. (b) Filtered hypothesis.

a few options, and the pointer to the output list to store the detections. Because application of the object classifier to a region of pixels doesn't depend on anything but the input pixels, all classifier applications can be performed in parallel. OpenCV takes this opportunity in case it was compiled with Intel Threading Building Blocks support enabled.

Usually a classifier finds many matches around the scope of the real object location (Figure 33.4a). This happens as a result of the insensitivity of the object classifier to tiny shifts, rotations, and scaling of the object of interest. This phenomenon is closely related to the generalization property of the object classifier — the ability to deal successfully with images of the same object that didn't participate in the training set. To get one final hypothesis per actual object representation, the detections have to be partitioned into equivalence classes and filtered. The partitioning is performed using the criterion of rectangular similarity, that is, if the area of intersection relative to their sizes is greater than some predefined threshold. Figure 33.4a contains two obvious classes: one in the top left corner, which comes from the detector's false-positive detections, and one close to the actual face location. The filtration of the detections classes is performed according to two simple rules:

- If the class contains a small amount of detections, then it is believed to be a false positive and is dropped.
- The rest of the classes are averaged, and the final hypotheses are presented as face detections (Figure 33.4b).

As can be seen, there are a lot of independent operations on the regions, telling target objects apart from nonobjects. But still the overall amount of computations is overwhelming. In order to speed up processing, Viola and Jones proposed the **cascade** scheme of the object classifier function. As shown in Figure 33.5, the idea is to represent an object classifier in a series of smaller object classifiers in order to reject nonobjects as fast as possible. To be detected by the cascade, an object has to pass all stages of the object classifier cascade. Such an early-termination processing scheme drastically reduces the overall workload.

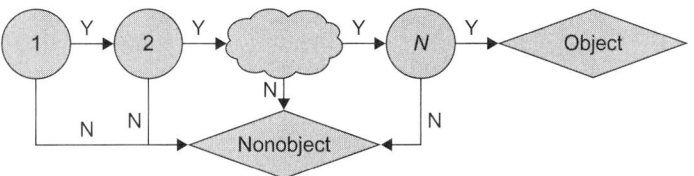

FIGURE 33.5

Strong classifiers cascade.

Table 33.1 Precision of the Lienhart frontal face classifier cascade.	
False alarm rate:	$0.5^{20} = 9.5 \times 10^{-7}$
Hit rate:	$(1.0 - 0.001)^{20} \cong 0.98$

As stated in [4], the frontal face classifier cascade of 20 stages is trained to reject 50% of non-faces on every stage. At the same time every stage falsely eliminates 0.1% of true face patterns. The integrate characteristics of such a cascade are given in Table 33.1.

33.2.2 Object Classifier Cascade Structure

The classifier cascade (Figure 33.5) consists of a chain of stages, also known as *Strong Classifiers* (in [1]) and the *"Committees" of Classifiers* (in [4]). Although these names were given to emphasize the complex structure of the entity, throughout the gem a stage will be referred to as simply the **classifier**. A classifier is capable of acting as an object classifier on its own account, and this had been a common approach before Viola and Jones proposed the cascade scheme. Having a solid object classifier represented by one classifier has the following disadvantages:

- It is much harder to train the monolithic classifier with acceptable detection rates compared with the cascade of classifiers with the same properties.
- There is no early termination when testing unlikely object-containing regions.

The OpenCV classifier (H) structure is presented in Figure 33.6. It encapsulates a set of K **weak classifiers** (h_i) and the stage threshold (T). A weak classifier got its name because it is not capable of classifying regions on the object level; all it does is calculate some function on the region of pixels and produce the binary response. For the sake of computation simplicity, the function was chosen to be based on Haar wavelets (features). The formula in Table 33.2 (left) contains the equation of the strong classifier (X denotes the region of pixels of the $M \times N$ size being tested).

As for the weak classifier, in the simplest case it consists of the threshold φ_i and one **Haar feature** f_i. A feature in the weak classifier is essentially a rectangular template, which is laid over the tested region in a specific location. The black-and-white coloring scheme of the template indicates the change of a sign when taking the sum of underlying pixel values of the input image: black pixels make a positive contribution, while white corresponds to a negative contribution. This summation evaluates

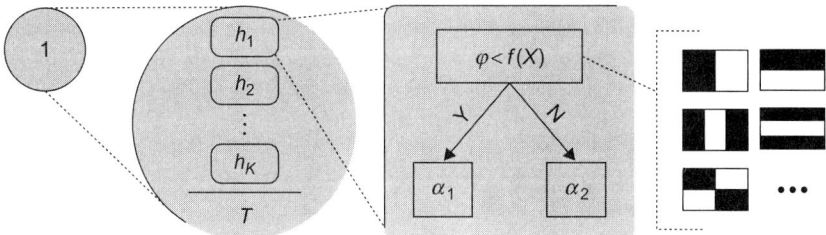

FIGURE 33.6

Left to right: the stage of the classifier cascade, the classifier, the weak classifier, and various Haar features.

Table 33.2 Classifier (left) and stump-based weak classifier (right) evaluation functions.

$$H(X) = \begin{cases} 1, & \sum_{i=1}^{K} h_i(X) \geq T \\ 0, & \text{otherwise} \end{cases} \qquad h_i(X) = \begin{cases} \alpha_1, & f_i(X) > \varphi_i \\ \alpha_2, & \text{otherwise} \end{cases}$$

$f_i(X)$, which is then compared with the threshold. The classifier that consists of such binary weak classifiers is called "stump-based." The formula in Table 33.2 (right) contains the equation of the weak classifier.

The OpenCV implementation of Haar features consists of a list of tuples (rectangle, weight). The rectangle corners coordinates are integers and must lie inside of the classifier $M \times N$ window. After summing the pixels under the rectangle, the sum is multiplied by the weight, which is represented by a floating-point value.

Generally, a weak classifier can be represented as a decision tree, where each node contains a Haar feature and the corresponding threshold, and leaves contain α values. Evaluation of such a weak classifier takes D times more time than a stump-based weak classifier, where D is the depth of the decision tree. An example of such a weak classifier is shown in Figure 33.7.

The illustration in Figure 33.8 helps to understand Haar features better. The two features are taken from the first stage of Lienhart's cascade for face detection; they are put over the 20×20 region, which actually contains a man's face. The first required feature can be described as the assumption that an image of the human face has a bright area on the forehead and a dark area on the eyes (due to shadowing, eyebrows, eyelashes, and iris). The second feature makes a similar assumption about the nose bridge area, which is always brighter than the eyes due to high local skin reflection properties. Of course, these two rules of thumb don't suffice to claim that the region is actually a face. According to [2], if provided with enough weak classifiers, each acting slightly better than random, one can train a strong classifier with as low a training error rate as one wishes. According to [1], the classifier of two presented features rejects over half of "non-faces" and passes ~100% "faces" to the next stages of the classifier cascade.

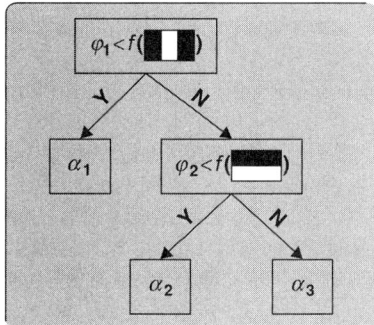

FIGURE 33.7

An example of a tree-based weak classifier.

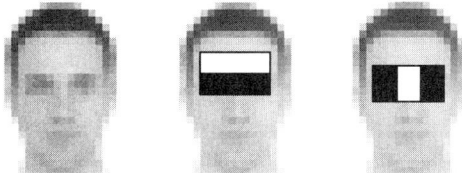

FIGURE 33.8

Haar features from the first stage classifier of the face detection cascade.

33.2.3 Integral Image Representation

In order to calculate the response of a weak classifier in a straightforward way, one would need to sum all values of pixels under the white part of the feature template and then calculate the same sum for the black part of the template and subtract the sums. For a feature of 10×10 pixels and the initial scale $S = 1$ this would require 100 memory accesses and 100 additions/subtractions. On the scale $S = 4$, the 10×10 feature will map to a region of 40×40 pixels, and its calculation will cost 1600 memory accesses and the same amount of additions/subtractions. The **integral image** representation was introduced to fight the complexity when calculating features on any scales. An input image (F) is converted to an integral image (I) using the first formula from Table 33.3.

As can be noted from the formula, the integral image representation is 1 pixel wider and higher than the original image. Each pixel of the integral image contains the sum of all pixels of the input image to the left and top of the location. Using this representation, any rectangular area of pixels can easily be summed with only four memory accesses and three additions/subtractions, as shown in the second formula in Table 33.3. For example, to calculate the sum of pixels under the eye rectangle (Figure 33.9), one needs to take the sum of pixels of both dark rectangles (with the solid black circle in the bottom-right corner) and subtract the sum of pixels of both light rectangles (which has the black-and-white circle). Here all four rectangles have their top-left corner in the image origin, and rectangular sums can be obtained from the integral image.

Table 33.3 Formulas for calculation of the integral image (top) and calculation of the rectangular sum of pixels, bounded by two points (bottom).

$$I(y,x) = \begin{cases} 0, & x = 0 \text{ or } y = 0 \\ \sum\limits_{(i,j)=(0,0)}^{(y-1,x-1)} F(i,j) = F(y-1,x-1) + I(y,x-1) + I(y-1,x) - I(y-1,x-1), & \text{otherwise} \end{cases}$$

$$Sum_{[y_0,x_0]}^{(y_1,x_1)} = I(y_1,x_1) - I(y_0,x_1) - I(y_1,x_0) + I(y_0,x_0), \qquad x_0 < x_1, y_0 < y_1$$

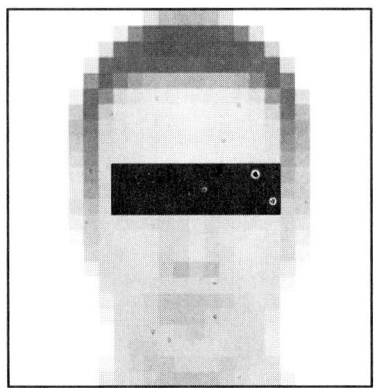 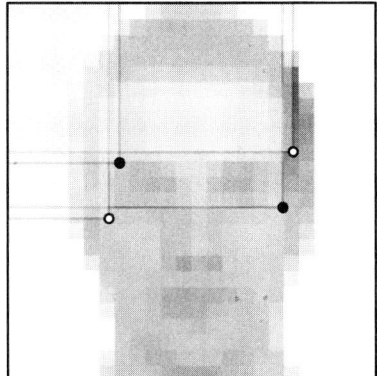

FIGURE 33.9

Visualization of rectangular area pixels sum calculation with the integral image. Integral image values at solid black circle positions give positive contribution, the values at black-and-white circles should be subtracted.

Table 33.4 Variance formulas.

$$Stddev^2(X) = Var(X) = E\left[(X - E[X])^2\right] = E[X^2] - E[X]^2$$

$$Var(X) = \frac{1}{MN} \sum_{i=0,j=0}^{M,N} X[i,j]^2 - \left(\frac{1}{MN} \sum_{i=0,j=0}^{M,N} X[i,j]\right)^2$$

To minimize the effect of varying lighting conditions, the original classifier cascade described in [1] was trained on variance-normalized images. A **variance-normalized image** can be obtained by dividing image pixels by the standard deviation of all pixels. The value can be easily calculated from the image pixels using the last formula from Table 33.4.

Variance calculation can also benefit from integral images, but it requires one more representation — the **squared integral image**, which represents the integral image of all pixel values squared. To calculate a variance of a pixels region using the formula shown in Table 33.4, one would calculate the mean using the integral image and the sum of squares using the squared integral image. The pixels of the region need to be divided by the standard deviation to become variance normalized, which is essentially a square root of the variance value. During the detection process the effect of normalization can be achieved by dividing feature values instead of the original pixel values.

Table 33.5 The object detection algorithm overview.

Build integral image $I(F)$ and squared integral image $I(F)$[1]
curScale $= 1.0$
For (all scales)[2]:
    curScale $* = S$
    For (curRegion in all regions X on the current scale)[3]:
        For ($H_i(x)$ in all cascade stages)[4]:
            StageSum=0.0
            For ($h_j(x)$ in all weak classifiers of $H_i(x)$)[5]:
                StageSum $+ =$ Calculate weak classifier $h_j(x)$ using $I(F)$ and $IS(F)$[6]
            If (StageSum $<$ StageThreshold):
                Mark region as non-object and proceed to next region
        Mark region as object
Partition and filter regions marked as objects

Table 33.6 Formulas for the operations count of the object detection algorithm.

a.	$\log_S \left(\min\left(\frac{H}{M}, \frac{W}{N} \right) \right)$
b.	$\dfrac{W \times H}{curScale^2}$

33.2.4 Overview of the Traditional Algorithm

The overview of the traditional algorithm for object detection using a cascade of classifiers is presented in the Table 33.5.

Given this algorithm, we can comment on the computation required for face detection. Assume the input image has dimensions $H \times W$ and it is processed by one of the traditional face detection classifiers of size $M \times N = 20 \times 20$ pixels, with 20 stages in the cascade and scaling factor $S = 1.2$, then:

1. It requires a limited amount of operations per pixel.
2. The exact amount of different scales at which the object detector will be applied to the input image can be calculated using the formula from Table 33.6a.
3. Assuming that on every scale iteration the input image is downscaled for further processing, we can calculate the amount of test regions on the current scale using the formula from Table 33.6b.
4. The typical amount of stages in the cascade is around 20.
5. The amount of weak classifiers in each stage varies depending on the stage *ID*. For example, in Lienhart's face-detection cascade the first stage consists of three weak classifiers (stumps), and the last stage contains 212 weak classifiers.
6. The calculation of the weak classifier value breaks up into calculation of D features of the decision tree (1 feature for a stump). Each feature consists of not more than three rectangles (refer to [1], [3], and [4] for additional constraints on the Haar features diversity).

33.3 OBJECT DETECTION PIPELINE WITH NVIDIA CUDA

One of the motivations for writing this gem is the emerging amount of fully GPU-resident pipelines. Full GPU residency of an algorithm helps to offload the CPU and eliminates excessive memory copies via the PCI-e bus.

In many cases CUDA acceleration of a few specific parts of the pipeline would not provide a tangible speedup because of the additional time overheads owing to maintaining data structures on both host and device (or even multiple devices!), memory copying overhead, and calls to driver API overhead. The first two overheads can be dealt with fully GPU-resident pipelines. The whole pipeline (both command flow and data flow) needs to be reorganized into the set of kernels that implement pipeline algorithms on the device with minor interaction with the host. This is often not a trivial task, but on the other hand, there are not so many classes of algorithms in computer vision and multimedia processing that require serial data execution.

The videoconferencing pipeline serves as a good example — video frames are fed into the encoder (which runs on the GPU, too), which performs traditional steps like motion estimation and rate control. The latter step decides how many bits to allocate for coding of each region of a frame. Here, face detection can fit into the pipeline to locate face regions and provide the encoder with information about more valuable regions of the frame.

When we are programming a GPU-resident pipeline, it is important to pay reasonable attention to the architectural peculiarities that can help to squeeze another 1–2% of the application performance. These low-level optimizations should never become the center of the universe because they all have a "best before" tag, which means that their life cycle is relatively short compared with the whole pipeline. A lot of effort has been put into existing CUDA applications to overcome high latency of the global memory on Tesla (SM 1.x) architecture, but with the new cached Fermi architecture (SM 2.x) these optimizations tend to slow down some of the applications. The best approach is to have a core SIMT algorithm that would work efficiently on a perfect (and thus, nonexisting) architecture, but also have a dispatcher for the fall-back paths to execute the kernel efficiently on the majority of contemporary architectures. This pattern can be implemented using C++ templates for compile-time kernel generation.

33.3.1 Integral Image Calculation

Implementing the integral image calculation with CUDA is the first step in porting the object detection algorithm to CUDA [5]. At a first glance the algorithm can be parallelized if one notices that the calculation of each pixel in the integral image requires the value of the input image pixel and three adjacent values of the integral image pixels, to the left, top, and top-left. This imposes a spatial data dependency, which can be potentially solved by applying the 2D-wave algorithm (Figure 33.10): the algorithm starts at the top-left corner of the input image, and on each step checks which pixels of the integral image can be calculated given the present data.

This algorithm, although simple to implement on the CPU, has some disadvantages when implementing it with CUDA:

1. It requires sparse nonlinear memory accesses.
2. It requires either several CUDA kernel launches (one for each slice of pixels) or a work pool, which in turn requires atomic operations on global memory.

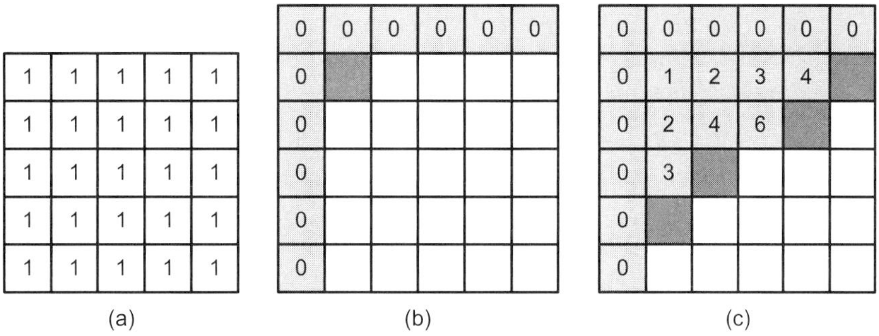

FIGURE 33.10

A 2-D-wave approach to integral image calculation. Dark gray — N-th stage pixels, Light gray — already calculated values, White — yet not processed pixels. (a) Original image. (b) Initialization. (c) After a few iterations.

Table 33.7 Separability of the integral image calculation.

$$I(x,y) = \sum_{(i,j)=(0,0)}^{(y,x)} F(i,j) = \sum_{i=0}^{y}\sum_{j=0}^{x} F(i,j)$$

Table 33.8 Prefix sums output vector.

$$I = \left[0, a_0, a_0 + a_1, ..., a_0 + a_1 + \cdots + a_{n-2}, \sum_{i=0}^{n-1} a_i\right]$$

A much better approach is to take into account the *separability* property of an integral image calculation (Table 33.7), which means that it can be performed on all rows and then all columns of an image sequentially.

The algorithm that takes a vector $F = [a_0, a_1, \ldots, a_{n-1}]$ of length n and produces the vector I of length $n+1$ (refer to Table 33.8), where each element appears to be a sum of all elements of the input vector to the left, is known as **scan** or **prefix sums**.

It has a very efficient implementation for CUDA which can be found in the CUDPP library, Thrust library, and CUDA C SDK ("scan" code sample). Thus, the algorithm for integral image calculation is as follows:

1. Perform scan for all rows of the image
2. Transpose the result
3. Perform scan for all rows of the transposed scan (corresponding to columns of the original image)
4. Transpose the last result and write to the output integral image

It should be noted that unlike the input image, which has its pixel values typically stored in 8 bits, an integral image for the object detection task needs 32 bits per pixel to store the values. The exact amount of bits per pixel for storing an integral image can be easily calculated by evaluating the size of the largest rectangular region of original image pixels that will be ever summed. For example, if it is known a priori that the size of regions will always be less than 16×16, then a 16-bit data type can be chosen to store the integral image because the maximum sum ($16*16*255 = 65280 = 0xFF00$) doesn't overflow 16 bits. Hence, for searching large faces in 1080p video frames with a square object classifier, there is an obvious need of a 32-bit integer data type to store the integral image.

As for the squared integral image, which cannot fit into 32 bits, Intel decided to store its values in 64-bit floating-point type (see the `ippiRectStdDev` function). This creates an additional problem when we are implementing the algorithm on early NVIDIA CUDA architectures (SM $<$ 1.3): G80, G84, G92, etc., which have no support for 64-bit double-precision floating-point values. The solution is to store squared integral image pixels in the 64-bit unsigned integer data type, which is supported by the CUDA-C compiler.

An efficient implementation of matrix transpose can be found in CUDA C SDK ("transpose" code sample).

Performing a scan for all rows/columns is a slightly different task compared with scanning of a single array. Launching scan *height* times to do scans of the image rows is not an efficient solution because a single row of an image doesn't contain enough data to provide sufficient workload for the device. This solution is also subject to additional time overhead caused by many API calls to the CUDA driver.

There are several ways to deal with a row-independent scan:

- CUDPP plans — an efficient tool for batching small similar tasks into the plan, which is then executed on the device. CUDPP takes care of optimal partitioning of the workload, if necessary.
- Thrust `exclusive_segmented_scan` function. This function, however, requires an additional array of the same type as the input image size. This array should be initialized with labels, indicating the beginning and end of each of the segments.
- Modify scan sample to work with independent rows in one kernel launch.

The modified scan kernel performs processing of an image row with one CUDA block; thus, the grid configuration contains *height* blocks (see example on Figure 33.11). Each CUDA block contains 128 threads, which perform (*width/blockDim.x*) iterations along the image row. On every iteration threads load 128 elements from the row in global memory (gmem) into the shared memory (shmem), perform an exclusive scan, and add the carrier value to the prefix sums. The initial carrier value is set to zero,

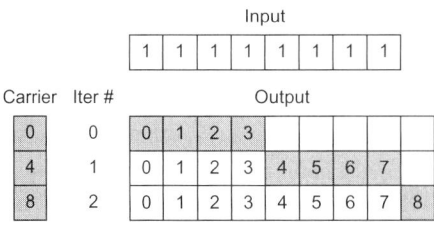

FIGURE 33.11

A modified scan algorithm for integral image generation (four-thread CUDA blocks for the sake of clarity).

but after the first iteration, it is updated with the sum of all elements being scanned up to the moment. Then the threads output values to the destination buffer in global memory.

One of the best practices guidelines (included with CUDA toolkit documentation) states that a GPU must be provided with enough workload of the finest granularity. A good CUDA kernel doesn't change its behavior depending on the size of the input data; the input size has to be handled by means of CUDA block and grid configurations. It is claimed that in order to cover global memory access latency, each streaming multiprocessor (SM) should be able to keep about six CUDA blocks on the fly. Thus, to guarantee that the hardware is not wasting its resources while executing a kernel, the grid size of the kernel configuration must be greater than the maximum known number of SMs (30 on an NVIDIA GTX 280) multiplied by six, which gives the minimum sufficient image height of 180 pixels. As soon as the majority of multimedia content is stored in formats larger than CIF (352 × 288), the kernel demonstrates good performance on all known NVIDIA GPUs.

After we implement a set of kernels for integral image calculation, the next step is to implement the calculation of the squared integral image. Obviously, this new set of kernels is subject to code reuse, and it is likely possible to generate all integral image-related kernels by means of C++ templates. The differences between the scan kernels are listed as follows:

- The initial rowwise scan for the integral image: input data is unsigned 8 bit (u8); output is unsigned 32 bit (u32).
- The second rowwise scan for integral image: input is previously scanned and transposed data in u32; output is u32.
- The initial rowwise scan for the squared integral image: input data is u8, but the input pixels must be squared before passing into the scan. Output can be u32 under the assumption that the row length (the input image maximum dimension) is sane and thus doesn't allow to overflow u32 type.
- The second rowwise scan for the squared integral image: input data is u32; no squaring is needed. Output data is u64.

To implement this using C++ templates, three template parameters need to be introduced: class T_in, class T_out, and bool bSquare. The changing parts of the kernel are lines where the input image of type T_in is read into shared memory, where the value is squared after reading, and where the output is stored to the destination buffer of type T_out. To read the value from the source buffer of u8 or u32 type it is convenient to create the __device__ function with the following signature:

```
template<class T>
static inline __device__ T readElem(T *d_src, Npp32u offs);
```

This function can have two explicit instantiations like below:

```
template<>
__device__ Npp8u readElem<Npp8u>(Npp8u *d_src, Npp32u offs)
{
    return tex1Dfetch(texSrcNpp8u, offs);
}

template<>
__device__ Npp32u readElem<Npp32u>(Npp32u *d_src, Npp32u offs)
{
 return d_src[offs];

}
```

This, of course, requires the unsigned char texture reference (texSrcU8) to be declared and bound to the region of global memory before the kernel execution.

33.3.2 Generation of the Normalization Values

As was mentioned previously, object classifiers are usually trained on the variance normalized data. To achieve this effect on the verification stage, one would need to calculate the pixels standard deviation of every region tested and divide each pixel value by the result.

The standard deviation of a rectangular region can be calculates from the formula in Table 33.4. For this, it requires four corner values of the region from the integral image and squared integral image, located either in global or texture memory.

The CUDA kernel configuration assumes a CUDA thread calculates one pixel of the normalization map, corresponding to the top-left corner of the $M \times N$ region of the original image. The configuration of CUDA block is not important unless it is possible to prefetch integral and squared integral images values by means of shared memory. For this purpose the block configuration is chosen as linear, 128×1 threads, and the shared memory of $(128 + N - 1) \times 2$ elements of type u64 are allocated. Before launch, N should be checked not to exceed the allowed amount of shared memory. This shmem segment is used for both integral images prefetching. The idea is to load elements from integral image and store in shmem in four copies: two for top and bottom 128 values and two for top and bottom $N - 1$ values. After that step, each thread addresses shared memory data four times at the correct corner positions and calculates the sum of pixels. The same applies to the squared integral image.

The calculation from Table 33.4 deals with big numbers, representing sums of pixels and their squared values. Thus, all intermediate variables should have a data type sufficient to store intermediate values.

For the sum of pixel values, u32 is sufficient for the square size less than 4096×4096 (to be precise, the maximum side is equal to sqrt(0xFFFFFFFF / 255)). The maximum squared pixels region has the side equal to sqrt(0xFFFFFFFF / 255^2) = 257, which is not enough for HD media content, and hence, u64 type is used.

Once the sum of pixels in the region (u32 sumPix) and sum of the squared pixels in the region (u64 sqsumPix) are calculated, the variance can be calculated using the formula from Table 33.9.

Here, both the terms require division by the number of pixels, or essentially the square of the rectangular region. If this were a constant depending only on the classifier window size ($M \times N$), then the simple solution would be to hard-code this division using multiplication and right shifts. But in practice the normalization values calculation has to be performed on every scale of the input image; thus, numPix stands for the classifier area, multiplied by the current scale parameter squared.

Table 33.9 Variance formula.

$$Var(X) = \frac{sqsumPix}{numPix} - \left(\frac{sumPix}{numPix} \right)^2$$

To avoid usage of division (either integer or float) in the CUDA kernel, the `invNumPix` value is passed as a parameter instead, which is the reciprocal of `numPix`, stored in the float 32-bit (`f32`) data type. With this variable the right term calculation is performed in two multiplications, while the left term leaves few issues unsolved.

Neither the hardware nor the compiler supports multiplication of `u64` by `f32`. The compiler won't generate any warnings, but one should be aware of implicit type casts — the `u64` value will be cast to `f32`, and after that, the multiplication will happen. The result calculation may be corrupt if the high word of the input `u64` was not empty.

To overcome this problem there are two possible solutions:

- Use double precision on systems that provide support to it (starting GT200) just to calculate this product. For the `u64` you need casting to double (`f64`), then the multiplication is done and the `f64` result can be stored in `u32`;
- Use two `f32` variables to operate on the `sqsumPix` variable. The first one is a result of conversion from `u64` to `f32`. The second is a correction value, which can be obtained by backward conversion of the `f32` result to `u64` and subtraction from the true value. The residual is then converted to `f32`. Thus, the original `u64` is represented by two `f32` words, and the multiplication can be performed using the distributive property of the operation. See the following code snippet:

```
Npp32f sqsum_val_base = __ull2float_rz(sqsum_val);
Npp64u sqsum_val_tmp1 = __float2ull_rz(sqsum_val_base);
Npp64u sqsum_val_tmp2 = sqsum_val - sqsum_val_tmp1;
Npp32f sqsum_val_residual = __ull2float_rn(sqsum_val_tmp2);
sqsum_val_base *= invNumPix;
sqsum_val_residual *= invNumPix;
Npp32f sqsum_val_res = sqsum_val_base + sqsum_val_residual;
```

This approach appears to be superior even compared with the native support of double-precision floating-point values on GT200 and Fermi architectures — the register consumption and the speed are much better.

One more technical pitfall is the usage of unions on SM 1.x architectures. Here, the unions are needed to provide texture-cached reading of the integral image (`u32`) and squared integral image (`u64`). As long as there is no valid texture reference to use with `u64` data type, the texture reference that is bound to the memory containing squared integral image is declared of `uint2` data type. When we are reading the element of squared integral image, there are several ways to get the `u64` value:

1. ```
   union
   {
   Npp64u ui1x64;
   uint2 ui2x32;
   } tmp;
   tmp.ui2x32 = tex1Dfetch(texSqr64u, x);
   return tmp.ui1x64;
   ```

2. ```
   uint2 ui2x32 = tex1Dfetch(texSqr64u, x);
   return *(Npp64u *)&ui2x32;
   ```

3. ```
   uint2 ui2x32 = tex1Dfetch(texSqr64u, x);
   return (((Npp64u)ui2x32.y) << 32) | ui2x32.x;
   ```
   ```

The first two ways lead the compiler to the excessive usage of local memory (lmem), because these approaches make use of casting of the structure types. Usage of local memory when not necessary has a pernicious effect on the kernel's performance, especially on the architectures without lmem cache. Thus the third approach appears to be optimal.

33.3.3 Working on the Range of Scales

OpenCV has two ways of handling an object search on different scales. The first way is scaling of the image: an image is downscaled by the current scaling factor; all integral images and the normalization maps are recomputed, and the object classifier is applied to the downscaled content as if it was working always on the identity scale. This is the most straightforward way and at the same time most precise and most computationally expensive.

The second OpenCV way is to scale the classifier. The input image as well as integral images remain intact all the way, but the $M \times N$ classifier window is upscaled by the current scaling factor. On every new scale the normalization map is updated according to the current window size, and the object detector is applied. The problem with this approach is that when upscaling the $M \times N$ classifier window by the real value, the features don't map to the pixels grid anymore. In order to prevent the precision loss that is due to coordinates rounding, the weights of all features in the classifier cascade have to be updated on every scale according to the changed area of the features' rectangles.

Both ways have pros and cons. The first way doesn't require changing the object classifier after its loading; it doesn't have problems with drifted feature area values, which may lead to the worse detection rate. However, it requires reconstructing the whole frame helper structures on every scale, which is a rather expensive operation. The second way needs to recalculate only the normalization map and adjust the classifier weights.

For the GPU implementation of the pipeline, one of the most important decisions to make is the data layout organization. The global memory access latency can be covered in several ways: access coalescing for direct access and spatial locality of adjacent accesses for cached access; it can be either texture cache or L1/L2 cache starting with Fermi architecture. The second approach doesn't fit into these requirements because with the growing scale factor, the distance between the adjacent accesses will only grow. The result is that such accesses can never be coalesced, and they also cause cache trashing. A limited amount of cache lines appear to be irrationally consumed to store one or a few elements of interest per line as shown in Figure 33.12.

The cons of the first way can be fought by the decision to work with only integer scales of the original image. This is the most valuable difference between the OpenCV processing pipeline and the one implemented with CUDA. The most tangible negative effect of this simplification is observed on the lowest scales, close to the identity. This implies worse detection rates for smallest faces. This should not be a big deal for the majority of applications that require only the largest face to be found. Table 33.10 contains two series of scaling factors from the OpenCV algorithm and from the algorithm for CUDA. As can be seen, the scaling factors do not differ too much after a few scale iterations.

Downscaling with an integer factor is essentially a decimation of the input, or nearest neighbor downsampling — a process, in which the output buffer receives one sample per N original samples.

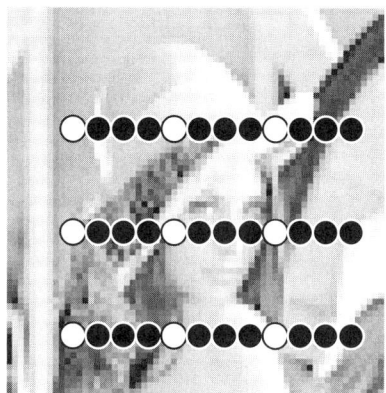

FIGURE 33.12

Cache trashing when addressing sparse pixels (cache line size is 4 pixels width for clarity). White points represent sparse accesses, black points stand for unused cached pixels in cache lines.

Table 33.10 Sequences of scaling factors for the scaling step of 1.2.												
Scale power	1	2	3	4	5	6	7	8	9	10	11	12	13
Scale factor	1.0	1.2	1.4	1.7	2.0	2.5	3.0	3.6	4.3	5.2	6.2	7.4	8.9
Rounded factor	1.0	miss	miss	miss	2.0	miss	3.0	miss	4.0	5.0	6.0	7.0	8.0

33.3.4 Classifiers Cascade

The next step is implementation of the CUDA kernel that performs the processing of a region of pixels at the original scale using the whole classifiers cascade. The kernel receives the classifier cascade, integral and squared integral images, normalization map, and a pointer to a segment of global memory where the output of classification is stored.

The very simplistic implementation of such a kernel has a simple mapping of the processing flow to CUDA grid and block configurations. The kernel is launched with as many threads as there are regions of the $M \times N$ size to be classified in the image, that is $(height - M + 1) \times (width - N + 1)$. Each CUDA thread works within the search region and sequentially calculates stages, classifiers, and features until the classification decision is done. After that it outputs the decision flag to the output detections mask of the same size as the input image.

The output mask should have a low amount of detections, so for the convenience of iteration over them, they are collected into the list of detections using the stream compaction algorithm.

Stream compaction is a data manipulation primitive that can be found in both CUDPP and Thrust libraries (in the Stream Compaction and Reordering section). The algorithm takes the input vector of values and the compaction predicate, which indicates if an element from the input vector should be in the output or not. The algorithm then outputs the "compacted" vector of only those values for which the predicate evaluated to true.

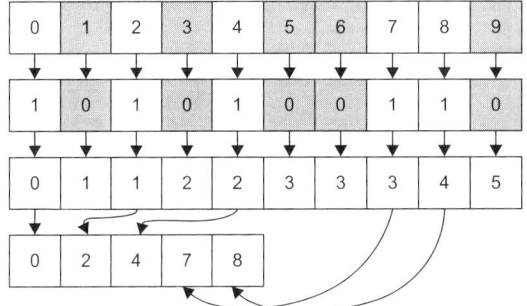

FIGURE 33.13

Stream compaction for object detections. Top to bottom: Input vector of elements, white are of interest; the mask of elements of interest; the prefix sums vector of the mask of interest (contains output offsets of the elements of interest); the compacted vector.

There are plenty of variations of stream compaction, such as taking different arguments, working with predicates or stencil masks, and outputting input elements themselves or their offsets from the beginning of the input vector. Figure 33.13 shows the process of stream compaction based on the scan operation.

The vector at the top contains integer elements; some of them are darkened which means that these elements are not of interest. The purpose of the algorithm is to take only elements of interest and put them into the new "compacted" vector in the following three steps:

- The mask of elements of interest is calculated. Each white element has 1 in the mask and all others have zeros.
- This mask is prefix summed, which produces a vector of addresses for where to put elements of interest.
- The compaction is then performed as a simple elementwise copy.

It has to be noted that under certain conditions if the input vector contains a very low amount of elements of interest, then the use of atomic operations on the global memory instead of scan may give better performance.

Processing Optimizations

The approach to the classifier cascade application with CUDA, which maps each region to one CUDA thread, is hereby called pixel-parallel processing (Figure 33.14). The CUDA block configuration is chosen to be linear for convenience. As a convention, the anchor of an $M \times N$ region will be represented by the top-left pixel (the middle pixel on the illustrations 33.15). Because all regions have to be processed by the kernel, all threads within the CUDA block will address the region of the $M \times (blockDim.x + N - 1)$ of the integral image. This leads to the idea that any kind of cache would be extremely helpful here for prefetching of the integral image values. The possibilities are shared memory, texture cache, and L1/L2 cache (starting with the Fermi architecture). As for shared memory, it will not be efficient on early architectures owing to the ratio of shared memory per multiprocessor to the amount of threads to launch.

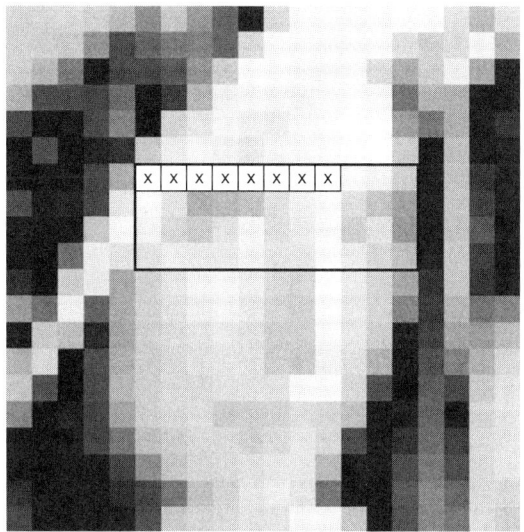

FIGURE 33.14

Pixel-parallel processing (x-marked pixels are anchors, corresponding to CUDA threads; the rectangular area of pixels is shared by all threads of the block). The CUDA block size is eight threads, M = N = 4.

The described processing is very simple to implement, but its performance is below any expectations. The reason for this phenomenon is so-called work starvation. Indeed, on each stage the classifier cascade is supposed to reject some percentage of the input hypotheses, which means that just after a few stages more than 50% of CUDA threads will become inactive (Figure 33.15). After all threads from the block terminate, the SM releases the CUDA block and its resources and proceeds with the new one. The worst-case scenario can happen if every CUDA block has one or more threads that will be discarded on the last stage of the cascade.

The efficiency of the processing may be improved if the classifier cascade is broken down into groups of stages (or even into separate classifiers), which are then executed in sequential kernel launches. The kernel needs to be modified to take the amount of stages to process before forced termination. This idea draws several problems that have to be overcome.

Configuring CUDA blocks for subsequent launches as before doesn't make work starvation go away because the same threads are addressing the same regions. This problem can be dealt with by means of the stream compaction algorithm that is applied to the output mask of detections after the first group of stages processing; it is capable of creating a list with indices of those anchors which passed through.

As a result, there is a need in some other kernel for the subsequent launches that takes the list of indices as an argument and assigns one thread per anchor passed to the moment. This new kernel differs from the previous in several ways. Instead of the direct computing of the anchor location from `threadIdx` and `blockIdx`, the new kernel has a one-dimensional block configuration and takes the anchor from the list (passed as input) at the absolute thread *ID* in the grid. In addition, the kernel can output detections to the same locations of the output vector, relying on the compaction kernel, or it can do compaction by itself (either each thread increments a global counter using `atomicAdd` and writes

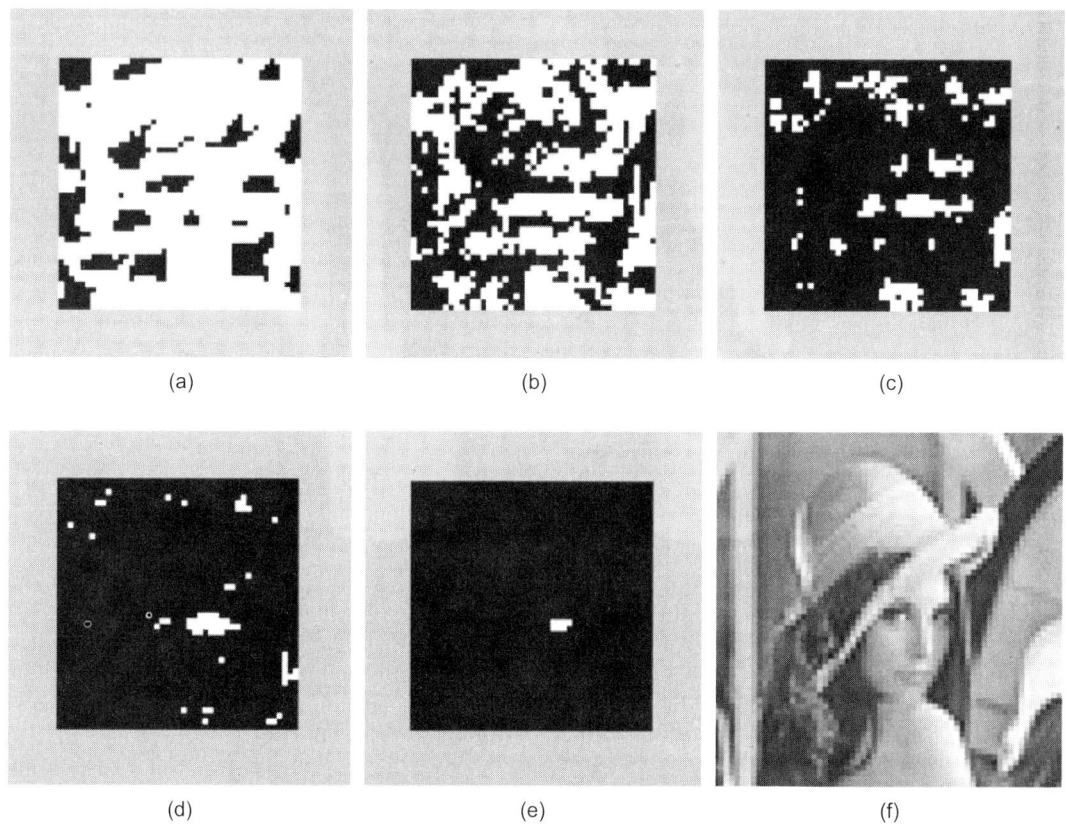

(a)   (b)   (c)

(d)   (e)   (f)

FIGURE 33.15

Lena image (bottom right) and masks of regions that passed through the first, second, third, sixth, and 20th stages of the face detection cascade.

to the slot, or the local compaction stage is held after all threads finish classification and the atomic operation is called only once from the CUDA block to reserve the needed amount of detections in the global array).

Although the latter processing scheme allows one to keep work starvation under the control, the situation can still be improved by revisiting the parallelism of the CUDA implementation. The two disadvantages of the latter CUDA kernel are

- The adjacent threads within the CUDA block share little (or don't share at all) areas of corresponding regions; hence, the access pattern to the integral image is quite sparse; and
- The work starvation at a smaller scale remains in place: still a possibility exists that all threads but one will reject the anchor and exit immediately, while the one left will do processing up to the end.

The proposed new scheme is called stage-parallel processing (Figure 33.16), which means that the parallelism has moved inside of the single-stage processing. The whole linear CUDA block is working

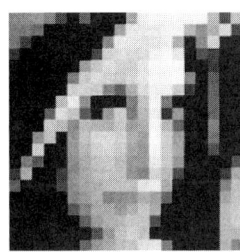

Stage 0 (2 weak classifiers, 4 threads in CUDA block) – underutilization example

0	1	2	3
0	1		

Stage *N* (amount of weak classifiers is greater than the number of CUDA threads)

0	1	2	3	4	5	6	7	8	9	10	11	12
0	1	2	3	0	1	2	3	0	1	2	3	0

FIGURE 33.16

Stage-parallel processing. One region 20×20 is processed by the whole CUDA block. Each white square represents one weak classifier with the absolute number in stage in the top field. The corresponding CUDA thread ID is in the bottom field.

with one region, and the processing of one classifier stage is performed in the following way. If we assume that the stage contains more weak classifiers than the value of CUDA block dimension, each CUDA thread picks one corresponding weak classifier from the beginning of the stage and calculates its value for the given region. Then it accumulates the value in the register and advances to the next weak classifier, located `blockDim.x` weak classifiers apart. When all weak classifiers are evaluated, all threads perform parallel reduction of the local accumulators, which results in the stage value, which in turn is compared with the stage threshold, and the classification decision is made.

The main advantage of this new kernel is the finest-grain parallelism, which completely solves the problem of work starvation and sparse memory accesses. It is also a disadvantage at the same time because the kernel is efficient only on the second part of the classifier cascade, where stages contain a large number of weak classifiers. Obviously, the performance of the kernel is low on the first stage of the face detection classifier cascade with a few weak classifiers.

The pros and cons of the two presented approaches certainly dictate the majority of usage restrictions. First, the pixel-parallel kernel executes several stages in one or a few launches. After that the stage-parallel kernel executes all hypotheses left up to the final classification. A good discussion topic would be "how to break down the cascade into groups of stages." As before, here is the bifurcation point:

- The analytical way is to hard-code the decision based on the information about each classifier cascade. For instance, switch to the stage-parallel kernel after the ratio of passed anchors goes below some percentage threshold. This kind of information can be obtained on the cascade-training phase or calculated from an exhaustive amount of tests.
- The formal way is to switch to the stage-parallel kernel as soon as the amount of weak classifiers becomes greater or equal to the number of threads with which the stage-parallel kernel is configured to run.
- The feedback way is to call the pixel-parallel kernel restricted to process *N* (parameter to tweak) stages at a time several times until the percentage of passed hypotheses goes below the threshold, or the amount of weak classifiers on the next stage is greater than the stage-parallel kernel block dimension. In this case the first pixel-parallel kernel works in the very traditional way and outputs the hypotheses count and the list of detections (or the mask, and then the host calls the compaction operation to generate the list). All subsequent pixel-parallel calls take input from the list, generated

by the previous kernel call (so-called kernel chaining). The feedback analysis is performed on the host by copying the hypotheses count value and comparing it against the total number of possible detections. Whenever it becomes possible to do the feedback analysis on the device and call the next kernel depending on some condition directly from the device, then it should work a bit faster.

In every particular case (the classifier cascade) the fastest way needs to be determined, but in general the feedback way is superior owing to its robust essence.

Cascade Layout Optimizations

The object classifier cascade is the cornerstone of the object-detection pipeline. It is the most intensively addressed structure, and thus it has to be stored in a compact but well-structured representation. The OpenCV XML classifier representation (Table 33.11) doesn't meet these requirements; its main purpose is to store the cascade in a pictorial, convenient for browsing way. In the OpenCV Haar classifier loader it is parsed to bits and stored in the RAM. The cascade structures being used in OpenCV after XML parsing can be found in the cv.hpp file. Although the internal representation is a structure of arrays that is an encouraged technique in GPU computing, there is still a lot of room for optimizations, especially GPU-specific.

The classifier adds up from stages, which in turn add up from trees (weak classifiers). Each tree consists of nodes, which encapsulate a number of rectangles with weights (the Haar feature), the feature threshold, and leaves. In Table 33.11 the leaves are the weak classifier response values. To store the tree-based classifier, the left_val and right_val tags might be changed to left_node and right_node, with the *ID* of the referenced node instead of the classifier response.

Table 33.11 OpenCV Haar classifier excerpt.

```
<opencv_storage><haarcascade_frontalface_alt type_id="opencv-haar-classifier">
        <size>20 20</size>
        <stages>
        <_>
                <!-- stage 0 -->
                <trees>
                <_>
                        <!-- tree 0 -->
                        <_>
                        <!-- root node -->
                        <feature>
                                <rects>
                                <_>3 7 14 4 -1.</_>
                                <_>3 9 14 2 2.</_></rects>
                                <tilted>0</tilted></feature>
                        <threshold>4.0141958743333817e-003</threshold>
                        <left_val>0.0337941907346249</left_val>
                        <right_val>0.8378106951713562</right_val></_></_>
                </trees>
        <stage_threshold>0.8226894140243530</stage_threshold>
        </stages>
</haarcascade_frontalface_alt></opencv_storage>
```

To facilitate caching of the whole classifier cascade data, it needs to be stored in the global memory with texture reference bound to it. It is worth noting that texture reference supports reading up to 16-byte (128-bit) data types (e.g., `uint4`), so the best approach is to pack the data to fit several arrays of structures (with elements of either 32, 64, or 128 bits in size), or to store it as several arrays of independent values.

Fortunately, all structures can be packed into the mentioned data types, not without hacks, though. The first array contains all feature rectangles with weights (Figure 33.17). As far as an average classifier window size does not exceed some value in any dimension, the rectangle's fields (top, left, width, height) can be stored in 8-bit unsigned integers. The weight is stored as a single-precision floating point, so the overall size of the rectangle with weight is 64 bits. The corresponding structure is named `HaarFeaturePart64`.

The second array contains descriptions of nodes. Each node is represented by the complete Haar feature, threshold, and two leaves (or pointers to other nodes). Because there are two leaves and one threshold, each stored as a 32-bit float (the leaf field can be interpreted as a 32-bit pointer to an other node, which agrees with the leaf size), this immediately leaves the only chance to fit "the complete Haar feature" into 32 bits to not exceed the allowed 128 bits for the total structure size. For this purpose the `HaarFeatureDescriptor32` structure is introduced. It contains the information about the number of rectangles in the feature (8 bits) and the offset from the beginning of the array of `HaarFeaturePart64` (24 bits). The whole 128-bit structure gets named `HaarClassifierNode128`.

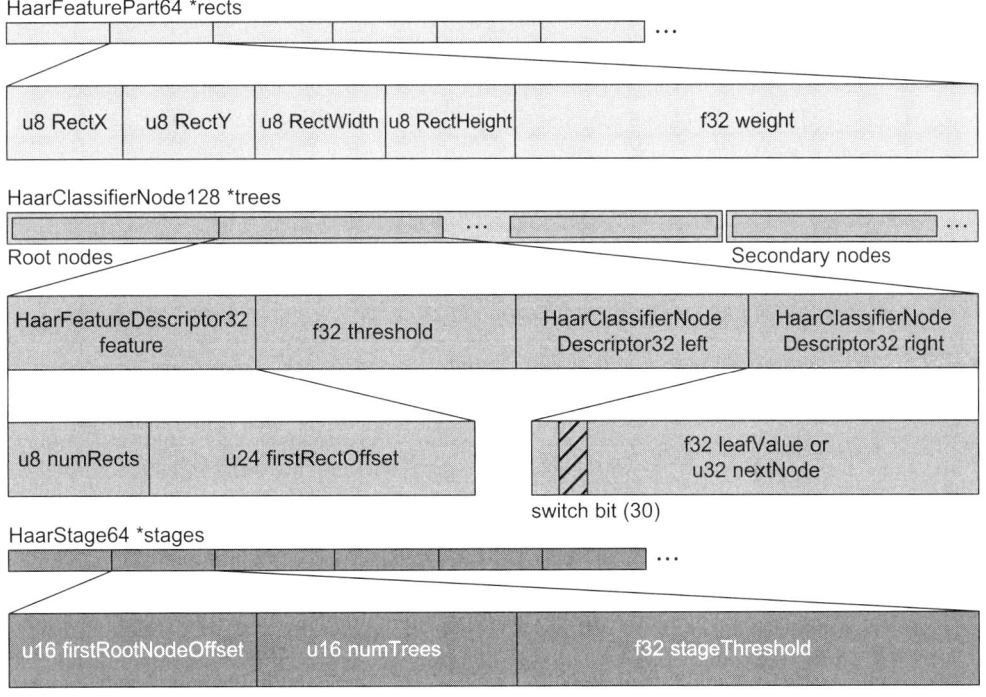

FIGURE 33.17

Classifier cascade GPU data layout.

It is important to store `HaarFeaturePart64` elements exactly in the same order as they appeared during the XML cascade parsing, because the `HaarFeatureDescriptor32` relies on their sequential order.

The final (third) array contains the description of the stages. Generally, a stage is characterized by the trees it contains and the stage threshold. The proposed representation of the stage is 16 bits for the amount of trees, 16 bits for the offset of the first tree root node in the array of `Haar-ClassifierNode128`, and 32 bits for the stage threshold. The corresponding data structure is named `HaarStage64`.

The `HaarStage64` representation relies on the solid indexing of the trees in the array of `HaarClassifierNode128`. Unlike the requirement of sequential filling of the array of `Haar-FeaturePart64`, the array of `HaarClassifierNode128` has to be handled slightly differently. In its first part all root nodes of the whole cascade are stored. After the last root node all intermediate nodes and leaves follow.

This layout allows keeping the size of `HaarStage64` without maintaining additional information about trees indexing. The opposite side of this storage scheme is a slightly more complex loading process, which has to maintain two separate arrays of nodes: one for root nodes and one for all others. After all nodes are loaded into the separate arrays, all far pointers to other nodes need to be corrected by adding the length of the root nodes vector.

One more bit-twiddling hack is storing the information about how to interpret the children of the node, that is, whether the 32-bit value is a floating-point leaf or integer pointer to some other node. Storing the single bit in the lowest bit of the integer (which is the least significant bit of the floating-point value at the same time) changes detection rates resulting from the precision loss. The safe location for this additional bit would be the highest bit of exponent (bit number 31) because it is never used in the values of weak classifier response. The highest exponent bit is used only for values with modulus greater or equal than 2, which rarely happens in practice, unless the classifier was trained with normalized weights.

Another potential placement for the classifier cascade is CUDA's constant memory. It is known to be one of the fastest memory types available on the GPU. The classifier cascade can be easily moved from global memory to constant memory. However, this enhancement has some application limitations.

First of all, constant memory is efficient only when a single location is addressed by all threads within a warp; otherwise, warp serialization occurs. Obviously, the worst warp serialization will happen in the stage-parallel kernel because every thread addresses a different weak classifier; thus, the optimization is not applicable here. However, the pixel-parallel kernel meets the addressing requirements because all threads address the same parts of the cascade simultaneously. The warp serialization still may happen while processing with a tree-based classifier, when different threads follow different paths depending on the calculations. No problems with serialization should happen when working with stump-based classifiers because of a lack of branching below the root node.

However, it appeared to be impossible to store the traditional face detection classifier cascade into the constant memory because the representation described earlier in this chapter required about 80 KB, whereas the capacity of constant memory is 64 KB (the size of the XML classifier representation is over 1 MB).

It appears that there is still a room for compression of the classifier cascade to increase chances for them to fit into the constant memory. This specific optimization covers only classifiers of limited window size ($M \times N$). The core idea is that the array of HaarFeaturePart64 takes about half of the total

Table 33.12 Constraints on the rectangle representation for storing in 2 bytes.

$x \in [0, N-1]$
width $\in [1, N]$
$x + \text{width} \in [1, N]$

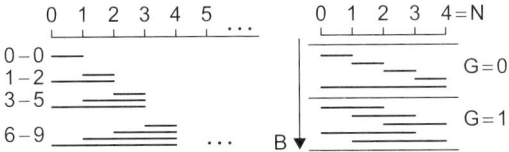

FIGURE 33.18

Schemes of solid enumeration (coding) of tuples (x, width) for N = 4.

size of the classifier cascade and by crunching it into 32 bits it is possible to achieve ~75% compression ratio. Two things need to be done: the first (trivial) is storing the rectangle weight in the IEEE 754 half float (16 bits).

The second step is to learn how to store a feature rectangle into 2 bytes. Because of the symmetry in the definition of rectangle $[(x, width), (y, height)]$, the problem can be reduced to storing a tuple $(x, width)$ in one byte (B), under the constraints from the Table 33.12.

The final step is to calculate the maximum N for which all possible tuples can be stored in 1 byte. The enumeration scheme for this is shown on Figure 33.18 (left). The increasing sum of elements from 1 to N evaluates to $(N+1)*N/2$, which yields the maximum for N equal to 22. This means that the maximum allowed classifier window size to use with this technique is 22×22 pixels.

The enumeration scheme can be used for building the conversion between $(x, width)$ and B, but it would require a square root operation involved. Figure 33.18 (right) demonstrates the alternative enumeration scheme for which a very simple conversion exists (see Table 33.13). The idea is to restructure the enumeration into groups, each containing $N+1$ elements, and perform conversion with the use of intermediate values — the number of group in which the element is located (G) and the number of element within the group (K). On the tuple decoding step the division can be replaced with multiplication followed by arithmetic shifts, or multiplication by the precalculated reciprocal.

33.4 BENCHMARKING AND IMPLEMENTATION DETAILS

The CUDA implementation of the algorithm discussed in the preceding sections differs from OpenCV in several ways. For the sake of truthfulness of the comparison, the OpenCV 2.1 implementation of the function was prepared for the comparison as follows:

- Processing on the different scales was restricted to the rounded factors instead of the original approach.

Table 33.13 Left — coding tuple pseudo code; right — decoding tuple pseudo code.

```if (width <= N / 2)```	```G = B / (N + 1);```
```{```	```K = B - G*(N + 1);```
``` G = width - 1;```	```if (K < N - G)```
``` K = x;```	```{```
```}```	``` x = K;```
```else```	``` width = G + 1;```
```{```	```}```
``` G = N - width;```	```else```
``` K = x + (N - G);```	```{```
```}```	``` x = K - (N - G);```
```B = G*(N + 1) + K;```	``` width = N - G;```
	```}```

- Instead of scaling the classifier, the implementation was made to perform image downsampling for every scale (controlled by the CV_HAAR_SCALE_IMAGE parameter).
- The initial region window size was set to the classifier window size.
- The "ystep" optimization was discarded because CUDA implementation processes all regions (this optimization forces the algorithm to skip processing every odd anchor along rows and columns if the current scale is less than 2, and results in 4 times less work on the particular scale).
- The library was compiled with Intel Threading Building Blocks support to enable the algorithm to use all CPU cores for parallel processing. OpenCV splits the image into horizontal slices and feeds them to the CPU cores, thus providing nearly 100% CPU load during processing.
- The amount of neighbors was set to 0 to exclude the hypotheses filtration stage from the processing time.
- Each image was loaded and processed several times to warm up command cache for the subsequent passes. The same was done for GPU processing.

All these restrictions are required to compare the algorithms, but in the real application, a lot of optimizations can be returned in place. For instance, when we are searching for the largest face, it is possible to early terminate after 10% of scales, providing a good speedup. All the optimizations reside on the top level of the pipeline, whereas the Haar classifier cascade application routine remains intact.

The results of the comparison can be found in Figure 33.19. The input data includes one group photo of large resolution, downsampled to several popular smaller resolutions (VGA, 720p, and 1080p). The hardware choice ranges from the low-end consumer GPUs and processors to the new high-end products. The plot demonstrates FPS (frames per second) of processing of each of the images by the selected GPUs and CPUs.

The ROC curve of the classifier should have not changed owing to the similarity of the results of OpenCV and GPU algorithms. All the discrepancies are studied and come from the difference between the hardware FP units and the order of floating-point operations.

Parts of the code are going to be available for free via OpenCV library GPU module. For questions regarding the chapter and the code send an email to the author.

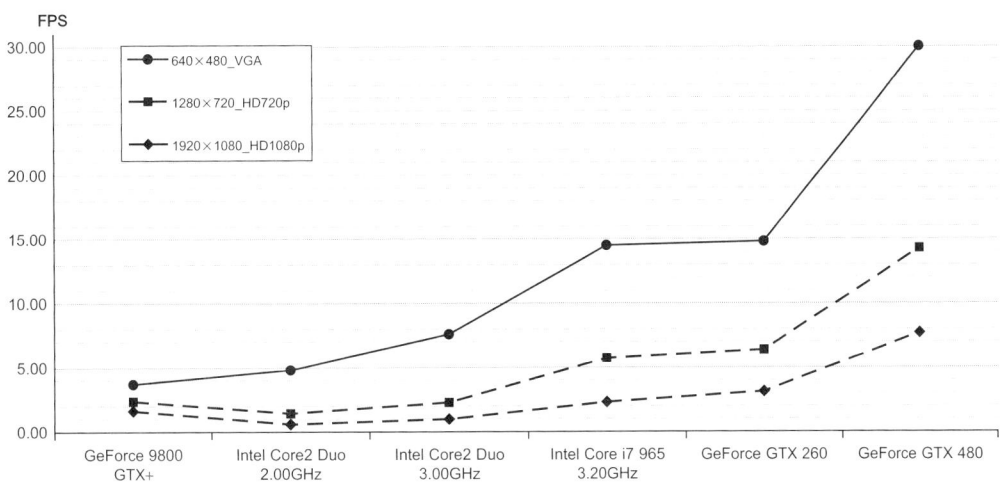

FIGURE 33.19

Benchmarking of the GPU implementation against OpenCV library (Full search algorithm).

33.5 FUTURE DIRECTION

At the time of active development of the classification-based object detection, Haar features appeared to be optimum of their computational complexity and the memory bandwidth, required for their computation. Since that time both compute capabilities and memory speed have grown, but the dynamics show that compute capabilities tend to grow faster.

Given this trend, the road map for creation of faster object detection algorithms for next-generation architectures should include revisiting of the low-level feature extraction algorithms and possibly changing simplistic Haar features to some higher-order correlation-based approach.

33.6 CONCLUSION

This gem has covered the history of the object detection approach, proposed by Viola and Jones. An efficient port of the object detection pipeline to NVIDIA CUDA architecture was presented, followed by a discussion of the implementation and possible sharp-tuned optimizations.

References

[1] P.A. Viola, M.J. Jones, Rapid object detection using a boosted cascade of simple features, in: Proceedings of the 2001 IEEE Computer Society Conference on Computer Vision and Pattern Recognition (CVPR 2001), Mitsubishi Electr. Res. Labs., Cambridge, MA, vol. 1, 2001, pp. 511–518.
[2] Y. Freund, R.E. Schapire, A short introduction to boosting, in: Proceedings of the Sixteenth International Joint Conference on Artificial Intelligence, AT&T Labs, Research Shannon Laboratory, Florham Park, NJ 07932 USA, 1999, pp. 771–780

[3] R. Lienhart, J. Maydt, An extended set of Haar-like features for rapid object detection, in: IEEE ICIP 2002, Intel Labs., Intel Corp., Santa Clara, CA, vol. 1, 2002, pp. 900–903.

[4] R. Lienhart, A. Kuranov, V. Pisarevsky, Empirical analysis of detection cascades of boosted classifiers for rapid object detection, MRL Technical Report, in: DAGM'03, 25th Pattern Recognition Symposium, Madgeburg, Germany, 2002, pp. 297–304 (revised December 2002).

[5] A. Obukhov, Face detection with CUDA, in: GPU Technology Conference, Fairmont Hotel, San Jose, 2009.

Video and Image Processing

Area Editor's Introduction

Timo Stich

34 Experiences on Image and Video Processing with CUDA and OpenCL 547

35 Connected Component Labeling in CUDA 569

36 Image De-Mosaicing 583

THE STATE OF GPU COMPUTING IN VIDEO AND IMAGE PROCESSING

GPUs have played a role in video and image processing for a long time. In the beginning they were used to display the processed results. Quickly, application developers picked up GPU computing, and GPUs are becoming the main processing devices in today's video- and image-processing applications. The ever-increasing amount of video and image data demands ever-increasing computational power while offering at the same time more potential for parallel computation. The GPU, with its many-core architecture, is the perfect match to these challenges and delivers the computational performance necessary to drive the image- and video-processing applications of today and the future.

GPU computing not only significantly speeds up existing workflows in video and image processing but also allows for more creativity by using the additional computational power to transform the workflows themselves. For example, with GPU computing, filters and operators can be performed in real time on full HD video, making low-resolution preview windows obsolete. At present, sophisticated video- and image-processing applications are only used off-line owing to long runtimes. When those applications take advantage of GPU computing, I expect even more breakthroughs. The transitioning of these applications into the real-time processing domain offers the opportunity for additional user interaction to be added, enabling the creation of new and more intelligent interactive tools in video- and image-processing applications.

IN THIS SECTION

Chapter 34, written by Temizel *et al.,* discusses different implementation choices for video-processing algorithms, including concurrent I/O operations, effective memory layout , and access, as well as kernel granularities, and gives general guidelines on achieving best performance.

Chapter 35, written by Šťava and Beneš, describes an implementation of the two-pass union-find algorithm to find connected components. The main concept is to first compute local solutions in shared memory and then merge these local results hierarchically to compute the final solution.

Chapter 36, written by Fung and Stam, describes implementations of various image de-mosaicing algorithms. The key to high performance is using separate arrays for the different color channels in shared memory to avoid bank conflicts and letting one thread compute four output pixels to avoid divergences.

Experiences on Image and Video Processing with CUDA and OpenCL

34

Alptekin Temizel, Tugba Halici, Berker Logoglu, Tugba Taskaya Temizel,
Fatih Omruuzun, Ersin Karaman

This chapter will be helpful to those, in particular academicians and professionals, who work with compute- and data-intensive image and video processing algorithms.

The chapter addresses the technical challenges and experiences associated with the domain-related algorithms implemented on GPU architectures specifically by using CUDA and OpenCL with an emphasis on real-time issues and optimization. We present a series of implementations on background subtraction and correlation algorithms, each of which addresses different aspects of GPU programming issues, including I/O operations, coalesced memory use, and kernel granularity. The experiments show that effective consideration of such design issues improves the performance of the algorithms significantly.

34.1 INTRODUCTION, PROBLEM STATEMENT, AND BACKGROUND

The importance of GPUs has recently been recognized for general-purpose applications such as video and image processing algorithms. An increasing number of studies show substantial performance gains with their GPU-adapted implementations. Video and image processing algorithms, in particular, real-time video surveillance applications, have gained ground owing to the growing need to ensure public security worldwide. They have now become viable to realize in high-camera-number cases, thanks to GPUs.

In this chapter, we implement two image and video processing applications on the CPU and the GPU to compare their effectiveness. As a video processing application, adaptive background subtraction, and as an image processing application, Pearson's correlation algorithms have been implemented.

Although there are studies showing parallel implementations for a myriad of image and video processing algorithms on GPUs, their performance evaluations are limited by specific platforms and computing architectures and without any concern for real-time issues. Moreover, they fail to guide the researchers and developers in terms of platform and computing architecture capabilities. For example, an algorithm is implemented using CUDA, and the performance comparison is often carried out between the CPU and the GPU mostly on a specific platform.

This study aims to guide users in implementing GPU-based algorithms using CUDA and OpenCL architectures by providing practical suggestions. In addition, we compare these two architectures to demonstrate their advantages over each other, in particular, for video and image processing applications.

34.2 CORE TECHNOLOGY OR ALGORITHM

In this study, we focus on two widely used algorithms in computer vision and video processing: adaptive background subtraction and Pearson correlation.

The first one is an adaptive background subtraction algorithm that can be used to identify moving or newly emerging objects from subsequent video frames. This information can then be used to enable tracking and deducting higher-level information that is valuable for automated detection of suspicious events in real time (see Figure 34.1). We selected the algorithm described in [1] because this cost-effective method is easy to implement and produces effective results. The algorithm is embarrassingly parallel in nature because the same independent operation is applied to each pixel in a frame.

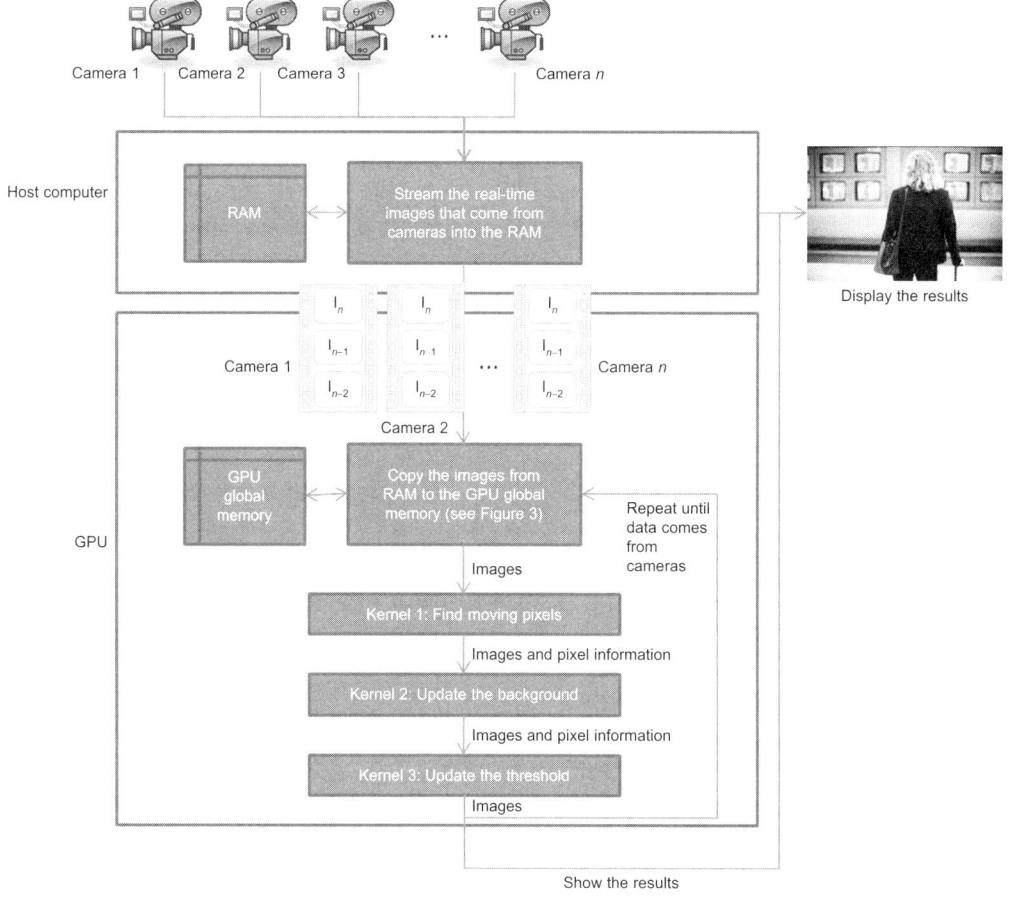

FIGURE 34.1

The flowchart of the background subtraction algorithm.

We have considered the following domain-specific constraints regarding a typical video surveillance application in our study. In order to achieve real-time processing with PAL (Phase Alternating Line) format videos, the number of frames processed per second (fps) was determined as 25. To perform this task in real time, we note that images from all cameras should be processed in 40 ms, prior to the arrival of the subsequent frames. The maximum number of cameras that can be supported in the GPU architecture is obtained by calculating the number of video frames that can be processed simultaneously in real time with this constraint.

Real-time processing is of great importance, particularly in the security domain. Until recently, officers have been able to deal with tracking suspicious cases in real time. However, a high number of cameras, combined with an increase in security risks in crowded public places, such as in airports, underground stations or terminals, and town squares, necessitate the automation of surveillance process in real time because it is no longer possible to carry out this process manually. Real-time processing is also required in other video applications, such as automated video content analysis and robotics.

The second algorithm is Pearson correlation, which is used to measure the similarity of two images. The application areas of the algorithm are numerous. For example, the algorithm may aid the security officers to compare registered cartridge cases in a database with one obtained in a crime scene. This computation can be carried out in parallel for N number of images independent of each other. To achieve good performance, however, it is important to avoid reaccessing the compared image many times from the global memory and to keep the interim correlation results in the local memory to have a better performance.

34.2.1 Background Subtraction

The algorithm consists of three main stages:

- Finding moving pixels
- Updating the background
- Updating thresholds

With each new image, moving pixels are found, and B_n and T_n are updated according to the following rules.

Finding Moving Pixels

$$|I_n(x,y) - I_{n-1}(x,y)| > T_n(x,y) \text{ and } |I_n(x,y) - I_{n-2}(x,y)| > T_n(x,y) \qquad (34.1)$$

Here, each pixel of the last two images I_{n-1} and I_{n-2} is compared against the corresponding pixels of the current image I_n. The algorithm keeps an adaptive threshold T_n for each pixel, and the pixel is said to be moving if the absolute difference is higher than this threshold.

Updating the Background

Background is updated with each new image, according to the following equation:

$$B_{n+1} = \begin{cases} \alpha B_n(x,y) + (1-\alpha)I_n(x,y), & \text{if } (x,y) \text{ is not moving} \\ B_n(x,y), & \text{if } (x,y) \text{ is moving} \end{cases} \qquad (34.2)$$

If the pixel is moving, background is updated using a time constant α; otherwise, it is kept the same. α, $(0 < \alpha < 1)$, determines how the new information updates older observations. An α value closer to 1 means that the older observations have higher weight and the background is updated more slowly.

Updating the Threshold

Threshold is updated with each new image according to the following equation:

$$T_{n+1}(x,y) = \begin{cases} \alpha T_n(x,y) + (1-\alpha)(c|I_n(x,y) - B_n(x,y)|), & \text{if } (x,y) \text{ is not moving} \\ T_n(x,y), & \text{if } (x,y) \text{ is moving} \end{cases} \tag{34.3}$$

Similar to the background update, if the pixel is moving, threshold is updated using the time constant α; otherwise, it is kept the same. The threshold c is a real number greater than one, analogous to the local temporal standard deviation of the intensity. In our experiments we used $c = 3$ and $\alpha = 0.92$.

Some examples from the background subtraction algorithm with the i-Lids dataset [2] are shown in Figure 34.2.

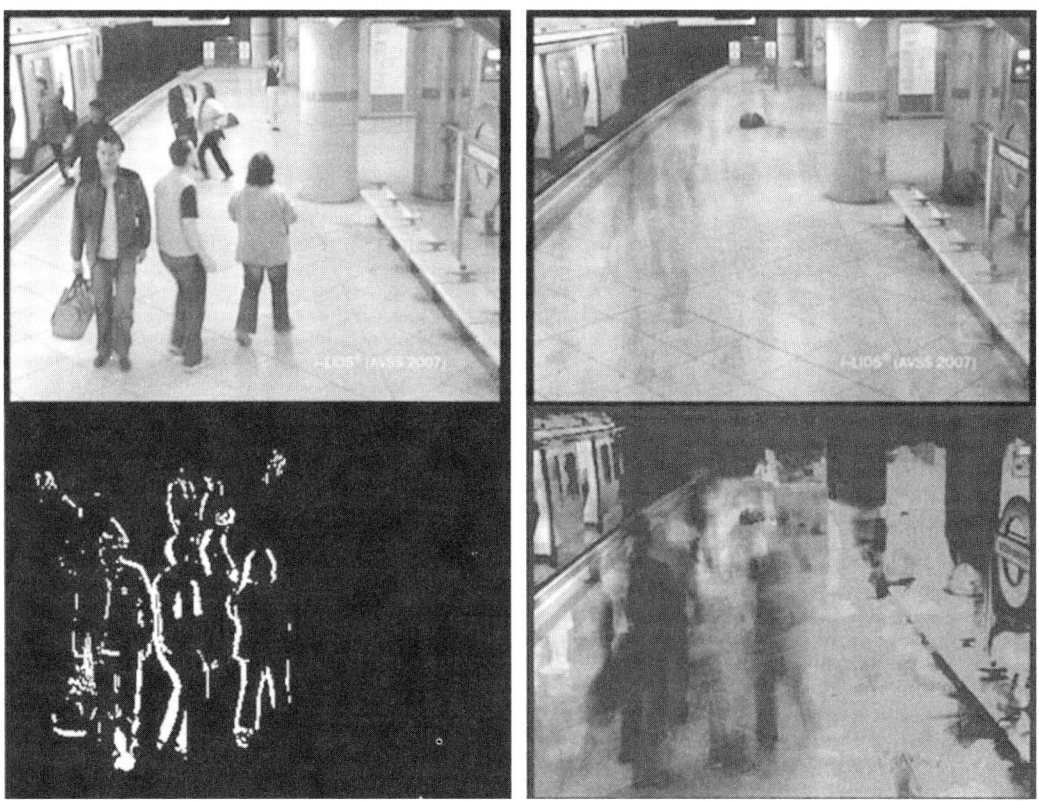

FIGURE 34.2

Images illustrating the background subtraction algorithm. The original image I_n (top left), extracted background image B_n (top right), moving pixels (bottom left), threshold image T_n (bottom right).

34.2.2 **Pearson's Correlation Coefficients**

Correlation is a technique for measuring the degree of relationship between two variables. It is used in a broad range of disciplines, including image/video processing and pattern recognition. The relationship between the variables is obtained by the calculation of coefficients of correlation. There are a number of different coefficients, including Kendall's tau correlation coefficient and Spearman's rho correlation coefficient, but the most popular and widely used one is that of Pearson's correlation coefficient (PMCC) aka sample correlation coefficient. It takes values between $[-1,1]$ where 1, 0 and -1 indicate a perfect match, that is, no correlation and perfect negative correlation, respectively.

PMCC is defined as the covariance of the variables that are to be compared, divided by their standard deviations:

$$\rho_{x,y} = \frac{cov(x,y)}{\sigma_x \sigma_y} \tag{34.4}$$

$$\rho_{x,y} = \frac{\sum_{i=0}^{n}(x_i - \mu_x)(y_i - \mu_y)}{\sqrt{\sum_{i=0}^{n}(x_i - \mu_x)^2}\sqrt{\sum_{i=0}^{n}(y_i - \mu_y)^2}} \tag{34.5}$$

$$\rho_{x,y} = \frac{n\sum_{i=0}^{n}x_i y_i - \sum_{i=0}^{n}x_i \sum_{i=0}^{n}y_i}{\sqrt{n\sum_{i=0}^{n}x_i^2 - \left(\sum_{i=0}^{n}x_i\right)^2}\sqrt{n\sum_{i=0}^{n}y_i^2 - \left(\sum_{i=0}^{n}y_i\right)^2}} \tag{34.6}$$

34.3 **KEY INSIGHTS FROM IMPLEMENTATION AND EVALUATION**

In this section, we discuss the two algorithms' performances in detail. Table 34.1 shows the parameters used in the experiments. Four different video sizes and three different GPUs have been used.

Table 34.1 Parameters, frameworks, and architectures used in the experiments.

Parameters		Values
CPU		Intel i7 920, 2.66 GHz, Windows 7 Professional (32 bit)
GPUs	GPU1	NVIDIA Quadro FX 5800, 240 cores, processor clock: 1.3 GHz Memory: (512 bit), 4 GB
	GPU2	NVIDIA GeForce GTX 285, 240 cores, processor clock: 1.476 GHz memory clock: 1.242 GHz (512 bit), 1 GB
	GPU3	NVIDIA GeForce 9800GT, 112 cores, processor clock: 1.5 GHz memory clock: 900 MHz (256 bit), 1 GB
	GPU4	ATI HD 5750, 720 stream processing units, engine clock: 700 MHz memory clock: 1.15 GHz, 1 GB
Programming Architectures		CPU applications implemented using Open MP 2.0, CUDA C/OpenCL driver version 197.13, C++ using Visual Studio 2008 CUDA SDK 3.0 ATI Catalyst Display Driver 10.5, v8.732.0.0 ATI Stream SDK 2.1 OpenCV 2.0

We implemented the algorithms on the GPU using OpenCL and CUDA and parallelized the algorithms on the CPU using OpenMP. OpenMP implementations were implemented using Visual Studio 2008.

34.3.1 Case Study 1: Real-Time Video Background Subtraction

In this case study, we implemented the background subtraction algorithm [1] that was explained in the previous sections on CPUs and GPUs. For the single-kernel case, all three steps of the algorithm are integrated in a single kernel. For the multikernel case, three separate kernels consisting of individual steps — namely, finding moving pixels, updating the background, and updating thresholds — are used. These three kernels are then run successively. In the experiments, we use four different image sizes: 160×120, 320×240, 640×480, and 720×576. The number of threads and block size are set to 64 and 512, respectively.

The main components of the algorithm (corresponding to Equations 34.1 to 34.3) are illustrated in Examples 34.1 to 34.3 with CUDA codes. Threshold pixels (Tn[]) are set to 127, and background pixels (Bn[]) are set to 0 at initialization.

Example 34.1 Finding the moving pixels

```
1  __global__ void FindMovingPixels(unsigned char *In, unsigned char*In_1,
   unsigned char *In_2, unsigned char *Tn, __global char *MovingPixelMap)
2  {
3      long int index = blockDim.x * blockIdx.x + threadIdx.x;
4      if( abs(In[i]-In_1[i]) > Tn[i] && abs(In[i]-In_2[i]) > Tn[i] ) {
5          MovingPixelMap[i] = 255;
6      }
7      else {
8          MovingPixelMap[i] = 0;
9      }
10  }
```

Example 34.2 Updating the background

```
1  __global__ void updateBackgroundImage(unsigned char *In, unsigned char *
   MovingPixelMap, unsigned char *Bn)
2  {
3      long int index = blockDim.x * blockIdx.x + threadIdx.x;
4      if(MovingPixelMap [i] == 0) {
5          Bn[i]=0.92*Bn[i] + 0.08*In[i];
6      }
7  }
```

Example 34.3 Updating the threshold

```
1  __global__ void updateThresholdImage(__global const char *In, __global char
   *Tn, __global char *MovingPixelMap, __global char *Bn)
```

```
2      {
3          long int index = blockDim.x * blockIdx.x + threadIdx.x;
4          int minTh = 20;
5          float th = 0.92* Tn[i] + 0.24 *(In[i] - Bn[i]);
6          if(moving_pixel_map[i]==0) {
7              if(th>minTh) {
8                  Tn[i] = th;
9              }
10             else {
11                 Tn[i] = minTh;
12             }
13         }
14     }
```

Figure 34.3 and Example 34.4 show the memory handling where redundant copies are avoided and three image buffers are used throughout the entire lifetime of the algorithm. With each new image, pointers are swapped, as shown in Example 34.4, and the new image is copied from the host to the GPU memory (the seventh line, which is shown in the light gray boxes in Figure 34.3). In performance calculations where I/O operation is excluded, this line is not taken into account.

Example 34.4 Swapping buffers

```
1    void SwapBuffers()
2    {
3      Unsigned char *tempMem;
4      tempMem = GPU_In_2;
5      GPU_In_1 = GPU_In;
6      GPU_In = tempMem;
7      CopyFromHostToDevice(GPU_In,CPU_In,sizeof(In));
8    }
```

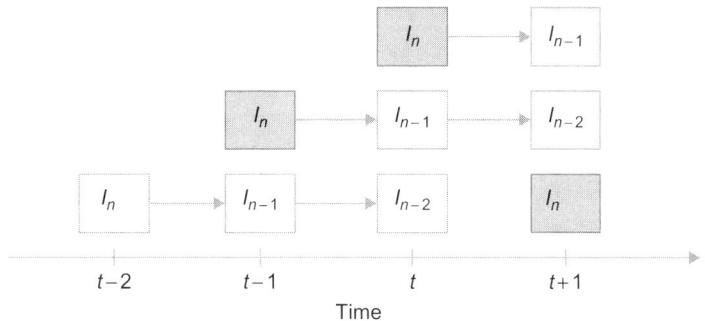

FIGURE 34.3

The relationship between current and former frames. Frames I_n and I_{n-1} at time $t-1$ are copied into I_{n-1} and $I_{n\ 2}$ at time t, respectively. Now I_n value is copied from the host computer's memory.

The images reside in global memory. We did not consider using shared memory because each pixel is accessed only once. Also, coalescing of the image data is not an issue for this algorithm because threads work on subsequent pixels.

In order to measure the performances, we calculate the maximum number of cameras that can be processed in real time. We assume a real-time constraint of 25 frames per second; hence, we calculate the number of images that can be processed in 40 ms to find out the number of cameras supported in real time.

34.3.2 Experiment 1: Single Kernel Only: Performance Gains with and without I/O Operations

In this experiment, we aim to measure how much speedup we get using various image resolutions on different GPU architectures compared with the CPU. We first find the maximum number of cameras supported with different image resolutions on Intel i7 920 architecture using OpenMP to utilize all four cores of this processor. Then, we measure the number of supported cameras on different GPU architectures. The performance gain is calculated by dividing the GPU results to the CPU results.

As can be seen from Figure 34.4, GPU2 (GTX 285) has achieved the highest performance, whereas GPU3 (9800 GT) has performed the lowest. CUDA is approximately two to three times faster than

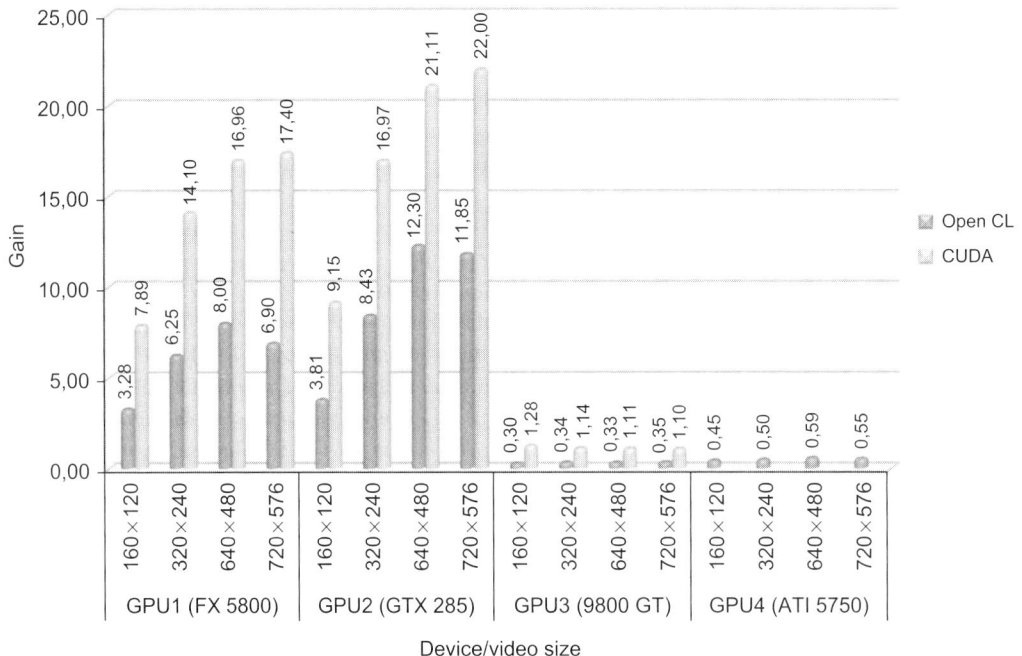

FIGURE 34.4

Performance gain ratio of various GPUs vs. OpenMP CPU (Intel i7 920) implementation (I/O not included).

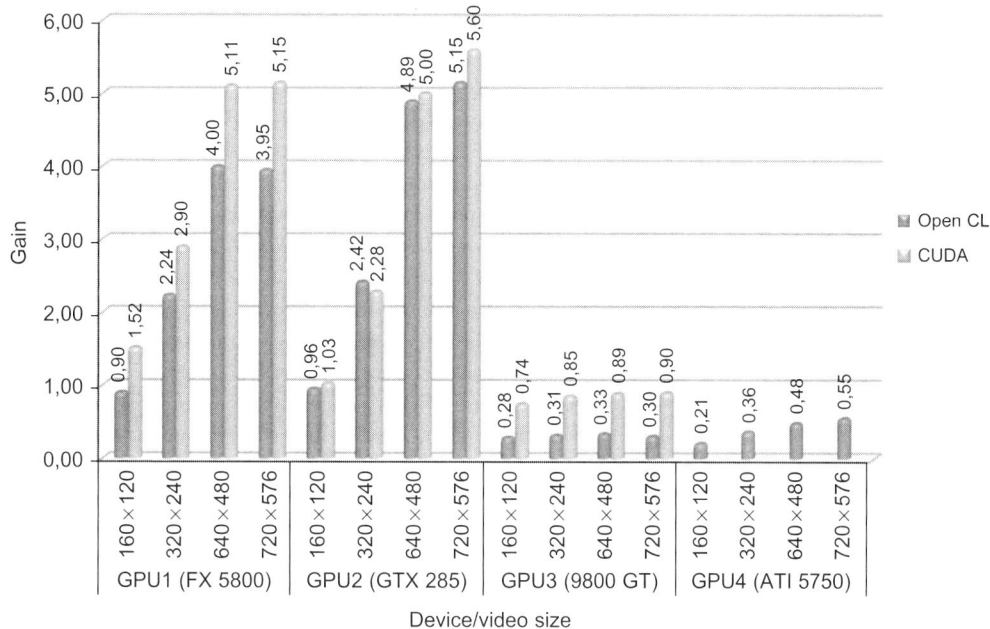

FIGURE 34.5

Performance gain ratio of various GPUs vs. OpenMP CPU (Intel i7 920) implementation (I/O included).

OpenCL for all cases. Figures 34.4 and 34.5 show the performance gain ratios for cases when I/O is not included and when I/O is included, respectively.

For the case where I/O time is included, even though CUDA has still higher performance, the gain decreases, and the performance gets closer to the OpenCL version. This is owing to the I/O operation time dominating over the processing time and making the effect of processing time less significant for the overall results. Although up to a 22x increase could be observed when I/O time is not included, this drops to 5.6x when the I/O time is included. This drop could be remedied to a degree by overlapping the memory copy operations with the processing, as will be described later.

An important parameter is the maximum number of cameras that can be supported for real-time operation. Figures 34.5 and 34.6 show the results for cases when an I/O was not included and when an I/O was included, respectively. These experiments have been conducted with a single-kernel version to get the best performance for all devices used in the experiment. Even though the cases when the I/O was not included give the theoretically highest performance, it is not realistic because the data needs to be copied from the host to the device memory. In order to make a fair comparison, the measurements should include the time spent for data transfer from the host to the device.

As can be observed from Figures 34.6 and 34.7, the I/O operation during which the image data are copied from the host to the device have a significantly adverse effect on performance. Hence, we implemented an asynchronous version in which the memory copy and processing operations are overlapped (i.e., an image is processed while the next image is copied from the host simultaneously). This asynchronous version is shown in Example 34.5. Here, the kernel operation *cuda_process_frames()* and

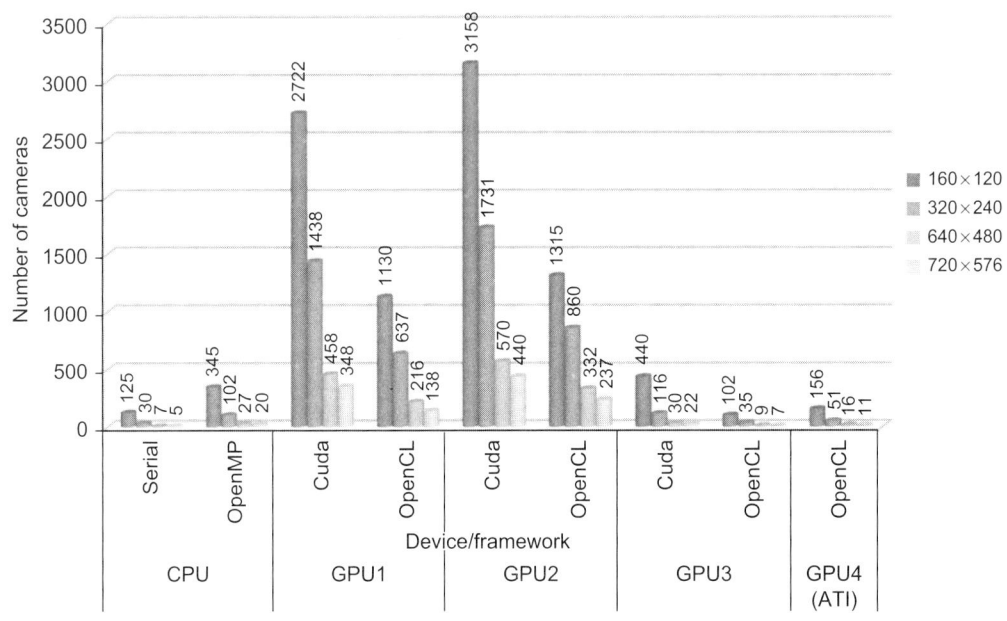

FIGURE 34.6

Maximum number of cameras that can be supported for real-time operation using CPU and GPUs (I/O not included).

memory copy *cudaMemcpyAsync()* are given two different stream parameters *stream1* and *stream2*. Each stream runs asynchronously independent of other streams.

Example 34.5 Asynchronous version

```
1   cudaStream_t stream1, stream2;
2   cudaStreamCreate(&stream1);
3   cudaStreamCreate(&stream2);
4   cuda_process_frames <<<dimGrid, dimBlock, stream1 >>>(In_D, In_1_D, In_2_D, Th_D, Bn_D,
    moving_pixel_map_D, framesize);
5   cudaMemcpyAsync(In_D_async, In, framesize, cudaMemcpyHostToDevice, stream2);
6   cudaThreadSynchronize();
7   char *tmp = In_D;
8   In_D = In_D_async;
9   In_D_async = tmp;
```

The results for this implementation are illustrated in Figures 34.8 and 34.9. It has been observed that up to 9x performance gain could be achieved for 720×576 images compared with the OpenMP CPU implementation. It has to be noted that this gain drops when the image sizes get smaller.

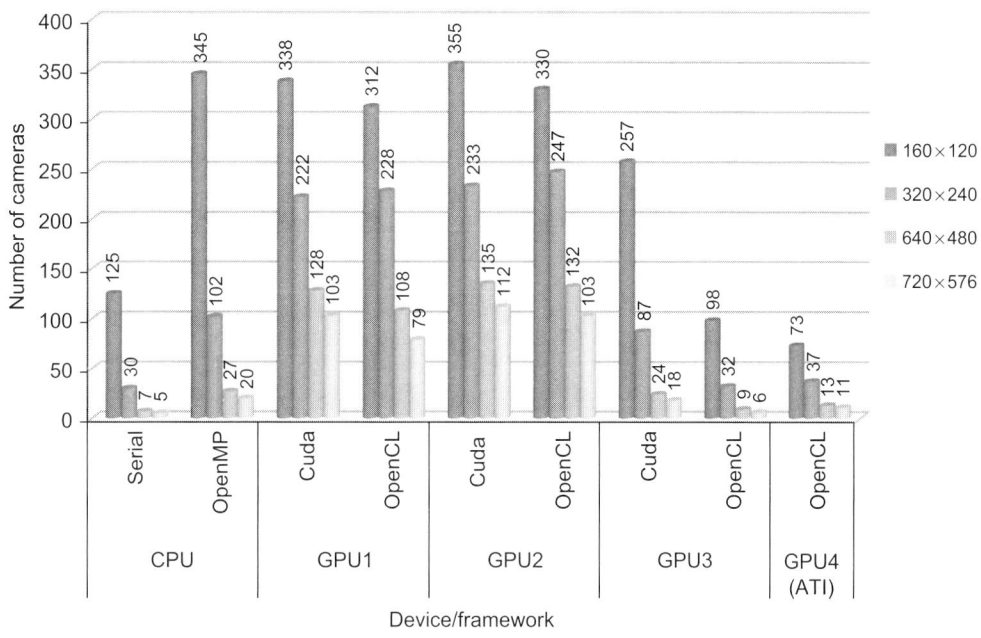

FIGURE 34.7

Maximum number of cameras that can be supported for real-time operation using CPU and GPUs (I/O included).

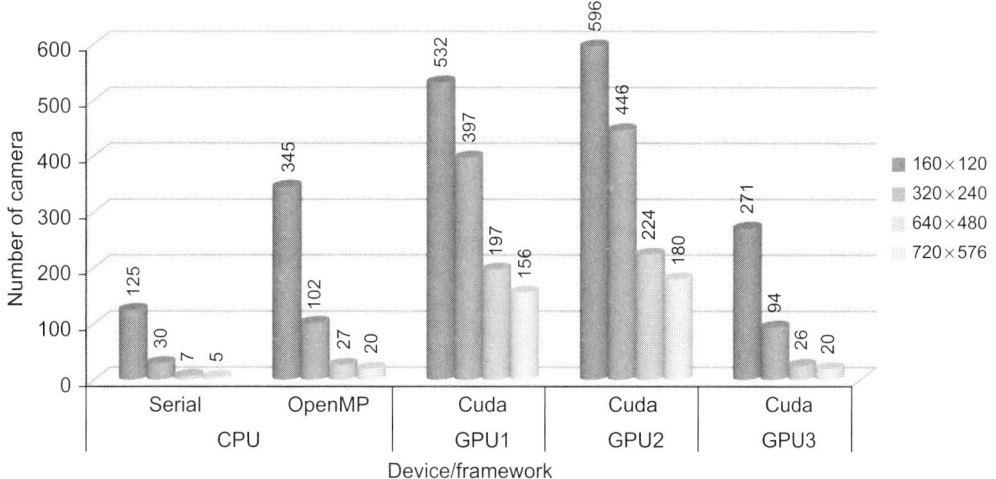

FIGURE 34.8

Maximum number of cameras that can be supported for real-time operation using CPU and GPUs (I/O included, asynchronous operation).

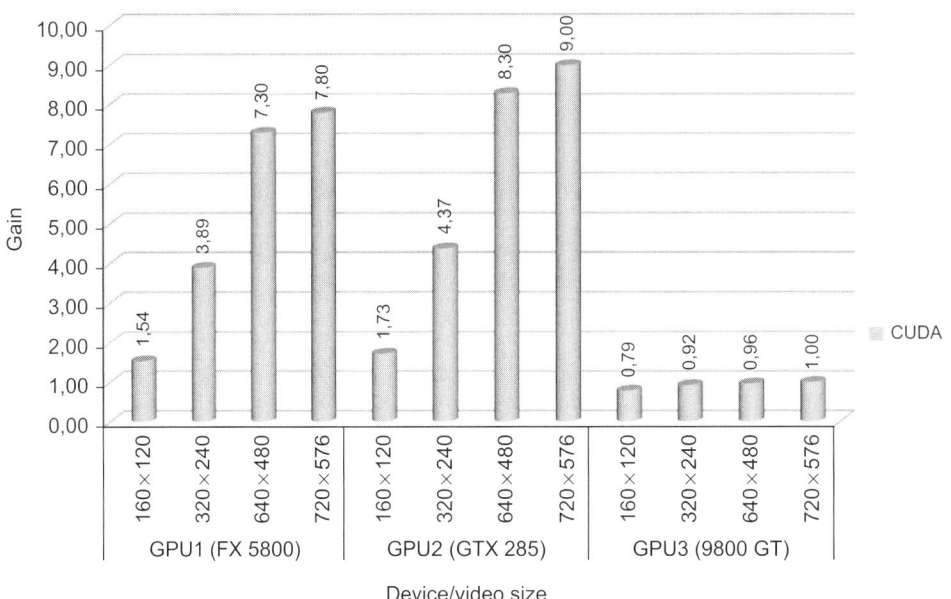

FIGURE 34.9

Performance gain ratio of various GPUs vs. OpenMP CPU (Intel i7 920) implementations (asynchronous).

34.3.3 Experiment 2: Single Kernel vs. Three Kernels: Performance Gains with and without I/O Operations

We have implemented a single-kernel version where all operations are gathered in a single kernel and a multiple-kernel version where the three main steps of the algorithms are implemented in three different kernels that are called subsequently. The total number of cameras that can be supported in this case is shown in Figure 34.10. As illustrated in this figure, increasing the number of kernels brings a significant overhead where the performance decreases as much as 43%. This is due to each kernel accessing the memory independently and hence requiring multiple accesses to the same data. On the other hand, in the single-kernel case, data is fetched once. It is also interesting to note that OpenCL suffers more heavily compared with CUDA. This performance difference is less when I/O time is included.

As a general rule, it is suggested that the number of kernels are kept at a minimum to avoid the performance penalty owing to multiple accesses to the memory and overhead in initiating kernel calls when the runtime of the kernel is relatively short.

34.3.4 Experiment 3: Single Kernel Only: Performance Gains with Serial I/O and Asynchronous I/O

Because the serial I/O case doesn't reflect real performance gains, and serial I/O is not the best method for achieving the best performance, an asynchronous version has been implemented, as illustrated in Example 34.5. The comparison of these versions is shown in Figure 34.11 (serial I/O vs. asynchronous I/O 8-bit reads).

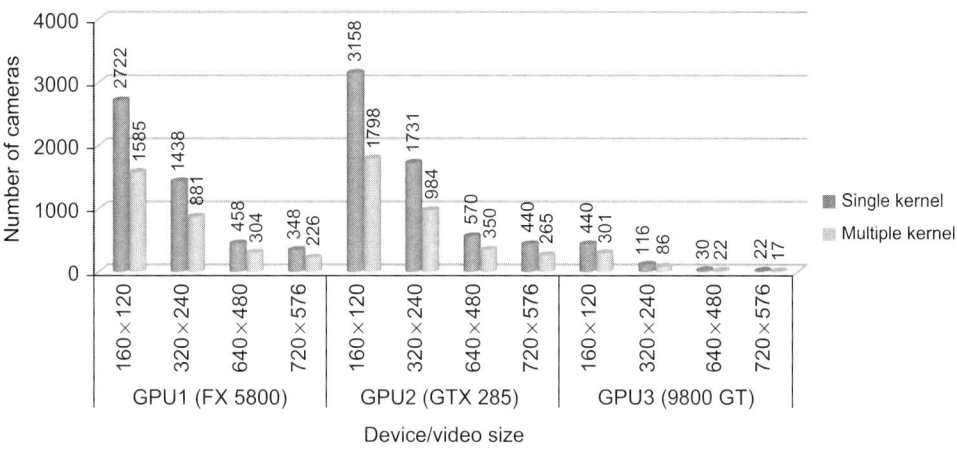

FIGURE 34.10

Comparison of the maximum number of cameras that can be supported for real-time operation using single-kernel and multiple-kernel GPU implementations.

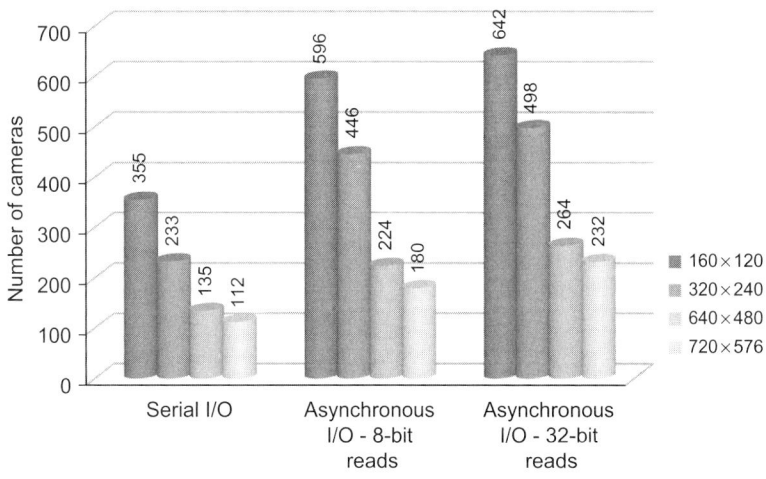

FIGURE 34.11

A comparison of the maximum number of cameras that can be supported for real-time operation using serial I/O, asynchronous I/O- 8-bit reads, and asynchronous I/O- 32-bit reads using GPU2.

The results show that a much higher number of cameras could be processed using asynchronous calls compared with using serial I/O. For example, with asynchronous calls, 68%, 91%, 66%, and 61% more cameras could be processed for 160×120, 320×240, 640×480, and 720×576 resolutions, respectively.

Although the performance gains were significant, they were not the same for all image sizes. For example, the highest gain was observed for images with 320×240 resolution. This is due to a lesser difference between the time spent on I/O operations required for copying images from the host computer's memory to the GPU's global memory and the processing time for background subtraction on GPUs as verified using Visual Profiler. If one of the operations takes more time than the other, latency will occur. For example, if I/O operations take more time than the computations, the kernel will wait for image transfer or vice versa.

As a result, I/O operations are essential parts of the applications, and they cannot be avoided in measuring performances. Asynchronous calls should always be preferred if the application logic is suitable.

34.3.5 Experiment 4: Reading 8 Bits vs. Reading 32 Bits from the Global Memory

In the previous experiments, we used *unsigned char* to access 8-bit image data from the global memory. Memory reads in GT200 are done for half-warps of 16 threads, and reads are done for 32, 64, or 128 bytes. In the previous cases, as each thread reads a byte, 16 bytes are read. For better utilization of global memory bandwidth, these reads have to be 32, 64, or 128 bytes. In the context of the problem in hand, this can be achieved by first reading 4 *chars* per thread and then processing each *char*, which results in $16*4 = 64$ bytes reads for each half-warp.

Example 34.6 demonstrates reading of data in 32-bit chunks processing 4- $\times$ 8-bit elements by each thread. Note that in this case only the current image In and the background Bn are loaded from the global memory, and Bn is written back to the global memory. For a complete implementation all the other images In_1, In_2, Bn, Tn, and MovingPixelMap should also be loaded in a similar fashion.

Example 34.6 Steps for 32-bit access to the global memory

```
1   __global__ void processImage(unsigned int *In, unsigned int *Bn) {
2   long int index = blockIdx.x * N + threadIdx.x * 4;
3   unsigned int packedIn = In[index]; // Read an int from the global memory
4   unsigned int packedBn = Bn[index]; // Read an int from the global memory
5   unsigned int bnout = 0;
6   for(int i=0;i<4;i++) {
7      unsigned int in = (packedIn & 0x0ffu); // read a char from packed data
8      int outdata = ...;// Process the data here, each thread processes 4-chars
9      bnout += ((unsigned int)(outdata)) << (i * 8); // pack the output
10     packedIn >>= 8; packedBn >>= 8;// Move to the next char
11     }
12  Bn[index] = bnout; // Copy the result back to the global memory
13  }
```

The results show that higher-number cameras could be processed using 32-bit reads, as shown in Figure 34.11 (asynchronous I/O 8-bit reads vs. asynchronous I/O 32-bit reads). Compared with 8-bit reads, 8%, 12%, 18%, and 29% more cameras could be processed for $160 \times 120, 320 \times 240, 640 \times 480,$ and 720×576 resolutions, respectively.

34.3.6 **Case Study 2: Cross-Correlation**

In this case study, we implement the Pearson correlation algorithm that was explained in previous sections on CPUs and GPUs. We have implemented two different approaches that differ on the memory types used for the calculation of $\rho_{x,y}$, the Pearson's correlation coefficient. The first approach is using only the global memory of the GPU, whereas the second utilizes the shared memory along with the global memory.

The GPU implementation of the algorithm significantly differs in parallelization from the background subtraction in the way that in this algorithm each worker cannot be assigned to each pixel of the image because the algorithm is composed of summations. The jobs are rather chosen as the individual image frames to be able to fully utilize the GPU. But it should be noted that this yields two constraints:

- A high number of images are needed for high-GPU utilization.
- The images to be compared should be available on the GPU memory.

Keeping the aforementioned constraints in mind, we diagramed the flowchart of the calculation of Pearson's correlation coefficients in Figure 34.12. The flowchart is valid for the both approaches that are utilized.

34.3.7 **Experiment 1: Global Memory Only**

As mentioned before, the first approach that uses only the global memory of the GPU is rather straightforward; the given one-pass version for the PMCC formula is directly implemented. Example kernel

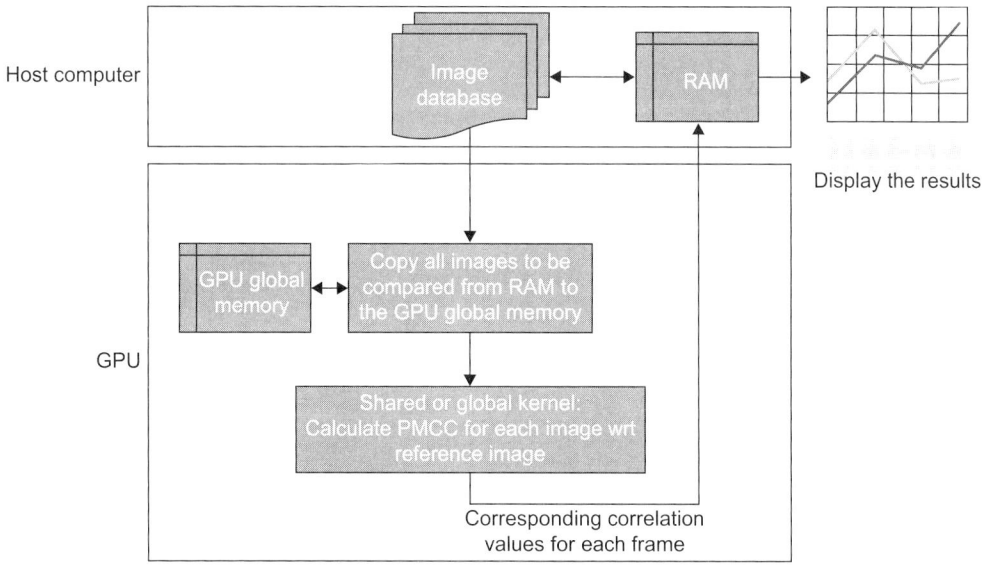

FIGURE 34.12

A flowchart of the calculation of Pearson's correlation coefficients.

code is very similar to the one given for the shared-memory version in Example 34.6; thus, the global memory version is not given to avoid duplication.

Experiments have been carried out for four different image sizes: 160×120, 320×240, 640×480, and 720×576. The approach is implemented using OpenCL and CUDA. The corresponding results for the comparison of 1024 images are shown in Figure 34.13. As seen, once again CUDA performs better than OpenCL at all times. Note that the ATI results are only given for 160×120 and 320×240 image sizes because the OpenCL implementation has a memory allocation limit and 1024 images of 640×480 exceeds this limit.

34.3.8 Experiment 2: Global Memory + Shared Memory with Coalesced Memory Access

One downside of the first approach is that every image to be compared accesses to the same memory space because they are all compared with the same reference image. The same memory that is written in global memory is read over and over again. An approach to overcome this inefficiency is using shared memory spaces that are much faster. The steps of the algorithm can be explained as follows:

1. Occupy a block of shared memory.
2. Calculate how many passes are required to process all the pixels in an image by dividing pixel number by the chosen shared memory block size.

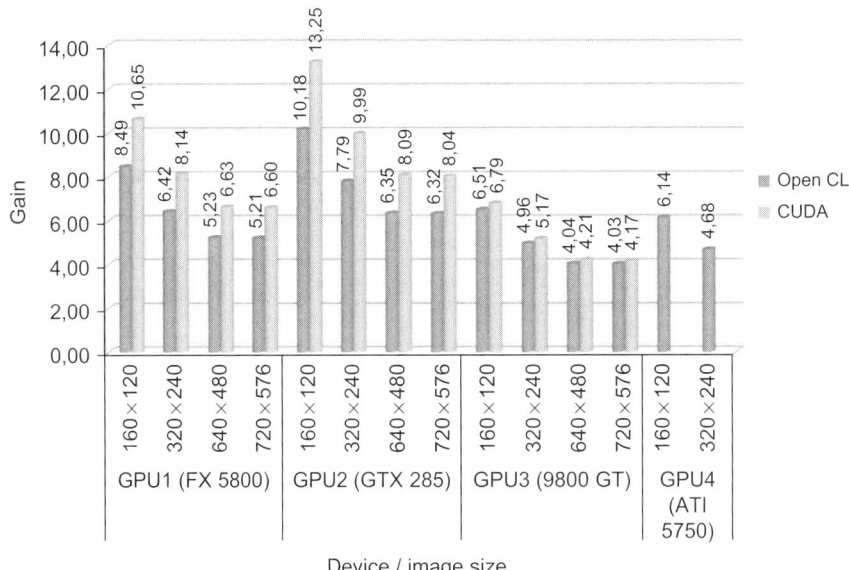

FIGURE 34.13

Performance gain of OpenCL and CUDA implementations over an OpenMP implementation on the CPU.

3. For each pass, first load a block of pixel values of reference image from global to shared memory. Calculate each element ($\sum_{i=0}^{n} x_i y_i$, $\sum_{i=0}^{n} x_i^2 \cdots$) in Equation 34.6 within the block using the values in the shared memory when needed. Note that the elements are added up in each step on top of previously calculated values.

4. At the end of the passes, we end up with calculated elements; thus, just putting the values in Equation 34.3, we obtain the correlation coefficient.

The corresponding CUDA kernel for the explained algorithm is given in Example 34.7.

Example 34.7 PMCC calculation using shared memory — CUDA implementation

```
1  __global__ void cudaPMCC(float *GPUcorrVal, unsigned char *GPUhostImg,
   unsigned char *GPUsampleImg, int ImageWidth, int ImageHeight, int
   GPUimgNumber){
2    int index = blockDim.x * blockIdx.x + threadIdx.x;
3    if(index < GPUimgNumber) {
4      float sum1=0.0f, sqrSum1=0.0f, sum2=0.0f, sqrSum2=0.0f, prodSum=0.0f;
5      __shared__ unsigned char temp[blockDim];
6      int BLOCK_LENGTH = blockDim;
7      int shotCount = (ImageWidth*ImageHeight + BLOCK_LENGTH  -1)/BLOCK_LENGTH;
8      for(int shotIndex = 0; shotIndex < shotCount; shotIndex += 1) {
9        int shotBegin = shotIndex * BLOCK_LENGTH;
10       int shotEnd = min(shotBegin + BLOCK_LENGTH, ImageWidth*ImageHeight);
11       int shotLength = shotEnd - shotBegin;
12       int shotRef = shotBegin + threadIdx.x;
13       temp[threadIdx.x] = (unsigned char)GPUhostImg[shotRef];
14       __syncthreads();
15       for(int i=0;i<shotLength;i++) {
16         float val1 = temp[i];
17         float val2 = GPUsampleImg[(shotBegin+i)*GPUimgNumber + index];
18         sum1    += val1;
19         sqrSum1 += val1*val1;
20         sum2    += val2;
21         sqrSum2 += val2*val2;
22         prodSum += val1*val2;
23       }
24     }
25   GPUcorrVal[index] = 0;
26   float count = ImageWidth*ImageHeight;
27   float variance1 = (count*sqrSum1)-(sum1*sum1);
28   float variance2 = (count*sqrSum2)-(sum2*sum2);
29   float covariance = (count*prodSum)-(sum1*sum2);
30   float energySqr = variance1*variance2;
31   if(energySqr > 0)
32   GPUcorrVal[index] = covariance/sqrt(energySqr);
33   }
34 }
```

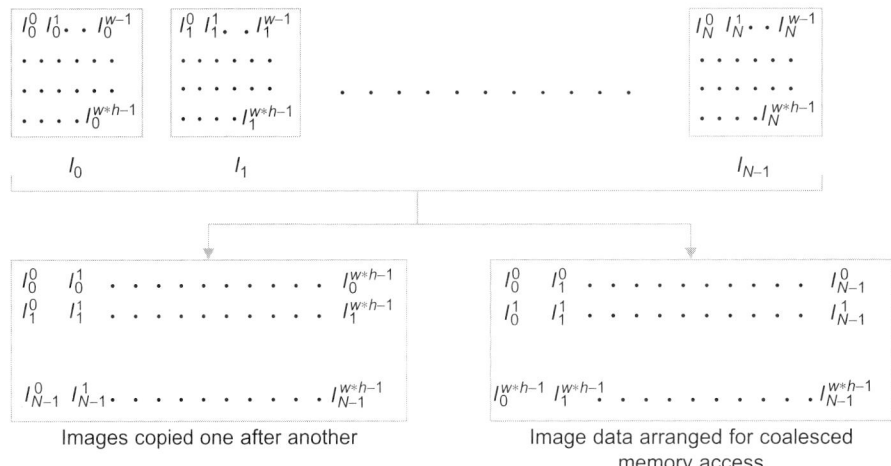

N is the total number of images where nth image is shown with
I_n, w and h are the image width and height, respectively.

FIGURE 34.14

Memory arrangement for coalesced memory access.

One more important issue that is considered in our study is the memory access. The images to be processed are arranged for coalesced memory access for optimal performance. The details of the memory arrangement are given in Figure 34.14.

Where N is the total number of images where nth image is shown with I_n, w and h are the image width and height, respectively.

The performance gains obtained by utilizing shared memory (vs. first approach) and coalesced access (vs. first approach) for images of size 320×240 are given in Figure 34.15. The tests are conducted for a comparison of 1024 images, as done in the first approach's experiment. It is observed that coalesced memory arrangement boosts the performance up to 4.34 times. Further performance improvements could be obtained by using shared memory in addition to using this approach.

34.3.9 Experiment 3: Effect of Increasing the Number of Images

This experiment's goal is to see the effect of the number of images on the performance gain. Four different image numbers are used for experiments: 1024, 2048, 4096, and 8192. Figure 34.16 shows the performance gains obtained for images of size 160×120 for both OpenCL and CUDA implementations using both shared-memory and coalesced-memory arrangements compared with OpenMP CPU implementation.

As seen from Figure 34.16, with the increasing number of images, the performance gain increases for GPUs with a high number of multicores because utilization increases for those GPUs. As a result of efficiency, comparison of 8192 images of size 320×240 was performed 89.84 times faster than the OpenMP CPU implementation.

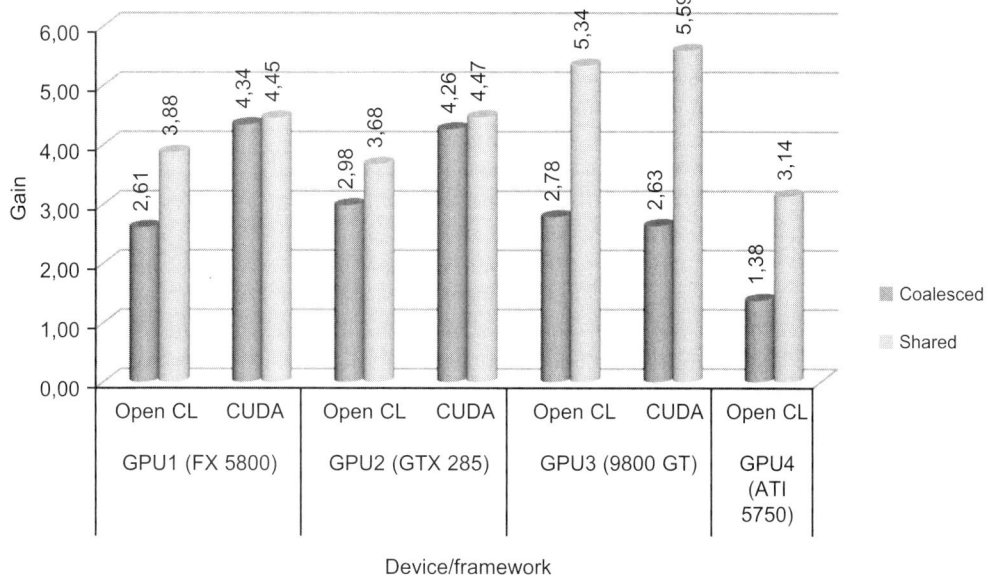

FIGURE 34.15

Performance gain of using shared-memory and coalesced-memory arrangements for 320×240 image sizes.

34.4 FINAL EVALUATION

In this chapter, we have compared the performance of background subtraction and correlation algorithms on the GPU using CUDA and OpenCL, and on the CPU by using OpenMP. We then discussed the results. We showed that up to 11.6x and 89.8x increases in performance could be achieved for these algorithms, respectively, compared with their CPU implementations. To get the most out of GPU-based computing, several issues need to be taken into consideration during the implementation of a parallelizable image and video processing applications on the GPU.

Because the memory I/O operations affect the performance of the application significantly, they have to be optimized, and data decomposition should be carried out with caution. Working with larger images (720×576) rather than smaller images (160×120) results in better performance gain. Asynchronous memory copying should be implemented wherever possible to overlap processing and data transfer. Algorithms need to be designed to prevent redundant memory copy operations. In certain video processing applications, preceding video frames might be required. So if one manages the image buffer using pointer swaps, rather than making copy operations, redundancy could be avoided.

Besides implementing efficient memory access between the CPU and GPU memories, we found that efficient GPU memory access is also vital for performance. Coalesced-memory access has to be preferred, and one should arrange the data for coalesced access whenever possible. For example, for the correlation algorithm, the image database could be arranged for coalesced access and retained as such

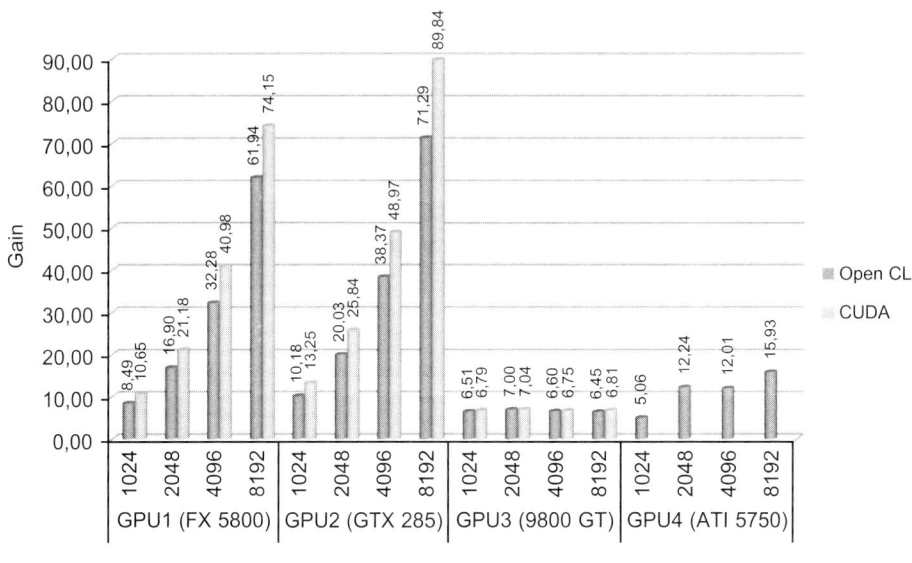

FIGURE 34.16

Performance gain for increasing image number over OpenMP implementation on the CPU for 160×120 image sizes.

permanently in the hard drive. One should employ 32-, 64-, or 128-byte reads per half-warp for better utilization of global memory bandwidth. This has been demonstrated for the background subtraction case, where 8-bit grayscale images are read/write as packed 32-bit data, resulting in 64-byte reads for half-warps. Shared-memory usage has to be preferred if the data is used more than once, and when one is using shared memory, bank conflicts should be avoided by arranging the access pattern of the threads properly.

The number of kernels affects the performance of the algorithm. The higher the number of kernels, the higher the number of required global memory accesses, degrading the overall performance. If multiple kernels require access to the same data, this code could be merged together in a single kernel to reduce the global memory accesses.

Regarding the API choice, whether it will be CUDA or OpenCL depends on the user's preferences. Although CUDA has outperformed OpenCL in all our experiments, and it has more comprehensive documentation and resources than OpenCL at present, it may change over time because OpenCL is a more recent programming API. Besides, OpenCL could be more appropriate for hybrid CPU/GPU applications because it supports both platforms. To provide cross-platform compatibility, OpenCL codes are built at runtime for the specific platform. On the other hand, CUDA code is built once, and the binary code is used similar to executables on the PC. This results in slow start-up times for the OpenCL codes. If the same code needs to be run on the same platform repeatedly, then the produced OpenCL binary needs to be stored on a disk to increase the start-up time. Updates are frequently released for both APIs, and it is recommended that the latest versions are used for the best performance.

References

[1] R. Collins, A. Lipton, T. Kanade, H. Fujiyoshi, D. Duggins, Y. Tsin et al., A system for video surveillance and monitoring: VSAM final report, technical report CMU-RI-TR-00-12, Robotics Institute, Carnegie Mellon University, 2000.

[2] i-LIDS dataset for AVSS 2007. http://www.elec.qmul.ac.uk/staffinfo/andrea/avss2007_d.html, 2010 (accessed 04.04.10).

Connected Component Labeling in CUDA

35

Ondřej Šťava, Bedřich Beneš

Connected component labeling (CCL) is a task of detecting connected regions in input data, and it finds its applications in pattern recognition, computer vision, and image processing. We present a new algorithm for connected component labeling in 2-D images implemented in CUDA. We first provide a brief overview of the CCL problem together with existing CPU-oriented algorithms. The rest of the chapter is dedicated to a description of our CUDA CCL method.

35.1 INTRODUCTION

The goal of a CCL algorithm is to find a unique label for every set of connected elements in input data. In other words, CCL is used to divide input elements, for example, pixels of a raster image, into groups where all elements from a single group represent a connected object. CCL can be thought of as topological clustering based on connectivity. CCL is often confused with segmentation, which is a closely related algorithm, but its purpose is different. Segmentation is used to detect all elements that describe some object or a feature of interest, whereas CCL is used to identify which of these elements belong to a single *connected* object. An example is a face recognition, where we can first use segmentation to detect all pixels that correspond to a human eye and then we can apply CCL to find a single group of pixels for every eye in the image. Another example of CCL is in Figure 35.1.

The CCL problem is usually solved on the CPU using sequential algorithms [1], but the speed of these algorithms is often not sufficient for real-time applications. Certain CCL algorithms can be parallelized, but as has been pointed out in [2], the sequential algorithms often outperform the parallel ones in real applications.

We propose a new parallel algorithm for CCL of 2-D data implemented in CUDA. The input is a 2-D grid of values where each value represents a unique segment in the input data. The output is a new 2-D array where all connected elements with the same segment value share the same label. Our implementation detects connected components with Moore neighborhood (8-degree connectivity) [3], and the method can be easily extended for N-dimensional grids and different connectivity conditions.

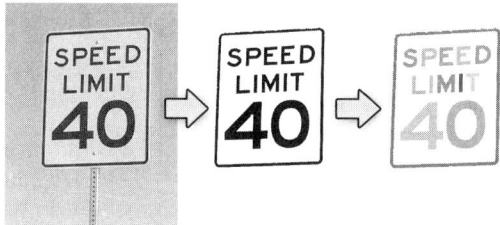

FIGURE 35.1

Connected component labeling as a part of a text recognition pipeline. The input image (left) is segmented, and all pixels that might represent a text are retrieved (middle). Connected component labeling is then used to separate pixels into groups that represent individual characters (right). Each detected group is depicted with a different color.

35.2 CORE ALGORITHM

The CCL problem has been a research topic for a long time, and algorithms that provide a solution in linear time have been presented [1]. Most of these CPU-oriented algorithms are sequential in nature, and they usually require multiple passes over the input data. The most commonly used algorithms use two passes where the first pass detects and stores equivalences between all connected neighboring elements, and the second pass analyzes the equivalences and assigns labels to individual elements. The equivalences between elements are usually stored in a disjoint set forest data structure that contains several equivalence trees where each tree represents a single connected component (see Figure 35.2). In these two pass algorithms, it is necessary to find an equivalence tree for every connected component of the input data in the first pass, as in the second pass the equivalence trees are used to assign labels to the input elements. To compute all equivalence trees in one pass, it is necessary to traverse the data in a fixed order and to gradually update the equivalence trees for each processed element. The most widely used method that is used to for this task is the *union-find* algorithm that ensures that the equivalence trees are always correct for all processed elements [1].

A pseudo code for a simplified version of a two-pass *union-find* CCL algorithm for 2-D raster data is described in Figure 35.3. Here, the equivalence trees are stored in a 2-D array with the same dimensions as the input data. All elements are identified by their 1-D address so that the root of an equivalence tree is the element with the entry in the equivalence array equal to the address of the element itself. The elements are processed in a scan-like fashion, and every analyzed element updates the equivalence array from its connections with other already-processed neighboring elements using the *Union* function (see Figure 35.4). In the second pass, all equivalence trees are flattened using the *FindRoot* function. After the flattening, each element is equivalent directly to the root of the tree (see Figure 35.2c) and the value of the root (address of the root element) is used as the label for the detected connected component. The labels generated by this algorithm are not consecutive because they are based on the address of the root element, but they can be easily relabeled.

35.2.1 Parallel Union Find CCL Algorithm

The algorithm from Figure 35.3 can be implemented on many-core devices such as GPUs. Hawick *et al.* [2] implemented the union-find CCL algorithm using three CUDA kernels. They demonstrated that

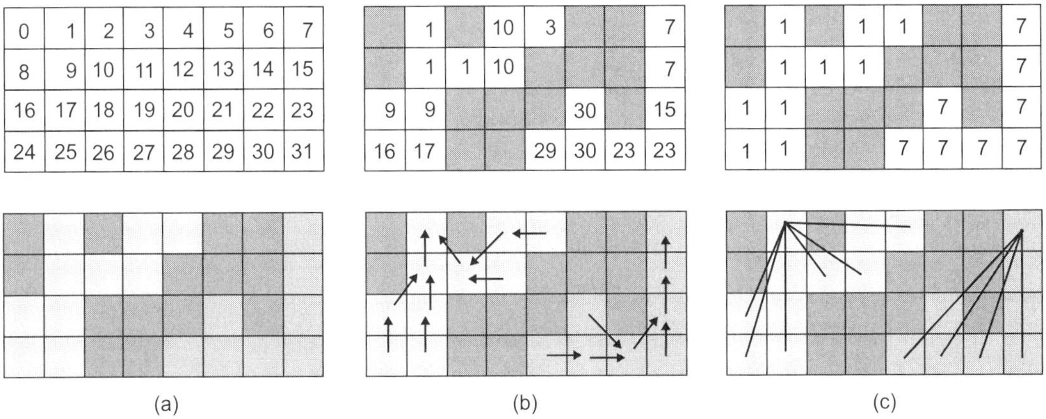

FIGURE 35.2

Equivalence trees representing two connected components. All equivalences are stored in a 2-D array where every element is identified by its address in the array (a). All elements from one equivalence tree represent a single connected component (b). To get the final labels of the components, the equivalence trees are simply flattened (c).

PSEUDO CODE FOR A TWO PASS UNION–FIND CCL ALGORITHM

```
INPUT:     elements     //2D array of input data
           labels       //2D array used to store equivalencies and the final labels
OUTPUT:    labels

// Pass 1
for y in 0:dimY
    for x in 0:dimX
        labels[x][y] <- to1DAddress(x,y);     //make the element the root of an equivalence tree
        for neighbor in 'all already processed neighboring elements of element[x][y]'
            if(elements[x][y] is connected to neighbor) Union(labels, to1DAddress(x,y), to1DAddress(neighborAddress));

// Pass 2
for y in 0:dimY
for x in 0:dimX
    labels[x][y] <- FindRoot(labels, to1DAddress(x,y));
return labels;
```

FIGURE 35.3

Pseudo code for a two pass union-find CCL algorithm.

their implementation provides a significant performance gain over an optimized CPU version for most of the tested data. The main drawback of the parallel two-pass CCL algorithms is that it is impossible to guarantee that a single equivalence tree is constructed for a single connected component of the input data in the first pass of the algorithm. The problem is that the equivalences of all elements are processed in parallel, and therefore, it is difficult to merge the new equivalences with the results from previously

```
//PSEUDO CODE: FUNCTIONS FINDROOT and UNION
FindRoot(equivalenceArray, elementAddress)
    while(equivalenceArray[elementAddress] != elementAddress)
        elementAddress <- equivalenceArray[elementAddress];
    return elementAddress;

Union(equivalenceArray, elementAddress0, elementAddress1)
    root0 <- FindRoot(equivalenceArray, elementAddress0);
    root1 <- FindRoot(equivalenceArray, elementAddress1);
    //connect an equivalence tree with a higher label to the tree with a lower label
    if(root0 < root1) equivalenceArray[root1] <- root0;
    if(root1 < root0) equivalenceArray[root0] <- root1;
```

FIGURE 35.4

Pseudo code for functions *FindRoot* and *Union*.

processed elements using the *Union* function. In many cases, the first pass of the algorithm will generate multiple disjoint equivalence trees for a single connected component of the input data, and to merge the trees into a single one, it is necessary to iterate several times. The exact number of the iterations is unknown because it depends on the structure of the connected components in the input data. Therefore, it is necessary to check after each iteration whether all connected elements have the correct labels. In the case of a CUDA algorithm, it is necessary to perform the check on the GPU and to upload the result back to the host, which can then execute another iteration of the kernels. Also, when the union-find CCL algorithm is directly mapped to CUDA, it is problematic to take advantage of the shared memory on the GPU because one kernel is used to compute equivalencies between all input data elements, and the resulting equivalence trees are too large for the shared memory of existing GPUs.

35.3 CUDA ALGORITHM AND IMPLEMENTATION

We present a new version the two-pass union-find algorithm where all iterations are implemented inside the kernels. The number of the executed kernels is fixed for a given dimension of the input data, and no synchronization between the host and device is needed. Our method also takes advantage of shared memory on the GPU as we divide the input data into smaller tiles where the CCL problem is solved locally. The tiles are then recursively merged using a treelike hierarchical merging scheme as illustrated in Figure 35.5. At each level of the merging scheme, we use border regions of neighboring tiles to merge the local solution of the CCL problem from lower levels.

All of the steps of our algorithm are implemented entirely on the GPU in four different kernels (see Figure 35.6). Kernel 1 solves the CCL problem for small tiles of the input data in shared memory. Then, the merging scheme is recursively applied on the border regions between the tiles. The merging scheme uses two different kernels. One merges together equivalence trees from a set of tiles, and the second one updates labels on border regions of the data tiles before each iteration of the merging scheme. The merging scheme is used only to merge equivalence trees from connected tiles; therefore, when all tiles on all levels are merged, it is necessary to find the final solution of the CCL problem by updating labels

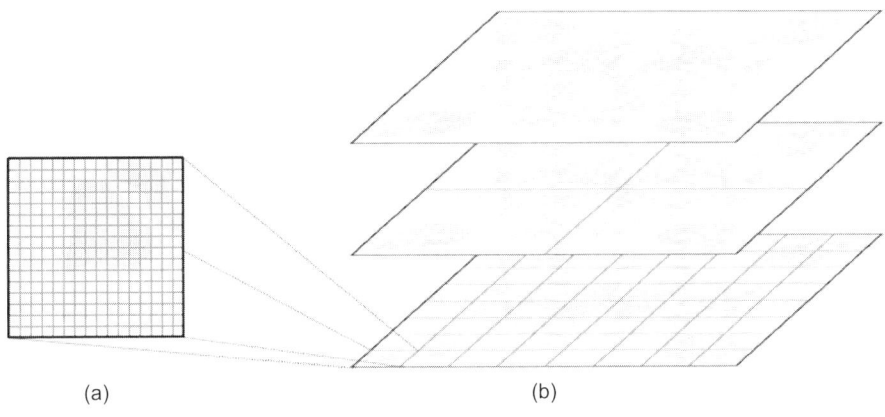

(a)   (b)

FIGURE 35.5

Two main steps of our algorithm. First, the CCL problem is solved locally for a small sub-set of input data in shared memory (a). The global solution is then computed by a recursive merging of the local solutions (b).

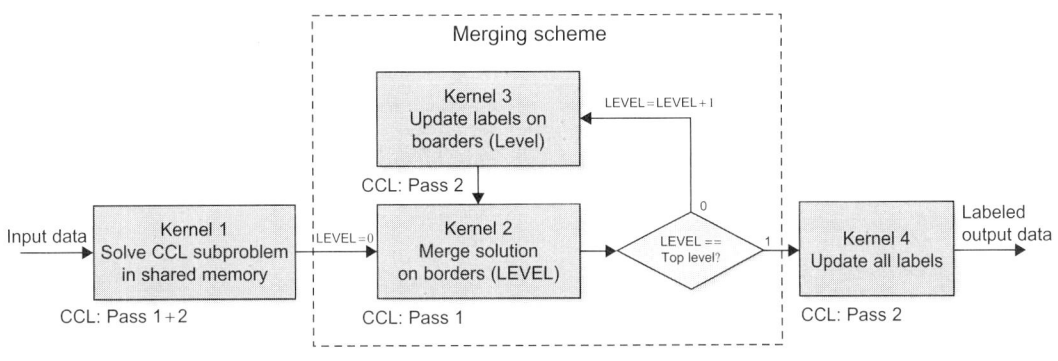

FIGURE 35.6

A flowchart of our CUDA CCL algorithm.

on all data elements. This process is done in the last kernel. Both the first kernel and the final kernel are called only once, while the merging scheme kernels are called for each level of the merging scheme. The number of levels is determined by the dimensions of the input data; therefore, it does not depend on the structure of the connected components in the analyzed data. This is a great advantage of our algorithm because it reduces the number of executed kernels, and it also eliminates all data transfer from the device to the host. Although the number of kernel calls is fixed for given dimensions of input data, it is still necessary to execute a different number of iterations of our CCL solver even if they have the same dimensions. However, all these iterations are performed directly inside the kernels 1 and 2, and they are effectively hidden from the host. The kernels are described in detail in the next sections.

35.3.1 **Implementation Remarks**

The CCL algorithm is written in CUDA 3.0 and C++, and all source code is available in an attached demo application. The CCL algorithm requires a GPU with computing capability 1.3 or higher because the kernels use atomic operations both on global and shared memory. The demo application also requires CUDA Toolkit 3.0 because it exploits the OpenGL interoperability functions introduced in this release.

35.3.2 **Input and Output**

The connectivity criterion must be first explicitly defined by the user, and it is one of the parameters of our algorithm. For example, we can say that two elements of an RGB image are connected if the difference between their luminance is below a given threshold value. Another way to define the connectivity criterion is to apply segmentation [5, 6] on the input data. In segmented data, two neighboring elements are connected only when they share the same segment value, and this is also the approach we chose in our implementation. The input data are stored in a 2-D array of 8-bit unsigned integers that contain the segment values for all elements with the exception of the segment value 0 that denotes the background and is ignored by our CCL algorithm.

The connected components are then detected for every nonbackground element using segment values from the Moore neighborhood. All connected components are represented by labels that are stored in a 32-bit integer 2-D array that has the same dimension as the input data. The same array stores the equivalence trees as described in Section 35.2.

35.3.3 **CCL in Shared Memory**

Kernel 1 finds first the local solution of the CCL problem for a small tile of the input data in the shared memory of the GPU (see the pseudo code for the kernel in Figure 35.8). Each tile is solved by one CUDA thread block, and each thread corresponds to a single element in the given tile. The local solution is obtained from a modified version of the two-pass CCL solver that has been described in Figure 35.3. The kernel executes a new iteration of the modified CCL algorithm whenever any two neighboring connected elements have a different label. Each iteration performs both passes of the algorithm, but the first pass is divided into two separate steps. First, each thread detects the lowest label from all neighboring elements. If the label from neighboring elements is lower than the label of the processed element (two connected elements belong to different equivalence trees), then we merge these equivalence trees using the *atomicMin* function. The atomic operation is necessary because the same equivalence tree could be updated by multiple threads at the same time. This CCL algorithm is demonstrated in a simple example in Figure 35.7. The final labels are related to the address space of the shared memory because it provides an easier addressing pattern for the memory access. Therefore, after all iterations complete, it is necessary to transfer the labels into the global address space and then store them in the global device memory.

35.3.4 **Merging Scheme**

To compute a global solution of the CCL problem, it is necessary to merge the local solutions from the previous step. We can use the connectivity between all border elements of the two tiles to merge the equivalence trees of the connected components in respective tiles. Because we want a parallel solution of the problem, it is usually necessary to perform several iterations of this merging operation

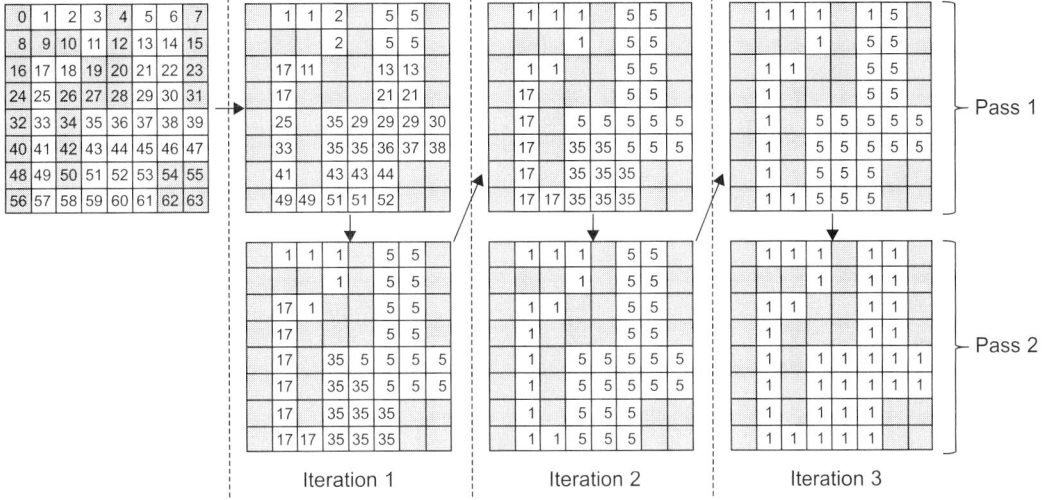

FIGURE 35.7

Application of the modified CCL algorithm for kernel 1 on a simple example.

because we cannot guarantee that all equivalence trees are merged after a single merge operation. This iterative mechanism needs synchronization between individual threads of a single thread block, but in general, it is not feasible to process all border elements in one thread block because there are neither enough threads, nor enough shared memory to store all the required data. Our solution of this problem is implemented in kernel 2 and illustrated in Figure 35.9. A given set of tiles is merged in one 3-D thread block where the x and y dimensions of the block are used to index individual tiles while the z dimension contains individual threads that are used to compare and merge equivalence trees on a given tile boundary using the *Union* function. Because the number of threads associated to each tile is not large enough to process all boundary elements of a given tile, all threads actually process multiple boundary elements sequentially. In the first stage, the threads process elements on both sides of the bottom horizontal boundary, and in the second stage, they process both sides of the right vertical boundary. If the boundary between two tiles is too long, the thread processes one boundary sequentially before proceeding to the next one. As we can see in Figure 35.9, the corner elements between four tiles are processed by multiple threads, but the number of these redundant threads is low and does not require special treatment.

One execution of kernel 2 can merge only a limited number of tiles together, so it is necessary to call the kernel multiple times where each iteration of the kernel takes the merged tiles from previous steps as an input. The number of tiles that are merged in each level can vary. We found out that merging 4×4 tiles produces good results. If we merge more tiles on one level, then the number of threads associated with each tile is too small, and the whole process becomes more sequential. On the other hand, if we merge fewer tiles, then the number of levels of the merging scheme increases — a result that is also not desirable. Pseudo code for kernel 2 is given in Figure 35.10. Connected component (equivalence trees) from neighboring tiles are merged using the *Union* function. The implementation of the *Union* functions follows the description from Figure 35.4 in Section 35.2. However, multiple threads might try to merge two equivalence trees at the same time, and that is why the merging operation is implemented using the

PSEUDO CODE OF KERNEL 1

```
INPUT:              dSegData              //2D array of segmented input data
OUTPUT:             dLabelsData           //2D array of labels (equivalence array)

shared sSegs[];                           //shared memory used to store the segments
shared sLabels[];                         //shared memory that is used to compute the local solution
localIndex <- localAddress(threadIdx);    //local address of the element in the shared memory
sSegs[localIndex] <- loadSegDataToSharedMem(dSegData, threadIdx.x, threadIdx.y);
sSegs[borders] <- setBordersAroundSubBlockToZero();
shared sChanged[1];
syncThreads();
label <- localIndex;
while(1) {
    //Pass 1 of the CCL algorithm
    sLabels[localIndex] <- label;
    if(threadIdx == (0,0)) sChanged[0] <- 0;
    syncThreads();
    newLabel <- label;
    //find the minimal label from the neighboring elements
    for(allNeighbors)
        ifl(sSegs[localIndex] == sSegs[neighIndex]) newLabel <- min(newLabel, sLabels[neighIndex]);
    syncThreads();
    //If the new label is smaller than the old one merge the equivalence trees
    if(newLabel < labal) {
        atomicMin(sLabels+label, newLabel);
        sChanged[0] <- 1
    }
    syncThreads();
    if(sChanged[0] == 1) break;           //the local solution has been found, exit the loop
    //Pass 2 of the CCL algorithm
    label <- findRoot(sLabels, label);
    syncThreads();
}
//store the result to the device memory
globalIndex <- globalAddress(blockIdx, threadIdx)
dLabalsData[globalIndex] <- transferAddressToGlobalSpace(label);
```

FIGURE 35.8

Pseudo code of kernel 1.

CUDA *atomicMin* function. When two connected elements are located in different equivalence trees (trees that have a different root label), we set the shared variable *sChanged* to 1, which indicates that another iteration of the algorithm is necessary.

It is important to mention that the output from kernel 2 is not a complete solution of the CCL problem for the given tiles because it only merges different equivalence trees together, but the labels on nonroot elements remain unchanged. However, it is guaranteed that each equivalence tree in the merged tile represents the largest possible connected component. The advantage of this approach is that the labels are updated only on a relatively small number of elements, and the amount of data written to global memory is usually small. The drawback is that as we merge more and more tiles together, the depth of equivalence trees on the border elements of the merged tiles may increase significantly, making

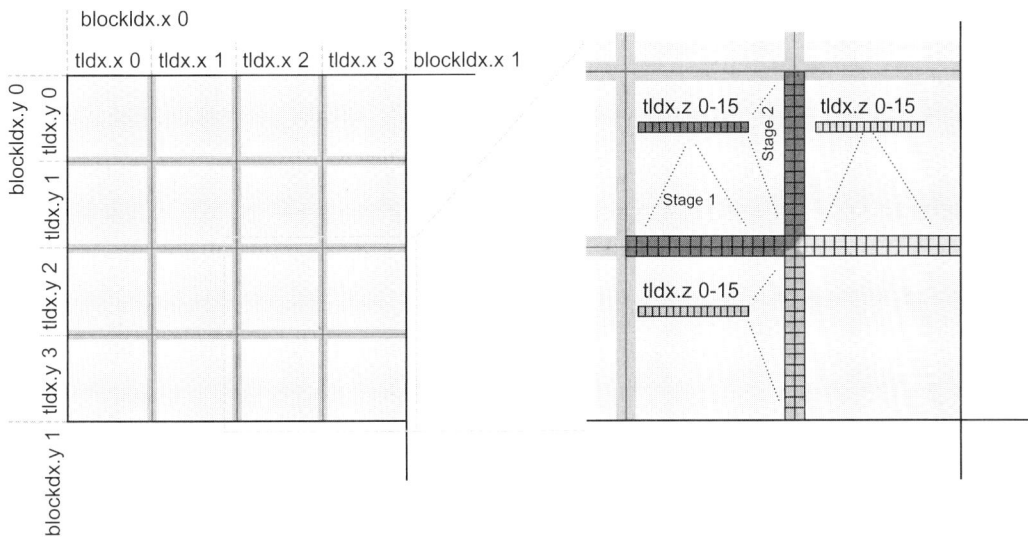

FIGURE 35.9

Left: One CUDA thread block is used to merge 16 tiles that contain local solutions to the CCL problem from previous steps of our algorithm. Right: Threads in the CUDA block are used multiple times to process different boundaries of the merged tiles.

the *Union* operation slower. To solve this problem we use kernel 3 to flatten the equivalence trees on border elements between tiles using the *FindRoot* operation (see Figure 35.4). The kernel is always executed between two consecutive kernel 2 calls as illustrated in Figure 35.6. Although our method would work even without kernel 3, the observed performance gain from using it is around 15–20%.

35.3.5 Final Update

When all tiles are merged, we can compute the global solution of the CCL problem. The labels in the final merged tile represent a disjoint equivalence forest where it is guaranteed that every tree corresponds to the largest possible connected component. To obtain the final solution, we flatten each equivalence tree using the *FindRoot* function that is called from kernel 4 for every element of the input data.

35.4 FINAL EVALUATION AND RESULTS

To evaluate the performance of our method, we measured throughput of our implementation and speedup over other CCL algorithms. Namely, we implemented an optimized CPU CCL algorithm described by Wu *et al.* in [1] and a CUDA-oriented algorithm by Hawick *et al.* in [2]. Because the input data were represented by 8-bit integers and output data by 32-bit integers, we decided to measure the throughput in megapixels per second where each pixel represented a single element in the input dataset. All measurements were performed on the same computer with 64-bit Windows 7, 3 GHz Intel

PSEUDO CODE OF KERNEL 2
INPUT: dSegData   //2D array of segmented input data
                    dLabelsData   //2D array of labels
                    dSubBlockDIm   //dimensions of the merged tiles
OUTPUT: dLabelsData   //2D array of labels

```
subBlockId <− threadIdx + blockIdx * blockDim;  //id (x,y) of the merged tile
repetitions <− subBlockDIm / blockDIm/z;        //how many times are the thread reused for the given subblock?
shared sChanged[1];                             //shared memory used to check whether the solution is final or not
while(1) {
        if(threadIdx == (0,0,0)) sChanged[0] <− 0;
        syncThreads();
        //process the bottomhorizontal border
        for(i in 0:repetitions) {
                x <− subBlockId.x * subBlockDim + threadIdx.z + i* blockDim.z;
                y <− (subBlockId.y+1) * subBlockDim − 1;

                if(!leftBorder) Union(dLabelsData, dSegData, globalAddr(x,y), globalAddr(x−1, y+1), sChanged)
                Union(dLabelsData, dSegData, globalAddr(x,y), globalAddr(x, y+1), sChanged)
                if(!rightBorder) Union(dLabelsData, dSegData, globalAddr(x,y), globalAddr(x+1, y+1), sChanged)
        }
        //process the right vertical border
        for(i in 0:repetitions) {
                x <− (subBlockId.x+1) * subBlockDim − 1;
                y <− subBlockId.y * subBlockDim + threadIdx.z + i* blockDim.z;
                if(!topBorder) Union(dLabelsData, dSegData, globalAddr(x,y), globalAddr(x+1, y−1), sChanged)
                Union(dLabelsData, dSegData, globalAddr(x,y), globalAddr(x+1, y), sChanged)
                if(!bottomBorder) Union(dLabelsData, dSegData, globalAddr(x,y), globalAddr(x+1, y+1), sChanged)
        }
        syncThreads();
        if(sChanged[0] == 0) break; //no changes −> the tiles are merged
        syncThreads();
}
```

FIGURE 35.10

Pseudo code of kernel 2.

Core 2 Duo CPU, and NVIDIA GeForce GTX 480 GPU. We didn't measure transfers of the input and output data between the host and the device as these operations are application dependent.

The complexity of a CCL problem depends on the structure of the connected components in the input data and the performance of each method can differ dramatically for different datasets. Hence, to perform an unbiased analysis, CCL algorithms should be tested on a variety of different input cases. There is no standardized set of input data designed for the performance testing, and therefore, we created several test cases that, in our opinion, represented common real-world scenarios. Results of all of our measurements are summarized in Figure 35.11.

First, we applied all tested algorithms in real-world settings in our application for defect detection in 3-D CT data of a wooden log (Figure 35.11a). The algorithm was used to detect potential defect regions in hundreds of main-axis parallel 2-D slices with resolution of 512×512 pixels. The second example (Figure 35.11b) is a scene with a small number of large objects that filled most of the analyzed data

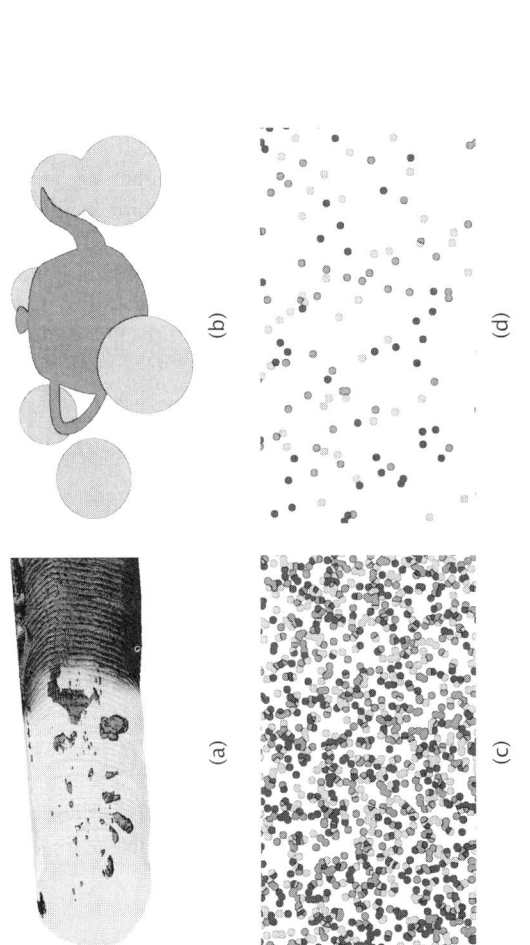

(a)

(b)

(c)

(d)

Method/Resolution	Example (a)	Example (b)			Example (c)			Example (d)		
Performance [MPixels/s]										
	512^2	1024^2	2048^2	4096^2	1024^2	2048^2	4096^2	1024^2	2048^2	4096^2
CPU – Wu et al. [2]	76	111	112	111	73	73	74	121	124	123
CUDA1 – Hawick et al. [1]	328	403	482	508	233	272	279	233	272	279
CUDA2 – Our method	1542	1049	1294	1553	647	735	834	1398	1740	1939
Speedup vs CPU	20.3x	9.4x	11.6x	14x	8.8x	10x	11.2x	11.5x	14x	15.7x
Speedup vs CUDA1	4.7x	2.6x	2.7x	3.1x	2.8x	2.7x	3x	2.5x	3.3x	3.5x

FIGURE 35.11

Performance of our algorithm compared with methods presented by Wu et al. [1] and Hawick et al. [2].

Kernel/Resolution	Relative performance of individual kernels [%]								
	Example (b)			Example (c)			Example (d)		
	1024^2	2048^2	4096^2	1024^2	2048^2	4096^2	1024^2	2048^2	4096^2
Kernel 1	34	40	46	41	45	50	44	48	53
Kernel 2	52	43	33	48	43	37	38	34	28
Kernel 3	7	8	9	6	6	5	8	7	7
Kernel 4	7	9	12	5	6	8	10	11	12

FIGURE 35.12

Relative work distribution among individual kernels for different examples from Figure 35.11.

space. The example was tested for different resolutions of input data, while the scene was rescaled to fit the dimensions of the data. For the final two examples, we generated a high number of small objects that were randomly scattered in the data space. Both cases were analyzed for different resolutions of input data, but in this case, we kept the scale of the objects locked and repeated the same pattern on a larger canvas. In the first case (Figure 35.11c) the base resolution (1024×1024) contained 2500 spheres that filled almost the entire canvas, whereas in the second case (Figure 35.11d), we generated only a sparse set of 250 spheres for the base resolution.

Results of all tested algorithms for all examples are summarized in the table in Figure 35.11. We can see that the speedup of our algorithm was about 10–15x compared with the tested CPU algorithm and on average about 3x compared with the Hawick's CUDA algorithm. We can also see that our algorithm performs best when the distribution of connected components in the analyzed data is sparse, as shown in Examples 1 (Figure 35.11a) and 4 (Figure 35.11d). On the other hand, the speedup is not so high when the connected components cover most of the input data (Figure 35.11b, c). If we compare results measured on different resolutions of a single experiment, we can observe that our algorithm had the best scalability of all three tested methods because the measured throughput [M pixels/s] increased significantly when we increased the resolution of the data. In the case of the CPU algorithm and the Hawick's CUDA algorithm, the throughput usually remained unaffected by the resolution.

35.4.1 Performance Analysis of Kernels

To further study the performance of our method, we also measured the relative time spent on individual kernels for examples from the previous section (see Figure 35.12). We can observe that for all tested examples, the most time-consuming kernels are kernels 1 and 2 that are used to compute the equivalence trees for individual connected components. The only purpose of kernels 3 and 4 is to flatten the equivalence trees (a relatively simple operation), and therefore, their contribution to the final computational time is rather small. Another interesting observation is that the relative time spent on merging of the equivalence trees from different tiles (kernel 2) decreases as the dimensions of the input data increases, thereby showing the effectiveness of our merging scheme.

35.4.2 Limitations

One drawback of our method is that it does not generate consecutive final labels because each label has a value of some element from a given connected component. In order to obtain consecutive labeling, we can apply the parallel prefix sum algorithm [7] on the roots of all detected equivalence trees, or we can reindex the labels on the CPU. Another limiting factor is that our implementation works only with arrays that have a size of power of two in both dimensions.

35.4.3 Future Directions

The current implementation of our CCL method provides a solid performance that is sufficient for most common cases, but still, some applications might be more demanding. A feasible solution for these cases would be to solve the CCL problem on multiple GPUs. To add support of multiple GPUs to our method, it would be necessary to modify the merging scheme by including an additional merging step that would be used to merge local solutions from different devices.

To increase the performance of our method itself, it might be interesting to explore possible optimizations of kernels 1 and 2. In the current implementation kernel 1 uses one CUDA thread to process one element, but it might be more optimal to use one thread for multiple elements because in that case we could take advantage of many optimizations proposed for sequential CCL algorithms [1]. The performance of kernel 2 could be potentially improved by using shared memory to speed up comparison of the equivalence trees on the boundaries of merged tiles.

References

[1] K. Wu, E. Otto, K. Suzuki, Optmizing two-pass connected-component labeling algorithms, Pattern Anal. Appli. 12 (2009) 117–135.

[2] K.A. Hawick, A. Leist, D.P. Playne, Parallel Graph Component Labelling with GPUs and CUDA, Parallel Comput. 36 (2010) 655–678.

[3] L. Gray, A Mathematician looks at Wolfram's new kind of science, Not. Am. Math. Soc. 50 (2003) 200–211.

[4] K. Suzuki, I. Horiba, N. Sugie, Fast connected-component labeling based on sequential local operations in the course of forward raster scan followed by backward raster scan, in: Proceedings of the 15th International Conference on Pattern Recognition (ICPR'00), vol. 2, IEEE Computer Society, Los Alamitos, 2000, pp. 434–437.

[5] R.M. Haralick, L.G. Shapiro, Image segmentation techniques, Comput. Vis. Graph. Image Process. 29 (1) (1985) 100–132.

[6] J. Shi, J. Malik, Normalized cuts and image segmentation, IEEE Trans. Pattern Anal. Mach. Intell. 22 (8) (2000) 888–905.

[7] M. Harris, S. Sengupta, J.D. Owens, parallel prefix sum (scan) with CUDA, in: M. Pharr, R. Fernando (Eds.), GPU Gems 3, Addison Wesley, 2007, pp. 851–576.

Image De-Mosaicing

36

Joe Stam, James Fung

36.1 INTRODUCTION, PROBLEM STATEMENT, AND CONTEXT

Digital imaging systems include a lens and an image sensor. The lens forms an image on the image sensor plane. The image sensor contains an array of light-sensitive pixels, which produce a digital value indicative of the light photons accumulated on the pixel over the exposure time. Conventional image sensor arrays are sensitive to a broad range of light wavelengths, typically from about 350 to 1100 nm, and thus do not produce color images directly. Most color image sensors contain a patterned mosaic color filter array over the pixels such that each pixel is sensitive to light only in the red, blue, or green regions of the visible spectrum, and an IR cut filter is typically positioned in the optical path to reflect or absorb any light beyond about 780 nm, the limit of the human visible spectrum.

The typical mosaic or Bayer [1] pattern color filter array (CFA) is shown in Figure 36.1. This figure shows a common RG-GB configuration used throughout this example. Other arrangements may be used, including horizontal or vertical stripes rather than a mosaic. Different optical methods also exist to create color images, such as the common "three-chip" configuration used in some professional cameras where dichroic beam splitters direct three different spectral bands of the image onto three different image sensor arrays. Color-imaging techniques all have advantages with respect to image quality, cost, complexity, sensitivity, size, and weight. Although the merits of different color-imaging techniques may be hotly debated, the Bayer filter pattern has clearly emerged as the most popular technique for virtually all consumer and most professional video and still cameras.

Because each pixel of a Bayer pattern filter responds to only one spectral band (red, green, or blue) the other two color components must be somehow computed from the neighboring pixels to create a full-color image. This process, commonly called *demosaicing,* or *de-Bayering*, is the subject of this chapter. Perhaps the simplest method is to reduce the effective resolution of the image by three quarters and treat each RG-GB 2×2 quad as a superpixel. Although simple, the lost resolution is undesirable, and artifacts remain because each pixel is not perfectly coincident with the other pixels in the quad. Many improved methods have been developed with various degrees of computational complexity. Simple linear interpolation between neighbors is probably the most commonly used, especially for video applications. Much more complex and higher-quality methods are preferred when postprocessing images from high-resolution digital still cameras on a PC — a tedious process typically referred to as RAW file conversion.

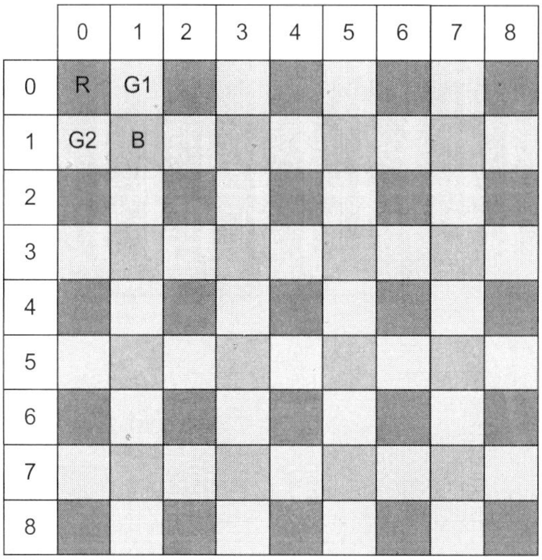

FIGURE 36.1

Bayer pattern color filter array (CFA).

De-mosaicing occurs either by an embedded processor within a camera (or even on the image sensor chip) or as part of a postprocess step on a workstation after acquisition. Simple on-camera implementations result in a substantial loss of quality and information. Using a high-power processor would consume too much of the camera's battery life and produce heat and electrical noise that could degrade the image quality. Although on-camera methods are acceptable for consumer applications, professional photographers and videographers benefit from storing the raw unprocessed images and reserving the color interpolation for a later stage. This allows the use of much higher quality algorithms and prevents the loss of any original recorded information. Additionally, the user may freely adjust parameters or use different methods to achieve their preferred results. Unfortunately, the raw postprocessing step consumes significant computational resources, and thus, proves cumbersome and lacks fluid interactivity. To date, use of full high-performance raw conversion pipelines is largely limited to use for still photography. The same techniques could be used for video, but the huge pixel rates involved make such applications impractical.

Graphics processing units (GPUs) have become highly programmable and may be used for general-purpose massively parallel programming. De-mosaicing is such an *embarrassingly parallel* process ideally suited for implementation on the GPU. This chapter discusses implementation of a few de-mosaicing algorithms on GPUs using NVIDIA's CUDA GPU computing framework. The de-mosaicing methods presented are generally known and reasonably simple in order to present a basic parallel structure for implementing such algorithms on the GPU. Programmers interested in more sophisticated techniques may use these examples as starting points for their specific applications.

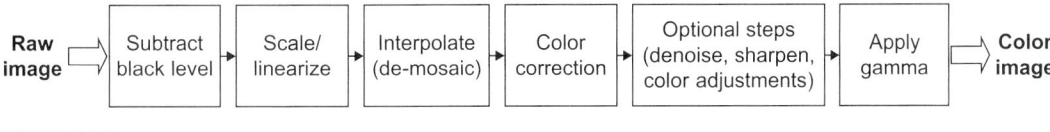

FIGURE 36.2

The raw image conversion process pipeline.

36.2 CORE METHOD

Figure 36.2 shows a typical pipeline for the entire raw conversion process. First, each pixel from the image sensor produces a digital output, assumed to be a 16-bit integer number for this entire example. This raw measurement may need to be modified in a few different ways. First the black level (the digital value equivalent to having no signal on the pixel) must be subtracted. It is usually not 0, owing to biasing of the pixels at some voltage above the minimum range of the A/D converter and because there may be some spatially dependent offset, commonly called fixed-pattern noise. If the black level is spatially dependent, a row- and/or column-dependent lookup table provides the black level to subtract; otherwise, a constant value is used.

After black-level compensation, the remaining signal is converted to a 32-bit floating-point value. For linear output sensors, simply scale to a 0.0-to-1.0 range by multiplying by the reciprocal of the white point value. If the output is nonlinear, then it must be converted through a function or a lookup table.

Next, the two missing color components are interpolated, the primary focus of this chapter discussed in detail. After interpolation the image must be adjusted for white balance and converted into the working color space. The color filter arrays on an image sensor are typically unique to a particular manufacturing process so the red, green, and blue values will not coincide with the color representation of a display or other standard color space. Simply multiplying the RGB components by a 3×3 matrix will suffice for this example, although more complex methods, such as a 3-D lookup table, provides more flexibility, particularly when dealing with out-of-gamut colors (for cameras capable of sensing colors outside the range of the chosen destination color space).

Numerous optional steps may be performed at this point such as denoising, sharpening, or other color adjustments. To stay concise, such enhancements are omitted from this sample, although the GPU is also very well suited for these tasks. Finally, the last stage applies a nonlinear gamma, if desired.

36.3 ALGORITHMS, IMPLEMENTATIONS, AND EVALUATIONS

Obviously, a GPU implementation of de-mosaicing benefits from the massive parallelism of GPUs. Equally important to achieve high throughput is proper memory management and memory access patterns. Although GPUs have tremendous memory bandwidth, in excess of 100 Gb/s on the fastest cards, with the sheer amount of calculation necessary per pixel, the limit to achieve real-time performance is quickly surpassed when reading directly from uncached memory. Graphics shader programmers, on the other hand, will be familiar with using textures to read image data. Texture reads are cached and provide significant improvement over reading directly, but the cache size is limited, not under programmer control, and there is no provision for storing or sharing intermediate calculations without writing back to the GPU's external DRAM, or global memory (GMEM). In the CUDA architecture, NVIDIA added shared memory (SMEM), an extremely fast user-managed on-chip memory that can be shared by multiple threads. SMEM is perfect for storing source pixel information and will form the backbone of our de-mosaicing implementation.

The provided source contains implementations of GPU de-mosaicing using a few different methods: bilinear interpolation, Lanczos [2] interpolation, a gradient-modified interpolation [3], and the Patterned-Pixel Group method [4]. The particular details of the methods will be discussed later after a look at the overall application. Start by examining the file `main.cpp`, which contains a single `main()` function with the entire application control. The first step is to create an OpenGL window to display the output image. The details of OpenGL display or CUDA/OpenGL interop are beyond the scope of this chapter and are not discussed here[1]; a simple `CudaGLVideoWindow` class contains all the code necessary to draw the image on the screen.

Next, CPU memory is allocated to store the original raw image prior to transfer to the GPU. Pinned host memory, allocated with `cudaHostAlloc()`, is selected to facilitate fast, asynchronous DMA (Direct Memory Access) transfers of data to the GPU. In a real-time system, pinned memory would facilitate simultaneous data transfer and processing so that one frame could be processed, while the next frame is read and uploaded to the GPU. To avoid convoluting this sample with lots of file-parsing code, no attempt is made to read any standard raw file format; rather, several images are provided in a flat binary file, and all image properties are hard-coded above the declaration of `main()`. Thus, users can easily replace this code with the necessary routines to acquire images from a particular source. Also, and consistent with our goal of simplicity, the sample implements only the common red-green1-green2-blue (or R-G1-G2-B) pixel arrangement shown in Figure 36.1. Best performance results when targeting the kernel to a specific pixel arrangement rather than including all the conditional logic to support possible variations.

The output image for this sample is an RGBA image with 32-bit/channel floating-point precision. GPUs efficiently handle 32-bit floating-point data, and this preserves the color precision and dynamic range of high-quality image sources; however, other output types are trivially substituted.

The quality of raw conversion algorithms is highly subjective. It is routinely debated, and depends on particular properties of specific cameras or the type of images acquired. Some algorithms, such as the PPG method, actually switch between calculations or vary coefficients based upon edge gradients or image content. Bilinear interpolation is chosen for simplicity and because it is regularly used when processing power is limited. Lanczos interpolation is also simple conceptually, but it provides superior output quality and can run on the GPU with only a modest decrease in throughput, despite a significant increase in overall computation load. The Malvar method [3] applies a gradient correction factor to the results of bilinear interpolation for dramatic improvement in quality with little additional complexity (and in this example we also apply the Malvar gradients to the Lanczos interpolation). Finally, the PPG method demonstrates a more complex conditional approach common in many of the most advanced

---

[1]CUDA/OpenGL interop is discussed in the NVIDIA CUDA Programming Guide. The user is also referred to a presentation entitled *What every CUDA programmer needs to know about OpenGL* from NVDIA'S 2009 GPU Technology Conference, available in the GTC 2009 archives at http://www.nvidia.com/object/gpu_technology_conference.html.

de-mosaicing methods. This chapter does not advocate for the use of any particular method, or make claims about the comparative quality of different methods. Rather, this sample demonstrates the techniques to achieve high-performance de-mosaicing on an NVIDIA GPU, and developers can easily substitute their own preferred algorithms if desired (also see [5]).

The file DeBayer.cu contains the CUDA C kernels along with the kernel launch functions. Examine DeBayer_Bilinear_16bit_RGGB_kernel(), the bilinear de-mosaicing kernel. In this method, the missing color components for each pixel are computed from the average of the neighboring adjacent pixels of the other colors. More precisely refer to Figure 36.3 and the following formulas:

For Red pixel $R_{2,2}$:

$$R_{2,2} = R_{2,2} \quad G_{2,2} = \frac{G_{2,1} + G_{1,2} + G_{3,2} + G_{2,3}}{4} \quad B_{2,2} = \frac{B_{1,1} + B_{3,2} + B_{1,3} + B_{3,3}}{4}$$

For Blue pixel $B_{1,1}$:

$$R_{1,1} = \frac{R_{0,0} + R_{2,0} + R_{0,2} + R_{2,2}}{4} \quad G_{1,1} = \frac{G_{1,0} + G_{0,1} + G_{2,1} + G_{1,2}}{4} \quad B_{1,1} = B_{1,1}$$

For Green Pixel $G_{2,1}$:

$$R_{2,1} = \frac{R_{2,0} + R_{2,2}}{2} \quad G_{2,1} = G_{2,1} \quad B_{2,1} = \frac{B_{1,1} + B_{3,1}}{2}$$

	0	1	2	3	4	5
0	$R_{0,0}$	$G_{1,0}$	$R_{2,0}$	$G_{3,0}$	$R_{4,0}$	$G_{5,0}$
1	$G_{0,1}$	$B_{1,1}$	$G_{2,1}$	$B_{3,2}$	$G_{4,1}$	$B_{5,1}$
2	$R_{0,2}$	$G_{1,2}$	$R_{2,2}$	$G_{3,2}$	$R_{4,2}$	$G_{5,2}$
3	$G_{0,3}$	$B_{1,3}$	$G_{2,3}$	$B_{3,3}$	$G_{4,3}$	$B_{5,3}$
4	$R_{0,4}$	$G_{1,4}$	$R_{2,4}$	$G_{3,4}$	$R_{4,4}$	$G_{5,4}$
5	$G_{0,5}$	$B_{1,5}$	$G_{2,5}$	$B_{3,5}$	$G_{4,5}$	$B_{5,5}$

FIGURE 36.3

Pixel computation layout.

Each thread will process one 2×2 pixel quad and outputs four RGBA F32 pixels. This strategy prevents thread divergence that would occur if each thread processed one output pixel and applied different formulas. Two pixels are read once as a `ushort2` value by each thread. The first two steps of the pipeline of Figure 36.2 are implemented in one simple code statement:

```
fval = CLAMP((float)((int)inPix.x − black_level) * scale, 0,1.0f);
```

In our example case the black level is assumed uniform across the image. As previously mentioned, the black level is commonly spatially dependent upon row or column location owing to fixed pattern noise from manufacturing variations in the row and column read-out circuitry and A/D converter variability in the image sensor. In this case the variable `black_level` may be replaced with a row or column lookup-table. The resulting integer value is then cast to float and multiplied by a pre-determined `scale` variable to convert the value to floating point in the 0.0f to 1.0f range. Again, for simplicity, the source data is assumed linear; if it is not then a linearization function may be applied. In this case a 1-D CUDA texture provides an ideal way to implement a lookup table with hardware linear interpolation.

The linear scaled floating-point raw values are now stored in the GPU's shared memory (SMEM). SMEM is extremely fast on-chip memory accessible to all threads within a thread block. It is analogous to CPU cache memory, but allocated and accessed under programmer control and thus can be relied upon for deterministic performance. SMEM serves the needs of de-mosaicing perfectly because the multiple threads in a block need to access the same source raw pixel values.

The thread block size dictates the input tile size stored. Additional apron source pixels are needed to interpolate pixels at edges of the tile, so the source reads are shifted up one row and left two columns with the left two threads in the thread block reading extra columns and the top two thread rows reading extra rows (two extra columns are read on each side rather than the one needed to maintain 32-bit read alignment).[2] For the first generation of NVIDIA GPUs with compute capability 1.x, a thread block size of 32×13 requires $34 \times 14 \times 4$ pixels, or 7616 bytes total, just less than 50% of the total 16 kilobytes of SMEM. Thus, two thread blocks run concurrently per SM, ensuring good overlap between memory access and computation. On the newest compute capability 2.x GPUs, 48 kB of SMEM is available, so a thread block size of 32×24 is chosen. SMEM is no longer the limiting factor; rather, 768 threads is 50% of the maximum 1572 threads per SM.

Reading the source data and storing the values into SMEM compose the majority of the code in the sample, and unfortunately complicates the implementation quite a bit. The performance benefit far outweighs the complexity that arises from shifting the reads for the extra row and column apron pixels, and properly clamping on the image boarders. Also, note that the raw source pixels are stored in SMEM as four different color planes rather than a contiguous tile. This prevents a two-way SMEM bank conflict that would arise because every thread processes two output pixels per row. The arrangement of the source reading and storage in SMEM is shown in Figure 36.4. Also note that the blue and green-2 SMEM tiles contain one extra apron row on top and the red and green-1 tiles contain their extra apron row on bottom.

---

[2] An observant programmer may notice that the global memory reads are not strictly aligned for proper coalescing; however, shifting the columns by one 32-bit word does not have a significant performance detriment, and further complication of the code is unwarranted. SM 1.2 and later architectures contain coalescing buffers or cache, thus eliminating the need for the complex read patterns needed to strictly coalesce memory.

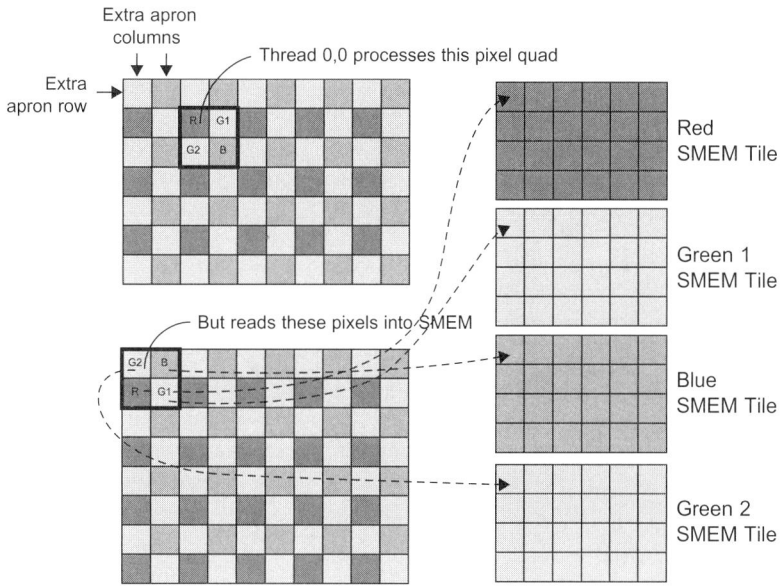

FIGURE 36.4

Source reading and storage.

The overall read process is diagramed in Figure 36.5.

The read process may also be understood by referring to the following pseudo code, which directly mirrors the code for the bilinear interpolation in the accompanying source code:

          Pseudo Code for Bilinear Interpolation reads to SMEM

Notes:
     X is the two—pixel column index in the image (Reading two 16—bit pixels
        at a time).
     References to 'X' or 'Column' below are two physical columns.

     Y is the row index.

     Tx and Ty are the thread indices.

     Boundary checking for off—of—image reads are omitted in this pseudo code for
        clarity.

```
// Step 1: Read Green2 and Blue pixels for the top left part of the tile
// Reads are shifted up one row and left one double—column
Column = X — 1
Row = Y — 1
Pixels = Image[Row][Column]
Linearize and Scale Pixels
Green2_SMEM_Tile[Ty][Tx] = Pixels[0]
Blue_SMEM_Tile[Ty][Tx] = Pixel[1]
```

```
// Step 2: Read the extra Green2 and Blue pixels for the right apron
If Tx< 2
        Column = X + Thread Block Width — 1
        Pixels = Image[Row][Column]
        Linearize and Scale Pixels
        Green2_SMEM_Tile[Ty][Tx + Thread Block Width] = Pixels[0]
        Blue_SMEM_Tile[Ty][Tx + Thread Block Width] = Pixel[1]

//Step 3: Read the Red and Green 1 pixels from the next row
Row = Y
Column = X — 1
Pixels = Image[Row][Column]
Linearize and Scale Pixels
Red_SMEM_Tile[Ty][Tx + Thread Block Width] = Pixels[0]
Green1_SMEM_Tile[Ty][Tx + Thread Block Width] = Pixel[1]

// Step 4: Read the extra Red and Green 1 pixels for the right apron
If Tx< 2
        Column = X + Thread Block Width — 1
        Pixels = Image[Row][Column]
        Linearize and Scale Pixels
        Green2_SMEM_Tile[Ty][Tx + Thread Block Width] = Pixels[0]
        Blue_SMEM_Tile[Ty][Tx + Thread Block Width] = Pixel[1]

// Step 5: Need to read two rows on the bottom to complete the apron
If Ty < 2
        Column = X — 1
        Row = (BlockIdx.y + 1) + BlockHeight*2 + Ty — 1
        Pixels = Image[Row][Column]
        Linearize and Scale Pixels
        If Ty = 0
                Green2_SMEM_Tile[Ty + Thread Block Height][Tx] = Pixels[0]
                Blue_SMEM_Tile[Ty + Thread Block Height][Tx] = Pixel[1]
        If Ty = 1
                Red_SMEM_Tile[Ty + Thread Block Height][Tx] = Pixels[0]
                Green1_SMEM_Tile[Ty + Thread Block Height][Tx] = Pixel[1]

// Step 6: Read the bottom right apron pixels
If Ty < 2 and Tx< 2
        Column = X + Thread Block Width — 1
        Row = (BlockIdx.y + 1) + BlockHeight*2 + Ty — 1
        Pixels = Image[Row][Column]
        Linearize and Scale Pixels
        If Ty = 0
                Green2_SMEM_Tile[Ty + Thread Block Height][Tx + Thread Block Width] =
                    Pixels[0]
                Blue_SMEM_Tile[Ty + Thread Block Height][Tx + Thread Block Width] =
                    Pixel[1]
        If Ty = 1
                Red_SMEM_Tile[Ty + Thread Block Height][Tx + Thread Block Width] =
                    Pixels[0]
                Green1_SMEM_Tile[Ty + Thread Block Height][Tx + Thread Block Width] =
                    Pixel[1]

Wait until all threads in thread block complete read.
```

Original layout: X and Y indices indicate the output pixels each thread is responsible for computing

Step 1: All threads read a G2 and B pixel pair which is shifted up one row and left two columns

Step 2: Threads with x index < 2 read extra G2-B pixel pairs on the right from this row

Step 3: All threads read an R and G1 pixel one row below the prior read, also shifted two columns left

Step 4: Treads with x index < 2 read extra R-G1 pixel pairs on the right from this row

Step 5: All threads with a y index < 2 read another row shifted left two columns at the bottom of this tile (twice the thread block y size rows down). Threads with y = 0 read the G2-B row, and threads with y = 1 read the R-G1 row below

Step 6: Threads with y index < 2 and x index < 2 read extra pixels pairs on the right for the same row read in step 5

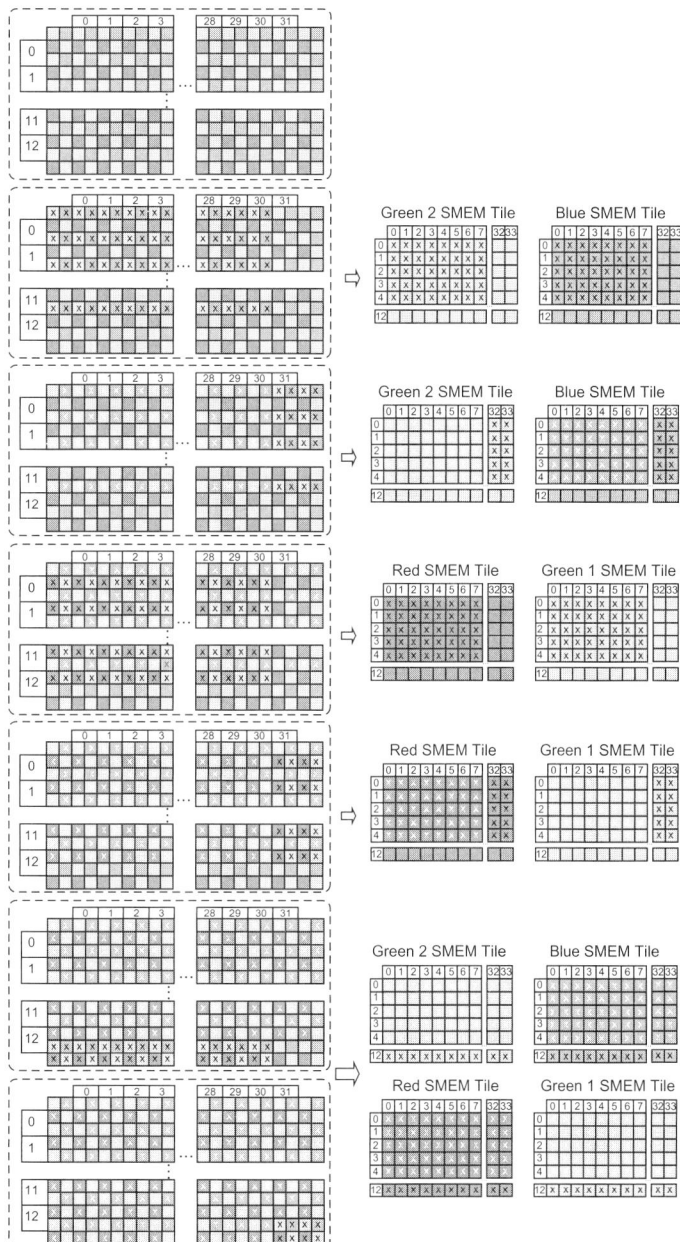

FIGURE 36.5

Read process.

Following the reading from global memory into SMEM, each thread block must synchronize with a __syncthreads() call to ensure all reads are complete before continuing. For this reason, the block sizes discussed previously are chosen to allow two blocks to run per SM, thereby giving the GPU compute work to do on one block, while another reads and waits for synchronization.

After synchronization each thread computes the missing color components for each output pixel in the 2×2 quad according to the preceding formulas. The output RGB value for each pixel is multiplied by the 3×3 color conversion matrix for the target output color space. More sophisticated color conversion methods, such as a 3-D lookup table using 3-D textures, may be substituted here to account for different rendering intent. Finally, the output gamma is applied and the result is clamped in the 0 to 1.0 range. Note that clamping may be omitted if out-of-gamut colors are permitted. Here is the CUDA-C code for the interpolation of additional color channels of the red filtered (northwest) pixel in the quad. The variables tile_R, tile_G1, tile_G2, and tile_B refer to the SMEM memory tiles containing the source pixel values for each color channel.

```
// Bilinear Interpolation
float4 NW;
NW.x = tile_R[sy][sx];
NW.y = 0.25f * (tile_G2[sy][sx] + tile_G2[sy+1][sx] + tile_G1[sy][sx-1] +
    tile_G1[sy][sx]);
NW.z = 0.25f * (tile_B[sy][sx-1] + tile_B[sy][sx] + tile_B[sy+1][sx-1] +
    tile_B[sy+1][sx]);
NW.w = 1.0f;

// color correction
float r = ColorMatrix[0] * NW.x + ColorMatrix[1] * NW.y + ColorMatrix[2] * NW.z;
float g = ColorMatrix[3] * NW.x + ColorMatrix[4] * NW.y + ColorMatrix[5] * NW.z;
float b = ColorMatrix[6] * NW.x + ColorMatrix[7] * NW.y + ColorMatrix[8] * NW.z;

// gamma
NW.x = CLAMP(__powf(r,gamma),0,1.0f);
NW.y = CLAMP(__powf(g,gamma),0,1.0f);
NW.z = CLAMP(__powf(b,gamma),0,1.0f);

// write output
pOut[Y*2*OutPitch_in_pixels + X*2] = NW;
```

Each thread writes each pixel of the 2×2 quad back out to GPU GMEM after computation is completed. Because each thread processes 2 pixels per row, only every other 128-bit word is written at a time, and strict coalescing does not occur. Alternatively, these values could be stored until the entire quad is processed, written back to SMEM (which can now be reused because the processing of the source raw data is complete), and then written to GMEM in a coalesced fashion. Experimentally, it has been determined that just writing the values immediately performs better because the writes of the first 3 pixels per thread can overlap the processing of the subsequent pixels. It is quite common to perform sharpening, noise reduction, or other color adjustments as part of the raw conversion process. After interpolation pixels may be stored back to the now free SMEM and filters applied. Performing this processing may be more efficient than running a separate kernel later because extra passes through

GMEM are eliminated.[3] When all additional filtering completes, then apply the final color conversion and gamma.

36.3.1 Improved Filtering

Bilinear interpolation leaves much to be desired in image quality that is especially noticeable at the edges in images. It is quickly evident that only a small portion of the kernel code in the preceding example relates to the actual interpolation computation, so presumably more complex methods may be used without a substantial performance penalty. Here, we discuss additional methods that improve upon the quality of the bilinear interpolation kernel.

In the sample, a second kernel, `DeBayer_Lanczos_16bit_RGGB_kernel()`, implements Lanczos interpolation. Lanczos interpolation is regarded as one of the highest-quality methods of image resampling. Coefficients for the Lanczos operator are given by:

$$L(x) = \begin{cases} \frac{a\sin(\pi x)\sin\left(\frac{x}{a}\right)}{\pi^2 x^2}, & |x| < 0, \ x \neq 0 \\ 1, & x = 0 \\ 0, & otherwise \end{cases}$$

Where x is the distance between each pixel in the neighborhood and the interpolated location and a is the order of the filter ($a = 2$ in our example). A plot of the Lanczos function is shown in Figure 36.6.

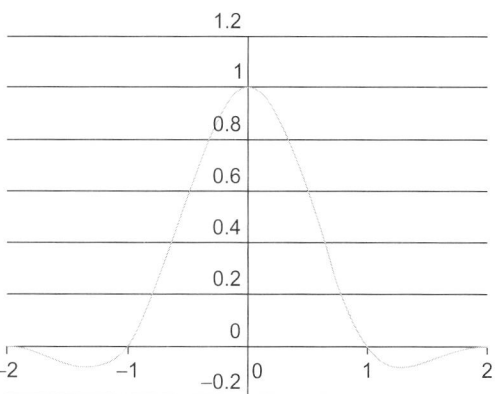

FIGURE 36.6

Plot of the Lanczos 2 function.

---

[3]The benefit of concatenating additional filtering into the de-mosaicing kernel is heavily dependent on the complexity of the additional operations. For computationally intensive filtering, the memory latency may be hidden by computation, and thus, breaking filters into separate kernels may prove easier to code and manage. For simple filters or additional color adjustments, memory latency and bandwidth constraints will bottleneck performance, and thus, adding the filter to the de-mosaicing kernel will likely provide superior performance.

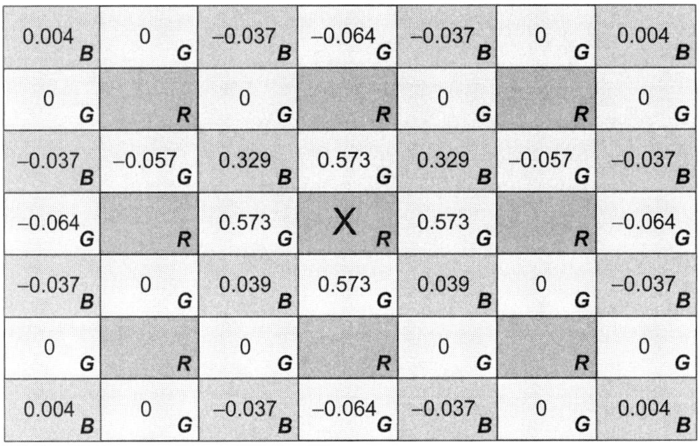

0.004 B	0 G	−0.037 B	−0.064 G	−0.037 B	0 G	0.004 B
0 G	R	0 G	R	0 G	R	0 G
−0.037 B	−0.057 G	0.329 B	0.573 G	0.329 B	−0.057 G	−0.037 B
−0.064 G	R	0.573 G	X R	0.573 G	R	−0.064 G
−0.037 B	0 G	0.039 B	0.573 G	0.039 B	0 G	−0.037 B
0 G	R	0 G	R	0 G	R	0 G
0.004 B	0 G	−0.037 B	−0.064 G	−0.037 B	0 G	0.004 B

FIGURE 36.7

Lanzcos filter coefficients.

To interpolate the missing color values for each pixel compute a weighted sum of the neighboring pixels filtered in the desired color. The weights are the product of the x and y Lanczos function values for the distance between the output pixel and the neighbors in each axis. Consider interpolating the blue and green color values for a red filtered pixel. Figure 36.7 shows the weights by which the neighboring green and blue pixels are multiplied and then summed to compute the corresponding blue and green color values. The sum is then normalized by multiplying by the reciprocal of the sum of the weights.

The Lanzcos interpolation CUDA kernel function is similar to the bilinear interpolation kernel, with the following substantial differences:

- A wider apron read is necessary to accommodate the larger neighborhood used to compute the interpolated values; thus, three extra rows above and below and four extra columns right and left are read. Because of the larger apron more SMEM is required, and thus, a smaller block size is used.
- The actual interpolation computation involves using several more input pixels and coefficients for each output pixel, but otherwise, follows the form for the bilinar kernel.

The CUDA-C code for computing the interpolated values of a red filtered pixel is as follows:

```
// Lanczos Interpolation
NW.x = tile_R[sy][sx];

NW.y = ( −0.063684f * tile_G2[sy−1][sx] +
         0.573159f * tile_G2[sy][sx] +
         −0.063684f * tile_G1[sy][sx−2] + 0.573159f * tile_G1[sy][sx−1] +
         0.573159f * tile_G1[sy][sx] + −0.063684f * tile_G1[sy][sx+1] +
         0.573159f * tile_G2[sy+1][sx] + −0.063684f * tile_G2[sy+2][sx] )
         * 0.490701f;

NW.z = ( 0.004056f * tile_B[sy−1][sx−2] + −0.036501f * tile_B[sy−1][sx−1] +
         −0.036501f * tile_B[sy−1][sx] + 0.004056f * tile_B[sy−1][sx+1] +
```

```
       −0.036501f * tile_B[sy][sx−2] + 0.328511f * tile_B[sy][sx−1] +
        0.328511f * tile_B[sy][sx] + −0.036501f * tile_B[sy][sx+1] +
       −0.036501f * tile_B[sy+1][sx−2] + 0.328511f * tile_B[sy+1][sx−1] +
        0.328511f * tile_B[sy+1][sx] + −0.036501f * tile_B[sy+1][sx+1] +
        0.004056f * tile_B[sy−2][sx−2] + −0.047964f * tile_B[sy+2][sx−1] +
       −0.047964f * tile_B[sy+2][sx] + 0.004056f * tile_B[sy+2][sx+1]) * 0.963151f;
NW.w = 1.0f;
```

Malvar, He, and Cutler improved upon basic interopolation by including a gradient-correction gain factor that exploits the correlation between the red, green, and blue channels in an image. A weighted luminance gradient of the actual filter color for each pixel is added to the output of the interpolated missing color. The specific gradient correction gain calculation forumulas for each particular interpolation case are given in [3] and in the accompanying source code. The gain correction factor uses an additional 5 to 9 additional pixel values in the calcualtion of the final interpolated color. However, because these values are already located in SMEM, the overall performance of the calcualtion is remarkably close to simple bilinear interpolation. We now list the calculation of the output of a red filtered pixel for comparison with the previously listed methods.

```
// Bilinear Interpolation + Gradient Gain Correction Factor
NW.x = tile_R[sy][sx];

NW.y = 0.25f * (tile_G2[sy][sx] + tile_G2[sy+1][sx] + tile_G1[sy][sx−1]
       + tile_G1[sy][sx]) + 0.5f * tile_R[sy][sx] +
      −0.125f * (tile_R[sy−1][sx] + tile_R[sy+1][sx] + tile_R[sy][sx−1]
       + tile_R[sy][sx+1]);

NW.z = 0.25f * (tile_B[sy][sx−1] + tile_B[sy][sx] + tile_B[sy+1][sx−1]
       + tile_B[sy+1][sx]) + 0.75f * tile_R[sy][sx] +
      −0.1875f * (tile_R[sy−1][sx] + tile_R[sy+1][sx] + tile_R[sy][sx−1]
       + tile_R[sy][sx+1]);

NW.w = 1.0f;
```

The Patterned Pixel gGrouping (PPgG) algorithm is used to interpolate red (R), green (G), and blue (B) values at each location, just as in the previous discussions, although the algorithm differs from the previous examples. PPG performs a two-phase computation that begins by interpolating all missing green values. For interpolation of the green values at blue or red pixels consider estimating $G_{2,2}$ at $R_{2,2}$. First, the method calculates gradients in four directions, centered at pixel $R_{2,2}$:

$$\Delta N = \left| R_{2,0} - R_{2,2} \right| \times 2 + \left| G_{2,1} - G_{2,3} \right|$$

$$\Delta E = \left| R_{2,2} - R_{4,2} \right| \times 2 + \left| G_{1,2} - G_{4,2} \right|$$

$$\Delta W = \left| R_{0,2} - R_{2,2} \right| \times 2 + \left| G_{1,2} - G_{4,2} \right|$$

$$\Delta S = \left| R_{2,2} - R_{2,4} \right| \times 2 + \left| G_{2,1} - G_{4,3} \right|$$

Next, the algorithm determines which direction has the minimum gradient and then uses that direction to estimate green values at the red locations, such as at $G_{2,2}$, as:

$$\text{If } \Delta N \text{ is minimum}: G_{2,2} = (G_{2,1} \times 3 + R_{2,2} + G_{2,3} - R_{2,0})/4$$

$$\text{If } \Delta E \text{ is minimum}: G_{2,2} = (G_{3,2} \times 3 + R_{2,2} + G_{1,3} - R_{4,2})/4$$

$$\text{If } \Delta W \text{ is minimum}: G_{2,2} = (G_{1,2} \times 3 + R_{2,2} + G_{3,2} - R_{0,2})/4$$

$$\text{If } \Delta S \text{ is minimum}: G_{2,2} = (G_{2,3} \times 3 + R_{2,2} + G_{2,1} - R_{0,2})/4$$

This fully fills in the green channel at all locations, and those results can now be used in the next steps. For interpolation of the blue and red values at green pixels, the algorithm estimates $B_{2,1}$ and $R_{2,1}$ at $G_{2,1}$ by a "hue transit" function, given a set of inputs:

$$B_{2,1} = \text{hue\_transit}\left(G_{1,1}, G_{2,1}, G_{3,2}, B_{1,1}, B_{3,2}\right)$$

$$R_{2,1} = \text{hue\_transit}\left(G_{2,0}, G_{2,1}, G_{2,2}, R_{2,0}, R_{2,2}\right)$$

where hue_transit() is defined as:

```
hue_transit(l₁, l₂, l₃, v₁, v₃){
    if (l₁ < l₂ < l₃ || l₁ > l₂ > l₃)
        return(v₁ + (v₃ − v₁) × (l₂ − l₁)/(l₃ − l₁))
    else
        return(v₁ + v₃)/2 + (l₂ × 2 − l₁ − l₃)/4
}
```

Finally, for interpolation of the blue or red values at red or blue pixels, consider estimating $B_{2,2}$ at $R_{2,2}$:

$$\Delta ne = \left|B_{3,2} - B_{1,3}\right| + \left|R_{4,0} - R_{2,2}\right| + \left|R_{2,2} - R_{0,4}\right| + \left|G_{3,2} - G_{2,2}\right| + \left|G_{2,2} - G_{1,3}\right|$$

$$\Delta ne = \left|B_{1,1} - B_{3,3}\right| + \left|R_{0,0} - R_{2,2}\right| + \left|R_{2,2} - R_{4,4}\right| + \left|G_{1,1} - G_{2,2}\right| + \left|G_{2,2} - G_{3,3}\right|$$

Then, the final values for $B_{2,2}$ and $R_{2,2}$ are determined as:

```
if Δne ≤ Δnw
```
$$B_{2,2} = \text{hue\_transit}\left(G_{3,2}, G_{2,2}, G_{1,3}, G_{3,2}, G_{1,3}\right)$$
```
else
```
$$B_{2,2} = \text{hue\_transit}\left(G_{1,1}, G_{2,2}, G_{3,3}, G_{1,1}, G_{3,3}\right)$$

Each pixel processed in the PPG method is dependent only on a neighborhood of pixels around it. As in the previous examples, multiple reads and writes are issued to this neighborhood, and it can be stored in shared memory for faster repeated read access. In the case of PPG, the size of the region must be somewhat extended to accommodate for generating apron green values to avoid any need for a global synchronization (which would require a new kernel launch).

A tile of Bayer data and surrounding apron region can be copied from global memory into shared memory, and a group of threads can process a tile. If the CUDA-C algorithm was written to have each thread process a single element of the Bayer pattern, this would result in divergence because the operations to interpolate values for different colors vary at each location. So, as in the previous methods, the algorithm can be written so that each thread is responsible for processing a 2×2 region of the data corresponding to a "quad" of four data element locations: $\{R_1 G_1 B_1 G_2\} = \{R_{0,0}, G_{1,0}, B_{1,1}, G_{0,1}\}$. This way, all threads execute interpolations for $R_{0,0}$, then $G_{1,0}$, and so on, and so avoid divergent paths.

The PPG algorithms require substantially more SMEM than the prior methods for storing the interpolated green values from phase 1, and bank conflicts must again be avoided. Thus, for PPG analysis, we examined an alternative case where the input data is stored in SMEM as 16-bit short integer data. Linearization and black-level subtraction may still be performed upon the read of the raw data, but then values are converted back to short integers to conserve SMEM. Conveniently, when 16-bit source Bayer pattern values are written into shared memory and with each thread processing a "quad" of data, it can be seen that successive threads will each access different and successive banks of shared memory. This is a result of the banks accommodating two 16-bit elements per bank, and a row of Bayer data consisting of two 16-bit elements per "quad" element on a row, meaning the next quad's R_1 value is spaced 32 bits, or one bank, away from the previous quad's R_1 value, and so on. Thus, operating on 2×2 regions of 16-bit elements avoids divergence and bank conflicts. Finally, as seen in the preceding formulas the PPG method does not require any computation with precise floating-point weights; all calculations use integer math. Thus, the entire calculation and final output are written using unsigned short values.

36.4 FINAL EVALUATION

Image de-mosaicing is extremely well suited for implementation on a graphics processor using NVIDIA CUDA. Several example algorithms are provided and serve as a framework that can be easily modified to suit a specific requirement.

Table 36.1 summarizes performance for several of the methods tested on an NVIDIA Quadro 5000 GPU. These metrics include timing of the entire raw conversion process outlined in Figure 36.2, which includes the final output color correction and write to memory as a full 32-bit float per color channel image. Timing does not include data transfer or drawing time because such requirements vary significantly for each application, transfer can likely be overlapped with computation, or live video feeds may be captured direct to GPU memory.

Such performance is easily sufficient for real-time high-quality demosaicing results on high-resolution images. In fact, at such rates even a stereo pair of ultra-high-definition 4 K video images can be processed in real time on a single GPU. Use of the GPU's shared memory facilitates such high performance by making neighboring pixel values instantly available for computation. Because of the shared memory and the GPU's overall high-computation performance, complex and high-quality

Table 36.1 Performance of de-mosaicing methods.

Method	Pixel Rate
Bilinear	2.1 Gpixels/s
Lanczos	1.7 Gpixels/s
Malvar	1.9 Gpixels/s
Lanczos + Malvar	1.6 Gpixels/s

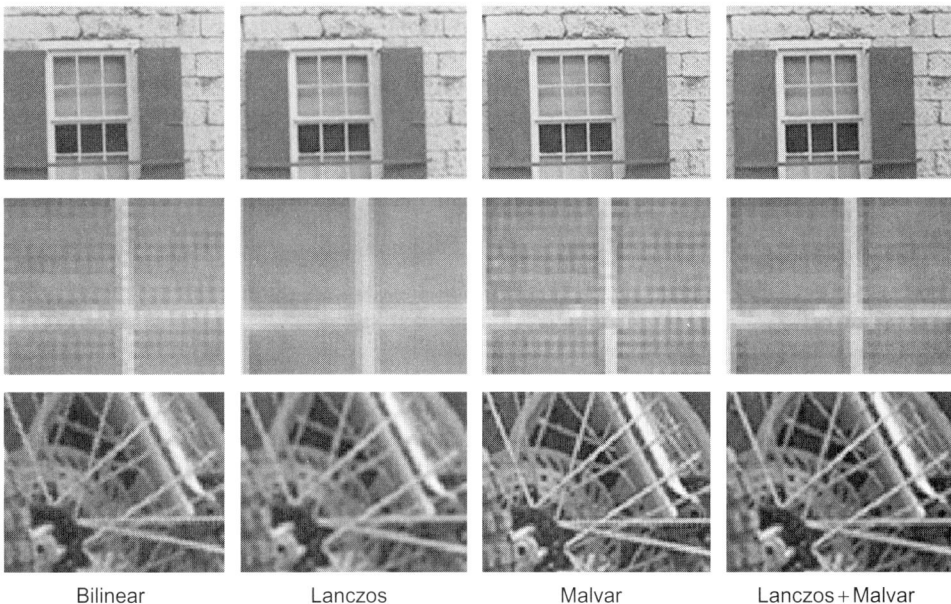

| Bilinear | Lanczos | Malvar | Lanczos + Malvar |

FIGURE 36.8

Results comparison on standard.

methods require only slightly more computation time than simple methods. For example, the Lanczos method runs only about 25% slower than simple bilinear interpolation, despite an approximately four-fold increase in calculation. Finally, Figure 36.8 shows the quality of each of these algoirthms in some particularly troublesome regions of test images from the Kodak test suite [6].

References

[1]   B.E. Bayer, U.S. Patent 3,971,065, 1975.
[2]   C.E. Duchon, Lanczos filtering in one and two dimensions, J. Appl. Meteor. 18 (1979) 1016–1022.
[3]   H.S. Malvar, L.-W. He, R. Cutler, High-quality linear interpolation for demosaicing of Bayer-patterned color images, Microsoft Research, 2004.
[4]   C.K. Lin, Pixel grouping for color filter array demosaicing. http://web.cecs.pdx.edu/~cklin/demosaic/.
[5]   A. Lukin, D. Kubasov, High-quality algorithm for Bayer pattern interpolation, Program. Comput. Software 30 (6) (2004) 347–358.
[6]   B.K. Gunturk, Y. Altunbasak, R.M. Merseau, Color plane interpolation using alternating projections, IEEE Trans. Image Process. 11 (2002) 997–1013.
[7]   M. McGuire, Efficent, high-quality Bayer demosaic filtering on GPUs, submitted to J. Graph. GPU Game Tools 13 (4) (2009) 1–16.

SECTION

Signal and Audio Processing
Area Editor's Introduction

John Roberts

9

37 Efficient Automatic Speech Recognition on the GPU 601

38 Parallel LDPC Decoding 619

39 Large-Scale Fast Fourier Transform 629

THE STATE OF GPU COMPUTING IN SIGNAL AND AUDIO PROCESSING

Inexorable growth in the volume of digital data available and the stunning advance of parallel computational power in GPUs is leading to application of GPU computing for signal processing in such areas as telecommunications, networking, multimedia, man-machine interfaces, signal intelligence, and data analytics.

Many of the computations involved in these domains lend themselves naturally to parallel computing, but others present challenges inherent in the organization, scale, or distribution of the data. Developers and authors such as those featured in this chapter find innovative approaches to address these and other issues to achieve unprecedented performance. Based on these results and the breadth of their applicability, extensive use of GPUs for computation in signal and audio processing should be expected in the future.

IN THIS SECTION

Chapter 37, written by Jike Chong, Ekaterina Gonina, and Kurt Keutzer, discusses GPU-accelerated automated speech recognition (ASR), the process of transcribing acoustic waveforms to word sequences in text form. Particular challenges addressed are handling irregular graph structures, eliminating redundant work, conflict-free reduction in graph traversal, and parallel construction of a global queue. The effective techniques presented to address these bode well for applications such as automatic meeting transcription, news broadcast transcription, and voice-activated multimedia systems in home entertainment systems.

In Chapter 38, Gabriel Falcao, Vitor Silva, and Leonel Sousa present GPU-accelerated low-density parity decoding (LDPC) codes for error correction. Using techniques such as a compact data structures representation for data access and optimum thread coarsening to balance computation and memory access, the authors achieve impressive throughputs previously attainable only by fixed-purpose VLSI-based systems.

In Chapter 39, Yifeng Chen, Xiang Cui, and Hong Mei detail the acceleration of large-scale FFTs without data locality on GPU clusters as an example of a class of processing problems. Such tasks are harder to accelerate given the bottlenecks represented by the PCI between main memory and GPU device memory and by the communication network between workstation nodes. The authors mitigate these hurdles and achieve significant speedups using such techniques as manipulating array dimensions during data transfer.

Efficient Automatic Speech Recognition on the GPU

37

Jike Chong, Ekaterina Gonina, Kurt Keutzer

Automatic speech recognition (ASR) allows multimedia content to be transcribed from acoustic waveforms to word sequences. This technology is emerging as a critical component in data analytics for a wealth of media data that is being generated every day. Commercial usage scenarios are already appearing in industries such as customer service call centers for data analytics where ASR is used to search recorded content, track service quality, and provide early detection of service issues. Fast and efficient ASR enables economic employment of text-based data analytics to multimedia contents. This opens the door to unlimited possible applications such as automatic meeting diarization, news broadcast transcription, and voice-activated multimedia systems in home entertainment systems.

This chapter provides speech recognition application developers with an understanding of specific implementation challenges when working with the speech inference process, weighted finite state transducer (WFST) based methods, and the Viterbi algorithm. It illustrates an efficient reference implementation on the GPU that could be productively customized to meet the needs of specific usage scenarios. To machine learning researchers, this chapter introduces capabilities of the GPU to handle large, irregular graph-based models with millions of states and arcs. Lastly, the chapter provides four generalized solutions for GPU computing researchers and developers to resolve four types of algorithmic challenges encountered during in the implementation of speech recognition on GPUs. These solutions include concepts that are generally useful for creating performance-critical applications on the GPU.

37.1 INTRODUCTION, PROBLEM STATEMENT, AND CONTEXT

It is well-known that automatic speech recognition (ASR) is a challenging application to parallelize [3, 4]. Specifically, on the GPU an efficient implementation of ASR involves resolving a series of implementation challenges specific to the data-parallel architecture of the platform. This section introduces the speech application and highlights four of the most important challenges to be resolved when implementing the application on the GPU.

37.1.1 The Speech Recognition Application

The goal of an automatic speech recognition application is to analyze a human utterance from a sequence of input audio waveforms in order to interpret and distinguish the words and sentences intended by the speaker. Its top-level software architecture is shown in Figure 37.1. The inference

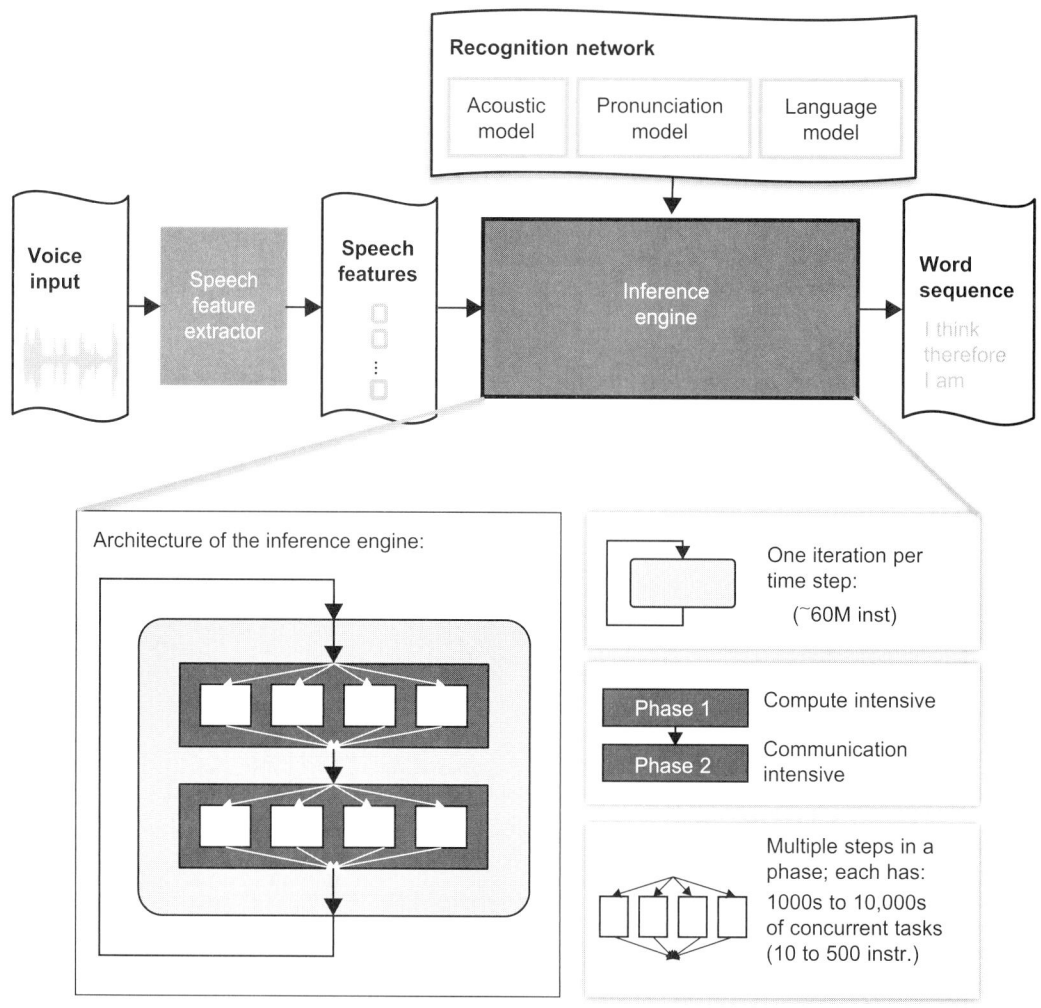

FIGURE 37.1

Architecture of a large vocabulary continuous speech recognition application.

process uses a *recognition network*, or a *speech model*, which includes three components: an acoustic model, a pronunciation model, and a language model. The acoustic model and language model are trained off-line using powerful statistical learning techniques. The pronunciation model is constructed from a dictionary. The *speech feature extractor* collects feature vectors from input audio waveforms using standard scalable signal processing techniques [8, 9]. The *inference engine* traverses the *recognition network* based on the Viterbi search algorithm [6]. It infers the most likely word sequence based on the extracted speech features and the recognition network. In a typical recognition process, there are significant parallelism opportunities in concurrently evaluating thousands of alternative interpretations of a speech utterance to find the most likely interpretation [12, 13].

Algorithmically, ASR is an instance of a machine-learning application where graphical models are used to represent language and acoustic information learned from large sets of training examples. In our implementation, the speech model used is a hidden Markov model (HMM) representing acoustic-, phone-, and word-level transitions, compiled into a unified state machine using WSFT techniques [5]. The model is represented as a graph with millions of states and arcs with probabilistic weights. The recognition process performs statistical inference on the HMM using the Viterbi beam search algorithm and iterates through a sequence of extracted input features. Each iteration is one time step and involves two phases of execution. Phase 1 computes the statistical likelihood for a match between an input feature and an element of a database of known phones. This operation is also known as "observation probability computation" and is compute intensive. Phase 2 uses the speech model to infer the most likely sequence seen so far. The computation in Phase 2 involves traversal through a large graph-based model guided by input waveforms. This computation has highly unpredictable control paths and data access patterns and is therefore communication intensive. The output is the most likely word sequence inferred from the input waveform.

37.1.2 The Implementation Challenges

In this chapter, we focus on discussing the four most important challenges when parallelizing the speech recognition inference engine on the GPU. Their solutions are described in Section 37.2, and elaborated on in Section 37.3. The four most important challenges are

1. *Handling irregular graph structures* with data parallel operations;
2. *Eliminating redundant work* when threads are accessing an unpredictable subset of the results based on input;
3. *Conflict-free reduction* in graph traversal to implement the Viterbi beam search algorithm; and
4. *Parallel construction of a global queue* while avoiding sequential bottlenecks when atomically accessing queue-control variables.

Resolving these implementation challenges allows for scalable data-parallel execution of speech recognition applications on the GPU.

37.2 CORE METHODS

There are efficient solutions for resolving the implementation challenges of speech recognition on the GPU that achieve more than an order of magnitude speedup compared to sequential execution. This chapter identifies and resolves four important bottlenecks in the GPU implementation. The techniques presented here, when used together, are capable of delivering 10.6× speedup for this challenging application when compared to an optimized sequential implementation on the CPU. The four solutions for the implementation challenges are:

1. *Constructing an efficient dynamic vector data structure* to handle irregular graph traversals (Section 37.3.1)
2. *Implementing an efficient find-unique function* to eliminate redundant work by leveraging the GPU global memory write-conflict-resolution policy (Section 37.3.2)

3. *Implementing lock-free accesses* of a shared map leveraging advanced GPU atomic operations to enable conflict-free reduction (Section 37.3.3)
4. *Using hybrid local/global atomic operations and local buffers* for the construction of a global queue to avoid sequential bottlenecks in accessing global queue-control variables (Section 37.3.4)

Each of the aforementioned solutions is described by first providing the context of the challenge within the automatic speech recognition application. We then proceed by defining the challenge in a generalized problem statement and presenting a solution to the implementation challenge. This allows the solutions to be applied more generally to a variety of machine-learning application areas.

37.3 ALGORITHMS, IMPLEMENTATIONS, AND EVALUATIONS

37.3.1 Constructing an Efficient Dynamic Vector Data Structure to Handle Irregular Graph Traversals

There exists extensive concurrency in the automatic speech recognition application. As shown in Figure 37.1, there are 1000s to 10,000s of concurrent tasks that can be executed at the same time in both phases 1 and 2 of the recognition engine.

In a sequential implementation of the speech-inference process, more than 80% of execution time is spent in phase 1. The computation in phase 1 is a *Gaussian mixture model* evaluation to determine the likelihood of an input feature matching specific acoustic symbols in the speech model. The structure of the computation resembles a vector dot product evaluation, where careful structuring of the operand data structures can achieve 16-20x speedup on the GPU. With phase 1 accelerated on the GPU, phase 2 dominates the execution time. Phase 2 performs a complex graph traversal over a large irregular graph with millions of states and arcs. The data-working set is too large to be cached and is determined by input available only at runtime.

Implementing phase 2 on the GPU is challenging [4], as operations on the GPU are most efficient when performed over densely packed vectors of data. Accessing data elements from irregular data structures can cause an order-of-magnitude performance degradation. For this reason, many have attempted to use the CPU for this phase of the algorithm with limited success [1, 2]. The suboptimal performance is mainly caused by the significant overhead of communicating intermediate results between phases 1 and 2.

One can implement both phases of the inference engine on the GPU by using a technique for dynamically constructing efficient vector data structures at runtime. As illustrated in Figure 37.2, this technique allows the intermediate results to be efficiently handled within the GPU subsystem and eliminates unnecessary data transfers between the CPU and the GPU.

Problem

One often has to operate on large, irregular graph structures with unpredictable data access patterns in machine-learning algorithms. How does one implement the data access patterns efficiently on the GPU?

Solution

The solution involves dynamically constructing an efficient data structure at runtime. Graph algorithms often operate on a subset of states at a time. Let this working set be the "active set." This active set

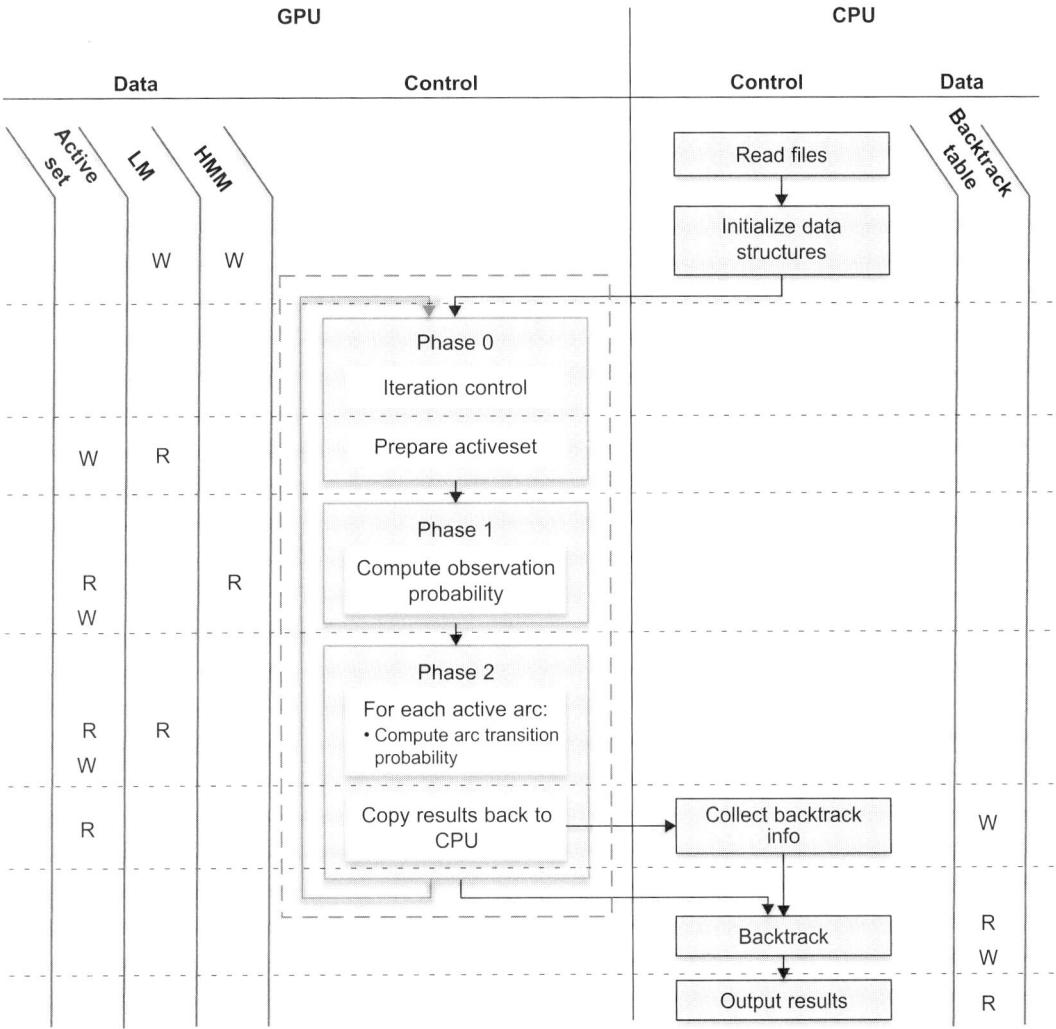

FIGURE 37.2

Summary of the data structure access and control flow of the inference engine on many core platforms.

information is often accessed multiple times within a sequence of algorithmic steps. This is especially true for information about the structure of the graph, such as the set of outgoing arcs emerging from the active states.

Active set information can be dynamically extracted from the overall graph and stored in a contiguous vector for efficient access. The cost of gathering the information is then amortized over multiple uses of the same piece of information.

In automatic speech recognition, this technique is used during aggregation of state and arc properties. As shown in Figure 37.2, the "Prepare ActiveSet" step gathers information from the speech model and dynamically populates a set of vectors summarizing the data-working set. This way, the following operations can execute on packed vectors of active states for the rest of the iteration.

The following code segment illustrates the usage of a dynamic runtime buffer:

```
1  % Gathering operands
2  int curr_stateID = stateID[i];
3  state_property0[i] = SpeechModel_state_property0[curr_stateID];
4  state_property1[i] = SpeechModel_state_property1[curr_stateID];
5  ...
6  % Utilizing gathered operands
7  stepA(stateID, state_property0);
8  stepB(stateID, state_property0, state_property1);
```

In the preceding code example, there is a *stateID* array that stores a list of the active states. On lines 2 and 3, the properties of an active state i are gathered from the graph data structures *SpeechModel_state_property*0 and *SpeechModel_state_property*1 into a consecutive vector of active state properties in the *state_property*0 and *state_property*1 arrays. In subsequent algorithm steps on lines 7 and 8, one can use the dynamically constructed data structure reusing the efficient data layout.

37.3.2 Implementing an Efficient Find-Unique Function to Eliminate Redundant Work

In phase 1 of the inference process, the algorithm computes the likelihood of a match between an input feature vector and elements in a database of known acoustic model units called "triphone states." In the speech model we used, there is a total of 51,604 unique triphone states making up the acoustic model. On average, only 20% of these triphone states are used for the observation probability computation in one time step.

In a sequential implementation, one can use memoization to avoid redundant work. As the active states are evaluated in phase 1, one can check if a triphone state likelihood has already been computed in the current iteration. If so, the existing result will be used. Otherwise, the triphone state likelihood is computed, and the result is recorded for future reference.

In the parallel implementation, active states are evaluated in parallel and implementing memoization would require extensive synchronization among the parallel tasks. Table 37.1 shows three approaches that could be used to compute the observation probability in each time step. One approach is to compute the triphone states as they are encountered in the graph traversal process without memoization. This results in a $13\times$ duplication in the amount of computation required. Even on a GTX280 platform, computing one second of speech would require 1.9 seconds of compute time. A slight improvement to this approach is to compute the observation probability for all triphone states, including the ones that may not be encountered in any particular time step. This results in $4.9\times$ redundancy in the necessary computation, which in turn results in 0.709 second of computation for phase 1 for each second of speech.

The more efficient approach is to remove duplicates in the list of encountered triphone states and compute the observation probabilities for only the unique triphone states encountered during the traversal. This approach requires a fast data-parallel find-unique function.

Table 37.1 Comparison of three approaches to determine observation probabilities to compute.

Approaches	Real-Time Factor*
1. Compute only encountered triphone with duplication and no memoization	1.900
2. Compute all triphone states once	0.709
3. Compute only encountered unique triphone states	0.146

*Real-time factor: the number of seconds required to compute for one second worth of input data.

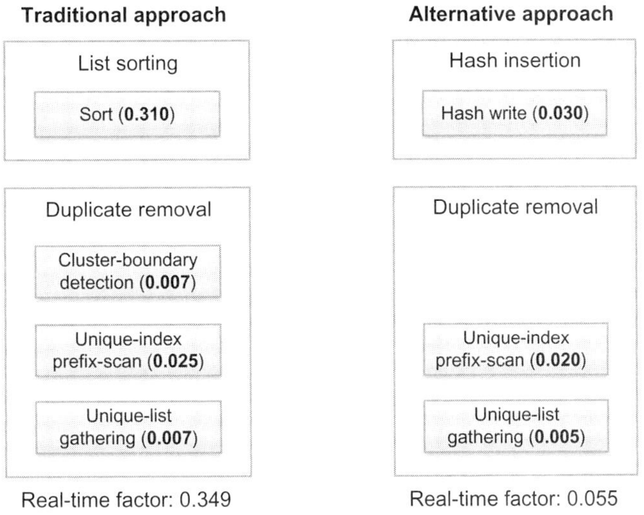

Traditional approach

List sorting

Sort (**0.310**)

Duplicate removal

Cluster-boundary detection (**0.007**)

Unique-index prefix-scan (**0.025**)

Unique-list gathering (**0.007**)

Real-time factor: 0.349

Alternative approach

Hash insertion

Hash write (**0.030**)

Duplicate removal

Unique-index prefix-scan (**0.020**)

Unique-list gathering (**0.005**)

Real-time factor: 0.055

FIGURE 37.3

Find unique function approaches.

Problem

How does one efficiently find a set of unique elements among tens of thousands of possible elements to eliminate redundant work on the GPU?

Solution

Traditionally, the find-unique function involves a process of "List sorting" and "duplication-removal." As shown in the left half of Figure 37.3, the "sort" step clusters identical elements together, and the "duplication-removal" process keeps one unique element among consecutive identical elements. On a data-parallel platform, Figure 37.3 illustrates further how the "duplication-removal" process expands into *cluster-boundary identification, unique-index prefix-scan*, and *unique list gathering* steps. Specifically, the *cluster-boundary identification* step flags a "1" for the elements that are different than their prior neighbor in the sorted list, and leaves all other positions as "0." The *unique-index prefix-scan* step computes the index of the cluster-boundary elements in the shortened unique list. The *unique list gathering* step transfers the flagged cluster boundary elements to the unique list. In this sequence of steps, sort is the dominant step with 89% of the execution time of the find-unique function. The sort step alone would take 0.310 seconds to process every second of input data.

An alternative approach is to generate a flag array based on the total number of unique triphone states in a speech model. This is illustrated in the right half of Figure 37.3. For the "Hash insertion" process, we leverage the semantics of conflicting writes for non-atomic memory accesses. According to the CUDA Programming Guide [8], at least one conflicting write to a device memory location is guaranteed to succeed. For the purpose of setting flags, the success of any one thread in write conflict situations can achieve the desired result. For the "Duplicate Removal" process, the flag array produced by the *hash write* step can be used directly for *unique-index prefix-scan* and *unique-list gathering* steps. This significantly simplifies the find unique function, providing an efficient way to eliminate redundant work with a small overhead.

37.3.3 Implementing Lock-Free Accesses of a Shared Map to Enable Conflict-Free Reduction

Phase 2 of the automatic speech recognition algorithm performs a parallel graph traversal that is equivalent to a one level expansion during breadth-first search. Starting from a set of current active states, one follows the outgoing arcs to reach the next set of active states. Each state represents an alternative interpretation of the word sequence recognized so far.

The generation of the next set of active states is done in two steps: (1) evaluating the likelihood of a word sequence when an arc is traversed, (2) recording the maximum likelihood of the traversed arc at the destination states (note that maximum likelihood is equal to minimum absolute value in negative log spaces). The first step involves computing the likelihood of particular transitions and is trivially data parallel. The second step involves a reduction over the likelihoods over all transitions ending in a destination state and recording only the transition that produced the most likely word sequence. This is the more challenging step to describe in a data-parallel execution environment.

One can organize the graph traversal in two ways: by *propagation* or by *aggregation*. During the graph traversal process, each arc has a source state and a destination state. Traversal by *propagation* organizes the traversal process at the source state. It evaluates the outgoing arcs of the active states and propagates the result to the destination states. As multiple arcs may be writing their result to the same destination state, this technique requires write conflict-resolution support in the underlying platform. Traversal by *aggregation* organizes the traversal process around the destination state. The destination states update their own information by performing a reduction on the evaluation results of their incoming arcs. This process explicitly manages the potential write conflicts by using additional algorithmic steps so that no write conflict-resolution support is required in the underlying platform.

There is significant overhead in performing the traversal by *aggregation*. Compared with traversal by *propagation*, the process requires three more data-parallel steps to collect destination states, allocate a result buffer for the incoming arcs, evaluate arcs to write to the designated result buffer index, and a final reduction over the destination state. The implementation of each step often requires multiple data-parallel CUDA kernels to eliminate redundant elements and compact lists for more efficient execution.

For traversal by *propagation*, one can implement a direct-mapped table to store the results of the traversal for all states, indexed by the state ID. Conflicting writes to a destination state would have to be resolved by locking the write location, checking if the new result is more likely than the existing result, and selectively writing into the destination state. The approach is illustrated in the following code segment:

```
1  float res = compute_result(tid);
2  int stateID = get_stateID(tid);
3  Lock(stateID);
4  if(res < stateProbValues[stateID]) {
5      stateProbValues[stateID] = res;
6  }
7  Unlock(stateID);
```

In the preceding code snippet, each transition evaluation is assigned to a thread. The result of the transition probability is computed by each thread (line 1). Then the *stateID* of the destination state is obtained by each thread (line 2). The *stateProbValues* array provides a lookup table storing the most likely interpretation of the input waveform that ends in a particular stateID. To conditionally update this lookup table, the memory location in the *stateProbValues* array is locked (line 3) to prevent write conflicts when multiple threads access the same state. The location then is updated if the probability computed represents a more likely interpretation of the input waveforms (lines 4–6), which mathematically is a smaller magnitude in log likelihood. Finally, after the update, the memory location for the state is unlocked (line 7).

This approach is not efficient, as recording a result involves two atomic operations guarding a critical section and multiple dependent long-latency memory accesses. In some platforms, because atomic and nonatomic memory accesses may execute out of order, the pseudocode as shown may not even be functionally correct.

Problem

How does one efficiently leverage CUDA capabilities to implement conflict-free reductions when handling large graphs?

Solution

Instead of having a locking/unlocking process for each state update, we take advantage of the *atomicMin()* operation in CUDA and implement a lock-free version of the traversal by *propagation*. The definition of *atomicMin()* is as follows:

```
1  float atomicMin(float* myAddress, float newVal);
```

From the CUDA manual [7], the instruction reads the 32-bit word *oldVal* located at the address *myAddress* in global or shared memory, computes the minimum of *oldVal* and *newVal*, and stores the result back to memory at the same address. These three operations are performed in one atomic transaction. The function returns *oldVal*.

By using the *atomicMin()* instruction, we implement a lock-free shared-array update. Each thread obtains the stateID of the corresponding state and atomically updates the value at that location. The accumulation of the minimum probability is guaranteed by the *atomicMin()* semantics.

```
1  int stateID = StateID[tid];
2  float res = compute_result(tid);
3  int valueAtState = atomicMin(&(destStateProb[stateID]), res);
```

In the preceding code snippet, each thread computes the likelihood of the transition ending at stateID (line 1) and obtains the stateID of the destination state for its assigned transition (line 2). Then, the destination state transition probability is atomically updated by keeping the smallest magnitude of log-likelihood using the the *atomicMin()* operation. This technique efficiently resolves write conflicts among threads (in the *destStateProb* array on line 3) and thus allows for lock-free updates to a shared array, selecting the minimum value at each array location. The resulting reduction in the write-conflict contention is at least $2\times$ because we have only one atomic operation instead of two locks. The actual performance gain can be much greater because the multiple dependent long-latency accesses in the original critical section between the locking and unlocking processes are also eliminated.

37.3.4 Using Hybrid Local/Global Atomic Operations and Local Buffers for the Construction of a Global Queue

During traversal of the recognition network in the speech-inference engine, one needs to manage a set of active states that represent the most likely interpretation of the input waveform. Algorithmically, this process is done by following arcs from the current set of active states and collecting the set of likely next active states. This process involves two steps: (1) computing the minimum transition probability and (2) collecting all new states encountered into a list. Section 37.3.3 discusses efficient implementation of the first step on the GPU. If we implement this as a two-step process, after the first step, we would have an array of states where some of the states are marked "active." The size of this array equals the size of the recognition network, which is on the order of millions of states, and the number of states marked active is on the order of tens of thousands. To efficiently handle graph traversal on the GPU, one needs to gather the set of active states into a dense array to guarantee efficient access of the state data in consequent steps of the traversal process.

One way to gather the active states is to utilize part of the routine described in Section 37.3.2, by constructing an array of flags that has a "1" for an active state and a "0" for a nonactive state and then performing a "prefix-scan" and "gather" to reduce the size of the list. However, the prefix-scan operation on such large arrays is expensive, and the number of active states is a less than 1% of the total number of states.

Instead, one can merge the two steps and actively create a global queue of states while performing the write-conflict resolution. Specifically, every time a thread evaluates an arc transition and encounters a new state, it can atomically add the state to the global queue of next active states. The resulting code is as follows:

```
1  float res = compute_result(tid);
2  int stateID = StateID[tid];
3  float valueAtState = atomicMin(&(destStateProb[stateID]), res);
4  if(valueAtState == FLT_MAX) {    //first time seeing the state, push it onto the queue
5      int head = atomicAdd(&Q_head, 1);
6      myQ[head] = stateID;
7  }
```

In the code snippet above, each thread evaluates the likelihood of arriving at a state (line 1) and obtains the stateID of the destination state for its assigned transition (line 2). Each entry of the *destStateProb* array is assumed to have been initialized to *FLT_MAX*, the largest log-likelihood magnitude (representing the smallest possible likelihood). In line 3, the value in the *destStateProb* array at the *stateID* position is conditionally and atomically updated with the evaluated likelihood. If the thread is the first to encounter the state at *stateID*, the returned value from line 3 would be the initial value of *FLT_MAX*. In that case, the new state is atomically added to the queue of destination states. This is done by atomically incrementing the queue pointer variable using the *atomicAdd* operation on the *Q_head* pointer (line 5). The value of the old queue head pointer is returned, and the actual *stateID* can be recorded at the appropriate location (line 6).

While the merged implementation is an efficient way to avoid instantiating numerous data parallel kernels for collecting active states in the two-step process, there is one sequentializing bottleneck that prevents this implementation from being scalable: when thousands of threads are executing this kernel concurrently, there are thousands of threads atomically updating the *Q_head* variable. As shown in Figure 37.4, the synchronization cost of a global queue implementation increases sharply as the number of state transitions evaluated increases.

Problem

How does one efficiently construct a shared global queue?

Solution

In order to resolve the contention on the head pointer, one can use a distributed queue implementation. Each CUDA thread block creates its own local shared queue and populates it every time a thread encounters a new state. After each block constructs its local queue of states, each block then merges its local queue into the global queue. The possible contention on the local queue head pointer is limited to the number of threads in a thread block (usually 64 to 512), and the contention on the global queue head pointer is thus reduced by 64× to 512×, greatly improving performance. Figure 37.4 shows that

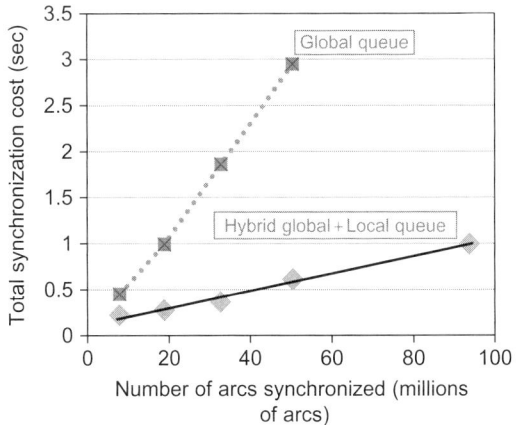

FIGURE 37.4

Comparison of the synchronization cost for global queue and hybrid global and local queue implementations.

the hybrid implementation scales gracefully with an increasing number of arcs. The resulting code is shown below:

```
1   // Local Q: shared memory data structure
2   // ----------------------------------------
3   extern __shared__ int sh_mem[]; // Q size is at most the number of threads
4   int *myQ = (int *)sh_mem;        // memory for local Q
5   __shared__ int myQ_head;          // local Q head ptr
6   __shared__ int globalQ_index;     // globalQ_index
7
8   if(threadIdx.x==0) {
9       myQ_head = 0;
10  }
11  __syncthreads();
12
13  int tid = blockIdx.x*blockDim.x + threadIdx.x;
14
15  if(tid<nStates) {
16      int stateID = StateID[tid];
17      float res = compute_result[tid];
18
19      if (res > pruneThreshold) {
20          res = FLT_MAX;
21      } else {
22          //if res is smaller than prune threshold
23          int valueAtState = atomicMin(&(destStateProb[stateID]), res);
24          if(valueAtState == FLT_MAX) {
25              //first time seeing the state, push it onto the local queue
26              int head = atomicAdd(&myQ_head, 1);
27              myQ[head] = stateID;
28          }
29      }
30
31      // Local Q -> Global Q transfer
32      // ----------------------------------------
33      __syncthreads();
34
35      if (threadIdx.x==0) {
36          globalQ_index = atomicAdd(stateHeadPtr, myQ_head);
37      }
38      __syncthreads();
39
40      if (threadIdx.x < myQ_head)
41          destStateQ[ globalQ_index + threadIdx.x] = myQ[threadIdx.x];
42
43  } // end if (tid<nStates)
```

In the preceding code snippet, lines 3–6 declare the shared-memory variables: local queue *myQ* and local queue head *myQ_head* index and the head index of the global queue, *globalQ_index*. Thread 0 initializes the local queue head for each block in lines 8–10. The thread ID is computed, and the bounds are checked in lines 13 and 15. Each thread obtains the destination state for its transition and computes the transition probability in lines 16 and 17, respectively. In lines 19–29, the probability for the destination state is updated as described earlier and in Section 37.3.3. This time, however, the new states encountered by the threads in each block are stored locally in the local queue (line 26). Once all threads in a thread block have completed their enqueuing operations to the local queue, the thread block adds the content of the local queue to the global queue as a block. Lines 35–37 update the global queue index, and line 41 copies the contents of the local queue to the global queue in parallel.

37.3.5 Performance Analysis

We achieved $10.6\times$ speedup on the GTX280 GPU compared with a highly optimized sequential baseline on a Core i7 CPU. The measurements are taken on the experimental platforms specified in Table 37.2. The theoretical upper limit for computation on the platforms are shown as "single-precision giga floating-point operations per second," or SP GFLOPS/s. The theoretical upper limit for memory bandwidth is shown as GB/s. For the manycore platform setup, we use a Core2 Quad-based host system with 8 GB host memory and a GTX280 graphics card with 1 GB of device memory. The sequential baseline uses one of the cores of a Core i7 CPU.

The speech models are taken from the SRI CALO real-time meeting recognition system [11]. The front end uses 13-dimensional perceptual linear prediction (PLP) features with first-, second-, and third-order differences, is vocal-track-length normalized and is projected to 39 dimensions using heteroscedastic linear discriminant analysis (HLDA). The acoustic model is trained on conversational telephone and meeting speech corpora using the discriminative minimum-phone-error (MPE) criterion. The language model is trained on meeting transcripts, conversational telephone speech, and web and broadcast data [10]. The acoustic model includes 52,000 triphone states that are clustered into 2613 mixtures of 128 Gaussian components.

The pronunciation model contains 59,000 words with a total of 80,000 pronunciations. We use a small back-off bigram language model with 167,000 bigram transitions. The recognition network is an $H \circ C \circ L \circ G$ model compiled using WFST techniques, and contains 4.1 million states and 9.8 million arcs.

The test set consists of excerpts from NIST conference meetings, taken from the "individual head-mounted microphone" condition of the 2007 NIST rich transcription evaluation. The segmented audio files total 44 minutes in length and comprise 10 speakers. For the experiment, we assumed that the

Table 37.2 Parameters for the experimental platforms.

Type	Sequential	Manycore
Processor	Core i7 920	GTX280 (+Core2 Q9550)
Cores	4 cores (SMT)	30 cores
SIMD width	4 lanes	8 physical, 32 logical
Clock speed	2.66 GHz	1.296 GHz
SP GFLOP/s	85.1	933
Memory capacity	6 GB	1 GB (8 GB)
Memory BW	32.0 GB/s	141.7 GB/s
Compiler	icc 10.1.015	nvcc 2.2

Table 37.3 Accuracy, word error rate (WER), for various beam sizes and corresponding decoding speed in real-time factor (RTF).

Avg. No. of Active States		32,820	20,000	10,139	3518
WER		41.6	41.8	42.2	44.5
RTF	**Sequential**	4.36	3.17	2.29	1.20
	GPU	0.40	0.30	0.23	0.18
Speedup		10.9×	10.6×	10.0×	6.7×

feature extraction is performed off-line so that the inference engine can directly access the feature files. The meeting recognition task is very challenging owing to the spontaneous nature of the speech.[1] The ambiguities in the sentences require a larger number of active states to keep track of alternative interpretations that lead to slower recognition speed.

Our recognizer uses an adaptive heuristic to adjust the search beam size based on the number of active states. It controls the number of active states to be below a threshold in order to guarantee that all traversal data fits within a preallocated memory space. Table 37.3 shows the decoding accuracy, that is, word error rate (WER) with varying thresholds and the corresponding decoding speed on various platforms. The recognition speed is represented by the real-time factor (RTF) that is computed as the total decoding time divided by the duration of the input speech.

As shown in Table 37.3, the GPU implementations can achieve significant speedup for the same number of active states. More important, we can improve both the speed and accuracy of the recognition process by using the GPU. For example, compared with the sequential implementation using an average of 3518 active states, the parallel implementation using an average of 32,820 active states can provide a higher recognition accuracy and at the same time see a 3× speedup.

For the next experiment, we choose a beam-width setting that maintains an average of 20,000 active states to analyze the performance implications in detail. The sequential implementation is functionally equivalent with negligible differences in decoding output.

We analyzed the performance of our inference engine implementations on the GTX280 GPU. The sequential baseline is implemented on a single core in a Core i7 quadcore processor. It uses a SIMD-optimized phase 1 routine and non-SIMD graph traversal routine for phase 2. Compared with this highly optimized sequential baseline, we achieve 10.6× speedup on the GTX280.

The performance gain is best illustrated in Figure 37.5 by highlighting the distinction between the compute-intensive phase (black bar) and the communication-intensive phase (white bar). The compute-intensive phase achieves 17.7× speedup on the GPU, while the communication-intensive phase achieves only 3.7× speedup on the GPU.

The speedup numbers indicate that synchronization overhead dominates the runtime as more processors need to be coordinated in the communication-intensive phase. In terms of the ratio between the compute- and communication-intensive phases, the pie charts in Figure 37.5 show that 82.7% of the

---

[1] A single-pass time-synchronous Viterbi decoder from SRI using lexical tree search achieves 37.9% WER on this test set.

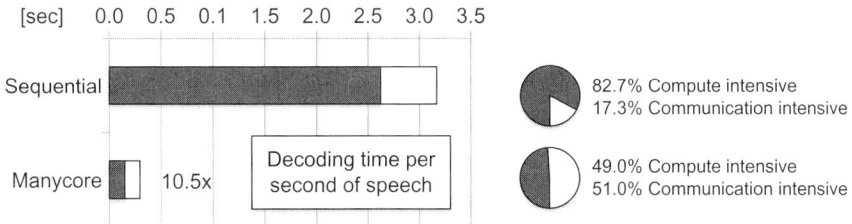

FIGURE 37.5

Ratio of computation-intensive phase of the algorithm vs. communication-intensive phase of the algorithm.

time in the sequential implementation is spent in the compute-intensive phase of the application. As we scale to our GPU implementation, the compute-intensive phase becomes proportionally less dominant, taking only 49.0% of the total runtime. The increasing dominance of the communication-intensive phase motivates a detailed examination of parallelization implications in the communication-intensive phases of our inference engine.

We found that the sequential overhead in our implementation is less than 2.5% of the total runtime even for the fastest implementation. This demonstrates that we have a scalable software architecture that promises greater potential speedups with more parallelism in future generations of processors.

37.4 CONCLUSION AND FUTURE DIRECTIONS

In this chapter, we demonstrated concrete solutions to mitigate the implementation challenges of an automatic speech recognition application on NVIDIA graphics processing units (GPUs). We described the software architecture of an automatic speech recognition application, posed four of the most important challenges in implementing the application, and resolved the four challenges with the corresponding four solutions on a GPU-based platform. The challenges and solutions are:

1. **Challenge:** *Handling irregular graph structures* with data-parallel operations
   Solution: *Constructing an efficient dynamic vector data structure* to handle irregular graph traversals
2. **Challenge:** *Eliminating redundant work* when threads are accessing an unpredictable subset of data based on input
   Solution: *Implementing an efficient find-unique function* by leveraging the GPU global memory write-conflict-resolution policy
3. **Challenge:** *Performing conflict-free reduction* in graph traversal to implement the Viterbi beam search algorithm
   Solution: *Implementing lock-free accesses* of a shared map leveraging advanced GPU atomic operations with arithmetic operations to enable conflict-free reduction
4. **Challenge:** *Parallel construction of a global queue* causes sequential bottlenecks when atomically accessing queue control variables
   Solution: *Using hybrid local/global atomic operations and local buffers* for the construction of a global queue to avoid sequential bottlenecks in accessing global queue control variables

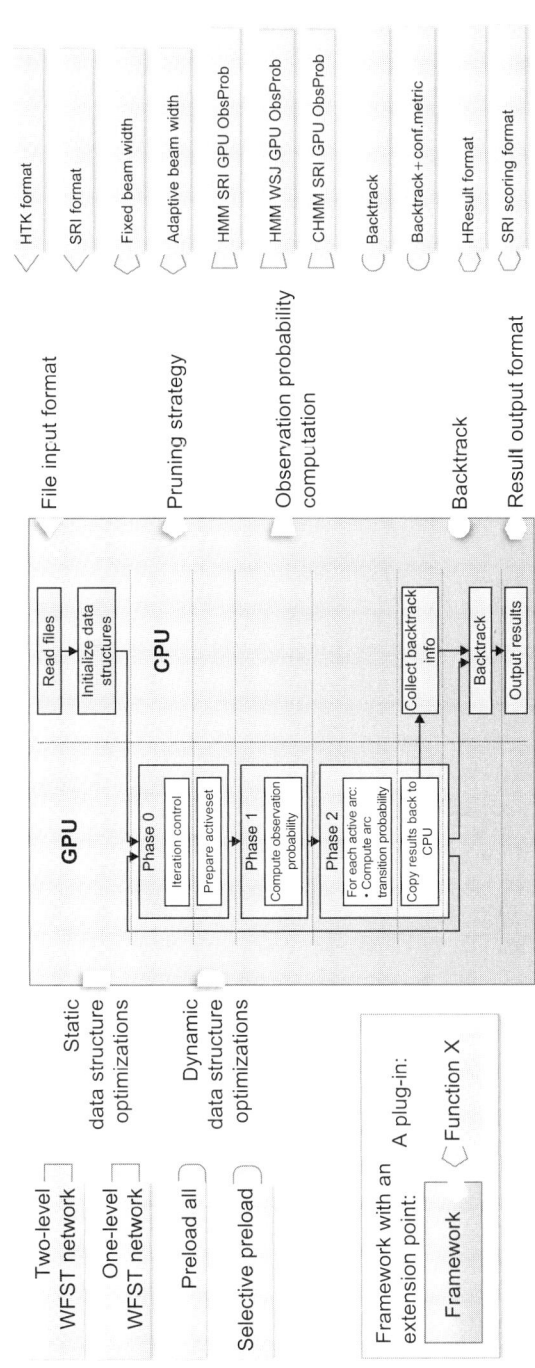

FIGURE 37.6

An automatic speech recognition inference engine application framework.

Our ongoing research is to incorporate these techniques in an automatic speech recognition inference engine framework that allows application developers to further customize and extend their speech recognizer within an optimized infrastructure for this class of applications. Figure 37.6 shows a framework with its reference implementation infrastructure at the center and extension points illustrated as notches along the border of the framework. The position of the extension points in the figure signifies the particular algorithm step that an extension point is extending. Each notch can have multiple interchangeable plug-ins. For example, an application developer is able to customize the pruning strategy either with adaptive beam-width thresholds or fixed beam-width thresholds.

The extension points listed on the left are execution speed-sensitive extension points that should be customized only by a parallel programing expert. The extension points listed on the right are extension points that provide good execution speed isolation, where any customization affects the speed of only that particular application step.

This kind of application framework provides an optimized infrastructure that incorporates all the techniques discussed in this chapter to allow efficient execution of the speech inference process on the GPU. By allowing flexible customizations of extension points without jeopardizing efficient execution, we believe such frameworks will provide application developers with significant implementation support for constructing efficient and scalable speech recognition applications on the GPU.

References

[1]   P. Cardinal, P. Dumouchel, G. Boulianne, M. Comeau, GPU accelerated acoustic likelihood computations, in: Proceedings of the 9th Annual Conference of the International Speech Communication Association (Interspeech), 22–26 September 2008, Brisbane, Australia, 2008, pp. 964–967.

[2]   P.R. Dixon, T. Oonishi, S. Furui, Fast acoustic computations using graphics processors, in: Proceedings of IEEE International Conference on Acoustics, Speech, and Signal Processing (ICASSP), 19–24 April 2009, Taipei, Taiwan, 2009, pp. 4321–4324.

[3]   A. Janin, Speech recognition on vector architectures, PhD thesis, University of California, Berkeley, CA, 2004.

[4]   A. Lumsdaine, D. Gregor, B. Hendrickson, J. Berry, Challenges in parallel graph processing, Parallel Process. Lett. 17 (1) (2007) 5–20.

[5]   M. Mohri, F. Pereira, M. Riley, Weighted finite state transducers in speech recognition, Comput. Speech. Lang. 16 (1) (2002) 69–88.

[6]   H. Ney, S. Ortmanns, Dynamic programming search for continuous speech recognition, IEEE Signal Process. Mag. 16 (5) (1999) 64–83.

[7]   NVIDIA CUDA Programming Guide, Version 2.2. http://developer.download.nvidia.com/compute/cuda/2_2/toolkit/docs/NVIDIA_CUDA_Programming_Guide_2.2.pdf, 2009.

[8]   A. Obukhov, A. Kharlamov, Discrete cosine transform for 8×8 blocks with CUDA, NVIDIA white paper, http://developer.download.nvidia.com/compute/cuda/sdk/website/C/src/dct8x8/doc/dct8x8.pdf, 2008.

[9]   V. Podlozhnyuk, FFT-based 2D convolution, NVIDIA white paper, http://developer.download.nvidia.com/compute/cuda/2_2/sdk/website/projects/convolutionFFT2D/doc/convolutionFFT2D.pdf, 2007.

[10] A. Stolcke, X. Anguera, K. Boakye, O. Cetin, A. Janin, M. Magimai-Doss, et al., The SRI-ICSI Spring 2007 meeting and lecture recognition system, in: Multimodal Technologies for Perception of Humans, 1 January 2008, vol. 4625, Springer, 2008, pp. 450–463.

[11] G. Tur, et al., The CALO meeting speech recognition and understanding system, in: Proceedings of the IEEE Spoken Language Technology Workshop, 15–19 December 2008, Goa, India, 2008, pp. 69–72.

[12] J. Chong, Y. Yi, A. Faria, N. Satish, K. Keutzer, Data-parallel large vocabulary continuous speech recognition on graphics processors, in: Proceedings of the 1st Annual Workshop on Emerging Applications and Many Core Architecture, 21 June 2008, Beijing, China, 2008, pp. 23–35.

[13] K. You, J. Chong, Y. Yi, E. Gonina, C. Hughes, Y. Chen, et al., Parallel scalability in speech recognition: inference engine in large vocabulary continuous speech recognition, IEEE Signal Process. Mag. 26 (2009) 124–135.

Parallel LDPC Decoding

38

Gabriel Falcao, Vitor Silva, Leonel Sousa

In this chapter we present a pair of kernels to decode a class of powerful error-correcting codes, known as low-density parity-check (LDPC) codes, on graphics processing units (GPU). The proposed parallel implementations adopt a compact data structures representation to access data, while the processing on the GPU grid efficiently exploits a balanced distribution of the computational workload. Moreover, we have analyzed different levels of thread coarsening and propose an efficient one, which balances computation and memory accesses. This case study shows that by adopting these practical techniques, it is possible to use the GPU's computational power to perform this type of processing and achieve significant throughputs, which until recently could be obtained only by developing very large scale integration (VLSI) dedicated microelectronics systems.

38.1 INTRODUCTION, PROBLEM STATEMENT, AND CONTEXT

In the past few years, LDPC codes have been adopted by several data storage and communication standards, such as DVB-S2 [1], WiMAX (802.16e) [2], Wifi (802.11n), or 10Gbit Ethernet (802.3an). As they present powerful error-correcting capabilities and also because the patent has expired, their successful exploitation is expected to continue. LDPC codes [3] decoding is a computationally intensive and iterative application that requires high-performance signal processing for achieving real-time decoding within a targeted throughput. Recovered back from the 1960s when they were invented by Gallager [3] at MIT, they recaptured the attention of academia and industry after the invention of Turbo codes in 1993 by Berrou *et al.* [4]. LDPC codes allow working close to the Shannon limit [5] and achieving excellent bit error rate (BER) performances.

Conventional approaches for LDPC decoding were, until recently, exclusively based on VLSI systems. Although they achieve excellent throughput [1, 2], they also represent nonflexible solutions with high nonrecurring engineering (NRE). Also, they apply low precision to represent data and use fixed-point arithmetic, which imposes quantization effects that limit coding gains, BER, and error floors. Thus, flexible and reprogrammable LDPC decoders can introduce important advantages, not only for real-time processing but also for researching new and more efficient LDPC codes. By developing suitable data structures and exploiting data parallelism with appropriate precision, it is possible to efficiently decode massive amounts of data by using multithreaded GPUs supported by CUDA.

38.2 CORE TECHNOLOGY

Belief propagation, also known as sum-product algorithm (SPA), is an iterative algorithm [5] for the computation of joint probabilities on graphs commonly used in information theory (e.g., channel coding), artificial intelligence, and computer vision (e.g., stereo vision). It has proved to be an efficient algorithm for inference calculation, and it is used in numerous applications, including LDPC codes [3], Turbo codes [4], stereo vision applied to robotics [6], or in Bayesian networks. LDPCs are linear (N, K) block codes defined by sparse binary parity-check $\mathbf{H}$ matrices of dimension $M \times N$, with $M = N - K$ and rate $= K/N$. They code messages of length K into sequences of length N and are usually represented by bipartite graphs formed by bit nodes (BNs) and check nodes (CNs) linked by bidirectional edges [5, 8] also called Tanner graphs [7]. The decoding process is based on the belief propagation of messages between connected nodes of the graph (as illustrated in Figure 38.1), which demands very intensive processing and memory accesses running the SPA [5].

The SPA applied to LDPC decoding is illustrated in Algorithm 1 and is mainly described by two (horizontal and vertical) intensive processing blocks [8] defined, respectively, by Eqs. 38.1 to 38.2 and Eqs. 38.3 to 38.4. Initially, the LDPC decoder receives the p_n channel probabilities, which represent the input data of Algorithm 1 (in the first iteration, q_{nm} values are initialized with p_n). Kernel 1 computes Eqs. 38.1 and 38.2, calculating the message update from CN_m to BN_n, which indicates the probability of BN_n being 0 or 1. In Eqs. 38.1 and 38.2 q_{nm} values are read and r_{mn} values are updated, as defined by the Tanner graph illustrated in Figure 38.1. Similarly, Eqs. 38.3 and 38.4 compute messages sent from BN_n to CN_m. In this case, r_{mn} values are read and q_{nm} values are updated. Finally, Eqs. 38.5 and 38.6 compute the a posteriori pseudo-probabilities and Eq. 38.7 performs the hard decoding. The iterative procedure is stopped if the decoded word $\hat{\mathbf{c}}$ verifies all parity-check equations of the code ($\hat{\mathbf{c}}\mathbf{H}^T = \mathbf{0}$), or if the maximum number of iterations (I) is reached.

Different levels of thread coarsening and data parallelism can be exploited, namely, by following an edge, node, or codeword processing approach. Although memory accesses in LDPC decoding are not regular, we propose a compact data representation of the Tanner graph suitable for stream computing. This type of processing can be efficiently handled by GPUs.

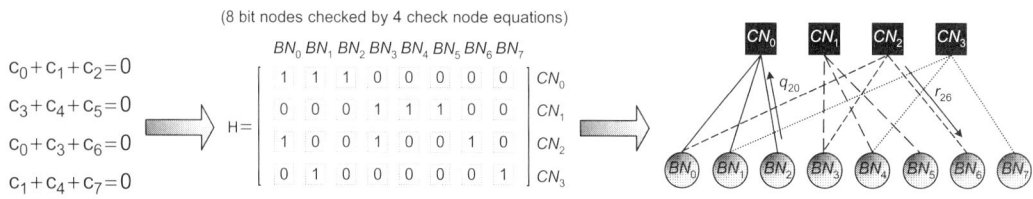

FIGURE 38.1

Linear block code [4, 8] example: parity-check equations, corresponding $\mathbf{H}$ matrix, and equivalent Tanner graph [7] representing an LDPC code.

Algorithm 1: Sum-product algorithm — SPA.

1: {Initialization}
$pn = p(yi = 1); q_{mn}^{(0)}(0) = 1 - p_n; q_{mn}^{(0)}(1) = p_n;$
2: **while** ($\mathbf{H}\hat{\mathbf{c}}^T \neq \mathbf{0} \wedge i < I$) {$\hat{\mathbf{c}}$-decoded word; I-Max. no. of iterations.} **do**
3:    {For all pairs (BN_n, CN_m), corresponding to $\mathbf{H_{mn}} = \mathbf{1}$ in parity-check matrix $\mathbf{H}$ of the code **do**:}
4:    {Compute messages sent from CN_m to BN_n, that indicate the probability of BN_n being 0 or 1:}

> *(Kernel 1 – Horizontal Processing)*

$$r_{min}^{(i)}(0) = \frac{1}{2} + \frac{1}{2} \prod_{n' \in \mathcal{N}(m)\backslash n} \left(1 - 2q_{n'm}^{(i-1)}(1)\right) \tag{38.1}$$

$$r_{min}^{(i)}(1) = 1 - r_{mn}^{(i)}(0) \tag{38.2}$$

{where $\mathcal{N}(m)\backslash n$ represents BNs connected to CN_m excluding BN_n.}
5:    {Compute message from BN_n to CN_m:}

> *(Kernel 2 – Vertical Processing)*

$$q_{nm}^{(i)}(0) = k_{nm}(1 - p_n) \prod_{m' \in \mathcal{M}(n)\backslash m} r_{m'n}^{(i)}(0) \tag{38.3}$$

$$q_{nm}^{(i)}(1) = k_{nm}p_n \prod_{m' \in \mathcal{M}(n)\backslash m} r_{m'n}^{(i)}(1) \tag{38.4}$$

{where k_{nm} are chosen to ensure $q_{nm}^{(i)}(0) + q_{nm}^{(i)}(1) = 1$, and $M(n)\backslash m$ is the set of CNs connected to BN_n excluding CN_m.}
6:    {Compute the *a posteriori* pseudo-probabilities:}

$$Q_n^{(i)}(0) = k_n(1 - p_n) \prod_{m \in \mathcal{M}(n)} r_{mn}^{(i)}(0) \tag{38.5}$$

$$Q_n^{(i)}(1) = k_n p_n \prod_{m \in \mathcal{M}(n)} r_{mn}^{(i)}(1) \tag{38.6}$$

{where k_n are chosen to guarantee $Q_n^{(i)}(0) + Q_n^{(i)}(1) = 1$.}
7:    {Perform hard decoding:}
$\forall n,$

$$\hat{c}_n^{(i)} = \begin{cases} 1 \leftarrow Q_n^{(i)}(1) > 0.5 \\ 0 \leftarrow Q_n^{(i)}(1) < 0.5 \end{cases} \tag{38.7}$$

8:    **end while**

38.3 ALGORITHMS, IMPLEMENTATIONS, AND EVALUATIONS

To obtain efficient parallel algorithms for programmable LDPC decoders, we have developed compact data structures to represent the sparse binary parity-check **H** matrices that describe the Tanner graph. They adequately represent data as streams to suit the parallel processing of the SPA in GPU stream-based architectures, which represents a different solution from the conventional compress row storage (CRS) and compress column storage (CCS) formats used to represent sparse matrices in a compact format. The edges of the Tanner graph are represented using the addressing mechanism depicted in Figure 38.2, which facilitates the simultaneous access to different data elements required by the SPA. The compact data structures herein proposed also suit parallel architectures that can impose restrictions owing to the size and alignment of data. Associated to these compact data structures, we adopted an adequate thread-coarsening level capable of supporting the GPU execution of both horizontal and vertical kernels described in Algorithm 1.

38.3.1 Data Structures and Memory Accesses

The first challenge when developing a parallel LDPC decoder on a GPU is related with the need of holding the addresses of the Tanner graph's edges in memory (like the one in Figure 38.1). In order to update r_{mn} and q_{nm} values as described from Eq. 38.1 to Eq. 38.2, we developed dedicated data structures to organize these addresses in memory, namely, $\mathbf{H}_{CN}$ and $\mathbf{H}_{BN}$, as illustrated in Figure 38.2 for the case of Figure 38.1. Before computation starts, the addresses are read from a file to initialize the data structures, which are then copied from host memory to the device. As Figure 38.2 indicates, $\mathbf{H}_{BN}$ and $\mathbf{H}_{CN}$ structures are used to write r_{mn} and q_{nm} data elements in kernels 1 and 2, respectively,

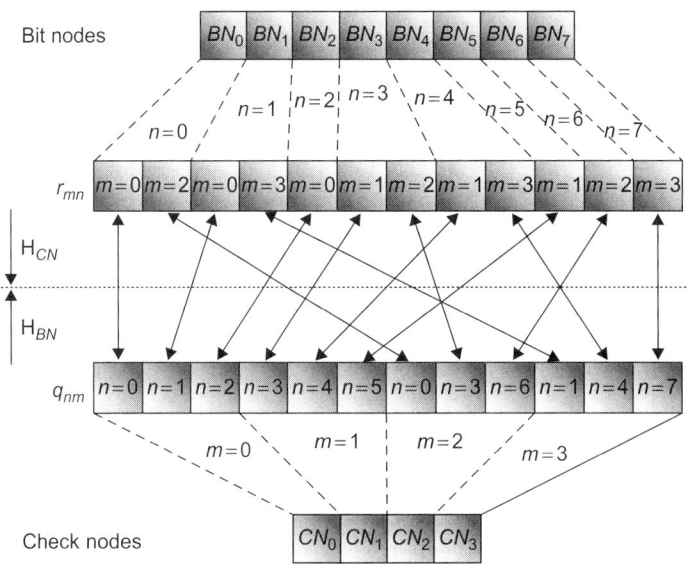

FIGURE 38.2

Data structures $\mathbf{H}_{CN}$ and $\mathbf{H}_{BN}$ that hold the addresses of $\mathbf{H}$'s edges, illustrating the example in Figure 38.1.

while reading operations are performed sequentially. According to Algorithm 1, q_{nm} data are read and processed to update r_{mn} values, and the reciprocal applies for updating q_{nm} values. Because the Tanner graph can be shared among distinct codewords, for simultaneously decoding multiple codewords in parallel, the data structures $\mathbf{H}_{CN}$ and $\mathbf{H}_{BN}$ can be shared, as Figure 38.3 illustrates. The parallel algorithm developed exploits parallelism $P = 6 \times 16$ by decoding six clusters of data, with 16 packed codewords per cluster. Data are represented with 8-bit precision, which allows 16 elements to be fetched/stored from/into memory on a single 128-bit access.

38.3.2 Coarse versus Fine-Grained Thread Parallelism

The second challenge is to balance computation with memory access communications in order to avoid idle periods. This leads to the development of a thread-per-BN and thread-per-CN approach based on the well-known forward-and-backward method [5] to minimize computation and memory accesses in LDPC decoding.

Figure 38.3 illustrates this approach, by showing each thread th_n processing a complete row or column of $\mathbf{H}$. The adoption of the forward-and-backward optimization becomes even more important in the context of parallel computing architectures, because it minimizes memory accesses that often constrain the GPU performance. The proposed parallelization is more efficient than having each thread updating a single edge of the Tanner graph, a situation where redundant communications would dominate. Figure 38.4 illustrates the procedure used in the thread-per-CN approach, with threads j, u, and v processing the example in Figure 38.1, where each thread updates a complete row of $\mathbf{H}$ (or r_{mn} data). Each block of threads of the GPU grid updates groups of nodes of $\mathbf{H}$.

38.3.3 An LDPC Decoding Kernel

Figure 38.5 shows the source code for the LDPC decoder on the host and depicts the execution of the kernels on the GPU. It initializes the GPU grid, programs the kernel, and fires execution. Each iteration of the decoder executes the kernel twice, with the pF flag indicating a request for horizontal (kernel 1) or vertical processing (kernel 2), respectively. For the example of LDPC code (8000, 4000) in Figure 38.5, the grid is programmed with 125 blocks and 64 threads per block. For the horizontal

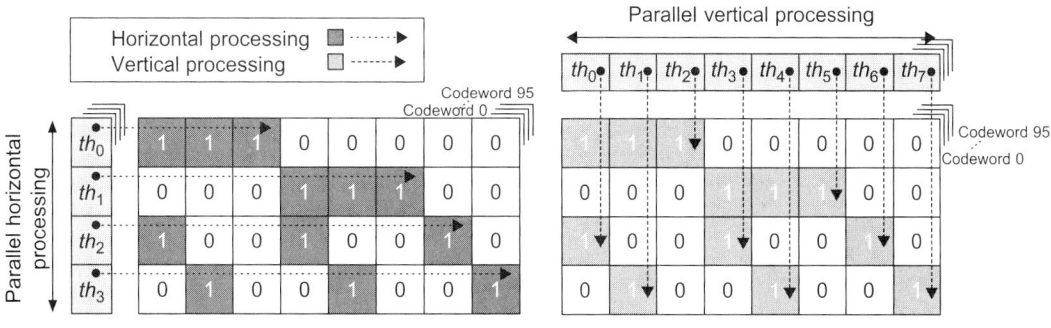

FIGURE 38.3

Task and data parallelism illustrating the example in Figure 38.1, where thread-per-CN (horizontal processing) and thread-per-BN (vertical processing) approaches are followed.

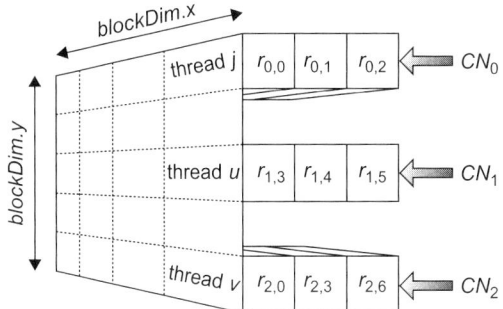

FIGURE 38.4

Block configuration of the GPU for the example in Figure 38.1. Each thread processes a complete row/column node of **H** according to Algorithm 1.

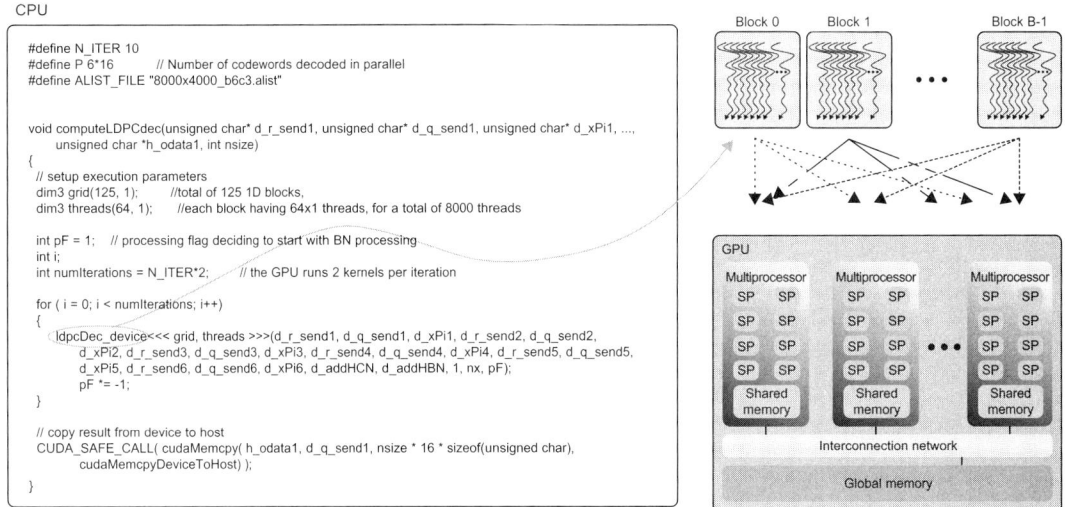

FIGURE 38.5

Host program launching parallel kernels on the device, where threads are grouped in blocks. The thread scheduler controls execution.

processing (kernel 1), the six input clusters of data are represented by elements d_q_send1 to d_q_send6, while processed data is stored in d_r_send1 to d_r_send6. The inverse applies for the vertical processing (kernel 2) where d_xPi1 to d_xPi6 represent the initial probabilities p_n in Algorithm 1 at the input of the decoder.

Listing 38.1 shows a segment of the device's kernel 1. The *update_rmn*() kernel in Listing 38.1 computes Eqs. 38.1 and 38.2 — the horizontal processing — and it updates and stores d_r1 elements in noncontiguous memory addresses obtained from the data structure d_HBN. At this point, d_q1 data is read sequentially, and the reciprocal applies for the *update_qnm*() kernel. Listing 38.1 shows the

```
update_rmn(uint4 *d_r1, uint4 *d_q1, ..., uint4 *d_r6, uint4 *d_q6,
                                short *d_HBN, int width, int height)
{
    unsigned int xIndex = blockDim.x * blockIdx.x + threadIdx.x;
    unsigned int yIndex = blockDim.y * blockIdx.y + threadIdx.y;
    unsigned int index_horiz = xIndex + width * yIndex;
    .
    .
    .
    // processing first subword (reading d_q1 and producing d_r1) using the forward−and−backward method
    .
    .
    .
    a2 = r−2.0 f*lei0; fin1 = r−2.0 f*lei1;
    fin2 = r−2.0 f*lei2; fin3 = r−2.0 f*lei3;
    fin4 = r−2.0 f*lei4; b5 = r−2.0 f*lei5;
    a3 = a2*fin1; b4 = b5*fin4;
    a4 = a3*fin2; b3 = b4*fin3;
    a5 = a4*fin3; b2 = b3*fin2;
    a6 = a5*fin4; b1 = b2*fin1;
    wm2 = a2*b2; wm3 = a3*b3;
    wm4 = a4*b4; wm5 = a5*b5;
    wm1_3 = b1*0.5 f+0.5 f; auxmul1_3 = wm2*0.5 f+0.5 f;
    auxmul2_3 = wm3*0.5 f+0.5 f; auxmul3_3 = wm4*0.5 f+0.5 f;
    auxmul4_3 = wm5*0.5 f+0.5 f; wm6_3 = a6*0.5 f+0.5 f;
    .
    .
    .
    d_r1[dHBN[index0]].x = (((unsigned char)(wm1_0*SCALE))<<24)|(((unsigned char)(wm1_1*SCALE))
                <<16)|(((unsigned char)(wm12*SCALE))<<8)|((unsigned char)(wm1_3*SCALE));
    d_r1[dHBN[index1]].x = (((unsigned char)(auxmul1_0*SCALE))<<24)|(((unsigned char)(auxmul1_1*SCALE))
                <<16)|(((unsigned char)(auxmul1_2*SCALE))<<8)|((unsigned char)(auxmul1_3*SCALE));
    .
    .
    .
    ... // processing next subword (reading d_q2 and producing d_r2), etc.
    .
    .
    .
}

__global__ void ldpcDec_device( uint4 *d_r1, uint4 *d_q1, uint4 *d_xPi1, ..., uint4 *d_r6, uint4 *d_q6,
                uint4 *d_xPi6, short *d_HCN, short *d_HBN, int width, int height, int procFlag )
{

    // procFlag decides between BN or CN processing
    if(procFlag>=0)                //BN processing
    {    // Fire kernel 1
        update_rmn(    d_r1,    d_q1, ..., d_r6, d_q6, d_HBN, width, height );
    }
    else                            // CN processing
    {    // Fire kernel 2
        update_qnm(    d_r1,    d_q1,    d_xPi1, ..., d_r6, d_q6, d_xPi6, d_HCN, width, height );
    }
}
```

Listing 38.1: Kernel code on the GPU.

level of parallelism $P = 96$ adopted. For each data element we allocate memory of type *unsigned char* (8 bits), while data buffers are of type *uint*4 (128 bits). In the beginning of processing, data are unpacked and normalized. After processing completes on the GPU, data elements are rescaled and repacked in groups of 8 bits in subword **x** (the type *uint4* disposes data into four 32-bit subwords **xyzw**). The same rule applies for the other codewords (**yzw** and also for data clusters 2, 3, 4, 5, and 6). This packing procedure optimizes data transfers between host and device, while at the same time increases the arithmetic intensity of the algorithm.

The same principle is followed for the computation of Eqs. 38.3 and 38.4 — vertical processing. Here, d_q1 to d_q6 data elements are processed and updated, after reading the corresponding d_r1 to d_r6 and d_xPi1 to d_xPi6 input elements.

38.4 **FINAL EVALUATION**

We adopt 8-bit data precision on the GPU, which contrasts with typical 5- to 6-bit representations used in VLSI, with advantages on BER. For example, for WiMAX code (1248, 624) [2] with an SNR = 2.5 dB, the BER performance with 8-bit precision is almost one order of magnitude better than by using 6-bit precision [10]. Furthermore, because it is programmable, the GPU allows using even higher precision to represent data (e.g., 16 or 32 bits) with superior BER results, at the cost of throughput performance.

The programming environments and platforms adopted for evaluating the proposed algorithm are the 8800 GTX GeForce GPU from NVIDIA with 128 stream processors (SP), each running at 1.35 GHz and with a total of 768 MB of video memory (VRAM), and the CUDA 2.0b programming environment. For comparison purposes, we have also programmed the LDPC decoder on an eight-core Intel Xeon Nehalem 2x-Quad E5530 multi-processor running at 2.4 GHz with 8 MB of L2 cache memory, by using OpenMP 3.0. The LDPC codes used represent regular codes with $w_c = 6$ edges per row and $w_b = 3$ edges per column. Table 38.1 presents the overall measured decoding throughputs running the SPA on the GPU and the speedup regarding the CPU [11, 12]. Experimental results in the table show that the GPU-based solution reports throughputs up to 35.1 Mbps for code (8000, 4000) (with 24,000

Table 38.1 LDPC decoding (SPA) throughput (Mbps) with an NVIDIA GPU using CUDA, and speedup regarding an Intel CPU (eight cores) programmed with OpenMP.

	LDPC code			
	(1024, 512)		(8000, 4000)	
No. of iterations	GPU	Speedup	GPU	Speedup
10	14.6	7.0	35.1	13.8
25	6.5	7.5	15.8	13.7
50	3.3	7.2	8.2	13.4

edges) running 10 iterations, while it achieves 2.5 Mbps for the same code decoded on the CPU using eight cores. The throughput values indicated for the GPU already consider computation time and data transfer time between host and device.

Algorithm 1 shows that the procedure to perform LDPC decoding is iterative and that each iteration executes two kernels. As illustrated in Figure 38.5 and Listing 38.1, each iteration implies calling the kernel *ldpcDec_device()* twice, with flag *pF* set to 1 or -1, respectively. This requires a number of communications between the host and the device that, under certain circumstances, may impact performance negatively, namely, if we are executing the application on a platform with multiple GPUs that share a bus with the host.

38.4.1 Conclusion

GPUs can be considered as reprogrammable and flexible alternatives to efficiently perform LDPC decoding. They report superior throughput performance when compared with multicore CPUs and also prove to be capable of competing with hardware-dedicated solutions [9] that typically involve high NRE costs. Also, they allow achieving BER performances that compare well against dedicated hardware systems because they permit higher precision to represent data.

All source code necessary to test the algorithm here proposed is available at *gpucomputing.net*, from where it can be downloaded.

38.5 FUTURE DIRECTIONS

The parallel algorithms here proposed have been validated under the context of CUDA. Nevertheless, if we run them on more recent GPU Tesla devices with a superior number of stream processors and larger global video memory, they expectedly will present higher throughputs, maintaining the BER performance. Also, research work can be done to improve the proposed algorithms in order to exploit the more powerful Fermi architectures.

Other improvements may still be achieved by using multi-GPU systems to exploit additional levels of data parallelism.

Moreover, the concept of belief propagation — namely, the SPA here described that holds the foundations of LDPC decoding — can be applied to other areas of computer science rather than error-correcting codes, such as stereo vision applied to robotics [6], or Bayesian networks among others. This chapter will also be of particular interest to researchers and engineers working on these topics.

References

[1] F. Kienle, T. Brack, N. Wehn, A synthesizable IP Core for DVB-S2 LDPC code decoding, in: Proceedings of the Design, Automation and Test in Europe (DATE'05), 7–11 March 2005, vol. 3, IEEE Computer Society, Munich, Germany, 2005, pp. 100–105.

[2] C.-H. Liu, S.-W. Yen, C.-L. Chen, H.-C. Chang, C.-Y. Lee, Y.-S. Hsu, S.-J. Jou, An LDPC decoder chip based on self-routing network for IEEE 802.16e applications, IEEE J. Solid-State Circuits 43 (3) (2008) 684–694.

[3] R.G. Gallager, Low-density parity-check codes, IRE Trans. Inf. Theory 8 (1) (1962) 21–28.

[4] C. Berrou, A. Glavieux, P. Thitimajshima, Near Shannon limit error-correcting coding and decoding: Turbo-codes (1), in: Proceedings of the IEEE International Conference on Communications (ICC '93), 23–26 May 1993, vol. 2, IEEE, Geneva, Switzerland, 1993, pp. 1064–1070.

[5] S.B. Wicker, S. Kim, Fundamentals of Codes, Graphs, and Iterative Decoding, Kluwer Academic Publishers, Norwell, MA 02061, 2003.

[6] A. Brunton, C. Shu, G. Roth, Belief propagation on the GPU for stereo vision, in: Proceedings of the 3rd Canadian Conference on Computer and Robot Vision (CRV'06), 7–9 June 2006, IEEE and IEEE Computer Society, pp. 76–76.

[7] R. Tanner, A recursive approach to low complexity codes, IEEE Trans. Inf. Theory 27 (5) (1981) 533–547.

[8] T.K. Moon, Error Correction Coding — Mathematical Methods and Algorithms, John Wiley & Sons, Inc., Hoboken, New Jersey, 2005.

[9] G. Falcao, V. Silva, L. Sousa, How GPUs can outperform ASICs for fast LDPC decoding, in: Proceedings of the 23rd International Conference on Supercomputing (ICS'09), ACM, New York, 2009, pp. 390–399.

[10] G. Falcao, V. Silva, L. Sousa, High coded data rate and multicodeword WiMAX LDPC decoding on Cell/BE, IET Electron. Lett. 44 (24) (2008) 1415–1417.

[11] G. Falcao, L. Sousa, V. Silva, Massive parallel LDPC decoding on GPU, in: S. Chatterjee, M.L. Scott (Eds.), Proceedings of the 13th ACM SIGPLAN Symposium on Principles and Practice of Parallel Programming (PPoPP'08), 20–23 February 2008, ACM, Salt Lake City, Utah, 2008, pp. 83–90.

[12] G. Falcao, L. Sousa, V. Silva, Massively LDPC decoding on multicore architectures, IEEE Trans. Parallel Distrib. Syst. (TPDS) (in press).

Large-Scale Fast Fourier Transform

39

Yifeng Chen, Xiang Cui, Hong Mei

Bandwidth-intensive tasks such as large-scale fast Fourier transfers (FFTs) without data locality are hard to accelerate on GPU clusters because the bottleneck often lies with the PCI bus or the communication network. Optimizing FFT for a single-GPU device will not improve the overall performance. This chapter shows how to achieve substantial speedups for these tasks. Three GPU-related factors contribute to better performance: first, the use of GPU devices improves the sustained memory bandwidth for processing large-size data; second, GPU device memory allows larger subtasks to be processed in whole and hence reduces repeated data transfers between memory and processors; and finally some costly main-memory operations such as matrix transposition can be significantly sped up by GPUs if necessary data adjustment is performed during data transfers. The technique of manipulating array dimensions during data transfer is the main technical contribution. These factors (as well as the improved communication library in our implementation) attribute to 24.3x speedup with respect to FFTW and 7x speedup with respect to Intel MKL for 4096 3-D single-precision FFT on a 16-node cluster with 32 GPUs. Around 5x speedups with respect to both standard libraries are achieved for double precision.

39.1 INTRODUCTION

A GPU cluster is a network-connected workstation cluster with one or more GPU devices on each node. Several such systems are now ranked among the top 20 fastest supercomputers (as of June 2010).

Computation-intensive tasks such as dense matrix multiplication and Linpack are often easy to accelerate by GPUs [1–3]. Memory-bandwidth-intensive tasks with a high degree of data locality such as finite-difference simulation are also suitable for GPU clusters [4]: the source data in 2-D or 3-D can be decomposed spatially and distributed over the device memories ("dmem") of GPUs, which only communicate with each other about state updates at the boundaries of the spatial decomposition so that the bandwidth between GPU devices (through PCI bus and Infiniband) will not form the performance bottleneck. Applications can benefit from the high bandwidth of dmem and achieve significant speedups. Memory-bandwidth-intensive tasks without data locality such as large-scale FFT [5], on the other hand, are much harder to accelerate.

Most existing codes [6–9] assume FFTs to have a "small scale" so that the entire user data can be held in one GPU's dmem. It fits an application scenario in which FFT is performed repeatedly on these data. Then the overhead to transfer the source data from and to the host memory (i.e., the main memory or simply hmem) is overwhelmed by the computation time.

In this chapter, we consider a "large-scale" FFT whose dataset is too large to fit in one GPU's dmem and requires multiple GPU nodes. The performance bottleneck then lies with either PCI bandwidth between hmem and dmem or the network's communication bandwidth between GPU nodes. Some applications, such as turbulence simulation, use FFT as large as 4096 3-D (total 512 GB complex-to-complex data in single precision). Compared with a single node, a cluster will provide multiplied memory bandwidth and memory capacity. FFT on a cluster requires transposition of the entire array over the network — an operation usually requiring communication of the entire dataset and slow hmem transpositions on each individual node [10]. It is not obvious how GPU with high-compute capability and on-card memory bandwidth can help accelerate such tasks.

In this chapter, we take on this challenge and design and implement an FFT code that achieves 24.3x speedup (using GPUs) with respect to FFTW (not using GPUs) and 7x speedup with respect to Intel MKL (not using GPUs) on a 16-node cluster with two GPU devices and two QDR infiniband adapters on each node. Around 5x speedups with respect to both standard libraries are achieved for double-precision FFTs.

Figure 39.1 illustrates the architecture of our test cluster with 16 nodes. Each node is connected with an NVIDIA Tesla C1060 GPU, a GTX 285 GPU, and two Mellanox ConnectX QDR Infiniband adapters with a combined peak duplex bandwidth of 80 Gbps. Motherboards are Supermicro X9DAH+F, each providing 18 DIMM slots, two IOH controllers, and multiple PCI-e 2.0-gen. Each node has one Xeon Quad-Core E5520 2.26G CPU and 36 GB 1066 MHz memory. The main characteristic of this cluster is its balanced bandwidth for PCI and the network.

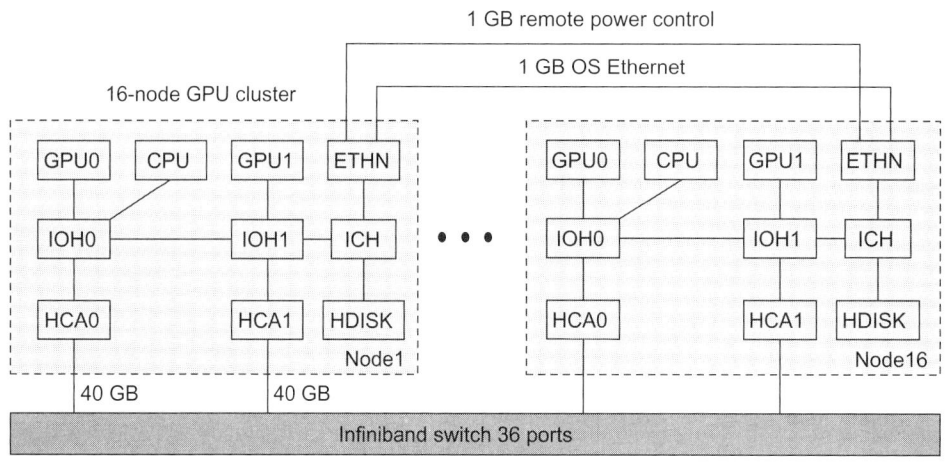

FIGURE 39.1

The architecture of PKU McClus cluster.

Several factors have contributed to the surprising performance of our FFT on PKU McClus: first, data processing by GPUs via PCI bus is faster than sustained large memory accesses (exceeding the cache size) by CPUs; second, dmem is much larger than CPU cache and hence allows larger sub-tasks to be processed in whole and reduces repeated data transfers between memory and processors; finally, array transposition on the GPU is much faster than that in hmem by CPUs. As a major technical contribution, we discover that by applying subtle data adjustments during data transfers (between dmem and hmem and between hmem and infiniband buffers), arrays no longer need hmem transposition. GPU transposition is up to 20 times faster than CPU transposition. For example, when copying a 512 MB array block from hmem to dmem, the algorithm partitions the data block and transfers it in 8 MB units. The source and destination addresses of these units are carefully permuted so that the effect of hmem transposition can be achieved by a combination of the permutation and some fast GPU transposition. This method of dimensional manipulation is also readily applicable to other algorithms of GPU clustering.

39.2 MEMORY HIERARCHY OF GPU CLUSTERS

The most notable characteristic of a GPU-accelerated workstation cluster is its exposed memory hierarchy. Different memory media have different sizes and bandwidth. There are two types of hmem: "pageable memory" and "pinned memory." Both can be very large (36 GB on PKU McClus), but relatively slow compared with other types of memory. The device memory of GPUs is smaller (e.g., 1 GB for GTX285 and 4 GB for C1060), but much faster. The bandwidth for data transfers between pinned hmem and dmem can be twice as fast as that between pageable hmem and dmem. L1 and L2 caches on CPU normally have several MBs and are faster than dmem. Memory components such as shared memory (or smem) and registers on GPU offer a combined throughput much higher than CPU caches. Instructions entirely operating on registers are known to outperform instructions with smem operands [3].

Figure 39.2 provides a convenient starting point for algorithm design. It illustrates the peak bandwidth of one-way singlex and two-way duplex data transfers on PKU McClus. Two-way singlex arrows are used if both directions of singlex data transfers have the same bandwidth. The bandwidth figures are all tested using real codes. In our tests, bandwidths of 73 GB/s and 122 GB/s are obtained on C1060 and GTX285, respectively, for properly coalesced dmem accesses. A common bottleneck for GPU acceleration lies with the PCI bus. The peak bandwidth from pinned hmem to dmem is 5.7 GB/s for one GPU device (either C1060 or GTX285). Bandwidth from dmem to pinned hmem can reach 5.4 GB/s. Bandwidth from or to pageable hmem is lower at 3.3 GB/s or 2.7 GB/s. When one is transferring data from pinned hmem to two GPUs simultaneously, the bandwidth can reach a combined 9.4 GB/s, while the opposite direction reaches 6.2 GB/s. The PCI of a GT200-based GPU works only in singlex mode. Thus, by overlapping computation and data transfers in streamed data processing, two GPUs can average 9.4*6.2/(9.4+6.2) = 3.7 GB/s. Note that the memcpy bandwidth within hmem is tested on a single-CPU thread. Multiple threads can reach about twice the bandwidth on our cluster.

Singlex infiniband communication through one Quad Data Rate (QDR) host channel adapter (HCA) on each node delivers 3 GB/s bandwidth using OpenMPI, while duplex communication only reaches 2.2 GB/s for either direction. OpenMPI is intended to be a transparent layer that handles the infiniband topology automatically. Ideally, the bandwidth using two HCA cards should be doubled, but our tests

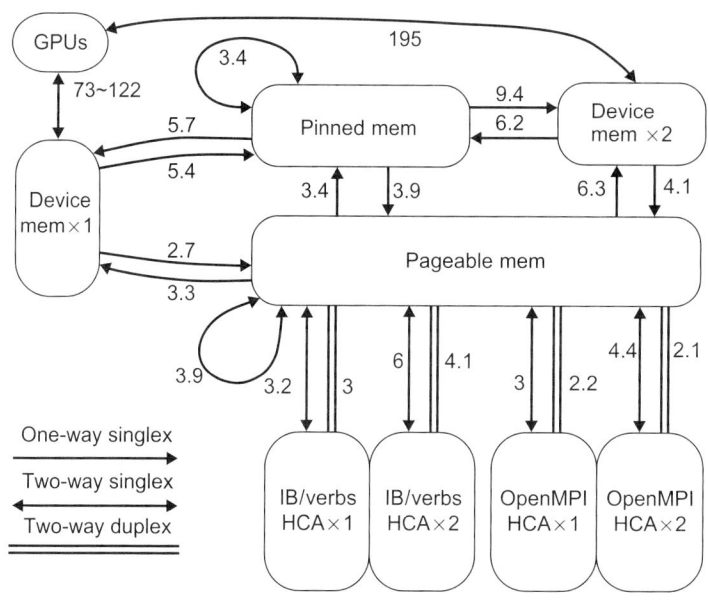

FIGURE 39.2

Bandwidth relations in GB/s between different memory media.

show that it only reaches 2.1 GB/s for either direction (under both OpenMPI 1.2.8 and OSU Mvapich2 1.2) in a so-called trunking, or link aggregation, mode. To maximize the bandwidth, we have developed an interface directly invoking IB/verbs's RDMA communication, achieving duplex 4.1 GB/s (for either direction), and singlex communication is improved to 6 GB/s as well. All tests are performed on direct HCA connections without switching. On our cluster, PCIs (with duplex 3.7 GB/s in combination) now reach a similar bandwidth as the infiniband's 4.1 GB/s. This is ideal for bandwidth-intensive tasks without data locality so that neither the PCI nor the network forms an obvious bottleneck.

Hardware and low-level software often require data to be transferred in certain restricted patterns. Failure to observe these patterns can yield very poor performances. For example, the GPU must access dmem in coalesced patterns. Noncoalesced dmem accesses can be exceedingly slow. In some algorithms it is advantageous to perform certain data adjustment during data transfers, which inevitably incur overheads. Our experiment shows that to reach near-peak bandwidth, data should be transferred in no-less-than 2 MB units between hmem and dmem. This provides a lower limit to the granularity of data transfers. Similarly, network bandwidth is also affected by message lengths (though much finer granularity is tolerated). Tests also show that duplex bandwidth about 4 GB/s seems to be as much as we can squeeze out of a typical 5500-series motherboard's PCI bus with 1066 MHz memory. That means when PCI bus and infiniband HCAs operate in parallel, their combined bandwidth will be capped. Streaming operations can overlap computation and communication, but the room for improvement is limited.

The software environment may also impose platform-related restrictions that further complicate the design and implementation of algorithms. Our FFT solution assumes CUDA 2.3 or higher because greater than 4 GB contiguous pinned hmem is needed. Another software restriction requires pinned memory not to be directly used as infiniband buffer. Our FFT solution works under this restriction.

39.3 LARGE-SCALE FAST FOURIER TRANSFORM

The process of data partition and distribution for traditional clusters is flat: the source data are distributed over all processes. GPU clusters, however, require data to be further decomposed according to the memory hierarchy.

39.3.1 A Naive Algorithm

To illustrate the design of our algorithm, we consider the largest FFT that the cluster can accommodate in the main memory. The source array is of three-dimensional 4096^3 complex-to-complex in single precision with total 512 GB data (32 GB on each of the 16 nodes), which is close to the total hmem size 576 GB. Note that storing data in GPU dmem will not improve performance because any communication with other GPUs will inevitably go through hmem and the network. The bottleneck still lies with PCI or the network.

Let us first consider a naive algorithm illustrated in Figure 39.3(a). At first glance, what we need to do is to decompose the 3-D array along one of the dimensions so that each node holds a $4096 \times 4096 \times 256$ subarray of complex numbers. In order to use both GPUs (which have separate pinned hmem), we further halve the subarray into two $4096 \times 4096 \times 128$ subarrays of 16 GB each. In the first phase of 3-D-FFT, each GPU performs 128 2-D (for the the first two dimensions) FFTs, which are grouped into a stream of 32 batches, each as $4096 \times 4096 \times 4$ of 512 MB (fitting in device memory). As the computation time is overwhelmed by data transfers in the streaming operation, we simply use CUFFT. The results from the first phase are swapped with other nodes via AllToAll infiniband communications. Data are copied to the outgoing infiniband buffer before communication and from the

for loop	for loop
pinned2d – 2D CUFFT – d2pinned	pinned2d – 2D CUFFT – d2IBbuf
memcpy pinned to IB buffer	AllToAll
AllToAll	| memcpy IB buffer to pinned (with adjustment)
memcpy IB buffer to pinned	for All
CPU hmem transposition	pinned2d (with adjustment)
for loop	**GPU dmem transposition**
pinned2d – 1D CUFFT – d2pinned	1D FFT kernel
CPU hmem transposition	**GPU dmem transposition**
for loop	d2pinned (with adjustment)
memcpy pinned to IB buffer	for loop
AllToAll	memcpy pinned to IB buffer (with adjustment)
memcpy IB buffer to pinned	| AllToAll
	| memcpy IB buffer to pinned
(a) Naive FFT algorithm	(b) PKUFFT algorithm

FIGURE 39.3

3D-FFT algorithms.

incoming buffer after communication. The purpose is to merge the results from different nodes so that the third dimension becomes continuous on each node, and then we can apply CUFFT again to perform batched 1-D-FFT for the third dimension. Note that AllToAll communications alone cannot completely transpose the first two dimensions with the third dimension. We need the CPU's local transposition in every individual node's hmem. For 32 GB of data, this is an expensive operation. After transposition, the data can then be grouped into $4096 \times 4 \times 4096$ subarrays so that we can use GPUs to compute their FFTs for the third dimension in a streaming operation. Another round of CPU-hmem transposition is needed before restoring the original element positions for the result array.

39.3.2 Optimized Algorithm

Our more optimized algorithm is illustrated in Figure 39.3(b). Several minor aspects of the naive algorithm are improved. Dmem data after the 2-D FFTs can be directly downloaded to the outgoing IB buffer. That saves one round of copying from hmem to the outgoing buffer. The data from the incoming IB buffer are transferred to the appropriate destinations in the hmem. The three steps of batched 2-D FFTs, AllToAll communications and transfers from buffer to hmem can be pipelined. Similarly after 1-D-FFT for the third dimension, transferring the batch to the outgoing buffer, AllToAll communications and transferring from the incoming buffer can be pipelined and parallelized. Our experiments show that parallelizing the PCI transfers with infiniband communication does not offer any performance gain, but parallelizing transfers from/to buffers with infiniband communication does. Experiments also show little performance advantage to perform FFTs on CPU and GPU at the same time owing to the capped overall bandwidth.

Notice that the naive algorithm performs two CPU transpositions in hmem. These operations make sure that data of the third dimension are aggregated in addresses close to each other. On modern clusters, the network bandwidth is in the same range as the hmem bandwidth. Hmem transpositions thus become comparably expensive.

Can better results be achieved, given that GPUs can perform very fast dmem transpositions owing to the high dmem bandwidth? It turns out that this is possible if certain data adjustments are performed during data transfers between hmem and dmem and between hmem and infiniband buffers. The idea is that when, for example, transferring 512 MB data from hmem to dmem just before the third dimension's FFT, we partition the data and transfer them in 8 MB units. The source and destination offsets are carefully permuted so that the data are moved to the right places convenient for the following operations. Such data adjustment, as well as various array partitioning for GPUs and infiniband buffers, requires sophisticated manipulation of array dimensions, which will be the topic of the next section. Note that GPU transpositions are still needed for data manipulation at smaller scales because data transfers between different memory media require a certain level of granularity. Thus, the transposition of an entire array over the network requires a combination of data adjustment and GPU transpositions.

Figure 39.4 shows the threads on a single node and the data flow. Two GPUs deliver a combined PCI bandwidth. As any pinned hmem is owned by the thread that allocates it, two separate areas of pinned hmem and two infiniband communication buffers are allocated and associated to the GPUs. Eight CPU threads run on each node: two for controlling the GPUs, two for infiniband communications, and another four for managing the infiniband buffers and moving data between pageable buffers and pinned memory.

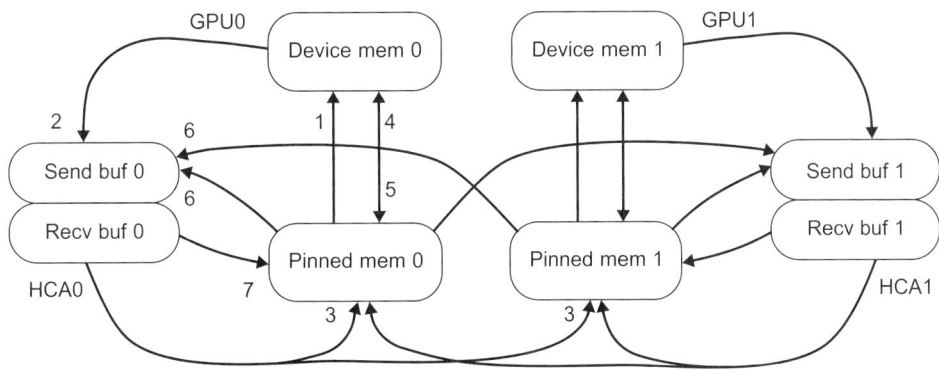

FIGURE 39.4

Data flow of 3-D-FFT on a single node.

39.4 ALGEBRAIC MANIPULATION OF ARRAY DIMENSIONS

We now study an algebraic method that can help algorithm designers determine the layouts of the array dimensions in intermediate steps of an algorithm. We first introduce the notation for simple FFT operations on traditional clusters (c.f. [10]).

39.4.1 Basics

An 8×8 array is shown in Figure 39.5(a) and represented as $\dfrac{y}{[8]} \dfrac{x}{[8]}$. The dimension of rows is named as x and that of columns as y. The array is assumed to be row major (which means the dimension x is stored continuously in memory). After a local transposition, it becomes like Figure 39.5(b) and represented as $\dfrac{x}{[8]} \dfrac{y}{[8]}$ in column-major order. In these expressions, each number in brackets under a line describes the size of the dimension, and the symbol above the line denotes the dimension's name. The example array can be partitioned along dimension y and distributed over four processes, as shown in Figure 39.5(c) and represented as $\dfrac{y_1}{[4]} \dfrac{y_0}{[2]} \dfrac{x}{[8]}$. Partition along dimension x for the transposed array is illustrated in Figure 39.5(d) and represented as $\dfrac{x_1}{[4]} \dfrac{x_0}{[2]} \dfrac{y}{[8]}$. It is also possible to partition the original array along both x and y dimensions. The result is a 4×4 array of 2×2 blocks: $\dfrac{y_1}{[4]} \dfrac{x_1}{[4]} \dfrac{y_0}{[2]} \dfrac{x_0}{[2]}$.

Three-dimensional FFT for traditional clusters can now be represented algebraically. Figure 39.6(b) shows the original 3-D array

$$\frac{x_1}{[4]} \frac{x_0}{[2]} \frac{y}{[8]} \frac{z}{[8]}$$

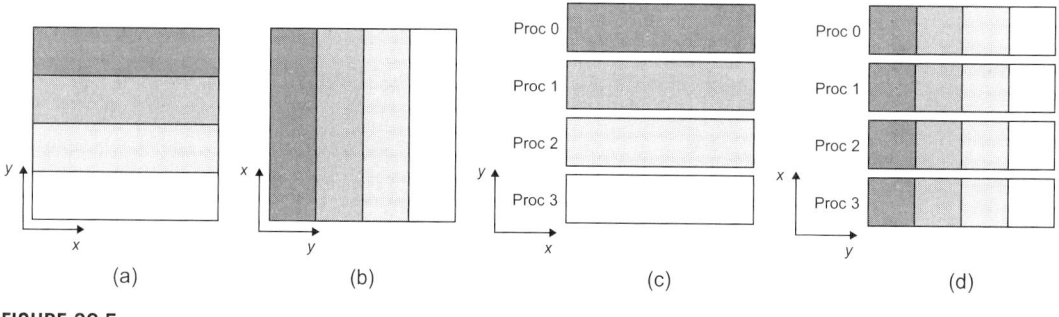

FIGURE 39.5

2-D arrays, transposition, and partition.

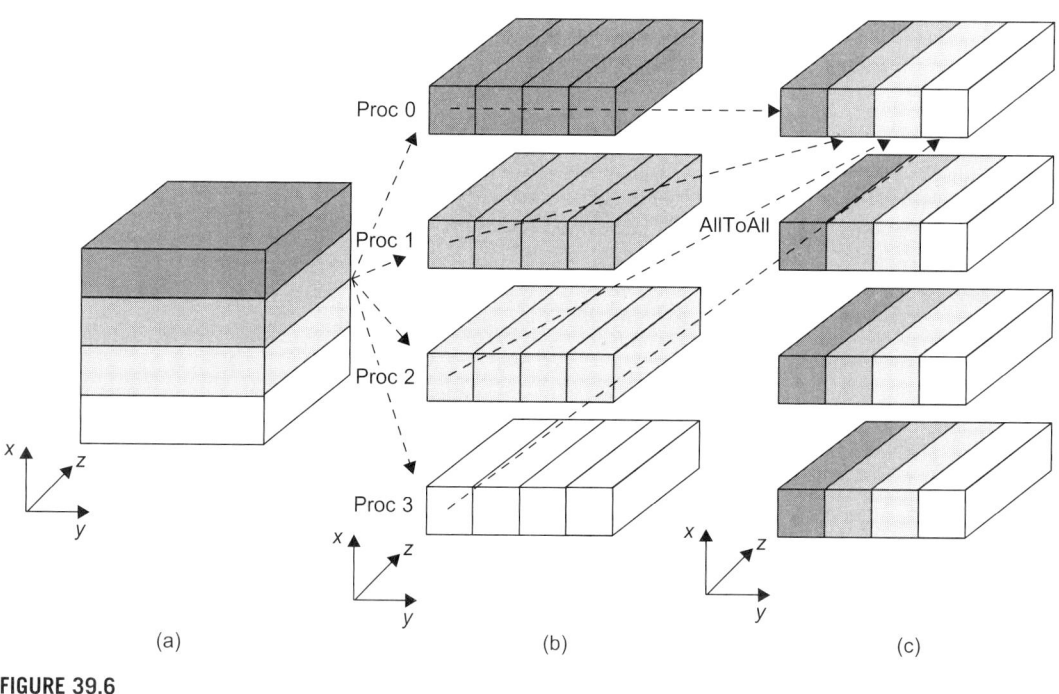

FIGURE 39.6

A three-dimensional FFT.

in which dimension x is partitioned and distributed over four processes. Batched 2-D FFTs are performed for the slice of the original array on each process. Before AllToAll communication, the results of 2-D FFTs are partitioned along dimension y for the four destination processes as

$$\frac{x_1}{[4]} \frac{x_0}{[2]} \frac{y_1}{[4]} \frac{y_0}{[2]} \frac{z}{[8]}.$$

After AllToAll communication, the array becomes

$$\frac{y_1}{[4]} \frac{x_0}{[2]} \frac{x_1}{[4]} \frac{y_0}{[2]} \frac{z}{[8]}.$$

The data are distributed along dimension y_1.

39.4.2 Avoiding Main-Memory Transpositions by Permuting Array Dimensions

We now introduce a method to adjust dimensions during data transfers (between different memory media) so that the combined effect of the adjustments together with GPU-based transpositions renders the expensive main-memory transpositions unnecessary (see Figure 39.7).

To support sophisticated parallelization, the source data are decomposed into a nine-dimensional array of complex numbers:

$$\frac{z_3}{[16]} \frac{z_2}{[2]} \quad \frac{z_1}{[32]} \frac{z_0}{[4]} \frac{y_3}{[16]} \frac{y_2}{[2]} \frac{y_1}{[32]} \frac{y_0}{[4]} \frac{x}{[4096]}$$

where dimension z_3 indicates that the array is partitioned along dimension z and distributed over 16 nodes. Dimension z_2 indicates that two separate pinned hmem areas are allocated for the two GPU devices (a restriction by CUDA for high-speed PCI data transfers).

In the first phase, each GPU computes 32 batches of four two-dimensional FFTs over dimensions x and y (which includes y_3, y_2, y_1, y_0). Each batch with four 4096^2 complex numbers of 512 MB data is computed in one round of hmem-to-dmem transfer, CUFFT and dmem-to-IBbuffer transfer. Thus, the data in all outgoing infiniband buffers (of $16 \times 2 = 32$ HCA adapters in total) have a layout:

$$\frac{z_3}{[16]} \frac{z_2}{[2]} \quad \frac{z_0}{[4]} \frac{y_3}{[16]} \frac{y_2}{[2]} \frac{y_1}{[32]} \frac{y_0}{[4]} \frac{x}{[4096]}.$$

Dimensions of the source data	[16][2] [32][4][16][2][32][4][4096]
Source data in pinned hmem	z_3 z_2 z_1 z_0 y_3 y_2 y_1 y_0 x
GPU batched 2-D FFT on x/y in dmem	z_0 y_3 y_2 y_1 y_0 x
Infiniband outgoing buffers	z_3 z_2 z_0 y_3 y_2 y_1 y_0 x
Infiniband incoming buffers	y_3 z_2 z_0 z_3 y_2 y_1 y_0 x
Pinned memory	y_3 y_2 z_1 y_1 z_3 z_2 z_0 y_0 x
GPU transposition in dmem	z_1 z_3 z_2 z_0 y_0 x
GPU batched 1-D FFT on z in dmem	x y_0 z_1 z_3 z_2 z_0

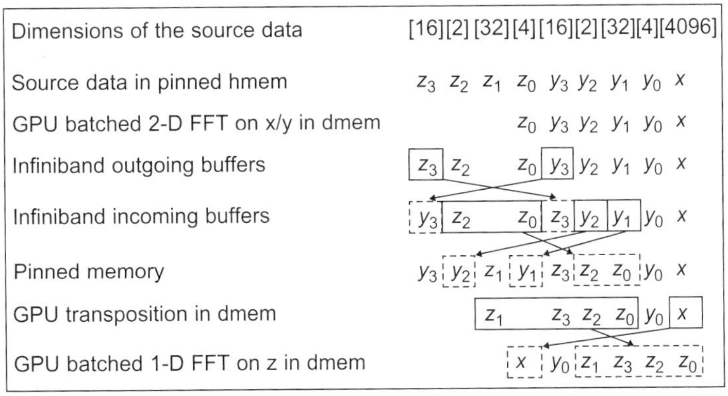

FIGURE 39.7

Permuted dimensions in the forward propagation.

In each of the 32 rounds, the AllToAll communication distributes data according to dimension y_3 over 16 nodes. Note that all HCA0 adapters communicate with each other, and so do HCA1 adapters. The layout in all incoming buffers then becomes:

$$\frac{y_3}{[16]} \frac{z_2}{[2]} \quad \frac{z_0}{[4]} \frac{z_3}{[16]} \frac{y_2}{[2]} \frac{y_1}{[32]} \frac{y_0}{[4]} \frac{x}{[4096]}.$$

As our FFT is performed in place (512 GB data in 576 GB memory), incoming data can be stored only in the memory just released after GPU computation in the first phase. When copying the data in the incoming buffers back to the pinned hmem, we perform some subtle data adjustment. The purpose is to move the subdimensions of z to the right so that the data of dimension z become more aggregated in hmem. We also try to sort the subdimensions of z as much as possible so that it is easier to coalesce dmem access for the later GPU computation. After 32 rounds, we will have a layout of the entire data as follows:

$$\frac{y_3}{[16]} \frac{y_2}{[2]} \quad \frac{z_1}{[32]} \frac{y_1}{[32]} \frac{z_3}{[16]} \frac{z_2}{[2]} \frac{z_0}{[4]} \frac{y_0}{[4]} \frac{x}{[4096]}.$$

The permutation is achieved by copying the data in 128 KB units of 4×4096 complex numbers. This granularity is determined by the rightmost unmoved dimensions y_0 and x in combination.

Adjustment is also needed when transferring data from pinned hmem to dmem for batched 1-D FFTs of dimension z, which also consists of 32 rounds according to dimension y_1. Thus, in each round, the data on each GPU have a layout:

$$\frac{z_1}{[32]} \frac{z_3}{[16]} \frac{z_2}{[2]} \frac{z_0}{[4]} \frac{y_0}{[4]} \frac{x}{[4096]}.$$

A slightly unconventional GPU transposition is then performed to swap the subdimensions of z and dimension x and reach a desirable layout for FFT:

$$\frac{x}{[4096]} \frac{y_0}{[4]} \frac{z_1}{[32]} \frac{z_3}{[16]} \frac{z_2}{[2]} \frac{z_0}{[4]}$$

from which 4096×4 1D-FFT over dimension z can be efficiently computed using our own single-GPU FFT code that handles the irregular order of the subdimensions of z. That code works in a semicoalesced manner that coalesces every 1/4 warp, and the distances between the subwarps are small. The GPU computation for FFT is well overlapped by PCI data transfers in our streaming-mode tests.

After FFT for z, the results need to be transferred back to the pinned hmem and communicated with other nodes to return to the original positions. The backward propagation of these intermediate steps is exactly the reversed forward propagation.

Thus, the permutations performed during data transfers have made it possible to aggregate elements of the third dimension z on individual GPUs so that GPU-based transposition can move the elements and achieve locality for them. CPU-based transpositions are then no longer necessary!

39.5 PERFORMANCE RESULTS

Our FFT code (using GPUs) is compared with FFTW version 2.1.5 and Intel MKL version 10.2.1.017 (not using GPUs) on PKU McClus. The performance is calculated by:

$$\frac{\sum_{d=1}^{D} M_d(5N_d log_2 N_d)}{\text{execution time}}$$

where D is the total number of dimensions, $M_d = E/N_d$ is the number of FFTs along each dimension, and E is the total number of data elements. The execution time is obtained by taking the minimum time over multiple runs.

Figure 39.8(a) shows the performance of our FFT, FFTW, and MKL when performing single-precision C2C 3-D-FFT on 4 or 16 nodes with different data sizes. The experiments for CPUs use all cores (e.g., 16 CPUs with 64 cores in total), which perform the best for FFTW and Intel MKL when running eight threads per node. GPU experiments do not use CPUs for computation. Instead, eight CPU threads are used for controlling GPUs, Infiniband buffers, and data transfers. On 16 nodes, our FFT reaches 209 GFLOPS and completes 4096 3D-FFT in 54 seconds; MKL does not process more than 256 GB data as out-place workspace of the same size is used; FFTW does not process more than 32 GB (for OS-related reasons). Figure 39.8(b) shows the performance of our FFT, FFTW, and MKL when performing 3-D-FFT of 32 GB data on different numbers of nodes. PKUFFT demonstrates a speedup 24.3× over FFTW and 7× over MKL. Figure 39.9 shows the corresponding performance results for double-precision complex-to-complex 3-D-FFT. PKUFFT achieves 5.4× speedup over FFTW and MKL. The dramatically improved performances are attributed to the following factors:

1. Data transfers through two PCIs are faster than sustained large-scale hmem accesses (exceeding the size of cache) by CPU.
2. The dmem is much larger than the CPU cache, and that means larger subtasks can be processed in whole, and this reduces the need for reloading data.
3. Algorithmic improvement that uses fast GPU transpositions and does not need expensive CPU transpositions in hmem.
4. An improved communication interface based on IB/verbs, which accounts for roughly 38.8% of the total time.

It is notable that three out of the four factors are related to GPU.

39.6 CONCLUSION AND FUTURE WORK

On GPU clusters, it is easy to achieve high speedups for computation-intensive tasks and bandwidth-intensive tasks with good data locality. Large-scale FFT is a bandwidth-intensive task without locality. Such a task initially appears to be hard for GPUs to accelerate. The surprising high performances reveal an interesting picture. Several GPU-related factors have helped us squeeze more memory

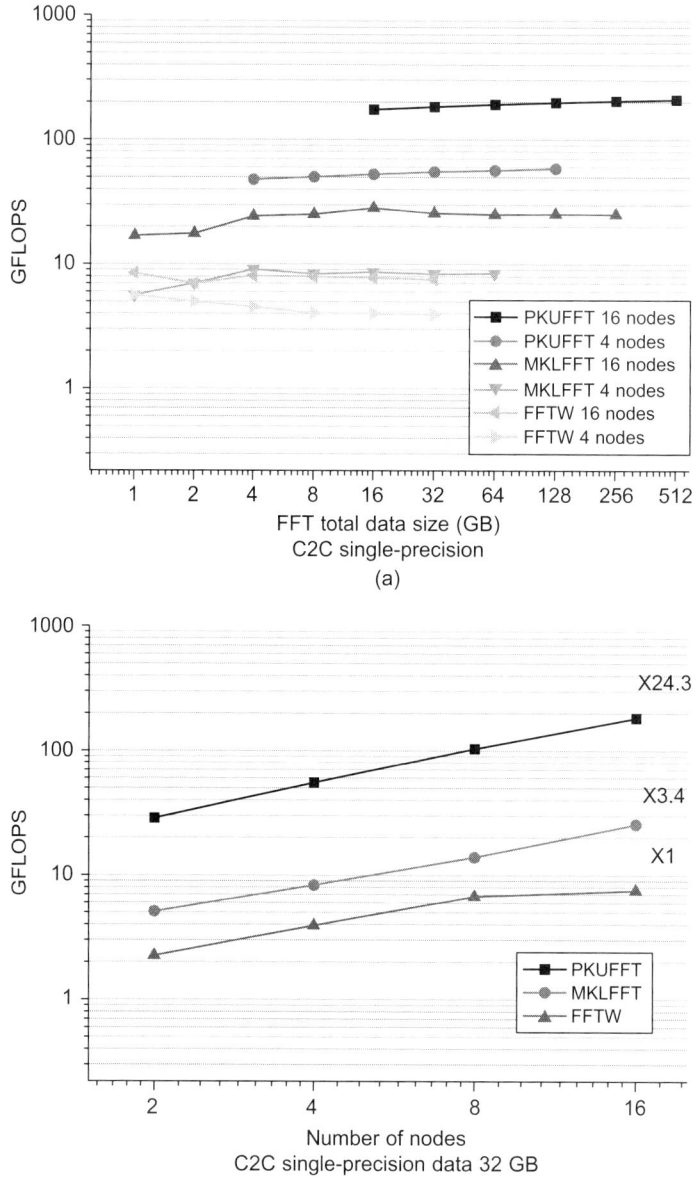

FIGURE 39.8

Single-precision 3D-FFT performance results of PKUFFT, FFTW 2.1.5, and Intel MKL 10.2.1.017.

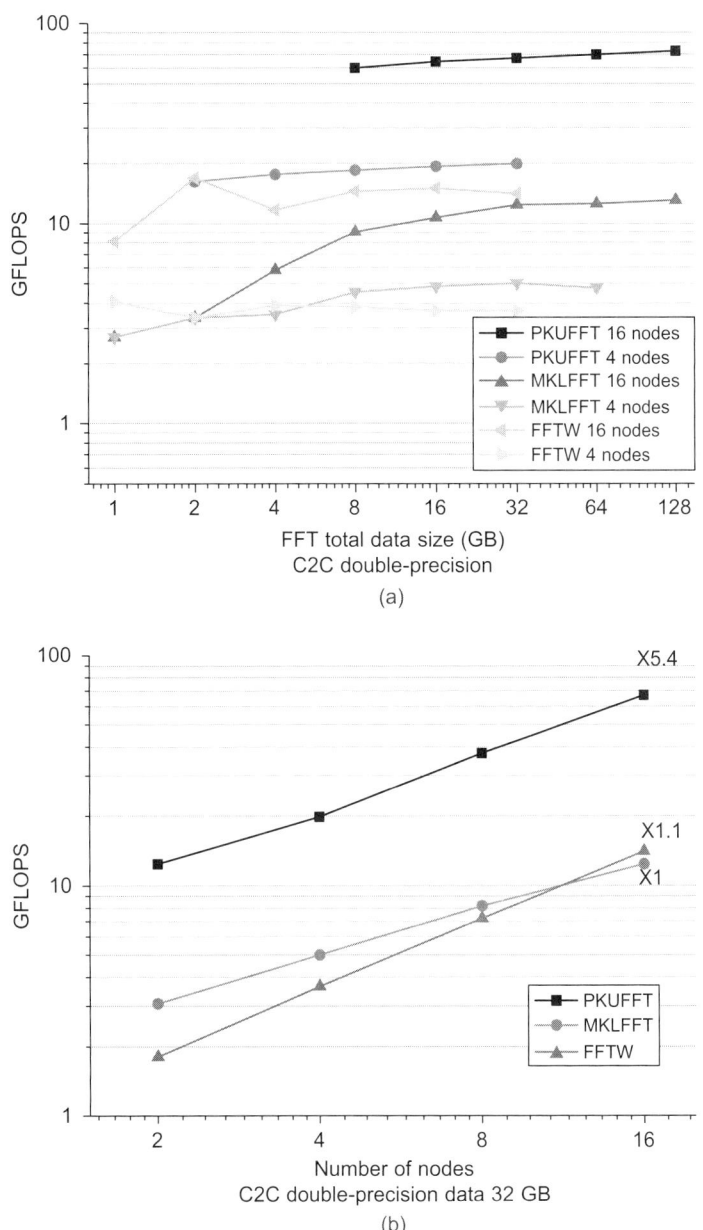

FIGURE 39.9

Double-precision 3-D-FFT performance results of PKUFFT, FFTW 2.1.5, and Intel MKL 10.2.1.017.

bandwidth out of each individual node. The main technical contribution is the algebraic manipulation of array dimensions. Without the method, it will be hard for a programmer to correctly determine various sophisticated index expressions. The exposed memory hierarchy of GPU clusters, on one hand, complicates programming, but on the other hand, presents an opportunity for optimization of data locality. The technique is readily applicable to a wide range of tasks.

Our design and implementation are based on the current restrictions of the hardware and software systems. If IB/verbs could use CUDA's pinned hmem directly as buffers, then data transfers from/to the buffers would be saved. Some progress (known as "GPU Direct") has been made to allow CUDA pinned hmem to become IB buffers directly (with certain size limits). The technique of dimension manipulation is still applicable to saving hmem transpositions. In that case, data adjustment in shorter messages can be performed during AllToAll communications.

A version of this chapter has been published at ACM Proceedings of ICS 2010 [11]. The authors would like to thank all anonymous referees for their helpful comments from which the preparation for this version has benefited.

References

[1]   X. Cui, Y. Chen, H. Mei, Improving performance of matrix multiplication and FFT on GPU, in: Proceedings of the 2009 15th International Conference on Parallel and Distributed Systems, 8–11 December 2009, Shengzhen, China, 2009, pp. 42–48.

[2]   M. Fatica, Accelerating linpack with CUDA on heterogenous clusters, in: Proceedings of 2nd Workshop on General Purpose Processing on Graphics Processing Units, 8–8 March 2009, Washington, DC, 2009, pp. 46–51.

[3]   V. Volkov, J.W. Demmel, Benchmarking GPUs to tune dense linear algebra, in: Proceedings of the 2008 ACM/IEEE conference on Supercomputing, 15–21 November 2008, Austin, Texas, 2008.

[4]   P. Micikevicius, 3D finite difference computation on GPUs using CUDA, in: Proceedings of 2nd Workshop on General Purpose Processing on Graphics Processing Units, 8–8 March 2009, Washington, DC, 2009, pp. 79–84.

[5]   E. Chu, A. George, Inside the FFT black box — serial and parallel fast Fourier transform algorithms, CRC Press, Boca Raton, Fla., 2000.

[6]   N.K. Govindaraju, B. Lloyd, Y. Dotsenko, B. Smith, J. Manferdelli, High performance discrete Fourier transforms on graphics processors, in: Proceedings of the 2008 ACM/IEEE conference on Supercomputing, 15–21 November 2008, Austin, Texas, 2008.

[7]   A. Nukada, S. Matsuoka, Auto-tuning 3-D FFT library for CUDA GPUs, in: Proceedings of the Conference on High Performance Computing Networking, Storage and Analysis, 14–20 November 2009, Portland, Oregon, 2009, pp. 1–10.

[8]   A. Nukada, Y. Ogata, T. Endo, S. Matsuoka, Bandwidth intensive 3-D FFT kernel for GPUs using CUDA, in: Proceedings of the 2008 ACM/IEEE conference on Supercomputing, 15–21 November 2008, Austin, Texas, 2008, pp. 1–11.

[9]   V. Volkov, B. Kazian, FFT prototype. http://www.cs.berkeley.edu/~volkov/, 2009.

[10]   R.C. Agarwal, F.G. Gustavson, M. Zubair, A high performance parallel algorithm for 1-D FFT, in: Proceedings of the 1994 conference on Supercomputing, December 1994, Washington, DC, United States, 1994, pp. 34–40.

[11]   Y. Chen, X. Cui, H. Mei, Improving performance of matrix multiplication and FFT on GPU, in: Proceedings of the 24th ACM International Conference on Supercomputing, 2–4 June 2010, Tsukuba, Ibaraki, Japan, 2010, pp. 315–324.

Medical Imaging
Area Editor's Introduction

Lawrence Tarbox

40 GPU Acceleration of Iterative Digital Breast Tomosynthesis 647

41 Parallelization of Katsevich CT Image Reconstruction Algorithm on Generic Multi-Core Processors and GPGPU 659

42 3-D Tomographic Image Reconstruction from Randomly Ordered Lines with CUDA 679

43 Using GPUs to Learn Effective Parameter Settings for GPU-Accelerated Iterative CT Reconstruction Algorithms 693

44 Using GPUs to Accelerate Advanced MRI Reconstruction with Field Inhomogeneity Compensation 709

45 $\ell 1$ Minimization in $\ell 1$-SPIRiT Compressed Sensing MRI Reconstruction 723

46 Medical Image Processing Using GPU-Accelerated ITK Image Filters 737

47 Deformable Volumetric Registration Using B-splines 751

48 Multiscale Unbiased Diffeomorphic Atlas Construction on Multi-GPUs 771

49 GPU-Accelerated Brain Connectivity Reconstruction and Visualization in Large-Scale
Electron Micrographs 793

50 Fast Simulation of Radiographic Images Using a Monte Carlo X-Ray Transport
Algorithm Implemented in CUDA 813

THE STATE OF GPU COMPUTING IN MEDICAL IMAGING

The use of GPU computing in medical imaging has exploded over the last few years. Early uses centered on using the texture-mapping capabilities of GPUs to do volume visualization of the 3-D datasets routinely created by modern medical imaging equipment. As people gained more experience with GPU computing and as GPUs became more capable, activity shifted to more sophisticated postprocessing techniques to better support medical diagnosis and research. Many of the visualization and image-processing techniques utilized in medical imaging, such as registration, segmentation, and classification, share methodologies with other disciplines, such as computer vision, and there is a significant amount of cross-pollination between those communities.

A flurry of recent activity has been in using GPU computing to do the initial reconstruction of measurement data into three-dimensional volume sets suitable for visualization and further processing. Before the advent of GPU computing, image reconstruction was done using digital signal and vector processors (DSPs), application-specific integrated circuits (ASICs), field-programmable gate arrays (FPGAs), and so on. The cost-effectiveness, speed, and programmability of GPU computing is a major driving force in this shift away from these more expensive, less flexible technologies towards image reconstruction on GPUs.

The processing techniques of medical imaging often include repetitive calculations done on large multidimensional arrays of data that are highly suited to the parallel-processing capabilities of GPUs. In fact, the speed and power of GPU computing has facilitated the clinical use of algorithms that previously were relegated to research laboratories due to their immense computational load. The principal challenge to using GPU computing in medical imaging is managing the massive amounts of data involved, which often overwhelms the memory capacity of existing GPU-based compute engines.

IN THIS SECTION

The first four chapters deal with tomographic image reconstruction, where the volumetric data is reconstructed from projection data collected by the measurement instrument at various angles around the object being scanned (i.e., the patient). Measurement instruments that utilize tomographic reconstruction include X-ray CT (computed tomography) where the projection data are attenuated X-ray beams passed through the object, and PET (positron emission tomography) where the projection data are decay events from radioactive isotopes

Chapter 40, written by Dana Schaa, Benjamin Brown, Byunghyun Jang, Perhaad Mistry, Rodrigo Dominguez, David Kaeli, and Richard Moore, describes the 3-D reconstruction of breast tissue using conventional X-ray images taken from a limited number of angles. This chapter provides a nice high-level description of the iterative reconstruction technique.

Chapter 41, written by Abderrahim Benquassmi, Eric Fontaine, Hsien-Hsin, and S. Lee, continues the discussion of iterative reconstruction techniques for improving the quality of CT reconstruction from dedicated CT measurement instruments.

Chapter 42, written by Guillem Pratx, Jing-Yu Cui, Sven Prevrhal, and Craig S. Levin, adds a new twist to the iterative reconstruction story by introducing methods for managing reconstruction of data generated from random events, such as the positron decay events measured in PET imaging. In this case, the projection rays are randomly distributed instead of regular.

Chapter 43, written by Wei Xu and Klaus Mueller, considers how to optimally select the parameter settings for reconstruction. In essence, these parameter settings drive algorithms such as those introduced in the first three chapters.

The next two chapters deal with reconstruction of magnetic resonance (MR) images, where data collected in the frequency space is transformed into spatial data.

Chapter 44, written by Yue Zhuo, Xiao-Long Wu, Justin P. Haldar, Thibault Marin, Wen-mei Hwu, Zhi-Pei Liang, and Bradley P. Sutton, describes how GPU computing has allowed them to improve the quality of MR reconstructions by correcting for distortions introduced by the measurement process, while still keeping reconstruction speeds at a clinically acceptable level.

Chapter 45, written by Mark Murphy and Miki Lustig, discusses methods for improving the scanning and reconstruction speed in creating MR images, making MR imaging more useful in pediatric medicine, where the restlessness of the young patients often inhibits its use.

The following three chapters describe the use of GPU computing to manipulate images after they have been collected and reconstructed.

Seamlessly adding GPU Computing capabilities to the popular Insight Tool Kit (ITK) is the subject of Chapter 46, written by Won-Ki Jeong, Hanspeter Pfister, and Massimiliano Fatica. Because ITK is used in many disciplines to segment, register, and massage image data, the methods introduced by this chapter have applicability well beyond medical imaging.

Chapter 47, written by James Shackleford, Nagarajan Kandasamy, and Gregory Sharp, details how they accelerated a B-spline-based deformable registration algorithm through GPU computing.

Many algorithms for processing medical images depend on well-constructed atlases. In one sense, atlases provide generalized reference images against which other images are compared. Chapter 48, written by Linh Ha, Jens Kruger, Claudio Silva, and Sarang Joshi, discusses how GPU computing can be used to create such atlases

Chapter 49, written by Won-Ki Jeong, Hanspeter Pfister, Johanna Beyer, and Markus Hadwiger, combines multiple techniques to help solve the tricky problem of tracking and reconstructing 3-D neural circuits (axons) in electron microscope images of brain tissue. From the standpoint of GPU computing, this is a particularly interesting problem in that such pathways are somewhat random, making their reconstruction difficult to parallelize for computation on a GPU. In addition, the electron microscope datasets are extremely large and difficult to manage on a GPU.

Unlike other chapters in this section, Chapter 50, written by Andreu Badal and Aldo Badano does not deal with actual image data, but describes how to simulate the image acquisition process. Although such simulations are primarily used by researchers trying to improve the image acquisition process, they potentially could be used as part of clinical image processing, for example, in the iterative reconstruction algorithms introduced in the beginning chapters of this section.

GPU Acceleration of Iterative Digital Breast Tomosynthesis

Dana Schaa, Benjamin Brown, Byunghyun Jang, Perhaad Mistry, Rodrigo Dominguez,
David Kaeli, Richard Moore, Daniel B. Kopans

Iterative digital breast tomosynthesis (DBT) is a technology that mitigates many of the shortcomings associated with traditional mammography. Using multiple low-dose X-ray projections with an iterative maximum likelihood estimation method, DBT is able to create a high-quality, three-dimensional reconstruction of the breast. However, the usability of DBT depends largely on making the time for computation acceptable within a clinical setting.

In this work we accelerate our DBT algorithm on multiple CUDA-enabled GPUs, reducing the execution time to under 20 seconds for eight iterations (the number usually required to obtain an acceptable quality reconstructed image). The algorithm studied in this work is representative of a general class of image reconstruction problems, as are the thread-mapping strategies, multi-GPU considerations, and optimizations employed in this work.

40.1 INTRODUCTION

In 2005, breast cancer claimed the lives of 41,116 women in the United States; it trailed only lung cancer as the leading cause of cancer mortality among US women [3]. However, this statistic belies the high five-year survival rate for patients treated for early-stage breast cancer [5]. This disparity illustrates the continuing need to improve breast cancer screening techniques.

Screening mammography has been shown by randomized-controlled trials to reduce breast cancer mortality rates in the range of 30–50% since 1985. In spite of its successes, mammography has been criticized for high false positives and imperfect sensitivity. Both of these can be largely attributed to structural noise (i.e., the superimposition of normal breast tissue), which can hide lesions. Although steps have been taken to improve the efficacy of conventional screening methods, the emotional, physical, and financial burdens caused by the low positive predictive value for biopsies, unnecessary callbacks, and undetected cancers remain high [7].

Digital breast tomosynthesis (DBT) is a technology that takes a series of X-ray projections to acquire information about the breast structure. A reconstruction method is required to combine these projections into a three-dimensional image. Figure 40.1 shows the data acquisition process used for DBT. Although clinical trials on DBT have shown promising results, the primary obstacle to using DBT in a clinical

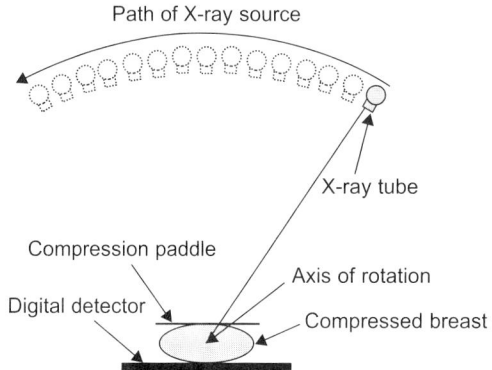

FIGURE 40.1

Setup of data acquisition for DBT. An X-ray source covers a ($40°$) arc emitting low-dose X-rays at 15 locations. Fifteen corresponding projections are acquired by a high-resolution digital detector.

setting is implementing a reconstruction process that is both accurate and fast. Note that this trade-off is not unique to DBT, but must be considered in many different medical imaging algorithms and domains [4, 6].

Traditionally, filtered backprojection (FBP) and its variants have been used for tomographic reconstruction. These methods have become standard reconstruction techniques owing to their ability to produce acceptable images and employ analytical models that simplify reconstructions by approximating the scanner geometry. In contrast, iterative methods use much more precise geometric models and iterate on error correction until they produce projections of high similarity to the original scans. As such, iterative techniques produce higher-quality images, but are much more computationally intensive. For DBT, a maximum-likelihood-based iterative method has been shown to be very effective at suppressing artifacts [2]. An overview of the algorithm is provided in Section 40.2.

Despite the advantages of iterative techniques for reconstruction, clinical acceptance has been slow owing to the high computational overhead associated with iterative reconstruction. Initial reconstructions performed at Massachusetts General Hospital took 48 hours on Pentium IV workstations. To overcome this barrier to clinical feasibility, parallel computing approaches were developed and implemented on Beowulf clusters [8].

Although the cluster-based parallel approach reduced reconstruction time, this speedup was achieved only through significant hardware cost, energy consumption, and hardware/software maintenance expense. In contrast to traditional parallel computing platforms, graphics processing units (GPUs) have gained acceptance owing to their low start-up cost, lower power demands, and low maintenance costs (versus a cluster of systems). GPUs are very well suited for data-parallel applications such as DBT. Advances in GPU hardware have been coupled with the development of software frameworks that have reduced the parallel programming effort associated with GPU computing. In this work, we highlight the benefits and trade-offs associated with migrating an iterative DBT reconstruction algorithm used in medical clinics to a GPU. We also explore the benefits obtained on different GPU platforms, as well as on systems equipped with multiple GPUs.

The next section describes the algorithm used for image reconstruction in DBT. Section 40.3 discusses issues related to porting and optimizing the code for single-GPU and multi-GPU acceleration and presents performance results, and Section 40.4 concludes this chapter.

40.2 DIGITAL BREAST TOMOSYNTHESIS

The iterative digital breast tomosynthesis (DBT) algorithm used in our work is an IRT that uses an iterative maximum likelihood estimation method (MLEM) [1]. The MLEM is a statistical method that continually corrects a guess of a 3-D image (representing patient tissue) until it produces simulated X-ray projections that highly correlate with the original X-ray projections that were received by the detector. The 3-D image consists of volumetric pixels (voxels) of attenuation coefficients that determine how that portion of the image affects X-ray intensity. The reconstruction has two phases, a forward projection and a backward projection, that are iteratively executed until the error level is below a quality threshold (typically requiring on the order of eight iterations). Figure 40.2 shows a flowchart of the iterative DBT algorithm used in this work.

The forward projection phase takes an initial guess of the 3-D image and uses it to generate simulated X-ray projections that would be obtained if this were the object actually being irradiated. The backward projection phase then uses the projected data from the forward phase to correct the guess of the image [7].

In the backward projection phase, the MLEM algorithm solves the likelihood function:

$$L = P(Y|u) \tag{40.1}$$

for the probability (P) of producing the projections (Y) received by the digital detector with the attenuation coefficients (u) for the reconstructed 3-D image. The maximized solution of Equation 40.1 defines

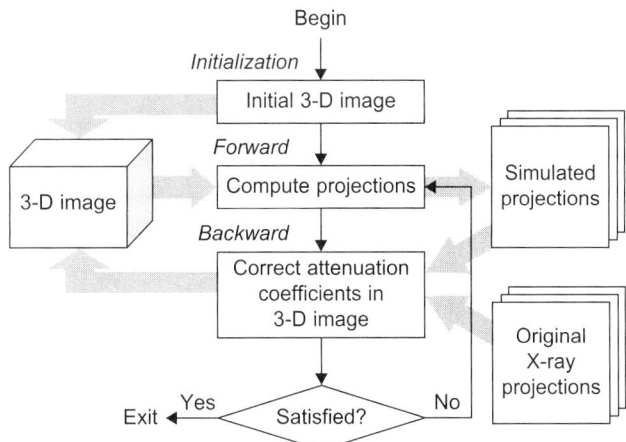

FIGURE 40.2

A high-level description of iterative digital breast tomosynthesis algorithm and data usage.

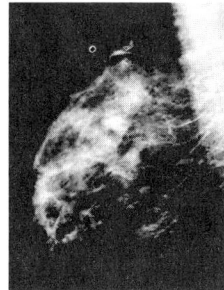

(a) Standard mammogram image

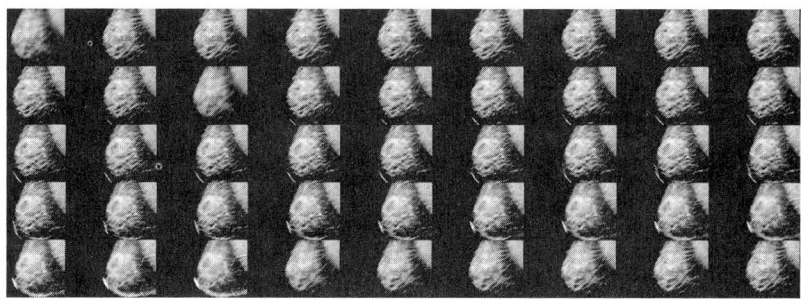

(b) Slices of the 3-D image reconstructed using iterative, MLEM-based DBT

FIGURE 40.3

A comparison of iterative DBT to traditional mammography. Although traditional mammography produces a 2-D composite of the breast tissue that introduces structural noise and can hide tumors, iterative DBT produces a 3-D image that enables the visualization of cross-sectional areas of the tissue.

an adjustment to the guess of the 3-D image whose projection data is the most similar to the projections obtained by the digital detector. The full details of the likelihood function can be found in [2].

After the desired error threshold is reached, the resulting 3-D image is then viewable by a physician, who can step through each cross-sectional region in search of tumorous tissue. Figure 40.3 compares a 2-D image obtained using traditional single-angle mammography with the 45 cross-sectional slices of the reconstructed image obtained using the iterative DBT algorithm that removes superimposed structures to permit detection.

40.3 ACCELERATING ITERATIVE DBT USING GPUs

40.3.1 Experimental Setup

NVIDIA's most popular computing framework is CUDA C, a general-purpose programming API that allows a programmer to utilize the GPU using an extension of the C programming language. The programming model is based on a massively multithreaded paradigm, where thousands or more threads are created, divided into groups, and run on single instruction multiple data (SIMD) hardware. The term *single instruction multiple thread* (SIMT) is used when referring to the fusion of the multithreaded execution model and SIMD hardware.

The test bed for our reconstruction algorithm is the Medusa GPU Cluster at Northeastern University. Each node of the cluster contains two quad-core Intel Xeon CPUs running at 2.27 GHz and has 24 GB of DDR3 RAM. A compute node is connected to two NVIDIA Tesla S1070 GPU units, allowing access to eight GPUs from a single node. Each of the four GPUs in the S1070 has 240 streaming processor cores divided among 30 streaming multiprocessors (SMs), and 4 GB of graphics memory.

40.3.2 Thread Mapping for GPU Execution

In GPU computing, thread mapping is a crucial decision point for hardware utilization, and therefore, performance. In the forward projection phase, we map threads to the dimensions of the detector cells of the X-ray detector. There is a one-to-one correspondence between detector regions and projection data; thus, roughly 3 million threads are created for each of the 15 forward projections. For GPUs with smaller amounts of memory (less than 2 GB), the data for the entire set of projections cannot fit into the GPU memory at once, so segmenting of the computation is required — this is naturally accomplished by computing each of the 15 projections one at a time and swapping them off of the GPU after computation is complete. This is not an issue for GPUs with larger memory capacities.

During the backward projection phase we map threads to image voxels, where a single thread computes the contributions of all X-ray source positions to the attenuation coefficient of a voxel. For the backward phase, creating one thread per voxel has a number of advantages over the detector-based mapping used in forward projection. If the detector-based mapping were used in the backward phase, each thread would compute a portion of the attenuation coefficient for all voxels it encountered on its path between source and detector. Doing so would require the use of atomic updates, which degrade performance, or require multiple 3-D images to be kept (one per projection) that would have to be merged to obtain the final image. Merging the data requires both extra calculation and larger data transfers. Further, because multiple rays from the same projection can impact a voxel, synchronization would still be required to ensure coherent updates. Using a voxel-based mapping avoids these limitations. Using the voxel-based approach also allows segmenting of the 3-D image into 2-D slices for GPUs with smaller memories and for multi-GPU execution.

Other data segmentation techniques are indeed possible (as shown in [8] for distributed environments), though the most effective require dynamically determining the boundaries of segments at runtime based on the geometry of the X-ray sources, or otherwise, suffer from blurred reconstruction at segment boundaries. Instead, the mappings presented here have proven to be very effective when targeting GPU and multi-GPU environments.

40.3.3 Optimizing with Texture Memory

When data on the GPU is accessed through the texture unit, additional data with spatial locality are automatically cached on chip in the texture cache. If cached data are accessed by a thread from the same SM, it can be retrieved from the cache without putting any pressure on the global memory bus.

In the backward projection algorithm used by DBT, when the path from the source to the detector cell falls between multiple vertices of the Cartesian grid, data from each vertex contribute to the calculation (as shown in Figure 40.4). Depending on the proximity to each vertex, the values retrieved

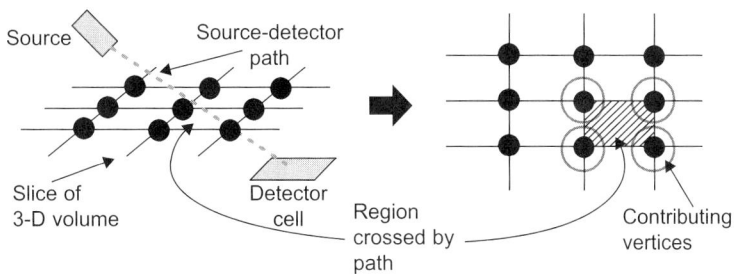

FIGURE 40.4

Calculating the intensity of X-rays from source to detector requires considering multiple voxel values in each cross-sectional slice of the image.

are given a weight to determine their influence on the final value. Because the weights of the values vary per thread and are determined live, we cannot take advantage of hardware interpolation that would otherwise reduce the number of accesses. However, if threads with spatial locality are grouped on the same SM, then multiple threads will end up accessing data from the same region, and using texture memory will serve to decrease pressure on the global memory bus.

Another benefit of texture memory is that boundary conditions can be handled automatically by hardware. For example, if an out-of-bounds index is accessed through the texture unit, the unit can be programmed to return the edge-pixel value, to return zero (using the CUDA C construct called *surfaces*), or to cause the kernel to fail. Aside from the obvious reduction of code complexity, removing conditional statements is generally an important optimization on current GPU SIMD hardware because conditionals cause thread divergence and prevent the processing units from performing meaningful work. Algorithms 1 and 2 show the code for bounds checking in DBT when global memory is used and the removal of conditionals when texture memory is used, respectively.

Algorithm 1: Snippet of code from a kernel accessing data in global memory.

```
// When accessing global memory, bounds must be checked before data can be
   retrieved.
// The pixels are weighted using the values w1, w2, w3, and w4,
   respectively.
```
if $x1 \geq 0$ AND $x2 < imageWidth$ AND $y1 \geq 0$ AND $y2 < imageHeight$ **then**
    $tmp = image(x1,y1) * w1 + image(x1,y2) * w2 + image(x2,y1) * w3 + image(x2,y2) * w4$
else if $x1 \geq 0$ AND $x2 < imageWidth$ AND $y2 == imageHeight$ **then**
    $tmp = image(x1,y1) * w1 + image(x1,y2) * w2$
else if $x1 \geq 0$ AND $x2 < imageWidth$ AND $y2 == 0$ **then**
    $tmp = image(x2,y1) * w3 + image(x2,y2) * w4$
else if $x2 == imageWidth$ AND $y1 \geq 0$ AND $y2 < imageHeight$ **then**
    $tmp = image(x1,y1) * w1 + image(x2,y1) * w3$
else if $x2 == 0$ AND $y1 \geq 0$ AND $y2 < imageHeight$ **then**
    $tmp = image(x1,y2) * w2 + image(x2,y2) * w4$
end if

In the case of DBT, using texture memory provided a very large performance gain on a CUDA architecture of compute capability 1.3 (Tesla S1070), and a significant (although much smaller) benefit on a Fermi architecture of compute capability 2.0 (GTX 480). The GTX 480 memory system features automatic caching for global memory that stores accessed data in a shared L2 cache and also in an on-chip, low-latency L1 cache. Because the automatic caching takes advantage of some spatial locality, it has an effect similar to the texture cache, and we see less benefit from using the texture unit on the GTX 480 than on the Tesla S1070 architecture.

Using the texture unit to handle boundary conditions, we were able to remove many of the conditional statements for the DBT kernel. Interestingly, removing these conditional statements actually showed a slight decrease in performance compared with the texture approach with conditionals in place. The reason for the decrease in performance is the memory-bound execution profile of the DBT application. Relative to the texture cache access time, the time to compute conditional outcomes is small

Algorithm 2: Snippet of code from a kernel accessing data in texture memory. The use of texture memory allows removal of bounds-checking code.

```
// When accessing texture memory, out-of-bounds indexes can be set to
   return 0
// using CUDA surfaces and the cudaBoundaryModeZero parameter.
// The pixels are weighted using the values w1, w2, w3, and w4,
   respectively.
```
$$val1 = surf2Dread(image, x1, y1, cudaBoundaryModeZero) * w1$$
$$val2 = surf2Dread(image, x1, y2, cudaBoundaryModeZero) * w2$$
$$val3 = surf2Dread(image, x2, y1, cudaBoundaryModeZero) * w3$$
$$val4 = surf2Dread(image, x2, y2, cudaBoundaryModeZero) * w4$$
$$tmp = val1 + val2 + val3 + val4;$$

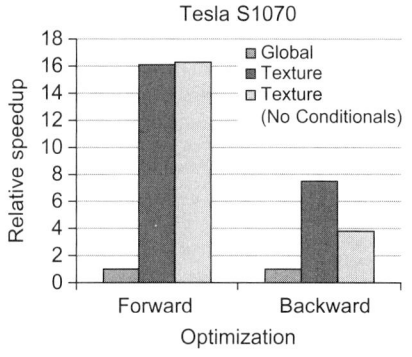

(a) Texture memory optimizations on Tesla S1070

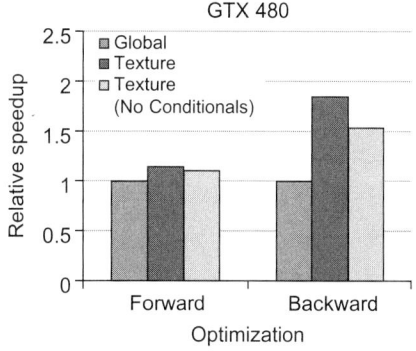

(b) Texture memory optimizations on GTX 480

FIGURE 40.5

A performance comparison across optimizations and hardware. The baseline algorithm (*Global*) reads data from global memory, the *Texture* optimization reads data from texture memory, and *Texture* (*No Conditionals*) uses the bounds-checking feature of the texture unit to remove conditional statements from the algorithm.

because the texture cache is not a low-latency cache. Leaving the conditionals in place could possibly save up to two texture accesses for many threads, and although accesses to texture cache decreases off-chip memory traffic, the time to access the cache is still on the order of an off-chip memory access. Figure 40.5 shows the performance benefits for the algorithm before and after mapping the forward and backward projections to texture memory on the S1070 and GTX 480 GPUs.

40.3.4 Acceleration with Multiple GPUs

Computing with multiple GPUs allows the computation to be split based on the properties of the thread mappings discussed previously, in which projections and image slices are treated as units (i.e., in forward projection, projections are split between GPUs, and in backward projection, slices of image voxels are split between GPUs). Figure 40.6 shows the distribution of slices on up to eight GPUs. If all GPUs

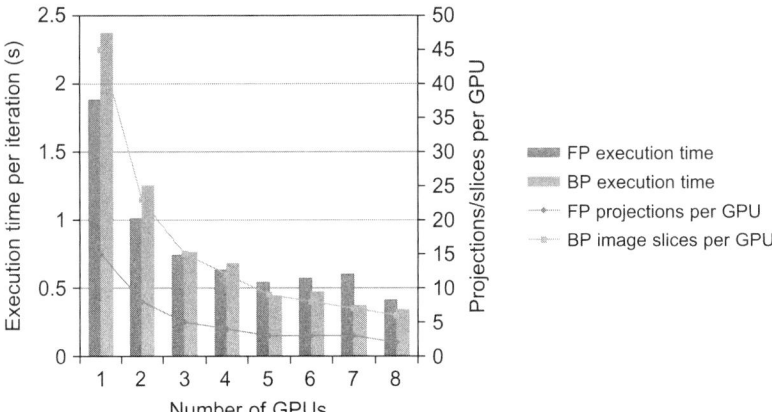

FIGURE 40.6

The distribution of two-dimensional data and computational speedup in a multi-GPU environment.

are not fed the same number of slices, then we are concerned only with the GPU with the largest number of slices because it will take the longest to execute. In addition to the number of slices per GPU, Figure 40.6 also shows the speedup for the computation of the algorithm when communication is not considered (this becomes relevant as the GPU moves on chip with the CPU and shares the same memory space). Notice that the forward projections per GPU line in Figure 40.6 show that for five to seven GPUs, at least one GPU must compute three projections. In these cases, we see no speedup for forward projection, and in fact, performance actually suffers slightly owing to the overhead of the extra devices.

In order for the thread mappings to work in multi-GPU execution, the results from both the forward and backward projection phases must be sent to the CPU for synchronization after the phase completes. Once the results are synchronized, they must then be broadcast to all GPUs to be used in the next phase. After the forward projection, locally computed projections along with corresponding absorption values (associated with each detector cell) must be synchronized and broadcast, and after the backward projection, the same must happen with the reconstructed image. Equations 40.2 and 40.3 describe the amount of data (S) that must be communicated based on the number of GPUs (N) in each algorithm phase, respectively. The first term in each equation is data that must be synchronized on the CPU (each GPU contributes a part), and the second term is the synchronized data that must be sent to each of N GPUs involved in the computation. Figure 40.7 represents these values graphically for up to eight GPUs.

$$S_{forward} = (S_{proj} + S_{absorb}) + N * (S_{proj} + S_{absorb}) \tag{40.2}$$

$$S_{backward} = S_{image} + N * S_{image} \tag{40.3}$$

Figure 40.8 shows a flowchart of the parallel DBT algorithm. This charts where computation can be parallelized between GPUs and when communication must occur.

There is the potential that the communication overhead may lead to performance degradation as more GPUs are added. For the DBT algorithm, the amount of data that needs to be communicated

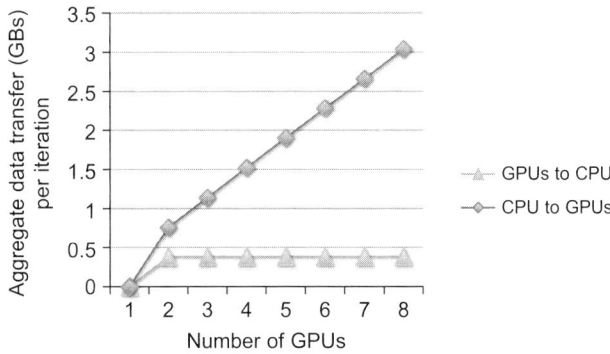

FIGURE 40.7

The amount of data that must be communicated in the iterative DBT algorithm as the number of GPU scales.

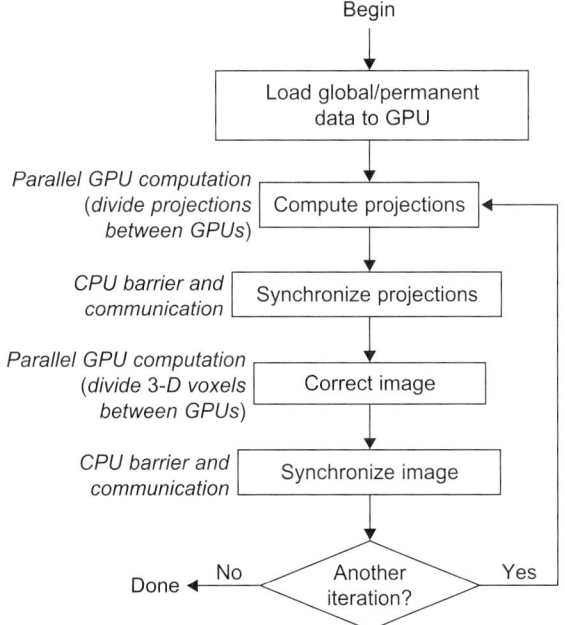

FIGURE 40.8

Diagram of the iterative multi-GPU DBT algorithm annotated with parallel computation and communication phases.

increases in a linear fashion as more GPUs are added (see Figure 40.7). However, after four GPUs are used, the communication overhead from this algorithm plateaus owing to the system configuration. The NVIDIA compute node of the Medusa cluster has two Tesla S1070s (four GPUs each) each on a dedicated x16 PCIe 2.0 slot. Because the S1070s are on separate PCIe lanes, using GPUs on the second

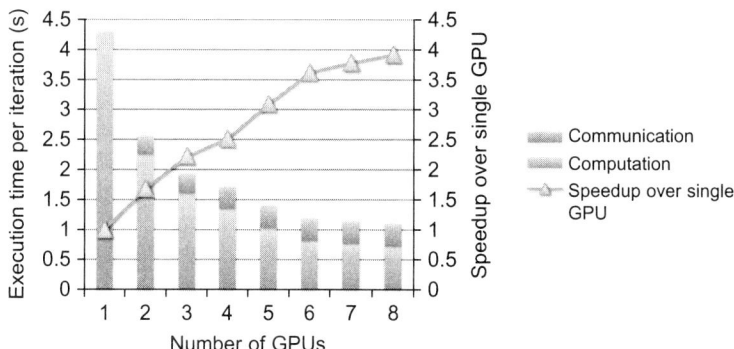

FIGURE 40.9

The execution time and speedup of iterative DBT on Tesla S1070s for up to eight GPUs.

S1070 does not contribute any additional communication overhead. Figure 40.9 shows the overall iteration time broken down into computation and communication for the algorithm as more GPUs are added.

40.4 CONCLUSIONS

DBT has demonstrated advantages over traditional mammography. Using roughly the same radiation dose as a 2-D mammogram (the current imaging standard), we can analyze breast tissue structure in three dimensions. This allows the radiologist to "peel away" layers of structural noise, reducing the likelihood of both false positives and false negatives. Through GPU acceleration, we have been able to reduce both the resources and time required to perform high-quality DBT reconstructions.

The performance gains obtained from using GPUs to accelerate iterative MLEM-based DBT reconstruction have been so impressive that time is no longer the dominant concern for clinical application. This work has demonstrated that DBT reconstruction can be less costly and more accurate, while also completing reconstruction in a reasonable amount of time. Given that we have been successful in addressing the computational demands of IRT for DBT, we can focus on additional ways to improve the quality of care for patients, such as consolidating the imaging and follow-up visits, enabling new technologies (such as computer-aided biopsies), or using redundant GPU execution to prevent errors.

Acknowledgments

This work was supported in part by an NSF ERC Innovation Award EEC-0909990, the Institute for Complex Scientific Software, NVIDIA for hardware donations, and The Bernard M. Gordon Center for Subsurface Sensing and Imaging Systems, under the Engineering Research Centers Program of the National Science Foundation (Award Number EEC-9986821). The authors would also like to thank Nicholas Moore at Northeastern University for his contributions and the editors for their constructive comments. The authors also acknowledge Volodymyr Kindratenko from the NCSA for providing access to the the Fermi-based system used in this work.

References

[1] L. Le Cam, Maximum likelihood — an introduction, ISI Rev. 58 (2) (1990) 152–171.

[2] T. Wu, A. Stewart, M. Stanton, T. McCauley, W. Phillips, D.B. Kopans, et al., Tomographic mammography using a limited number of low-dose cone-beam projection images, Med. Phys. 30 (2003) 365.

[3] Centers for Disease Control and Prevention, 1999–2005 Cancer incidence and mortality data. `http://apps.nccd.cdc.gov/uscs/`, 2009.

[4] B. Jang, D. Kaeli, S. Do, H. Pien, Multi-GPU implementation of iterative tomographic reconstruction algorithms, in: ISBI'09: Proceedings of the Sixth IEEE International Conference on Symposium on Biomedical Imaging, IEEE Press, Piscataway, NJ, 2009, pp. 185–188.

[5] D.B. Kopans, Breast imaging, third ed., Lippincott, Williams & Wilkins, Philadelphia, PA, 2007.

[6] J.-B. Thibault, K.D. Sauer, C.A. Bouman, J. Hsieh, A three-dimensional statistical approach to improved image quality for multislice helical CT, Med. Phys. 34 (11) (2007) 4526–4544.

[7] T. Wu, R. Moore, E. Rafferty, D. Kopans, A comparison of reconstruction algorithms for breast tomosynthesis, Med. Phys. 31 (9) (2004) 2636–2647.

[8] J. Zhang, W. Meleis, D. Kaeli, T. Wu, Acceleration of maximum likelihood estimation for tomosynthesis mammography, in: International Conference on Parallel and Distributed Systems (ICPAD'06), IEEE Computer Society, Minneapolis, MN, 2006, pp. 291–299.

Parallelization of Katsevich CT Image Reconstruction Algorithm on Generic Multi-Core Processors and GPGPU

Abderrahim Benquassmi, Eric Fontaine, Hsien-Hsin S. Lee

41.1 INTRODUCTION, PROBLEM, AND CONTEXT

Medical imaging is one of the most computationally demanding applications. Radiologists and researchers in related areas such as image processing, high-performance computing, 3-D graphics, and so on, have studied this subject extensively by using different computing facilities, including clusters, multicore processors, and more recently, general-purpose graphics processing units (GPGPU) to accelerate various 3-D medical image reconstruction algorithms. Because of the nature of these algorithms and the cost-performance consideration, recent works have been concentrating more on how to parallelize these algorithms using the emerging, high-throughput GPGPUs. An interesting medical imaging modality widely used in clinical diagnosis and medical research is computed tomography (CT). CT scanners have been the focus of studies attempting to accelerate the reconstruction of their acquired images. CT scanners are classified into parallel fan-beam and cone-beam devices. The cone-beam type can be labeled as circular or helical, based on the path its X-ray source traces. In circular CT scanners, the X-ray source completes one circular scan, then the platform holding the patient is moved forward by a certain amount, and a new circular is performed, and so on. The length that the table was moved determines the CT scanner slice thickness. In the case of helical scanners, the X-ray source keeps rotating while the platform holding the patient continuously slides inside the scanner's gantry. The movement of the table is a linear function of the X-ray source rotation angle. In the Cartesian frame reference attached to the table, the X-ray source traces a helical path whose axis is parallel to the scanner's table, as depicted in Figure 41.1. The helical type of scanner is preferred in medical imaging, but it comes with the cost of a complicated reconstruction algorithm. The source emits X-ray beams that traverse the patient's body and get attenuated by a factor that depends on the medium density. The attenuation factors are recorded as the acquired data from the detectors. These attenuations are used to infer the density of the different tissues constituting the travel medium.

41.2 CORE METHODS

Feldkamp *et al.* [2] proposed an efficient algorithm to perform filtered back projections for 3-D CT. Unfortunately, their algorithm was approximate and could introduce certain undesirable artifacts in

Cylindrical volume of interest f(x,y,z)

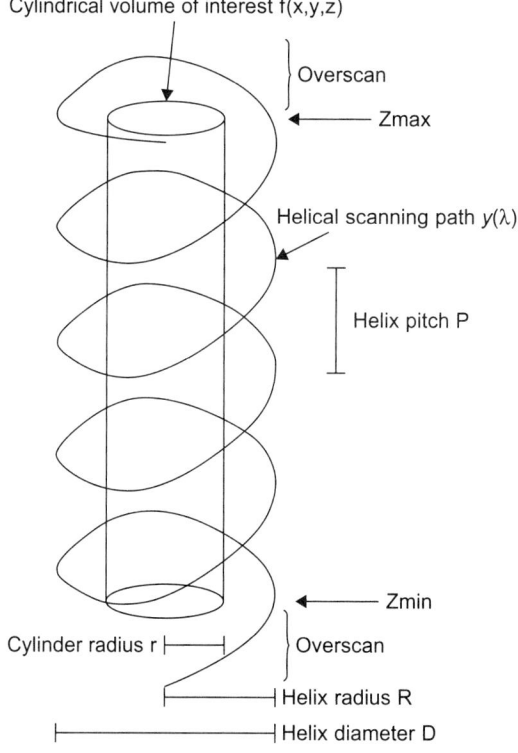

Overscan

Zmax

Helical scanning path y(λ)

Helix pitch P

Zmin

Overscan

Cylinder radius r

Helix radius R

Helix diameter D

FIGURE 41.1

Helical path of the X-ray source around the volume of interest.

the final reconstructed image. Katsevich [4] devised the first mathematically exact algorithm to reconstruct helical cone-beam CT images. The exactitude of the algorithm is before discretization. As for any mathematical algorithm, the computer precision will have an effect on the final result. A drawback of this algorithm is its computational complexity — when a volume of side N (i.e., $N \times N \times N$ volume) is reconstructed from M projections, its computational complexity will be of $O(M \times N^3)$ order. This article addresses the computation time to reconstruct the images acquired by the cone-beam CT scanner by using start-of-the-art processing systems. We present parallelized and optimized implementations of the Katsevich algorithm on two popular platforms: generic IA-based multicore processors and the general-purpose graphics processing units (GPGPU) and then perform competitive analysis on their respective performance. The goal of this work is twofold. First, we will provide methodology, parallelization strategies, and coding optimization techniques to practitioners in the field of medical imaging. Second, we will shed new insight with regard to present performance glass jaws in the GPGPU hardware and provide recommendations to architects for improving future GPGPU designs.

41.3 ALGORITHMS, IMPLEMENTATIONS, AND EVALUATIONS

In [3], Fontaine and Lee provided details about the mathematical models of the Katsevich algorithm and demonstrated its basic implementation and parallelization, with several architectural optimizations at the algorithm level. We adopt similar parallelization strategy in this work. Figure 41.2 depicts a high-level overview of the algorithm.

Briefly, image reconstruction is performed in three main steps, the differentiation, the filtering, and the back projection. The differentiation and the filtering steps prepare the acquired projections' data to be back-projected onto the volume being reconstructed. X-ray beams that originate from the source, traverse the volume being imaged, and hit the detectors plane where their respective attenuations are measured. The acquired signal is known as projection data. The density of each element of the volume determines the attenuation factor, and therefore, the signal's value at a (u, ω) location on the detector's plane. The reverse process, starting from the signal measured and determining the density of the medium traversed, is known as back projection. Listing 41.1 shows a pseudo code of the steps taken from the acquired signal to the reconstructed volume. The differentiation step performs the multidimensional derivative along u, ω and the angle λ. When a flat detector screen is used, the X-rays that hit the screen's corners travel a longer distance than those that hit closer to the center. To account for this fact the differentiation step corrects the values by multiplying them by a weighting factor of $\dfrac{D}{\sqrt{u^2 + w^2 + D^2}}$.

Filtering the projections after differentiation is acomplished in three steps: the forward mapping, the convolution with the kernel of the Hilbert transform, and the backward mapping. Any noncolinear three points in space uniquely define a plane. For a helical path defined by $y(\lambda) = \left(R\cos(\lambda), R\sin(\lambda), P\frac{\lambda}{2\pi}\right)$ any three points located on it and separated by the same length $(y(\lambda), y(\lambda + \psi)$, and $y(\lambda + 2\psi)$, where $\psi \in \left(-\frac{\pi}{2}, \frac{\pi}{2}\right)$), will define a plane called a κ-plane. This plane intersects the detector's plane in a line known as Kappa line (κ-line). There are $P = 2L + 1$ discrete κ-lines defined by the angular increments $\psi_l = l\Delta\psi$ where $l \in [-L, L]$ and $\Delta\psi = \dfrac{\pi + 2\arcsin(\frac{r}{R})}{2L}$; R and r are the radii of the helix and the volume of interest, respectively. Because the convolution needs to be performed along these lines, we need an operation that aligns the κ-lines onto horizontal rectilinear segments. This operation is known as the forward height re-binning. Figure 41.3 shows these lines and the forward mapping. For a given projection, the forward mapping will be done according to the formula:

$$\omega(u, \psi_l) = \frac{DP}{2\pi R}\left(\psi_l + \frac{\psi_l}{\tan(\psi_l)}\frac{u}{D}\right) \tag{41.1}$$

where u is the coordinate along the horizontal axis on the detectors plane, D is the distance from the X-ray source to the detector's plane, P and R are the pitch of the helix and its radius, respectively, and ψ_l is the angular discrete sampling as described earlier in this chapter.

After this remapping, the Hilbert transform is done on a row-by-row basis via a 1-D convolution with a special kernel[1] known as the Hilbert Transform Kernel. When all rows are convolved, the backward remapping step transforms the horizontal lines back to κ-lines. The backward mapping is done

---

[1]The *kernel* term is as used in mathematical convolution, not as in the CUDA sense.

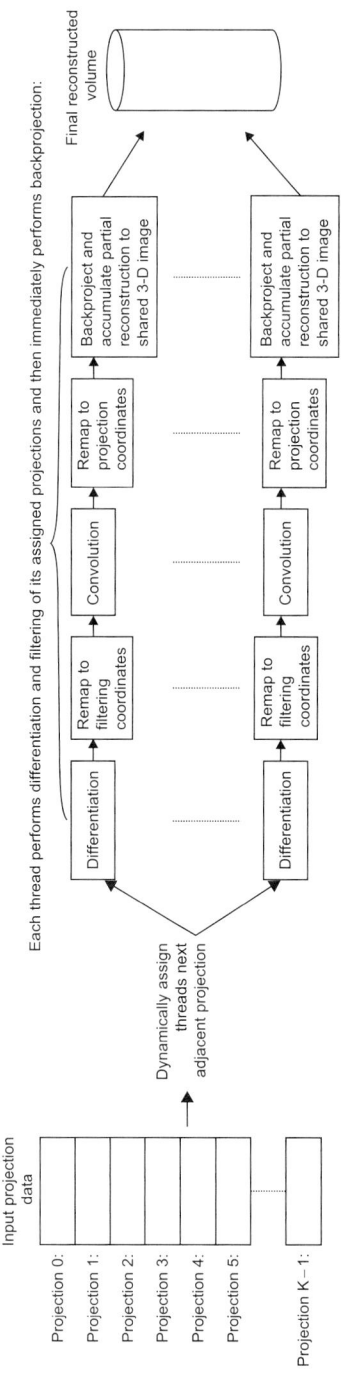

FIGURE 41.2

Parallelization strategy for the cone-beam cover method.

```
1
2
3    ReconstructVolume(int VolumeSide,
4        int NumProjections, int NumRows, int NumColumns)
5    {
6        for(P=0; P<NumProjections − 1; P++)
7        {
8            // differentiate the projections first
9            DiffProj[P] = Differentiate(Projections[P], Projections[P+1]);
10
11
12   // Filtering is done through Forward Mapping, Convolution with a special kernel and the Backward Mapping
13           // map from the detectors plane coordinate to filtering coordinates
14           FwdMapped[P] = DoForwardMapping(DiffProj[P]);
15
16           // perform Hilbert transform by convolving the Hilbert Kernel
17           FilteredProj[P] = Convolve1D(FwdMapped[P], HilbertKernel);
18
19           // map from filtering coordinates back to projection coordinate (i.e. detectors plane reference)
20           BkwdMapped[P] = DoBackwardMapping(FilteredProj[P]);
21
22
23           // for this filtered projection, add its partial contribution to each voxel of the volume
24           Backproject(BkwdMapped[P]);
25       }
26   }
```

Listing 41.1: Pseudo code of the algorithm's implementation.

using a function $\widehat{\psi}(u,\omega)$, which is the inverse of $\omega(u,\psi)$ defined by Eq. 41.1. At this stage, the projections are filtered and ready to be back-projected to construct the final volume. The second major step, and also the most time-consuming part of the entire computation, is the back projection. For any horizontal slice orthogonal to the z-axis of the volume under construction, there are a number of filtered back projections that will partially contribute to the final intensity value of each of the slice's voxels. We started by a single thread C implementation. After verifying its correctness we used its output as a reference against which we verified the results of the parallel implementations, on both a multicore CPU and the GPGPU. The filtering phase lends itself easily to parallelization.

41.3.1 Projections' Filtering

It may be helpful to consider a volume example so that we can refer to its dimension throughout the chapter. Let's consider reconstructing a volume of $512 \times 512 \times 512$ voxels from 2560 projections, each of them 128 rows by 512 columns. In case of single-precision storage, the projection data size is 671,088,640 bytes large. The filtering operations cannot be done in place, and need temporary storage memory space. This shows the memory space requirements such applications put on the machine.

Differentiation

When the GPGPU board has enough memory for all the projections and the temporary storage, we can process all the acquired data in a single kernel launch. Otherwise, we need to do it in a number

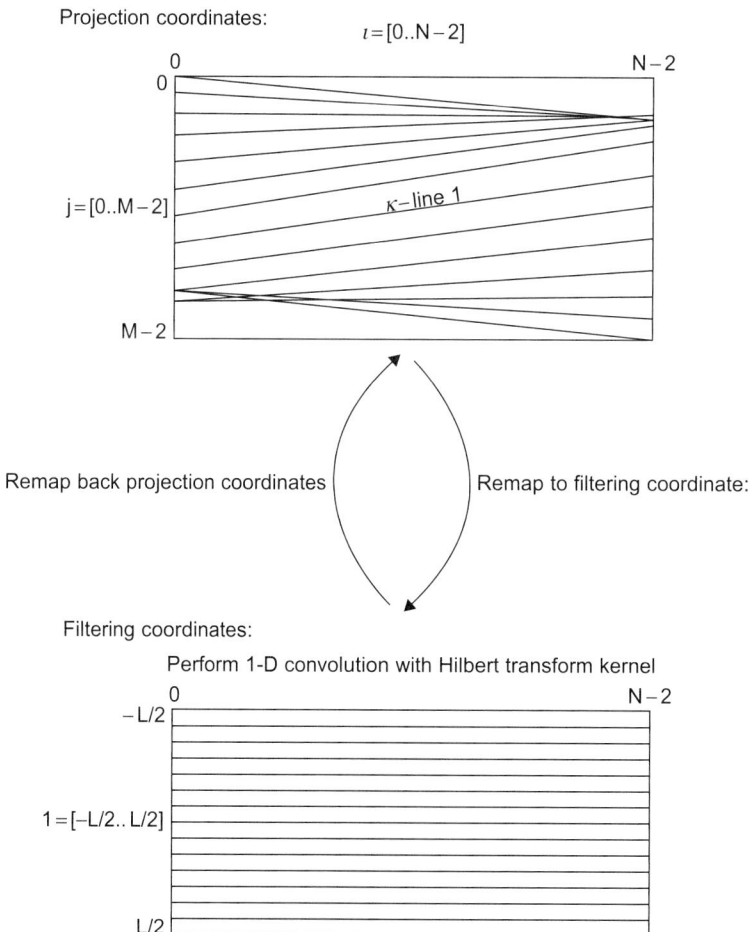

FIGURE 41.3

Kappa lines are mapped to parallel lines and back to Kappa lines.

of steps determined by the size of the data and the amount of available memory. Listing 41.3 shows the excerpt of the differentiation kernel code. The dParams is a structure holding different needed parameters, and it is placed in the constant memory. We made this choice because all threads read the same parameters because they execute exactly the same code in a lockstep manner. The different parameters are computed on the host side from the information about the volume dimensions, and the projections it will be reconstructed from. Listing 41.2 shows the code snippet that loads the initialized structure to the constant memory using `cudaMemcpyToSymbol` CUDA API. When certain information needs to be computed only once and can fit inside the constant memory, it may help performance to compute them a priori and store. The different threads reference a location rather than recomputing the value. This approach helps when the cost to compute the values in the saved table is higher than the cost

```
1
2    void InitializeParameters(int VolumeSide,
3        int NumProjections, int NumRows, int NumColumns)
4    {
5        // details omitted
6
7        // copy the Parameters structure to device memory
8        int ParamsSize = sizeof(InitialParams);
9        cutilSafeCall( cudaMemcpyToSymbol(dParams, hParameters, ParamsSize) );
10   }
```

Listing 41.2: Parameters initialization code.

```
1
2    __global__ void DiffKernel(float* source, float* destination)
3    {
4        int projection = blockIdx.x;
5        int col = blockIdx.y;
6        int row = threadIdx.x;
7
8        int elementsPerProjection = dParams.NumRows * dParams.NumColumns;
9
10       // compute differentiation result for (x,y)=(col, row)
11       // diff is a __device__ function that computes
12       // the multi−dimensional differentiation at (x,y) point
13       // here the depth z is between current projection and the next
14       float result = diff(row, col, projection, projection+1);
15
16       // save result into destination
17       float* pDest = &destination[projection*elementsPerProjection];
18       pDest[row*dParams.NumColumns + col] = result;
19   }
```

Listing 41.3: Differentiation kernel code.

to read it from the constant memory. For our example implementation, we saved trigonometric values for the projections' angles in the constant memory. But when we applied the `--fast-math` flag to the compiler, the generated instruction for sin() and cos() were as fast as reading from the table.

The differentiation is done using the chain rule along the row, column, and neighboring projection, as Figure 41.4 shows. This computation is implemented in the `diff` device function, which is called by the `DiffKernel`.

The limits of the maximum number of threads per block and the maximum extents on each dimension put restrictions on how to configure the computation grid on the GPGPU. For example, when differentiating 128×512 column projections, one cannot use `dim3 diffBlock(128, 512, 1)` because the maximum threads per block is 1024. Therefore, a valid kernel configuration needs to be something like `dim3 diffBlock(128, 1, 1); dim3 diffGrid(2560, 512)`.

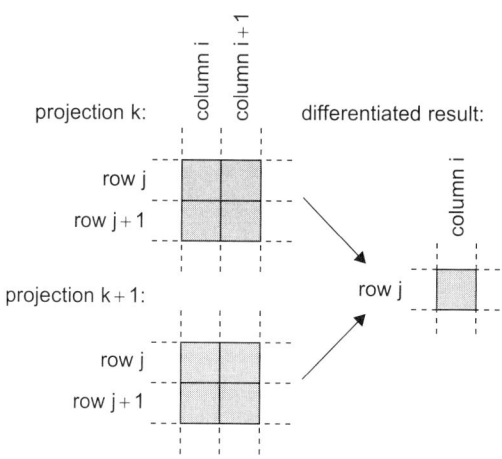

FIGURE 41.4

Eight texels are required to compute the differential result.

Forward Mapping

As mentioned earlier, we need to map the detectors that fall on the helical path into a horizontal line before we can apply the convolution with the Hilbert transform kernel. The forward-mapping tables can be computed a priori and stored, as done in the multicore CPU implementation. But for the GPGPU implementation, the constant memory is not large enough to hold the tables for a volume like 512^3, and the global memory access is costly, so we adopted the approach of computing them on the fly as needed while performing the forward-mapping operation. The forward-mapping CUDA kernel is configured in a very similar way to the differentiation kernel, as can be seen from Listings 41.4 and 41.5.

`computeForwardMappingCoordinates` implements the core of computing the forward mapping as described by the equation mentioned earlier and is listed in Listing 41.6.

Convolution

After differentiation and forward-mapping operations, the projection is ready for the 1-D convolution for each of its rows. Each thread of a given block will compute the convolution result for a single pixel along a given row. The block will operate on each single row. Therefore, the kernel configuration will have a number of threads equal to the number of columns in each row. The configuration grid will be two-dimensional with the number of projections as the X dimension and the number of rows per projection as the Y dimension. Since the threads of a single block will operate on neighboring pixels, using textures to benefit from their caching support was an obvious choice. Therefore, the convolution step makes usage of a 3-D texture bound to the output memory of the forward-mapping operation as listed in Listing 41.7. The X and Y dimension matched the rows and columns of a projection, while the Z dimension matched the number of projections. It is worth noting that when the number of projections exceeds 2048, which is the limit on a 3-D texture, it is necessary to adopt a blocking approach and process the projections in subsets. A `cudaArray` was allocated and the results from the forward-mapping step copied to it. This device-to-device copying is necessary because of the use of `cudaArray` type. On the device side, the CUDA kernel that applies the convolution looks like Listing 41.8. Since the Hilbert transform kernel (`dHilbertIdeal` in Listing 41.8) will be accessed by

```
1
2    __global__ void doForwardMapping(float* source, float* destination)
3    {
4        int projection = blockIdx.x;
5        int col = blockIdx.y;
6        int row = threadIdx.x;
7
8        int elementsPerProjection = dParams.NumRemmapedRows * dParams.NumColumns;
9        int srcStep = dParams.xRebinWidth;
10
11       float xs = 0;
12       float ys = 0;
13
14       computeForwardMappingCoordinates(row, col, &xs, &ys);
15
16       // interpolate the needed value from the neighboring locations
17       int xs0 = (int)xs;
18           int ys0 = (int)ys;
19       int xs1 = xs0 + 1;
20           int ys1 = ys0 + 1;
21
22       int index1 = xs0 + (ys0*srcStep);
23           int index2 = xs1 + (ys0*srcStep);
24           float I0 = source[index1]*(xs1 − xs) + source[index2]*(xs − xs0);
25
26       index1 = xs0 + (ys1*srcStep);
27           index2 = xs1 + (ys1*srcStep);
28       float I1 = source[index1]*(xs1 − xs) + source[index2]*(xs − xs0);
29
30
31           float result = I0*(ys1 − ys) + I1*(ys − ys0);
32
33       float* pDest = &destination[projection*elementsPerProjection];
34       pDest[row*d_Params.NumColumns + col] = result;
35    }
```

Listing 41.4: Forward-mapping kernel code.

```
1
2        dim3 fwdMapBlock(NumRows, 1, 1);
3        dim3 fwdMapGrid(NumProjections, NumColums, 1);
4
5        doForwardMapping<<< fwdMapGrid, fwdMapBlock >>>(source, destination);
6        cutilSafeCall( cudaThreadSynchronize() );
```

Listing 41.5: Forward-mapping kernel launch configuration.

all threads, it was loaded into the constant memory to benefit from the fact that the threads of a warp accessing the same address will result in a single read. The read will be broadcast to all the thread members of the warp.

```
1
2    __device__ void computeForwardRemapCoordinates(int i, int l, float* pX, float* pY)
3    {
4            // implementing the forward mapping fomula
5         float u = (float(i) − float(dParams.N)/2.0f + .5) * dParams.delta_u;
6         float psi = −PI / 2.0f − dParams.alpha_m + float(l)*dParams.delta_psi;
7         float w_k = dParams.D * dParams.h / dParams.R * (psi + psi/tan(psi) * u / dParams.D);
8         float k = w_k / dParams.delta_w + dParams.M/2;
9
10        if( k < 0 )
11            *pY = 0;
12        else if( k > d_Params.M−2 )
13            *pY = dParams.M−2;
14        else
15            *pY = k;
16
17        *pX = i;
18
19   }
```

Listing 41.6: Implementation of the forward-mapping formula.

```
1
2    // details omitted
3
4        cudaChannelFormatDesc channelDesc = cudaCreateChannelDesc<float>();
5        cudaExtent conv_volumeSize =
6            make_cudaExtent(NumElementPerRow, NumRows, NumProjections);
7
8        cutilSafeCall( cudaMalloc3DArray(&d_convTextureData,
9                    &channelDesc,
10                   conv_volumeSize) );
11
12       // memory copy details omitted
13
14       // set texture parameters, Non−Normalized, No−Interpolation, Clamp
15       ConvTextureRef.normalized     = false;
16       ConvTextureRef.filterMode     = cudaFilterModePoint;
17       ConvTextureRef.addressMode[0] = cudaAddressModeClamp;
18       ConvTextureRef.addressMode[1] = cudaAddressModeClamp;
19       ConvTextureRef.addressMode[2] = cudaAddressModeClamp;
20
21       // bind array to 3-D texture
22       cutilSafeCall(cudaBindTextureToArray(
23           ConvTextureRef, d_convTextureData, channelDesc));
```

Listing 41.7: Binding a 3-D texture to convolution input memory.

```
1
2    __global__ void convolutionRow(int KernelRadius, float* d_Result)
3    {
4        const int x = threadIdx.x;
5        const int y = blockIdx.y;
6        const int projection = blockIdx.x;
7
8        // details omitted
9
10       int destOffset = NumElementsPerProjection * projection;
11       float* pResultDest = &d_Result[destOffset];
12       float sum = 0;
13       for(int k = -KernelRadius; k <= KernelRadius; k++)
14       {
15           float val = tex3D(ConvTextureRef, x + k, y, projection);
16           sum += val * dHilbertIdeal[KernelRadius - k];
17       }
18
19       pResultDest[IMUL(y, NumElementPerRow) + x] = sum;
20   }
```

Listing 41.8: Convolution kernel code.

Backward Mapping

The backward-mapping step brings the elements from the horizontal lines to the κ-lines. It is very similar in kernel launch configuration. The only difference is that it makes a call to the `computeBackwardRemapCoordinates` function instead of the forward-mapping one. This function[2] runs a loop to find the value of $\widehat{\psi}(u, \omega)$. After this step is completed, the projections can be sampled to add their respective contributions to each voxel of the volume under reconstruction.

41.3.2 Back Projection

To reconstruct the 512^3 volume mentioned earlier, in a single shot, we need to allocate enough memory to hold it, in addition to the memory required to hold the filtered projections. Therefore, we need:

$$sizeof(float) \times \left(512^3 + 2560 \times 128 \times 512\right) = 1,207,959,552 \quad Bytes$$

which is well above 1 GB of the device memory. This imposes the back projection to be performed in a blocked manner in the case of devices with less than 1.5 GB. The use of 3-D texture was motivated by the need to use the caching mechanism underlying the textures. The Katsevich algorithm uses sine and cosine trigonometric function to compute the sampling coordinates. These sampling coordinates are then used to read from the filtered projections. The use of trigonometric function in generating the memory access coordinates makes it very difficult, if not impossible, to come up with coalesced memory access pattern. When the size of the data working set can fit into the constant memory, it can help the performance to copy the data into the constant memory for reducing the cost of memory accesses. However, in this type of application, where a single projection in the example mentioned

---

[2]See companion source code

above is of size 256 kB, the use of constant memory is not possibile owing to the 64 kB size constraint. Therefore, we opted to use textures to take advantage of their underlying cache. But using textures comes with its constraints imposed by the GPGPU architecture and/or the CUDA API. For instance, in our implementation, the blocked approach we adopted was not because of the memory limitation, but owing to the fact that 3-D texture's coordinates cannot exceed 2048 in any given dimension. Because we use the Z-depth as the projection index, we had to constrain the number of projections loaded at once to be less than 2048. We reconstructed the volume in slices of a given thickness. When a slice between Z_1 and Z_2 coordinates is being reconstructed, not all projections are needed. In fact, only projections between a half-pitch under-scan below Z_1 and half-pitch over-scan above Z_2 are needed. For example, in the context of the 512^3 volume, a slice the thickness of 64 pixels requires 768 projections, not the whole 2560.

   The parallelization of this step can be done in several different ways. First, we can set a block of threads to reconstruct a subvolume ($[x_0\,x_1],[y_0\,y_1],[z_0\,z_1]$). The block of threads is set with dimensions $(x_1 - x_0 + 1, y_1 - y_0 + 1, 1)$, while the grid of blocks is set with (*NumBlocksX*, *NumBlocksY*, 1) for its dimensions, where `NumBlocksX` and `NumBlocksY` are the number of sub-blocks in the X and Y directions, respectively. Each thread in a given block will reconstruct the column $[z_0\,z_1]$ at location (x,y) such that $x_0 \le x \le x_1$ and $y_0 \le y \le y_1$. A second way of doing this is to have all the threads of the same block reconstruct the same column $[z_0\,z_1]$, and each block is set to build a given location (x,y). The launch grid is configured as `dim3 BPGrid(volumeX, volumeY, 1)`, where `volumeX` and `volumeY` are the volume dimensions in the X and Y directions, respectively. The latter method rendered better performance than the former. This is due mainly to the fact that the coordinates (x,y) affect the values of the sampling coordinates, while the z level does not. When the threads of a given block are constructing the column $[z_0\,z_1]$, they sample a given projection at the same (u,w) position. This benefits from the spatial locality offered by the cache underlying the textures. This method reconstructed the volume in one-third of the time taken by the former one. To summarize, each thread of a block (x,y) reconstructs the voxel at level z by looping through all the necessary projections. A third way of reconstructing a slice of the volume is to parallelize the computation along the projections, in other words, to make each thread compute the partial contributions of a subset of the projections. This approach requires reduction to generate the final density value of a given voxel. Besides the location (x,y), the other factor that affects sampling coordinates values is the angle at which the projection was taken. Because these threads handle different projections, they use different sampling coordinates and, hence, they cannot take advantage of memory locality. These are part of the reason why this third approach runs slower than the second. The other factor is the fact that the needed reduction step to generate voxel densities is to be done in the shared memory; hence, the number of threads per block is limited by the size of the shared memory and the number of elements per column being reconstructed. Another reason that the second approach performed better than the other two is the complete elimination of the need for global synchronization. This absence of interdependence between the threads allows them to make forward progress as fast as the GPU clock permits. For GPU applications, any algorithm's implementation that needs to take care of memory coherency will suffer significantly because the memory accesses will become a serialization point in the computation flow. Eliminating, or at least reducing, the need for global synchronization is a key optimization for GPGPU applications.

   Listing 41.9 shows the second method described earlier. Each thread loops through all projections and reconstructs a single voxel of the volume; therefore, we avoided the coherency issue that arises from the cooperative construction of a voxel by multiple threads.

```
1
2   __global__ void doBackprojectionKernel(int zOffset, int firstProj, int lastProj, float* pVolume)
3   {
4       // threads of bllock (i,j) will reconstruct subvolume (i,j, [zOffset .. zOffset+blockDim.x]
5       int i = blockIdx.x + threadIdx.y*dParams.ImageX/2;
6       int j = blockIdx.y + threadIdx.z*dParams.ImageY/2;
7
8       float y=dParams.Ymin + (j*dParams.delta_y);
9       float x=dParams.Xmin + (i*dParams.delta_x);
10
11      // if point falls outside the volume of interest, do nothing
12      if( (x*x + y*y) > dParams.radius_2)
13          return;
14
15      // each thread reconstructs a single voxel (x,y,z)
16      int m = zOffset + threadIdx.x;
17
18      // pixelValue will accumulate the density value
19      float pixelValue = 0;
20
21
22      SamplingCoordinates sc_prev;
23      SamplingCoordinates sc_curr;
24      SamplingCoordinates sc_next;
25
26      // initialize sc_prev, sc_curr
27      // details omitted
28
29
30      int textureZDepth = 0;
31      for(int projection = firstProj; projection < lastProj; projection++)
32      {
33          // compute the next sampling coordinates
34          computeSamplingCoordinates(angle_next, x, y, sc_next);
35
36          addContribution(x, y, m, zDepth, angle, sc_prev, sc_curr, sc_next, pixelValue);
37
38          // increment the textureZDepth to match the current projection in the texture Z coordinate
39          textureZDepth++;
40
41          // current becomes previous and next becomes current
42          sc_prev = sc_curr;
43          sc_curr = sc_next;
44
45          // increment the projection angle
46          angle += dParams.delta_s;
47          angle_next += dParams.delta_s;
48
49      }
50
51      // write the density to volume memory
52      int pos = threadIdx.x + (j + i*dParams.ImageY)*blockDim.x;
```

```
53        pVolume[pos] += pixelValue;
54    }
```

Listing 41.9: The back projection kernel.

The function addContribution[3] samples the 3-D texture and returns the contribution from a particular filtered projection to the current (x, y, z) voxel. We organized the 3-D texture by making each filtered projection a slice in it. When the GPGPU device's global memory can hold all the projections for the volume being reconstructed, we load all of them. If not, we load just a number of them per kernel launch, and we perform a number of launches to complete the back projection. Even when there is enough memory to hold all the filtered data, we could not do it because the CUDA implementation does not allow more than 2048 per dimension. It would be helpful to have a flexible texture extension setup. For example, to have a $2048 \times 2048 \times 2048$ 3-D texture or a $512 \times 512 \times 8192$. The texture-sampling facility offers two types of cudaTextureFilterMode, cudaFilterModePoint and cudaFilterModeLinear. When the linear interpolation mode is set, the type of interpolation is determined by the dimensionality of the texture. CUDA provides a template to declare texture reference objects of different dimensions. The statement texture < float, 2, cudaReadModeElement-Type > texRef2D, for example, declares a 2-D texture reference object using floats as the underlying type. The statement texRef.filterMode = cudaFilterModeLinear; is used when the programmer wants to use hardware interpolation. The type of linear interpolation, that is, 1-D, 2-D, or 3-D interpolation, is inferred from the texture type, which is defined by the dimension parameter passed to the texture template. It is very common to use 3-D textures for the sole purpose of stacking a number of 2-D textures. In this case the programmer may still want to use hardware linear interpolation in the 2-D sense even if the texture object is declared of type 3-D, because the intent of using 3-D texture is just to stack many 2-D textures, not to use it for 3-D sampling. But setting the filter mode to linear will cause the hardware interpolator to use eight elements, four elements from each of two neighboring 2-D textures. It would be a good addition to CUDA to let the programmer specify the dimensionality of interpolation when 2-D or 3-D texture references are used. A call like texRef3D.filterMode = cudaFilterModeLinear2D, where the texture reference is declared as texture<float, 3, cudaReadModeElementType> texRef3D; would mean that 2-D linear interpolation is wanted on the X-Y plane only. The hardware interpolator would pick the nearest 2-D texture to the given Z level and sample it using the 2-D linear interpolation.

The statment float sample = tex3D(texRef3D, u, v, w); should return the 2-D linearly interpolated value of the four neighbors of position (u, v) on the 2-D projection corresponding to the Z level closest to w.

41.4 FINAL EVALUATION AND VALIDATION OF RESULTS, TOTAL BENEFITS, AND LIMITATIONS

Different GPGPU devices were used to test our implementation, including a Tesla C870 containing 16 streaming multiprocessors (SMs) with eight cores on each that amounts to a total of 128 cores,

---

[3] See companion source code

a Tesla C1060 containing 30 SMs with eight cores on each, and the new Fermi-based GTX 480 with 480 cores distributed between 60 SMs. We performed comparison among the implementations of the same algorithm. In this case, the cone-beam cover method was implemented on the multicore CPU using OpenMP and Intel Compiler and Intel's IPP library. The multicore CPU speedup numbers are for the cone-beam cover method between a single thread and eight-thread parallel version. The performance of the eight-thread multicore version was measured on a dual-socket quad-core Clovertown processor running at 2.33 GHz. Table 41.1 summaries our performance measurement for the CPU implementation and the best of the breed GPGPU implementation running on GTX 480.

The results collected from the GTX 480 with comparison to the basic single-core and the multicore CPU implementations are presented for different cubic volumes in the same table. In ideal conditions (i.e., assuming a perfect memory subsystem), the multithreaded version should manifest the same speedup no matter what the volume size is. For the cases running on the multicore CPU, the cache hierarchy plays a critical role in the whole performance; therefore, the program suffers a certain penalty when large data is handled to reconstruct the image. Because the cache capacity misses are responsible for the penalty, having many threads available to perform computation alleviates the penalty by partially hiding it through parallelism. Hence, a part of the speedup from the multithreaded CPU code is due to the number of threads running in parallel; the other part of the speedup is due to partially hiding the cache misses penalty. For this reason, the 8T CPU code shows a superlinear speedup with reference to the single-thread version. In the cases of GPGPU, the existence of level of parallelism and a high enough ratio of computation-to-memory access can hide the memory access penalty. Because our implementation on the GPGPU is completely parallelized, the reconstruction time looks more interesting when large volumes are used. Nonetheless, it is noticeable that the speedup trend did not continue when we reconstruct the largest volume in our experiment: 1024^3. Reconstructing such large volume incurs many more round-trips between the host and the device than for smaller volumes. Copying memory by small chunks carries some penalty compared with moving all the data at once. In addition, making many trips between the host and the device requires synchronization using the `cudaThreadSynchronize` API. As an example the reconstruction of 1024^3 costs 160 seconds just for copying memory between the host and device.

To see how the performance of GPGPU implementation scales with the number of cores, we collected the results from several GPGPUs with a different number of cores. The Tesla C870 has 128 cores, the Tesla C1060 has 240 cores, and the GTX 480 has 480 cores. To show only the effect of the number of cores per device over the speedup, the same memory loads are used on all devices. For example, when we reconstruct a 1024^3 volume, memory is a decisive parameter on speedup; for this reason, even when it is possible to load larger datasets at once onto the Tesla C1060 that has a larger

Table 41.1 Reconstruction time (in seconds) for different volumes.

Volume	Single-Core CPU (Baseline)	8T CPU	8T CPU Speedup	GPGPU (GTX 480)	GPGPU Speedup
$128 \times 128 \times 128$	7.18	0.81	8.8x	0.23	30.6x
$256 \times 256 \times 256$	96.79	10.3	9.3x	1.97	49.2x
$512 \times 512 \times 512$	1515	108.8	13.9x	22	68.8x
$1024 \times 1024 \times 1024$	23,789	1412.8	16.8x	490	48.5x

Table 41.2 Speedups achieved on different GPGPU devices.

Volume	Tesla C870 (128 Cores)	Tesla C1060 (240 Cores)	GTX-480 (480 Cores)
128 × 128 × 128	10.3x	21.5x	30.6x
256 × 256 × 256	14.1x	28.3x	49.2x
512 × 512 × 512	20x	36.5x	68.8x
1024 × 1024 × 1024	21x	42.2x	48.5x

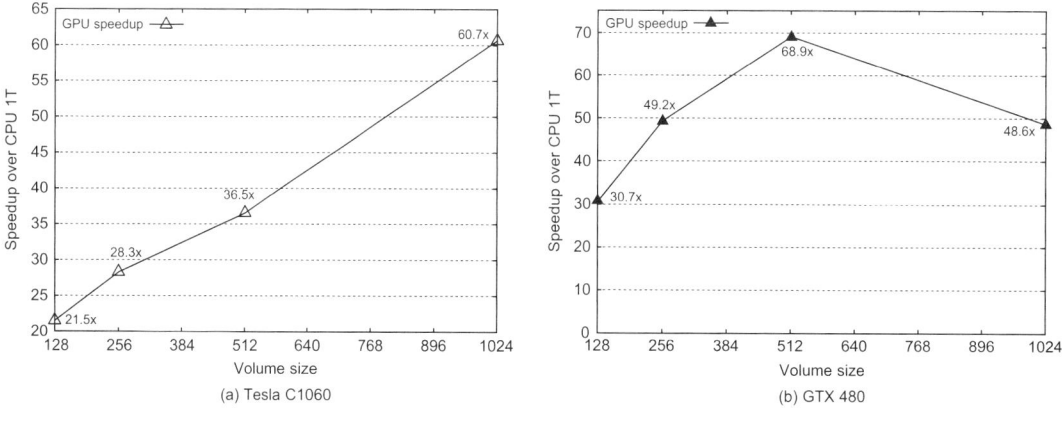

FIGURE 41.5

GPGPU speedup trend.

global memory size of 4 GB, we restricted the partial datasets to be of the same size as on the Tesla C870 and the GTX 480, both of which have only 1.5 GB of global memory. Table 41.2 shows how the same application code performs on GPGPU devices with a different number of cores and shows their corresponding scaling trend. The speedups as a function of the volume are reported in Figures 41.5(a) and 41.5(b) for the Tesla C1060 and the GTX 480, respectively.

When we are reconstructing large volumes, a good amount of time is spent in transferring data because it is done in partial amounts that can fit in the GPU device memory. For example, the 1024^3 volume reconstruction consumes 152 seconds in data transfer and extra round-trips between the host and the device.

Unlike the case of the Tesla C1060 with 4 GB memory (Figure 41.5(a)), the speedup chart of the GTX 480 (Figure 41.5(b)) did not continue the trend at the 1024^3 volume. This is mainly due to the multiple round-trips penalty of 152 seconds. If we consider reconstruction time only, the speedup would be a little more than 60 times.

41.4.1 A Note on Energy Consumption

The multithreaded multicore CPU version was run on a dual-socket Clovertown processor at 2.33 GHz (each processor has a total power consumption of 80 watts as stated on Intel's Web site). The best

Table 41.3 Energy savings from using Tesla C870, Tesla C1060, and GTX-480.

Volume	8T CPU Energy (j)	C870 Energy (j)	C1060 Energy (j)	GTX-480 Energy (j)	C870 Energy Savings	C1060 Energy Savings	GTX-480 Energy Savings
$128 \times 128 \times 128$	129	117	62	57	9.5%	51.9%	55.8%
$256 \times 256 \times 256$	1657	1162	642	492	29.9%	61.3%	70.3%
$512 \times 512 \times 512$	17412	12818	7798	5500	26.4%	55.2%	68.4%
$1024 \times 1024 \times 1024$	225920	187510	103651	122500	17.1%	54.1%	45.8%

performance on the GPGPU was given by the GTX-480 board, which has a total power consumption of 250 watts. The Tesla C870 has a total power consumption of 170 watts, while the Tesla C1060 board is rated at 187.8 watts. The maximum power dissipations for the different GPUs are collected from their respective brochures provided by NVIDIA. We used the maximum power dissipation as a ballpark estimate for the energy consumed. These numbers are by no means definitive, nor are they measured experimentally. They are simply a rough guess of the energy consumption neighborhood. There is an implicit assumption that the CPU or GPU will dissipate the peak power value while performing the computation. Table 41.3 shows how many joules it took to reconstruct each volume for the eight-threads CPU version and for the GPGPU version. Even though the power consumption of the GPGPU is much higher than that of the CPU multicore system, the energy dissipated to accomplish the same job, nonetheless, is much smaller on the GPGPU. This is not surprising because the SM design of a GPGPU is much more computationally efficient. On average, we observed energy savings from 9.5% to 70.3% depending on the size of volume being reconstructed and the GPU device used. The GTX-480 shows the highest energy savings except for the 1024^3 volume where C1060 GPU was better. This is because the GTX-480 board used in the experiments has only 1.5 GB of memory, and more seconds were paid for the extra transfers. The energy cost benefits of using GPUs for applications that can be implemented in a heavily parallel ways are quite evident. This also justifies the current industry trend of integrating more diversified accelerators on chip to improve the overall energy efficiency of computation.

41.5 RELATED WORK

Owens *et al.* [7] surveyed and categorized the development of general-purpose computation on graphics processors and demonstrated the potential of their enormous computation capability. Regarding the CT image reconstruction work, Noo *et al.* [6] discussed the Katsevich algorithm for both the curved and flat panel detectors and presented an implementation strategy for these two types of CT scanners. Deng *et al.* [1] describe a parallel implementation scheme of the reconstruction algorithm on a 32-node cluster of 64-bit AMD Opteron processors. Fontaine and Lee [3] studied the parallelization of the Katsevich CT image reconstruction method using Intel multicore processors. Their OpenMP implementation was used in this chapter for comparison against the CUDA results on three different GPGPUs. Lee *et al.* [5] present a comparative study of applications on GPU and multicore CPU platforms. Results from a set of throughput computing kernels are presented to show how the performance of an Intel Core i7-960 processor compares with that of an NVIDIA GTX280. The optimizations on each platform are also discussed. Recently, more works have been done by using GPGPU to improve the performance of medical imaging reconstruction. For example, Stone *et al.* [9] presented the use of GPGPUs in the acceleration of image reconstruction from the magnetic resonance imaging (MRI) machines. Sharp *et al.* [8] studied the acceleration of the cone-beam CT image reconstruction method using the Brooks programming environment on an NVIDIA 8800 GPU, but adopted the older, nonexact FDK algorithm in their study. Xu *et al.* [10] studied the feasibility of real-time 3-D reconstruction of CT images using commodity graphics hardware. A parallel implementation of the Katsevich algorithm on GPU is presented in [11]. Yan *et al.* developed a minimal overscan formula and explained an implementation using both CPU and GPU. Their application performed the projection's filtering on the CPU and the back projection on the GPU graphics pipeline. Zhou and Pan [12] proposed an algorithm based on the filtered back-projection approach that requires less data than the quasi-exact and exact algorithms.

41.6 FUTURE DIRECTIONS

The presented work shows how a fully parallel implementation of a given algorithm takes full advantage of the GPGPU architectures and how it scales with no need to change the code. A similar experiment can be done for the symmetry method proposed in [3]. This method requires rearrangement of the projections after filtering to make the ones that are separated by an angle of $\frac{\pi}{2}$ column interleaved. After this shuffling, the sampling can be done in 128-bit wide elements (i.e., `float4`), and four voxels will be reconstructed at once. Fontaine and Lee's paper provides detailed explanations with respect to how it was done with their algorithmic level optimization (inherent symmetry), as well as the application of SIMD ISA provided by the IA-based processors. It is expected that this algorithm will show similar speedups.

41.7 SUMMARY

Medical image processing applications are not just computation intensive; they also require a large amount of memory for both original data storage and temporary data processing. When the implementation of a given algorithm can completely be parallelized, it will likely benefit from the availability of more processing cores to scale performance given the memory overheads are negligible. It may even be beneficial to sacrifice certain optimization opportunities to allow full parallel implementation of the algorithm. In this article, we used the Katsevich CT image reconstruction algorithm as an application to demonstrate how modern multicore and GPGPU processors can substantially improve the performance of medical image processing. We also identified the limited size of device memory to be a performance glass jaw that prevents the scalability of speedup as the input data set becomes larger. Not having enough memory to hold all the volumes being reconstructed and their intermediate results requires high bandwidth between the host and the GPGPU, leading to substantial performance degradation.

References

[1]   J. Deng, H. Yu, J. Ni, T. He, S. Zhao, L. Wang, et al., A parallel implementation of the Katsevich algorithm for 3-D CT image reconstruction, J. Supercomput. 38 (1) (2006) 35–47.

[2]   L. Feldkamp, L. Davis, J. Kress, Practical cone-beam algorithm, J. Opt. Soc. Am. A 1 (6) (1984) 612–619.

[3]   E. Fontaine, H.-H.S. Lee, Optimizing Katsevich image reconstruction algorithm on multicore processors, in: Proceedings of 2007 International Conference on Parallel and Distributed Systems, vol. 2, Kaohsiung, Taiwan, 2007, pp. 1–8.

[4]   A. Katsevich, Theoretically exact filtered backprojection-type inversion algorithm for Spiral CT, SIAM J. Appl. Math. 62 (2002) 2012–2026.

[5]   V. W. Lee, C. Kim, J. Chhugani, M. Deisher, D. Kim, A.-D. Nguyen, et al., Debunking the 100X GPU vs. CPU myth: an evaluation of throughput computing on CPU and GPU, in: ISCA '10: Proceedings of the 37th Annual International Symposium on Computer Architecture, ACM, New York, 2010, pp. 451–460.

[6]   F. Noo, J. Pack, D. Heuscher, Exact helical reconstruction using native cone-beam geometries, Phys. Med. Biol. 48 (23) (2003) 3787–3818.

[7]   J. D. Owens, D. Luebke, N. Govindaraju, M. Harris, J. Kruger, A. Lefohn, et al., A survey of general-purpose computation on graphics hardware, Comput. Graph. Forum 26 (1) (2007) 80–113.

[8]   G. Sharp, N. Kandasamy, H. Singh, M. Folkert, GPU-based streaming architectures for fast cone-beam CT image reconstruction and demons deformable registration, Phys. Med. Biol. 52 (2007) 5771.

[9]   S. Stone, J. Haldar, S. Tsao, W. Hwu, B. Sutton, Z. Liang, Accelerating advanced MRI reconstructions on GPUs, J. Parallel Distrib. Comput. 68 (10) (2008) 1307–1318.

[10] F. Xu, K. Mueller, Real-time 3D computed tomographic reconstruction using commodity graphics hardware, Phys. Med. Biol. 52 (12) (2007) 3405.

[11] G. Yan, J. Yian, S. Zhu, C. Qin, Y. Dai, F. Yang, et al. Fast Katsevich algorithm based on GPU for helical cone-beam computed tomography, IEEE Trans. Inf. Technol. Biomed. 14 (4) (2010) 1053–1061.

[12] Y. Zhou, X. Pan, Exact image reconstruction on PI-lines from minimum data in helical cone-beam CT, Phys. Med. Biol. 49 (2004) 941–959.

3-D Tomographic Image Reconstruction from Randomly Ordered Lines with CUDA

42

Guillem Pratx, Jing-Yu Cui, Sven Prevrhal, Craig S. Levin

We present a novel method of computing line-projection operations along sets of randomly oriented lines with CUDA and its application to positron emission tomography (PET) image reconstruction. The new approach addresses challenges that include compute thread divergence and random memory access by exploiting GPU capabilities such as shared memory and atomic operations. The benefits of the CUDA implementation are compared with a reference CPU-based code. When applied to PET image reconstruction, the CUDA implementation is 43X faster, and images are virtually identical. In particular, the deviation between the CUDA and the CPU implementation is less than 0.08% (RMS) after five iterations of the reconstruction algorithm, which is of negligible consequence in typical clinical applications.

42.1 INTRODUCTION

42.1.1 List-Mode Image Reconstruction

Several medical imaging modalities are based on the reconstruction of tomographic images from projective line-integral measurements [1]. For these imaging modalities, typical iterative implementations spend most of the computation performing two line-projection operations. The *forward projection* accumulates image data along projective lines. The *back projection* distributes projection values back into the image data uniformly along the same lines. Both operations can include a weighting function called a "projection kernel," which defines how much any given voxel contributes to any given line. For instance, a simple projection kernel is 1 if the voxel is traversed by the line, otherwise, it is zero.

As a result of the increasing complexity of medical scanner technology, the demand for fast computation in image reconstruction has exploded. Fortunately, line-projection operations are independent across lines and voxels and are computable in parallel. Early after the introduction of the first graphics acceleration cards, texture-mapping hardware was proposed as a powerful tool for accelerating the projection operations for sinogram datasets [2]. In a sinogram, projective lines are organized according to their distance from the isocenter and their angle. The linear mapping between the coordinates of a point in the reconstructed image and its projection in each sinogram view can be exploited using linear

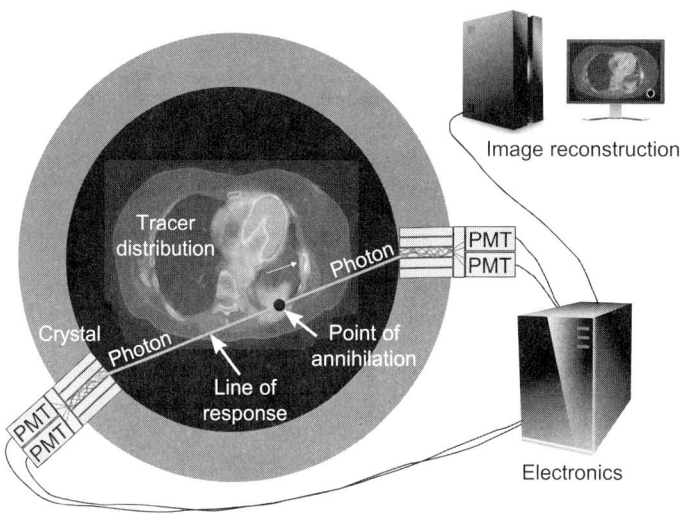

FIGURE 42.1

A basic principle of PET imaging.

interpolation hardware built into the texture mapping units, which is the basis for almost every GPU implementation [3–6].

Although many tomographic imaging modalities such as X-ray computed tomography (CT) acquire projection data of an inherent sinogram nature, others — in particular, positron emission tomography (PET) — are based on spatially random measurements.

In clinical practice, PET scanners are used mainly in the management of cancer [7, 8]. The purpose of a PET scan is to estimate the biodistribution of a molecule of interest — for instance, a molecule retained by cancerous cells. A radioactive version of the molecule is administered to the patient and distributes throughout the body according to various biological processes (Figure 42.1). Radioactive decay followed by positron-electron annihilation results in the simultaneous emission of two anticollinear high-energy photons (labelled on Figure 42.1). These photons are registered by small detector elements arranged in a ring around the measurement field. Detection of two photons in near-temporal coincidence indicates that a decay event likely occurred on the line (called line of response, or LOR) that joins the two detector elements involved. The stream of coincidence events is sent to a data acquisition computer for image reconstruction.

Although coincidence events provide line-integral measurements of the tracer distribution, histogramming these events into a sinogram is often inefficient because the number of events recorded is much smaller than the number of possible measurements, and therefore, the sinogram is sparsely filled. Instead, reconstruction is performed directly from the list-mode data, using algorithms such as *list-mode ordered-subsets expectation-maximization* (OSEM) [9–12], a variation of the popular OSEM algorithm [13], itself an accelerated version of the EM algorithm [14]. List-mode OSEM computes the maximum likelihood estimate by iteratively applying a sequence of forward- and back-projection operations along a list of lines (Figure 42.2).

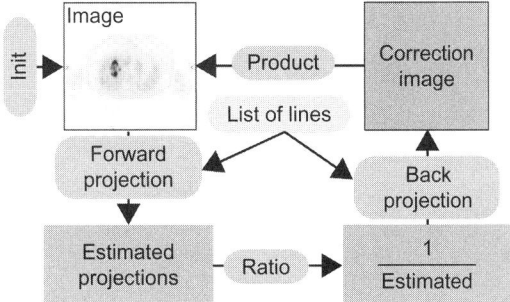

FIGURE 42.2

Iterative update mechanism in list-mode OSEM [9–12]. The forward- and back projection operations are performed along individual lines, taken from a list representing recorded coincidence events. The image is typically initialized with ones.

Table 42.1 Possible computation models for line-projection operations in tomography.

	Forward Projection	**Back Projection**
Line driven	Gather	Scatter
Voxel driven	Scatter	Gather

42.1.2 Challenges

List-mode OSEM, a computationally demanding algorithm, cannot be implemented using GPU texture-mapping approaches [2–6] because the linear mapping between image space and projection space does not apply to a list of randomly oriented lines. Instead, lines must be processed individually, and this issue raises new, complex challenges for a GPU implementation.

One of the major obstacles is that list-mode reconstruction requires scatter operations. In principle, forward- and back-projection operations can be performed either in a *voxel-driven* or *line-driven* manner. In GPGPU language, output-driven projection operations are gather operations, whereas input-driven projection operations are scatter operations (Table 42.1). A gather operation reads an array of data from an array of addresses, whereas a scatter operation writes an array of data to an array of addresses. For instance, a line-driven forward projection loops through all the lines and for each line, reads and sums the voxels that contribute to the line. A voxel-driven forward projection loops through all the voxels in the image and, for each voxel, updates the lines that receive contributions from the voxel. Both operations produce the same output, but data write hazards can occur in scatter operations. It has been previously suggested that, for best computing performance, the computation of line-projection operations for tomography should be output driven (i.e., gather) [12].

In list mode, the projection lines are not ordered; therefore, only line-driven operations may be utilized. As a result, list-mode back projection requires scatter operations. In the previous version of our list-mode reconstruction code, implemented using OpenGL/Cg, the scatter operations are performed

FIGURE 42.3

An axial slice, showing the back projection of nine randomly oriented lines using a 3-D "tube" model and a radially symmetric Gaussian kernel.

by programming in the vertex shaders where the output is written [15]. In that approach, a rectangular polygon is drawn into the frame-buffer object so that it encompasses the intersection of the line with the slice. This chapter presents a new approach where the output of the back projection is written directly to the slice, stored in shared memory.

Another challenge arising when performing list-mode projections on the GPU is the heterogeneous nature of the computations. As we have seen, lines stored in a list must be processed individually. However, because of the variable line length, the amount of computation per line can vary greatly. Therefore, to achieve efficient load balancing, computation must be broken down into elements smaller than the line itself.

Lastly, PET image reconstruction differs from X-ray CT because in order to reach high image quality, back projection and forward projection must model the imperfect response of the system, in particular, physical blurring processes — such as positron range and limited detector resolution. These blurring processes are implemented by projecting each line using a volumetric "tube" (Figure 42.3) and wide, spatially varying projection kernels [16, 17]. As a result, the number of voxels that participate in the projection of each line increases sharply, resulting in higher computational burden and increased complexity.

42.2 CORE METHODS

To address the challenges described in the previous section, we present several novel approaches based on CUDA.

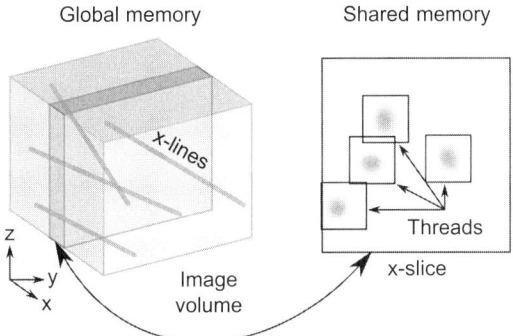

FIGURE 42.4

Depiction of a CUDA-based line projection for a set of lines in the x class. The image volume and the line geometry are stored in global memory. Slices are loaded one by one into shared memory. One thread is assigned to each line to calculate the portion of the projection involved with the current slice, which involves a 2-D loop with constant bounds.

1. Lines are first presorted into three classes, according to their predominant direction — that is, the Euclidian direction (x, y, or z) that has the largest absolute inner product with the line.
2. The image volume, which needs to be accessed randomly, is too large ($>1\,\text{MB}$) to be stored in shared memory. Therefore, line-projection operations traverse the volume slice by slice, with slice orientation perpendicular to the predominant direction of the lines (Figure 42.4). The three classes of lines are processed sequentially. Streaming multiprocessors (SM) load one slice at a time into shared memory, which effectively acts as a local cache (Figure 42.4). The calculations relative to the shared slice are performed in parallel by many concurrent threads, with each thread processing one line.
3. Because lines have different lengths, more threads are assigned to longer lines. By distributing the workload both over slices and over lines, we can balance the computation load.
4. All threads execute a double for-loop over all the voxels participating in the projection (Figure 42.4). Because lines are predominantly orthogonal to the slice, a for-loop with fixed bounds reaches all the voxels that participate in the projection while keeping the threads from diverging. More specifically, because the slice-based approach guarantees that the angle between the slice normal and the line is less than 45 degrees (Figure 42.5), these bounds are set to $\sqrt{2}(T_W + S)$, where T_W is the width of the projection tube and S the slice thickness, within the for-loop, the threads read (write to) all the voxels that participate for the current slice, weighting them by a kernel value computed on the fly on the GPU. The double for-loop can sometimes reach voxels that are outside the projection tube; these voxels are rejected based on their distance to the line.
5. Because lines can intersect, atomic add operations must be used to update voxels during back projection to avoid write data races between threads. Currently, these operations are performed in integer mode, but with the recently-released Fermi architecture, atomic operations can now be applied to floating-point values.
6. The list of lines is stored in global memory. Data transfers are optimized because the line geometry is accessed in a sequential, and therefore coalesced, manner.

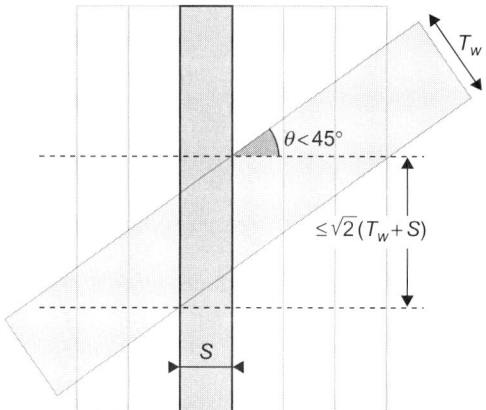

FIGURE 42.5

Intersection of a projection tube (in gray) with a slice. Because the obliquity of the line is less than 45 degrees, the volume of intersection is bounded, and a fixed number of iterations suffice to enumerate all the voxels that participate in the projection for the current slice.

42.3 IMPLEMENTATION

42.3.1 Overview

As discussed previously, projecting a list of randomly ordered lines on the GPU raises many challenges. To our knowledge, the only implementation of list-mode reconstruction on the GPU was done by our group using OpenGL/CG [15].

However, using OpenGL for GPGPU has several drawbacks: The code is difficult to develop and maintain because the algorithm must be implemented as a graphics-rendering process; performance may be compromised by OpenGL's lack of access to all the capabilities of the GPU, for example, shared memory; and code portability is limited because the code uses hardware-specific OpenGL extensions. CUDA overcomes these challenges by making the massively parallel architecture of the GPU more accessible to the developer in a C-like programming paradigm.

Briefly, the CUDA execution model organizes individual threads into thread blocks. The members of a thread block can communicate through fast shared memory, whereas threads in different blocks run independently. Atomic operations and thread synchronization functions are further provided to coordinate the execution of the threads within a block. Because the runtime environment is responsible for scheduling the blocks on the streaming multiprocessors (SMs), CUDA code is scalable and will automatically exploit the increased number of SMs on future graphics cards.

The methods described in this chapter were developed as part of our GPU line-projection library (GLPL). The GLPL is a general-purpose, flexible library that performs line-projection calculations using CUDA. It has two main features: (1) Unlike previous GPU projection implementations, it does not require lines to be organized in a sinogram and (2) A large set of voxels can participate in the projection; these voxels are located within a tube a certain distance away from the line and can be weighted by a programmable projection kernel. Collaborating with Philips Healthcare, we are currently investigating using the GLPL with their newest PET system, the Gemini TF, with so-called time-of-flight capabilities that require list-mode processing [18]. The GLPL is flexible and can be used for image reconstruction for other imaging modalities, such as X-ray CT and single-photon emission computed tomography (SPECT).

The GLPL implements GPU data structures for storing lines and image volumes, and primitives for performing line-projection operations. Using the GLPL, the list-mode OSEM reconstruction algorithm (Figure 42.2) can be run entirely on the GPU. The implementation was tested on an NVIDIA GeForce 285 GTX with compute capability 1.3.

42.3.2 Data Structures

Image volumes are stored in global memory as 3-D arrays of 32-bit floats. For typical volume sizes, the image does not fit in the fast shared memory. For instance, the current reconstruction code for the Gemini TF uses matrices with $72 \times 72 \times 20$ coefficients for storing the images, thus occupying 405 kB in global memory. However, individual slices can be stored in shared memory, which acts as a managed cache for the global memory (Figure 42.4).

By slicing the image volume in the dimension most orthogonal to the line orientation, the number of voxels included in the intersection of the projection tube with the current slice is kept bounded (Figure 42.5). To exploit this property, the lines are divided into three classes, according to their predominant orientation which is determined by calculating an inner product. Each of the three classes is processed sequentially by different CUDA kernels. Because PET detectors are typically arranged in a cylindrical geometry, with axial height short compared with diameter, the z class is empty and only slices parallel to the $x - z$ or $y - z$ planes are considered. For the image volume specifications used in this work, these slices are 5.6 kB and easily fit in 16 kB of shared memory.

The list of lines is stored in the GPU global memory, where each line is represented as a pair of indices using two 16-bit unsigned integers. A conversion function maps the indices to physical detector coordinates. The Philips Gemini TF PET system has, for instance, 28,336 individual detectors, organized in 28 modules, with each module consisting of a 23×44 array of $4 \times 4 \times 22 \, \text{mm}^3$ crystals [15]. A 5 minutes. PET dataset can contain hundreds of millions of lines and occupy hundreds of megabytes in global memory.

Lines are processed sequentially and, therefore, the geometry data are coherently accessed by the threads. To perform a projection, each thread first reads the two detector indices that define the line end points from global memory. The memory access is coalesced; hence, on a device of compute capability 1.3, two 128-bit memory transactions are sufficient for a half-warp (i.e., eight threads running concurrently on the same SM). The indices are then converted into geometrical coordinates by arithmetic calculations.

42.3.3 Forward Projection

The line-forward projection, mathematically a sparse matrix-vector multiplication, is a gather operation. The voxel values contained in a tube centered on the line are read, weighed by a projection kernel, and accumulated. A basic CPU implementation would employ three levels of nested loops with variable bounds.

However, such an approach is not efficient in CUDA because the computational load would be unevenly distributed. Instead, the outer level of the nested loops is performed in parallel by assigning one thread per line and per slice. Because the lines have been partitioned according to their orientation, the angle between the slice normal and the line is less than 45 degrees (Figure 42.5), and all the voxels in the tube (of width T_W) can be reached when the number of iterations in each of the two inner for-loops is set to $\sqrt{2}(T_W + S)$. Hence, the computation load is homogeneously distributed onto the many cores. Having all the threads run the same number of iterations is a critical feature of our implementation. If threads ran a different number of iterations, their execution would diverge. Furthermore, having constant bounds allows the 2-D for-loop to be unrolled, providing additional acceleration.

Source code for the forward-projection kernel is given in Figure 42.6. First, the threads collaboratively load the image slice into shared memory. After each thread reads out the coordinates of the line, the 2-D for-loop is performed. Within the loop, voxel values are read from shared memory. These values are weighted by a projection kernel, computed locally, and accumulated within a local register. In our implementation, we used a Gaussian function, parameterized by the distance between the voxel center and the line, as a projection kernel. The Gaussian kernel is computed using fast GPU-intrinsic functions. The final cumulative value is accumulated in global memory.

42.3.4 Back Projection

Back projection, mathematically the transpose operation of forward projection, smears the lines uniformly across the volume image (Figure 42.3). Back projection is therefore, in computation terms, a scatter operation. Such scatter operations can be implemented explicitly in the CUDA programming model because write operations can be performed at arbitrary locations.

The CUDA implementation of line back projection is modeled after the forward projection. There are, however, two basic differences. First, the current slice is cleared beforehand and written back to the global memory thereafter. Second, the threads update voxels in the slice instead of reading voxel data. Because multiple threads might attempt to update simultaneously the same voxel, atomic add operations are used.

42.4 EVALUATION AND VALIDATION OF RESULTS, TOTAL BENEFITS, AND LIMITATIONS

42.4.1 Processing Time

The GLPL was benchmarked for speed and accuracy against a CPU-based reference implementation. The processing time was measured for the back projection and forward projection of one million spatially random lines, using an image volume of size $72 \times 72 \times 20$ voxels and included the transfer of line and image data from the CPU to the GPU. The CPU implementation was based on the ray-tracing function currently employed in the Gemini TF reconstruction software. The hardware used in this comparison was a GeForce 285GTX for the GPU and an Intel Core2 E6600 for the CPU. The GPU and CPU implementations processed one million lines in 0.46 s and 20 s, respectively. The number of thread blocks was varied and the total processing time split into GPU-CPU communication, GPU processing, and CPU processing (Figure 42.7).

In the current implementation of the GLPL, most of the processing time is spent on GPU computation (Figure 42.7). Furthermore, data is transferred only once from the CPU to the GPU and used multiple times by the GPU over multiple iterations. Likewise, some of the preprocessing tasks are performed by the CPU only once for the entire reconstruction.

```
__global__ void ForwardprojectHorizontal(float *image, float *lines, int linesN){
        // current slice
        __shared__ float slice[Ny * Nz];
        int slsz = Ny * Nz;
        float max_dist = TOR_WIDTH * TOR_WIDTH / 2.0f;

        for (int current_slice = 0; current_slice < Nx; ++current_slice){
                // Load slice into shared memory
                int offset = current_slice * slsz;
                for (int vi = threadIdx.x; vi < slice_size; vi += blockDim.x){
                        slice[vi] = image[vi + offset];
                }
                __syncthreads();

                for (int line = threadIdx.x + blockIdx.x * blockDim.x; line < linesN; line += blockDim.x * gridDim.x) {

                        // line structure
                        CUDALor *the_line = (CUDALor*)lines + line;

                        // line direction
                        float   l1 = the_line->dy,
                                        l2 = the_line->dz;

                        float   t = (current_slice - the_line->x0) / the_line->dx;
                        float   y = the_line->y0 + t * l1,
                                        z = the_line->z0 + t * l2;
                        int             centerY = floor(y), centerZ = floor(z);
                        float   sum = 0;

                        for (int yy = centerY - TOR_WIDTH; yy <= centerY + TOR_WIDTH; ++yy)
                        for (int zz = centerZ - TOR_WIDTH; zz <= centerZ + TOR_WIDTH; ++zz) {
                                if ( yy >= 0 && yy < Ny && zz >= 0 && zz < Nz) {
                                        float   dy = yy - y,
                                                        dz = zz - z;
                                        float   inner = dy * l1 + dz * l2;

                                        // Distance to the line, squared
                                        float d2 = dy * dy + dz * dz - inner * inner;

                                        float kern = (d2 < max_dist) ? exp(-d2 * ISIGMA) : 0;

                                        sum += slice[yy + Ny * zz] * kern;
                                }
                        }

                        // Write the value back to global memory
                        the_line->value += sum;
                }
                __syncthreads();
        }
}
```

FIGURE 42.6

A CUDA kernel used to perform forward projection of horizontal lines.

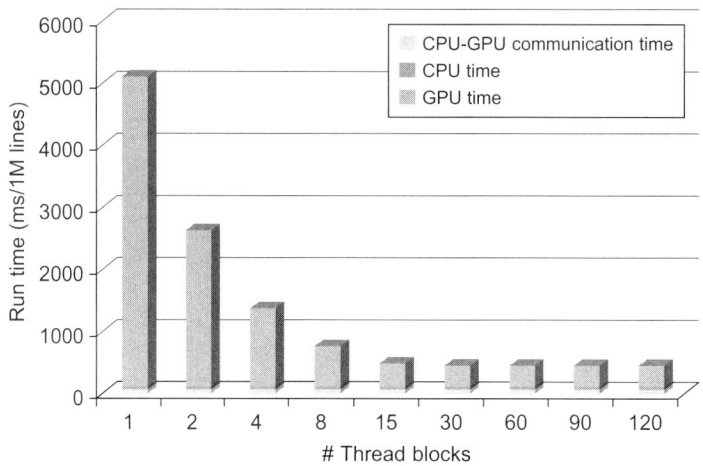

FIGURE 42.7

Runtime for processing 1 million lines with CUDA as a function of the number of thread blocks.

As expected, only the GPU computation time depends upon the number of thread blocks. The total throughput (expressed in number of lines processed per second) improves with increasing number of blocks, until reaching a plateau at 30 blocks (Figure 42.8). This result is expected because the GeForce 285 GTX can distribute thread blocks onto 30 SMs. When fewer than 30 blocks are scheduled, the overall compute performance is decreased because some of the SMs are idle. At the peak, the GLPL is able to process 2 million lines per second.

In order to gain more insight, we modeled the processing time T_{proc} as the sum of three components:

$$T_{proc} = S/N + C + kN$$

where S is the scalable computation load, N the number of SM used, C the constant overhead (including CPU processing and CPU-GPU communication), and k the computation overhead per SM used. We found that for one million lines, the scalable computation load was $S = 5027$ ms, the constant overhead $C = 87$ ms, and the overhead per SM $k = 6$ ms. The goodness of the fit was $r^2 = 0.9998$. Hence, 95% of all computation is scalable and runs in parallel.

42.4.2 Line-Projection Accuracy

The accuracy of the GLPL was compared with a standard CPU implementation of line-projection operations by running list-mode OSEM on both platforms. Because the development of data conversion tools for the Philips Gemini TF is still under way, we measured the accuracy of the line projections on a dataset acquired with another system installed at Stanford, the GE eXplore Vista DR, a high-resolution PET scanner for small animal preclinical research.

A cylindrical "hot rod" phantom, comprising rods of different diameters (1.2, 1.6, 2.4, 3.2, 4.0, and 4.8 mm) was filled with 110 μCi of a radioactive solution of Na^{18}F and 28.8 million lines were acquired. Volumetric images, of size $103 \times 103 \times 36$ voxels, were reconstructed using the list-mode 3-D OSEM

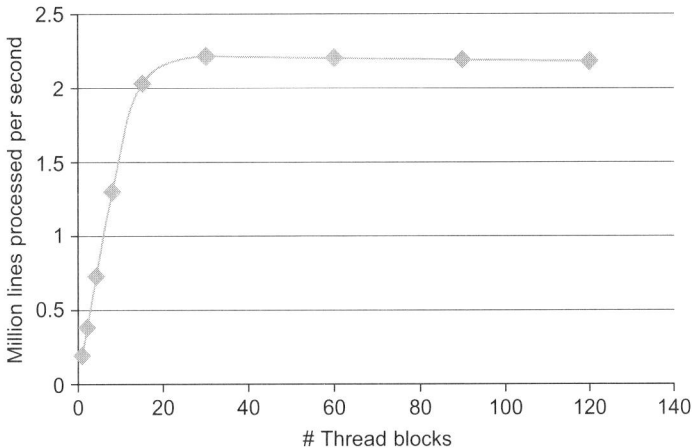

FIGURE 42.8

Performance of the GPU implementation, measured in million lines per second, as a function of the number of thread blocks.

algorithm. For simplicity, the usual data corrections (for photon scatter, random coincidences, photon attenuation, and detector efficiency normalization) were not applied. For this image configuration, each subiteration (forward projection, back projection, and multiplicative update) took 746 ms per million LORs, including 489 ms for calculation on the GPU, 210 ms for preprocessing on the CPU, and 46 ms for communication between the CPU and the GPU. The entire reconstruction took 1.3 minutes on the GPU and about 4.3 hours on the CPU. Note that for the accuracy validation, the reference CPU reconstruction was performed with nonoptimized research code because the fast ray-tracing functions used in the Gemini TF system (and used for measuring processing time) could not be easily ported to the eXplore Vista system.

Transaxial image slices, reconstructed using the CPU and the GPU, are visually identical (Figure 42.9). The RMS deviation between both images is 0.08% after five iterations, which is negligible compared with the statistical variance of the voxel values in a typical PET scan (>10%, from Poisson statistics). Higher image quality can be achieved by decreasing the number of subsets and increasing the number of iterations (Figure 42.9c). Such reconstruction is only practical on the GPU because of the increased computational cost.

We believe that the small deviation that we measured was caused by small variations in how the arithmetic operations are performed on the CPU and GPU. For example, we have observed that the exponential function produces slightly different results on each platform. These differences are amplified by the ill-posed nature of the inverse problem solved by the iterative image reconstruction algorithm.

As an example of a real application, a mouse was injected with $Na^{18}F$, a PET tracer, and imaged on the eXplore Vista (Figure 42.10). Image reconstruction was performed with 16 iterations and five subsets of list-mode OSEM using the GLPL.

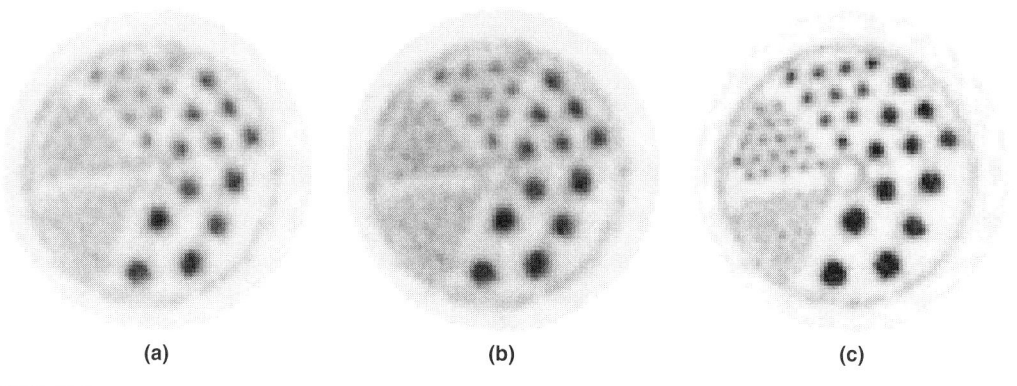

(a)   (b)   (c)

FIGURE 42.9

Hot rods phantom, acquired on a preclinical PET scanner with two iterations and 40 subsets of list-mode OSEM, using CPU-based projections (a) and the GLPL (b). A better image can be obtained using five subsets and 20 iterations on the GPU (c).

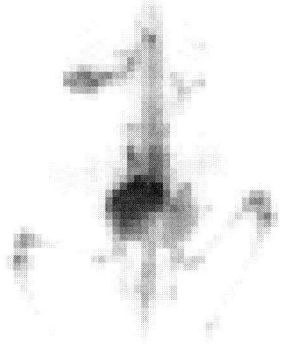

FIGURE 42.10

Mouse PET scan (maximum intensity projection), reconstructed with 16 iterations and five subsets of list-mode OSEM using the GLPL.

42.5 FUTURE DIRECTIONS

A current limitation of our implementation is the size of the GPU shared memory. In particular, in high-resolution PET, images are stored with finer sampling, and slices might not be fit in shared memory (16 kB). As the amount of shared memory increases with the release of new GPUs, the GLPL will be able to process larger images and/or process multiple contiguous image slices simultaneously. With the recent release of the Fermi architecture, which offers 48 kB of shared memory, slices taken from image volumes as large as $175 \times 175 \times 60$ voxels can be loaded into shared memory. Alternatively, the image volume can be processed directly in global memory, or the image slices can be subdivided into smaller blocks that fit within shared memory. Both approaches, however, would diminish compute efficiency.

The number of line events generated in a typical PET scan — approximately 20 million per minute — raises tremendous challenges for distributing, storing, and processing such a large amount of data. Hence, we are designing a parallel architecture that distributes the stream of line events onto a cluster of GPU nodes for reconstruction.

References

[1]   G.T. Herman, Fundamentals of Computerized Tomography: Image Reconstruction from Projections, second ed., Springer, London, UK, 2009.

[2]   B. Cabral, N. Cam, J. Foran, Accelerated volume rendering and tomographic reconstruction using texture mapping hardware, in: A. Kaufman, W. Krueger (Eds.), Proceedings of the 1994 Symposium on Volume Visualization, 17−18 October 1994, Washington, DC, ACM, New York, 1994.

[3]   F. Xu, K. Mueller, Accelerating popular tomographic reconstruction algorithms on commodity PC graphics hardware, IEEE Trans. Nucl. Sci. 52 (2005) 654.

[4]   J. Kole, F. Beekman, Evaluation of accelerated iterative X-ray CT image reconstruction using floating point graphics hardware, Phys. Med. Biol. 51 (2006) 875.

[5]   F. Xu, K. Mueller, Real-time 3D computed tomographic reconstruction using commodity graphics hardware, Phys. Med. Biol. 52 (2007) 3405.

[6]   P. Despres, M. Sun, B.H. Hasegawa, S. Prevrhal, FFT and cone-beam CT reconstruction on graphics hardware, in: J. Hsieh, M.J. Flynn (Eds.), Proceedings of the SPIE, 16 March 2007, San Diego, CA, SPIE, Bellingham, WA, 2007, p. 6510.

[7]   J.M. Ollinger, J.A. Fessler, Positron-emission tomography, IEEE Signal Process. 14 (1) (1997) 43.

[8]   S. Gambhir, Molecular imaging of cancer with positron emission tomography, Nat. Rev. Cancer 2 (2002) 683–693.

[9]   L. Parra, H.H. Barrett, List-mode likelihood: EM algorithm and image quality estimation demonstrated on 2-D PET, IEEE Trans. Med. Image 17 (1998) 228.

[10] A.J. Reader, S. Ally, F. Bakatselos, R. Manavaki, R.J. Walledge, A.P. Jeavons, P.J. Julyan, S. Zhao, D.L. Hastings, J. Zweit, One-pass list-mode EM algorithm for high-resolution 3-D PET image reconstruction into large arrays, IEEE Trans. Nucl. Sci. 49 (2002) 693.

[11] R.H. Huesman, List-mode maximum-likelihood reconstruction applied to positron emission mammography (PEM) with irregular sampling, IEEE Trans. Med. Image 19 (2000) 532.

[12] A. Rahmim, J.C. Cheng, S. Blinder, M.L. Camborde, V. Sossi, Statistical dynamic image reconstruction in state-of-the-art high-resolution PET, Phys. Med. Biol. 50 (2005) 4887.

[13] H. Hudson, R. Larkin, Accelerated image reconstruction using ordered subsets of projection data, IEEE Trans. Med. Image 13 (1994) 601.

[14] L.A. Shepp, Y. Vardi, Maximum-likelihood reconstruction for emission tomography, IEEE Trans. Med. Image 2 (1982) 113.

[15] G. Pratx, G. Chinn, P.D. Olcott, C.S. Levin, Fast, accurate and shift-varying line projections for iterative reconstruction using the GPU, IEEE Trans. Med. Image 28 (3) (2009) 435.

[16] A. Alessio, P. Kinahan, T. Lewellen, Modeling and incorporation of system response functions in 3-D whole body PET, IEEE Trans. Med. Image 25 (2006) 828.

[17] V.Y. Panin, F. Kehren, C. Michel, M.E. Casey, Fully 3D PET reconstruction with system matrix derived from point source measurements, IEEE Trans. Med. Image 25 (7) (2006) 907.

[18] S. Surti, S. Karp, L. Popescu, E. Daube-Witherspoon, M. Werner, Investigation of time-of-flight benefits for fully 3-D PET, IEEE Trans. Med. Image 25 (2006) 529.

Using GPUs to Learn Effective Parameter Settings for GPU-Accelerated Iterative CT Reconstruction Algorithms

43

Wei Xu, Klaus Mueller

43.1 INTRODUCTION, PROBLEM STATEMENT, AND CONTEXT

In computed tomography (CT), the filtered backprojection (FBP) algorithm is most widely used for the reconstruction of an object from its X-ray projections. It considers each projection only once and is therefore fast to compute. FBP requires a great number of projection images to be acquired, and within a highly constrained scanning orbit. Recently, more awareness has been placed on reducing the patient X-ray dose. This limits the number of projection images per scan, among other factors. Here, FBP methods are less applicable and iterative reconstruction methods produce significantly better results (Figure 43.1). However, iterative methods are computationally expensive, but they are now becoming feasible owing to the vast computational performance of GPUs.

Iterative methods typically offer a diverse set of parameters that allow control over quality and computation speed, often requiring trade-offs. The interactions among these parameters can be complex, and thus effective combinations can be difficult to identify for a given data scenario. As a result their choice is often left to educated guesses, which in most cases leads to suboptimal speed and quality performance. In addition, we have also found that the specific parallel architecture of GPUs further influences this parameter optimization, modifying some of this conventional wisdom.

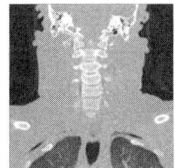

(a) FBP 0°–360°   (b) FBP ±60°   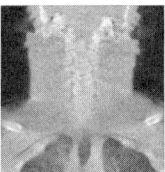 (c) Iterative ±60°   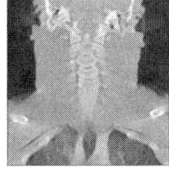 (d) Regularized
iterative ±60°

FIGURE 43.1

Reconstructions of the visible human neck area, coronal cuts. (a) FBP − 360 projections, 0°–360°, (b) FBP − 60 projections, ±60°, (c) iterative − 60 projections, ±60°, (d) regularized iterative − 60 projections, +60°

Determining the optimal parameter settings, similar to iterative CT reconstruction, is a high-dimensional search problem, and we seek to make this search computationally feasible with GPUs taking part in this process. We further aim to learn these optimal parameter settings in the context of specific imaging tasks and then port these settings to other similar imaging scenarios to achieve equally optimal results.

43.2 CORE METHOD(S)

As an interesting observation in the context of parallel computation, we have found [11] that iterative reconstruction methods used in medical imaging, such as EM (expectation maximization) or algebraic methods, such as SIRT (simultaneous iterative reconstruction method), have special properties when it comes to their acceleration on GPUs. This is particularly well expressed when the data is divided in subsets, with each forming an atomic iterative step in a so-called *ordered subsets* algorithm. Although splitting the data used within each iterative update into a larger number of smaller subsets has long been known to offer greater convergence and computation speed on the CPU, it can be vastly slower on the GPU. This is a direct consequence of the thread fill rate in the projection and backprojection phase. Larger subsets spawn a greater number of threads, which keeps the pipelines busier and also reduces the latencies incurred by a greater number of passes and context switches. This is different from the behavior on CPUs where this decomposition is less relevant in terms of computation overhead per iteration. So we seek to optimize the number of subsets for best speed of computation.

On the other hand, from a quality perspective the best subset size is one that most optimally balances the noise compensation offered by larger subsets (many projections in one subset) and the smaller number of iterations required for convergence offered by smaller subsets (many corrective updates within one iteration). Having noticed that on GPUs the speed of convergence is not necessarily related to actual wall clock time, our focus was to provide a mechanism by which one can balance GPU *runtime performance* (which is convergence as measured in wall-clock time) with noise cancelation (for better reconstruction quality).

A second parameter that can be used to mitigate noise effects in the data is to co-optimize the relaxation factor for the iterative updates (see the discussion later in this chapter). It can be used to restore the theoretical convergence advantage of data decompositions into smaller ordered subsets. Finally, using only a small number of projections in the backprojection causes streak artifacts, whereas noisy projections acquired in low-dose acquisition modes lead to a significant amount of noise in the reconstructions. Both can be reduced by ways of regularization between iterative updates. Regularization entails an edge-preserving smoothing operation, which also has parameters that trade quality and speed.

We describe a framework that not only targets GPU-acceleration of iterative reconstruction algorithms but also exploits GPUs to optimize their parameters for a given quality/speed performance objective. In essence we use GPUs to help us reason about GPUs within a machine-learning framework. Our optimization procedure exploits fast GPU-based computation to generate computation products that it then automatically evaluates using a perceptually based fitness function, implementing a simulated human observer, together with the recorded execution time, to steer the optimization.

We offer two different approaches. In the first, we compute a large number of CT reconstructions for all possible parameter combinations and then search this population to recommend parameter settings under two different labeling criteria: (1) "best quality, given a certain time limit" or (2) "best reconstruction speed, given a certain quality threshold." A weighting scheme is applied to combine the candidate parameters: either a fast-decaying Gaussian function or the max function. In the second approach, we treat the problem as a multi-objective optimization problem, optimizing the settings for desired speed/quality trade-off (or compromise). Genetic algorithms are well suited for this class of problems. Instead of computing all parameter combinations beforehand, we randomly generate a subset as the initial population and then guide the creation of new generations with selection, recombination, and mutation operators on the parameter settings, improving the fitness values until the nondominated optimal solutions set has been determined. With this approach, the suggested parameters are no longer one specific value, but a group of mutually nondominated values comprising objectives. Both approaches require a massive number of reconstructions to be computed, which is only economically feasible with GPU support. Finally, besides the two approaches, an interactive parameter selection interface is introduced to assist evaluation of the behavior of different parameter settings.

43.3 ALGORITHMS, IMPLEMENTATIONS, AND EVALUATIONS

43.3.1 GPU-Accelerated Iterative Ordered-Subset Algorithms

Iterative CT reconstruction methods can broadly be categorized into projection onto convex sets (POCS) algorithms and statistical algorithms. The method we devised, OS-SIRT [7], is a generalization of the simultaneous algebraic reconstruction technique (SART) [2] and the simultaneous iterative reconstruction technique (SIRT) [4], two traditional iterative algorithms belonging to the first category. It groups the projections into a number of equal-size subsets and for each subset, iteratively applies the three-phase computation — forward projection, corrective update computation, and backprojection until convergence. We describe this algorithm next.

Most iterative CT techniques use a projection operator to model the underlying image-generation process at a certain viewing configuration (angle) φ. The result of this projection simulation is then compared with the acquired image obtained at the same viewing configuration. If scattering or diffraction effects are ignored, the modeling consists of tracing a straight ray r_i from each image element (pixel) and summing the contributions of the (reconstruction) volume elements (voxels) v_j. Here, the weight factor w_{ij} determines the contribution of a v_j to r_i and is given by the interpolation kernel used for sampling the volume. The projection operator is given as

$$r_i = \sum_{j=1}^{N} v_j \cdot w_{ij} \quad i = 1, 2, \ldots, M \tag{43.1}$$

where M and N are the number of rays (one per pixel) and voxels, respectively. Because GPUs are heavily optimized for computing and less for memory bandwidth, computing the w_{ij} on the fly, via bilinear interpolation (possibly using the GPU fixed-function pipelines), is by far more efficient than storing the weights in memory. The correction update is computed with the following equation:

$$v_j^{(k+1)} = v_j^{(k)} + \lambda \frac{\sum_{p_i \in OS_s} \frac{p_i - r_i}{\sum_{l=1}^{N} w_{il}} w_{ij}}{\sum_{i=1}^{N} w_{ij}} \quad r_t = \sum_{l=1}^{N} w_{il} \cdot v_l^{(k)} \tag{43.2}$$

Here, the p_i are the pixels in the M/S acquired images that form a specific (ordered) subset OS_s where $1 \leq s \leq S$ and S is the number of subsets. The factor λ is the relaxation factor that scales the corrective update to each voxel (reducing oscillations). The factor k is the iteration count, where k is incremented each time all M projections have been processed. In essence, all voxels v_j on the path of a ray r_i are updated (corrected) by the difference of the projection ray r_i and the acquired pixel p_i, where this correction factor is first normalized by the sum of weights encountered by the (backprojection) ray r_i. Because a number of backprojection rays will update a given v_j, these corrections need also to be normalized by the sum of (correction) weights. In practice, only the forward projection uses a ray-driven approach, where each ray is a parallel thread and interpolates the voxels on its path. Conversely, the backprojection uses a voxel-driven approach, where each voxel is a parallel thread and interpolates the correction image. Thus, the weights used in the projection and the backprojection are slightly different, but this turns out to be of less importance in practice.

The high performance of GPUs stems from its multicore structure, enabling parallel execution of a sufficiently large number of SIMD (single instruction, multiple data) computing threads. Each such thread must have a target that eventually receives the outcome of the thread's computation. In the forward projection the targets are the pixels on the projection images receiving the outcome of the ray integrations (Eq. 43.1). The corrective update computation is a simple weighted subtraction operation between computed and scanned projections that has the same targets as forward projections. In the backprojection the targets are the reconstructed volume voxels receiving the corrective updates (Eq. 43.2). At any phase, the computation of each target (pixel or voxel) is independent of the outcomes of other targets. This feature allows us to manage the three phases as three passes in the GPU and inside each pass the threads with corresponding targets can be executed in parallel. For details, the reader is referred to our papers [7–11].

43.3.2 GPU-Accelerated Regularization for OS-SIRT

A regularization step is needed when the reconstruction becomes severely ill posed, in cases when the data is sparse or the angular coverage is limited. This is often the case in low-dose CT applications. The regularization operator is added as the fourth phase to "clean up" the intermediate reconstruction between iterations. Here, the targets are the volume voxels and the computation can also be accelerated on the GPU. We have used the bilateral filter (BF) to remove noise and streaking artifacts that emerge in these situations, while at the same time keeping sharp edges as the salient features. The bilateral filter uses a combination of two Gaussians as a weighting function to average the values inside a target voxel neighborhood. One of the Gaussian functions operates as a domain filter to measure the spatial difference, while the other operates as a range filter to measure the pixel value difference. Because the BF-filter is noniterative, it is by nature much faster than the (iterative) TVM algorithm and, as shown earlier in this chapter, offers the same or even better regularization results, except in extremely noisy situations.

43.3.3 Approach 1: Learning Effective Reconstruction Parameters Using Exhaustive Sampling

With the projection data, we compute a representative set of reconstructions, sampling the parameter space in a comprehensive manner. The parameters include number of subsets S, the relaxation factor λ, and number of iterations. If the regularization operator is applied, then three more parameters are added: two Gaussian standard deviations and a neighborhood size. We then evaluate these reconstructions with a perceptual quality metric as discussed later in this chapter to obtain a fitness (quality) score for each reconstruction. Adaptive sampling can be used to drive the data collection into more "interesting" parameter regions (those that produce more diverse reconstruction results in terms of the quality metrics). Therefore, each reconstruction has both a quality score and a computation time. Having acquired these observations, we label them according to certain criteria, such as "quality, given a certain wall-clock time limit," or "reconstruction speed, given a certain quality threshold." The observations with the higher marks, according to some grouping, subsequently receive higher weights in determining the reconstruction algorithm parameters. Currently, we either use the max function or a fast-decaying Gaussian function to produce this weighting.

43.3.4 Approach 2: Learning Effective Reconstruction Parameters Using Multi-Objective Optimization

For OS-SIRT, the best quality and minimum time are the two objectives that are conflicting in nature with one another. Essentially, there is no single solution to satisfy every objective. Finding the optimal solutions is to make good compromises or trade-offs of the objectives. Therefore, this parameter-learning problem is actually a multi-objective optimization (MOO) [3, 5]. Generally speaking, there are two classes of approaches to this problem: combining objective functions to a single composite function or determining a nondominated optimal solution set (a so-called Pareto optimal set). The kernel of Approach 1 described previously belongs to the former class of multi-objective optimization problems. The two objectives are weighted together to form a single objective function by selecting different labeling criteria. However, when the user does not have a specific quality or time demand, but is curious about the level of potential progress toward each objective when the reconstruction continues, a nondominated Pareto optimal set is more helpful and reasonable.

To solve the MOO problems, genetic algorithms (GA) are well suited. Genetic algorithms inspired by the evolutionary theory about the origin of species have been developed for decades. They mimic the species evolutionary process in nature that strong species have higher opportunity to pass down their genes to the next generations, and at the same time, random changes may occur to bring additional advantages. By natural selection, the weak genes will be eliminated eventually. GA operates in a similar way by evolving from a population with individuals representing initial solutions with operators such as selection, crossover, and mutation to create descending generations. The fitness function is used to evaluate an individual that determines its probability of survival for the next generation. For MOO several fitness functions are used. Numerous GA methods have been described, such as weighted-based genetic algorithm (WBGA), vector evaluated genetic algorithm (VEGA), multi-objective genetic algorithm (MOGA), and nondominated sorting genetic algorithm (NSGA) [3]. Approach 1 is a customized application of the combination of fitness functions of WBGA to accommodate our special requirements. VEGA is limited owing to the "middling" problem, whereas MOGA is highly dependent on an appropriate selection of the sharing factor. NSGA progresses more slowly than MOGA and is shown to be computationally inefficient.

In our work, we have selected NSGA-II [1], which is the improved version of NSGA as the method to find the Pareto optimal set. This method uses elitism and a crowded comparison operator to keep both the inheritance from well-performing chromosomes and the diversity of the found optimal solutions, while keeping the computational efficiency. We execute the learning process in this way: after generating the initial population, the reconstruction algorithm OS-SIRT and the parameter searching algorithm NSGA-II are run alternatively until the stopping criterion has been satisfied (for instance, after a sufficient number of generations). This scheme falls into the category of a master-slave model of parallel genetic algorithms [6]. Within each generation, OS-SIRT is executed as a parallel fitness values evaluator, while NSGA-II combines these values to find the current solution set with a user-defined set size. Time is recorded as one objective and reconstruction quality is evaluated by a perceptual metric E-CC introduced later in this chapter. To cast the optimization into a minimization problem, we modify the quality metric to its distance to unity. The process stops until the solutions in the current set are nondominated to each other. For the selection, crossover, and mutation operators, we use binary tournament selection, real coded blend crossover, and a nonuniform mutation. Although the parameters we found may not be substantially better for a specific user demand, they provide a pool of candidates that are trade-offs of time and quality. More important, they are obtained considerably faster because fewer reconstructions need to be computed. With Approach 1 we need to perform every combination of the representative parameters, whereas with Approach 2, the computational complexity is the number of generations multiplying twice the size (user defined) of Pareto optimal solutions, which is usually much smaller.

43.3.5 Perceptual Metric as Automated Reconstruction Quality Evaluator

As mentioned before, a reliable quality metric is needed to evaluate the reconstruction results. Most popular for the assessment of image quality in CT have been statistical metrics such as mean absolute error (MAE), root mean square (RMS), normalized RMS (NRMS), cross-correlation coefficient (CC), and R-factor. However, these metrics do not consider the fact that human vision is highly sensitive to structural information. These properties are well captured in the gradient domain, by ways of an edge-filtered image calculated via a Sobel Filter operator. We have labeled this group of metrics by prefix E-. Further, shifting effects caused by the CT reconstruction backprojection step can be alleviated by Gaussian-blurring the reconstruction image before edge filtering. We have labeled this group of metrics with prefix "BE-." Another method to gauge structural information is structural similarity (SSIM), which combines luminance, contrast, and structure [8].

We tested the evaluation of these methods with four images whose rankings are determined by a human observer (in the order NF 140, NF 180, SNR 10, SNR 5, with NF 140 being the best) shown in Figure 43.2. Only the edge-based metrics (E-MAE, E-NRMS, and E-CC), as well as SSIM, can reproduce this ranking. In this chapter, the E-CC metric standing for the CC of two edge images is used as the perceptual quality metric as automated human observer owing to its efficiency in computation.

43.3.6 An Interactive Parameter Selection Interface

Users often like to see what will happen when some parameters are slightly changed to express their personal trade-offs better. We devised an effective parameter space navigation interface [10] allowing users to interactively assist parameter selection for iterative CT reconstruction algorithms (here for OS-SIRT). It is based on a 2-D scatter plot with six display modes to show different features of the reconstruction results based on user preferences. It also enables a dynamic visualization by gradual parameter alteration for illustrating the rate of impact of a given parameter constellation.

For OS-SIRT, there are seven parameters to represent one reconstruction: SNR-level, relaxation factor λ, number of subsets S, number of iterations, time, CC, and RMS. With the given projections, we selected a representative set of integer subsets, λ (plus three simulated relaxation factor functions) and SNR-levels, respectively. For each combination of "< S, λ, SNR-level>" (called grid points), <time,

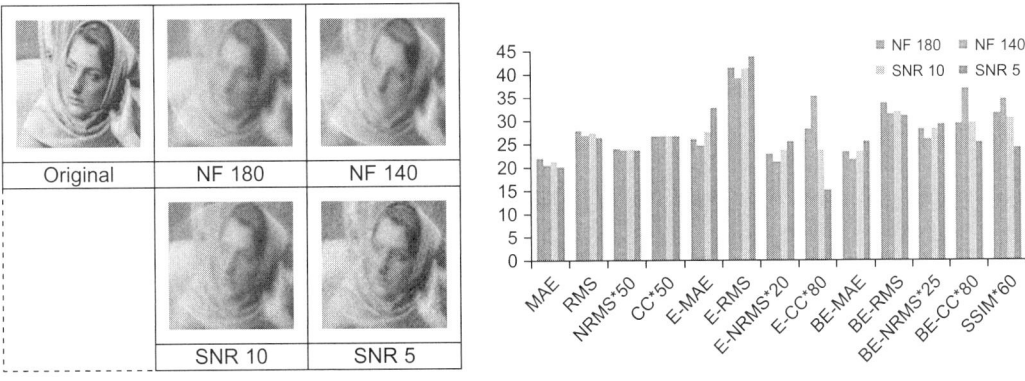

FIGURE 43.2

A metrics comparison.

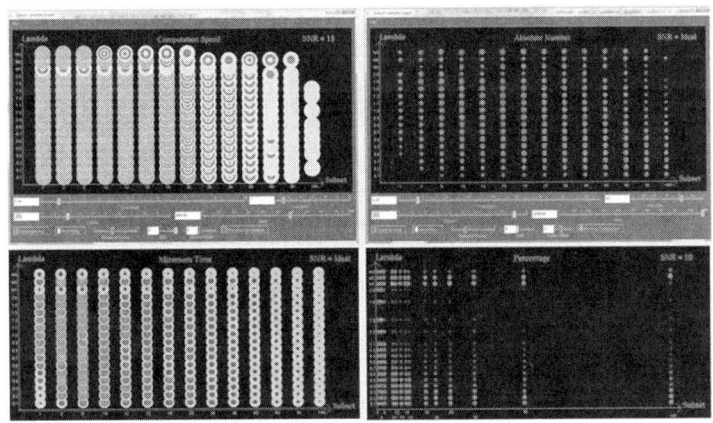

FIGURE 43.3

Parameter space navigator.

CC, RMS> (called tuples) were recorded every five iterations. With this pool of tuples, we use our parameter space visualizer to visualize the parameters with user control.

The interface of the parameter space visualizer is composed of a main window and a control panel (see the first row of Figure 43.3). The main window is a 2-D scatter plot of number of subsets (x coordinate) and relaxation factor (y coordinate) with different sizes and colors of circles to show the features of tuples. The size and color of the circle represent the number of tuples satisfying current parameter settings controlled by users in the control panel. In the control panel, users could change the values of the time, CC, and RMS bars to set boundary values to sift tuples and switch visualizations among different SNR-levels. There are six modes showing various features of the tuples: computation speed mode, percentage mode, absolute number mode, minimum time mode, maximum CC mode, and starting CC mode. The interface assists users to quickly find the preferred parameter settings and provide a dynamic view of parameter changes by moving the control bars.

43.4 FINAL EVALUATION AND VALIDATION OF RESULTS, TOTAL BENEFITS, AND LIMITATIONS

In this section, we tested the performance for every algorithm mentioned previously: the OS-SIRT reconstruction with regularization and the two parameter learning approaches. All computations used an NVIDIA GTX 280 GPU/Intel 2 Quad CPU 2.66 GHz. Cg/GLSL with OpenGL API is used for the coding of GPU acceleration parts.

43.4.1 Performance Gains of Our Iterative CT Reconstruction Algorithms

An application where very large volumes are frequently reconstructed from projections is electron microscopy. Here, the maximal dose (and therefore number of projection images) is limited by the amount of energy that the biological specimen can tolerate before decomposition. This application forms an excellent test bed for our high-performance iterative reconstruction framework.

We find that our GPU-accelerated iterative ordered-subset (OS) algorithm is able to decrease the running time from hours to minutes for the reconstruction large 3-D volumes. Tables 43.1 and 43.2

Table 43.1 Comparing 2-D reconstruction performance.

Number of Iterations	Slice Resolution	(Diez et al.) Quadro 4500	7800GTX	Speedup	GTX 280	Speedup
10	256 × 256	N/A	0.41s	N/A	0.13s	N/A
50	256 × 256	N/A	2.05s	N/A	0.66s	N/A
10	512 × 512	9s	1.23s	7.3	0.34s	26.0
50	512 × 512	39s	5.32s	7.3	1.75s	22.2
10	1024 × 1024	32s	4.30s	7.5	1.23s	25.8
50	1024 × 1024	146s	21.89s	6.7	6.44s	22.7
10	2048 × 2048	123s	17.39s	7.1	5.06s	24.3
50	2048 × 2048	567s	85.30s	6.7	26.94s	21.0

Table 43.2 Comparing 3-D reconstruction performance.

	SIRT		OS-SIRT 5		SART	
Volume Resolution	**1-ch**	**4-ch**	**1-ch**	**4-ch**	**1-ch**	**4-ch**
356 × 506 × 148	2.642	2.103	3.672	2.278	15.867	5.712
712 × 1012 × 296	12.822	10.665	14.625	11.053	47.993	19.341
1424 × 2024 × 591	75.708	58.471	82.055	62.135	192.337	87.042

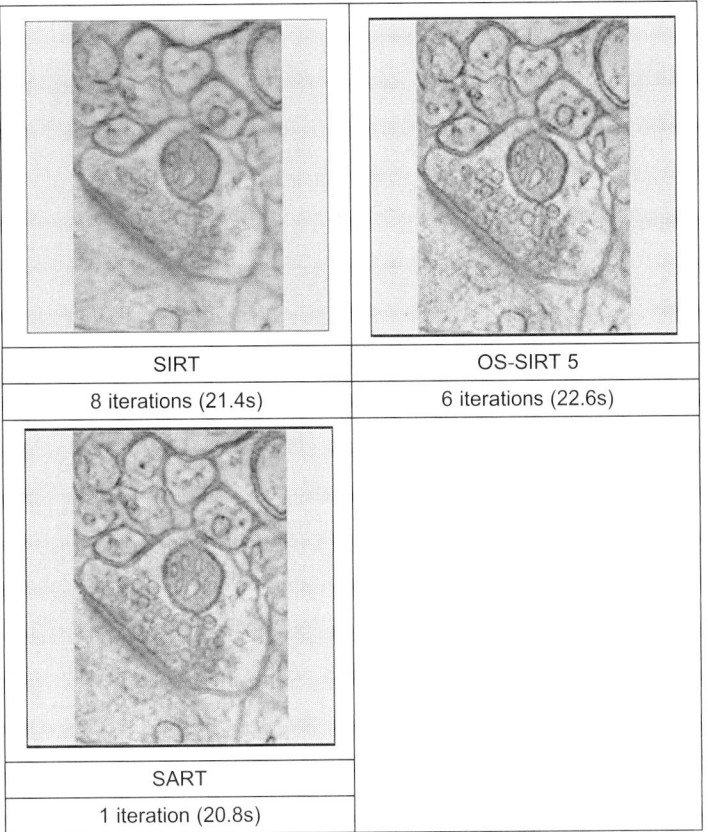

SIRT	OS-SIRT 5
8 iterations (21.4s)	6 iterations (22.6s)
SART	
1 iteration (20.8s)	

FIGURE 43.4

Comparing electron microscopy reconstructions (HPFcere2 dataset) obtained at similar wall-clock times, but different qualities (OS-SIRT 5 is best).

demonstrate the speedup for both 2-D (Table 43.1 comparing ours with timing reported by others) and 3-D (Table 43.2) [11]. The reconstruction results for SART (N subsets of size 1 projection), SIRT (1 subset with size N projections), and our ordered subsets SIRT (OS-SIRT) with the optimal number of subsets, 5 (OS-SIRT 5), as determined by our optimization procedure, are shown in Figure 43.4.

Figure 43.5 compares the three different algorithms (SIRT, OS-SIRT 5, and SART) quantitatively using the R-factor (the R-factor compares the absolute error of the actual projections with the simulated projections). Although the R-factor still improves beyond the images we have shown here, we found that these improvements are not well perceived visually, and so, we have not shown these images here. To visualize the aspect of computational performance in the context of a quantitative reconstruction quality measure (here, the R-factor), we have inserted into Figure 43.5 a metric that we call the "computation time iso-contour." Here, we used 22 s for this contour — the approximate time required for 1 SART, 6 OS-SIRT, and 8 SIRT iterations (see Figure 43.4), which yielded reconstructions of good

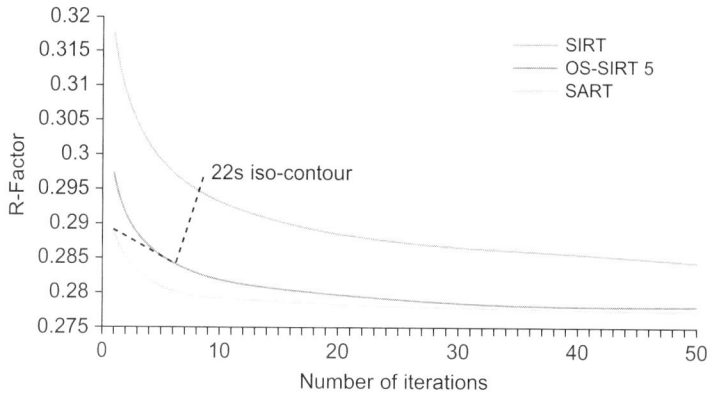

FIGURE 43.5

Comparing different subsets algorithms in terms of speed and quality. The 22s iso-contour shows that OS-SIRT achieves the best quality (R-factor).

Table 43.3 Comparing bilateral filtering performance.

Test Size	Window Size	CPU Time (s)	GPU (Cg) Time (s)	GPU (CUDA) Time (s)
256 × 256	11 × 11	0.622	0.007	0.005
	31 × 31	4.891	0.013	0.011
	61 × 61	18.626	0.037	0.033
	91 × 91	39.031	0.069	0.066
512 × 512	11 × 11	2.652	0.011	0.007
	31 × 31	19.998	0.038	0.032
	61 × 61	74.319	0.119	0.112
	91 × 91	164.065	0.253	0.241
1024 × 1024	11 × 11	10.811	0.033	0.017
	31 × 31	84.618	0.133	0.098
	61 × 61	> 300	0.452	0.368
	91 × 91	> 300	0.983	0.823
256 × 256 × 256	3 × 3 × 3	46.831	0.492	N/A
	7 × 7 × 7	592.969	1.535	N/A
	11 × 11 × 11	> 600	4.823	N/A

quality for OS-SIRT 5. We observe that OS-SIRT 5 offers a better time-quality performance than SART, and this is also true for other such time iso-contours (although not shown here) because the time per iteration for OS-SIRT is roughly 1/6 of that for SART. SIRT, on the other hand, converges at a much higher R-factor.

43.4.2 Performance Gains of Our Regularization Scheme

As mentioned, for few-view, limited-angle, and noisy projection scenarios, the application of regularization operators between reconstruction iterations seeks to tune the final or intermediate results to some a priori model. Total variation minimization (TVM) is a commonly used method for medical imaging regularization. It has the effect of flattening the density profile in local neighborhoods and thus is well suited for noise and streak artifact reduction. However, in the context of high-performance computing, owing to its iterative procedure, TVM is quite time-consuming, even when accelerated on GPUs. To speed up the computation we aim to devise a method that is not iterative, but has the same goals as TVM, that is, the reduction of local variations (noise, streaks) while preserving coherent local features. We found that a bilateral filtering (BF) scheme can behave just as good or better than TVM, but without the need for iterative application. In our scheme each kernel performs a convolution operation inside a neighborhood with two textures used as lookup tables of weights to combine the nearby and similar pixels. The performances of CPU and GPU are compared in Table 43.3. We observe that GPU acceleration leads to speedups of two orders of magnitude, reducing it to only 10% of an iterative update, making regularization a computationally affordable operation. The effects of filtering for both BF and TVM are shown in Figure 43.6 [9].

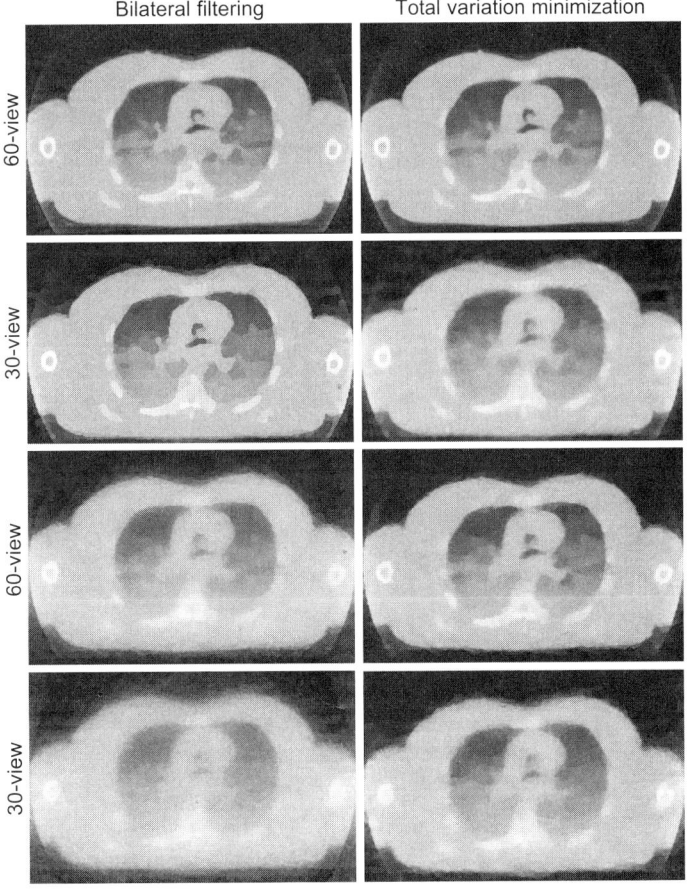

FIGURE 43.6

A slice of a CT few-view reconstructed torso with lung: (top two rows) noise free; (bottom two rows) SNR 10.

43.4.3 **Performance of Approach 1**

To test the effectiveness of the learned parameters using Approach 1, we first simulated, from the test image (here is baby head CT scan), 180 projections at uniform angular spacing of $[-90°, +90°]$ in a parallel projection viewing geometry. We then added different levels of Gaussian noise to the projection data to obtain SNRs (signal-noise ratio) of 15, 10, 5, and 1. The first column of Figure 43.7 presents the best reconstruction results (using the E-CC between the original and the reconstructed image) for each SNR in terms of the "reconstruction speed, given a certain quality threshold" criterion. In other words, the images shown are the reconstructions that could be obtained at the shortest wall-clock time given a certain minimal E-CC constraint. This constraint varies for each projection dataset (low SNR cannot reach high E-CC levels), and this is also part of the process model. Figure 43.8 summarizes the various parameters obtained for the various aforementioned data scenarios. The "Best Subset" and "Best λ" values denote the parameter settings that promise to give the best results, in terms of the given quality metric and label criterion. The "Lowest λ" and "Turning Point" values describe the shape of

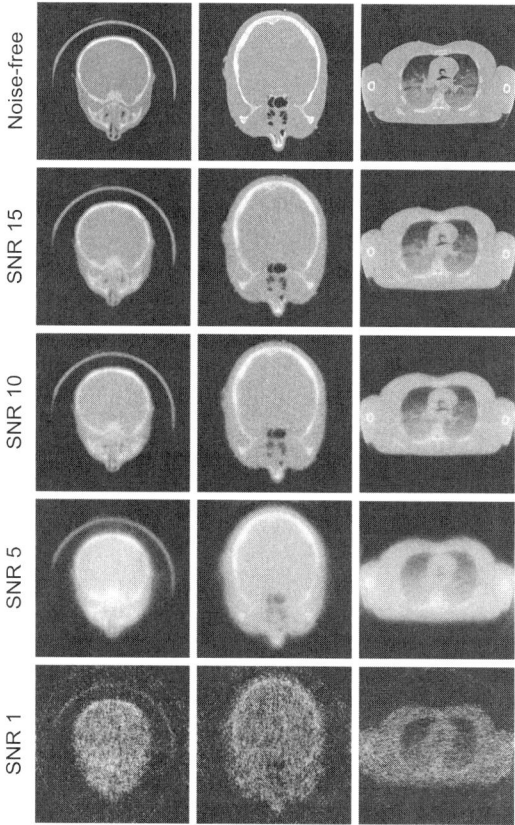

FIGURE 43.7

Applying learned parameter settings for different imaging scenarios.

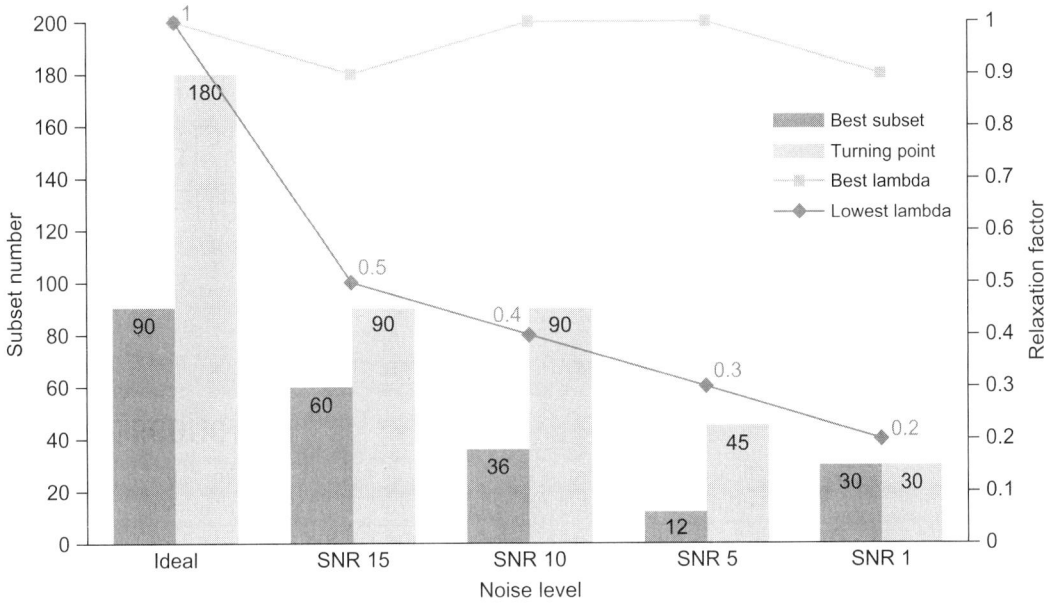

FIGURE 43.8

Optimal learned parameter settings for different SNR.

the λ-curve as a function of the number of subsets. The λ-factor is always close to 1 for small subsets and then linearly (as an approximation) falls off at the "Turning Point" to value "Lowest λ" when each subset only consists of one projection.

We then explored if the knowledge we learned translates to other similar data and reconstruction scenarios. Columns 2 and 3 of Figure 43.7 show the results obtained when applying the optimal settings learned from the baby head to reconstructions of the visible human head (size 256^2) and visible human lung (512^2), from similar projection data. We observe that the results are quite consistent with those obtained with the baby head, and this is promising. As future work, we plan to compare the settings with those learned directly from these two candidate datasets.

43.4.4 Performance of Approach 2

To test the performance of the second approach, the visible human head (size 256^2) with different noise levels (ideal, SNR 10, and SNR 5) is used. We set the size of any Pareto optimal set to 20 and obtained the corresponding sets for parameters (number of iterations, number of subsets, and relaxation factor λ) after adequate generations (here until any solution is nondominated by others in the same set). The results for different noise levels are shown in Figure 43.9. For each noise level, the gradual evolutions of the fitness values after a selected number of generations are plotted. We observed that when the generation develops, the fitness values are closer to the axes that means closer to its optimal value. The solutions pool is listed in Table 43.4. It demonstrates that when the noise level increases the reconstruction is more difficult, while at the same time, the needed numbers of iterations and subsets are getting smaller. This is confirmed by Approach 1 as well [8].

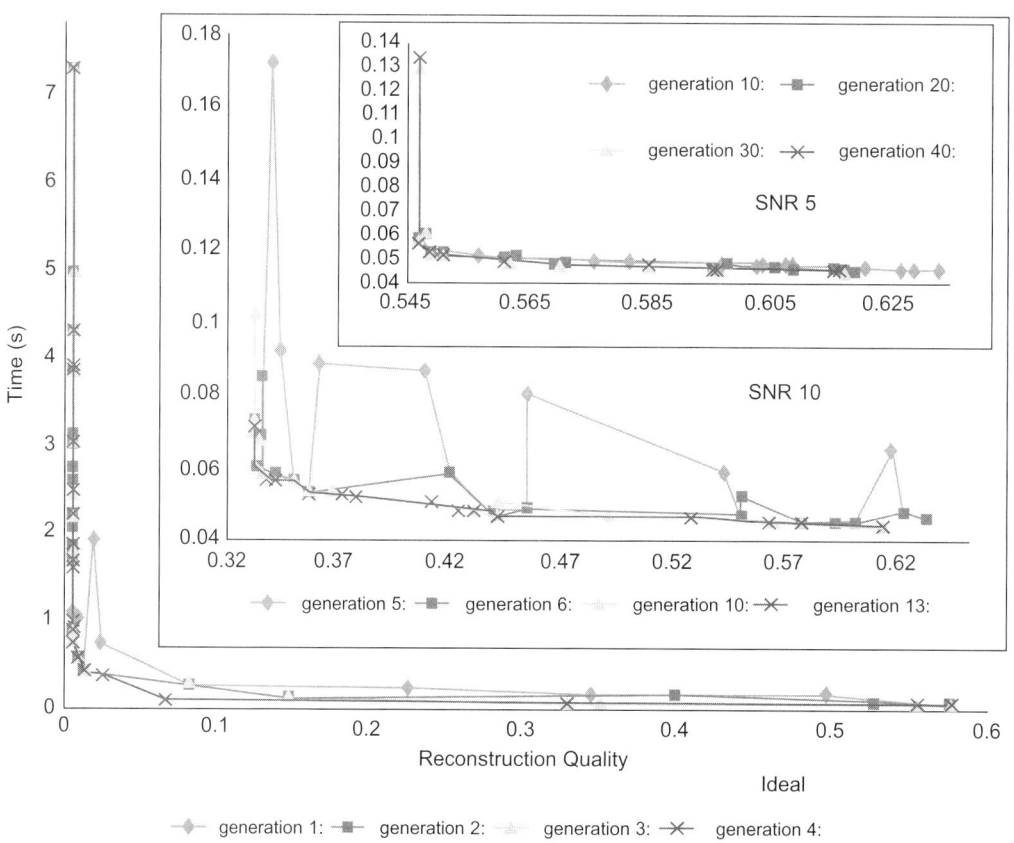

FIGURE 43.9

Fitness values of solutions set evolutions for different SNR.

The limitation of this approach is that the genetic algorithm itself includes a few parameters to control selection, crossover, and mutation operators. A more careful study exploring suitable settings, as well as the various choices of operators, would better tune the solutions.

43.5 FUTURE DIRECTIONS

In this chapter, we introduced a framework based on a GPU-accelerated iterative reconstruction platform with regularization to search the optimal parameter settings for the reconstruction process itself satisfying multiple performance objectives. In essence, we use GPUs to help us reason about GPUs within a machine-learning framework. As future work, the machine-learning procedure could further be accelerated in GPUs, and the regularization parameters could also be studied in the same way. We believe that our parameter-learning approach has many more general applications than shown here. Parameters are commonplace in many applications, and finding optimal settings for these can be a

Table 43.4 Pareto optimal set learned by Approach 2.

Index	Ideal			SNR 10			SNR 5		
	No. Iter	No. Subset	λ	No. Iter	No. Subset	λ	No. Iter	No. Subset	λ
1	55	180	0.84	2	30	0.755	2	90	0.162
2	76	90	0.997	2	30	0.82	2	90	0.167
3	68	90	0.92	2	20	0.982	2	15	0.884
4	56	90	0.87	2	20	0.892	2	15	0.909
5	53	90	0.87	2	18	0.938	2	12	0.961
6	43	90	0.952	2	15	0.991	2	15	0.975
7	48	60	0.787	2	15	0.862	2	12	0.99
8	50	45	0.902	2	12	0.978	2	12	0.966
9	47	45	0.974	2	10	0.966	2	10	0.995
10	38	60	0.811	2	10	0.896	2	10	0.993
11	16	90	0.965	2	9	0.732	2	10	0.883
12	19	60	0.923	2	6	0.998	2	6	0.998
13	20	45	0.969	2	6	0.943	2	6	0.995
14	19	30	0.964	2	6	0.894	2	6	0.998
15	8	60	0.83	2	6	0.877	2	5	0.984
16	17	15	0.997	2	3	0.913	2	4	0.923
17	2	60	0.875	2	2	0.973	2	3	0.998
18	3	10	0.459	2	2	0.764	2	3	0.993
19	2	30	0.033	2	2	0.739	2	2	0.999
20	2	4	0.175	2	2	0.288	2	2	0.972

laborious task. By using GPUs to test all possible parameter settings in parallel, optimal settings can be found fast and accurately. Because the result we optimize is ultimately meant for human consumption, an important component we have devised and integrated into our optimization framework is the simulated human observer. At the same time, we also use the interactive performance of GPUs to allow users to formulate and test trade-offs on the fly, by way of the parameter visualization framework that we also presented here.

References

[1] K. Deb, S. Agrawal, A. Pratap, T. Meyarivan, A fast elitist non-dominated sorting genetic algorithm for multi-objective optimization: NSGA-II, in: Proceedings of the Sixth International Conference on Parallel Problem Solving from Nature (PPSN VI), 18–20 September 2000, Springer, Paris, France, 2000, pp. 849–858.

[2] A.H. Andersen, A.C. Kak, Simultaneous algebraic reconstruction technique (SART): a superior implementation of the ART algorithm, Ultrason. Imaging 6 (1984) 81–94.

[3] C.A. Coello, A short tutorial on evolutionary multiobjective optimization, in: Proceedings of the 1st International Conference Evolutionary Multi-Criterion Optimization (EMO'01), 7–9 March 2001, Springer-Verlag, Zurich, Switzerland, 2001, pp. 21–40.

[4] P. Gilbert, Iterative methods for the 3D reconstruction of an object from projections, J. Theor. Biol. 36 (1) (1972) 105–117.

[5] A. Konak, D.W. Coit, A.E. Smith, Multi-objective optimization using genetic algorithms: a tutorial, Reliab. Eng. Syst. Saf. (Special Issue – Genetic Algorithms and Reliability) 91 (9) (2006) 992–1007.

[6] E. Cantu-Paz, A Survey of Parallel Genetic Algorithms, Technical Report 97003, Illinois Genetic Algorithms Laboratory, Department of General Engineering, University of Illinois, Urbana, Illinois, 1997.

[7] F. Xu, W. Xu, M. Jones, B. Keszthelyi, J. Sedat, D. Agard, K. Mueller, On the efficiency of iterative ordered subset reconstruction algorithms for acceleration on GPUs, Comput. Methods Programs Biomed. 98 (3) (2010) 261–270.

[8] W. Xu, K. Mueller, Learning effective parameter settings for iterative CT reconstruction algorithms, in: 10th International Meeting on Fully Three-Dimensional Image Reconstruction in Radiology and Nuclear Medicine (Fully3D'09) 5–10 September 2009, Beijing China, 2009, pp. 251–254.

[9] W. Xu, K. Mueller, A performance-driven study of regularization methods for PU-accelerated iterative CT, in: 10th International Meeting on Fully Three-Dimensional Image Reconstruction in Radiology and Nuclear Medicine, 2nd High Performance Image reconstruction Workshop (HPIR'09), 6 September 2009, Beijing China, pp. 20–23.

[10] W. Xu, K. Mueller, Parameter space visualizer: an interactive parameter selection interface for iterative CT reconstruction algorithms, in: SPIE on Medical Imaging, 13–18 February 2010, vol. 7625, San Diego, CA, SPIE, Bellingham, WA, 2010, pp. 76251Q.

[11] W. Xu, F. Xu, M. Jones, B. Keszthelyi, J. Sedat, D. Agard, et al., High-performance iterative electron tomography reconstruction with long-object compensation using Graphics Processing Units (GPUs), J. Struct. Biol. 171 (2) (2010) 142–153.

Using GPUs to Accelerate Advanced MRI Reconstruction with Field Inhomogeneity Compensation

Yue Zhuo, Xiao-Long Wu, Justin P. Haldar, Thibault Marin,
Wen-mei W. Hwu, Zhi-Pei Liang, Bradley P. Sutton

Magnetic resonance imaging (MRI) is a flexible diagnostic tool, providing image contrast relating to the structure, function, and biochemistry of virtually every system in the body. However, the technique is generally slow and has low sensitivity, which limits its application in the clinical environment. Several significant advances in the past 10 years have created potential solutions to these problems, greatly increasing imaging speed and combining information from several acquisitions to increase sensitivity. But the computational time required for these new techniques has limited their use to research settings. In the clinic, images are needed at the conclusion of a scan to immediately decide if a subject moved, if the correct location was imaged, or if sufficient signal and contrast were obtained. Therefore, to achieve clinical relevance, it is necessary to accelerate the advanced MRI image reconstruction techniques.

In this chapter, we focus on a GPU implementation for a fast advanced non-Cartesian MRI reconstruction algorithm with field inhomogeneity compensation. The parallel structure of the reconstruction algorithms makes it suitable for parallel programming on GPUs. Accelerating this kind of algorithm can allow for more accurate image reconstruction while keeping computation times short enough for clinical use.

44.1 INTRODUCTION

MRI is a relatively new medical imaging modality developed by Professor Paul Lauterbur in the early 1970s, for which he was awarded a Nobel Prize in 2003. MRI can be used to measure the structure and function of tissue inside of living subjects, such as human brain tissue, by manipulating the magnetization of nuclei (typically hydrogen nuclei in water) placed in a highmagnetic field. MRI is a noninvasive technique that can be manipulated to obtain different types of image contrast. Nowadays, MRI has become a mature medical imaging technology with many different clinical applications, for example, functional neuroimaging of the brain and cardiovascular imaging.

However, several challenges exist that limit the application of MRI in the clinical environment. Traditionally, the main limitations in MRI have been due to the manner in which data are sampled in clinical scans. Clinical data have been sampled in a Cartesian (i.e., rectilinear) manner to facilitate image reconstruction through the use of the fast Fourier transform (FFT). Cartesian sampling can place a significant limit on acquisition speed. In addition, image artifacts can also exist in MRI owing to susceptibility-induced magnetic field inhomogeneity. Accurate spatial localization in MRI relies on having a uniform magnetic field across the region of the patient's anatomy that is being imaged. Disruptions to this uniformity (called magnetic field inhomogeneity) can cause artifacts in reconstructed images, such as spatial distortions and signal loss. Because good acquisition efficiency and image quality have always been important objectives in MRI, advanced reconstruction techniques that can accommodate non-Cartesian data acquisition and field inhomogeneity have also become critical issues.

In this chapter, we introduce an MR imaging toolbox that implements a fast reconstruction algorithm using parallel programming on GPUs. This chapter is designed to assist researchers working in medical imaging and reconstruction algorithm development, especially in the area of MR image reconstruction. Many advanced acquisition and reconstruction strategies exist in research environments, but their implementation in the clinic has been impeded by their large computational requirements. Thus, this chapter describes a platform for the translation of these advanced schemes to the clinic by enabling clinically-relevant computational times. Furthermore, the speedup of image reconstruction will significantly influence the application and future development of imaging in a variety of application areas (e.g., functional brain imaging of depression and memory, detection of cancer, and evaluation of heart disease). The rest of this chapter is organized as follows: First, we describe recent technologies in MRI that are easily ported to the GPU to enable clinically useful computational times. Second, the implementation of the advanced MRI reconstruction algorithm on GPUs is presented. Finally, we will provide the implementation results and an evaluation on a sample acquisition of a brain slice for functional imaging.

44.2 CORE METHOD: ADVANCED IMAGE RECONSTRUCTION TOOLBOX FOR MRI

44.2.1 Non-Cartesian Sampling Trajectory

Traditional MRI data acquisition can be viewed as sampling information in the spatial frequency domain (k-space), and images can be reconstructed using the Fourier transform (FT). For Cartesian trajectories (Figure 44.1(a)), image reconstruction can be performed using the fast Fourier transform (FFT) algorithm. Using the FFT can reduce the computational complexity from $O(N^2)$ to $O(N \cdot \log(N))$

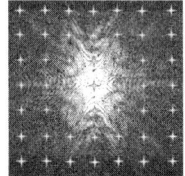
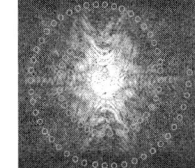

(a) Cartesian sampling trajectory   (b) Non-Cartesian sampling trajectory (spiral)

FIGURE 44.1

Cartesian and non-Cartesian MRI sampling trajectories in k-space.

for two-dimensional images, where N is the total number of pixels in the final reconstructed image. Although the FFT is an efficient reconstruction method, additional techniques are required for the reconstruction of data sampled on non-Cartesian sampling trajectories. Non-Cartesian sampling trajectories (e.g., the spiral trajectory) might be preferable in some situations because they can offer more efficient coverage of k-space (Figure 44.1(b)) and shorter acquisition times, and provide additional opportunities for balancing the spatial and temporal resolution in data acquisition. To maintain some of the speed advantage of the FFT, the gridding method for non-Cartesian reconstruction [11] allows for interpolation of non-Cartesian data onto a Cartesian grid. However, this method suffers from inaccuracies introduced by interpolation. In addition, gridding methods that use the FFT in reconstruction do not inherently allow for the modeling of additional physical effects during the data acquisition process. Thus, gridding can lead to image artifacts, including geometric distortions and signal loss. Compensating for physical effects such as magnetic field inhomogeneity in the gridding reconstruction requires further approximations and interpolations. Recently introduced inverse-problem approaches to image reconstruction formulate a physical model that can incorporate additional physical effects in order to correct images and reduce distortion.

44.2.2 Susceptibility-Induced Magnetic Field Inhomogeneity Compensation

In MRI reconstruction, advanced imaging models can correct for geometric distortion and some of the signal loss that is due to susceptibility-induced magnetic field inhomogeneity. Field inhomogeneity is due to the fact that air and tissue in the human brain have very different magnetic susceptibilities, which leads to large deviations in the local magnetic field. The susceptibility-induced magnetic field inhomogeneity near the interface of air/tissue (e.g., in the orbitofrontal cortex) can cause geometric distortions and signal loss in reconstructed images as reported in [12, 15, 16, 18]. As illustrated in Figure 44.2, signal loss results from susceptibility-induced magnetic field inhomogeneity gradients (called susceptibility gradients), which cause dephasing of the signal within a voxel. Methods exist

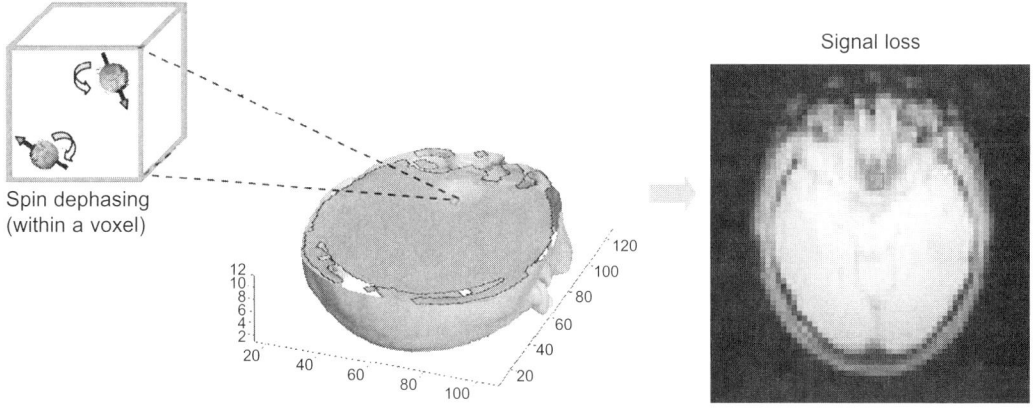

FIGURE 44.2

Signal loss (one kind of susceptibility-induced field inhomogeneity artifact) caused by spin dephasing within a voxel.

for compensating for these susceptibility artifacts. Noniterative, Fourier-transform-based correction methods cannot compensate for signal loss, but only for geometric distortion. Statistical estimation (using a physical model including the effects of susceptibility gradients on the received signal) is a natural alternative, and reconstructions can be obtained in this framework using iterative algorithms.

Our previous work builds a physical model that accounts for field inhomogeneity and both the within-plane and through-plane susceptibility gradients to correct for geometric distortions and signal loss [21, 22], as shown in Eq. 44.1.

$$d(\mathbf{k}(t_m)) = \int \rho(\mathbf{r})e^{-i2\pi\omega(\mathbf{r})t_m}e^{-2\pi\mathbf{k}(t_m)\cdot\mathbf{r}}\mathrm{d}\mathbf{r}, \tag{44.1}$$

where d denotes the complex k-space signal; $\rho(\mathbf{r})$ is the object at location $\mathbf{r}$; $\mathbf{k}(t_m)$ is the k-space sampling trajectory (which can include the Z-shimming imaging gradient [9]) at time t_m; and $\omega(\mathbf{r}) = \omega(x,y,z)$ represents the magnetic field inhomogeneity map (including the susceptibility gradients in X, Y, Z directions), which can be parameterized in terms of 3-D rectangle basis functions as in Eq. 44.2.

$$\omega(x,y,z) = \sum_{n=0}^{N-1}\left(\omega_n + G_{x,n}(x-x_n) + G_{y,n}(y-y_n) + G_{z,n}(z-z_n)\right)\cdot\phi_n(x,y,z). \tag{44.2}$$

N is the number of spatial image voxels; ω_n is off-resonance frequency for each voxel (in Hz); $G_{x,n}, G_{y,n}$ are the within-plane susceptibility gradients and $G_{z,n}$ is the through-plane susceptibility gradient (in Hz/cm); $\varphi_n(x,y,z)$ represents the basis function; and (x_n,y_n,z_n) denotes the location of the center of the nth voxel. Using this model, geometric distortion and signal loss induced by both within-plane and through-plane susceptibility gradients [21, 22] can be compensated simultaneously.

44.2.3 Advanced MR Imaging Reconstruction Using Parallel Programming on GPU

The motivation of this work is to reduce computation time by implementing our advanced MRI reconstruction method (that compensates for magnetic field inhomogeneity and accommodates non-Cartesian sampling trajectories) using parallel programming with CUDA on GPUs. On a typical CPU, the iterative reconstruction method requires long computation times that are not tolerable for clinical applications. Fortunately, the iterative MRI reconstruction framework can greatly benefit from a fast GPU-based implementation. Our implementation used techniques to optimize the memory management and computation, including use of constant memory with tiling, and use of fast hardware math functions. These and several other optimization techniques will be discussed in Section 44.3.2. Our implementation makes use of the iterative conjugate gradient algorithm [6] for matrix inversion. Our implementation also includes a regularization term that can contain prior information (we use a spatial smoothness constraint in our implementation using the prior knowledge that MR images are typically smooth). The computation related to this regularization term was implemented on the GPUs using sparse matrices (see Section 44.3.2). In contrast to our previous work that implemented regularized image reconstruction without field inhomogeneity compensation [19], we have currently implemented the entire conjugate gradient algorithm on the GPU to avoid time-consuming data transfers between the CPU and the GPU. Finally, we have developed a MATLAB toolbox to facilitate the access to the GPU reconstruction algorithm, and to visualize the reconstructed images (see Section 44.3.3). This toolbox was designed to enhance the accessibility of the distributed version of the GPU implementation.

We will show that our implementation on GPUs achieved a significant speedup with clinically viable reconstruction times.

44.3 MRI RECONSTRUCTION ALGORITHMS AND IMPLEMENTATION ON GPUS

In this section, we first introduce the algorithms used for the advanced MRI reconstruction. Then we present the details of the fast implementation of the algorithm on GPUs using CUDA-based parallel programming.

44.3.1 Algorithms: Iterative Conjugate Gradients

The implementation of the iterative conjugate gradient (CG) algorithm used in this work is based on [21], and solves the optimization problem shown in Eq. 44.3:

$$\hat{\rho} = \arg\min_{\rho} \|\mathbf{G}\rho - \mathbf{d}\|_2^2 + \beta R(\rho), \tag{44.3}$$

where $\mathbf{G}$ (also called the forward operator) is the system matrix modeling the MR imaging process (including non-Cartesian sampling and a model for the effects of field inhomogeneity), R is a penalty functional that encourages spatially smooth reconstructions, and β is a weighting factor. In our imaging model, $\mathbf{G}$ includes the zero order (causing geometric distortion) and first order (causing signal loss) effects of magnetic field inhomogeneity. These terms modify the relationship between $\mathbf{d}$ and ρ so that a direct FFT is not a good approximation of $\mathbf{G}$ even when data is sampled with a Cartesian trajectory. The process of directly calculating and storing $\mathbf{G}$ leads to storage problems with large datasets and long computation times. Moreover, because the FFT cannot be used (without additional approximations and algorithmic complexity [7]), reconstruction cannot benefit from the GPU implementations of the FFT in the CUDA library. Thus, one key point of this work is to solve the problem of calculating the system matrix $\mathbf{G}$ in a reasonable amount of time while keeping storage requirements within the constraints imposed by the GPU. Our solution for limiting memory usage is to compute the entries of $\mathbf{G}$ as they are used during matrix-vector multiplications and to store the final results of matrix-vector multiplication rather than the full $\mathbf{G}$ matrix. Similarly, in implementation of the CG algorithm (see Table 44.1), we also only store the entries of $\mathbf{G}^{\mathbf{H}}\mathbf{d}$ instead of $\mathbf{G}^{\mathbf{H}}$ for each voxel (the so-called backward operator), where $^{\mathbf{H}}$ denotes the complex conjugate transpose.

A solution to reducing computation time is to use multiple threads on the GPU to calculate the forward/backward operator for each voxel in parallel because the computations for each voxel are independent. Our CG implementation is composed of several subfunctions, including the forward operator, the backward operator, sparse matrix multiplications, and dot products.

In the implementation of the CG algorithm, the most computationally intensive operations are the matrix-vector multiplications involving $\mathbf{G}$ and $\mathbf{G}^{\mathbf{H}}$. Other than the forward/backward operators, significant computational slowdown occurs if data is transferred between the CPU and the GPU before and after each call to the forward/backward operators. For example, a data transfer time of 157 ms was observed for a dataset with $N = 64^2$. This is a large amount of time relative to the computation time, which was 0.152 ms for the forward operator with this dataset (on an NVIDIA G80 GPU). This suggests that all CG computations should be ported to the GPU, with data stored in GPU

Table 44.1 Operators in conjugate gradients (CG) algorithm.

Title	Content
	$Gx = \boxed{G \cdot x}$
	$Cx = \boxed{C \cdot x}$
	oldinprod = 0
	for i = 1 num_iter
	$grad = \boxed{G^H \cdot \overline{(y - Gx)}} - \boxed{C^H \cdot Cx}$
Conjugate graduate algorithm	newinprod = $\boxed{grad^H \cdot grad}$
	gamma = newinprod / oldinprod
	if i == 2
	dir = grad
	else
	dir = $\boxed{grad + gamma * dir}$
	end
	oldinprod = newinprod
	$Gdir = \boxed{G \cdot dir}$
	$Cdir = \boxed{C \cdot dir}$
	step = $(dir^H \cdot grad) / \boxed{(Gdir^H \cdot Gdir + Cdir^H \cdot Cdir)}$
	$Gx = \boxed{Gx + step \cdot Gdir}$
	$Cx = \boxed{Cx + step \cdot Cdir}$
	$x = \boxed{x + step \cdot dir}$
	end
Input variables	x – Initial image estimate (typically, a uniform image with value of 0)
	y – Acquired k-space data
	G – System matrix
	C – Sparse matrix for regularization constraint
	num_iter – Number of iterations (typically 8)
Output variable	x – Final image estimate
Operator markers	☐ Forward operator (Fourier transform)
	⌐ ¬ Backward operator (inverse Fourier transform)
	☐ Sparse matrix-vector multiplication
	☐ Vector-vector addition
	⌐ ¬ Dot product

memory. This can tremendously reduce the data transfer between the GPU and CPU during the CG iterations.

Note that a transpose sparse matrix-vector multiplication is not needed because switching rows and columns in the sparse matrix representation reduces the problem to just sparse matrix-vector multiplication. As a result, we conclude that there are five CUDA-based kernels that need to be implemented. They are (1) the forward operator, (2) the backward operator, (3) a sparse matrix-vector multiplication, (4) a vector dot product, and (5) vector-vector addition. For simplicity, we describe only two of the important functions in this chapter, namely, the backward operator (the forward operator implementation is similar), and the regularization term with a sparse representation. Additional implementation details can be found by examining the code distributed with this book [24].

44.3.2 High-Speed Implementations of the Iterative CG Algorithm on GPU

In this section, we describe the important functions for high-speed implementation of the CUDA-based image reconstruction on the GPUs. We mainly focus on the implementation of the two kernels, which are the most representative in terms of GPU technique: the backward operator function and the regularization term (which uses sparse matrix representation). The brute-force approach to the calculation of the modified Fourier forward/backward transform operators is a good match to the low-memory bandwidth and high-computational capacity of GPU-based implementations, and it eliminates the need for any interpolation approaches in order to include the additional physics in the signal model. In addition, we briefly describe a multi-GPU implementation for reconstruction of multiple slices.

Kernel Functions on the GPU

In our MRI application, we applied several well-known CUDA optimization techniques from levels of algorithm implementation to program coding style and performance tuning. Regarding algorithmic level optimization, we first analyzed the overall program execution process on a CPU and located two hot spots, the forward/ backward kernels, which take nearly 100% of the whole execution time. However, as mentioned earlier, because we need multiple iterations for each slice (e.g., eight iterations in the example used in this chapter), data are potentially transferred back and forth to the GPU side several times. This justifies our choice to move the data to the GPU memory and perform all calculations on the GPU.

Backward Operator

The simplified code segment of the backward operator function is shown in Figure 44.3. The outer loop processes each voxel, and the inner loop performs the calculations for each voxel with time-consuming mathematical operations (e.g., multiplication, division, and sin/cos functions). As mentioned earlier, the computation for each image-space voxel is independent of the computation for the other voxels, and thus, is a good match for parallel programming on the GPU.

To further optimize, the implementation groups together data variables, such as fm, fmgx, fmgy, and fmgz (the magnetic field map and susceptibility gradients the X, Y, Z directions) to benefit from memory coalescing because they are often fetched together. And kx, ky, and kz (k-space sampling trajectories in kx, ky, kz directions) are placed in constant memory to speed up memory access time. An additional consideration for the memory implementation is data tiling. For example, let us assume that the number of image-space voxels is $N = 64^2$, and the number of k-space samples is $M = 3770$

```
for (j = 0; j < N; j++) {
    for (i = 0; i < M; i++) {
        scx = sinc(kx[i]/N+ t[i]*fmgx);   Field map gradients in X,Y,Z
        scy = sinc(ky[i]/N+ t[i]*fmgy);
        scz = sinc(kz[i]/N+ t[i]*fmgz);
        k-space trajectory    Time              Field map
        arg = (kx[i]*ix + ky[i]*iy + kz[i]*iz) + (fm[j]*t[i]);
        cosarg = cos(arg);
        sinarg = sin(arg);             Image space trajectory
        iData_r[j]+=scx*scy*scz*((cosarg*kData_r[i])-(sinarg*kData_i[i]));
        iData_i[j]+=scx*scy*scz*((sinarg*kData_r[i])+(cosarg*kData_i[i]));
        Image space data (complex)              k-space data (complex)
    }
}
```

FIGURE 44.3

Backward operator in conjugate gradient algorithm.

(for spiral sampling trajectory). For kx, ky, and kz (three vectors with 3770 samples each, and 4 bytes of storage for each sample), storage uses 45,240 bytes ($3770 \times 3 \times 4$ bytes), which almost fills up the 64 kB of constant memory available on an NVIDIA G80 GPU. And this case is small compared with typical clinical datasets. Data tiling in constant memory, coincident with coalescing commonly fetched variables, solves this problem. We list some of the main optimizations in the following to improve the GPU performance.

1. Use fast hardware math functions to replace sin and cos. This could cause some accuracy loss, but speeds up the computation significantly. We have previously shown that there is no significant decrease in accuracy from the use of the fast hardware math functions in [23].
2. Take advantage of memory coalescence by storing variables used by the same portion of code in a structure.
3. Replace the division operations with right-shift operations.
4. Group kx, ky, and kz and store them as a structure in constant memory with a data tiling technique if their size exceeds the constant memory capacity.
5. Use registers to hold variables with multiple uses, like kData_r and kData_i (the real and imaginary parts of the complex k-space data from the acquisition).
6. Use multiple GPUs for reconstruction of multiple slices to further parallelize the computations (this avoids communication between GPUs, since reconstruction of a given slice is completely independent from reconstruction of the other slices).

Additionally, though not currently implemented, additional optimizations could potentially further increase the performance.

7. Unroll the loop to remove additional branch instructions and use double buffering to get better mixing of computation and memory accesses. However, when using this technique, one must be aware that the number of needed registers will increase and that could lower the number of active blocks on an SM.
8. Dividing the kernel into two parts could lower the computation to memory access ratio (the original ratio is 32/15 if taking sin/cos as one operation), but allows for reuse of the constant memory for

Table 44.2 Summary of optimizations used in different versions of our MRI Toolset.

MRI Toolset Versions	Optimizations for the GPU Code
Version 0.1	Using constant memory (Tiling)
	Moving out loop constant variables
	Using registers
	Using fast math functions
Version 0.2a	Moving out branches to the CPU side
	Loop unrolling
	Array of structures vs. Structure of arrays
	Computation between double and float values: float literals

the second half kernel. For example, we could let the first four statements, scx, scy, scz, and arg be the first half kernel and the remaining be the second half kernel. Then, we can reuse constant memory to store kData_r and kData_i. This method can be applied in conjunction with method 7.

Table 44.2 shows a summary of optimizations used in different versions of our MRI Toolset.

Sparse-Matrix Vector Multiplication (SpMV)

Sparse matrix-vector multiplications are widely used for many scientific computations, such as graph algorithms [1], graphics processing [2, 3], numerical analysis [10], and conjugate gradients [14]. This problem is essentially a simple multiplication task where the worst case (dense matrix) has a complexity of $O(N^3)$. The key feature of the problem is that the majority of the elements of the matrix are zero and do not require explicit computation. In this section, we will focus on the format-selection according to sparse data format. We surveyed several recent research works on SpMV done on NVIDIA GPU platforms, including [1–5, 8]. The algorithms for SpMV are greatly affected by the sparse matrix representation so we considered several popular formats, such as the Intel MKL and BSR (block compressed sparse row) sparse matrix storage formats [10], CSR (Compressed Sparse Row) [8] and CSC (Compressed Sparse Column) formats, and Matrix Market Coordinate Format (MMCF) [14]. We aim at finding a balance between programmability for parallelism and efficiency for speed. The main objective of these representations is to remove the redundant elements (namely, zero values), while keeping the representations readable, easy to manipulate, and compact enough during operations to handle extremely large matrix sizes. Because each format is designed for specific matrix characteristics in order to have the best performance, it is important to choose the right format. For our application, we chose the CSR format and the corresponding GPU CSR vector kernel implementation.

In the CSR vector kernel, the nonzero elements of each row in a matrix are served by one warp (32 threads). Thus, each row is manipulated in the unit of 32 nonzero elements, and 32 multiplication results are added into the final sum of each row. Therefore, if the standard deviation of the numbers of nonzeros in all rows is higher than a warp size, the load imbalance can degrade performance. Each row of the sparse matrix in our regularization term contains roughly a similar number of nonzero elements. This is due to the form of the spatial regularization, which places local constraints on neighboring voxels. Because of this characteristic, the CSR format is very suitable for our case because little load imbalance can happen. Developers should choose a suitable sparse matrix format based on their application.

Multi-GPU Implementation

The multi-GPU-based MRI reconstruction method is implemented on an NVIDIA Tesla S1070 that contains four GT200 GPUs. As mentioned earlier, to reduce the problem of memory bandwidth bottlenecks caused by communications between the GPU and CPU, we reconstruct each slice of the MRI data on one GPU. Therefore, a multithread approach is employed. Each CPU thread is assigned a slice to process, and a GPU that will be used for the kernels. Assignments are designed to preserve a balanced load for all GPUs, as shown in Figure 44.4. We are currently working on a dynamic queue to optimize this multi-GPU implementation. This dynamic queue will replace static assignment of slices to GPUs by dynamically dispatching slices to available GPUs [20]. Significant improvement is expected to be obtained, especially if the GPUs have different performance levels.

44.3.3 **MATLAB Toolbox for MRI Reconstruction**

In order to allow easy use of our GPU reconstruction program, we have developed a MATLAB (a widely used computational environment [13]) toolbox to perform GPU-enabled reconstruction and

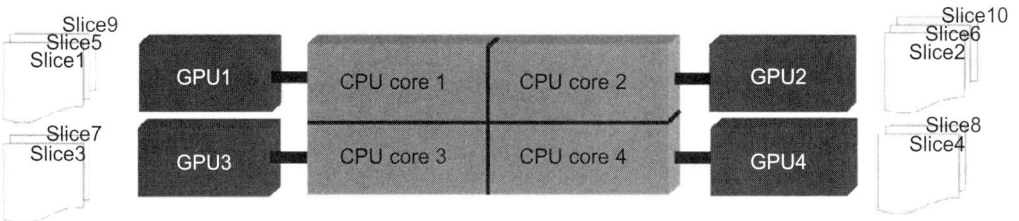

FIGURE 44.4

Assignment is designed to keep a balanced load among multi-GPUs (e.g., four GPUs connected with a quad-core CPU).

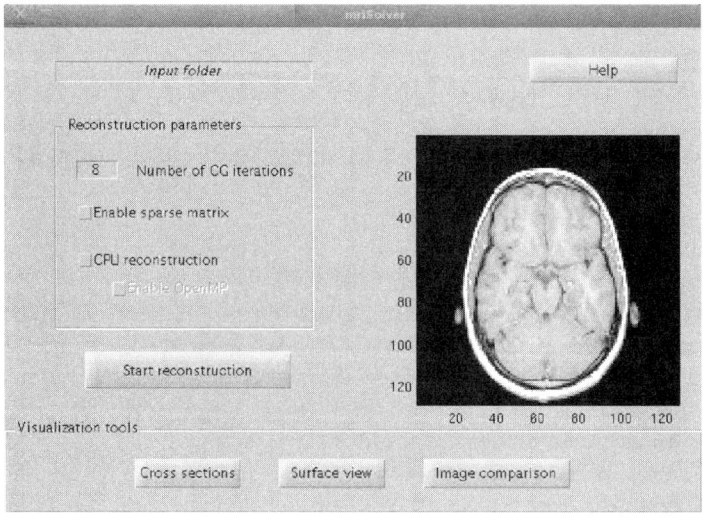

FIGURE 44.5

MATLAB graphic user interface (GUI) to perform iterative MR image reconstruction from MATLAB.

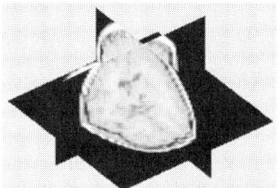

(a) 3-D cross-section view

(b) Head contours and
surface view

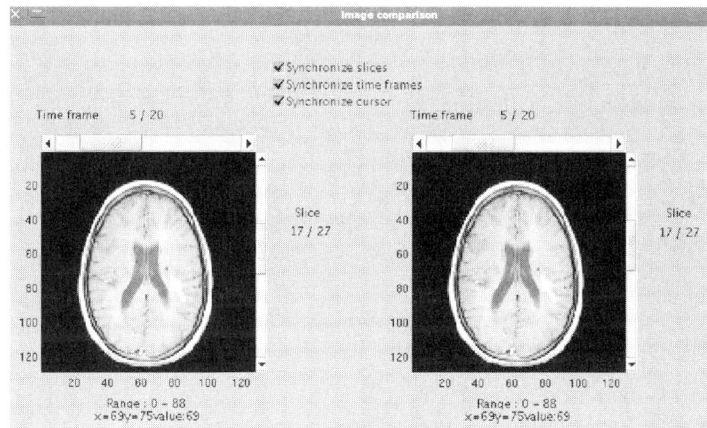

(c) Comparison between two datasets with values
for synchronized cursors

FIGURE 44.6

Visualization functions in the advanced MR imaging toolbox.

conveniently visualize the reconstruction results without exporting binary files from the reconstruction program to a separate visualization program. The first part of the toolbox consists of a MATLAB interface to the GPU program (Figure 44.5). This interface aims to decrease the effort required for new users to start using the reconstruction code, and increase the likelihood of widespread use of our code (in particular) and GPUs in MRI reconstructions (in general). By incorporating the reconstruction code into MATLAB, the iterative reconstruction can be called from MATLAB as part of a complex program (including data pre- or post-processing) with little effort. Additionally, we provide visualization tools (Figure 44.6) for MATLAB along with export tools to common visualization formats.

44.4 FINAL RESULTS AND EVALUATION

In this section, we present the results obtained with our GPU-based reconstruction method. The CPU and GPU code from our MRI Toolset version 0.1 is available at [24]. In this release, we applied the techniques of tiling with constant memory, loop invariant code motion, storing variables in registers, and using single-precision floating-point computations on the GPU kernels. In the CPU kernels, we

Table 44.3 Performance comparison between CPUs and GPUs.

a. Execution time of the key kernels with single thread enabled

Kernels	CPU Execution Time (ms)	CPU Execution Time (%)	GPU Execution Time (ms)	Speedup (CPU/GPU)
Forward operator	25,648.82	52.29	70.41	364.28
Backward operator	23,401.77	47.71	45.12	518.66
Total execution time	49,051.58	100.00	123.15	**398.31**

b. Execution time of the key kernels with four threads enabled

Kernels	CPU Execution Time (ms)	CPU Execution Time (%)	GPU Execution Time (ms)	Speedup (CPU/GPU)
Forward operator	6,698.27	52.41	69.69	96.12
Backward operator	6,080.66	47.58	44.98	135.19
Total execution time	12,780.04	100.00	121.31	**105.35**

tried to use OpenMP to parallelize the CPU reconstruction because it accelerates processing time for CPU code. However, the error rate caused by an OpenMP-enabled CPU kernel was not acceptable compared with that of the single-thread version. The normalized root mean squared error measured between CPU and GPU reconstruction was around 10^{-3} when using a single-threaded CPU code, and up to around **0.03** when using OpenMP.

For evaluation, a computation time comparison between CPUs and GPUs is shown in Table 44.3 (for matrix size of 64^2 with 8 iterations). This comparison uses our MRI Toolset v0.2a, running on a dual-core AMD Opteron Processor 2216 (CPU) and an NVIDIA GTX 280 (GPU). As shown in Table 44.3, the speedups of our implementation (for the advanced MRI reconstruction) on the GPU reach **398x** compared with a single-thread-enabled CPU, and **105x** compared with a four-thread-enabled CPU.

44.5 CONCLUSION AND FUTURE DIRECTIONS

Through the use of GPU hardware, we were able to accelerate an advanced image reconstruction algorithm for MRI from around a minute to around a tenth of a second. This reconstruction speed would provide images in the time frames necessary for clinical application. Thus, the use of GPUs will enable improved trade-offs between data acquisition time, signal-to-noise ratio, and the severity of artifacts owing to nonideal physical effects during the MRI imaging experiment.

Follow-up directions include CUDA-based parallel programming on GPUs for an advanced MR imaging reconstruction method combining field inhomogeneity compensation with parallel imaging (e.g., the SENSE algorithm [17]). In parallel imaging, information is collected simultaneously from multiple receivers, and this additional information can be used to significantly reduce sampling requirements and greatly accelerate data acquisition.

References

[1]   R.E. Bank, C.C. Douglas, SMMP: Sparse matrix multiplication package, Adv. Comput. Math. 1 (1993) 127–137.

[2]   N. Bell, M. Garland, Efficient Sparse Matrix-Vector Multiplication on CUDA, NVIDIA Technical Report NVR-2008-004, December 2008.

[3]   J. Bolz, I. Farmer, E. Grinspun, P. Schroder, Sparse matrix solvers on the GPU: conjugate gradients and multigrid, ACM Trans. Graph. 22 (3) (2003) 917–924.

[4]   L. Buatois, G. Caumon, B. Lévy, Concurrent number cruncher — A GPU implementation of a general sparse linear solver, Int. J. Parallel, Emergent Distrib. Syst. 24 (3) (2009) 205–223.

[5]   M. Christen, O. Schenk, H. Burkhart, General-Purpose Sparse Matrix Building Blocks using the NVIDIA CUDA Technology Platform, Book of Abstracts for First Workshop on General Purpose Processing on Graphics Processing Units, October 4, 2007, Boston.

[6]   J.A. Fessler, Penalized weighted least-squares image reconstruction for positron emission tomography, IEEE Trans. Med. Imaging 13 (2) (1994) 290–300.

[7]   J.A. Fessler, S. Lee, V.T. Olafsson, H.R. Shi, D.C. Noll, Toeplitz-based iterative image reconstruction for MRI with correction for magnetic field inhomogeneity, IEEE Trans. Signal Process, 53 (9) (2005) 3393–3402.

[8]   M. Garland, Sparse matrix multiplications on manycore GPU's, in: Proceedings of the 45th Annual Conference on Design Automation, Annual ACM IEEE Design Automation Conference, 8–13 June 2008, Anaheim, ACM, New York, 2008, pp. 2–6.

[9]   G.H. Glover, 3D z-shim method for reduction of susceptibility effects in BOLD fMRI, Magn. Reson. Med. 42 (2) (1999) 290–299.

[10] Intel Corporation, Sparse Matrix Storage Formats, http://www.intel.com/software/products/mkl/docs/webhelp/appendices/mkl_appA_SMSF.html.

[11] J.I. Jackson, C.H. Meyer, D.G. Nishimura, A. Macovski, Selection of a convolution function for Fourier inversion using gridding, IEEE Trans. Med. Imaging 10 (3) (1991) 473–478.

[12] G. Liu, S. Ogawa, EPI image reconstruction with correction of distortion and signal losses, J. Magn. Reson. Imaging 24 (3) (2006) 683–689.

[13] Matlab, http://www.mathworks.com/products/matlab.

[14] The Matrix Market, Website: http://math.nist.gov/MatrixMarket/.

[15] D.C. Noll, C.H. Meyer, J.M. Pauly, D.G. Nishimura, A. Macovski, A homogeneity correction method for magnetic resonance imaging with time-varying gradients, IEEE Trans. Med. Imaging 10 (4) (1991) 629–637.

[16] D.C. Noll, J.A. Fessler, B.P. Sutton, Conjugate phase MRI reconstruction with spatially variant sample density correction, IEEE Trans. Med. Imaging 24 (3) (2005) 325–336.

[17] K.P. Pruessmann, M. Weiger, M.B. Scheidegger, P. Boesiger, SENSE: Sensitivity encoding for fast MRI, Magn. Reson. Med. 42 (1999) 952–962.

[18] K. Sekihara, K. Masao, H. Kohno, Image restoration from non-uniform magnetic field influence for direct Fourier NMR imaging, Phys. Med. Biol. 29 (10) (1984) 15–24.

[19] S.S. Stone, J.P. Haldar, S.C. Tsao, W.W. Hwu, B.P. Sutton, Z.-P. Liang, Accelerating advanced MRI reconstructions on GPUs, J. Parallel Distrib. Comput. 68 (2008) 1307–1318.

[20] J. Stone, J. Saam, D.J. Hardy, K.L. Vandivort, W.W. Hwu, K. Schulten, High performance computation and interactive display of molecular orbitals on GPUs and multi-core CPUs, in: ACM International Conference Proceeding Series, vol. 383, 8 March 2009, Washington, DC, ACM, New York, 2009, pp. 9–18.

[21] B.P. Sutton, D.C. Noll, J.A. Fessler, Fast, iterative image reconstruction for MRI in the presence of field inhomogeneities, IEEE Trans. Med. Imaging 22 (2) (2003) 178–188.

[22] Y. Zhuo, B.P. Sutton, Effect on BOLD sensitivity due to susceptibility-induced echo time shift in spiral-in based functional MRI, in: Proc of IEEE Engineering in Med and Biol Society 2009, 2–6 September 2009, Minneapolis, IEEE, Piscataway, NJ, 2009, pp. 4449–4452.

[23] Y. Zhuo, X. Wu, J.P. Haldar, W. Hwu, Z. Liang, B.P. Sutton, Multi-GPU Implementation for Iterative MR Image Reconstruction with Field Correction, in: Proceedings of International Society for Magnetic Resonance in Medicine (ISMRM 2010), 1–7 May 2010, Stockholm, 2010, p. 2942.

[24] Y. Zhuo, X. Wu, J.P. Haldar, W. Hwu, Z. Liang, B.P. Sutton, GPU/CPU Code is available for download at the following Web sites: http://impact.crhc.illinois.edu/mri.php or http://mrfil.bioen.illinois.edu/index_files/code.htm.

ℓ1 Minimization in ℓ1-SPIRiT Compressed Sensing MRI Reconstruction

45

Mark Murphy, Miki Lustig

Magnetic resonance imaging (MRI) is a rich, multidisciplinary topic whose modern success is due to a synthesis of knowledge from many fields: medicine, physics, chemistry, engineering, and computer science. This chapter discusses the successful Cuda parallelization of an algorithm (ℓ1-SPIRiT [5]: ℓ1-regularized **iT**erative **S**elf-consistent **P**arallel **I**maging **R**econstruction) for reconstructing MR images acquired using two advanced methods: compressed sensing and parallel imaging (CS+PI).

The issues discussed in this chapter are simlilar to those faced by many MRI and statistical signal processing applications. Computationally, ℓ1-SPIRiT requires solving many independent convex optimization problems, each of which is a substantial computational burden on its own. All algorithms for solving the optimization problems are iterative, requiring repeated application of several linear operators that implement interpolations and orthonormal transformations.

45.1 INTRODUCTION, PROBLEM STATEMENT, AND CONTEXT

The acquisition of MR images in clinical contexts is inherently slow. MRI examinations are long and uncomfortable for patients; they also are expensive for hospitals to provide. MRI is an incredibly flexible imaging modality with many medical applications. The lengthiness and expense of MRI exams limits MRI's applicability in many contexts, however. MRI scans are inherently slow for two reasons. First, MRI data must be sampled sequentially, and each sample is expensive. An MRI scanner produces discrete samples of k-space[1] one at a time by applying a series of time-varying magnetic fields in the presence of a very strong constant magnetic field. There are unavoidable physical limits on the rate of change of these magnetic fields, as well as the rate at which the molecules in the patient's body can respond to the fields. Second, MRI is plagued by an inherently low signal-to-noise ratio (SNR). If too little time is spent acquiring the MRI data, then the image will be dominated by the unavoidable noise generated by the MR system and the patient's body.

Compressed sensing (CS) is an approach to ameliorating the first cause: A CS MRI scan simply acquires fewer data points. However, as we will discuss briefly, one must be careful to acquire the *right* data points. Parallel imaging (PI) ameliorates the second cause: redundantly acquiring the MR

---

[1]In MRI and related fields, the Fourier-domain representation of an image is usually called "k-space."

data from multiple receive channels improves the signal-to-noise ratio. With PI, one can effectively trade SNR for scan time. In either case, $\ell1$-SPIRiT's approach to combining these two techniques can substantially increase the quality and speed of MR imaging. Although combining CS+PI results in less MRI data being collected, we still desire high-resolution images. Thus, $\ell1$-SPIRiT must estimate the values of the data that weren't collected.

Typically, SPIRiT is applied to 3-D volumetric scans acquired redundantly from 8–32 receive channels. In resolution, each of the dimensions varies between 128 and 512, and we undersample by approximately $4\times$. Each voxel is a single-precision complex number, and these datasets range in size from hundreds of MB to several GB. The iterative algorithms for performing SPIRiT reconstruction, combined with the massive datasets, produce long runtimes that threaten SPIRiT's clinical usability. The original research prototype of $\ell1$-SPIRiT requires over an hour to reconstruct these images. However, a radiologist directing an MRI examination must have the images from each scan before prescribing the next: the reconstruction must execute "instantaneously." As we will discuss in later sections, our implementation of $\ell1$-SPIRiT reconstructs these MRI scans in fewer than 30 seconds on a multi-GPU system, running faster even than serial implementations of competing, simpler techniques. The code described in this chapter has been deployed at Lucile Packard Children's Hospital, and is used to reconstruct dozens of scans per week. C++ source code is available on-line from the author's Web site: http://www.eecs.berkeley.edu/~mjmurphy/llspirit/html.

45.1.1 Compressed Sensing

Compressed sensing [4] is a general approach for reconstructing a signal when it has been sampled significantly below the Nyquist rate. To develop intuition of the usefulness and mechanics of compressed sensing, Figure 45.1 provides a detailed example of its application to a toy signal. In this section, we provide a brief treatment of the mathematical formalism.

First, we must discuss *sparsity*. A vector x is considered *sparse* if it has very few nonzero elements. A vector itself that is not sparse may be sparse when represented via some other basis. This will occur, for example, when the vector is simply a linear combination of a few of the vectors in the basis. For example a sine wave is not sparse, but has a very compact representation in the Fourier domain. Some vectors may not be sparse, but may be *compressible* — the magnitudes of their coefficients in some basis decay rapidly. Such a vector is nearly sparse, except for a large number of small coefficients.

In MRI, we wish to produce an image of the density of tissues on a patient's body. We can denote an image as $x \in \mathbb{C}^n$: an n-dimensional complex-valued vector. n is the number of voxels in our 3-D images — typically 100 million or more. Using the MRI scanner we want to take m samples of the k-space (i.e., Fourier domain) representation of our image, with $m \ll n$ to accelerate the scan. We can represent the process of taking these measurements as multiplication of x with a matrix Φ, constructed by selecting some subset of the rows of a discrete Fourier transform (DFT) matrix. We'll denote the undersampled k-space data $y = \Phi x$. Because $m \ll n$, the problem of inverting the equation $y = \Phi x$ is highly underdetermined: a solution can be drawn from an entire $(m - n)$-dimensional subspace of $\mathbb{C}^n$.

Real-world images such as the ones produced by MRI tend to be compressible: image compression algorithms such as JPEG [6] leverage this fact. In particular JPEG uses a wavelet transform to expose compressibility, as real-world images tend to be nearly sparse in the wavelet domain. Compressed sensing provides a means of selecting a particular solution $\tilde{x} \in \mathbb{C}^n$ (of the many which satisfy $\Phi x = y$): the

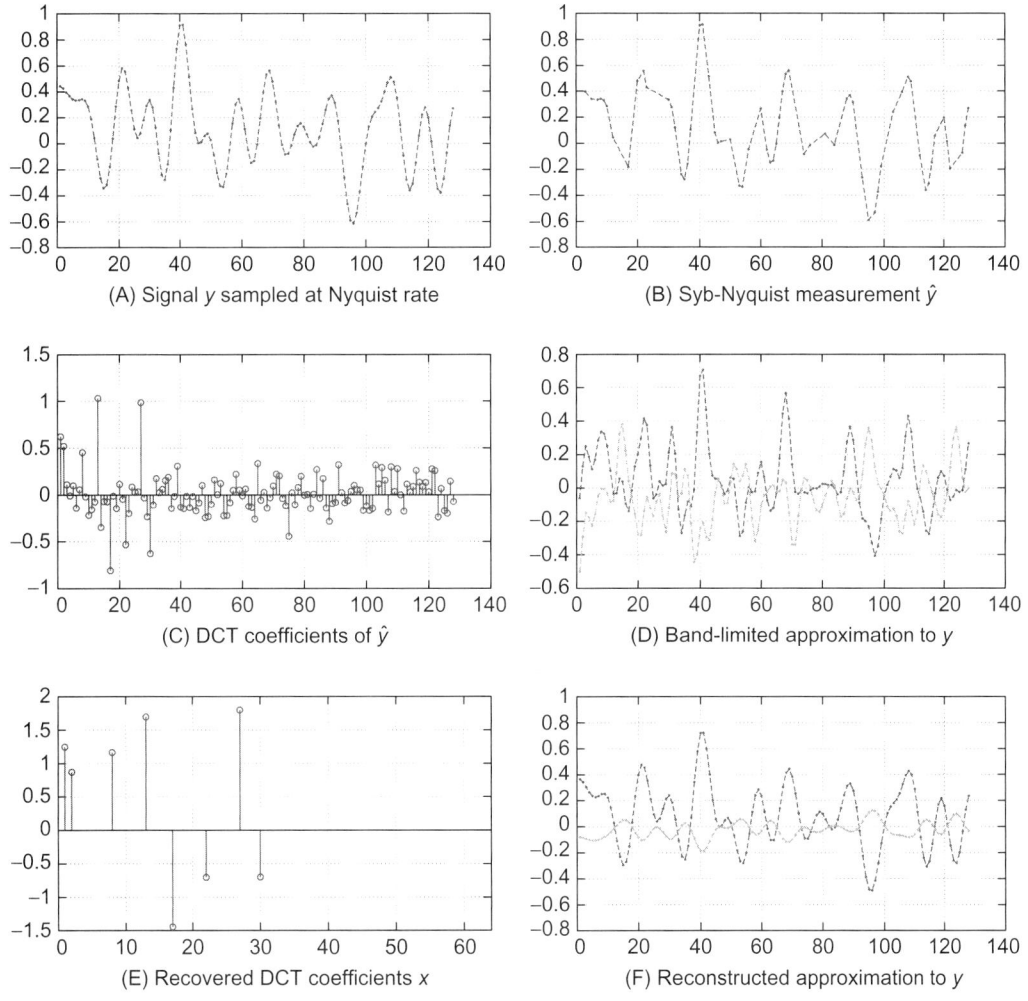

FIGURE 45.1

A simple example of a compressed sensing recontsruction. Panel A shows a length-128 signal y, which we wish to sample below the Nyquist rate. Panel B shows $\hat{y}$, a random subsampling of y at $\frac{1}{2}$ the Nyquist rate — 64 samples. One approach to recontruction of the signal is to assume that 64 samples is the Nyquist rate: that is, assume that we only need 64 coefficients in a Fourier basis. We can compute the discrete cosine transform (DCT) of $\hat{y}$, yielding the coefficients in panel C. We can low-pass filter the acquired signal to produce the very poor approximation to y displayed in panel D. A compressed sensing reconstruction, however, notes that the signal y is *sparsified* via a (DCT): as panel E shows, only a few (8) DCT coefficients are necessary to represent y in the DCT domain. That is, the coefficients x shown in panel E are the solution x to the convex optimization problem: Minimize $||x||_1$ subject to $\hat{y} = \mathrm{DCT}^{-1}x$. The equality $\hat{y} = \mathrm{DCT}^{-1}x$ is enforced only at the samples that were actually acquired. Finally, panel F depicts the resulting compressed sensing reconstruction of y — the inverse DCT of the coefficients in E.

image which is maximally sparse. Formally, our desired image can be found by solving the following optimization problem:

$$\text{Minimize} \quad \|Wx\|_1$$
$$\text{Subject to} \quad y = \Phi x$$

Where the $\ell 1$ norm is defined as the sum of the absolute value of a vector's components: $\|x\|_1 = \sum_{i=1}^{n} |x_i|$; and Wx is the representation of x in a wavelet basis. The compressed sensing reconstruction problem is convex, and thus, it is possible to design tractable algorithms for its solution [3]. However, these algorithms will necessarily be iterative and, given the large size of our datasets, very computationally expensive.

45.1.2 Parallel Imaging

Parallel Imaging (PI) refers to the redundant acquisition of an MR image from multiple receive coils. Parts of the patient's body closer to a given coil will produce a stronger signal in that coil, so the 8–32 receive coils in a PI acquisition are arranged to provide good coverage of an entire region of the body. Because each coil receives a high signal-to-noise ratio (SNR), the scan can be performed substantially faster — frequently in $2 - 4\times$ less time. Each channel produces only a partial image, but much of the volume is imaged redundantly from the many coils. The SPIRiT reconstruction leverages this redundancy as an additional constraint in the $\ell 1$ minimization required by compressed sensing.

In particular, given a nonacquired k-space location $x(i, j, k)$, SPIRiT computes a set of weights to be applied to all k-space voxels within some radius (typically 2–3 voxels) surrounding $x(i, j, k)$. The value of the nonacquired k-space location is estimated as the sum of the weights times the neighboring voxels from all coils' images — i.e., missing k-space data are estimated by convolving the known data with a shift-invariant filter. However, the undersampling patterns used by SPIRiT produce adjacent missing k-space data. Thus, SPIRiT seeks a fixed point of this convolution operation: i.e., a set of estimates for the missing k-space data that is self-consistent with respect to these interpolation kernels.

More formally, because convolution is a linear operation we can represent the application of interpolation kernels to an image x as a linear transformation Gx. We'll refer to G as the "Calibration Operator" because it encodes all information about our multicoil calibration. The self-consistency formulation is equivalent to requiring that x be a fixed point of G: $Gx = x$. We can further constrain the compressed sensing problem with this additional linear equality, producing the final specification of the $\ell 1$-SPIRiT reconstruction:

$$\begin{aligned} \text{Minimize} \quad & \|Wx\|_1 \\ \text{Subject to} \quad & \Phi x = y \\ & Gx = x \end{aligned} \tag{45.1}$$

45.2 CORE METHODS (HIGH LEVEL DESCRIPTION)

In this section, we discuss the algorithm we currently use to solve the $\ell 1$-SPIRiT reconstruction in Equation 45.1. Our algorithm is a "Projections-Over-Convex-Sets" (POCS) method. That is, we iteratively apply projections onto three convex sets corresponding to the three terms in Equation 45.1: images which are "wavelet sparse" (i.e., $\|Wx\|_1$ is small); images which are "Measurement Consistent" (i.e., $\Phi x = y$); and images which are "calibration consistent" (i.e., $Gx - x$). The POCS algorithm is most succinctly described in pseudocode:

```
do {
        k = k + 1
(1)     z_k = Gz_{k-1}                    % Enforce calibration consistency
(2)     z_k[acquired] = y                 % Enforce Data consistency
(3)     z_k = ΦW^{-1}S_λ{WΦ^{-1}z_k}      % Wavelet soft-threshold
} until convergence
```

The three lines marked (1), (2), and (3) are the sources of computational intensity in the algorithm. Here we have used z_k to denote the k-space representation of the image, G and Φ as the Calibration and Fourier operators, and W as the wavelet transform operator, thus the effect of lines (1) and (2) should be clear. We have used S_λ to denote a *soft-thresholding* operation. S_λ is defined elementwise on a vector as $S_\lambda(x_i) = \frac{x_i}{|x_i|+\epsilon} \cdot \max(|x_i| - \lambda, 0)$. That is, $S_\lambda(x_i)$ has the same phase as x_i, but a slightly smaller magnitude. The effect of soft thresholding is to remove wavelet coefficients owing to aliasing resulting from the k-space undersampling: thus, the soft-thresholding removes aliasing noise and prevents image artifacts from appearing.

45.3 ALGORITHMS, IMPLEMENTATIONS, AND EVALUATIONS (DETAILED DESCRIPTION)

Most of the computation involved in the algorithm described in the previous section manifests itself as simple elementwise operations on the image data. Given the availability of the highly optimized CUFFT library, the parallelization and optimization of our code is fairly straightforward. The exception is the wavelet transform, which required substantially more optimization than the other operations.

Our MRI pulse sequence only undersamples the data in two of the three dimensions. Undersampling in the first dimension, the *readout direction*, is not sensible. This is a consequence of the use of gradient fields by MRI scanners to manipulate k-space: acquiring an entire readout line is no more expensive than acquiring a single point along that line. Consequently, we can decouple the 3-D problem into many independent 2-D problems by performing an inverse Fourier transform along the readout direction. Each independent 2-D problem can be solved in parallel. Each 2-D problem itself is a substantial computation, and our implementation parallelizes the 2-D solver across a single GPU. In systems with multiple GPUs, we distribute 2-D problems round-robin to ensure load balance.

45.3.1 Calibration Consistency Operator

As described in Section 45.2, the application of the Calibration Consistency operator G is a convolution in the Fourier domain. It is well known that convolutions in the Fourier domain are equivalent to elementwise multipication in the image domain. If the convolution kernel has m coefficients, and the image has n voxels, then the the implementation of G in the Fourier domain is $O(mn)$, while the implementation in the Image domain is only $O(n)$ after incurring an $O(n \log n)$ cost of performing Fourier transforms. Note that we must perform the Fourier transforms anyway — otherwise, we could not compute the wavelet transform and perform the soft-thresholding operation. Thus, the Fourier transforms effectively cost nothing, and an image domain implementation is clearly more efficient. Furthermore,

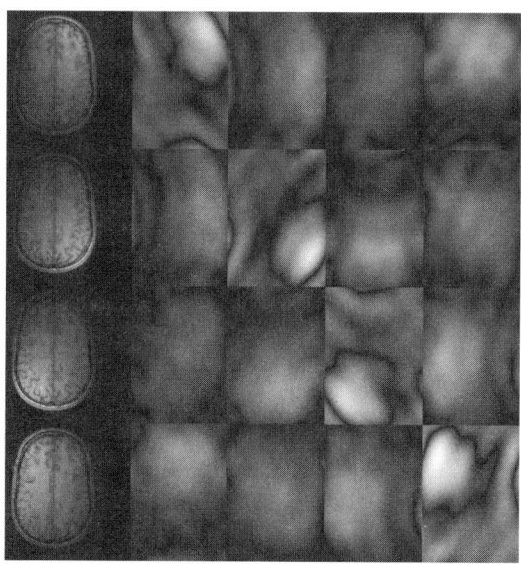

FIGURE 45.2

An example 2-D slice of four channels of a brain MRI, and the image-domain masks used to implement the k-space calibration-consistency convolution efficiently. To estimate the nonacquired k-space samples for a given channel, each pixel in the images on the left would be multiplied by the four weights from the desired row of mask images.

convolutions are more difficult to optimize than elementwise operations, and we can more easily produce a near-peak-performance image-domain implementation. Figure 45.2 shows an example of the image-domain elementwise masks that are used to compute the Fourier-domain convolutions.

However, the image-domain implementation requires a substantially higher memory footprint than does the Fourier-domain implementation. In the Fourier domain, the convolution kernels are very small. Each kernel is typically 7^3, and we have typically 8×8 of them. However, to represent these kernels in the image domain, we must zero-pad them to the size of the image (at least 128^3) and perform an inverse Fourier transform. This increasess memory usage by approximately three orders of magnitude: we must carefully manage this data, or we will overrun the memory capacity of the GPUs.

If there are eight channels in the MRI acquisition (typically there are eight, but there can be as many as 32), then we have 64 convolution kernels. For a typical volume size of $384 \times 256 \times 100$ with eight channels, precomputing and all of the image-domain masks would require $384 \times 256 \times 100 \times 8 \times 8$ complex-valued, single-precision: 4.6 GB of data. For a 32-channel acquisition, this would balloon to 75 GB. However, because the 3-D problem decouples into independent 2-D problems, we need to store the image-domain covolution masks only for as many 2-D problems as we have in flight simultaneously. Currently, we have one 2-D problem in flight per GPU in the system. This may change in future versions of the code, however, as we will discuss in Section 45.5. For each 256×100 2-D problem of a 32-channel acquisition, the 2-D convolution masks require 200 MB of memory and fit in the DRAM of any reasonably sized CUDA-capable GPU.

Our implementation of the calibration consistency operator uses neither the texture cache, nor the shared memory because there is little data reuse that can be exploited. All data (the convolution masks and the image data itself) are stored in the GPU's DRAM and streamed through using standard coalesced memory operations. Because the code performs just under 1 complex floating-point operation per complex float loaded from DRAM, the computation rapidly becomes DRAM bandwidth bound and no further optimization is necessary.

45.3.2 Data Consistency Projection

The data consistency projection serves the purpose of ensuring that our estimate of the image does not diverge from the data produced during the MRI scan. Our implementation of this projection is simple. First we transform our current estimate x_k into the Fourier domain, for which we use the highly optimized CUFFT libary. The Fourier transform of our estimate will include "estimated" values for the k-space voxels acquired from the MRI scan. However, we know that these estimates are wrong: these k-space voxels should have the values produced by the MRI scan. Thus, the second step of the data-consistency projection is simply to overwrite these voxels with the known values.

Much as in the case of the Calibration Consistency projection, this step is trivially parallel and rapidly becomes bandwidth bound. Furthermore, the bulk of the work is in computing the Fourier transforms. As discussed in Section 45.5, reliance on CUFFT in this step has overly constrained our current parallelization of the SPIRiT algorithm possibly leading to substantial inefficiency.

45.3.3 Soft Thresholding

As discussed in Section 45.2, the soft-thresholding step can be intuitively understood as a denoising operation that decreases the $\ell 1$ norm of the wavelet representation of the image. This step has the effect of pushing to zero wavelet coefficients that are very small and consolidating the energy of the signal about a sparse set of coefficients. In our context, we consider the magnitude of a wavelet coefficient to be the sum across all 8–32 channels of the magnitude of the channels' individual wavelet coefficients. Our implementation serializes the sum for each voxel, instead exploiting the more abundant voxel-wise parallelism. After computing the sum, we can compute what the new magnitude should be for each wavelet coefficient and update in place the data.

Much as in the implementation of the data-consistency and calibration-interpolation operations, little optimization is needed in order to achieve efficient execution. Soft thresholding is very easily written via standard CUDA programming practice to achieve near-peak memory bandwidth utilization. Because the runtime of this step is dominated by memory access, and no reuse can be exploited, we need not optimize the code any further.

45.3.4 Wavelet Transform

Figure 45.3 shows an example of the application of a wavelet transform to an MR image. The forward and inverse wavelet transforms are the most intricately optimized steps of our implementation. The algorithm we are using to compute the wavelet transforms in $\ell 1$-SPIRiT is $O(n \lg n)$ (n is the number of pixels in the image) and repeatedly convolves the image with high- and low-pass filters, downsampling at every step. The result is a spatial separation of the image content corresponding to high- and low-frequency Fourier coefficients. The algorithm performs $O(\lg n)$ steps, during which the image undergoes several $O(n)$ convolutions.

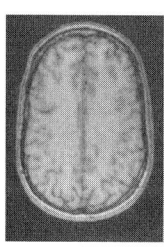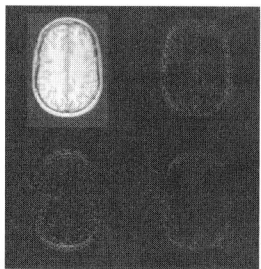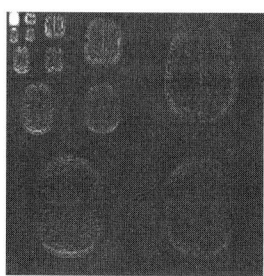

FIGURE 45.3

On the left is a typical MRI image. The center is the image after one step of a wavelet transform. Note that the image has been spatially high-pass filtered in both X and Y and downsampled to produce the bottom-right quarter; low-pass filtered in both X and Y for the top-left quarter; and a combination of high- and low-pass filtering was used to produce the other two quarters. On the right is the image after four steps of the wavelet transform.

If during one step of a wavelet transform, the image is H pixels tall and W pixels wide[2], our goal is to produce four $H/2$ by $W/2$ pixel images, one of which is high-pass filtered in both the X and Y dimensions, one of which is low-pass filtered in both dimensions, and two which are a combination of low- and high-pass filtered in the two dimensions. This could be achieved by performing four 2-D convolutions, and downsampling by a factor of two. However, a more efficient implementation leverages the separability of the wavelet filters. In particular, the 2-D convolutions are performed as pairs of 1-D convolutions: first convolving each length W row with high- and low-pass filters, then convolving each length H column. The downsampling operation can be combined with the convolution to reduce computation by a factor of $2\times$.

While we are performing a convolution on a row (or column) of the image, it is crucial to cache the input data to leverage the data reuse inherent in convolution. We are using length-P (usually four) filters and performing two down-sampling convolutions, so effective caching will reduce memory bandwidth requirements by a factor of $P\times$. Again, we expect that an efficient implementation of the wavelet transform should be memory bound owing to the extremely high floating-point throughput of the GPU. Note that when we are convolving in the nonunit stride dimension (in our case, convolving the rows of the image), it is also necessary to block in the unit-stride dimension. In order for memory accesses to be coalesced, we must load up to 16 rows at a time into the GPU's shared memory. In fact, we found that blocking increased the performance of both our row and column convolutions, likely because of the increased thread block size the blocking transformation enabled. Once the blocked data is in shared memory, we can then perform our convolutions rapidly on the cached data.

The implementations of the row- and column-convolutions for both the forward and inverse transforms are similar. Here, we provide a partial listing of the source for the forward transform's row convolution, with some details omitted for clarity. Note that the `shared_rows` variable represents the data we are caching in the GPU's shared memory, and the constant K determines how many rows we load into a single thread block's memory. Because the data is column major, K must be large enough

---

[2]Our implementation is of a *dyadic* wavelet, requiring that both the width and height be zero-padded to powers of two so that downsampling by a factor of two is always legal.

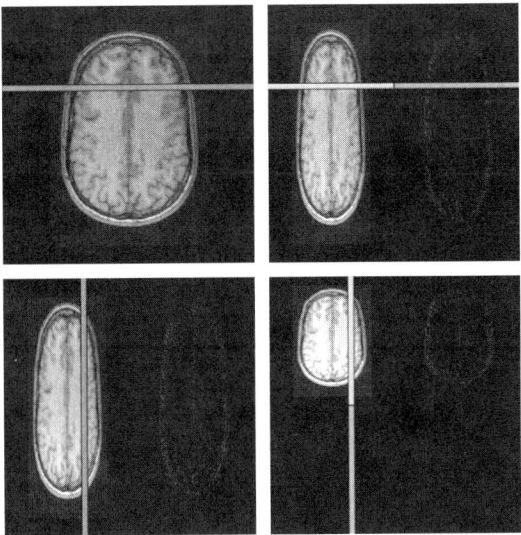

FIGURE 45.4

Illustration of the convolutions performed during the wavelet transform. The horizontal and vertical lines on the left are convolved with a quadrature-pair of high- and low-pass filters and downsampled to produce the corresponding portions of the images on the right. In order for the GPU hardware to coalesce the memory accesses for the row-convolutions, we must combine the convolutions for at least eight rows into a single thread block and load the resulting image strip into shared memory. The same blocking transformation also improves the columnwise convolutions (which are unit stride, and would coalesce anyway) by increasing thread-block size.

to ensure that global memory accesses are coalesced. The high- and low-pass filters are stored in the GPU's constant memory in arrays named hpf and lpf, respectively. Also, note that while the MRI data is complex valued, our wavelet filters are real valued. Thus, we perform the transform independently on the real and imaginary components of the data.

```
__global__ void forward_wavelet_rows ()
{
    // some initializaion omitted for bevity

    extern __shared__ float shared_rows[];

    for (int j = threadIdx.y; j < n; j += blockDim.y)
        shared_rows[threadIdx.x + j*blockDim.x] = X[i + M*j];

    __syncthreads();

    // Low-pass Downsample
    for (int j = threadIdx.y; j < n/2; j += blockDim.y){
        float y = 0;
        for (int k = 0; k < P; k++)
            y += shared_rows[threadIdx.x + K*(2*j+k)&(n-1)]*lpf[k];
        X[i + j*M] = y;
```

```
    }

    // High-pass Downasmple
    for (int j = threadIdx.y; j < n/2; j += blockDim.y){
        float y = 0;
        for (int k = 0; k < P; k++)
            y += shared_rows[threadIdx.x + K*mod(2*j+1-k,n)]*hpf[k];
        X[i + (n/2)*M + j*M] = y;
    }
}
```

This code parallelizes the computation of each row's convolution among $\frac{1}{K}^{th}$ of the threads in a thread block. Since K rows are loaded, the entire thread block computes K convolutions in parallel. However, a wavelet transform of a single image is insufficient to saturate the GPU for any appreciable amount of time. Additional parallelism is found in performing the transforms for all 8–32 channels simultaneously. Additionally, our wavelet filters are real valued and transforms of the complex-valued MRI images further decompose into real and imaginary transforms which can be performed in parallel.

```
void forward_wavelet (float *X_real, float *X_imag,
                      int M, int N, C, int L)
{
    T = 256; // threads per Thread Block
    int min_size = (1 << L);

    // other variable initializaion omitted for clarity

    for (int m = M, n = N, j = J, j > L; j--)
    {
        if (m > min_size)
        {
            for ( K = MAX_K
                ; K*m*sizeof(float) > SHARED_MEM_SIZE
                ; K >>= 1);

            forward_wavelet_cols <<< dim3(2, C*(n/K)), dim3(T/K, K)
                                     K*m*sizeof(float) >>>
                                 (X_real, X_imag, M, m, N, n, C);
        }

        if (n > min_size)
        {
            for ( K = MAX_K
                ; K*n*sizeof(float) > SHARED_MEM_SIZE
                ; K >>= 1);

            forward_wavelet_rows <<< dim3(2*(m/K), C), dim3(K, T/K),
                                     K*n*sizeof(float) >>>
                                 (X_real, X_imag, M, m, N, n, C);
        }
```

```
        if (m > min_size) m = m/2;
        if (n > min_size) n = n/2;
    }
}
```

In the preceding code, we have called the column and row convolutions as separate kernels: all convolutions are performed in place in global DRAM, and the output of the column convolutions is the input to the row convolutions. The grid dimensions of `dim3(2,C*(n/K))` and `dim3(2*(m/k),C)` specify that we want to perform convolutions for all C image channels in parallel, that we are grouping the n column convolutions (or m row convolutions) into groups of K, and we multiply by two in order to process the real and imaginary components separately.

45.4 FINAL EVALUATION AND VALIDATION OF RESULTS, TOTAL BENEFITS, AND LIMITATIONS

The original research prototype implementation of ℓ1-SPIRiT was a Matlab script, relying on Matlab's efficient implementations of Fourier transforms and matrix/vector operations, as well as an external C implementation of wavelet transforms. Our CUDA implementation is 100 to 200 times faster than this code, although the comparison is hardly fair. Instead, we shall use an optimized C++ implementation as a performance baseline, running on the CPU cores of our reconstruction machine. Our reconstruction machine is a dual-socket Intel Xeon X5650 Westmere system, with six dual-threaded cores per socket running at 2.67 GHz. The six cores in each socket share a 12 MB L3 cache, and have private 256 kB L2 caches and 64 kB Ll caches. The machine also has four Tesla C1060 GPGPUs in PCI Express x16 slots. Each Tesla C1060 has 240 single-precision execution pipelines running at 1.3 GHz, organized into 30 streaming multiprocessors (SMs), with 4 GB of dedicated graphics DRAM capable of approximately 100 GB/s bandwidth. Each of the 30 SMs has a 16 kB shared scratchpad memory accessible by all threads in the SM, and a 64 kB register file partitioned among threads. All CUDA tools used were version 2.3. All non-CUDA C++ code was compiled with GNU G++ 4.3.3.

We'll discuss the runtime of ℓ1-SPIRiT for three different high-resolution eight-channel 3-D acquisitions. Table 45.1 summarizes several important characteristics of these datasets. The "Seq. ℓ1-Min Time" column reports the runtime of our optimized C++ code running on a single core of the recon machine. The "#2-D Problems" column is the readout dimension, which determines the number of independent 2-D reconstructions that must be performed. Dataset A is typical of a very high-resolution scan, typically performed of a pediatric patient's abdomen under general anesthesia. Scans B and C are typical resolutions for other applications, for example in 4-D Flow [2], where the scan resolution is lower but a large number (approximately 100) of individual 3-D volumes are acquired over a period of time. 4-D Flow reconstructions require each individual 3-D volume to be reconstructed, and total reconstruction time can be many hours.

The end-to-end MRI reconstruction requires some computations not discussed in the previous sections. For all datasets, there are approximately 11 seconds of runtime not spent `int` the POCS iterations: 7 seconds solving linear systems of equations to produce the calibration operator G, 3 seconds performing Fourier transforms of the readout direction, and the remaider in miscellaneous minor computations. Because of space limitations, we shall not discuss these computations further.

Table 45.1 Characteristics of our three example datasets.

Dataset	#2-D Problems	2-D Problem Size	Data Size	Seq. $\ell1$-Min Time
A	320	260×132	670 MB	42 min 54 s
B	192	320×56	210 MB	6 min 28 s
C	192	256×62	186 MB	5 min 52 s

Table 45.2 A comparison of the runtimes of the sequential and parallel CPU implementations with one- and four-GPU implementations.

Dataset	1GPU	12CPUs	1GPU	4CPUs
A	42:54 m	5:36 m (7.64x)	3:57 m (10.8x)	59.6 s (43.1x)
B	6:28 m	37.9 s (10.2x)	54.2 s (7.2x)	14.3 s (27.1x)
C	5:52 m	34.8 s (10.1x)	42.9 s (8.2x)	11.5 s (30.6x)

Table 45.2 compares the runtimes of our various parallel implementations of the $\ell1$ minimization code. It is worth noting that our one-CPU implementation is fairly well optimized: this code itself is approximately $4\times$ faster than the original Matlab implementation. The "12CPUs" column is the same source code as the one-CPU implementation, but parallelized using OpenMP [1]. In all cases, the CPU parallelization is fairly efficient. The smaller two datasets, B and C, achieve $10\times$ speedup using 12 CPU cores.

Interestingly, although the hyperthreading on the Intel Nehalem architecture can provide approximately a 30% performance boost for some codes, in this case, using more than 12 CPU threads substantially hurts performance — increasing runtime by approximately 50% for problem A. This effect is due to contention for cache and memory bandwidth. The large caches on the CPU platform are in large part responsible for the good scaling of the CPU code: note that the smaller problems (B and C) scale more efficiently on the CPU than does the larger problem (A). The size of the 2-D datasets for B and C are 1.1 and 0.95 MB, respectively. Most operations in the algorithm are out of place, so two copies of the data must be allocated. With 12 2-D problems in flight simultaneously, and a working set size of about 2 MB per problem, the algorithm will run almost entirely in the 24 MB of CPU cache in the system.

However, the GPU implementation scales better for the large dataset (A). Our GPU implementation is 50% more efficient for dataset (A) than for dataset (B). This effect is due to synchronization overhead and GPU utilization. The larger problem is simply more work, with longer average runtimes for all kernels and less frequent pipeline flushes owing to global synchronizations. Given that the small shared memories are not sufficient to cache the large 2 MB working set, almost all computations must stream their inputs and outputs to/from the GPU's DRAM. As discussed in the previous section, memory bandwidth is the most important microarchitectural resource for all of this algorithm's operations. If there is not enough concurrency to adequately compensate for the large DRAM access latency, performance will suffer. This is precisely the reason for the relative inefficiency of the GPU parallelization.

45.5 DISCUSSION AND CONCLUSION

In the previous section, we discussed how our GPU implementation is more efficient with larger problem sizes, as smaller problems are less capable of saturating the GPU's execution and memory access pipelines. This leads one to wonder why we did not implement the reconstruction so that multiple 2-D problems could be in flight simultaneously on each GPU. The "one problem per GPU" decision is due to the relative inflexibility of the CUFFT 2.3 API. In particular, in CUFFT 2.3 2-D transforms cannot be batched, and they cannot be non-unit stride. Additionally, the CUFFT optimized routines can be called only from the CPU host, rather than from inside device code. As a result of these restrictions, the only practical way to perform Fourier transforms in our context is to "serialize" our many 2-D transforms, and allow CUFFT to leverage the moderate parallelism within each transform. FFTs require substantial synchronization, and our 2-D FFTs are not very large — in particular, the size of the 2-D problems listed in Table 45.1. Thus, the FFTs are relatively inefficient.

One particularly interesting alternate parallelization strategy is to execute each 2-D problem in a single thread block. Each 2-D problem typically requires less than 100 MB of DRAM, and the GPU's global memory capacity can easily support hundreds of 2-D problems in flight simultaneously. A 32-channel problem requires substantially more memory, but would still allow for nearly full occupancy, especially if the memory footprint is reduced by implementing the calibration interpolation in the Fourier-domain, as discussed in Section 45.3.1.

The recently released CUFFT 3.0 allows batched FFTs of any dimensionality, via the `cufftPlanMany` API. Thus, we could have many 2-D Fourier transforms in flight simultaneously; however, the 2-D problems must synchronize at least twice per iteration: the CUFFT routines can be called only from the CPU host, and two transforms (forward and inverse) are preformed per iteration. Thus, CUFFT presents a middle-ground solution that could provide higher FFT performance, but still require frequent global syncrhonizations.

Despite the inefficiency of the current parallelization strategy, the $40\times$ speedup for the largest (and most important) datasets has proven sufficient for clinical applicability of the ℓ1-SPIRiT technique. Our software has been deployed in a clinical setting for six months at the time of this writing and has reconstructed thousands of MRI scans. The largest of datasets, e.g., dataset A in Table 45.1, reconstruct in under a minute, and most datasets reconstruct in 20–30 seconds. Such runtimes are short enough that the radiologist prescribing scans will scarcely notice them.

References

[1] OpenMP: an API for shared-memory parallel programming in C/C++ and FORTRAN, http://www.openmp.org.

[2] M.T. Alley, P.J. Beatty, A. Hsiao, S.S. Vasanawala, Reducing the scan time of time-resolved, 3d phase contrast imaging with 2d autocalibrated parallel imaging, in: ISMRM, 2010.

[3] S. Boyd, L. Vandenberghe, Convex Optimization, Cambridge University Press, 2004.

[4] E. Candes, J. Romberg, T. Tao, Robust uncertainty principles: exact signal reconstruction from highly incomplete frequency information (2004).

[5] M. Lustig, J.M. Pauly, SPIRiT: iterative self-consistent parallel imaging reconstruction from arbitrary k-space, Magn. Reson. Med. (2010).

[6] M.W. Marcellin, M.J. Gormish, A. Bilgin, M.B. Boliek, An overview of JPEG-2000, 2000.

Medical Image Processing Using GPU-Accelerated ITK Image Filters

46

Won-Ki Jeong, Hanspeter Pfister, Massimiliano Fatica

46.1 INTRODUCTION

In this chapter we introduce GPU acceleration techniques for medical image processing using the insight segmentation and registration toolkit (ITK) [1]. ITK is one of the most widely used open-source software toolkits for segmentation and registration of medical images from CT and MRI scanners. It consists of a collection of state-of-the-art image processing and analysis algorithms that often require a lot of computational resources. Although many image processing algorithms are data-parallel problems that can benefit from GPU computing, the current ITK image filters provide only limited parallel processing for certain types of image filters. The coarse-grain parallel multithreading model employed by the current ITK implementation splits the input image into multiple chunks and assigns a thread for each piece, taking advantage of the capabilities of multiprocessor shared-memory systems (Figure 46.1). However, the performance increase as the number of cores grows is sublinear owing to memory bottlenecks.

Because many ITK image filters are embarrassingly parallel and do not require interthread communication, we can exploit the fine-grain data parallelism of the GPU [4]. To validate these ideas we implemented several low-level ITK image processing algorithms, such as convolution, statistical, and PDE-based de-noising filters, using NVIDIA's CUDA. We have two main goals in this work:

- Outlining a simple and easy approach to integrate CUDA code into ITK with only minimal modification of existing ITK code
- Demonstrating efficient GPU implementations of spatial-domain image processing algorithms.

We believe that our approach gives developers a practical guide to easily integrate their GPU code into ITK, allowing researchers to use GPU-accelerated ITK filters to accelerate their research and scientific discovery.

46.2 CORE METHODS

We implemented three widely used spatial-domain image processing algorithms [2]: linear convolution, median filter, and anisotropic diffusion (Figure 46.2).

Thread 1

Thread 2

Thread n

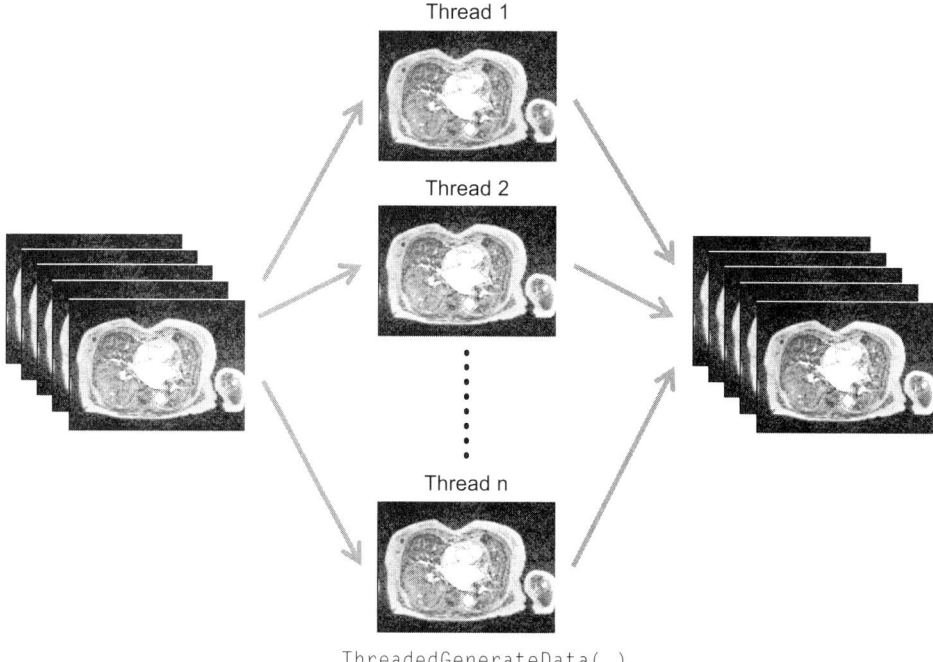

ThreadedGenerateData( )

FIGURE 46.1

Coarse-grain parallelism implemented in current ITK image filters.

Linear convolution: Linear convolution is the process of computing a linear combination of neighboring pixels using a predefined set of weights, that is, a weight *mask*, that is common for all pixels in the image (Figure 46.3). The Gaussian, mean, derivative, and Hessian of Gaussian ITK filters belong to this category. Linear convolution for a pixel at location (x, y) in the image I using a mask K of size $M \times N$ is computed as:

$$I_{new}(x, y) = \sum_{s=-a}^{a} \sum_{t=-b}^{b} K(s, t) I(x + s, y + t), \tag{46.1}$$

where I_{new} is the new image after filtering. Assuming without loss of generality that the domain is a two-dimensional image, the mask K is symmetric along the x and y axis, and M and N are odd numbers, then $a = (M - 1)/2$, and $b = (N - 1)/2$. Figure 46.3 shows the linear convolution process in the image domain using a 3×3 mean filter mask as an example.

This type of filter maps very effectively to the GPU for several reasons. First, convolution is an embarrassingly data-parallel task because each pixel value can be independently computed. We can assign one GPU thread per pixel, and there is no interthread communication during the computation. Second, the same convolution mask K is applied to every pixel, leading to SIMD (single instruction multiple data)-friendly computation. Last, only adjacent neighbor pixels are used for the

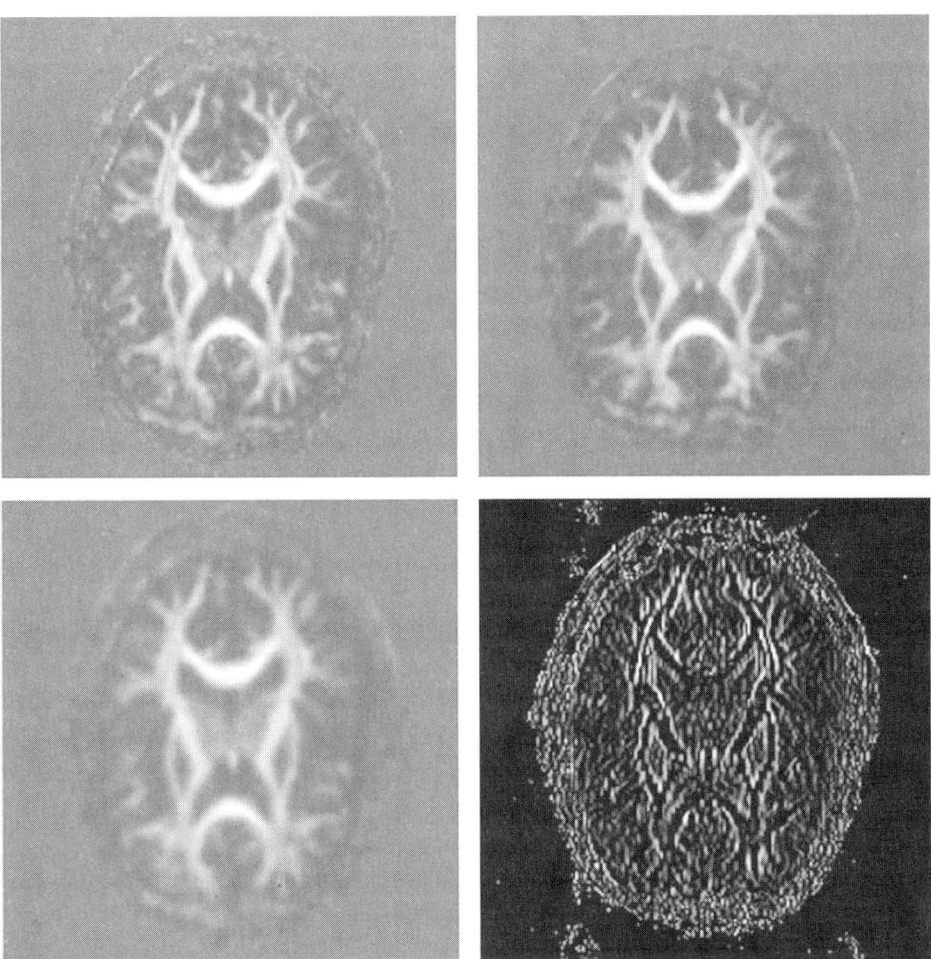

FIGURE 46.2

ITK image filtering results. Top left: Input image. Top right: Median filter. Bottom left: Gaussian filter. Bottom right: Magnitude of gradient filter.

computation, leading to highly spatial coherent memory access. See Section 46.3.2 for implementation details.

Median filter: The ITK median filter belongs to the category of statistical filters where the new pixel value is determined based on the local nonlinear statistics; that is, the median of neighboring pixels. The filter is mainly used to remove salt-and-pepper noise while preserving or enhancing edges (Figure 46.2). Although each pixel value can be computed independently, computing nonlinear statistics is not a GPU-friendly task. We overcome this problem by employing a bisection search technique that can be implemented more efficiently on the GPU than naive per-pixel histogram computation (see Section 46.3.3).

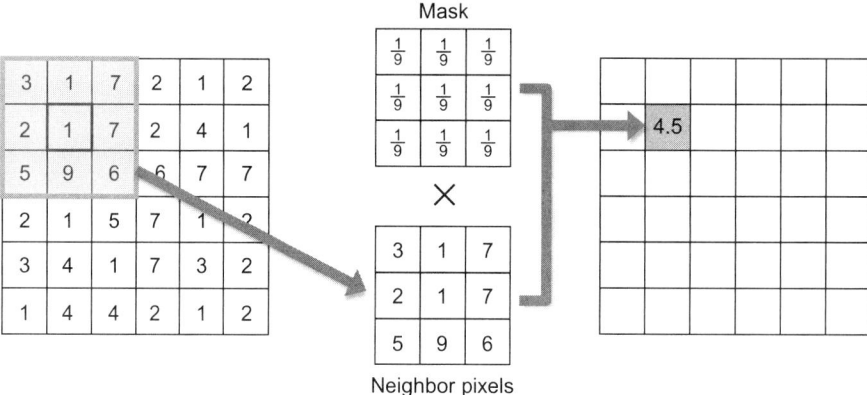

FIGURE 46.3

Linear convolution with a mean filter mask.

Anisotropic diffusion: The anisotropic diffusion filter we implemented solves a gradient-based non-linear partial differential equation (PDE) first introduced by Perona and Malik [5]. The filter mimics the process of heat dispersion in inhomogeneous materials to remove image noise while preserving important features. The PDE is defined as follows:

$$\frac{\partial I}{\partial t} = \nabla \cdot (c(||\nabla I||)\nabla I). \tag{46.2}$$

The amount of diffusion per pixel is anisotropically defined by the diffusivity term $c(x)$. This is a fall-off function; for example, $c(x) = e^{-\frac{x^2}{k^2}}$ applied to the gradient magnitude $||\nabla I||$ at each pixel. There are several different implementation variants of Perona and Malik's diffusion PDE, but we follow the approach proposed in the original paper. In order to solve the PDE we discretize the equation using a finite difference method and employ an iterative Euler integration method to calculate the solution. Our GPU numerical solver can be applied to a wide range of partial differential equations (see Section 46.3.4).

46.3 IMPLEMENTATION

In this section, first we will describe how to integrate GPU code written in NVIDIA CUDA into existing ITK code. Then, we will discuss the GPU implementation details of each ITK image filter.

46.3.1 Integration of NVIDIA CUDA Code into ITK

To integrate GPU code into ITK we needed to modify some common ITK files and add new files into the ITK code base. We have edited or added source code into the `Code/BasicFilters` and `Code/Common` directories and added a new directory `Code/CUDA` where all CUDA source code (.cu) as well as related headers are located. Two new functions, `checkCUDA()` and `initCUDA()`, are introduced to check the availability of a GPU and to initialize it, respectively.

Our approach to integrate CUDA code into ITK is to make it transparent to the users so that any application program written using the previous ITK library does not need to be modified. To use GPU functionality the application code needs only to be re-compiled and linked against our new ITK library. To selectively execute either CPU or GPU versions of the ITK filters, the user sets the operating system environment variable ITK_CUDA accordingly. The entry points for each ITK image filter are the new member functions ThreadedGenerateData() (for multithreaded filters) or GenerateData() (for single-threaded filters) that implement the actual filter operations. Inside these functions we check the ITK_CUDA flag using the checkCUDA() function to branch the execution path to either the CPU or GPU at runtime. Figure 46.4 shows a code snippet of ThreadedGenerateData() in itkMean-ImageFilter.txx that shows how existing ITK filters can be modified to selectively execute GPU or CPU code.

```
Template<class TInputImage, class TOutputImage>
void
MeanImageFilter<TInputImage, TOutputImage>
::ThreadedGenerateData(const OutputImageRegionType& outputRegionForThread,
                        int threadId)
{
      unsigned int i;
      ZeroFluxNeumannBoundaryCondition<InputImageType> nbc;

      ConstNeighborhoodIterator<InputImageType> bit;
      ImageRegionIterator<OutputImageType> it;

      // Allocate output
      typename OutputImageType::Pointer output = this->GetOutput();
      typename InputImageType::ConstPointer input = this->GetInput();

      if( checkCUDA() )                              Check GPU flag and launch CUDA code
      {
            cudaMeanImageFilter<InputImageType, OutputImageType,
               InputSizeType>(input, output, m_Radius);
      }
      else
      {

            // Find the data-set boundary "faces"
            typename NeighborhoodAlgorithm::ImageBoundaryFacesCalculator<
               InputImageType>::FaceListType faceList;
            NeighborhoodAlgorithm::ImageBoundaryFacesCalculator<InputImageType>bC;
            faceList = bC(input, outputRegionForThread, m_Radius);
                                                         ⋮
                                                     Original ITK code
```

FIGURE 46.4

Code snippet of the modified itkMeanImage Filter.txx that incorporates CUDA code.

Each GPU filter consists of host code written in C++ that runs on the CPU with calls to the CUDA runtime and GPU kernel code written in CUDA that is called by the host code. When a GPU ITK filter is launched, the host code dynamically allocates GPU memory, copies the input ITK image and filter parameters to GPU memory (e.g., `input`, `output`, and `m_Radius` in Figure 46.4), and launches the GPU kernel to perform the actual computation. Once kernel execution has finished, the host code copies the results from GPU memory to the output ITK image.

In the GPU kernel code we have to pay special attention to dealing with different pixel formats and input image dimensions. The current CUDA ITK implementation can handle two- and three-dimensional images and 8-bit unsigned char or 32-bit float pixel types. In older versions of CUDA, each type of conversion has to be explicitly done by implementing a separate GPU kernel for each possible input and output pixel type. However, this limitation no longer exists in the newer CUDA compilers (version 3.0 and beyond) that support C++ templates.

We now describe the details of the GPU data structures and parallel algorithms for the different image filters discussed in Section 46.2.

46.3.2 Linear Convolution Filters

The linear convolution filters we implemented — mean, Gaussian, derivative, and Hessian of Gaussian — are separable. Therefore, an n-dimensional convolution can be implemented as a product of one-dimensional convolutions along each axis, which reduce the per-pixel computational complexity from $O(m^n)$ to $O(nm)$, where m is the kernel size along one axis and n is the dimension of the input image. We implemented a general one-dimensional CUDA convolution filter and applied it along each axis successively using the corresponding filter mask weights.

For a filter mask of size n, there are $2n$ memory reads (n mask reads, n neighbor pixel value reads), and $2n - 1$ floating-point operations (n multiplications and $n - 1$ addition). Because a global memory fetch instruction is more expensive compared with a single floating-point instruction and there are roughly the same number of memory and floating-point instructions, our problem is memory bound. Therefore, we mainly focus on optimizing memory access in our GPU filter implementation.

Data layout: The convolution filters use local neighbors to compute the weighted average, and each pixel is used multiple times by its neighbors. Therefore, bringing spatially close pixel values into the fast GPU shared memory or texture cache and sharing them between threads in the same thread block reduces global memory bandwidth. In our filter implementations we use shared memory. In addition, the filter mask is identical for every pixel. We precompute the filter mask weights in the host code and copy them to the GPU's constant memory so that all GPU threads can share it via a cache.

To further minimize the data transfer time between global and shared memory, we configure the dimension of the CUDA thread block such that adjacent kernels do not overlap. Figure 46.5 (upper row) shows an example of splitting the domain into regular-shaped blocks, which results in additional global memory access in the region where kernels overlap (between the dotted lines). Instead, we can split the domain into elongated blocks (bottom left) to eliminate kernel overlap (bottom right).

Filter weight computation: The weights for a mean filter mask are 1/(kernel size) and the one-dimensional Gaussian weights are normalized (e.g., (0.006, 0.061, 0.242, 0.383, 0.242, 0.061, 0.006) for unit standard deviation). We use central-difference weights (0.5, 0, −0.5) and (0.25, −0.5, 0.25) for

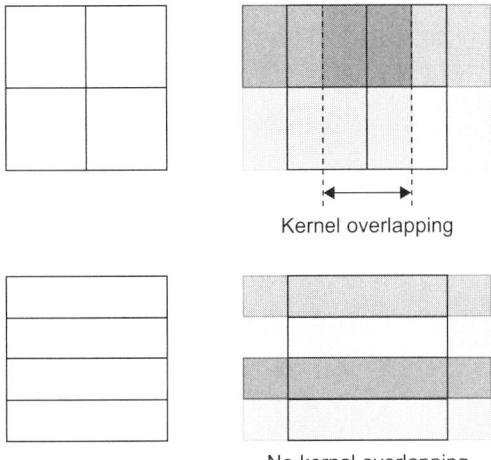

Kernel overlapping

No kernal overlapping

FIGURE 46.5

Kernels overlap on regular shaped blocks (top). No kernel overlapping on elongated blocks (bottom). Rectangles on the left column are CUDA blocks. Shaded rectangles on the right column are memory regions to be copied to shared memory for each block.

the first and second derivative filters, respectively. The Hessian of Gaussian filter computes the second derivatives of the Gaussian. For example, a 3-D Hessian of Gaussian matrix is defined as follows:

$$H(G \star I) = \begin{bmatrix} \dfrac{\partial^2(G \star I)}{\partial x^2} & \dfrac{\partial^2(G \star I)}{\partial x \partial y} & \dfrac{\partial^2(G \star I)}{\partial x \partial z} \\[2ex] & \dfrac{\partial^2(G \star I)}{\partial y^2} & \dfrac{\partial^2(G \star I)}{\partial y \partial z} \\[2ex] & & \dfrac{\partial^2(G \star I)}{\partial z^2} \end{bmatrix}$$

Each tensor component is the second derivative of the image convolved with a Gaussian filter mask. This can be naively implemented by successively applying Gaussian and derivative filters. However, it is better to combine two convolutions into a single convolution filter because the combination of two separable filters is also separable. Therefore, each tensor component can be computed by applying the corresponding 1-D convolution filter along each axis. For example, $\frac{\partial^2(G \star I)}{\partial x^2}$ can be computed by applying a 1-D second-order derivative of Gaussian filter along the x-axis followed by applying a 1-D Gaussian filter along the y and z axes. The weights for the 1-D derivative Gaussian filter can be calculated algebraically, as shown in Figure 46.6.

46.3.3 Median Filter

The median filter is a nonlinear statistical filter that replaces the current pixel value with the median value of pixels in the neighboring region. A naive implementation first creates a cumulative histogram

```
float kernelsum = 0;
```

```
for(int i=0; i<=halfKernelWidth; i++)                    Compute Gaussian filter weights
{
    float val;
    float _x = i;     // distance from the center
    val = 1.0f/exp((_x*_x)/(2.0f*w_sigma*w_sigma));
    kernelsum += val;
    if(i > 0) kernelsum += val;
    h_kernel[0][halfKernelWidth+i] = h_kernel[0][halfKernelWidth-i] = val;
}
```

```
for(int i=0; i<maxKernelWidth; i++)              Compute first/second derivatives of Gaussian
{
    float _x = i - halfKernelWidth;
    h_kernel[0][i] /= kernelsum;     // normalization
    h_kernel[1][i] = (_x/(-(w_sigma*w_sigma)))*h_kernel[0][i];
    h_kernel[2][i] = ((1-(_x/w_sigma)*(_x/w_sigma))/(-(w_sigma*w_sigma)))
                    *h_kernel[0][i];
}
```

FIGURE 46.6

Computing weights for the zero-, first-, and second-order derivatives of a Gaussian filter.

for the neighbor region and then finds the first index beyond half the number of pixels in the histogram. The major problem of this approach on the GPU is that each thread needs to compute a complete histogram, and therefore 256 histogram bins have to be allocated per pixel for an 8-bit image. This is inefficient on current GPUs because there are not enough hardware registers available for each thread, and using global memory for histogram computation is simply too slow.

To avoid this problem, our implementation is based on a bisection search on histogram ranges proposed in [6]. This method does not compute the actual histogram but iteratively refines the histogram range that includes the median value. During each iteration, the current valid range is divided into two halves, and the half that has the larger number of pixels is chosen for the next round. This process is repeated until the range converges to a single bin. This approach requires $\log_2$(number of bins) iterations to converge. For example, an image with an 8-bit pixel depth (256 bins) requires only eight iterations to compute the median. Figure 46.7 shows an example of this histogram bisection scheme for eight histogram bins.

Because we do not want to store the entire histogram but want to keep track of only a valid range for each thread, we have to scan all the neighbor pixels in each iteration to refine the range. This leads to a computational complexity of $O(m \log_2 n)$, where n is the number of histogram bins (a constant for a given pixel format) and m is the number of neighboring pixels to compute the median (a variable depending on the filter size). To minimize the $O(m)$ factor, we store neighboring pixels in shared memory and reuse them multiple times. Similar performance can be achieved using texture memory instead of shared memory.

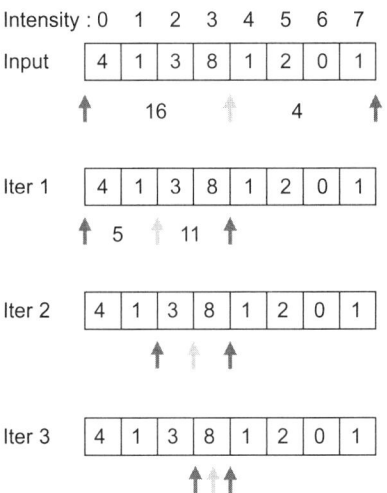

```
// Current block (input) is in shared memory

min = 0;
max = 255;
pivot = (min+max)/2.0f;
For(i=0; i<8; i++)
{
    count = 0;
    For(j=0; j<filtersize; j++)
    {
        if(input[j] > pivot) count++;
    }

    if(count < filtersize/2) max = floor(pivot);
    else min = ceil(pivot);
    pivot = (min + max)/2.0f;
}

return floor(pivot);
```

FIGURE 46.7

A pictorial example (left) and pseudocode (right) of the histogram bisection scheme. This example is based on eight histogram bins (i.e., 3 bits per pixels). Left: Dark grey arrows indicate the current valid range, and the light grey arrow (described as `pivot` in the pseudocode on the right) indicates the location of the median bin.

46.3.4 Anisotropic Diffusion Filter

A numerical solution of Equation 46.2 can be calculated using a standard finite difference method [3], where time discretization is approximated by a forward explicit Euler method as follows:

$$\frac{I^{k+1} - I^k}{dt} = \nabla \cdot (c(||\nabla I^k||)\nabla I^k). \tag{46.3}$$

We approximate the right side of Equation 46.3 using one-sided gradients and conductance values defined at the center of adjacent pixels (light grey crosses in Figure 46.8). The solution can be computed by iteratively updating the image using the following formula (for the 2-D case):

$$I^{k+1} = I^k + dt(c(||I_{x+}||)I_{x+} - c(||I_{x-}||)I_{x-} + c(||I_{y+}||)I_{y+} - c(||I_{y-}||)I_{y-}), \tag{46.4}$$

where $I_{\pm}$ are one-sided gradients computed using forward/backward differences along an axis. For example, the one-sided gradients at the pixel location (i,j) along the x-axis can be computed as follows:

$$I_{x+}(i,j) = \frac{I(i+1,j) - I(i,j)}{h_x}$$

$$I_{x-}(i,j) = \frac{I(i,j) - I(i-1,j)}{h_x},$$

where h_x is the grid spacing along the x-axis (Figure 46.8).

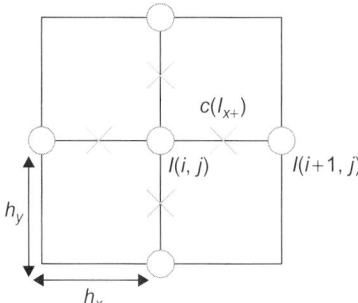

FIGURE 46.8

The grid setup for the derivative approximation and conductance computation in the 2-D case. The circles are pixel values, and crosses are conductance values defined in the middle between adjacent pixels.

Each pixel value is used multiple times — for example, four times for 2-D and six times for 3-D — to compute the one-sided gradients and conductance values. We precompute the one-sided gradients and conductance values per pixel and store them in shared memory to eliminate redundant computation and to reduce global memory access. The preprocessing step is done per block right before the actual Euler integration in the same CUDA kernel. Note that $I_{x+}(i,j) = I_{x-}(i+1,j)$. Therefore, we need to precompute only one one-sided gradient image per axis instead of computing all forward and backward gradients. For example, for an $n \times n$ 2-D block, we first copy $(n+2) \times (n+2)$ pixels (current block and its adjacent neighbor pixels) from global to shared memory and then compute four $(n+1) \times (n+1)$ lookup tables for forward gradients and conductance values for the x and y directions, respectively. We thereby reduce not only the shared memory footprint but also the computation time by half. Backward gradients and their conductance values can be accessed by simply shifting the index by -1.

We use the Jacobi method to iteratively update the solution. In the Jacobi method, each pixel can be independently processed without communicating with others, mapping naturally to the GPU's massively parallel computing model. For each update iteration we use a source and a target buffer. The GPU kernel is allowed to read only from the source buffer and to write only to the target buffer to ensure data consistency. Because a single iteration is running a GPU kernel, the new result must be written back to global memory at the end of each GPU kernel call. The time step dt needs to be set properly so that the iterative process does not diverge. In our experience $dt = 0.25$ for 2-D and $dt = 0.16$ for 3-D work well.

46.4 RESULTS

We tested our GPU ITK filters on a Windows PC equipped with an NVIDIA Quadro FX 5800 GPU, two Intel Xeon Quad-core (total eight cores) CPUs running at 3.0 GHz, and 16 gigabytes of main memory. We used NVIDIA CUDA 2.3 and ITK 3.12 to build the GPU ITK filters. Although this is a first attempt to assess the usability of current GPUs to accelerate existing ITK code, the results look very promising. We measure wall clock time for each filter execution, including CPU-to-GPU data transfer times, to compare the actual application-level performance. Timings are measured in seconds

# iter	2	4	8	16
GPU	0.225	0.308	0.479	0.82
1 CPU	14.9	29.7	59.3	122
2 CPU	9.78	18.6	38.2	76.7
3 CPU	7.89	17	32.2	64.2
4 CPU	7.13	13.7	27.7	58.2
5 CPU	6.3	12.5	25.2	48.2
6 CPU	5.76	10.4	22.4	43.9
7 CPU	4.89	9.86	20.1	40.2
8 CPU	4.08	9.49	19.2	36.9
Speedup	18x	30.8x	40x	45x

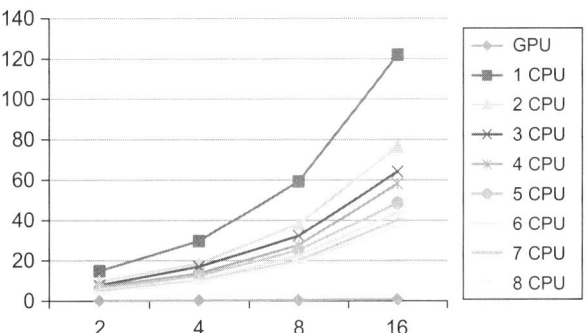

FIGURE 46.9

Running time comparison of the anisotropic diffusion filter.

Variance	1	2	4	8
GPU	0.177	0.178	0.176	0.177
1 CPU	3.51	4.11	5.01	7.07
2 CPU	2.96	3.21	5.04	6.18
3 CPU	1.36	2.94	4.12	5.5
4 CPU	1.09	2.9	3.24	5.03
5 CPU	0.934	2.82	2.86	4.6
6 CPU	0.811	2.9	3.08	4.35
7 CPU	0.738	2.84	2.48	4.24
8 CPU	0.785	2.65	2.39	3.33
Speedup	4.1x	14.8x	13.5x	18.8x

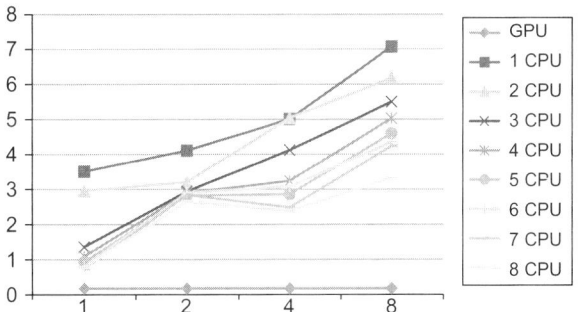

FIGURE 46.10

Running time comparison of the Gaussian filter.

for a $256 \times 256 \times 256$ 3-D volume dataset. Our GPU ITK filters on a single GPU are up to 45 times faster than the multithreaded ITK filters on *eight* CPU cores.

We observed the biggest speedup for the anisotropic diffusion filter. As clearly visible in Figure 46.9, the iterative Jacobi update on a regular grid is an embarrassingly parallel task, resulting in a huge speedup on the GPU. In addition, we have observed that the current ITK anisotropic diffusion filter does not scale well to many CPU cores (only up to 4× speedup on eight CPU cores).

Convolution filters also map well on the GPU. Figure 46.10 shows the running times of the ITK discrete Gaussian filter and our GPU implementation. The GPU version runs up to 19 times faster than the CPU version on eight CPU cores. In addition, the GPU version runs much faster for large kernel sizes because more processor time is spent on computation rather than I/O. Similar to the anisotropic filter, the current ITK Gaussian filter does not scale well to multiple CPU cores.

Finally, our GPU median filter runs up to eight times faster than the current ITK median filter (Figure 46.11). Because statistical filters cannot be easily parallelized on SIMD architectures, the performance of our GPU median filter is acceptable. In addition, the GPU version is still roughly 20× faster if it is compared with the result on a single CPU core.

Kernel size	3	5	7	9
GPU	0.279	0.929	2.24	4.42
1 CPU	6.55	14.4	42.3	99.5
2 CPU	4.03	11.2	21.4	48.4
3 CPU	3.14	7.35	16.5	34.4
4 CPU	2.24	5.88	12.8	28.1
5 CPU	6.3	5.91	11	23.6
6 CPU	5.16	4.94	9.04	20.3
7 CPU	4.72	4.65	8.32	18
8 CPU	4.46	3.99	7.92	16.6
Speedup	8x	4.2x	3.5x	3.7x

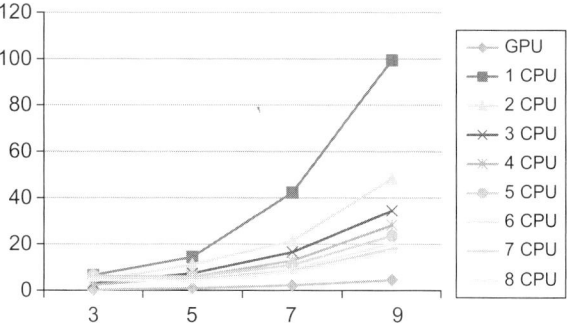

FIGURE 46.11

Running time comparison of the median diffusion filter.

In summary, we demonstrated that GPU computing can greatly boost the performance of existing ITK image filters. In addition, we introduced a simple approach to integrate CUDA code into the existing ITK code by modifying the entry point of each filter. Using only a single GPU easily beats eight CPU cores for all tests we performed, thus confirming the great potential of GPUs for highly parallel computing tasks. The current implementation is open source and can be downloaded at http://sourceforge.net/projects/cudaitk/ and used freely without any restriction for non-commercial use.

46.5 FUTURE DIRECTIONS

Although our prototype GPU ITK filters have shown promising results, we have found several fundamental problems in the current implementation that may degrade their efficiency in a more complicated setup. First, our GPU implementation does not provide a native ITK GPU image class or data structure that supports the pipelining of ITK filters — a common strategy in ITK workflows. Therefore, in the current implementation, the entire image data must be copied between CPU and GPU memory at the end of each filter execution. This may become a significant bottleneck for pipelining multiple filters for large images because the data must travel through the PCI-e bus repeatedly. Developing a new ITK native GPU image class that supports pipelining on GPU memory would solve this issue. Another problem is that the current ITK image filters had to be rewritten from scratch to run on the GPU because easy-to-use GPU template code is not readily available. Another target for future work will be GPU image filter templates or operators that provide basic functions to access and manipulate image data and that may help developers to easily implement additional GPU filters.

46.6 ACKNOWLEDGMENTS

This work was supported in part by the National Science Foundation under Grant No. PHY-0835713 and through generous support from NVIDIA. Won-Ki Jeong accomplished this work during his summer internship at NVIDIA in 2007.

References

[1] The Insight Segmentation and Registration Toolkit. http://www.itk.org, 2010.

[2] R.C. Gonzalez, R.E. Woods, Digital image processing, second ed., Prentice-Hall, Saddle River, NJ, 2006.

[3] K.W. Morton, D.F. Mayers, Numerical solution of partial differential equations: an introduction, Cambridge University Press, New York, 2005.

[4] J.D. Owens, D. Luebke, N. Govindaraju, M. Harris, J. Krger, A.E. Lefohn, et al., A survey of general-purpose computation on graphics hardware, Comput. Graph. Forum 26 (1) (2007) 80–113.

[5] P. Perona, J. Malik, Scale-space and edge detection using anisotropic diffusion, IEEE Trans. PAMI 12 (7) (1990) 629–639.

[6] I. Viola, A. Kanitsar, M.E. Groller, Hardware-based nonlinear filtering and segmentation using high-level shading languages, in: G. Turk, J.J. van Wijk, R.J. Moorhead (Eds.), Proceedings of the 14th IEEE Visualization 2003 (VIS'03), 19–24 October 2003, Seattle, WA, IEEE Computer Society, Washington, DC, 2003, p. 41.

Deformable Volumetric Registration Using B-Splines

James Shackelford, Nagarajan Kandasamy, Gregory Sharp

This chapter shows how to develop a B-spline-based deformable registration algorithm within the single instruction multiple thread (SIMT) model to effectively leverage the large number of processing cores available in modern GPUs. We focus on improving processing speed without sacrificing quality to make the use of deformable registration more viable within the medical community. Performance results on a Tesla C1060 show that for large images, our GPU algorithm achieves a speedup of 15 times over a single-threaded CPU implementation. Moreover, the CPU and GPU versions achieve near-identical registration quality.

47.1 INTRODUCTION

Modern imaging techniques such as X-ray computed tomography (CT), positron emission tomography (PET), and magnetic resonance imaging (MRI) provide physicians with 3-D image volumes of patient anatomy that convey information instrumental in treating a wide range of afflictions. It is often useful to register one image volume to another in order to understand how anatomy has changed over time or to relate image volumes obtained via different imaging techniques.

The volumetric registration process consists of aligning two or more 3-D images into a common coordinate frame. Fusing multiple images in this fashion provides physicians with a more complete understanding of patient anatomy and function. A registration is called *rigid* if the motion or change is limited to global rotations and translations, and is called *deformable* when the registration includes complex local variations. Rigid matching is appropriate for serial imaging of the skull, brain, or other rigidly immobilized sites. Deformable registration is appropriate for almost all other scenarios and is useful for many applications within medical research, medical diagnosis, and interventional treatments. Ideally, deformable registration will replace rigid registration to improve the geometric precision of a variety of medical procedures.

To date, several deformable registration algorithms have been proposed and validated, including demons registration [9], viscous fluid registration [3], B-spline registration [5], and thin-plate splines [2]. Spline-based registration methods are popular because their flexibility and robustness provide the ability to perform both uni-modal and multimodal registration. However, spline-based registration is computationally intensive and reports of algorithms requiring hours to compute for high-image resolutions are not uncommon, even on modern CPUs [1, 4]. Therefore, these registration techniques are not generally accepted in clinical practice.

A key element in accelerating medical imaging algorithms is the use of parallel processing because, in many cases, operations can be performed independently on different portions of the image. For deformable registration, a number of GPU implementations focus on uni-modal registration using demons or optical flow [7, 8]. Recent work has also focused on accelerating B-spline interpolation using GPUs [6].

This chapter develops a data-parallel method of performing deformable image registration using uniform cubic B-splines. The methods and data structures developed herein provide the means to leverage the fine grain parallelism provided by the CUDA programming model, allowing the deformable registration process to be accelerated significantly.

47.2 AN OVERVIEW OF B-SPLINE REGISTRATION

The B-spline deformable registration algorithm maps each and every voxel in a fixed image F to a corresponding voxel in a moving image M. This mapping is described by a deformation field v, which is defined at each and every voxel within the fixed image. An optimal deformation field accurately describes how the voxels in the moving image have been displaced with respect to their original positions in the fixed image. Naturally, this assumes that the two images are of the same scene taken at different times using similar or different imaging modalities. As we will see, finding such an optimal deformation field is an iterative process.

47.2.1 Using B-Splines to Represent the Deformation Field

In the case of B-spline registration, the dense deformation field v is parameterized by a sparse set of control points, which are uniformly distributed throughout the fixed image's voxel grid. This results in the formation of two grids that are aligned to one another: a dense voxel grid and a sparse control point grid. In this scheme, the control point grid partitions the voxel grid into many equally sized regions called *tiles*. A spline curve is a type of continuous curve defined by a sparse set of discrete control points. The number of control points required for each dimension is $n + 1$ where n is the order of the employed spline curve. Because we are working with cubic B-splines, we require four control points in each dimension, which results in a 64 (4^3) control point requirement for each tile. The deformation field at any given voxel within a tile is computed by utilizing the 64 control points in the immediate vicinity of the tile. Furthermore, because we are working in three dimensions, three coefficients (P_x, P_y, and P_z) are associated with each control point, one for each dimension. Mathematically, the x-component of the deformation field for a voxel located at coordinates (x, y, z) in the fixed image can be described as:

$$v_x(x, y, z) = \sum_{l=0}^{3} \sum_{m=0}^{3} \sum_{n=0}^{3} \beta_l(u) \beta_m(v) \beta_n(w) P_x(i + l, j + m, k + n). \tag{47.1}$$

The y- and z-components are defined similarly. Here, (i, j, k) denote the coordinates of the tile within the volume, β is the B-spline basis function and (u, v, w) are the local coordinates of voxel (x, y, z) within its housing tile. It should be noted that the B-spline basis function is defined only within the range between 0 and 1, and so, the local coordinates are appropriately normalized to fall within this range. The symbols l, m, and n are used to index the control points in the neighborhood of the tile — for the 3-D case there are 64 l, m, n combinations.

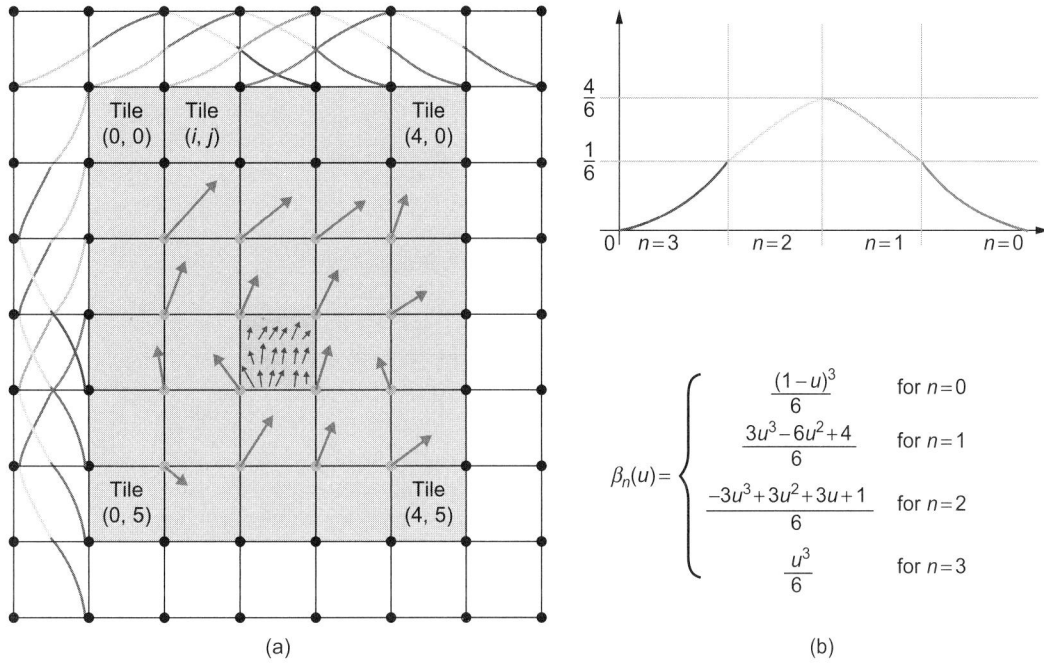

FIGURE 47.1

A graphical example of computing the deformation field from B-spline coefficients in two-dimensions. (a) The 16 control points needed to compute the deformation field within the highlighted tile are shown in gray. The smaller arrows represent the deformation vectors associated with each voxel within the tile. (b) Uniform cubic B-spline basis function plotted (top) and written as a piecewise algebraic equation (bottom).

Figure 47.1 visualizes the computation of the deformation field within a single tile for a two-dimensional image. Because this example is 2-D, only 16 (4^2) control points are required to compute the deformation field for any given tile — the 16 needed to compute the deformation field within the highlighted tile have been drawn in gray, whereas all the other control points are drawn in black. Each of these control points has associated with it two coefficients (P_x and P_y), which are depicted as the x and y components of the larger arrows. The B-spline basis functions β_l and β_m have been superimposed on the grid's x and y axis, respectively, to aid in understanding. The smaller arrows represent the deformation field, which is obtained by computing v_x and v_y for each voxel within the tile. The 3-D case is similar, but requires the additional computation of v_z at each voxel.

47.2.2 Computing the Cost Function

Now that we have a working understanding of how the deformation field can be described in terms of a sparse array of B-spline coefficients, we can begin to search for the optimal deformation field. This is accomplished by optimizing the B-spline coefficients, but in order to do this, we must first quantitatively define what makes a set of coefficients either favorable or unfavorable. We set these criteria by employing a cost function.

The cost function is a single quantity that is computed for a given set of B-spline coefficients to determine their favorability. It is constructed such that coefficients yielding better registrations produce a lower cost, while coefficients producing poorer registration result in a higher cost. Recall that a better registration results in a mapping between the fixed and moving images, causing them to appear more similar. As a result, the cost function is sometimes also referred to as a similarity metric. Here, we will employ the sum of squared differences (SSD) cost function C, which should be suitable for a large majority of applications:

$$C = \frac{1}{N} \sum_z \sum_y \sum_x (M(x + v_x, y + v_y, z + v_z) - F(x, y, z))^2, \tag{47.2}$$

where N denotes the total number of voxels in the moving image M after the application of the deformation field v.

47.2.3 Optimizing the B-Spline Coefficients

Although evaluating the cost function provides a metric for determining the quality of a registration for a given set of coefficients, it provides no insight as to how we can optimize the coefficients to yield an even better registration. However, by taking the derivative of the cost function C with respect to the B-spline coefficients P, we can determine how the cost function changes as the coefficients change. This provides us with the means to conduct an intelligent search for coefficients that cause the cost function to decrease and, thus, obtain a better registration. Such a method of optimization is known as gradient descent and, in this context, the derivative of the cost function is referred to as the cost function gradient. As we move along the cost function gradient, the cost function will decrease until we reach a global (or local) minimum. Although there are more sophisticated methods for optimization, a simple method would be to employ:

$$P_{i+1} = P_i - a_i \frac{\partial C}{\partial P_i} \quad i = 1, 2, 3, \ldots \tag{47.3}$$

where P is a vector comprising the P_x, P_y, and P_z B-spline coefficients, i is the iteration number, and a_i is a scalar gain factor that regulates how fast we descend along the gradient.

To compute the cost function gradient, we begin by utilizing the chain rule to separate the expression into two terms:

$$\frac{\partial C}{\partial P} = \sum_{(x,y,z)} \frac{\partial C}{\partial \vec{v}(x, y, z)} \frac{\partial \vec{v}(x, y, z)}{\partial P}. \tag{47.4}$$

The first term describes how the cost function changes with the deformation field, and because the deformation field is defined at every voxel, so is $\partial C / \partial v$. When using the SSD as the cost function, the first term becomes

$$\frac{\partial C}{\partial \vec{v}(x, y, z)} = [M(x + v_x, y + v_y, z + v_z) - F(x, y, z)] \nabla M(x, y, z). \tag{47.5}$$

Here, $\nabla M(x, y, z)$ is the moving image's spatial gradient. This expression is very similar to the SSD cost function. As a result, the two are best calculated together.

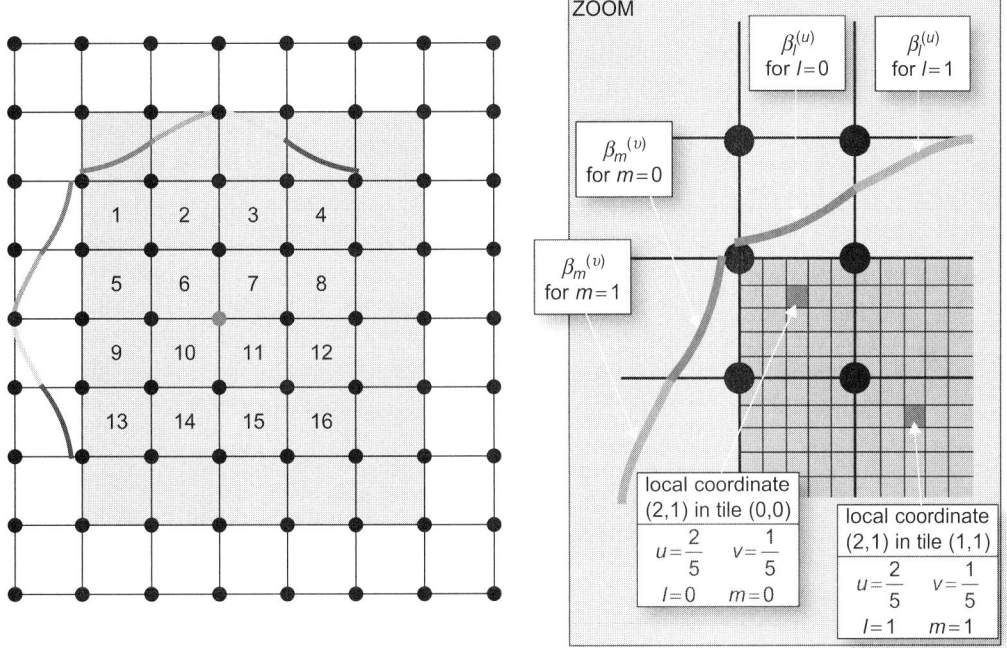

FIGURE 47.2

A 2-D example of parameterizing the cost function gradient using B-splines. Local coordinates are normalized by the number of voxels in the corresponding tile dimensions. This normalization is necessary since the B-spline basis functions are only defined within zero and one.

The second term of the cost function gradient describes how the deformation field changes as the coefficients change. By taking the derivative of v, we find that this term is dependent only on the B-spline basis function:

$$\frac{\partial \vec{v}(x,y,z)}{\partial P} = \sum_{l=0}^{3}\sum_{m=0}^{3}\sum_{n=0}^{3} \beta_l(u)\beta_m(v)\beta_n(w). \tag{47.6}$$

Notice that "transforming" the change in the cost function from being in terms of the deformation field to being in terms of the coefficients requires us to employ the B-spline basis functions once again — essentially the reverse operation of what we did when computing the deformation field. Figure 47.2 graphically depicts the operation of computing the cost function gradient at a single control point (marked in gray). Here, $\partial C / \partial v$ has been computed at all voxels, including the voxel shown in the zoom view at local coordinates $(2, 1)$ in tile $(0, 0)$. The location of this voxel's tile with respect to the gray control point results in the evaluation of the B-spline basis function in both the x and y dimensions. These evaluations are performed at the normalized local coordinates of the voxel; for our voxel this would result in evaluating $\beta_0(2/5)$ for the x-dimension and $\beta_0(1/5)$ for the y-dimension. These two results and the value of $\partial C / \partial v$ at the voxel in question are multiplied together and the product is stored away for later. Once this procedure is performed at every voxel for each tile in the vicinity of the control point, all of the resulting products are summed together. This results in the value of cost function gradient at the control point in question.

Because this example is in 2-D, 16 (4^2) control points are required to parameterize how the cost function changes at any given voxel with respect to the deformation field. As a result, when computing the value of the cost function gradient at a given control point, the 16 tiles the control point affects must be included in the computation — these tiles have been highlighted. Also, notice how each of the highlighted tiles have been marked with a number between 1 and 16. Each number represents the specific combination of B-spline basis function pieces used to compute a tile's contribution to the cost function gradient at the control point. In the 2-D case, it should be noted that each tile will affect exactly 16 control points and will be subjected to each of the 16 possible B-spline combinations exactly once. This is an important property we exploit when parallelizing this algorithm on the GPU.

47.3 IMPLEMENTATION DETAILS

Optimizing the B-spline coefficients is an iterative process. As a result, for every iteration the deformation field must be computed at every voxel, the cost function must be evaluated, the cost function gradient must be computed, and then the optimizer must be invoked to descend along the gradient to produce a new set of coefficients. This entire process is repeated until the cost function reaches a global (or local) minimum or until a user-specified number of iterations have completed. The flow of the algorithm is shown in Figure 47.3. Of the various iterative processes, the only step performed on the CPU is the optimization.

47.3.1 Input, Output, and State

The registration algorithm requires two primary inputs: the moving image M and the fixed image F. The output of the iterative process is P, which holds the set of B-spline coefficients the algorithm is attempting to optimize. Additionally, this array is updated every iteration and essentially represents the current state of the registration. If we wanted to stop the registration and restart it on another computer, for example, we would save the current set of coefficients in order to maintain the state. We use the following variable names for these key elements throughout the code listings: f_img[ ] for the fixed image F (stored in GPU global memory), tex_moving_image for the moving image M (mapped to a texture), and tex_coeff for the coefficient set P (mapped to a texture).

47.3.2 Leveraging the Symmetry Among Tiles

The uniform spacing of control points throughout the voxel grid results in many geometrically identical tiles. This is important because the B-spline basis functions are evaluated at the local coordinates of a voxel within a tile. Because all tiles are geometrically identical, they each possess the same local coordinate system. This results in needing to evaluate the B-spline basis functions for only a single tile because all tiles exhibit symmetry. Furthermore, these function evaluations will remain constant across all registration iterations, so they may be precomputed and stored into a lookup table (LUT) during the initialization phase of the algorithm. We refer to this table as the B-spline LUT, whose construction

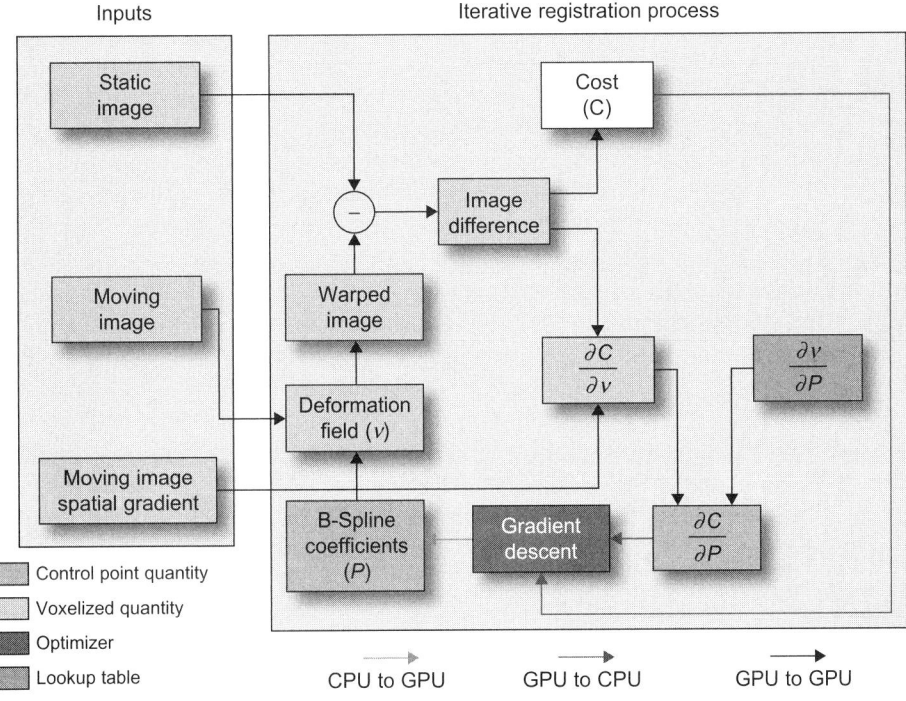

FIGURE 47.3

A flowchart demonstrating the iterative B-spline registration process.

is demonstrated in Listing 47.1. This data structure is used to accelerate both the computation of the deformation field and the cost function gradient.

47.3.3 Initialization

Before the iterative registration process can begin on the GPU, several initialization processes must first be carried out on the CPU in preparation. This consists primarily of initializing the coefficient array P to all zeros, copying data from host memory to GPU memory, and precomputing reusable intermediate values. These precomputed values are stored in lookup tables residing in global memory. The B-spline LUT is bound to a texture reference for accelerated access on the GPU.

Specifically, three lookup tables are generated in the initialization stage: B-spline LUT, the Tile Offset LUT, and the Knot LUT. The B-spline LUT (LUT_Bspline) contains the precomputed B-spline basis function evaluations discussed in Section 47.3.2. The Tile Offset LUT (LUT_Tile_Offsets) is used by the kernel that computes the cost function gradient. Its role is to provide thread blocks with an offset into global memory that defines where their input data begins. The Knot LUT (LUT_Knot) is also used by the kernel computing the cost function gradient. Its role is to provide threads with an offset into global memory that defines where their output data should be written.

```
1    float compute_basis_function (int l, vox_idx, tile_dim)
2    {
3        float u = (float)vox_idx / tile_dim; // normalized coordinate of a voxel within its tile
4        float B;
5
6        switch(l) {
7        case 0:
8            B = (1.0/6.0) * (− 1.0 * u*u*u + 3.0 * u*u − 3.0 * u + 1.0);
9            break;
10       case 1:
11           B = (1.0/6.0) * (+ 3.0 * u*u*u − 6.0 * u*u            + 4.0);
12           break;
13       case 2:
14           B = (1.0/6.0) * (− 3.0 * u*u*u + 3.0 * u*u + 3.0 * u + 1.0);
15           break;
16       case 3:
17           B = (1.0/6.0) * (+ 1.0 * u*u*u);
18           break;
19       default:
20           B = 0.0;
21           break;
22       }
23       return B;
24   }
25
26       ...
27
28       float* LUT_Bspline_x = (float*) malloc (sizeof(float) * tile_dims[0] * 4);
29       float* LUT_Bspline_y = (float*) malloc (sizeof(float) * tile_dims[1] * 4);
30       float* LUT_Bspline_z = (float*) malloc (sizeof(float) * tile_dims[2] * 4);
31
32       int i, j;
33       for (j = 0; j < 4; j++) {
34           for (i = 0; i < tile_dims[0]; i++)
35               LUT_Bspline_x =[j*tile_dims[0] + i] = compute_basis_function (j, i, tile_dims[0]);
36
37           for (i = 0; i < tile_dims[1]; i++)
38               LUT_Bspline_y =[j*tile_dims[1] + i] = compute_basis_function (j, i, tile_dims[1]);
39
40           for (i = 0; i < tile_dims[2]; i++)
41               LUT_Bspline_z =[j*tile_dims[2] + i] = compute_basis_function (j, i, tile_dims[2]);
42       }
43
44       ...
```

Listing 47.1: Building the B-spline LUT.

Lastly, to reduce redundant computations associated with evaluating the cost function C, the spatial gradient of the moving image ∇M (m_grad) is computed (not to be confused with the cost function gradient $\partial C/\partial P$). ∇M is a three-dimensional image volume and does not change throughout the registration process.

47.3.4 **Combining the Cost and $\partial C/\partial v$ Computations**

The evaluation of the cost function C and the computation of its derivative with respect to the deformation field $\partial C/\partial v$ are computed side by side within a single kernel. Both terms are primarily dependent on the computation of $M(x + v_x, y + v_y, z + v_z) - F(x, y, z)$. In the code we call this quantity `diff`, and it is computed for each and every voxel in parallel. This is accomplished by Listing 47.2, which is executed with one thread per each voxel within the fixed image.

Computing the deformation vector field: The majority of the work performed by the preceding kernel is found within the `__device__` function `find_correspondence()` in line 27 and shown in Listing 47.3. This function is responsible for: (1) computing the deformation vector `d` at a thread's assigned fixed image coordinates, (2) computing the corresponding coordinates `m` within the moving image after applying the deformation, and (3) notifying the calling function of voxels that have mapped outside of the moving image. Lines 13–32 perform the operation outlined in Section 47.2.1, namely, computing a single point in the deformation field from the parameterization offered by the B-spline coefficients. Notice that the computation of this single point requires 64 (4^3) control points (i.e., B-spline evaluations) and involves reading 192 (64×3) coefficient values. The B-spline LUTs are intentionally separated in order to take advantage of the caching benefits offered by the texture unit for the inner two loops of the computation (lines 15 and 17). Had we precomputed and stored the products in the lookup table instead (i.e., removed the need for line 18), each load from the lookup table would then be unique, and the caching provided by the texture unit would underutilized. Although this technique requires three table lookups and two multiplies, it is faster than perfoming single loads from a similar lookup table consisting of premultiplied values.

Cost function evaluation: Returning to Listing 47.2, we note that the SSD is computed by writing the squared difference between the fixed image voxel value the executing thread is assigned and its corresponding moving image voxel value to `score[thread_idxg]`, which is an array residing in global memory consisting of as many elements as there are fixed image voxels (lines 42 and 43). After the kernel has completed, a simple sum reduction kernel is employed to sum all of the squared differences, which results in an un-normalized SSD. To obtain the normalized SSD, we divide the result by the number of voxels falling within the moving image. This is obtained by sum reducing `skipped[ ]` and subtracting the result from the number of voxels in the fixed image.

Computation of $\partial C/\partial v$: The change in the cost function with respect to the deformation field $\partial C/\partial v$ is computed within `__device__` function `write_dc_dv()` (line 45) at each voxel by simply multiplying `diff` by the value of the moving image gradient `m_grad[ ]`. Here, `m_grad[ ]` is indexed by `n`, which is the voxel coordinate within the moving image that was obtained by applying the deformation vector `d` to the fixed image coordinate `f`. The computation must be performed three times for each voxel that maps within the moving image, once for each dimension. The results are written to global memory allocated to the arrays `dc_dv_x[ ]`, `dc_dv_y[ ]`, and `dc_dv_z[ ]`. Each dimension is alloted a separate area within the global memory in order to facilitate coalesced memory writes. Additionally, `write_dc_dv()` populates the `dc_dv` arrays according to which tile the thread's assigned voxel fell within. This means that $\partial C/\partial v$ values for voxels falling within the first tile are lumped together in global memory before all of the values for voxels falling within the second tile, and so on. Furthermore, `write_dc_dv` guarantees that the tiles stored within memory in this fashion will contain a multiple of

```
1    // Setup thread attributes
2    int threadsPerBlock = (blockDim.x * blockDim.y * blockDim.z);
3    int blockIdxInGrid  = (gridDim.x * blockIdx.y) + blockIdx.x;
4    int thread_idxl     = (((blockDim.y * threadIdx.z) + threadIdx.y) * blockDim.x) + threadIdx.x;
5    int thread_idxg     = (blockIdxInGrid * threadsPerBlock) + thread_idxl;
6
7    if (thread_idxg > fdim.x * fdim.y * fdim.z) {      // Only process threads that map to voxels
8        return;
9    }
10
11   int4 p;       // tile index
12   int4 q;       // local voxel index (within tile)
13   float3 f;     // distance from origin (in mm )
14
15   float3 m;     // voxel displacement (in mm )
16   float3 n;     // voxel displacement (in vox)
17   int3 n_f;     // voxel displacement floor
18   int3 n_r;     // voxel displacement round
19   float3 d;     // deformation vector
20   int fv;       // fixed voxel
21   fv = thread_idxg;
22
23   // compute tile index and local index of voxel within tile
24   setup_indices (&p, &q, &f, fv, fdim, vpr, rdim, img_origin, img_spacing);
25
26   // compute the deformation vector for the current voxel
27   int fell_out = find_correspondence (&d, &m, &n, f, mov_offset, mov_ps, mdim, cdim, vpr, p, q);
28
29   if (fell_out) {          // vector mapped our voxel outside the moving image.
30       skipped[fv]++;       // this will affect the cost function normalization,
31       return;              // so we record the incident and return
32   }
33
34   // because the voxel is probably mapped between voxels in the moving image,
35   // we retrieve a tri−linearly interpolated intensity value from the moving image
36   float3 li_1, li_2;
37   clamp_linear_interpolate_3d (&n, &n_f, &n_r, &li_1, &li_2, mdim);
38
39   float m_val = get_moving_value (n_f, mdim, li_1, li_2);
40
41   // compute the score and dc_dv
42   float diff = m_val − f_img[fv];
43   score[fv] = diff * diff;
44
45   write_dc_dv (dc_dv_x, dc_dv_y, dc_dv_z, m_grad, diff, n_r, mdim, vpr, pad, p, q);
```

Listing 47.2: kernel_bspline_ssd_dcdv( ).

```
1    __device__ inline int
2    find_correspondence (float3 *d, float3 *m, float3 *n, float3 f, float3 mov_offset,
3                        float3 mov_ps, int3 mdim, int3 cdim, int3 vpr, int4 p, int4 q)
4    {
5        int i, j, k, z, cidx;
6        float A,B,C,P;
7
8        d->x = 0.0f; d->y = 0.0f; d->z = 0.0f;
9
10       // compute the deformation vector of this particular voxel
11       z = 0;
12       for (k = 0; k < 4; k++) {
13       C = tex1Dfetch (tex_LUT_Bspline_x, k * vpr.z + q.z);
14           for (j = 0; j < 4; j++) {
15           B = tex1Dfetch (tex_LUT_Bspline_x, j * vpr.y + q.y);
16               for (i = 0; i < 4; i++) {
17                   A = tex1Dfetch (tex_LUT_Bspline_x, i * vpr.x + q.x);
18                   P = A * B * C;
19
20                   cidx = 3 * ((p.z + k) * cdim.x * cdim.y + (p.y + j) * cdim.x + (p.x + i));
21
22                   d->x += P * tex1Dfetch (tex_coeff, cidx + 0);
23                   d->y += P * tex1Dfetch (tex_coeff, cidx + 1);
24                   d->z += P * tex1Dfetch (tex_coeff, cidx + 2);
25                   z++;
26               }
27           }
28       }
29
30       // get corresponding voxel coordinates in moving image
31       m->x = f.x + d->x;   // Displacement in mm
32       m->y = f.y + d->y;
33       m->z = f.z + d->z;
34
35       // Displacement in voxels
36       n->x = (m->x - mov_offset.x) / mov_ps.x;
37       n->y = (m->y - mov_offset.y) / mov_ps.y;
38       n->z = (m->z - mov_offset.z) / mov_ps.z;
39
40       if (n->x < -0.5 || n->x > mdim.x - 0.5 || n->y < -0.5 || n->y > mdim.y - 0.5 || n->z < -0.5 || n->z >
41           mdim.z - 0.5) {
42           return 1;          // mapped outside moving image
43       }
44       return 0;              // mapped inside moving image
45   }
```

Listing 47.3: __device__ find_correspondence( ).

64 elements by zero padding between tiles if necessary, as shown in Figure 47.4. This data restructuring from row major to "padded tile row major" provides the kernel responsible for computing $\partial C/\partial P$ with three dense input arrays indexed by tile that can be read back from GPU global memory with perfect data coalescence. The zero padding between tiles serves to standardize the data in a way that allows us to design a single kernel to calculate $\partial C/\partial P$ efficiently for any arbitrary tile configuration with no significant penalty in execution speed or need to perform special handling for edge tiles.

47.3.5 Computing the Cost Function Gradient

The kernel that calculates the cost function gradient $\partial C/\partial P$ is designed to operate on tiles of data instead of individual voxels. Here, we assign one thread block of 64 threads to each tile in the fixed image. For a given tile with $\partial C/\partial v$ values defined at each voxel location, the 64 threads work together to parameterize these derivative values in terms of B-spline control-point coefficients, namely, a set of $\partial C/\partial P$ values. Because it takes 64 control points to parameterize the contents of a 3-D tile using cubic B-splines, the thread block will contribute to the gradient values defined at the 64 control points in the tile's immediate vicinity. In fact, each control point in the grid will receive such gradient value contributions from exactly 64 tiles (thread blocks). The final value of the cost function gradient at a given control point is the sum of these 64 contributions that it has received from its surrounding tiles.

One may find visualizing this portion of the registration algorithm difficult owing to the large number of data dependencies — especially since each dependency is determined by a three-dimensional

kernel_bspline_mse_score_dc_dv( ) output:

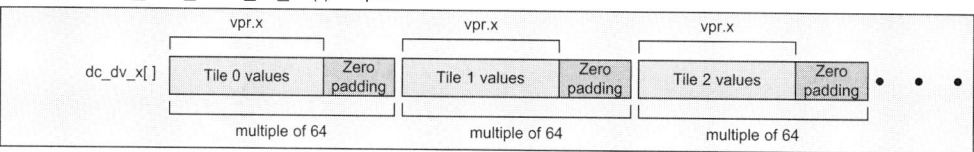

kernel_bspline_gradient( ) output:

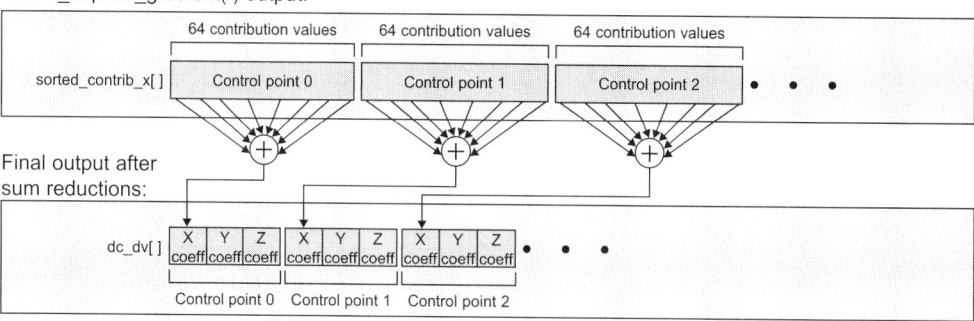

FIGURE 47.4

The data structure used to organize kernel output. The input to each kernel is the output of the kernel drawn above it. The inputs to `kernel_bspline_ssd_dcdv()` are the inputs shown in Figure 47.3. Notice that `kernel_bspline_gradient()` takes voxel-centric data as input and produces control-point-centric data as output. This shift in focus is key to the efficient parallelization of the registration algorithm.

geometric proximity. Figure 47.2 serves to aid visualizing the situation for 2-D, demonstrating that each tile will be parameterized using each of the 16 possible B-spline piecewise function combinations exactly once. For the 3-D case there are 64 possible piecewise combinations, but the same idea still holds — each tile uses each combination exactly once. Further inspection of Figure 47.2 reveals that the different piecewise combinations are linked to specific locations surrounding a control point. It is, therefore, reasonable to conclude that given a specific piecewise combination to apply to a tile, you can easily determine which control point within the tile's vicinity will experience a contribution to its gradient. This is exactly what the cost function gradient computation kernel does.

Listing 47.4 presents the entire gradient computation kernel. The operation of this code is also graphically illustrated in Figure 47.5. The first action performed by the kernel is a table lookup based on the executing thread block's index within the grid. This lookup returns the starting offset of the thread block's associated tile in the dc_dv arrays produced by kernel_bspline_ssd_dcdv(). LUT_Tile_Offsets[ ] is one of two lookup tables generated in the initialization stage of the algorithm — the other being the B-spline LUT.

Once the thread block knows the starting offset of its assigned tile, two nested for-loops dubbed *stage 1* and *stage 2* volley the control of the algorithm:

Stage 1 is the loading stage. In this stage each of the 64 threads works in unison to fetch 64 contiguous dc_dv values from global memory, and these values are then immediately stored into registers (lines 7–9). This contiguous set of 64 $\partial C / \partial v$ values is called a *cluster* and serves as the fundamental work unit for the kernel. Because we are working in three dimensions, each cluster will result in three loads. Once a cluster has been loaded, stage 1 ends with each thread computing the local coordinates within the tile for the cluster *element* it is responsible for (lines 12–15). We will use the term "element" instead of "dc_dv value" because it abstracts away the dimensionality of the problem. The three-dimensional case simply results in two more operations per element than the one-dimensional case.

As shown in Figure 47.4, the input dc_dv values are zero padded to 64, which was purposefully chosen to make the tiles a multiple of the employed cluster size. This zero padding prevents a cluster from partially reading into the next tile when the control-point configuration results in tiles that are not naturally a multiple of the cluster size. With the zero padding, elements that would have read outside the bounds of their assigned tile will now just read a zero. When an element reads a zero pad value, the local coordinates it computes at the end of stage 1 possess no meaning.

Stage 2 is the processing stage. This stage sequentially cycles through each of the 64 possible B-spline piecewise function combinations, which are based on the local coordinates computed in stage 1. Each function combination is applied to each element in the cluster in parallel; the result is stored into a temporary sum reduction array comprising of 64 floating-point numbers located in shared memory s_reduction. Once stored, the array is reduced to a single sum, which is then accumulated into a region of shared memory indexed by the piecewise function combination – s_contrib_x[ ], s_contrib_y[ ], and s_contrib_z[ ]. Stage 2 ends once these operations have been performed for all possible 64 piecewise combinations. Upon completion, control is returned to stage 1, which proceeds to begin another cycle by loading the next cluster.

Stage 2 discards elements who have read a zero pad mathematically. This approach removes the need for introducing control logic that would ultimately lead to thread divergence within one of the two warps comprising the cluster. Here, a B-spline function combination is applied to an element via multiplication, as shown in lines 32–35 of Listing 47.4. It is also here that the result of this

```
 1    // First, get the offset of where our tile starts in memory.
 2    tileOffset = LUT_Tile_Offsets[blockIdxInGrid];
 3
 4    // STAGE 1
 5    for (cluster=0; cluster < tile_dim.w; cluster+=64) {
 6        // pulldown the current cluster. each thread pulls down 1 set of 3 values (x,y,z)
 7        val.x = dc_dv_x[tileOffset + cluster + threadIdx.x];
 8        val.y = dc_dv_y[tileOffset + cluster + threadIdx.x];
 9        val.z = dc_dv_z[tileOffset + cluster + threadIdx.x];
10
11        // local coordinates within the current tile for the dc_dv value this thread is processing.
12        voxel_idx = (cluster + threadIdx.x);
13        voxel_loc.z = voxel_idx / (tile_dim.x * tile_dim.y);
14        voxel_loc.y = (voxel_idx − (voxel_loc.z * tile_dim.x * tile_dim.y)) / tile_dim.x;
15        voxel_loc.x = voxel_idx − voxel_loc.z * tile_dim.x * tile_dim.y − (voxel_loc.y * tile_dim.x);
16
17        // STAGE 2: subject the cluster to all 64 B−spline basis products
18        tile_pos.w = 0; // Current tile position within [0,63]
19        for (tile_pos.z = 0; tile_pos.z < 4; tile_pos.z++) {
20            C = TEX_REF(LUT_Bspline_z, tile_pos.z * tile_dim.z + voxel_loc.z);
21            for (tile_pos.y = 0; tile_pos.y < 4; tile_pos.y++) {
22                B = C * TEX_REF(LUT_Bspline_y, tile_pos.y * tile_dim.y + voxel_loc.y);
23                for (tile_pos.x = 0; tile_pos.x < 4; tile_pos.x++) {
24                    s_reduction_x[threadIdx.x] = 0.0f;
25                    s_reduction_y[threadIdx.x] = 0.0f;
26                    s_reduction_z[threadIdx.x] = 0.0f;
27
28                    A = B * TEX_REF(LUT_Bspline_x, tile_pos.x * tile_dim.x + voxel_loc.x);
29
30                    s_reduction_x[threadIdx.x] = val.x * A;
31                    s_reduction_y[threadIdx.x] = val.y * A;
32                    s_reduction_z[threadIdx.x] = val.z * A;
33                    __syncthreads();
34
35                    // All 64 elements in the current cluster have been processed
36                    // for this B−spline function piece combination (out of 64).
37                    // sum reduce these 64 elements down to one value (partial contribution).
38                    for(unsigned int s = 32; s > 0; s >>= 1) {
39                        if (threadIdx.x < s) {
40                            s_reduction_x[threadIdx.x] += s_reduction_x[threadIdx.x + s];
41                            s_reduction_y[threadIdx.x] += s_reduction_y[threadIdx.x + s];
42                            s_reduction_z[threadIdx.x] += s_reduction_z[threadIdx.x + s];
43                        }
44                        __syncthreads();
45                    }
46
47                    // accumulate the partial contribution into the area of
48                    // shared memory correlating to the current tile position.
49                    if (threadIdx.x == 0) {
50                        s_contrib_x[tile_pos.w] += s_reduction_x[0];
51                        s_contrib_y[tile_pos.w] += s_reduction_y[0];
52                        s_contrib_z[tile_pos.w] += s_reduction_z[0];
```

```
53                          }
54                      __syncthreads();
55
56                      // Continue to work on the current cluster, shift to the next tile position
57                      tile_pos.w++;
58                  }
59              }
60          }
61      }
62
63      // STAGE 3
64      int cp_num = LUT_Control_Points[64*blockIdxInGrid + threadIdx.x];
65
66      sorted_contrib_x[ (64*cp_num) + threadIdx.x ] = s_contrib_x[threadIdx.x];
67      sorted_contrib_y[ (64*cp_num) + threadIdx.x ] = s_contrib_y[threadIdx.x];
68      sorted_contrib_z[ (64*cp_num) + threadIdx.x ] = s_contrib_z[threadIdx.x];
```

Listing 47.4: kernel_bspline_gradient( ).

multiplication is fed into the series of summations that ultimately lead to the accumulation of this product into the shared-memory location that holds the intermediate solutions produced by the current cluster. The result of this product for an element assigned to a zero pad will naturally be zero, and because all subsequent operations are additions, the zero-pad values will ultimately hold no influence over the solution.

Stage 3 is the distribution stage. Once stage 2 has processed all the clusters within a tile, we will have 64 gradient contributions stored within shared memory that need to be distributed to the control points they influence. Because these contributions are indexed in shared memory based on a piecewise combination number, and because we know we easily determine the location of the influenced control point based on this combination number, distribution is a simple sorting problem. Incidentally, we have 64 threads and 64 gradient contributions that require distribution. Stage 3 assigns one contribution to each thread and distributes them appropriately based on their combination number. Observe from lines 76–78 in Listing 47.4 that each control point has 64 "slots" to store the 64 contributions that they will each receive. This is done in order to avoid possible race conditions when multiple threads attempt to write to the same memory location. Once kernel_bspline_gradient() completes, a simple sum reduction kernel is employed to add up each control point's slots, as depicted in Figure 47.4, which results in the cost-function gradient $\partial C/\partial P$. As depicted in the figure, the array dc_dp[ ] used to hold the cost-function gradient is organized in an interleaved fashion, as opposed to using separate arrays for each component. This provides better cache locality when these values are read back by the optimizer, which is executed using the host system's CPU. The time required to copy the gradient array dc_dv[ ] from GPU memory to host memory over the PCIe bus is negligible. For example, registering two $256 \times 256 \times 256$ images with a control-point spacing of $10 \times 10 \times 10$ voxels requires 73, 167 B-spline coefficients to be transferred between the GPU and the CPU per iteration, incurring about 0.35 ms over a PCIe 2.0 x16 bus.[1]

---

[1]The PCIe 2.0 x16 bus provides a maximum bandwidth of 8 gigabytes per second.

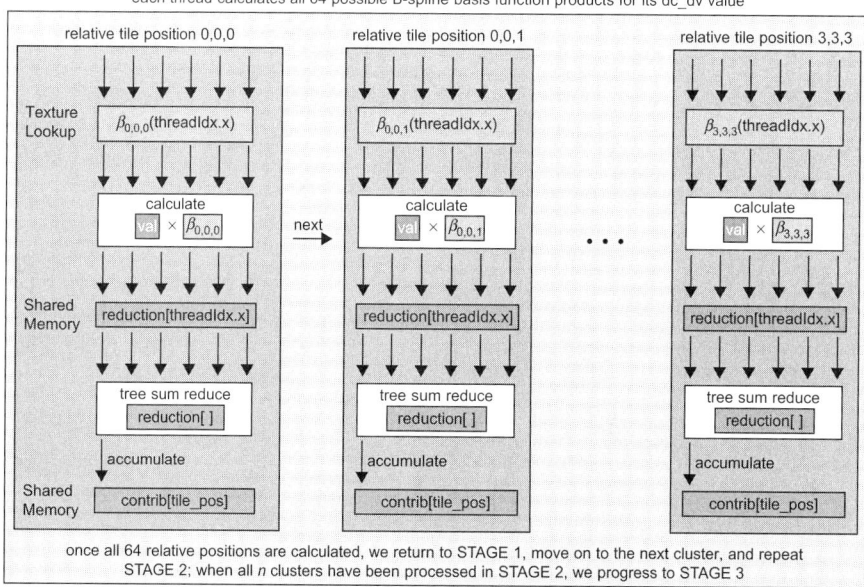

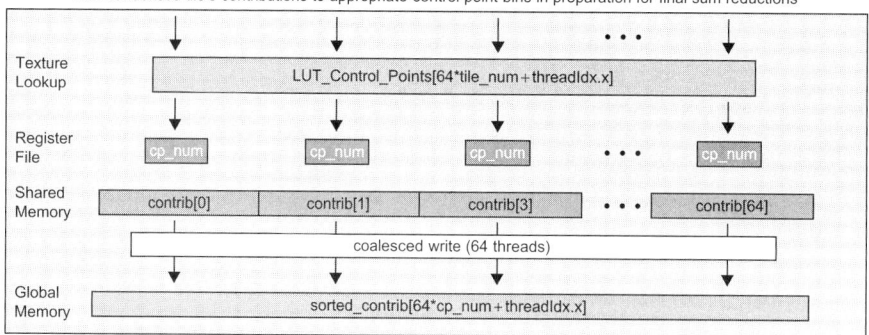

FIGURE 47.5

A graphical depiction of the cost-function gradient computation carried out by `kernel_bspline_gradient()`.

47.4 **RESULTS**

Here, we present performance results obtained for the GPU implementation, and to provide a basis for comparison, we contrast the performance achieved by the GPU implementation with a highly optimized single-core CPU implementation. Each implementation's sensitivity to both volume size as well as control-point spacing (i.e., the tile size) is quantified. The tests reported in this section were performed on a machine possessing a 2.5 GHz Intel Xeon E5540 processor, 24 GB of RAM, and an NVIDIA Tesla C1060.

47.4.1 **Registration Quality**

Figure 47.6(a) shows the registration of two CT images of a patient's thorax on the GPU. The image on the left is the reference image, captured as the patient was exhaling, and the image on the right is the moving image, captured after the patient had fully inhaled. The resulting vector field after registration is overlaid on the inhale image. Figure 47.6(b) is a zoomed-in view of Figure 47.6(a), focusing on just the left lung. To determine the registration quality, we generate the deformation field by running the registration process for 50 iterations and then compare the results against the reference implementation. The CPU and GPU versions generate near-identical vector fields with an RMS error of less than 0.014.

47.4.2 **Sensitivity to Volume Size**

The algorithm's performance in regard to input volume size is tested by holding the control point spacing constant at 10 voxels in each physical dimension while increasing the input volumes size in $10 \times 10 \times 10$ voxel steps. For each input volume size we record the time taken for a single B-spline registration iteration to complete. We look at single iteration time instead of the total time required to obtain a "good" registration because the time taken to perform an iteration will remain constant throughout the registration, whereas the number of iterations required to obtain a suitable registration is somewhat subjective and will vary depending on several factors, such as the application, the initial difference between the images being registered, and what the user deems to be a suitable registration for the given application. The left panel in Figure 47.7 shows that the execution time for a single iteration scales linearly with the number of voxels in the fixed image volume. Because the GPU implementation utilizes texture references to accelerate reads from the moving image volume during the cost computation, this input volume may contain no more than 2^{27} voxels owing to limitations imposed by the 27-bit addressing scheme used by the texture unit. In terms of cubic input volumes, this translates to a maximum moving image resolution of $512 \times 512 \times 512$ voxels, which is appreciably high.

The GPU implementation achieves a speedup of 15 times over the CPU for large volumes. Moreover, the kernels are compute bound because their memory accesses have been thoroughly optimized. Therefore, we expect to achieve a linear speedup with increasing number of cores with no changes to our design.

47.4.3 **Sensitivity to Control-Point Spacing**

Another important metric used to evaluate the robustness of our implementation is its sensitivity to the control-point spacing specified by the user. This issue is of specific interest because tile size is directly affected by control-point spacing. Our implementation achieves its short iteration times by assigning individual tiles to thread blocks for the gradient computation. As a result, changes in the

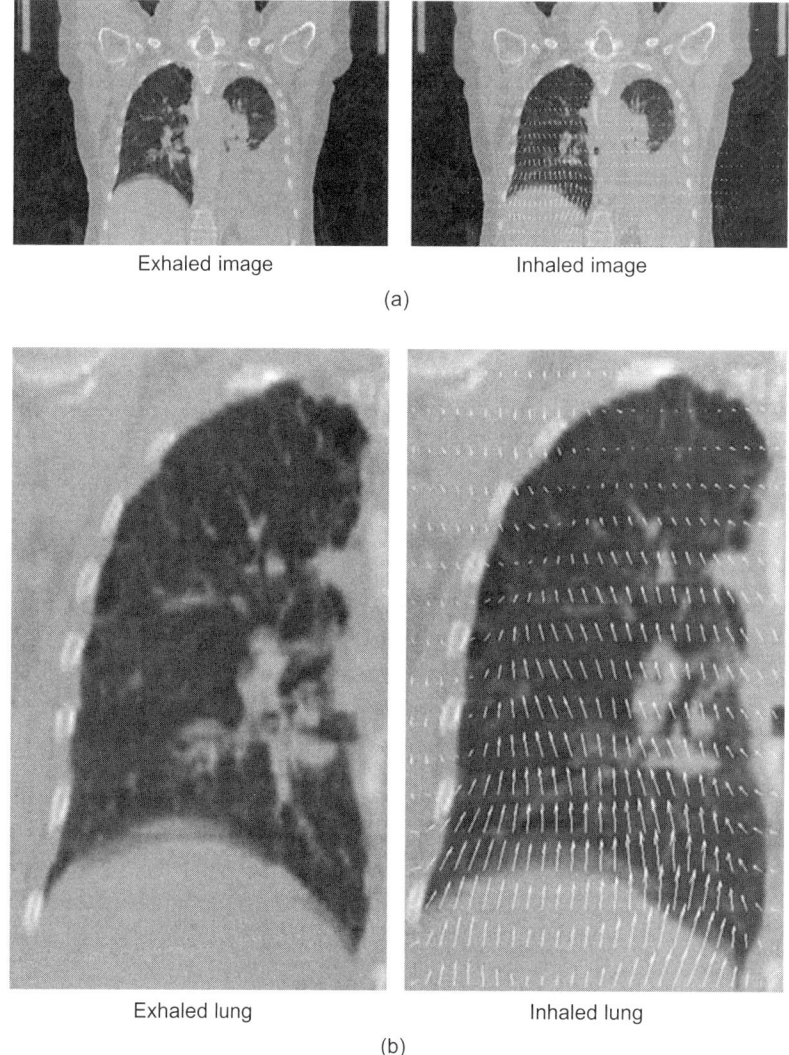

FIGURE 47.6

(a) Deformable registration of two 3-D CT images on the GPU. (b) A zoomed-in view of (a) focusing on the left lung.

control-point spacing affects the configuration of the thread-block grid, which ultimately dictates how work is scheduled to the GPU. We show in the right panel of Figure 47.7 how our implementation is affected by varying the control-point spacing for a fixed image volume of $256 \times 256 \times 256$ voxels. As shown, reasonable control-point spacings have little affect on overall execution time. Furthermore, because the gradient computation processes individual tiles in clusters of 64 elements, shared-memory resources remain the same for any arbitrary control-point spacing. Larger tiles, therefore, simply result

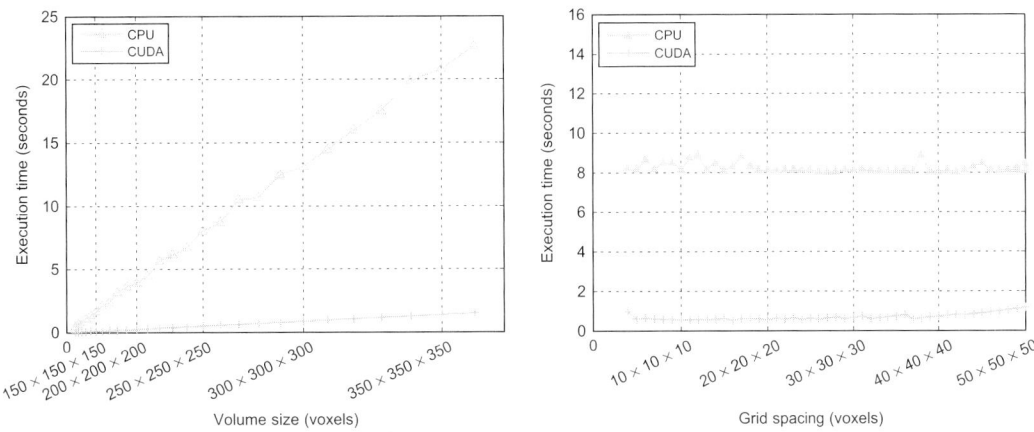

FIGURE 47.7

(Left plot): The execution time for a single registration iteration is shown as a function of volume size. The control-point spacing is fixed at $10 \times 10 \times 10$ voxels. (Right plot): Execution time versus control-point spacing for a volume size of $256 \times 256 \times 256$ voxels.

in more clusters being processed before a given thread block completes. This may explain the upward trend in execution time shown in Figure 47.7 for tiles around 37^3 and larger. In such a configuration, the thread-block grid becomes populated with fewer, yet larger thread blocks. As a result, each block requires many more memory operations than a smaller block, and latency hiding becomes increasingly difficult for the hardware owing to the sparsely populated thread-block grid. Fortunately, this effect manifests itself as only a very minor degradation in performance for low-resolution control-point grids. Special care was taken to mitigate the need for such latency hiding by ensuring that all kernels exhibit 100% coalesced global memory accesses for any arbitrarily sized input volume.

47.5 CONCLUSIONS

We have introduced a grid-alignment technique to greatly reduce the complexity of B-spline-based registration. We have then used the main ideas underlying the aligned-grid method to develop a highly parallel design for the GPU. When compared with a highly optimized CPU implementation, the GPU version achieves a speedup of approximately 15 times when executed on the Tesla 1060 GPU. Our experiments also demonstrated a fairly strong independence between the B-spline grid resolution and execution time for our parallel algorithms.

References

[1] S. Aylward, J. Jomier, S. Barre, B. Davis, L. Ibanez, Optimizing ITK's registration methods for multi-processor, shared-memory systems in: MICCAI Open Source and Open Data Workshop, 29 October 2007, Brisbane, Australia, 2007.

[2] F. Bookstein, D. Green, A feature space for derivatives of deformations, in: H.H. Barret, A.T. Gmitro (Eds.), Information Processing in Medical Imaging, Lecture Notes in Computer Science, vol. 687, Springer, Berlin, 1993, pp. 1–16.

[3] G.E. Christensen, R.D. Rabbitt, M.I. Miller, Deformable templates using large deformation kinematics, IEEE Trans. Image Proc. 5 (10) (1996) 1435–1447.

[4] G. Rohde, A. Aldroubi, B. Dawant, The adaptive bases algorithm for intensity based nonrigid image registration, IEEE Trans. Med. Imaging 22 (2003) 1470–1479.

[5] D. Rueckert, L.I. Sonoda, C. Hayes, D.L. Hill, M.O. Leach, D.J. Hawkes, Nonrigid registration using free-form deformations: application to breast MR images, IEEE Trans. Med. Imaging 18 (8) (1999) 712–721.

[6] D. Ruijters, B.M. ter Haar Romeny, P. Suetens, Efficient GPU- accelerated elastic image registration, in: Proceedings of Sixth IASTED International Conference on Biomedical Engineering, 13–15 February 2008, Innsbruck, Austria, 2008, pp. 419–424.

[7] S.S. Samant, J. Xia, P. Muyan-Özçelik, J.D. Owens, High performance computing for deformable image registration: Towards a new paradigm in adaptive radiotherapy, Med. Phys. 35 (8) (2008) 3546–3553.

[8] G. Sharp, N. Kandasamy, H. Singh, M. Folkert, GPU-based streaming architectures for fast cone-beam CT image reconstruction and demons deformable registration, Phys. Med. Biol. 52 (19) (2007) 5771–5783.

[9] J.P. Thirion, Image matching as a diffusion process: an analogy with Maxwell's demons, Med. Image Anal. 2 (3) (1998) 243–260.

Multiscale Unbiased Diffeomorphic Atlas Construction on Multi-GPUs

48

Linh Ha, Jens Krüger, Sarang Joshi, Cláudio T. Silva

In this chapter, we present a high-performance multiscale 3-D image-processing framework to exploit the parallel processing power of multiple graphic processing units (multi-GPUs) for medical image analysis. We developed GPUs algorithms and data structures that can be applied to a wide range of 3-D image-processing applications and efficiently exploit the computational power and massive bandwidth offered by modern GPUs. Our framework helps scientists solve computationally intensive problems that previously required supercomputing power. To demonstrate the effectiveness of our framework and to compare it with existing techniques, we focus our discussions on atlas construction — the application of understanding the development of the brain and the progression of brain diseases.

48.1 INTRODUCTION, PROBLEM STATEMENT, AND CONTEXT

48.1.1 Atlas Construction Problem

The construction of population atlases plays a central role in medical image analysis, particularly in understanding the variability of brain anatomy. The method projects a large set of images to a common coordinate system, creating a statistical average model of the population, and doing regression analysis of anatomical structures. This average serves as a deformable template that maps detailed atlas data, such as structural, developmental, genetic, pathological, and functional information, on to the individual or entire population of the brain. This transformation encodes the variability of the population understudy. Likewise, the statistical analysis of the transformation between populations reflects the interpopulation differences. Apart from providing a common coordinate system, the atlas can be partitioned and labeled, thus providing effective segmentation via registration of anatomical labels.

The brain atlas construction is a powerful technique to study the physiology, evolution, and development of the brain, as well as disease progression. Two desired properties of the atlas construction are that it should be diffeomorphic and nonbiased.

In nonrigid registration problems, the desired transformations are often constrained to be diffeomorphic, that is, continuous, one to one (invertible), and smooth with a smooth inverse so that the topology is maintained. Connected sets remain connected; disjoint sets remain disjoint; neighbor relationships between structures, as well as smoothness of features, such as curves, are preserved; and coordinates are transformed consistently.

Preserving topology is important for synthesizing the atlas because the knowledge base of the atlas is transferred to the target anatomy through topology preserving transformation providing automatic labeling and segmentation. Moreover, important statistics such as the total volume of a nucleus, the ventricles, or the cortical subregion can be generated automatically. The diffeomorphic mapping from the atlas to the target can be used to study the physical properties of the target anatomy, such as mean shape and variation. Also, the registration of multiple individuals to a standard atlas coordinate space removes the individual anatomical variation and allows information to be combined with a single conical anatomy. Figure 48.1 shows that the diffeomorphic setting results in a high-quality deformation field that is infinitely smooth on a non-self-crossing grid.

The nonbias property guarantees that the atlas construction is consistent. Our atlas construction framework, first proposed by Joshi *et al.* [9], is based on the notion of Frechet mean to define a geometrical average. On a metric space M, with a distance $d : M \times M \to R$ the intrinsic average μ of a collection of data x_i is defined as a minimizer of the sum-of-square distances to each individual, that is

$$\mu = \underset{p \in M}{\operatorname{argmin}} \sum_{i=1}^{N} w_i d^2(p, x_i)$$

As the computation of the Frechet mean is independent from the order of the inputs, the atlas is inherently nonbiased. The Frechet mean is also rational in terms of minimizing the total energy to deform an average to all images in a population.

The combination of both diffeomorphic and nonbias property results in a minimization energy template problem which is formulated as

$$\{\hat{h}_i, \hat{I}_i\} = \underset{h_i, I}{\operatorname{argmin}} \sum_{i=1}^{N} \int_{\omega} (I_i \circ h_i - I)^2 + \int_{0}^{1} \int_{\omega} ||Lv_i(x,t)||^2 dx dt \tag{48.1}$$

subject to $h_i(x) = \int_0^1 v_i(h_i(x,t),t)dt$ (*)

FIGURE 48.1

A small part of the letter "C" deforming into a full "C" using 2-D greedy iterative diffeomorphism. From left to right: (1) Input and target image. (2) Deformed template. (3) Grid showing the deformation applied to the template.

Algorithm 1: Atlas construction framework.

1: **Input** : N volume inputs
2: **Output**: Template atlas volume
3: **for** $k = 1$ to *max_iters* **do**
4:     Fix images I_i^k, compute the optimal template $\hat{I}^k = \frac{1}{N} \sum_{i=1}^{N} I_i^k$
5:     **for** $i = 1$ to N **do** {loop over the images}
6:         Fix the template $\hat{I}^k$, solve pairwise-matching problem between I_i^k and $\hat{I}^k$
7:         Update the image with optimal velocity field
8:     **end for**
9: **end for**

This is a dual-optimization problem on the image matching (the first term) and deformation energy (the second term). The L-operator is a partial differential operator that controls the smoothness of the deformation field. The constraint (*) comes from the theory of large deformation diffeomorphism that the transformations h_i are generated by integrating velocity field v_i forward in time. The method is the extension of elastic registration to handle large deformations.

Although the optimization seems intractable, by noting that for fixed transformation h_i the best estimation of the average $\hat{I}$ is given by $\hat{I}(x) = \frac{1}{N} \sum_{i=1}^{N} I_i(h_i)$, we come up with a simple solution based on an alternating optimization, as shown on Algorithm 1. In each step, we estimate the atlas by averaging the deformed images, then compute the optimal velocity fields by solving optimization problems on deformation energy, and finally update the deformed images. This process is repeated until convergence. Note that, with the assumption of a fixed template on the second step, the optimal velocity of an image can be computed independently from the others. This velocity is determined by solving the pairwise matching problem. By tightly coupling the atlas construction problem with basic registration problems — the pairwise matching algorithms — our framework allows us to implement different techniques and even to combine multiple techniques into a hybrid approach.

48.1.2 **Challenges**

As shown in the preceding section, unbiased diffeomorphic atlas construction is a powerful method in computational anatomy. However, the impact of the method was limited because of two main challenges: the extensive memory requirement and the intensive computation.

The extensive memory requirement is one of the major obstacles of 3-D volume processing in general because the size of a single volume often exceeds the available memory on a processing node. This becomes more challenging on GPUs because they have less memory available. In addition, the atlas construction process requires not just a single volume, but a population of hundreds of volumes, thus easily exceeding the available memory of pratically any computational system.

The massive size of the problem is compounded with the complexity of the computation per element. These computations are often not just simple local kernels, but global operations, for example, an ODE integration using a backward mapping technique.

Generating a brain atlas at an acceptable resolution for a reasonably sized population took an impractically long time even with a fully optimized implementation on high-end CPU workstations or small CPU clusters [6]. Acceptable run times could only be obtained by utilizing supercomputer resources [3, 4]. Hence, the technique was restricted to the baseline research community. Fortunately, the development of GPUs in recent years, especially the introduction of a general processing model and a unified architecture, brings a more accessible solution. Our results show that an implementation on the GPU can handle practical problems on a single desktop with a substantial performance gain, on the order of 20 to 60 times faster than a single CPU.

Our multi-GPU implementation on a 32-node GPU cluster is roughly 1000 times faster than a 32-core CPU workstation. We are able to handle a large dataset of 315 T1 brain images at size $114 \times 192 \times 160$ using only eight cluster nodes. The ability to solve the problem on small-scale computing systems opens opportunities for researchers to fully understand practical impacts of the method and to enhance their knowledge of anatomical structures.

In addition to providing a practical solution to a specific problem, we also present a general image processing framework and optimization techniques to exploit the massive bandwidth and computational power of multi-GPU systems and to handle compute-expensive problems previously available only on a supercomputer.

Although we have integrated a number of different techniques into our system, such as the greedy iterative diffeomorphism, large deformation diffeomorphic metric mapping (LDDMM), and metamorphoses, in this chapter we focus on the implementation of the greedy method on GPUs.

48.2 CORE METHODS

The greedy iterative diffeomorphism was proposed by Christensen [5]. The method separated the time dimension from the space dimension of the problem. At each iteration, a new optimal velocity field is computed, given that the current deformation is fixed (i.e., the past velocity fields are fixed). The solution is computed by integrating the optimal solution at each step forward in time in a gradient descent approach. The method is locally in-time optimal; thus, in general, it will not produce the shortest path connecting images through the space of diffeomorphism. However, it is generally preferred in practice because it can produce good results with less computational expense than the other approaches. The greedy iterative diffeomorphism is built on the general framework with the greedy pairwise matching algorithm at its core (Algorithm 2).

There are several performance keys of a GPU implementation: high-throughput data structures and basic functions; high-performance advance functions, such as optimal ODE integration and PDE solvers; and multiresolution and multi-GPU strategies. We will discuss in detail how to achieve the peak performance in the following section.

Algorithm 2: Greedy pairwise matching step.

1: **Input** : Original image I_0, target I_1, deformed image $I_0(t)$, deformation field h
2: **Output**: New deformed image $I_0(t)$, deformation field h
3: Compute the force $F = -[I_0(t) - I_1] \triangledown I_0(t)$
4: Solve the PDE $Lv(x) = F(x)$ where $L = \alpha \nabla^2 + \beta \nabla \nabla + \gamma$
5: Update the deformation $h_{new} = h_{cur}(x + \epsilon v(x))$
6: Update the transform image $I_0(t) = I_0(h_{new}(x))$

48.3 ALGORITHMS, IMPLEMENTATIONS, AND EVALUATIONS

48.3.1 Data Structures

Although it is typically recommended to have volume data padding so that the volume dimensions are multipliers of the GPU warp size, our experiment showed that it has a negligible effect on improving the performance. The reason is that as GPU data-parallel fetching strategies become more sophisticated and efficient, the coalesced condition is greatly relieved from CUDA 1.0 to CUDA 2.0 hardware, so it is easy to achieve with regular image functions. Moreover, data padding significantly increases the storage requirement, especially in 3-D, and requires extra processing steps. For these reasons, we chose a tight 3-D volume representation that can represent a 3-D volume as a 1-D vector; thus, most of the basic operations on 1-D can be directly applied to 3-D. Additionally, we often save two integer shared-memory locations and operations per kernel by passing a single-volume value instead of three-dimensional numbers.

We also define a special structure for 3-D vector fields based on a structure of array representation. Instead of allocating three separated GPU pointers, we allocate a single memory block and use an offset to address the three components. This presentation allows us to optimize basic operations on the vector field, most of the time as a single-image operation. Moreover, it helps us save one shared-memory pointer per kernel.

48.3.2 Basic Image Operators

The goal of our system design is to be able to run the entire processing pipeline on GPUs. This allows one to maximize the computational benefit from GPUs and minimizes idle time. We keep data flow running on the GPUs and use only CPUs for cross-GPU and cross-CPU operations. With the design goal in mind to be optimal, even on a per-function level, we provide n-ary basic-3-D functions.

The performance of the basic function is constrained by the global memory bandwidth. To improve the performance we need to minimize the bandwidth usage. Most of the functions provided by regular processing libraries such as Thrust [8] or NPP (http://developer.nvidia.com/object/npp_home.html) are unary or binary functions that involve one or two arguments as the inputs. Although any n-argument function can always be decomposed into a set of unary and binary functions, this decomposition requires extra memory to store intermediate results, and increases bandwidth utilization by saving and/or reloading the data. Our n-ary operators, on the other hand, load all the components of an n-argument function to the register files at the same time; hence, no extra saving/loading is required. This process allows for optimal memory bandwidth usage. For example, if we consider the image-loading operator being one memory bandwidth unit, then the linear interpolation $x = a * y + b * z$ requires seven units with binary decomposition, while optimal bandwidth is three units, which is achievable with n-ary operators. The bandwidth ratio is also our expected speedup of our n-ary versus binary functions. In terms of storage requirements, the binary decomposition doubles the memory requirement by introducing an extra template memory per operation, whereas n-ary functions require no extra memory.

In addition to providing all the basic operations similar to those of the Thrust library [8], we implement n-ary functions combining up to five operations. We also offer n-ary in-place operators that consume fewer registers and less shared memory. Naming of these functions reflects their functionality to preserve the readability and maintainability of the code and to allow further automatic code generation and optimization by the compiler. As shown in Figure 48.2, our normalization function

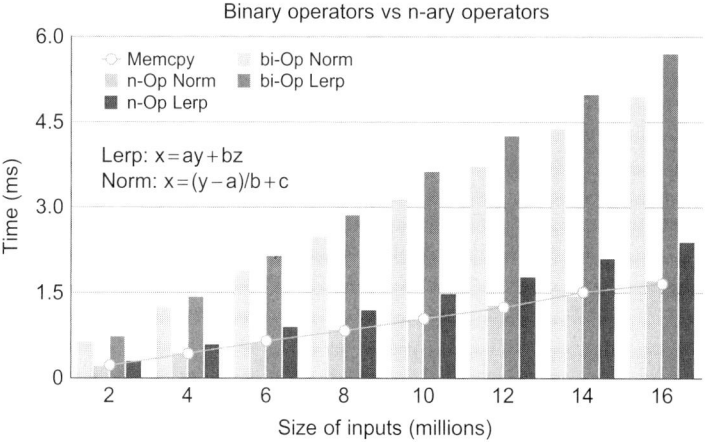

FIGURE 48.2

n-ary versus binary operator with linear interpolation and range normalization function in comparision with the device device memory copy. Note the efficiency of our n-ary approach as compared against the classic binary operator approach.

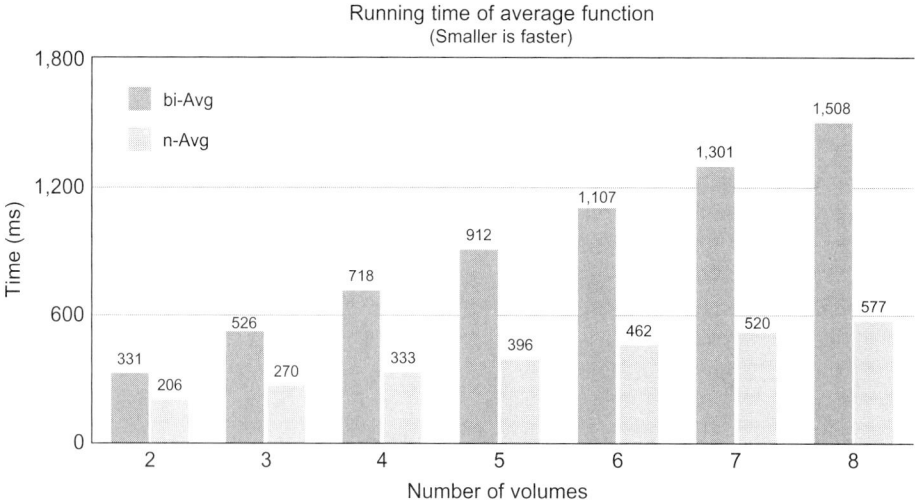

FIGURE 48.3

n-ary average function versus binary average operator.

and linear interpolation achieve speedup factors of up to 2-3 over the implementation using optimized binary operators.

Based on the same strategy of n-ary operators, we propose a parallel efficient average function with hand-tuned performance for all number of inputs from 1 to 8, as illustrated in Figure 48.3.

Gradient computation is a frequently used and essential function in image processing. Based on the locality of the computation, several optimization techniques may be applied, such as 1-D linear texture cache, 3-D texture, or implicit cache through shared memory. Among these techniques, we found the 3-D stencil method [11] using the shared memory the most effective. Table 48.1 shows the runtime comparison in milliseconds of different gradient computations: simple approach, linear 1-D texture, 3-D texture, and our shared-memory implementation.

The result shows that gradient computation on shared memory exploiting the 3-D stencil technique is twice as fast as using the linear texture cache.

48.3.3 ODE Integration

The ODE integration computes the deformation field by integrating velocity along the evolution path. A computationally efficient version of ODE integration is the recursive equation that computes the deformation at time t based on the deformation at time $t-1$; that is, $h_t = h_{t-1}(x + v(t-1))$. This computation could be done by the reverse mapping operator (Figure 48.4), which assigns each destination grid point a 3-D interpolation value from the grid neighbor points in the source volume. Fortunately, on GPUs, this interpolation process is fully hardware accelerated with 3-D texture volume support from CUDA 2.0 APIs. This optimization greatly reduces the computational cost of the ODE integration.

Table 48.1 Runtime comparison of different gradient computation

Gradient Method	Simple	1-D Linear	3-D Texture	Shared
$160 \times 224 \times 160$	3.4	3.0	6.8	1.6
$256 \times 256 \times 256$	9.5	8.9	21	5.2

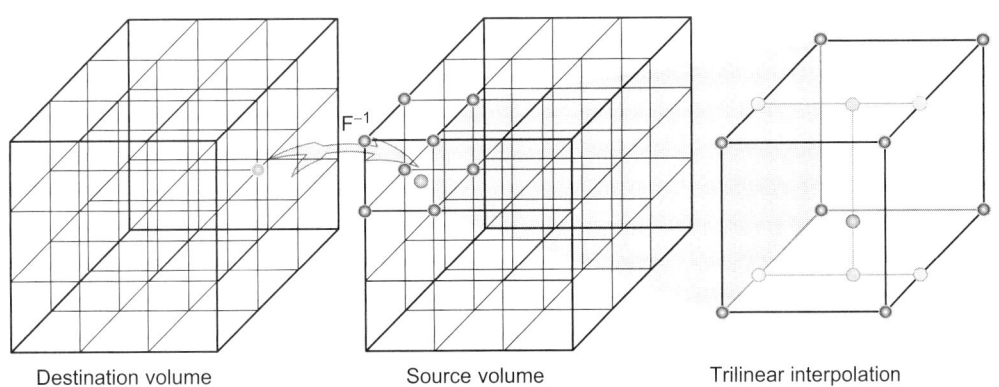

Destination volume   Source volume   Trilinear interpolation

FIGURE 48.4

Reverse mapping based on 3-D trilinear interpolation.

48.3.4 **PDE Solver**

As shown in Algorithm 2, optimal velocity is computed from the force function by solving the Navier-Stokes equation

$$\alpha \nabla^2 v(x) + \beta \nabla \nabla v(x) + \gamma v(x) = F(x) \tag{48.2}$$

Often β is negligible, and Equation 48.2 simplifies to the Helmholtz equation

$$\alpha \nabla^2 v(x) + \gamma v(x) = F(x) \tag{48.3}$$

where $\alpha = 0.01$ and $\gamma = 0.001$ are generally used in practice. Note that there is no crossing term in the Helmholtz equation; that means the solver could independently run on each dimension.

Although the ODE computation can be easily optimized simply by utilizing the 3-D hardware interpolation, the PDE solver is less amenable to GPU implementation. The PDE is a sparse linear system with size $N^3 \times N^3$, where N^3 is the volume of the input. A direct dense linear package such as CUDA BLAS cannot handle the problem. What we need is a sparse solver. There are many different methods to solve a sparse linear system. The two most common and efficient ways are explicit solvers in the Fourier domain and implicit solvers using iterative refinement methods such as conjugate gradient (CG), successive over relaxation (SOR), or multigrid.

In our framework we support different methods such as FFT, SOR, and CG. There are multiple reasons to support multiple techniques, rather than a single method. Although the FFT solver is the slowest, it produces an exact PDE solution. Although the others are significantly faster, they produce only approximate solutions, which often have local smoothing effects. The inability to account for the influence of spatially distant data points in the initial solution slows down the convergence rate of these methods in the long run. Consequently, they require more iterations to achieve the same result as the FFT approach. Because of smoothing properties of the velocity field, the variance in the solution of the PDE solver between two successive steps is often small. This variance can be captured adequately by the iterative solvers in a few iterations. This is made possible by using the previous solution as an initial guess for the iterative solver in the next step. For the first iteration, without a proper guess, iterative solvers are often slow to converge, so they require a large number of iterations and may quickly become slower than the FFT approach. Therefore, we use an FFT solver in the first iteration and then switch to iterative methods. Our experiments show that the hybrid CG solver that starts with an FFT step produces exactly the same results as an FFT method, but is almost three times faster.

For the details on the FFT solvers we refer the reader to [12]. Here, we will discuss the implementation of SOR and CG methods.

48.3.5 **Successive Over Relaxation Method**

The successive over-relaxation (SOR) is an iterative algorithm proposed by Young for solving a linear system [13]. Theoretically, the 3-D FFT solver has a complexity of $O(n \log(n))$ versus $0\left(n^{5/3}\right)$ for SOR. However, the complexity analysis does not account for the fact that SOR is an iterative refinement method whose convergence speed largely depends on the initial guess. With a close approximation of the result as the initial value, it normally requires only a few iterations to converge. The same argument is true for other iterative methods such as CG.

We observe that in the elastic deformable framework with steady fluids, the changes in the velocity field are quite small between greedy steps. The computed velocity field of the previous step is inherently

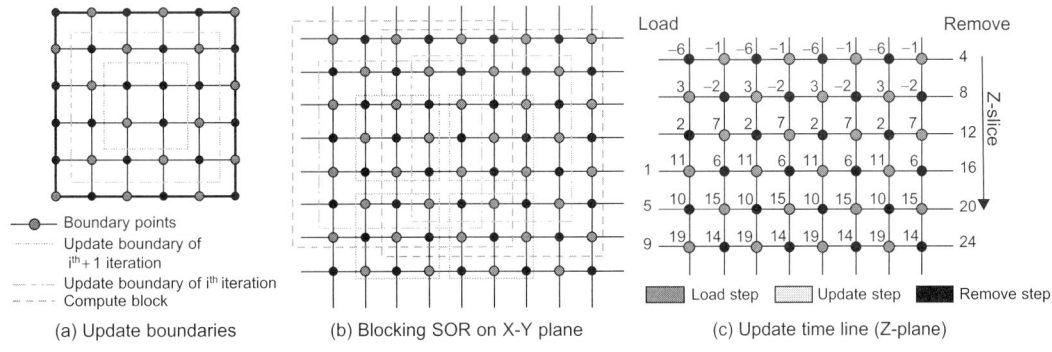

FIGURE 48.5

Parallel block SOR; we assign each CUDA thread block a block of data to compute the black points inside the boundary shown by ──●──, ⋯⋯, and use that result to compute the point inside the boundary shown by ⋯⋯, ────. Two neighboring compute blocks share a four-grid-point-wide region.

a good approximation for the current one. In practice, we typically need 50 to 100 SOR iterations for the first greedy step, but only four to six iterations for each subsequent step.

Our framework provides an SOR implementation with red-black ordering, as shown in Figure 48.5. This strategy allows for efficient parallelism because we update only points of the same color based on their neighbors, which have a different color. Also, red-black decoupling is proved to have a well-behaved convergence rate with the optimal over-relaxation factor ω defined in 3-D as $\omega = \dfrac{2}{1+\sqrt{1-\frac{1}{3}[\cos\frac{\pi}{w}+\cos\frac{\pi}{h}+\cos\frac{\pi}{l}]^2}}$.

We incorporate optimization techniques from the 3-D stencil buffer problem to exploit the fast shared memory available in CUDA and improve the register utilization of the algorithm (Algorithm 3). We further improve the performance by increasing the arithmetic intensity of the data. This is done with merging steps of SOR that combines red-update steps and black-update steps of traditional SOR in one execution kernel. We also proposed *block-SOR* algorithms that we divide input volume into blocks, each fitting onto one CUDA execution block. We then exploit the shared memory to perform the merging step locally on the block. For simplicity, we illustrate the idea in 2-D in Figure 48.5, but it is generalized to arbitrary dimensions.

As shown in Figure 48.5 the updated volume is two cells smaller in each dimension than the input. This reduction in size explains why we cannot merge an arbitrary number of steps in one kernel. To update the whole volume, we allow data overlaps among processing blocks, as shown in Figure 48.5(b). Here, we allow data redundancy to increase memory usage. The configuration shown in Figure 48.5(b), having a four-point-wide boundary overlap, is able to update one red-black merging step over a M^2 block using $(M+4)^2$ input. Likewise, a k-merging step needs a data block of size $(M+4*k)^2$. To quantify the benefit of SOR merging steps, we compute a trade-off factor α such that:

$$\alpha = \frac{\text{Minimum needed data size}}{\text{Actual processing data size}} * \text{Speed\_up\_factor} \qquad (48.4)$$

Algorithm 3:   Efficient CUDA PDE block-SOR solver.

1: **Input** : Old velocity field v and new force function F
2: **Output**: Compute new velocity field v
3: Allocate 4 shared mem arrays $s_{prev}, s_{cur}, s_{next}, s_{next2}$ to store 4 slices of data
4: Load F of 3-first slices to the registers of current thread
5: Load v of 3-first slices to registers and shared memory
6: The boundary thread load the padding data of v
7: Update the black point of the second slice s_{cur}
8: **for** $k = 1$ to $Z - 2$ **do** {loop over Z direction}
9:     Load the F and v of the next slice to the free shared-mem array s_{next2}
10:     Update the black points of the s_{next} slice
11:     Update the red points of the s_{cur} slice
12:     Write the s_{prev} to the global output, s_{prev} buffer is free to load the next slice
13:     Shift the value of v and F in the registers, $cur \rightarrow prev, next \rightarrow cur, next2 \rightarrow next$
14:     Circular shift the shared memory array pointers, s_{prev} becomes s_{next2}
15: **end for**
16: Update the red points on the last slice close to boundary
17: Write out the last slice

In 3-D, to update the volume block M^3, we need $(M + 4k)^3$ volume inputs; the trade-off factor is $\alpha = \left(\frac{M+1}{M+4k}\right)^3 * k$. Note that the size of shared memory constraints the block size M and merging level k. In practice, we see benefits only if we merge one black and red update step per kernel call.

Algorithm 3 shows the pseudocode of our block-SOR implementation on CUDA. We further leverage the trade-off by limiting block-SOR in the 2-D plane only and exploit the coherence between consecutive layers in the third dimension to minimize data redundancy. On the Tesla, our block-SOR implementation using shared memory is two times faster than an equivalent version using 1-D texture cache. Figure 48.5(c) shows the updating time line in Z-dimension; it is clear that each node is computed by its neighbors, which are updated in previous steps.

48.3.6 Conjugate Gradient Method

Although the SOR method is specialized for solving PDEs on a regular grid, in practice the conjugate gradient approach is often the preferred technique because of several advantages:

- It is capable of solving a PDE on an irregular grid as well.
- It is simple to implement because it is built on top of basic linear operations.
- In general, it converges faster than the SOR method.

As shown in Figure 48.7, the CG algorithm is implemented in our framework as a template class with T being the matrix presentation of the system. The only function required from T is a matrix vector multiplication. The template allows for the integration of any sparse matrix vector multiplication package using an explicit presentation such as ELL, ELL/COO [2] and CRS [1], or an implicit presentation that encodes the system matrix with constant values in the kernel.

Figure 48.6 is the implementation of the implicit matrix vector multiplication with Helmholtz Matrix and zero-boundary condition. The texture cache is used to access neighboring information to

```
__global__ void helmholtz3D_MV(float* b, float* x,
        float alpha, float gamma, int sizeX, int sizeY, int sizeZ){
    uint xid     = threadIdx.x + blockIdx.x * blockDim.x;
    uint yid     = threadIdx.y + blockIdx.y * blockDim.y;
    uint id      = xid + yid * sizeX, planeSize= sizeX * sizeY;
    if (xid < sizeX && yid < sizeY){
        float zo = 0, zc = fetch(id, x), zn;
        for (uint zid=0; zid<sizeZ; ++zid, id += planeSize){
            zn = (zid + 1 < sizeZ) ? fetch(id + planeSize, x) : 0;
            float r = zo + zn;
            r += (xid > 0)           ? fetch(id − 1, x)      : 0;
            r += (xid + 1 < sizeX)? fetch(id + 1, x)       : 0;
            r += (yid > 0)           ? fetch(id − sizeX, x) : 0;
            r += (yid + 1 < sizeY)? fetch(id + sizeX, x)  : 0;
            b[id] = zc * (6 * alpha + gamma) − alpha * r ;
            zo = zc; zc = zn; // shift values on Z−dir
            }
        }
}
```

FIGURE 48.6

Matrix vector multiplication CUDA kernel with implicit Helmholtz Matrix.

```
template< class T>
void CG_impl(float* d_b, T& d_A, float* d_x, int imax,
                float* d_r, float* d_d, float* d_q){
    int n = d_A.getNumElements();
    computeResidual(d_r, d_b, d_A, d_x); // r = b − Ax
    copyArrayDeviceToDevice(d_d, d_r, n); // d = r
    float delta_new = cplvSum2(d_r, n);       // delta_new = r^Tr
    float delta0 = delta_new, delta_old, eps=1e−4, alpha, beta;
    for (i=0; (i < imax) && (delta_new > eps * delta0); ++i)
        maxtrixMulVector(d_q, d_A, d_d);      // q = Ad
        alpha = delta_new/cplvDot(d_d, d_q, n); // alpha = delta_new/d^Tq
        cplvAdd_MulC_I(d_x, d_d, alpha, n) ;   // x = x + alpha * d
        cplvAdd_MulC_I(d_r, d_q, −alpha, n);   // r = r − alpha * q
        delta_old = delta_new;
        delta_new = cplvSum2(d_r, n);          // delta_new = r^Tr
        beta = delta_new / delta_old;          // beta = delta_new / delta_old
        cplvMulCAdd_I(d_d, beta, d_r, n);      // d = beta * d + r
    }
}
```

FIGURE 48.7

CG solver template.

achieve maximal memory bandwidth. Our experiments showed that in the case of the regular grid, the implicit approach allows for a more efficient matrix vector multiplication because the matrix does not consume memory bandwidth. As shown in Table 48.2, it is up to 2.5 times faster than explicit implementations [2]. The performance is measured in GFLOPs with Helmholtz Matrix vector multiplication.

Table 48.2 Performance comparison in GFLOPs between our implicit method and explicit implementations [2] (larger is faster)

Matrix size	64^3	96^3	128^3	160^3	192^3	224^3	256^3
Implicit	17	37	53	42	54	51	59
Explicit Dia	25	27	27	25	25	25	27
Explicit Ell	16	17	17	16	16	16	16

Algorithm 4: Multiscale atlas construction.

1: **Input** : N volume inputs, multi-scale information
2: **Output**: Template atlas volume
3: **for all** $s = 1$ to N_s **do** {loop over the scales}
4:   Read $factor_s$, $nIters_s$, fluid registration parameters at the scale
5:   **for** $i = 1$ to N **do** {loop over the images}
6:     **if** $factor_s = 1$ **then** {first level scale - original image}
7:       $I_{is} \leftarrow I_i$
8:     **else** {down sample the image}
9:       Blur the image $I_i(blur) = GaussFilter(I_i)$
10:       Down sample $I_{is} = DownSample(I_i(blur))$
11:     **end if**
12:     **if** $s = 1$ **then** {first iteration}
13:       $h_{is} \leftarrow Id, v_{is} \leftarrow 0$
14:       Copy the sample image $I_{is}^0 = I_{is}$
15:     **else**
16:       Up sample deformation field $h_{is}(x) = UpSample(h_{is}(x))$
17:       Up sample velocity field $v_{is}(x) = UpSample(v_{is}(x))${if needed}
18:       Update deformed image $I_{is}^0 = I_{is}(h_{is}(x)))$
19:     **end if**
20:   **end for**
21:   **Apply the atlas construction procedure at this scale**
22: **end for**

48.3.7 Multiscale Framework

The concept of our multiscale framework is derived from the multigrid technique, which computes an approximate solution on a coarse grid and then interpolates the result onto the finer grid. As the solution on the coarse grid generates a good initial guess of solution on the finer grid, it speeds up the convergence on the finer level. In addition to reducing the number of iterations, multiresolution increases the robustness with respect to noise in the input data because it is capable of handling local optimums inherent to gradient-descent optimization. We design a multiscale GPU interface (Algorithm 4) based on two main components: the downscale Gaussian filter and the upscale sampler.

Table 48.3 Performance comparison in us between different optimization strategies to implement 3D-Gaussian Filter with different kernel sizes

Half-Kernel Size	Separable	Dim-Shift	Recursive	FFT
2	14	17	10	85
4	26	28	10	85
8	49	47	10	80

The downscaled filter is composed of a low-pass filter followed by a down sampler. The low-pass filter is a 3-D-Gaussian filter that is implemented using 1-D-Gaussian separable filters along each axis. We discovered that it is more efficient to implement this 3-D filter based on the separable-recursive Gaussian filter, rather than convolution-based or FFT-based approaches. Our recursive version is generalized from the 1-D recursive version (see NVIDIA SDK *RecursiveGaussian*) with a circular-dimension shifting 3-D transpose. As shown in Table 48.3 the 3-D recursive version is the fastest, and its runtime, measured in milliseconds, is independent of the kernel size. The other methods in comparison are: a separable filter, a circular-dimension shifting combined with the 1-D filter in the fastest dimension, and an FFT-based filter.

While the down sampler simply fetches values from the grid, the up sampler is the reverse-mapping operation from the grid point of the finer scale to the point value of the coarser grid based on the trilinear interpolation. Here, we used the same optimization as for the ODE integration.

Our multiresolution framework can be employed in any 3-D image-processing problem to improve both performance and robustness.

48.3.8 Multi-GPU Processing Model

Computing systems in practice have to deal with a large amount of data that cannot be processed directly and efficiently by a single-processing system. GPUs are no exception to this limitation. Hence, the development of a parallel multi-GPU framework is necessary, especially for exploiting the total power of multi-GPU systems (multi-GPU desktops) or GPU cluster systems.

In the following, we address the two main bottlenecks of multi-GPUs and cluster implementations: the limited CPU-GPU bandwidth, which is about 20 times slower than the local GPU memory bandwidth, and the limited network bandwidth between compute nodes, which is an order of magnitude slower than CPU-GPU bandwidth. Our computational model aims at minimizing the amount of data transfer over the slow media, exploiting existing APIs such as MPI, and moving most of the computation from the CPUs to the massively parallel GPUs.

Multi-GPU Model

We first proposed a multiple-input multi-GPU model [7]. The key idea was to maximize the total volume of inputs that the system can handle. In other words, by maximizing the number of inputs per node, we increase the *arithmetic intensity* of each processing node.

We divide the inputs between GPU nodes and assign a GPU memory buffer at each node to serve both as an accumulation buffer and an average input buffer. The output buffer is used to sum up the local deformed volumes; the input buffer contains the new average and is shared among volumes of the node.

At each iteration, we compute the local accumulation buffers and send the result to the server to compute the global accumulation buffer. The new aggregate volume is read back to GPU nodes. Next, we perform a volume division on the GPUs to update the average.

Our aggregate model is more efficient than our previous average model [7] because it yields the same memory bandwidth, but moves the computation from CPUs to GPUs; hence, it is able to exploit the computational power of the GPU. This strategy minimizes both the overall cost per volume element as well as the data transfer over the low-bandwidth channel.

GPU Cluster Model

We generalize the multiple-input multi-GPU model to a higher level to build a computationally efficient framework on GPU clusters. As displayed in Figure 48.8, we maintain two buffers on a CPU-multi-GPU processing node: an output accumulation buffer and an input aggregate buffer that is shared among the members of the buffer's GPUs. These two CPU memory buffers are used as the interface memory to other processing nodes through the MPIs. As we used the aggregated model instead of the average, we can directly exploit the MPI all-reduce function to efficiently compute and update the accumulated volume to all processing nodes. Next, we address the load distribution problem of the GPU cluster implementation.

Load Balancing

We consider load balancing on a system with homogeneous GPUs with N_i, N_g, N_p being the number of inputs, GPUs, and CPUs. Our test system is a Tesla S1070 cluster, with each node having dual-GPUs, thereby implying that $N_g = 2 * N_p$.

On the cluster, the total runtime per iteration is computed by $T = T_{GPU} + T_{CPU} + T_{Network}$. As the number of GPUs per node is fixed, T_{CPU} — the amount of time to compute the aggregate among GPUs of the same node — is fixed. Consequently, we must reduce T_{GPU} and/or $T_{Network}$ to improve the runtime.

First, we assume that N_p is fixed, then $T_{Network}$ — the amount of time to accumulate and distribute the result between CPUs — is defined. T_{GPU} depends on the maximum number of inputs per GPU, which is at least $N_{ig} = \left\lceil \dfrac{N_i}{N_g} \right\rceil$. This number is optimal if inputs are distributed evenly between GPUs, not CPUs because CPUs may have a variable number of GPUs attached. So our first strategy is distributing

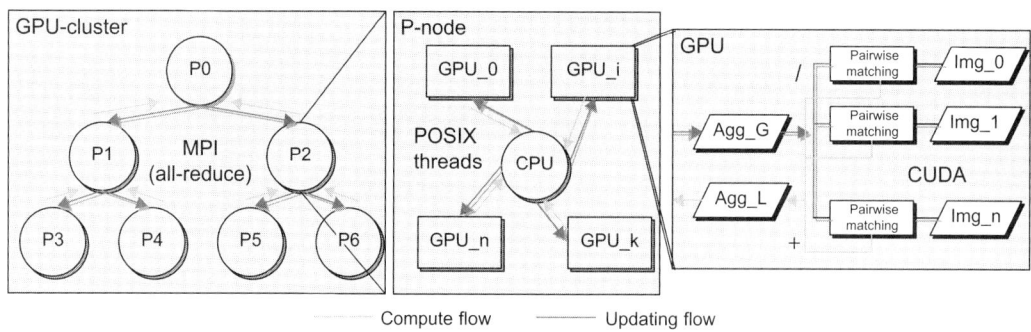

Compute flow   Updating flow

FIGURE 48.8

Multi-GPU framework on the GPU cluster.

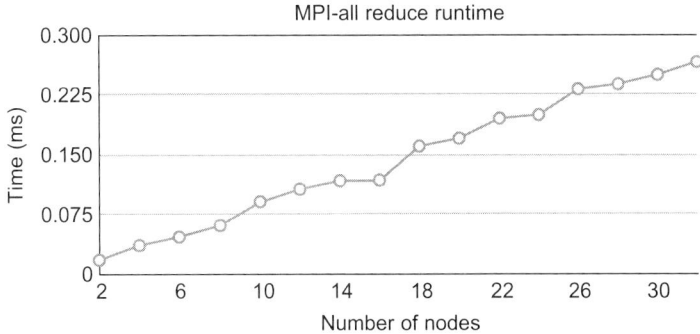

FIGURE 48.9

MPI-all reduce runtime on an infiniband network with OpenMPI 1.3 shows a linear dependency on the number of nodes.

inputs evenly among GPU nodes. With this strategy, there is at most one unbalanced GPU, and the GPU runtime with synchronization is optimal.

Second, it is highly likely that the MPI all-reduce function performs the binary tree down-sweep to accumulate the volume and binary tree up-sweep to distribute the sum to all nodes, as shown in Figure 48.8. This yields a minimal amount of data transferred over the network, that is, $2 * N_p$. It is suggested that the amount of data transfer over the network increases linearly with the number of CPU nodes, and therefore, fewer CPUs implies smaller delay. This hypothesis is confirmed in our cluster in the experiment (see Figure 48.9).

To reduce the number of CPU nodes, we increase the GPU workload. Note that from the first strategy we want to increase all GPUs with the same number of volumes so that the computation is balanced. Let us increase this number by one; the total runtime then is

$$T = T_{GPU} * \frac{N_{ig} + 1}{N_{ig}} + T_{CPU} + T_{Network} * \frac{N_p - N_{ps}}{N_p}$$

where N_{ps} is the number of GPUs reduced by increasing the workload. This equation gives us an approximation of running time as the number of volumes per GPU changes. Hence, we can vary the capability on the GPU node to achieve a better configuration. Note that in the dual-GPU system, if the number of volumes per GPU is less than N_g, when we increase the number of volumes per GPU by one, we can decrease the number of CPUs at least by two.

Our load-balancing strategy is as follows: First, the users choose the number of nodes. Based on this choice the system computes the number of inputs per GPU. The components' runtime is then determined with a one-iteration dry run on the zero-initialized volumes that require no data from the host. Next, the optimizer varies the number of volumes per GPU, recomputes the number of CPU nodes, and computes the total runtime. This heuristic yields an optimal configuration to handle the problem.

48.3.9 Performance Tuning

To further improve the performance, we now present a volume-clipping optimization and the scratch memory model. Those techniques are specially applied for multi-image-processing problems.

Volume Clipping Optimization

Volume clipping is the final step of the preprocessing, which includes

- Rigid alignment and affine registration
- Intensity calibration and normalization
- Volume clipping

The rigid alignment and affine registration guarantee all inputs to be in the same space, while the preprocessing distances between them are minimal. This strategy significantly speeds up the convergence of the image registration process. The intensity calibration ensures that the intensity range of the inputs are matched and are normalized for visualization purposes. Although these two preprocessing steps are generally applied in a regular image registration framework, the volume clipping is a special optimization scheme applied for the brain image to reduce processing time.

Pointwise computations on zero-data usually return zero; we call this data redundant. This redundancy happens near the boundary of the volume. The volume-clipping strategy first computes the nonzero data-bounding boxes and then tightly clips all the volumes to the common bounding box with guarded boundary conditions. In practice, the volume of clipping inputs can be significantly smaller than a typical input volume; for example, the 256^3 brain images in our experiment have a common volume of size $160 \times 192 \times 160$, a volume ratio of three. Because the runtime of a function is proportional to the volume of the inputs, we experienced three to four times speedup just by applying this volume-clipping strategy. Note that this optimization is more effective at PDE SOR solvers than FFT-based solvers because the latter require a power of two volume size to be computationally efficient.

Scratch Memory Model

It is always a challenge to implement 3-D processing frameworks on GPUs as the parallel processing scheme often requires more memory than it would on CPUs. To deal with this memory problem, we proposed a scratch memory model, a shared-temporary memory space, coupled with different optimization techniques including:

- Zero-copy operation based on pointer swapping to reduce the redundant memory copy from scratch memory (Figure 48.10(a))
- A circular buffer technique to reduce memory copy redundancy and also memory storage requirements for computation in a loop (Figure 48.10(b))

The use of the scratch memory model helps us to significantly reduce the memory requirement. In particular, in the case of the greedy iterative atlas construction, we only need a single image buffer and two 3-D-vector buffers for an arbitrary number of inputs on a single GPU device. Consequently, we are able to process 20 brain volumes with 4 GB global memory, or 40 brain volumes on a single dual-GPU node.

48.4 FINAL EVALUATION AND VALIDATION OF RESULTS, TOTAL BENEFITS, AND LIMITATIONS

The system we used in our experiment is a 64-node Tesla S1070 cluster, each containing two GPUs. Communication from the host to GPU was via the external x16 PCIe bus, and inter-node

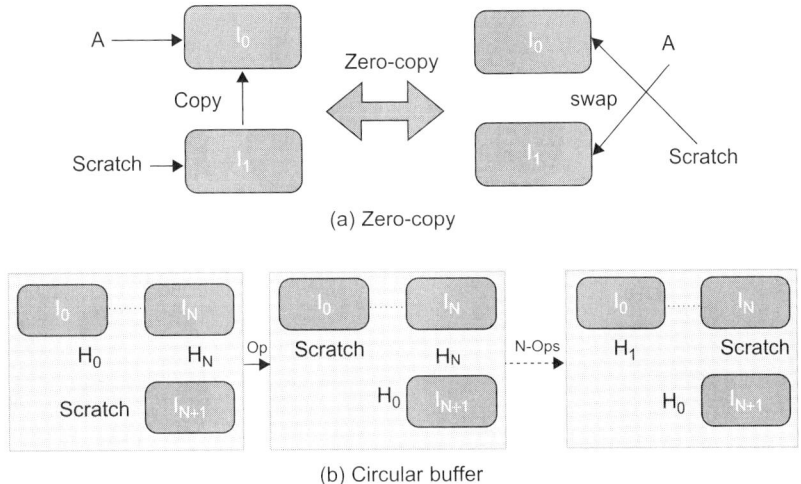

FIGURE 48.10

Optimization strategies with the scratch memory model.

communication was implemented through a 20 Gb 4x DDR infiniband interconnect. The program was compiled with CUDA NVCC 2.3. For multiresolution, we performed a two-scale computation with 25 iterations in the coarse level and, 50 iterations in the finer level, with parameters set $\alpha = 0.01$, $\gamma = 0.001$, and *maximum step size* $= 1$. The three solvers used in the comparison were FFT solver, the block-SOR, and conjugate gradient(CG). The runtime did not include the data-loading time that depends on the hard disk system.

48.4.1 Quality Improvements

To evaluate the robustness and stability of the atlases, we use the random permutation test proposed by Lorenzen *et al.* [10]. The method is capable of estimating the minimum number of inputs required to construct a stable atlas by analyzing mean entropy and the variance of the average template. We generated 13 atlas cohorts, $C_{l,l=2\cdots14}$, each including 100 atlases constructed from l input images chosen randomly from the original dataset. The 2-D mid-axial slices of the atlases are shown in Figure 48.11. The normal average atlases are blurry, and ghosting is evident around the lateral ventricles, as well as near the boundary of the brain. In this case, the greedy iterative average template appears to be much sharper, preserving anatomical structures.

The quality of the atlas construction is visibly better than the least MSE normal average. The entropy results shown in Figure 48.12 also confirm the stability of our implementation. As the number of inputs increases, the average atlas entropy of the simple averaging intensity increases, while the greedy iterative average template decreases owing to much higher individual sharpness. This quantitatively asserts the visible quality improvement in Figure 48.11. The atlases become more stable with respect to the entropy as the standard deviation decreases with an increasing number of inputs. After cohort C_8, the atlas entropy mean appears to converge. So we need at least eight images to create a stable atlas representing neuroanatomy.

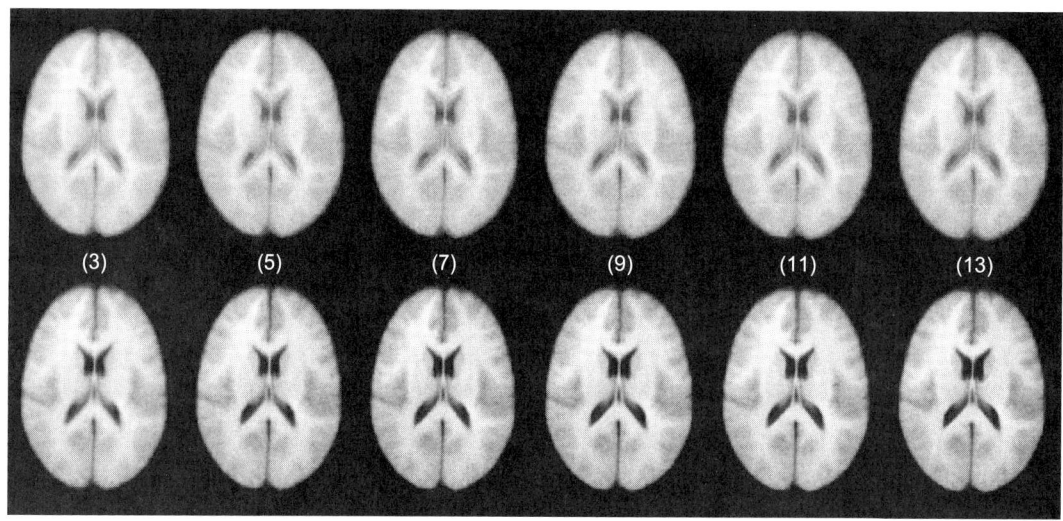

FIGURE 48.11

Atlas results with 3, 5, 7, 9, 11, and 13 inputs constructed by arithmetically averaging rigidly aligned images (top row) and greedy iterative average template construction (bottom row).

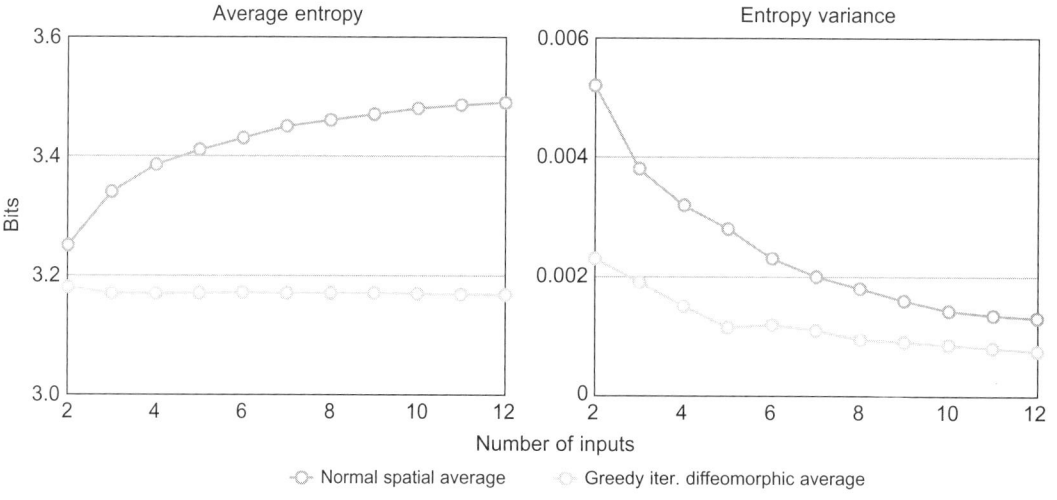

FIGURE 48.12

Mean entropy and variance of atlases constructed by arithmetically averaging and the greedy iterative average template.

48.4.2 Performance Improvement

We compare the speedup of the multiscale framework to the single-scale version with a pairwise matching problem to produce comparable results. Experiments show that we generally need 25 iterations in

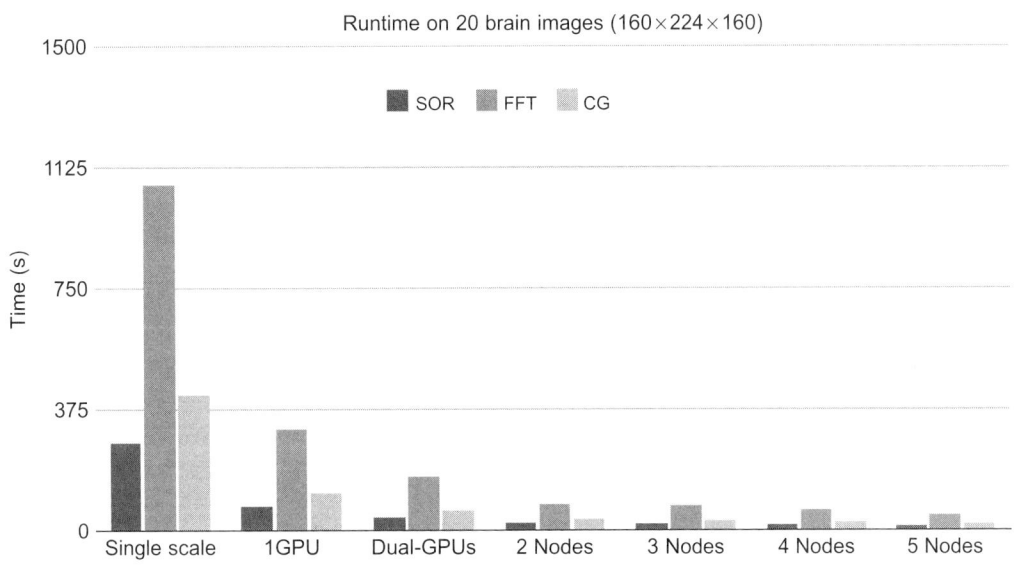

FIGURE 48.13

Runtime to compute the average atlas of the 20 T1 brain images (144 × 192 × 160) with multiscale and/or multi-GPUs, cluster implementation in reference to one-scale version.

the second level and 50 iterations in the first level to produce similar results, whereas we need 200 iterations with a single-scale implementation. The speedup factor is about 3.5 and comes primarily from lowering the number of iterations in the finest level.

We quantify the compute capability and scalability of our system in two cases. First, by applying the scratch memory technique, we are able to handle 20 T1 images of size 160 × 224 × 160 on a single GPU device. We measure the performance with one GPU device (multiscale), one single node with dual-GPUs (multiscale multi-GPUs), and two, four, and five GPU nodes (multiscale cluster) in reference to a single-scale version on the 20-brain input set. As shown in Figure 48.13 the multiscale version is about 3.5 times faster than the single-scale version, whereas our multi-GPU version is twice as fast as a single device. The cluster version shows a linear performance improvement to the number of nodes.

Second, we experiment with the full dataset of 315 volumes of T1 input size 144 × 192 × 160. For the first time we handle the whole dataset on eight nodes of the GPU cluster. We measure the performance with 8, 12, 16, 20, 24, 28, and 32 nodes. On the 32-core Intel Xeon server X7350, 2.93 GHz with 196 GB of shared memory, which is able to load the whole dataset in the core, the CPU-optimized greedy implementation took 2 minutes for a single iteration. As shown on Figure 48.14, it only takes the SOR solver about 70 seconds to compute the average on eight nodes of the GPU cluster and only 20 seconds on 32 nodes, which is two orders of magnitude faster than the 32-core CPU server.

48.5 FUTURE DIRECTIONS

In this chapter we have presented our implementation of the unbiased greedy iterative atlas construction on multi-GPUs; however, this is only a showcase to illustrate the computing power and efficiency of our

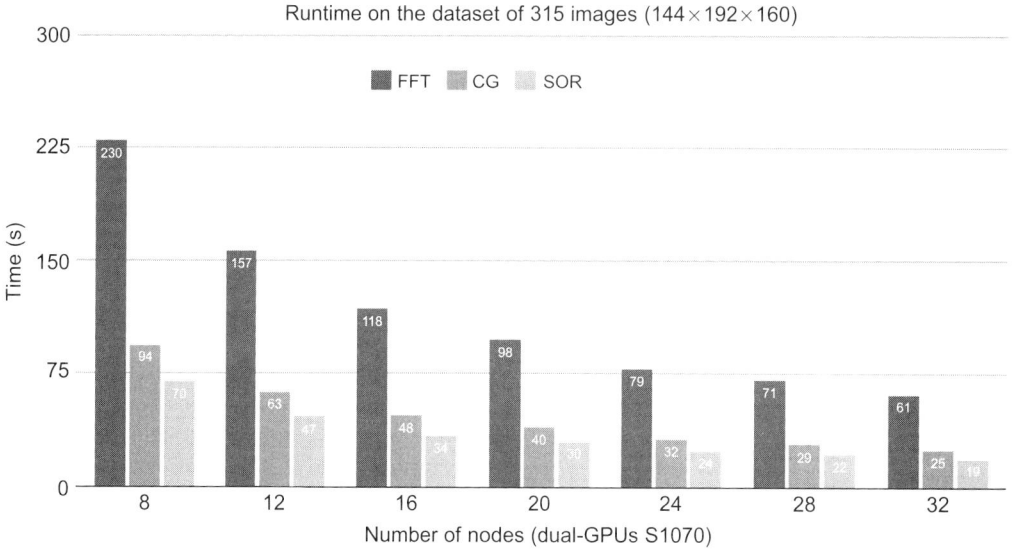

FIGURE 48.14

Multiscale runtime to compute the average atlas of the 315 T1 brain images (144 × 192 × 160) with different PDE solver.

processing framework. As we mentioned in the introduction, the atlas construction problem is a basic foundation for a class of diffeomorphic registration problems to study the intrapopulation variability and interpopulation differences. The ability to produce the result in real time enables us to understand the research influence of this powerful technique. Also the framework allows us to implement more sophisticated registration problems, such as LDDMM, metamorphosis, or image current. Although each technique has a different trade-off between quality of results and the computation involved, our framework is capable of quantifying those trade-offs to suggest a good solution for the practical problem suitable with inputs and the accessible computational power.

Although the system has the capability to handle large amounts of data, it requires a single matching pair to be completely solvable on a single-GPU node; however, such compute power is not always available. So we are considering extending the processing power of a single-GPU system using an out-of-core technique. This requires a major redesign of our system; however, it is a required feature of our processing system to handle the ever-growing amounts of data in the future.

Note that our code is a part of the AtlasWerks project, which is free for research purposes and is available to download at http://www.sci.utah.edu/software.html.

Acknowledgments

This research has been funded by the National Science Foundation grant CNS-0751152 and National Institute of Health Grants R01EB007688 and P41-RR023953. L. Ha was partially supported by the Vietnam Education Foundation fellowship. Specially, the authors thank Sam Preston, Marcel Prastawa, and Thomas Fogal for their time and feedback on the work.

References

[1] M.M. Baskaran, R. Bordawekar, Optimizing sparse matrix-vector multiplication on GPUs, IBM Technical Report, 2008. Available from: http://domino.watson.ibm.com.

[2] N. Bell, M. Garland, Implementing sparse matrix-vector multiplication on throughput-oriented processors, in: SC '09: Proceedings of the Conference on High Performance Computing Networking, Storage and Analysis, 2009, Portland, Oregon, ACM, New York, 2009, pp. 1–11.

[3] M. Bro-Nielsen, C. Gramkow, Fast fluid registration of medical images, in: VBC '96: Proceedings of the 4th International Conference on Visualization in Biomedical Computing, 1996, Springer-Verlag, London, UK, 1996, pp. 267–276.

[4] G.E. Christensen, M.I. Miller, M.W. Vannier, U. Grenander, Individualizing neuroanatomical atlases using a massively parallel computer, Computer 29 (1996) 32–38.

[5] G.E. Christensen, R.D. Rabbitt, M.I. Miller, Deformable templates using large deformation kinematics, Image Proc. IEEE Trans. Image Proc. 5 (10) (1996) 1435–1447.

[6] B.C. Davis, P.T. Fletcher, E. Bullitt, S. Joshi, Population shape regression from random design data, in: Proceeding of the 11th IEEE International Conference on Computer Vision (ICCV 2007), 2007, pp. 1–7.

[7] L.K. Ha, J. Krüger, P.T. Fletcher, S. Joshi, C.T. Silva, Fast parallel unbiased diffeomorphic atlas construction on multi-graphics processing units, in: EUROGRAPHICS Symposium on Parallel Graphics and Visualization, 2009. Available from: http://www.sci.utah.edu/~csilva/papers/egpgv2009.pdf.

[8] J. Hoberock, N. Bell, Thrust: A Parallel Template Library, Version 1.3, 2009. Available from: https://www.ohloh.net/p/thrust.

[9] S. Joshi, B. Davis, M. Jomier, G. Gerig, Unbiased diffeomorphic atlas construction for computational anatomy, neuroimage 23 (Suppl.) (2004) S151–S160.

[10] P. Lorenzen, B. Davis, S. Joshi, Unbiased atlas formation via large deformations metric mapping, in: J.S. Duncan, G. Gerig (Eds.), Medical Image Computing and Computer Assisted Intervention (MICCAI), Int. Conf. Med. Image Comput. Comput. Assist. Interv. (MICCAI), vol. 8 (Pt. 2), 2005, pp. 411–418.

[11] P. Micikevicius, 3D finite difference computation on GPUs using CUDA, in: Proceedings of 2nd Workshop on General Purpose Processing on Graphics Processing Units, GPGPU2, 2009, New York, 2009, pp. 79–84.

[12] NVIDIA, CUDA Technical Training, Technical report, NVIDIA Corporation, 2009.

[13] D. Young, Iterative Solution of Large Linear Systems, Academic Press, 1997.

GPU-Accelerated Brain Connectivity Reconstruction and Visualization in Large-Scale Electron Micrographs

Won-Ki Jeong, Hanspeter Pfister, Johanna Beyer, Markus Hadwiger

49.1 INTRODUCTION

The reconstruction of neural connections to understand the function of the brain is an emerging and active research area in neuroscience. With the advent of high-resolution scanning technologies, such as 3-D light microscopy and electron microscopy (EM), reconstruction of complex 3-D neural circuits from large volumes of neural tissues has become feasible. Among them, only EM data can provide sufficient resolution to identify synapses and to resolve extremely narrow neural processes. Current EM technologies are able to attain resolutions of three to five nanometers per pixel in the x-y plane. Because of its extremely high resolution, an EM scan of a single section from a tiny brain tissue of only a half cubic millimeter in size can easily reach up to tens of gigabytes, and the total scan of the tissue sample can be as large as several hundred terabytes of raw data. Figure 49.1 is an example of a high-resolution EM image in different zoom levels.

These high-resolution, large-scale datasets pose challenging problems, for example, how to process and manipulate large datasets to extract scientifically meaningful information using a compact representation in a reasonable processing time. Among all, reconstructing a wire diagram of neuronal connections in the brain is the most important challenge we tackle. In this chapter, we introduce a GPU-accelerated interactive, semiautomatic axon segmentation and visualization system [1]. There are two challenging problems we address: (1) interactive 3-D axon segmentation and (2) interactive 3-D image filtering and rendering of implicit surfaces. We exploit the high-throughput, massively parallel computing power of recent GPUs to make the proposed system run at interactive rates. The main focus of this chapter is introducing the GPU algorithms and their implementation details, which are the core components of our interactive segmentation and visualization system.

49.2 CORE METHODS
49.2.1 Semiautomatic Axon Segmentation

Axons are pathways that serve as a communication network to connect distant cell bodies, and are presented as thin, elongated tubes in 3-D space. Our approach [1] to extract such long and thin 3-D tubular structures is combining 2-D segmentation and 3-D tracking methods. Each 2-D segmentation is

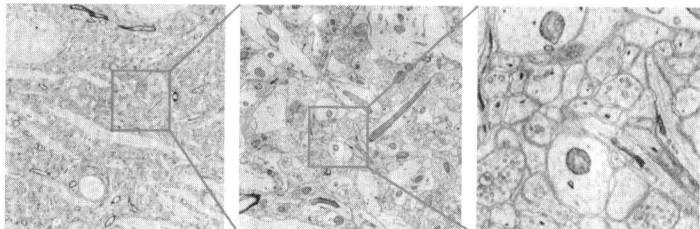

FIGURE 49.1

An example of a high-resolution EM scan of a mouse brain. From left to right: A zoomed-out view of an EM image, 4× magnification, and 16× magnification. The pixel resolution of an EM image that we are dealing with is around three to five nanometers; this resolution allows scientists to look at nanoscale cell structures, such as synapses or narrow axons, as shown in the image on the right.

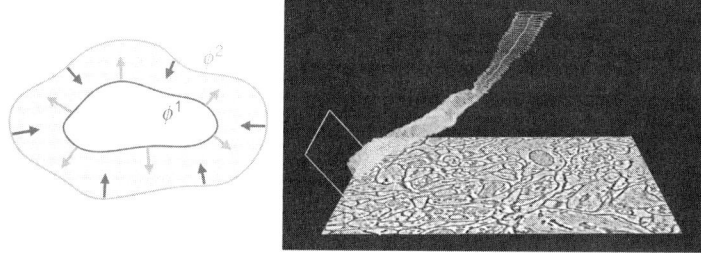

FIGURE 49.2

3-D axon segmentation consists of 2-D cell membrane segmentation and 3-D tracking. Left: The active ribbon model. Right: 3-D tracking of an axon as a collection of 2-D ribbons.

done on a small 2-D region-of-interest (ROI) image sampled from the input 3-D volume. Therefore, it scales well to the large EM images we are acquiring. We use the active ribbon model [10] to segment the outer boundary of the axon membrane on each 2-D ROI. As each cell membrane is extracted, we trace the center of each axon cross-section using a forward Euler integration method to finally create a 3-D model of the axon. Figure 49.2 (left) is a pictorial description of the active ribbon model, and (right) is a screenshot of our 3-D axon segmentation in action.

The active ribbon model consists of two deformable interfaces, ϕ^1 and ϕ^2 in Figure 49.2 (left), that push or pull against each other until they converge to the inner and outer wall of the cell membrane. The deformable model we employed is a multiphase level set [11], where the n-level set is a set of points whose distance is n. We use two level sets whose partial differential equations (PDE) are defined by various internal and external forces to enhance the smoothness of the interfaces and to preserve the band topology as follows:

$$\frac{d\phi^i}{dt} + (\alpha \mathbf{F}_D + \beta \mathbf{F}_R + \gamma \mathbf{F}_K + \delta \mathbf{F}_C)|\nabla \phi^i| = 0, \qquad (49.1)$$

where $\mathbf{F}_D$ is the data-dependent speed to move the interface toward the membrane, $\mathbf{F}_R$ is the ribbon consistency speed to keep the distance between two level sets constant, $\mathbf{F}_K$ is the mean curvature speed to maintain the shape of the interface as smooth as possible, and $\mathbf{F}_C$ is the image correspondence speed to enforce the level sets to transfer from one slice to the next correctly.

Solutions to Equation 49.1 can be computed using an iterative update scheme. To keep the topology of the active ribbon consistent during the level set iteration, we need to evaluate the distance between the two zero level sets. Because the active ribbon does not guarantee the correct distance after deformation owing to the combination of various force fields, we need to correct the error by computing the signed distances from the level sets after the level set equation update. We also include an image correspondence force into the level set formulation to robustly initialize the location of the interfaces on subsequent slices. The computational challenges we address are

- Multiphase level set computation;
- Re-initialization of level sets using distance transform; and
- Image correspondence computation using nonrigid image registration.

We implemented those time-consuming numerical methods on the GPU to achieve interactive performance.

Solving PDEs using an iterative solver on parallel systems is a well-studied problem [3]. However, mapping it on massively parallel architectures, such as GPUs, has been attempted only recently [4]. Although many iterative solvers are based on global update schemes (e.g., the Jacobi update), the most efficient approach to solve the level set PDE is using adaptive updating schemes and data structures, such as narrow band [9] or sparse field [12] approaches. Such adaptive schemes are typically not good candidates for parallelization on the GPU, but we overcome the problem by employing data structures and algorithms that exhibit spatially coherent memory access and temporally coherent executions. Our approach is using a *block-based* data structure and update scheme as introduced in [1, 2, 4]. The input domain is divided into blocks of predefined size, and only the blocks containing the zero level set, that is, the *active blocks*, will be updated. Entire data points (or nodes) in a block are updated concurrently using parallel threads on the GPU. This parallel algorithm can be used to update level set PDEs and to compute distance transforms.

On the other hand, the GPU nonrigid image registration that we implemented is a standard global energy minimization process using the Jacobi update, which is a gradient descent method implemented on the GPU. The energy function we minimize is:

$$E_I = \frac{1}{2} \int_\Omega (\widetilde{I}_i - I_{i+1})^2 + \alpha \|\nabla \mathbf{v}\|^2, \tag{49.2}$$

where I_i and I_{i+1} are two input images, Ω is the image domain, $\widetilde{I}_i$ is the image I_i deformed by the vector field $\mathbf{v}$, and α is a regularization parameter. The solution vector field $\mathbf{v}$ that minimizes Equation 49.2 gives pixel-to-pixel correspondence between I_i and I_{i+1}. In order to find $\mathbf{v}$, we use a gradient flow method along the negative gradient direction of E_I with respect to $\mathbf{v}$.

49.2.2 3-D Volume and Axon Surface Visualization

For the visualization of the high-resolution and extremely dense and heavily textured EM data, we support the inspection of data prior to segmentation, as well as the display of the ongoing and the final segmentation.

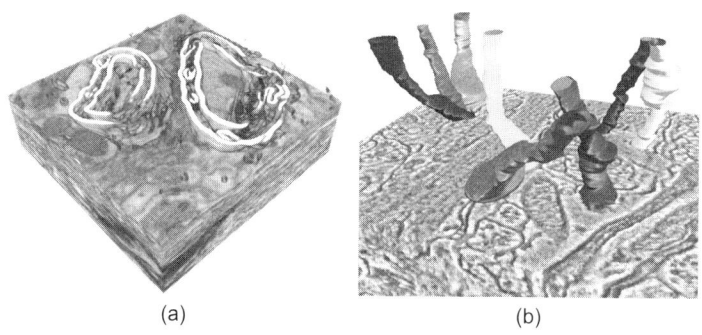

(a)   (b)

FIGURE 49.3

Volume rendering of electron microscopy (EM) data to depict neural processes. (a) On-the-fly boundary enhancement. (b) 3-D visualization of segmented neural processes embedded in the volume.

To visualize the complex structure of interconnected nerve cells and to highlight regions of interest (e.g., myelinated axons) prior to segmentation, we have implemented on-the-fly nonlinear noise removal and boundary enhancement (Figure 49.3(a)). To display the ongoing and final neural process segmentation, we combine direct volume rendering with implicit surface ray casting in a single rendering pass (Figure 49.3(b)).

Our visualization approach is built upon a GPU-based raycaster [8] that supports bricking for handling of large datasets. *Bricking* is the process of splitting up a single volume into several individual volume bricks. Bricking by itself does not reduce overall memory consumption; however, it can reduce memory consumption on the GPU by downloading only currently active bricks (i.e., the current working set of bricks) to GPU memory.

On-Demand Volume Filtering Using the GPU

To improve the visual quality of the volume rendered EM data and to highlight regions of interest prior to segmentation, we have implemented on-the-fly nonlinear noise removal and boundary enhancement filters. A local histogram-based boundary metric [5] is calculated on demand for currently visible parts of the volume and cached for later reuse. During ray casting we use the computed boundary values to modulate the current sample's opacity with different user-selectable opacity weighting modes (e.g., min, max, alpha blending), thereby enhancing important structures like myelinated axons, while fading out less important regions. For noise removal, we have implemented Gaussian, mean, median, bilateral, and anisotropic diffusion filters in both 2-D and 3-D with variable neighborhood sizes.

We have implemented a general on-demand volume-filtering framework entirely on the GPU using CUDA, which allows for changing filters and filter parameters on the fly, while avoiding additional disk storage and bandwidth bottlenecks for terabyte-sized volume data.

Filtering is performed only on currently visible 3-D bricks of the volume, depending on the current viewpoint, and the computed bricks are stored directly on the GPU, using a GPU caching scheme. This avoids costly transfers to and from GPU memory, while at the same time, avoiding repetitive recalculation of already filtered bricks. During visualization, we display either the original volume, the de-noised volume, the computed boundary values, or a combination of the above.

GPU Implicit Surface Ray Casting

For visualizing segmented neural processes in 3-D, we depict the original volume data together with semitransparent iso-surfaces that delineate segmented structures such as axons or dendrites in a single front-to-back ray casting step implemented in CUDA [1].

Keeping our large dataset sizes in mind, we store the segmentation results in a very compact format, where each axon is represented as a simple list of elliptical cross sections. For an ongoing segmentation, the list of elliptical cross sections is continuously updated. For rendering, we use standard front-to-back ray casting with the addition of interpolating implicit surfaces from the set of ellipses on the fly. If, during ray casting, a sample intersects an implicit surface, the color and opacity of the surface are composited with the previously accumulated volume rendered part, and volume rendering is continued behind the surface. Therefore, during ray casting, we need to compute the intersections of rays with the implicit surface. The implicit surface itself is interpolated between two successive elliptical cross sections, which enclose the given sample position on a ray. We efficiently combine direct volume rendering with iso-surface ray casting [8], using a single ray-casting CUDA kernel.

49.3 IMPLEMENTATION

We implemented the most time-consuming and computationally expensive components in our system using NVIDIA CUDA and have tested our implementation on NVIDIA GPUs.

49.3.1 GPU Active Ribbon Segmentation

Our GPU active ribbon segmentation consists of two parts: GPU level set update and GPU distance computation. GPU level set update is an inner loop of the main iteration and is iterated multiple times before the re-distance step corrects the errors incurred by the level set update. The entire process is depicted in Figure 49.4.

Level Set Updating Using the GPU

Our GPU multiphase level set method manages two sets of signed distance fields, one for each active ribbon boundary, and updates each level set concurrently in order to preserve the topology of the active ribbon. Each individual level set is implemented using a streaming narrowband level set method [4] that updates the solution only in the active regions using a block-based GPU data structure. However, we do not explicitly check the boundary of each block for activation as in the original method. Instead, we simply collect all the blocks whose minimum distance to the zero level set is within the user-defined narrowband width. The distance to the zero level set is computed in the re-distance step, so we only need to find the minimum value per block using a parallel reduction scheme. In addition, each level set uses the other level set to update its value, so both level sets must be updated concurrently using the Jacobi update scheme and ping-pong rendering using extra buffers. Interblock communication across block boundaries is handled implicitly between each CUDA kernel call because the current level set values are written back to global memory at the end of each level set update iteration.

We efficiently manage the active list by storing and updating the entire list on the GPU, and only the minimum information is transferred to the CPU that is required to launch a CUDA kernel accordingly. The first element of the active list is the total number of active blocks, followed by a list of active

CPU host code

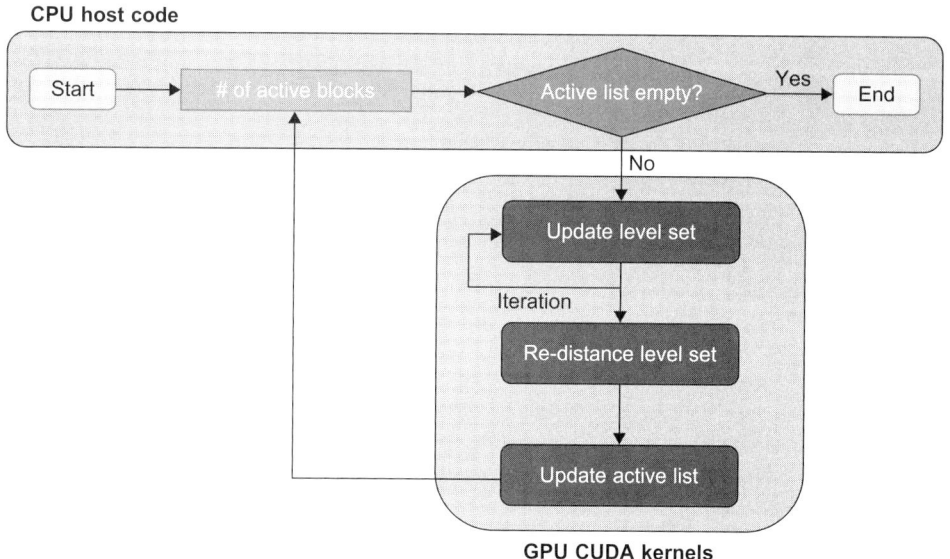

FIGURE 49.4

A flowchart of the GPU active ribbon segmentation process.

block indices. Therefore, the host code reads only the first element in the active list to launch a CUDA kernel with the grid size equal to the number of active blocks. To retrieve a correct block from global memory in the CUDA kernel code, we perform a one-level indirect access, i.e., reading an active block index from active list and computing the actual memory location of the block in global memory. The process is described in Figure 49.5. Updating the active list is performed in parallel on the GPU. If any pixel in the current block touches the narrowband, i.e., the minimum distance to the zero level set is smaller than the narrowband width, then the current block index is added to the active list in global memory. The active list is implemented as a preallocated 1-D integer array and an unsigned integer value that points to the last element in the array. To add a new active block index to the active list, we use `AtomicAdd()` to mutually exclusively access the last active list element index and increase it by one because many blocks can access it simultaneously.

We implemented the level set solver using an explicit Euler integration scheme with a finite difference method. Because the curvature term in our level set formulation is a parabolic contribution to the equation, we use a central difference scheme for curvature-related computations; otherwise, an upwind scheme is used to compute first- and second-order derivatives [9]. Therefore, the update formula for Equation 49.1 can be defined as follows:

$$\phi_{new}^i = \phi_{old}^i - dt(((\alpha \mathbf{F}_D + \beta \mathbf{F}_R)|\nabla \phi^i|)_{up} + (\gamma \mathbf{F}_K |\nabla \phi^i|)_{central} + \delta \mathbf{F}_C) \quad (49.3)$$

$$\mathbf{F}_D = (c_2 - c_1)\left(I - \frac{(c_1 + c_2)}{2}\right)$$

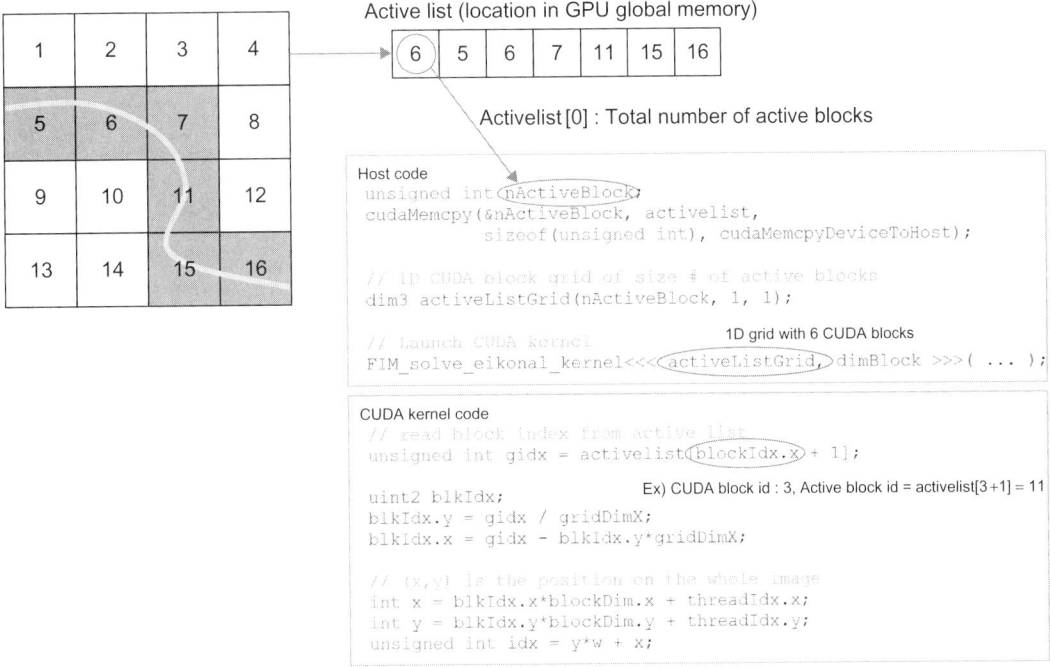

FIGURE 49.5

An example of the host and CUDA kernel code showing how to use the active list. Six blocks among 16 blocks are active (left, colored in grey). The active list is stored in GPU global memory, and only the first element of the list (the total number of active blocks) will be copied to CPU memory. Then the host code launches the CUDA kernel with the 1-D grid size equal to the number of active blocks.

$$\mathbf{F}_R = \sigma_i(\phi^j)\nabla\phi^j \cdot \frac{\nabla\phi^i}{|\nabla\phi^i|}$$

$$\mathbf{F}_K = \nabla \cdot \frac{\nabla\phi^i}{|\nabla\phi^i|}$$

$$\mathbf{F}_C = \text{sign}\left(\phi^i - \widetilde{\phi}^i_{prev}\right)\left|\phi^i - \widetilde{\phi}^i_{prev}\right|,$$

where c_1 and c_2 are the average pixel intensity of inner cell region and cell membrane, respectively, ϕ^j is the other level set in the active ribbon, $\sigma_i(\phi^j)$ is the function that returns a positive value if two level sets ϕ^i and ϕ^j are too close and a negative value otherwise, $\widetilde{\phi}^i_{prev}$ is the level set solution deformed by the vector field $\mathbf{v}$ (in Equation 49.2) from the previous slice, and $(\cdot)_{central}$ and $(\cdot)_{up}$ are approximated by the central difference and one-sided upwind difference scheme, respectively. Because pixel values are reused multiple times during derivative computation, we load the current block and its adjacent pixels into shared memory and reuse them to minimize global memory access. Figure 49.6 shows the code snippet of the level set update code implemented in CUDA.

```
//
// Finite difference calculation
//
float dx, dy, dxx, dxy, dyy, dxp, dyp, dxn, dyn;

dx  = (smem[cPos.x+1][cPos.y] − smem[cPos.x−1][cPos.y])*0.5f;
dy  = (smem[cPos.x][cPos.y+1] − smem[cPos.s][cPox.y−1])*0.5f;
dxp = (smem[cPos.x+1][cPox.y] − smem[cPos.x][cPox.y]);
dyp = (smem[cPos.x][cPos.y+1] − smem[cPos.x][cPos.y]);
dxn = (smem[cPos.x][cPos.y] − smem[cPos.x−1][cPos.y]);
dyn = (smem[cPos.x][cPos.y] − smem[cPos.x][cPos.y−1]);
dxx = (smem[cPos.x+1][cPos.y] − 2.0f*smem[cPos.x][cPos.y] + smem[cPos.x−1][cPox.y]);
dyy = (smem[cPos.x][cPos.y−1] − 2.0f*smem[cPos.x][cPos.y] + smem[cPos.x][cPos.y+1];
dxy = (−smem[cPos.x−1][cPos.y+1] − smem[cPos.x+1][cPos.y−1] +
        smem[cPos.x−1][cPos.y−1] + smem[cPos.x+1][cPos.y+1])*0.25f;

gradMag = sqrt(dx*dx + dy*dy);

float sgn = (isInner) ? 1.0f : −1.0f; // inside/outside level set in Active Ribbon
float wt = (sgn > 0) ? 4.0f : 1.0f;   // more data term weights to inner level set

// Compute speed functions
float FD, FR, FK, FC;

FR = sgn*sigma (−minRibbonWidth, −maxRibbonWidth, sgn*phi2[idx]);
FD = wt*sgn*(c1−c0)/255.0f*(input[idx] − (c0+c1)*0.5f)); // simplified chan and vese

if((dx*dx + dy*dy) > EPS) FK = (dy*dy*dxx − 2.0f*dx*dy*dxy +
                                    dx*dx*dyy)/powf(dx*dx + dy*dy, 1.5f);
else FK = 0;

FC = smem[cPos.x+1][cPos.y] − phiTarget;

// Upwind gradient magnitude
if (FD > 0)
{
    upwindGradMag = sqrtf( fmaxf(dxn,0.0f)*fmaxf(dxn,0.0f) +
                           fminf(dxp,0.0f)*fminf(dxp,0.0f) +
                           fmaxf(dyn,0.0f)*fmaxf(dyn,0.0f) +
                           fminf(dyp,0.0f)*fminf(dyp,0.0f) );
}
else
{
    upwindGradMag = sqrtf( fminf(dxn,0.0f)*fminf(dxn,0.0f) +
                           fmaxf(dxp,0.0f)*fmaxf(dxp,0.0f) +
                           fminf(dyn,0.0f)*fminf(dyn,0.0f) +
                           fmaxf(dyp,0.0f))*fmax(dyp,0.0f) );
}

// save output
inc[idx] = (alpha*FD + beta*FR)*upwindGradMag + gamma*FK*gradMag + delta*FC;
```

FIGURE 49.6

A code snippet of the level set update code written in CUDA. smem[] is a float array allocated in shared memory that holds the current block and its neighboring pixels.

Re-Distancing Level Sets Using the GPU

To quickly re-initialize the distance field using correct signed distance values after a number of level set updates, we employ a fast iterative method (FIM) [2] and solve the Eikonal equation on the GPU. The solution to the Eikonal equation gives the weighted distance to the source (seed) region. In our case we have a Euclidean distance because the speed value is one. We run the Eikonal solver four times, twice per level set, because the positive and negative distances from the zero level set should be computed independently. For example, to compute the positive distance, we set the distance value for all the pixels currently having negative values to zero. Those pixels are marked as source pixels and are treated as the boundary condition of the Eikonal equation.

FIM belongs to a class of label-correcting algorithms, which are well-known shortest path algorithms for graphs. Label-correcting algorithms do not use ordered data structures or special updating sequences that are common to label-setting algorithms such as the fast marching method [9]. Therefore, they map well to GPUs. FIM algorithms employ a list to simultaneously update multiple points in the active list using a Jacobi update step. To implement FIM on the GPU efficiently, we use a block-based data structure similar to our GPU level set implementation described in the previous section. Each active block is iteratively updated until it converges, and GPU threads update all the points in the same active block simultaneously. When an active block is converged, its neighboring blocks are checked, and any nonconvergent neighboring blocks are added to the active list. To check the convergence of a block we perform parallel reduction. Algorithm 1 shows the pseudocode description of our GPU FIM, where $U(\mathbf{b})$ represents a set of discrete solutions of the Eikonal equation, $g(\mathbf{b})$ represents a

---

Algorithm 1: GPU FIM$(V, L.)$.

---

comment: Update blocks $\mathbf{b}$ in active list L, V: set of all blocks

while L is not empty

$\mathbf{do}$ $\begin{cases}$
  comment: Step 1 - Update Active Blocks

  for each $\mathbf{b} \in L$ in parallel

  $\mathbf{do}$ $\begin{cases} \textbf{for } i = 0 \textbf{ to } n \\ \quad \mathbf{do} \ \{(U(\mathbf{b}), C_n(\mathbf{b})) \leftarrow \text{ solution of } g(\mathbf{b}) = 0 \\ C_b(\mathbf{b}) \leftarrow \text{reduction}(C_n(\mathbf{b})) \end{cases}$

  comment: Step 2 - Check Neighboring Blocks

  for each $b \in L$ in parallel

  $\mathbf{do}$ $\begin{cases} \textbf{if } C_b(b) = \text{TRUE} \\ \quad \textbf{then} \begin{cases} \textbf{for each} \text{ adjacent neighbor } \mathbf{b}_{nb} \text{ of } \mathbf{b} \\ \quad \mathbf{do} \begin{cases}(U(\mathbf{b}_{nb}), C_n(\mathbf{b}_{nb})) \leftarrow \text{ solution of } g(\mathbf{b}_{nb}) = 0 \\ C_b(\mathbf{b}_{nb}) \leftarrow \text{reduction}(C_n(\mathbf{b}_{nb})) \end{cases} \end{cases} \end{cases}$

  comment: Step 3 - Update Active List

  clear(L)

  for each $\mathbf{b} \in V$

  $\mathbf{do}$ $\begin{cases} \textbf{if } C_b(\mathbf{b}) = \text{FALSE} \\ \quad \textbf{then} \ \{\text{insert } \mathbf{b} \text{ to } L \end{cases}$
$\end{cases}$

---

block of Godunov discretization of the Hamiltonian for a grid block **b**, and C_n (a grid of boolean values that is same size as **b**) and C_b (a scalar boolean value) represent the convergence for nodes and a block **b**, respectively.

49.3.2 3-D Axon Tracking Using Image Correspondence

We use an image registration method to compute slice-to-slice correspondence to robustly initialize the current level set using the previous segmentation result. We implemented a nonrigid (deformable) image registration method on the GPU that minimizes a regularized intensity-difference energy (Equation 49.2). To compute the optimal **v** that minimizes E, we used a gradient flow method with discrete updates on **v** along the negative gradient direction of E. We implemented the gradient flow using semi-implicit discretization as a two-step iterative process as follows:

$$\mathbf{v} \leftarrow \mathbf{v} + dt(I_{i+1} - \widetilde{I}_i)\nabla\widetilde{I}_i \tag{49.4}$$

$$\mathbf{v} \leftarrow G \star \mathbf{v}, \tag{49.5}$$

where G is a Gaussian kernel and $\star$ is the convolution operator.

The first step, the iterative update process, is an explicit Euler integration method over time, and maps naturally to the GPU. Efficient GPU implementation of the iterative process is done using texture memory. $\widetilde{I}_i$ and $\nabla\widetilde{I}_i$ are the deformed image I_i and gradient of I_i by the vector field **v**, respectively. Because of the regularization term in the energy function E, the vector field **v** smoothly varies from one point to another. Therefore, $\widetilde{I}_i$ and $\nabla\widetilde{I}_i$ are, in fact, spatially coherent random memory accesses, and this memory access pattern can benefit from using a hardware-managed texture cache and pixel interpolation. The second step, Gaussian convolution on the vector field **v**, is implemented as consecutive 1-D Gaussian filtering along the x and y directions on a two-channel vector image **v**.

49.3.3 GPU-Based Volume Brick Filtering Framework

Our on-demand volume-filtering algorithm for EM data works on a bricked volume representation and consists of several steps:

1. Detection of volume bricks that are visible from the current viewpoint
2. Generation of a list of bricks that need to be computed
3. Noise removal filtering for selected bricks, storing the results in the GPU cache
4. Calculation of histogram-based boundary metric on selected bricks, storing the results in the GPU cache
5. High-resolution ray casting with opacity modulation based on computed boundary values

To reduce communication between CPU and GPU, we perform all of the preceding steps on the GPU and only transfer the minimum information needed to launch a CUDA kernel back to the CPU.

To store bricks that have been computed on the fly we use a dynamic GPU caching scheme. Two caches are allocated directly on the GPU: one cache to store de-noised volume bricks and the second cache to store bricks containing the calculated boundary values. First, the visibility of all bricks is updated for the current viewpoint in a first ray casting pass and saved in a 3-D array corresponding to the number of bricks in the volume. Next, all bricks are flagged as either: visible/not visible and present/not present in cache. Visible bricks that are already in the cache do not need to be recomputed. Only visible bricks that are not present in the cache need to be processed. Therefore, the indices of "visible, but not present" bricks are stored for later calculation. During filtering/boundary detection the computed bricks are stored in the corresponding cache. A small lookup table is maintained for mapping between brick storage space in the cache to actual volume bricks. Unused bricks are kept in the cache for later reuse. However, if cache memory gets low, unused bricks are flushed from the cache using an Lease-Recently-Used (LRU) scheme and replaced by currently visible bricks.

49.3.4 GPU Volume Brick Boundary Detection

As described in Section 49.3.3, for every view we determine a list of visible bricks in the volume during ray casting. We then perform filtering and boundary detection only for these visible bricks.

The boundary detection algorithm that we are using is based on the work of Martin *et al.* [5], which introduced a very robust method for detecting boundaries in 2-D images based on comparisons of local half-space histograms. In contrast to simpler edge detectors, this approach works very well in the presence of noise and can be used with arbitrary neighborhood sizes for computing the local histograms. For our EM data this boundary detection produces very good results, for example, in highlighting the boundaries of axons. The general idea is to go over all possible boundary directions for any given pixel, and compute a boundary value for each of the directions. The boundary value corresponds to the strength or probability of there being a boundary across the tested direction. The boundary value is computed by comparing the local histogram of the neighborhood on one side of the boundary with the local histogram of the neighborhood on the other side. The boundary in a given direction is strong when the two histograms are very different and weak when the two histograms are similar. The difference of the two histograms and thus the boundary value can be computed using the L1-norm or the χ^2 distance metric between histograms. In practice, of course, the space of all possible boundary directions is discretized to just a few directions, for example, 8 or 16 in 2-D.

Instead of using this boundary detection algorithm for 2-D images, we implement it in 3-D for volume bricks. For an efficient implementation in CUDA, we compute local histograms in a 3-D neighborhood around each voxel. The neighborhood size can be chosen by the user. For our experiments we use a neighborhood of $8 \times 8 \times 8$ voxels, but smaller neighborhood sizes could be used just as well. From the computed histograms, we calculate the brightness gradient of a voxel for every tested boundary direction. Each voxel's neighborhood is separated into two half-spaces that are determined by the boundary direction to check. For each half-space, the local histogram is computed. Finally, for each voxel the maximum difference of all boundary directions is stored in the volume brick and subsequently used as the scalar boundary value of the voxel during rendering. The boundary value can be used to determine the opacity of a voxel, for example.

We have implemented two different approaches for computing histogram-based boundary values in CUDA.

The first approach (*HistogramVoxelSweep*), illustrated in Figure 49.7, sets up an array of threads that work together to compute one output voxel at a time. This array of threads is then swept over the grid of all voxels in a volume brick in order to compute the output for the entire brick. During this sweep, many of the input voxels of the previous neighborhood, as well as major parts of the neighborhood histograms, can be reused for the next output position, because adjacent neighborhoods have significant overlap.

The second approach (*HistogramVoxelDirect*), illustrated in Figure 49.9, is much simpler. Here, a single thread evaluates the entire neighborhood of one voxel using an explicit loop over (x, y, z), and

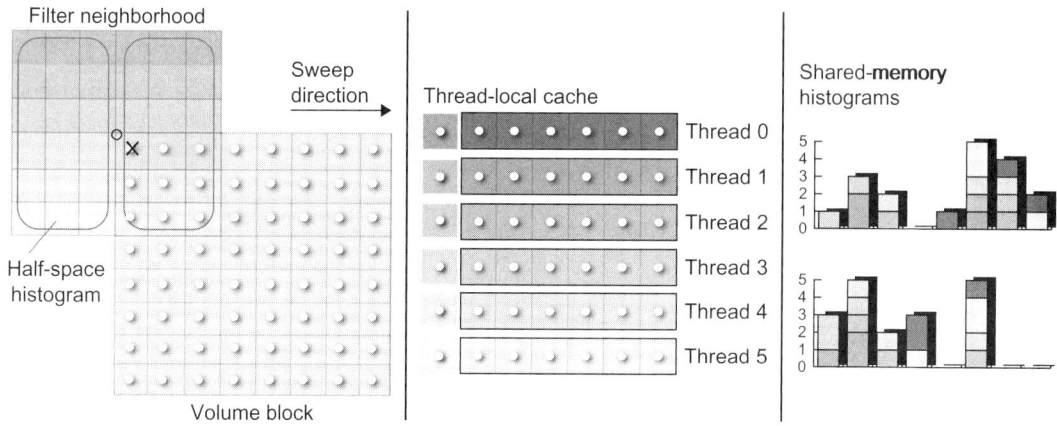

FIGURE 49.7

HistogramVoxelSweep for a 2-D image. For processing a neighborhood size of 6×6 voxels, a thread block with six threads is used. All threads in the block jointly work on the evaluation of one neighborhood at a time, each thread responsible for the six voxels in the horizontal direction, before the sweep or sliding window proceeds to the next neighborhood/output voxel. The thread block is swept over the 8×8 grid of voxels in a volume brick, first sweeping horizontally along each row, then advancing to the next row. This way, most of the computed histogram data can be reused from one neighborhood to the next, by explicitly caching and updating it in shared memory. For every neighborhood, the two half-space histograms are updated incrementally by removing the voxels leaving the neighborhood and adding the voxels entering it. Atomic operations must be used to allow multiple threads to update the same histogram simultaneously.

several such threads independently evaluate different neighborhoods, that is, output voxels. There is no explicit sharing of data between adjacent neighborhoods. As we will see later, this approach can only perform well by exploiting both a texture cache and an L1 cache for implicit data reuse. However, when an L1 cache is present, the simple *HistogramVoxelDirect* algorithm outperforms the more sophisticated *HistogramVoxelSweep* algorithm. Because *HistogramVoxelDirect* results in repeated reads on the same volume brick location we also implemented an extension to this algorithm by first fetching the source volume data into shared memory for faster data access.

Section 49.4.2 presents performance results and comparisons of the two algorithms on two different hardware architectures, that is, the GT200 and GF100/Fermi, without and with an L1 cache, respectively. We now in turn describe each of the two approaches in more detail.

Algorithm 1: HistogramVoxelSweep. Because we want all threads in a block to jointly process the entire neighborhood of a single voxel, the CUDA thread block size is set corresponding to the user-specified neighborhood size. However, in order to avoid exceeding hardware resource limits and to enable incremental updates on the shared histograms, we use a thread block size and shape of one dimension lower than the actual neighborhood. That is, for a 3-D neighborhood of $8 \times 8 \times 8$ voxels, a 2-D CUDA thread block of 8×8 threads is used. The third dimension is then handled via an explicit loop in the kernel for the third axis. This is very similar to a "sliding window," as it is described in CUDA's SDK examples for convolution filtering [6]. Because each thread block is swept over all the voxels in a volume brick that we want to compute, we launch the CUDA kernel with a grid size corresponding to the number of volume bricks that need to be processed. That is, each thread block computes an entire volume brick, one voxel at a time in every iteration of the sweep. For simplicity, this is illustrated in Figure 49.7 for the 2-D case, where the neighborhood is 6×6 voxels and a 1-D CUDA thread block with six threads is used. In the figure, the volume brick size is 8×8 voxels.

In this algorithm, each thread is responsible for only a part of a voxel's neighborhood. Every sample in a voxel's neighborhood is counted in one of the two local half-space histograms. A simple dot product of the sample position with the edge equation of the tested edge determines which of the two half-spaces and thus histograms counts the sample. The histograms are stored in CUDA shared memory so that they can be accessed by all threads processing the same neighborhood. We store each histogram with 64 bins, with one integer value per bin. More histogram bins would consume too much memory on current GPUs, but in our experience 64 bins provide a good trade-off between accuracy and memory usage. Both half-space histograms are updated during the sweep by removing the values that are not part of the current neighborhood anymore from their respective histogram and adding the new values that were not part of the previous neighborhood. To reduce redundant texture fetches, each thread locally caches a history of the values it has previously fetched. The necessary size of the corresponding thread-local cache array is determined by the neighborhood size in one dimension; for example, a history of eight values is needed for a neighborhood of $8 \times 8 \times 8$ voxels. The cached history enables the aforementioned incremental neighborhood histogram updates because in order to perform these updates the values to be removed from the histograms must be known. Using this history caching strategy, in each iteration of the sweep each thread needs to perform only one new texture fetch, also updating the history cache array accordingly. After both histograms have been updated, their difference is computed using a parallel reduction step that evaluates either the L1-norm of the difference of the two histograms viewed as 1-D vectors, that is, the sum of their component wise absolute differences, or the χ^2 metric [7].

Figure 49.8 illustrates this algorithm in pseudocode. The main steps executed by each thread for each iteration of the sweep are

1. Remove the values that have exited the neighborhood from both half-space histograms using atomic operations;
2. A texture fetch is performed to obtain the new value that has entered the neighborhood. Next, this value is stored in the thread-local history cache by overwriting the value that has left the neighborhood; and
3. Add the values that have entered the neighborhood to both half-space histograms using atomic operations.

After they have performed the preceding steps, all threads are synchronized. Then, the histogram difference for the current neighborhood is computed using parallel reduction, storing the resulting boundary value in the current output voxel.

Algorithm 2: HistogramVoxelDirect. A much simpler approach than setting up a thread block for jointly computing a single output voxel, which we were doing in the previously described *HistogramVoxelSweep* algorithm, is to use only a single thread for evaluating the entire neighborhood of a voxel, which we call the *HistogramVoxelDirect* algorithm. In this algorithm, we conceptually set the number of threads in a thread block corresponding to the size of a volume brick, instead of the size of the neighborhood. However, although we conceptually process all neighborhoods in parallel, usually we cannot

```
/* HistogramVoxelSweep:
All threads of a CUDA block collaborate on calculating the local histograms for one voxel (in each
iteration step). Threads are set up in 2D and sweep along the 3rd dimension (sliding window). The
threads iterate over an entire volume brick by sweeping along the x-direction. Each thread locally
stores the preceding density values of the kernel neighborhood in a history, and at each step, only
fetches one new density value. Each step, the thread removes the old density value (that exited the
kernel neighborhood) to the histogram. Histograms are stored in shared memory, and are updated by
atomic operations.
*/

//kernel setup
dim3 blockSize( filterKernelSize.x, filterKernelSize.y, 1);
dim3 gridSize( numVolumeBricks.x, numVolumeBricks.y, numVolumeBricks.z);
kernel_histogram_voxel_sweep<<< gridSize, blocksize >>>;

_shared_ int s_histo_1[ NUM_HISTOGRAM_BINS ];
_shared_ int s_histo_2[ NUM_HISTOGRAM_BINS ];
//kernel function for HistogramVoxelSweep algorithm
_global_ void Kernel_histogram_voxel_sweep() {
    //thread-local history for tracking the neighborhood values along the
        x-direction
    float localHistoryArray[ filterKernelSize.x ];
    int3 kernelOffset = make_int3( 0, -filterKernelSize.y/2, -filterKernelSize.z/2 );
    //iterate over entire volume brick, to calculate the boundary value for each voxel
    for ( int zPos = 0; zPos < VOLUME_BRICK_SIZE_Z; zPos++ ) {
        for ( int yPos = 0; yPos < VOLUME_BRICK_SIZE_Y; yPos++ ) {
            for ( int xPos = 0; xPos < VOLUME_BRICK_SIZE_X; xPos++ ) {
                if ( !initDone ) {
                    initThreadLocalHistoryArray();
                    initHistograms();
                } else {
                    //remove elements from shared histograms that have left the neighborhood
                    removeHistogramEntryAtomic( s_histo_1, localHistoryArray[ idx_histo1_oldest ] );
                    removeHistogramEntryAtomic( s_histo_2, localHistoryArray[ idx_histo2_oldest ] );
                    //advance indices for tracking the histogram elements in the localHistoryArray
                    advanceHistoIndexes() ;
                    // fetch current thread's volume sample into localHistoryArray
                    localHistoryArray[ idx_histo2_newest ] = fetchVolumeSample( xPos +
                            filterKernelSize, yPos + kernelOffset.y + threadIdx.y,
                            zPos + kernelOffset.z + threadIdx.x);
                    //add elements to shared histograms that have just entered the neighborhood
                    addHistogramEntryAtomic( s_histo_1, localHistoryArray[ idx_histo1_newest ] );
                    addHistogramEntryAtomic( s_histo_2, localHistoryArray[ idx_histo2_newest ] );
                }
                _syncthreads();
                //calculate histogram difference in parallel using a reduce operation
                float boundaryValue = compareHistogramsReduction( s_histo_1, s_histo_2 );
                //save boundary value for current iteration in global memory
                if( tId == 0 ) {
                    saveBoundaryValue ( boundaryValue );
                }
            }
        }
    }
}
```

FIGURE 49.8

Pseudocode illustrating the **HistogramVoxelSweep** algorithm.

have one thread per neighborhood for larger volume brick sizes without exceeding hardware resource limits. Therefore, we use different thread block sizes and shapes depending on the volume brick size and empirical performance tests. For example, for a 3-D volume brick with $16 \times 16 \times 16$ voxels, we can set up a 2-D CUDA thread block of 16×16 threads. However, for a brick size of $64 \times 64 \times 64$, we cannot use 2-D CUDA thread blocks of 64×64. In those cases, we use 2-D CUDA thread blocks of size 64×4 or 64×8, for example. Tables 49.2 and 49.3 list the thread block sizes we have used for best performance.

Irrespective of the thread block size we use, each of the threads evaluates the full neighborhood for its corresponding output voxel, using a full loop over (x, y, z). For example, for a neighborhood of $8 \times 8 \times 8$ voxels, each thread loops over 512 voxels. If there are fewer threads in the thread block than voxels in the volume brick, each thread has to compute multiple neighborhoods instead of just one, which is simply done sequentially. For example, in order to compute a full volume brick of $32 \times 32 \times 32$ voxels using a 32×8 thread block, $256 \, (= 32 * 8)$ neighborhoods are evaluated simultaneously, and each thread in turn processes one of $128 \, (= 32 * 32 * 32/256)$ neighborhoods one after the other. For simplicity, we illustrate this in Figure 49.9 for the 2-D case, where the neighborhood is 6×6 voxels and the volume brick size is 8×8 voxels. For illustration, a 1-D CUDA thread block with eight threads is used in this figure although in reality the full grid of 8×8 voxels could easily be processed simultaneously by 64 threads.

In order to cache the input voxels needed by all threads in the thread block, as a first step we fetch all voxels covered by the thread block into shared memory. Additionally, we also fetch a surrounding apron of half the neighborhood size on each side into shared memory. This is also illustrated in Figure 49.9. Note that although this prefetching into shared memory is simple to implement and achieves a slight performance improvement, in practice, it did not make a significant difference in our performance measurements. This illustrates the effectiveness of the texture cache.

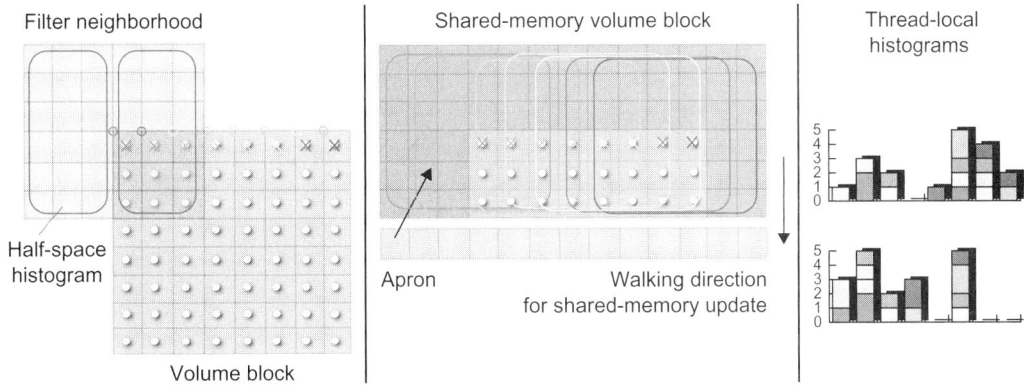

FIGURE 49.9

HistogramVoxelDirect. For computing an 8×8 grid of output voxels in a volume brick, a thread block with eight threads is used. Each thread in the block evaluates the entire 6×6 neighborhood of a given voxel, via a loop in (x, y) over all 6×6 voxels. No information or histograms are shared between different neighborhoods. This avoids the need for atomic operations because each histogram is only accessed by a single thread. However, this is only fast when an L1 cache is available, like on the GF100/Fermi architecture.

```
/* HistogramVoxelDirect:
Each thread calculates in every iteration step the boundary value for one voxel. Threads of a
cudaBlock are set up to work on a specified number of rows (numRows) of the volume brick
concurrently. The threads iterate over all rows and the depth of the volume brick. To speed up
global memory accesses, volume brick data is fetched into shared memory. To reduce shared memory
consumption, this is done in an iterative manner, one row slice at each iteration step along the
y-axis, while the old slice is released.
*/

// kernel setup
dim3 blockSize( volumeBrickSize.x, noRows, 1 );
dim3 gridSize( numVolumeBricks.x, numVolumeBricks.y, numVolumeBricks.z );
Kernel_histogram_voxel_direct<<< gridSize, blockSize >>>;

// kernel function for HistogramVoxelDirect algorithm
_global_ void Kernel_histogram_voxel_direct() {
    unsigned char histo_1[ NUM_HISTOGRAM_BINS ];
    unsigned char histo_2[ NUM_HISTOGRAM_BINS ];
    //iterate over voxels in volume brick (cannot be done in parallel due to hardware constraints)
    for ( int zPos = 0; zPos < VOLUME_BRICK_SIZE_Z; zPos++ ) {
        //fetch volume data that is needed by all threads of the cudaBlock into shared memory
        fetchRowsOfVolumeDataIntoSharedMemory( init );

        for ( int yPos = 0; yPos < VOLUME_BRICK_SIZE_Y; yPos = yPos + blockDim.y ) {
            //fetch position of voxel that is processed by current thread
            Int3 volumeSamplePosition = make_int3( threadIdx.x, ypos + threadIdx.y, zPos );
            //create local half-space histograms for voxel
            createLocalHistograms( volumeSamplePosition, histo_1, histo_2 );
            //calculate histogram difference (L1 or chi^2 metric)
            float boundaryValue = compareHistograms( histo_1, histo_2 );
            //save boundary value for current voxel in boundary cache in global memory
            saveBoundaryValue( boundaryValue );
            //fetch new row of volume data into shared memory, for next iteration step
            fetchRowsOfVolumeDataIntoSharedMemory( no_init );
        }
    }
}

//create local half-space histograms for voxel, by iterating sequentially over filterkernel neighborhood
_device_ void createLocalHistograms ( int3 volSamplePos, uchar* histo_1, uchar* histo_2 ) {
    clearLocalHistograms( histo_1, histo_2 );
    //iterate over filterkernel neighorhood
    for( int zkernel = -filterKernelSize.z/2; zkernel < filterKernelSize.z/2; zkernel++ ) {
        for( int ykernel = -filterKernelSize.y/2; ykernel < filterKernelSize.y/2; ykernel++ ) {
            for( int xkernel = -filterKernelSize.x/2; xkernel < filterKernelSize.x/2; xkernel++ ) {
                int3 curSamplePos = make_int3( volSamplePos.x + xkernel,
                                               volSamplePos.y + ykernel, volSamplePos.z + zkernel );
                //fetch current sample's density value
                float density_value = fetchVolumeSample( curSamplesPos );
                //add density value to correct half-space histogram
                uchar* histo = chooseHistogramForSamplePosition( curSamplePos, histo_1, histo_2 );
                addValueToHistogram( density_value, histo );
            }
        }
    }
}
```

FIGURE 49.10

Pseudocode illustrating the **HistogramVoxelDirect** algorithm.

The *HistogramVoxelDirect* algorithm is illustrated by the pseudocode in Figure 49.10. Every thread computes its neighborhood completely independently of all the other threads. Histograms are stored locally with each thread and not shared between threads. This makes the implementation much simpler and avoids the need for atomic operations, which were necessary in the *HistogramVoxelSweep* algorithm to allow multiple threads access to the same histogram. However, avoiding atomic operations results in performance improvements. On the other hand, not sharing overlapping histograms between threads neglects potential performance optimizations. Also, because histograms are too large to be stored in thread-local registers, they are automatically placed in global memory, even if they are so-called local variables. This again requires an L1 cache to achieve good performance. On a GPU architecture without an L1 cache (e.g., the NVIDIA GT200 architecture), the more sophisticated *HistogramVoxelSweep* algorithm clearly outperforms the simpler *HistogramVoxelDirect* algorithm. However, when an L1 cache is present (e.g., the NVIDIA GF100/Fermi architecture), the performance of the simpler algorithm significantly increases and even clearly surpasses the performance of the more complex algorithm. The main reasons for this are that the L1 cache compensates for the lack of explicit sharing of data between threads, and that no atomic operations are required in the *HistogramVoxelDirect* algorithm. The performance analysis in Section 49.4.2 illustrates that the *HistogramVoxelDirect* algorithm consistently performs better on an architecture with an L1 cache.

49.4 RESULTS

49.4.1 Performance of GPU Axon Segmentation

We measured the running time of the multiphase level set segmentation method on the CPU and GPU. The CPU version is implemented using the ITK image class and the ITK distance transform filter. The numerical part of the CPU implementation is similar to the GPU implementation for fair comparison. The running time includes both updating and re-distancing times. Table 49.1 shows the level set running time on a 512×512 synthetic circle dataset. Our GPU level set solver runs up to 13 times faster than the CPU version on a single CPU core (NVIDIA Quadro 5800 vs. Intel Xeon 3.0 GHz). On a real EM image (using a 512×512 region of interest) our GPU level set solver usually takes less than a half-second to converge in contrast to the CPU version, which takes five to seven seconds. Our GPU nonrigid image registration runs in less than a second on a 512×512 image (500 iterations). The application-level runtime of our segmentation method per slice, without user interaction, is only about an order of a second on a recent NVIDIA GT200 GPU, which is sufficiently fast for interactive applications.

Table 49.1 Running time (in seconds) comparision of CPU and GPU active ribbon segmentation.

Radius	No. of Iters	CPU	GPU	Speedup
50	120	1.5	0.18	8x
100	130	5.8	0.48	12x
150	100	9.7	0.74	13x
200	110	18.7	1.4	13x

49.4.2 Performance of Histogram-Based Boundary Detection

To measure the performance of our histogram-based boundary detection we compared the running time of both algorithms (i.e., *HistogramVoxelSweep* and *HistogramVoxelDirect*) on two different NVIDIA GPU architectures, namely, the GT200 architecture and the new GF100/Fermi architecture, which introduced L1 and L2 caches. We measured the performance of filtering a 256^3 bricked volume, using varying brick sizes of 16^3, 32^3, and 64^3 and varying thread block sizes. All measurements were taken using the CUDA 3.0 event API.

Table 49.2 shows performance results on an NVIDIA GTX 285. It can be seen that *HistogramVoxelSweep* outperforms the simpler *HistogramVoxelDirect* algorithm. The low performance of *HistogramVoxelDirect* is due to the fact that on the GTX 285 there is no L1 cache and only a maximum of 16 kB of shared memory available. Therefore, thread-local histograms, which are too large to be stored in registers, have to be stored either in global memory, which results in high-latency accesses, or in shared memory, which results in shared memory being the bottleneck for parallel execution of multiple CUDA blocks on a streaming multiprocessor on the GPU.

Table 49.2 Performance results on the GT200 architecture, measured on an NVIDIA GTX 285. We have experimented with different neighborhoods, as well as different thread block sizes that do not exceed hardware resource limits, and in this table we list the size that achieved the highest performance. We list the time it takes to process a single-volume brick, as well as a full subvolume of 256^3. On the GT200 architecture, the sophisticated *HistogramVoxelSweep* algorithm is clearly faster than the simpler *HistogramVoxelDirect* algorithm, because it performs explicit caching using shared memory. The performance difference for a small neighborhood size (4^3) is much less apparent than with a large neighborhood size (8^3).

Algorithm	Neighborhood Size	Volume Brick Size	Thread Block Size	Time per Brick [ms]	No. Bricks in 256^3 Subvolume	Time for Full 256^3 Subvolume [ms]	Relative Speed
Histogram-VoxelDirect	8^3	$16 \times 16 \times 16$	16×16	0.77	4096	3162	1.00 x
		$32 \times 32 \times 32$	32×8	6.06	512	3103	1.02 x
		$64 \times 64 \times 64$	64×4	62.19	64	3980	0.79 x
Histogram-VoxelSweep	8^3	$16 \times 16 \times 16$	8×8	0.12	4096	495	6.40 x
		$32 \times 32 \times 32$	8×8	1.28	512	655	4.83 x
		$64 \times 64 \times 64$	8×8	28.47	64	1822	1.74 x
Histogram-VoxelDirect	4^3	$16 \times 16 \times 16$	16×16	0.13	4096	524	1.00x
		$32 \times 32 \times 32$	32×8	0.92	512	470	1.12x
		$64 \times 64 \times 64$	64×4	9.73	64	623	0.84x
Histogram-VoxelSweep	4^3	$16 \times 16 \times 16$	4×4	0.08	4096	324	1.62x
		$32 \times 32 \times 32$	4×4	0.82	512	418	1.25x
		$64 \times 64 \times 64$	4×4	24.59	64	1574	0.33x

Table 49.3 Performance results on the GF100/Fermi architecture, measured on an NVIDIA GTX 480. We have experimented with different neighborhoods, as well as different thread block sizes that do not exceed hardware resource limits, and in this table we list the size that achieved the highest performance. We respectively list the time it takes to process a single-volume brick, as well as a full subvolume of 256^3. On the GF100/Fermi architecture, the simple *HistogramVoxelDirect* algorithm is clearly faster than the sophisticated *HistogramVoxelSweep* algorithm, which illustrates the effectiveness of the L1 and texture caches.

Algorithm	Neighborhood Size	Volume Brick Size	Thread Block Size	Time per Brick [ms]	No. Bricks in 256^3 Subvolume	Time for Full 256^3 Subvolume [ms]	Relative Speed
Histogram-VoxelDirect	8^3	$16 \times 16 \times 16$	16×8	0.066	4096	271	1.00 x
		$32 \times 32 \times 32$	32×8	0.508	512	260	1.05 x
		$64 \times 64 \times 64$	64×8	7.313	64	468	0.58 x
Histogram-VoxelSweep	8^3	$16 \times 16 \times 16$	8×8	0.102	4096	417	0.65 x
		$32 \times 32 \times 32$	8×8	0.955	512	489	0.55 x
		$64 \times 64 \times 64$	8×8	18.828	64	1205	0.23 x
Histogram-VoxelDirect	4^3	$16 \times 16 \times 16$	16×16	0.014	4096	57	1.00x
		$32 \times 32 \times 32$	32×16	0.119	512	61	0.95x
		$64 \times 64 \times 64$	64×16	1.281	64	82	0.70x
Histogram-VoxelSweep	4^3	$16 \times 16 \times 16$	4×4	0.068	4096	278	0.20x
		$32 \times 32 \times 32$	4×4	0.703	512	360	0.16x
		$64 \times 64 \times 64$	4×4	14.656	64	938	0.06x

Table 49.3 shows performance results on an NVIDIA GTX 480. The new GF100/Fermi architecture has an L1 cache for speeding up global memory transactions, and it also allows the user to adapt the sizes of the shared memory and L1 cache for each kernel individually, depending on the kernel's properties. As this table shows, the speedup of the *HistogramVoxelDirect* algorithm between the GTX 285 and the GTX 480 is almost 12x, whereas the speedup of the *HistogramVoxelSweep* algorithm between the GTX 285 and the GTX 480 is not even 2x. This again shows the performance improvement of the simpler *HistogramVoxelDirect* algorithm owing to the new L1 cache.

49.5 FUTURE DIRECTIONS

We are planning to extend the current segmentation and tracking method to handle merging and branching of neural processes. Simultaneous tracking of multiple neural processes in a GPU cluster system would be another interesting future work. We would like to integrate a variety of edge-detection approaches into our on-demand volume filtering framework. One of the biggest challenges is the large z-slice distance in EM images. The integration of shape-based interpolation or directional coherence methods into the volume rendering would be a promising direction to solve this problem. Another interesting future direction is developing distributed GPU ray-casting and volume-filtering methods in a GPU cluster system to handle tera-scale volumetric datasets. We are currently using the proposed segmentation method to trace axons in a large-scale 3-D EM dataset ($16,384 \times 16,384 \times 1,800$ pixels, about 5 nm in x-y and 29 nm in z distance).

Acknowledgments

This work was supported in part by the National Science Foundation under Grant No. PHY-0835713, the Austrian Research Promotion Agency FFG, Vienna Science and Technology Fund WWTF, and the Harvard Initiative in Innovative Computing (IIC). The work also had generous support from Microsoft Research and NVIDIA. We thank our biology collaborators Prof. Jeff Lichtman and Prof. R. Clay Reid from the Harvard Center for Brain Science for their time and the use of their data. The international (PCT/US2008/081855) and U.S. patent (12/740,061) applications for the Fast Iterative Method [2] have been filed and are currently pending.

References

[1]   W.-K. Jeong, J. Beyer, M. Hadwiger, A. Vazquez, H. Pfister, R.T. Whitaker, Scalable and interactive segmentation and visualization of neural processes in EM datasets, IEEE Trans. Vis. Comput. Graph. 15 (6) (2009) 1505–1514.

[2]   W.-K. Jeong, R.T. Whitaker, A fast iterative method for Eikonal equations, SIAM J. Sci. Comput. 30 (5) (2008) 2512–2534.

[3]   G.M. Karniadakis, R.M. Kirby, Parallel Scientific Computing in C++ and MPI, Cambridge University Press, New York, 2003.

[4]   A.E. Lefohn, J.M. Kniss, C.D. Hansen, R.T. Whitaker, Interactive deformation and visualization of level set surfaces using graphics hardware, in: Proceedings of the 14th IEEE Visualization 2003 (VIS'03), 19–24 October 2003, Seattle,WA, IEEE Computer Society, Washington, DC, 2003, pp. 75–82.

[5]   D. Martin, C. Fowlkes, J. Malik, Learning to detect natural image boundaries using local brightness, color, and texture cues, IEEE Trans. Pattern Anal. Mach. Intell. 26 (1) (2004) 530–549.

[6]   V. Podlozhnyuk, Image convolution with CUDA, NVIDIA CUDA SDK Whitepapers, 2007.

[7]   J. Puzicha, J. Buhmann, Y. Rubner, C. Tomasi, Empirical evaluation of dissimilarity measures for color and texture, in: Proceedings of International Conference on Computer Vision (ICCV), 1999, pp. 1165–1172.

[8]   H. Scharsach, M. Hadwiger, A. Neubauer, K. Bühler, Perspective isosurface and direct volume rendering for virtual endoscopy applications, in: B.S. Santos, T. Ertl, K.I. Joy (Eds.), Proceedings of Eurovis 2006, EuroVis06: Joint Eurographics – IEEE VGTC Symposium on Visualization, 8–10 May 2006, Eurographics Association 2006, Lisbon, Portugal, 2006, pp. 315–322.

[9]   J. Sethian, Level Set Methods and Fast Marching Methods, Cambridge University Press, New York, 2002.

[10] A. Vazquez-Reina, E. Miller, H. Pfister, Multiphase geometric couplings for the segmentation of neural processes, in: Proceedings of the IEEE Conference on Computer Vision and Pattern Recognition (CVPR), 20–25 June 2009, Miami, FL, IEEE Computer Society, Los Alamitos, CA, 2009, pp. 2020–2027.

[11] L.A. Vese, T.F. Chan, A multiphase level set framework for image segmentation using the Mumford and Shah model, Int. J. Comput. Vis. 50 (3) (2002) 271–293.

[12] R. Whitaker, A level-set approach to 3-D reconstruction from range data, Int. J. Comput. Vis. 29 (3) (1998) 203–231.

Fast Simulation of Radiographic Images Using a Monte Carlo X-Ray Transport Algorithm Implemented in CUDA

50

Andreu Badal, Aldo Badano

In this chapter, we describe a Monte Carlo algorithm for the simulation of x-ray transport and show how this algorithm can be efficiently implemented in a Graphics Processing Unit (GPU). The main application of our new simulation code is the evaluation of medical radiographic imaging systems. Example simulations of projection imaging and compute tomography (CT) using a realistic voxel-based human anatomy model are presented. MC-GPU [1–3], the C/CUDA [4] code implementing the presented algorithm, is in the public domain and is openly and freely distributed at the website: `http://code.google.com/p/mcgpu/`.[1]

50.1 INTRODUCTION, PROBLEM STATEMENT, AND CONTEXT

The use of x-rays to visualize structures inside the human body has been an essential medical tool for over a century. In spite of the evident benefits of the noninvasive imaging of internal organs for the diagnosis of disease, it is a known fact that the exposure to ionizing radiation is hazardous and may increase the lifetime probability of developing cancer. Therefore, imaging systems have to be optimized to provide sufficient image quality for the particular diagnostic tasks, while minimizing the amount of radiation received by the patients. The minimization of radiation dose in medical imaging is of special importance considering the current trend of an increase in the number of radiological examinations performed every year, which has resulted in a significant increase in the average annual dose received by the population from man-made sources [5].

Computer simulations play a significant role in the study of the performance of imaging systems and in the estimation of the radiation doses received by patients. The Monte Carlo (MC) method provides a natural and elegant way to simulate radiation transport in complex systems and is accepted by the community to be the simulation approach in best agreement with experimental measurements. Several general-purpose MC simulation codes for the transport of ionizing radiation in matter are available and extensively used in medical physics, such as Geant4 (GATE), EGS, MCNP, and PENELOPE [6].

---

[1] This work was developed at the Food and Drug Administration (FDA) by employees of the federal government in the course of their official duties and is not subject to copyright protection. FDA assumes no responsibility whatsoever for use by other parties of this software and its documentation. The mention of commercial products herein is not to be construed as either an actual or an implied endorsement of such products by the U.S. Department of Health and Human Services.

However, the simulations performed with these codes usually require large computing times because a large number of particle tracks have to be simulated to estimate the parameters of interest (pixel values, for example) with low statistical uncertainty. Moreover, each track may involve the simulation of multiple atomic interactions in different materials. Exceedingly long computing times limit the application of detailed simulation codes and may force the users to apply grossly simplified models that may lead to inaccurate results.

In the following sections, we describe a GPU-accelerated MC code that simulates a complete x-ray imaging system and generates synthetic radiographic images reproducing clinical medical imaging protocols much faster than previously possible. The presented algorithm can be efficiently executed in one or multiple GPUs. The speedup provided by the GPU technology permits the detailed simulation of imaging modalities such as CT, where hundreds of radiographic projections are used to reconstruct a 3-D volume. This kind of simulation was possible in the past only with large CPU clusters or using approximate methods such as ray tracing. An ideal ray-tracing image can be generated by integrating the attenuation of the radiation beam in a straight line from the source to the detector. Two problems of ray tracing are that it can introduce some aliasing artifacts if the space is not consistently sampled and, more importantly, that it does not reproduce the effects of the stochastic scattering events that change the energy and direction of the x-rays. The MC method is the most suitable simulation technique to estimate the contribution of the randomly scattered radiation to the radiographic image, which is one of the main processes that degrade the contrast of the medical images. A MC simulation also provides the ability to differentiate the scatter generated by different kinds of atomic events or created in different parts of the body and can be used to estimate the radiation dose deposited in the organs of the virtual patient.

Many clinical applications could benefit from fast MC simulations. Some examples in medical imaging are iterative image reconstruction, scatter and beam-hardening correction or patient-specific optimization of imaging protocols. Apart from x-ray imaging, the new code may also be useful to study imaging modalities such as SPECT, PET, and portal imaging because the implemented atomic interaction models are also valid for the transport of high-energy photons. Extensions of this code including charged particle transport could also be used in radiotherapy treatment planning, but this feature is not currently implemented.

50.2 CORE METHODS

In the following section we describe a state-of-the-art MC algorithm for the transport of x-rays and an efficient voxelized geometry tracker technique. The implemented x-ray interaction physics models are based on those used in the PENELOPE code [6], which are recognized as one of the most accurate in the field of particle transport simulation. The PENELOPE models can be used to transport particles with energy between 50 eV and 1 GeV, and in any material. The voxelized geometry is handled using the virtual interaction (or Woodcock) model [7], which significantly speeds up the transport by allowing x-rays to cross multiple voxels of different material and density in a single step. With Woodcock tracking the simulation time is independent of the voxel size and, therefore, highly detailed anatomic models can be used without any reduction in the computational performance.

A combined multiplicative linear congruential pseudorandom number generator [8] has been adapted to the GPU to sample the stochastic events that occur during the particle track. A rigorous and efficient sequence-splitting technique [9] is used to initialize the generator used by each GPU thread in a location far enough from the others within the generator cycle. Using this technique, we can safely employ the congruential generator in parallel by any number of threads because the generated subsequences will not overlap and, hence, will be uncorrelated.

50.3 ALGORITHMS, IMPLEMENTATIONS, AND EVALUATIONS

50.3.1 Modeling an X-Ray Imaging System

In order to simulate a medical x-ray imaging system we need to separately model the three main components of the imaging system: the radiation source, the detector, and the material "universe" found between the source and the detector (in our case, the patient body).

The radiation source can be easily modeled as a point focal spot emitting x-rays in every direction with a uniform probability. To improve the efficiency of the simulation and to be closer to the design of a real system, we have extended this simple model, allowing the user to select a polar and an azimuthal aperture angle that define a square field of radiation. In a clinical system, the beam size is conformed equivalently using lead blocks (collimators), which we assume absorb 100% of the incident radiation. Entering a negative angle, the code automatically computes the optimum angles to illuminate the whole sensitive surface of the detector. The energy of the x-rays emitted by the source could be sampled from available energy spectra experimentally measured from clinical x-ray tubes. The current version of the code simulates a simple monoenergetic beam, but the possibility to use an energy spectrum will be added in future releases. Because all the primary x-rays have the exact same energy, beam-hardening effects cannot be directly studied with the current code.

An ideal energy-integrating x-ray detector has been modeled defining a completely absorbent surface divided in a 2-D grid of pixels in front of the source. The distance between the source and the detector, the detector size, and the number of pixels are selected by the user in the input file. The radiographic signal in each pixel is estimated by adding the energy of all the x-ray quanta that enter the pixel. Before reporting the results at the end of the simulation, the pixel values are normalized by the total number of x-rays that were simulated and by the pixel area. Thus, the values in the final image have units of eV/cm^2 per x-ray. The pixel values do not depend directly on the number of x-rays that were simulated, but the statistical uncertainty in the estimation of the values still depends on the number of particles. The uncertainty decreases inversely proportional to the number of particles squared. Although the uncertainty is not tallied, it can be easily estimated by simulating multiple realizations of the same image. The implemented detector model could be improved by taking into account the detection efficiency at the incident x-ray energy and by incorporating sophisticated counting statistics models. However, the resulting model would be valid only for a particular design and material composition of the detector, and we prefer to model a generic idealized detector. Postprocessing filters, such as Gaussian blurring or additive noise, can be applied to the simulated images to add features found in images produced by real detectors.

Finally, the third component of the medical imaging system that has to be modeled is the material "universe" where the x-rays move, also called the geometry or the phantom. In medical applications the geometry includes the patient body and, optionally, beam modifiers and other relevant objects located near the radiation beam. The most common way to describe the human anatomy in medical physics simulations is the use of volume elements called voxels, that is, giving the density and material composition at each element of a uniform 3-D grid enclosing the patient. The voxel values can be inferred

```
[SECTION VOXELS HEADER v.2008-04-13]
  3    1    2    No. OF VOXELS IN X,Y,Z
 10.0 10.0 15.0  VOXEL SIZE (cm) ALONG X,Y,Z
  1               COLUMN MATERIAL ID
  2               COLUMN MASS DENSITY
  1               BLANK LINES X,Y—CYCLES: 1=YES,0=NO
[END OF VXH SECTION]
  1 1.50
  1 1.00
  1 0.50


  2 1.50
  2 1.00
  2 0.50
```

FIGURE 50.1

A sample voxelized geometry file for MC-GPU (compatible with the penEasy 2008 code). This file defines a simple $30 \times 10 \times 30$ cm^3 object composed of six voxels, with two materials and three different densities.

from a CT scan of an actual patient. However, the segmentation of a CT to determine the material composition and density of each voxel is a challenging task. A better alternative is the use of publicly available computational models of the human anatomy such as the Virtual Family [10] or others [11]. Some advantages of using standard models include a representative anatomy for the average population, clinician-validated organ segmentation and, in some cases, higher resolution (smaller voxel size) than regular CT scans.

In our code, the voxelized geometry is read from an external text file, such as the sample file shown in Figure 50.1 (the format is compatible with the general-purpose MC code penEasy 2008). This sample geometry defines a $30 \times 10 \times 30$ cm^3 object composed of six voxels, with two materials and three different densities (an example simulation with this object is shown in Section 4.1). As can be seen in the figure, the text file is divided into two parts: (1) a header section that defines the number and size of the voxels in the X, Y, Z dimensions and (2) a two-column list with the material and density of each and every voxel. Optionally, blank lines can be added after each X column and between XY planes to facilitate the visualization of the geometry using the popular GNUPLOT software. To speed up the localization of points inside the voxelized region, the lower-back corner of the voxelized volume (corresponding to the lower-back corner of the first voxel) is assumed to be located at the origin of the coordinate system, and the coordinate axes are aligned with the edges of the voxels.

50.3.2 Monte Carlo Algorithm to Generate X-Ray Tracks

The MC code described in this chapter [1–3] simulates a radiographic image by averaging the individual contributions to the image from a large number of x-ray tracks across the patient's body. From 10^9 to 10^{12} tracks may be required to obtain a single image reproducing a realistic clinical setting. The total number of tracks depends mostly on the size of the irradiation field, the pixel size, and the level of noise acceptable in the image.

The iterative algorithm that is used to simulate a particle track can be summarized in five steps: (1) creating an x-ray according to the implemented source model, (2) sampling the distance the x-ray will move before suffering an atomic interaction using a random number generator and the energy- and material-dependent interaction probability models, (3) moving the x-ray to the interaction location taking care of material changes, (4) simulating the atomic interaction (Compton, Rayleigh, or photo-electric), and going back to step 2 unless the particle was absorbed (photoelectric effect), escaped the voxel geometry bounding box, or entered the detector, in which case (5) the contribution of this track to the radiographic image is tallied according to the implemented detector model.

The distance that an x-ray will travel before the next interaction can be easily sampled as

$$\text{distance} = -\lambda * \ln(\xi),$$

where λ is the total interaction mean free path (which is inversely proportional to the interaction probability) for the current energy, material, and density, and ξ is a random number between 0 and 1 generated with a generator such as the one described in the following section. In a voxelized geometry each voxel may have a different material or density, and therefore, the simulation code may have to stop the particle after crossing each voxel interface and sample a new distance to interaction. Because the sampled distances are typically much larger than the voxel size for x-rays (not the case for electrons), moving the particle from voxel to voxel and resampling is a very inefficient process.

In the presented code, the voxelized geometry is not modeled using the inefficient method previously described, but using the virtual interaction, or Woodcock, algorithm [2, 7]. This algorithm assumes that the whole voxelized volume is uniformly filled with the most attenuating material found in the voxelized phantom. With a uniform composition, it is not necessary to find the intersections between the trajectory of the ray and the voxel interfaces, or to access the slow GPU global memory to find out the composition of the multiple voxels that the particle crosses before interacting. After the distance to the next interaction is sampled, the code can readily move the particle from the current position to the interaction point. Then, the code has to determine inside which voxel the interaction takes place and find the voxel material and density. When we use voxels of constant size and aligned with the coordinate axes, determining the voxel that contains a given point in space is straightforward. In case the particle escaped the voxelized region before the interaction, no interaction occurs (the voxels are assumed to be surrounded by empty space). If the particle is pointing to the detector after exiting the voxels, the detector function is called to add the particle's energy to the corresponding pixel counter.

The artificially high attenuation used by the Woodcock method is compensated by introducing "virtual" interactions that do not have any effect on the particle energy or direction. The probability of having a virtual interaction is given by the ratio between the total mean free path in the most attenuating material (called the Woodcock mean free path) and the actual total mean free path in the voxel where the interaction takes place. In medical imaging simulations, with relatively low material densities and energies of the order of 100 keV, the Woodcock tracking gives a speedup to approximately one order of magnitude. Larger speedups can be obtained at higher energies because more voxels are traversed between interactions. Notice that with the virtual interactions, the tracking speed is independent of the voxel size, and for this reason, the virtual interactions make a big difference in the simulation of high-resolution voxel phantoms. An important drawback of this technique is that the performance can be largely reduced if the phantom contains a few highly attenuating voxels, such as a metallic implant in a human anatomical model. In such cases, other approaches, such as a mixed geometry handler (voxels and quadric surfaces) or the use of an octree structure to separate regions with different maximum attenuations, may prove optimal.

The x-rays in the diagnostic imaging energy range interact with matter through three different mechanisms. Compton (or inelastic) interactions modify the energy and direction of the x-ray quanta and result in the emission of a secondary electron. Rayleigh (or elastic) interactions change the direction of the x-ray, but not its energy. Finally, in a photoelectric effect the x-ray is absorbed by an atom and an electron with the same energy of the incident photon — minus the atomic ionization energy — is emitted. Our current code does not model the transport of charged particles. Therefore, the electrons created by Compton and photoelectric interactions are not transported, and the particle's energy is assumed to be locally deposited at the creation location. This is a good approximation for imaging simulations because the secondary low-energy electrons travel a very short range inside the body materials (of the order of a few microns) and will not arrive at the detector-sensitive area. The fluorescence photons that may be emitted after the ionization of an atom and the bremsstrahlung photons emitted by secondary electrons are not simulated because they do not contribute significantly to the image. The presented code could be extended to simulate electron transport, but this would not affect the simulated images and would increase very much the simulation time. Because electrons would interact several times inside each voxel, the Woodcock tracking algorithm is not expected to be optimal in this case.

In our code, the Compton and Rayleigh interactions are sampled using the algorithms from the PENELOPE code [6]. Tables with the interaction probabilities as a function of material composition and energy are obtained from the PENELOPE database and linearly interpolated for the actual photon energy during the x-ray tracking. Naturally, it is possible to implement other interaction models in the simulation. In particular, the Compton events can be easily sampled using the Klein-Nishina model, and the Rayleigh events could be sampled from tabulated data. However, the PENELOPE models are more sophisticated and produce more accurate results at the x-ray energy range.

A detailed diagram of the implemented MC algorithm is given in Figure 50.2. This figure shows the execution flow that each GPU thread follows. To reduce the total number of threads and compensate for the time spent initializing them, each thread simulates a batch of thousands of x-ray tracks instead of a single track. After we have simulated all the requested particle tracks in the GPU, the host code retrieves the image data from the GPU and reports the final image in absolute units of eV/cm^2 per primary x-ray in an external text file. The contributions to the image by those x-rays that were scattered before being detected and those that were not scattered are reported separately. The contributions by the different kinds of interactions are also separated. The output file can be easily visualized using a provided GNUPLOT script.

50.3.3 Simulation of CT Scans in Multiple GPUs

In order to facilitate the simulation of the hundreds of projection images required to reconstruct a 3-D volume with a CT scan, our code includes an option to automatically generate multiple images around a static object. The projections at different angles are simulated calling the GPU kernel multiple times inside a loop in the host code. The location and orientation of the source and the detector for each angle and the large voxel data are copied to the GPU memory only once at the beginning of the execution.

To speed up the CT simulations, the code is able to generate different images in parallel in multiple GPUs. The GPUs are accessed from multiple CPU threads created in the host CPU using the message passing interface (MPI) library. Each GPU is initialized independently and generates a fraction of the total number of images in a way that avoids any communication between the CPU threads (for example, if we use n GPUs, the i-th GPU will generate the projections i, $i + n$, $i + 2n$, etc.). Apart from using

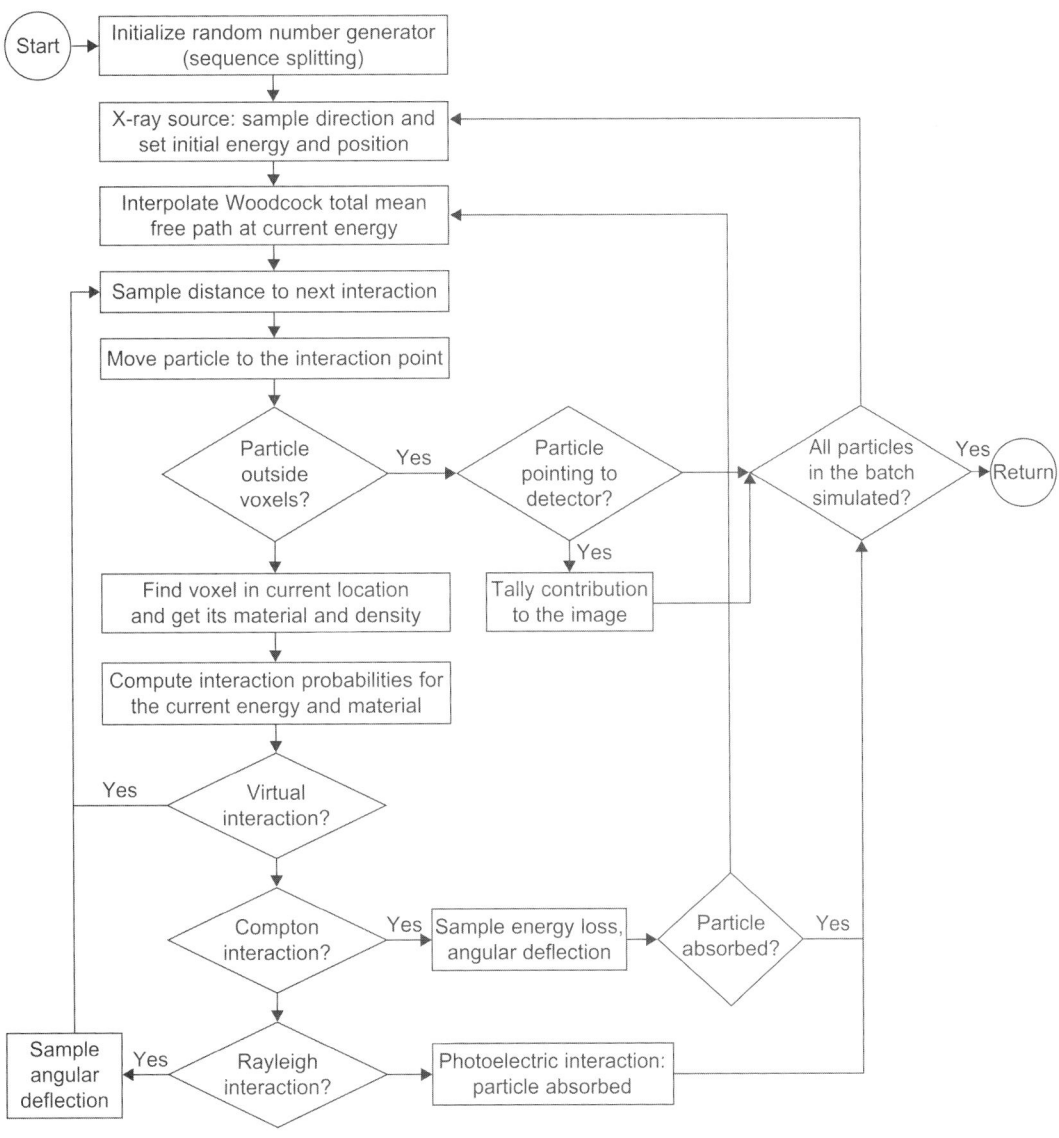

FIGURE 50.2

Diagram of the Monte Carlo transport algorithm executed in each GPU thread.

multiple GPUs to simulate different images, it could be possible to speed up the simulation of a single projection distributing its x-rays to multiple GPUs. Currently, we do not follow this strategy because the time spent waiting for all the GPUs to complete the execution and the communication overhead to reduce the results in a single image could decrease the performance of the code.

50.3.4 Random Number Generation

To sample the stochastic events that take place in the x-ray tracks, we have implemented in the GPU the combined multiplicative linear congruential pseudorandom number generator used by PENELOPE. This classic generator, called RANECU [8], is based on the combination of the sequences of two multiplicative congruential generators. The C/CUDA code of this generator is provided in Figure 50.3. A version returning double-precision values is also used in the code. As all congruential generators, RANECU produces a cyclic sequence of pseudorandom numbers. The repetition cycle of RANECU is $2.3 \cdot 10^{18}$ values [9], long enough for even the most demanding simulations, as we will show later. The randomness of congruential generators has some limitations, but their mathematical basis is well understood, and they have been used in MC transport successfully for decades.

```
//////////////////////////////////////////////////////////
//! Pseudo-random number generator RANECU, combining
//! two multiplicative congruential generators.
//!
//!   @param[in,out] seed Two integer values.
//!   @return Random value in the open interval (0,1)
//!
//////////////////////////////////////////////////////////
#ifdef USING_CUDA
_device_
#endif
inline float ranecu(int2* seed)
{
  int i1 = (int)(seed->x/53668);
  seed->x = 40014*(seed->x-i1*53668)-i1*12211;

  int i2 = (int)(seed->y/52774);
  seed->y = 40692*(seed->y-i2*52774)-i2*3791;

  if (seed->x < 0) seed->x += 2147483563;
  if (seed->y < 0) seed->y += 2147483399;

  i2 = seed->x-seed->y;
  if (i2 < 1) i2 += 2147483562;

  #ifdef USING_CUDA
    return (_int2float_rn(i2)*4.65661305739e-10f);
  #else
    return ((float)(i2)*4.65661305739e-10f);
  #endif
}
```

FIGURE 50.3

C/CUDA source code of the pseudorandom number generator RANECU [8] used in the simulations. The preprocessor *if* statements allow the compilation of the code using CUDA (defining "USING_CUDA" at compile time) or using any standard C compiler for the CPU. The int2 data type is a structure containing two integer variables.

In order to use this generator in parallel in hundreds of threads, avoiding any correlation between the random subsequences generated in parallel, each thread initializes the generator in a location far enough from the others in the generator cycle (sequence-splitting parallelization method). The mathematical algorithm used to split the sequence of RANECU has been adapted from the seedsMLCG code [9]. In the current version of the code, the initial seeds for each GPU thread are calculated so that each thread can use up to 256 random numbers for each simulated x-ray track before repeating the values generated by the following thread. On average, only 20 to 50 random numbers are used to sample each track, and therefore, the subsequences in different threads will never overlap.

50.3.5 Technical Details and Evaluation of the CUDA Implementation

As it was previously mentioned, we implemented the algorithm described in the previous sections using the CUDA programming model [4] that allows the execution of the simulations in the massively multiprocessor GPUs manufactured by the NVIDIA Corporation. This code is in the public domain and is distributed as free and open software.

The program is essentially coded in standard C, and the CUDA extensions are only called to initialize the GPU and to move the data to the video memory at the beginning of the simulation and to retrieve the results at the end. To allow the use of the simulation code in CPUs, all the CUDA calls were enclosed within preprocessor *if* statements and equivalent code for the GPU and the CPU was programmed. The code can be compiled for the GPU defining the parameter "USING_CUDA" at compilation time; otherwise, the code can be compiled with any C compiler and executed in a CPU. Having a GPU and a CPU version of the same code is very useful to debug the code and to estimate the speedup provided by the GPU architecture. Most of the operations in the code are performed in single precision and using 32-bit floating-point variables. However, the sampling of some deflection angles, as well as the rotation of the particles and some sensitive parts of the interaction sampling, are performed in double precision.

The MC algorithm can be efficiently executed in the GPU architecture because each x-ray track is independent of the others and, therefore, it is possible to simulate hundreds of tracks simultaneously. But there are two main limitations in the performance of the algorithm in the GPU. The first limitation is the fact that the algorithm depends on accessing large amounts of data (interaction mean free paths and voxels composition). The latency of memory access is partially compensated by executing multiple thread blocks in each microprocessor of the GPU at the same time. The second limitation is branching: the x-ray tracks simulated in parallel in the same microprocessor may suffer different kinds of interaction that then have to be sampled sequentially. This means, for example, that the threads that suffer a virtual interaction will have to wait for the sampling of Compton and Rayleigh events to be completed before moving to the next interaction. In spite of this, the algorithm still produces a remarkable speedup in the GPU architecture because many steps of the simulation are still executed in parallel (source sampling, database interpolations, and image tally). Also, multiple Compton events, which are by far the most time-consuming part of the code, are sampled in parallel at each iteration.

A characteristic of the detector model implementation in CUDA that is worth noting is that when multiple particle tracks are simulated in parallel in the GPU, there is the possibility of multiple threads updating the value of the same pixel at the same time. To avoid any loss of information, the pixel values have to be updated using atomic operations that prevent the access to a memory location from any other thread until the current one has updated the value of the variable stored in this location. As a practical note, because the CUDA *atomicAdd()* function is not available for floating-point values in devices of compute capability 1.3, we tally the pixel values using 64-bit integers (*unsigned long long int*). To reduce the possible loss of accuracy in the conversion to integers, the pixel values are scaled by 10,000 before rounding to integers. A problem of using integers instead of floats is that the pixel signal counters can overflow if the signal is too large. Knowing that the maximum integer value that can be represented in 64 bits is of the order of 10^{19}, we can estimate that, given a 100 keV x-ray source, a pixel can overflow only after detecting more than 10^9 x-rays. This order of particle fluence in a single pixel is much larger than the common fluence in any clinical application. However, we have observed overflow problems in some testing simulations using ideal pencil beams where all the x-rays point to the same pixel of the image. Fortunately, the new Fermi GPUs can perform atomic operations with floats in the GPU global memory, and in addition, the atomic operations are supposed to be much faster in Fermi than in previous generations. This will speed up the simulation, but just slightly because the overall time spent in the image tally is little, and very seldom x-rays in the same GPU warp are detected at the same pixel owing to the random sampling of the initial x-ray direction.

A key point of any CUDA code is optimizing the use of the different memory levels available in the GPU. We use the large — and rather slow — GPU global memory to store the interaction mean free paths and the voxelized geometry data (typically several hundreds of Mbytes large). The material and density values of each voxel are stored as a float2 variable (a C structure containing two float variables) and read in a single instruction; the mean free paths are stored as float3 and read also in a single instruction to reduce the number of memory accesses. Some of the data could be stored in the texture memory and linearly interpolated using the GPU built-in functions, but this feature is not currently implemented in the code. The data defining the source, the detector, and the bounds of the tables that have to be interpolated (mean free paths) are stored in the GPU constant memory for fast cached access. Finally, the constant data required to sample the time-consuming Compton events are stored in the shared memory for maximum access speed. The amount of shared memory that is used by each thread block depends mostly on how many different materials are defined in the simulation. Because this memory is limited, defining many materials may bound the number of blocks that can run simultaneously in each multiprocessor of the GPU. In most cases fewer than 10 materials are required and the resulting memory use is moderate, allowing the execution of several blocks in parallel.

With regards to the random number generator described in the previous section, it is interesting to note that the state of the generator is described by only two integer values (the seeds of the two congruential generators). These two values are stored in the register space of each thread and passed to the generator at each call. Other generators, such as the Mersenne Twister, are known to generate random values faster than RANECU, but require much more memory resources.

50.4 FINAL EVALUATION AND VALIDATION OF RESULTS, TOTAL BENEFITS, AND LIMITATIONS

50.4.1 Code Testing in a Simple Geometry

We tested our code simulating a projection image of the simple six-voxel object defined in Figure 50.1. A volume rendering of this object is displayed in Figure 50.4(a). The lower three voxels of the object are composed of water with the artificial densities 1.5, 1.0, and 0.5 g/cm^3; the upper voxels are filled with

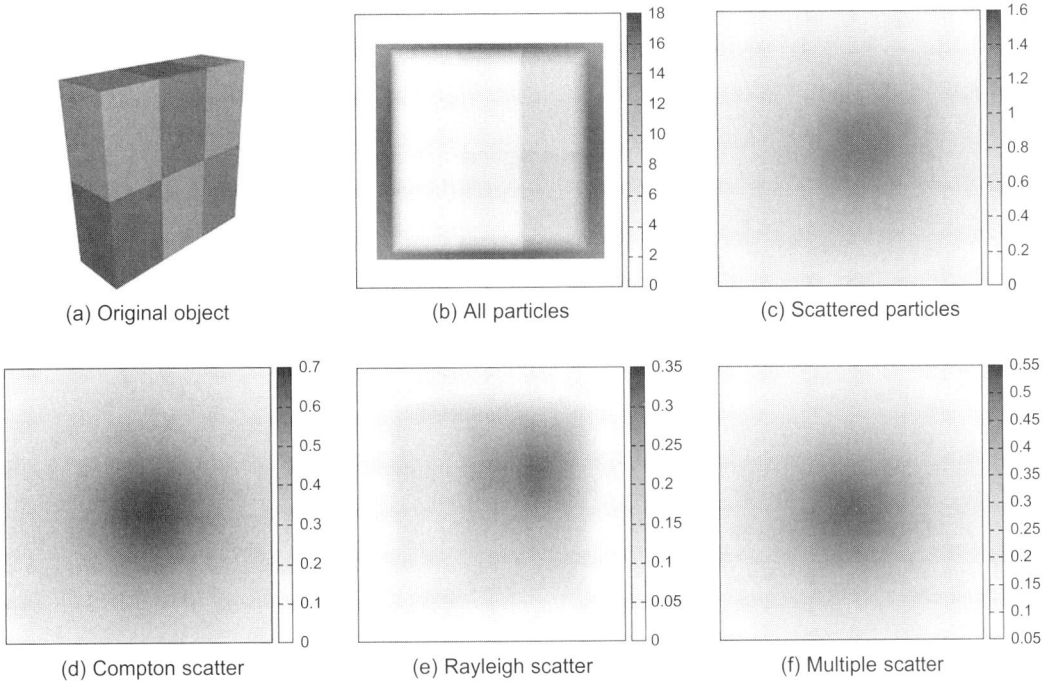

FIGURE 50.4

Radiographic projection image of a simple six-voxel object: (a) volume rendering of the original object (as defined in Fig. 50.1); (b) tallied x-ray projection image (with 300 × 300, 3 mm pixels); (c) total scatter signal in the image; (d) Compton scatter; (e) Rayleigh scatter; (f) multiple scatter. The gray scales have units of eV/cm^2 per x-ray; darker pixels have a larger signal, meaning that the x-rays encountered less attenuating materials in the track.

a material equivalent to bone with the same three densities. Figure 50.4(b) presents the radiographic projection of this object with 90 keV x-rays and Figure 50.4(c) shows the part of the image generated only by those x-rays that suffered an atomic interaction before being detected. The lower three images in Figure 50.4 display the different components of this scatter image: the image produced by x-rays that suffered only one Compton event (d), one Rayleigh event (e), or multiple scattering events (f).

This simulation was executed in an NVIDIA GeForce GTX 480 (Fermi) GPU using $2 \cdot 10^{10}$ histories. The total simulation time was 17.8 minutes, giving a simulation speed of 18,759,790 x-rays/second. The code was compiled using NVIDIA's CUDA compiler (NVCC), CUDA 3.0 and the Linux 64-bit driver 195.36.31. The code used 63 registers, 256 bytes of local memory, 4036 bytes of shared memory, and 58,804 bytes of constant memory. With 64 threads per block, the GPU occupancy was 33%, with eight blocks executed in each microprocessor and a total of 7680 threads (thus, x-rays) being active in the GPU at the same time. Naturally, only 480 threads can be actually executed in parallel, one in each computing core of the GPU, but the remaining threads may be waiting for memory accesses meanwhile, effectively hiding the memory latency. In this particular simulation each thread simulated a batch of 25,000 x-ray tracks and in total 800,000 threads, divided in 12,500 blocks of 64, were executed in the GPU. This is a good example of the data parallelism required to get a good speedup in the GPU architecture.

Analyzing the images in Figure 50.4, and similar ones generated with different densities and materials, we confirmed that the Woodcock ray tracing and the detector and source models were correctly implemented. Comparing the results with equivalent simulations with PENELOPE, we validated that the atomic interactions were correctly sampled, too. Observing the scatter images, we can readily see how the x-rays scattered by the Rayleigh effect suffer mostly small angle deflections that preserve some anatomical information — as expected — while the Compton scatter is more uniformly distributed at all angles (the signal is larger at the center for geometric reasons). We can also see that the upper voxels made of bone are more attenuating (lighter in 50.4(b)) and produce more scatter (darker in 50.4(e)) than the water voxels with the same density, owing to the higher content in high atomic number elements like calcium.

This sample simulation was repeated in one GPU of a GeForce GTX 295 card, giving a speed of 3,259,346 x-rays/second. Therefore, in this case, the Fermi architecture is 5.75 times faster than the previous architecture. The two simulated images are identical. The code was compiled with the "fast math" option to use faster mathematical functions with reduced numerical accuracy. If the simulation is performed without "fast math," the pixel values are not exactly the same even when using the same random number seeds because small changes in the precision of the floating-point operations modify some of the x-ray tracks. For example, a tiny difference in the sampled deflection angle may change the pixel where a particle is detected. The average relative difference (in absolute value) between the images with and without fast operations was 0.08%. Because this numerical error is several orders of magnitude below the statistical uncertainty in the estimation of the pixel values, the numerical inaccuracies are not expected to affect in any practical way the quality of the simulated images.

50.4.2 Example Simulation with a Realistic Human Phantom

The main reason to develop the software presented in this chapter was the study of clinical imaging systems and, in particular, to create synthetic CT scans, a type of simulation that is too time-consuming to be performed with accurate general-purpose MC transport codes. In this final section we present two example simulations of medical imaging using a realistic adult male phantom from the Virtual Family [10].[2]

The first example application is a whole-body radiographic projection image of a version of the male phantom adapted to the MC code using 1 mm voxels and 10 different body materials. The size of this phantom is $61 \times 31 \times 186$ cm^3, resulting in more than 350 million voxels that occupy 2.6 GB of global memory in the GPU. To show the anatomical detail of the phantom, we defined a detector much larger than any common clinical detector, with a sensitive area of 100×200 cm^2 and 500×1000, 0.2×0.2 cm^2 pixels. Figure 50.5 presents the results of the simulation, with scatter (a) and without scatter (b), for 10^{10}, 50 keV x-rays. Because of the large memory requirements this simulation was only performed in a Tesla C1060 GPU. The simulation lasted 112 minutes, with an average speed of 1,487,676.8 x-rays/second.

---

[2]The high-resolution anatomical models of the Virtual Family are freely distributed for scientific purposes at: www.itis.ethz.ch/virtualfamily.

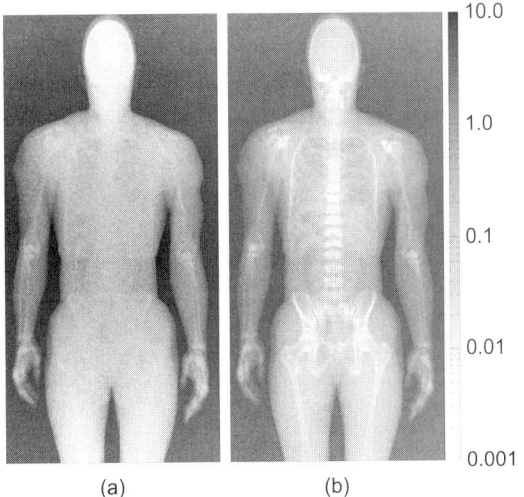

10.0

1.0

0.1

0.01

0.001

(a)   (b)

FIGURE 50.5

A simulated whole-body radiographic projection of the adult male phantom from the Virtual Family: (a) image including primary and scatter radiation; (b) image without scatter. The same logarithmic grayscale is used in both images, with units of eV/cm^2 per x-ray.

As a second example, we simulated a clinically realistic eight-row head CT scan using a version of the male phantom's head with $400 \times 500 \times 480$, 0.5 mm voxels and 11 different biological tissues (732.4 MB in memory). The CT simulation consisted of 720 projections (one every 0.5 degrees) performed in a full 360-degree rotation around the phantom at the height of the nose. For each projection, we simulated $2.2 \cdot 10^9$, 50 keV x-rays (the mean energy in a clinical 90 kVp x-ray spectrum). The detector had 900, 0.6 mm pixels in the horizontal direction and 8, 3 mm pixels in the vertical direction, with a source-to-detector distance of 100 cm and a source-to-object distance of 50 cm (twofold magnification). The CT was reconstructed with a Feldkamp cone-beam CT reconstruction algorithm. The simulated sinogram is displayed in Figure 50.6(a). The sinogram was created concatenating the signal detected at the third row of the detector (900 pixels) for the 720 projections taken in a full rotation around the patient. The third slice of the reconstructed volume (with 900×900, 0.3 mm pixels) is shown in Figure 50.6(b), next to a density map of the equivalent plane in the original voxelized phantom (c).

The CT was simulated in parallel in two Linux workstations with a total of 16 GPUs (four GeForce GTX 295 dual-GPUs in each computer). The time required to simulate the total $1.6 \cdot 10^{12}$ x-rays was 13 hours, giving a collective simulation speed of 17 million x-rays/second for the 16-GPU cluster. The average time per projection (in one GPU) was 17 minutes, with an average speed of 2,117,647 x-rays/second.

To evaluate the performance of the code, the first (lateral) projection of the CT was simulated using different GPU models and an Intel Xeon W3520 quad-core CPU at 2.67 GHz. The obtained timing results are summarized in Table 50.1. The CPU code was compiled with the GNU compiler (gcc) and with the Intel compiler with the auto-parallelization and SSE optimizations enabled. The code

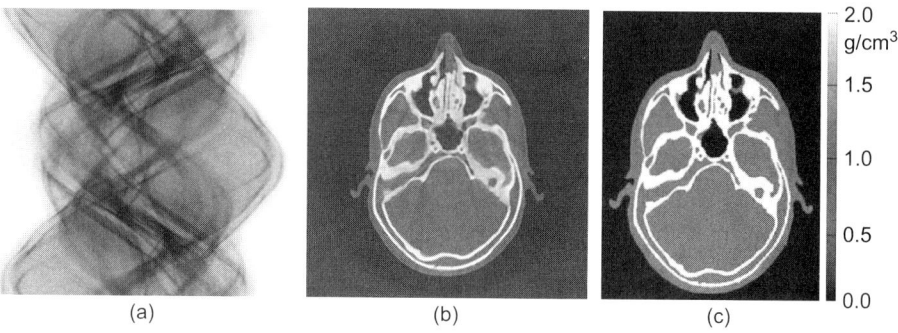

FIGURE 50.6

GPU-simulated head CT scan: (a) sinogram with the 720 rows of data generated in a full rotation around the head (log scale); (b) reconstructed slice with 900 × 900, 0.3 mm pixels; (c) density map of the equivalent plane in the original phantom (with 0.5 mm voxels).

Table 50.1 Performance of a sample simulation in a single core of an Intel Xeon CPU and in four GPUs from NVIDIA. The CPU code was compiled with the GNU compiler (gcc) and with the Intel compiler (all optimizations enabled). The GPU code was compiled targeting three different compute capabilities: sm_12 (32-bits, single precision only), sm_13 (32-bits, double precision), and sm_20 (64-bits, double precision). For the Fermi GPU (sm_20), the code was tested twice: setting a large cache (+L1) and setting a large shared memory (+Sh.).

	Intel Xeon CPU core		GeForce GTX 285		GeForce GTX 295		Tesla C1060		GeForce GTX 480 (Fermi)			
	Intel	gcc	sm12	sm13	sm12	sm13	sm12	sm13	sm12	sm13	sm20 +L1	sm20 +Sh.
Speed [x-rays/sec]	297848.9	72966.1	4421843.9	2168962.2	3800836.2	1783644.0	3800114.0	1957905.0	10141119.2	9087209.3	5407719.8	8524970.2
Speedup vs. CPU	1.0	0.25	14.9	7.3	12.8	6.0	12.8	6.6	34.0	30.5	18.2	28.6

with the Intel compiler was four times faster than gcc and was used as a reference. The GPU code was compiled with NVCC 3.0 using "fast math" and targeting three different compute capabilities. The differences between the compute capabilities are the use of 32 or 64 bits of memory addresses and the availability of double-precision operations. For the Fermi architecture, the code was tested setting a large L1 cache (small shared memory) and also setting a large shared memory (small cache). A maximum 34-fold speedup in the Fermi GPU compared with the CPU was measured. Of course, the results would have looked better for the CPU if we had used the four computing cores of the CPU. In fact, we can expect a linear reduction of the computation time for each extra CPU because the algorithm scales very well in the massively multiprocessor architecture of the GPU. The GPU is still 8.5 times faster than the four cores of the CPU. Naturally, if a large cluster of CPUs is available, the simulations will be faster in the CPUs, but the GPUs are much more efficient in terms of cost, energy consumption, and space.

Incidentally, we found out that compiling the code in Fermi with a large L1 cache instead of a large shared memory was significantly slowing down our code, probably because less thread blocks were able to share each microprocessor. Our code does not benefit much from a global memory cache because the initial direction of the x-rays and the interaction points are randomly sampled and therefore the accesses to the large voxel data are mostly incoherent. As an exception, caching may speed up a simulation using a very simple geometry such as the one used in the first example of the previous section if the whole voxel data can be fit inside the cache, which could explain the bigger speedup observed with the Fermi card in that example.

In the CT simulation we estimated that there were on average 894 virtual interactions, 51 photoelectric absorptions, 112 Compton interactions, 15 Rayleigh events, and 3527 random numbers generated for every 100 simulated x-rays. Therefore, fewer than 10^{14} random numbers were generated in the whole simulation, which is about 0.004% of the RANECU generator cycle.

A practical issue that we faced when using the eight-GPU workstations was the extraordinary power that these systems consume and the heat that they produce. We kept the computers in a special room with an air-conditioning system blowing directly on the GPUs through the lateral case aperture. With this setting, the maximum temperature of the GTX 295 GPU during the simulations was 85 degrees Celsius. The electrical power drawn by each computer was just below one kilowatt at full load. The new Fermi cards run even warmer and require more power. An example plot of the temperature of the GPUs during a sample simulation is shown in Figure 50.7.[3] In this case we simulated at the same time 10^{10} x-rays in a GeForce GTX 480 card (Fermi) and $5 \cdot 10^9$ x-rays in each one of the two GPUs of a GeForce GTX 295 card. As we can observe in the plot, the Fermi card runs above 90 degrees, more than 10 degrees warmer than the previous generation of GPUs. In spite of this, the new card required half the time to simulate double the number of particles — an impressive performance improvement. Preliminary tests with a workstation with four GeForce GTX 480 GPUs from EVGA show that the heat pipes built in the cards succeed, with adequate ventilation, in keeping the temperatures of the four-GPU system similar to a single GPU and below 100 degrees Celsius.

50.5 FUTURE DIRECTIONS

The code described in this chapter is being actively developed to extend the available features and increase the imaging modalities that can be simulated. Some features that we are implementing are the use of multi-energetic x-ray beams and the capability to tally the dose deposited in the voxelized phantom. We are also preparing a comprehensive benchmark of the GPU code with the original PENELOPE code, to validate the accuracy of the new code and analyze the effect of the few modifications in the

---

[3]The data for the temperature plot was generated with the utility *nvidia-smi*, provided with the NVIDIA CUDA driver for Linux. To get the GPU temperature every two seconds, the following shell command was executed: "nvidia-smi -a -q -l -i 2 > temp.dat". The accuracy of the temperature measurements was not verified.

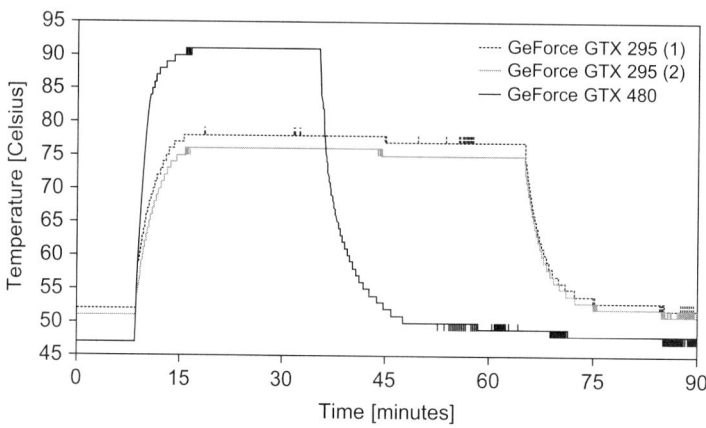

FIGURE 50.7

Temperature of two GPUs during a sample simulation: 10^{10} x-rays were simulated in the GeForce GTX 480 card (Fermi architecture) and $5 \cdot 10^9$ x-rays were simulated at the same time in each one of the two GPUs of a GeForce GTX 295 card (blue and red).

sampling models that were introduced to port the PENELOPE algorithms to the GPU architecture (for example, single-precision operations).

References

[1] A. Badal, A. Badano, Accelerating Monte Carlo simulations of photon transport in a voxelized geometry using a massively parallel Graphics Processing Unit, Med. Phys. 36 (2009) 4878–4880.

[2] A. Badal, A. Badano, Monte Carlo Simulation of X-Ray Imaging Using a Graphics Processing Unit, in: B. Yu (Ed.), IEEE NSC-MIC, Conference Record, HP3–1, 25–31 October 2009, Orlando, Florida, 2009, pp. 4081–4084.

[3] A. Badal, I. Kyprianou, D. Sharma, A. Badano, Fast cardiac CT simulation using a Graphics Processing Unit-accelerated Monte Carlo code, in: E. Samei, N.J. Pelc (Eds.), Proceedings of the SPIE Medical Imaging Conference, Medical Imaging 2010: Physics of Medical Imaging, 15 February 2010, SPIE, San Diego, California, USA, 2010, p. 762231.

[4] NVIDIA Corporation, NVIDIA CUDA Programming Guide, Technical Report. http://www.nvidia.com/cuda, 2010.

[5] R. Fazel, H.M. Krumholz, Y. Wang, J.S. Ross, J. Chen, H.H. Ting et al., Exposure to low-dose ionizing radiation from medical imaging procedures, N. Engl. J. Med. 361 (2009) 849–857.

[6] F. Salvat, J.M. Fernandez-Varea, J. Sempau, PENELOPE – A code system for Monte Carlo simulation of electron and photon transport, NEA-OECD, Issy-les-Moulineaux. http://www.nea.fr/tools/abstract/detail/nea-1525, 2010.

[7] E. Woodcock, T. Murphy, P. Hemmings, S. Longworth, Techniques used in the GEM code for Monte Carlo neutronics calculations in reactors and other systems of complex geometry, in: Proceedings of the Conference on Applications of Computing Methods to Reactor Problems, Argonne National Laboratories Report ANL-7050, 1965.

[8]   P. L'Ecuyer, Efficient and portable combined random number generators, Commun. ACM 31 (1988) 742–749.

[9]   A. Badal, J. Sempau, A package of Linux scripts for the parallelization of Monte Carlo simulations, Comput. Phys. Commun. 175 (6) (2006) 440–450.

[10] A. Christ, W. Kainz, E. Hahn et al., The Virtual Family—development of surface-based anatomical models of two adults and two children for dosimetric simulations, Phys. Med. Biol. 55 (2010) N23.

[11] Handbook of anatomical models for radiation dosimetry, in: X.G. Xu, K.F. Eckerman (Eds.), Series in Medical Physics and Biomedical Engineering, CRC Press, Taylor & Francis, 2009.

Index

A

ABINIT software package, BigDFT, 133–134
ABM, *see* Agent-based modeling (ABM)
Absorption sampling, photon transport, 254
Accumulation function, photon transport, 258
ACO, *see* Ant colony optimization (ACO)
Activation rate, macro-gates, 355, 359–362
Activity-based clustering, gate-level simulation, 362
Adaptive (ADP) extensions, programmable graphics pipeline in CUDA, 434
Adaptive Poisson-Boltzmann Solver (APBS), electrostatics algorithms
    MDH method, 45–47
    overview, 44
Adaptive windows, real-time stereo on GP-GPU
    algorithms, implementations, evaluations, 475–485
    basic problem, 473–474
    core method, 475
    cross-checking, 484–485
    foreground *vs.* full image, 490–493
    Middlebury evaluation, 486–487
    multiresolution background modeling, 475–478
    multiresolution *vs.* single resolution, 487–490
    multiresolution stereo matching, 478–479
    performance evaluation, 486–493
    single CUDA kernel, 479–485
ADULT dataset, SVM evaluation, 307–309
Agent-based modeling (ABM), with CUDA
    algorithms and implementations, 314
    basic problem, 313–320
    communication and transition function behavior scripting, 317–319
    core method, 314
    future work, 324
    overview, 313–314
    performance evaluation, 321–323
    real-time instanced agent visualization, 319–320
    state-based agent simulation, 314–315
    XML-driven CUDA code generation, 315–317
Aggregation
    ASR graph traversal, 608–610
    pseudocode, 95–96, 98
    real-time stereo on GP-GPU, 475
    as spectral synthesis step, 94
ALAP, *see* As-late-as-possible (ALAP) levelization
Albedo
    clouds rendering, 390
    definition, 247
    lighting models, 390

photon transport, 251, 254, 258
    random walk path regeneration, 402, 404–406, 408–410
Algorithmic transformation, LINGO, 27–30
AllToAll infiniband communications, large-scale FFT, 638
    algebraic manipulations, 636–637
    naive algorithm, 633–634
    optimized algorithm, 634
All-vs-All, multiclass SVM, 295–296
Alpha-expansion algorithms, Graph Cuts for computer vision, 449–450
Alpha kernel function, SMO, 297, 302
ALU, *see* Arithmetic logic unit (ALU)
Angular momentum
    black hole simulations, 104–106
    CGTOs, 9
    unrolled-type-specific code, 14
Anisotropic diffusion filter
    brain connectivity reconstruction, 796
    ITK-based medical imaging, 740, 745–747
Ant colony optimization (ACO)
    basic problem, 325–326
    basic scheme, 326
    core method, 326
    operation and implementation, 330–337
    optimization, 327–330
    pseudocode overview, 327
Antidiagonal approach, pattern matching acceleration, 188–189
Antimonotonicity, temporal data mining, 213
AntMinerGPU
    basic operation, 330–337
    classification rules, 328
    construction graph, 328–329
    CPU/GPU control flow, 332
    data point removal, 337
    data structures, 331–332
    edge probabilities, 333–334
    future work, 340
    heuristic value computation, 333
    overview, 327–330
    performance evaluation, 337–339
    pheromone deposition, 337
    pheromone evaporation, 335
    pheromone initialization, 332–333
    pheromone updating, 330
    pseudocode overview, 331
    solution construction phase, 329–330
    solution evaluation, 335–337
    solution generation, 334
APBS, *see* Adaptive Poisson-Boltzmann Solver (APBS)

Arithmetic logic unit (ALU)
GPU-based parallelization, 368–369
parallel gate implementation evaluation, 372–373
Arithmetic optimization, GSO calculations, 22–23
Array-based data structures, Barnes Hut *n*-body algorithm, 78–79
Array dimensions, FFT algebra
basic manipulations, 635–637
main-memory transpositions, 637–638
Arrival times (AT), fast circuit optimization, 366–368
As-late-as-possible (ALAP) levelization, gate-level simulation, 348
ASR, *see* Automatic speech recognition (ASR)
Asteroseismology
definition, 93
future GRASSY work, 101
spectral synthesis, *see* Stellar spectral synthesis
Astrophysics, GRASSY work, 101
Asynchronous input/output operations, image/video processing, 558–560
AT, *see* Arrival times (AT)
Atlas construction
basic image operators, 775–777
basic problem, 771–773
CG method, 780–782
challenges, 773–774
core methods, 774
data structures, 775
future work, 789–790
GPU cluster model, 784
load-balancing, 784–785
multi-GPU model, 783–784
multiscale framework, 782–783
ODE integration, 777
PDE solver, 778
performance analysis, 786–789
performance improvement, 788–789
performance quality, 787–788
performance tuning, 785–786
scratch memory model, 786–787
SOR method, 778–780
volume clipping optimization, 786
Atom bins, short-range cutoff electrostatics, 52–54
Atomic densities
and Becke kernel, 40
as indicator functions, 20
Atomic operations
ASR, 604, 610–613
Barnes Hut *n*-body algorithm via CUDA, 80
CCL in CUDA, 574, 576
Graph Cuts for computer vision, 441–443
MaxEnt with, 284–285

MaxEnt without, 283–284
programmable graphics pipeline in CUDA, 429–433
radiographic image simulation, 821–822
temporal data mining, 223
Audio processing, GPU computing status, 599–600
Automatic speech recognition (ASR)
algorithms, implementations, evaluations, 604–615
atomic operations, 610–613
core methods, 603–604
dynamic vector data structure, 604–606
find-unique function, 606–608
future work, 615, 617
implementation challenges, 603
inference engine framework, 616
lock-free accesses, 608–610
performance analysis, 613–615
speech recognition application, 601–603
Axon segmentation, brain connectivity reconstruction, 809
Axon surface visualization, brain connectivity reconstruction, 795–797
Axon tracking, brain connectivity reconstruction, 802
Azimuth angle, photon transport, 247–248, 254–255

B

Back-face culling test, programmable graphics pipeline, 428
Background modeling, real-time stereo, 475–478
Background subtraction algorithm, image/video processing, 548–550, 552–554
Backprojection
CT projection filtering, 669–672
image reconstruction method, 686
list-mode image reconstruction, 679
list-mode OSEM, 681
Backward mapping, CT projection filtering, 669
Backward operator, MRI reconstruction, 715–717
Backward propagation, FFT, 638
Baker-Campbell-Hausdorf (BCH) expansion, MD calculations, 61, 70–71
Barnes-Hut multiple acceptance criteria, fast *N*-body simulations, 121–122
Barnes-Hut *n*-body algorithm, CUDA implementation
algorithm overview, 76–77
basic problem, 75–76
evaluation methodology, 88–89
global optimizations, 78–79
kernel 1 optimization, 79–80
kernel 2 optimization, 80–81
kernel 3 optimization, 81–83
kernel 4 optimization, 83
kernel 5 optimization, 84–86
kernel 6 optimization, 86
limitations, 91

optimizations overview, 86–88
  results, 89–90
Base pairs (BPs)
  genome-matching acceleration, 174, 178–179
  RNA folding problem, 199–200
Basis functions
  B-spline registration, 752–753, 755–758, 766
  DFT, 134–136, 138
  electronic structure, 60, 65, 69
  fine-scale facial deformation, 419–420
  high-resolution facial details, 420–421
  large-scale deformation, 416–417
  MO computations, 8–11
  MRI, 712
  multiclass SVM, 307
Basis sets
  basic concept, 8
  DFT calculations, 133, 137
  MO algorithms, 10–14, 16–18
Bayer pattern color filter array (CFA), 583–584
BBH, *see* Binary black hole (BBH) systems
BC, *see* Boundary condition (BC)
BCH, *see* Baker-Campbell-Hausdorf (BCH) expansion
BDP2, programmable graphics pipeline in CUDA, 434
Becke kernels
  comparison, 40–41
  serial triple loop pseudo-code, 38
Becke weight, quadrature grid DFT calculations
  core method, 36–37
  implementation, 37–39
  kernel comparison, 40
Belief propagation
  LDPC, 620, 627
  real-time stereo, 487
BEM, *see* Boundary element methods (BEM)
BER, *see* Bit error rate (BER)
BF, *see* Bilateral filter (BF)
BFGS algorithm, GSO calculations, 23, 25–27
BFS, *see* Breadth-first search (BFS)
BH, *see* Black hole (BH) simulations
Bidirectional reflectance distribution function (BRDF), random
    walks in path tracing, 409–410
Bidirectional scattering distribution function (BSDF), random
    walks in path tracing, 402–403, 406
BigDFT code
  benefits and limitations, 144–145
  BLAS routines, 140–143
  code structure, 138
  convolutions, 138–139
  core method, 135–138
  CPU code, 145
  Daubechies wavelets, 134

definition, 133–134
  efficiency developments, 149
  hybrid code performance, 145–147
  implementation, 140
  kinetic convolution and preconditioner, 139
  kinetic operator, 136
  local potential, 136
  magic filters, 136
  molecule simulation domain example, 135
  multiple core calculations, 148
  operations, 136–137
  overview, 134
  parallel distribution, 147
  performance evaluation, 140, 150
  3D operators, 140–143
Bijection, MaxEnt with, 284–285
Bilateral filter (BF), CT reconstruction, 696, 702–703
Bilinear interpolation, de-mosaicing
  algorithms, 586–593
  filtering enhancements, 593–597
  performance, 597–598
Binary black hole (BBH) systems, 103
Binary support vector machine, 294–295
Biomolecular systems, electrostatics algorithms
  core method, 45
  direct Coulomb summation, 47–51, 56–57
  MDH method, 45, 54–56
  overview, 43–44
  short-range cutoff, 50–55, 57–58
Bit error rate (BER), LDPC, 619, 626
Bit nodes (BN), LDPC, 620, 622–623
Biweight Tuckey test, visual saliency motion estimator kernel,
    460
Black hole (BH) simulations
  GPU implementation, 106–107
  GPU supercomputing clusters, 107–109
  numerical algorithm, 105
  overview, 103–104
  performance results, 107–108
  PN approximation, 104–105
  statistical results, 109
BLAS routines
  atlas construction, 778
  BigDFT code, 138, 140–145, 147
  MaxEnt model, 287–290
  MD calculations, 67–68
BLAST, pattern matching acceleration, 192
Block-based data structures, brain connectivity reconstruction,
    795
Block compressed Sparse Row (BSR), MRI reconstruction, 717
Block-per-point method, quadrature grid DFT calculations, 38
BN, *see* Bit nodes (BN)

Born-Oppenheimer approximation
    basic approach, 59
    direct MD, 60
    MD calculations, 72
Bottom-up visual saliency model
    definition, 451
    schematic, 452
Boundary condition (BC)
    atlas construction, 780–781, 786
    BigDFT code, 137, 139–140, 149
    brain connectivity reconstruction, 801
    DBT, 652
    real-time speed-limit-sign recognition, 506
Boundary element methods (BEM), and FMM, 114
Bounding box kernel, Barnes Hut *n*-body algorithm, 76–77
Box-Muller transform, random number generator performance, 243
BPTI, quadrature grid calculations, 41–42
Brain connectivity reconstruction, in EM
    axon surface visualization, 795–797
    core methods, 793–797
    future work, 811–812
    GPU active ribbon segmentation, 797–802
    GPU axon segmentation, 809
    GPU-based volume brick filtering, 802–803
    GPU implicit surface ray casting, 797
    GPU volume brick boundary detection, 803–809
    histogram-based boundary detection, 810–811
    HistogramVoxelDirect algorithm, 805, 807–809
    HistogramVoxelSweep algorithm, 804–805
    implementation, 797–809
    level set re-distancing, 801–802
    level set updating, 797–800
    on-demand volume filtering, 796
    overview, 793
    performance analysis, 809–811
    semiautomatic axon segmentation, 793–795
    3D axon tracking, 802
    3D volume visualization, 795–797
BRDF, *see* Bidirectional reflectance distribution function (BRDF)
Breadth-first search (BFS), Graph Cuts for computer vision, 446–447
Breast cancer screening, overview, 647–649
Bricking, brain connectivity reconstruction, 796
Brute-force message group loading, ABM communication, 319
BSDF, *see* Bidirectional scattering distribution function (BSDF)
B-splines, deformable registration algorithm
    coefficient optimization, 754–756
    cost function, 753–755
    cost function with deformation field, 759–762
    cost function gradient, 762–766

deformation field, 752–753
implementation, 756–766
initialization, 757–758
input, output, state, 756
overview, 751–752
performance analysis, 767–769
process flowchart, 757
tile symmetry, 756–757
BSR, *see* Block compressed Sparse Row (BSR)
Butterfly reduction, MaxEnt model, 283–285
BX cells, RNA folding algorithm, 204

C

CA, *see* Cellular automata (CA)
Calibration Consistency operator, SPIRiT MRI, 727–729
Calibration Operator, SPIRiT MRI parallel imaging, 726–727
Carbon-60 calculations
    multi-GPU performance, 18
    single-GPU performance, 17
Carbon nanotubes, MD calculations, 65–68
Car-Parrinello molecular dynamics (CPMD), 59
Cartesian sampling, and MRI, 710
CC, *see* Cross-correlation coefficient (CC)
CCS, *see* Compress column storage (CCS) format
CDF, *see* Cumulative probability distribution (CDF)
Cellular automata (CA), LB methods, 382–383
Center-of-gravity kernel, Barnes Hut *n*-body algorithm, 78
CFA, *see* Bayer pattern color filter array (CFA)
CG, *see* Conjugate gradients (CG)
Cg
    CT reconstruction, 700, 702
    and list-mode OSEM, 681–682
    tomographic image reconstruction, 684
    VSM, 469
CGTOs, *see* Contracted Gaussian type orbitals (CGTOs)
Chaos Game algorithm
    Fractal Flames, 263–264
    memory-access patterns, 267–269
    Monte Carlo, 265
    performance evaluation, 270–272
    phases, 267
    static data, 270
Chapman-Enskog expansion, 396
Character recognition, and machine learning, 289–290
Check nodes (CN), decoding kernel, 622–623
Chemical informatics, similarity evaluation
    core methods, 22
    GSO
        CPU/GPU balancing, 25–27
        data-parallel objective function, 23–25
        kernel fusion, 25–27

overview, 20–21
  parallelization and arithmetic optimization, 22–27
  LINGO, 21–22
    algorithmic transformation and memory optimization,
      27–30
    SIML, 31–33
    SIML and memory tuning, 28–30
  overview, 19–20
  performance comparison, 30, 32
  3D shape molecule overlay, 21
CLAHE, *see* Contrast Limited Adaptive Histogram
      Equalization (CLAHE)
Classifier cascade
  layout optimizations, 538–541
  object-detection with CUDA, 533–541
  structure, 521–522
Closing phase, path regeneration for random walks, 408
Clouds, LB methods example, 390–391
Cluster-boundary identification, ASR, 608
CMRG, *see* Combined multiple recursive generators (CMRGs)
CN, *see* Check nodes (CN)
Coalesced memory accesses
  Barnes Hut *n*-body algorithm via CUDA, 86, 88
  fast *n*-body algorithms, 118
  image/video processing, 562–565
  pattern matching acceleration, 196–198
  VSM, 457, 460
Coarse-grain parallelism
  fast circuit optimization, 365
  medical image processing, 738
Coefficient arrays, wavefunction, HCl, 11
Collision matrix
  LB method OpenCL implementation, 386
  LB methods, 384–385
  plant rendering, 390
Column-parallel scan, pattern matching acceleration, 188–191
Combinatorial logic, gate-level simulation, 348
Combined multiple recursive generators (CMRGs), 232–233
Composite filters, speed-limit-sign recognition, 501–502
Compress column storage (CCS) format, LDPC, 622
Compressed sensing (CS), MRI
    approach, 724–725
    basic problem, 723–726
Compressed Sparse Row (CSR), MRI reconstruction, 717
Compressibility, CS MRI, 724
Compress row storage (CRS) format, LDPC, 622
Compton interactions, radiographic image simulation, 818, 823
Compton law, photon transport, 248, 255, 257
Computed tomography (CT)
  deformable registration algorithm, 751–752, 767–768
  parallelization
    algorithms, implementations, evaluations, 661–672

backprojection, 669–672
backward mapping, 669
basic problem, 659
convolution, 666, 668–669
core methods, 659–660
differentiation, 663–666
forward mapping, 666–668
future work, 676
performance evaluation, 672–675
projection's filtering, 663–669
related work, 675–676
steps, 661–663
radiographic image simulations, 815–816, 818–819,
      824–826
reconstruction parameters
  algorithms, implementations, evaluations, 695–700
  basic problem, 693–694
  core methods, 694–695
  exhaustive sampling, 696–697
  future work, 706–707
  iterative algorithms performance, 700–702
  multi-objective optimization, 697–698
  OS-SIRT, 695–696
  parameter selection interface, 698–700
  performance evaluation, 700–706
  quality metric, 698
  regularization scheme performance, 702–703
Computer simulations
  black holes, 103–109
  event-driven logic, 344, 346–347, 355
  gate-level with GP-GPUs, 347–363
  n-bodies with CUDA, 113–131
  oblivious logic, 344, 346, 352–354
  radiographic images, 813–828
  state-based agent simulation, 314–315
Computer vision
  GPU computing status, 437–438
  Graph Cuts
    algorithms, implementations, evaluations, 440–447
    core method, 439–440
    evaluation, validation, 447–448
    global relabeling, 446–447
    multilabel Graph Cuts, 448–450
    parallel push implementation, 441–444
    workload management, 444–445
  real-time stereo, *see* Real-time stereo
Compute Unified Device Architecture, *see* CUDA (Compute
      Unified Device Architecture)
Concurrent gate group, definition, 370, 372
Concurrent thread array (CTA), CUDA, stereo matching,
      479–482, 485
Cone-beam cover method, CT parallelization, 662

Conflict-free reduction, ASR, 608–610
Conjugate gradients (CG)
  atlas construction, 778, 780–782
  MRI reconstruction, 713–715
    high-speed implementations, 715–718
    kernel functions, 715–717
Connected component labeling (CCL), in CUDA
  algorithms, implementations, 572–577
  CCL definition, 569
  core algorithm, 570–572
  future work, 581
  I/O, 574
  kernel analysis, 580
  limitations, 580–581
  merging scheme, 574–577
  overview, 569–570
  parallel union find, 570–572
  performance evaluation, 577–581
  in shared memory, 574
Constant cache
  CUDA, 17
  fast circuit optimization, 372–373
  genome search algorithms, 177
  GPU MO algorithms, 11
  molecular electrostatics, 47–48
Constant memory
  Barnès-Hut n-body algorithm, 79, 87–88
  CMRGs, 234
  CT image reconstruction, 664–667, 669–670
  facial animation, 423–424
  fast circuit optimization, 373
  genome-matching acceleration, 175, 179–180
  iterated function systems, 266, 270
  LB model, 386, 389
  LINGO, 28
  medical image processing, 742
  MO computations, 8, 11, 13
  molecular electrostatics, 47–49, 51–52, 54
  MRI reconstruction, 712, 715–717, 719
  n-body algorithms, 129
  object detection, 540
  programmable graphics pipeline in CUDA, 428–429
  radiographic image simulation, 822–823
  sequence database scanning, 170
  SPIRiT compressed sensing MRI, 731
Construction graph
  and ACO, 326
  AntMinerGPU, 328–329
    data structures, 331–332
    solution generation, 334
Contracted Gaussian type orbitals (CGTOs), MO calculations,
    9, 10

Contrast Limited Adaptive Histogram Equalization (CLAHE),
    speed-limit-sign recognition, 502–504, 509–510
Control-point spacing, B-spline registration, 765, 767–769
Convolutions
  BigDFT code, 138–140
  CT projection filtering, 666, 668–669
  ITK-based medical imaging, 738–739, 742–743
  SPIRiT MRI, 730–733
Cornell box scene, random walks in path tracing, 409–410
Cost function, B-spline registration, 753–755, 759–762
Cost function gradient, deformable registration algorithm
    distribution stage, 765
    loading stage, 763
    overview, 762–763
    processing stage, 763, 765
CountScanWrite approach, temporal data mining, 222, 224
CPMD, *see* Car-Parrinello molecular dynamics (CPMD)
CPU/GPU architectures, object detection, 517
CPU/GPU balancing, and GSO, 25–27
CPU/GPU bandwidth, atlas construction, 783
CPU/GPU communication
    brain connectivity reconstruction, 802
    tomographic image reconstruction, 686, 688
CPU/GPU comparison
    MRI reconstruction, 720
    n-body algorithms, 90
CPU/GPU control flow
    ant colony optimization, 332
    AntMinerGPU, 332
CPU/GPU copy, chemical informatics, 32
CPU/GPU hybrid clusters, DFT, 133, 148
CPU/GPU partitioning
    DFT, 147
    image/video processing, 566
    SW algorithm, 155
CPU/GPU transfers
    Barnes Hut n-body algorithm, 88
    chemical informatics, 19, 27
    n-body algorithms, 87–88
Cross-checking, stereo matching, 476, 479, 484–485
Cross-correlation, image/video processing, 561
Cross-correlation coefficient (CC), CT reconstruction
    parameters, 698
CRS, *see* Compress row storage (CRS) format
CS, *see* Compressed sensing (CS)
CSR, *see* Compressed Sparse Row (CSR)
CTA, *see* Concurrent thread array (CTA)
CUBLAS routines
    BigDFT code, 141, 143–145, 147
    electronic structure, 59, 61–62, 64, 66–67, 71–72
    machine learning, 282, 287, 289
    MD calculations, 66–67, 71

multiclass SVM, 299, 303
SMO reduce step, 299
CUDA (Compute Unified Device Architecture)
    ABM, 313–324
    ASR, 609, 611–612
    atlas construction, 775, 777–781
    Barnes Hut n-body algorithm, 75–76, 78–86, 88–91
    basic architecture, 345
    black hole simulations, 103–109
    brain connectivity reconstruction, 796–809
    CCL, 569–581
    chemical informatics, 23–27, 29–30
    CT image reconstruction, 664, 666, 670, 672, 675
    DBT, 652
    de-mosaicing, 584, 587, 594, 596–598
    dynamical quadrature grids, 38–39
    electronic structure, 61–65
    facial animation, 413, 422–426
    fast circuit optimization evaluation, 374
    FFT, 632, 637
    Fractal Flames with IFS, 266–270
    gate-level simulation, 345–347, 352, 361–363
    genome matching, 173–183
    Graph Cuts for computer vision, 439–450
    GRASSY platform, 97–98
    image/video processing, 547–566
    LB model, 385–390
    LDPC, 626–627
    machine learning, 278, 280–287
    medical imaging, 737–743, 746
    MO computations, 5–6, 11–12, 15–17
    molecular electrostatics, 43–44, 46–47, 53, 55–58
    MRI reconstruction, 712–713, 715–718
    n-body simulations, 113–114, 116–131
    object detection, 526–543
    photon transport, 258–259
    programmable graphics pipeline, 427–435
    radiographic image simulation, 813–828
    random number generators, 231–232, 240, 242–245
    real-time stereo, 477–485
    speed-limit-sign recognition, 499, 505
    SPIRiT MRI, 728–729, 733
    SW algorithm, 156–169
    temporal data mining, 215, 217–218, 224–226
    tomographic image reconstruction, 679–691
    VSM, 457–458, 464, 466–467, 469
CUDPP (CUDA Data Parallel Primitives) Library
    integral image calculation, 526–530
    stream compaction, 533–534
    temporal data mining, 215, 218–219, 222
CUFFT library
    interaction kernel, 458

large-scale FFT, 637–638
large-scale FFT naive algorithm, 633–634
speed-limit-sign recognition, 507
SPIRiT MRI, 727, 729, 735
Cumulative probability distribution (CDF), photon transport,
        248–250
Current gate, definition, 370
Cutoff function
    quadrature grid DFT calculations, 36–37
    short-range, *see* Short-range cutoff
Cyclic dependencies, macro-gate segmentation, 349

D

DAG, *see* Directed acyclic graph (DAG)
Data consistency projection, SPIRiT MRI, 729
Data hazards, Graph Cuts for computer vision, 441–443
Data-intensive applications, GPU computing, 275–276
Data layout
    ASR, 606
    genome-matching, 179
    ITK-based medical imaging, 742
    object detection, 532, 539
Data mining, temporal data, *see* Temporal data mining
Data-parallel interaction kernel, block diagram, 458
Data parallelism
    chemical informatics, 22, 25, 27–28, 32
    LDPC, 619–620, 627
    medical image processing, 737
    molecular electrostatics, 43, 49
    n-body simulation, 122
    radiographic image simulation, 824
    SW algorithm, 157
Data-parallel objective function, GSO, 23–25
Data structures
    AntMinerGPU, 331–332
    ASR, 603–606, 612, 615–616
    atlas construction, 771, 774–775
    Barnes-Hut n-body algorithm, 75, 78, 91
    brain connectivity reconstruction, 795, 797, 801
    B-spline registration, 752, 757, 762
    CCL, 570
    facial animation, 420, 423
    gate-level simulations, 344, 347, 361
    genome-matching, 179
    image reconstruction, 685
    LDPC, 619, 622–624
    medical image processing, 742, 748
    molecular electrostatics, 53
    multiclass SVM, 310
    neuroscience data mining, 213–214
    object detection, 526, 540
    programmable graphics pipeline, 428

Data structures (*continued*)
    SMILES, 22
    tomographic image reconstruction, 685
Data training, MaxEnt model, 281
Daubechies wavelets, BigDFT code, 134, 136, 149
DBT, *see* Digital breast tomosynthesis (DBT)
De-Bayering, *see* De-mosaicing
Decoding kernel, LDPC, 623–626
Deformable registration algorithm, B-splines
    coefficient optimization, 754–756
    cost function, 753–755
    cost function with deformation field, 759–762
    cost function gradient, 762–766
    deformation field, 752–753
    implementation, 756–766
    initialization, 757–758
    input, output, state, 756
    overview, 751–752
    performance analysis, 767–769
    process flowchart, 757
    tile symmetry, 756–757
Deformation field, B-spline registration
    with cost function, 759–762
    cost function gradient, 762–766
    field representation, 752–753
Deformation model, facial animation
    fine-scale
        CUDA kernel code, 422
        high-resolution details, 419
        implementation, 417–420
        local blending, 420
        memory access strategy, 423–424
        overview, 417–418
        precomputation, 420
        skin strain, 418–419
    future work, 425–426
    large-scale
        background, 414
        core technology, 414–425
        equations, 416
        examples, 415
        implementation, 416–417
        memory access strategy, 423
        performance evaluation, 424–425
        system overview, 413
De-mosaicing
    algorithms, implementations, evaluations,
        585–597
    basic problem, 583
    core method, 585
    definition, 583
    filtering enhancements, 593–597

    implementation methods, 586–593
    memory considerations, 586, 588, 592, 594–595, 597
    performance evaluation, 597–598
    pixel composition layout, 587
    read process, 591
    source reading and storage, 589
Dense matching, real-time stereo, 473, 475, 480–482
Density functional theory (DFT) calculations
    BigDFT
        benefits and limitations, 144–145
        BLAS routines, 140–143
        code structure, 138
        convolutions, 138–139
        core method, 135–138
        CPU code, 145
        Daubechies wavelets, 134
        definition, 133–134
        efficiency developments, 149
        hybrid code performance, 145–147
        implementation, 140
        kinetic convolution and preconditioner, 139
        kinetic operator, 136
        local potential, 136
        magic filters, 136
        molecule simulation domain example, 135
        multiple core calculations, 148
        operations, 136–137
        overview, 134
        parallel distribution, 147
        performance evaluation, 140, 150
        3D operators, 140–143
    KS formalism, 133
    quadrature grids
        core method, 36–37
        implementation, 37–39
        overview, 35–36
        performance enhancement, 39–41
Density functional tight-binding (DFTB) theory
    MD calculations, 63, 69, 71
    nanotubes, 65
Density matrix propagation, MD calculations, 62–65, 69
Dependency requirements, pattern matching acceleration,
    187–188
Depth test, programmable graphics pipeline in CUDA,
    429–434
Device memories (dmem), large-scale FFT, 629, 634
DFA method, chemical informatics, 22, 27–29, 32–33
DFT, *see* Density functional theory (DFT) calculations;
    Discrete Fourier transform (DFT) matrix
DFTB, *see* Density functional tight-binding (DFTB) theory
Diffusion approximation, Lattice-Boltzmann lighting
    models, 382

Diffusion equation
  derivation, 395–398
  LB model, 384, 394
  Monte Carlo photon transport, 259
Diffusion filters
  brain connectivity reconstruction, 796
  medical imaging, 739–740, 743–748
Digital breast tomosynthesis (DBT)
  basic technology, 647–649
  data acquisition setup, 648
  definition, 647
  experimental setup, 650
  GPU acceleration, 650–656
  high-level description, 649
  vs. mammography, 650, 656
  multiple GPUs, 653–656
  overview, 649–650
  texture memory optimization, 651–653
  thread mapping, 650–651
DirectCompute, and facial animation, 426
Direct Coulomb summation
  electrostatics calculations, 47–51, 56–57
  short-range cutoff electrostatics, 50–53
Directed acyclic graph (DAG)
  AntMinerGPU, 328
  fast circuit optimization, 366
Direction numbers, Sobol quasi-random generator, 235
Direct molecular dynamics, overview, 60–61
Discrete cosine transform (DCT), CS MRI
        reconstruction, 725
Discrete Fourier transform (DFT) matrix, CS MRI, 724
Discrete ordinates method, Lattice-Boltzmann lighting
        models, 381–382
Disparity-sweeping process, stereo matching, 481–482
dmem, *see* Device memories (dmem)
Dormand-Prince method, black hole simulations, 105
Double-precision (DP)
  BigDFT code, 141, 143–144
  black hole simulations, 106–107
  DFT, 133, 141–144, 149
  dynamical quadrature grids, 39–40
  electronic structure, 69, 71
  FFT, 630, 639, 641
  MD methods, 69
  object detection, 528, 531
  radiographic image simulation, 820, 826
  template-driven agent-based modeling, 323
Down-Sweep, pattern matching acceleration, 197
DP, *see* Double-precision (DP); Dynamic programming (DP)
DRAM
  de-mosaicing, 586
  fast circuit optimization, 369

SPIRiT MRI, 728–729, 733–735
  template-driven agent-based modeling, 319
Duplication-removal process, ASR, 607
Dynamic grids, and LB methods, 395
Dynamic pathway, VSM, 453, 455–457, 464, 467–469
Dynamic programming (DP)
  fast circuit optimization, 366–367
  pattern matching, 185
  real-time stereo, 487
  RNA folding algorithm, 199–201
  in SW algorithm, 155–156, 163
Dynamic vector data structure, ASR, 603–606

E
Edge probabilities, AntMinerGPU, 329, 332–334
Electronic design automation (EDA), GPU computing status,
        341–342
Electronic structure propagation
  basic problem, 59–61
  building blocks and implementation, 65–68
  calculations, 69–72
  density matrix, 69
  Fock matrix, 69
  hardware considerations, 69
  matrix operations, 66–68
  overview, 59
  technology basics, 61–65
Electron microscopy (EM), brain connectivity reconstruction
  axon surface visualization, 795–797
  core methods, 793–797
  future work, 811–812
  GPU active ribbon segmentation, 797–802
  GPU-based volume brick filtering, 802–803
  GPU implicit surface ray casting, 797
  GPU volume brick boundary detection, 803–809
  HistogramVoxelDirect algorithm, 805, 807–809
  HistogramVoxelSweep algorithm, 804–805
  implementation, 797–809
  level set re-distancing, 801–802
  level set updating, 797–800
  on-demand volume filtering, 796
  performance analysis, 809–811
  semiautomatic axon segmentation, 793–795
  3D axon tracking, 802
  3D volume visualization, 795–797
Electrostatics algorithms
  core method, 45
  direct Coulomb summation, 47–51, 56–57
  MDH method, 45–47, 54–56
  overview, 43–44
  as Poisson problems, 113
  short-range cutoff, 50–55, 57–58

EM, *see* Electron microscopy (EM); Expectation maximization (EM)
Embedded speed-limit-sign recognition
    compute power adjustments, 511–512
    fast-radial symmetry, 505–506
    feature-based pipeline, 499–501
    FFT correlation with nonlinear filters, 507
    future work, 513–514
    implementation, 505–507
    methods, 499–505
    overview, 497–498
    pipeline evaluation, 508–511
    pipeline scalability, 512–513
    recognition results, 508
    results, 507–513
    SIFT-based pipeline, 505
    template-based pipeline, 500–505
Energy consumption, Katsevich CT image reconstruction parallelization, 674–675
Enumeration scheme, classifier cascades, 541
Episodes, temporal data mining, 212–217, 219–226
Error-correcting codes, multiclass SVM, 295
Euler method
    black hole simulations, 105
    brain connectivity reconstruction, 794, 798–799, 802
    medical image processing, 740, 745–746
Event-driven logic simulation
    definition, 344
    hybrid simulator, 346
    macro-gate sizing heuristics, 355
    simulator overview, 346–347
Expectation maximization (EM)
    CT reconstruction, 694
    tomographic image reconstruction, 680
Extinction coefficient
    LB model, 381
    photon transport, 247, 250–254, 261

F

FABS, *see* Fixed-size A-buffer scheme (FABS)
Face detection
    cascade stages, 536–537
    cascade structure, 521–523
Facial animation
    background, 414
    core technology, 414–425
    examples, 415
    fine-scale deformation, 417–420
    future work, 425–426
    high-resolution details, 420–421
    large-scale deformation, 416–417
    memory access strategy, 423–424

    parallelization, 423
    performance evaluation, 424–425
    results and evaluation, 421
    skin strain, 418–419
    system overview, 413
FASTA, pattern matching acceleration, 192
Fast circuit optimization
    algorithms, implementations, evaluations, 369–373
    basic problem, 365–367
    core method, 367–369
    future work, 376
    gate-level task scheduling, 369–372
    gate sizing/assignment, 367–368
    GPU-based parallelization, 368–369
    parallel gate implementation evaluation, 372–373
    performance evaluation, 373–375
Fast Fourier transform (FFT)
    array dimension algebra, 635–638
    atlas construction, 778
    feature-based pipeline, 501–502
    future work, 639, 642
    GPU cluster memory hierarchy, 631–632
    MRI reconstruction, 710–711
    naive algorithm, 633–634
    optimized algorithm, 634
    overview, 629–631
    performance evaluation, 639–641
    speed-limit-sign recognition, 507
    SPIRiT MRI, 735
Fast Fourier transform in the West (FFTW)
    and FFT, 630
    large-scale FFT, 639–641
    VSM, 465
Fast iterative method (FIM), brain connectivity reconstruction, 801
Fast multipole method (FMM)
    Helmholtz equations, 113–114
    n-body simulations, 114–116
        advanced techniques, 129, 131
        CUDA implementation, 116–120
        M2L kernel implementation, 125–130
        performance enhancements, 120–122
        P2P kernel implementation, 122–125
Fast spectral synthesis, with texture interpolation
    basic problem, 93–95
    flux calculation and aggregation, 95–96
    future work, 101
    GRASSY platform, 97–100
    testing, 100
Feature-based pipeline, speed-limit-sign recognition, 499–501, 512–514
FEMs, *see* Finite-element methods (FEMs)

FFT, *see* Fast Fourier transform (FFT)
FFTW, *see* Fast Fourier transform in the West (FFTW)
Field inhomogeneity compensation, MRI reconstruction, 711–712
Filtered backprojection (FBP)
    CT reconstruction, 693–694
    tomographic reconstruction, 648
Filtering
    atlas construction, 782–783
    Bayer pattern color filter array, 583–584
    BigDFT code, 136, 138–143
    brain connectivity reconstruction, 796, 802–803
    CT projections, 663–669
    CT reconstruction, 693–694, 696, 702–703
    de-mosaicing, 593–597
    medical imaging, 739–740, 742–748
    OS-SIRT, 696
    speed-limit-sign recognition, 501–502, 507
    tomographic reconstruction, 648
    VSM, 453, 455–465
Filter weights, ITK-based medical imaging, 742–744
FindRoot function, CCL in CUDA, 570, 572, 576
Find-unique function, in ASR, 603
Fine-grain parallelism, B-spline registration, 752
Fine-scale facial deformation
    CUDA kernel code, 422
    high-resolution details, 419
    implementation, 417–420
    local blending, 420
    memory access strategy, 423–424
    overview, 417–418
    precomputation, 420
    skin strain, 418–419
Finite-element methods (FEMs), LB methods, 383
Fixed-size A-buffer scheme (FABS), programmable graphics pipeline, 433
FLAME GPU, for ABM with CUDA
    communication, 317, 319
    future work, 324
    performance, 321–323
    state-based agent simulation, 314–315
    visualization, 320
    XML-driven CUDA code generation, 315–317
Flux aggregation
    pseudocode, 95–96, 98
    as spectral synthesis step, 94
Flux calculation
    pseudocode, 95–96
    as spectral synthesis step, 94
FMM, *see* Fast multipole method (FMM)

Fock matrix
    MD calculations, 61–65, 69
    MD problem, 60–61
Force calculation kernel, Barnes Hut n-body algorithm, 78, 85
Foreground detection algorithm, stereo matching, 475–478, 490–493
Fortran, MD calculations, 61–65, 71
Forward mapping, CT projection filtering, 666–668
Forward-projection, image reconstruction
    list-mode, 679
    list-mode OSEM, 681
    method, 685–687
Forward propagation, FFT, 637
Fourier transforms
    SPIRiT MRI, 727–728
    VSM, 465
Fractal Flames algorithm, with IFS
    components, 264–265
    core technology, 266–267
    functions, 265–266
    implementation, 266–270
    memory-access patterns, 267–269
    performance evaluation, 270–272
    phases, 267
    problem overview, 263–264
    rendering, 269
    static data, 270
Frechet mean, atlas construction, 772
Free path sampling, photon transport on GPU, 250–254
Frustrum clipping, programmable graphics pipeline in CUDA, 428
Function condition, state-based agent simulation, 314–315
Fusion
    DBT, 650
    VSM, 452–453, 455–456, 465, 468–469

G

Gabor filtering kernel, VSM, 462–465
    CUDA kernels, 457
    dynamic pathway, 455–457
    motion estimator kernel, 458–462
    static pathway, 453
Game of Life, 382–383
GAMESS, carbon-60 single-GPU performance, 17–18
Gaps, genome-matching acceleration, 181–182
Gap values, macro-gate sizing heuristics, 355
Gate assignment, fast circuit optimization, 367–368
Gate-level simulation
    compilation phase, 347–351
    design compilation, 358–359
    future work, 362–363
    macro-gate activity, 359–361

Gate-level simulation (*continued*)
   macro-gate balancing, 350–351
   macro-gates, 356–358
   monitored nets, 358–359
   overview, 343–347
   performance evaluation, 361–362
   performance results, 355–362
   related work, 363
   simulation phase, 351–355
   simulator organization, 347
   system-level compilation, 348–350
Gate-level task scheduling, fast circuit optimization, 369–372
Gate sizing, fast circuit optimization, 367–368
Gaussian filter
   ITK-based medical imaging, 742–743, 747
   multiscale atlas construction, 782–783
   OS-SIRT, 696
   VSM, 455–456
Gaussian mixture model, ASR, 604
Gaussian noise, CT reconstruction performance, 704
Gaussian shape overlay (GSO), chemical similarity evaluation
   core methods, 22
   CPU/GPU balancing, 25–27
   data-parallel objective function, 23–25
   definition, 19
   kernel fusion, 25–27
   molecule examples, 21
   overview, 20–21
   parallelization and arithmetic optimization, 22–27
   performance comparison, 30, 32
Gaussian type orbitals (GTOs), MO calculations, 9
General-purpose graphics processing units (GP-GPUs)
   ACO acceleration
      algorithms, implementations, evaluations, 327–337
      AntMinerGPU, 327–340
      basic problem, 325–326
      basic scheme, 326
      core method, 326
      data structures, 331–332
      operation and implementation, 330–337
      optimization, 327
      pseudocode overview, 327
   CT image reconstruction
      algorithms, implementations, evaluations, 661–672
      backprojection, 669–672
      basic problem, 659
      core methods, 659–660
      future work, 676
      performance evaluation, 672–675
      projection's filtering, 663–669
      related work, 675–676
      steps, 661–663
   gate-level simulation
      compilation phase, 347–351
      design compilation, 358–359
      future work, 362–363
      macro-gate activity, 359–361
      macro-gate balancing, 350–351
      macro-gates, 356–358
      monitored nets, 358–359
      overview, 343–344
      performance evaluation, 361–362
      performance results, 355–362
      related work, 363
      simulation phase, 351–355
      simulator organization, 347
      simulator overview, 345–347
      system-level compilation, 348–350
   real-time stereo
      algorithms, implementations, evaluations, 475–485
      basic problem, 473–474
      core method, 475
      cross-checking, 484–485
      foreground *vs.* full image, 490–493
      Middlebury evaluation, 486–487
      multiresolution background modeling, 475–478
      multiresolution *vs.* single resolution, 487–490
      multiresolution stereo matching, 478–479
      performance evaluation, 486–493
      single CUDA kernel, 479–485
General relativity (GH), numerical solutions, 103–104
Genome encoding, in genome-matching acceleration, 177–178
Genome-matching acceleration, with massive parallel computing
   algorithms, implementations, evaluations, 176–183
   basic problem, 173–174
   benefits and limitations, 183
   core methods, 174–176
   CUDA-CPU execution, 181
   CUDA kernel parameter settings, 180–181
   data layout, 179–180
   future work, 183
   gaps and mismatches, 181–182
   genome encoding, 177–178
   hashing, 182
   performance scaling, 182–183
   smaller threads, 181
   target headers, 178–179
   target processing, 180
GEO600, as gravitational wave detector, 103
Global-best rule, AntMinerGPU, 330–332, 337
Global optimizations
   Barnes Hut *n*-body algorithm, 78–79

chemical informatics, 23
real-time stereo, 473
Global queue, ASR, 603–604, 610–613, 615
Global reduce, SVN, 297, 299
Global relabeling, Graph Cuts for computer vision, 446–447
GLPL, *see* GPU line-projection library (GLPL)
GLSL, *see* Open Graphics Library Shading Language (GLSL)
GP-GPUs, *see* General-purpose graphics processing units
(GP-GPUs)
GPU-accelerated computation
ant colony optimization, 325–337
brain connectivity reconstruction, 793–812
computed tomography reconstruction, 693–707
DFT calculations, 133–134, 144
medical image processing, 737–748
memory hierarchy, 631
MO computations, 8–13
radiographic image simulation, 814
speed-limit-sign recognition, 505–506, 514
GPU hardware architecture, 369
GPU line-projection library (GLPL), tomographic image
reconstruction, 684–686, 688–691
Gradient calculations
atlas construction, 777
B-spline registration, 763, 766–768
chemical informatics, 21, 33
machine learning, 280, 282, 287
MaxEnt model, 287
Gradient-modified interpolation, de-mosaicing, 586, 595
Graph Cuts, for computer vision
algorithms, implementations, evaluations, 440–447
basic problem, 439
core method, 439–440
evaluation, validation, 447–448
global relabeling, 446–447
multilabel Graph Cuts, 448–450
parallel push implementation, 441–444
workload management, 444–445
Graph traversals, ASR, 604–606, 608–610, 614–615
GRASSY (Graphics Processing Unit — Accelerated Spectral
Synthesis)
definition, 95
division of labor, 97–98
future work, 101
interpolation decomposition, 97
overview, 97
performance model, 100
precision issues, 98–99
pseudo-code, 98–99
testing, 100
texture packing, 97
Gravitational problems, 113

Gravitational radiation, 103
Gravitational wave detectors, 103
Greedy iterative diffeomorphism, atlas construction, 772, 774
Grid potentials, molecular electrostatics, 51–52, 54
Grid size
brain connectivity reconstruction, 798–799, 805
LB model, 395
object detection, 528
SVM, 303–304
GSO, *see* Gaussian shape overlay (GSO)
GTECH library, gate-level simulation, 348
GTFold, RNA folding, 203, 208
GTOs, *see* Gaussian type orbitals (GTOs)

H

Haar features
classifier cascade layout, 538–540
object classifier cascade structure, 521–523
Hairpin loop, RNA folding problem, 200–202
Hamiltonian matrix
BigDFT, 134
electronic structure, 59
Hamiltonian operator
BigDFT, 135–138, 140, 145
brain connectivity reconstruction, 802
MO calculations, 8
quadrature grid DFT, 35
Hammersley point
Chaos Game algorithm, 268
Fractal Flames algorithm, 270
Hanning function, VSM, 463
Hanning mask, VSM, 455, 465
Hard-sphere model, and GSO, 20
Hardware description language (HDL), gate-level simulation,
344
Hashing
ASR, 607
genome-matching, 174, 181–182
molecular electrostatics, 51–53
Hash tables
genome-matching, 175
pattern matching, 192, 196
HCA, *see* Host channel adapter (HCA)
HDL, *see* Hardware description language (HDL)
Heap objects, Barnes Hut *n*-body algorithm, 78–79, 86
Helmholtz equations
atlas construction, 778, 780–782
BigDFT, 134, 139
FMM, 113–114
Henyey-Greenstein parameter, LB model, 385, 390, 392
Heteroscedastic linear discriminant analysis (HDLA), speech
models, 613

Hidden Markov Models
  speech recognition application, 603
  speed-limit-sign recognition, 512
Hierachical decomposition kernel, Barnes Hut *n*-body
    algorithm, 77
High-performance computing (HPC), *vs.* ABM, 313
High-performance enabled secure copy (HPN SCP), black hole
    simulations, 109
Hilbert transform, CT image reconstruction, 661
Hilbert Transform Kernel, CT image reconstruction, 661,
    663–664, 666
Histogram-based boundary detection, brain connectivity
    reconstruction, 810–811
HistogramVoxelDirect algorithm
  basic method, 803–804
  brain connectivity reconstruction, 805, 807–809
  performance, 810–811
  pseudocode, 808
HistogramVoxelSweep algorithm
  basic method, 803–804
  brain connectivity reconstruction, 804–805
  performance, 810–811
  pseudocode, 806
HLDA, *see* Heteroscedastic linear discriminant analysis
    (HDLA)
hmem, large-scale FFT, 630, 634
Homogenous computing clusters, BigDFT code, 145
Homologous protein identification, with SW algorithm
  long sequences, 168–169
  overview, 156–157
  registers and loop unrolling, 163–168
  shared memory implementation, 160–162
  simple CUDA implementation, 157–160
Host channel adapter (HCA), FFT, 631–632, 637–638
Host-device interface
  machine learning, 282, 286
  MO computations, 13
Host-mapped memory, MO computations, 13
HPC, *see* High-performance computing (HPC)
HPN SCP, *see* High-performance enabled secure copy (HPN
    SCP)
HSV space, multiresolution background modeling,
    475–476
Human phantom, radiographic image simulation, 824–827
Hutchinson's recursive set equation, IFS, 264–265
hybrid-ss-min (Unafold), recurrence equations, 201–202

I

ICGs, *see* Independent current gates (ICGs)
Illumination buffer, photon transport, 256–258
Image correspondence, brain connectivity reconstruction, 795,
    802

Image operators, atlas construction, 775–777
Image processing
  CCL in CUDA
    algorithms, implementations, 572–577
    core algorithm, 570–572
    overview, 569–570
    performance evaluation, 577–581
  with CUDA/OpenCL
    background subtraction, 549–550
    basic problem, 547
    core technology, 548–551
    cross-correlation, 561
    global memory only, 561–562
    global memory reads, 560
    global/shared/coalesced memory access, 562–565
    implementation/evaluation, 551–565
    number of images, 564
    Pearson's correlation coefficients, 551
    performance evaluation, 565–566
    real-time video background subtraction, 552–554
    single kernel and I/O operations, 554–555
    single kernel and serial/asynchronous I/O operations,
      558–560
    single/three kernel and I/O operations, 558
  GPU computing status, 545–546
Image reconstruction
  CT
    algorithms, implementations, evaluations, 661–672,
      695–700
    backprojection, 669–672
    basic problem, 659, 693–694
    core methods, 659–660, 694–695
    exhaustive sampling, 696–697
    future work, 676, 706–707
    iterative algorithms performance, 700–702
    multi-objective optimization, 697–698
    OS-SIRT, 695–696
    parameter selection interface, 698–700
    performance evaluation, 672–675, 700–706
    projection's filtering, 663–669
    quality metric, 698
    regularization scheme performance, 702–703
    related work, 675–676
    steps, 661–663
  MRI
    algorithms and implementations, 713–719
    core method, 710–713
    with field inhomogeneity compensation, 711–712
    future work, 720–721
    iterative conjugate gradients, 713–715
    MATLAB toolbox, 718–719
    multi-GPU implementation, 718

non-Cartesian sampling trajectory, 710–711
overview, 709–710
with parallel programming, 712–713
performance analysis, 719–720
SpMV, 717
from randomly ordered lines with CUDA
algorithms, implementations, evaluations,
684–686
backprojection, 686
challenges, 681–682
core methods, 682–684
data structures, 685
forward-projection, 685–687
future work, 690–691
line-projection accuracy, 688–690
list-mode image reconstruction, 679–681
overview, 684–685
processing time, 686, 688
Incremental alpha-expansion algorithms, Graph Cuts for
computer vision, 449–450
Independent current gates (ICGs), definition, 370–371
Indicator functions, atomic densities as, 20
Inference engine, ASR, 602–605, 610, 614–617
Initialization function, photon transport, 257
Input/output operations
CCL in CUDA, 574
image/video processing
single kernel, 554–558
single kernel and serial/asynchronous I/O operations,
558–560
single/three kernel and I/O operations, 558
Insight segmentation and registration toolkit (ITK), medical
imaging
anisotropic diffusion, 740, 745–746
core methods, 737–740
CUDA integration, 740–742
definition, 737
filter comparison, 746–748
future work, 748
implementation, 740–746
linear convolution, 738–739
linear convolution filters, 742–743
median filter, 739, 743–745
Integral image calculation
object detection, 522–534, 536
real-time stereo, 475, 483
Intel Math Kernel Library (MKL)
electronic structure, 66–71
FFT, 629–630, 639–641
MRI reconstruction, 717
random number generators, 232, 242, 244–245

Intel Threading Building Blocks
object detection with CUDA, 542
Viola-Jones object-detection, 520
Interactions kernel
block diagram, 458
VSM, 457–460
Inter-GPU communication
pattern matching, 186, 191
VSM, 463–466
Interior loops
LB model, 387
RNA folding problem, 199–202, 209
Internal loops, RNA folding problem, 202–203, 207
Interpolation decomposition, GRASSY platform, 97
Interpolation methods
de-mosaicing, 586–598
fast spectral synthesis, 93–101
GRASSY platform, 97, 101
Inversion method, photon transport, 248
Irradiance
photon transport, 258
random walk path regeneration, 401
Isotropic scattering, LB models, 381, 384–385
Iterated Function Systems (IFS), and Fractal Flames algorithm
components, 264–265
core technology, 266–267
functions, 265–266
implementation, 266–270
memory-access patterns, 267–269
performance evaluation, 270–272
phases, 267
problem overview, 263–264
rendering, 269
static data, 270
Iterative conjugate gradients, MRI reconstruction
algorithm, 713–715
high-speed implementations, 715–718
kernel functions, 715–717
Iterative Self-consistent Parallel Imaging Reconstruction
(SPIRiT), MRI
algorithms, implementations, evaluations, 727–733
basic problem, 724
Calibration Consistency operator, 727–729
core methods, 726
data consistency projection, 729
overview, 735
parallel imaging, 726
performance analysis, 733–734
soft thresholding, 729
wavelet transform, 729–733
ITK, *see* Insight segmentation and registration toolkit (ITK)

J

JIT, *see* Just-in-time (JIT) kernel compilation
Joint Relaxation and Restriction (JRR) algorithm
    fast circuit optimization, 366, 373–374
    gate-level task scheduling, 371
    gate sizing/assignment, 367–368
    outline, 367
JRR, *see* Joint Relaxation and Restriction (JRR) algorithm
Just-in-time (JIT) kernel compilation, GPU MO algorithms, 16

K

Kappa lines, CT image reconstruction, 661, 664
Katsevich algorithm, CT image reconstruction, parallelization
    algorithms, implementations, evaluations, 661–672
    backprojection, 669–672
    basic problem, 659
    core methods, 659–660
    future work, 676
    performance evaluation, 672–675
    projection's filtering
      backward mapping, 669
      convolution, 666, 668–669
      differentiation, 663–666
      forward mapping, 666–668
    related work, 675–676
    steps, 661–663
Kernel definition, 76
Kernel functions
    ant colony optimization, 331–332, 336–337
    brain connectivity reconstruction, 806, 808
    facial animation, 417
    fast circuit optimization, 368–369, 373
    image de-mosaicing, 594
    machine learning, 282
    MRI reconstruction, 715–717
    random number generators, 240
    real-time stereo, 477, 479, 483–484
    sequence database scanning, 169
    SVM, 294, 298–299, 301–304
Kernel fusion, and GSO, 25–27
Kernel optimizations
    Barnes Hut *n*-body algorithm via CUDA
      implementation results, 89–90
      kernel 1, 79–80
      kernel 2, 80–81
      kernel 3, 81–83
      kernel 4, 83
      kernel 5, 84–86
      kernel 6, 86
      optimizations overview, 86–88
    genome-matching acceleration, 180–181
    SW algorithm, 163–168

Kinetic convolution, BigDFT, 139
Kinetic operator, BigDFT code, 136, 140–143
Klein-Nishina formula
    photon transport, 247, 255, 259, 261
    radiographic image simulation, 818
Knot lookup table, B-spline registration, 757–758
Knudsen number, diffusion equation derivation, 396
Kohn-Sham (KS) formalism
    BigDFT
      code structure, 138
      core method, 135–136
      Daubechies wavelets, 134
      overview, 134
    DFT, 133
    quadrature grid DFT, 35–36
KS, *see* Kohn-Sham (KS) formalism
k-space
    CS MRI, 723
    MRI reconstruction, 710–712, 714–716
    SPIRiT MRI, 724, 726–729

L

Lagrange multipliers, SMO, 297, 299, 301
Lanczos interpolation, de-mosaicing, 586, 593–595, 597–598
LAPACK routines
    BigDFT code, 138, 145, 147
    MaxEnt model, 287–290
Large-scale facial deformation
    background, 414
    core technology, 414–425
    equations, 416
    examples, 415
    implementation, 416–417
    via matrix multiplication, 418
    memory access strategy, 423
    performance evaluation, 424–425
    system overview, 413
Lattice-Boltzmann (LB) lighting models
    algorithms, implementations, evaluation, 383–393
    basic problem, 381–382
    cloud rendering, 390–391
    core methods, 382–383
    diffusion equation derivation, 395–398
    examples, 390–393
    future work, 395
    OpenCL implementation, 385–390
    overview, 383–385
    performance evaluation, 393–395
    plant rendering, 390–392
    plastics rendering, 392–393
LDPC, *see* Low-density parity check (LDPC) encoder

L'Ecuyer's multiple recursive generator MRG32k3a
    formulation, 232–233
    implementation, 234–235
    overview, 231–232
    parallelization, 233–234
    performance evaluation, 242–245
Legendre polynomials, FMM M2L kernel implementation, 126
LETTER dataset, SVM evaluation, 308
Levelization
    definition, 345
    gate-level simulation, 348
Level set method, brain connectivity reconstruction
    re-distancing, 801–802
    semiautomatic axon segmentation, 794–795, 809
    updating, 797–800
LIBSVM, 293, 306, 308–310
Lid values, gate-level simulation, 355–357, 363
Life sciences, GPU computing status, 153–154
Lighting models, *see* Lattice-Boltzmann (LB) lighting models
LIGO, as gravitational wave detector, 103
Lincoln supercomputer, pattern matching acceleration, 193–196
Linear convolution, ITK-based medical imaging, 738–739
Linear convolution filters, medical imaging, 740, 742–743
Line-driven forward projection, PET, 681
Line of response (LOR), and PET, 680
LINGO
    chemical informatics, 20–22, 27–33
    definition, 19
Liouville-von Neumann molecular dynamics (LvNMD)
    MD calculations, 62, 70, 72
    overview, 59
List-mode image reconstruction
    basic problem, 679–681
    tomographic image reconstruction, 685, 688–690
L2L, *see* Local to local treecode (L2L)
Load balance
    atlas construction, 784–785
    Barnes Hut *n*-body algorithm, 83, 86
    random number generators, 242
    SPIRiT MRI, 727
Local potential, BigDFT, 134–137
Local reduce, SVM, 297, 299–300, 303
Local to local treecode (L2L), fast *n*-body simulations, 115–116, 122
Local to particle treecode (L2P), fast *n*-body simulations, 115–116, 120, 122
Lock-based compaction, temporal data mining, 217–218
Lock-free access, ASR, 604, 608–610
Lock-free compaction, temporal data mining, 218–219
Locks, Barnes Hut *n*-body algorithm, 80–81, 88
Logic simulators
    gate-level, *see* Gate-level simulation

    vs. GPU-based, 360
    test benches, 357
    types, 344
Lookup table (LUT)
    B-spline registration, 756–758
    LINGO calculations, 27–28
Loop unrolling
    DFT, 140
    molecular electrostatics, 49, 53
    MRI reconstruction, 717
    n-body simulation, 125
    SW algorithm, 155, 163–168
LOR, *see* Line of response (LOR)
Low-density parity check (LDPC) encoder
    algorithms, implementations, evaluations, 622–626
    basic problem, 619
    core technology, 620–621
    data structures, 622–623
    decoding kernel, 623–626
    definition, 619
    future work, 627
    gate-level simulation, 355–356, 358
    memory accesses, 622–623
    performance evaluation, 626–627
    thread parallelism, 623
L2P, *see* Local to particle treecode (L2P)
LUT, *see* Lookup table (LUT)
LvNMD, *see* Liouville-von Neumann molecular dynamics (LvNMD)

M
MACE, *see* Minimum average correlation energy (MACE)
Machine learning (large-scale)
    algorithm and implementation, 280–287
    with atomics and bijection, 284–285
    base algorithm, 279–280
    butterfly sum reduction, 285
    character recognition application, 289–290
    core technology, 278–280
    energy calculation, 282
    future work, 290
    gradient calculation, 287
    host-device interface, 282
    overview, 277
    performance enhancements, 287–290
    probability normalization, 282–286
    theoretical background, 278–279
    training overview, 281
    value summing, 286–287
    without atomics, 283–284
MacMolPlt, MO visualization, 8

Macrocells
    photon transport, 253–254
    radiation dose visualization, 260
Macro-gates
    activation rate, 359–361
    event-driven simulation, 352
    future work, 362–363
    oblivious simulation, 352–354
    segmentation process, 356–358
    simulation phase, steps, 351–355
    sizing heuristics, 355
    system-level compilation
        balancing, 347, 350–351
        definition, 347
        segmentation, 349–350
        steps, 348–350
MAE, *see* Mean absolute error (MAE)
Magic filters, BigDFT code, 136–143
Magnetic resonance imaging (MRI) reconstruction
    B-spline registration, 751–752
    definition, 709, 723
    with field inhomogeneity compensation
        core method, 710–713
        future work, 720–721
        high-speed implementations, 715–718
        kernel functions, 715–717
        MATLAB toolbox, 718–719
        multi-GPU implementation, 718
        non-Cartesian sampling trajectory, 710–711
        overview, 709–710
        with parallel programming, 712–713
        performance analysis, 719–720
        SpMV, 717
        susceptibility-induced, 711–712
    SPIRiT, compressed sensing
        algorithms, implementations, evaluations, 727–733
        approach, 724–725
        basic problem, 723–726
        Calibration Consistency operator, 727–729
        core methods, 726–727
        data consistency projection, 729
        overview, 735
        parallel imaging, 726
        performance analysis, 733–734
        soft thresholding, 729
        wavelet transform, 729–733
Main memory access
    Barnes Hut n-body algorithm, 75–76, 82–88, 90
    fast spectral synthesis, 95
    FFT, 629–630, 633, 637
    medical image processing, 746
    MO computations, 13

    molecular electrostatics, 53
    VSM, 465
Malvar method, de-mosaicing, 586, 595, 597–598
Mammography
    breast cancer screening technology, 647
    vs. DBT, 650, 656
Map step, SMO, 297–298
Markov-Random-Fields (MRF), Graph Cuts, 439
Mass-charge, fast n-body simulations, 115–116, 118
Massively parallel hybrid CPU-GPU clusters, BigDFT code
    benefits and limitations, 144–145
    BLAS routines, 140–143
    code structure, 138
    convolutions, 138–139
    core method, 135–138
    CPU code, 145
    Daubechies wavelets, 134
    definition, 133–134
    efficiency developments, 149
    hybrid code performance, 145–147
    implementation, 140
    kinetic convolution and preconditioner, 139
    kinetic operator, 136
    local potential, 136
    magic filters, 136
    molecule simulation domain example, 135
    multiple core calculations, 148
    operations, 136–137
    overview, 134
    parallel distribution, 147
    performance evaluation, 140, 150
    3D operators, 140–143
Massive parallel computing, genome-matching
    algorithms, implementations, evaluations, 176–183
    basic problem, 173–174
    benefits and limitations, 183
    core methods, 174–176
    CUDA-CPU execution, 181
    CUDA kernel parameter settings, 180–181
    data layout, 179–180
    future work, 183
    gaps and mismatches, 181–182
    genome encoding, 177–178
    hashing, 182
    performance scaling, 182–183
    smaller threads, 181
    target headers, 178–179
    target processing, 180
Matching error, real-time stereo, 475, 479, 485–486, 490
Math Kernel Library (MKL), *see* Intel Math Kernel Library
    (MKL)

MATLAB toolbox
  MaxEnt model
    base algorithm, 280
    character recognition application, 289–290
    performance enhancements, 287–290
    training overview, 281
  MRI reconstruction, 712, 718–719
  VSM, 465–466
Matrix Market Coordinate Formal (MMCF), MRI
    reconstruction, 717
Matrix multiplication
  atlas construction, 781
  electronic structure, 59, 61–62, 64–68, 71
  facial animation, 417
  FFT, 629
  for large-scale facial deformation, 418
  machine learning, 287–290
  Mersenne Twister MT19937, 237
  MRI reconstruction, 713, 717
  RNA folding, 205–206
Matrix transposition
  electronic structure, 62, 65–66
  FFT, 629
  MD calculations, 66
  object detection, 528
Maximum entropy (MaxEnt), machine learning
  algorithm and implementation, 280–287
  with atomics and bijection, 284–285
  base algorithm, 279–280
  butterfly sum reduction, 285
  core technology, 278–280
  energy calculation, 282
  future work, 290
  gradient calculation, 287
  host-device interface, 282
  overview, 277
  performance enhancements, 287–290
  probability normalization, 282–286
  theoretical background, 278–279
  training overview, 281
  value summing, 286–287
  without atomics, 283–284
Maximum likelihood estimation method (MLEM), DBT,
    649–650, 656
maxScore, SW algorithm, 156
Max-succeeding-group problem
  gate-level task scheduling, 372
  NP-completeness, 376–378
Max-throughput problem, gate-level task scheduling, 372
MDH, see Multiple Debye-Hückel (MDH) method
MDTS, see Multidepth test scheme (MDTS)
Mean absolute error (MAE), CT reconstruction parameters, 698

MEAs, see Multielectrode arrays (MEAs)
Median diffusion filter, medical imaging, 739, 743–745,
    747–748
Medical imaging, see also Computed tomography (CT);
    Magnetic resonance imaging (MRI) reconstruction
  GPU computing status, 644
  with ITK
    anisotropic diffusion, 740
    anisotropic diffusion filter, 745–746
    core methods, 737–740
    CUDA integration, 740–742
    filter comparison, 746–748
    future work, 748
    linear convolution, 738–739
    linear convolution filters, 742–743
    median filter, 739, 743–745
    overview, 737
Memory-access patterns
  brain connectivity reconstruction, 802
  Chaos Game algorithm, 267–269
  CT image reconstruction, 669–670
  facial animation, 417, 423
  image de-mosaicing, 585
  integral image representation, 523
  iterated function systems, 267–270
  LDPC, 622–623
  MO computations, 10, 15
  molecular electrostatics, 51–52
  real-time stereo, 475
  RNA folding, 209
  temporal data mining, 219
Memory access strategy, facial animation, 423–424
Memory fence, Barnes Hut n-body algorithm, 82
Memory hierarchy
  FFT, 631–633, 642
  gate-level simulation, 347
Memory latency
  Barnes-Hut n-body algorithm, 86
  chemical informatics, 23
  image de-mosaicing, 593
  object-detection with CUDA, 532–533
  programmable graphics pipeline, 428, 433–434
  radiographic image simulation, 823–824
  temporal data mining, 225
  VSM, 456–457, 462
Memory optimization
  chemical informatics, 2, 19, 27–30
  DBT, 653
Memory tuning, chemical informatics, 28–30
Mersenne Twister random number generator
  and Chaos game algorithm, 270
  formulation, 237–238

Mersenne Twister random number generator (*continued*)
  overview, 231–232, 237
  parallelization, 238
  performance evaluation, 242–245
  point generation, 238–240
  random walks in path tracing, 406
  serial implementation, 239
  skip-ahead algorithm, 240–242
  state updates, 238–240
Mesh building, as spectral synthesis step, 94
Mesh rendering, as spectral synthesis step, 94
MEX functions, MaxEnt model, 281
Middlebury evaluation
  Graph Cuts for computer vision, 448
  real-time stereo, 486–488, 491
Minimum average correlation energy (MACE), feature-based
    pipeline, 501–504
Minimum-phone-error (MPE) criterion, speech models, 613
Mismatches
  genome matching, 176, 181–183
  pattern matching, 185
MKL, *see* Intel Math Kernel Library (MKL)
M2L, *see* Multipole to local treecode (M2L)
MLEM, *see* Maximum likelihood estimation method (MLEM)
M2M, *see* Multipole to multipole treecode (M2M)
MMCF, *see* Matrix Market Coordinate Formal (MMCF)
MNIST dataset, SVM evaluation, 307–308
MO, *see* Molecular orbital (MO) computations
MOGA, *see* Multi-objective genetic algorithm (MOGA)
Molecular dynamics (MD) methods
  basic problem, 59–61
  building blocks and implementation, 65–68
  calculations, 69–72
  density matrix, 69
  direct, *see* Direct molecular dynamics
  Fock matrix, 69
  hardware considerations, 69
  matrix operations, 66–68
  overview, 59
  technology basics, 61–65
Molecular orbital (MO) computations
  algorithms, 6–7, 10–16
  carbon-60 multi-GPU performance, 18
  carbon-60 single-GPU performance, 17
  constant cache, 13
  core method, 6
  CPMD, 59
  hardware global memory cache, 15
  isosurfaces example, 6
  JIT kernel generation, 17
  kernel comparison, 8
  mathematical background, 8–10

  multilevel parallel decomposition, 11–13
  overview, 5–6
  single-machine multi-GPU, 8
  tiled-shared memory, 13–14
  visualization, 6–7
  zero-copy host-device I/O, 15
Monitored nets, gate-level simulation, 358–359
Monte Carlo (MC) algorithm
  Chaos Game, 265
  Fractal Flames, 269
  radiographic image simulation
    algorithms, implementations, evaluations, 815–822
    basic problem, 813–814
    code testing, 822–824
    core methods, 814–815
    future work, 827–828
    MC for x-ray tracks, 816–818
    multiple-GPU CT scan simulations, 818–819
    performance analysis, 822–827
    random number generation, 820–821
    realistic human phantom, 824–827
    technical details, 821–822
    x-ray imaging system model, 815–816
Monte Carlo photon transport
  absorption sampling, 254
  basic physics, 247–249
  complete system, 256–258
  free path sampling, 250–254
  future work, 259, 261
  implementation results, 258–259
  overview, 249–250
  parallel random number generation, 256
  path divergence, 249
  radiation dose visualization, 260–261
  scattering direction, 254–256
  scattering in media, 248
MOO, *see* Multi-objective optimization (MOO)
Motion estimator kernel, VSM, 453, 455–464, 468
MovingPixelMap, 560
M2P, *see* Multipole to particle treecode (M2P)
MPE, *see* Minimum-phone-error (MPE) criterion
MPIs, atlas construction, 784–785
MRF, *see* Markov-Random-Fields (MRF)
MRI, *see* Magnetic resonance imaging (MRI) reconstruction
Multiclass support vector machine, core method, 295
Multidepth test scheme (MDTS), programmable graphics
    pipeline in CUDA, 432–434
Multielectrode arrays (MEAs), temporal data mining
  core methodology, 212–214
  datasets and testbed, 222
  one thread per occurrence performance, 222–224
  one thread per occurrence strategy, 215–219

overview, 211–212, 214–215
serial episode mining, 214
two-pass elimination approach, 219–222
two-pass elimination performance, 224–226
Multi-GPU calculations
ant colony optimization, 340
atlas construction, 771–790
Carbon-60, 17
CT scan simulations, 818–819
DBT, 647, 649, 651, 654–655
DFT, 147
LDPC, 627
MO computations, 8, 11, 13
molecular electrostatics, 57
Monte Carlo photon transport, 258
MRI reconstruction, 715, 718
n-body simulation, 131
SPIRiT MRI, 724
SVM, 304–305, 307, 310
template-driven agent-based modeling, 324
VSM, 451–471
Multilabel Graph Cuts, for computer vision, 448–450
Multilevel parallel decomposition, MOs, 13
Multiloop, RNA folding problem, 200–204, 207
Multinomial logistic regression, *see* Maximum entropy
(MaxEnt)
Multi-objective genetic algorithm (MOGA), OS-SIRT, 697
Multi-objective optimization (MOO), OS-SIRT, 697–698
Multiple Debye-Hückel (MDH) method
vs. direct Coulomb summation, 47
electrostatics calculations, 45–47, 54–56
Multipole to local treecode (M2L), fast *n*-body simulations,
115–116, 119–120, 122, 125–130
Multipole to multipole treecode (M2M), fast *n*-body
simulations, 115–116, 122
Multipole to particle treecode (M2P), fast *n*-body simulations,
115–116, 120, 122
Multiprocessor memory schematic, 372
Multiresolution background modeling, real-time stereo,
475–478
Multiresolution stereo matching, process, 478–479

N

Naive path tracing (NPT), random walks, 406–410
Nanotubes, MD calculations, 65–68
n-body algorithm, Barnes-Hut
algorithm overview, 76–77
CUDA implementation
basic problem, 75–76
evaluation methodology, 88–89
global optimizations, 78–79
implementation limitations, 91

implementation results, 89–90
kernel 1 optimization, 79–80
kernel 2 optimization, 80–81
kernel 3 optimization, 81–83
kernel 4 optimization, 83
kernel 5 optimization, 84–86
kernel 6 optimization, 86
optimizations overview, 86–88
n-body simulations
advanced techniques, 129, 131
fast, 114–120
M2L kernel implementation, 125–130
overview, 113–114
performance enhancements, 120–122
P2P kernel implementation, 122–125
Neuronal spike streams, data mining
core methodology, 212–214
definition, 211
GPU parallelization
datasets and testbed, 222
one thread per occurrence performance, 222–224
one thread per occurrence strategy, 215–219
overview, 214–215
two-pass elimination approach, 219–222
two-pass elimination performance, 224–226
overview, 211–212
serial episode mining, 214
Neuroscience, temporal data mining
core methodology, 212–214
GPU parallelization
datasets and testbed, 222
one thread per occurrence performance, 222–224
one thread per occurrence strategy, 215–219
overview, 214–215
two-pass elimination approach, 219–222
two-pass elimination performance, 224–226
overview, 211–212
serial episode mining, 214
Next-generation sequencing (NGS) technology, and GPU
computing, 153–154
NGS, *see* Next-generation sequencing (NGS) technology
Nonlinear filters, speed-limit-sign recognition, 507
Nonrecurring engineering (NRE), LDPC problem, 619
Normalization values
CGTOs, 9
FFT for speed-limit-sign recognition, 507
MaxEnt model, 282–286
object-detection pipeline with CUDA, 530–532
Normalized root mean square (NRMS), CT reconstruction
parameters, 698
Normalized Scanpath Saliency (NSS), VSM evaluation, 470
Normal updates, facial animation, 423–424

NP-completeness, fast circuit optimization, 370, 376–378
NPT, *see* Naive path tracing (NPT)
NRE, *see* Nonrecurring engineering (NRE)
NRMS, *see* Normalized root mean square (NRMS)
NSGA-II, OS-SIRT, 697–698
NSS, *see* Normalized Scanpath Saliency (NSS)
Numerical analysis
    GRASSY work, 101
    MRI reconstruction, 717

O

Object classifier
    layout optimizations, 538–541
    object detection, 517–521, 528, 530, 532–541
Object detection
    benchmarking and implementation, 541–543
    cascade layout optimizations, 538–541
    classifiers cascade, 533–541
    future work, 543
    integral image calculation, 526–530
    normalization value generation, 530–532
    overview, 517, 526
    scaling, 532–533
    Viola-Jones framework
        core algorithm, 519–520
        integral image representation, 523–525
        object classifier cascade structure, 521–522
        overview, 517–519
        traditional algorithm, 525
Objective functions
    chemical information, 21, 23–26, 30
    CT reconstruction, 697
    machine learning, 278–279, 281–282, 288, 290
Oblivious logic simulation
    definition, 344
    within macro-gates, 352–354
    simulator overview, 346
Octrees, Barnes Hut *n*-body algorithm via CUDA
    core methods, 76–77
    kernel 3 optimization, 81–83
    kernel 4 optimization, 83
ODEs, *see* Ordinary differential equations (ODEs)
On-demand volume filtering, brain connectivity reconstruction, 796
One-dimensional convolutions, BigDFT code, 138–139
One thread per occurrence strategy, temporal data mining
    algorithmic enhancements, 216–217
    basic idea, 215–216
    lock-based compaction, 217–218
    lock-free compaction, 218–219
One-vs-All (OVA), multiclass SVM, 295–296

Open Computing Language (OpenCL)
    and BigDFT, 149
    and facial animation, 426
    and GSO, 23
    image/video processing
        background subtraction, 549–550
        basic problem, 547
        core technology, 548–551
        cross-correlation, 561
        global memory only, 561–562
        global memory reads, 560
        global/shared/coalesced memory access, 562–565
        implementation/evaluation, 551–565
        number of images, 564
        Pearson's correlation coefficients, 551
        performance evaluation, 565–566
        real-time video background subtraction, 552–554
        single kernel and I/O operations, 554–555
        single kernel and serial/asynchronous I/O operations, 558–560
        single/three kernel and I/O operations, 558
    LB method implementation, 385–390
    MDH electrostatics, 55–56
    and VMD, 16
OpenCV, *see* Open Source Computer Vision (OpenCV)
OpenEye ROCS *vs.* PAPER, 32
Open Graphics Library (OpenGL)
    Chaos Game algorithm, 268
    de-mosaicing, 586
    facial animation performance, 424
    Fractal Flames algorithm, 269
    and list-mode OSEM, 681–682
    speed-limit-sign recognition, 505
    tomographic image reconstruction, 684
    VSM, 469
Open Graphics Library Shading Language (GLSL)
    CT reconstruction, 700
    instanced agent rendering, 320
Open Message Passing Interface (OpenMPI)
    atlas construction, 785
    FFT, 631–632
Open Multi-Processing (OpenMP)
    facial animation performance, 424–425
    image/video processing, 554–556, 558, 562, 564–566
    Katsevich CT image reconstruction parallelization, 673, 675
    MRI reconstruction, 720
    RNA folding problem, 203
    SPIRiT MRI, 734
Open Source Computer Vision (OpenCV), object detection
    benchmarking and implementation, 541–543
    cascade layout optimizations, 538
    core algorithm, 519–520

object classifier cascade structure, 521–522
scaling, 532–533
OpenSPARC project, gate-level simulation, 356
OpenVIDIA
speed-limit-sign recognition, 506
VSM, 468–470
Optical depth, photon transport on GPU, 251, 253
Ordered-subsets algorithm, CT reconstruction parameters,
694–695
Ordered-subsets expectation-maximization (OSEM), list-mode
challenges, 681–682
image reconstruction, 680–681
line-projection accuracy, 688–690
tomographic image reconstruction, 685
Ordered-subsets simultaneous iterative reconstruction technique
(OS-SIRT)
exhaustive sampling, 696–697
GPU-accelerated regularization, 696
iterative CT reconstruction algorithms, 700–702
method, 695–696
multi-objective optimization, 697–698
parameter selection interface, 698–700
quality metric, 698
Order-independent transparency, programmable graphics
pipeline in CUDA
algorithms, implementations, evaluations, 428–433
basic problem, 427–428
core method, 428
fixed-size A-buffer scheme, 433
future work, 435
multidepth test scheme, 432–433
performance evaluation, 433–434
pseudocode, 431
system overview, 428–431
Ordinary differential equations (ODEs)
atlas construction, 777
black hole simulations, 104–107
OSEM, *see* Ordered-subsets expectation-maximization (OSEM)
OS-SIRT, *see* Ordered-subsets simultaneous iterative
reconstruction technique (OS-SIRT)
Overlapping search, pattern matching acceleration, 191–192

P

PAPER
chemical informatics, 21–27
future work, 33
vs. OpenEye ROCS, 30, 32
Parallel computing techniques
brain connectivity reconstruction, 793
DBT, 648
fast circuit optimization
basic problem, 365–367

core method, 367–369
future work, 376
gate-level task scheduling, 369–372
GPU-based, 368–369
parallel gate implementation evaluation, 372–373
performance evaluation, 373–375
genome-matching
algorithms, implementations, evaluations, 176–183
basic problem, 173–174
benefits and limitations, 183
core methods, 174–176
CUDA-CPU execution, 181
CUDA kernel parameter settings, 180–181
data layout, 179–180
future work, 183
gaps and mismatches, 181–182
genome encoding, 177–178
hashing, 182
performance scaling, 182–183
smaller threads, 181
target headers, 178–179
target processing, 180
LDPC, 623
medical image processing, 746, 748
programmable graphics pipeline, 427
Parallel distribution, BigDFT code, 147
Parallel imaging (PI)
CS MRI, 723–724, 726
SPIRiT MRI, 735
Parallelism
ant colony optimization, 325
ASR, 603, 615
atlas construction, 779
Barnes Hut *n*-body algorithm, 75, 86, 89
B-spline registration, 752
chemical informatics, 19–20, 22–23, 25, 27–28, 32
CT image reconstruction, 673
DFT, 38, 140
fast circuit optimization, 365–366, 368–370, 376
Fast Graph Cuts, 440, 447
gate-level simulation, 343–344, 349, 361–363
image de-mosaicing, 585
LDPC, 619–620, 623, 626–627
machine learning, 282, 290
medical image processing, 737–738
molecular electrostatics, 43, 49
MRI reconstruction, 717
n-body simulation, 113, 116, 122
object detection, 536–537
pattern matching, 185, 190–192, 196
photon transport, 249
programmable graphics pipeline, 434

Parallelism (*continued*)
   radiographic image simulation, 824
   real-time speed-limit-sign recognition, 498, 514
   SPIRiT MRI, 729, 732, 735
   SVM, 296, 304, 310
   SW algorithm, 157
   template-driven agent-based modeling, 313
Parallelization techniques
   ASR, 615
   black hole simulations, 106
   brain connectivity reconstruction, 795
   B-spline registration, 762
   CT image reconstruction
      algorithms, implementations, evaluations, 661–672
      backprojection, 669–672
      backward mapping, 669
      basic problem, 659
      convolution, 666, 668–669
      core methods, 659–660
      differentiation, 663–666
      forward mapping, 666–668
      future work, 676
      performance evaluation, 672–675
      projection's filtering, 663–669
      related work, 675–676
      steps, 661–663
   DFT, 145, 149
   facial animation, 423
   fast circuit optimization, 366–368, 376
   FFT, 637
   Graph Cuts for computer vision, 440, 442–443, 446
      push operation, 441–443
      relabel operation, 443–444
   GSO calculations, overview, 22–23
   image/video processing, 561
   iterated function systems, 264–265
   LB model, 383
   LDPC, 623
   L'Ecuyer's multiple recursive generator MRG32k3a, 233–234
   machine learning, 281, 288
   Mersenne Twister MT19937, 238
   molecular electrostatics, 47
   n-body simulation, 129
   radiographic image simulation, 821, 825
   random number generators
      L'Ecuyer's multiple recursive generator MRG32k3a, 232–235
      Mersenne Twister MT19937, 237–242
      overview, 231–232
      performance evaluation, 242–245
      Sobol generator, 235–236

   RNA folding problem, 194, 203–205
   Sobol quasi-random generator, 235–236
   SPIRiT MRI, 727, 729, 732, 734–735
   SVM, 310
   temporal data mining, 214–215, 217, 219, 221–222
Parallel local tracking, temporal data mining, 216–217
Parallel programming
   ASR, 617
   DBT, 648
   fast circuit optimization, 374
   image de-mosaicing, 584
   MRI reconstruction, 709–710, 712–713, 715, 720
Parallel scan, pattern matching, 188–192, 195–198
Pareto optimal set, CT reconstruction performance, 707
Park-Miller pseudorandom number generator, 334
Partial differential equations (PDEs)
   atlas construction, 778
   brain connectivity reconstruction, 794–795
   ITK-based medical imaging, 740
   LB methods, 383
Particle to multipole treecode (P2M), fast n-body simulations, 115–116, 120
Particle to particle treecode (P2P), fast n-body simulations, 115–117, 120, 122–125
Path regeneration, random walks
   implementation, 406–408
   overview, 401–406, 410
   path regeneration, 404–406
   processing unit utilization, 403
   research results, 408–410
   sparse warps, 404
Patterned-Pixel Group method (PPG), de-mosaicing, 586, 595–597
Pattern matching acceleration, with supercomputer clusters
   algorithms, implementations, evaluations, 187–192
   antidiagonal approach, 188–189
   basic problem, 185–186
   core method, 186–187
   data packing, 192
   future work, 196
   hash tables, 192
   overlapping search, 191–192
   overview, 193–196
   reduced dependency, 187–188
   row/column parallel approach, 188–191
PBE, *see* Poisson-Boltzmann Equation (PBE)
PDEs, *see* Partial differential equations (PDEs)
Peak-to-sidelobe ratio (PSR), speed-limit-sign recognition, 502
Pearson's correlation coefficient (PMCC), image/video processing, 547–551, 561–563
PENELOPE, radiographic image simulation, 814–815, 818, 820, 824, 827–828

Perceptual linear prediction (PLP), speech models, 613
Performance analysis
    ABM with CUDA, 321–323
    AntMinerGPU, 337–339
    ASR, 613–615
    atlas construction, 786–789
    atlas construction tuning, 785–786
    BigDFT code, 140, 145–147, 150
    brain connectivity reconstruction, 809–811
    B-spline registration, 767–769
    CCL in CUDA, 577–581
    Chaos game algorithm, 270–272
    CT reconstruction, 672–675, 700–703
    de-mosaicing, 597–598
    facial animation, 424–425
    fast circuit optimization, 373–375
    gate-level simulation, 355–362
    genome-matching acceleration, 182–183
    Graph Cuts for computer vision, 447–448
    GRASSY platform, 100
    image/video processing, 551–552, 554–560, 565–566
    large-scale FFT, 639–641
    LB methods, 393–395
    LDPC, 626–627
    MRI reconstruction, 719–720
    object-detection with CUDA, 541–543
    programmable graphics pipeline in CUDA, 433–434
    radiographic image simulation, 822–827
    random number generators, 242–245
    speed-limit-sign recognition, 507–513
    SPIRiT MRI, 733–734
    stereo matching, 486–493
    SVM, 306–310
    temporal data mining, 222–226
PET, *see* Positron emission tomography (PET)
Pheromone
    and ACO, 326
    AntMinerGPU, 330, 332–333, 335, 337
Photon buffer, photon transport, 256
Photon density, LB methods, 384–386
Photon transport
    absorption sampling, 254
    basic physics, 247–249
    complete system, 256–258
    free path sampling, 250–254
    future work, 259, 261
    implementation results, 258–259
    LB lighting model, 394
    overview, 249–250
    parallel random number generation, 256
    path divergence, 249
    radiation dose visualization, 260–261

scattering direction, 254–256
scattering in media, 248
PI, *see* Parallel imaging (PI)
Pipeline model, VSM, 465–466
Pixels
    brain connectivity reconstruction, 793–795, 798–803, 812
    CCL, 569–570, 578–580
    character recognition application, 289
    CT image reconstruction, 666, 670–672, 695–696, 703
    DBT, 652–653
    Graph Cuts for computer vision, 439, 442, 446–449
    image de-mosaicing, 583–597
    image/video processing, 548–550, 552, 554, 556, 560–563
    iterated function systems, 269
    medical image processing, 738–740, 742–746
    MRI reconstruction, 711
    object detection, 517, 519–530, 532–535, 537, 540–541
    order-independent transparency, 428–434
    radiographic image simulation, 814–817, 821–826
    random walk path regeneration, 401–403, 406
    real-time stereo, 473, 475, 477–485, 487–489, 491–492
    speed-limit-sign recognition, 499, 505–507
    SPIRiT MRI, 728–730
    volumentric, *see* Voxels
    VSM, 453, 458, 460–462, 466–467
PKU McClus cluster
    architecture, 630–631
    large-scale FFT, 639–641
Planck constant, photon transport, 248
Plant rendering, 390–392
Plastics rendering, 392–393
Playable Universal Capture, 414
PLP, *see* Perceptual linear prediction (PLP)
P2M, *see* Particle to multipole treecode (P2M)
PMCC, *see* Pearson's correlation coefficient (PMCC)
PMMA, *see* Polymethyl methacrylate (PMMA)
POCS, *see* Projections-Over-Convex-Sets (POCS) method
Pointer-chasing memory operations, Barnes Hut *n*-body
        algorithm via CUDA, 75–76
Point-generation kernel, Chaos Game algorithm, 267
Poisson-Boltzmann Equation (PBE), electrostatics
        algorithms, 44
Poisson equation, and BigDFT code, 134, 137
Poisson problems, gravitation/electrostatics, 113
Poisson process, temporal data mining, 222
Poisson statistics, tomographic image reconstruction, 689
Polymethyl methacrylate (PMMA), rendering, 392–393
Population size, and AntMinerGPU performance, 338–339
Positron emission tomography (PET)
    basic principle, 680
    deformable registration algorithm, 751–752

Positron emission tomography (*continued*)
    image reconstruction from randomly ordered lines
        algorithms, implementations, evaluations, 684–686
        backprojection, 686
        challenges, 681–682
        core methods, 682–684
        forward-projection, 685–687
        future work, 690–691
        line-projection accuracy, 688–690
        list-mode image reconstruction, 679–681
        overview, 684–685
        processing time, 686, 688
        vs. x-ray CT, 682
Post-Newtonian (PN) approximation, overview, 104–105
P2P, *see* Particle to particle treecode (P2P)
PPG, *see* Patterned-Pixel Group method (PPG)
Precision issues, *see also* Double-precision (DP);
        Single-precision (SP)
    astrophysics, 101
    black hole simulations, 106
    B-spline registration, 751
    CT image reconstruction, 660
    dynamical quadrature grids, 35, 39–40
    GRASSY platform, 97–99
    image de-mosaicing, 586
    LDPC, 619, 623, 626–627
    molecular electrostatics, 55–56
    object detection, 521, 532, 540
    radiographic image simulation, 824
    real-time stereo, 475
    VSM, 466–467
PreElim algorithm, temporal data mining, 220–222,
        224–226
Prefix sums
    CCL, 581
    iterated function systems, 270
    object detection, 527–528, 534
    template-driven agent-based modeling, 314–315, 320
    temporal data mining, 218–219
Processed gate, definition, 370–371
Programmable graphics pipeline, for order-independent
        transparency
    algorithms, implementations, evaluations, 428–433
    basic problem, 427–428
    core method, 428
    fixed-size A-buffer scheme, 433
    future work, 435
    multidepth test scheme, 432–433
    performance evaluation, 433–434
    pseudocode, 431
    system overview, 428–431

Progressive multiresolution adaptive windows, real-time stereo
        on GP-GPU
    algorithms, implementations, evaluations, 475–485
    basic problem, 473–474
    core method, 475
    cross-checking, 484–485
    foreground *vs.* full image, 490–493
    Middlebury evaluation, 486–487
    multiresolution background modeling, 475–478
    multiresolution *vs.* single resolution, 487–490
    multiresolution stereo matching, 478–479
    performance evaluation, 486–493
    single CUDA kernel, 479–485
Projection kernel
    definition, 679
    image reconstruction, 685
    tomographic image reconstruction, 682, 684–686
Projections-Over-Convex-Sets (POCS) method
    OS-SIRT, 695
    SPIRiT MRI, 726–727, 733
Propagation
    ASR graph traversal, 608–610
    belief propagation, 487, 620, 627
    electronic structure, 59–72
    fast circuit optimization, 365–367
    FFT, 637–638
    gate-level simulation, 345, 363
    information in computer vision, 447
    random walk path regeneration, 401–402
Prospective gate, fast circuit optimization, 370–371, 377
Pseudoknots, RNA folding, 200
Push operation, Graph Cuts for computer vision
    overview, 440–441
    parallel push implementation, 441–443
    parallel relabel implementation, 443–444

Q
QDR, *see* Quad Data Rate (QDR)
QM kernel, RNA folding algorithm, 202, 205, 207
QP, *see* Quadratic programming (QP)
Quad Data Rate (QDR), FFT, 631–632
Quadratic programming (QP), and SMO, 296–297
Quadrature grids, DFT calculations
    core method, 36–37
    implementation, 37–39
    overview, 35–36
    performance enhancement, 39–41
Quad variables, stellar spectral synthesis, 94
Quantum chemistry calculations
    MO visualization, 6
    Schrödinger equation basics, 8

R

Radial basis functions (RBFs), facial animation, 419–420
Radial symmetry voting, speed-limit-sign recognition, 505–506
Radiation dose, visualization, 260–261
Radiographic image simulation
  algorithms, implementations, evaluations, 815–822
  basic problem, 813–814
  code testing, 822–824
  core methods, 814–815
  future work, 827–828
  MC for x-ray tracks, 816–818
  multiple-GPU CT scan simulations, 818–819
  performance analysis, 822–827
  random number generation, 820–821
  realistic human phantom, 824–827
  technical details, 821–822
  x-ray imaging system model, 815–816
Radiosity
  definition, 381
  LB models, 395
  random walk path regeneration, 410
Random function selection, iterated function systems, 263–265, 272
Randomly ordered lines, tomographic image reconstruction
  algorithms, implementations, evaluations, 684–686
  backprojection, 686
  challenges, 681–682
  core methods, 682–684
  data structures, 685
  forward-projection, 685–687
  future work, 690–691
  line-projection accuracy, 688–690
  list-mode image reconstruction, 679–681
  overview, 684–685
  processing time, 686, 688
Random number generators
  L'Ecuyer's multiple recursive generator MRG32k3a, 232–235
  Mersenne Twister MT19937, 237–242
  overview, 231–232
  parallel, photon transport, 256
  performance evaluation, 242–245
  radiographic image simulations with MC x-ray transport in CUDA, 820–821
  Sobol generator, 235–236
Random walks, path tracing
  implementation, 406–408
  overview, 401–406, 410
  path regeneration, 404–406
  processing unit utilization, 403

  research results, 408–410
  sparse warps, 404
RANECU, radiographic image simulation, 820–821, 827
Raster operations (ROP)
  algorithms, implementations, evaluations, 428–433
  basic problem, 427–428
  core method, 428
  fixed-size A-buffer scheme, 433
  future work, 435
  multidepth test scheme, 432–433
  performance evaluation, 433–434
  pseudocode, 431
  system overview, 428–431
RAT, *see* Required arrival times (RAT)
RAW hazards, Graph Cuts for computer vision, 441
Ray casting, brain connectivity reconstruction, 796–797, 802–803, 812
Rayleigh interactions, radiographic image simulation, 817–819, 821, 823–824, 827
Rayleigh scattering, photon transport, 247, 255, 259, 261
Ray marching, photon transport, 251, 254
Ray tracing
  GPU computing status, 379–380
  iterated function systems, 265
  LB models, 385, 390
  order-independent transparency, 427–428
  radiographic image simulation, 814
  tomographic image reconstruction, 686, 689
RBFs, *see* Radial basis functions (RBFs)
Read process, image de-mosaicing, 589–591
Real-time factor (RTF), ASR, 607, 614
Real-time stereo
  algorithms, implementations, evaluations, 475–485
  basic problem, 473–474
  core method, 475
  cross-checking, 484–485
  foreground vs. full image, 490–493
  Middlebury evaluation, 486–487
  multiresolution background modeling, 475–478
  multiresolution vs. single resolution, 487–490
  multiresolution stereo matching, 478–479
  performance evaluation, 486–493
  single CUDA kernel, 479–485
Real-time video background subtraction, image/video processing, 552–554
Real-time visualization, ABM, 319–320
Recognition network, ASR, 602, 610, 613
Recursive Gaussian filter
  altlas construction, 783
  VSM, 455–456, 464
Reduce step, SMO, 297, 299–302
Reduction split, RNA folding algorithm, 204–206

Reflective properties
  plant rendering, 391
  plastics rendering, 392–393
Regeneration phase, random walk path regeneration, 407–408
Region-of-interest (ROI) image, brain connectivity
    reconstruction, 794
Relabel operation, Graph Cuts for computer vision
  global relabeling, 446–447
  overview, 440–441
  parallelization, 443–444
Rendering, *see also* Path regeneration
  clouds example, 390–391
  Fractal Flames algorithm, 269
  GPU computing status, 379–380
  plants example, 390–392
Required arrival times (RAT), fast circuit optimization, 366
Reverse topological order traversal, gate-level task scheduling,
    369–370
R-factor, iterative CT reconstruction algorithms performance,
    701–702
RGB, de-mosaicing, 585, 592, 595–597
RGBA buffers
  de-mosaicing, 586, 588
  stereo matching, 481
RG-GB, de-mosaicing, 583, 593–595
RHS, *see* Right-hand-side (RHS) expressions
Riemann sum approximation, photon transport, 251
Right-hand-side (RHS) expressions, black hole simulations,
    106
RMS, *see* Root mean square (RMS)
RNA folding algorithm
  algorithms, implementations, evaluations, 201–206
  basic problem, 199
  core method, 200–201
  future work, 209
  GPU implementation comparison, 208
  and GTfold, 203
  implementation comparison, 208
  internal loops, 203
  multiloops, 203–208
  parallelization scheme, 203
  recurrence equations, 201–202
  related algorithms, 206
ROI, *see* Region-of-interest (ROI) image
Root mean square (RMS)
  B-spline registration, 767
  CT reconstruction parameters, 698
ROP, *see* Raster operations (ROP)
Row-parallel scan, pattern matching acceleration, 188–191,
    196–198
rsqrtf function, Barnes Hut *n*-body algorithm, 85–86

RTF, *see* Real-time factor (RTF)
Russian roulette, random walk path regeneration, 401–402,
    404–410

S
SA, *see* Slack allocation (SA)
SAD image, stereo matching, 483
SART, *see* Simultaneous algebraic reconstruction techniques
    (SART)
Scalability
  atlas construction, 789
  CCL, 580
  CT image reconstruction, 676
  fast circuit optimization, 375
  MO computations, 8
  speed-limit-sign recognition, 498, 508, 512–513
  SVM, 293
Scale Invariant Feature Transform (SIFT), speed-limit-sign
    recognition, 505, 508–510
Scaling
  black hole simulations, 107–108
  CT image reconstruction, 674
  DFT, 135–137, 145–146
  dynamical quadrature grids, 37, 40–41
  electronic structure, 65, 67, 71–72
  fast circuit optimization, 375
  genome matching, 182–183
  Graph Cuts for computer vision, 445, 447
  MO computations, 18
  molecular electrostatics, 50
  object detection, 520, 524, 532–533, 542
  pattern matching acceleration, 194–195
  SPIRiT MRI, 734
  VSM, 458
Scaling coefficient, LB models, 396–397
Scan algorithms
  integral image calculation, 526–530
  pattern matching acceleration, 188–191, 196–198
Scatter-gather iterations, Multi-GPU Cascade SVM, 305
Scattering angle, photon transport, 247, 254–255
Scattering direction
  LB methods, 384–385
  photon transport, 254–256
Scheduling kernel, macro-gate event-driven simulation, 352
Schrödinger equation
  electronic structure, 59
  MO computations, 8
Scientific simulation, GPU computing status, 2
Scratch memory model, atlas construction, 786–787
Scripting, ABM transition function behavior, 317–319
Secondary structure, RNA folding problem, 199–200
Seed buffer, photon transport, 256

Segmentation
    atlas construction, 771–772
    brain connectivity reconstruction, 793–797, 802, 809,
        811–812
    CCL, 569, 574
    DBT, 651
    Graph Cuts for computer vision, 439, 447–448
    macro-gates, 349–350, 356–358
    medical imaging, 737
    radiographic image simulation, 815–816
    real-time stereo, 475, 487
Segmentation algorithm, gate-level simulation, 347–350,
        355–360, 363
Semiautomatic axon segmentation, brain connectivity
        reconstruction, 793–795
Sensitivity list, macro-gate event-driven simulation, 352
Separability property, integral image calculation, 527
Sequence database scanning, with SW algorithm
    long sequences, 168–169
    overview, 155–157
    registers and loop unrolling, 163–168
    shared memory implementation, 160–162
    simple CUDA implementation, 157–160
Sequential minimal optimization (SMO)
    future work, 310
    map step, 298
    reduce step, 299–302
    SVM, 296–297
    testing phase, 302–303
Serial input/output operations, image/video processing,
        558–560
SGEMM
    character recognition, 289
    SVM, 303
Shared map, ASR, 604, 608–610, 615
Shooting function, photon transport, 258
Short-range cutoff, electrostatics calculations, 50–55, 57–58
SHUTTLE dataset, SVM evaluation, 308
Sierpinski triangle, IFS, 264
SIFT, see Scale Invariant Feature Transform (SIFT)
Signal-to-noise ratio (SNR)
    black hole simulations, 103
    CT reconstruction, 704–706
    MRI reconstruction, 720, 723–724, 726
    SPIRiT MRI, 723–724, 726
Signal processing
    ASR, 602–603
    GPU computing status, 599–600
    LDPC, 619
    real-time stereo, 473–474
    speed-limit-sign recognition, 514
    SPIRiT MRI, 723

SIMD, see Single instruction multiple data (SIMD)
Similarity evaluation, chemical informatics
    algorithmic transformation and memory optimization,
        27–30
    core methods, 22
    data-parallel objective function, 23–25
    LINGO overview, 21–22
    overview, 19–21
    parallelization and arithmetic optimization, 22–27
    performance comparison, 30, 32
    SIML, 31–33
    3D shape molecule overlay, 21
SIML, chemical informatics, 19, 22, 28–33
SIMT, see Single-instruction multiple-thread (SIMT)
Simulation kernel, gate-level simulation, 352, 354
Simulation phase, gate-level simulation
    event-driven, 352
    oblivious simulation, 352–354
    overview, 351–355
    test benches, 354–355
Simultaneous algebraic reconstruction techniques (SART)
    iterative CT reconstruction algorithms, 700–702
    and OS-SIRT, 695
Simultaneous iterative reconstruction techniques (SIRT), CT
        reconstruction, 694, 700–702
Single instruction multiple data (SIMD)
    CT image reconstruction, 676
    DBT GPU acceleration, 650
    fast circuit optimization, 366–367
    GPU-based parallelization, 368
    ITK-based medical imaging, 738
    and OS-SIRT, 696
    path tracing for random walks, 401, 403
    speech models, 614
    stereo matching, 489
Single-instruction multiple-thread (SIMT)
    DBT GPU acceleration, 650
    gate-level simulation, 345–346
    genome-matching acceleration, 174
Single-photon emission computed tomography (SPECT),
        tomographic image reconstruction, 685
Single-precision (SP)
    ASR, 613
    black hole simulations, 105–107
    CT image reconstruction, 663
    dynamical quadrature grids, 39
    electronic structure, 67, 69, 71
    FFT, 629, 640
    MD methods, 69
    MRI reconstruction, 720
    n-body simulations, 131
    object detection, 539–540

Single-precision (*continued*)
 radiographic image simulation, 828
 SPIRiT MRI, 724, 728, 733
Single resolution adaptive window, stereo matching, 487–491
SIRT, *see* Simultaneous iterative reconstruction techniques (SIRT)
Sizing heuristics, macro-gates, 355
Skin strain
 CUDA kernel code, 422
 and facial pose, 418–419
Skip-ahead algorithm, Mersenne Twister MT19937, 240–242
Slack allocation (SA), fast circuit optimization evaluation, 374
SMILES string, and LINGO, 21–22, 28
Smith-Waterman (SW) algorithm
 pattern matching
  algorithms, implementations, evaluations, 187–192
  antidiagonal approach, 188–189
  basic problem, 185–186
  core method, 186–187
  data packing, 192
  future work, 196
  hash tables, 192
  overlapping search, 191–192
  overview, 193–196
  reduced dependency, 187–188
  row/column parallel approach, 188–191
 protein identification
  long sequences, 168–169
  overview, 156–157
  registers and loop unrolling, 163–168
  shared memory implementation, 160–162
  simple CUDA implementation, 157–160
  sequence database scanning, 155–156
SMO, *see* Sequential minimal optimization (SMO)
SMs, *see* Streaming-multiprocessors (SMs)
SNR, *see* Signal-to-noise ratio (SNR)
SO, *see* Spin-orbit (SO) interactions
Sobol quasi-random generator
 formulation, 235
 implementation, 236
 overview, 231–232, 235
 parallelization, 235–236
 performance evaluation, 242–245
Soft-thresholding, SPIRiT MRI, 727, 729
Solution construction phase, AntMinerGPU, 329–330
Solution-evaluation kernel, AntMinerGPU, 335–337
SOR, *see* Successive overview relaxation (SOR) method
Source reading, de-mosaicing, 588–589
SP, *see* Single-precision (SP); Stream processors (SP)
Sparse-matrix vector multiplication (SpMV), MRI reconstruction, 717
Sparse warps, random walks in path tracing, 404

Sparsity, SPIRiT MRI, 724
Speech feature extactor, speech recognition application, 602
Speech model
 performance analysis, 613–615
 speech recognition application, 602
Speech recognition, *see* Automatic speech recognition (ASR)
Speed-limit-sign recognition
 compute power adjustments, 511–512
 fast-radial symmetry, 505–506
 feature-based pipeline, 499–501
 FFT correlation with nonlinear filters, 507
 future work, 513–514
 implementation, 505–507
 methods, 499–505
 overview, 497–498
 pipeline scalability, 512–513
 recognition results, 508
 results, 507–513
 SIFT-based pipeline, 505
 template-based pipeline, 500–505
Spin-orbit (SO) interactions, black hole simulations, 109
SPIRiT, *see* Iterative Self-consistent Parallel Imaging Reconstruction (SPIRiT)
SpMV, *see* Sparse-matrix vector multiplication (SpMV)
Spring forces, and LB methods, 395
SSD, *see* Sum of squared differences (SSD)
Stage-parallel processing, object detection, 536–537, 540
State-based agent simulation, ABM with CUDA, 314–315
Static pathway, VSM, 452–453, 455–457, 459, 466–467
Statistical modeling
 GPU computing status, 229
 speed-limit-sign recognition, 512
Stellar spectral synthesis
 basic problem, 95
 flux calculation/aggregation, 95–96
 GRASSY platform
  division of labor, 97–98
  interpolation decomposition, 97
  overview, 97
  performance model, 100
  precision issues, 98–99
  pseudo-code, 98–99
  testing, 100
  texture packing, 97
 steps, 94–95
Stereo matching
 algorithms, implementations, evaluations, 475–485
 basic problem, 473–474
 core method, 475
 cross-checking, 484–485
 foreground *vs.* full image, 490–493
 Middlebury evaluation, 486–487

multiresolution background modeling, 475–478
multiresolution *vs.* single resolution, 487–490
multiresolution stereo matching, 478–479
performance evaluation, 486–493
single CUDA kernel, 479–485
Stream compaction, object detections, 533–535
Streaming-multiprocessors (SMs)
    CT image reconstruction, 672–673, 675
    DBT GPU acceleration, 650–652
    speed-limit-sign recognition, 512–513
    tomographic image reconstruction, 684
Stream processors (SP)
    gate-level simulation, 345
    LDPC performance, 626
Strong classifiers, object detection, 521–522
Structure of Array (SoA) format
    ABM communication, 318
    XML-driven CUDA code generation, 316–317
Stump-based classifier, definition, 521–522
Successive overview relaxation (SOR) method, atlas
    construction, 778–780
Sum-product algorithm (SPA), LDPC, 620–621, 626
Sum of squared differences (SSD), B-splines, 754
Supercomputing clusters
    black hole simulations, 107–109
    pattern matching acceleration, 185–196
Support vector machine (SVM)
    algorithms, implementations, evaluations, 296–306
    basic problem, 293
    binary SVM, 294–295
    block/grid sizes, 303–304
    core method, 294–295
    future work, 310
    GPU performance, 308–310
    instance port, 306
    multiclass SVM, 295
    Multi-GPU cascade SVM, 304–305, 307, 310
    performance evaluation, 306–310
    SMO, 296–297
    SMO map step, 298
    SMO reduce step, 299–302
    testing phase, 302–303
SVM, *see* Support vector machine (SVM)
SW, *see* Smith-Waterman (SW) algorithm
SwissProt database
    pattern matching, 186
    and SW algorithm, 157, 168
Synthesizable test benches, gate-level simulation, 354–355
System-level compilation, gate-level simulation
    combinatorial logic extraction, 348
    definition, 347
    levelization, 348

macro-gate segmentation, 349–350
steps, 348–350
synthesis, 348

T

Tanner graphs, LDPC, 620, 622–623
Target headers, genome-matching acceleration, 178–179
Target processing, genome-matching acceleration, 180
Task parallelism, chemical informatics, 23
Task scheduling
    gate-level, 369–372
    GPU-based parallelization, 369
Taylor series, diffusion equation derivation, 395
TBO, *see* Texture buffer object (TBO)
TDSE, *see* Time-dependent Schröedinger equation (TDSE)
Template-based pipeline, speed-limit-sign recognition,
    500–505, 508–514
Template-driven code, for ABM
    algorithms and implementations, 314
    communication and transition function behavior scripting,
        317–319
    core method, 314
    future work, 324
    overview, 313
    performance evaluation, 321–323
    real-time instanced agent visualization, 319–320
    state-based agent simulation, 314–315
    XML-driven CUDA code generation, 315–317
Temporal data mining
    core methodology, 212–214
    datasets and testbed, 222
    one thread per occurrence performance, 222–224
    one thread per occurrence strategy, 215–219
    overview, 211–212, 214–215
    serial episode mining, 214
    two-pass elimination approach, 219–222
    two-pass elimination performance, 224–226
Temporal filtering, VSM, 453
Tentative collision point, photon transport, 252
Test benches
    gate-level simulation, 347–348, 354–357, 363
    GPU-based logic simulator, 357
Testing phase, SVM, 302–303, 305–306
Test reduce step, SVM, 303–304, 308
Texture buffer object (TBO), ABM visualization, 320
Texture interpolation, fast spectral synthesis
    basic problem, 93–95
    flux calculation and aggregation, 95–96
    future work, 101
    GRASSY platform, 97–100
    testing, 100

Texture memory
    brain connectivity reconstruction, 802
    DBT GPU acceleration, 651–653
    genome-matching, 179–180
    medical image processing, 744
    object detection, 530
    photon transport, 259
    radiographic image simulation, 822
    visual saliency motion estimator kernel, 462
Texture packing, GRASSY platform, 97
TGFSR, *see* Twisted generalized feedback shift register
    (TGFSR)
Thread block
    ASR, 611, 613
    atlas construction, 779
    Barnes-Hut *n*-body algorithm, 91
    black hole simulations, 107
    brain connnectivity reconstruction, 804–805, 807, 810–811
    B-spline registration, 757, 762–763, 767–769
    CCL, 574–575, 577
    chemical informatics, 23–24, 32
    de-mosaicing, 588, 590–592
    electronic structure, 62
    fast circuit optimization, 369, 372–373
    fast spectral synthesis, 97–98, 100
    gate-level simulation, 345–348, 350–352, 354–355
    LB model, 388
    medical image processing, 742
    MO calculations, 11, 13, 15, 17
    molecular electrostatics, 45–49, 51–55
    n-body simulation, 116–120, 124–125
    pattern matching, 186, 198
    radiographic image simulation, 821–822, 827
    random number generators, 231–232, 244
    real-time stereo, 476–477, 479–481, 483–484
    RNA folding, 205
    SPIRiT MRI, 730–732, 735
    SVM, 297, 303
    SW algorithm, 157, 168
    template-driven agent-based modeling, 319, 322–323
    tomographic image reconstruction, 684, 686, 688–689
    VSM, 461
Thread divergence
    Barnes Hut *n*-body algorithm, 75, 80, 82, 84–87
    black hole simulations, 105–106
    B-spline registration, 763
    DBT, 652
    image de-mosaicing, 588
    photon transport, 250
    quadrature grids, 39
    tomographic image reconstruction, 679
Thread mapping, DBT, 647, 650–651, 653–654

Thread-per-point method, quadrature grid DFT calculations,
    38–39
Three-dimensional axon tracking, brain connectivity
    reconstruction, 802
Three-dimensional convolutions, BigDFT code, 138–139
Three-dimensional DDA algorithm, photon transport, 253
Three-dimensional lattice
    direct Coulomb summation, 48
    GPU MO algorithms, 10–11
    LB methods, *see* Lattice-Boltzmann (LB) lighting models
Three-dimensional operators, and BigDFT code, 140–143
Three-dimensional volume visualization, brain connectivity
    reconstruction, 795–797
Thrust libraries
    atlas construction, 775–776
    object detection, 527, 533–534
Tic-Tac-Toe dataset, AntMinerGPU evaluation, 337–339
Tiled-shared memory
    GPU MO algorithms, 13–14
    schematic representation, 15
Tile Offset lookup table, B-spline registration, 757–758
Tiles, B-spline registration, 752, 756–757, 768–769
Tiling scheme, RNA folding algorithm, 205–208
Time-dependent Schröedinger equation (TDSE), direct MD, 60
Timing-constrained power optimization, fast circuit
    optimization, 366
Total variation minimization (TVM), CT reconstruction
    performance, 703
Training phase
    object detection, 537
    SVM, 293, 305–306, 308, 310
Transition functions, template-driven agent-based modeling,
    314–315, 317–321
Transmissive properties
    plant rendering, 391
    plastics rendering, 392–393
Tree-based data structures, Barnes Hut *n*-body algorithm
    algorithm overview, 76–77
    basic problem, 75–76
    evaluation methodology, 88–89
    global optimizations, 78–79
    implementation limitations, 91
    implementation results, 89–90
    kernel 1 optimization, 79–80
    kernel 2 optimization, 80–81
    kernel 3 optimization, 81–83
    kernel 4 optimization, 83
    kernel 5 optimization, 84–86
    kernel 6 optimization, 86
    optimizations overview, 86–88
Treecode calculations, fast *n*-body simulations, 115–117,
    122–125

treediv, VSM, 469–470

treetran, VSM, 469–470

Triphone states, ASR, 606–607

TTT, *see* Tic-Tac-Toe dataset

TVM, *see* Total variation minimization (TVM)

Twisted generalized feedback shift register (TGFSR), 237–242

Two-dimensional estimation, VSM, 453

Two-pass elimination approach, temporal data mining
    algorithmic enhancements, 220–222
    basic problem, 219–220
    performance evaluation, 224–226

U

Unafold
    algorithms, implementations, evaluations, 201–206
    core method, 200–201
    and GTfold, 203
    implementation comparison, 208
    internal loops, 203
    multiloops
        first implementation, 204
        GPU implementation, 205–206
        overview, 203–204
        reduction split and reordering, 204–206
        tiling scheme, 205–208
    parallelization scheme, 203
    recurrence equations, 201–202
    related algorithms, 206
    RNA folding problem, 199–200

Unbiased diffeomorphic atlas construction
    basic image operators, 775–777
    basic problem, 771–773
    CG method, 780–782
    challenges, 773–774
    core methods, 774
    data structures, 775
    future work, 789–790
    GPU cluster model, 784
    load-balancing, 784–785
    multi-GPU model, 783–784
    multiscale framework, 782–783
    ODE integration, 777
    PDE solver, 778
    performance analysis, 786–789
    performance improvement, 788–789
    performance quality, 787–788
    performance tuning, 785–786
    scratch memory model, 786–787
    SOR method, 778–780
    volume clipping optimization, 786

Union-find algorithm, CCL problem, 570–572

Union function, CCL in CUDA, 570, 572, 575–576

Unique-index prefix-scan, ASR, 608

Unique list gathering lists, ASR, 608

UNROLLFACTOR, direct Coulomb summation, 48–50

Upper-bounding coefficient, photon transport, 252–253

Upscale sampler, multiscale atlas construction, 782–783

Up-Sweep, pattern matching acceleration, 197

USPS dataset, SVM evaluation, 307–308

V

Variance calculations, integral image representation, 524

Variation functions, Fractal Flames, 265–266

Vector evaluated genetic algorithm (VEGA), OS-SIRT, 697

Vector statistical library (VSL), random number generator performance, 243

VEGA, *see* Vector evaluated genetic algorithm (VEGA)

Vertex buffer object (VBO)
    Chaos Game algorithm, 267
    speed-limit-sign recognition, 505

Very large scale integration (VLSI), LDPC, 619, 626

Video memory (VRAM), LDPC, 626

Video processing
    with CUDA/OpenCL
        background subtraction, 549–550
        basic problem, 547
        core technology, 548–551
        cross-correlation, 561
        global memory only, 561–562
        global memory reads, 560
        global/shared/coalesced memory access, 562–565
        implementation/evaluation, 551–565
        Pearson's correlation coefficients, 551
        performance evaluation, 565–566
        real-time video background subtraction, 552–554
        single kernel and I/O operations, 554–555
        single kernel and serial/asynchronous I/O operations, 558–560
        single/three kernel and I/O operations, 558
    GPU computing status, 545–546

Video reframing process, VSM, 471

Viola-Jones object-detection framework
    core algorithm, 519–520
    integral image representation, 523–525
    object classifier cascade structure, 521–522
    overview, 517–519
    traditional algorithm, 525

Virgo, as gravitational wave detector, 103

Virtual particles, photon transport, 252–253

Virtual point lights (VPL), random walks in path tracing, 411

Visual attention models, definition, 451

Visual Molecular Dynamics (VMD)
    and CUDA, 16
    electrostatics algorithms, 43–44
    MO display, 5–6
Visual saliency model
    CUDA kernels, 457–458
    definition, 451
    dynamic pathway, 453, 455–457
    fusion, 453
    Gabor kernel, 462–463
    GPU implementation, 454–465
    interactions kernel, 457–458
    motion estimator kernel, 458–462
    multi-GPU implementation, 463–465
    NSS evaluation, 470
    pipeline model, 465
    precision, 467–468
    real-time streaming solution, 470–471
    results, 454
    results evaluation, 469–470
    schematic, 452
    static pathway, 453, 455, 466–467, 470
Viterbi search algorithm, speech recognition application, 602–603
VLSI, *see* Very large scale integration (VLSI)
VMD, *see* Visual molecular dynamics (VMD)
Volume brick boundary detection, brain connectivity reconstruction, 803–809
Volume brick filtering framework, brain connectivity reconstruction, 802–803
Volume clipping, atlas construction, 786
Volume filtering, brain connectivity reconstruction, 796
Volume rendering, brain connectivity reconstruction, 795–797
Volume size
    atlas construction, 786
    B-spline registration, 767, 769
    CT image reconstruction, 673–674
    SPIRiT MRI, 728
    tomographic image reconstruction, 685
Volumetric pixels, *see* Voxels
Von Neumann equation, direct MD, 60
Voxel-driven forward projection, PET, 681
Voxels
    brain connectivity reconstruction, 803–811
    B-spline registration, 752–762, 764–765, 767–769
    CT reconstruction, 663, 669–672, 676, 695–696
    DBT, 649, 651, 653, 655
    LB models, 390
    Monte Carlo photon transport, 248–251, 253–254, 259–261
    MRI reconstruction, 711–713, 715, 717

radiographic image simulation, 813–819, 821–827
    SPIRiT MRI, 724, 726–727, 729
    tomographic image reconstruction, 679, 681–686, 689–690
Voxel-wise parallelism, SPIRiT MRI, 729
VPL, *see* Virtual point lights (VPL)
VRAM, *see* Video memory (VRAM)

W
WAR hazards, Graph Cuts for computer vision, 441
Warm-up kernel, Chaos Game algorithm, 267
Warp
    Barnes Hut *n*-body algorithm via CUDA, 80–81
    definition, 80
    random walks in path tracing, 404
Wavefunction
    BigDFT, 134–138, 140–141, 143–144, 147
    electronic structure, 59–60
    MO calculations, 8–14, 16–17
Wavelet transform, SPIRiT MRI, 729–733
WBC, *see* Wisconsin Breast Cancer (WBC) dataset
WBGA, *see* Weighted-based genetic algorithm (WBGA)
Weak classifiers
    cascade layout optimizations, 538
    Viola-Jones object-detection, 521–523
WEB dataset, SVM evaluation, 307–308
Weighted-based genetic algorithm (WBGA), OS-SIRT, 697
WER, *see* Word error rate (WER)
Wisconsin Breast Cancer (WBC) dataset, AntMinerGPU evaluation, 337–339
Woodcock tracking
    Monte Carlo for x-ray tracks, 817
    photon transport, 253–254, 259
    radiographic image simulation, 814, 817–819, 824
Word error rate (WER), speech models, 614
Workload management, Graph Cuts for computer vision, 444–445
Work size, LB OpenCL implementation, 386–389
Work starvation, classifiers cascade, 535
Workstation clusters
    atlas construction, 784
    FFT, 629, 631–632
Wrinkle formation
    facial animation system overview, 413
    and skin strain, 418–419
WSFT techniques, speech recognition application, 603

X
X-Machine
    ABM communication, 317
    state-based agent simulation, 314–315
    XML-driven CUDA code generation, 316

XML
  for ABM
    core method, 314
    CUDA code generation, 315–317
    overview, 313
    performance evaluation, 321–323
  classifier cascade layout optimizations, 538, 540
X-ray imaging system, radiographic image simulation, 815–816
X-ray projections
  DBT, 647, 649
  PET *vs.* CT, 682
X-ray transport algorithm, MC, radiographic image simulation
    in CUDA
  algorithms, implementations, evaluations, 815–822
  basic problem, 813–814
  code testing, 822–824

core methods, 814–815
future work, 827–828
MC for x-ray tracks, 816–818
multiple-GPU CT scan simulations, 818–819
performance analysis, 822–827
random number generation, 820–821
realistic human phantom, 824–827
technical details, 821–822
x-ray imaging system model, 815–816
XSLT (Extensible Stylesheet Transformations), XML-driven
    CUDA code generation, 316

Z

Zero-copy host-device I/O, GPU MO algorithms, 15
Zero-copy kernels, and CUDA, 17
Zero-copy memory access techniques, CUDA methods, 8